Ch 1
122-136
190-203
233-257
283-313
323-330
417-436

Ch. 12
548-578
617-632
654-666
793-808
Nadkarni/Shaw
Bancroft art.
Bas Parent
Ch. 2
3
5
6
7
9

DOMESTIC VIOLENCE LAW

By

Nancy K. D. Lemon

Lecturer
Boalt Hall School of Law
University of California, Berkeley

AMERICAN CASEBOOK SERIES®

WEST
GROUP

ST. PAUL, MINN., 2001

American Casebook Series, and the West Group symbol
are registered trademarks used herein under license.

COPYRIGHT © 2001 By WEST GROUP
       610 Opperman Drive
       P.O. Box 64526
       St. Paul, MN 55164–0526
       1–800–328–9352

ISBN 0–314–24841–2

*TEXT IS PRINTED ON 10% POST
CONSUMER RECYCLED PAPER*

Preface

History of This Book and Course

This book began in 1988, when I was first hired to teach a seminar on Domestic Violence Law at Boalt Hall School of Law, at the University of California at Berkeley, my alma mater. I made many transcontinental phone calls to find a text for the course, only to discover that not only was there no such book in existence, but there had been no courses offered on this subject at that point.

Consequently, I spent many weeks that summer compiling materials to create a photocopied reader. I have continued to teach the course each year. It has grown to three units and up to forty-five students, and has included auditors who are judges, domestic violence activists, scholars from other countries, social welfare students, etc. In 1989, I added an optional companion clinical course for students who wish to gain practical experience in this field. Each year between 1988 and 1995 I updated the substantive materials and tested them in the classroom.

After using photocopied readers for many years, I arranged for publication of the first edition of this book, the first law school textbook on the topic of domestic violence law, in 1996. This coincided with a rapid expansion in the number of law schools offering some type of course or clinical on this topic, from none in 1987 to fifty-seven in 1997 ("When Will They Ever Learn? Educating to End Domestic Violence: A Law School Report," American Bar Association Commission on Domestic Violence, 1997).

Purpose and Uses of These Materials

The changes in the materials I included over the years have reflected a change in my philosophy of teaching. When I started, I saw my role primarily as imparting information to students, and at times, I am afraid, may have lapsed into basically expecting them to learn "the party line." However, I soon came to realize that a more useful approach is to present students with an overview of the policy issues presented in the area of domestic violence law, including the most controversial ones, and to help them think critically about those issues. I now see the class as a "domestic violence think tank," where we are all free to express any opinion or point of view, and there are seldom clear answers. This is why the materials include pieces which are in direct contradiction to each other. As a teacher, I find this approach exciting and dynamic, an opportunity to be instrumental in the development of the academic arm of the domestic violence movement.

As someone who spent most of my professional life from 1981-1993 in the trenches as a practicing attorney working in non-profit agencies, this domestic violence law seminar is a luxurious opportunity to step back a

iii

bit and reflect on the larger picture, to think about where we've come from and where we're going. One of my goals as a teacher is thus to bridge the gap between theory and practice. I hope that this bridge contributes both to the law school curriculum and to the larger domestic violence movement. In the law school context, it is my desire that both the first and second editions of this book contribute to the numerical growth and sophistication of law school classes focusing on domestic violence issues, as well as to increased awareness of domestic violence issues in other law school classes (e.g. family law, torts, immigration, criminal law, evidence, constitutional law, etc.).

In other educational settings, these materials can be assigned as the main textbook for a class, or as supplemental readings in any graduate or upper-level undergraduate course designed to address issues of gender, critical approaches to law and the legal system, or jurisprudence and social policy. Please share it with your colleagues in other disciplines.

Finally, I also hope that this book will be useful to attorneys, advocates, and policymakers in the sometimes daunting task of making the legal system more responsive to the needs of survivors of domestic violence and their children.

Overview of Materials

This book is a collection of articles, book excerpts, cases, and statutes focusing on the role of the legal system in regard to domestic violence. I am defining domestic violence as the various types of abuse occurring in an intimate partner relationship; thus, I am not focusing on other types of family violence, such as elder abuse and child abuse.

My primary goal is not to impart knowledge of what the actual laws are with regard to domestic violence, which would be impossible in one volume, and would need to be updated monthly. Instead, it is to provide an overview of the principal legal issues raised by domestic violence situations, and to enable the reader to think critically about those issues.

The materials are quite interdisciplinary, especially in the introductory chapters. This is because the phenomenon of domestic violence cannot be understood in purely legal terms. In addition, it is important for the reader to be aware of the complexity and variety in terms of who victims of domestic violence are, so that proposed solutions (e.g. mandatory arrest, issuance of restraining orders, physicians reporting abuse to law enforcement, no-drop prosecution policies, etc.) can be evaluated with that awareness in mind.

The four introductory chapters cover some of the history of the legal system's treatment of domestic violence, both in the US and internationally. They also ask what causes domestic violence, what effects the abuse has on the victims, and what approaches are effective in trying to rehabilitate perpetrators; obviously, one's approach to rehabilitation will vary depending on one's analysis of the cause of the problem, and the reader is thus encouraged to think critically about the various treatments which are described.

The third chapter looks at the issue of racism as related to the domestic violence movement and to the legal system's response to domestic violence. The increased emphasis placed on this topic in this edition is partly due to an increased awareness on my part and on the part of the battered women's movement of the issue of racism and its major impact on US society. The women's movement generally and the battered women's movement in particular have struggled with this issue, and need to struggle more, until we all can look squarely at the differences between battered women, as well as at the commonalities. If proposed solutions to the problem of domestic violence do not work for all victims, rather than attempting to implement these solutions and ignoring potential adverse consequences, we need to go back to the drawing board. We as a movement are strong enough to withstand close examination of the hardest issues, racism being one such issue, and to critique how the movement itself has addressed these.

The introductory materials conclude with a chapter focusing on gay and lesbian domestic violence issues. In my opinion, the most interesting aspect of these materials is the way they invite us to question our basic analysis as to what causes domestic violence. Are sex roles actually key in causing this problem? If so, how do we explain such abuse in same-sex couples? This is an example of an area where there is no easy answer.

The second section of the book deals with the response to domestic violence by the civil legal system in the US. These four chapters focus on tort actions between victim and perpetrator, civil restraining orders, children in homes where domestic violence takes place, and alternative dispute resolution. The materials highlight the current issues in each of these areas; two of the most challenging include the response of the legal system to mothers who allegedly have "failed to protect" their children from witnessing the mother's own battering, and the questions which arise when attempting to resolve domestic violence cases outside the courtroom setting, using mediation or peacemaking.

The five chapters in the third section of the book focus primarily on the response of the criminal justice system. Again, policy issues are replete throughout. The chapter on law enforcement response looks at the issue of mandatory arrest in the context of domestic violence, a very controversial issue. The chapter on prosecution questions whether no-drop policies further empower or disempower victims of domestic violence, as well as discussing innovations in the nuts and bolts of prosecuting such cases. The materials on judges invite the reader to examine the development and usefulness of domestic violence courts. The final chapter, on victims of domestic violence as criminal defendants, analyzes the concept and term "Battered Woman Syndrome," and argues for another approach, namely the typical effects of intimate partner abuse upon its victims.

The four chapters in the fourth and last section of the book deal with issues which do not fit neatly into the "civil" or "criminal" categories typically used in the US legal system. They start with current federal responses to domestic violence, including the Violence Against Women Act (VAWA) and restrictions on possession of firearms by batterers. As this book went to press, the US Supreme Court issued its opinion finding unconstitutional the civil rights remedy provided for in VAWA, possibly the most important domestic violence issue the high court has ever addressed. The next chapter looks at confidentiality issues affecting victims of domestic violence, including the controversial question whether medical personnel should be mandated to report domestic violence to law enforcement. Domestic violence victims as welfare recipients and workers is the topic of the following chapter; this is another new area of law, which is just starting to be developed. This book concludes with the issues presented by immigration and international human rights laws as these impact victims of domestic violence; again we see a controversial issue being debated in the appellate courts, namely whether being a victim of domestic violence can be the basis for a request for asylum. The book thus comes full circle, starting and finishing with an international perspective.

A Final Note, An Apology to Some Readers, and An Invitation

Creating this second edition, while sometimes difficult and time-consuming, was also a labor of joy. It is inspiring to see the wealth of legal scholarship bursting forth all over this country, on dozens of domestic-violence related topics. It is exciting to have so much to choose from, and to see the ways practitioners, scholars, and students have been able to build on each other's work to create a body of sophisticated literature.

Some of the users of this book may be dismayed by the deletion of most of the endnotes, tables, references, and internal citations. This decision was made due to space constraints, so that the book could include more substantive pieces. I trust that readers who would like to see the omitted material will be able to access the original articles and cases. If this is very difficult, I would be happy to send a copy of a particular piece.

As a book like this is always a work in progress, I also welcome suggestions from readers or other teachers for what materials to include in the next edition, as well as comments on these materials and how they were useful to you.

Nancy K. D. Lemon

2000
Berkeley, California

Acknowledgements

The production of this edition of this book has required the commitment, skill, and energy of many people.

Thanks to my wonderful students at Boalt Hall School of Law, who invariably teach me while I teach them, and who help sharpen and update my thinking with every class.

I am indebted to all the publishers and authors who allowed me to reprint their work.

I am thankful to my husband, Blaine R. Devine, and my son, Ryan L. Devine, for their patience and major contributions to keeping our household running while I was engaged in this process. I am also indebted to my son for his technical assistance when my computer seriously crashed twice in a four-month period while I was preparing this edition. Thanks go also to my brother, John A. Lemon, to Fidel Dolorier of the Boalt computer lab, and to the numerous other tech support people who assisted me in repeatedly resuscitating my computer.

Major gratitude is due to Susan Peabody, who worked for many hours figuring out the complex technical aspects of preparing this edition, made numerous corrections on various drafts, gave me useful advice on style issues, and was generally by my side through thick and thin.

And thanks to my mother, Adelle E. Lemon, for meticulously proofreading every single word, comma, and asterisk, and for being outraged by some of the stories she read here. She was supported by my father, Robert L. Lemon, who cooked for her the many days she volunteered her time to help me.

Finally, I am deeply grateful to the thousands of battered women who overcame fear and shame enough to tell their stories through these cases and articles. I hope this book will inspire more of them to come forward and further educate the rest of us about this very important topic.

*

Summary of Contents

		Page
PREFACE		iii
ACKNOWLEDGEMENTS		vii
TABLE OF CASES		xix
TABLE OF AUTHORITIES		xxi

Chapter 1. History And Overview ... **1**

Chapter 2. Domestic Violence: Causes, Effects, And Treatment ... **42**

Chapter 3. Cross-Cultural Issues: Survivors of Heterosexual Domestic Violence Who Face Multiple Oppressions ... **132**

A. Overview ... 133
B. Asian Immigrant Women ... 136
C. African American Women ... 142
D. Latinas ... 155
E. Native American Women ... 171
F. Traditional Jewish Women ... 178
G. Disabled Women ... 182

Chapter 4. Gay and Lesbian Battering ... **190**

Chapter 5. Suing Batterers in Tort Actions ... **232**

Chapter 6. Civil Restraining Orders ... **283**

A. Issuance, Mutual Orders ... 284
B. Enforcement ... 309
C. Full Faith and Credit ... 323

Chapter 7. Children in Homes Where Domestic Violence Takes Place ... **330**

A. Custody and Visitation ... 331
B. Leaving With the Children: Abduction, UCCJA/UCCJEA, Hague Convention, Relocation ... 359
C. Response of Juvenile and Criminal Courts to "Failure to Protect" ... 391

Chapter 8. Alternative Dispute Resolution ... **417**

Chapter 9. Rape of Intimate Partners ... **442**

Chapter 10. Law Enforcement ... **489**

A. Overview ... 489
B. Mandatory Arrest ... 493
C. Suing the Police ... 548
D. Dual Arrest ... 572

Page

Chapter 11.   Prosecutorial Response ------------------------ **578**
A. Overview, No Drop Policies------------------------------- 579
B. Evidentiary Issues -------------------------------------- 595
C. Heat Of Passion, Cultural Defenses---------------------- 614

Chapter 12.   Judges and Courts-------------------------- **632**
Chapter 13.   Victims of Domestic Violence as Criminal De-
                fendants ------------------------------- **666**
Chapter 14.   Federal Responses: Violence Against Women
                Act, Restrictions on Firearms----------- **713**
A. Overview--- 714
B. VAWA's Civil Rights Remedy ----------------------------- 725
C. Firearms Restrictions----------------------------------- 753

Chapter 15.   Confidentiality Issues, Including Mandatory
                Reporting of Domestic Violence --------- **770**
Chapter 16.   Victims of Domestic Violence As Welfare Re-
                cipients and Workers-------------------- **792**
A. Welfare Issues--- 793
B. Workplace Violence-------------------------------------- 821

Chapter 17.   Immigration and Human Rights Issues ------- **838**
A. Immigration -- 839
B. Domestic Violence as a Human Rights Issue-------------- 863
C. Asylum --- 879

Table of Contents

	Page
PREFACE	iii
ACKNOWLEDGEMENTS	vii
TABLE OF CASES	xix
TABLE OF AUTHORITIES	xxi

Chapter 1. History and Overview **1**

Cheryl Ward Smith, "The Rule of Thumb," A Historic Perspective? 1

Virginia H. Murray, a Comparative Survey of the Historic Civil, Common, and American Indian Tribal Law Responses to Domestic Violence 2

Reva B. Siegel, "The Rule of Love": Wife Beating as Prerogative and Privacy 7

Calvin Bradley v. The State 10

Joan Zorza, Women Battering: High Costs and the State of the Law 11

Martha R. Mahoney, Legal Images of Battered Women: Redefining the Issue of Separation 16

Deborah Epstein, Redefining the State's Response to Domestic Violence: Past Victories and Future Challenges 28

Judith Armatta, Getting Beyond the Law's Complicity in Intimate Violence Against Women 39

Chapter 2. Domestic Violence: Causes, Effects, And Treatment **42**

Power and Control Wheel 43

Kathleen Waits, Battered Women and Their Children: Lessons From One Woman's Story 43

Mary Ann Dutton and Catherine L. Waltz, Domestic Violence: Understanding Why It Happens and How to Recognize It 66

Lenore E. Walker, The Psychosocial Theory of Learned Helplessness 74

Edward Gondolf & Ellen Fisher, The Survivor Theory 80

Jacquelyn C. Campbell, Wife–Battering: Cultural Contexts Versus Western Social Sciences 92

David Levinson, Societies Without Family Violence 94

William E. Mitchell, Why Wape Men Don't Beat Their Wives: Constraints Toward Domestic Tranquility in a New Guinea Society 99

Barbara Corry, ABC's of Men Who Batter 105

Joan Zorza, Batterer Psychopathology: Questions and Implications 111

Edward W. Gondolf and Associates, Do Batterer Programs Work?: A 15 Month Follow–Up of Multi–Site Evaluation 117

screening

                                                                    Page
Kerry Healey, Christine Smith, and Chris O'Sullivan, Batterer
    Intervention: Program Approaches and Criminal Justice Strate-
    gies --- 122 –

**Chapter 3. Cross-Cultural Issues: Survivors of Heterosexu-
    al Domestic Violence Who Face Multiple Oppressions   132**
A. Overview--- 133
    Angela Browne, Reshaping the Rhetoric: The Nexus of Violence,
        Poverty, and Minority Status in the Lives of Women and
        Children in the United States------------------------------------ 133
B. Asian Immigrant Women--- 136
    Karen Wang, Battered Asian American Women: Community
        Responses from the Battered Women's Movement and the
        Asian American Community ------------------------------------- 136
C. African American Women --------------------------------------- 142
    Angela Mae Kupenda, Law, Life, and Literature: A Critical
        Reflection of Life and Literature to Illuminate How Laws of
        Domestic Violence, Race, and Class Bind Black Women, Based
        on Alice Walker's Book the Third Life of Grange Copeland 142
    Zanita E. Fenton, Domestic Violence in Black and White: Ra-
        cialized Gender Stereotypes in Gender Violence ----------------- 147
    Linda Ammons, Mules, Madonnas, Babies, Bathwater, Racial
        Imagery and Stereotypes: The African–American Woman and
        the Battered Woman Syndrome ---------------------------------- 151
D. Latinas -- 155
    Jenny Rivera, Domestic Violence Against Latinas by Latino
        Males: An Analysis of Race, National Origin, and Gender
        Differentials -- 155
E. Native American Women --- 171
    Virginia H. Murray, A Comparative Survey of the Historic Civil,
        Common, and American Indian Tribal Law Responses to
        Domestic Violence --- 171
F. Traditional Jewish Women-- 178
    Beverly Horsburgh, Lifting the Veil of Secrecy: Domestic Vio-
        lence in the Jewish Community ---------------------------------- 178
G. Disabled Women-- 182
    Margaret A. Nosek, Carol A. Howland, and Mary Ellen Young,
        Abuse of Women With Disabilities: Policy Implications --------- 182

Chapter 4. Gay and Lesbian Battering ------------------------ **190**
Kathleen Finley Duthu, Why Doesn't Anyone Talk About Gay and
    Lesbian Domestic Violence?--- 191
Nancy J. Knauer, Same–Sex Domestic Violence: Claiming a Domes-
    tic Sphere While Risking Negative Stereotypes --------------------- 203
Nancy E. Murphy, Queer Justice: Equal Protection for Victims of
    Same–Sex Domestic Violence------------------------------------- 213
Ruthann Robson, Lavender Bruises: Intralesbian Violence, Law and
    Lesbian Legal Theory --- 218
Valli Kanuha, Compounding the Triple Jeopardy: Battering in
    Lesbian of Color Relationships------------------------------------- 228

Page

Chapter 5. Suing Batterers In Tort Actions **232**
Clare Dalton, Domestic Violence, Domestic Torts and Divorce: Constraints and Possibilities 233
Jessie E. Thompson v. Charles N. Thompson 257
Moran v. Beyer 263
Jean Marie Cusseaux v. Wilson Pickett, Jr. 266
Joy Lee Stuart v. Ronald T. Stuart 270
Merle H. Weiner, Domestic Violence and the Per Se Standard of Outrage 275
Daisy Annette Santiago v. Osvaldo Rios Alonso 280

Chapter 6. Civil Restraining Orders **283**
A. Issuance, Mutual Orders 284
Kit Kinports and Karla Fischer, Orders of Protection in Domestic Violence Cases: An Empirical Assessment of the Impact of the Reform Statutes 284
V.C. v. H.C., Sr., Et Al. 294
Joan Zorza, What is Wrong With Mutual Orders of Protection? 299
Karen Ann Mechtel v. Allen David Mechtel 304
B. Enforcement 309
Joan Zorza and Nancy K. D. Lemon, Two–Thirds of Civil Protection Orders are Successful; Better Court and Community Services Increase Their Success Rates 309
David M. Zlotnick, Empowering the Battered Woman: The Use of Criminal Contempt Sanctions to Enforce Civil Protection Orders 313
United States v. Alvin J. Dixon and Michael Foster 321
C. Full Faith and Credit 323
Susan B. Carbon, Peter MacDonald and Seema Zeya, Enforcing Domestic Violence Protection Orders Throughout the Country: New Frontiers of Protection for Victims of Domestic Violence 323

Chapter 7. Children In Homes Where Domestic Violence Takes Place **330**
A. Custody and Visitation 331
Joan Zorza, Protecting the Children in Custody Disputes When One Parent Abuses the Other 331
Stephen E. Doyne, Janet M. Bowermaster, J. Reid Meloy, Donald Dutton, Peter Jaffe, Stephen Temko, and Paul Mones, Custody Disputes Involving Domestic Violence: Making Children's Needs a Priority 340
Lynne R. Kurtz, Protecting New York's Children: An Argument for the Creation of a Rebuttable Presumption Against Awarding a Spouse Abuser Custody of a Child 348
Maureen Sheeran and Scott Hampton, Supervised Visitation in Cases of Domestic Violence 352
B. Leaving With The Children: Abduction, UCCJA/UCCJEA, Hague Convention, Relocation 359
Barbara J. Hart, Parental Abduction and Domestic Violence 359

Licata brief

Page

B. Leaving With The Children: Abduction, UCCJA/UCCJEA, Hague Convention, Relocation—Continued

Billie Lee Dunford–Jackson, The Uniform Child Custody Jurisdiction and Enforcement Act: Affording Enhanced Protection for Victims of Domestic Violence and Their Children 366

Regan Fordice Grilli, Domestic Violence: Is it Being Sanctioned by the Hague Convention? ------------- 372

Janet M. Bowermaster, Relocation Custody Disputes Involving Domestic Violence ----------------- 378

C. Response of Juvenile and Criminal Courts to "Failure to Protect" ------------- 391

G. Kristian Miccio, A Reasonable Battered Mother? Redefining, Reconstructing, and Recreating the Battered Mother in Child Protective Proceedings ----------------- 391

Lesley E. Daigle, Empowering Women to Protect: Improving Intervention With Victims of Domestic Violence in Cases of Child Abuse and Neglect; A Study of Travis County, Texas 406

Bryan A. Liang and Wendy L. MacFarlane, Murder by Omission: Child Abuse and the Passive Parent ---------------- 409

Amy Haddix, Unseen Victims: Acknowledging the Effects of Domestic Violence on Children Through Statutory Termination of Parental Rights ----------------- 412

Audrey E. Stone and Rebecca J. Fialk, Criminalizing the Exposure of Children to Family Violence: Breaking the Cycle of Abuse ----------------- 414

Chapter 8. Alternative Dispute Resolution ----------------- **417**

Vogt v. Vogt ----------------- 417

Holly Joyce, Mediation and Domestic Violence: Legislative Responses ----------------- 421

Joanne Fuller and Rose Mary Lyons, Mediation Guidelines ---------- 428

Jessica Pearson, Mediating When Domestic Violence Is a Factor: Policies and Practices in Court–Based Divorce Mediation Programs ----------------- 434

Donna Coker, Enhancing Autonomy for Battered Women: Lessons From Navajo Peacemaking ----------------- 436

Chapter 9. Rape Of Intimate Partners ----------------- **442**

Lisa R. Eskow, The Ultimate Weapon?: Demythologizing Spousal Rape and Reconceptualizing Its Prosecution ----------------- 442

The People of the State of New York v. Mario Liberta ----------------- 462

Cassandra M. Delamothe, Liberta Revisited: A Call to Repeal the Marital Exemption for All Sex Offenses in New York's Penal Law ----------------- 472

Garth E. Hire, Holding Husbands and Lovers Accountable for Rape: Eliminating the "Defendant" Exception of Rape Shield Laws ----------------- 476

Model Penal Code, Part II. Definition of Specific Crimes, Offenses Involving Danger to the Person, Article 213. Sexual Offenses 482

Marnie Shiels, Spousal Rape Laws: 20 Years Later ---------------- 485

Page

Chapter 10. Law Enforcement --- **489**
A. Overview -- 489
    Barbara J. Hart, Arrest: What's the Big Deal ---------------------------- 489
B. Mandatory Arrest -- 493
    Lawrence W. Sherman, The Influence of Criminology on Crimi-
        nal Law: Evaluating Arrests for Misdemeanor Domestic Vio-
        lence -- 493
    Joan Zorza, The Criminal Law of Misdemeanor Domestic Vio-
        lence, 1970–1990 -- 526
    Barbara Fedders, Lobbying for Mandatory–Arrest Policies:
        Race, Class, and the Politics of the Battered Women's Move-
        ment -- 543
C. Suing the Police --- 548
    Joan Zorza, Suing the Police After Deshaney ------------------------ 548
    Anthony Mastroianni v. County of Suffolk ---------------------------- 562
    Debra Culberson v. Vincent Doan -------------------------------------- 566
D. Dual Arrest -- 572
    Wisconsin Statutes Annotated, Criminal Procedure, Chapter
        968, Commencement of Criminal Proceedings -------------------- 572
    Andrea D. Lyon, Be Careful What You Wish For: An Examina-
        tion of Arrest and Prosecution Patterns of Domestic Violence
        Cases in Two Cities in Michigan ------------------------------------ 573

Chapter 11. Prosecutorial Response ------------------------------- **578**
A. Overview, No Drop Policies --- 579
    Donna Wills, Domestic Violence: The Case for Aggressive Prose-
        cution -- 579
    Linda G. Mills, Intuition and Insight: A New Job Description
        for the Battered Woman's Prosecutor and Other More Modest
        Proposals -- 585
    Susan B. Breall and Deborah Adler, Guidebook for Prosecutors
        Working With Battered Immigrant Women ---------------------- 593
B. Evidentiary Issues -- 595
    Heather Fleniken Cochran, Improving Prosecution of Battering
        Partners: Some Innovations in the Law of Evidence ----------- 595
    The People v. Mark Anthony Hoover -------------------------------- 599
    The People v. Gabriel Louis Hernandez ---------------------------- 605
    Paula Finley Mangum, Reconceptualizing Battered Woman Syn-
        drome Evidence: Prosecution Use of Expert Testimony on
        Battering -- 610
C. Heat of Passion, Cultural Defenses --------------------------------------- 614
    Victoria Nourse, Passion's Progress: Modern Law Reform and
        the Provocation Defense -- 614
    Leti Volpp, (Mis)identifying Culture: Asian Women and the
        "Cultural Defense" -- 617

Chapter 12. Judges and Courts ------------------------------------- **632**
Cheryl Hanna, The Paradox of Hope: The Crime and Punishment
    of Domestic Violence --- 632
Amy Karan, Susan Keilitz, and Sharon Denaro, Domestic Violence
    Courts: What Are They and How Should We Manage Them? 640

                                                                    Page
Deborah Epstein, Effective Intervention in Domestic Violence
    Cases: Rethinking the Roles of Prosecutors, Judges, and the
    Court System -- 654
Jacqueline St. Joan, Sex, Sense, and Sensibility: Trespassing Into
    the Culture of Domestic Abuse ------------------------------- 662

Chapter 13. Victims of Domestic Violence as Criminal De-
    fendants -- **666**
Mary Ann Dutton, Validity of "Battered Woman Syndrome" In
    Criminal Cases Involving Battered Women --------------------- 666
Janet Parrish, Trend Analysis: Expert Testimony on Battering and
    Its Effects in Criminal Cases (Highlights) ------------------ 683
Ellen Leesfield & Mary Ann Dutton– Douglas, "Faith and Love":
    Use of the Battered Woman Syndrome to Negate Specific Intent 685
The People v. Evelyn Humphrey ----------------------------------- 690
Denise Bricker, Fatal Defense: An Analysis of Battered Woman's
    Syndrome Expert Testimony for Gay Men and Lesbians Who Kill
    Abusive Partners --- 704
Linda L. Ammons, Mules, Madonnas, Babies, Bath Water, Racial
    Imagery and Stereotypes: The African– American Woman and
    the Battered Woman Syndrome (Part II) ---------------------- 709

Chapter 14. Federal Responses: Violence Against Women
    Act, Restrictions on Firearms ------------------------ **713**
A. Overview --- 714
    George B. Stevenson, Federal Antiviolence and Abuse Legisla-
        tion: Toward Elimination of Disparate Justice for Women and
        Children --- 714
    Jenny Rivera, The Violence Against Women Act and the Con-
        struction of Multiple Consciousness in the Civil Rights and
        Feminist Movements ----------------------------------- 718
B. VAWA's Civil Rights Remedy --------------------------------- 725
    Victoria F. Nourse, Where Violence, Relationship, and Equality
        Meet: The Violence Against Women Act's Civil Rights Reme-
        dy --- 725
    Julie Goldscheid, Gender–Motivated Violence: Developing a
        Meaningful Paradigm for Civil Rights Enforcement ------ 728
    Reva B. Siegel, "The Rule of Love": Wife Beating as Preroga-
        tive and Privacy (Part II) --------------------------- 733
    United States v. Antonio J. Morrison Et Al. ---------------- 738
C. Firearms Restrictions -------------------------------------- 753
    Maria Kelly, Domestic Violence and Guns: Seizing Weapons
        Before the Court Has Made a Finding of Abuse --------- 753
    Susan Carbon, Peter MacDonald and Seema Zeya, Enforcing
        Domestic Violence Protection Orders Throughout the Coun-
        try: New Frontiers of Protection for Victims of Domestic
        Violence (Part II) ----------------------------------- 755
    United States of America v. Timothy Joe Emerson ----------- 760
    United States of America v. James L. Boyd III ------------- 765

Page

Chapter 15. Confidentiality Issues, Including Mandatory Reporting of Domestic Violence ---------------------------------- **770**
Joan Zorza, Recognizing and Protecting the Privacy and Confidentiality Needs of Battered Women----------------- 770
Mia M. McFarlane, Mandatory Reporting of Domestic Violence: An Inappropriate Response for New York Health Care Professionals 781
James T. R. Jones, Kentucky Tort Liability for Failure to Report Family Violence----------------- 787

Chapter 16. Victims of Domestic Violence As Welfare Recipients and Workers----------------- **792**
A. Welfare Issues----------------- 793
   Jody Raphael, Domestic Violence and Welfare Receipt: Toward a New Feminist Theory of Welfare Dependency ---------- 793
   Maria L. Imperial, Self–Sufficiency and Safety: Welfare Reform for Victims of Domestic Violence----------------- 796
   Wendy Pollack and Martha F. Davis, The Family Violence Option of the Personal Responsibility and Work Opportunity Reconciliation Act of 1996: Interpretation and Implementation ---------- 808
   Joan Meier, Domestic Violence, Character, and Social Change in the Welfare Reform Debate----------------- 814
   Eloise Anderson v. Brenda Roe and Anna Doe ------------- 817
   Rita L. Saenz v. Brenda Roe and Anna Doe ------------- 820
B. Workplace Violence----------------- 821
   Robin R. Runge and Marcellene E. Hearn, Employment Rights Advocacy for Domestic Violence Victims ------------- 821
   Jill C. Robertson, Addressing Domestic Violence in the Workplace: An Employer's Responsibility ------------- 828

Chapter 17. Immigration and Human Rights Issues ----------- **838**
A. Immigration ----------------- 839
   Tien-Li Loke, Trapped in Domestic Violence: The Impact of United States Immigration Laws on Battered Immigrant Women ----------------- 839
   Cecelia M. Espenoza, No Relief for the Weary: VAWA Relief Denied for Battered Immigrants Lost in the Intersections 856
   Lee J. Teran, Barriers to Protection at Home and Abroad: Mexican Victims of Domestic Violence and the Violence Against Women Act ----------------- 860
B. Domestic Violence As a Human Rights Issue ----------------- 863
   Dorothy Q. Thomas & Michele E. Beasley, Domestic Violence As a Human Rights Issue----------------- 863
   Radhika Coomaraswamy, Violence Against Women in the Family, Integration of the Human Rights of Women and the Gender Perspective: Violence Against Women ----------------- 877
C. Asylum ----------------- 879
   In Re R–A–, Brief of Amici Curiae in Support of Request for Certification and Reversal of the Decision of the Board of Immigration Appeals ----------------- 879

*

Table of Cases

The principal cases are in bold type. Cases cited or discussed in the text are roman type. References are to pages. Cases cited in principal cases and within other quoted materials are not included.

Anderson v. Roe, 1998 WL 847246 (U.S.Amicus.Brief 1998), **817**

Boyd III, United States v., 52 F.Supp.2d 1233 (D.Kan.1999), **765**

Bradley v. State, 1 Miss. 156 (Miss.1824), **10**

Culberson v. Doan, 65 F.Supp.2d 701 (S.D.Ohio 1999), **566**

Cusseaux v. Pickett, 279 N.J.Super. 335, 652 A.2d 789 (N.J.Super.L.1994), **266**

Dixon and Foster, United States v., 509 U.S. 688, 113 S.Ct. 2849, 125 L.Ed.2d 556 (1993), **321**

Emerson, United States v., 46 F.Supp.2d 598 (N.D.Tex.1999), **760**

Harris v. State, 71 Miss. 462, 14 So. 266 (Miss.1894), 10

Hernandez, People v., 83 Cal.Rptr.2d 747 (Cal.App. 4 Dist.1999), **605**

Hoover, People v., 92 Cal.Rptr.2d 208 (Cal.App. 4 Dist.2000), **599**

Humphrey, People v., 56 Cal.Rptr.2d 142, 921 P.2d 1 (Cal.1996), **690**

Liberta, People v., 485 N.Y.S.2d 207, 474 N.E.2d 567 (N.Y.1984), **462**

Mastroianni v. County of Suffolk, 668 N.Y.S.2d 542, 691 N.E.2d 613 (N.Y. 1997), **562**

Mechtel v. Mechtel, 528 N.W.2d 916 (Minn.App.1995), **304**

Moran v. Beyer, 734 F.2d 1245 (7th Cir. 1984), **263**

Morrison, United States v., ___ U.S. ___, 120 S.Ct. 1740, 146 L.Ed.2d 658 (2000), **738**

People v. _____ (see opposing party)

Saenz v. Roe, 526 U.S. 489, 119 S.Ct. 1518, 143 L.Ed.2d 689 (1999), **820**

Santiago v. Alonso, 66 F.Supp.2d 269 (D.Puerto Rico 1999), **280**

Stuart v. Stuart, 143 Wis.2d 347, 421 N.W.2d 505 (Wis.1988), **270**

Thompson v. Thompson, 218 U.S. 611, 31 S.Ct. 111, 54 L.Ed. 1180 (1910), **257**

United States v. _____ (see opposing party)

V.C. v. H.C., Sr., 257 A.D.2d 27, 689 N.Y.S.2d 447 (N.Y.A.D. 1 Dept.1999), **294**

Vogt v. Vogt, 455 N.W.2d 471 (Minn. 1990), **417**

*

Table of Authorities

References are to pages.

Adler, Deborah and Susan B. Breall, Guide-book for Prosecutors Working With Battered Immigrant Women, Volcano Press (forthcoming, 2000), 593

Ammons, Linda, Mules, Madonnas, Babies, Bathwater, Racial Imagery and Stereotypes: The African–American Woman and the Battered Woman Syndrome, 1995 Wis. L. Rev. 1003 (1995), 151, 709

Armatta, Judith, Getting Beyond the Law's Complicity in Intimate Violence Against Women, 33 Willamette L. Rev. 773 (1997), 39

Beasley, Michele E. and Dorothy Q. Thomas, Domestic Violence as a Human Rights Issue, 58 Albany L. Rev. 1119 (1995), 863

Bowermaster, Janet M., Relocation Custody Disputes Involving Domestic Violence, 46(3) U. of Kansas L. Rev. 433 (1998), 378

Bowermaster, Janet M., Stephen E. Doyne, J. Reid Meloy, Donald Dutton, Peter Jaffe, Stephen Temko and Paul Mones, Custody Disputes Involving Domestic Violence: Making Children's Needs a Priority, 50(2) Juv. & Fam. Ct. J. 1 (Spring 1999), 340

Breall, Susan B. and Deborah Adler, Guidebook for Prosecutors Working With Battered Immigrant Women, Volcano Press (forthcoming, 2000), 593

Bricker, Denise, Fatal Defense: An Analysis of Battered Woman's Syndrome Expert Testimony for Gay Men and Lesbians Who Kill Abusive Partners, 58 Brook. L. Rev. 1379 (1993), 704

Browne, Angela, Reshaping the Rhetoric: The Nexus of Violence, Poverty, and Minority Status in the Lives of Women and Children in the United States, 3 Geo. J. on Fighting Poverty 17 (1995), 133

Campbell, Jacquelyn C., Wife–Battering: Cultural Contexts Versus Western Social Sciences, Sanctions and Sanctuary: Cultural Perspectives on the Beating of Wives, edited by Dorothy Ayers Counts, Judith K. Brown, and Jacquelyn C. Campbell, Westview Press (1992), 92

Carbon, Susan B., Peter MacDonald and Seema Zeya, Enforcing Domestic Violence Protection Orders Throughout the Country: New Frontiers of Protection for Victims of Domestic Violence, 50(2) Juv. & Fam. Ct. J. 39 (1999), 323, 755

Cochran, Heather Fleniken, Improving Prosecution of Battering Partners: Some Innovations in the Law of Evidence, 7 Tex. J. Women & L. 89 (1997), 595

Coker, Donna, Enhancing Autonomy for Battered Women: Lessons from Navajo Peacemaking, 47 UCLA L. Rev. 1 (1999), 436

Coomaraswamy, Radhika, Violence Against Women in the Family, Report of the Special Rapporteur on Violence Against Women, Its Causes and Consequences, UN Doc. E/CN, 4/1999/68 (March 10, 1999), 877

Corry, Barbara, ABC's of Men Who Batter, unpublished (2000), 105

Daigle, Lesley E., Empowering Women to Protect: Improving Intervention with Victims of Domestic Violence in Cases of Child Abuse and Neglect; A Study of Travis County, Texas, 7 Tex. J. Women & L. 287 (1998), 406

Dalton, Clare, Domestic Violence, Domestic Torts, and Divorce, 31 New England Law Rev. 319 (1997), 233

Davis, Martha F. and Wendy Pollack, The Family Violence Option of the Personal Responsibility and Work Opportunity Reconciliation Act of 1996: Interpretation and Implementation, April/May 1997 Clearinghouse Rev. 1079 (1997), 808

Delamothe, Cassandra M., *Liberta* Revisited: A Call to Repeal the Marital Rape Exemption for all Sex Offenses in New York's Penal Law, 23 Fordham Urban Law J. 857 (1996), 472

Denaro, Sharon, Amy Karan and Susan Keilitz, Domestic Violence Courts: What Are They and How Should We Manage Them?, 50(2) Juv. & Fam. Ct. J. 75 (Spring 1999), 640

Doyne, Stephen E., Janet M. Bowermaster, J. Reid Meloy, Donald Dutton, Peter Jaffe, Stephen Temko and Paul Mones, Custody Disputes Involving Domestic Violence: Making Children's Needs a Priority, 50(2) Juv. & Fam. Ct. J. 1 (Spring 1999), 340

Dunford–Jackson, Billie Lee, The UCCJEA: Affording Enhanced Protection for Victims of Domestic Violence and Their Children, 50(2) Juv. & Fam. Ct. J. 55 (Spring 1999), 366

Duthu, Kathleen Finley, Why Doesn't Anyone Talk About Gay and Lesbian Domestic Violence?, 18 Thomas Jefferson L. Rev. 23 (1996), 191

Dutton, Donald, Stephen E. Doyne, Janet M. Bowermaster, J. Reid Meloy, Peter Jaffe, Stephen Temko and Paul Mones, Custody Disputes Involving Domestic Violence: Making Children's Needs a Priority, 50(2) Juv. & Fam. Ct. J. 1 (Spring 1999), 340

Dutton, Mary Ann, Validity of "Battered Woman Syndrome" in Criminal Cases Involving Battered Women, edited by Malcolm Gordon, National Institute of Justice, The Validity and Use of Evidence Concerning Battering and Its Effects in Criminal Trials, U.S. Dept. of Justice 1 (1996), 666

Dutton, Mary Ann and Catherine Waltz, Domestic Violence: Understanding Why It Happens, and How to Recognize It, 17–WTR Fam. Adv. 14 (Winter 1995), 66

Dutton–Douglas, Mary Ann and Ellen Leesfield, Faith and Love: Use of the Battered Woman Syndrome to Negate Specific Intent, The Champion (April 1989), 685

Epstein, Deborah, Effective Intervention in Domestic Violence Cases: Rethinking the Roles of Prosecutors, Judges, and the Court System, 11 Yale J. L. & Feminism 3 (1999), 654

Epstein, Deborah, Redefining the State's Response to Domestic Violence: Past Victories and Future Challenges, 1 Geo. J. Gender & L. 127–143 (1999), 28

Eskow, Lisa R., The Ultimate Weapon?: Demythologizing Spousal Rape and Reconceptualizing Its Prosecution, 48 Stanford L. Rev. 677 (1996), 442

Espenoza, Cecelia M., No Relief for the Weary: VAWA Relief Denied for Battered Immigrants Lost in the Intersection, 83 Marq. L. Rev. 163 (1999), 856

Fedders, Barbara, Lobbying for Mandatory-Arrest Policies: Race, Class, and the Politics of the Battered Women's Movement, 23 N.Y.U. Rev. L. & Soc. Change 281 (1997), 543

Fenton, Zanita E., Domestic Violence in Black and White: Racialized Gender Stereotypes in Gender Violence, 8 Colum. J. Gender & L. 1 (1998), 147

Fialk, Rebecca and Audrey Stone, Criminalizing the Exposure of Children to Family Violence: Breaking the Cycle of Abuse, 20 Harv. Women's L. J. 205 (1997), 414

Fischer, Karla and Kit Kinports, Orders of Protection in Domestic Violence Cases: An Empirical Assessment of the Impact of the Reform Statutes, 2 Tex. J. Women and the Law 163 (Spring 1993), 284

Fisher, Ellen and Edward Gondolf, The Survivor Theory, Battered Women as Survivors: An Alternative to Treating Learned Helplessness, Lexington Books (1988), 80

Fuller, Joanne and Rose Mary Lyons, Mediation Guidelines, 33 Willamette L. Rev. 905 (1997), 428

Goldscheid, Julie, Gender–Motivated Violence: Developing a Meaningful Paradigm for Civil Rights Enforcement, 82 Harvard Women's L. J. 123 (1999), 728

Gondolf, Edward and Associates, Do Batterer Programs Work?: A 15 Month Follow–Up of Multi–Site Evaluation, 3(5) D. V. R. 65 (June/July 1998), 117

Gondolf, Edward and Ellen Fisher, The Survivor Theory, Battered Women as Survivors: An Alternative to Treating Learned Helplessness, Lexington Books (1988), 80

Grilli, Regan Fordice, Domestic Violence: Is It Being Sanctioned by the Hague Convention?, 4 Sw. J. L. & Trade Americas 71 (1997), 372

Haddix, Amy, Unseen Victims: Acknowledging the Effects of Domestic Violence on Children Through Statutory Termination of Parental Rights, 84(3) Cal. L. R. 757 (1996), 412

Hampton, Scott and Maureen Sheeran, Supervised Visitation in Cases of Domestic Violence, 50(2) Juv. & Fam. Ct. J. 13 (Spring 1999), 352

Hanna, Cheryl, The Paradox of Hope: The Crime and Punishment of Domestic Violence, 39 Wm. & Mary L. Rev. 1505 (1998), 632

Hart, Barbara, Arrest: What's the Big Deal, 3 Wm. & Mary J. of Women and the Law 189 (1997), 489

Hart, Barbara, Parental Abduction and Domestic Violence, unpublished (1992), 359

Healey, Kerry, Christine Smith and Chris O'Sullivan, Batterer Intervention: Program Approaches and Criminal Justice Strategies, National Institute of Justice (1998), 122

Hearn, Marcellene E. and Robin Runge, Employment Rights Advocacy for Domestic Violence Victims, 5(2) D. V. R. 17 (Dec./Jan. 2000), 821

Hire, Garth E., Holding Husbands and Lovers Accountable for Rape: Eliminating the "Defendant" Exception of Rape Shield Laws, 5 S. Cal. Rev. L. & Women's Stud. 591 (1996), 476

Horsburgh, Beverly, Lifting the Veil of Secrecy: Domestic Violence in the Jewish Community, 18 Harvard Women's L. J. 171 (Spring 1995), 178

Howland, Carol A., Margaret A. Nosek and Mary Ellen Young, Abuse of Women with Disabilities: Policy Implications, 8 Journal of Disability Policy Studies 154 (1997), 182

Imperial, Maria, Self–Sufficiency and Safety: Welfare Reform for Victims of Domestic Violence, 5 Georgetown J. on Fighting Poverty 3 (1997), 796

Jaffe, Peter, Stephen E. Doyne, Janet M. Bowermaster, J. Reid Meloy, Donald Dutton, Stephen Temko and Paul Mones, Custody Disputes Involving Domestic Violence: Making Children's Needs a Priority, 50(2) Juv. & Fam. Ct. J. 1 (Spring 1999), 340

Jones, James T. R., Kentucky Tort Liability for Failure to Report Family Violence, 26 N. Ky. L. Rev. 43 (1999), 787

Joyce, Holly, Mediation and Domestic Violence: Legislative Responses, 14 Journal of the American Academy of Matrimonial Lawyers 447 (1997), 421

Kanuha, Valli, Compounding the Triple Jeopardy: Battering in Lesbian of Color Relationships, Diversity and Complexity in Feminist Therapy (Haworth Press, 1990), 228

Karan, Amy, Susan Keilitz and Sharon Denaro, Domestic Violence Courts: What Are They and How Should We Manage Them?, 50(2) Juv. & Fam. Ct. J. 75 (Spring 1999), 640

Keilitz, Susan, Amy Karan and Sharon Denaro, Domestic Violence Courts: What Are They and How Should We Manage Them?, 50(2) Juv. & Fam. Ct. J. 75 (Spring 1999), 640

Kelly, Maria, Domestic Violence and Guns: Seizing Weapons Before the Court Has Made a Finding of Abuse, 23 Vt. L. Rev. 349 (1998), 753

Kinports, Kit and Karla Fischer, Orders of Protection in Domestic Violence Cases: An Empirical Assessment of the Impact of the Reform Statutes, 2 Tex. J. Women and the Law 163 (Spring 1993), 284

Knauer, Nancy J., Same–Sex Domestic Violence: Claiming a Domestic Sphere While Risking Negative Stereotypes, 8 Temp. Pol. & Civ. Rts. L. Rev. 325 (1999), 203

Kupenda, Angela Mae, Law, Life, and Literature: A Critical Reflection of Life and Literature to Illuminate How Laws of Domestic Violence, Race, and Class Bind Black Women, 42 Howard L. J. 1 (1998), 142

Kurtz, Lynne, Protecting New York's Children: An Argument for the Creation of a Rebuttable Presumption Against Awarding a Spouse Abuser Custody of a Child, 60 Alb. L. Rev. 1345–1375 (1997), 348

Leesfield, Ellen and Mary Ann Dutton–Douglas, Faith and Love: Use of the Battered Woman Syndrome to Negate Specific Intent, The Champion (April 1989), 685

Lemon, Nancy K. D. and Joan Zorza, Two–Thirds of Civil Protection Orders Are Successful; Better Court and Community Services Increase Their Success Rates, review of Susan L. Keilitz, Paula L. Hannaford, & Hillery S. Efkeman, Civil Protection Orders: The Benefits and Limitations for Victims of Domestic Violence, Nat. Center for State Courts (1997), 2(4) D. V. R. 51 (April/May 1997), 309

Levinson, David, Societies Without Family Violence, Family Violence in Cross–Cultural Perspective, Sage (1987), 94

Liang, Bryan A. and Wendy L. MacFarlane, Murder by Omission: Child Abuse and the Passive Parent, 36 Harv. J. on Legis. 397 (1999), 409

Loke, Tien–Li, Trapped in Domestic Violence: The Impact of United States Immigration Laws on Battered Immigrant Women, 6 Boston U. Public Interest L. J. 589 (1997), 839

Lyon, Andrea D., Be Careful What You Wish For, 5 Mich. J. Gender & the Law 254 (1999), 573

Lyons, Rose Mary and Joanne Fuller, Mediation Guidelines, 33 Willamette L. Rev. 905 (1997), 428

MacDonald, Peter, Susan B. Carbon and Seema Zeya, Enforcing Domestic Violence Protection Orders Throughout the Country: New Frontiers of Protection for Victims of Domestic Violence, 50(2) Juv. & Fam. Ct. J. 39 (1999), 323, 755

MacFarlane, Wendy L. and Bryan A. Liang, Murder by Omission: Child Abuse and the Passive Parent, 36 Harv. J. on Legis. 397 (1999), 409

Mahoney, Martha R., Legal Images of Battered Women: Redefining the Issue of Separation, 90(1) Mich. L. Rev. 1 (1991), 16

Mangum, Paula Finley, Reconceptualizing Battered Woman Syndrome Evidence: Prosecution Use of Expert Testimony on Battering, 19 B. C. Third World L. J. 593 (1999), 610

McFarlane, Mia M., Mandatory Reporting of Domestic Violence: An Inappropriate Response for New York Health Care Professionals, 17 Buff. Pub. Interest L. J. 1 (1998–1999), 781

Meier, Joan, Domestic Violence, Character, and Social Change in the Welfare Reform Debate, 19(2) Law & Policy 205 (1997), 814

Meloy, J. Reid, Stephen E. Doyne, Janet M. Bowermaster, Donald Dutton, Peter Jaffe, Stephen Temko and Paul Mones, Custody Disputes Involving Domestic Violence: Making Children's Needs a Priority, 50(2) Juv. & Fam. Ct. J. 1 (Spring 1999), 340

Miccio, G. Kristian, A Reasonable Battered Mother?: Redefining, Reconstructing, and Recreating the Battered Mother in Child Protective Proceedings, 22 Harv. Women's L. J. 89 (1999), 391

Mills, Linda, Intuition and Insight: A New Job Description for the Battered Woman's Prosecutor and Other More Modest Proposals, 7(2) UCLA Women's Law J. 183 (1997), 585

Mitchell, William E., Why Wape Men Don't Beat Their Wives: Constraints Toward Domestic Tranquility in a New Guinea Society, Sanctions and Sanctuary: Cultural Perspectives on the Beating of Wives, edited by Dorothy Ayers Counts, Judith K. Brown, and Jacquelyn C. Campbell, Westview Press (1992), 99

Mones, Paul, Stephen E. Doyne, Janet M. Bowermaster, J. Reid Meloy, Donald Dutton, Peter Jaffe, Stephen Temko, Custody Disputes Involving Domestic Violence: Making Children's Needs a Priority, 50(2) Juv. & Fam. Ct. J. 1 (Spring 1999), 340

Murphy, Nancy E., Queer Justice: Equal Protection for Victims of Same–Sex Domestic Violence, 30 Val. U. L. Rev. 335 (1995), 213

Murray, Virginia H., A Comparative Survey of the Historic Civil, Common, and American Indian Tribal Law Responses to Domestic Violence, 23 Okla. City U. L. Rev. 433 (1998), 2, 171

Nosek, Margaret A., Carol A. Howland and Mary Ellen Young, Abuse of Women with Disabilities: Policy Implications, 8 Journal of Disability Policy Studies 154 (1997), 182

Nourse, Victoria, Passion's Progress: Modern Law Reform and the Provocation Defense, 106 Yale L. J. 1331 (1997), 614

Nourse, Victoria, Where Violence, Relationship, and Equality Meet: The Violence Against Women Act's Civil Rights Remedy, 11 Wis. Women's L. J. 1 (1996), 725

O'Sullivan, Chris, Kerry Healey and Christine Smith, Batterer Intervention: Program Approaches and Criminal Justice Strategies, National Institute of Justice (1998), 122

Parrish, Janet, Trend Analysis: Expert Testimony on Battering and its Effects in Criminal Cases (Highlights), National Institute of Justice, The Validity and Use of Evidence Concerning Battering and Its Effects in Criminal Trials, U.S. Dept. of Justice ix (1996), 683

Pearson, Jessica, Mediating When Domestic Violence is a Factor: Policies and Practices in Court–Based Divorce Mediation Programs, 14(4) Mediation Quarterly 319–335 (1997), 434

Pollack, Wendy and Martha F. Davis, The Family Violence Option of the Personal Responsibility and Work Opportunity Reconciliation Act of 1996: Interpretation and Implementation, April/May 1997 Clearinghouse Rev. 1079 (1997), 808

Raphael, Jody, Domestic Violence and Welfare Receipt: Toward a New Feminist Theory of Welfare Dependency, 19 Harv. Women's L. J. 201 (1996), 793

Rivera, Jenny, Domestic Violence Against Latinas by Latino Males: An Analysis of Race, National Origin, and Gender Differentials, 14 Boston College Third World L. J. 231 (1994), 155

Rivera, Jenny, The Violence Against Women Act and the Construction of Multiple Consciousness in the Civil Rights and Feminist Movements, 4 J. of Law & Policy 371 (1996), 718

Robertson, Jill C., Addressing Domestic Violence in the Workplace: An Employer's Responsibility, 16 Law & Ineq. J. 633 (1998), 828

Robson, Ruthann, Lavender Bruises: Intra–Lesbian Violence, Law and Lesbian Legal Theory, 20 G. G. U. L. Rev. 567 (1990), 218

Runge, Robin and Marcellene E. Hearn, Employment Rights Advocacy for Domestic Violence Victims, 5(2) D. V. R. 17 (Dec./Jan. 2000), 821

Sheeran, Maureen and Scott Hampton, Supervised Visitation in Cases of Domestic Violence, 50(2) Juv. & Fam. Ct. J. 13 (Spring 1999), 352

Sherman, Lawrence W., The Influence of Criminology on Criminal Law: Evaluating Arrests for Misdemeanor Domestic Violence, 83 J. Crim. L. 1 (1992), 493

Shiels, Marnie, Spousal Rape Laws: 20 Years Later, 5(4) Victim Policy Pipeline 5, National Center for Victims of Crime (Winter 1999/2000), 485

Siegel, Reva, The Rule of Love: Wife Beating as Prerogative and Privacy, 105 Yale L. J. 2117 (1996), 7, 733

Smith, Cheryl Ward, The Rule of Thumb, A Historic Perspective?, 1(7) Focus, Los Angeles County Domestic Violence Council (April 1988), 1

Smith, Christine, Kerry Healey and Chris O'Sullivan, Batterer Intervention: Program Approaches and Criminal Justice Strategies, National Institute of Justice (1998), 122

Stevenson, George, Federal Antiviolence and Abuse Legislation: Toward Elimination of Disparate Justice for Women and Children, 33 Willamette L. Rev. 847 (1997), 714

St. Joan, Jacqueline, Sex, Sense, and Sensibility: Trespassing into the Culture of Domestic Abuse, 20 Harv. Women's L. J. 263 (1997), 662

Stone, Audrey and Rebecca Fialk, Criminalizing the Exposure of Children to Family Violence: Breaking the Cycle of Abuse, 20 Harv. Women's L. J. 205 (1997), 414

Temko, Stephen, Stephen E. Doyne, Janet M. Bowermaster, J. Reid Meloy, Donald Dutton, Peter Jaffe and Paul Mones, Custody Disputes Involving Domestic Violence: Making Children's Needs a Priority, 50(2) Juv. & Fam. Ct. J. 1 (Spring 1999), 340

Teran, Lee J., Barriers to Protection at Home and Abroad: Mexican Victims of Domestic Violence and the Violence Against Women Act, 17 B. U. Int'l L. J. 1 (1999), 860

Thomas, Dorothy Q. and Michele E. Beasley, Domestic Violence as a Human Rights Issue, 58 Albany L. Rev. 1119 (1995), 863

Volpp, Leti, (Mis)Identifying Culture: Asian Women and the "Cultural Defense," 17 Harvard Women's L. J. 57 (1994), 617

Waits, Kathleen, Battered Women and Their Children: Lessons from One Woman's Story, 35 Houston L. Rev. 29 (1998), 43

Walker, Lenore, The Psychosocial Theory of Learned Helplessness, The Battered Woman, Harper & Row (1979), 74

Waltz, Catherine and Mary Ann Dutton, Domestic Violence: Understanding Why It Happens, and How to Recognize It, 17–WTR Fam. Adv. 14 (Winter 1995), 66

Wang, Karen, Battered Asian American Women: Community Responses From the Battered Women's Movement and the Asian American Community, 3 Asian Law Journal 151 (1996), 136

Weiner, Merle H., Domestic Violence and the Per Se Standard of Outrage, 54 Md. Law Rev. 183 (1995), 275

Wills, Donna, Domestic Violence: The Case for Aggressive Prosecution, 7(2) UCLA Women's Law J. 173 (1997), 579

Young, Mary Ellen, Margaret A. Nosek and Carol A. Howland, Abuse of Women with Disabilities: Policy Implications, 8 Journal of Disability Policy Studies 154 (1997), 182

Zeya, Seema, Susan B. Carbon and Peter MacDonald, Enforcing Domestic Violence Protection Orders Throughout the Country: New Frontiers of Protection for Victims of Domestic Violence, 50(2) Juv. & Fam. Ct. J. 39 (1999), 323, 755

Zlotnick, David M., Empowering the Battered Woman: The Use of Criminal Contempt Sanctions to Enforce Civil Protective Orders, 56 Ohio St. L. J. 1153 (1995), 313

Zorza, Joan, Batterer Psychopathology: Questions and Implications, unpublished, National Center on Women and Family Law (1993), 111

Zorza, Joan, Protecting the Children in Custody Disputes When One Parent Abuses the Other, 29 Clearinghouse Review 1113 (April 1996), 331

Zorza, Joan, Recognizing and Protecting the Privacy and Confidentiality Needs of Battered Women, 29 Fam. L. Q. 273 (1995), 770

Zorza, Joan, Suing The Police After DeShaney, National Center for Women and Family Law (unpublished, 1995), 548

Zorza, Joan, The Criminal Law of Misdemeanor Domestic Violence, 1970–1990, 83 J. Crim. L. 46 (1992), 526

Zorza, Joan, What is Wrong With Mutual Orders of Protection?, 4(5) D. V. R. 67 (June/July 1999), 299

Zorza, Joan, Woman Battering: High Costs and the State of the Law, Special Issue, Clearinghouse Review 383 (1994), 11

Zorza, Joan and Nancy K. D. Lemon, Two-Thirds of Civil Protection Orders Are Successful; Better Court and Community Services Increase Their Success Rates, review of Susan L. Keilitz, Paula L. Hannaford, & Hillery S. Efkeman, Civil Protection Orders: The Benefits and Limitations for Victims of Domestic Violence, Nat. Center for State Courts (1997), 2(4) D. V. R. 51 (April/May 1997), 309

*

DOMESTIC VIOLENCE LAW

*

Chapter 1

HISTORY AND OVERVIEW

This chapter introduces the topic of this book, domestic violence law in the United States.

Starting with Roman Law, where the term "rule of thumb" originated, the materials trace the development of the response of the Roman and Anglo–American legal system to domestic violence, and the influence of Judeo–Christian religion on this response. A nineteenth century US case illustrates the fact that at that time, it was typical for our legal system to not only tolerate domestic violence, but to actually condone it. The materials start to examine the repudiation of this "doctrine of chastisement," but question whether real change took place, asking whether what occurred was merely a change in the rationale for non-interference in cases of domestic violence.

The second half of the chapter focuses on contemporary issues. One article raises the issue of the enormous cost of domestic violence to the US today. The term "separation assault" is introduced, a key concept which we will see illustrated throughout many of the later articles and cases in this book. The materials also look at the role of the state generally, noting that government actors in the US are much more involved in addressing the problem of domestic violence than ever before, but that this also creates additional challenges.

The chapter concludes with an excerpt bringing an international perspective to these questions, and noting that legal changes alone are not sufficient to end domestic violence, though such changes are a key part of the solution.

CHERYL WARD SMITH, "THE RULE OF THUMB," A HISTORIC PERSPECTIVE?

Focus, Vol. 1, No. 7 (Los Angeles Domestic Violence Council) (April 1988).

Wife abuse and child abuse, contrary to current opinion, are not merely symptoms of modern day stress which disturb family tranquility, and cause the breakdown of a formerly non-violent family structure. The history of women's abuse began over 2,700 years ago in the year 753

B.C. It was during the reign of Romulus in Rome that wife abuse was accepted and condoned under The Laws of Chastisement. The tradition continues to a certain extent even today.

Under The Laws of Chastisement, the husband had an absolute right to discipline his wife physically for various unspecified offenses. This authority was vested in the husband as the sole head of each household: wives were seen as necessary and inseparable possessions of their husbands. Because the man and wife were viewed as one person under the law, the husband could be held liable for any crimes the wife might commit. Thus, The Laws of Chastisement were designed to allow the husband to protect himself from harm caused by his wife's misdeeds. The husband was authorized to protect himself by inflicting physical punishment on his wife. The laws permitted a man to beat his wife with a rod or switch so long as its circumference was no greater than the girth of the base of the man's right thumb. This law became commonly known as "The Rule of Thumb." These laws established a tradition which was perpetuated in English Common Law and in most of Europe.

About 202 B.C., with the ending of the Punic Wars, there were many changes in the family structure resulting in more freedom for women. Women were recognized as property owners, and obtained the right to sue their husbands for unjustified beatings.

VIRGINIA H. MURRAY, A COMPARATIVE SURVEY OF THE HISTORIC CIVIL, COMMON, AND AMERICAN INDIAN TRIBAL LAW RESPONSES TO DOMESTIC VIOLENCE

23 Okla. City U. L. Rev. 435–443 (1998).

II. THE HISTORIC RESPONSE OF CIVIL AND COMMON LAW TO DOMESTIC VIOLENCE

"By the old law, a husband might give his wife moderate correction ... but it is declared in black and white that he may not beat her black and blue, (though the civil law allowed) a man to bestow in moderation his fist upon any woman who had bestowed upon him her hand."[11]

Women in European and American societies have traditionally held a subordinate position to men, a status that dates back to the early Greeks, Romans, and Hebrews. Male dominance in these societies was a result of social and legal structures and religious beliefs. Thus, male dominance and domestic violence in western civilization is not new, nor is it a rarity. Instead, it is an expression of traditional cultural and religious norms. As one author has noted, "it has been with us for more than two thousand years ... seeded the fields of law from which our notions of justice were harvested. It is rooted in the denial of equality to women."[12]

11. Gilbert Abbot & A. Beckett, The Comic Blackstone 121–22 (1985).

12. Michael G. Dowd, Domestic Violence and the Law, 16 Pace L. Rev. 1 (1995).

A. The Influence Of Judeo–Christian Religion

Historic Roman, Hebrew, European, and American societies were vertically structured because they were modeled after, and in some cases controlled by, Judeo–Christian religion. Early Judeo–Christian religion, like Muslim and Hindu beliefs, taught that societies should be based on the model of the patriarchal family, with men holding positions of power and authority.

In addition, several prominent religious leaders such as Saint Augustine, Calvin, and Martin Luther believed in the male right to dominate and control women and in the subservient nature of women. The Old and New Testaments instruct the subordination of women, beginning with the creation of Eve from the rib of Adam. Biblical women who were not considered docile, chaste, and passive were subject to death by mutilation or stoning. Women were the property of men, and rape was an encroachment of the father or husband's property interest.

Through the twelfth century, the Christian church's position toward women remained unchanged. Medieval canon law, based in part on Roman law, argued that women were the subjects of men, and as such, should be deprived of all authority.

In the fourteenth century, the Christian church recognized a husband's right of chastisement, adopted in the English common law. Father Cherubino wrote The Rules of Marriage, later officially sanctioned by the Catholic Church, in which he stated that when a wife committed an offense against her husband, he should "scold her sharply, bully and terrify her. And if this still doesn't work ... take up a stick and beat her soundly...."

Like early Christian teachings, Hebrew religious leaders taught that Hebrew society must be vertically structured, with men holding positions of power and authority at the top. Hebrew women were controlled by men and their value connected to childbearing. Some early Hebrew teachers argued that men could compel their wives to perform household chores, take care of the children, and perform her duties, through wife-beating. A Hebrew husband possessed the power to condemn his wife to death for committing adultery. In the sixteenth century, Solomon Luria stated in Yam Shel Shelomo, a commentary on the Talmud, that a husband is permitted to beat his wife "in any manner when she acts against the laws of the divine Torah. He can beat her until her soul departs, even if she transgresses only a negative commandment."

Some commentators argue that even in the modern era, religious beliefs and the authority of religious institutions perpetuate domestic violence in Europe and America. The basic social and legal structures initially instituted pursuant to the influence of Judeo–Christian religion are still in place, and although women have gained considerable rights in recent decades, men continue to overwhelmingly control the governmental and church hierarchy.

For example, one commentator who studied domestic violence in Ireland noted that traditional cultural and religious influences still encourage Irish women to "take your oil." In addition, most conservative Irish religious dogma continues to "extol[ ] the virtues of preserving the marriage bond, which takes priority over the happiness and security of women's lives."

In modern Jewish society, unequal treatment of men and women continues in at least one form, the issuance of a Get, or bill of divorce. Traditional Hebrew law allowed a man to divorce his wife without cause, and the woman was unable to protest. About A.D. 200, women were also allowed to request a Get in limited circumstances, but a man could not be forced to accept the divorce.

Today, Jewish men can still apply for a Get without cause and a wife can be forced to accept the divorce against her will. However, the traditional restrictions on a woman obtaining a Get continue, including the rule that a husband cannot be forced to accept a Get obtained by his wife.

B.   Domestic Violence In Roman Society And Civil Law

European and American societies and legal systems have been greatly influenced by the Romans. Roman society was structured vertically in pyramid form. Slaves constituted the broad base of the pyramid, with men who were Roman citizens in positions of power and authority at the top.

Throughout Roman history, *patria potestas*, or paternal power, was the legal authority of the paterfamilias, the oldest male head of a Roman family. The paterfamilias had control over all members of his family, including *ius vitae necisque*, the power of life and death. The legal concept of *patria potestas* made the wife and mother a legal sister to her own children, and daughter to her husband or master. The Roman wife, like her children, was legally subject to the paterfamilias' power of life and death.

Roman marriages were not regulated by the law, with the exceptions of requiring an individual to have the mental capacity to marry, be of a certain age, and to obtain their father's consent. Subject to these conditions, all that was required for a valid marriage was a manifestation of an intention to be married. Divorce was also without legal regulation. By the time of Justinian in a.d. 527–65, women had increased freedoms and legal rights, and either party could terminate a marriage by simply indicating they no longer wished to be married.

Under early Roman civil law, however, a husband could beat, divorce, or murder his wife for offenses she committed that disparaged his honor or threatened his property rights. In addition, a husband's family could likewise kill his wife for adultery, without participation by the husband. During the Augustan era, the husband or his family members who killed his wife for adultery would be acquitted of murder.

The evolution of the crime of rape in Roman civil law is indicative of the status of women in early Roman society. Rape arose from the early Roman law of *raptus*, a form of violent theft applied to both property and persons. Women, like children, were the property of men in Roman society, and under Roman civil law, injury for rape was based on damages to a father, husband, or brother. In other words, rape was an economic crime against property, and not a crime against the female victim.

With the advent of Christianity as the official religion of the Roman Empire, much of the social and legal progress benefitting women was reversed. For example, in a.d. 542 Justinian changed the Roman divorce laws, forbidding divorce by consent of either party. Although the new law was repealed after five years, it was eventually reinstated in addition to other Canon Law.

C. *Domestic Violence And The Common Law*

1. *England*

Historic English common law sanctioned two contradictory roles for husbands: first, husbands were to act as their wives' disciplinarians, and second, husbands were to be their wives' protectors. These roles developed due to women's legal subordination and perceived inferiority.

Unlike Roman civil law, English common law required a man and woman seeking to be married to go through certain legal "formalities." Marriage was a contract, changing the legal status of both parties, and divorce was rarely obtained, and only through legal means. Under the "chattel theory," introduced around the sixth century, a woman was first the property of her father and then, upon marriage, the property of her husband. Two important customs developed from this theory, "bride capture" and "stealing an heiress." In the former a man could conquer a woman through rape; in the latter, a man could literally kidnap a woman for marriage.

Early common law rape laws were similar to those of Roman civil law, and derived from "bride capture" and "stealing an heiress." These laws protected the "property rights" of the male relatives of the female victim. For example, if a man raped a young unmarried woman, he was guilty of stealing her father's property, and not guilty of a crime against the victim herself. To the contrary, if a husband raped his wife, he was merely "using his property."

Under the feudal doctrine of coverture, which prevailed from the eleventh to sixteenth centuries, women lost their legal identity upon marriage. At that time, the husband and wife became one—the husband. This legal fiction was referred to as the "unities theory," and pursuant to it, a wife could not own personal property, make a will, nor be a party to a contract. In fact, it was recognized that a husband did not make contracts with his wife since it was tantamount to making a contract with himself.[57]

The chattel and coverture theories combined to make husbands legally responsible for their wives' misbehavior. This responsibility, along with the desire to maintain family discipline and order, and the influence of Christianity, brought about the doctrine of "chastisement," which allowed a husband to beat his wife. Sir William Blackstone wrote about the doctrine of chastisement in the late eighteenth century, stating: "as he is to answer for her misbehavior, the law thought it reasonable to intrust him with this power of restraining her, by domestic chastisement, in the same moderation that a man is allowed to correct his apprentices or children. . . ."[58] The only limits placed on a husband's right to beat his wife were that he do so in a moderate manner. In accord with the doctrine of chastisement, English jurists in 1782 developed the "rule of thumb," whereby a husband could beat his wife with a rod no thicker than his thumb.

During the late nineteenth century, an era of feminist agitation for reform began in England. Influential women such as Frances Power Cobbe persuaded the English Parliament to pass laws rejecting chastisement, making domestic violence illegal. Although these new laws were a marked departure from the traditional English common law, and a victory for the women's movement in England, the "marital rape exemption" and the rule of primogeniture limiting women's property rights continued well into the twentieth century.

2. The United States

Early American colonies enacted laws proscribing wife abuse, believing it to be a threat to a settlement's orderliness and stability. These laws were not strictly enforced, and domestic assaults were typically excused if a husband could "justify" his behavior. Shortly after settlement, Colonial courts were pressured to follow English jurisprudence.

So long as it did not conflict with the Constitution or state statutes, new states after the Revolutionary War generally incorporated English common law. For example, Blackstone's Commentaries played an important role in shaping American legal thought. Courts in the United States, particularly in the mid-Atlantic region and the South, began adopting the "chastisement" doctrine articulated by Blackstone and accepting the English "rule of thumb." For example, in 1824 the Supreme Court of Mississippi stated that in exercising his right to chastise his wife, a husband should not be subjected to "vexatious prosecutions" by his wife, and that courts should be hesitant to expose such private conduct to public scrutiny. Likewise, courts in North Carolina, Alabama, and Pennsylvania, among others, recognized the doctrine of chastisement.

57. 1 William Blackstone, Commentaries On The Laws Of England: Of the Rights of Persons 430 (1765) * * *

58. Id. at 445.

In the mid-nineteenth century, changes in conceptions of authority and family structure occurred in American society.

For example, many experts argued that corporal punishment of children was an ineffective method of instilling respect for authority and bringing about good behavior. Eventually, the fledgling American women's movement adopted these views regarding the doctrine of chastisement. In 1848, the movement's leaders publicly denounced the common law doctrines of marital status and the hierarchical, vertical structure of American society and marriage in a formal Declaration of Sentiments.

In addition to the women's movement, several nineteenth century American legal scholars issued treatises on American common law recognizing a "softened" right of chastisement. For example, in 1827 James Kent wrote: "As the husband is the guardian of the wife, and bound to protect and maintain her, the law has given him a reasonable superiority and control over her person, and he may even put gentle restraints upon her liberty, if her conduct be such to require it."

Although changes in the law were initially heralded by women's groups as a success, it soon became clear that for the immediate future, true reform was limited. For example, a relatively liberal state such as Massachusetts rejected all remedies for domestic violence that allowed wives to separate from their violent husbands. In many states that did pass laws allowing a wife to petition for divorce to escape abuse, husbands could defeat the petition by claiming their behavior was "provoked," or their wife delayed petitioning and thus "condoned" the abuse.

It was not until the modern women's movement of the 1960s that domestic violence once again became a national issue. As a result, the federal and state governments enacted new laws in the 1970s, 1980s, and 1990s, and existing laws were revised. In some respects, these changes in the American legal system reflected an international legal movement against domestic violence.

REVA B. SIEGEL, "THE RULE OF LOVE": WIFE BEATING AS PREROGATIVE AND PRIVACY

105 Yale L. J. 2117, 2118–2120 (1996).

INTRODUCTION

The Anglo–American common law originally provided that a husband, as master of his household, could subject his wife to corporal punishment or "chastisement" so long as he did not inflict permanent injury upon her.

During the nineteenth century, an era of feminist agitation for reform of marriage law, authorities in England and the United States declared that a husband no longer had the right to chastise his wife. Yet, for a century after courts repudiated the right of chastisement, the American legal system continued to treat wife beating differently from other cases of assault and battery. While authorities denied that a husband had the right to beat his wife, they intervened only intermittently in cases of marital violence: Men who assaulted their wives were often granted formal and informal immunities from prosecution, in order to protect the privacy of the family and to promote "domestic harmony." In the late 1970s, the feminist movement began to challenge the concept of family privacy that shielded wife abuse, and since then, it has secured many reforms designed to protect women from marital violence. Yet violence in the household persists. The U.S. Surgeon General recently found that "battering of women by husbands, ex-husbands or lovers [is] the single largest cause of injury to women in the United States."[5] "[T]hirty-one percent of all women murdered in America are killed by their husbands, ex-husbands, or lovers."[6]

The persistence of domestic violence raises important questions about the nature of the legal reforms that abrogated the chastisement prerogative. By examining how regulation of marital violence evolved after the state denied men the privilege of beating their wives, we can learn much about the ways in which civil rights reform changes a body of status law. In the nineteenth century, and again in the twentieth century, the American feminist movement has attempted to reform the law of marriage to secure for wives equality with their husbands. Its efforts in each century have produced significant changes in the law of marriage. The status of married women has improved, but wives still have not attained equality with their husbands—if we measure equality as the dignitary and material "goods" associated with the wealth wives control, or the kinds of work they perform, or the degree of physical security they enjoy. Despite the efforts of the feminist movement, the legal system continues to play an important role in perpetuating these status differences, although, over time, the role law plays in enforcing status relations has become increasingly less visible.

As this Article will show, efforts to reform a status regime do bring about change—but not always the kind of change advocates seek. When the legitimacy of a status regime is successfully contested, lawmakers and jurists will both cede and defend status privileges—gradually relinquishing the original rules and justificatory rhetoric of the contested regime and finding new rules and reasons to protect such status privileges as they choose to defend. Thus, civil rights reform can breathe new life into a body of status law, by pressuring legal elites to translate it into a more contemporary, and less controversial, social idiom. I call this kind of change in the rules and rhetoric of a status regime "preservation through transformation," and illustrate this modernization dynamic in a case study of domestic assault law as it evolved in rule structure and rationale from a law of marital prerogative to a law of marital privacy.

---

5. Joan Zorza, The Criminal Law of Misdemeanor Domestic Violence, 1970–1990, 83 J. Crim. L. & Criminology 46,46 (1992) * * *

6. Zorza, supra note 5, at 46. * * *

Parts I–III of this Article illustrate that as the nineteenth-century feminist movement protested a husband's marital prerogatives, the movement helped bring about the repudiation of chastisement doctrine; but, in so doing, the movement also precipitated changes in the regulation of marital violence that "modernized" this body of status law. A survey of criminal and tort law regulating marital violence during the Reconstruction Era reveals that the American legal system did not simply internalize norms of sex equality espoused by feminist critics of the chastisement prerogative; instead, during the Reconstruction Era, chastisement law was supplanted by a new body of marital violence policies that were premised on a variety of gender-, race-, and class-based assumptions. This new body of common law differed from chastisement doctrine, both in rule structure and rhetoric. Judges no longer insisted that a husband had the legal prerogative to beat his wife; instead, they often asserted that the legal system should not interfere in cases of wife beating, in order to protect the privacy of the marriage relationship and to promote domestic harmony. Judges most often invoked considerations of marital privacy when contemplating the prosecution of middle and upper-class men for wife beating. Thus, as I show, the body of formal and informal immunity rules that sprang up in criminal and tort law during the Reconstruction Era was both gender-and class-salient: It functioned to preserve authority relations between husband and wife, and among men of different social classes as well.

These changes in the rule structure of marital status law were justified in a distinctive rhetoric: one that diverged from the traditional idiom of chastisement doctrine. Instead of reasoning about marriage in the older, hierarchy-based norms of the common law, jurists began to justify the regulation of domestic violence in the language of privacy and love associated with companionate marriage in the industrial era. Jurists reasoning in this discourse of "affective privacy" progressively abandoned tropes of hierarchy and began to employ tropes of interiority to describe the marriage relationship, justifying the new regime of common law immunity rules in languages that invoked the feelings and spaces of domesticity. Once translated from an antiquated to a more contemporary gender idiom, the state's justification for treating wife beating differently from other kinds of assault seemed reasonable in ways the law of chastisement did not.

As the history of domestic violence law illustrates, political opposition to a status regime may bring about changes that improve the welfare of subordinated groups. With the demise of chastisement law, the situation of married women improved—certainly, in dignitary terms, and perhaps materially as well. At the same time, the story of chastisement's demise suggests that there is a price for such dignitary and material gains as civil rights reform may bring. If a reform movement is at all successful in advancing its justice claims, it will bring pressure to bear on lawmakers to rationalize status-enforcing state action in new and less socially controversial terms. This process of adaptation can actually revitalize a body of status law, enhancing its capacity to legitimate social inequalities that remain among status-differentiated groups. Examined from this perspective, the reform of chastisement doctrine can teach us much about the dilemmas confronting movements for social justice in America today.

CALVIN BRADLEY v. THE STATE

1 Miss. (Walker) 156 (1824), [Overruled In *Harris
v. State*, 71 Miss. 462, 14 South. 266].

This cause was tried in the circuit court before the honorable Judge Turner, at the April term of 1824. The defendant was indicted for a common assault and battery, and upon his arraignment, pleaded not guilty, *son assault demesne*, and that Lydia Bradley was his lawful wife & c. Issue was taken upon all the pleas. After the evidence was submitted, and before the jury retired, the counsel for the defendant moved the court to instruct the jury. If they believed the person named in the bill of indictment, and upon whom the assault and battery was committed, was the wife of the defendant, at the time of the assault and battery,—that then and in such case they could not find the defendant guilty. The court refused to give the instructions prayed for by the defendant, and charged the jury, that a husband could commit an assault and battery on the body of his wife, to which opinion of the court, a bill of exceptions was filed, and the case comes up by writ of error upon petition.

The only question submitted for the consideration of the court, is, whether a husband can commit an assault and battery upon the body of his wife. This, as an abstract proposition, will not admit of doubt. But I am fully persuaded, from the examination I have made, an unlimited license of this kind cannot be sanctioned, either upon principles of law or humanity. It is true, according to the old law, the husband might give his wife moderate correction, because he is answerable for her misbehavior; hence it was thought reasonable, to intrust him, with a power, necessary to restrain the indiscretions of one, for whose conduct he was to be made responsible. Strange, 478, 875; 1 H.P.C. 130. Sir William Blackstone says, during the reign of Charles the first, this power was much doubted.— Notwithstanding the lower orders of people still claimed and exercised it as an inherent privilege, which could not be abandoned, without entrenching upon their rightful authority, known and acknowledged from the earliest periods of the common law, done in a case before Mr. Justice Raymond, when the same doctrine was recognised, with proper limitations and restrictions, well suited to the condition and feelings of those, who might think proper to use a whip or rattan, no bigger than my thumb. In order to enforce the salutary restraints of domestic discipline, I think his lordship might nave narrowed down the rule in such a manner, as to restrain the exercise of the right, within the compass of great moderation, without producing a destruction of the principle itself. If the defendant now before us, could shew from the record in this case, he continued himself within reasonable bounds, when he thought proper to chastise his wife, we would deliberate long before an affirmance of the judgment.

The indictment charges the defendant with having made an assault upon one Lydia Bradley, and then and there did beat, bruise, & c.—and the jury have found the defendant guilty, which never could have taken place, if the evidence supported either the second or third pleas of the accused. It was not necessary for the defendant below to introduce his second and third pleas, as we think he could have made a full and ample defence, upon the same matter, under the plea of the general issue. However abhorrent to the feelings of every member of the bench, must be the exercise of the remnant of federal authority, to inflict pain and suffering, when all the finer feelings of the heart should be warmed into devotion, by our most affectionate regards, yet every principle of public policy and expediency, in reference to the domestic relations, would seem to require, the establishment of the rule we have laid down, in order to prevent the deplorable spectacle of the exhibition of similar cases in our courts of justice.—Family broils and dissensions cannot be investigated before the tribunals of the country, without casting a shade over the character of those who are unfortunately engaged in the controversy. To screen from public reproach those who may be thus unhappily situated, let the husband be permitted to exercise the right of moderate chastise-ment, in cases of great emergency, and use salutary restraints in every case of misbehavior, without being subjected to vexatious prosecutions, resulting in the mutual discredit and shame of all parties concerned. *Judgment affirmed.*

JOAN ZORZA, WOMEN BATTERING: HIGH COSTS AND THE STATE OF THE LAW

Clearinghouse Review, Special Issue (1994) 383–388.

I. THE HIGH COST OF WOMEN ABUSE

Although society pays dearly for domestic violence, we are so used to thinking of women battering as a private matter that we have hardly begun to put a price on the problem for either the victim or society.

Battered women spend at least twice as much time in bed due to illness as women who have never been battered. Noticing the higher health expenses, the Pennsylvania Blue Shield Initiative recently esti-mated that domestic violence costs that state $326.6 million per year, which would amount to at least $6.5 billion annually for the entire United States. Yet other studies suggest how very conservative their estimate was.

Between 20 percent and 35 percent of women seeking medical care in emergency rooms in America are there because of domestic violence, totaling 1,453,437 medical visits per year. Based on an average cost of $1,633 for direct medical services for those seeking medical care due to interpersonal violence at Chicago's Rush Presbyterian–St. Luke's Medi-cal Center, New York City hospital emergency room costs for battered women are calculated to be $506 million annually. Assuming that this amounts to only half of the city's medical costs (it excluded private physician, psychosocial, counseling, and follow-up care costs), New York City, with a population of eight million people, must spend one billion per year in medical costs for domestic violence. This translates to $31 billion per year nationally, or $124 annually for each living person.

Even these figures do not tell the whole story. Many women's injuries are never connected to their prior abuse (e.g., 53 percent of female chronic pain sufferers were previously abused by their partners before the onset of their chronic pain condition). Also omitted are the high medical and counseling costs of the many children injured or traumatized when their mothers are beaten.

Many other costs to society have never been determined. Although the March of Dimes found that women battered during pregnancy have more than twice the rate of miscarriages and give birth to more babies with more birth defects than women who may suffer from any immunizable illness or disease, the extra costs of raising these children and traumatized "normal" children, including their special education and counseling costs, are borne by the nation as a whole due to their effects on the government and the economy.

The mental health costs related to abuse of women must be staggering. The effects of emotional abuse or the psychological effects of any abuse are even more severe than the effects of physical abuse. Battered women are 15.3 times more likely than nonabused women to want seriously to commit suicide. Because of abuse and the resulting suicide attempts, 26 percent of all abused females, and half of all black females, in the nation end up in hospitals. Yet, before these women were battered, their risk of suicide was no different from that of women never battered. Battering is the single greatest context identified for—and possibly associated with half of—female alcoholism. After the onset of violence, women are 16 times more likely to become alcoholics and 9 times more likely to abuse drugs than women who are not abused. Virtually all females in alcohol rehabilitation programs are victims of partner or parental abuse. About half of all female mental health clients—of whom 37 percent are diagnosed as depressed and 10 percent have suffered a psychotic break—are abused. Because doctors frequently fail to recognize the abuse and to intervene appropriately, the cumulative cost and impact of the *sequelae* of abuse far exceed the initial abuse-related injury, often resulting in dozens and even hundreds of medical and mental health visits—obviously at enormous cost to the victims and society.

The entire medical costs are so great that Pennsylvania's medical insurance companies, having finally begun to document them, are now rejecting battered women as bad insurance risks or refusing to cover their injuries on the theory that the injuries are a preexisting condition.

Society also pays to shelter women and children made homeless as a result of domestic violence, the largest cause of homelessness in America, accounting for up to half of all homeless families. New York City conservatively estimated that it spent $30–40 million annually, assuming that only 21 percent of its homeless families and 40 percent of its homeless women had no place to live because of domestic violence. Yet the New York State Office for the Prevention of Domestic Violence documented that battered women and their children comprised 40 percent of those in the state's homeless shelters in 1987, and this did not even include the 7,700 women and children housed that year by the state's domestic violence programs.

In addition to sheltering homeless children with their mothers, society also pays to keep many children in foster care who would not be there if their mothers were not abused. New York City spends $71.5 million annually on foster care benefits, which average $13,600 per child per year, for the 40 percent of its children who would be home if their mothers were not abused, plus all of the costs of the child protective service agencies involved.

Like the medical profession, employers have been very slow to recognize how domestic violence affects the workplace. Yet an occupational impact study done on the 69.5 percent of Tulsa, Oklahoma, shelter residents who were employed when they were abused found that 96 percent of them experienced problems at work from their abusers. Over half of their abusers frequently harassed them on the telephone at work, expressing jealousy of male coworkers. Over half of the women missed work, had trouble performing their jobs, were reprimanded, or received low job performance evaluations because of the abuse. New York and Minnesota studies have found that abusive husbands and lovers harass in such a manner 74 percent of employed battered women at work, so that each year 54 percent of them miss work at least 18 days, 56 percent are late for work at least 60 days, 28 percent leave early at least 60 days, and 20 percent lose their jobs altogether. Seventy-five percent of working battered women must also use company time to call doctors, lawyers, shelters, counselors, family, and friends because they cannot do so at home. All of these costs to their employers amount to at least $13 billion annually. A far more conservative Bureau of National Affairs estimate concluded that employers spend only from $3 billion to $5 billion each year in lost work time, increased health care costs, higher turnover, and lower productivity.* * *

Law enforcement constitutes another big cost of domestic violence. Domestic violence calls are the largest category of calls to police each year. One-third of all police time is spent responding to domestic disturbance calls. The New York City Police Department made 12,724 domestic violence arrests in 1989 at an average cost of $3,241 per arrest. Although the cost of indigent defense attorneys was not included, the city had paid at least $41 million in police, court, and detention time arising from these arrests.

Of course, not all reported intimate partner incidents result in arrest; indeed, only about 10 percent of spouses who are abused ever call the police, and 47 percent [of] the female victims are abused more than three times a year. Also, a son who sees his mother beaten is more likely to become a delinquent or a batterer himself than if his father beat him instead. Children who see their mothers abused are six times more likely to commit suicide and 24 times more likely to assault someone sexually than children who grow up in nonviolent homes. Sixty-three percent of all males in America between the ages of 11 and 20 who are serving time for homicide are incarcerated because they killed their mother's abuser. All of these secondary effects of domestic violence further inflate the country's criminal justice costs.

Amazingly, our institutions continue to treat domestic violence as an essentially "private" problem involving only the perpetrator and his victim. While it is true that the victim bears the greatest price for the abuse (many batterers cause their victims enormous further expense by stealing their money, welfare checks, and food stamps; and by destroying, damaging, or selling their clothing, furniture, household belongings, and their home), much of the cost is borne by society at large. Our institutions have hardly begun the task of reducing and eliminating what is ultimately a shared public and preventable burden or, even, of holding each abuser accountable for what he has done. Instead of trying to examine what society needs to do to eliminate the abuse of women, we have largely left each victim to solve her own problem.

II. Nature And Frequency Of Domestic Violence

Until recently, domestic violence, although unstudied, was believed to be an exceedingly rare phenomenon. Indeed, in 1972, only five social science papers were written on the topic—papers based on major misconceptions about spousal abuse that have continued to confuse people's thinking about the subject up to the present. Those papers were based on studies of battered women in mental hospitals, whom the authors wrongly believed had provoked their husbands' abuse. From those few women, it was assumed that all battered women had major pathologies. We now know that battered women have no profile and that they do not differ from nonbattered women until after they have been abused. Thus, the sole determinant of whether a woman will be battered depends upon who her partner is: whether he is a batterer. Being female is her greatest predictor of being abused. Even the early statistics suggesting that her chance of being abused later in life depended upon her exposure to family violence while growing up proved wrong because it failed to realize how very common family violence actually is. Many of these early misconceptions have contributed to our persistence in asking why battered women do not leave their abusers instead of why men batter them. Most battered women do not leave because they have no housing, child care, or money, and they justifiably fear retaliation against themselves and their children if they leave.

In contrast to the victims, men who batter were believed to be normal. Nevertheless, there has been some indication recently in psychological literature that far more batterers (although not all of them) have psychopathologies, which may be both a risk factor for abusiveness and a factor that makes treatment for their violence harder.

In any year in America, more women are abused by their husbands than get married. Over the course of their marriages, more than one quarter, perhaps as many as half, of all couples experience at least one incidence of domestic violence. Overall, four million women in the United States are beaten annually, with women in dating relationships beaten about as often as married women, and cohabiting women even more often victimized. However, the most frequently and seriously battered women are those who are separated or divorced from their partners; although they comprise only 10 percent of all women, they account for 75 percent of all battered women and are 14 times more likely to be battered than women still cohabiting. Half of these women—two million in all—are severely beaten. Weapons are used in 30 percent of domestic-violence incidents.

The injuries that all battered women receive are at least as severe as those suffered in 90 percent of violent felonies, although the overwhelming number of domestic-violence injuries is considered to be only misdemeanors in most states. Conjugal assaults, although they account for only 5 percent of all reported assaults in the United States, account for 12 percent of all assaults that result in serious injury, 16 percent of assaults requiring medical care, and 18 percent of assaults that result in loss of at least a full day of work. Women are more than ten times more likely to be victimized by their intimate partners than men.

Virtually no difference exists between the rates of violence that husbands and lovers inflict on white women and those inflicted on black women. Rates of intimate partner violence hardly differ on the basis of whether the woman lives in a central city, a suburban area, or in a rural area. But the rate of intimate partner abuse for women college graduates is less than half the rate for women with less education. Women making less than $10,000 were five times more likely to experience violence from an intimate partner than those with family incomes over $30,000, and seven and one-fourth times more likely than those with family incomes above $50,000. Women are more than twice as likely to be injured in an assault by an intimate partner than by an assault by a stranger (59 versus 27 percent). While almost six times as many women victimized by intimate partners as those victimized by strangers (18 percent versus 3 percent) did not report the incident to the police, police responded to just over three-fourths of female victimization calls without regard to the identity of the victimizer. But police responded much faster when the assailant was a stranger than when he was an intimate partner, and they were more likely to search the scene for evidence if the victim had been victimized by a stranger. Although women were as likely to try to protect themselves against intimates as against strangers, more women felt that their protective efforts helped them if their assailant was a stranger than if he was an intimate (70 percent versus 61 percent), with almost a quarter of the women feeling that their self-protective measures had made their situation worse.

In this country, 31.5 percent of women killed—three women per day—are murdered by their husbands. Almost three out of four women killed in America are murdered by current or former husbands or lovers, usually when they were trying to leave or had already left. Women murdered by intimate partners frequently experienced prolonged, brutal deaths after years of violence. A study of homicides in Philadelphia found that one-fourth of the women killed died by means of her killer's hands, fists, and feet. At least 64 percent of women killed by intimate partners were known by the police to have been physically abused by their partners before their deaths, and over two-thirds of the men had been known to have histories of physical brutality to others before they killed their partners.

Twenty years ago, about half of spousal homicide victims were men. Since the advent of shelters and abuse prevention laws in the 1970s, wives have killed fewer husbands so that husbands now constitute only 34 percent of spousal homicides. While women, if given options, take them instead of killing, their abuser men have not reduced their rate of killing women since the 1970s. Unlike men who murder their lovers, women are almost never sadistic when they kill their partners and only rarely kill them after they separate. Yet abusive men who kill their partners serve an average of 2–6 years for their crimes, whereas women, who kill their partners mainly in self-defense, serve an average of 15 years. Black women who kill in self-defense are twice as likely to be convicted as white women for the same crime.

MARTHA R. MAHONEY, LEGAL IMAGES OF BATTERED WOMEN: REDEFINING THE ISSUE OF SEPARATION

90 Mich. L. Rev. 1, 2–10, 71–79, 93–94 (1991).

INTRODUCTION

I am writing about women's lives. Our lives, like everyone's, are lived within particular cultures that both reflect legal structures and affect legal interpretation. Focusing on domestic violence, this article describes an interrelationship between women's lives, culture, and law. This relationship is not linear (moving from women's lives to law, or from law to life) but interactive: cultural assumptions about domestic violence affect substantive law and methods of litigation in ways that in turn affect society's perceptions of women; both law and societal perceptions affect women's understanding of our own lives, relationships, and options; our lives are part of the culture that affects legal interpretation and within which further legal moves are made. Serious harm to women results from the ways in which law and culture distort our experience.

The courtroom is the theater in which the dramas of battered women have been brought to public attention. Trials like that of Francine Hughes, whose story became the book and movie The Burning Bed, create a cultural and legal spotlight that has in some ways benefited women by increasing public knowledge of the existence of domestic violence. However, the press has emphasized sensational cases that have a high level of terrorism against women and a grotesque quality of abuse. These cases come to define a cultural image of domestic violence, and the women in these cases define an image of battered women.

These images disguise the commonality of violence against women. Up to one half of all American women—and approximately two thirds of women who are separated or divorced—report having experienced physical assault in their relationships. However, litigation and judicial decision making in cases of severe violence reflect implicit or explicit assumptions that domestic violence is rare or exceptional.

For actors in the courtroom drama, the fiction that such violence is exceptional allows denial of the ways in which domestic violence has touched their own lives. Perhaps most damagingly, the fiction of exceptionality also increases the capacity of women to deny that the stories told in the publicized courtroom dramas have anything to do with our own lives. Therefore, it limits the help we may seek when we encounter trouble, the charges we are willing to file, our votes as jurors when charges have been filed by or against others, and our consciousness of the meaning of the struggles and dangers of our own experience.

Although domestic violence is important in many areas of legal doctrine, including family law and torts, the criminal justice system places the greatest pressures on cultural images of battered women. The self-defense cases in which women kill their batterers are small in number compared to the overall universe of domestic violence, yet they are highly emotionally charged as well as highly publicized. In many states, the right to expert testimony on behalf of these defendants has been won through much dedicated feminist litigation. The justification for admitting expert testimony is determined in large part by cultural perceptions of women and of battering; therefore, many points made by experts respond to just these cultural perceptions. Yet the expert testimony on battered woman syndrome and learned helplessness can interact with and perpetuate existing oppressive stereotypes of battered women.

Academic expertise on women has thus become crucial to the legal explanation of women's actions and the legal construction of women's experience. Psychological analysis, in particular, has responded to the sharp demand for explanation of women's actions in the self-defense cases. Yet the sociological and psychological literature still reflect some of the oppressive cultural heritage that has shaped legal doctrines. Even when expertise is developed by feminists who explain that women act rationally under circumstances of oppression, courts and the press often interpret feminist expert testimony through the lens of cultural stereotypes, retelling a simpler vision of women as victims too helpless or dysfunctional to pursue a reasonable course of action. These retold stories affect other areas of law, such as custody cases, which share the problems of professional evaluation of women and the incorporation of cultural stereotypes. The portrait of battered women as pathologically weak—the court's version of what feminists have told them—therefore holds particular dangers for battered women with children.

Legal pressures thus distort perceptions of violence in ways that create real problems for women. Many of us cannot recognize our experience in the cultural picture that develops under the influence of legal processes. The consequence is that we understand ourselves less, our society less, and our oppression less, as our capacity to identify with battered women diminishes ("I'm not like that"). Before the feminist activism of the early 1970s brought battering to public attention, society generally denied that domestic violence existed. Now, culturally, we know what it is, and we are sure it is not us.

Recent feminist work on battering points to the struggle for power and control—the batterer's quest for control of the woman—as the heart of the battering process. Case law and the popular consciousness that grows from it have submerged the question of control by psychologizing the recipient of the violence or by equating women's experience of violence with men's experience. We urgently need to develop legal and social explanations of women's experience that illuminate the issue of violence as part of the issue of power, rather than perpetuating or exacerbating the images that now conceal questions of domination and control.

As one example of a strategic effort to change both law and culture, this article proposes that we seek to redefine in both law and popular culture the issue of women's separation from violent relationships. The question "why didn't she leave?" shapes both social and legal inquiry on battering; much of the legal reliance on academic expertise on battered women has developed in order to address this question. At the moment of separation or attempted separation—for many women, the first encounter with the authority of law—the batterer's quest for control often becomes most acutely violent and potentially lethal. Ironically, although the proliferation of shelters and the elaboration of statutory structures facilitating the grant of protective orders vividly demonstrate both socially and legally the dangers attendant on separation, a woman's "failure" to permanently separate from a violent relationship is still widely held to be mysterious and in need of explanation, an indicator of her pathology rather than her batterer's. We have had neither cultural names nor legal doctrines specifically tailored to the particular assault on a woman's body and volition that seeks to block her from leaving, retaliate for her departure, or forcibly end the separation. I propose that we name this attack "separation assault."

Separation assault is the common though invisible thread that unites the equal protection suits on enforcement of temporary restraining orders, the cases with dead women that appear in many doctrinal categories, and the cases with dead men—the self-defense cases. As with other assaults on women that were not cognizable until the feminist movement named and explained them, separation assault must be identified before women can recognize our own experience and before we can develop legal rules to deal with this particular sort of violence. Naming one particular aspect of the violence then illuminates the rest: for example, the very concept of "acquaintance rape" moves consciousness away from the stereotype of rape (assault by a stranger) and toward a focus on the woman's volition (violation of her will, "consent"). Similarly, by emphasizing the urgent control moves that seek to prevent the woman from ending the relationship, the concept of separation assault raises questions that inevitably focus additional attention on the ongoing struggle for power and control in the relationship.

Because of the interactive relationships between law and culture in this area, law reform requires such an approach to simultaneously reshape cultural understanding. Separation assault is particularly easy to grasp because it responds to prevailing cultural and legal inquiry ("why didn't she leave") with a twist emphasizing the batterer's violent quest for control. However, meaningful change requires rethinking the entire relationship of law and culture in the field of domestic violence and developing many approaches to revealing power and control. Otherwise, since separation assault is so resonant with existing cultural stereotypes, it may be understood as justifying or excusing the woman's failure to leave rather than challenging and reshaping legal and social attitudes that now place this burden on the woman.

To illustrate the contrast between women's lives and legal and cultural stereotypes, and to accomplish a translation between women's lives and law, this article offers narratives and poems from the lives of survivors of domestic violence, and a few from the stories of non-survivors, as part of its analysis and argument.[27] Seven women's stories have come to me through their own accounts. Five of these have at some time identified themselves as battered women. Three of these women were Stanford Law School students or graduates; another was an undergraduate student at Stanford. One was an acquaintance in a support group. One is black, the rest are white. All but two were mothers when the violence occurred. Though our class backgrounds vary, only one was a highly educated professional before the battering incidents described, but several have acquired academic degrees since the marriages ended.

---

27. Conversations with women are cited several times in the footnotes of this article. * * * This citation form is deliberately chosen and consistent with the method of the article. * * * There are three reasons for my choice of citation form. The first is honesty. * * * The second reason is methodological. * * * Finally, the third reason for citing women's conversations is political: women may not have published their thoughts because of constraints on their time and effort imposed by uniquely womanly responsibilities. This article had its roots in conversations between Kim Hanson and myself, neighbors in family student housing, when I was a first-year and she a third-year law student at Stanford. Our children played together, and we talked around them over the back fence, encountering each other while hanging laundry, while carrying groceries in from the car. This work is in part the product of that shared work and thought. Since then, Kim has litigated for a major law firm, started her own firm, become known as a battered women's advocate, and remarried. She has had two more babies since we first met. I hope some day she writes her own articles. Until then, I acknowledge her thought in my work as a way of acknowledging her work as part of my own.

The other women's voices in this paper are drawn from identified published sources.

One of these stories is my own. I do not feel like a "battered woman." Really, I want to say that I am not, since the phrase conjures up an image that fails to describe either my marriage or my sense of myself. It is a difficult claim to make for several reasons: the gap between my self-perceived competence and strength and my own image of battered women, the inevitable attendant loss of my own denial of painful experience, and the certainty that the listener cannot hear such a claim without filtering it through a variety of derogatory stereotypes. However, the definitions of battered women have broad contours, at least some of which encompass my experience and the experiences of the other strong, capable women whose stories are included here.

In fact, women often emphasize that they do not fit their own stereotypes of the battered woman:

> The first thing I would tell you is that very little happened. I am not one of those women who stayed and stayed to be beaten. It is very important to me not to be mistaken for one of them, I wouldn't take it. Besides, I never wanted to be the one who tells you what it was really like.

The rejection of stereotypes, the fear of being identified with these stereotypes, is expressed by lesbian women as well as heterosexual women:

> First I want you to know that I am an assertive and powerful woman. I do not fit my stereotype of a battered woman. I am telling you this because I never thought it could happen to me. Most lesbians I know who have been battered impress me with their presence and strength. None of them fit my stereotype. Do not think that what happened to me could not happen to you.

Although there is relatively little published material on lesbian battering, this literature can shed light on the ways in which we conceptualize the battering process. Although lesbian battering is similar to heterosexual battering, the analysis of lesbian battering is unique in two ways that are significant for this paper: it has been generated entirely by feminist activists, and it has developed in isolation from the legal system. Therefore, it provides one clue to the question, "[W]hat would this ... landscape look like if women had constructed it for ourselves?"

Part I of this article discusses violence in the ordinary lives of women, describing individual and societal denial that pretends domestic violence is rare when statistics show it is common, and describing the ways in which motherhood shapes women's experience of violence and choices in response to violence. Part II examines definitions of battering and evaluates their effectiveness at disguising or revealing the struggle for control at the heart of the battering process. I then describe in Part III the pressures that self-defense and custody cases place on legal and cultural images of battered women and contrast the development of an analysis of lesbian battering, an analysis generated outside the legal system. In Part IV, I discuss battering as a struggle for power and control and show how legal analysis can help reveal the control issue by naming separation assault and building litigation strategies to redefine the issue of separation. Finally, in Part V, I identify separation assault in the cases where women have been killed or harmed, as well as cases in which women killed in self-defense, and explain how the concept of separation assault is consistent with the particular needs of expert testimony in the self-defense cases. I demonstrate how naming separation assault can intervene in the inter-relationship between law and culture in the field of domestic violence to change both the questions asked and the answers found by courts in several areas of law.

* * *

V.   The Uses of A Name: Separation Assault and Legal Doctrine

Naming separation assault is an attempt to use a social definition, a cultural concept, to resolve doctrinal problems in law. It should not articulate a new test for women's behavior ("did this woman in fact leave and how shall we judge the energy with which she attempted separation?") but rather promote a new understanding of violence against women. As it intervenes in cultural consciousness, separation assault allows legal actors (including attorneys, prosecutors, judges, jurors, social workers, and legal scholars) to reconceive many legal questions that depend on an understanding of women's lives and experiences. Our understanding of "objective" reasonableness depends on our cultural intuitions about normal experience and normal response. By reflecting a consciousness of power and control, and by emphasizing the dangers attendant on separation, separation assault helps make women's experience comprehensible in law.

In the following sections, I show how separation assault can be identified in cases in many areas of legal doctrine, and then explain how understanding separation assault can help resolve troubled areas in law. My review of the cases and doctrines is necessarily partial and suggestive, rather than comprehensive. It is a beginning. It is intended both to invite more discussion of the ways in which litigation can help expose in both law and culture the power and control at the heart of battering, and to invite further analysis of the particular dangers to women at separation.

A.   *Recognizing Separation Assault in the Cases:*
The Problem of the Dead Woman's Voice

There is a two-layered problem in seeing through the criminal cases involving abuse of women. First, these cases appear in various doctrinal guises, and few explicitly acknowledge that they concern domestic violence at all. Second, on closer examination, many of the "wife-murder" cases turn out to be "ex-wife murder," the most extreme violence turned against women at separation. Many of the women killed by their husbands are killed after they have separated. Ironically, since those women are not alive to tell their stories, their voices disappear into the narrative voices of the courts, where the women are not usually identified as battered:

> On a day in early September in 1977, the petitioner and his wife of 28 years had a heated argument in their home. During the course of this altercation, the petitioner, who had consumed several cans of beer, threatened his wife with a knife and damaged some of her clothing. At this point, the petitioner's wife declared that she was going to leave him, and departed to stay with relatives. This was not the first time that he and his wife had been separated as a result of his violent behavior. That afternoon she went to a justice of the peace and secured a warrant charging the petitioner with aggravated assault. A few days later, while still living away from home, she filed suit for divorce. A court hearing date was set and several efforts to persuade the wife to return home were rebuffed. At some point during this period, his wife moved in with her mother.... several angry phone calls were exchanged, while she refused to reconcile.
>
> At this juncture, the petitioner got out his shotgun and walked with it down the hill from his home to the trailer where his mother-in-law lived. Peering through a window, he observed his wife, his mother-in-law, and his 11–year-old daughter playing a card game. He pointed the shotgun at his wife through the window and pulled the trigger. The charge from the gun struck his wife in the forehead and killed her instantly. He proceeded into the trailer, striking and injuring his fleeing daughter with the barrel of the gun. He then fired the gun at his mother-in-law, striking her in the head and killing her instantly.[310]

Godfrey v. Georgia presents an almost perfect picture of the dangers for women at separation: Mrs. Godfrey had resolutely separated from her husband and energetically sought the protection of the law. However, her story does not enter the criminal law casebook as a domestic violence case. Rather, Godfrey is a death penalty case presenting the issue of whether this murder was unambiguously "outrageously or wantonly vile, horrible or inhuman," or whether the case revealed ambiguity and vagueness in the death penalty statute. The Supreme Court essentially found Mrs. Godfrey's death to be quite an ordinary murder. I believe the majority was correct—this was an ordinary murder—but the facts were even more ordinary than the majority realized.

Mary McNeill has shown that several torts cases on duty are actually domestic violence cases in disguise. However, once the domestic violence is perceived, separation assault appears to be a further hidden issue in at least one of the cases. In *Jablonski by Pahls v. United*

310. Godfrey v. Georgia, 446 U.S. 420, 424–25 (1980).

States,[315] Melinda Kimball had repeatedly approached the psychologists who examined the man she lived with, telling his doctors that she was afraid of him. They failed to commit him or to seek his medical records, which would have revealed that he had ten years earlier been diagnosed as schizophrenic and had then had homicidal ideas about his wife. One doctor told Kimball that she should avoid Jablonski if she feared him. Kimball left after a priest also urged her to separate from Jablonski. She was murdered when she returned to the apartment to pick up some baby diapers. Since there is no record of any attempt to kill her before she left, separation appears to be at least a precipitating factor in Kimball's death.

In *Garcia v. Superior Court,* Grace Morales was killed by Napoleon Johnson, Jr., the man from whom she had recently separated.[319] According to the complaint, Johnson's parole officer was aware that Johnson had killed his first wife after she left him. Although he was notified that Johnson had threatened to kill Morales and that Morales was filing a temporary restraining order, the parole officer advised Morales that Johnson would not come looking for her. Johnson kidnapped Morales and killed her; her children sued. The court distinguished the parole officer's "negligent representations" from a failure to warn for which the officer might have been liable under *Tarasoff v. Regents of the University of California,*[323] and held that the plaintiffs must allege that Morales reasonably relied on the parole officer's advice.

The California case of *People v. Berry,* doctrinally significant for its holding on cooling off periods when killers claim provocation by their victims, also concerns a hidden separation assault.[325] The only account of the marriage is the one Berry gave the police and at trial. According to Berry's story, his wife, Rachel Pessah, had gone to Israel within days of their marriage; on her return, she taunted him about her love for another man and her plans to leave Berry. After repeated arguments and threats or attempts to separate, he tried to strangle her. He called a cab to take her to a hospital, and she later filed a police report that resulted in a warrant for his arrest. He told her he was leaving their home and going to stay with a friend. Two days later, he returned to the apartment and waited overnight. She returned the next day and said she supposed he had come to kill her. He was indecisive, but said he had. She screamed. He strangled her.

Even feminist literature on battering may overlook the particularity of attacks on women's autonomy. For example, the feminist newsletter *Response* cites the 1988 case of *Balistreri v. Pacifica Police Department*[330] in a short article entitled "Court Rules in Favor of Abused Wife." The one-paragraph article describes Balistreri

315. 712 F.2d 391 (9th Cir.1983).

319. 789 P.2d 960, 961–62 (Cal.1990).

323. 551 P.2d 334 (Cal.1976), distinguished in Garcia, 789 P.2d at 963.

325. 556 P.2d 777 (Cal.1976).

330. 855 F.2d 1421 (9th Cir.1988), amended on other grounds, 901 F.2d 696 (9th Cir.1988).

As an abused wife who sued police for not protecting her. . . . Police had refused to arrest the batterer when summoned following a beating, failed to offer medical assistance, and did not protect the woman over a 3–year period during which she reported incidents to police and obtained a restraining order.

Most of the facts of *Balistreri* concern attacks after separation. When Balistreri's husband beat her severely in February 1982, officers failed to help her. She divorced her husband—apparently promptly, because "throughout 1982" she complained to police of vandalism and harassing phone calls by the husband "from whom she was now divorced." In November that year, her "former husband" crashed his car into her garage, and in March 1983, a firebomb was thrown through the window of her house. From 1983 to 1985, telephone harassment and vandalism continued. Balistreri emerges as a woman of great strength—resisting her ex-husband's repeated attacks and pursuing her complaint within the legal system when her lawyer would go no further. "Abused wife," the term used by *Response*, captures neither her determined resistance nor her separation as the keys to the repeated violence she suffered.

B. *Recognizing the Danger to Women at Separation*

Recognizing the assault on separation can help disentangle a number of complex legal issues in cases in which women have been killed or harmed. In some areas of substantive law, identifying separation assault will change the questions posed by the court in its decision making process. In other doctrinal areas, the shift in time frame made possible by highlighting the assault on separation can change judicial comprehension of the assault on the woman or of the probability that more assaults may occur. Separation assault may also, as in contested custody actions, help reveal underlying motivations in the legal action itself.

Restraining Orders: In some jurisdictions, when women seek orders of protection against violent men, courts routinely grant mutual orders of protection rather than orders specifically protecting the women. Mutual orders of protection direct each party not to assault, endanger, or threaten the other. If mutual orders are violated, police officers believe they must either arrest both parties or do nothing. The New York Task Force on Women in the Courts concluded that a woman with a mutual order of protection is in a worse position than a woman with no order at all, since the mutual order makes her look equally violent in the eyes of the courts, and the husband may not be held responsible if there is another violent incident. Also, it may be harder for her to obtain a more restrictive order if the violence recurs. The Task Force concluded that this was particularly dangerous if the mutual order was granted when the woman had requested protection for herself at the same time she filed an action to end the marriage—an especially dangerous period. Even in jurisdictions that do not routinely grant mutual orders, battering men may make cross-accusations of violence against battered women. While many battered women do fight back against their husbands, their violence is largely defensive and less severe than the men's violence—yet since it is also described as "violence," these allegations can prove troubling and confusing to judges.

If we understood better the particular attacks women face at separation, courts could sort both cross-accusations of violence and requests for mutual orders of protection by examining the nature of current threats and the history of violence in relation to the issue of separation. The question then becomes: "Which of these people needs her [or his] capacity to separate protected?" Answering this question will help sort the dangers and should result in the grant of appropriate protective orders.

Duty to Warn: Recognizing the common occurrence of separation assault may also clarify professionals' duty to warn potential victims. For example, the *Jablonski* court upheld the district court's finding that the psychiatrists committed malpractice in failing to get Jablonski's records and failing to warn Kimball of his potential for violence. Applying the concept of separation assault does not disturb this holding. Her foreseeability as a victim would be even clearer. However, the clergyman and doctors who advised Kimball to leave Jablonski might also have had a duty to warn her about extra care to be exercised in separating from a homicidal man, as well as a duty to warn her of his dangerousness.

In *Garcia v. Superior Court*, Johnson's murder of his first wife was a separation assault of exactly the type that Johnson had threatened against Morales. The parole officer misrepresented Johnson's danger to Morales with respect to the very issue of measures regarding separation. Although the parole officer was legally barred from telling anyone the exact crime for which Johnson had previously been imprisoned, the court fails to reckon with the implications of the outright falsehood embodied in the parole officer's statement that Johnson's prior conviction was not for anything that endangered Morales' children.

A telling quote in the *Garcia* dissent shows that judges may inappropriately assume that separation assaults will inevitably culminate in murder: the court below had concluded "it [was] highly speculative to assume that [Morales] could have accomplished any improvement in her security. The frightening reality is that for one in Morales's position there is frequently nothing she can do to protect herself." When courts rely on their own intuitions to state "truths" regarding violence against women, the dangers of cultural stereotyping are severe. A sense of the dangers of separation should have led the court to emphasize the need not to mislead Morales as to her safety and to recognize the implications of consciously identifying the assault on separation.

Custody Determinations: Understanding Dominance and Time–Framing Assault. The concept of separation assault provides insight into the difficult bargains women strike during custody determinations. Women may accept mutual orders of protection, rather than orders that specifically protect them against their batterers, in exchange for the husband's agreement not to contest custody. Courts often award joint custody to batterers, and some courts that do not perceive violence against the mother as an aspect of the custody determination may even award them sole custody. The problem is exacerbated for battered women by the professional analyses of the social workers in whom the court vests the power to evaluate women, and by the possibility that the judge will share a stereotypical, stigmatizing image of battered women.

Separation assault provides a link between past violence and current legal disputes by illuminating the custody action as part of an ongoing attempt, through physical violence and legal manipulation, to force the woman to make concessions or return to the violent partner. It reveals the potential for continuing danger from a batterer who may not have struck out physically in the recent past. Threats against the woman's separation attempts may reveal that the "domestic" violence has outlasted the marriage. Recognizing separation assault can therefore help judges understand the relevance of past violence and threats, and the relevance of the nature of present attacks, to custody cases. Also, when there is evidence of violent separation assault, a judge could give more intense scrutiny to the motives behind custody disputes and reconsider the appropriateness of joint custody awards or liberal visitation decrees. This would help diminish "legal separation assault" in custody cases. Finally, by remaking the cultural concept of separation, we may hope to affect positively the evaluation of women by the social workers in whom the legal system places so much power.

Judging the Wife–Killer: Time–Framing, Provocation, and the Nature of the Assault: In *Berry*, the defendant's arguments for a jury instruction on provocation depended entirely upon his statements that his wife had taunted him sexually and provoked her own murder. In fact, he did not kill her when she taunted him, but when she left him. Recognizing separation assault expands the relevant time frame to show his behavior was consistent with numerous prior assaults that seem at least as responsive to her departure as to sexual provocation. He had violently assaulted his first wife as well. *Berry* is cited for its holding that twenty hours of waiting in the apartment—some days after his wife's last "provocative" conduct—was not as a matter of law too long a period to permit an instruction on provocation. The court might have viewed the case differently had the assault on separation been as cognizable as his response to her alleged sexual taunts: it is difficult to find "heat-of-passion" in a repeatedly attempted assault carried out over a period of time.

A short time frame favors men in these cases, as it does in many types of cases, by removing violence from a context of power and struggle. Prior attacks on the woman's attempts to separate may essentially be rehearsals for the final killing. Alternatively, the long-term assault on her separation may be perceived as one ongoing attack. If only the final, deadly assault is cognizable, the nature of the assault as an attack on separation, rather than on the woman's sexual provocation, may remain disguised. Separation assault can therefore change the time frame within which the man's mental state is to be evaluated by changing the perception of the ways in which the woman's autonomy is under attack.

* * *

CONCLUSION

Violence is a way of "doing power" in a relationship; battering is power and control marked by violence and coercion. A battered woman is a woman who experiences the violence against her as determining or controlling her thoughts, emotions, or actions, including her efforts to cope with the violence itself. Many, many women experience such violence in our society. The precise response of any woman is likely to be determined by her life circumstances and family situation.

We should know this. Nothing in the preceding paragraph should make women ashamed of being battered. However, the interrelationship among cultural images, legal images, litigation, and substantive law has made it difficult for women to understand our experience of violence. The stereotypical image of a battered woman—dysfunctional, helpless, dependent—is alien to the self-image and self-knowledge of most women who encounter violence from our partners. Attempts to counter these stereotypes have interacted with other contemporary social and legal developments: each block of legal reform (such as the development of expert testimony on battered women) has interacted with the rest of the legal structure (such as the advent of no-fault divorce, or the evidentiary rules governing the admission of expert testimony) to pose continued difficulties in recognizing women's experience in law.

These reciprocal, mutually reinforcing forces of popular perception, law, and litigation have made it difficult for women to identify ourselves and our experience as part of a continuum of power and domination affecting most women's lives. The challenge is to identify legal and social strategies that will allow us to change law and culture simultaneously, by illuminating the context of power and control within which a woman lives and acts. Naming separation assault can help reveal the overall struggle for power that is the heart of the battering process: it describes a particularly dangerous attack hitherto hidden in the phrase "domestic violence," emphasizes the assault on the woman's autonomy and volition, and offers insights that can help resolve several troubled areas of law. This intervention is both legal and cultural, a way to rewrite legal doctrine by changing the way we understand the questions and categories involved.

I offer the theory of separation assault as part of a feminist approach to law reform in this area: working from women's experience, we must develop legal and cultural strategies that more clearly reveal the struggles we face. We need many such interventions. The key to more widespread change lies in the way transformed legal and social images of women will in turn affect women's experience and understanding of our lives, allowing women to recognize our experience as part of a larger system of subordination so that we can structure our understanding of our needs in relation to those of other women facing oppression. Women's recognition of our own oppression has been slowed by the images that law has helped create. As we come to recognize our experiences as oppression, rather than personal insufficiency, weakness, or "unhappiness" in marriage—for example, recognizing separation assault rather than "failure" to leave a relationship—we will be better able to address the dangers we face and realize our individual and collective capacity for change.

DEBORAH EPSTEIN, REDEFINING THE STATE'S RESPONSE TO DOMESTIC VIOLENCE: PAST VICTORIES AND FUTURE CHALLENGES

1 Georgetown J. of Gender and the Law 127–143 (1999).

INTRODUCTION

What role should the state play in the fight against domestic violence? Although most activists in the early domestic abuse movement viewed government institutions with a robust dose of suspicion, over time they began to look to the state for substantial assistance. During this period—the late sixties and seventies—increased hope for a positive governmental role appeared to be well-founded. The civil rights, feminist, and labor movements had pushed the federal government into expanding civil liberty guarantees and economic protections. Laws were enacted prohibiting sex-and race-based discrimination, health care got a strong boost through the creation of Medicaid and Medicare, and workplace safety guarantees were expanded. And in the seventies and eighties, on the domestic violence front, state legislatures enacted civil protection order statutes that were the first laws specifically designed to protect victims of intimate abuse.

As legislatures moved ahead in establishing civil rights for women—and battered women in particular—activists focused on the corresponding need for a strong legislative and executive response from the criminal justice system. They called upon the state to mandate improved police response to domestic violence calls, to form special prosecutorial units dedicated to pursuing these cases, and to "treat domestic violence like any other crime." Government actors have responded and are now beginning to improve their records in imposing criminal sanctions in family abuse cases.

But as the state escalates its response to domestic violence, activists need to reassess their dependence on and trust in state power. Criminal prosecutions of batterers are occurring despite victim opposition and without regard to victims' wishes about the future of their families. Survivors who decline to testify voluntarily are being compelled to do so by subpoena, even when their testimony could result in a retaliatory assault. And battered women who have relied on a government safety net for survival are now being pushed off the welfare rolls, pressured to find jobs that often do not exist, and threatened with sanctions for failing to comply with these requirements.

This essay seeks to renew the energy of the domestic violence movement by taking stock of the significant victories that have been achieved in improving the state's response to family abuse over the past thirty years. It then encourages activists concerned about victims' rights to identify strategies to reduce the movement's profound dependence on state action and meet the critical challenges ahead. We can begin by working within the private sector to increase social support for victims and to strengthen their residential and economic communities. Such changes could reduce family violence and lessen the need for state intervention. But even if such efforts are successful, there will always be a need for government action in some cases. Activists, therefore, must find ways to strengthen the victim's role in the context of an exercise of state power. They must ensure that the government obtains the information necessary to permit and encourage a response that honors a survivor's personal view of the best course for herself and her family.

In addition, activists need to focus on the largely neglected third branch of the state—the judiciary. While legislatures and executives have responded strongly to the problem of intimate abuse, most judges lack formal education in the field and find it difficult to sympathize with victims who frequently return to their abusive partners. Judicial failure to understand the dynamics of intimate violence often results in hostile treatment of litigants and a refusal to award the full range of protections to which victims are entitled. If movement activists can find ways to train judges and improve the justice system's response to the special problems created by family abuse cases, victims will be far better served by the laws that exist on the books.

I. Recent Victories in Redefining The State's Response to Domestic Violence

The United States' battered women's movement grew out of the broader feminist movement of the late 1960s and early 1970s. During that period, activists perceived violence against women as integrally linked to gender inequality and viewed the political and legal establishment with suspicion, maintaining that it perpetuated institutional forms of sexism. This perception led the movement to focus initially outside of the governmental sphere, on the establishment of shelters, empowerment groups, and community education workshops.

This distrust of the state was a natural consequence of a long history of the American legal system's approval of and complicity in violence against women. From the early colonial period onward, American courts followed British common law by affirming the husband's right of domestic chastisement. In the words of the Mississippi Supreme Court, this rule allowed a husband to "use salutary restraints in every case of a [wife's] misbehavior, without being subjected to vexatious prosecutions, resulting in the mutual discredit and shame of all parties concerned."[5]

It was not until the late nineteenth century that states finally began to move away from actually condoning a husband's use of physical force to discipline his wife. But many still clung to the position that in the absence of "serious" violence, the government should not interfere in the private, family realm. As late as 1873, the North Carolina Supreme Court stated: "if no permanent injury has been inflicted, nor malice, cruelty nor dangerous violence shown by the husband, it is better to draw the curtain, shut out the public gaze, and leave the parties to forget and forgive."[7] This view prevailed in most states well into the twentieth century.

Given this history, it comes as no surprise that the domestic violence movement began by refusing to work cooperatively with the state. But gradually, as the enormity of the problem of intimate abuse became clear, feminist activists realized that government resources could be an essential component of an effective solution. Movement strategy shifted to a push for increased legislative and executive involvement, at first through civil protection order legislation and later through mandatory arrest laws and no-drop prosecution policies.

Despite numerous frustrations and failures over the past thirty years, the domestic violence movement has made enormous strides. The country has moved from a time when no term for intimate abuse existed in the national lexicon to an era of substantial public awareness and political will to intervene. Every jurisdiction has now enacted civil protection order legislation, and the vast majority of these statutes authorize the essential relief necessary for battered women to leave abusive relationships. These "basics" include provisions for emergency *ex parte* relief, so that victims have court-ordered protection during the potentially volatile period between the time of filing a lawsuit and trial. This is the period when the abusive partner is served with court papers demonstrating the victim's intent to leave him which often triggers a particularly severe "separation assault."

Modern laws governing civil protection orders also authorize fairly comprehensive post-trial relief. In addition to the basic provisions requiring the abuser to cease his assaults and stay away from the victim, these orders may award temporary child custody, safe visitation arrangements for the non-custodial parent, and child support. Rapid resolution of these latter issues is critical, because one of the primary reasons that victims return to their abusive partners is the pressure created by the loss of economic support. For a woman with children, a child support award may be the key to freedom. Similarly, because the potential for renewed violence is greatest during visitation, carefully structured pick-up and drop-off provisions, designed to eliminate victim-perpetrator contact, also can have a significant prophylactic effect.

5. Bradley v. State, 1 Miss. (1 Walker) 156, 157 (1824) * * *

7. State v. Oliver 70 N.C. 60, 61–62 (1873) * * *

Finally, thirty-four states have adopted criminal contempt laws to help enforce protection orders, and forty-five jurisdictions have made violating a protection order a statutory crime. Effective enforcement is essential to ensure meaningful compliance; otherwise, a civil protection order becomes no more than a piece of paper that a batterer can, and often will, ignore with impunity. As one study of the civil protection order process concluded, "[E]nforcement is the Achilles' heel of the ... process, because an order without enforcement at best offers scant protection and at worst increases the victim's danger by creating a false sense of security."[17]

The federal government has taken action as well. In 1994, Congress enacted the Violence Against Women Act (VAWA), and the "daughter of VAWA" is currently pending in Congress. Among other things, these laws condition state receipt of sizable federal funding on the creation of systems that (1) ensure that protection orders are given full faith and credit by all sister states, (2) provide government assistance with service of process in protection order cases, and (3) criminalize violations of protection orders. Although the specifics of protection order legislation vary from state to state and gaps in coverage for battered women certainly remain, legislation is no longer an obstacle, but a source of hope. Enormous legal strides have been made in a relatively short period of time.

The responsiveness of the criminal justice system also has improved. Although increased criminalization has become controversial as a strategic matter, this increase has been far more successful than most people would have thought possible ten years ago. Across the country, police are arresting offenders and prosecutors are pressing charges more frequently. Finally, intimate abuse is beginning to be treated as a problem with serious criminal implications.

II.　Future Challenges in Improving the State's Response to Domestic Abuse

Despite recent improvements in the state's response to domestic violence, crucial challenges remain. I will focus on two of them here. First, how can we improve state efforts to deter crimes of intimate abuse without undermining victims' control over their lives? Second, how can we restructure the judicial system and educate individual judges so that the intolerable failure to respond to family violence is reduced?

A.　The Complexities of Criminalizing Domestic Violence

Perhaps the most fundamental question raised by this symposium echoes a long-familiar ambivalence in feminist theory about state power: have recent efforts to increase state responsiveness resulted in an "overcriminalization" of domestic violence, with an almost automatic initiation of criminal prosecution occurring regardless of the needs and desires of the victim and her family? This question is complex, and no

---

17.　Finn & Colson, supra note 14, at 49.

snapshot examination of the current state of affairs can provide a sufficiently nuanced answer. The issue must be examined through a lens that allows consideration of the criminal justice system's relationship with the issue of intimate abuse over time.

For many years, battered women's advocates called upon police and prosecutors to treat domestic violence like any other crime. This plea was voiced in response to the state's long-standing failure to recognize any criminal dimension to family abuse. Police officers frequently ignored domestic violence calls or delayed their response to such calls by several hours. When they did respond, they were trained to mediate rather than to arrest.

The experience of the District of Columbia is typical. A study conducted in 1990 showed that the police were arresting accused batterers in only five percent of all intimate abuse cases. They failed to arrest in more than eighty-five percent of cases in which the victim had sustained serious injuries that were visible when the police arrived on the scene. Instead, police were most likely to arrest the perpetrator in situations where he insulted an officer or damaged a vehicle.

Activists across the country have used studies like this one to convince state legislatures to enact mandatory arrest laws. These statutes terminate police discretion in domestic violence cases; if probable cause exists, the officer must arrest. In Washington, D C., soon after the local mandatory arrest law went into effect, police were arresting perpetrators in forty-one percent of domestic violence calls. This jump, from five to forty-one percent, reflects a sea change for victims of family abuse. Putting the problem of unwilling victims aside for the moment, those who seek access to the criminal justice system are far more likely to succeed with the advent of mandatory arrest.

But mandatory arrest policies alone have not been sufficient. Even when presented with more domestic violence arrests, prosecutors nationwide rarely pressed charges, and when they did, they rarely followed through with the case. In the District of Columbia, for example, the charging rate was approximately fifteen percent of arrest cases, and very few of these proceeded to plea or trial. The low prosecution rates were the result of a special policy for intimate abuse cases, in which charges would be dropped at the victim's request, at any time, with no questions asked. The rationale was the belief that convictions could not be obtained without victim cooperation and testimony. Although some prosecutors recognized that batterers were pressuring victims into making the request to drop the charges, they claimed that they could not distinguish between a battered woman who was communicating her true feelings and one who had a literal or figurative gun to her head. Thus, they adopted a uniform approach and dropped charges in every case.

This "automatic drop" policy ceded to perpetrators an enormous degree of control over the criminal justice process. All a batterer had to do was coerce his victim—through violence or threats of violence—into asking the prosecutor to drop the charges; once she did so, the risk of incarceration instantly vanished.

During the 1980s and 1990s, victim advocates lobbied aggressively to change these policies, and they have finally begun making inroads in a growing number of jurisdictions. Still citing the difficulty in distinguishing between those who "really" want to drop charges and those who do not, many prosecutors have adopted "no drop" policies, pursuant to which a case proceeds regardless of the victim's wishes, as long as sufficient evidence exists to prove criminal conduct.

Early data indicate that these no-drop policies yield substantial positive results, including the reduction of homicides. In San Diego, for example, officials found that under the old policy levels of violence increased when abusers learned that a case would be dismissed if the victim refused to cooperate. In 1985, however, the city implemented a no-drop policy and domestic homicides fell from thirty in 1985, to twenty in 1990, to seven in 1994. No-drop policies also appear to lower recidivism and strengthen the message that intimate abuse will not be tolerated.

After years of community pressure in the District of Columbia, the U.S. Attorney's Office finally adopted an aggressive approach to prosecution, including a no-drop policy. Prosecutors assigned to the newly-created Domestic Violence Unit view intimate violence as a crime against the state and seek to vindicate the government's interests regardless of the individual victim's wishes. Perpetrators no longer are able to manipulate the system by coercing the victim into dropping the charges; control has been shifted from the perpetrator to the government.

As in San Diego, D.C.'s no drop-policy led to a radical shift in domestic violence prosecutions. In 1989, the office prosecuted approximately five misdemeanor cases out of 19,000 family abuse calls to 911 emergency services. From 1996–1997, the first year of the new regime, the Domestic Violence Unit filed approximately 6,000 misdemeanor cases. The statistics for the following year are closer to 8,000. An even more telling statistic is that the Unit now presses charges in approximately sixty-seven percent of arrest cases, precisely the same rate as in stranger violence arrests. Similarly, the conviction rate in domestic violence cases now closely approximates that in other misdemeanor non-jury trials in the District of Columbia, ranging between sixty-five and sixty-seven percent.

Mandatory arrest laws and no-drop prosecution policies have moved domestic violence criminal prosecutions to a position of rough parity with crimes perpetrated by non-intimates, and have expanded greatly the tools available to battered women seeking to escape abuse. In addition, these forms of targeted criminal legislation carry a degree of symbolic power and moral authority for which civil rulings can offer no real equivalent. The concept of treating family abuse "like any other crime" is finally within reach.

But by embracing the state as an ally, victims find themselves seeking redress from a criminal justice system that can perpetuate the kinds of power and control dynamics that exist in the battering relationship itself. In many cases, prosecutors take complete control over the case, functioning as the sole decision-maker and ignoring the victim's voice, wishes, and ideas. If a victim changes her mind mid-way through the litigation and seeks to drop charges so that the father of her children can continue to work and provide financial support, a prosecutor may refuse to do so, on the ground that this would not serve the interests of the state in punishing violations of the social contract. Such revictimization can thwart the survivor's efforts to regain control over her life and move past the abusive experience.

Increased intervention by the criminal justice system has been particularly problematic for many subgroups of victims, in particular immigrant populations and racial minorities. For example, recent reforms in United States immigration laws create strong disincentives for immigrant women to press criminal charges against their batterers. The new laws dictate that an immigrant convicted of a domestic violence offense, stalking, or a protection order violation becomes deportable, even if he has previously obtained lawful permanent resident status. Many women are reluctant to expose their partners to the risk of deportation, and be ostracized from their communities for doing so, particularly if the perpetrator might be subjected to political persecution if forced to return to his home country. Deportation of a batterer also may adversely affect the victim's own petition for legal residency.

Similarly, women of color often choose to remain silent about abuse. Kimberle Crenshaw, whose writing explores the "intersectionality" of experiences of racism and sexism on battered women of color, argues:

> Women of color are often reluctant to call the police, a hesitancy likely due to a general unwillingness among people of color to subject their private lives to the scrutiny and control of a police force that is frequently hostile. There is also a more generalized community ethic against public intervention, the product of a desire to create a private world free from the diverse assaults on the public lives of racially subordinated people. The home is not simply a man's castle in patriarchal sense, but may also function as a safe haven from the indignities of life in a racist society.[53]

In an extensive focus group study in New York, African American participants expressed the view that reporting batterers to the police was a breach of loyalty, since such reporting could further contribute to the social stereotyping of black men as particularly violent.[54] In one woman's words, "the ideas behind ... how Black boys are feared by White people,

---

53. Kimberle Crenshaw, Mapping the Margins: Intersectionality, Identity Politics, and Violence Against Women of Color, 43 Stan. L. Rev. 1241, 1257 (1991).

54. See Violence in the Lives of African American Women, supra note 50, at 18–19;

see also Beth Richie, Battered Black Women: A Challenge for the Black Community, The Black Scholar, March–April 1985, at 40, 43–44.

and how police beat Black men ... it's a bad time to be Black and it's an even worse time to talk about the problems we face in our community."[55]

B. *Possibilities for Progress*

How can we find a satisfactory way to enhance deterrence of intimate abuse while adequately protecting the safety and autonomy of individual victims and reducing their reliance on historically discriminatory state institutions? A promising development is the extensive common ground between two symposium speakers who ultimately reach opposite conclusions: Robert Spagnoletti, Chief of the D.C. U.S. Attorney's Office Domestic Violence Unit and a strong supporter of mandatory arrest and no-drop prosecution, and Professor Linda Mills, known for her empathic, victim-centered work and opposition to increased criminalization. Mr. Spagnoletti explains that he adopted a no-drop prosecution policy because he found it impossible to distinguish between victims who genuinely wished to drop charges and those who were being coerced. Professor Mills claims that we can, and must, learn to make such distinctions by adopting a variety of victim-centered intervention policies. These positions differ less in principle than in rhetoric and in perspective on the availability of resources.

The common ground lies, at least in part, in an increased focus on the role that private individuals and communities can play in diminishing the incidence of violence and the need for state intervention, and in ensuring that the victim plays a greater role in those cases in which government response remains necessary. A growing body of research indicates that civil society has an important role to play here.

A recent study in East Lansing, Michigan,[59] for example, compared two groups of battered women leaving a domestic violence shelter. One was a control group; in the other, each woman was assigned a college student volunteer who served as her advocate for six hours a week, over a ten-week period. The advocates had no prior experience working in the domestic violence field, but received ten weeks of training before embarking on the project. Each student worked with a woman to help her assess her personal needs and goals, and then assisted her in obtaining limited or difficult to access community resources. These resources included housing, employment, legal assistance, transportation, child care, health care, counseling for the children, and social support.

Both groups of women were interviewed every six months for two years. Women in the advocacy group reported less physical violence—in fact, over twice as many women in the advocacy group experienced no violence whatsoever during the two-year period. These women also experienced less depression and a higher quality of life, and those who wished to end their abusive relationships were more effective in doing so. Of particular importance is the fact that women with advocates per-

---

55. Id. at 18–19.

59. See Chris Sullivan et al, Promising Findings of a Community–Based Advocacy Project for Women with Abusive Partners: Two Year–Follow–Up, J. Consulting and Clinical Psych. (forthcoming 1999).

ceived themselves as significantly more effective in obtaining community resources and assistance as well as interpersonal social support.

Similar results were reached in a study of the role of social support from family, friends, neighbors, and coworkers in determining victim follow-through in domestic violence criminal prosecutions.[68] Where "follow through" was defined as cooperating in the prosecution of a batterer (after the initial decision to press charges) by providing necessary information to prosecutors and expressing a willingness to testify, survivors able to access more interpersonal support were approximately twice as likely to cooperate voluntarily with the prosecution.

These results are quite exciting. They indicate that, in many cases, an increase in victim support from family, friends, and trained personnel can be enough to empower victims to exit the cycle of violence. Advocacy services apparently reduce some victims' dependency on the criminal justice system, by helping them find the strength to escape on their own. And for those who need prosecutorial intervention, the presence of an advocate or supporter enables them to better assert themselves in obtaining the help they need. By amplifying victims' voices, advocates can help the government better respond to individual concerns, and better discern those cases in which the survivor seeks to drop charges because of a considered decision that the course of action is best for herself, her family, and the larger community to which she belongs. Certainly, domestic violence is a crime against the state and generally should be treated as such; but victim advocates could be a key to transforming one-size-fits-all prosecution policies into responses that also are tailored to the concerns of individual women.

These studies and others like them indicate that as we work to increase state accountability for violence, we must put equivalent energy into providing individual advocates and creating communities that can provide victims more social support. In so doing, we may lessen the need for state intervention and, where such intervention is necessary, amplify victims' voices to enable the state to better respond to individual concerns.

C.　The Role of the Judicial Branch

The current debate about state accountability for intimate violence has focused primarily on the legislative and executive branches of government. Questions arise about the appropriate legislative response to domestic abuse and whether and to what extent the federal government should play a role in regulating an area traditionally left to the states. Local, regional, and national conferences are being held to discuss implementation strategies adopted by the executive branch, in the form of police department arrest protocols and prosecutorial no-drop policies. Far less attention has been paid to the possibilities offered by the third branch of government—the judiciary. A fundamental restructuring of the traditional justice system's approach to the social problem of domes-

68.　See Lisa A. Goodman et al., Obstacles Women Face in Prosecuting their Batterers: The Role of Social Support, Violence and Victims (forthcoming 1999).

tic abuse is, in my view, the critical next generation of work needed to improve the state's response.

The ability of the judicial system to deal with specialized forms of violence matters at least as much as the applicable substantive law. Improvements on the legislative front are doomed if judges continue to view these issues as private matters that do not belong in a courtroom, or actions that are not "really" criminal in nature.

Domestic violence activists have recently begun to focus on judicial reform, and the District of Columbia has been a leader in this movement. In November 1996, the District inaugurated a new, integrated Domestic Violence Court, in which a small number of trained judges are assigned to spend a year hearing civil protection order cases, prosecutions of crimes between intimates, and family law matters between parties where an active protective order is in place. Many interesting issues have grown out of this reform experiment, but one of the most important is the effort to combat a general failure of judicial neutrality in domestic violence cases.

Most judges come to the bench with no real understanding of the social and psychological dynamics of domestic violence and, instead, bring with them a lifetime of exposure to the myths that long have shaped the public's attitude toward the problem. The most persistent of these myths is the belief that intimate abuse is somehow acceptable, or at least insignificant, and therefore not deserving of a serious public response, and the belief that battered women could leave their relationships with relative ease if they simply chose to do so. Lack of information about these basic aspects of domestic violence causes many judges to become frustrated with petitioners whom they perceive as filing inappropriate cases and "refusing" to leave abusive relationships. State gender bias task forces across the country consistently report that the result is a persistent anti-victim bias among judges hearing family violence cases.

For example, in 1994, Kenneth Peacock found his wife in bed with another man. Several hours later, he shot her in the head with a hunting rifle. When Peacock pleaded guilty to voluntary manslaughter, the Maryland judge who presided over his case commented, "the most difficult thing that a judge is called upon to do ... is sentencing noncriminals as criminals." He imposed an eighteen-month sentence, to be served on a work release program, which allowed Peacock to reenter the community within two weeks of sentencing. In another case, a Florida judge heard testimony that a man had doused his wife with lighter fluid and set her on fire. The judge burst into song in open court crooning, "You light up my wife," to the tune of "You Light Up My Life." And a New York judge began a hearing with the comment, "Well, well, well, we had a little domestic squabble, did we? Naughty, naughty. Let's kiss and make up, and get out of my court." These are just a few, particularly egregious examples culled from numerous gender bias task force reports. They may be somewhat atypical in terms of the extent of the insensitivity exhibited, but they demonstrate how deeply ingrained the problem is.

The District has attempted to respond to this problem by requiring judges on the new Domestic Violence Court to undergo formal judicial training on intimate abuse. These judges must also accept a year-long assignment, which allows them to build a reservoir of experience in the area. Although the training opportunities have been sorely limited, the advocacy community already has witnessed substantial positive changes in judicial treatment of these cases. A telling example lies in the change in judicial response to requests for custody and child support in civil protection order cases. As discussed in Part I, rapid resolution of these issues is of extreme importance in domestic violence cases, where perpetrators commonly use financial leverage to manipulate and control their victims.

Prior to the Domestic Violence Court's formation, D.C. judges awarded temporary custody in fewer than half of the civil protection order cases in which the parties had a child together, despite clear statutory authorization to grant such relief. Further, they awarded child support in only 2.6% of civil protection order cases where the parties had a child together, and 4.9% of those cases involving a custody order, although such an award is authorized by statute and case law. This kind of track record is typical nationwide; forty-three percent of domestic violence service providers report that judges are unwilling to consider awarding remedies that are clearly authorized by statute, especially custody, child support, and other forms of financial relief.

In the new Domestic Violence Court, however, judges now routinely award custody based on the best interest of the child standard as well as child support based on D.C.'s financial guidelines. Judges even occasionally take the time to talk to people who appear before them about the harmful impact that witnessing adult-on-adult abuse can have on children and about the intergenerational nature of domestic violence.

In my view, this counts as a substantial success, far beyond what I believed possible. I am beginning to conclude that targeted judicial education can be an extraordinarily effective means of accomplishing social change. The judiciary is a relatively small population to work with in the effort to debunk larger societal mythologies and stereotypes, and every judge who gains a broader understanding of the issue can have an impact on a large number of families who appear before her. Therefore, judicial training and court reform is a crucial next step if we seek to deliver on the promise of the new generation of domestic violence legislation.

CONCLUSION

The domestic violence movement has been one of the most successful sociopolitical movements of this century. The past thirty years have witnessed not only enormous improvements in societal consciousness-raising, but also a dramatically improved state response, through the availability of legal remedies and the responsiveness of the criminal justice system. But new challenges accompany this increase in the focus of state power. As the police grow more likely to arrest and prosecutors grow more likely to press charges, we must find new and innovative ways to ensure that victims' voices are not silenced and that survivors are not forced to sacrifice their autonomy in exchange for government assistance. In addition, renewed energy must be focused on helping judges purge the stereotypes they bring to the bench, comprehend the dynamics underlying intimate abuse, and deliver appropriate relief. Activists must continue to press the state to respond to the intimate abuse crisis, while simultaneously shoring up support for individual victims.

JUDITH ARMATTA, GETTING BEYOND THE LAW'S COMPLICITY IN INTIMATE VIOLENCE AGAINST WOMEN

33 Willamette L. Rev. 773, 842–845 (1997).

IV. CONCLUSION

From an international perspective, domestic violence is a nearly universal phenomenon. It exists in countries with unduly varying political, economic, and cultural structures. The extensiveness of domestic violence establishes that the problem does not originate with the pathology of an individual person. Rather, domestic violence is embedded in the values, relationships, and social and institutional structures of society. Its roots are found in a hierarchical social structure of male dominance and female subordination. To end domestic violence, societal models based on dominance must be changed.

While change will not occur through legal reform alone, legal structural change is a necessary component of broader social change. At the very least, legal approval of domestic violence must be ended. Moreover, to end the legal system's complicity in domestic violence, the legal system cannot lend itself to use by an abuser seeking to control and harm another. Nor can the law act as an impediment to women seeking safety and well-being. As a survey of women's advocates in ninety-four countries concluded, there is a "need for gender specific, comprehensive and systematically integrated domestic violence legislation."[418]

Ending legal complicity in domestic violence requires abolishing the laws of a gender-neutral stance. Justice must remove her blindfold and see the context that shapes people's lives. The principle of neutrality cannot provide justice between groups with a great disparity in power and resources without taking the disparity into account. Gender-conscious laws are necessary to make the law less of a tool in the hands of abusers.

The issue of family, family privacy, and legally sanctioned violence also must be addressed in any legal reform strategy. Domestic violence

---

418. State Responses, supra note 4, at 91. * * *

takes root in a family structure that gives men power over women and approves of violence as a disciplinary and conflict resolution method, but then declares itself off-limits from state interference. While the state should not unnecessarily interfere in personal relationships, the state must interfere to protect its citizens from harm.

Any legal reform effort must take an integrated approach to the problem of not only domestic violence but all forms of violence against women.

"[M]ost legal systems have not displayed a synthetic approach to the problem [of violence against women]." In other words, the laws of most legal systems address the various manifestations of violence against women separately, with no suggestion that they may have a uniform or even related structural cause. This has meant that, practically speaking, laws concerning different forms of such violence are located in different legal remedies and texts. From a theoretical viewpoint, this failure to adopt a synthetic legal approach has resulted in a general failure to link the various manifestations of violence against women to subordination of and discrimination against women generally. The failure to adopt a synthetic approach in legal remedy has affected other areas, so that service provision and other strategies employed to address the problem have also developed in a fragmented way.[419] It cannot be overemphasized that a fragmented approach practically ensures that root causes will be ignored. Addressing domestic violence in isolation from other forms of violence and discrimination against women has resulted in characterizing domestic violence as a problem of family systems, rather than a problem rooted in a patriarchal social structure. In the same way, this fragmented approach has led to viewing sexual assault as the pathological acts of a few individuals without any understanding of social conditioning, and addressing female poverty as a social service instead of a political issue.

> It is highly likely that the various forms of violence against women are linked and are based on a common cause—the subordination of women. It is likely, therefore, that many of the measures that are now employed to address this violence are merely treating the symptom, rather than the cause of the phenomenon. Work is now required to ensure that all measures interrelate and encompass effective approaches to address the legal, social and economic injustices that women face.[420]

The international human rights community has formulated international standards of behavior. Recently, the international community declared its consensus that violence against women is a human rights violation, and that states have an affirmative duty to protect women from such violence. Further, the international community has recognized that neither family privacy nor religious or cultural traditions should outweigh a woman's right to safety, health, and well-being.

419. Connors, supra note 55, at 183–84.   **420.** Id. at 199.

The Beijing Platform for Action, agreed to by all participating countries at the Fourth World Conference on Women in 1995, clarifies the interrelatedness of all forms of violence and discrimination against women. "Developing a holistic and multidisciplinary approach to the challenging task of promoting families, communities and States that are free of violence against women is necessary and achievable. Equality, partnership between woman and men and respect for human dignity must permeate all stages of the socialization process."[423] The Beijing Platform for Action further sets out a comprehensive program for addressing the different manifestations of women's subordination. As such, it provides an important guide for any strategy designed to address domestic violence.

Law reformers at the national and local levels should follow the leadership of the international community and declare that violence against women is a serious and widespread problem that must be addressed for the well-being and progress of the entire world community. And they should make addressing it a priority.

---

423. Beijing Platform for Action, Chapter IV. D. paragraph 119.

Chapter 2

DOMESTIC VIOLENCE: CAUSES, EFFECTS, AND TREATMENT

This chapter starts by raising the questions, What is domestic violence?; What types of abuse are incorporated into this term?; What are typical experiences of victims of domestic violence, and typical reactions to those experiences? It also explores conflicting theories about the causes of domestic violence, and conflicting descriptions of typical responses of survivors.

Continuing to ask what causes domestic violence, the materials then take a cross-cultural perspective, looking at whether domestic violence occurs in all societies, and if not, what is different about those societies where we do not find it.

The third part of the chapter looks in more depth at batterers, examining typical behaviors, possible reasons for that behavior, and whether batterer treatment programs are effective in stopping the abuse.

Note that these are not traditional "legal" materials. However, the issues they raise—conflicting theories as to causes of this phenomenon, differing descriptions of typical responses of those subjected to domestic violence, and whether current treatment programs are effective—have major policy implications for how the US legal system attempts to solve this problem.

POWER AND CONTROL WHEEL

Domestic Abuse Intervention Project, Duluth, MN.

KATHLEEN WAITS, BATTERED WOMEN AND THEIR CHILDREN: LESSONS FROM ONE WOMAN'S STORY

35 Hous. L. Rev. 29–67 (1998).

II. MARY'S STORY

A. *Background and Methodology*

Mary is an attractive, forty-year-old white woman. She has lived her whole life in a mid-size southwestern city. She is a computer systems analyst and works for one of the major employers in her home town. * * *

B. *Mary's Story*

I was twenty-three years old when I started my relationship with Russ. He was thirty-five and also a computer analyst where I worked.

The year was 1980. When I met Russ, my first marriage had recently failed and my son from that marriage, Richard, was three years old.

The end of my first marriage was very traumatic for me because I had been raised a strong Catholic. I felt as though I had failed. In retrospect, I think Russ sensed my vulnerability and took advantage of it. He acted the part of a "knight in shining armor." He wined me and dined me. I was very impressed.

Russ and I broke up a number of times while we were dating. I saw some of his anger and controlling behavior, and they frightened me. I even left the company where we both worked to get away from him. But he pursued me and won me back, and we were married in 1984. He was never physically violent during our courtship.

I became pregnant soon after we were married. I had severe morning sickness during the first seven months of the pregnancy. I felt very weak. Also, while I was pregnant, Russ announced that he was quitting his job and was going to raise horses. He said this was something he had always dreamed about. Despite the fact that raising horses is rarely profitable, he made this incredibly important decision without consulting with me at all. Going without Russ's salary scared me. I was pregnant and also had my son Richard to support.

Russ's first physical abuse occurred when I was pregnant. I have since learned that this is often the case. He had quit his job. I tried to discuss with him my fears about our financial situation, especially with the baby coming. We argued. All of a sudden, he came at me like a rocket launcher. He pushed me against the wall and, holding me there, started to strangle me. He screamed, "You don't tell me what I need to do."

I was shocked. I slid down the wall and fell to the floor, crying. He stood over me and berated me, saying that I was crying because I was "weak."

I can still remember vividly what Russ looked like during this first attack. Words cannot describe it; it was so frightening. His face was distorted, inhuman, and filled with rage; his eyes bugged out. He did not look like the Russ I thought I knew; he seemed like a rabid dog.

I know there is this idea of the "cycle of violence" and that batterers express remorse after a battering episode. I have heard of a "honeymoon" period following the abuse where the batterer is extra nice. Well, that may happen in some cases, but it certainly did not happen in mine. Russ never apologized for this incident or any of the more violent ones that came later. He did not even acknowledge what he had done or that there was anything wrong with it. He never promised, "Honey, it won't happen again." He would, however, sometimes give me gifts after a beating. But even these supposed "gifts" were selfish and controlling. After a severe beating in which he tore up my right arm and shoulder, he bought me a waterbed so I could sleep more comfortably. The purchase angered me because we could not afford it. When I asked him to take it back to the store, he blew up and said my bitching about my shoulder and inability to sleep on my right side was boring. He called me a whiner.

It occurred to me to leave him at this point, but I was much too ashamed to consider it seriously. I thought to myself, "Well, you've dug a hole for yourself—now you have to live in it." I was much too ashamed and embarrassed to even think about calling the police. If I had, everyone in our neighborhood would have known that we were not a perfect couple. I wanted to keep up appearances.

Though Russ never apologized for the violence, we did have many good times together, at least during the early years of our marriage. I am a very affectionate person, and he could be affectionate too.

During the pregnancy, I went to work at the second shift to make more money. This left Russ taking care of Richard, my son from my first marriage. I later learned that, while caring for Richard, Russ hit him with a paddle board. After the beating, to intimidate Richard, Russ said mockingly, "Are you going to run to Mommy?" Richard did not reveal this to me until I had left Russ for good. He knew Russ would just beat him again if he told me. Richard figured one beating was better than two.

Naturally, the abuse from his stepfather has led to a lot of anger from Richard, now age twenty. However, the anger has not been directed toward me.

In 1985, I gave birth to our first child together, a daughter, Elizabeth. Russ was obviously disappointed that it was a girl. He pressured me to have another child right away. Because of the abuse and my fear of Russ, I was willing to do anything to appease him. So, I became pregnant when Elizabeth was just five months old, even though I was neither physically or emotionally ready for another child. Our son Daniel was born fourteen months after Elizabeth.

Getting back to the issue of Russ's abuse of me. After the choking incident when I was pregnant, Russ just had to give me "the look," and I would try to make peace. I worked to keep the kids quiet; we all worked hard to keep from upsetting Russ. Everyone walked on eggshells. When the kids heard his truck coming, they would run and hide.

While I was pregnant with our second child, Daniel, Russ twisted my arm so violently that it permanently damaged my shoulder. I cannot even remember now what the fight was about. A doctor later told me he was shocked to see an injury like mine in a layperson. He told me the damage done to my shoulder was so severe that it was similar to what he would expect from a professional baseball pitcher after years of throwing and stress.

The shoulder injury prevented me from full participation in athletics. This was devastating to me. I have always been a superb athlete and enjoyed doing physical things. Because of who I am, the shoulder injury was not just physically painful. It was a way of taking away my identity.

I did not initially seek medical help for the shoulder injury. I was ashamed and thought it was all my fault. Of course, Russ was always telling me that everything was my fault. I did not want anyone to know.

Russ also set up a number of rules for our house. The children and I were to follow the rules "or else." For instance, I was not allowed to watch comedies such as "Cheers" and "M*A*S*H" on television. Instead, we always watched the blood-and-guts action shows that Russ liked. My sense of humor is an important part of who I am and an important part of my self-image. Once again, as with the shoulder injury, Russ was chipping away at the very core of my being.

There were always a lot of guns in our house. At one point, while in a face-to-face argument with my son Richard, who by then was about eleven or twelve, Russ shot a twelve-gauge shotgun straight up in the air, doing major damage to the ceiling and roof of our house. Obviously, this was a terrible act of intimidation and abuse. But, as I will discuss later, Russ did not see it this way, and the judge and custody evaluators did not take this incident seriously either.

As I now know is typical, I was subjected to an unending stream of degrading comments. Russ was always saying things to me like, "Your thighs are fat. Your boobs are too small. No one else would want you. You're lucky to have me." I cannot express the horrible, demeaning, and damaging effects these comments had on me. After all, they were coming from someone I loved and who supposedly loved me. I thought they had to be true. I could not help but internalize them. I had always felt good about my body, but the constant stream of criticism tore away at that. At one point, Russ almost convinced me to have my breasts enlarged, an operation that would have been completely unnecessary.

The tearing away at my self-image and self-esteem is hard to describe. I like to draw an analogy to an artichoke. You can pull one leaf off an artichoke and it's no big deal. But you slowly pull away one leaf and then another and then another, and before long, you're down to the artichoke heart. It's not an artichoke anymore with the leaves gone. And, once the leaves are off, you can stab the artichoke in the heart, no problem. Russ really knew where the insults would hurt, and he tore away at me.

Still, I always kept up a good front. I was able to keep information about the abuse away from my family for a long time. The only exception was one sister who lives in Colorado. (I have five brothers and two sisters; we are a very close and loving family). One time, when she and I were talking over the phone, she heard Russ's angry screaming in the background. She asked one of my brothers, who lives locally, to follow up with me. When he did, I sloughed it off and said, "I'm fine."

I think a lot of people saw the look of terror in the children's eyes when Russ was around. But they either thought nothing of it or did not do anything. In retrospect, I also think various people in my life knew about Russ's anger but did not allow themselves to see the abuse and did not come forward to help me.

My son Richard was not the only child who was abused. When Elizabeth was three, Russ's ten-year old son from a previous marriage (Russ Jr., known as Chip) molested her. Chip would stay with us for part of the summer. One day, when I was not there and Russ was supposedly in charge, Chip went into Elizabeth's bedroom, pulled the blanket over her head, pulled down her pants and started fondling her. When I returned home, Elizabeth was sitting on her bed crying. Unfortunately, it was not unusual for the kids to be crying when I got home after Russ had been caring for them.

When I asked Elizabeth what had happened, she told me what Chip had done. I went and told Russ. He immediately became a maniac and started hitting Chip and pounding him against the wall. I later learned that Russ's supposed anger toward Chip was just a show for my benefit. Years later when I had left Russ, and Elizabeth finally felt safe, she told me what had really happened. After Chip had molested her, and before I came home, Elizabeth had told her father what Chip had done. Russ yelled at Elizabeth. That was the real reason she was crying when I got home. When Russ later talked about the incident, he referred to Elizabeth as a "manipulative bitch."

After Chip's molestation of Elizabeth, I never let him be alone in the house with her. Russ refused to send Chip home to his mother in Illinois. To Russ, what Chip had done to Elizabeth was no big deal, since it had happened in private. Interestingly, the next summer, when Chip was caught shoplifting, Russ was genuinely furious and did want to send him back to his mother. The shoplifting was a public event and a potential public embarrassment to Russ. People might find out about the shoplifting and think less of Russ.

Russ beat me severely for the first time in January 1989, right after the Super Bowl. We had had an argument three days before (I have forgotten over what) and he had not spoken to me since. This was a common way for him to punish me after a fight. Whenever he was giving me the "silent treatment," he would typically "make up" by having sex with me. It was rape or near-rape, really, since it did not matter whether or not I wanted to have sex. Russ did not care if I wanted to make up in that way. He would also punish me by staying out all night, presumably with other women.

Well, I had been sleeping on the couch for several nights. It was after the Super Bowl, and I thought he had passed out on our bed, drunk (Russ is an alcoholic). I wanted to get a good night's sleep, so, thinking he was asleep, I climbed into our bed. He immediately grabbed my hair very violently and started ripping off my clothes, trying to rape me. He twisted my breasts severely. The pain was excruciating. I screamed in pain but I fought back; I'm pretty strong.

Hearing my screams, Elizabeth (age four) came to the bedroom door and yelled, "Daddy stop!" He chased her out of the room. Meanwhile, I ran to the laundry room at the other end of the house, naked and crying hysterically. I closed the laundry room door behind me and tried to keep him out. Russ is 6'4" tall and weighs 240 pounds, so he easily pushed the door open. He shoved me against the wall and repeatedly beat my head against it. Finally, I slid down the wall, exhausted. As he had done before, he stood over me and called me names like "bitch" and "cunt." Then, satisfied that he had proven his power over me, he went back to bed and fell asleep.

One thing I remember vividly from this incident is seeing a hammer in the laundry room while Russ was beating me. I could have reached it. I remember thinking to myself, "Maybe I should use it on him." But I did not. In that split second, I thought of how Russ had told me many times that most women who tried to defend themselves were killed by the very weapon they had tried to use. I imagined that if I did not kill Russ with that hammer, he would use it to kill me. I thought to myself, "I'm getting beaten, but I'm not dead. And I sure as hell don't want to die and leave the kids with him."

After Russ had gone back to bed, I gathered up all three kids and went to my brother-in-law's house. He is the former husband of one of my sisters and like another brother to me. As I was leaving our house, Russ woke up and tried to keep me from taking the kids, but I managed to get away.

I was too ashamed to call the police. My brother-in-law said, "Don't go back." I replied, "I have to go back or else I'll be stuck with all the bills." What did I mean by that? Well, the IRS had ruled that Russ's horse raising scheme had been a hobby and not a business. So the IRS had disallowed all those expenses and we had been hit with a bill for back taxes of $20,000. I thought to myself, "If I don't go back, Russ will leave and I'll be stuck with paying back all the money we owe. But if I go back, he'll stay and help me pay it off." Ironically, in the end, I ended up paying it all back anyway.

I look back on it now and my thinking seems ridiculous. But people need to understand that battered women often do not think straight because of post-traumatic stress. Who could or would think clearly under such circumstances? And I was also thinking that it would be disgraceful to be divorced a second time. I knew that society would think I was unstable, probably a bad person, and certainly a bad mother.

There is another reason, in addition to post-traumatic stress, for why I found it hard to assess my situation clearly. Like most batterers, Russ had isolated me from my family and friends. When they came over, he was very rude and would always play the television loudly. He acted as if they were not there or were a bother. I was always the peacemaker and did my best to make us look good. I would say, "He's had a bad day" or "He's really tired." But naturally, given his obnoxious behavior and my obvious discomfort, many of my friends stopped coming over.

I know that some batterers are always charming to everyone outside the family. That was not really true of Russ. He was sometimes intimidating, condescending, and mean to my friends. He would often put me down in front of them.

Actually, I was luckier than many battered women, as I continued to have contact with family and friends. Plus, my family was always very supportive and never gave up on me. They did not blame me for the abuse or insist that I leave Russ before I was ready. I was even able to confide in one of my sisters about the abuse. I am also grateful to a good friend from work who asked me about the bruises on my arm. She had seen Russ be psychologically abusive to me and mean to other people. I told her the truth and she listened and believed me and cared and supported me.

Still, even with the support I received, Russ had succeeded in isolating me. And it is hard to think clearly when you feel all alone with your problems. I now see how effective Russ's isolation techniques were.

Even after the January 1989 beating, I would not have considered myself an abused woman, but going to my brother-in-law's house was important because it was my first time out. It was also the first time I'd talked about the abuse with a man.

The laundry room beating marked the end of any good times between Russ and me. After this, it seemed he wanted to hurt me just about all the time.

I think battered women stay with their abusers out of both hope and fear. They hope the batterer will change; they fear what might happen if they leave. After this incident, hope was gone for me; fear was all that remained. How could I hope, when Russ showed no remorse and never apologized? He sometimes claimed to have "blacked out" during this and other incidents. I know he is an alcoholic, but his blackouts were just too convenient for my tastes.

After the Super Bowl beating, he never again made me cry. In order to survive, I shut out my emotions.

In terms of the health care system: shortly after Elizabeth was born, Russ complained to our family doctor about me. The doctor responded by putting both of us on thyroid medicine. This later led Russ to tell me that I was "crazy" because I was on this medicine; somehow his being on the medicine did not make him crazy. There were always two sets of rules, one for him and one for me. Whatever he did was fine; whatever I did was wrong.

It was the same way with money. Russ could spend money however he wanted and could buy whatever he wanted. His check was exclusively for him to spend. One of his favorites tricks was to get something he wanted (like a gun or rifle) and say to me, "Look what I bought for you."

My check was to take care of everything else in the house. If we were short of money, it was always my fault, never his fault for his extravagant, selfish purchases.

The doctor never asked me about domestic violence. At one point, I said to him, "Russ gets real angry with me." I wanted the doctor somehow to pick up on what I was saying and offer me help. Yet, I was also terrified that he would repeat to Russ whatever I said. I knew that

Russ would respond violently to that, so I was very circumspect. The doctor's response was, "Is he manic-depressive?" I mumbled in response, "I don't know," and the doctor pretty much dropped the subject.

I think it was the doctor's job to make a diagnosis of Russ, not mine. Plus, he should have taken the time to earn my trust and to talk to me about the underlying facts, Russ's abuse, that were causing my medical problems. He should have assured me that he would keep what I told him confidential.

I also felt the doctor should have noticed that I was incredibly exhausted and depressed. True, I had three young children to care for and a demanding job; however, my exhaustion went way beyond what could be explained by those circumstances. If he had ever asked, "Why are you so exhausted?" in a way that indicated he really wanted to know the answer, I think I might have poured out my heart to him.

Today, I have a doctor who starts every visit by sitting down and asking me, "How are things going, Mary? What is happening in your life? How are the kids doing?" And it is clear that he really cares about the answers. He is not looking at his watch or edging toward the door from the minute he comes in. And I think that, as a result, he can provide me with better medical care because he understands the context in which my medical problems are occurring.

The incident that caused me to leave for good happened in June 1990. It started on a Thursday night. I had long planned on going to a bridal shower on Friday evening. I had asked, and Russ had agreed, that he would look after the kids on Friday night. As far as I was concerned, it was all arranged. That Thursday night I reminded Russ, "You'll have the kids tomorrow night so I can go to the shower." He was furious and screamed in my face, "I made plans for tomorrow night. I made them before yours. You can't go. And don't hire a babysitter because we can't afford it." All that night, he kicked me while we were in bed together. He turned the lights on and off all night. I hardly got any sleep. (I have since learned that sleep deprivation is a common batterers' tactic).

I remember how relieved I was when he got up in the morning to take his shower to go to work. For those few minutes while he was in the shower, I could sleep and rest. Of course, it was not nearly long enough. It was clear that he was still enraged. As he left for work, he said to me, "No one deserves a beating more than you. You're going to get the worst beating of your life when I get home tonight."

That was it for me. I thought to myself, "It's time for this to be over." After Russ had gone to work, I grabbed some stuff for myself and my children. We left the house and went into hiding. This was also the point at which I finally called the local battered women's program, HomeSafe. Only after this June 1990 incident did I identify myself as an abused woman.

The first night the kids and I stayed at a friend's house. My oldest son, Richard, slept on the floor and the two little ones slept with me on a spare bed. After that I began networking with people I had met through Al–Anon. We moved to a different place every night. My counselor from HomeSafe advised me to stay on the move—just like the North Vietnamese. Sometimes we stayed with people we knew; sometimes we met them for the first time at their door.

Just a few days after leaving, I sought and received an order of protection. The judge gave me what I wanted, but belittled me and minimized my safety concerns in the process. In my petition, I detailed Russ's "you're going to get a beating when I get home" threat. I also stated that the last severe beating had occurred in January 1989 (the Super Bowl/laundry room incident). The judge said, in a dismissive way, "It's been a year and a half since he last beat you. Is last week's threat really serious?"

After I'd gotten the order of protection, Russ was warned by our babysitter that I had some papers that were going to be served on him. He tried to hide from the sheriff and police. On Monday evening (three days after I'd fled), he trashed our house. I went by the house the next day and found the house destroyed. I then bought a camera and went back to the house and took pictures. After I took pictures, I started cleaning up the house. Later that evening (Tuesday) I saw that Russ had been to the house again. This time he wrote hateful messages on the walls and mirror in the master bath. He also tore up my underclothes and took all of my business suits and dresses (my Al–Anon friends helped me get spare clothes to wear to work). Russ urinated on the walls of the master bedroom and ejaculated on my pillow.

My big mistake was not taking pictures of the second incident. Later in the custody proceedings, Russ's lawyer ridiculed me and said that I had to be making it all up. The reason I didn't take pictures was because my children were with me. I cleaned up everything so they would not see it. I did have two witnesses with me to the urination/ejaculation incident, but the judge ignored them.

We stayed in hiding for three weeks, then we moved back into our house (after changing the locks). I had a girlfriend move in with me. I was too afraid to be alone. Plus, I wanted a witness for anything else Russ might do to me.

Soon after going into hiding, I hired the first of what would be several lawyers. Overall, I am very dissatisfied with how both the lawyers and the legal system handled my situation. I feel that my lawyers did not understand what I had experienced. They did not understand because they would not or could not listen to what I had to say. They did not seem to care about what I wanted and why. Most had a predetermined outcome in mind and a predetermined approach of how they were going to accomplish that outcome. I could not get them to listen to me or to budge from their preconceptions.

I was always very up front with my lawyers about the abuse that had occurred. I also told them very clearly about my fears for myself and my children.

My first lawyer (I will call her Lawyer #1) was a woman and an experienced family lawyer. When I explained to her that I was very afraid of Russ, her response was completely egotistical: "Just let him come after me, and I'll kick his ass." Her focus was on what she was going to do, not what was best for me. She also said, "You're my client, we'll screw that bastard." This was not what I wanted. I wanted to be safe. I did not want to go "one on one" with Russ, and I did not want my lawyer to do that either. I felt that taking him on like this would increase the danger to me and my children. I felt that this lawyer just did not listen to me or take my concerns seriously.

Lawyer #1 was also my first introduction to how people in the legal system—people who should know better—completely dismiss abuse of women and children. At one point, after I had told her my story, she said, "So he slapped you around and beat the kids. What's your point?" She acted as if these facts were irrelevant to the divorce and custody proceedings.

Russ's lawyer said to my lawyer, "Let's sit Russ and Mary together in the pretrial conference. That'll help work things out." I strongly objected to this. I told my lawyer that sitting next to Russ would be scary and intimidating for me. My lawyer responded, "Don't be gutless like they say you are." I also asked that Russ be searched for possible weapons, but my lawyer said that she would not ask for this.

This lawyer talked tough, but she spent most of her time flirting with Russ's lawyer. She did not stand up to Russ. She was also just plain incompetent; she gave away a key issue to Russ and his lawyer. When we were negotiating over money, Russ and his lawyer wanted his payments to be labeled "house payments" instead of "child support." My lawyer said, "Fine, no problem." I was not happy about this, but my lawyer said to me, "money is money." I later learned, when Russ didn't make the payments, that there are special enforcement mechanisms that are available only for child support payments. In this context, all money is not the same. So the lawyer's mistake deprived me and my children of valuable rights.

After I left Russ, he had no real interest in the kids. He did not care about seeing them, much less having custody. He only became interested when I insisted on supervised visitation. That was a challenge to his power and authority; plus, his ego could not tolerate the public embarrassment of being allowed only supervised visitation. That is when he demanded custody of Elizabeth and Daniel.

I sometimes wonder if I made a mistake in seeking supervised visitation. Not because the kids did not need it or deserve it, given his abuse of them. But maybe he would have left the kids and me alone if I had just "let sleeping dogs lie." I will never know. Of course, if the legal system had responded properly and effectively to my request for supervised visitation, that would have made a big difference too.

While we were fighting over supervised visitation, my lawyer said, "We'll get psychological testing for both of you." She did not listen when

I responded, "He'll pass the test with flying colors. He's very slick and impressive."

When I sought supervised visitation, I was focused on the kids' safety. After I left him, I thought Russ would leave me alone. Boy was I wrong! I wish my lawyer would have alerted me to the continued danger that I would face. I did not know—and my lawyer never told me—that separation often increases the danger to battered women.

Lawyer #1 demanded and received a large up front retainer fee. Then she sent me to a psychologist, which cost even more money. This psychologist was very strange and later had a mental breakdown.

Other psychologists were not much better. My kids and I went through a bunch of them. One psychologist called me "an air head." I confronted him about that, and he did not like how assertive I was.

Russ claimed that I was a lesbian and an alcoholic. Both of these accusations are completely false. I do not want to sound as if I believe that being a lesbian is bad; I do not. However, most judges are very homophobic, especially in a fundamentalist-dominated city like mine. Accusing a woman of being a lesbian is, unfortunately, a very effective weapon in a custody battle and a very common one. Russ also claimed that he had really raised the kids, which was absurdly untrue.

Russ's tactics worked. The lawyers and psychologists, as well as the judge, all concentrated on me and what I had supposedly done wrong. They let Russ off the hook.

I am really angry that the legal system allows batterers to set the agenda through their wild accusations against victims. Russ played the game of "the best defense is a good offense" to perfection. The system allowed him to put the focus on me, instead of on his abuse of me and the children. My lawyers never fought effectively against this tactic.

Eventually, I fired Lawyer #1. From what I could tell, she was spending most of her time and energy flirting with Russ's lawyer, and I was very unhappy with her malpractice on the child support/house payments allocation. I then interviewed another female lawyer who had been recommended by HomeSafe, the local battered women's program. This lawyer told me about a specific psychologist in town who is often called as an expert witness in custody fights. The lawyer said, "We'll pay him off and he'll say what we want." I thought this was wrong and refused to hire this lawyer. This same psychologist ultimately testified for Russ in the custody hearing and is the one who referred to me as an "airhead." I do not know if Russ and his lawyer "paid him off," but I cannot help but wonder. I hired another female lawyer (Lawyer #2) instead.

Russ brought in the police to supervise the exchange of the children for visitation. He claimed that he called in the police because I was abusive. I have learned that batterers often claim that they are being abused.

Elizabeth did not want to visit with her dad, so I did not force her to go. This was later held against me as showing that I was uncooperative with Russ's rights as a father. The judge tried to compare a visit with an abusive father with a trip to the dentist: a good mother will make her child go.

An important incident occurred when Russ came to a football game where my oldest son, Richard, was playing. Russ was not his father. It was my birthday, and obviously the game was an important event for my son and me.

Russ showed up, followed closely by my first husband, Chris, Richard's father. I was surprised to see Chris at the game, since he had shown only sporadic interest in Richard. I suspect Russ got Chris to come to the game as a further way to torture me. When Chris got out of his car, they shook hands and did not look at all surprised to see each other.

This was ironic, since the two of them had always hated each other. When I was living with Russ, he and Chris had fought over control of Richard. Russ had asserted his right to act as Richard's father, not out of love, but out of his need to dominate. Chris, even though he was not an involved father, had resisted somewhat. It is my guess that Russ used their mutual hatred of me to manipulate Chris. I think Chris was a willing pawn in Russ's mind games with me.

When I retreated to my car after seeing Russ, he pointed at me in a taunting way. Chris went along. The two of them appeared to be having a good laugh at my expense. They were enjoying my fear and discomfort.

It was clear to me that Russ's only purpose in coming was to scare me. He had never shown any interest in Richard.

I had learned by now to always have my protective order with me. I showed it to the police who were working at the game. I asked them to order Russ to leave. The police responded that my protective order did not cover this situation because the game was a public event. I certainly was not going to stay there while Russ was there. So I had to leave the stadium without seeing the game.

This was an example of how Russ, like most batterers, always stayed right "on the line." That is, he did things that would intimidate me but would not get him in trouble with the authorities.

Something I remember vividly from the football game incident was one police officer whose kindness and sensitivity meant a lot to me. The other officers, after determining that they could not or would not remove Russ from the game, just basically left. This police officer, however, came over to me and explained why the police thought they were unable to remove Russ from the game. He looked me in the eye and really talked to me. He dealt with me as a person. He was clearly empathetic and sympathetic with my fear and my anger that Russ was keeping me from attending Richard's game. I still think fondly of this officer, even though he did not do anything concrete to help me. It meant a lot that he talked to me and acknowledged the legitimacy of my fears and the unfairness of what was happening.

Another person who helped me was a very good psychologist who had a reputation for understanding battered women and their children. My counselor at HomeSafe had recommended her. Unfortunately, at the time I was seeking help, this psychologist was feeling very burned out and could not accept me or my children as patients. However, she came and babysat for my children one night. Afterward, we spoke briefly. Even that short exchange was very meaningful to me. The psychologist validated my perceptions and concerns. She told me, "What you want for yourself and your kids is right."

This affirmation was important. All the discouragement I had received from my lawyers and other professionals had really taken its toll. When I first left Russ, I had felt strongly that I was right in my perceptions of Russ, myself, and my children. I thought the safety I wanted was reasonable and fair. But the lawyers and psychologists had been so disempowering. They did not listen. They undermined everything I thought and said. They did not take my safety concerns seriously. Consequently, my confidence in my own judgment had been stripped away. This psychologist, even in a very brief session, helped restore my faith in my abilities and judgment.

The evening of the football game fiasco, I called my lawyer (Lawyer #2) to discuss what could be done. It was clear to me that she was very intoxicated. She did not respond at all to my outrage and to my safety concerns. I fired her shortly thereafter. I was tired of paying big retainers and getting nowhere.

I then went looking for a male lawyer. I want to acknowledge that I did not yet trust women. Russ had constantly belittled women, and so I did not really believe that women professionals could be competent. I also still bought into the idea that women were natural rivals with each other. In saying this, I do not mean to excuse what my first two lawyers did. I think I was more than justified in firing them. But I think I fired them much more quickly than I would have if they had been men.

Attorney #3, a man, represented me through the trial that eventually ended in my losing custody of my son Daniel. Attorney #3 sent me to a psychologist whose attitude reminded me of Lawyer #1. This psychologist, a woman, said "we'll get him," referring to Russ's psychologist. That is, the psychologist saw this as a personal battle with Russ's psychologist. The key was for her to "win"; she did not focus on the safety or well-being of my children and me. Perhaps because she was focused on herself and not me, ultimately she was charmed by Russ and came to believe his lies. She was so self-absorbed. I can still picture her tossing her hair flirtatiously as she made remarks that destroyed me and my children.

This psychologist had a very dismissive attitude. She never really believed my story of abuse. Because I was a professional and a strong person, I think she identified with me, but that identification hurt me. I think she did not want to confront the possibility that someone like her could ever be abused, or would stay in an abusive relationship. The fact that I was a strong person seemed to make my story less credible to her. She virtually said to me, "Mary, you're a strong person. Because you're a strong person, I don't believe you'd put up with the abuse, if it was really as bad as you say. Therefore, you must be lying."

She did not understand domestic violence at all. Like the judge who reluctantly granted my protective order, she was puzzled and troubled by the fact that I was so scared by Russ's "you're going to get the beating of your life" threat. She focused on the fact that it had been a year and a half since the last severe physical incident when he made that threat. She even asked me at one point, "When he threatened to beat you [in June 1990], did he say it in a playful way?" She did not understand that physical violence is just one tool batterers use to control their victims. She did not understand the non-physical techniques (degradation, isolation, sleep deprivation) that Russ used. She did not understand that the physical violence does not have to be frequent or severe to be effective.

Russ's psychologist—the one who I had once been told was for sale— really did a number on me, too. According to him, I was an "angry woman," and this was bad. He thought Russ should have custody of both children.

He completely bought Russ's lies about me. He suggested—based on nothing other than Russ's statements and, perhaps, my assertiveness— that I might indeed have lesbian tendencies. He criticized me for having "an agenda," which I suppose referred to the fact that I was doing my best to keep my children and myself safe. On the other hand, the fact that Russ had never paid a dime in child support was dismissed. His failure somehow did not indicate any lack of interest in the children's welfare.

The same denial/minimization occurred around Russ's sexual abuse of me, including the brutalizing of my breasts. The psychologists bought Russ's explanation that "Mary likes rough sex that way."

No one cared about Russ's ongoing intimidation of me either. During the divorce proceedings, Russ would leave angry messages on my answering machine, saying things like "I will get you." He would even threaten to kill me and make it look like a suicide. He would say, "I could do that without any problem. You know how good I am with guns." I told my family and friends over and over, "No matter how bad it gets, I'm telling you that I would never commit suicide. I would never leave my kids without a mother. If they find me dead and it looks like a suicide, don't you believe it. If that happens, make sure the police investigate Russ." I told the lawyers and psychologists about Russ's threats, but they did not take them seriously.

It also bothers me that psychologists will not investigate the true facts, yet they assert that they know the truth. I repeatedly offered to put them in touch with other witnesses who would support my story.

They declined, saying that was not their job. Yet, they would claim to know what actually happened. Apparently, they felt they were such experts that they knew who was telling the truth, Russ or me. Russ, with his charming batterer's demeanor, won every time.

Both the psychologists and the judge failed to understand how the abuse affected the children. For instance, the children were scared to death of Russ. This is not surprising, given what they had seen him do to them and to me. As a result, they were very well-behaved when they were with him; they just wanted to avoid getting hurt more. Then when the kids were with me, in a comfortable, safe environment, they were often out of control. It just makes sense. They needed some place where they could safely express the trauma and stress they were experiencing. Yet, the psychologists, and ultimately the judge, held it against me that the kids did not always behave well when they were with me. They thought that Russ was a good parent because the kids were so well-behaved when they were with him. They thought I was a bad parent because the kids misbehaved when I was in charge. The psychologists and the judge never looked at the causes of the kids' problems. They never held Russ responsible for the behavior that was causing the kids to feel out of control in the first place.

Most fundamentally, the psychologists and judge bought the idea that Russ's abuse of me was irrelevant to child custody issues. They did not see any reason why the abuse should keep Russ from having full custody of the children. My own psychologist said, "So he's abused you. But he loves those kids." Even when I reminded her that the kids, especially Elizabeth, had seen the abuse, the psychologist responded, "She's young, she'll get over it."

I never got supervised visitation. At my insistence, my lawyer put a request for supervised visitation in my divorce petition. But he never fought for it or seemed to understand why the children and I needed it. In trying to discourage me from even asking for supervised visitation, he said, "Don't do that. It'll make the judge mad."

From what I have said, it should not surprise you to learn that both psychologists opposed supervised visitation. They both thought Russ was a good parent and that supervised visitation was unnecessary for both me and the kids.

Overall, I found the lawyers and psychologists very self-promoting and egotistical. It seemed as if everyone was having a good time, playing the game of litigation and psychology. All the while, my life was on the line. My children and I did not matter. I also felt like the lawyers and psychologists were running a cash register business at my expense. They were a lot more interested in my money than my welfare. The first two years of my divorce proceedings cost me more than twenty-five thousand dollars.

As incredible as it might sound, the judge who heard my custody case had an outstanding protective order against him by his ex-wife. I also sensed very strongly that the judge did not like me. For these reasons, I told my lawyer I wanted to seek the judge's recusal. My lawyer dismissed me, saying, "You'll just get someone worse."

At the custody hearing, Russ denied everything. He said he had never done anything to me physically. My psychologist did testify that he had admitted the laundry room beating to her in a private session. However, Russ had obviously minimized the severity of that beating. His admission did not change my psychologist's opinion that Russ was a good father. Russ also denied yelling at Elizabeth after his son Chip had molested her. Besides, he said, the molestation had never been proven.

He testified that he had been the primary caretaker of the children. The key evidence supporting this allegation was that he had usually taken the kids to and from the babysitter's house. It did not seem to matter that the babysitter was close to his workplace and far away from mine. This piece of evidence alone seemed to outweigh the fact that I did practically everything else for the kids.

Russ's testimony was so slick and manipulative. He laughed at the right times and misted up with tears at the right times. He acted the part of the "good ol' boy." That goes a long way where I live; I could tell the judge really liked him. Russ referred to Elizabeth and Daniel, by now ages 5 and 4, as "my babies" and talked about how much he loved them. He said things like, "They mean the world to me" and "I can't live without them." He made a particular point of saying, "I'm so close to Daniel." Russ came across as intelligent and very stable, as someone who really had his act together.

Russ's most outrageous testimony was reserved for the shotgun incident with my son Richard. He said that the gun went off by "accident." He also testified, "It was an old gun," as if that somehow made a difference. He probably would have denied this incident too, but I had photographs of the damage done to the ceiling and roof. My lawyer tried to discredit Russ's testimony, but Russ never budged. And it is clear that the judge never saw through Russ's lies and manipulations.

I testified to the abuse of the children and me. I am sure I did not seem as calm or collected as Russ. Given what I had been through, and given the fact that I was fighting for my children's lives and my own, I think that is understandable. I cried at one point, but overall I was very matter-of-fact, even low-key in my testimony. That is just the kind of person I am. I am not going to be emotional in front of strangers or in a formal setting like a courtroom. I also think it came across in my testimony that I am a strong person with good self-esteem.

I feel that the judge held against me that I was strong and matter-of-fact. I think that, in his mind, I did not portray the proper image of a "real" victim of domestic violence. Yet, at the same time, my crying and emotionalism hurt me, too. The judge seemed bored and annoyed when I started to cry. He asked, "How much longer is this going to take? Are we almost done here?" He had never said that during Russ's testimony. Indeed, throughout the trial, the judge seemed biased against my attorney and me. He often interrupted my attorney to ask, "How much longer is this going to take?'' but never interrupted Russ's attorney or asked him to hurry up.

I think it also probably hurt me that I was a professional. The judge did not seem to believe that a woman of my education and achievement would take the abuse I described.

I tried to offer testimony from other people whom Russ had abused. Shortly before the custody trial, I had learned that Russ abused his first wife. The judge refused to hear this testimony. I later learned that this was a typical pattern for this judge when hearing cases where women were claiming domestic violence.

Both psychologists' testimony damaged my case. Russ's psychologist said I had ''drug addict tendencies,'' picking up on Russ's false accusation of alcoholism. He said that Russ had been very active in raising the kids and that I was an angry woman who would not cooperate fairly with Russ's rights as a father if I were given custody of Daniel. I thought my lawyer did a good job of cross-examining Russ's psychologist.

The worst damage was done by my psychologist. She testified that I was feigning the abuse. She also made a big deal about a phone conversation we had had. I was suffering from an allergy attack and had the sniffles. During the conversation, we laughed. She later testified that I had quickly gone from crying to laughing. As a result, she said, she questioned my stability. Of course, she had never said anything to me about this, nor had she asked why I was sniffling. She just assumed she knew it all.

My psychologist testified that I should have custody of Elizabeth but was wishy-washy about Daniel. She testified that he would do okay with either Russ or me. She also criticized me for just giving ''lip service'' on providing Russ with visitation. Along with the judge, she is the person I most blame for my losing custody of Daniel.

I must emphasize again how everything I did was scrutinized with a microscope and everything Russ did was excused. I had entered into evidence pictures of how Russ had totally destroyed our house after being served with the protective order. The Judge's response: ''But he was hurt.'' Just like Russ had two sets of rules—one for himself and one for me—the court seemed to have completely different rules for batterers and victims.

Similarly, the judge completely bought Russ's explanation about the shotgun business. The fact that it had been an old 12–gauge shotgun made it okay. And the judge believed that the gun had gone off by accident. Even if that were true, I will never understand why the judge did not ask himself, ''What was a grown man doing face to face with an 11–year old with a shotgun in his hand, even if it was pointing straight up?'' Why did this not count as child endangerment? Why did it not reflect badly on Russ's fitness as a parent?

I do not know how I could have gotten through this period without the support of my family and HomeSafe. I am also very lucky that my priest was supportive and understanding.

The judge ordered that Russ be given custody of our son Daniel, then age four. The judge said that Russ was a good parent. He agreed with the psychologists that I would be a bad custodial parent because I was angry and could not get along with Russ with regard to visitation. The judge said that he was unable to determine my "sexual deviancy," thus giving credence to Russ's false claims that I was a lesbian.

To make matters worse, the judge told me that I was getting custody of Elizabeth for a six-month probationary period. I will never forget his warning from the bench: "If you do one thing to disrupt visitation, I'll take your daughter and give your ex-husband custody of her too."

As if losing Daniel weren't bad enough, the lawyer who accompanied me to the final hearing made it worse. My own lawyer was not there; he sent one of his associates instead. After hearing that I had lost custody of my son, I broke down in tears. The associate angrily took me into the court conference room and said, "Shut the fuck up. You'll lose the other kid."

The night that I lost custody of Daniel was the worst night of my life. I came very close to going back to Russ, just to protect my son. When I got home that night, there was a message on my phone from Russ. It said, "Well, this isn't exactly the way I wanted it, but I'm willing to take you back." He said it like he would be doing me a big favor.

I called my counselor from HomeSafe and told her I was thinking about returning to Russ. I had absolutely no positive feelings toward him and no delusions about what it would be like. The idea of taking more abuse from him made me sick, but I could not stand the idea of him abusing Daniel either. If I went back, I thought maybe I could protect Daniel, if not myself.

The counselor told me, "Mary, you've saved two of your three kids [meaning Richard and Elizabeth]. If you go back, everyone loses." I knew she was right, but it was still a horrible feeling, like I was sacrificing Daniel for the sake of myself and the other two children. I mean, if a parent saves two of her three children from a burning house, does she feel good about rescuing two, or terrible that she could not rescue all three? I cannot tell you how angry I am that the legal system required me to make that choice.

Needless to say, during that probationary period, Russ was in abuser's heaven. He could do anything he wanted. If I expressed any upset or disagreement, I knew it would be held against me and I might lose Elizabeth too. During this period, Russ would not return the kids as scheduled following visitation, so I had to get someone to go with me to his house and retrieve the children.

I did not appeal the custody decision because by this point, I had no money left to pay the lawyer. It was certainly clear that the lawyer would not pursue the appeal without more up-front money.

I probably never would have gotten Daniel back, except that Russ's live-in girlfriend (with whom he is still living) contacted the children's psychologist to report that he was abusing Daniel. This was four or five months after Russ had gained custody of Daniel. I think the girlfriend made her revelation partly because I had told her that Russ was planning to seek full custody of Elizabeth, too. Russ was not really taking care of the kids; the girlfriend was. When she learned that he would be going after Elizabeth too, she said, "WHAT___!!!" I think she cared about the children and knew that Russ's having custody would be harmful and dangerous for them, plus, I doubt she was interested in being the caretaker for both kids.

After learning about Russ's abuse of Daniel, I immediately went to my lawyer (Lawyer #3), demanding an immediate petition for a change of custody. He said we could not seek a modification of custody because it was too soon. He said, "Let the ink dry on the judge's custody order." That was the last straw and I fired him.

I got a new lawyer and a new psychologist. I recorded a telephone conversation with Russ's girlfriend about the abuse of Daniel. Russ's girlfriend was subpoenaed, and because of the recording, I knew—and Russ knew—that the abuse of Daniel would come out. Even if Russ intimidated her into changing her testimony, I think he knew that the tape was credible.

Faced with a situation he could not win, Russ folded. He agreed to a modification and I regained custody of Daniel. I grabbed at the chance to get custody back, even though I had to agree that Russ could have unsupervised visitation with the children. I knew Russ would never agree to supervised visitation. I did not want, and could not pay for, another long, drawn-out battle in court. Besides, based on what I had seen, I did not want to risk what a judge might do.

As far as I am concerned, Russ agreed to the change of custody to save face. No one in authority ever held him accountable for his abuse. People in authority, like the judge and the psychologists, always supported him and held a good opinion of him. Russ wanted to maintain his good image at all costs. By giving up custody of Daniel without a fight, he could avoid the public humiliation of being outed as an abuser.

He portrayed the custody change to the children as a sacrifice he was making because he loved them so much. "This is what's best for you," he said. Once again, he took no responsibility for doing anything wrong in abusing Daniel. He showed no remorse.

Even after I had custody of both kids, Russ continued to engage in repeated violations of my protective order through phone harassment and stalking. Additionally, his son, Chip, was there unsupervised when the kids visited Russ. Apparently, though, Chip did not abuse either child further.

Finally, in March 1996, about four years after returning Daniel to me, Russ lost visitation. He had put the children in the back of his pickup truck. He was driving fast and hit a bump. Elizabeth flew out and Daniel was dragged behind the truck. Elizabeth scraped her side, hit her head, and hurt her back. She had to have her back manipulated by the doctor and had to take muscle relaxants. Daniel did not want to admit the incident had even occurred, but he did limp for a few days. Because he had directly endangered the children, the judge took away visitation (this was a different judge from the one who had given Russ custody of Daniel).

Eliminating visitation was a proper result, and I am glad about it. Still, I cannot help but feel a little bitter that no one ever really cared about my safety and its effect on our children. In the court's eyes, Russ only became a bad father and a bad person when he injured the children personally and individually. He was never a bad father or a bad person because he had abused their mother. My word about his abuse of the children never counted. The court listened only after I had concrete, outside proof, such as their injuries from being thrown from the pickup truck.

Russ has never paid a dime in child support since I left him. He owes more than twenty-five thousand dollars. I could pursue various state and even federal legal action against Russ, but so far I have not. I have the paperwork all ready to file against him any time I need to. But I consider this my "ace in the hole" against him. I am sure he knows that if he does anything really harmful to me or the kids, I am in a position to have him jailed for willful non-support. This keeps him away from us, and that is a lot more important to me than the money. However, on two separate occasions, he has spent a month in jail for non-payment of child support. Another time, he was arrested for criminal violation of my order of protection; however, he posted bail immediately. Though he was found guilty on two counts, he received a suspended sentence.

In the course of one of the trials for criminal non-support, I learned an amazing story about my original custody judge. God knows why, but apparently the judge finally "got it" about Russ. I have it on good authority that the original judge said to an attorney who had been appointed to represent the children, "This case is like Sleeping with the Enemy [the Julia Roberts movie about domestic violence]. This guy is crazy. There should be an automatic protective order for the children." He also said to the new custody judge, "This guy [Russ] is a ticking bomb."

It has taken me a long time to come back emotionally from the trauma of what Russ did to me and the children. As a child and young woman, I was a happy and light-hearted person. The years of abuse by Russ and then the legal system turned me into someone very different.

For many years, I rarely smiled or laughed. I was often short-tempered, especially at work. I walked around with my head down, burdened by my fears, just doing my best to get through the day.

As I said, it reached the point where Russ could no longer make me cry. But you do not just turn off your emotions toward one person; you turn them off for everything. Several years after I left Russ, one of my brothers died. I could not cry at his funeral. Slowly my ability to feel is coming back; recently I have been able to cry again, at least sometimes. But I will never be the jovial person I once was. Russ's abuse robbed me of many moments of both joy and sorrow that I should have experienced.

My children and I have a pretty good life. I am now forty years old. I recently bought a new house and we are settling in pretty well. For the past five years, I have had a new man in my life, Ken. He is wonderful, kind, and gentle with me and the kids.

However, Russ still affects our lives. He lives in a nearby county, so I am still afraid of what he might do to me or the children. Wherever I go, I always want to face the door so I can see him if he should come in. I'll never be free until one of us—Russ or me—is dead.

Elizabeth, now twelve, has not seen Russ since he lost visitation. She understands the kind of person he is and she does not want to have anything to do with him. All things considered, she is pretty well adjusted. Still, it hurts. We were shopping at Kmart this year shortly before Father's Day. The checkout clerk said cheerfully to Elizabeth, "What are you getting your Dad for Father's Day?" Elizabeth responded bitterly, "The same thing that he's gotten for me the last two Christmases and my last two birthdays: nothing." (Russ did, however, give both children a twenty dollar gift certificate for Christmas this past year.) The clerk responded quietly, "Oh, I guess your dad is like my son's father."

I worry that, because of Russ, Elizabeth will find it hard to trust people, especially men. I have made it a point to have good, kind, and gentle men around my children, not just Ken but also my brothers, men I work with, etc. And I do not allow gender bashing in my house or on the sports teams I coach. I do not allow boys to say bad things about girls, and I do not allow the girls to put down all boys either.

Still, Elizabeth is wary of what men might do in intimate relationships. When I have talked with Elizabeth about the possibility that Ken and I might get married, she says, "Mom, I'm worried that he'll turn out to be like Dad." I encourage her to look at how Ken treats people and how it is so different from Russ. But I understand her fear.

It's even harder on Daniel, now eleven. Of all my children, I worry about him the most. Daniel goes back and forth about Russ. He still wants to have a relationship with his father. That is only natural for a boy approaching adolescence, I guess. Besides, Russ had custody of him; that led to a certain closeness, even if Russ did abuse him. Though there's no visitation, Daniel and Russ continue to talk on the phone and Russ continues to manipulate him.

I know Daniel is holding in a lot of anger and confusion. I worry what that is doing to him. Sometimes he lets the anger go, and that is very scary, especially now that he is getting bigger. It will not be long until he will be bigger, probably much bigger, than I am. I worry whether or not I will be able to control him.

At times Daniel completely denies the abuse. Other times, he says, "I hated Dad when he did that." Daniel is mad at me for having Russ's visitation terminated. He also blames himself, not Russ, for the pickup truck injuries that led to the termination; he says, "I asked Dad to go fast." I do not know how much Russ has encouraged Daniel to blame himself, but I certainly know that Russ takes no responsibility for endangering his children.

Sometimes, Daniel defends Russ to me. Sometimes he will even say, "I'm just like my Dad and I want to be just like my Dad." When he does that, I reply, "I disagree," and try to point out the many ways that Daniel is caring and kind. It is a tightrope. I do not want to put Russ down so much that Daniel feels he must protect him. If you put the father down too much, the son can start to feel like he is no good too. On the other hand, I cannot let Daniel romanticize Russ.

Daniel does not remember Russ's physical abuse of me. He was too young. Sometimes Daniel indicates that he believes Russ and not me about the abuse. This hurts me so much, and scares me too. I try not to disparage Russ. Instead, I tell Daniel, "Keep an open mind. See whether things really support your dad's story or mine." I hope he comes to see his father realistically before it is too late.

As I mentioned, Russ continues to manipulate Daniel. He has said to Daniel, "Take money from your mother, lie to her about where you're going, and run away and come live with me." When Daniel told this to the children's psychologist, she was very firm, "Parents shouldn't teach their children to lie and steal."

Russ does other things to hurt and control Daniel. For instance, Daniel recently tried to call Russ from our home phone. He kept getting a busy signal despite repeated tries. When I called Russ from my office to see what was going on, I got right through. Russ then told me, as casual as could be, that he was blocking calls from our home phone number. How could a supposedly loving father do that to his child?

Recently, Daniel snuck out on the babysitter and met his father. I know Russ had arranged the meeting, showing his disregard for the legal order against visitation. I grounded Daniel for that incident.

I allow Daniel to call Russ sometimes. I think cutting off all communication against Daniel's wishes would make matters worse. I do record the conversations sometimes. I know Russ is always trying to get to me through what he tells Daniel. For instance, Daniel once said to me out of the blue, "Even if you and Ken get married, I'll never call him Dad." Well, I had never suggested that to Daniel. I am sure Russ told Daniel, "You know, if your mother marries Ken, you'll have to call him

Dad." Interestingly, Daniel has said he thinks Ken and I should get married. He thinks it would be best if we all lived under one roof.

I cannot help but feel that Daniel's problems are tied to the years that Russ had custody of him. Those were such important, impressionable years when Russ had him and abused him.

To make matters even worse, Daniel has had such horrible experiences with therapists that he does not trust any of them. The therapist he sees now is someone I trust, and I make him go, but I understand his mistrust of therapy. The kids were so poked and prodded and mistreated during the custody battle; that is not something that magically goes away. This therapist has gained Daniel's trust somewhat, but progress is still hard.

I also worry about Richard, the child of my first marriage. He experienced so much abuse from Russ, as well as seeing the abuse of me when he was at a very impressionable age. Like Elizabeth, he finds it hard to trust Ken. Some time ago, he said to me, "I don't think you should marry Ken while Elizabeth and Daniel are still at home." He knows firsthand what stepfathers can do. Richard and I both realize that he has shown some abusive tendencies. Between the role modeling and the anger that Richard feels, I guess this is understandable. I worry that he might become an abuser. I hope he will continue to work hard to see that does not happen.

People do not always understand the impact on our society of children who have witnessed and experienced abuse. Sometimes I meet people whose attitude seems to be, "Gee, it's terrible what happened to Mary's children, but it really doesn't affect me." I tell them, "Your children are playing next to my children. If my child has behavioral problems because some judge gave him to his abusive father, you'd better believe it affects your children."

Besides my job and my kids, HomeSafe is a big part of my life. I am on the Board of Directors. I volunteer on the twenty-four-hour crisis line at least one night every month. I think there have been times when I have really helped a woman by listening to her and saying "I've been there myself." People at work also know about my experience as an abused woman and sometimes seek me out for advice.

My kids are very supportive of my HomeSafe work. On nights when I am on the crisis line, they understand it is important. They like to hear my stories about women I have helped on the crisis line.

The children really came through during a recent period when a battered woman stayed at our house for six weeks. She was someone I worked with. Other people at work had learned about the abuse and came to talk to me. They asked me to talk to her, even though I did not know her well. I said, "I'm not going to force myself on her. She's already got someone doing that at home; I'm not going to add to her burden. But tell her that I would be happy to talk to her if she would like to talk to me." Just a few hours later, she came to talk. She desperately needed to leave her abuser, and I said, "Why don't you come stay at my house?" She accepted and I called my kids and told them about her situation. Daniel could not have been sweeter or more supportive. He said, "Tell her everything will be okay. Tell her we've been through all this." He even offered to let her stay in his room.

From my work at HomeSafe, I know now how lucky I am compared to most battered women. In addition to supportive family, friends, and clergy, I had a good job and some money. In contrast, most battered women I have met through HomeSafe are trying to escape their batterers without any money or support from family or friends. Indeed, their family and friends have either encouraged them to stay in the relationship, have blamed them for the abuse, or have commanded them to leave before the women were ready. I also hear terrible stories about clergy telling women that "Marriage is sacred," or "This wouldn't be happening to you if you were right with the Lord," or "You must forgive him and reconcile your marriage." Additionally, I talk to women who might leave their abuser if they could be sure that they and their children would still have a roof over their heads and food on the table.

I give many speeches in the community about my experience as a battered woman. I share my story so people will understand that domestic violence happens to all kinds of women. I want them to know that there is still a lot we need to do to change the system. It is bad enough to be abused by someone who says he loves you; unfortunately, women today, like me, are often abused a second and third time by lawyers, psychologists, and judges.

I am public about the abuse for another, more selfish reason. I figure if I put myself in the spotlight, more people—domestic violence workers, police, friends—will be watching my back. If anything happens to me or my children, they will go looking for Russ.

I agreed to share my story with Professor Waits for the same reason that I speak in the community. If just one person reading this story comes away with a better understanding of abuse, it will be worth it. I am not going to go down quietly. I feel that Russ and the legal system took away my children, my money, and my life. They will not take away my voice.

* * *

MARY ANN DUTTON AND CATHERINE L. WALTZ, DOMESTIC VIOLENCE: UNDERSTANDING WHY IT HAPPENS AND HOW TO RECOGNIZE IT

17–WTR Fam. Advoc. 14–18 (Winter, 1995).

Domestic violence is a pattern of coercive interaction that inevitably changes the dynamics of the intimate relationship within which it occurs. Once the pattern of coercive control is established, both parties understand differently the meaning of specific actions and words within the context of a continually changing relationship. It is similar to what occurs when we come to understand the meaning of seemingly innocuous behaviors within our families: the "silent treatment," a glaring look or a critical tone when we visit for the holidays, are late for dinner, or miss an important family event.

The meaning of these behaviors extend far beyond what is said or done at the moment. Rather, meaning is garnered from an accumulated history of interaction within which we acquire a continually refined ability to discriminate subtle nuances of communication. This principle also applies when the communication involves anger, fear, threat, injury, or loss, and where the lessons have been taught through a history of violence and abuse.

Typically, battered women are not easily recognized, and batterers are even harder to identify. Even when there is evidence of injury or threats of severe violence, the complex dynamics of domestic violence and the secrecy and distortions that shroud it can lead professionals to minimize or fail to recognize it altogether. Effectively recognizing domestic violence requires an examination of efforts both batterers and victims use to hide the violence; strategies battered women use to protect themselves and their children; and the psychological, physical, economic, and social impact of the violence.

Although historically the focus has been on heterosexual relationships, domestic violence also occurs between same-sex partners and throughout all social and economic levels of society. Research data shows that women in heterosexual relationships engage in violence at rates similar to those of men. However, this data must be considered in context. "Physical menace" and fear cannot be separated from an understanding of domestic violence. Recognizing not just who is hit, but who is afraid of being hit, creates a more accurate picture of victimization.

Data indicate that violence toward women by their male partners results in physical injury, the need for medical care, absence from work, and psychological injury (e.g., stress and depression) at higher rates than violence toward men by their female partners. * * *

TYPES OF VIOLENCE

Within the social science literature, behaviors constituting a pattern of coercive control have been categorized as physical, sexual, and psychological abuse, including abuse toward property and pets. Examples of physical violence include throwing objects, pushing, physical restraint by forcefully holding or tying up, slapping, hair pulling, punching, kicking, burning, choking, strangling, smothering, slamming a head against a hard object, beating, hitting with an object, running over with an automobile, subjecting another's skin or eyes to a dangerous substance (e.g., gasoline or bleach), and using a weapon.

Regardless of type, the function of violent or abusive behavior is the same: to gain control over another's actions, thoughts, and feelings.

Although legal definitions of sexual assault typically require specific elements (e.g., lack of consent, force or threat of force, and sexual penetration), abusive behaviors include a much broader range that may include forced nudity, provocative dressing, viewing pornographic films, or other types of sexual activity. Likewise, a batterer may use subtle and implicit threats to coerce sexual compliance when those threats are credible based on previous violence.

Psychological abuse may accompany both physical and sexual abuse, or it may occur alone. There is a distinction, however, between "negative" interactions found in nonviolent relationships and "psychologically abusive" interactions characteristic of violent relationships. In Treating Men Who Batter: Theory, Practice, and Programs. New York: Springer (1989), Ganley distinguishes psychologically abusive behavior by the existence of a credible threat of violence derived from prior violence. Such knowledge may refer to violence directed toward the victim, a previous mate, the children, or someone else.

Like physical and sexual violence, psychological abuse also seeks control over another. Examples include:

- Coercion and threats—to kill the battered woman or others, take children away, destroy financially, coerce illegal activity, such as drug trafficking or prostitution;

- Intimidation—displaying weapons, destroying objects, making menacing gestures;

- Isolation—limiting use of a telephone, contact with others, or access to transportation;

- Minimization, denial, and blaming—the abuser denies the violence, will not acknowledge that it is a problem, or blames the victim ("We're both guilty");

- Use of children to control—relaying intimidating threats through children or using custody or visitation proceedings to gain access to the battered woman or control her whereabouts;

- Use of economic resources—unilaterally maintaining exclusive access to cash, credit cards, bank accounts; accruing debt in battered woman's name; withholding child support payments;

- Use of "male privilege"—making unilateral decisions about where to live, major purchases, and whether the woman is employed outside the home;

- Induced debility—through deprivation of sleep or food;

- Monopolization of perceptions—limiting access to information;

- Emotional abuse and degradation—resorting to name-calling and insults;

- Induced altered states of consciousness—through hypnotic induction or forced alcohol or drug use; and

- Occasional indulgences—designed to perpetuate the victim's hope that the violence and abuse will end.

Stalking is a more recently recognized form of abusive behavior. Although not limited to intimate relationships, it often occurs when the battered victim attempts to leave or has already left the relationship. Stalking includes sending a series of threatening letters; appearing at a spouse's work-place or home when ordered or asked not to; making incessant, intimidating telephone calls or employing other types of coercion to induce the victim to return to the batterer.

Assessing the seriousness of domestic violence often requires determining the context in which the behavior occurred, since neither the type of aggression nor the potential criminal charge adequately predicts the seriousness of the injury. For example, "pushing" may appear to be a relatively innocuous form of violence unless it is a push down a flight of stairs during pregnancy, in front of an oncoming vehicle, into a glass door, or out an upper-level window. Conversely, although a gun may result in a superficial wound, the potential risk of serious physical injury or death and the likelihood of psychological damage make the use of a gun a serious form of domestic violence.

A sensitive and skilled interviewer who has established a basis for trust and collaboration may make it possible for a victim to reveal information about her abuse. However, victims may attempt to withhold information in an effort to protect battering partners from embarrassment and social disapproval; to protect themselves from increased violence or the loss of their children; or to protect others from injury or legal sanctions for attempting to help them.

Posttraumatic stress reactions may cause battered women to avoid thinking, feeling, or remembering some aspects of the violence. If the prior abuse included coercing her to engage in illegal behavior, such as nude dancing, prostitution, selling illegal items, child abuse, or forgery, the obstacles to disclosure may be even greater.

In gathering information from a batterer, questions that are specific, concrete, and direct are more likely to get results. Perpetrators are generally reluctant to disclose the violence unless they are feeling guilty or remorseful or are fearful of losing family relationships or being forced to go to jail or undergo treatment.

Factors that encourage batterers to deny or distort their violent behavior include:

- Reluctance to give up personal power by acknowledging wrongdoing;

- Threat to one's self-image as a right, strong, powerful, and in-control person; and

- Fear of criminal charges, disapproval of family or friends, and the potential loss of a job.

Profile of a Batterer

Studies have revealed no single personality profile of a batterer. Nonetheless, a risk-marker profile is useful in identifying the types of individuals and situations that increase the risk of battering. The profile cannot, however, be used to predict violence, nor do risk factors necessarily suggest a causal link to battering.

Risk markers for battering include witnessing and/or experiencing violence in the childhood home, chronic alcohol abuse or illicit drug use, status inconsistency (e.g., occupational attainment or income is lower than expected based on educational achievement), and status incompatibility (e.g., educational or occupational attainment and income is less than a partner's), as well as depression and low self-esteem.

It is important to note, however, that psychopathology and other psychological problems have not been consistently associated with battering. Some risk factors may be the product of engaging in domestic violence per se or consequences that follow from it (e.g., divorce or separation), rather than being linked etiologically to battering.

Empirical studies identify higher rates of domestic violence by men with less education, higher unemployment, and lower incomes. However, these results may reflect the fact that virtually all studies rely either on the police records or on the batterer to voluntarily identify himself, and thus socially and economically advantaged men are much less likely to be identified.

Battered women commonly respond to the violence and abuse they experience by actively or passively resisting it. A woman's resistance is influenced by cultural factors, socioeconomic resources, social support, history of prior victimization, and her individual strengths and vulnerabilities.

A recent national crime victim survey reported that 80 percent of female victims who suffered violence at the hands of an intimate partner used some means of self-protection. Of those, 40 percent responded physically and 40 percent used passive/verbal means. Only 53 percent reported that their efforts helped the situation, whereas 23 percent indicated that resistance made the situation worse. See Violence Against Women. Washington, D.C.: U.S. Department of Justice, Office of Justice Programs, Bureau of Justice Statistics. Publication No. NCJ–145325 (1994).

The overused question, Why did she stay? is too narrow a perspective from which to understand a battered woman who remained in an abusive home. This question is less productive than, and deflects attention from, the real issue of how she responded to the violence. Likewise, the question erroneously implies that leaving the batterer necessarily increases the woman's safety. Separating or deciding to separate may actually increase the risk of violence to the battered woman. In the most extreme cases, battered women are more likely to be killed after the separation. Thus, remaining in the relationship may actually save the victim's life and protect her children, at least short-term.

Battered women's attempts to stop, escape, and avoid the violence are influenced by many factors (e.g., economic resources, social status, social support, children, physical and emotional vulnerabilities). These help-seeking strategies have been grouped as follows:

- Personal—hiding or disguising one's appearance, compliance with demands, fighting back, deliberately showing no resistance;
- Informal—telling family or friends, seeking shelter, seeking some kind of support group;
- Formal—calling police, filing for divorce or legal separation, seeking mental health or medical intervention.

Mapping the range of strategies that a battered woman has used to resist the violence and abuse against her and her children inevitably reveals someone other than the stereotypical helpless, passive victim. However, even battered women who fit the stereotype engage in repeated efforts to protect themselves and their children from ongoing abuse. As professionals, we often fail to recognize these efforts and even assume that a battered woman can stop the violence if only she does the "right" thing. A recent study demonstrated, however, that once the violence starts, only the batterer can stop it. See Jacobson, N.S. et al., Journal of Consulting and Clinical Psychology, 63(3), 982–988 (1994).

Sometimes a batterer will stop the violence in response to his partner's threats to separate or call the police. In other cases, however, even successful criminal prosecution is not enough to protect a battered woman from repeated injury or even death. In all cases, understanding a battered woman's response to violence means recognizing:

- The cumulative pattern of violent and coercive behavior;
- The chronology of her efforts or strategies to resist the violence and abuse against her, her children, and others around her;
- The emotional, economic, social, and physical cost of engaging in these efforts;
- Others' responses to how the battered woman deals with the violence;
- The short-and long-term outcomes of these efforts with reference to safety from violence and abuse;
- The obstacles to strategies the battered woman did not choose; and
- The overall context of her life.

Psychological Impact

The psychological effects of domestic violence impact not only the battered woman but her children as well. Seeing, hearing, and knowing about violence in the childhood home is a major risk factor that distinguishes male batterers and female victims from their cohorts. * * *

The psychological impact of violence cannot be understood on the basis of the violence or abuse alone. The meaning of the behavior, derived in part from the context in which it occurred, influences its psychological impact. Thus, when a battered woman believes that her partner is willing and likely to seriously injure or kill her or her children, the psychological impact of the violence will be greater than would have resulted from the violent behavior or injury alone.

The nature of the psychological impact of domestic violence varies among battered women and may include:

- Emotional reactions—anger, fear, shame;

- Symptoms of psychological distress or dysfunction—disassociation, somatic complaints, depression or grief, anxiety, substance abuse;

- Multifaceted syndromes—post-traumatic stress disorders or a variety of acute stress disorders;

- Trauma-related cognitive schema—low self-esteem, a distrust of others, and a belief that the world is unsafe.

A battered woman's psychological reactions to violence may influence the strategies she uses to respond to it. For example, in some cases, more fearful reactions may increase the likelihood or the intensity of a battered woman's resistance to violence. Conversely, intense feelings of terror may paralyze her as she attempts to protect herself.

EFFECTIVE TREATMENT

Evaluation of batterer treatment has focused primarily on group approaches. The efficacy of couples' intervention or individual psychotherapy for domestic violence is at this point inconclusive. Some argue that couples' intervention in the early stages of treatment increases the risk of violence and fails to make the batterer accountable for his behavior.

A recent study found a 40 percent recidivism rate among batterers five years after treatment. (Recidivism is defined as a conviction for domestic violence assault, an order of protection due to domestic violence, or police contact on suspicion of domestic violence.) * * *

Further, a literature review of 16 group treatment studies revealed that "the majority of men stop their physically abusive behavior subsequent to intervention." * * * Successful outcomes, defined as cessation of violent behavior, ranged from 53 to 85 percent.

Several factors are important in considering effectiveness. The first is the length of follow-up. Most of the studies employed a six-month follow-up period, though the range was four months to three years. Studies have shown, however, that the outcome at six months is not necessarily consistent with that at 18 months. * * *

The second factor to consider is the source of the data. Follow-up data may vary considerably, depending on whether it is based on batterers' self-reporting, report by the victim, or police records.

Third, the term "successful outcome" may mean a reduction of violent behavior, cessation of violent behavior, or cessation of both violent and psychologically abusive or controlling behavior.

Fourth, most studies report data only for participants who remain in the treatment group and who can be located for follow-up. Batterers who drop out of treatment are typically excluded from follow-up contact. Thus, reported success rates may overestimate treatment effectiveness since dropouts are not considered.

Finally, many treatment programs are court mandated and thus imply legal consequences for those who fail to complete treatment. There is sufficient data to suggest that treatment is effective for the majority of male batterers who successfully complete the program and are available for follow-up. However, continued research is needed to develop a more sophisticated understanding of which batterers will respond to treatment and the length, intensity, and types of treatment that are effective for individual batterers. Likewise, we need to look at how the batterer's treatment was integrated into the court system, how long the treatment was effective, and whether the results were transferable to new relationships.

Because research suggests that a substantial number of "successful completers" are, nevertheless, recidivists (15–47 percent), continued effort is needed to better understand both deterrents to and effective treatment for battering.

EXPERT TESTIMONY

Expert testimony about domestic violence and its psychological effects can be relevant to a variety of legal issues involving battered women in both criminal and civil cases. An expert evaluation should include an analysis of (1) the violence and abuse, (2) the battered victim's psychological reactions to domestic violence, and (3) the victim's strategies for resisting and protecting herself and the children. Such an analysis is not complete without incorporating relevant contextual factors that influence the victim's psychological reactions and strategies.

Effective use of expert testimony requires a focus on the link between these factors (e.g., the nature of violence, psychological effects of violence, strategies used, context) and the legal elements of the particular case (e.g., self defense, duress, failure to protect).

Although the social science literature provides a theoretical and empirical foundation for understanding the dynamics between batterer and victim, no amount of research data or theory can adequately articulate an understanding of a particular battered woman in relation to a particular batterer. That perspective is gained from a careful analysis of case-specific information framed against the backdrop of scientific knowledge and professional experience.

LENORE E. WALKER, THE PSYCHOSOCIAL THEORY OF LEARNED HELPLESSNESS

The Battered Woman 44–54 (Harper & Row, 1979).

RESPONSE–OUTCOME

Most plants and animals have little voluntary control over what happens to them in their environment. Much of the time they merely react to events that happen. For example, if you place a plant on a windowsill, its leaves and stem will grow toward the light. The way in which it grows has nothing to do with whether or not the plant can change the direction from which the light comes; thus its movements do not change the relationship between the response and the outcome. Growing toward the light is not a voluntary response; the plant will grow that way regardless. Such behavior cannot be changed or modified. However, since human beings are not plants, we make many voluntary responses which can be changed or modified, depending upon the outcome. If a voluntary response makes a difference in what happens, or operates on the environment in a successful way, we will tend to repeat that voluntary response. This is the principle of reinforcement. If we expect that a response we make is going to produce a certain outcome, and our expectations are met when we make that response, we then feel that we have had control over that situation. To check whether or not we have actually had some control over a particular situation, we choose to make the same response the next time, and if that outcome happens again, we verify our ability to control it. We can then choose not to make the response and the outcome does not happen. Human beings thus can decide whether or not to make that voluntary response again, depending upon whether or not they want their expectations met. This gives us a certain amount of power or control over our lives. If, on the other hand, we expect certain things to occur when we make a certain response, and they do not, we will often look for explanations as to *why* such expectations did not take place. If we cannot find any logical explanations, after a time we assume we have no control over the outcome. In this way, we learn what kinds of things in our environment we can control and what kinds of things are beyond our control.

LOSS OF VOLUNTARY CONTROL

Laboratory experiments have shown that if an organism experiences situations which cannot be controlled, then the motivation to try to respond to such events when they are repeated will be impaired. Even if later on the organism is able to make appropriate responses which do control events, the organism will have trouble believing that the responses are under its control and that they really do work. Furthermore, the organism will have difficulty in learning how to repeat those responses.

This results in an apparent disturbance in the organism's emotional and physical well-being. Both depression and anxiety seem to be the characteristics of such an organism's behavior.

LEARNED HELPLESSNESS

The area of research concerned with early-response reinforcement and subsequent passive behavior is called learned helplessness. Experimental psychologist Martin Seligman hypothesized that dogs subjected to noncontingent negative reinforcement could learn that their voluntary behavior had no effect on controlling what happened to them. If such an aversive stimulus was repeated, the dog's motivation to respond would be lessened.

Seligman and his researchers placed dogs in cages and administered electrical shocks at random and varied intervals. These dogs quickly learned that no matter what response they made, they could not control the shock. At first, the dogs attempted to escape through various voluntary movements. When nothing they did stopped the shocks, the dogs ceased any further voluntary activity and became compliant, passive, and submissive. When the researchers attempted to change this procedure and teach the dogs that they could escape by crossing to the other side of the cage, the dogs still would not respond. In fact, even when the door was left open and the dogs were shown the way out, they remained passive, refused to leave, and did not avoid the shock. It took repeated dragging of the dogs to the exit to teach them how to respond voluntarily again. The earlier in life that the dogs received such treatment, the longer it took to overcome the effects of this so-called learned helplessness. However, once they did learn that they could make the voluntary response, their helplessness disappeared.

Similar experiments have been performed on other species, including cats, fish, rodents, birds, and primates and humans, with the same kind of results. Some animals learned to be helpless at a faster rate and became more helpless across a greater number of situations. For some, the learning was discriminate and occurred in only one situation. For others, the sense of powerlessness generalized to all behavior.

An experiment demonstrating the generalization of learned helplessness phenomenon occurred in rats. Newborn rats were held in the experimenter's hand until all voluntary escape movements ceased. They were then released. This procedure was repeated several more times. The rats were then placed in a vat of water. Within thirty minutes, the rats subjected to the learned helplessness treatment drowned. Many did not even attempt to swim, and sank to the bottom of the vat immediately. Untreated rats could swim up to sixty hours before drowning. The sense of powerlessness was generalized from squirming in order to escape handholding to swimming in order to escape death. Since the rats were all physically capable of learning to swim to stay alive, it was the psychological effect of learned helplessness which was theorized to explain the rats' behavior.

The learned helplessness theory has three basic components: information about what will happen; thinking or cognitive representation about what will happen (learning, expectation, belief, perception); and behavior toward what does happen. It is the second or cognitive representation component where the faulty expectation that response and outcome are independent occurs. This is the point at which cognitive, motivational, and emotional disturbances originate. It is important to realize that the expectation may or may not be accurate. Thus, if the person does have control over response-outcome variables but believes she/he doesn't, the person responds with the learned helplessness phenomenon. If such a person believes that she/he does have control over a response-outcome contingency, even if she/he doesn't, the behavior is not affected. Therefore, the actual nature of controllability is not as important as the belief, expectation, or cognitive set. Some people will persevere longer than others in attempting to exert control; however, they will give up when they really believe the situation is hopeless. Witness the patient who loses the "will to live" and dies when she/he could have lived. The patient believes that nothing can save her/him, whether or not a cure is in reality feasible.

Once we believe we cannot control what happens to us, it is difficult to believe we can ever influence it, even if later we experience a favorable outcome. This concept is important for understanding why battered women do not attempt to free themselves from a battering relationship. Once the women are operating from a belief of helplessness, the perception becomes reality and they become passive, submissive, "helpless." They allow things that appear to them to be out of their control actually to get out of their control. When one listens to descriptions of battering incidents from battered women, it often seems as if these women were not actually as helpless as they perceived themselves to be. However, their behavior was determined by their negative cognitive set, or their perceptions of what they could or could not do, not by what actually existed. The battered women's behavior appears similar to Seligman's dogs, rats, and people.

In addition to the way they perceive or think about what happens, people also differ in how they explain normal occurrences. Different people have different predispositions to believing in the causations of events. For example, some people believe that most of the events that occur in their life are caused by factors outside themselves. We call these people "externalizers." Deeply religious people fall into this category, as do people who believe in strictly following rigid rules and regulations. People who believe that they have a lot of influence over what happens in their life are called "internalizers." It has been found that externalizers tend to become victims of learned helplessness more easily than internalizers. Research remains to be done to discover whether battered women can be classified as externalizers.

As in the experiment with rats, feelings of helplessness among humans tend to spread from one specific aversive situation to another. A battered woman therefore does not have to learn that she cannot escape one man's battering, but rather that she cannot escape men's overall coercion.

Helplessness also has a debilitating effect on human problem solving. Experiments with college students show that while the damage is not irreversible, it does alter one's motivation to initiate problem-solving actions. Thus, learning ability is hampered and the repertoire of responses from which people can choose is narrowed. In this way, battered women become blind to their options. People who feel helpless really believe that they have no influence over the success or failure of events that concern them. Women who have learned to expect battering as a way of life have learned that they cannot influence its occurrence.

The time sequence experienced by battering victims seems to be parallel to the time sequence experienced by victims of a major traumatic disaster. It has been shown that many people who experience a disaster immediately volunteer their time and energy in order to attempt to combat their feelings of helplessness. Some become Red Cross helpers over a large area; others become volunteers in the immediate vicinity. The feeling of being able to do something generally helps the volunteer as much as it helps the victim. This phenomenon is also seen in self-help groups such as Alcoholics Anonymous and Reach for Recovery. The general reaction to major traumas such as hurricanes, earthquakes, airplane crashes, or catastrophic fires is a feeling of powerlessness. However, unless such trauma is repeated, these feelings will usually dissipate over time. On the other hand, if there are repeated traumas within a short period of time, then people become immune, passive, and convinced that they cannot do anything to help themselves. Witness the results in concentration camps. A chronic feeling of powerlessness takes over which does not dissipate. The response of victims of repeated disasters is similar to battered women's perception of powerlessness. It is also probable that helplessness is learned on a relative continuum. There may be different levels of learned helplessness that a woman learns from an interaction of traditional female-role standards and individual personality development. The male-female dyadic relationship may be a specific area affected by this interactive developmental process. Battered women seem to be most afflicted with feelings of helplessness in their relationships with men. Women with responsible jobs and careers resort to traditional female-role stereotyped behavior with their men, even though such behavior is not present in other areas of their lives.

Thus, in applying the learned helplessness concept to battered women, the process of how the battered woman becomes victimized grows clearer. Repeated batterings, like electrical shocks, diminish the woman's motivation to respond. She becomes passive. Secondly, her cognitive ability to perceive success is changed. She does not believe her response will result in a favorable outcome, whether or not it might. Next, having generalized her helplessness, the battered woman does not believe anything she does will alter any outcome, not just the specific situation that has occurred. She says, "No matter what I do, I have no influence." She cannot think of alternatives. She says, "I am incapable and too stupid to learn how to change things." Finally, her sense of emotional well-being becomes precarious. She is more prone to depression and anxiety.

Are battered women "clinically" depressed? Many of the new cognitive theories in psychology define clinical depression as a state in which a person holds an exaggerated belief that whatever he or she does, it will not be good enough. Such people also believe that their inadequacies preclude them from controlling their lives effectively. A person who believes that she is helpless to control a situation also may believe that she is not capable enough to do so. The small number of women I have interviewed do not provide the basis for any scientific conclusions about depression; however, it does appear that much of their behavior is designed to ward off depression. For example, many of them attempted to exert a degree of control over their batterings. Although they accepted the batterings as inevitable, they tried to control the time and place. This small measure of control seemed to be an effort not to feel totally helpless. For example, when a woman begins to nag at a man after she knows he has had a hard day at work, she can justify her belief that she really deserved the battering she anticipated all along because she started it. Although she appears to be masochistically setting up her own victimization, such behavior may well be a desperate attempt to exercise some control over her life.

Another point we observed relative to depression concerned anxiety levels of battered women. When these women discussed living under the threat and fear of battering, there was less anxiety than we expected. In fact, in many cases it seemed that living with the batterer produced less anxiety than living apart from him. Why? She often feels that she has the hope of some control if she is with him. Another explanation is that a fear response motivates a search for alternate ways of responding that will avoid or control the threat. Anxiety is, in essence, a call to danger. Physiologically the autonomic nervous system sends out hormones that are designed to cope with the immediate stress. Once this stress is under control, anxiety returns to a normal level. Or higher levels of hormones are constantly emitted in order to live under such pervasive stress. This reaction will also occur when certain threats are considered uncontrollable. What also happens in this situation is that anxiety does not return to a normal level; rather, it decreases and depression takes over.

How Battered Women Become Victimized

There seems to be little doubt that feelings of powerlessness by both men and women contribute to the cause and maintenance of violent behavior. However, although many men do indeed feel powerless in relation to their control over their lives, it is my contention that the very fact of being a woman, more specifically a married woman, automatically creates a situation of powerlessness. This is one of the detrimental effects of sex-role stereotyping.

Women are systematically taught that their personal worth, survival, and autonomy do not depend on effective and creative responses to life situations, but rather on their physical beauty and appeal to men. They learn that they have no direct control over the circumstances of their lives. Early in their lives, little girls learn from their parents and society that they are to be more passive than boys. Having systematically trained to be second best, women begin marriage with a psychological disadvantage. Marriage in our patriarchal society does not offer equal power to men and women. The notion that marriage laws protect women is questionable when statistics reveal the mental health problems and criminal behavior married women suffer from. On the contrary, the law seems to perpetuate the historical notion of male supremacy. In most states a husband cannot be found guilty of raping his wife. The husband still has the legal right to decide where the family will live, restricting the woman's freedom of movement. Power in marriage also is related to economic and social status. Since men more often than women hold higher-paying jobs with more status, their occupational prestige gives them decision-making powers they can use to engage in physical and psychological one-upmanship. Finally, most men are also superior in physical strength, another source of masculine power and confidence.

Cultural conditions, marriage laws, economic realities, physical inferiority—all these teach women that they have no direct control over the circumstances of their lives. Although they are not subjected to electrical shocks as the dogs in the experiments were, they are subjected to both parental and institutional conditioning that restricts their alternatives and shelters them from the consequences of any disapproved alternatives. Perhaps battered women, like the dogs who learn that their behavior is unrelated to their subsequent welfare, have lost their ability to respond effectively.

Consequences of Learned Helplessness

One result of learned helplessness can be depression, as discussed previously. Another result seems to be a change in the battered woman's perception of the consequences of violence. Living constantly with fear seems to produce an imperviousness to the seriousness of violence.

There is an unusually high incidence of guns, knives, and other weaponry reported in the battering attacks. I am constantly amazed that more people are not accidentally killed during these incidents. The women interviewed declared that they did not fear death, although they also did not really believe they would die, either. Those women interviewed who murdered their husbands all stated they had no idea they had killed them until the police informed them. One woman fought furiously with police when they took her to the homicide precinct for booking. She felt her husband would recover from the severe bullet wounds that had been inflicted. Several men reported surprise that their rage had inflicted any pain or injuries to the women. Both the men and the women involved in this violence repeatedly reassured other people that they wouldn't really hurt each other. As we begin to see more battered women, we also realize the high probability that as the violence escalates, they will eventually be killed by or kill their men.

STOPPING LEARNED HELPLESSNESS

If battering behavior is maintained by perceptions of helplessness, can this syndrome be stopped? Turning back to the animal studies, we see that the dogs could only be taught to overcome their passivity by being dragged repeatedly out of the punishing situation and shown how to avoid the shock. Just as the dogs have helped us understand why battered women do not leave their violent situations voluntarily, perhaps they can also suggest ways the women can reverse being battered. A first step would seem to be to persuade the battered woman to leave the battering relationship or persuade the batterer to leave. This "dragging" may require help from outside, such as the dogs received from the researchers. The safe houses for battered women are very effective here. Secondly, battered women need to be taught to change their failure expectancy to reverse a negative cognitive set. They need to understand what success is, to raise their motivation and aspiration levels, to be able to initiate new and more effective responses, so they can learn to control their own lives. Self-esteem and feelings of competence are extremely important in protecting against feelings of helplessness and depression. Women must be able to believe that their behavior will affect what happens to them. Counseling or psychotherapy can teach women to control their own lives and to be able to erase that kind of victim potential.

Battering behavior must cease. We cannot afford the toll it takes in our society. A thorough study of some of the particulars occurring in battering relationships may lead us to effective methods to reverse this tragic process. By examining in this book some of the techniques the batterers use, how they victimize women and cause further psychological destruction, I hope to improve the understanding of battering.

EDWARD GONDOLF & ELLEN FISHER, THE SURVIVOR THEORY

Battered Women as Survivors: An Alternative to Treating Learned Helplessness 11–18, 20–24 (Lexington Books, 1988).

Our assertion that battered women are active survivors raises a fundamental theoretical issue. It appears to contradict the prevailing characterization that battered women suffer from learned helplessness. According to learned helplessness, battered women tend to "give up" in the course of being abused; they suffer psychological paralysis and an underlying masochism that needs to be treated by specialized therapy. Our survivor hypothesis, on the other hand, suggests that women respond to abuse with help-seeking efforts that are largely unmet. What the women most need are the resources and social support that would enable them to become more independent and leave the batterer. (See table 2–1.)

In this chapter, we examine in more detail the theoretical basis for these two contrasting characterizations of battered women. First, the assumptions of learned helplessness are discussed. We consider also the experimental research underlying learned helplessness and its application to battered women. Second, we present the basis of a survivor theory with an overview of our survivor hypothesis, a summary of the supportive empirical research, and a redefinition of the symptoms of learned helplessness.

Finally, the implications of the alternative survivor theory are raised. There appears to be learned helplessness among the help sources designed to aid the battered women. The help sources need to be "treated," and the patriarchal assumptions that debilitate the available help sources need to be addressed.

LEARNED HELPLESSNESS

The Prevailing Characterization

The battered woman has been typically characterized as a helpless and passive victim. Lenore Walker's ground-breaking book, *The Battered Woman* (1979), noted that the battered woman becomes "psychologically paralyzed" as a result of learned helplessness. As animal experiments have demonstrated, there is a tendency to become submissive in the face of intermittent punishments or abuse. Similarly, the battered woman is immobilized amidst the uncertainty of when abuse will occur. She begins to feel that she has no control over her experience. No matter what she does, she "gets it." In the process, the victim begins to blame herself for the abuse. This self-blame implies some recourse or control over the otherwise unpredictable abuse. "If only I change myself, then the abuse will stop."

Lenore Walker (1979:49–50) summarizes the victimization this way:

> In applying the learned helplessness concept to battered women, the process of how the battered woman becomes victimized grows clearer. Repeated batterings, like electrical shocks (in animal experiments), diminish the woman's motivation to respond. She becomes passive. Secondly, her cognitive ability to perceive success is changed. She does not believe her response will result in a favorable outcome, whether or not it might. Next, having generalized her helplessness, the battered woman does not believe anything she does will alter any outcome, not just the specific situation that has occurred. she says "no matter what I do, I have no influence." She cannot think of alternatives. She says, "I am incapable and too stupid to learn how to change things." Finally, her sense of emotional well-being becomes precarious. She is more prone to depression and anxiety.

Battered women, therefore, appear to need specialized counseling to address their debilitated psychological state. A number of clinical studies have, in fact, prescribed treatment for the battered woman's lack of self-esteem and fragmented identity, feelings of loss and inadequacy, or isolation and anxiety that is traced to abuse as a child. Feminist critics, however, have strongly objected to the implication that battered women provoke or prolong abuse and generally require psychological counseling.

Table 2-1

Learned Helplessness	Survivor Hypothesis
Severe abuse fosters a sense of helplessness in the victim. Abuse as a child and the neglect of help sources intensifies this helplessness. The battered woman is consequently severely victimized.	Severe abuse prompts innovative coping strategies from battered women and efforts to seek help. Previous abuse and neglect by help sources lead women to try other help sources and strategies to lessen the abuse. The battered woman, in this light, is a "survivor."
The victim experiences low self-esteem, self-blame, guilt, and depression. The only way to feel some sense of control over what is otherwise an unpredictable environment is to think that "if I change my ways, things will get better." But the abuse continues.	The survivor may experience anxiety or uncertainty over the prospects of leaving the batterer. The lack of options, know-how, and finances raise fears about trying to escape the batterer. The battered woman may therefore attempt to change the batterer instead of attempting to leave.
The victim eventually becomes psychologically paralyzed. She fails to seek help for herself and may even appear passive before the beatings. When she does contact a help source she is very tentative about receiving help and is likely to return to the batterer despite advice or opportunity to leave.	The survivor actively seeks help from a variety of informal and formal help sources. There is most often inadequate or piecemeal helpgiving that leaves the woman little alternative but to return to the batterer. The helpseeking continues, however.
This vulnerability and indecisiveness prolongs the violence and may contribute to its intensification. Some observers argue that this tendency may reflect an underlying masochism in the battered woman. The woman may feel that she deserves to be beaten and accepts it as a fulfillment of her expectations.	The failure of help sources to intervene in a comprehensive and decisive fashion allows abuse to continue and escalate. The inadequacy of help sources may be attributed to a kind of learned helplessness experienced in many community services. Service providers feel too overwhelmed and limited in their resources to be effective and therefore do not try as hard as they might.
Battered women as victims need primarily psychological counseling to treat their low self esteem, depression, and masochism. Cognitive therapy that addresses attributions of blame for the abuse may also be particularly effective in motivating the victim.	Battered women as survivors of abuse need, most of all, access to resources that would enable them to escape the batterer. Community services need to be coordinated to assure the needed allocation of resources and integrated to assure long-term comprehensive intervention.

* * *

Explanations of Battered Women

It is not surprising, then, that the notion of learned helplessness has become a fixture in the domestic violence field as well. Battered women, as the theory goes, typically are conditioned to tolerate the abuse as a result of persistent and intermittent reinforcement from the batterer. The community lack of response to the abuse, and frequent accusation that the woman contributed to the abuse, further the helplessness. The cage door is shut, so to speak, and the women have no apparent way out.

Additionally, studies have suggested that learned helplessness may be rooted in childhood exposure to violence. Exposure to violence as a child may, in fact, predispose a woman to an abusive relationship as an adult. She may grow up thinking that abuse is normal, or feel such shame and rejection that she expects and accepts the worst. The relationship between abuse as a child and as an adult may, however, be spurious or inevitable given the amount of violence in and around our homes. Perhaps a more acceptable position is that the batterers appear to be "violence prone," and not battered women.

Another popular explanation for what appears as learned helplessness is the "brainwashing" that a woman experiences in an abusive relationship as an adult. The batterer's manipulation and control of the woman has, in fact, been likened to the tactics used by brainwashers in prisoner-of-war camps. Eventually the captive is psychologically broken down to the point of relinquishing any sense of autonomy and complying to all the wishes of the captor.

Psychologists Donald Dutton and Susan Painter have similarly applied the theory of "traumatic bonding" to battered women. They point out that the abuse leaves the victim emotionally and physically drained and in desperate need of some human support or care. She is therefore likely to respond to the batterer's apologies and affection after the abuse. In this vulnerable state, she may sympathize and overidentify with the batterer, much as some prisoners of war or concentration camps have become sympathetic toward their guards. In essence, the trauma makes the woman prone to a kind of masochism.

Helplessness as Masochism

Although the initial application of learned helplessness to battered women was not intended to implicate masochism, it has been explicitly extended to do so.

* * *

In Dr. Natalie Shainess's conception, however, masochism is learned developmentally and culturally, rather than predestined as the Freudians suggest. This may in part be related to growing up in abusive homes and thinking, as a result, that abuse is normal, or to internalizing the persistent subjugation and degradation of women in society at large. The masochism can be unlearned, therefore, by being more assertive and decisive in interpersonal relations. The popularity of books like *Women*

Who Love Too Much appears to speak to this notion that women make themselves vulnerable and dependent and can solve this problem by simply being more assertive.

Reformulations of Helplessness

The learned helplessness theory has admittedly been critiqued and reformulated in recent years. Its earlier versions reflected the assumptions of behaviorist conditioning. Like the animals in Seligman's experiments, humans appeared to be "trained" into submission and learned helplessness. Their situation appeared to determine their behavior. In sum, learned helplessness was a conditioned reaction to the unpredictable punishments one received.

The advent of cognitive psychology has introduced the role of individual expectations and attributions in mediating learned helplessness. In this view, one's perceptions of the environment are what most influence one's reaction to it. If an individual perceives a series of punishments or failures as outside of his or her control, then learned helplessness is more likely.

Similarly, several qualitative studies of battered women have shown that their assumptions about their social environment contribute to their reactions to abuse. However, rather than confirm learned helplessness, these studies actually open the door to alternative explanations. The women, rather than being passive recipients of the violence, appear instead as participants in the definition of the relationship and of themselves. If anything, the battered women learn, as the abuse escalates, that the self-blame associated with learned helplessness is inappropriate.

Interviews with self-identified battered women show that the women are more likely to blame themselves for the abuse after the first incident. Consequently they may attempt to change their behavior to please their batterers and avoid further abuse. As is usually the case, the violence recurs and escalates despite the women's efforts to please their batterers. They begin, therefore, to increasingly blame the batterer (that is, attribute the cause to him) and seek ways to change him. When these fail, the women then seek more decisive intervention and means to establish their own safety.

There is some suggestion, however, that there is a limit to this initiative. After repeated unsuccessful attempts to control the battering, some women may then begin to give up and lessen their helpseeking. This resignation, after an intermediate phase of active helpseeking, differs from the conventional notion of learned helplessness in which there is a progression toward total brainwashing. (See table 2–2 for a summary of this attributional helpseeking progression.)

Another interview study, with a small sample of shelter residents, suggests that the women experience a loss of self; for example, they mention feeling like a zombie, a robot, or simply numb amidst the violence. They begin to lose their "observing self" as well, in that they doubt and question their judgment and interpretation of events. However, the battered women continue to have "insights" about their relationship and their batterers' definition of the situation. They occasionally act on these insights by seeking verification of or response to them. The women also creatively and valiantly develop coping strategies intended to reduce the severity of the abuse. Eventually, with sufficient confirmation of the insights, they begin to define themselves as "survivors,"—as individuals who are aware of their strength in enduring the abuse. They muster self-respect for that endurance and attempt to improve their situation.

This shift in perception begins to occur after any one of a variety of catalysts: a change in the level of violence, a change in resources, a change in the relationship, severe despair, a change in the visibility of violence, and external interventions that redefine the relationship. Any of these prompt a rejection of the previous rationalizations or denials of abuse, according to a qualitative study by Kathleen Ferraro and John Johnson.

Not only are the women's perceptions seen as basic to their reaction, these perceptions also evolve and change. In fact, the tentative findings suggest that battered women are rational in their response. They hold to societal conceptions of their duty in a relationship until that conception is no longer plausible. The catalysts for change are not "treatment" of the symptoms of learned helplessness but rather a change in situational evidence or events that necessitates an adjustment in one's perceptions and attribution. As has been argued about other oppressed or victimized people, the women's "grievance" has to be confirmed and resources made available in order for them to become "mobilized."

Table 2–2

Attributional and Helpseeking Progression

First Incidents:

The woman blames herself for the abuse. This is in part the result of the expectations of marriage in which she is to be a nurturer. The woman therefore attempts to change her own behavior and adequately please the batterer. The woman may attempt to get some advice from some informal help sources, such as family or friends. If she fails to get sufficient support and proper advice, she may begin to doubt her own judgment.

Recurring Abuse:

The battered woman begins to realize that there is more to the abuse than her displeasing the batterer. She begins therefore to blame the batterer for some of the abuse and seeks to change him. She may call the police or contact a shelter. Her attempts fail and the abuse escalates. Her "insights" into the dynamics continue to grow, however.

Escalating Abuse:

The battered woman eventually realizes that the batterer is not likely to change. She seeks more decisive intervention through legal assistance and explores ways to live separate from the batterer. If these efforts fail, the battered woman may continue in the abusive relationship and personally cope with the abuse as best she can. If the woman does receive appropriate support, she begins to accept herself as a "survivor" and continues the long process of helpseeking required to live safely on her own.

Toward a Survivor Theory

The Survivor Hypothesis

The alternative characterization of battered women is that they are active survivors rather than helpless victims. As suggested above, battered women remain in abusive situations not because they have been passive but because they have tried to escape with no avail. We offer, therefore, a survivor hypothesis that contradicts the assumptions of learned helplessness: Battered women increase their helpseeking in the face of increased violence, rather than decrease helpseeking as learned helplessness would suggest. More specifically, we contend that helpseeking is likely to increase as wife abuse, child abuse, and the batterer's antisocial behavior (substance abuse, general violence, and arrests) increase. This helpseeking may be mediated, as current research suggests, by the resources available to the woman, her commitment to the relationship, the number of children she has, and the kinds of abuse she may have experienced as a child.

The fundamental assumption is, however, that woman seek assistance in proportion to the realization that they and their children are more and more in danger. They are attempting, in a very logical fashion, to assure themselves and their children protection and therefore survival. Their effort to survive transcends even fearsome danger, depression or guilt, and economic constraints. It supersedes the "giving up and giving in" which occurs according to learned helplessness. In this effort to survive, battered women are, in fact, heroically assertive and persistent.

Empirical Research

There are at least a few empirical studies that substantiate this hypothesis that battered women are survivors. The studies by Lee Bowker (1983), Mildred Pagelow (1981), and Lenore Walker (1984) indicate quantitatively that the helpseeking efforts of battered women are substantial.

Perhaps the most significant of these empirical works is Walker's *The Battered Women's Syndrome* (1984), designed to verify the author's original learned helplessness and "cycle of violence" theorization. Walker found, however, that the women in her Rocky Mountain sample were not necessarily beaten into submissiveness; rather, helpseeking increased as the positive reinforcements within the relationship decreased and the costs of the relationship in terms of abusiveness and injury increased.

* * *

Self-Transcendence in Helpseeking

These assertions about women survivors may reflect a more fundamental philosophical assumption about human nature in general. The survivor tendency we see in battered women is more than self-assertion, self-actualization, or self-determination. It may reflect what Frankl and others have referred to as "self-transcendence." An inner strength, yearn for dignity, desire for good, or will to live appears despite one's previous conditioning and present circumstances. Even in the midst of severe psychological impairment, such as depression, many battered women seek help, adapt, and push on. This is not to say that we should expect battered women, or other survivors of misfortune, to bounce back on their own. Rather, by receiving the proper supports, one's inner strength can be realized, resiliency demonstrated, and a new life made.

This process is one that must be supported by helpers rather than invoked by them. This is accomplished by what some call a reflexive approach; that is, helpers accentuate the potential for self-transcendence in others by displaying it in themselves. The challenge is, therefore, for helpers to express resiliency, determination, and optimism, rather than succumb to the learned helplessness of so many bureaucratized help sources. As a result, so-called clients are more likely to discover and express their own resiliency. This approach is not some Pollyanna or positive thinking. It is a matter of community building—that is, creating a place where positive role models promote mutual support.

Shelters have afforded one of the most promising experiments in this regard. Women and children, by virtue of their circumstances, are joined in a kind of intentional community where not only emotions and experience are shared but also the common tasks of daily life. The "muddling with the mundane" in the communal living arrangements of shelters—the negotiating and even haggling over food, shelter, and children—potentially teaches much in itself. If managed effectively, shelter life may encourage women to assert themselves in new ways, clarify issues and fears, and collaborate with other women in need. In the process, the intimidating isolation that so many battered women experience is broken and an internal fortitude released.

Redefining the Symptoms

This is not to deny the observations of shelter workers that some battered women do experience severe low self-esteem, guilt, self-blame, depression, vulnerability, and futility—all of which are identified with learned helplessness. Some battered women may even appear to act carelessly and provocatively at times, as the proponents of masochism argue. But cast in another light, these "symptoms" take on a different meaning, as well as a different proportion.

The so-called symptoms of learned helplessness may in fact be part of the adjustment to active helpseeking. They may represent traumatic shock from the abuse, a sense of commitment to the batterer, or separation anxiety amidst an unresponsive community. All of these are quite natural and healthy responses but not entirely acceptable ones in a patriarchal (or male-dominated) society that values cool detachment. Not to respond with some doubts, anxiety, or depression would suggest emotional superficiality and denial of the real difficulties faced in help-seeking.

First, the symptoms of learned helplessness may be a temporary manifestation of traumatic shock. Many of the women arriving at shelters have suffered severe physical abuse equivalent to what one might experience in a severe auto accident. What appears as physical unresponsiveness or psychological depression may therefore be more an effort of the body and mind to heal themselves. The women, rather than being passive and withdrawn personalities, are going through a necessary healing process. They need not so much psychotherapy as time and space to recuperate.

Second, the symptoms may reflect an effort by battered women to save the relationship. Seeking help represents, in some sense, an admission of failure to fulfill the traditional female role of nurturing and domesticity. It appears to some women, too, as a breach of the marriage vow to love and honor one's spouse. As several of the interview studies show, battered women do initially blame themselves for not being nurturing, supportive, or loving enough to make the marriage work. It is important, however, to distinguish this initial sense of failure from the sense of an uncontrollable universe which underlies learned helplessness.

Third, the depression and guilt in some shelter women may be an expression of separation anxiety that understandably accompanies leaving the batterer. The women face tremendous uncertainty in separating even temporarily from the batterer. They fear reprisals for leaving, loss of custody of the children, and losing their home and financial support. The unknown of trying to survive on one's own can be as frightening as returning to a violent man. The prospects of obtaining employment sufficient to support oneself and children are minimal for most shelter women, especially considering their lack of previous experience and education. This coupled with the feminization of poverty in contemporary America makes a return to the batterer the lesser of the two evils. At least there is a faint hope that the batterer will change, whereas the prospects for change in the larger community seem less favorable.

TREATING THE HELPERS

Helplessness Among Helpers

In sum, many battered women make contact with a variety of helping sources in response to their abuse. As the abuse becomes more severe and the batterer more apparently beyond change, the diversity of the woman's contacts actually increases. We argue that this represents a survivor tendency of strength and resiliency. Depression, guilt, and shame may accompany a battered woman, but these should not be used to characterize battered women in general or to label them as victims of learned helplessness.

The prevailing notion of learned helplessness may, in fact, be misleading. Learned helplessness suggests that it is the woman who needs to be diagnosed and treated. Admittedly, some women do need tremendous emotional support and mental health care in the wake of devastating abuse. However, we believe that there is a more important side to consider: the insufficient response of community help sources.

If learned helplessness is a valid conception, it is ironically prevalent in the system of helping sources. It is more likely that agency personnel suffer from insufficient resources, options, or authority to make a difference, and therefore are reluctant to take decisive action. Too often, community services respond singularly to a problem rather than in some coordinated and mutually reinforcing fashion. This too cannot help but cause a sense of diffusion and duplication. There remains, furthermore, a reductionism that would treat abuse as a symptom of some other disorder or accident. In fact, emergency room staff have been accused of "cooling out" the abused woman with tranquilizer medications that actually reduce the woman's ability to respond effectively to her abuse.

It is our community systems of care and intervention that need treatment. Granted, the battered woman's contact with the clergy, human services, police, and legal assistance may at times be tentative. But the women meet an equally tentative response from the helpers. Malpractice suits, no-risk clauses, privatization of services, severe funding cutbacks, and a laissez-faire public attitude have brought reluctance rather than initiative to the helping professions.

Certainly more than new community programs are needed to counteract the impact of this state of affairs. Many of the social problems we face today—pockets of severe unemployment, generations of poverty among minority groups, increased immigration and opposing discrimination—require governmental leadership, if not activism, and perhaps some personal intrusions.

"Getting Tough"

We have seen recently a promising "get tough" trend with drug use and drunk driving. However expedient and superficial, the government-supported intervention and intrusion in these areas are decisive and apparently are having some impact. Domestic violence will require no less. The boundaries of family privacy will have to be crossed, not only to assure the safety of women and children but also to prevent the long-term side effects of domestic violence—impoverished, single-parent households; emotionally hampered children; and generational recurrence of violence. The cost to society for these latter problems is simply too great to tolerate.

This call to action is not meant to be an alarmist outburst overstepping reasoned restraints. What is needed is basically a better use and deployment of the existing services and interventions available in our respective communities. Community services need to be coordinated and integrated in a fashion that brings a decisive and comprehensive response to abuse. Essentially, a woman's contact with one helping source should be sufficient to call forth the response of the entire helping system. The helpers within the system, of course, need more than just a widened and reinforced "dragnet" in order to accomplish this. They need to become more acutely aware of the survivor character of battered women and of their own learned helplessness. As a result of self-examination and restructuring within the helping professions, not only will battered women be better served, but the prospects of their feeling helpless will also be eliminated.

Addressing Patriarchal Assumptions

There is a temptation to leave the survivor critique of community services at this practical level. That is, there are deficiencies in our help sources that need to be remediated to better support the helpseeking efforts of battered women. But this critique fails to expose the underlying assumptions that contribute to the preoccupation with learned helplessness in the first place and to the breakdown of help sources in the second.

According to feminist analysis, patriarchy—a system of male dominance—underlies much of the tendency to characterize women as deficient and to respond insufficiently. But it emerges in the helpseeking of battered women not so much as a conscious conspiracy of males against females but as a style of thought and interaction that is "masculine" in its deference to hierarchy, expertise, technique, and individualism. This approach has emphasized a pathological analysis of problems, a medical model of treatment, and privatization of family life.

The first patriarchal assumption rooted deep in our society is that problems are caused by some individual pathology. Our social policies tend to address deviance and dysfunction in individuals or families rather than in the structures of society as a whole. In fact, social policy is more often used to preserve that social structure rather than change it. The result is that individuals are to be restrained or managed for the social well-being. Our social science must therefore identify what is "wrong" with individuals and find ways to "fix" them or bring them back to the norm. Allocating resources to women in a way that would increase their social status or power is therefore resisted.

A second patriarchal assumption is that the medical model of professional expertise is the most appropriate form of treatment. The medical model has loosely been characterized as experts treating the problem "within" the person. That is, there is some dysfunction in the body or mind that is responsible for socially deviant acts. This orientation has given rise to an abundance of clinical psychologies that look for the root of our problems in the dysfunction of our thought processes and seek to right them through expert persuasion. Most of these "treatments" are technique-based; they impersonalize the helping process by slighting the emotional nurturing, mutual self-disclosure, and long-term commitment that are so fundamental to the feminine perspective.

A third patriarchal assumption at odds with the survivor notion is the continued privatization of family life. At a time of tremendous social transition and dislocation, there is a tendency to allow and expect families to fend for themselves in the name of autonomy. While families or individual family members may receive "treatment," it is increasingly difficult to obtain adequate housing, child care, income assistance, and meaningful employment. This is especially the case for single women attempting to enter the work force while caring for children. The "masculinized" systems have been short particularly on credit, alimony, and child support for single-parent women whose standard of living tends to collapse after divorce or separation. The point is this: In order to more substantially and realistically address social problems on the order of wife abuse, we ultimately need to relax our underlying masculine assumptions about "the way it spozed to be." We must dare to confront the demands of social reform from a more feminine point of view. That doesn't necessarily connote some radical overturning or autocratic governmental scheme. It is more likely to come, as many realignments have come throughout history, in a social "awakening" and realignment of values. Some might argue that it could be the outgrowth of a continued "feminization of America" in which women and feminine values continue to play a fuller role in society.[1]

---

1. There is of course some qualification that might be made to this female survivor explanation. it is plausible that the help-seeking we observed is exceptional rather than gender-based. the shelter women may be a group of resilient personalities. that is, they may be individuals who defied the learned helplessness and underlying masochism of the majority of battered women to obtain help. one noted longitudinal study of resilient children shows how family circumstances contributed to the children's latter adaptability, despite debilitating poverty that would have them at risk of learned helplessness and social pathology. the presence of surrogate parents (extended social support while growing up) was associated with resiliency in the adults. the battered women in shelters could be similar individuals. however, our preliminary evidence suggests that a substantial portion of the battered women experienced abuse as a child, rather than the kinds of social encouragement that were found in the childhood of the resilient individuals.

The study of exceptional resiliency nonetheless poses some principles that may lend support to our gender-based conception of the survival instinct. The resilient individuals were in moderately large families where they were expected to help take care of brothers and sisters, as well as cooperate in some selfless way for the benefit and survival of the family as a whole. The shelter women have similarly had to exercise tremendous nurturing and selflessness in their adult families in order to overcompensate for their batterers' abuse of them and their children. They need to survive themselves in order to take care of their children. Consequently, they as women must attempt to survive.

JACQUELYN C. CAMPBELL, WIFE–BATTERING: CULTURAL CONTEXTS VERSUS WESTERN SOCIAL SCIENCES

Sanctions and Sanctuary: Cultural Perspectives on the Beating of Wives, edited by Dorothy Ayers Counts, Judith K. Brown, and Jacquelyn C. Campbell, 233–234, 244–246 (Westview Press, 1992)

EXPLANATORY THEORIES

Western social sciences have developed a variety of hypotheses to explain the occurrence of wife-beating. These can be divided into the broad categories of psychological and socio-cultural. Various forms of stress theory, social learning theory, and exchange theory are currently receiving the most empirical support and attention in psychology. Researchers have also proposed psychoanalytic and neuropsychological reasons for wife-beating, but these explanations are only infrequently endorsed by current scholars and activists. They are less well accepted partly because their logical extension is to excuse the perpetrator and/or blame the victim and partly because of a lack of consistent empirical support. Scholars have also used sociobiological theory to explain female homicide which can be conceptualized as the extreme end of the continuum of wife-beating * * * I will review the following theories which use a wider societal perspective: feminist theory, resource theory, subculture of violence theory, and systems theory. I will also examine the societal factors identified in social learning and exchange theories.

* * *

CONCLUSIONS

Anthropology can contribute significantly to both the scholarly formulations explaining wife-battering and the practical solutions derived from them. The evidence from the societies presented in this volume does not clearly support any one of the theoretical models over the others. Instead it suggests that no Western social science theory explains all of the patterns of wife-beating and battering we describe. Specifically, I found only limited support for the culture/subculture of violence, resource, and social learning theories as they are now articulated. Data from our sample provide only mixed support for exchange theory, especially the social control premise. Feminist theory offered many important insights for understanding our evidence. However, feminist theory should distinguish between wife-beating, wife-battering and mutual violence (and admit the latter exists) and discriminate more carefully between the various forms of violence against women. Finally, systems theory needs either to treat wife and child abuse as separate phenomena or to differentiate between child beating and child battering if it is to have cross-cultural validity.

This review demonstrates the importance of societal level influence on violence, an insight that is significant for policy initiatives to prevent violence. One widespread if not universal phenomenon is the struggle of young men between 15 and 30 to define their roles and achieve manhood status, however it is defined. There are similarities between the young married Ujelang male who wishes he could play the role of an unmarried warrior and the young married American who yearns to be either Rambo or Donald Trump. Both go out to drink with the guys and envy their unmarried and apparently free counterparts. Both may go back home and attack their wives. We cannot explain the individual act, but the society's response to the beating is based on cultural differences. In the Ujelang village, the man will be chastised if he does more than hit; in the United States, usually only his female partner will rebuke him, and his violence will probably escalate. In Ujelang, political leaders scrutinize and evaluate the actions of both husband and wife; in the United States, probably no one will analyze the situation until it becomes severe. In both places the man blames the woman's behavior for his actions. His sexual jealousy and her failure to adhere to prescribed female role behavior are widespread reasons given for wife-beating. However, communities vary in their acceptance of these reasons (or excuses) for violence against wives.

Where negative sanctions against battering are combined with a sense of group honor based on nonviolence (as among the Ujelang) and the decent treatment of women (as the Kaliai are trying to establish), there is a chance to limit battering. If women are not to be battered it is essential that they have options including personal autonomy, economic opportunity, and the ability to form close linkages with other women. Among the Ujelang, Garifuna and Ecuadorian villagers, and in Mayotte, options for female power in at least one of these spheres, combined with community sanctions against violence, seem to override norms of male dominance and verbal bravado. In these societies wife-beating seldom escalates to wife-battering. Efforts to control wife-beating are also enhanced if the cultural (or subcultural) definition of a "real man" does not include the idea of controlling women by force. It is apparent, however, that social and cultural constraints against wife-beating can overcome individual propensities to violence.

The current calls from feminists and activists to change societal structures which allow or facilitate battering are supported by our anthropological data. Sanctuary for beaten women is necessary in all cultures and is provided by wife abuse shelters in most industrialized countries. Much more needs to be done in this regard in Iran, India, and Taiwan. There should also be strong sanctions against wife-beating and battering, but our data shows that community action can be more effective than official sanctions in preventing battering. Community action that is consistent with the society's level of industrialization and with established custom is a more realistic and effective strategy than expecting to change basic religious precepts or social practices such as marital exchanges or post marital residence.

In the United States and Canada we have publicized nationally the plight of battered women, passed laws prohibiting marital assault, and provided wife abuse shelters, and we are in the process of increasing the economic and political status of women. Although work in those areas must continue, perhaps it is time to start applying sanctions at the neighborhood level. Let us make individual batterers known to their communities, their churches, their schools, and their job sites for public censure. Let us work toward forming community and neighborhood level groups of women, both for economic solidarity and solidarity against men who batter. When a woman is being beaten, her neighbors can call the police for her if they are alerted to watch for danger signs before the violence begins. In this way, we can borrow ideas from Wape and Garifuna women and the *compadres* of Ecuador, imitate intercession by kin and community courts as among the Nagovisi, and pattern ourselves after the !Kung who help their neighbors. All these societies have mechanisms to limit the harm done by wife-beating and they all have much to teach us.

DAVID LEVINSON, SOCIETIES WITHOUT FAMILY VIOLENCE

Family Violence in Cross–Cultural Perspective 102–107 (Sage Publications, 1987).

As pointed out in Chapter 1, one of the major benefits of the cross-cultural comparative approach is that it enables us to examine ways of life that are different from our own. I rely on the comparative approach here to help provide us with a sociocultural profile of societies in which family life is free of violence. In Table 7.3, I list the 16 societies in our sample that are relatively free of family violence. Freedom from family violence is indicated by the family violence scale score in the second column of the table. This score, which ranges from 1.00 to 3.66, indicates the combined level of wife beating, husband beating, physical punishment of children, and sibling fighting that occurs in each society in the sample. Societies with a score of 1.00 have no or rare family violence. These 16 societies provide an interesting subsample of the full society sample on which this book is based. The 16 are representative of all seven major geographical regions of the world. However, South America is overrepresented with four societies (Ona, Siriona, Pemon, and Toba), while Africa (Bushmen) and Asia (Andamans and Central Thai) are underrepresented. Similarly, a broad range of economic systems (hunter-gatherers, horticulturalists, herders, agriculturalists) are covered, but hunter-gatherers (Ona, Andamans, Siriono, Bushmen) are overrepresented, perhaps because hunter-gatherers rarely mistreat their children (Rohner, 1986).

Table 7.3: Societies Without Family Violence

	FVS	1	2	3	4	5	6	7	8	9
Fox	1.25	2	*3*	*3*	1	1	*5*	1	1	2
Iroquois	1.00	2	2	2	1	1	*4*	1	1	
Papago	1.25	2	2	2	2	2	3	3	1	1
Ona	1.00	2	2	1	1	1	1	3	*3*	1
Siriona	1.25	3	—	*4*	1	1	1		1	1
Pemon	1.20	2	2	2	1	1	1	—	—	2
Toba	1.25	2	—	2	1	1	*4*	—	1	
Javanese	1.25	1	1	2	1	2	3	1	1	1
Ifugao	1.00	2	2	*4*	1	1	3	—	2	*4*
Trobriands	1.33	2	2	2	1	1	3	2	1	2
Bushmen	1.00	3	2	2	1	1	1	—	1	1
Andamans	1.33	2	2	2	1	1	1	1	2	1
Central Thai	1.00	2	2	2	1	1	3	4	1	2
Kurd	1.33	2	*3*	3	1	1	—	—	1	1
I. Bedouin	1.00	2	*3*	2	1	2	1	3	2	
Lapps	1.33	1	*3*	2	1	1	1		1	1

FVS = family violence scale
1 = domestic decision making
2 = control of fruits of family labor
3 = divorce freedom
4 = type of marriage
5 = premarital sex double standard
6 = divorce frequency
7 = intervention type
8 = male fighting
9 = husband/wife sleeping NOTE: Italicized codes deviate from the typical pattern across these societies.

The nine columns of numbers in the table are the ratings for nine factors that seem especially typical of societies without family violence (italicized codes are ones that deviate from the typical pattern across these societies). In general, it seems that in societies without family violence, husbands and wives share in domestic decision making, wives have some control over the fruits of family labor, wives can divorce their husbands as easily as their husbands can divorce them, marriage is monogamous, there is no premarital sex double standard, divorce is relatively infrequent, husbands and wives sleep together, men resolve disputes with other men peacefully, and intervention in wife beating incidents tends to be immediate. Some of these findings are as I would expect, since they are simply the reverse of our findings regarding the causes of family violence. One should not be surprised, for example, to find that shared decision making in the household predicts the absence of wife beating since we already know that male dominance in decision making predicts wife beating. However, some of these findings do not follow this pattern, and, in fact, our earlier analysis indicated that they were unrelated to family violence. The three factors of interest in this regard—premarital double standard, the divorce rate, and husband-wife sleeping—are especially significant since they suggest that equality and closeness in the marital relationship lead to low rates of family violence.

The central conclusion I reach from these findings is that family violence does not occur in societies in which family life is characterized by cooperation, commitment, sharing and equality. While these factors do not ensure that wives will not be beaten or children physically punished, it is clear that if they guide family relationships, family violence will be less frequent.

It should be noted, however, that some factors have been left out of the table because they seem to predict the absence of only one form of violence and have little or even an adverse effect on other forms. The best example of this class of factors is household organization, with extended-family households associated with the nonphysical punishment of children but unrelated to wife beating. Thus while it is possible, as I have done here, to produce a list of sociocultural characteristics of a family violence-free society, these factors, as a group, may be of limited predictive value when applied to a specific form of family violence.

THE CENTRAL THAI

It seems fitting to close by traveling to the Far East to describe the Central Thai, a society free of family violence. The Central Thai are a group of some 10 million people who speak the Central Thai dialect, live in central and southern Thailand, and are predominantly of the Buddhist faith. About 85% of the Central Thai live in rural communities where they grow rice for their own consumption and for cash sale. Our focus here is one of those rural agricultural communities—Bang Chan—a village of about 1,700 people about an hour's travel from Bangkok by road or three hours by canal. * * *

Life in Bang Chan is much like life in hundreds of other Central Thai communities except that the proximity to Bangkok has made Bang Chaners more comfortable with urban ways and more reliant on some of the conveniences and pleasures of modern life. The 1,771 Bang Chaners live in some 296 distinct households. The majority of households are nuclear (59%), although a variety of extended-family arrangements (35%) are also common. Both men and women have much freedom in choosing mates. Marriages tend toward the unstable, with divorce considered justifiable for virtually any reason and preferred to remaining in a marriage filled with discord and conflict. Flexibility governs household living arrangements and many nuclear families often have an extra relative or two as members. Some families are also without the husband/father who may spend as much as six months each year working in Bangkok. The basic rule is that people can live together so long as they all get along peacefully and each does his or her share. Bang Chan families are remarkable for their absence of any meaningful division of labor by sex.

In contrast to all other known cultures, in Thailand both men and women serve equally as midwives and do plowing. They both own and operate farms, inherit property equally, share equally in the property brought to a marriage and divide it equally in the case of divorce. It is not uncommon to find men tending babies while women are off on a business deal; nor is it unusual, as indicated earlier, to see women paddling right along with men as crew members in a boat race.

Individualism is a basic value in Bang Chan "1,771 individualists—polite, gentle, nonaggressive, but nevertheless individualists—pursuing their own purposes" (Phillips, 1966). Equally strong is a basic respect for others: "every individual regardless of his position in the hierarchy, deserves respect. The first is respect associated with the proper performance of one's role; the second, a recognition of the essential dignity of every human being." Along with individualism and mutual respect goes a strong need to control overt signs of aggression: "Because the volatility of a dispute is what is often most feared, one rarely hears of any actual argument accompanying the disagreement; instead, villagers say, 'We had a few words and he left. That's all.' " This need to control aggressive feeling governs family relationships as well.

Parents try[ing] to come to terms with, or overcome [the child's] preordained characteristics by inculcating good habits through example, coaxing, and whipping (the three modes of socialization, in order of priority, although villagers are more prone to talk about whippings than actually give them; most are too tenderhearted, and the rare whipping is almost always the result of sudden rage).

Other than in horseplay, children do not push each other around; in my twenty-two months in Thailand, I saw not one case of young children in a serious fight, despite the fact that I looked for it. Very rare indeed is the parent who uses force or the threat of force on his child; there is no Siamese equivalent of the American intimidation, "You had better do that or else...."

In another place, this same informant says of his relationship with his wife: "My wife and I never quarrel. If we quarreled, we would have to separate" [Phillips, 1966: 34, 35, 185].

While physical violence is rare in Bang Chan, the emotions that lead to violence in so many other societies are also felt by Bang Chaners. How do they deal with these feelings? Mainly by expressing them indirectly. Gossip is rampant, in fact so rampant and so predictable that it serves to resolve old conflicts rather than lead to new ones. People often flee from conflict-prone encounters, giggle in the face of awkward requests, are self-effacing, and use humor to smooth rough situations. And Bang Chaners express hostility in what we would call passive aggressive ways. They sometimes steal another's property and return it only after the victim has shown sufficient concern over his loss to make the perpetrator feel better. And last, men will occasionally make public suicide attempts by hanging, which inevitably fail.

Many of the households are isolated in the center of wet rice fields, connected to one another and the local Buddhist monastery and government school by a series of canals. Other households are strung along the banks of major canals. As suggested by the desire to avoid conflict as just described, community relations are governed to a large extent by the belief that "if people live far away from each other, there will not be any trouble." This isolation, combined with the division of Bang Chan into nine administrative units by the Thai government, reflects an absence of any strong sense of community identity by the Bang Chaners. While they all feel mutual ties based on loyalty to the local monastery and school, and there are ambiguously defined kin groups beyond the family, the community can be described only as "loosely structured."

There are some important lessons in the Central Thai way of life for preventing family violence. Actually, it is somewhat surprising to be able to say this, as the Bang Chan community displays many of the sociocultural features commonly assumed to be tied to high levels of family violence. Bang Chaners live in isolated nuclear family households. Husbands may be away from the home for extended periods of time. The divorce rate is high. Household composition is unstable. And individuality is more important than is a shared sense of community identity. This could be a description of many communities in the contemporary United States as well as Bang Chan. But unlike the United States, family violence does not exist in Bang Chan. Why the difference? Three Bang Chan psychosocial patterns seem most important: first, the goal of avoiding disputes and the range of nonviolent techniques available to deal with aggressive feelings; second, the basic respect Bang Chaners have for one another, based on the belief that all people are entitled to such respect regardless of their role, status, or power; and third, and most important, the virtual absence of a division of labor by sex in the household. To a large extent, there is no men's work and women's work, but simply work.

When analyzed in the context of factors I have found linked to family violence, such as husband dominance in domestic decision making, sexual economic inequality, single-parent caretakers, mens' houses, and violent conflict resolution, the absence of a household division of labor by sex can tell us much about how to prevent family violence. First, it tells us that with two regular caretakers in the home, there will be regular relief from the pressures that often accompany caretaking and less chance that those pressures will boil over into violence directed at the children. Second, given our earlier finding that sibling violence is often modeled on parent-child violence, it tells us that alternative caretakers in the home will indirectly control fighting between siblings. Third, the absence of a clear division of labor by sex tells us that adult male and female roles are not rigidly defined. Thus manifestations of an unresolved male sex identity conflict both outside and within the family are unlikely. And, last, it tells us that since sexual equality accompanies the shared division of labor, each party will have the emotional and economic independence to withdraw from a potentially violent relationship.

The Central Thai, with their nonviolent ways, are living proof of the central conclusion of this study—family violence will be more common in societies in which men control women's lives, it is acceptable to resolve conflicts violently, and the mother bears the major responsibility for child rearing. The Central Thai are also living proof that it doesn't have to be this way.

WILLIAM E. MITCHELL, WHY WAPE MEN DON'T BEAT THEIR WIVES: CONSTRAINTS TOWARD DOMESTIC TRANQUILITY IN A NEW GUINEA SOCIETY

Sanctions and Sanctuary: Cultural Perspectives on the Beating of Wives, edited by D.A. Counts, J.K. Brown, and J.C. Campbell, 89–98 (Westview Press 1992).

The West, as we know, is fascinated with violence. Western journalists, film makers, and anthropologists working in New Guinea have made the island famous for head-hunting, cannibalism and male-female antagonism. The range of New Guinea societies, however, is great. While the gentler societies lack the riveting appeal of those that are more flamboyantly aggressive, they can be instructive. The Wape of Papua New Guinea's Sandaun (formerly West Sepik) Province are a case in point. Like many other Melanesian peoples, the egalitarian Wape live in a mountainous tropic forest habitat in sedentary villages and are slash-and-burn horticulturalists. Marriage occurs through bridewealth payments, polygyny is allowed but rare, postmarital residence is generally virilocal, and patrilineal clans are ideally exogamous while patrilineages are strictly so. But the Wape differ from a number of the societies with whom they share these customs: Wape men do not beat their wives. This does not mean that conjugal relations are always harmonious, but it is unusual for a man to slap his wife and I know of no instances where a woman suffered an injurious beating from her husband.

Because wife-beating is an accepted custom in many parts of Papua New Guinea and considered by the government to be a serious public health problem, in this paper I identify some of the factors or constraints that help explain the comparative tranquility of Wape domestic life. These constraints—located on various but intersecting sociocultural, psychological, historical, ecological and physiological levels of analysis—are inextricably bound together in a complex circular relationship. Our present knowledge of this relationship does not warrant the postulating of constraints operating on one level as being more important than those on another, so the general tranquility of Wape domestic life cannot be explained by a simple "cause and effect" model favored by an experimental positivistic science. The explanatory model proposed here is an associational one, more descriptive than causal, whose very circularity is essential to the explanation.

The data for this study, including a review of relevant court records, were collected during an eighteen month field trip in 1970–1972 and brief revisits in 1982 and 1989. Although I have visited many of the villages of the approximately 10,000 Wape during my three trips to Wapeland, my view of Wape society and culture is as seen from Taute village, my principal fieldwork site.

CORRELATES OF WAPE DOMESTIC TRANQUILITY

Ethos and Emotions

The ethos of Wape society is markedly pacific. Although the society is not without its points of stress and the people not without passion concerning their personal relationships, the overall affective thrust of social life is to keep emotions, especially those that might lead to violence, under control. Even before Western contact, when enemy villages engaged in pay-back killings, the attacks might be years apart. Some Wape villages, on learning that the invading whites had banned warfare, abandoned the custom even before government patrols could intervene. During my fieldwork, I never saw a physical fight between men, between women, or even between children. The preferred Wape response to potential violence is conciliatory, not confrontational. When dissension in village life does occur, as it inevitably does, quarrels tend to be defused before culminating in physical violence or, if someone does strike another, he or she does not strike back. As a stranger to Wape-land, I had the first of several personal lessons in their gentle interaction style a few days after I moved into Taute village. When I shouted at a group of children crowding onto the raised and rotting veranda of our temporary house to get off, a man who had befriended me said reprovingly, "Speak softly!" The Wape perceive expatriates, especially men, as unpredictable and potentially bellicose. To gain some control over expatriate emotions, villagers place magical ginger under the house ladder of a visiting patrol officer—and I imagine a visiting anthropologist as well—to soothe him as he climbs down into the village. Another time, when I rebuked a group of men during the building of our house for cutting down the ornamental shrubs that hid the outhouse, they simply turned and silently walked away.

Enculturating a resident anthropologist or Wape children is not always an easy task, but the methods are identical. Aggressive acts are met with disinterest. An enraged toddler is left alone to kick and scream on the ground until her or his reason returns. Children and anthropologists soon learn that public aggression is an embarrassing and non-rewarding activity. Consequently, the Wape restrain the expression of negative emotions toward others and are generally friendly in their everyday village activities. Antipathy toward another person is rarely expressed directly in public though it may be expressed privately to a confidant.

Still, there are times when adults feel so personally transgressed and furious that they must do something more drastic than confiding their anger to a friend. Several alternatives are available. An offended person may gossip openly to others about the offense or, as everyone knows some sorcery, privately execute a punitive ritual. Or, for example, if a man's dog attacks and cripples a woman's piglet and the man makes no attempt to correct the wrong, in desperation she might go to his house and, standing outside, deliver a self-righteous harangue heard by all the neighbors while the transgressor and his family sit silently within. If the problem escalates, a meeting of the entire village is called by one of the concerned parties and anyone remotely involved with the problem should attend; not to go is to compromise one's integrity or innocence. Gathered on the front verandas of the houses surrounding the central plaza, men, women, and even children have their say until finally, perhaps several hours later, a consensus is reached.

I have stressed here the pacific ethos of Wape culture as well as indicated some of the actions resorted to when an individual's emotions must be expressed outwardly, namely, gossiping, sorcery, haranguing, and public meetings. However, none of these actions—regardless of the degree of aggressive intent—usually involve direct physical violence. Later I will discuss two exceptions to this finding that document a darker side of Wape emotions.

The Gaze of the Ancestors

The Wape are not conciliatory solely because they have been socialized to believe that public anger is often unrewarding or humiliating. There is a powerful sanctioning agent that helps to keep their behavior in check: the spirits of their dead ancestors. As Hollan has similarly observed for the Toraja of Indonesia, "Fear of supernatural retribution and social disintegration motivate the control of anger and aggression." The Wape believe that at death, an adult's spirit returns to lineage lands in the forest. The spirit is also believed to be a frequent visitor to the village, where it looks after its descendants by sending illness and bad luck to family enemies. There is a high incidence of illness in Wapeland, testimony enough to ancestral power.

One night while visiting on a neighbor's veranda, I idly inquired about a slight, unidentifiable sound and learned that it was my host's dead father benevolently signaling his presence. Ancestral spirits are believed to see and hear all. This strongly discourages arguments among villagers because a spirit may avenge a descendant by negatively influencing an opponent's hunting, gardening or personal health. For this reason also, individuals occasionally express their anger publicly in Tok Pisin, the region's *lingua franca*, so the older ancestors who never learned it can't understand what is being said.

Frequent disagreements among family members or neighbors can jeopardize the welfare of the entire village. To appease the ancestors, a conciliatory ritual must be held where the opponents speak out to them, announcing that they are now friends and asking the spirits to desist in the punitive interventions. A husband also knows that his wife's agnates as well as her classificatory mother's brothers are concerned about her welfare and, if he mistreats her, may resort to their ancestors or sorcery.

Gender Proximics

Another important factor pertaining to the absence of wife-beating is that Wape society, while acknowledging male-female differences in terms of dress and division of labor, is organized not to polarize gender differences but to de-emphasize them. Husbands and wives use the same paths and sleep together in the same house with their children. Village boys and girls, including teenagers, play at ease with one another. The lightly constructed homes are close together so that aural privacy is at a minimum; even a modestly raised voice is heard by all the neighbors who are also relatives. Menstruating mothers and daughters are not secluded in menstrual huts but remain at home where husbands, if they are not going hunting, continue to eat their wives' food. At puberty, boys begin to sleep separately in a village bachelors' house but they still interact daily with their parents and siblings and usually take their meals with them at home. Nor are boys or youths secluded from their mothers and sisters for initiation into manhood as in some New Guinea societies, where, often brutally, they are cleansed of female contamination in preparation for a warrior's career.

Female Status and Strategies

This is also a society where women and girls do not provide all of the child care. My tape-recorded interviews with male informants are penetrated with a baby-sitting father's asides to his restless toddler or the hungry cries of his infant. Fathers, as well as sons, take an active part in the care of infants and toddlers, especially when the mother is in the forest processing sage or collecting firewood.

This brings us to another important factor to explain why Wape husbands do not beat their wives: Wape women produce most of the food eaten. A typical meal consists of sage jelly with boiled greens—both the result of women's labor—and, with luck, a scrap of meat. While hunting is of great ritual and social importance to men, the introduction of the shotgun has seriously, and in some areas ruinously, depleted wild game. Pigs, of which there are few, are killed primarily for ceremonial exchanges among kin. As monogamy, both in the known past and present, is the Wape norm, a husband is dependent upon a single wife to feed him.

Another point is that a young woman has considerable say in the choice of a husband, signalling a young man in whom she is interested by slipping him a small present of food or tobacco. If possible, women prefer to marry within their natal village and rarely marry into a village that is more than an hour or two walk from their father and brothers. Throughout a wife's marriage—and divorce is unusual—she and her husband are in close contact with her agnatic kin through a continuing series of economic exchanges that necessitates back-and-forth visiting while her brothers hold special ritual sanctions over her children, members of her husband's lineage. By the same token, she is tied to her mother's lineage too, especially to her classificatory mother's brothers who, as already indicated, watch over her well-being and whose homes are available as a place of refuge. A woman who feels that her husband is abusive to her does not hesitate to move in with relatives, where she may stay for a week or more until they return with her to her husband's house. In no case may he seek her return. In the meantime, he becomes dependent on his agnates' wives to feed him or must find his own food. Neither choice is a pleasant one.

The women of a hamlet, or at least the one in which I lived, develop strong solidarity bonds, something I only learned through observation. In the unlikely event that a couple becomes so angry during a quarrel that they begin to shout at each other, women of the hamlet, a few sometimes armed with large sticks, descend upon the house and stand around it until the woman joins them outside.

A factor that relates to the interaction style of women is that they usually do not act in ways to further provoke or escalate a husband's anger towards them but are able to terminate his abuse with a very dangerous and ritualized action. While both Wape men and women are highly sensitive to personal shaming, when a wife is deeply humiliated or shamed by her husband's behavior towards her, she usually does not return the insult but instead attempts suicide. While female suicide attempts are not uncommon in Papua New Guinea, in most communities they appear to be more frequently precipitated by a husband's brutal beatings, as among the Gainj and Kaliai, than by his shaming words.

Three young wives of our small hamlet unsuccessfully attempted suicide while I lived there by drinking poison made from the root of the deadly derris vine. Interestingly, in each case the woman lived in a household with her husband and one of his parents. In two of the cases a precipitating event was criticism by her husband for not supplying enough food for the family.

There are no reliable suicide statistics for Wape society. But, on the basis of my own data and that of Dr. Lynette Wark Murray, the experienced missionary physician who patrolled Wapeland during my initial fieldwork, suicide attempts by unhappy wives, although hushed up by the community, do occur and follow a definite cultural pattern. Because an in-marrying wife's suicide is deeply stigmatizing to the husband's lineage, a woman who survives an attempted suicide finds herself the center of solicitous community attention. It is a desperate way to "get even" with an overly critical or abusive husband but, in the cases I observed, most effective, with the added compensation that it generated a favorable change in his domestic demeanor.

Although Wape men do not often commit suicide (I heard of only one inexplicable case), there is a corresponding dark side to men's behavior. While in the field I observed two instances and learned of several others where a man, said to be temporarily possessed by a wandering ghost, attempted to attack fellow villagers with his bow and arrows. These amok attacks occur only to men and are episodic, often with long periods of lucidity between them. A man so possessed is considered "crazy" by other villagers and is not held completely responsible for his actions. Although the target of a man's attack is socially diffuse with the opportunity to direct part of his aggression toward his wife, he never does.

Diet and Drugs

While the use of drugs, including alcohol, cannot alone make wife-beaters out of husbands, it should be noted that the Wape do not have easy access to alcohol, as is true in some parts of Papua New Guinea where wife-beating is culturally accepted. The addictive substances that are available to the Wape, namely tobacco and betel nut, are not gender differentiated: men and women alike are heavy users of both substances.

Severe protein and caloric deficiency are characteristic of the Wape diet and may, in a highly generalized way, be related to their pacific temperament and domestic tranquility. Sago is notoriously low in nutrients and the mountain-dwelling Wape, unlike most sago eaters who live on the coast or along large rivers, cannot obtain adequate protein from fish. Wape soils are poor and, although sago is supplemented with seasonal garden produce, gardens are small, unfenced and poorly cultivated. Medical growth and development studies indicate the birth weight of the Wape infant is one of the lowest reported in the world and subsequent growth in height and weight is slow with the onset of secondary sex characters correspondingly delayed. For example, a girl's first menstrual period occurs at a mean age of 18.4 years. There also is a progressive and marked loss of weight with age in both male and female adults. Many villagers suffer from chronic upper respiratory infections and malaria is holoendemic and uncontrolled. Recent studies indicate that the health problems of the Wape are still severe. It is hardly surprising that Wape ceremonial life is centered upon curing festivals.

Christian Mores and Government Law

Finally, we must consider the influence of the Catholic and Protestant missionaries and local government officials in respect to the absence of wife-beating in Wapeland. All Wape villages are under the influence of either Christian Brethren or Franciscan missionaries while, more recently, an indigenous fundamentalist church, New Guinea Revival, has also gathered considerable support. All of these churches are strong advocates of a harmonious family life and marital amity. The laws of the country further support these values and government and health officials distribute literature and lecture to villagers about them. But, as we already have seen, "domestic peace" is not a new idea to the Wape people. The importance of the churches' and state's moral rhetoric and sanctions regarding domestic life is not one of innovation, but the reinforcement on another level of the contemporary Wape society's own tradition of domestic tranquility.

CONCLUSIONS

To answer the question of why Wape men don't beat their wives in a country where wife-beating is a major public health problem, I have noted and discussed some of the implicated constraints. These can be summarized as follows:

- A pacific and conciliatory cultural ethos supported by churches and the state
- Non-polarization of gender differences
- Punitive intervention by watchful ancestral spirits
- Women instrumental in selecting their husbands
- Monogamy
- Married couples domiciled among watchful relatives
- Wives as principal food providers
- Near absence of alcohol
- Nutritionally deficient diet
- Solidarity bonds among hamlet women
- Threat of a wife's suicide if her husband shames her
- Women's agnates and classificatory mother's brothers responsive to their welfare

None of these constraints alone can explain the relatively tranquil nature of Wape domestic life. When viewed as an interrelated cluster, though, these constraints help us understand the absence of wife-beating. If a society has very poor nutrition, a pacific conciliatory ethos, low access to alcohol, watchful and succoring neighbors and relatives, vengeful ancestors, husbands dependent on a single wife for sustenance, non-polarization of the sexes, and the threat of a wife's suicide if shamed by her husband, it is difficult to conceive of a marital relationship progressing to a state where a wife is being beaten.

However, this inquiry into the absence of Wape wife-beating has uncovered another form of Wape domestic violence—attempted suicide by females—with a cultural scenario of its own. In desperation, wives humiliated by their husbands "beat up" on themselves and, indirectly, their spouses by attempting to poison themselves. The difference is that attempted suicide, unlike being beaten, is a self-empowering act of rectitude, an aggressive action against one's person that, if one survives, may reshape a damaged husband-wife relationship more equitably. To Wape men, the possibility of a wife's attempted suicide is a sobering symbol for the limits of oppression. To women, it is a desperate act fraught with peril, an act some know is worth the risk.

BARBARA CORRY, ABC'S OF MEN WHO BATTER
Unpublished (2000).

Abused as Children: Most batterers were beaten, verbally abused, or sexually abused as children. The majority of batterers also were "under-fathered" i.e., they had fathers who neglected or rejected them, or fathers whom they could never please. Treated like objects, batterers were taught, by example, specific techniques to hurt and humiliate others. In addition, batterers learned that violence is "normal" in families: they were taught that bigger people get to hit and abuse smaller people (women/children). In turn, batterers discipline their children with violence, thus perpetuating the cycle of abuse.

Believe in Traditional Sex Roles: Batterers hold to traditional sex roles (i.e., macho men, subservient women). They believe that a woman is there to take care of them, feed them, bear their children, keep their house clean, accept their infidelities, and tolerate their drinking. Batterers believe that women should be disciplined if they "disobey their husband" or "forget their place." Abusive men often talk about their "rights" as husbands and their role as "head" of the family. They believe that women exist to serve men, and that their "wives are theirs to do with as they wish." Batterers also hold attitudes consistent with male privilege such as, "a little slap will do her good," or "I'll show her who's boss," or "What she needs is for someone to teach her a good lesson."

Controlling: Battering is purposefully controlling behavior by someone who wants total control. A man who batters may control where his spouse goes, whom she sees, what she reads, when she eats, and what she buys. He may monitor her phone calls, mileage, clothing, and make-up. A batterer fears abandonment and, therefore, he tries to control his mate's actions by controlling the money and by limiting her access to family and friends. These men control their partners in order to feel like they have some control in their lives and some power in the world. Their need to dominate stems from a need to reassure themselves that they are special, valued by others, and worthy of appreciation—all things they did not get as children. A batterer's fear of not being in control also is related to the fear of death or injury he experienced as a child in a violent home.

Deny, Minimize, and Blame: A batterer does not want to be responsible for his violent actions or for the harm he causes. Abusive men learn to deny wrongdoing, minimize injury, and blame others.

Men who batter will BLAME others for their actions and say things like "If she didn't want a beating, why did she interrupt me while I was on the phone," or "She knew not to disrespect me in public," or "You're really asking for it when you make me crazy like this," or "I don't get this way with anyone else, it's your fault."

Batterers will also DENY hurting their partners with comments like "She tripped and fell," or "I was swinging at the air, and she walked into it," or "I was just trying to push her away," or "She's fair skinned and bruises easily."

Finally, batterers will MINIMIZE their violent actions with excuses like, "It was just a bump," or "I just twisted her arm a bit," or "I only slapped her a couple of times last year," or "Compared to what some other men do, it's not so bad." A batterer also may say, "I didn't know what I was doing," or "I was out of control," as if someone else was responsible. In reality, battering is target specific (i.e., the batterer aimed at his spouse—not the mailman or the grocer), and he even may have aimed for specific parts of his partner's body (e.g., her pregnant belly or body parts not visible to the outside world).

Emotionally Abusive: Battering is not limited to physical abuse. Emotional abuse may include repeatedly criticizing his spouse; shouting at her; swearing at her; putting down her opinions; blaming or shaming her; making her feel stupid; treating her like a servant; accusing her unjustly; undermining her self-confidence; calling her names; insulting her family; embarrassing her in front of others; withholding encouragement; flirting openly or having affairs; and not discussing events which damage the relationship.

Feel Powerless: Batterers are actually frightened men who are afraid to be alone in the world (i.e. they are very scared and extremely insecure on the inside.) Feeling powerless as children, batterers learned how to bully and dominate in order to feel less afraid and avoid being victimized any further. Bullies are cowards, and bullying is a blustering, protective mechanism. Batterers resort to their belief in male authority over women when they feel impotent or insecure.

Grew Up With Violence: Batterers learned early on that they could gain control and get power by throwing things or by raising their voice. Violence became an acceptable way to express their emotions or to get what they wanted. Slapping, punching, etc. became normal, taken-for-granted ways for spouses to relate to one another, and perfectly acceptable means to resolve conflicts. They also learned early on, by example, that "men get to hit" and that "women tolerate it."

Have a Negative Belief System About Women: Batterers lump "all women" together and do not see women as individuals. In addition, they have negative stereotypes about women such as: "all women are manipulative," or "all women see men as paychecks." Batterers also dismiss women's ideas and opinions. Furthermore, they believe that "a man must control his woman or she will control him."

Insecure: Abusive men have a deeply rooted fear that they are inadequate. They don't believe they have a lot to offer. Batterers are unhappy with who they are and see themselves as failing to live up to their image of manhood. All of their bullying and intimidation serve as a smokescreen to keep others from seeing how insecure they really feel. Their violence is controlling behavior designed to keep themselves from feeling inadequate and powerless. Batterers are actually very lonely, alienated men.

Jealous: Batterers tend to be extremely jealous and have difficulty trusting others. They believe that "jealousy is natural in men."

Kill or Torture What They Cannot Possess: In the worst cases, battering involves extreme physical or mental cruelty, such as tying up the woman's hands and feet; beating her so badly that you break a shotgun in three pieces; stabbing her repeatedly so that she requires hundreds of stitches; cutting her throat; fracturing the roof of her mouth; and making cigarette burns on her breasts. Other batterers stalk and kill what they can no longer possess. These tragedies are usually portrayed as crimes of passion caused by the man's intense love for and inability to live without the woman. However, murder is actually the ultimate expression of the batterer's need to control the woman.

Lack Relationship Skills: Men who batter have had very poor role models for important relationship skills such as problem solving, conflict resolution, and establishing intimacy with a partner. If they do not learn new skills, batterers tend to repeat the destructive patterns which they observed in their respective families. Batterers do not know how to ask directly for what they need. They also do not know how to tell their partners that they are not feeling appreciated or that they are not feeling heard. Batterers have poor skills to resolve differences over money, sex, disciplining the children, etc.; without intervention, these areas often become major battle grounds. It is important to note, also, that in the context of an unequal and violent relationship, the woman is usually discounted and often unable to be more assertive. And, with both parties unable to express themselves effectively, little communication or conflict resolution occurs in battering relationships.

Master Manipulators: A batterer is someone who knows exactly how to convince his partner to feel sorry for him. He becomes very skilled at telling his partner exactly what she wants to hear. He will beg and plead and promise and say all the right things. The batterer's worst fear is that his partner will leave, and he tries to be charming enough to make sure this doesn't happen. Just as his violence was overblown, so are his apologies and gifts. However, unless the batterer is made to be accountable for his violence and unless he becomes committed to personal change, his manipulation and his abusive behavior will not end.

Not Able to Nurture: Batterers have difficulty giving and receiving love. They find it hard to make themselves vulnerable and, without treatment, are not able to empathize with their spouse's pain.

Overly Dependent on Their Spouses: Batterers become overly dependent on their partners for their unmet emotional needs. They seek from their mates the nurturing and security they did not receive as children. When his mate cannot meet his needs, the batterer becomes frustrated. As one man put it, "I felt I needed her to 'make' me happy; if I wasn't happy, it was her fault."

Prior History of Violence: If you listen carefully, you might hear a batterer's friends say that he is frequently "moody" or "has a hot temper." He may have a history of being a bully at work or school. He may also have an obvious or subtle track record of mistreating other women. If a man's anger is out of proportion or if he acts impulsively when he is angry, e.g., by punching walls, throwing things, or breaking objects, these signs say that he needs professional help to control his rage and express his anger in non-violent ways.

Quickly Change From Dr. Jekyll to Mr. Hyde: Batterers can be extremely passive and very charming one minute and explode in anger the next. The violence can be triggered if he feels threatened, shamed, powerless, or humiliated. Drugs or alcohol are often used as an excuse for "losing control."

Regard Spouses as Easy Targets: Most batterers would not think of doing to other men what they do to their spouses. A batterer knows he can easily vent his anger on his spouse in the privacy of his own home and that she probably won't tell anyone. A female partner is most likely someone smaller and weaker, someone who is economically dependent on him, someone who cares about him, and someone whom he can bully into not going to the police. If he intimidates her sufficiently, and she doesn't tell anyone, he knows he can get away with abusing her.

Self-Centered/Narcissistic: Batterers lack consideration for others. As one batterer put it, "I had the 'Do what I want, when I want, why I want, and because I want' syndrome." No one matters apart from the batterer and his needs. They also believe "If someone slights or hurts me, I have the right to attack them back."

Try to Punish and Control With Subtle Forms of Abuse: Batterers often use subtle forms of abuse to punish, humiliate, and control their partners. A batterer may say things to create fear such as: "If you EVER gain weight, I will leave you." or "If you EVER let the housework go, you'll be sorry." In addition, a batterer's verbal abuse and criticism often become chronic. He will repeatedly complain about the way his spouse takes care of him or the children, and he will find other things wrong— even after his partner has turned herself inside out to lose weight, stay within the budget, cook his favorite foods, etc. A batterer feels so small inside (i.e., he has such low self-esteem), that he will repeatedly put his spouse and/or children down in order to feel more important or feel better about himself.

Unable to Identify or Express Their Feelings Directly: Men who batter are unable to differentiate between their feelings and they do not have a vocabulary to express their emotions. All of a batterer's emotions are funnelled through anger. In addition, batterers have learned to use violence—instead of words—to communicate their feelings. For example, a slap literally says "You humiliated me!" A punch stands-in for "I loved you and you betrayed me!" Choking her equals "Shut up and get out of my face NOW!"; and sitting on her chest may mean "You are NOT leaving me!", "I want you to listen to me!", or "You're making me crazy, and I hurt this much!"

Vary By Type: Men who batter vary by type: "The Good," "The Bad," and "The Ugly" (Gondolf, 1989):

"The Good"—Men who abuse women only emotionally or verbally. A "Good Guy" may speak of women's equality and claim he likes women, but may control and pressure his spouse, and his remarks often are laced with snide remarks about women. Moreover, he expects a reward for being nice and he is courteous as long as a woman treats him well.

"The Bad"—Men who physically abuse their mates but not other people. "Bad Guys" may be sporadic batterers or chronic (frequent) batterers. They may even be very charming to those outside the family, making it hard for others to believe ill of them.

"The Ugly"—Men who are violent inside and outside the home, including anti-social and sociopathic men. Antisocial men cause severe injuries and have severe drug or alcohol problems. Sociopathic men have long criminal records, problems with both drugs and alcohol, and have a sadistic attitude in general.

Will Get What They Want Through Physical Violence: Batterers tell us that their violence is a convenient tool to get what they want and to make things go the way they want. Physical beatings are a way to control a disagreement or put an end to a fight. Asserting one's physical superiority is a way to MAKE one's spouse stay, or make one's mate hurt as much as the batterer is hurting inside. Physical violence may include shoving, slapping, kicking, punching, choking, tripping, arm twisting, hair pulling, raping, or physical confinement.

Xenophobic: A batterer is someone who fears, distrusts, and dislikes that which is foreign to him. This includes his mate, and women in general. In practice, this means that while a batterer may listen to other men, he does not regard women as equals or take women seriously. Like racists, batterers fear and dislike those who are different from themselves (in this case, women). Also like racists, abusive men act out of insecurity. Some batterers hurt others for sport, others because it satisfies something in them. These characteristics also tell us that it is important to see domestic violence as a broader social problem which is woven into the fabric of a patriarchal society rather than as only an "individual shortcoming" or a "private family matter." In addition to creating effective batterer's treatment programs, we must identify and change the social forces which condone violence generally, tolerate violence against women, and allow sexism to flourish.

You Must Follow His Orders—Or Else—and No Matter What You Do, He is Impossible to Please: As one battered woman put it, "You have to follow his commands (e.g., take his shoes off, stay away from his electronic equipment, heat his dinner, NOW), or else, like he was king and this was his domain and everybody else in the family were little ants made to serve him." Batterers trigger-off whenever they are ready and for whatever reason they have at the moment. Often, battering occurs over the most trivial things. Batterers will beat or verbally demolish their mates for forgetting to put the butter on the table, burning the meat, not ironing the shirts correctly, not sewing clothes to his satisfaction, making scrambled eggs instead of eggs over-easy, serving limp lettuce on a sandwich, or not dressing fast enough. No matter what his mate does, a batterer is never satisfied.

Zero in on Spouses' Vulnerabilities: Men who batter often betray the trust of their spouses and break their confidences. Batterers also attack their mate's vulnerabilities, and they become skilled at using things their partners have shared in confidence against them.

JOAN ZORZA, BATTERER PSYCHOPATHOLOGY: QUESTIONS AND IMPLICATIONS

National Battered Women's Law Project of the National
Center on Women and Family Law (1993).

Before the early seventies there was virtually no study of spouse abuse. Only five brief studies of the problem existed in the social sciences, and all incorrectly implied that it was the wife who caused the problem by provoking her mate. It was not until 1972 that "spouse abuse" was given a heading in social science indexes.

Battering between intimate partners is now known to be perpetrated overwhelmingly by men against women, with women sustaining the greater and more severe injuries. When women batter it is almost always in an effort to defend themselves.

There is general agreement that whether a woman will be victimized is independent of her characteristics and behaviors; it is even unrelated to how much exposure she had to family violence as a child. Studies comparing abused women with nonabused women in relationships fail to find significant differences. It is a woman's being in a relationship with a batterer that determines whether she will be battered. For most battered women, recovery from the effects of repeated traumatic abuse happens once she lives in a violence-free atmosphere, particularly if she is supported by a domestic violence program or social, family and work relationships. Therapy is generally unnecessary for battered women to recover.

Much of the literature about domestic violence has claimed that batterers differ little from the general male population, with very few of them being psychopaths. The best predictor of a man's violent behavior toward his partner, according to this literature, was his history of past violence, including his having witnessed or experienced violence while growing up. Of men in treatment for battering their current partner, 93% had battered a previous partner. Most batterers were believed to have no behaviors which would permit any DSM–III diagnosis. Rather, batterers learned to be violent and were rewarded for their behavior over time. Their coercive battering behavior worked and was reinforced by socialization. Unlike other violent offenders, whose violent acts diminish as they grow older, batterers become more violent in both frequency and intensity over time. Batterers are resistant to treatment and have high recidivism rates even when treated for their abuse: at least half of treated male batterers continue their violence with new partners.

While we may not know what causes battering we do know that hormones have little effect on male violence against women. Similarly, alcohol, though strongly correlated with wife beating, does not cause it. Social learning is believed to be the crucial intervening variable that enables those who ingest mood altering substances to abuse their family members. However, some drugs such as barbiturates, cocaine, amphetamines and phencyclidine (PCP) may cause some users to become violent.

New Theory That Most Batterers Have Pathology

In contrast to the old view that saw batterers as mostly normal, some of the recent literature on batterers claims that most and possibly all batterers do have psychopathologies. "Psychopathy is a personality disorder defined by a constellation of affective, interpersonal, and behavioral characteristics, central to which are a profound lack of empathy, guilt, or remorse, and a callous disregard for the feelings, rights, and welfare of others.... psychopaths typically are glib, egocentric, selfish, callous, deceitful, manipulative, impulsive, sensation-seeking, irresponsible, and without 'conscience'."[21]

Edleson and Tolman have worked for over a decade with many hundreds of men who batter in Alaska, New York, Minnesota, Chicago, Israel and Singapore. They found that men with psychological disorders constitute a large proportion of batterers they have seen in treatment, especially those who have drug or alcohol problems.[22] They describe an empirical typology of three profiles of batterers based on personality test data:

> The first profile, associated with the borderline personality disorder, describes an individual who is asocial, withdrawn, moody, and hypersensitive to interpersonal slights. A man with this profile is viewed by others as volatile and overreactive. He may vacillate from calm one minute to extreme anger in the next. The men in this group exhibit high levels of anxiety, depression, and alcohol problems.

> The second profile, a cluster associated with narcissistic and anti-social personality disorders, describes a self-centered person who uses others to meet his needs and reciprocates only when it meets his advantage. Men with this profile insist their perceptions, values, and rules be accepted by others. Hesitation by others to respond to the self-centered man's demands violates his sense of entitlement to be treated according to his standards, and he responds with threats and aggression.

> The third profile describes a tense, rigid individual who behaves in a passive or ingratiating manner and is associated with a dependent/compulsive personality cluster. These men lack self-esteem and have a strong sense of need for one or a few significant others.

21. Robert D. Hare, Adelle E. Forth, Katy E. Strachan, "Psychopathy and Crime Across the Life Span" in Aggression and Violence Throughout the Life Span, Ray DeV. Peters, Robert J. McMahon & Vernon L. Quinsey eds. (Newbury Park, CA: Sage Publications 1992) 285.

22. Jeffrey L. Edleson & Richard M. Tolman, Intervention for Men Who Batter: An Ecological Approach (Newbury Park, CA: Sage Publications 1992), 41.

Rebellious hostile feelings can result from failure to meet those needs. The men in this group exhibited low anger and moderate depression. An understanding of these patterns may help in, among other things, prediction of situations in which men may be more likely to use abusive behavior, in identifying core cognitive patterns that may support their abuse, and in assessing the need for concurrent treatment."[23]

Vaselle–Augenstein and Ehrlich are clearer that both the clinical and empirical evidence suggests that "there is psychopathology in many, if not all, batterers," with batterers as a group having "an identifiable set of personality characteristics: dependence, depression, anxiety, low self-esteem, paranoia, dissociation from their own feelings, poor impulse control, antisocial tendencies, and hostility toward women."[24] Batterers differ from non-batterers who are maritally unhappy in exhibiting far more psychopathology.[25] They cite findings of Hamberger and Hastings based on administering the Milton Clinical Multiaxial Inventory to batterers. Hamberger and Hastings found three main factors that indicated personality disorders in the abusers: borderline or schizoid, narcissistic or antisocial, and passive-dependent/compulsive.[26] They divided batterers into eight subgroups, seven of which were pathological:

> Group 1 was volatile and overreactive with poor impulse control. Men in this group had the Jekyll–Hyde personality and conformed to the DSM–III diagnostic category of borderline personality. Group 2 was rigid about rules and regulations; for them, punishment was administered unemotionally. they conformed to the DSM–III category of narcissistic or antisocial personality. Group 3 was rebellious, hostile, dependent, and low in self-esteem. They conformed to the DSM–III category of dependent or compulsive personality. Group 4 was the classic psychopathic personality—angry, aggressive, and antisocial. Group 5 had pronounced mood swings and a borderline personality. Group 6 was superficially charming but sensitive to rejection and apt to respond aggressively when dependency needs were not met. Group 7 was characterized by marked dependency needs, anxiety, and depression. Group 8 was low on all factors, and it was the only group that showed no clear pathology.[27]

Hamberger and Hastings' data are derived from their two studies of men in batterer treatment programs. The first study involved 105 abusive men in a court-mandated program and their second replication study involving 99 abusive men attending a domestic violence abatement program. All but 15% of the men in the first study and 12% of the men in the second study had clear pathology. This 85–88% rate for batterers with psychopathology compares with an 80% rate for incarcerated male offenders in Canada's prisons.

23. Id. at 42.

24. Vaselle–Augenstein & Ehrlich, supra note 3, at 147.

25. Id.

26. Id. at 147–48 * * *.

27. Id. at 148.

In evaluating well over 1,000 cases of domestic violence, Maiuro describes uncovering diagnosable profiles of batterers similar to those found by Hamberger and Hastings. Many of Maiuro's abusers met the criteria for personality disorders, depression, impulse control disorder, unresolved learning disabilities or attention deficits, alcohol abuse, cyclic mood or arousal disorders, adjustment reactions, organic personality syndromes, and, to a lesser extent, formal thought disorders. However, although Maiuro did not include any numerical breakdown, he states that batterers as a group have more psychopathology, especially personality disorders, than the general population.

Vaselle–Augenstein and Ehrlich also note the similarity to Gondolf's findings based on interviews with more than 500 battered women. Gondolf found that 7% of batterers were "sociopathic" and were likely to be sexually as well as physically abusive and to have been arrested for violent and drug-related crimes; 41% of batterers were "anti-social" and were physically and verbally abusive but were less violent and less likely to have been arrested; and 52% of batterers were "typical batterers" who engaged in less severe verbal and physical abuse, were more likely to be apologetic after the battering, and most likely to have their victims return to them.

Troubling Questions About Implications of Pathology

Vaselle–Augenstein and Ehrlich, citing positions held by most battered women's advocates, note that there has been considerable resistance to characterizing batterers as having pathology and not being normal men because calling the batterer pathological (1) seems to ignore the larger social context in which battering occurs, including the violence in society and social approval for violence against women; (2) absolves the batterer of responsibility for his behavior; (3) diverts attention from the main issue of needing to end the man's violence; and (4) cannot explain the high prevalence of violence. Furthermore, characterizing batterers as having pathology does not explain why most batterers do not abuse their coworkers or strangers, and why many men with pathologies do not abuse their partners. While acknowledging that such objections are by no means trivial they state that:

> recognition of the role played by individual pathology in battering does not necessarily mean that social-cultural factors, developmental history, environmental factors, and other important contributing causes need to be ignored or discounted. Neither is it necessary to adopt the extreme position that nothing is important other than individual pathology. Nor does acceptance of the existence of individual pathology in batterers mean that they should not be held responsible for their actions.[36]

Nor does it mean that sanctions will not work to stop their abusive behavior.

36. Id. at 149.

WHAT DO THESE FINDINGS MEAN?

Lawyers lack the expertise to determine the validity of these studies and their claims that almost all batterers have pathology. It is possible that the batterers studied, all of whom either volunteered for or were court-ordered into treatment, are not representative of all batterers. It is likely that those in treatment would have more pathology than the average batterer. Yet, even if these claims are true, battering may still be learned behavior which is socially sanctioned. That is, for someone to become a batterer, he may have to both have pathology and live in a society which tolerates or even encourages the abuse. Even Hamberger acknowledges that at present we cannot presume that pathology causes men to batter women. The pathology may only be "part of a final common pathway of a constellation of factors," which include both societal and interpersonal ones, that lead some men to batter their partners. Maiuro argues that battering behavior has many causes "and that psychopathology variables should be viewed as vulnerability factors rather than causal entities."

IMPLICATIONS FOR BATTERER TREATMENT

However, if it is true that batterers have pathology, it should require rethinking what types of batterer treatment programs are needed, including whether there should be different programs for different types of batterers. Most current treatment programs are short-term, yet short-term programs are highly unlikely to cure personality disorders. Furthermore, cojoint therapy is unlikely to work when the abuser has pathology. Even the proponents of family systems therapy acknowledge that it is not very effective in cases where there are significant personality disorders, especially sociopathy, or exhibited psychotic behavior.

IMPLICATIONS FOR CRIMINAL CASES AGAINST BATTERERS

If most batterers have pathology, an extremely troubling ramification is that batterers will argue that their pathology is a defense to their battering crimes. Yet the vast majority of criminals have psychopathology and the criminal justice system does not permit them to use this excuse as a defense or justification. Even if the criminal justice system were to treat batterer psychopathology as some kind of insanity defense, the argument would remain that any batterer so out of control because of his pathology is a real danger to society, and hence must be committed to a mental institution. However, the fact that most batterers are, in fact, able to control when, where, how severely and whom they beat argues strongly that their pathology is not really a defense to their battering because it is not a cause of their criminal behavior.

IMPLICATIONS FOR CUSTODY

Yet it is also true that recognizing that batterers have pathology should help battered mothers win more custody fights. For too long courts (and therapists) saw the abusive father as basically a normal man, perfectly able to parent effectively even though he was violent towards his children's mother. They also incorrectly believed that children were not affected by seeing their mothers beaten.

But any batterer pathology has to be seen as relevant towards the abuser's parenting ability and relationship with his children. Even Hamberger and Hastings' Group 8 batterers, who show no clear pathology, would be likely to have poor parenting ability because, while they scored below 75 on all factors, they scored just below 75 on the narcissistic, aggressive and conforming scales, indicating some deficiencies.

Courts (and therapists) must still catch up and recognize that the victims of domestic violence are not sick but undergoing a normal stress which will most likely end if the court can protect them from their abusers. Whether or not batterers have pathology, we need to educate the judiciary and medical professionals to know that virtually every battered woman can effectively parent once the batterer is removed from the household and that batterers make poor parents. This will insure that we are not helping to set up mothers to lose custody fights. We need to emphasize that battered women are experiencing this normal reaction to the abnormal stress caused by the batterer's outrageous behavior, and that any children in the home are also being traumatized by the batterer's abuse. Regardless of whether batterers are seen as having pathology, it also goes against all equitable principles to allow the batterer to take advantage of his wrongdoing, even in a custody case.

Courts can protect the abused mother by awarding her sole custody of her children and ordering, at most, visitation supervised by an impartial person who understands the dynamics of domestic violence. Many courts (and therapists) are still unaware that 53–70% of women batterers deliberately physically abuse their children. Similarly, they are unaware that even when the children are not beaten themselves, the children are seriously traumatized by seeing their mother beaten. Divorce and separation do not end this traumatization as spouse abuse generally increases after a couple separates. Most abusive men ultimately stop abusing their former partner, although they generally go on to beat their new partner. Even the majority of the small number of men who complete batterer training programs go on to beat new partners after they leave treatment.

CONCLUSION

The resolution of the question of whether most batterers have pathology will not change the fact that the tried and true legal strategies must still be pursued to help battered women. Were woman abuse not so rewarding, many batterers would stop their abusive behavior. This suggests that courts can do much to stop the battering by awarding a battered woman restitution whenever it is permitted for any damages resulting from her abuser's battery, in addition to always granting her an order of protection, with custody and support orders, where appropriate. Given that battering can be lethal for the victim and her children but that mental health professionals agree that they are unable to predict lethality in individual cases, judges must err on the side of overprotecting battered women and their children once abuse is established. Above all, judges should not be permitted to give mutual restraining orders, which greatly increase the likelihood of serious violence.

EDWARD W. GONDOLF AND ASSOCIATES, DO BATTERER PROGRAMS WORK?: A 15 MONTH FOLLOW–UP OF MULTI–SITE EVALUATION

3(5) Domestic Violence Report 65–66, 78–79 (June/July 1998).

INTRODUCTION

One of the most pressing questions for policy makers and practitioners in the domestic violence field is whether counseling programs for men who assault their female partners or "batterer programs" are effective in preventing further assaults on women. A second inquiry also being vigorously debated is what is the most effective referral procedure, program length, and program format? For instance, are 9–month programs, that are mainly discussion sessions for men who have been convicted for assaulting their female partners, more effective than 3–month programs, that are mainly instructional classes for men sent to the program as part of pre-trial diversion? A third emerging question is whether different types of batterers warrant specialized treatment or intervention. Related to the quest of "batterer types" is whether we can identify "risk markers" or predictors of who will reassault.

Based on previous research and practitioner experience, our initial expectations were that batterer programs do help interrupt the violence for the majority of men referred to them and that the longer, more comprehensive programs have lower rates of reassault, especially given the social reinforcement for abuse and compounding problems of many batterers (e.g., alcohol abuse). Finally, we might expect "antisocial" men and men with more severe psychopathology to be the most likely to reassault. We posed a situational model of reassault, however, which suggests that contact with the woman, additional services or intervention, unemployment, and further drinking would influence the outcome.

METHOD INVOLVING FOUR MULTI–SYSTEMS

We evaluated four batterer intervention systems using a naturalistic, comparative research design, as opposed to a clinical trial or experimental design. Over 30 program evaluations have been published in recent years, but most of these are limited by their single-site design and low-response rates. Few studies comparing programs or program approaches have been conducted, and there remain some difficult questions about the ethics, feasibility, and reliability of experimental or "clinical trials" in this field.

Selection of Four Sites: Four research sites were selected to represent a continuum of intensive and extensive interventions that included: (1) a pre-trial, 3–month, didactic program with court liaisons (Pittsburgh); (2) a post-conviction, 3–month, process program with women's services (Dallas); (3) a post-conviction, 5–month, didactic program associated with a legal advocacy program for victims (Houston); and (4) a post-conviction, 9–month, process program with complementary services including substance abuser treatment, individual mental health counseling, and women's services coordinators (Denver). The programs all approximated the gender-based cognitive behavioral approach endorsed by most states that have standards for batterer programs. A background questionnaire, an alcohol test (MAST), and a personality test (MCMI) were administered to 210 men at each of the four sites for a total sample of 840 (82% of the sample were court-ordered as opposed to being "voluntary" participants). The men's partners were also interviewed by phone at the time of intake.

Partner Interviews for 15 months: The men and their battered partners, as well as 170 identified new partners, were interviewed by phone every three months for 15 months. Police arrest reports, program records and participation reports, rearrest records during the follow-up, and women's medical records were reviewed and analyzed to help verify self-reports. Site visits, which included staff interviews and observation of group sessions, were conducted to verify the program approach and system.

A female partner was interviewed for 79% of the batterers at least once during the 15–month follow-up, and 68% of the women were contacted for the full follow-up period. The women respondents are slightly biased toward program completers and Anglo subjects. A similar response rate was achieved for the men. In 64% of the cases, both the men and their partners were interviewed. The outcome findings are based on women's reports, unless otherwise indicated.

Major Findings

Reassaults and Injuries: The reassault rate for the participants in the four programs fell between 32% and 39%. Nearly one-third (32%) of the men reassaulted a female partner according to the women's reports. Adjusting the women's reports with available reports of their male partners increased the reassault rate to 36%, and adjusting for male reports and arrest records increased the rate to 39%. A capture-recapture analysis of all available men, women, and arrest reports projects a reassault rate of 39% for the entire sample.

A much lower percentage of women was actually physically injured during the follow-up. Over half of the men (60%) who reassaulted a partner (19% of the total with responding partners) physically bruised or injured their partner, but only 20% of the injured partners (4% of the total respondents) sought medical attention for their injuries. In addition, we found no significant difference in victim safety, or danger, based on whether a program had contact with the women. However, the Denver program, which attempted to contact partners, did increase the women's involvement in services. That program was only able to contact about 30% of women and most of those contacted did not maintain contact with the program for long.

A surprising number of the reassaults occurred shortly after program intake. Nearly half (44%) of the men who reassaulted a partner did so within three months of program intake. The total percentage of new reassaults dropped from 14% at the 3–month follow-up to 3% at the 9–month follow-up and continued at that level through the remainder of the follow-up. However, over half (59%) of the men who reassaulted (19% of the total with responding partners) committed more than one reassault, and a third (32%) of the men who reassaulted a partner did so during more than one of the 3–month follow-up intervals. It is clear that there is a small portion of men who are unresponsive to the intervention and continue to be severely abusive.

Other Abuse and Arrests: A higher percentage of women reported other forms of abuse. Fully 70% of the men were verbally abusive, nearly half (45%) used controlling behaviors, 43% threatened their partners, and 16% stalked them. The men's arrest records indicate that only 10% of the batterers had been rearrested for domestic violence, 14% had been arrested for some other violence, and 16% had been arrested from some other offense during the follow-up. During the entire follow-up, 40% of the men had been rearrested for some offense.

Most Women Felt Better: Notwithstanding the high emotional abuse and lesser abuse rates against the women, two-thirds of them (66%) indicated at the 15–month follow-up that they were "better off" overall than when their partner was sent to the batterers' program, although 12% indicated they were "worse off." The area least likely to have improved was financial. Almost three-fourths (72%) of the women reported feeling "very safe" at each follow-up interval.

PROGRAM COMPARISONS AND BATTERER TYPES

Participating in the program appears to contribute to reducing reassaults. The program dropouts (35% of the respondent sample) were approximately 13% more likely to have reassaulted their partners (40% vs. 28% * * *). The dropouts were also more likely to have been rearrested for domestic violence (20% vs. 5%). Program attendance remained a significant predictor when controlling for background factors in a logistic regression for reassault. Moreover, the voluntary participants were significantly more likely to drop out of the programs and more likely to reassault than the court-ordered men. We were furthermore able to compare arrest records of Pittsburgh men who were court-ordered to the batterers program to those who were only fined or whose cases were dismissed or withdrawn. The demographics and case characteristics of the non-program men did not significantly differ from those sent to the program, yet the non-program subjects had twice the recidivism (rearrests) rates of the program completers for domestic violence, other assaults and the other offenses during the 15–month follow-up.

No Outcome Differences Among Program or Batterer Types: There was no significant difference in the outcomes of the four different programs, e.g., in the rates for reassaults, men's threats, domestic violence rearrests, or victims' "quality of life" satisfaction. While the longer, more comprehensive program did have a significantly lower rate of "severe" reassault, this apparent "site effect" disappeared when background variables (i.e., demographics, personality, behavioral, and relationship status variables) were controlled in a logistic regression and "survival" analysis.

The outcomes also did not significantly vary for different personality types. A factor analysis of scores on the MCMI subscales was used to generate four types that reflect the prevailing personality types for batterers. The types might be characterized as (1) little psychopathology, (2) antisocial/narcissistic, (3) avoidant/dependent, and (4) severe pathology. Also, there was no evidence that one "type" of batterer did better in one program approach or another (i.e., didactic vs. process). Separate subscales for antisocial, borderline, or avoidant tendencies were not of themselves predictive of reassault.

The only substantial predictor of outcome was whether a man was drunk during the follow-up period. General estimating equations were used to test situational variables (e.g., unemployment of the man or woman, additional services for the batterer, victim services for the woman) for longitudinal data (each of the 3–month follow-up intervals). Men who were reportedly "drunk" during the follow-up were three times more likely to reassault than those who were not drunk. Behavioral and personality factors assessed at program intake and the situational factors during follow-up were not significant or substantial predictors.

CONCLUSIONS AND IMPLICATIONS

Summary: Our evaluation of four batterer programs produced some unexpected findings. The reassault rate is comparable to that reported in previous single-site evaluations and may be a substantial accomplishment given the personality problems, criminal history, and substance abuse among substantial portions of the men. Moreover, there does appear to be a "program effect" in that program completers are significantly less likely to reassault than the dropouts even when controlling for background factors. The severest reassault is committed by those who reassault early and repeatedly during the follow-up. Unfortunately, we cannot readily identify these more "dangerous" men or the reoffenders in general.

The rate of new reassaults during the follow-up decreased substantially rather than increased as deterrence theories might suggest. We may find that this rate of reassault increases beyond a threshold of a year and a half, and after the chronic offenders (i.e., those who reassault early and repeatedly) are removed.

The most surprising finding is that the shorter programs appear to be as "effective" as the longer, more comprehensive ones. The benefits of the longer programs may not become evident until after our relatively short 15–month follow-up. Furthermore, the longer programs may be compromised by other features in their communities, such as the slow response of the police to men who drop out, or the delays in some courts between arrest and referral to a batterer program. Some programs may be unique to their communities. That is, they reflect the resources, personnel, legal procedures, and expectations of their particular locale.

Our findings also reinforce how difficult it is to predict reassault among clinical populations. Different personality types did not have worse outcomes than others and did not appear to do better in one program or another. Additionally, behavioral characteristics assessed at intake and situational factors during follow-up were not significantly and substantially related to program outcome. Only "drunkenness" during follow-up was significantly or substantially related to program outcome. This finding does not necessarily mean that alcohol abuse is the "cause" of reassaults. "Drunkenness" may be an indicator of unresponsiveness and defiant men.

Program Implications: The programmatic implications of our findings remain tentative without a longer follow-up and additional confirming research. The 15–month follow-up does suggest that program format in terms of length, court-linkages and curriculum may be as effective as longer programs faced with court delays and uncertain sanctions for dropout or reassault. Additionally, more intensive (e.g., 3–4 days a week for three months) rather than extensive (e.g., once a week for nine months) programming might be warranted for the potential early and repeat assaulters identified in our study. We did not, however, find evidence for specialized programming to address different personality types, beyond the prevailing gender-based cognitive-behavioral approach. There may be a need to more carefully monitor alcohol abuse after the program and sustain alcohol treatment for some men over the long term.

Future Research: We are continuing our investigation into a number of other topics related to the batterers and victims in our study. These topics include several studies about the characteristics of the batterers and their victims, including the reliability of alcohol assessments, the reliability and validity of abuse self-reports, the structure and topics of incident narratives, and the women's use of services. We are also examining more about the programs and their outcomes in topics, such as, the variations in program structure and linkages, the influence of race on program participation and outcome, the outcome of "voluntary" participants as opposed to court-mandated participants, predictors of injury and medical assistance, predictors of program dropout, the perceptions of sanctions and outcome, and violence avoidance techniques used by batterers.

We are also beginning an additional 3–year grant that will extend our 15–month follow-up to four years, and reveal the long-term impact of the programs for the initial and new partners of the men. This new research will additionally explore the reasons for the relatively small portion of women who receive additional services or support. This research will, furthermore, examine the effect of the new welfare reform on the relationships between the men and women in our initial study. The overall purpose of the new research is to confirm or revise our current findings based on a relatively short-term follow-up.

KERRY HEALEY, CHRISTINE SMITH, AND CHRIS O'SULLIVAN, BATTERER INTERVENTION: PROGRAM APPROACHES AND CRIMINAL JUSTICE STRATEGIES

US DOJ, National Institute of Justice 17–23, 26–31 (1998).

OVERVIEW OF THEORIES AND RELATED INTERVENTIONS

Feminist (or profeminist), family systems, and psychotherapeutic theories of domestic violence offer divergent explanations of the root causes of battering and lead to distinct intervention models. The following section outlines the basic tenets of each theory, illustrates how these assumptions influence the choice of intervention strategies, and notes the advantages and disadvantages of each theoretical and treatment approach. As noted previously, however, examples of programming based exclusively on one theory are becoming increasingly rare.

FEMINIST APPROACHES: THE SOCIAL PROBLEM APPROACH

Batterer intervention programs originated in the early 1970's, as feminists and others brought to public attention the victimization of women and spawned grass roots services such as rape hot lines and battered women's shelters. According to Anne Ganley of Seattle's Veteran Administration Medical Center and David Adams of EMERGE in Boston, providers of services to battered women felt that victims who had received services either returned home to face the same destructive environment or left the relationship—and the batterer found a new victim. To help victims, advocates realized, it was also necessary to address the root cause of their problems—the perpetrators of violence. Profeminist men concerned with sexism in themselves and society felt a particular responsibility for working with male abusers. As a result, some of the first systematic interventions for batterers developed from a profeminist perspective.

WHAT IS A FEMINIST MODEL OF BATTERING?

Central to the feminist perspective on battering is a gender analysis of power. According to this view, domestic violence in intimate relationships mirrors the patriarchal organization of society in which men play a dominant role in most social institutions. Along with verbal, emotional, and economic abuse, violence is a means of maintaining male power in the family when men feel their dominance is being threatened. Economic roles have left women dependent on men and unable to escape abusive situations. Men's superior physical strength may enable them to dominate women through violence.

Feminists argue that a consequence of the social arrangement in which men hold the positions of respect and power is that men and women alike devalue the feminine and overvalue the masculine. To the batterer, women are childlike and incompetent. It is not uncommon for batterers to convince their wives that they are not capable of adult activities, such as driving a car or holding a job. For example, a former victim reported that her husband had convinced her that she could not turn on the washing machine without breaking it, so she had to wait until he returned from work before she could do the laundry for their seven children. Similarly, in disputed custody cases when a batterer and partner separate, the husband often contends that his wife is incapable of taking care of the children.

In the feminist view, batterers feel that they should be in charge of the family: making decisions, laying down rules, disciplining disobedient wives and children, and correcting unsatisfactory performance of duties. Batterers may typically exercise control over the family in nonviolent, coercive ways and only sometimes resort to violence. As men, batterers feel entitled to gender-based respect and obedience; therefore, what they perceive to be disrespect and disobedience infuriates them. Batterers often rationalize their violence on the grounds that it was necessitated by their partner's actions: she provoked or caused it, and they simply reacted as any man would.

Feminist programs attempt to raise consciousness about sex role conditioning and how it constrains men's emotions and behavior (through education around sexism, male privilege, male socialization). Programs with a feminist philosophy present a model of egalitarian relationships along with the benefits of nonviolence and of building relationships based on trust instead of fear. Most feminist approaches support confronting men over their power and control tactics in all domains of the relationship, including verbal and psychological abuse, social isolation, the undermining of the victim's self-confidence, and sexual coercion. A particular concern of profeminist male group facilitators is the constant risk and temptation of colluding with batterers. For example, a male facilitator at Family Services of Seattle reported that when his female cofacilitator was absent at one session, the men in the group expected him to drop his profeminist "guise" and participate in or agree with their negative characterizations of women.

ADVANTAGES AND CRITICISMS OF THE FEMINIST MODEL

Perhaps because work with batterers was originated by battered women's advocates and feminists, the feminist perspective has influenced most programs. A national survey conducted in 1986 found that 80 percent of programs attempt to change sex role attitudes, stop violence, and increase self-esteem. Even programs adopting a family systems model (see below) may advocate an egalitarian and democratic relationship to couples in treatment. Support for the feminist analysis of the role of power in domestic violence comes from the observation that most batterers are able to control their anger and avoid resorting to violence when "provoked" by someone more powerful than they, such as their work supervisors, police officers, or judges. Further support for the feminist analysis comes from research showing that batterers are less secure in their masculinity than nonbatterers—the theory being that men who do not feel masculine will need to to assert their masculinity more forcefully to compensate for their sense of inadequacy. Other studies have documented the sense of entitlement that batterers feel in controlling their partners' behavior and in justifying violence if these women deviate from the female sex role.

Critics have claimed that the feminist perspective overemphasizes sociocultural factors, such as patriarchal values, to the exclusion of individual factors like growing up abused. Men's behavior in intimate relationships varies across individuals and broad cultural factors cannot explain this variability. Feminist theory predicts that all men in our society will be abusive, claim its critics, adding that besides being untrue, this theory makes it impossible to predict which men will be violent. To make individual predictions, a model must assign a role to other factors including, but not limited to, psychological deviance.

Other criticisms center not on the validity of feminist explanations of battering but on the translation of that theory into programming. For example, some observers argue that feminist educational interventions are too confrontational in tone and, as a result, are ultimately self-defeating, alienating batterers, increasing their hostility, and making them less likely to become engaged in treatment. It is possible that the goal of the feminist model—to rebuild the batterer's belief system in order to achieve nonviolence—may be unnecessarily ambitious and adversarial. Batterers' existing value systems may be more easily fine-tuned to emphasize nonviolence (e.g., building on religious convictions or humanism) without a feminist overlay.

Another concern is that educational programs may effectively transmit information without deterring violent behavior. A 1991 evaluation of three short-term psychoeducational batterer programs in Baltimore found that while batterers considered the curriculum helpful, they recidivated at a higher rate than batterers who did not receive treatment. A study of graduates of Duluth's Domestic Abuse Intervention Project found that completion of the feminist educational intervention had no impact on recidivism after five years. Outcomes such as these point to the need for broader evaluations that examine the impact of systemic factors—arrest and prosecution policies, court procedures, and probation supervision—on intervention effectiveness, as well as a clarification of the goals of feminist-based interventions. If deterrence is not a likely outcome of an intervention, other goals, such as punishment, education, behavioral monitoring, or social change, must be explicitly advanced. (A few practitioners are in fact shifting their primary focus away from individual change in batterers in favor of social change through a coordinated community response).

The Family Systems Model

The family systems model regards individual problem behaviors as a manifestation of a dysfunctional family unit, with each family member contributing to the problem. Rather than identifying one individual as the cause of the violence and removing that person from the home or singling that person out for treatment, the model advocates working with the family or couple together, providing support with the goal of keeping the family intact.

According to the family systems (or "interactional") model, both partners may contribute to the escalation of conflict, with each striving to dominate the other. Family systems theorists believe that most abuse is verbal and emotional, but as the conflict escalates, either partner may resort to violence. Because, from this perspective, *interactions* produce violence, no one is considered to be the perpetrator or victim, even if only one person is physically violent. Family systems theory also suggests that interactions may permit or facilitate abusive behaviors in one person, such as a nonabusive parent's failure to intervene in child abuse or a family member's failure to establish appropriate personal boundaries, thus setting the stage for their own victimization. Family systems therapists criticize psychological approaches that focus on individual deficits (low self-esteem, dependence, anger) while neglecting to teach interpersonal skills that could promote safety. Family systems theory leads to treatment that involves improving communication and conflict resolution skills. Both members of the couple can develop these skills through "solution-focused brief therapy" that

- locates the problem in the interaction rather than in the pathology of one individual;

- focuses on solving the problem, rather than looking for causes; and

- accentuates the positive—for example, examining occasions when the couple avoided violence.

Advantages and Criticisms of the Family Systems Model

Advantages of the family systems approach note that many violent couples would like to remain together and that there may be positive aspects to the relationship that counseling can build on. However, while some observers report that over half of domestic violence couples remain together, a study of abused wives whose husbands did become nonviolent found that most of the women subsequently terminated the marriage because of other marital problems that became apparent after the violence ended.

Both feminist and cognitive-behavioral approaches agree that partner abuse does not involve shared responsibility. Both approaches firmly hold that batterers bear full responsibility for the violence, victims play no causal role, and no one incites violence. Of particular concern to both feminist and cognitive-behavioral proponents is the format of couples counseling: encouraging each partner to discuss problems openly with the other partner can put the victim at risk after the session if the woman expresses complaints. Furthermore, no frank exchange between counselor and victim concerning the abuse is likely to be possible in the presence of the batterer. Moreover, the format is conducive to victim blaming. Finally, if the court prohibits the batterer from contacting the victim, the family systems approach will violate the court order. For these reasons couples counseling is expressly prohibited in 20 State standards and guidelines. Judges involved with partner abuse cases that also involve child abuse need to pay particular attention to safety issues raised by family systems interventions, which may be the treatment approach recommended by child welfare workers who are working toward a goal of family reunification. In such cases, issues of victim and child safety must be weighed carefully, and if a family systems approach is chosen, close monitoring is needed.

Psychological Approaches: A Focus on Individual Problems

Psychological perspectives hold that personality disorders or early experiences of trauma predispose some individuals to violence. Being physically abusive is seen as a symptom of an underlying emotional problem. Parental abuse, rejection, and failure to meet a child's dependence needs can be the psychological source of battering. People with these underlying problems may choose partners with whom they can reenact the dysfunctional relationship they had with their parents. Two forms of batterer intervention have evolved from this perspective: individual and group psychodynamic therapy and cognitive behavioral group therapy.

Individual and Group Psychodynamic Counseling

Psychoanalysis can be undertaken not only in individual counseling but also in unstructured batterer groups that allow members to explore their life experiences. Psychodynamic therapies involve uncovering the batterer's unconscious problem and resolving it consciously. Proponents of psychodynamic therapy for batterers believe that other interventions are superficial: since other therapies are unable to eliminate the abuser's deep-rooted and unconscious *motive* for aggression, they cannot end violence but only suppress it temporarily. Long-term change requires exposing and resolving the root cause of the violent behavior.

Advantages and Criticisms of Psychodynamic Approaches

Browne and Saunders recently conducted a study comparing a "process psychodynamic treatment model" with a feminist/cognitive-behavioral intervention and found no difference in recidivism rates based on partners' reports. Nevertheless, they argue:

> [T]here were two advantages to the process-psychodynamic model. it retained a significantly higher percentage of men in treatment and it was more successful with men who had dependent personality disorder. *Regardless of the treatment approach used, more self-*

disclosure and less lecturing were related to greater group cohesion, which in turn was related to lower recidivism rates.[20] [Emphasis added]

Critics argue that psychodynamic therapy merely assigns a psychiatric label to people who batter (e g., insecure, narcissistic, dependent, compulsive, or suffering from intermittent explosive disorder) without explaining how they got that way or what can be done about it. The psychodynamic approach has also been criticized for allowing batterers to continue the behavior until the underlying psychological problem is resolved. David Adams, director of EMERGE, gives the example of a batterer mandated to treatment who had already learned in individual psychotherapy that he battered because he was insecure. At the intake interview for the batterer program, the counselor asked the man whether he was going to continue to choose to be violent until he resolved his insecurity. The man said that he had never thought of battering as a choice, but now he would reconsider the notion. Feminists argue that labeling batterers as having psychological problems not only exonerates them in their own eyes but also ignores the cultural acceptability of male dominance in the family and how it serves to keep the batterer in control of his partner. The approach pays attention to *internal* psychological functions of abuse for the batterer but ignores the *interpersonal* function of controlling the other person's behavior.

In practice, many psychologically oriented programs have moved away from the original stance that battering is caused primarily by psychological disorder and always indicates an emotional problem. Instead, they have integrated social explanations with psychological explanations. For example, some psychologically oriented theorists propose that it is the combination of a man's low self-esteem and a cultural expectation that men should be dominant and successful that produces a batterer.

COGNITIVE-BEHAVIORAL MODEL OF CHANGE

Cognitive-behavioral therapy is used in the treatment of violent offenders. Whereas the psychoanalytic tradition focuses on psychological disorders based in the unconscious and early childhood experiences, the cognitive-behavioral model focuses on conscious material in the present: therapy is intended to help individuals function better by modifying how they think and behave in current situations. The theory behind cognitive-behavioral batterer interventions maintains that behaviors are learned as a result of positive and negative reinforcements (rewards and punishments) for engaging in particular behaviors under particular circumstances (e. g., parental pride or praise for aggressive behavior). Behavior is also influenced by how people mentally construct and interpret their environment and experiences—that is, the way they think

20. Browne, Saunders, and Straecker,   Who Batter."
"Process–Psychodynamic Groups for Men

about themselves, other people, and their relationships. The cognitive-behavioral theory postulates that men batter because:

- they are imitating examples of abuse they have witnessed during childhood or in the media;

- it enables the batterer to get what he wants; and

- abuse is reinforced through victim compliance and submission.

Cognitive-behavioral interventions focus on "cognitive restructuring" and skill building. Counselors focus on identifying the chain of events that lead each batterer to violence, starting with beliefs and "self-talk"—the way we talk to ourselves in our minds. For example, a batterer whose partner is ten minutes late may tell himself, "She's out with her boyfriend" or "She can't be trusted." The programs attempt to restructure the beliefs and "self talk" that lead to violence; for example, "I don't know why she's late, but I'm sure she's trying to get here." The programs help batterers to analyze the thought patterns underlying violent reactions (e. g., "Dinner isn't ready because my wife doesn't respect me") and learn new ways of understanding situations that trigger violence (e.g. "Dinner isn't ready because my wife had a busy day"). The program teaches nonviolent alternative behaviors, such as conflict-resolution tactics, relaxation techniques, and communication skills.

* * *

ADVANTAGES AND CRITICISM OF THE COGNITIVE-BEHAVIORAL MODELS

One advantage of the cognitive-behavioral model is that its analysis of battering and its intervention strategy are compatible with a criminal justice response to domestic violence. The approach holds the batterer fully responsible for his violence and fully responsible for learning and adopting nonviolent alternatives. Without trying to solve larger issues of social inequality on the one band, or delving into deep-seated psychological issues on the other, the cognitive-behavioral approach simply focuses on the violent acts themselves and attempts to change them. The model also offers a straightforward intervention that can be implemented in a limited period of time.

The feminist perspective criticizes the cognitive-behavioral approach for failing to explain why many men with thought patterns or skills deficits that allegedly explain their domestic violence are not violent in other relationships, how culture or subcultures influence patterns of violence, and why some men continue to abuse women even when the behavior is not rewarded. These criticisms are usually moot because most cognitive-behavioral programs integrate the feminist analysis of domestic violence, both in the cognitive component (for example, by examining thoughts that encourage wife-beating, such as "She should obey me. I'm the man of the household") and the social learning aspects (for example, by discussing how sexism in the media and in society provides models of social support for abusing and degrading women).

COMPATIBILITY OF THE MODELS WITH CRIMINAL JUSTICE GOALS

The feminist educational approach to batterer intervention is theoretically more compatible with a criminal justice perspective than either the family systems or psychotherapeutic approaches in several respects.

● The feminist educational view of domestic violence is that the behavior is criminal, not just the result of faulty couple interactions or mental illness.

● The feminist educational view is that consequences are appropriate. By contrast, the psychotherapeutic explanation results in a treatment approach that is designed to modify the inner emotional life of the batterer through insight and possibly medication. Changing the inner person and prescribing medication to alter behavior may be considered by some to be beyond the scope of a criminal justice intervention.

● The primary goal of feminist educational programs is to hold batterers responsible for their violence. While most psychological programs also make this claim, feminists believe that the psychotherapeutic view of batterers as victims of childhood trauma or other mistreatment undercuts a program's ability to hold batterers responsible. The family systems approach—unlike the criminal justice system—holds the victim as well as the batterer accountable.

● The explicit goal of feminist educational approaches is to end the abusive behavior rather than to heal the batterer (the psychotherapeutic goal) or to improve relationships (the family systems goal).

A case can be made, however, that psychological interventions can also meet the needs of the criminal justice system. The aim of the criminal justice system in sending men to batterer programs is to reduce recidivism; for this to happen, the intervention has to be effective. While advocates of the feminist educational model criticize the psychotherapeutic model for failing to hold batterers responsible for their behavior, advocates of the psychotherapeutic approach respond that educational interventions are not successful in deterring or rehabilitating batterers because they are too short and superficial and do not address the needs of batterers with severe mental illness, who may comprise up to 25 percent of all batterers. Indeed, the "confrontational" and didactic process of the feminist model—as well as the feminist rhetoric in which it is framed—may alienate the batterer and increase his hostility and resistance. For example, an assistant group facilitator for the Compassion Workshop in Silver Spring, Maryland, reported that, when he was in treatment, feminist interventions had only increased his anger and denial, while subsequent, nonconfrontational, compassion-based treatment had helped him become nonviolent. His wife, a cofacilitator of the group whose role was to give the perspective of the victim, agreed that the feminist education model had exacerbated her husband's abuse but that after psychologically oriented counseling, he was now violence free.

While the narrow treatment goals of the strictly educational feminist programs are compatible with the criminal justice view—simply stopping the abusive behavior as expeditiously as possible and holding the batterer responsible—the feminist theory of domestic violence also has broad social goals that may be seen as going beyond the purview of the criminal justice system. Because feminist theory locates the cause of domestic violence in social structures and the organization of society, social change may be seen as the ultimate goal of the curriculums. In a sense, though, even this broad goal is consistent with a criminal justice agenda in that it suggests that broad-based community education and a coordinated community response are necessary for preventing domestic violence. In contrast, it is difficult to identify a broad prevention strategy that follows from either the individualistic psychotherapeutic theory of domestic violence or the systems model.

Finally, some practitioners and criminal justice professionals are beginning to regard any form of batterer intervention as a proxy for intensive probation. While the curriculum may not deter reoffenses over time, at least during program participation batterers are being monitored closely, and their victims are receiving at least minimal attention and referrals. This heightened vigilance with regard to the batterer's behavior and the victim's welfare is compatible with criminal justice goals.

As will be seen in the following chapters, however, theoretical compatibility with the criminal justice system is not the only important factor in selecting a batterer intervention. On a practical level, interventions must be able to retain batterers in treatment and address any obstacles to program participation.

CONCLUSION: MULTIDIMENSIONAL MODELS DOMINATE THE FIELD

Many practitioners accept that there are compelling features in more than one theoretical model. In practice, regardless of their primary perspective, most programs have adopted some tenets of the feminist model. For example, they view sexual inequality and masculine role expectations of dominance as core issues to address—along with cognitive-behavioral techniques for modifying behavior—and they teach batterers to use "time-outs" (a behavioral technique for controlling emotional outbursts). Longer-term programs may progress through the feminist and cognitive models in stages, and some even progress to a psychotherapeutic group process model for aftercare. These programs have a brief initial phase using a feminist educational model to tackle denial of responsibility, a longer second phrase teaching cognitive-behavioral techniques for skill-building, and a third phase delving into individual psychological issues in an unstructured format for those men identified as having psychological problems contributing to battering. Other programs blend treatment modalities and approaches by combining individual, group, and couples treatment sequentially over an extended period of two to three years.

Programs may also use different models or materials to accommodate the special needs of specific types of batterers, most commonly substance abusers, African Americans, Asians, Latinos, recent immigrants, female offenders, gay and lesbian batterers, or batterers with poor literacy skills.

Some practitioners may resist incorporating consideration of individual psychology and cultural differences in interventions because they are concerned that the individual approach will eclipse consideration of the sociological factors emphasized by the prevailing feminist model. However, the critical issue from a criminal justice perspective is simply "what works"; if mixed-model interventions that incorporate psychotherapeutic elements or cultural competence are shown to be more effective in retaining and engaging batterers in treatment, questions of theory are likely to become secondary.

* * *

Chapter 3

CROSS-CULTURAL ISSUES: SURVIVORS OF HETEROSEXUAL DOMESTIC VIOLENCE WHO FACE MULTIPLE OPPRESSIONS

This chapter focuses on how domestic violence is experienced by particular groups in the US, including women of color, Orthodox Jewish women, and disabled women. It starts with an article which looks at the intersections between violence, poverty, and minority status in the US.

In the section on Asian American battered women, the author notes the substantial barriers which immigration difficulties raise in terms of victims of domestic violence being able to escape their abusers. This article also critiques the battered women's movement for not adequately addressing the needs of Asian American victims, and simultaneously calls for the Asian American community to deal with the issue of domestic violence in its midst.

Several African American writers discuss domestic violence in the lives of battered women in that community, discussing the failure of both the anti-racism and feminist movements to address the intersections of race and gender. The materials look at the history of the treatment of African American women, noting the ways that racist attitudes and policies based on that history impact legal decision making, access to resources, and community response to domestic violence.

The article on Latinas in the US notes the problems with using a law enforcement approach to domestic violence in this community, the lack of Spanish-speaking services, and the problems Latinas face due to immigration laws. Domestic violence in the lives of Native American women is discussed in the context of three tribes: Cheyenne, Navajo, and Cherokee, with differing approaches to this issue.

Orthodox Jewish women in the US also are in a minority status, and consequently deal with many of the same issues: their relationship to the majority culture's legal system, how this system interacts with religious

132

law and practice, loyalty to the community, etc. The chapter concludes with excerpts from an article looking at disabled women and domestic violence, comparing the abuse this population experiences with that of non-disabled women and making policy recommendations.

The inclusion of these materials in one chapter is not intended to imply that these issues can be addressed on only one occasion. On the contrary, the intent is that the reader will use the information from this chapter to continue to examine the issues raised in the rest of this book. In every area of law, it is important to ask how current and proposed policies and practices affect all victims of domestic violence, and to design solutions which meet the needs of all groups.

A. OVERVIEW

ANGELA BROWNE, RESHAPING THE RHETORIC: THE NEXUS OF VIOLENCE, POVERTY, AND MINORITY STATUS IN THE LIVES OF WOMEN AND CHILDREN IN THE UNITED STATES

3 Geo. J. on Fighting Poverty 19–21 (1995).

ETHNICITY AND VIOLENCE

In working with extremely poor and incarcerated populations in recent years, I am increasingly concerned with the nexus of poverty and violence in women's and children's lives, and with the continuing neglect of minority populations and issues in research and in the feminist movement, as well as in social policy. Although many assumptions are made, little is known about the prevalence of violence against women and children in most minority groups. Research based on national random samples has clarified that race alone does not distinguish violent and nonviolent couples. Much of the increased risk faced by minority women is associated with poverty and isolation. For example, when factors such as family income and the man's occupation are controlled, rates of partner assault for African–American couples are not significantly different than the rates for Caucasian husbands and wives. Levels of lethal violence and homicide, however, are much higher among African–Americans. Similarly, one of the few comparative analyses to be done with Hispanic and non-Hispanic Caucasians in Los Angeles found that there were no differences in the level of physical violence toward a spouse or other intimate adult partner between Mexican–American and Caucasian couples. However, Mexican-born Mexican–American men had significantly lower rates of violence in partner relationships than either Caucasians or U.S.-born Mexican–Americans. This finding is in itself troubling, as it suggests that early socialization into United States society plays a critical role in the development of aggression.

Assumptions about the prevalence of violence among some minority populations may, in themselves, work directly against prevention. For example, beliefs that African–Americans are ''just violent people'' seriously affect the responsiveness of formal help sources including how victims and perpetrators are treated by the police, how seriously partner assault or assaults against children are viewed, how victims are counseled, how medical and social service personnel treat and refer both victims and perpetrators, and the proportion of early interventions and other resources devoted to addressing violence within African–American communities. Thus, expectations that some minority populations will be more violent than the Caucasian majority become self-fulfilling. The risk of homicide, for example, increases proportionately with the denial of protection against assault.

Minority status may also present special problems for women faced with aggression inside or outside of the family. Immigrant status and little knowledge of the English language are critical factors in the responses of some minority women to the dangers they face. For many immigrant women, maintaining residency and attaining citizenship is dependent upon staying married to their husbands. Women residing in the country without legal documents are particularly inhibited from seeking help, since identification could lead to arrest and deportation. Immigrant women also may be in the country without family or friends who might otherwise provide important sources of protection and psychological or financial support.

Cultural values also may suppress help-seeking by ethnically diverse women. For example, little is known about Asian–American women's experiences of violence at home, and virtually no studies are funded to address this gap in knowledge or pave the way for culturally-appropriate interventions. Asian–Americans consider family problems highly private matters; preventing a "loss of face" and protecting the privacy of the family unit are strongly-held values. Divorce is uncommon among Asian–American couples, and separation is not usually considered to be an option by assaulted women. Language may be especially difficult for Asian–Americans as well. Although most police forces, hospital settings, and social service agencies have Spanish-speaking staff, interpreters for other languages are not readily available in many locales. Even Spanish-speaking interpreters are not available in many court settings.

Similarly, information on the lives of Native American women comes primarily from anecdotal data. Male violence against women appears to be at frightening levels throughout many Native American populations, but reliable estimates are nonexistent. Sanctions for informing on a husband or assailant or contacting external help sources are typically more severe than sanctions against abuse. Allen contends that the assault of Native American women by Native American men was almost nonexistent until the introduction of alcohol and patriarchal belief systems by the conquering Western culture. The relationship between the extreme subjugation, isolation, and poverty of Native Americans within U.S. society is also a critical contributor to the catastrophic levels of violence in many Native American communities. Native American women face overall levels of physical jeopardy scarcely imagined by the rest of the American population. Homicide rates are three times higher than for other Americans, and suicide rates are more than double. At a time when many Americans are living into their seventies or beyond, the average life expectancy for Native American women is around forty-seven years old.

POVERTY, POLICIES, AND VIOLENCE

In thinking about violence within impoverished populations, we often reverse the temporal ordering of events and their effects in our discussions and our interventions. The oppression we ignore; the poverty we deem too big to solve; the violence and other outcomes we punish and decry, and seem mystified when our choices for intervention coincide only with their increase. Societally we emphasize what are effects of events or conditions as though they were independent behaviors or mood states. For example, in urban settings, we talk about drug use, high rates of aggression, and fatalities among poor and minority populations and spend our resources to punish drug use and aggression after the fact, without a serious investment in causes of the problem or remediation of known precursors. The irony of this approach comes in the focus on cost-savings since the cost of crime and punishment, including incarceration—carried on the backs of the tax payers—is far greater than the costs of prevention and adequate community-based interventions.

Nationally, we say it is the prevalence and effects of violence on individuals and society with which we are concerned. Yet we cannot ignore or promote poverty among our citizens and reduce violence at the same time. Poverty has consistently been found to constitute a serious risk factor for child abuse and neglect, as well as for partner violence. Although it is distributed across all income categories, violence often occurs in the context of other debilitating factors, such as a lack of resources to meet basic family needs and the presence of other emotionally or physically abusive interactions within the community. For children raised in economically distressed homes, the likelihood of exposure to physical or sexual abuse by parental figures, other relatives or acquaintances, or other children, is inordinately high. For both women and children living in poverty, the necessity to "double-" or "triple-up" with others to maintain a dwelling exacerbates the risk of physical and sexual abuse by other persons living in that environment.

Levels of poverty have worsened significantly in this nation over the past fifteen years. As economist Edward Wolff has noted, in the 1980s, there was a dramatic shift in household wealth in this country, with the top 1% of wealth holders enjoying two-thirds of all the increases in financial assets and an absolute decline in the bottom 80% of households. This recent shift has led to the greatest wealth inequality since the 1920s. For the first time, the United States now has greater wealth inequality than exists in traditionally class-ridden European countries. Escalating cutbacks in benefits coupled with severe shortages of low-income housing and increases in unemployment have jeopardized the stability of all people with reduced or fixed incomes. From 1991 to 1992 alone, 2.8 million more Americans became poor.

* * *

B. ASIAN IMMIGRANT WOMEN

KAREN WANG, BATTERED ASIAN AMERICAN WOMEN: COMMUNITY RESPONSES FROM THE BATTERED WOMEN'S MOVEMENT AND THE ASIAN AMERICAN COMMUNITY

3 Asian L. J. 151–154, 157–158, 160–161, 162, 167–168, 173–174, 177, 182–184 (1996).

INTRODUCTION

He hit me, held a knife to my throat, a gun to my head, and choked me with a golf club. My arms, legs, and body were often covered with bruises. He would kiss them, cry and say, "Baby, I didn't mean to hit you. I don't know why ... I lost my temper."[1]

He would drag me by my hair down the stairs, smash my head into the wall, throw me down on the floor then kick and hit me all over.... He would spit on me when I got dressed....[2]

These brutal experiences are familiar to many battered women, but these two stories belong to battered Asian American women. Their stories are unique, not because Asian American women necessarily experience domestic violence differently from non-Asian American women, but because the stories of battered Asian American women are still relatively unheard and unknown. While the movement against domestic violence has made tremendous gains in the past twenty years, not all battered women have benefited equally. Women of color have gained less from the progress of the anti-domestic violence movement, which has been primarily "white-centered." And within communities of color, including Asian American communities, domestic violence has yet to become a priority issue.

Although battered women experience universally similar abuse, the needs and concerns of Asian American domestic violence victims require special attention. Battered Asian American women are situated differently than other battered women in the United States, especially white women. Domestic violence is a complex psychological and sociological phenomenon which is further complicated in Asian American communities by other factors such as language, immigrant status, culture, and racial stereotypes. Battered Asian American women stand at the inter-

1. Jacqueline R. Agtuca, A Community Secret: For the Filipina in an Abusive Relationship 6 (1994) (quoting a battered Filipina American woman).

2. Sonia Chopra, The New New Yorkers: Silent No More, South Asian Women Get Help to Escape Domestic Abuse, Newsday, May 22, 1994, at 1 (quoting a battered Asian Indian woman).

section of multiple identities, not only as women and domestic violence victims, but also as Asians and often as immigrants. However, American society and laws, which are constructed largely along binary lines (e.g., the "black-white" paradigm of race), have great difficulty recognizing intersectionalities and effectively ignore those—such as battered Asian American women—who exist at intersections of identity.

* * *

b. *The "White–Centeredness" of the Anti–Domestic Violence Movement*

Win Ha first sought help last year after her husband beat her three times during her first month in the U.S. A Vietnamese friend gave her the number of an advocacy group, and Ha was placed in a mainstream women's shelter. But she stayed only three days. "There was no Vietnamese food in the shelter," says Ha, and no one spoke Vietnamese, so when Ha's children became sick, she didn't know what to do.

The anti-domestic violence movement is largely a white women's movement. It is part of a broader women's rights movement, a movement which historically has been racist and nativist. As such, contemporary feminism has been criticized for failing to embrace a vision that speaks to American women of all races.

By focusing on gender alone, the anti-domestic violence movement falls into the same trap as other feminist movements: it ends up privileging white women. In American society and laws, gender and race both operate hierarchically. Men are privileged over women, and white is privileged over non-white. In a hypothetical world where gender is the only basis of oppression, the subordination of women to men might be the only battle women need to fight. However, in the very real world where race is also a basis of oppression, where oppressions are not discrete and insular, and where white is the privileged race, white women possess an "unearned advantage" and a "conferred dominance" over non-white women by virtue of being white. White privilege allows white women to examine gendered issues such as domestic violence from a color-blind perspective. The current anti-domestic violence discussion privileges those for whom gender is the primary basis of oppression and does not speak to women who face conflating oppressions of gender and race.

* * *

Furthermore, the current language of the anti-domestic violence discussion perpetuates white-centeredness by making race a non-issue. For example, much of the research, studies, and literature on domestic violence fails to reveal any relevant demographics about battering victims and perpetrators, other than their gender. Women of color are "virtually invisible," at least in the sense that available domestic violence data is often color-blind. For example, most domestic violence data describes "women" without any racial context. Yet such numbers are cited repeatedly to illustrate the pervasiveness and seriousness of battering for all American women, regardless of race. By not further defining "women" (or, for that matter, "men"), it is unclear who is actually reflected in domestic violence data. The lack of statistics which describe battered women beyond gender, and occasionally class, is a result of the failure to research domestic violence according to race or ethnicity. In our numbers-oriented society, the absence of specific empirical data on battered women of color marginalizes non-white domestic violence victims. One manifestation of this marginalization is the difficulty in obtaining or justifying the funding of specific services for battered Asian American women. By presenting color-blind and race-less domestic violence statistics, the anti-domestic violence movement affirms the status quo of white domination.

II. DEFINING AND SITUATING ASIAN AMERICAN WOMEN IN THE DOMESTIC VIOLENCE CONTEXT

* * *

The common factors which distinguish battered Asian American women from white women are: (1) the overwhelmingly immigrant character of Asian American communities, (2) the existence of similar cultural patterns across most Asian American communities, and (3) the existence of harmful stereotypes about Asian Americans collectively and Asian American women specifically.

* * *

As a result of recent immigration patterns, Asian American women are predominantly foreign-born, which creates several inherent obstacles for battered Asian American women that do not exist for battered white women. Specifically, the immigrant character of Asian American communities presents unique language and immigration law problems.

* * *

B. The Existence of Similar Cultural Patterns Across Many Asian American Communities

My sister's death did not begin with her murder—it began years ago where he first called her a whore. It started with the pushing, the hitting and kicking.... He broke her nose, bent her finger back so far it broke and gave her bruises, but everyone always pitied him. Now that he's killed her, people still pity him. They still say: we have to help him.... He's a Filipino.... He just lost control....[95]

Because most Asian Americans are immigrants, most Asian American communities retain, at least in part, the culture of their country of origin. Although treating all Asian American communities as fungible can be dangerous, the diverse Asian American subgroups do share certain cultural commonalities which have important implications for battered Asian American women. In general, modern American society

95. Agtuca, supra note 1, at 46 * * *.

and laws value individualism and grant women significant rights, however many Asian American communities emphasize the family and place women in subordinate roles. This is not to say that Asian American communities are more misogynistic than other American communities; American society, after all, is rooted in European notions of patriarchy and male privilege. Furthermore, "culture" is not static, but fluid and ever-evolving—both for each individual Asian subgroup and for Asian Americans as a whole. However, the cultural beliefs which permeate the many Asian American communities do influence the status and condition of battered Asian American women. Constant evolution and change may someday eliminate any substantive differences in culture, but until that day, the cultural differences which do exist must be recognized and confronted.

* * *

C. Harmful Stereotypes About Asian Americans Collectively and Asian American Women Specifically

Although Asian America is comprised of many diverse communities, Asian American communities are commonly perceived by outsiders as a singular whole. While commonalities among diverse Asian American communities must necessarily be recognized in order to unite Asian Americans politically, the danger of linking together all Asian American communities must also be recognized. In the context of domestic violence against Asian American women, two common stereotypes of Asian Americans illustrate the dangers of assuming a singular Asian American whole. [The author states that these are the model minority myth and the ultra-femininity myth.]

* * *

III. THE FAILURE OF THE ASIAN AMERICAN COMMUNITY TO MOVE BEYOND ITS "MALE-CENTERED" PERSPECTIVE TO ADDRESS VIOLENCE AGAINST ASIAN AMERICAN WOMEN

Battered Asian American women belong to multiple communities. Part I examined the failure of the anti-domestic violence movement to progress beyond its historical white-centeredness to accommodate the needs and concerns of women of color, especially Asian American women. Similarly, the Asian American community must be critiqued for singularly focusing along racial lines to the exclusion of gender issues.

Because race and racism are integral to the functioning of American society, Asian Americans, as a racial minority in this country, have understandably been involved in race-based civil rights struggles from the time Asians first came to this country. Race has defined the context in which the Asian American community has organized politically, an approach which makes sense for Asian American men, who do not face gender subordination and who thus organize around race issues. However, Asian American women have also tended to organize around race issues, because American society focuses on singular axes of oppression.

Women of color are forced to rank their oppressions and in this hierarchy of oppression, race usually comes out ahead of gender. Any criticism of the Asian American community's failure to address women's issues affirmatively must be viewed against this race-gender hierarchy.

* * *

CONCLUSION

Differently situated from battered white women and on unequal footing with Asian American men, battered Asian American women continue to fall through the cracks despite gains in both battered women's rights and Asian American civil rights. Battered Asian American women are disadvantaged because both the battered women's movement and Asian American civil rights struggles are currently defined along singular, linear axes: the former, of gender, and the latter, of race.

Such linear paradigms are limited by essentialist notions of gender and race. Essentialism is the idea that within any particular community, there exists one "essential" experience which purports to represent all members of that community. The white-centeredness of the anti-domestic violence movement focuses on the white woman as the essential battered woman while the male-centeredness of the Asian American civil rights movement establishes the experience of the Asian American man as the essential Asian American experience. Although some categorization is needed for understanding experience, essentialism is ultimately dangerous because it privileges certain voices and silences others, usually those voices which have traditionally been ignored. In the anti-domestic violence movement, white women are privileged at the expense of non-white women; in the Asian American community, men's voices are heard over women's. As a result, Asian American women are silenced in both communities.

These limited paradigms fail to include battered Asian American women, who are neither "just women" nor "just Asian Americans." The dangers of essentialism do not mean that categories should be completely eliminated, but rather that there should be an accommodation of multiple consciousness as opposed to any rigid categorization. To overcome the current essentialist paradigms, both the anti-domestic violence movement and the Asian American civil rights movement must affirmatively recognize a broader, non-linear vision which embraces the intersectionality of multiple, co-existing identities. In adopting an inclusive vision, each movement must recognize that battered Asian American women are uniquely situated from other battered women and from Asian American men.

Embracing an intersectional perspective will allow the anti-domestic violence movement to escape its white-centeredness. By viewing domestic violence as a problem that affects different women differently, domestic violence advocates will be able to remove the blinders of white privilege and to adopt color-conscious programs which address the unique needs and concerns of Asian American women. This would mean not only hiring bilingual and culturally-sensitive staff and volunteers for existing shelters and programs, or conducting research specifically investigating domestic violence against Asian American women. It would also mean involvement in campaigns to eradicate stereotypes of Asian American women as sexually exotic and submissive beings, in recognition that such racist stereotypes condone sexual violence against Asian American women. By assisting in the battle against racial images which help perpetuate domestic violence against Asian American women, anti-domestic violence advocates, who are predominantly white, will aid in eliminating battering against Asian American women.

Similarly, the adoption of an intersectional framework by the Asian American community will enable its civil rights struggles to progress beyond the current male-centered focus. By recognizing that racism cannot be so easily separated from other "-isms," the Asian American community can begin to adopt a gender-conscious civil rights agenda. Asian American civil rights organizations must also recognize that violence against Asian Americans manifests itself in more than purely race-based ways. For example, while some victims, like Vincent Chin, are victims of aggressors who have been motivated purely or primarily by racist beliefs, other Asian American victims of violence are targeted for intersecting reasons: race, gender, sexual orientation, economics, among others. In addition, the Asian American community must move beyond beliefs which subordinate Asian American women, in order to allow the community as a whole to address violence which victimizes Asian American women. This would be the first step toward bringing domestic violence into the Asian American civil rights agenda; such violence will no longer be able to be ignored and treated as a non-civil rights issue. Including violence against women and domestic violence in the Asian American civil rights agenda will provide battered Asian American women access to a great many existing resources, including legal, cultural, and social resources which have historically been reserved for racial civil rights issues such as hate violence.

It is important to push both the battered women's movement and the Asian American community towards an intersectional framework because battered Asian American women face certain unique obstacles which are rooted in both their gender and race. These obstacles must be addressed together, not in discrete and insular packages of race as separate from gender. Only within such an intersectional paradigm can the unique needs and concerns of Asian American women be adequately addressed.

I conclude this Comment with a quotation from two women who are both battered women's advocates and Asian American community activists. Their vision is one which I hope both the anti-domestic violence movement and the Asian American civil rights community will adopt as their motto in addressing domestic violence and other gendered issues affecting Asian American women:

This is a wake-up call to APA activists fighting on the frontlines for the civil rights of Asian Pacific Americans, as well as all peoples. We as a community can never hold our heads high and claim a righteous struggle for civil rights unless we fight hand-in-hand for the rights of our sisters to be free from violence of the body, mind, the spirit.... There will never be a strong and healthy community unless violence in the home ... is eradicated. We can never reach the potential that is our birthright unless we stop denying the impact of domestic violence on our own lives and start dealing with its effects. It is futile to hope and work for a better society when we pass on a legacy of violence and dysfunction.[187]

C. AFRICAN AMERICAN WOMEN

ANGELA MAE KUPENDA, LAW, LIFE, AND LITERATURE: A CRITICAL REFLECTION OF LIFE AND LITERATURE TO ILLUMINATE HOW LAWS OF DOMESTIC VIOLENCE, RACE, AND CLASS BIND BLACK WOMEN, BASED ON ALICE WALKER'S BOOK THE THIRD LIFE OF GRANGE COPELAND

42 How. L. J. 14–21 (1998).

[The author is discussing states in which a spouse must prove fault in order to be granted a divorce, and the different standards applied to black women vs. white women seeking a divorce based on cruelty.]

It is not my intent here to completely ignore the sanctity of marriage. Rather, the intent is to promote the true sanctity of the home by promoting the sanctity of all individuals whether they are married women or men, black women or white women. The true sanctity of the home is upheld when all individuals within the home are respected. Protecting only the structural sanctity of the home, fault divorce laws that value some women—as more able to take "minor blows to the body" and less worthy of freedom—less than other women provide a cultural defense to divorce that reinforces negative stereotypes that some groups are entitled to less justice or peace than others. This stereotyping can be disastrous to non-white women (and even perhaps some poor white women) who do not fit the traditional concept of the "conventionally virtuous spouse." For example, under the law, a black woman who has had to be exceptionally strong to deal with racial and economic realities would not be entitled to the same non-abusive marriage as a white woman who has had a gentle life and who is seen as delicate and soft. This is a preposterous law.

Not only is this problematic for black women, but it is also problematic for any woman who is perceived as having neither the "tradition-

187. Lin & Tan, supra note 13, at 322–323.

al" type of refinement nor traditional cultural sensitivities. Perhaps it is
even problematic for any non-white woman, as will be discussed later.

Domestic abuse alone, even without the support of the law, has
always been especially oppressive for black women. Even if a black
woman seeks help, society and law enforcement workers have found it
difficult to believe that she is really in need of, or deserving of, help like
"other" women.

Unfortunately, she may not even seek help because forces may have
already persuaded her that she is not deserving of such help. One
therapist who treats black women described these forces:

> Black women learn early in their social development to deny the
> sexism to which they are subjected. They are in an unusual predica-
> ment. Often, by the time a black girl reaches adolescence, the
> expectation that relationships with black men will be harsh, oppres-
> sive, and intense has been ingrained in her mind. The black women
> I see have a subconscious attitude that I call 'internalized oppres-
> sion,' an almost tacit acceptance that they as [black] women will be
> mistreated by both society and black men.[78]

Moreover, racial guilt imposed on a woman already stressed from
abuse may be the chain that keeps one linked to even more abuse.
Multiply oppressed, gagged and bound, black women in troubled relationships actually need more assistance from helping agencies and more
protection by the law, not less as is currently the standard.

It would seem then that feminists who strive to eliminate domestic
violence would be cognizant of these problems and would urge for
changes in the legal system for more effective help for all women.
Unfortunately, feminist attempts to eradicate domestic violence, though
possibly well meaning, have generally worked to the disadvantage of
black women. A myth has been that black women are battered more
than white women. To their credit, feminists and even police departments have set out to dispel this myth—to stop the perpetuation of the
stereotype that all black men are violent.[82] White feminists have also
had, however, some questionable motives for seeking to dispel this myth.
They have been afraid that, if people view domestic abuse as only a
minority problem, people will not be interested in solving the problem
and in saving black women from abuse. Consequently, abused white
women would continue to suffer. White feminists fear that society will
"dismiss domestic violence as a minority problem ... not deserving of
aggressive action."[83] Stories by white women that "begin with a statement like, 'I was not supposed to be a battered wife,' " imply that black
and other nonwhite women were supposed to be the battered wife.[84]
Similarly, divorce laws, like those challenged here that allow the delicate
and cultured woman, but not the hardened woman, to be set free from

78. Audrey B. Chapman, Getting Good
Loving: How Black Men and Women Can
Make Love Work 18 (1995).

82. Crenshaw, supra note 57, at 1256.

83. Id. at 1253.

84. Id. at 1258.

abuse, are probably attempts to help the abused white woman who has difficulty proving enough abuse to be set free. When the law helps these "virtuous" white women, black women are once again regarded as not deserving enough to receive the law's generous sweep of protections.

But this is not a new phenomenon, nor is it a phenomenon particular to domestic violence issues. Even when all other factors are held constant, for example, the rapists of black women receive less severe punishment than the rapists of white women.[85] One scholar reports that in a "case involving the rape of a young black girl, one juror argued for acquittal [of the rapist] on the grounds that a girl her age from that kind of neighborhood probably wasn't a virgin anyway."[86] And, society is less outraged and engaged over the rape of black women than it is over the rape of white women. This reveals, "a sexual hierarchy in operation that holds certain female bodies in higher regard than other [female bodies]."[87]

And again this is not a new phenomenon. Tracing back to the early days of slavery and the years following, images of black women were degraded and sexualized as black women were labeled as "bad" women deserving of the bad treatment they were receiving. Black women were falsely depicted as immoral to justify the rape of black women by white men and the whole scale system of forcing the children of black women into an uncompensated and abused workforce for building America. To justify the workloads placed on them in the master's house and in the fields with the men, black women were depicted as unusually strong, masculine, and tough. They were pictured as "able to endure hardship no 'lady' is supposed to be capable of enduring." As further indication that black women were different from the white women who were deserving of better treatment, colonial white America placed black women in the fields in roles that white America saw as "surrogate" male roles.

Sojourner Truth attempted to blast some of these misconceptions in her famous speech, Ain't I a Woman, when she asserted that although she was black, not white; poor, not rich; and independent, not helpless, her claim to equal treatment was as just as that of white men and women. This "strength," that some regard as a virtue of black womanhood, is often used as a sword or as a whip to keep black women in "their" place. For example, the laws questioned in this paper (the movement for fault divorce and the high standard of proving fault for some women) suggest that strong or hardened women should be left in an abusive marriage because they can take it. Understandably, even black women continue to question whether their "strength" is really a plus or virtue. For "[a]lthough black slave[ ] [women] often boasted of their work ability, they longed to be treated with the same regard and consideration they believed was due them as a woman's privilege in a

85. Id. at 1275–76.
86. Id. at 1279.

87. Id. at 1268–69 * * *.

patriarchal society."[95] Even after slavery ended, the myth of the bad black woman continued to justify her exploitation. The differences in the way black and white women were also addressed and regarded by society continuously reinforced the myth. The myth even gained force with the hardworking efforts of black women being acknowledged by society, but only as back-handed compliments. bell hooks stated that "[society] labeled hard-working, self-sacrificing black women who were concerned with creating a loving, supportive environment for their families, Aunt Jemima's, Sapphires, Amazons—all negative images that were based upon existing sexist stereotypes of womanhood."[97]

To be honest, the cases do not specifically state that "black" women will not be set free. So on the surface it appears that, under the cases, a black women who is delicate, educated, and highly cultured will receive the same consideration regarding freedom from abuse as a similarly situated white lady. That scenario, however, is unlikely; consider a frank remark and realistic appraisal of societal views from an honest black woman: "There are two kinds of females in this country—colored women and white ladies. Colored women are maids, cooks, taxi drivers, crossing guards, school teachers, welfare recipients, bar maids, and the only time they become ladies is when they are cleaning ladies."[98]

As a group, black women are portrayed, especially in the media, as "fallen" and undeserving women. Unfortunately society believes this portrayal or wants to believe it to justify the continued ranking of black women at the bottom of the heap and the continued labeling of black women as less deserving, which perhaps makes white women more deserving.

For black women in abusive relationships, the problem is further magnified. The "law" will leave her in the abusive marriage, but if she stays (for the sanctity of the home) and later injures her own abusive spouse, the legal system will again likely see her as "hardened" and not as a victim. If she urges that her "crime" is a result of the abuse and the battered woman syndrome, her defense will fail because she is not seen as a "normal—weak, passive and proper" woman. Race plays a role in these conceptions, or rather misconceptions or limited conceptions, of true and deserving womanhood. As we culturally define what a normal woman is, "African–American women are viewed as angry, masculine, domineering, strong and sexually permissive—characteristics which do not denote 'victim'" or normal woman.[102] If a real or true deserving woman is seen as pious, pure, gentle, submissive, domestic, and middle class, "then a white woman is automatically more like the 'good' fairy tale princess stereotype than a black woman who as the 'other' may be

---

95. hooks, supra note 2, at 48; see generally Audrey Edwards, Black and White Women: What Still Divides Us?, Essence, Mar. 1998, at 77, 77 * * *.

97. hooks, supra note 2, at 70.

98. Lerner, supra note 96, at 217 (quoting Louise D. Stone, What It's Like to be a Colored Woman, Wash. Post, Nov. 13, 1966).

102. Moore, supra note 89, at 302–03.

seen as the 'bad' witch.''[103] Therefore, labeling black women as strong has provided a disservice. For that label, without deeper observation, "ignore[s] the reality that to be strong in the face of oppression is not the same as overcoming oppression, that endurance is not to be confused with transformation.''[104]

To be honest, the law only prevents the "divorce" of "hardened" women but does not stop them from leaving the marital home for safety. However, if cultured white women are legally freed based on "minor" violence, black women ought to be given the same freedom whether they are culturally similar or differently cultured or not cultured at all.

This continued negative stereotyping and devaluing of women who do not fit the image of the virtuous female deserving of protection brutalizes "other" women by leaving them legally tied to abusive situations and by possibly leading them to internalize this brutalization or brutalize others. The best example of this internal and external brutalization is seen in the honest and real world of literature. In Toni Morrison's book, The Bluest Eye, one of the little black girl characters makes this confession:

> I Destroyed white baby dolls. but the dismembering of dolls was not the true horror. the truly horrifying thing was the transference of the same impulses to little white girls.... To discover what eluded me: the secret of the magic they weaved on others. What made people look at them and say, "Awwwww," but not for me?[108]

An evasive answer to the character's piercing question is that the same thing that will make judges set them free but not you. In The Bluest Eye, Pecola, another little black girl, wishes for "blue eyes" because she thinks that then she will be like the little white girls and will have a happier life. Under the present laws and the present movement of the law, it is a sad commentary if one's accidental inheritance of blue eyes could mean the difference between suffering and freedom.

But these "delicate, virtuous women" whom the law seeks to save from even "minor" abuse are not the enemy. The enemies are those who will use unenlightened laws and legal and societal mores to continue to perpetuate domination and supremacy that make "refined" women deserving, but not women like Mem and girls like Pecola. Consider the thoughts of another character from The Bluest Eye as she responds to an ugly verbal attack from a little white girl named Maureen:

> We were sinking under the wisdom, accuracy, and relevance of Maureen's last words. If she was cute ... then we were not. And what did that mean? We were lesser. nicer, brighter, but lesser....
> And all the time we knew that Maureen Peal was not the enemy and

103. Allard, supra note 101, at 193–94; see also Moore, supra note 89, at 324

104. hooks, supra note 2, at 6.

108. Toni Morrison, The Bluest Eye 22 (1970).

not worthy of such intense hatred. The thing to fear was the Thing that made her beautiful, and not us.[110]

These unenlightened laws and movements, therefore, are potentially a real death sentence for black women. Arguably a black woman can still "leave" the violent home, she just may be unable to obtain a divorce. This point of view is especially troublesome, for to leave but still be legally bound, along with all the other pressures to return to the home and man, could force her back into a situation that is as real as the fate of Mem. Black women already have a tremendous amount of pressure imposed both internally and externally to return to the relationship. Like white women, black women are susceptible to the emphasis placed on maintaining the structure and "sanctity" of the family unit. In addition, black women are well aware of the prison of racism and are protective of the images of their men. They are hesitant to name the violence and call attention to problems in their relationships evolving from sexism. Protective of their homes, which are a necessary haven from societal racism, black women may be reluctant to call the police for help—the same police who may be hostile towards them, their families, and communities. The black woman, therefore, sees explanations for her man's behavior based on the indignities he suffers from greater society. It is difficult, therefore, for her to name the violence because she is afraid she will be seen as betraying her already oppressed race.

The intent, though, is not to further point fingers at black men. Black malehood is not the enemy. The enemy is the system of supremacy and domination that establishes the pecking order (of whiteness then nonwhiteness, maleness then femaleness) that keeps us trying to excel by keeping others under foot. Although some white women fare better than black women under the law, they are not the enemy either. Although some black men (just like white men) abuse, they are not the enemy. The enemy is deeper and is cored in supremacy, patriarchy, and their manifestations—the need for structural appearance over true sanctity.

* * *

ZANITA E. FENTON, DOMESTIC VIOLENCE IN BLACK AND WHITE: RACIALIZED GENDER STEREOTYPES IN GENDER VIOLENCE

8 Colum. J. Gender & L. 1–4, 48–55 (1998).

I. Introduction

The media attention given to the criminal[1] and civil[2] trials of Orenthal James Simpson has focused the attention of mainstream soci-

---

110. Id. at 74. Cf. id. at 124–25 * * *.

1. People v. Simpson, No. BA097211, 1995 WL 704381 (Cal. Super. Ct. Oct. 3, 1995) (lasting fifteen months between June 1994 and October 1995).

2. Rufo v. Simpson, No. SC03197; Goldman v. Simpson, No. SC036340; Brown v. Simpson, No. SCO3687; 1997 WL 114574 (Cal. Super. Ct. Mar. 10, 1997).

ety on the issues surrounding domestic violence. Unfortunately, instead of prompting greater awareness of the magnitude of the issues, the media and the actors in the legal proceedings manipulated stereotypes and obscured the issues of domestic violence.

Through the lens of the media focus on the O.J. trials, the issue of domestic violence has implicitly become "black and white." Literally, beliefs about justice in these cases were portrayed by media polls as divided by race. For example, a Los Angeles Times poll conducted near the end of the civil trial indicated that "71% of whites said they thought Simpson committed the murders, while 70% of blacks said they thought he was innocent."[5] There were no polls broken down by gender. In fact, we don't know if the polls that were done by race included proportional numbers of men and women of either race. Would it have been more or less significant if men and women (regardless of race) held the same views about the issues of domestic violence? There were also no polls broken down by income or social status. Would it have mattered if people's belief in Simpson's innocence or guilt correlated to their relative income? Most significantly, these polls did not reveal the basis for the responses of the pollees. Do we know if their perceptions of justice were based on race, or on gender, or on class, or on the available evidence, or on all of the above?

The criminal trial was portrayed as a defeat for battered women and simultaneously as a victory for the African American community and the civil trial as a vindication of the rights of battered women and retributive of mainstream (read white) justice. Implicit in this characterization is the understanding that the battered women imagined were white. This conceptualization existed, most obviously, because Nicole Brown Simpson was white and the defendant was black. Notwithstanding the obvious, the "racial divide" reflected a misuse of the disbelieving opinions of black women, particularly those on the jury of the criminal trial, to indicate that the issues of the trial had import only as determined by race. Also important in the representations of domestic violence was that it was only a "woman's issue." Thus, with the foregoing characterizations, the battle-lines concerning domestic abuse were not drawn in terms of gender, but primarily in terms of race.

* * *

B. *Applying Context*

African American women are affected by mainstream culture and popular media just like everybody else. Indeed, most Americans have little or no understanding of domestic violence issues. The most common reaction to the plight of a women affected by battered women's syndrome is disbelief and the question, "Why didn't she just leave?" That African American women are a part of greater society and feed into its biases and ignorances is at least one partial explanation for some

---

5. Abigail Goldman and Mary Curtius, Simpson Civil Case: For Many It's as Sim- ple as Black and White Reaction, L.A. Times, Feb. 5, 1997, at A14.

reactions. In fact, one could easily suggest that the failure of the justice system is not so much in this one, rather overly publicized, case where the defendant was acquitted and the issues of domestic violence obscured, but in the multitude of cases year after year where violence in the domestic context is overlooked or under-penalized, marginalizing the plight of victims of domestic abuse. American society is in a collective state of denial concerning the issues of domestic violence and has been for many years.

Consistent with the understanding that African American women are part of a societal whole, many African American women have had exposure to, or experience with, domestic violence. Thus, some reactions may be of understanding, consistent with empathy based on a similar experience to Nicole's. Despite the lack of media attention given to these women, I am sure there were many African American women who were also watching the O.J. trials for its potential impact on issues of domestic violence in this country as they may have had to deal with its aftermath. In fact, there is a lack of media attention to domestic violence issues in general and to those specifically in minority and poor communities. One black woman pointed out, "There has been domestic violence going on in South–Central Los Angeles for years.... How come when it happens in Brentwood it's such a big issue?"[196] Why aren't we interested in the violence that occurs among the poor of same race? Are we only intrigued by the implication of power created stereotypes of wealth and interracial relationships?

Because of the interaction of gender, race, and class, creating a personal dynamic quite different from that of Nicole, some African American women may have been inclined to disbelief. In addition to the classic victim's cycle of domestic abuse, which is almost a paralyzing force preventing a woman from leaving her abuser, many African American women also stay in abusive relationships to "present a unified front." That is, because the national media and politicians have historically assaulted the black family as degenerating in a "tangle of pathology," many African American women feel the need to stay in their relationships, keep their families together, and be unified against outside oppressions and stereotypic representations. They feel that to break up their families would just add to the problems of both their own families and the problems of the black community.

African Americans are also disproportionately represented among the poor. Breaking up the family means breaking up the potential resources. Because Nicole would not have had to deal with the same kinds of oppression in her life (i.e., she experienced white privilege and an affluent lifestyle), it may have been just as difficult for an African American woman experiencing domestic abuse to understand why Nicole didn't stay away from her abuser.

196. Charrisse Jones, Nicole Simpson, In Death, Lifting Domestic Violence to the Forefront as National Issue, N.Y. Times, Oct. 13, 1995, at A28.

Just as Nicole's personal dynamic was different from those of many black women subjected to domestic abuse, O.J. also was not subject to the same personal dynamic and oppressions to which most African American men are subjected. O.J.'s affluence allowed him to escape much of the stress associated with racism in society, eliminating one of the pressures that contributes to the cycle of violence in communities of color. In fact, because of his celebrity status, O.J. was not viewed as "black" by mainstream Americans. Taking this in tandem with the historic reverence for white womanhood (or, for the stereotypes there associated), many African American women may understand that O.J.'s relationship with Nicole was part of the indicia of his success. So, even if African American women believed that Nicole would not necessarily have stayed away from her abuser, they may not have believed that O.J. would abuse his "prize."

Interaction of the justice system, especially the police, with communities of color is a major factor contributing to a dynamic that cannot be ignored in understanding the broad picture of domestic violence as it pertains to women of color. There is a general distrust of the justice system by people of color that is well founded in history. This includes both legal and extra-legal persecution of the hyper-sexualized black male for perceived indiscretions with chaste white women, an ideology which permitted an entire era of extrajudicial lynching. Violence perpetrated on people of color by the police or other persons of authority is not a new or waning phenomenon. We have only scratched the surface when we consider the high profile cases of police brutality against people of color. Thus, there is the very real possibility of inviting violence against men accused, extending and exacerbating the violence. There is also reticence in reinforcing gender specific racial stereotypes of the inherently violent black male. Inviting police involvement would provide one more reason for the perpetuation of such stereotypes, and would in turn perpetuate racism and continue the conceptual cycle of societal violence.

Second, women of color often have a lack of confidence in the system's ability to serve their needs. There is both a real and perceived lack of interest by the police in the complaints of black women. Generally, there is a pattern of not treating very seriously the complaints of domestic related violence by any women, as it is usually dismissed as a private affair. For black women the problem is exacerbated by the racialized gender stereotypes of them: the uncontrollable, promiscuous black woman who is capable of sustaining greater physical abuse than her white counterpart, and who is herself capable of violence.

This is also compounded by a belief that shelters and institutions established to help battered women are only for the needs of white women. Understandings, real and perceived, that resources are primarily available for white women and the necessity that they themselves take care of their domestic problems without such resources, would make it difficult to believe that Nicole could not have dealt with her own situation with greater ease.

In addition there is no confidence in a public outcry for wrongs against women of color as there would be for wrongs against a white woman by a black man. The visceral nature of mainstream white responses to the acquittal of the O.J. criminal trial reaffirms this conceptualization. It is also interesting to note that the same responses did not exist for the acquittals of William Kennedy Smith for the rape of a white woman or of the affluent Claus Von Bulow for the murder of his white wife. The juxtaposition of these responses to cases should at least give us pause.

Even more disturbing are the media choices in which cases are "news," formulating our collective perception of reality for us. In 1990, during the same week as the Central Park rape of a white woman jogger, the rape of a woman of color, who was also sodomized and thrown from the top floor of a four story building, was relegated to the back pages.

* * *

LINDA AMMONS, MULES, MADONNAS, BABIES, BATHWATER, RACIAL IMAGERY AND STEREOTYPES: THE AFRICAN–AMERICAN WOMAN AND THE BATTERED WOMAN SYNDROME

1995 Wis. L. Rev. 1017–1030 (1995).

A. The Plight of Battered Black Women

Women in America are violated by their current or former partners at such an alarming rate that domestic violence is considered epidemic. Annually, women, as compared to men, experience over ten times as many incidents of violence by an intimate. According to the National Institute of Health, in the mid–1980s homicide was the leading cause of death among African–Americans. Some studies indicate that black women rank second in the frequency of arrests for murder. The typical victim of a black female who kills is a black male with whom she had a relationship.

Until recently, the public, criminal justice agencies, and the courts have ignored the plight of the battered woman. Battered women are not believed either because society has historically been in denial about the terrorism that occurs in the home, or because abused women who do not leave their partners are thought to be lying about the seriousness of the abuse they suffered. Black women face similar hurdles, but additionally they must overcome the presumption that their race predisposes them to engage in and enjoy violence. "[P]olice trainees are frequently told that physical violence is an acceptable part of life among ghetto residents." In other words, blacks are "normal primitives," or violence-prone. African–American women who are battered face unique challenges in getting relief and support. For example, when black women are treated for domestic violence related injuries in inner-city hospitals, protocols for wife beating are "rarely introduced or followed." Trusting health-care providers with their stories of abuse is difficult because black women have often felt that systems do not have their best interests at heart. However, when the provider is sensitive to their needs they will reveal their stories of abuse. Julie Blackman, a psychologist, illustrated how the mental health system deals with black and white women in abusive relationships by contrasting the Hedda Nussbaum–Joel Steinberg case with that of Frances and Herman McMillian.[78] Nussbaum was the battered lover of Steinberg. Lisa, Steinberg's daughter, was also abused. When Lisa was killed in a battering episode, Nussbaum turned state's evidence against her lover. Steinberg was convicted of manslaughter in the first degree, and sentenced to a maximum term of eight and one-third to twenty-five years. Nussbaum was never charged and was given the psychiatric and social services support she needed.

On the other hand, Frances McMillian, a poor black woman who was arrested for endangering the welfare of her children, was denied treatment by the same facilities. McMillian and her nine children lived in a two-room apartment in the Bronx with an abusive husband and father, Herman McMillian. The family was discovered because of a fire. When Blackman attempted to get Mrs. McMillian admitted to the treatment facilities that had treated Nussbaum, they would not accept her. Blackman says:

> I tried repeatedly to reach the psychiatrist who had been most directly involved in Hedda's treatment. Hedda's lawyer encouraged him to take Hrances and reminded him that he ought not exclude Frances just because she was black. I never did speak to Hedda's psychiatrist about Frances, but his treatment facility decided to reject her anyway.[79]

The district attorney took nine misdemeanor counts to a grand jury even though he was "sympathetic to her condition." McMillian was indicted.

Battered African–American women are also particularly vulnerable because of the lack or the underutilization of resources. For example, African–American women hesitate to seek help from shelters because they believe that shelters are for white women. Because the shelters are associated with the women's movement, and many black women are estranged from women's politics, they may feel that only white women's interests are served in the shelters. African–American women are not totally mistaken in this assumption. A study of the shelter movement in America led a researcher to conclude that black women are ignored in the policymaking, planning and implementation of shelter services. The lack of community outreach in black neighborhoods by the shelters also contributes to the perception that the safe havens are not for women of

78. See Julie Blackman, Emerging Images of Severely Battered Women and the Criminal Justice System, 8 Behav. Sci. & L. 121 (1990).

79. Id. at 125 n.1.

color. Finally, black women have found the shelter environment inhospitable to their cultural differences.

When leaving shelters, black women are more likely to need health care, material goods and help with their children. A National Institute of Health funded study of sixty battered African–American women over an eight month period found that black women remained in shelters for a significantly longer time than their white counterparts before they could get the necessary resources to start over. Racism also affected the ability of some black women to leave. For example, African–American women would be quoted an apartment rental price over the phone, only to have that price raised when the landlord met the women. White social service personnel would sometimes patronize, ignore or exhibit hostility toward black women.

African–American women depend on informal networks and seek support through prayer, personal spirituality, and the clergy. The African–American church is a traditional source of strength. Pastors (typically male), are a central authority figure in many black communities. However, misinformed ministers may overemphasize the value placed on suffering as a test from God. Further, some clergy have misconstrued biblical principles of love, forgiveness and submission to reinforce sexism and subordination which can be used to justify abuse. Black female parishioners are often told from the pulpit to protect the black male because he is an endangered species.

The inconsistency of police intervention and the lack of other community resources, including hospitals, contribute to the acuteness of violence in African–American neighborhoods. Black women may have to resort to more extreme violence to resolve a battering situation because the police are not interested. African–American women have no historical basis for believing that the world is just and fair and therefore traditional institutions are viewed with great skepticism. Professionals who work with black, battered women provide a unique perspective on how race affects the issue.[94] Kenyari Bellfield, a shelter worker, describes the predicament of battered African–American women:

> [A]long with the actual experience of psychological and physical abuse, women of color suffer from the complex phenomenon of racism. The translation of racial oppression to women of color who are battered stems from the basic assumption that people of color are inherently more violent. For a woman of color who is battered, an overwhelming sense of hopelessness and low self-esteem are the result. The effects of racism and sexism seem too great to tackle in the face of having been victimized by a loved one. The very system which has historically served to subjugate and oppress her is the

94. See Congressional Hearing on Domestic Violence Prevention and Treatment Act: Hearings Before the Subcomm. on Se-   lect Education of the House Comm. on Education and Labor, 95th Cong., 2d Sess. (1978) (statement of Kenyari Bellfield).

only system which can save her from the immediate abusive situation.[95]

Cooperating with authorities in prosecuting her abuser could result in community abandonment or scorn because of the perception that black men are selectively penalized. Further, black battered women may connect the physical abuse with racism. Some feel that they become the object of their partner's rage triggered by the persistent maltreatment of black males by the greater society, and therefore the abuser is less culpable. Novelist Alice Walker describes the motivation and rationalization of an abusive male character in her work, The Third Life of Grange Copeland:[98]

> His crushed pride, his battered ego, made him drive Mem away from school teaching.... It was his rage at himself, and his life and his world that made him beat her for an imaginary attraction she aroused in other men, crackers, although she was not a party to any of it. His rage and his anger and his frustration ruled. His rage could and did blame everything, everything on her.[99]

The loyalty trap affects the ability of black women to seek protection and effective counseling. For example, African–American women do not feel comfortable discussing their problems in integrated settings. The fear is that disclosure in some way may hurt the community. Therefore the prohibition against airing dirty laundry becomes more important than healing. Emma Jordan Coleman describes the dilemma abused black women face as a "Hobbesian choice between claiming individual protection as a member of her gender and race or contributing to the collective stigma upon her race if she decides to report the ... misdeeds of a black man to white authority figures."[102]

The justice system has not rushed to protect black women who have been beaten. Analogies to rape and other gender discriminatory practices illustrate how black female victimization has been and remains unimportant. White men have had carte blanche access to all women. Heinous crimes have been committed in the name of protecting white womanhood. Interracial sexual or physical assault (e.g., minority male/white female) still produces outrage that is not comparable to any other kind of inter-or intra-racial adult abuse. For example, the same week that the highly-publicized rape of the affluent, white Central Park jogger by several Hispanic and black males took place, twenty-eight other first-degree rapes or attempted rapes took place in New York City. Donald Trump purchased full-page ads in the New York Times, The Daily News, The New York Post, and New York Newsday to denounce the men who had committed the violent acts. Trump spent $85,000 for the advertisements. In response to Trump, black clergy published their own ad,

---

95. Id. at 520–21.

98. Alice Walker, The Third Life of Grange Copeland (1970).

99. Id. at 55.

102. Emma Jordan Coleman, The Power of False Racial Memory and the Metaphor of Lynching, in Race, Gender and Power in America: The Legacy of the Hill–Thomas Hearings 37, 40 (Anita Faye Hill & Emma Coleman Jordan eds., 1995)

stating that Trump was trying to divide the city into two camps with a thinly veiled polemic. Another article reported that two weeks after the Central Park incident, a thirty-eight year old black woman was forced off a Brooklyn street at knife-point by two men, taken to a rooftop, raped, beaten, and thrown fifty feet to the ground. The woman sustained abdominal injuries, two broken ankles, and a fractured right leg. This attack did not receive the national notice of the Central Park jogger case and there was no ad from Donald Trump. Three men went to prison for the crime.

Assumptions about sexual stratification explain why reactions to sexual assault differ.[114] Criminologist Anthony Walsh provides the following analysis:

1. Women are viewed as the valued and scarce property of the men of their own race.

2. White women, by virtue of membership in the dominant race, are more valuable than black women.

3. The sexual assault of a white by a black threatens both the white man's "property rights" and his dominant social position. This dual threat accounts for the strength of the taboo attached to inter-racial sexual assault.

4. A sexual assault by a male of any race upon members of the less valued black race is perceived as nonthreatening to the status quo, and therefore less serious.

5. White men predominate as agents of social control. Therefore they have the power to sanction differently according to the perceived threat to their favored social position.[115]

In other words, black women's bodies are not as valuable as their white female counterparts. The history of the devaluation of black women in general provides insight into understanding the circumstances of the battered African–American female. The following discussion on slavery's legacy provides that context.

* * *

D. LATINAS

JENNY RIVERA, DOMESTIC VIOLENCE AGAINST LATINAS BY LATINO MALES: AN ANALYSIS OF RACE, NATIONAL ORIGIN, AND GENDER DIFFERENTIALS

14 B. C. Third World L. J. 231–257 (1994).

After about two months he started … hitting me again. This time I was going to do something, so I told Yolanda, my best friend. The

---

114. See Anthony Walsh, The Sexual Stratification Hypothesis and Sexual Assault in Light of the Changing Conceptions of Race, 25 Criminology 153 (1987).

115. Id. at 155.

said, and i'll never forget it, "so what, you think my boyfriend doesn't hit me? That's how men are." It was like I was wrong or weak because I wanted to do something about it. Last time he got mad he threatened me with a knife. That really scared me.[1]

Te voy a dar una ojera
Y como llegaste a mi
Alejate, bandolera
Si te tiro por la ventana
Tu subes por la escalera.[2]

I. INTRODUCTION

In 1991, the United States Surgeon General announced that domestic violence was the single greatest cause of injury to young women. Today, violence against women by their current or former male partners accounts for thirty percent of all homicides of women in the United States. In fact, ten women die every day as a result of "domestic violence," and studies indicate that fifty percent of all women in the United States will suffer some form of family violence in their lifetimes.

Violence against women is so prevalent and widespread that in 1992 the American Medical Association (AMA) released guidelines suggesting that doctors screen women for signs of domestic violence.[7] The guidelines define domestic violence as a pattern of coercion that "could include repeated battering and injury, psychological abuse, sexual assault, progressive social isolation, deprivation and intimidation."[8] These guidelines further recognize that the violence "cuts across all racial, ethnic, religious, educational and socio-economic lines."[9]

Although the general issue of domestic violence has received tremendous attention, the specific issue of violence inflicted upon Latinas by their spouses and male partners has not been comprehensively examined and discussed within the mainstream battered women's movement or in literature on domestic violence. This specific issue deserves consideration because differences of gender, race, and national origin shape Latinas' experiences with domestic violence.

This Article represents an effort to shed light on the violence against Latinas within the Latino community. It examines the various factors unique to the political, social, and economic status of Latinas, and includes a critique of the most significant efforts currently within the

1. Myrna M. Zambrano, Mejor Sola Que Mal Acompanada 140 (1985).

2. Hector Lavoe, Bandolera, on Comedia (Fania Records 1976). This verse is an excerpt from a popular song by one of the best-known Latino male recording artists. The quote in the text says:

I Am going to hit you

I Am going to give you a black eye

And the same way you came to me

Go away, thief

If I throw you out the window

You climb up the stairs.

Id.

7. Doctors Are Advised to Screen Women for Abuse, N.Y. TIMES, June 17, 1992, at A26 [hereinafter Doctors Are Advised].

8. Id.

9. Id.

legal and social service sectors to assist battered women. In addition, this Article explores the impact of culture and community, and the role of language, as these serve as points of departure for understanding the experiences of Latinas.

* * *

II. BACKGROUND

A. *Latinas' Experiences and Expressions of Male Violence*

Racial and cultural differences are critical considerations in analyzing and responding to the crisis of domestic violence. These differences are not merely cosmetic or superficial, nor are they simply grounds to support demands for assistance. Differences based on race and culture are both internal and external, and represent primary factors affecting the experiences of violence by women of color.

Latinas are best situated to describe the nature of the violence against them by their male partners. The following excerpt, in a Latina's own words, reflects some of these feelings of anger, fear and isolation.

> I have never called the police here because [he] told me that they will deport us if I do. I've thought about learning some English, but between work and the kids there is hardly any time. So I've never really asked anybody for help. Anyway sometimes he goes months without hurting me and I try to forget about it and just work.

Studies and statistics have established that Latinas are differently situated from white and black women. Indeed, many factors converge to place boundaries on battered Latinas. They experience vulnerability and helplessness because of a dearth of bilingual and bicultural services from social service providers and shelters. In addition, Latinas commonly found in the United States may experience cultural isolation. The impact of these differences on Latinas' lives has led one researcher to conclude that Latinas need support services—targeted to their specific needs—to a greater extent than other battered women. Understanding the dynamic interplay of race and ethnicity in Latinas' lives first requires an analysis that focuses on the intersection of Latina experiences and needs.

B. *Selected Demographic and Statistical Data*

Without an understanding of the economic, social, and political factors that impact Latinas' lives, an analysis of domestic violence against Latinas would be incomplete. This section includes data on the Latino community, Latino males, Latinas, and other women. The information regarding Latinas and other women provides a statistical basis for comparing Latinas' status within the Latino community with those outside. The data suggest that Latinas' comparatively poor economic and political position places them at a distinct disadvantage, thus causing Latinas to experience and respond to domestic violence differently than other women.

1. Latino Community: During the 1980s, the Latino population increased at approximately five times the rate of the total United States population and continues to be the fastest growing ethnic group in the nation. Twenty-nine percent of Latino families had at least five members, whereas only 13% of non-Latino families were this size. The Latino population is younger than the non-Latino population, with a median age of 26.2 years, as compared to 33.8 years for non-Latinos.

For the most part, however, this population increase has not resulted in commensurate gains in economic status. Indeed, Latinos continue to be one of the poorest populations in the United States. In 1990, 25% of Latino families fell below the poverty line, as compared to 9.5% of non-Latino families. Moreover, although they represented only 11% of the total population of children, Latino children represented 21% of the children living in poverty. As of 1990, one in every six persons living in poverty was Latino.

Employment statistics indicate that Latinos have the highest rates of both unemployment and labor force participation. The unemployment rate is 10%, as compared to 6.9% for the non-Latino population. The labor force participation rate, however, is 78% for Latinos, as compared to 74% for non-Latinos.

Educational attainment data, as an indication of employability, socioeconomic mobility, and potential for financial stability and growth, demonstrate the limitations on the economic and political growth of Latinos. In 1991, only 51% of Latinos had completed at least four years of high school, and a mere 10% had completed at least four years of college. Even more disturbing was the national 31.3% high school dropout rate for Latinos.

Three final factors often limit Latinos' economic and political strength. First, because a large number of Latinos are neither citizens nor legal permanent residents, their economic existence is often based on "underground" employment sources and markets. They remain unable to fully utilize critical services such as social and medical assistance programs. Second, many Latinos are not native English speakers and have limited English language comprehension. Although fluent in Spanish, their lack of English language skills places them at a competitive disadvantage in the employment market and acts as a barrier to obtaining an equal education. Third, Latino families are more likely than non-Latino families to be headed by a single woman. Although being raised by a single mother may not impact negatively on personal development or career attainment, to the extent that these rates correlate positively with poverty rates, they are important indicators of actual and potential socioeconomic status.

2. Race and Gender Differentials Affecting Latinas' Status: Data specific to Latinas suggests differences based on race between Latinas and other women, as well as differences based on gender between Latinas and Latino men. The most glaring differentials are reflected in the data on labor force participation and occupation distribution.

Labor force participation rates for Latinas are less than those for non-Latinas: 51% and 57%, respectively. Most women hold jobs in the technical, sales, and administrative support occupations, and only 16% of Latinas hold managerial and professional specialty positions, compared to 28% of non-Latinas. Latinos' overrepresentation in the lowest paying, nonmanagerial, and nonprofessional jobs further compounds their tenuous employment status. For example, 26% of Latinas worked in service occupations, as compared to 17% of non-Latinas; and more Latinas work as operators, fabricators, and laborers than non-Latinas. Such jobs translate into a significant income differential based partially on race: the median annual income for Latinas was $10,100 compared to $12,400 for other women.

Gender also influences these income differentials. In 1991, half of all Latinas earned less than $10,000, whereas only one third of all Latino men earned less than this amount. Furthermore, whereas 23% of Latino men earned at least $25,000 in 1991, only 12% of Latinas reported such earnings.

Latinas' educational attainment rates mirror those of the general Latino community, but are noticeably poorer compared to other females. Data from 1988 reveal that one third of thirteen-year-old Latinas are at least one year behind their classmates in learning, and this rate increases at the high school level. Due to high rates of teenage pregnancy among adolescent Latinas, they are also less likely than other females to complete their high school education or to subsequently pursue completion of an education or job training program. In addition, recent studies suggest that Latinas' experiences in school could negatively impact their educational attainment and ability to reap the benefits of a quality education.

3. *Summary of the Data:* The data reveal that the Latino community is in a precarious economic position. Moreover, statistics specific to Latinas indicate that, as a class, they are particularly susceptible to external economic fluctuations and occupy a marginal financial existence within the market economy structure. Latinas have lower earning potential and power compared to all men, regardless of race or national origin. Latinas are in an acutely weak position, because of their low rates of educational attainment and their high rates of sole stewardship of families. Latinas are not merely unemployed and underemployed, but also unemployable at higher rates.

Latinas' limited socioeconomic mobility can be traced both to the overall economic depression within the Latino community and to individual Latinas' scarce economic resources. Latinas are the lowest paid population, and are concentrated in jobs least likely to provide opportunities for mobility or economic improvement and stability.

This economic gap is not a unilateral problem of patriarchal market structures; Latinas also have a lower earning status among women. Thus, the interplay and intersection of race and gender issues acts dynamically on Latinas, greatly influencing their experiences and forging their inferior economic, political, and social status.

C. Stereotypes Based on Race and National Origin: "El Macho" and the Sexy Latina

Historically, Latinos have been stereotyped as violent and alien. This misrepresentation of the "Latino character" has developed during the past century, and non-Latino society today continues to express and exploit inaccurate images of Latinos and Latino family life.

Popular myth has become accepted as truth; Latino males are believed to be irrational and reactive. The standard description of Latino males as hot-blooded, passionate, and prone to emotional outbursts is legendary. "Macho" is the accepted—and expected—single-word description synonymous with Latino men and male culture. Consequently, it is natural to expand and apply this construct to the entire Latino community, and thereby justify the assumptions that Latinos are violent.

The outer boundaries of stereotypes and expectations of Latinas are emphasized by juxtaposing the image of the Latina against this stereotype or "profile" of the Latino male. Latinas are presented as both innocent virgins and sexy vixens. The Latina is regarded as accepting of the patriarchal structure within her community. Accustomed to a male-centered community, the Latina is constructed as docile and domestic. In order to satisfy her hot-blooded, passionate partner, however, the Latina must also be sensual and sexually responsive. One commentator succinctly summarized these caricatures as they developed through film: "[They] established and repeated other stereotypes, including the violent-tempered but ultimately ineffective Puerto Rican man; the mental inferior; the innocent, but sensual Puerto Rican beauty; and the 'loose', 'hot-blooded mama.' "[54]

These images are not relegated solely to celluloid characterizations. Portrayals of Latino males as uncontrollably destructive persist, and are promoted broadly as examples of "real" Latinos. What was at one time illusory is made to appear genuine through narrow presentations of violent, often marginal sectors of a community—for example, gang cultures.

Within the Latino community, Latinas' identities are defined on the basis of their roles as mothers and wives. By encouraging definitions of Latinas as interconnected with and dependent upon status within a family unit structure, the Latino patriarchy denies Latinas individuality on the basis of gender. For Latinas, cultural norms and myths of national origin intersect with these patriarchal notions of a woman's role and identity. The result is an internal community-defined role, modified by external male-centered paradigms.

This intersection of gender, national origin, and race denies Latinas a self-definitional, experiential-based, feminist portrait. Those within the

---

54. Perez, supra note 47, at 13.

Latino community expect Latinas to be traditional, and to exist solely within the Latino family structure. A Latina must serve as a daughter, a wife, and a parent, and must prioritize the needs of family members above her own. She is the foundation of the family unit. She is treasured as a self-sacrificing woman who will always look to the needs of others before her own. The influence of Catholicism throughout Latin America solidifies this image within the community, where Latinas are expected to follow dogma and to be religious, conservative, and traditional in their beliefs.

The proliferation of stereotypes, which are integral to institutionalized racism, obstructs the progress and mobility of Latinas. Assumptions about Latinas' intellectual abilities and competence are formed on the basis of stereotypes, and justified by pointing to poor educational attainment statistics. Unless these myths and misconceptions are revealed and dispelled, the reality of Latinas as targets of Latino violence will remain unexplored, and Latinas' critical problems will remain unsolved.

III. STRATEGIES IN RESPONSE TO VIOLENCE AGAINST WOMEN

As American society struggles to address violence against women, feminist discourse and methodology collides with traditional patriarchal approaches to concerns termed "women's issues." Advocates who demand practical and successful programs for battered women are often presented, instead, with pilot programs and temporary services that cannot ensure a woman's safety or provide her with a permanent escape from violence.

History repeats itself, and as is true of other struggles for equality by women, many of the strategies and responses to domestic violence evidence a lack of understanding of the needs of Latinas and other women of color. When Latinas are treated differently by law enforcement officials or denied access to domestic violence shelters because of language and cultural differences, or when Latinas do not even take the first step of seeking assistance because there is no place to turn, the domestic violence movement fails.

This section explores some of the more significant responses to domestic violence and explains how these responses often fail to provide Latinas with the necessary means and services to escape domestic violence and gain control of their lives.

A. Legal Initiatives in Response to Violence Against Women

1. Legislation: Several states have passed legislation that criminalizes spousal abuse and marital rape. The extent of the protection afforded to women under these statutes is varied and diverse. As of 1992, provisions requiring mandatory arrest for a domestic violence incident existed in fifteen states, and nineteen states required arrest for violation of an order of protection.

The effectiveness of state and local legislation must be evaluated by considering the numerous obstacles that Latinas must surmount in order to exercise their rights to security and protection. First, state law enforcement officers and judicial personnel continue to reflect the Anglo male society. Latinos and bilingual personnel are rarely found within the legal system, and women continue to represent only a small percentage of the police force.

Second, the nature of the protection or sanctions set forth in state laws notwithstanding, domestic violence legislation remains susceptible to poor enforcement by police and judicial personnel. Indeed, one study in Milwaukee revealed that 95% of domestic violence cases were not prosecuted. Thus, even in states with a legal basis for prosecuting batterers, it remains incumbent upon women's advocates to monitor the utilization and enforcement of these hard-won legal rights.

2. *Law Enforcement:* Law enforcement officials' failure to respond appropriately to violence against women has received harsh criticism as it negatively impacts on women and on efforts geared toward ending domestic violence. Studies have documented the refusal by the police to respond to complaints of domestic violence, or to treat such complaints seriously. The police are notorious for their casual attitude toward women who file charges of violence against their male partners. This constitutes an institutional barrier to women seeking assistance, and is another form of "violence" against these women.

The general discourse surrounding appropriate techniques and mechanisms for ensuring women's protection have failed to address Latinas as a specific group. Instead, the debate has focused on women as a monolithic class with similar patterns of conduct and common concerns. When women of color have been considered, they have been treated as an homogeneous group, without reference to race-specific differences and experiences.

The treatment of women of color has focused primarily on their economic status, and has lacked a detailed analysis of the role of race— including the entrenched racism of law enforcement institutions nationally. As a result, the different experiences and realities of women of color are not considered when designing effective guidelines on enforcement in domestic violence situations. This absence creates the risk that prophylactic and penological strategies aimed at all women will fail to adequately address the needs of Latinas.

Various reforms have been suggested and implemented to ensure that police officers adequately respond to violence against women. These reforms range from narrowly drafted legislation directed toward police officers' official duty in domestic violence situations to police sensitivity training and education about the nature of domestic violence. Although some of these reforms have been successful, others are the subject of much criticism and debate.

Existing efforts to reform law enforcement policies exemplify the consequences of a narrow and myopic approach to domestic violence issues. Reforms are guided by the social construct of law enforcement officials' roles as peacemakers and protectors of the common good. The idealized image of the police officer as a kind, governmental guardian, however, is not a common experience among either ethnic groups or whites in this country. The violence perpetrated against people of color and the double standard applied in law enforcement were dramatically exemplified in the beating of Rodney King by Los Angeles police officers. Cases involving Latino victims of police abuse include the Jose Garcia case in Washington Heights and the Federico Pereira case in Queens, New York.

Latinos in the United States have had a long, acrimonious history of interaction with local police and federal law enforcement agencies. This history is marked by abuse and violence suffered by the Latino community at the hands of police officers who have indiscriminately used excessive physical force against Latinos. The resulting tension between the community and the police is further exacerbated by denials from law enforcement organizations and monitoring agencies that the police act abusively or beyond the scope of appropriate authority.

The history of racism and current racial tensions affects the success of any domestic violence enforcement strategy. For example, Latinas are suspicious of police who have acted in a violent and repressive manner toward the community at large. In addition, a Latina must decide whether to invoke assistance from an outsider who may not look like her, sound like her, speak her language, or share any of her cultural values.

This dissimilarity is critically important because it reflects the linguistic, cultural, and political barriers facing Latinas. In situations where Latinas must rely on law enforcement officials for assistance, they usually meet officers who are not bilingual and bicultural, and who are unable to communicate with people who speak little or no English. The women, therefore, are left to care for themselves—to seek translation at a time of extreme danger and urgency. A Latina in such a position cannot be expected to devise an alternative plan to compensate for the lack of appropriate personnel. This burden should be borne by the institutions and officials assigned the responsibility of protecting the rights of all members of society.

The failure of domestic violence enforcement strategies—as manifested by Latinas' suspicions, hesitance, and concern—can be addressed through comprehensive, intensive education of both enforcement personnel and the Latino community about domestic violence and arrest policies. Officials must develop such education strategies with input from community-based organizations and Latino advocates. Otherwise, education programs will reflect ingrained stereotypes and replicate the same problems that the programs are designed to address. To be successful, community education projects must be founded and located within the target communities. Advocates and members of community-based organizations should set the pace and the tone of these projects. These leaders should ensure that the projects are culturally specific and reflect the community's level of knowledge and sensitivity about domestic violence. Latina advocates must be at the forefront of these efforts to ensure that patriarchal structures are not integrated into the dialogue.

A second factor affecting current enforcement strategies is the failure of activists to consider the impact of racist attitudes on police behavior. Officers often fail to make an arrest, minimize the seriousness of the situation, or treat the woman as if she was responsible for the violence. Battered women's activists have criticized male police officers for their sympathetic attitudes toward batterers. This criticism, however, reveals a major flaw in the approach of the activists: such an approach does not consider the race of the batterer, which is a relevant factor in the police response to a domestic violence situation. The history of aggression toward Latino males by police officers cannot be ignored, nor can the police's collegial mentality of "them against us" be denied in assessing institutional enforcement.

There may be a sense among police officers that violent behavior is commonplace and acceptable within the Latino community, and that both men and women expect Latinos to react physically in situations of domestic conflict. There is no definitive research on the impact of these stereotypes on arrest patterns. The perceptions of police and individual Latinos about their motivations and routine behavior, however, are important factors in patterns of arrest for domestic violence.

Arguably, a mandatory arrest policy represents one solution to this problem. Restricting a police officer's discretion by requiring an arrest in all cases where probable cause exists would minimize the disparate treatment that Latinos receive. Under such a policy, Latinas would receive fairer treatment in response to their requests for assistance. By focusing on the ultimate arrest of the batterer, however, a mandatory arrest policy ignores the dynamics among police officials, Latinas, and batterers.

The history of police abuse toward the Latino community makes the content of the interaction a relevant issue. If a Latina or her male partner is physically or verbally abused during the arrest, or if she is not given any further information concerning her rights or available support services, a Latina gains only a temporary benefit. Nevertheless, some activists argue that a mandatory arrest policy can empower women by providing them with some control over their situation.

Several aspects of the Latinas' status, however, diminish the possible empowering effects of a mandatory arrest policy. First, Latinas face the precarious, often untenable situation of the "double bind"—empowerment through the disempowerment of a male member of the community. The internal conflict and external pressure to cast police officials as outsiders, hostile to the community, frustrates the development of the Latinas' empowerment. Second, when the officer does not speak Spanish and the woman speaks little or no English, the empowerment potential again is diminished. Third, evidence suggests that police officers react to such arrest policies by arresting both the man and the woman—so called "dual arrests." Empowerment is unlikely when women are treated as if they have acted illegally, are as culpable as their batterers, or cannot be believed. Finally, subsequent official responses, as well as resources available to the woman, determine her ability to end the violence and take control of her situation. Latinas have neither access to, nor the benefit of, extensive resources to ensure their safety.

The political status of Latinos in the United States poses a more difficult issue—both practically and theoretically. The Puerto Rican experience is representative of the complex issues of ethnic group identification and cultural solidarity. Puerto Ricans, despite being United States citizens, are often treated as "foreigners." As a consequence, and in part because of the unequal treatment they receive, Puerto Ricans have a "dual" status and identity vis-a-vis their political and social position in the United States and their cultural status in Puerto Rico.

Not surprisingly, nationalistic fervor and a longing to "connect" with Puerto Rican culture shape both individual perceptions and behavioral patterns in the United States. Any conduct that can be characterized as contrary to the group's cultural or social ideology is thus eschewed as undermining efforts for equality, and is regarded as an individual attempt to assimilate or "Americanize."

Against this backdrop, the first issue regarding the impact of Latinas' political status becomes clear: if a Latina decides to go beyond the perimeters of her community and seek assistance from outsiders—persons already considered representatives of institutional oppression—the community may view her acts as a betrayal. A Latina, therefore, may tolerate abuse rather than call for outside help. This hesitance to seek assistance provides the community with an excuse for ignoring or denying violence against Latinas, as well as for trivializing and resisting Latina activists' efforts to create a community strategy to end the violence.

Second, law enforcement officials may not give adequate consideration to calls received from poor neighborhoods and neighborhoods with significant populations of people of color. Domestic violence calls from these communities may be less likely to draw attention and interest because officials consider such work either highly dangerous or unrewarding. Although a misperception, this attitude engenders a sense within the community that seeking police assistance is futile.

3. The Criminal Justice System: Many of the same concerns and issues manifested in the development of policies designed to ensure proper police enforcement also exist with respect to the role of the prosecutor's office and the judiciary. Local prosecutors may charge defendants in domestic violence cases with a lesser crime, or propose and accept plea bargains involving minimal penalties. Plea bargains, which usually provide either a token sentence or no sentence, fail to communicate a sense that the prosecutor's office recognizes the serious nature of the charges or the severity of the batterer's conduct.

Local prosecutors and judges react differently to domestic violence cases than to other criminal cases. They often treat these cases as inconsequential or private matters, ill suited to state intervention. Gender bias in the courts therefore results in the disparate treatment of domestic violence crimes compared to other crimes of violence.

The Latino community's long-standing fear that, in general, Latinos are prosecuted more frequently and more vigorously than whites, mitigates perceptions that Latinos will be treated less harshly because the crime involves domestic violence. In order for Latinas to feel that they have been treated justly—and to give them actual just treatment—reforms must address traditional institutional racist structures.

There are numerous obstacles, based on language and culture, which must be removed in order for a Latina to use the criminal justice system effectively and ensure a criminal prosecution against her batterer. First, the shortage of bilingual and bicultural personnel—prosecutors, judges, clerks, and psychologists, all of whom are crucial and can influence the ultimate outcome of a Latina's case—creates a system unprepared for and unwilling to address claims by Latinas. Second, Latinas have limited resources to fill the gaps in available support services to assist them.

Third, Latinas face racial and ethnic barriers. Neither white women victims nor white male batterers receive discriminatory treatment on account of their race. In contrast, Latinas receive different treatment because of stereotypes and myths about Latinas and about Latinos generally. Latinas are devalued and dehumanized in this process, having no connection to those who have been assigned to prosecute and adjudicate their complaints.

Fourth, the "cultural defense" raised by men in response to prosecution for killing their wives represents another barrier to Latinas. The defendant's theory in each of these cases is that violence against women, or the particular violent act at issue, is sanctioned by the culture and may, in fact, be a recognized cultural norm. This defense seeks to mitigate the punishment of the defendant.

At first, the concept of a legal system—in particular a criminal justice system—that recognizes and incorporates cultural factors into its proceedings and decisions appears attractive. Such an approach, by requiring legal institutions to consider all relevant factors and to judge the defendant from his or her actual perspective, appears inherently more fair and just. In the context of cases of violence against women, however, a "cultural defense" serves only to promote violence within the community.

The cultural defense tactic's fundamental premise—that a particular norm or set of norms is culturally inherent to an identifiable group of persons—is problematic, because defining and identifying culture, or specific aspects of culture, is difficult. Furthermore, a victim's response that the conduct is certainly not "cultural" is equally credible.

Furthermore, even if violent actions against women are inherent to a particular culture in certain situations, such conduct or norms are often based on patriarchal structures. Legitimizing violent actions as cultural norms only reinforces the patriarchy, and would only lead to further abuse of women. The actions must also be rejected because they run counter to a legal system allegedly founded on the equality of all individuals.

B. Social Services

Any legal initiatives designed to address domestic violence must be complemented by social services and programs designed to address the economic, social, psychological, and emotional needs of women seeking to escape or reduce the violence in their lives. These services include counseling, assistance in securing entitlements and health coverage, and temporary or permanent housing for women who leave their homes. Because of linguistic, cultural, and institutional barriers, Latinas have limited access to such services. These social services are especially critical for Latinas, whose access to and utilization of judicial and law enforcement remedies are also limited. A recent study found that Latina shelter residents were the least likely, in comparison to white and African–American shelter residents, to contact a friend, minister, or social service provider for assistance prior to entering the shelter. The study also found that Latinas' actions comported with marital norms, which differed from those of other shelter residents. Specifically, Latinas appear bound by a norm of "loyal motherhood." They tend to get married younger, have larger families, and stay in relationships longer. They are correspondingly poorer, have completed fewer years of formal education, and suffer more extensive periods of abuse than their non-Latina counterparts.

In general, an insufficient number of battered women's shelters exist. For every woman who seeks shelter, five are turned away, and ninety-five percent of shelters do not accept women with children. Moreover, when Latinas try to enter shelters, many are turned away because they speak little or no English. Indeed, the lack of bilingual and bicultural personnel among these service providers represents a major barrier to Latinas' access to programs and shelters.

Shelters without bilingual and bicultural personnel claim that they would do a disservice to Latinas by accepting them, because the language barrier would prevent personnel from providing Latinas with adequate services. In a sense, Latinas are therefore denied access to shelters on the basis of national origin. Unfortunately, the shelter is often the only resource available to Latinas, thus compounding the negative impact of this exclusionary practice.

When they are accepted into a shelter, Latinas find themselves in foreign and unfamiliar surroundings, because a shelter rarely reflects a Latina's culture and language. For purposes of safety, women are often placed in shelters outside their community, which contributes to Latinas' sense of loneliness and isolation. Without bilingual and bicultural personnel and a familiar community environment, these shelters can provide only the barest services and temporary shelter. Insensitivity based on racism or on a lack of knowledge about or exposure to other cultures, by both shelter personnel and other residents, further isolates Latinas and escalates their sense of unwelcomeness.

Nor do shelters facilitate the Latina's return to her own community. Because there are insufficient numbers of Spanish-speaking personnel, the Latina cannot develop the skills and strengths necessary to escape the violence permanently and establish a new, independent life. These shelters currently provide only temporary, short-term services; and Latinas cannot hope to become empowered when they are placed in such a disempowering, dependent position.

These circumstances illustrate the particularly difficult position of Latinas in battered women's shelters. Such women face obstacles associated with language differences, discrimination, limited personal income, marital norms, and limited mobility because of their larger families. These factors have practical implications for the development of adequate strategies to respond to violence against Latinas. Experts conclude that the concerns of Latinas deserve high priority.

> The Hispanic women, in particular, need more economic and educational support to help them in their crisis, as well as in general. They need to be given priority in terms of housing, social welfare benefits, child care, and transportation. This need is compounded by the fact that a substantial number of hispanic women in the[se] shelters are "undocumented citizens" and are not eligible for public assistance. Much of their aid therefore must come from church or private groups devoted to assisting "undocumented" worker families.[119]

Research supports the argument that women of color, in this case Latinas, should be placed at the center of feminist reform movements. The current lack of services available to Latinas reflects the consequences of failing to place the unique differences of women of color in a central position in feminist discourse.

Historically, the Latino community has not had the opportunity to participate fully and to compete for contracts with state and local governments. As a result, few Latino community-based organizations or service providers, whether nonprofit or for-profit, are capable of successfully securing contracts with local government administrations to provide services to battered Latinas. Often, the process of securing a contract to establish a shelter or to provide bilingual counseling and advisory services to battered women is so daunting that organizations opt out of the process. With no state-funded Latino providers, contracts will go to other providers that will not service Latinas adequately.

An organization that plans to open a shelter providing bilingual services must turn instead to private sources of revenue. As these organizations struggle to secure sufficient funding, they remain vulnerable to fluctuations in financial support from foundations and private

119. Racial Differences Among Shelter Residents, supra note 90, at 48–49. * * *

funders, and dependent on individual and corporate benefactors' continued interest in domestic violence issues. Because of the lack of Latino government contracts, as well as the precarious nature of private funding sources, it appears unlikely that expansive and comprehensive services uniquely designed for the Latino community can be provided without resources mandated by federal and state legislation.

IV. RESPONSES

The Latino community has not yet begun to develop a comprehensive strategy to end violence within the community. This failure reflects more than mere oversight. Historically, activists and leaders within the community have confronted racism and national origin discrimination with clear, focused strategies. Moreover, Latinos have vehemently opposed the characterization of those in their community as violent and uneducated. This commitment to equality and civil rights stops short, however, of addressing issues such as "women's rights" that are of specific importance to Latinas. Struggles within the Latino community to recognize the pervasiveness of domestic violence and its impact upon the lives of women and their families must continue. Unfortunately, demands for a community response to the violence have been met with claims that such issues are private matters that cause division within the community, and consequently impact negatively on the larger struggle for equality. These references to solidarity obfuscate the real issue: Latinas are physically, emotionally, and psychologically abused on a daily basis by the men who are closest to them. These are not private matters—just as the lack of adequate health care, and the struggles for an equal education and a decent living wage do not constitute "private matters."

Latina advocates have established programs that reflect the culture and language of Latinas. By focusing on models of empowerment and incorporating long-term goals, Latina advocates hope to establish an environment in which battered Latinas can escape the violence and restructure their lives.

Latina advocates continue to work within the community through the existing institutions and media to educate one another on the nature of domestic violence. They also work within the battered women's movement to educate other activists on the unique needs of Latinas, and to demand that the larger movement be responsive to these needs. Their efforts to politicize what is often considered a "private" issue will help ensure that the concerns of Latinas are factored into the equation of feminist reform of domestic violence discourse.

V. CONCLUSION

Consideration of and responsiveness to cultural and racial differences must be central to any strategy in the domestic violence movement. In the past, reforms have been drafted and implemented without consideration of the status of the Latino community. The historical relationship between law enforcement institutions and the Latino community has not been considered in the promotion of tactics such as mandatory arrest policies. Currently, these policies do not fully serve the needs of the Latino community, and may place Latinas in increased danger.

Extensive educational efforts therefore must be linked to mandatory arrest policies to inform the community of the policy and of the duties imposed on the police. Good faith and trust must be established by having the police work with Latino organizations and Latina advocates whose reputations and commitment to the community are well established.

Much of the movement against domestic violence has centered on the establishment and maintenance of shelters and increased social services. These are recognized as critical provisions for battered women. Yet, Latinas have not received sufficient resources and services to address their multiple needs. Not only are resources scarce and in great demand, but the resources that are available are parcelled out in a manner that discriminates among women based on their cultural and racial characteristics. Latinas have suffered harsh consequences as a result of these practices.

Sufficient financial and technical support must be provided to community-based shelters and service providers. Programs developed in and by the community will likely be more sensitive and responsive to the cultural and racial differences that are unique to the Latina experience.

Stereotypes about Latino men and women proliferate and create obstacles to full participation and utilization of programs and enforcement mechanisms. Monolinguistic xenophobia denigrates those with Spanish language skills to an inferior position—one synonymous with ignorance and illiteracy. Latinas, therefore, are considered to be either uneducated or undereducated. They receive little and are believed to merit little. Efforts both within the Latino community and in the domestic violence movement must be devoted to eradicating such stereotypes.

The most significant aspect of any reform, however, is the extent to which it is based on a philosophy of empowerment and a rejection of traditional patriarchal structures. Programs or services that offer temporary relief from violence, but do not provide women with the tools or opportunity to develop the necessary skills and monetary and emotional resources to gain control of their lives permanently, are insufficient.

Activists are not constrained to choose either to incorporate with the existing anti-domestic violence movement—with all of its flaws and weaknesses—or to push forward with a separatist agenda focused solely on Latinas. Rather, the opportunity exists to learn from prior efforts and mistakes in both the civil rights and women's movements. A convergence of the successes of both can provide guidance and direction.

The development of strategies to address domestic violence must be grounded in the reality and experiences of all women, recognizing that there may be tensions and conflicts associated with developing reforms. It must be accepted that Latinas face multiple barriers because of their race, national origin, and gender; that this multiple discrimination factors into how Latinas experience and respond to domestic violence; and that institutional racism and patriarchal structures are interrelated in the experience of Latinas. A reform movement that recognizes these realities and experiences will acknowledge the need to work in unison, but only from a strong base. Latino community-based organizations must be strengthened and provided with the financial and political flexibility to develop and establish domestic violence shelters and services. The Latino community must prioritize domestic violence initiatives. The lives of women and the well-being of an entire community depend on it.

E. NATIVE AMERICAN WOMEN

VIRGINIA H. MURRAY, A COMPARATIVE SURVEY OF THE HISTORIC CIVIL, COMMON, AND AMERICAN INDIAN TRIBAL LAW RESPONSES TO DOMESTIC VIOLENCE

23 Okla. City U. L. Rev. 443–457 (1998).

III. HISTORIC AMERICAN INDIAN RESPONSES TO DOMESTIC VIOLENCE: CHEYENNE, NAVAJO, AND CHEROKEE LAW

[T]he basic principle applicable to the relationship of a man and woman is that of *hozho*, or that state of affairs where everything is in its proper place and functioning in harmonious relationship to everything else. Inherent in that concept is proportionality, reasonableness, and individual dignity.[79]

A. *Domestic Violence in Indian Communities Today*

Approximately two million Indian, Eskimo, and Aleut persons live in the United States today. For most of those people, a totally male-dominated, hierarchical social and legal structure, with its accompanying abuse of power, was unknown prior to non-Indian contact in North America.

In the modern era, however, increases in domestic violence in Indian communities are even greater than in non-Indian America. Two outside influences specifically play a role in this phenomena: first, the racist stereotyping of Indians, which unfortunately, many Indian people themselves have come to believe and act out, and second, the adoption of vertical social systems and male dominance in societal arrangements.

European and American literature inaccurately portrayed accounts of Indian life for many years, rather than observing and reporting the

---

79. Kuwanhyoima v. Kuwanhyoima, No. TC–CV–334–84 (Tuba City Dist. Ct., April 9, 1990), aff'd on other grounds, but opinion approved, No. A–CV–13–90 (Navajo Nation S. Ct., Dec. 5, 1990).

actual state of relations between Indian men and women. In reality, traditional roles for Indian men and women were often the reverse of roles in non-Indian society. Many Indian tribes were matrilineal, with women owning the property and holding positions of leadership. Even in patrilineal tribes, abuse of women, like abuse of children or the elderly, was extremely rare and in many cases criminal.

The influence of traditional non-Indian patriarchal views had a profound effect on many Indian people, particularly in the late-nineteenth and early-twentieth centuries. United States government programs such as allotment, which divided Indian land into 160–acre plots given to the male head of the household, educational programs that taught men to become farmers and women housewives, governmental demands for a single "headman" to make decisions with the United States on behalf of a tribe, which centralized power in one individual— nearly always a man, and Indian inheritance and property laws that skewed traditional Indian notions. All of these were not only confusing to many Indian people, but reversed the traditional roles of men and women in many Indian communities.

Certainly, outside factors cannot completely explain the increase in domestic violence in Indian communities in the modern era. The same problems occurring in non-Indian relationships, including economic and job troubles, jealousies, and adultery, must be considered when determining why spousal abuse has become a problem. However, it cannot be overly stressed that the influence of traditional Anglo–American male dominance is the primary culprit. As one Navajo woman stated: "A lot of women are having trouble with their husbands. The only model the men have is the macho white man. They try to copy him and Navajo women object."[89]

B. *The Traditional Legal Responses*

At first glance, the Cheyenne, Navajo, and Cherokee appear to have little in common. The Cheyenne were nomadic people living primarily in South Dakota, Nebraska, Kansas, and Colorado. Like most other plains tribes, they benefited greatly from the introduction of horses to North America by the Spanish, as they moved frequently throughout the warm months following game.

The Navajo are located in what is today the southwestern United States and were heavily influenced by Spanish language, religion, and culture after 1600. The Navajo are currently the largest Indian tribe in North America.

Prior to their nineteenth century removal to present-day Oklahoma, the Cherokee were located in northern Georgia, North Carolina, South Carolina, Tennessee, and Alabama. They lived in towns and villages, built permanent log homes, grew crops throughout the year, and prac-

89. Zion, supra note 82, at 421.

ticed commercial trade among themselves prior to dealing with non-Indian traders and businessmen.

For all their differences, however, traditional Cheyenne, Navajo, and Cherokee societies used similar approaches to domestic violence. Reactive methods of dealing with domestic violence existed, particularly for the Cheyenne and Navajo. Most importantly, however, all three organized their societies and legal institutions in ways that greatly emphasized avoiding domestic violence from the outset.

1. The Cheyenne

At first glance, the patrilineal, seemingly male-dominated society of the Cheyenne might lead one to assume that domestic violence was a common problem with little recourse available to an abused wife. However, known cases illustrating Cheyenne reaction to such occurrences, along with an understanding of Cheyenne family law in general, require a contrary conclusion.

Marriage in traditional Cheyenne society was a contractual arrangement. It could occur in a formal way, with the eldest brother (or other family member) of a girl arranging her marriage, or through elopement. However, in either case marriage was validated by the exchange of gifts, offered initially by the husband and his family, with items of equal or greater value given by the brother and family of the bride in return.

Courtship, accompanied by gift exchanging, frequently extended over four or five years. As a result, everyone in the camp knew of the impending marriage, including other possible would-be suitors of the bride. This alleviated potential conflicts that might develop due to mistaking the "status" of a yet-unmarried girl. More importantly, with regard to husband and wife compatibility, the extended courtship period gave both parties and their families more time to become acquainted, and for the girl's brother, to ensure the accuracy of his decision.

Although it might appear that a bride's brother would succumb to the temptation of a possible husband's largesse, and force his sister to marry an unfit man for the sake of receiving presents, contemporary Cheyenne accounts of traditional marriage practices assure us that the norms of proper family life unquestionably called for a girl's future welfare to be considered. At the same time, however, once a final decision was made regarding the engagement, "her duty to submit (was) quite plain...." Girls refusing to marry their fiance following engagement and courtship were severely punished through disownment by their families, especially when the girl eloped with another man. Punishment by the fiance himself in these instances was not unusual.

The status of married Cheyenne women was one of considerable strength. There were few legal "disabilities," while at the same time there existed positive checks against cruelty by husbands. For example, wife abuse was automatic grounds for divorce. The wife could leave and go "home to mother," or alternatively, a family member of the wife could declare her divorced and demand her husband leave the couples' home. In either case, final decision-making authority rested with the brother (or other family member) who arranged the marriage at the outset. The parents of a girl returning home might remind her of her commitment, but could not force her to return to her husband. However, the girl's brother, if approached by the husband with a second gift offering, would "cross-examine" the girl to determine the truthfulness and seriousness of her story. A final decision would be made following careful consideration. If divorce was declared, the husband's new gifts were returned, and the brother would send word to the husband's warrior society and throughout the camp, ensuring that no confusion regarding his sister's legal status ensued. If the marriage contract were renewed, the girl would return to her husband with new gifts from her brother and family.

In addition to fear of divorce or retribution by a woman's family members, other traditional Cheyenne customs lessened the likelihood that a man would abuse his wife. Among these was matrilineal owner-ship of property. If a woman divorced her husband, she had legal claim to the home, its contents, and the children. In addition, the husband gave up all right to inherit this property from his ex-wife, including property she might inherit from her own family members in the future, if she preceded him in death.

An additional, though often controversial, Cheyenne custom that many argue lessened the incidence of domestic violence was the practice of polygamy. Like the Navajo and Cherokee, Cheyenne women outnum-bered the men, especially after contact with non-Indians. Although this was one practical consideration that made polygamy acceptable, another practical consideration was that adultery and jealousy were avoided by the practice. Thus, the likelihood of domestic disputes arising from these issues was lessened.

Most importantly, a Cheyenne man who could provide food for multiple wives, and who chose to marry again, usually married the sister or cousin of his first wife. Like the Navajo, the Cheyenne believed this provided additional physical protection for the women from possibly abusive husbands. In addition, if a wife was abused and returned to her family, her "testimony" of what had occurred during "cross-examina-tion" by her brother could be corroborated.

Although married Cheyenne women endured few legal "disabilities," the balance of legal prerogatives belonged to the men. For example, a wife could divorce her husband for cause, including domestic violence. However, the abused wife had no right to punish him herself, that role usually belonging to her family members. In addition, husbands could divorce their wives without cause. The divorce announcement, or "throwing away" of a wife, could be made publicly during a warrior society ceremony or dance, and thus was a great disgrace to any woman.

Although men held the upper hand regarding when and how a divorce could be obtained, Cheyenne society and legal norms, like those of the Navajo and Cherokee, lessened the likelihood of domestic violence in the first instance. To be sure, retribution frequently awaited husbands who abused their wives. More importantly, however, is the fact that the Cheyenne, like the Navajo, sought to avoid domestic violence at the outset by condemning the practice, giving married Cheyenne women legal rights to property and children, and establishing protective practices such as polygamy. It was through these traditional methods that the Cheyenne not only dealt with domestic violence, but also lessened the likelihood of its occurring altogether.

2. *The Navajo*

In traditional matrilineal Navajo society, married women shared equal rights with their husbands, and often had superior authority. Women planted crops and contributed equally to their family's economic welfare. Navajo property law reflected these important contributions through women's property ownership and control. Traditional Navajo family law also reflected these contributions, and there is little dispute that under Navajo law, violence toward women, or mistreatment of them in any way, was illegal.

Little information exists regarding the reactive legal consequences of domestic violence. Whether or not a husband faced severe retribution at the hands of his wife's relatives, as existed in Cheyenne society, is unknown. What is known is that married men and women, for the sake of familial and clan stability, were strongly encouraged to reconcile their differences in extended-family meetings. Whether the couple stayed together as husband or wife, or an agreed-upon divorce was arranged, "setting things straight" and restoring harmony was an important goal.

Traditional Navajo custom, like the Cheyenne, sought to avoid domestic violence in the first instance. This was done through women's property ownership mentioned above, belief in a variety of important deities represented by women, ceremonies honoring women's role in Navajo society, and engagement and marriage laws aimed at reflecting the importance and protection of women.

Traditional Navajo marriages were arranged by clan elders or leaders. Elders sought to bring together prospective husbands and wives that were compatible, while at the same time creating marriages that would bring economic benefits and good relations between clans. Because domestic violence disrupted family and inter-clan survival, thereby bringing shame to the families of the erring husband and wife, family and clan leaders had a strong interest in counseling against spouse abuse.

For example, prior to marriage, engaged Navajo men and women were required to attend meetings with elders and clan relations. These people taught the future husband and wife the rights and duties of spouses. The man and woman were admonished "Don't get mad at each other"; "Don't talk back to each other"; "Don't divorce each other"; and, "Stay together nicely." During these meetings, and throughout the traditional Navajo marriage ceremony, domestic violence was specifically addressed, with elders telling a young man that he should "never take his hand to his wife...."

The traditional Navajo, like the Cheyenne and Cherokee, practiced polygamy. In Navajo society, one specific purpose of polygamy was avoidance of adultery and its accompanying jealousies and damaging effects on a relationship. A Navajo man usually married the sisters of his first wife, or would take a divorced or widowed woman as his first wife, and then marry her daughters from her prior marriage after they reached adulthood. This type of female-controlled family arrangement, especially where all of the women were closely related, offered protection to the women, making it nearly impossible for a man to abuse one or all of his wives.

In addition to pre-and post-marriage "counseling" and polygamy, traditional Navajo communities took part in an additional custom that lessened the likelihood of domestic violence: matrilocal residence, or the husband going to live with his wife's mother's clan and family.

Pursuant to Navajo law, a woman's family had an obligation to take her in and offer protection from an abusive spouse, if necessary. Matrilocal residence made fulfillment of the obligation easier, and the prospect of losing a wife and having to answer to her family probably kept many men from becoming violent. Even in those rare instances where a husband and wife lived away from her family, a protective custom existed that did not allow the new couple to live alone during their first year of marriage.

Traditional Navajo law, like that of the Cheyenne, offered some reactive methods for dealing with domestic violence. Counseling was used to solve domestic problems, and great pressure and influence to mend disputes and live in peace was brought by family and clan leaders. Most importantly, however, the Navajo sought to avoid domestic violence altogether by creating a society in which a married woman had a legal status equal to her husband and a cultural status that possibly exceeded that of men. In addition, traditional Navajo customs offered protective measures against domestic violence such as inter-family polygamy and matrilocal residence.

3. *The Cherokee*

Prior to the late 1700s, the Cherokee lived in small villages, practiced commercial trade among themselves, and in this way were interdependent and relied heavily upon one another to obtain various foods, clothing, tools, building materials, and other necessary items. However, the traditional Cherokee, when compared to other American Indians (and most of their contemporary non-Indians), were probably the premier "civil libertarians" of their time. Equality, personal rights, and individual freedoms were paramount, and it has been said that one individual could put his or her entire village at military risk in the name of upholding their personal liberty.

Traditional Cherokee society, like that of the Navajo, was clearly matrilineally structured. However, Cherokee family law, especially laws of engagement and marriage, were heavily influenced by the independence of the individual Cherokee. As a result, engagement and marriage among the traditional Cherokee has been described as "amorphous, straining to the limit our tolerance with comparative jurisprudence."[137]

Traditional Cherokee marriage practices offer no definitive patterns. This is because the Cherokee, unlike most Indians (and non-Indians, for that matter), had no formal marriage "ceremonies" or celebrations, and no engagement "contracts" or "arranged" marriages. In addition, no family member, be it a mother, brother, father, or clan leader, could compel a girl to marry a particular man. Cherokee marriage was not legally binding on either the husband or wife. Marriage occurred simply by cohabitating, and divorce when either the husband or wife moved out of the home. In either case, no legal "rights" were granted or lost, and no change of legal status for either party occurred.

Added to this individual-oriented society were the property rights of women. A Cherokee woman owned the house in which she lived, all of its contents, and the crops she planted and harvested. In addition, children were raised by their mother and her clan, particularly her brothers and uncles. Fathers had no legal right to "family planning." In other words, the practice of infanticide, by a mother, was allowed. In the case of divorce, children stayed with their mother, and she looked to her brothers for support and protection.

Given the independent, equality-driven society in which the traditional Cherokee lived, it is not surprising that domestic violence was extremely uncommon. In fact, very little evidence exists of reactive methods of dealing with domestic violence. Even such marital problems as adultery and its accompanying jealousies and mistrust did not frequently cause violent outbursts from either a husband or wife. This may be because adultery was a private matter in an "open-minded" society, was not a crime, or because divorce was easily and frequently obtained for those who were no longer happy in an existing relationship.

In any event, traditional Cherokee society was structured in such a way that incidence of domestic violence was the exception and not the norm. Unlike the Cheyenne and Navajo, however, it does not appear that the Cherokee created customs and laws that purposefully sought to avoid domestic violence. Instead, Cherokee notions of personal freedom, independence, and equality naturally resulted in lessening the likelihood of marital abuse.

IV. Conclusion

The social and legal response of a society to domestic violence is reflective of its religious beliefs, traditions and customs, and social and

---

137. Reid, supra note 93, at 113. For information on current Cherokee marriage and divorce laws, see 2 Cherokee Nation Code, Marriage and Family tit. 43 (West 1993).

governmental structures. Those societies with purely patriarchal religious beliefs and customs are more likely to have vertical social and governmental structures with men occupying positions of power and authority. In these societies, abuse of women is not only common, it is also usually legal.

The Roman civil law and Anglo–American common law share similar historic responses to domestic violence. Although these legal systems have diverse origins, they have many similarities, including the influence of Judeo–Christianity and vertical social and governmental structures. The legal subordination and perceived inferiority of women was common in both legal systems, and domestic violence was not illegal.

The traditional societies and legal systems of the Indian tribes, bands, and nations living in North America prior to non-Indian contact were as diverse as civil and common law societies. However, the Cheyenne, Navajo, and Cherokee had similar means of addressing domestic violence. These included organizing their societies and legal institutions in ways that greatly emphasized avoiding domestic violence from the outset. In addition, in the case of the Cheyenne and Navajo, reactive methods for dealing with abusive husbands also existed.

Although recent reports of domestic violence statistics in newspapers, magazines, and television news shows have once again attracted attention to the problem of domestic violence in the United States, most Americans do not understand why domestic violence occurs, nor are they familiar with how legal systems around the world historically addressed this problem. Knowing why domestic violence occurs, and how certain societies and legal systems have responded in the past, may help prevent domestic violence in the future. In addition, modern legal scholars and practitioners can use this information to aid in further developing laws to combat what some experts believe has been, and continues to be, a national crisis.

F. TRADITIONAL JEWISH WOMEN

BEVERLY HORSBURGH, LIFTING THE VEIL OF SECRECY: DOMESTIC VIOLENCE IN THE JEWISH COMMUNITY

18 Harv. Women's L. J. 177–180, 192–194 (1995).

Although commentators have discussed some of the particular and general problems associated with domestic violence, relatively little attention has been paid to Jewish battered women. Even a well-publicized case, such as the tragic story of Hedda Nussbaum, prompted little public interest. Contrary to the idealized vision of Jewish family life as warm, loving, and nurturing, in many Jewish homes a woman experiences physical violence, emotional abuse, and terror. Like other battered women, a Jewish woman must deal with the general problem of sexism. She is ashamed to admit she is abused and worries that the police will fail to protect her. She also worries that she will lose custody of her children as well as her only means of support if she should divorce her abuser. In addition, Jewish women encounter anti-Semitic stereotyping in the outside world. Stamped as an abrasive, emasculating, and over-bearing mother or a pampered, demanding, and self-centered shrew, a Jewish woman hardly evokes sympathy from the public or a court of law. She also incurs hostility within her own community in accusing a Jewish man of physical abuse. Exposing Jewish misconduct to the Christian majority is a *shanda*, a shame that brings disgrace upon all Jews in that each shoulders the burden of representing an entire people. To some Jews, she is nothing short of a traitor who undermines efforts to combat the more pressing issue of anti-Semitism.

For an Orthodox Jewish woman, the problems are even more overwhelming. In naming herself battered and identifying with other non-Jewish women, she must risk the loss of her Jewish self and the fulfillment that comes from belonging to a religious community with deeply felt shared values. She might have few contacts with the outside world. She could actually fear representation by a non-Jewish lawyer or even a non-Orthodox Jewish lawyer. In many cases, regardless of secular law reforms and despite her courageous willingness to end her marriage and obtain a restraining order, she might never be able to extricate herself from her batterer. She is anchored to him for the rest of her life, unless he dies or is willing to grant her a divorce according to Jewish law.

The Jewish woman's problems are exacerbated by the scarcity of statistical evidence on domestic violence among Jews. Both the Jewish and non-Jewish worlds make her officially nonexistent. Although studies document domestic violence in fifteen to thirty percent of Jewish families, as far as both cultures are concerned, Jewish men never abuse the women in their lives. Popular images enshrine them as the perfect husbands. The popular culture also assumes Jewish women to be spoiled by their fathers, catered to by their mates, and that they exercise control over their intimate relationships. As a result, Jewish women suffer the stigma of supposedly dominating their meek, obliging boyfriends and husbands. Jewish women internalize the stereotyping of Jewish male/female relationships and are less able to picture themselves as battered. They are also unlikely to be believed by family, friends, social workers, or the courts. Many rabbis discount their claims of abuse, telling them to try harder, for the sake of *shalom bayit* ("peace in the home"). The Jewish community's denial of domestic violence and the tendency to hide the issue within the confines of religious courts contribute to the oppression of Jewish women and underscore the ineffectiveness of secular authorities to combat woman-beating on their own. In the end, fewer social services are available to these women.

Furthermore, Jewish academics, who are uniquely in a position to publicize the plight of battered Jewish women and thereby educate others to understand their situation, have ignored the issue. Law professors who are drawn to Jewish law in their scholarship minimize or ignore altogether the degree to which rabbinical justice is an expression of patriarchy. The very same regime of law that refuses to release a battered Jewish woman from her pain is extolled by Jewish intellectuals in the academy as a paradigm of enlightenment and a source of inspiration for the secular legal system. Ignored by the Jewish intelligentsia, alienated by her religious leaders, friends, and family, as well as unknown in the outside world, a Jewish battered woman can be truly alone.

It is important to lift the veil of secrecy, render visible what has been made invisible and tell the stories of Jewish battered women. To help these women we must first get to know them through their narratives and through exploring Jewish law, traditions, and social practices that are contributing factors in the development of a battering culture. In this Article, I attempt to accomplish this task and to introduce you to the world of Jewish battered women. I believe I am obligated because, as Robert Cover has put it, I am Jewish and thereby personally responsible for all that occurs in the family of Jews.

If I am not for myself, who will be?

If I am only for myself, what am I?

If not now, when?[8]

In this Article, I examine the blatant and more subtle forms of intragroup oppression in Jewish culture that foster the mistreatment of women. In Part I, I discuss Jewish law (*halakhah*) and Jewish religious/social practices from a feminist perspective, indicating the many ways in which certain interpretations of the law reflect a belief in the inferior status of women and sustain an environment conducive to woman-abuse. I focus on the exclusion of women as meaningful participants in the Jewish tradition, the toleration of woman-beating in the rabbinical commentary, and the inability of women to initiate a divorce under *halakhah*. In Part II, I attempt to describe the recurring problems facing Jewish battered women. In Part III, I criticize the writings of Jewish law professors who present an idealistic picture of Jewish law, omitting its gender bias and indifference to women's needs. I argue that academics, by romanticizing the Jewish tradition, increase the difficulties of Jewish battered women.

My purpose is to introduce a seldom discussed topic and to broaden the inquiry of those who work in the area of domestic violence. Change must come from within the Jewish community if domestic abuse among Jews is to end. As we become more aware of the dynamic interplay between the secular law and the religious law, and as Jewish feminists strive to create a new, inclusive understanding of the Torah, we will be better able to protect battered Jewish women. In tempering our appreciation for traditional Jewish law by listening to the voices it silences, we also extend the dialogue between particularity and generality in feminist legal thought.

* * *

8. Hillel, Aboth, ch. 1, Mishna 14.

C.   THE IMPACT OF THE JEWISH DIVORCE SYSTEM ON WOMAN-ABUSE

The refusal of the rabbinical authorities to permit *halakhic* changes has also caused serious problems for the many Jewish women who need to obtain a Jewish divorce. No area of *halakhah* has been more contested by Jewish women. Furthermore, although Jewish law and secular law seldom are at odds in this country, a Jewish religious divorce raises secular issues. Many Jewish women, who require both a civil and a religious divorce, ask the state to intervene in the religious tribunal's proceeding and redress their grievances. The interaction between religious law and secular law in the divorce arena demonstrates the limits on state power to empower Jewish battered women. They are sacrificed by the secular system out of constitutional respect for private religious practices and forsaken by the religious authorities for the sake of upholding tradition. Caught between both legal systems, abused women, who surmounted other obstacles to obtain civil restraining orders and civil divorce decrees, find they are still chained to their abusers under Jewish law.

Halakhah permits divorce under certain conditions. This has been an advantage for both women and men in that some unhappy unions may be dissolved. To protect a woman, Jewish law requires that she consent to a divorce proceeding. In addition, it mandates an elaborate premarital agreement (*ketubah*) in which the man promises to pay the woman a sum of money if he should divorce her. In the Jewish legal system, however, only a man creates the marriage and only he has the unilateral power to end it. A marriage cannot dissolve until the husband delivers a *get* to his wife. Both parties must appear before the Bais Din (usually composed of rabbis, or a male rabbi and two male witnesses). A scribe writes in Aramaic:

> I release and set aside you, my wife, in order that you may have authority over yourself to marry any man you desire.... You are permitted to every man.... This shall be for you a bill of dismissal, a letter of release, a *get* of freedom.... [98]

The husband then literally places the *get* into the woman's hands and she formally receives it. After the ceremony, the *get* is sliced with a knife so that it cannot be used again and turned over to the custody of the officiating rabbi. Both parties receive a *petur*, a statement of release attesting that they have received a Jewish divorce.

Since battering is a means of control, Jewish law places the Jewish batterer in a unique position to ensure that a woman's fate remains in his hands. Some battered Jewish women, knowing that only the husband is empowered to divorce, view their situation as hopeless. For them, there is no point even in attempting to leave. A civil divorce cannot save her from a tragic and humiliating fate, for without a *get*, she is an *agunah*, a woman enchained. An *agunah* has virtually no standing in the

---

98. Blu Greenberg, Jewish Divorce Law: Lilith, Summer 1977, at 26, 27.
If We Must Part, Let's Part as Equals,

community. As a woman who is neither married nor unmarried (under Jewish law), she still legally belongs to her husband, although they no longer live together as husband and wife.

Unless she has been issued a *get*, an *agunah* is not free to enter into a Jewish marriage even if she has acquired a civil divorce and even if the first marriage only involved a civil ceremony. Any children born of a second marriage, without having first acquired a *get*, are *mazerim* ("bastards"), the offspring of an adulterous union. *Mazerim* are shunned and forbidden to marry Jews (although they are Jews) for ten generations and may only marry other *mazerim* or converts to Judaism. In contrast, the children of a Jewish father who has not obtained a Jewish divorce are not illegitimate. In Jewish law the status of the children depends on the status of the mother. For observant Jewish women whose very identities are centered in marriage and children, obtaining a *get* is a matter of great importance. They are trapped, unable to rebuild their lives as long as the *get* issue remains unresolved.

G. DISABLED WOMEN

MARGARET A NOSEK, CAROL A. HOWLAND, AND MARY ELLEN YOUNG, ABUSE OF WOMEN WITH DISABILITIES: POLICY IMPLICATIONS

8 Journal of Disability Policy Studies 161–170 (1997).

RECENT FINDINGS

In 1992, the Center for Research on Women with Disabilities (CROWD) was funded by the National Institutes of Health (NIH) to study the broad range of sexuality issues facing women with physical disabilities. The study began with a qualitative interview study of 31 women with physical disabilities. The qualitative data analysis revealed six thematic domains: (a) sense of self, (b) relationships, (c) barriers, including environmental and attitudinal barriers and emotional, physical, and sexual abuse, (d) sexuality information, (e) sexual functioning, and (f) general and reproductive health. The theme of abuse arose so often and with such intensity that it was impossible to ignore it as a factor that substantially affected the sexual functioning and self-esteem of the women with disabilities. Twenty-five of the 31 women reported being abused in some way. * * * The second phase of the NIH study was an extensive quantitative assessment of the sexuality of women with disabilities, covering multiple areas of concern, such as sexual functioning, reproductive health care, dating, marriage, and parenting issues, and developmental issues, including family influences and a woman's sense of self as a sexual person. Data were collected by means of a national survey based on the findings from the qualitative study. * * * Women were asked if they had ever experienced emotional, physical, or sexual abuse. Emotional abuse was defined as being threatened, terrorized, corrupted, or severely rejected, isolated, ignored, or verbally attacked. Physical abuse was defined as any form of violence against her body, such as being hit, kicked, restrained, or deprived of food or water. Sexual abuse was defined as being forced, threatened, or deceived into sexual activities ranging from looking or touching to intercourse or rape. If the woman responded positively to the abuse question, she was asked to indicate the type(s) of abuse, who the perpetrator was, and at what age the abuse began and ended.

* * * A total of 946 completed questionnaires were received, 504 from women with disabilities and 442 from members of the comparison group, a 45% response rate. Analyses were run on a subset of 860 women, 439 with disabilities and 421 without disabilities, after eliminating those who did not meet the age criterion, did not respond to the abuse questions, or experienced abuse before the onset of disability

* * * The prevalence of any abuse (including emotional, physical or sexual abuse) for women with and without disabilities was 62.0% vs. 62.2%. About the same proportion of women with disabilities compared to women without disabilities reported emotional abuse (51.7% vs. 47.5 %), physical abuse (35.5% vs. 35.6%), or sexual abuse (39. 9% vs. 37. 1%). When the categories of physical and sexual abuse were combined, 51.9% of women with disabilities and 50.6% of women without disabilities responded positively. None of these types of abuse was significantly different for women with or without disabilities. Thirteen percent of the women with disabilities had experienced physical or sexual abuse within the past year.

More husbands abused women (both with and without disabilities) emotionally (25.5% and 26.1%) and physically (17.3% and 18.5%) than other perpetrators. Mothers and fathers were the next most common perpetrators of emotional and physical abuse for both groups of women. Strangers were the most often cited perpetrators of sexual abuse for both groups (10.5% for women with disabilities and 11.6% for women without disabilities).

Women with disabilities were significantly more likely to experience emotional abuse by attendants, strangers, or health care workers than women without disabilities. There was a trend for more women with disabilities to experience emotional abuse by mothers, brothers, and other family members, as well. Women with disabilities were more likely to experience physical (1.6% vs. 0%) or sexual (2.3% vs. 0.5%) abuse by attendants. There was a trend for women with disabilities to be more likely to experience sexual abuse by health care workers.

Women who had experienced abuse that lasted longer than a single incident (n=534 or 62%) were examined to determine differences in the duration of abuse. Women with disabilities experienced abuse (emotional, physical, or sexual abuse categories combined) for significantly longer periods of time than women without disabilities (7.4 years versus 5.6 years). When looking at physical or sexual abuse alone, women with disabilities also had such experiences for significantly longer durations than women without disabilities (3.9 years vs. 2.5 years).

POLICY IMPLICATIONS

Findings in the literature and recent studies can be explained in part by many factors related to the life situation of women with physical disabilities that increase their vulnerability to abuse. First and most damaging is the general devaluation of women with disabilities. There is a social stereotype that they are asexual, passive, unaware, and therefore, easy prey. This stereotype also contributes to the attraction of romantic partners who are controlling and searching for women they can dominate. Second, many women who have been victims of abuse for most of their lives may accept it as normal behavior. The lack of peer role models who enjoy more functional relationships, plus isolation and segregation, leave them with no evidence to refute claims by abusers that different standards apply to them because of their disability. Third, difficulty financing and obtaining adaptive equipment leaves many women trapped in immobility and unnecessarily dependent on abusers. Such situations severely reduce escape options. Fourth, inaccessible home and community environments further reduce escape options and intensify the social isolation of women with physical disabilities. Fifth, due to their need for medical attention for chronic conditions, many women with disabilities experience increased exposure to medical and institutional settings. These settings may reinforce passive behaviors and compliance with authority, and may force women into situations of isolation where family and mobility equipment are taken away. Sixth, the large majority of persons who have activity limitations depend on family for personal assistance. Whether or not the person providing the assistance is the perpetrator of abuse, the situation generates perceptions that this is the only living option for the woman, that no one else would take care of her, and that abuse is the price she must pay for survival. Finally, women with disabilities have extreme difficulty finding and maintaining employment. Many women with or without disabilities are financially dependent on their abusers. Women with disabilities may be in the situation of receiving funds through government benefit programs which they are coerced by physical threats into handing over to abusive family members.

All of these factors contribute to the fact that the few options for escaping abusive situations that are available to women in general are not always available to women with disabilities. Because many of these factors can be moderated only by changing society-wide attitudes toward women with disabilities and increasing the importance we place on the delivery of social services, people tend to believe that nothing can be done to change this situation. The feeling of helplessness and hopelessness toward the abuse of women with disabilities can be remedied to some extent by changes in policies that govern the delivery of social services and by the enforcement of existing accessibility and non-discrimination laws. We would like to offer the following observations and recommendations on how these changes can be implemented.

Programs for battered women commonly have architectural, attitudinal, and policy barriers. For women who are in life-threatening abusive situations, crisis intervention includes escaping temporarily to a woman's shelter, escaping permanently from the abuser, and having an escape plan ready in the event of imminent violence if the woman chooses to remain with the perpetrator. These options may be problematic for the woman with a disability if the shelter is inaccessible or unable to meet her needs for personal assistance with activities of daily living, if there is no accessible transportation to the facility, if the shelter staff are unable to communicate with a deaf or speech-impaired woman, if she depends primarily on the abuser for assistance with personal needs and has no family or friends to stay with, or she is physically incapable of executing the tasks necessary to implement an escape plan, such as packing necessities and driving or arranging transportation to a shelter or friend's home. She may also be unable to make arrangements to take her children with her, and worry about leaving them alone with the perpetrator. She may have to devise a safety plan with a trusted friend or relative to help her make arrangements to escape.

Andrews and Veronen (1993) list four requirements for effective victim services for women with disabilities. First, service providers need to provide adequate assessment of survivors, including questions about disability-related issues. Second, survivor service providers should be trained to recognize and effectively respond to needs related to the disability, and disability service providers should be trained in recognizing and responding to physical and sexual trauma. Third, barriers to services should be eliminated by providing barrier-free information and referral services, by ensuring physical accessibility to facilities, by providing 24–hour access to transportation, to interpreters, and to communication assistance, and by providing trained personnel to monitor risks and respond to victims receiving services through disability programs. Finally, persons with disabilities who are dependent on caregivers, either at home or in institutions, may need special legal protection against abuse.

According to the National Coalition Against Domestic Violence and the National Coalition Against Sexual Assault, inaccessibility in battered women's shelters is a serious problem. These programs generally operate on very thin budgets and covering the cost of accessibility modifications and services is a substantial challenge. There is currently a very high and growing demand for these shelters, making bed availability a problem for all women. According to Veronica Robinson, former director of the abuse program at Access Living in Chicago, making shelters accessible and generating an expectation that women with disabilities can be served there will only create cynicism when no beds are available. Vigorous advocacy is needed to increase funding for these programs and to expand options for temporary or transitional housing.

Despite these serious financial barriers, quality standards must be implemented for battered women's programs. Buildings must comply with the architectural requirements of the Americans with Disabilities Act, state laws, and local ordinances. Auxiliary aids and services must be made available. Program staff should receive training on basic disability facts, ways to communicate with women with disabilities, and the unique vulnerabilities and reduced escape options faced by women with disabilities living in the community and in institutions. In this way they can increase their sensitivity to disability issues and be more effective counselors. Women with disabilities should be hired as program staff and administrators.

A point of debate is whether every shelter needs to be accessible or is it acceptable to establish a limited number of fully accessible shelters that serve only women with disabilities. One side of the argument is that one accessible shelter is better than none, which is the unfortunate reality for most communities. Also, the needs of women with disabilities would be met more effectively by a highly trained staff and totally accessibility facility. The other side claims that segregated facilities create the perception that general programs are absolved of their responsibilities to accommodate women with disabilities. Further, the demand is so great that one program in a community could never meet the needs of abused women with disabilities seeking help.

Service providers often fail to recognize abusive situations, are silent when abuse is recognized, and are unable to refer abused individuals appropriately. Anecdotal evidence indicates that providers of social services, including Social Security workers, human services workers, and rehabilitation counselors, do not generally believe that addressing the abuse-related needs of their clients is within their role or responsibility. The same can be said for physicians and the whole spectrum of health care workers. Information about abuse prevention and intervention, and the availability of community resources for battered women, was rarely included in the professional training for any of these disciplines. Service providers are often unaware of the degree to which abuse can interfere with their clients' achievement of program goals. In-service trainings are called for to enable service providers to increase their skills in discussing abuse with their clients and to establish an information base for referring their clients appropriately to community resources. Research is needed to identify the extent of this problem and to discover training techniques that would be the most effective.

Churches may be the first point of contact and first point of rejection for abused women with disabilities who are reaching out for help. This statement by the Reverend Nancy Lane, Ph D, an Episcopal priest who has cerebral palsy, illustrates the desperation of many abused women with disabilities. Churches generally offer counseling and some social services to their members, but for women with disabilities, the effectiveness of these services is sometimes diminished by religious stereotypes about disability. In some religious traditions women are devalued and women with disabilities are devalued even more. Obedience and submission to the husband is expected. Disability may be associated with punishment for past deeds or sins of the family. Since many churches place a high value on the authority and integrity of the family, they are silent when issues of abuse come to their attention. Their preoccupation with the disability may obscure their recognition of abuse within the family. They may even convince women with disabilities who have been abused to remain silent and seek resolution of their problems through prayer.

Dr. Lane found that the literature on abuse of power by the clergy over women never mentions disability, and that the literature on church and disability never mentions abuse. She cites a fundamental need to change church attitudes toward disability before this problem can approach resolution. Policy declarations about recognizing and addressing the abuse of women, including women with disabilities, must be made from the highest levels of church hierarchies and implemented uniformly through the ranks of community congregations. Although churches are familiar with and refer to battered women's shelters, there is rarely such communication between churches and independent living centers and other disability advocacy organizations. The involvement of religious organizations in community coalitions and organized disability advocacy will increase the breadth of outreach. Churches are the first and main point of contact for many people in minority communities and individuals who are in no other way connected to service providing systems. Their role in abuse prevention and intervention could be invaluable.

Protective services are overwhelmed and often unresponsive. Adult Protective Services in most states have a mandate to protect only those adults with disabilities who reside in institutional environments; adults living in the community have to be at least 65 years old to receive protective services. These services, while generally regarded as well intended, are compromised by limited funding and very large case loads. The bureaucracy in place to administer protective services often further compromises effectiveness. Short cuts in the bureaucracy are necessary in order to reduce the response time when police calls are received about women with disabilities who are in danger. A more investigative approach is necessary in order to identify feasible living alternatives for abuse victims. Field workers and program administrators should receive extensive training to increase their awareness and sensitivity to the vulnerabilities and realities of living with a broad range of physical, intellectual, mental, and sensory disabilities. Advocacy is needed to expand the mandate of these services to cover a larger age range and variety of living situations, as well as to increase the resources available for the delivery of services.

The lack of options for personal assistance forces dependence on abusive caregivers. The dynamics of receiving personal assistance from a family member or unrelated, hired person are very complex. Persons with severe physical disabilities depend on another individual to assist them with intimate daily survival needs, such as toileting, bathing, dressing, transferring, and eating. It is very easy to abuse such individuals by assisting in a way that causes pain, threatening not to assist with essential tasks, or abandonment altogether. The National Study received numerous reports of women whose assistants withheld medication or refused to give them their orthotic devices, such as wheelchairs, crutches, or braces, until money, sex, or other favors were given. Opportunities are ample for voyeurism and contact with genitals when assistance with toileting and bathing is necessary. Other types of non-contact abuse, such as stealing and extortion, are also made easy when the individual cannot directly control their possessions.

In some cases, emotional and physical violence is not deliberate. Family members may resent their responsibility to provide assistance, or may feel stress, fatigue, jealousy, or displaced anger due to dysfunctional relationships. Paid assistance may, out of incompetence, insensitivity, or general carelessness, be rough or inattentive to special needs resulting from painful limbs or joints, vulnerability to skin breakdowns, lack of sensation, hypersensitivity, osteoporosis, or susceptibility to respiratory or other types of infections. In many cases, despite repeated efforts to train and reinforce correct behaviors, assistants are unable or unwilling to change.

Tolerating abuse in these situations may be the only way to survive. Many women with congenital disabilities have lived with family all of their lives and were raised to believe that no other living options were available to them. Women who depend on their spouses for personal assistance are told by their spouse that they must tolerate the abuse because no one else would ever marry them. The small percentage of women who have resources to hire assistants from outside the family sometimes develop a high tolerance for abuse because the alternative of finding new assistants is too daunting. Advertising, interviewing, running background checks, trial work periods are all very time consuming and physically and emotionally stressful. It is very difficult to fire an abusive assistant and pursue the course of finding another of better quality without some type of backup system from family, friends, or a reliable, affordable agency.

On the personal level, the solution to this problem is to develop a tight network of family and friends to check up on one's well being and be available if emergency assistance is necessary. On the societal level, we must expand affordable and feasible options for providing high quality, reliable assistants. Plans for a national system for funding and providing long-term, respite, and emergency personal assistance services have been under discussion by the National Council on Independent Living, The Coalition of Citizens with Disabilities, the Administration for Developmental Disabilities and the U. S. Department of Health and Human Services for decades; however, little progress has been made beyond local and statewide demonstration programs. National legislation with ample funding allocation is necessary before a uniform national system of services can be made available. Only then will women with disabilities have a feasible and attainable alternative to abuse as the price of survival.

Police have received little training in the special needs of women with disabilities. Crime statistics make no record of disability. To do so would require police officers to be able to identify the wide variety of disabling conditions using only superficial information. This is an almost impossible challenge; however, some documentation is necessary before violence against women with disabilities will gain the attention it deserves. Standards for reporting should require some indication of functional limitations, such as mobility, sensory, or mental impairment.

Police officers, court justices, and other law enforcement staff should receive training in accommodations needed by persons with disabilities. Some progress has been made in increasing awareness of the needs of persons who have hearing impairments or developmental disabilities. Children should never be used as interpreters and non-disabled individuals should never be asked to speak in place of a disabled person who is capable of rendering the necessary information.

The courts have not proven friendly toward women with disabilities. There is a tendency to order mediation, which forces women to confront their abusers and risk the possibility that the abuser will twist the facts to make her appear to be an abuser or harasser. When children are involved, there is a long and unfortunate tradition in the courts of judgments that the woman is not competent to serve as a mother solely on the basis of her disability. Solutions to these problems will come about when judges acknowledge the civil rights of women with disabilities and understand the principles of the Americans with Disabilities Act.

There is a serious lack of affordable legal services. Many women with disabilities do not see legal representation as an affordable option. The extraordinary expenses associated with living with a disability combined with the financial exploitation suffered by many women make the cost of legal services out of reach. There is a serious need to expand the amount of pro bono and low cost services available to women with disabilities who are entitled to seek legal recourse to resolve cases of violence and long-term abuse.

Community services are not well integrated. The array of needs experienced by women with disabilities is very complex. The fragmentation of social services and the lack of communication among community-based helping resources feeds the perception that no help is available and, therefore, abuse must be tolerated. According to Sharon Johnson, a rehabilitation counselor in Duluth, Minnesota, who deals often with abuse among her clients, the integration of social services is a key to providing women with disabilities alternatives to abusive living situations. She cites the following factors that contribute to the supportive environment in her community: 1) Protective orders are easy to get, 2) the police receive sensitivity training about disability issues, 3) the police know how to get interpreters quickly and easily, 4) perpetrators who are caught must go to "anger" management classes, 5) there are many high quality battered women's programs, 6) service providers know about these programs and use them as resources for their clients, 7) there are crisis centers for children of battered women, 8) there is a county program that funds and refers individuals to serve as personal assistants, 9) there are various options for affordable housing, and 10) there is good communication among social service systems. Long term solutions to the problem of fragmentation depend on funding availability. In communities around the country, advocacy is needed to increase funding resources for disability-related social services, to encourage service providers to follow an integrated service model, and to train consumers on techniques to make the system work for them.

Chapter 4

GAY AND LESBIAN BATTERING

This chapter is similar to Chapter 3 in that it focuses on a particular group in the US, here gay men and lesbians. Some of the same themes we saw in Chapter 3 arise again: a historically problematic relationship between the specific community and law enforcement in particular and the justice system generally; a community ethic of not airing one's dirty laundry in public, so as not to give the majority culture excuses for further oppression; and a lack of resources meeting the needs of particular groups of victims of domestic violence.

New themes in this chapter include issues of equal protection when statutes specifically exclude same-sex victims, and the lack of a domestic sphere or domestic privacy in same-sex relationships. Additionally, one of the articles raises the question whether and under what conditions battered lesbians or gay men can effectively utilize the US legal system for protection, and what alternatives might be available. Another excerpt points out the multiple issues and oppressions faced by battered lesbians of color.

This chapter also returns to the question, "What causes domestic violence?"—and the answers proposed are complex. The previous chapters tended to analyze domestic violence as primarily based on male and female conditioning, stressing the great differences between the sexes in that conditioning. The similarity of that sex-role conditioning across many different ethnic and cultural groups was noted. But that analysis does not explain the phenomenon of gay or lesbian domestic violence. To answer the question, "What causes domestic violence?" when the parties are in a same-sex relationship may require that the reader re-examine previously held assumptions about the root causes of domestic violence generally.

KATHLEEN FINLEY DUTHU, WHY DOESN'T ANYONE TALK ABOUT GAY AND LESBIAN DOMESTIC VIOLENCE?

18 Thomas Jefferson L. Rev. 23–40 (1996).

I. INTRODUCTION

Despite the epidemic of crime and violence in our society, people expect their home to be a refuge where they feel comfortable and secure, especially when surrounded by those they love and who love them. Unfortunately, many domestic violence victims face the disturbing reality that they are actually more in fear and at risk of emotional and physical harm in their own home by an intimate partner than on the street by a stranger. The double murder charges filed against O.J. Simpson in June 1994 catapulted domestic violence into the public eye. The nation faced the startling possibility that an American hero living in Brentwood repeatedly abused and even killed his former wife and the mother of his children.

During the double murder case, the media repeatedly informed the public about domestic violence, including the fact it occurs in approximately one in four to one in three couples and exists in every socioeconomic, racial and cultural group. However, discussion of domestic violence in gay and lesbian relationships was noticeably absent from the mainstream media even though approximately ten percent of the national population is homosexual and the prevalence and dynamics are very similar to those of heterosexual battering. Even the gay and lesbian communities have been very reluctant to recognize and talk about same sex domestic violence.

Although it is generally accepted that domestic violence occurs in at least the same proportion in homosexual relationships, the crimes appear to be even more underreported than in heterosexual relationships and much less research and fewer resources have been dedicated in the area. Even the 1995 National Crime Prevention Council report addressing violence against women acknowledged that researchers, service providers, and law enforcement officers have paid far less attention to the issue of domestic violence in gay and lesbian relationships. This fact needs to change. Like heterosexual domestic violence, society must recognize gay and lesbian domestic violence as an important public concern rather than just a private matter, homosexual issue, or relationship problem. The gay, lesbian and heterosexual communities must recognize the problem and work together to more effectively help stop violence in all intimate relationships.

II. DEFINING GAY AND LESBIAN DOMESTIC VIOLENCE

A. *Formulating Definitions Specifically For Gay Men And Lesbians*

Most people are unaware that domestic violence exists in gay and lesbian relationships. It is less surprising to learn that very little has been published about same sex domestic violence. This is especially true when one realizes that American psychologist Lenore Walker first introduced the term "battered woman" in 1973, and the first book ever written about battered wives was not published until 1974 in England. Since Del Martin published her landmark American work on the subject of battered wives in 1976, citizens, courts and legislators have continued to struggle to reject and modify the Anglo–Saxon common law attitudes and practices of treating wives as property. Domestic violence is generally referred to synonymously as spousal abuse or wife abuse and victims are often called battered wives or battered women. These types of references have placed the focus of domestic violence on heterosexual marital relationships, and inaccurately imply that domestic violence does not apply to gay and lesbian relationships.

The terms typically used to describe domestic violence should be modified and expanded to include gay and lesbian relationships. For lesbians, "[d]eveloping a vocabulary that defines and describes the experience of abuse at the hands of another woman is an integral part of [their] recovery process. It is also fundamental to [lesbians'] political and personal understanding of abusive lesbian relationships." The National Coalition Against Domestic Violence Lesbian Task Force has presented a definition of lesbian battering:

> Lesbian battering is that pattern of violent and coercive behaviors whereby a lesbian seeks to control the thoughts, beliefs, or conduct of her intimate partner or to punish the intimate for resisting the perpetrator's control over her.

> Individual acts of physical violence, by this definition, do not constitute lesbian battering.[10] Physical violence is not battering unless it results in the enhanced control of the batterer over the recipient. If the assaulted partner becomes fearful of the violator, if she modifies her behavior in response to the assault or to avoid future abuse, or if the victim intentionally maintains a particular consciousness or behavioral repertoire to avoid violence, despite her preference not to do so, she is battered.[11]

Contrary to these assertions, two British authors reject the term "battering" because it has become synonymous with male battering against heterosexual women and does not fully describe the ranges of physical, sexual, and psychological violence. They prefer the term "abusive lesbian relationship," and use "abuser" rather than "batterer" to represent the violent partner. These descriptions emphasize the power and control dynamic which includes much more than physical battering. They have also chosen the word "survivor" rather than "victim" to emphasize the woman's strength and courage.

10. Joelle Taylor & Tracey Chandler, Lesbians Talk Violent Relationships 12 (1995).

11. Barbara Hart, Lesbian Battering: An Examination, in Naming the Violence: Speaking Out About Lesbian Battering 173, 173 (Kerry Lobel ed., 1986).

The definition of abuse in this context is similar to the definition of lesbian battering:

> Abuse is the conscious manipulation of another through the use of threats, coercion, psychological disempowerment, sexual humiliation, and/or force. Abuse is used to elevate one party's sense of personal power at the expense of another's. Abuse is the deliberate disregarding of another's needs and wants in favour of the abuser's own, regardless of the emotional consequences for her partner.[15]

Similarly, gay men's domestic violence is "any unwanted physical force, psychological abuse, material or property destruction inflicted by one man on another," and assumes that the two men are involved in some sort of formal or informal, dating or sexual relationship. Like the definitions of heterosexual and lesbian battering and abuse, the central element is power because the batterer deliberately uses various forms of abuse and violence to maintain power and control over the victim.

In the first in-depth study of gay men's domestic violence, authors David Island and Patrick Letellier also emphasize the importance of the language used to describe, discuss and define domestic violence. They advocate avoiding the terms "violent relationship," "abusive relationship," and "battering relationship" because such words suggest mutual or shared responsibility for violence and abuse. They prefer the expression that "a man is in a relationship with a violent man" rather than "in a violent relationship." This terminology clarifies that gay men's domestic violence is not a relationship problem but rather deliberate, violent, and criminal acts by one man against his partner.

B.   But My Partner Never Leaves Any Marks

In any intimate relationship, physical battering is the most obvious form of control and coercion an abuser uses to maintain the power imbalance. It is easy to recognize black eyes, bleeding gashes, and large bruises as signs of domestic violence. However, focusing on the physical injury to the victim detracts from the many less apparent and more wide-spread forms of abuse that usually precede or occur in combination with physical abuse, as the batterer feels he or she needs to maintain power and control.

These less recognizable forms of abuse include acts that do not cause any physical injury: destruction of personal possessions, sexual acts against the partner's will, threats and intimidation, social isolation from family and friends, and deprivation of decision making power and financial control. "The debilitating effects of such psychological abuse as continual ridicule, humiliation, and threats of physical violence should not be underestimated."[22]

---

15. Taylor & Chandler at 13.

22. Island & Letellier, supra note 5, at 25.

C. Domestic Violence Is A Mental Health Disorder

Most batterers suffer from some kind of diagnosable, progressive, psychological disorder or mental condition. However, they are usually not insane, crazy, or psychotic. Those extreme diagnoses improperly excuse batterers' violence and suggest that they cannot change or control their behavior. Although there are various diagnostic categories to apply to the many different types of batterers, at the very least they are all dysfunctional as they make completely rational, conscious decisions about their intentions and acts to inflict harm on their partners. "The commission of violent, criminal acts in the home is all the evidence needed to conclude a lack of psychological well-being in the perpetrator and an unsatisfactory adjustment to society and the ordinary demands of living."[26]

Some people in the domestic violence movement and mental health field argue that labeling gay and lesbian batterers with a psychodiagnostic category will cause bigots to further stigmatize and victimize gay men and lesbians. Some persons still mistakenly believe that homosexuality itself is a psychological disorder.

However, Island and Letellier believe that proper psychodiagnostic categorizing of batterers will place responsibility on the individual to change and acknowledge that violence is a choice. This point is best illustrated with an analogy to drunk drivers. Just as drunk drivers, rather than alcohol, cause traffic accidents, individual batterers, rather than the victims' conduct, alcohol, drugs, patriarchal society, violence in society, or any other excuse, cause domestic violence. Batterers must seek treatment to cure their mental illness and choose nonviolent behavior.

III. Recognizing Gay and Lesbian Domestic Violence

A. It Could Happen to Anyone

Many heterosexuals and homosexuals cling to the belief that domestic violence simply could not occur in their relationships, family, circle of friends, or even community. In reality, domestic violence is non-discriminatory. It crosses all racial, ethnic, geographic, religious, educational, and socio-economic class boundaries. It even crosses the boundaries of sexual orientation, occurring in approximately the same proportion among gays and lesbians as among heterosexuals. Some researchers even postulate that gay men's domestic violence may occur at a greater rate than in the heterosexual community and affect an estimated 500,000 victims each year.

Like victims of heterosexual domestic violence, gay and lesbian victims are generally normal and find themselves trapped in committed relationships with partners who become increasingly abusive. These victims are not masochistic or co-dependent. Most victims could not have predicted their partner would later batter them. The batterer is initially

26. Id. at 61.

charming, romantic, and attentive, and the violence usually does not occur until after the couple has become more seriously involved or is living together.

Both heterosexuals and homosexuals need to dispel the myth that domestic violence does not exist in gay and lesbian relationships. Lesbians can no longer afford to view violence as a male phenomenon rather than a power and control issue. "It is crucial that lesbians abused by other lesbians are given the space and support to define their experiences, to name the issues involved and to evolve a critique which points towards a resolution, both practical and political."[35] There is even greater denial and silence about gay battering than lesbian battering.[36] Our sexist culture needs to overcome the socialization that men are victimizers and not also victims. "The gay community needs to recognize that wealthy, white, educated, 'politically correct' gay men batter their lovers as much as does any other group in society."[37] Just like AIDS, hate crimes, and political oppression, the problem of gay and lesbian domestic violence will not simply go away if society ignores it.

B.   It Is Not Fair Fighting Between Equal and Consenting Participants

Both the heterosexual and homosexual communities entertain the common misperception that two men or two women involved in a violent incident are "just fighting" or engaged in "mutual battering." Everyone, including the victim, may fail to recognize the problem as domestic violence. Abused lesbians and gay men also tend to use physical force to defend themselves against their batterers more frequently than abused heterosexual women do. As a result, the victim and others, such as friends, police officers, prosecutors, doctors, and counselors, may inaccurately believe the victim was the aggressor, does not deserve help, or shares responsibility for the abuse. Batterers will often label the victim as "mutually abusive" in order to take advantage of the victim's guilt and confusion surrounding the incident and to avoid accepting full responsibility for their own actions. Other batterers will claim to be the victim to police, victim advocates, or friends, exploiting the fact that it is more difficult to identify the batterer in same sex relationships, particularly when the partners are approximately the same size, age, and strength.

Same sex relationships force both heterosexuals and homosexuals to avoid gender stereotypes and to re-evaluate the validity of assumptions about physical characteristics. "Size, weight, butchness, queeniness, or any other physical attribute or role are not good indicators of whether or not a man will be a victim or a batterer."[43]

Many battered lesbians are physically more powerful than their batterers, but chose not to use their physical prowess to control the

---

35. Taylor & Chandler at 9.

36. Island & Letellier, supra note 5, at 36.

37. Id. at 24.

43. Island & Letellier, supra note 5, at 18.

perpetrator or would only do so to protect themselves. The myth that the batterer will always be bigger and physically stronger than the victim only focuses on physical abuse and fails to recognize that domestic violence is really about power and control maintained by numerous forms of abuse in the relationship.

IV. How Is Gay and Lesbian Domestic Violence Different Than and Similar to Heterosexual Domestic Violence?

A. The Cycle of Violence

With the exception of a few important differences, the dynamics of lesbian and gay domestic violence are very similar to the dynamics of male-to-female battering. The cycle of violence, first identified by Lenore Walker in her book The Battered Woman, applies to heterosexual, gay and lesbian couples. The three phase cycle begins with tension building that includes minor battering incidents and verbal and psychological abuse. The victim will usually try to control the batterer's anger by trying to anticipate his or her every whim and staying out of the way.

The next phase is an acute battering incident. The batterer will beat the victim regardless of the victim's actions, but will try to justify his or her own behavior by blaming it on the victim. The batterer will then beg for forgiveness and shower the victim with love, gifts and attention in the honeymoon phase. The batterer promises to change and the victim wants to believe that the caring, romantic person he or she fell in love with has returned and the abuse will stop. The victim stays in the relationship for a variety of reasons, then the cycle repeats itself escalating in frequency and severity. The victim responds with increasing hopelessness, fear, minimization, denial, and learned helplessness as he or she struggles to rationalize and cope with the partner's violent behavior.

B. Using Homophobia to Control and Oppress

Use of homophobia is the crucial difference between gay and lesbian domestic violence and heterosexual domestic violence. Society's fear and hatred of homosexuality causes isolation and increases the vulnerability of gay men and lesbians to domestic abuse. The same sex batterer frequently uses homophobia as a powerful tool to maintain the control and power imbalance in the relationship in a variety of ways. For example, the batterer may threaten "to out" the victim to family, friends, co-workers and ex-spouses who are not aware of and will not accept his or her sexuality. When forced "out of the closet," victims may lose child custody, prestigious careers, and valued personal relationships. Since there are few positive gay and lesbian role models, batterers may convince "newly out" partners that their relationship is normal and abuse occurs in all gay or lesbian relationships. They may also take advantage of their partners' own internal homophobia and guilt to convince them that they do not deserve any better because they are homosexual.

Batterers also exploit the myth and misconceptions of "just fighting" and "mutual battering" when talking about an incident with the victim, friends, or police to avoid full responsibility for the abuse, especially when the victim has fought back in self-defense. Abusers also convince their partners that gays or lesbians are not entitled to legal protection and will be treated badly by the homophobic doctors, shelters, police and court system if he or she seeks help.

A victim's prior unpleasant experiences with members of heterosexual society often lend credibility to batterers' claims. For example: a shelter may have refused to admit or help the gay man; a restraining order clinic advocate may have asked the battered lesbian for her husband's name; the hot line worker may not have believed that the male caller really is a domestic violence victim; or the police officers may have referred to the gay male victim as "she" and called the abuse mutual combat. Gay and lesbian batterers may also use law enforcement and the court system to perpetuate the abuse by falsely claiming to be the victim and obtaining restraining orders against the victim.

As a result of homophobia, some people believe that gay and lesbian victims are less deserving of assistance and intervention because their lifestyles are immoral. Victims are reluctant to report violence that will only reinforce the homophobic attitudes that all "unnatural relationships" have such problems because gay men and lesbians have worked so hard to validate their relationships to heterosexual society. Other people mistakenly believe that because gay men and lesbians are not as emotionally committed as heterosexual partners, it should be easier to leave the abusive relationship, especially since they are not legally married and usually do not have children. Such beliefs demonstrate a serious lack of understanding about homosexuality and the dynamics of domestic violence.

C. Isolation of Gay and Lesbian Victims

In addition to the typical characteristics of a domestic violence situation, "the fact alone of being lesbian or gay tends to increase one's distance from the larger society and from its resources."[58] Gay and lesbian victims often do not have a strong support system, causing them to feel they do not have many options to help them stop the violence. People with AIDS or who are HIV positive particularly may believe they have no viable alternatives to staying with their abusive partners. If victims are geographically separated from other gay men and lesbians, they may think their partners are the only ones who can understand and accept their sexuality. The gay man or lesbian may be concealing his or her sexual orientation or facing disapproval from other people, including his or her own family. Both gay men and lesbians are less likely than heterosexual women to turn to family members for emotional support.

"Abused same-sex partners also are less likely to turn to friends for support than are heterosexual women, even—and sometimes particular-

---

58. Lundy at 281.

ly—if these friends are lesbian or gay." Lesbians prefer to see their community as a peaceful, women-centered utopia that does not include abuse. They may actually discourage victims from publicly "airing dirty laundry" and from participating in patriarchal institutions such as the courts. Similarly, gay men prefer to believe they would not batter their partners because they are more enlightened than heterosexuals and have left the paternalistic dominant society. Gay men would rather not discuss or know about domestic violence in their community.

As a result of the silence, it is not surprising that very few support services for gay and lesbian victims or treatment programs specifically for gay and lesbian batterers exist anywhere with the exception of San Francisco, Seattle, Minneapolis and New York. Lesbian victims can try to utilize services for heterosexual battered women, but may have to pretend that they were abused by a man to avoid homophobia from both service providers and other victims. Even if gay victims want help, they have fewer options available because they will not be accepted by women's shelters, support groups, or counseling programs. Batterer treatment programs, victim support groups, hot lines, and emergency shelters should be created to address the specific needs of gay men and lesbians.

V. How Should Law Enforcement and the Court Systems Get Involved?

As examined above, there are significant obstacles and misconceptions to overcome before victims, friends, neighbors, treating physicians and nurses, and others who come in contact with victims will recognize and report gay and lesbian domestic violence when it occurs. However, society must treat gay and lesbian domestic violence as a serious crime as well as morally and socially unacceptable behavior. Unfortunately, there has been widespread mistreatment of gay men and lesbians in the legal system. These individuals need better protection, support and understanding from police, prosecutors, and judges. The distinct but intertwining roles and contributions of the police, prosecutors, and criminal court will be discussed separately.

A. The Police Department

In recent years, more than half of the police departments in major cities across the country have established policies directed at arresting batterers in domestic violence cases. States such as California and Massachusetts have also mandated a minimum of eight hours of police training focusing on handling domestic violence calls. While these are encouraging steps, increased mandatory training on the complicated dynamics of domestic violence and effective intervention is necessary for all officers, and should include comprehensive information about gay and lesbian domestic violence and combatting homophobia.

A victim's 911 call may be the first time he or she has reported the abuse to authorities or reached out for help from anyone. The police department's response is critical to the victim's safety and perception of how he or she will be treated by the criminal justice system. Although experienced in dealing with people during a crisis, the 911 dispatcher should ask questions to determine whether he or she is dealing with a gay or lesbian domestic violence victim without making assumptions or comments that will offend or alienate the victim. Even in San Francisco, with a large gay and lesbian population, some police officers' ignorant, homophobic and bigoted attitudes have further victimized the victim. Rather than presuming mutual combat or ignoring the problem, the police officers should take the time to carefully assess the situation, identify the victim and the suspect, and determine applicable charges.

The officers should comply with mandatory arrest policies that shift responsibility for the criminal charges from the victim to the police department, as in all other types of serious crimes. Also, an officer can often obtain an emergency protective order at the scene for the victim by completing a form and calling a judge. The order will be valid for several days, allowing the victim time to file a petition for a civil restraining order in Family or Domestic Relations Court. Officers should provide victims a domestic violence referral sheet that includes restraining order information and gay and lesbian resources.

Officers should also prepare comprehensive reports, photograph injuries and property damage, and impound any torn clothing, damaged property, or weapons. California law even requires officers to complete an informational report whenever they respond to a domestic violence call but cannot determine whether a violation of the penal code has been committed.[71] These reports can become valuable evidence of a history of domestic violence, such as emotional and verbal abuse, if later violent crimes are reported. The field officers should forward their reports to a domestic violence investigations unit where specially trained detectives can conduct further investigations and contact the victims to provide any referrals or information concerning the criminal case.

B. The Prosecutor's Office

Prosecutors receive reports from the local police department to review and determine which, if any, criminal charges to file against the suspect. The nature of the relationship between the victim and defendant, rather than the specific criminal act, usually determines whether a case will be categorized as domestic violence. For example, the California Penal Code defines domestic violence as "abuse committed against an adult or a fully emancipated minor who is a spouse, former spouse, cohabitant, former cohabitant, or person with whom the suspect has had a child or is having or has had a dating or engagement relationship."[72] This definition is gender-neutral and includes homosexual couples." 'Abuse' means intentionally or recklessly causing or attempting to cause bodily injury, or placing another person in reasonable apprehen-

---

71. Cal. Penal Code § 13701 (West 1996).

72. Id. § 13700(b).

sion of imminent serious bodily injury to himself or herself, or another.''[73]

In 1994, the California Legislature made the penal code section prohibiting willful infliction of corporal injury, commonly referred to as the spousal abuse statute, applicable to gay men and lesbians by deleting the requirement that cohabitants in an intimate relationship be ''of the opposite sex.''[74] A variety of other offenses, such as battery, assault with a deadly weapon, homicide, dissuading a witness from testifying, vandalism, terrorist threats, burglary, stalking, and even homicide, can be categorized as domestic violence cases depending on the relationship of the parties involved. New Jersey's Prevention of Domestic Violence Act is also gender-neutral and expansive enough to include same sex, non-related cohabitants or former cohabitants, along with specifically designating thirteen criminal offenses as domestic violence.

Prosecutors must exercise their discretion to objectively evaluate the cases and charge as many applicable offenses as possible in each criminal complaint. The attorney, rather than the victim, should sign the criminal complaint. The victim's opinion about whether the State should prosecute the suspect should be considered but not be ultimately determinative. For example, the bank teller does not decide if the bank robber who held a gun to her head and demanded money should be prosecuted for his crime. The teller is not asked if she wants to sign the complaint because society recognizes bank robbery as a serious crime that should be prosecuted even if the victim does not want to ''press charges.'' It would make even more sense not to demand that the bank teller victim sign the complaint if she had been repeatedly harassed, threatened, and beaten by the bank robber and feared retaliation.

Responsibility for criminal cases should be shifted from the victims to the prosecutors for all crimes. Each District Attorney's, City Attorney's, or Commonwealth Attorney's Office should have a specialized vertical prosecution unit to handle domestic violence cases. The same attorney should handle the case throughout the criminal proceedings to ensure consistency and develop a rapport with the victim. Victim advocates working in the prosecutor's office domestic violence unit should also provide consistent contact, support, and service referrals for victims involved in the various stages of the criminal process. The prosecutors and staff in these units also must be trained in the dynamics of domestic violence and learn to be sensitive to all victims, including gay men and lesbians.

Casey Gwinn of the pioneering San Diego City Attorney's Office has identified five major positive trends in domestic violence prosecution which have been recognized by the National Crime Prevention Council:

    (1) Prosecutors assume an increasingly active role in community-based coordinating councils;

73. Id. § 13700(a).   **74.** Id. § 273.5(a).

(2) Early intervention at the misdemeanor level before violence escalates into aggravated assaults or homicides;

(3) Policies and protocols that focus on the abuser rather than the victim and shift the responsibility for the criminal case from the victim to the prosecutor;

(4) Elimination of victim-blaming policies and procedures; and

(5) Increasing emphasis on long-term accountability for the abuser rather than quick fixes like fines or diversions.

Ideally, participation in community based coordinating councils should include prosecutors and police officers working with gay and lesbian organizations and task forces to help educate members of the gay and lesbian community about domestic violence and alleviate fears about the criminal justice system. Judges, prosecutors, and police officers should receive training about gay and lesbian domestic violence and eliminating homophobia to properly handle these types of cases. Medical service providers, including paramedics, emergency room doctors and nurses, and hospital social workers should also be educated so they will recognize abuse, offer the victims appropriate assistance and referrals, and not alienate or offend the victims.

C. The Criminal Courts

Judges must provide the real teeth to the criminal justice system to reinforce that all domestic violence is a serious crime and public concern. Just as police and prosecutors, judges should not treat any case less seriously because of the sexual orientation of the victim and defendant. When the defendant is arraigned on charges filed by the prosecutor, the judge should set bail to keep the defendant in jail if the defendant poses a danger to the victim's safety or the community, has a criminal history, has previously failed to appear in court, or may flee the jurisdiction. The judge may also order the defendant to stay away from the victim as a condition of release on his or her own recognizance or bail. Civil protective orders and restraining orders are actually issued by separate Family or Domestic Relations Courts, although violations of the orders may be prosecuted as criminal offenses. Even if the defendant is not in jail while the case is pending, the judge should increase bail and order a warrant for arrest if the defendant continues to harass or harm the victim or attempts to dissuade the victim from testifying truthfully.

When gay and lesbian cases go to trial, the judge should conduct extensive voir dire of prospective jurors to determine if their personal feelings, prejudices, or religious beliefs about gay and lesbian relationships will affect their ability to be fair and impartial jurors and apply the law to the facts of the case. The judge or attorneys may want to minimize or exclude the nature of the relationship, but the defendant's criminal conduct and the victim's behavior may make little sense outside the context of a batterer's pattern of abuse of an intimate partner. Similar to Battered Women's Syndrome and Rape Trauma Syndrome testimony, the court should allow the prosecution to introduce expert testimony to explain the existence and dynamics of gay and lesbian domestic violence to dispel the pervasive myths and misconceptions that would preclude a fair trial.

The criminal justice system should prosecute all domestic violence cases regardless of the sexual orientation of the victim or defendant. Judges and prosecutors should avoid quick fixes such as diversion programs and fines. California recently repealed its statute that previously authorized judges to order defendants to participate in diversion programs which stayed and eventually dismissed criminal charges in certain misdemeanor domestic violence cases. Rather, judges are required to impose mandatory minimum probation terms in most domestic violence cases. These terms include three years probation to the court or under the supervision of a probation officer, a minimum one year batterer's treatment program, and restitution to the victim.

Although the facts of each individual case must be considered, the courts should also order defendants to serve substantial time in custody or perform public work service. However, mandatory batterer's counseling should be the most important element of the sentence since battering is a curable mental disorder requiring a minimum of one to two years in treatment. The judges need to order defendants to jail and reassign them if they do not attend mandatory counseling sessions or violate any other terms of probation.

VI. Conclusion

Gay men don't want to hear about it and lesbians don't want to discuss it. Straight men and women don't even want to know about it because most heterosexuals are uncomfortable with homosexuality. No one really likes to discuss domestic violence, especially if it is happening to themselves or someone they know. So why do we suddenly need to talk gay and lesbian domestic violence?

Gay and lesbian domestic violence is not a new problem. Rather, it is a newly discovered one that deserves increased attention, research and resources. As a heterosexual prosecutor, I eagerly joined the San Diego City Attorney's Office's Child Abuse and Domestic Violence Unit to help those countless battered women and put the bad guys in jail. I had never really thought about whether domestic violence existed in gay and lesbian relationships, until I sporadically received police reports to review involving two gay men or two lesbians. Despite my training and experience, I had never heard, read or talked about gay and lesbian domestic violence. I only found out that it happened because I read the police reports, talked to the victims, listened to the tapes of the emotional 911 calls, and saw the photographs of bruises, gashes, and bite marks. Since the gay and lesbian cases looked very similar to my other domestic violence cases, I treated them the same way. The only exception was that I would ask the court to order gay and lesbian defendants to attend one year of counseling with a private therapist since there is no certified batterer's treatment program for gay men or lesbians in San Diego County.

Eventually, I volunteered to handle all of the same sex domestic violence cases for the Unit. With the support and encouragement of the City Attorney's Office, I began to educate myself and others about the issue. With the help of a gay therapist and a lesbian therapist who have been working in the field, our office conducted a training session for prosecutors, staff, and others interested in learning about same sex domestic violence. People began talking and asking questions about a topic that had never been openly discussed. Dedicated gay and lesbian leaders, therapists, victim advocates, prosecutors, police officers, and other volunteers in San Diego County began working together to stop the violence and end the silence in the gay and lesbian community.

The most immediate needs and goals for San Diego County are probably very similar to those throughout the country: gay and lesbian victim support groups, gay and lesbian friendly safe-houses, County certified gay and lesbian batterer treatment programs, a 24–hour hot line, informational pamphlets and posters specifically addressing gay men and lesbians, statistics of all reported gay and lesbian domestic violence, regular training sessions for police, prosecutors, judges, and emergency room staff, and a community awareness campaign including coverage by the gay and lesbian press. Public funds and resources, as well as the cooperation of the gay and lesbian communities and the heterosexual domestic violence movement, will be necessary to accomplish these ambitious projects. Most importantly, the dialogue and research about gay and lesbian domestic violence must continue and expand. Now we know hundreds of thousands of gay and lesbian victims are suffering in silence each year—let's not just lock this problem back in the closet.

NANCY J. KNAUER, SAME–SEX DOMESTIC VIOLENCE: CLAIMING A DOMESTIC SPHERE WHILE RISKING NEGATIVE STEREOTYPES

8 Temp. Pol. & Civ. Rts. L. Rev. 325–350 (1999).

INTRODUCTION

The lesbian and gay communities have been reluctant to discuss same-sex domestic violence for fear of validating negative stereotypes of same-sex relationships and detracting from the push for the legal recognition of such relationships. The relative silence on this issue continues despite the fact that individuals in same-sex relationships are more likely to be abused by their partners than beaten in an act of anti-gay violence and despite recent legislative efforts to restrict domestic violence laws to cover only opposite-sex couples. Nor has it stopped anti-gay organizations from using same-sex domestic violence to bolster their assertions that homosexuality is a dangerous lifestyle and that same-sex relationships are unhealthy, unstable, violent, and sick.

The political downside of discussing same-sex domestic violence is obvious. By reinforcing negative stereotypes, the recognition of same-sex violence risks destabilizing the emerging positive image of same-sex relationships popularized by the media and the on-going legal fight for equal marriage rights. Same-sex domestic violence forces a discussion of same-sex relationships that is not crafted solely for political advantage, but instead reflects the multivalent nature of identity and the lived experiences of individuals in same-sex relationships whether they identify themselves as gay, lesbian, bisexual, heterosexual, or queer. It demands a picture of same-sex relationships that leaves room for the separations, the custody battles, and the fact that violence occurs in same-sex relationships with the same frequency that it does in opposite-sex relationships.

Same-sex domestic violence also challenges our highly gendered (and heteronormative) understanding of domestic violence because it cannot be explained by reference to gender difference, the historical subjugation of women, or the private nature of family violence. For years feminists have argued that the boundaries of the domestic or private sphere act as a shield for domestic violence. Now, domestic violence laws provide special services and enhanced protections precisely because the violence occurs in the domestic sphere.

A domestic or private sphere is something that same-sex couples have never enjoyed. To claim domestic violence protections, lesbian and gay advocates must first argue for something that feminists have identified as a situs of oppression—a private sphere of family life. This is because the recognition of same-sex domestic violence requires the recognition of same-sex relationships. However, after arguing that same-sex relationships are worthy of such recognition, advocates must then explain the violence that can occur within these relationships.

Part I outlines the current, albeit limited, information on same-sex domestic violence and discusses how it destabilizes the emerging gay-positive model of same-sex relationships and the prevailing gendered (and heteronormative) paradigm of domestic violence. Part II summarizes the current state of the law regarding same-sex domestic violence and efforts of state legislators to restrict domestic violence laws to opposite-sex couples. Part III asserts that even if domestic violence laws are extended to cover same-sex couples, there remain serious obstacles to individuals who would otherwise benefit from such protections, including internalized homophobia and the perceived homophobia on the part of the police, the judiciary, social service workers, and even domestic violence advocates.

I. SAME-SEX DOMESTIC VIOLENCE

Same-sex domestic violence is a difficult topic. It has received little attention from the lesbian and gay communities or the domestic violence movement. For the lesbian and gay communities which are currently exerting so much time, energy, and money into securing the legal recognition and protection of same-sex relationships, raising the issue of violence risks reinforcing negative stereotypes. For the domestic violence movement, the existence of domestic violence in the absence of gender differences presents a direct challenge to the feminist construction of domestic violence as a gender-specific deployment of power and violence. Finally, to the extent that both the lesbian and gay communities and the domestic violence movement have been influenced by feminism, the discussion of female-to-female violence shakes the very foundations of cultural or "different voice" feminism.

A. *The Numbers*

Despite the fact that same-sex domestic violence has been discussed since the 1980s, there remains little empirical work upon which to base conclusions regarding same-sex domestic violence. However, one thing that does seem clear is that same-sex domestic violence occurs with the same frequency as opposite-sex domestic violence. It manifests as the same exercise of control through the use of coercion, violence, threats, and verbal and psychological abuse. It can be just as debilitating as opposite-sex domestic violence and just as deadly. In the year preceding this Symposium, the Philadelphia newspapers reported three separate incidents of suicide and/or murder stemming from abusive lesbian relationships. By now we are all familiar with "battered woman's syndrome," but the published reports explained that these women who killed were the batterers and not the abused.

The most comprehensive study of same-sex domestic violence was conducted by the National Coalition of Anti–Violence Programs. Released in 1997, the study compiled accounts of domestic violence reported by twelve different organizations which monitor anti-gay violence. The study defines domestic violence as "verbal, physical, financial, and/or sexual abuse occurring in the context of a romantic relationship." It estimates that between 25% and 33% of same-sex relationships involve physical or psychological abuse. This is comparable to estimates of the incidence of violence in opposite-sex relationships. It is these findings that have led to the conclusion that an individual in a same-sex relationship is more likely to be abused by his or her partner than beaten in an act of anti-gay violence.

It also seems clear that as public awareness regarding same-sex domestic violence increases, so too do the number of reported cases. A survey released in October 1998 shows a 41% nationwide increase in reported cases of same-sex domestic violence. The increase was 67% in San Francisco where the District Attorney's Office has hired a victims' advocate specifically to deal with instances of same-sex domestic violence. Of course, increased public awareness and official recognition have their limits. As discussed below in Part III, even where the law recognizes same-sex domestic violence, homophobia will continue to present significant obstacles for the victims who may be reluctant to reveal their sexual orientation to family, social workers, the police, or court personnel.

* * *

C.   Challenging a Gendered (and Heteronormative) Paradigm of Domestic Violence

Authors have long ago discarded the term "wife-abuse" or "wife-beating" for the apparently gender neutral "spousal" or "partner" abuse. For example, a New York Times headline reads: "Woman's Killer Likely to Be Her Partner, A Study Finds."[43] "Partner" certainly sounds gender neutral, but the first line reports: "More women in New York City are killed by their husbands or boyfriends than in robberies, disputes, sexual assaults, drug violence, random attacks, or any other crime in cases where the motive for the murder is known."[44] There is no mention of same-sex domestic violence or any hint that a woman's "partner" is not necessarily male.

Same-sex domestic violence forces a re-examination of our image of domestic violence which assumes a male batterer and a female victim. It is this gendered understanding of domestic violence that in turn renders the violence necessarily heterosexual. Thus, the absence of gender difference produces two related conceptual problems: how to explain domestic violence without reference to gender roles and how to view it outside a heteronormative frame and within a context of homophobia.

Commentators frequently point to the following practical concerns presented by same-sex domestic violence, all of which illustrate the interpretive force of gender. First, in the absence of gender difference, who is the presumed aggressor? When the police officers arrive at the scene how do they know whom to arrest? Often the police solve this dilemma by arresting both parties on the assumption that they are "mutual combatants." In the case of woman-on-woman domestic violence, how does the battered women's shelter know which woman to admit? The battered women's movement has consistently stressed that it is important to believe the woman, but how does one determine which woman to believe?

These questions arise because same-sex domestic violence does not fit the existing gendered model of domestic violence where a male batterer seeks to control and dominate a female victim with the support of patriarchal institutions and constructs such as the family and privacy. For example, the National Research Council includes the following factors under a discussion of the "causes" of violence against women: "attitudes and gender schema;" "patriarchal family structures;" and the historical "status of women as property." The historical subjugation of women and the private nature of domestic violence, however, cannot explain same-sex domestic violence. To the contrary, same-sex couples

43. Pam Belluck, Woman's Killer Likely to Be Her Partner, A Study Finds, N.Y.Times, Mar. 31, 1997, at B1.

44. Id.

have never enjoyed any state sanctioned veil of privacy surrounding their relationships and the legal recognition of same-sex relationships remains a hotly contested social goal.

1. Battering as "Male" Behavior

Same-sex domestic violence shows women as batterers, men as victims, and gender as irrelevant. If gender is irrelevant, then so too is much of the existing theoretical work on domestic violence. What remains is a relatively blank slate to begin to conceptualize the deployment of power in the absence of gender difference. Before dismissing the explanatory force of gender, however, it is important to acknowledge the fluidity of gender and the fact that gender specific (or expected) behavior need not track biological sex. Accordingly, one way to preserve the gendered paradigm is to define battering as "male" behavior that can be committed, regardless of the biological sex of the offender. This maintains the constructs of male verses female behavior, but allows that gender does not necessarily follow sex. The batterer remains "male" even though she is a biological female. Conversely, the victim remains "female" even if he is a biological male. As Christine Littleton explains, it "is not that battering is non-sexual, but rather that sexual roles are non-biological."[60]

Eaton dismisses this approach as the "imposition of a heteronormative framework upon lesbian relationships."[61] She notes that not only is it "insulting, [but] it is especially dangerous as a cognitive device for understanding lesbian battering, because it feeds the common myth about abusive lesbian relationships that 'butches' are batterers and 'femmes' their victims."[62]

Leaving aside the contemporary resurgence of gender play within the lesbian communities, the continued reliance on gender seems at best a misdescription. It maintains gender difference where there is none—at least none that is respected or acknowledged by larger societal institutions. By adhering to a "dominant resistance discourse," it fails to question how power is mediated and deployed in the absence of gender difference. For example, what impact does sexual orientation have on the violence or abuse? Do other factors such as race, class, education, age, and/or ability, come into sharper relief in the absence of gender difference? How do these multiple identifications intersect, combine, and conflict? Finally, how do gender expectations continue to impact on the parties to the extent that they exist in a same-sex relationship within a gendered and heteronormative world?

2. Homophobia: "An Extra Weapon in Their Arsenal"

As Phyllis Goldfarb correctly points out, gender is only one proxy for power. It represents only one vector of oppression—race, class, ability,

---

60. Christine A. Littleton, Women's Experience and the Problem of Transition: Perspectives on Male Battering of Women, 1989 U. Chi. Legal F. 23, 28 n.20.

61. Eaton, supra note 11, at 207.

62. Id. For a discussion of the use of this type of argument in order to explain a battered woman who killed her female batterer, see Goldfarb, supra note 15, at 623 * * *.

and sexual orientation are others. In the absence of gender difference, same-sex domestic violence offers insights regarding patterns of power and dominance and new overlays of stigma. Although Part III discusses the consequences of experiencing domestic violence in the context of homophobia, studies indicate that homophobia itself can factor directly in the type of abuse perpetrated by same-sex partners. For the abusers, homophobia becomes "an extra weapon in their arsenal" as they threaten their partners with "outing." This represents a form of abuse that is "without heterosexual equivalent."

Homophobia in the United States often prompts (or forces) individuals in same-sex relationships to conceal their relationship or at least the sex of their partner. This concealment requires extraordinary skills in information management because the extent to which an individual chooses to be "out" may vary greatly in different aspects of her life. For example, Mary Eaton notes that "[m]any lesbians, even if 'out' in other aspects of their lives, may decide not to disclose their sexual orientation to friends, family, or employers, for fear of loss of emotional support or the ability to sustain themselves financially."[73]

Threats to reveal the true nature of the relationship can provide the abuser with considerable psychological (and economic) leverage because of the perceived costs associated with being gay in a homophobic society. These costs range from loss of employment, family, friends, or custody of children, to the threat of anti-gay stranger violence. In addition, threats of "outing" can relate not simply to sexual orientation, but also to HIV status.

II. SAME-SEX DOMESTIC VIOLENCE AND THE LAW: CLAIMING A DOMESTIC OR PRIVATE SPHERE

Anti-gay legislation has become a staple on the national, state, and local levels. In recent years, this legislation has focused on rescinding anti-discrimination provisions and refusing to recognize same-sex relationships and the families they produce. While these measures have met with only varying degrees of success, the same-sex marriage laws passed by twenty-five states have been the most widespread and have received the most media attention. The anti-gay family laws also include measures limiting adoption and eligibility for the foster parent program. The latest entrant in this category is the attempt to restrict domestic violence protections to individuals with an opposite sex abuser.

This last development is not surprising because, as stated earlier, the recognition of same-sex domestic violence necessarily entails the recognition of same-sex relationships. "Pro-family" forces argue that extending domestic violence protections to include same-sex couples legitimizes same-sex relationships and extends "special rights" to homosexuals. Reasons to restrict domestic violence protections include appeals to history and Biblical teachings, the bans on same-sex marriage, and the existence of criminal sodomy laws. Currently, up to nine states restrict

73. See Eaton, supra note 11, at 206–07.

the protections to opposite-sex couples. The majority of the states have gender-neutral domestic violence statutes. However, it is not always clear whether the long-fought protections currently afforded by these gender neutral statutes apply to same-sex couples.

A. Feminist Theory and the Domestic

For decades feminists have tried to undo the private nature of domestic violence. Many commentators even elect not to use the term "domestic" in relation to intimate violence for fear that it trivializes the violence. Paradoxically, the legal rules which now exist to address domestic violence exist precisely because of the private or domestic nature of the crime. These protections include: civil protection from abuse orders, publicly financed shelters for abused women, enhanced punishments, police training, and mandatory arrest on probable cause in the absence of a warrant or a police witness. For same-sex couples to gain the same protections, they must first assert the private nature of their relationship and in the same breath invite, or demand, state intrusion and protection.

Same-sex couples exist outside of a state recognized private or domestic sphere. For example, the case of Michael Hardwick illustrates that in nineteen states, the police can arrest same-sex partners for consensual, noncommercial sex, in the privacy of their own home. The case of Robin Shahar shows that an individual can be fired from her state job as a result of her and her partner's private religious commitment ceremony. Same-sex marriage is not an option in any state, which means that no state will recognize the inheritance rights or health care decision-making authority of a same-sex partner. The only protections available are those that can be secured by private contract.

B. The State of the Law

There are currently five states which specifically exclude same-sex couples from protection by affirmatively limiting domestic violence to opposite-sex couples: Arizona, Delaware, Indiana, Montana, and South Carolina. Two additional states require that a couple who is not married or related by blood must have a child in common to be protected by the statute. Finally, Mississippi limits its statute to "spouses, former spouses, [and] persons living as spouses...."[98] Protection from abuse orders are specifically available to same-sex couples in only four states: Hawaii, Illinois, Kentucky, and Ohio.

The remainder of the states have ambiguous gender-neutral laws that refer to "partners," "cohabitants," or "household members," but do not restrict applicability on account of sex. It is probably fair to say that the vast majority of these states have not actually considered whether same-sex couples qualify. Perhaps the most disturbing twist is

98. Miss. Code Ann. § 93–21–3 (1972 & Supp. 1998). Although a same-sex marriage ban would make it unlikely that this language would be interpreted to include same-sex partners, an Ohio appellate court did interpret similar language to include same-sex couples. See infra note 105.

that many of the states with gender-neutral statutes are also sodomy states. This presents a potential catch–22 where a victim of domestic violence may first have to assert that he or she is a criminal in order to qualify for protection.

1. The Extension of Protections

Gradually, same-sex domestic violence has received official recognition in a variety of ways. Appellate court decisions in Ohio and Kentucky and statutory changes, such as those in California and North Carolina, have extended domestic violence protection to same-sex couples. Numerous police departments now include same-sex domestic violence issues in sensitivity training sessions. In addition, both the San Francisco and San Diego District Attorney's Offices have hired victims' advocates. The District Attorney of San Francisco declared that, "lesbian and transgender victims of domestic violence are no different from straight victims in the eyes of the law here in San Francisco." In New York, Governor Pataki issued an executive order, over the objection of the state Senate, authorizing a study of domestic violence that would include same-sex couples.

Many moves that appeared favorable to individuals in same-sex relationships signaled the beginning of longer debates regarding the proper scope of domestic violence protections. For example, after North Carolina approved a bill allowing a same-sex partner to secure a restraining order, opponents stalled a victims' rights bill because they wanted to exclude same-sex victims of domestic violence. The argument was that the victims' rights bill should not include "people breaking state laws forbidding adultery, fornication and sodomy."

In California, the first attempt to drop the requirement that the parties be of the "opposite sex" was unsuccessful. In 1990, opponents argued that domestic violence legislation was designed to protect the traditional family unit and that unmarried partners could leave the relationship at any time. Further, opponents noted that the lack of gender inequities in the case of same-sex domestic violence made it less important for the state to intervene and duplicate the services that were already available by simply calling 911. Despite the fact that the California law was changed in 1994, surveys on same-sex domestic violence continue to list California as one of the states with gender neutral language where same-sex protection is considered "uncertain."

2. The Argument Against "Special Rights" for Homosexuals

The efforts to extend domestic violence protections to include same-sex couples have met with opposition, which labels these attempts to gain "special rights" for a sexual minority. The "special rights" argument is not new and parallels those arguments used against equal marriage rights and employment discrimination protections. The most extreme example of the "special rights" argument was presented by a criminal defendant, an alleged abuser, who asserted that his state's domestic violence law denied him equal protection because it did not cover same-sex couples.

In 1997, a Kentucky Court of Appeals ruled that orders of protection from domestic violence should be issued to same-sex couples, noting the gender neutral language of the statute which applies to "any family member or member of an unmarried couple."[120] Before the case was decided, State Senator Tim Philpot proposed a revision to the law limiting the definition of an unmarried couple to individuals of the opposite sex.[121] He stated that the purpose of the protection from abuse orders was "to protect women and children from abuse and protect a traditional family unit."[122]

Again, he linked the exclusion of same-sex couples to the ban on same-sex marriage.[123] In 1997, the state legislature held hearings on both the proposed ban on same-sex marriages and the exclusion of same-sex couples from domestic violence protection. Noting that any victim of violence is free to file criminal charges, State Senator Philpot stated, "I do not agree that gay couples fit the definition of family. It hasn't happened in the history of the world."[125]

The debate in Arizona was particularly intense and resulted in a broad based reform bill for domestic violence not being enacted. A comprehensive revision to the protection afforded victims of domestic violence was held up because of concerns that the new provisions could apply to same-sex couples. The proposed law would have changed the relevant statutory language to "intimate partnership." Although it passed the Arizona State House, it was defeated in the Senate. As a result, the laws covering protection from abuse orders, arrest on probable cause, removal of a weapon from the home without an arrest, and appearing before a judge before release, are not available to same-sex couples in Arizona.

State Senator John Kaites argued against the bill on the grounds that Arizona does not recognize same-sex marriage.[130] (Of course, the same can be said of every state and the District of Columbia.) Referring to same-sex marriages, Kaites said, "And they shouldn't be recognized.... If a man assaults another man, it's still assault whether they live together or not."[131] He continued that "[w]e should not create a special classification for homosexuals living together."[132]

The Arizona State Senate ultimately approved the revisions to the domestic violence laws, but did not extend coverage to same-sex couples.[133] State Senator David Peterson made explicit the connection between recognizing same-sex relationships and extending domestic vio-

---

120. Mark R. Chellgren, Ruling Protects Same-sex Partners Court Applies Violence Law, Cin. Enquirer, Dec. 13, 1997, at B2.

121. See id.

122. Id.

123. See Gil Lawson, Gay-marriage Ban Would be 'Attack on Our Families,' Courier–Journal (Louisville, KY), Aug. 20, 1997, at B1 (describing hearings).

125. Id.

130. See David Madrid, Bill Would Crack Down on Domestic Abuse, Tucson Citizen, Feb. 27, 1998, at C1.

131. Id.

132. Id.

133. See Howard Fischer, Domestic Violence Proposal Excludes Gays, Ariz. Daily Star, Apr. 9, 1998, at B3. See also Sarnataro, supra note 129, at B1.

lence protection when he stated, "[f]or those of us who are opposed to that type of lifestyle, the mere fact that you start to break down the laws [against sodomy] on the books and say that's OK is a step in the wrong direction."[134]

Often there are other laws related to domestic violence, including treatment, services, and research, that may be limited in their application to opposite-sex couples. For example, in Minnesota, General Assistance will provide reimbursement for services provided to women who are abused by a man. This means that shelters which provide services to lesbians must do so out of additional or separate funding. The recently enacted Indiana Domestic Violence Prevention and Treatment Fund limits its services to individuals who have been assaulted by, or fear imminent serious bodily injury from their "spouse or former spouse."

Finally, the effect of the failure to recognize same-sex domestic violence can go beyond the specific cases of domestic violence to the extent it reflects the public policy of the jurisdiction. For example, the lack of recognition of same-sex domestic violence was used in a recent child custody case between two lesbian co-parents. The couple lived together in Washington where one gave birth to the child and the other adopted the child the following year. After two years the couple moved to North Carolina and separated the following year. The biological mother argued that an out-of-state second parent adoption was invalid under North Carolina law. Her attorney argued that the lack of recognition of same-sex domestic violence was evidence of the public policy of the state of North Carolina.

* * *

CONCLUSION

* * *

A more realistic view of same-sex relationships will also call into question the prevailing gendered (and heteronormative) understanding of domestic violence. It will require domestic violence activists and feminists to uncouple their concepts of power and dominance from the frame of gender difference and consider the role of other identifications, such as race, age, sexual orientation, and disability, in the deployment of power and violence. Only then will domestic violence services live up to the promise of the gender-neutral vocabulary currently in use by domestic violence activists.

* * *

---

134.   Fischer, supra note 133, at B3.

NANCY E. MURPHY, QUEER JUSTICE: EQUAL PROTECTION FOR VICTIMS OF SAME-SEX DOMESTIC VIOLENCE

30 Val. U. L. Rev. 346–351, 354, 356, 357–362, 365–369, 379 (1995).

III. THE EQUAL PROTECTION CHALLENGE

"The equal protection of the laws is a pledge of the protection of equal laws."[63]

This Section raises an equal protection challenge to domestic violence statutes that discriminate against same-sex couples. The Section begins by showing that *de jure* and *de facto* discrimination against gay men and lesbians makes this type of legislation inherently suspect under the Equal Protection Clause. Then the Section analyzes the constitutionality of state domestic violence statutes under each of the three standards of review that have developed in traditional judicial interpretation of the Constitution. * * *

Legislation challenged under the Equal Protection Clause of the Fourteenth Amendment may be analyzed with reference to either the *de jure* or the *de facto* discrimination alleged to be at work in the statute. The *de jure* discrimination against gay men and lesbians in domestic violence statutes occurs in two distinct ways. First, three state domestic violence statutes violate the Equal Protection Clause directly with the explicit language that specifically excludes same-sex couples by affording protection solely for persons abused by members of the "opposite sex." Second, seven additional state domestic violence statutes exclude same-sex couples by implication, through a definitional use of the term "spouse". The legal restrictions imposed by these facially discriminatory statutes renders them inherently suspect as violative of the Equal Protection Clause.

De facto discrimination against gay men and lesbians occurs in states where domestic violence statutes appear facially neutral in their language, but are applied only to opposite-sex couples. These statutes fall under the rule set forth over a century ago in *Yick Wo v. Hopkins:*[77] a statute which is neutral on its face violates the Constitution if it is "applied and administered by public authority with an evil eye and an unequal hand."[78] The equal protection challenge to these facially neutral domestic violence statutes can be distinguished from cases requiring proof of discriminatory intent or purpose because the arbitrary application of these statutes is at issue, not merely a disparate impact that results from the equal application of the laws.[81] The two leading cases propounding the doctrine of discriminatory purpose, *Washington v. Davis* and *Arlington Heights v. Metropolitan Housing Development Corporation*, are inapposite to the equal protection challenge being made here, since those cases dealt with laws that were applied equally to all but had an adverse impact on certain individuals or groups.[82] When domestic violence statutes are not applied or administered with an even hand to both same-sex and opposite-sex couples, states draw the kind of

---

63. Yick Wo v. Hopkins, 118 U.S. 356, 368 (1886).

77. 118 U.S. 356 (1886). * * *

78. Id. at 373.

81. 426 U.S. 229 (1976).

82. 429 U.S. 252 (1977).

intolerable, arbitrary distinctions that the Court struck down in *Yick Wo*.

Domestic violence statutes that discriminate between opposite-sex and same-sex couples, either *de jure* by their language or *de facto* in their application, may not withstand an equal protection challenge under any of the three standards of review that the Supreme Court has developed. The Court, in interpreting the constitutionality of state statutes, applies either strict scrutiny, intermediate scrutiny, or rational basis analysis. Under strict scrutiny analysis, the government must show that it is pursuing a compelling or overriding interest and that the legislation is narrowly tailored to promote that interest. The intermediate scrutiny standard requires that the government action must bear a substantial relationship to an important government interest in order to be upheld. The third standard of review analyzes government action under the rational relationship test, requiring only that the government interest bear a reasonable or rational relationship to the challenged government action. The remainder of this Section analyzes existing domestic violence statutes under each of the three standards of review.

A. Strict Scrutiny Analysis

If gay men and lesbians were determined to be members of a suspect class, then domestic violence legislation that discriminates against them would be subject to a strict scrutiny analysis. Strict scrutiny is applied whenever a law affects a fundamental right or discriminates against a suspect class. The Supreme Court has identified three factors that aid in determining whether a class qualifies as suspect. * * * First, the Supreme Court considers whether the group in question has suffered a history of purposeful discrimination. * * * Second, the Supreme Court considers whether the discrimination against the group is invidious. This analysis involves asking several questions: whether the trait has bearing on the group's ability to contribute to society; whether the group experiences unique disabilities due to inaccurate stereotypes; and whether the trait is immutable. * * * Third, in determining whether a group should be a suspect class, the Supreme Court considers whether the group in question is politically powerless. The Court has maintained that those excluded from the democratic process are in need of special judicial protection because they cannot expect to receive help elsewhere. * * *

In summary, the sexual orientation of gay men and lesbians has resulted in a history of purposeful discrimination against them. Gay men and lesbians have experienced invidious discrimination in all areas of their lives. Gay men and lesbians also lack the political power to remedy their situation without judicial intervention. It would, therefore, comport with the standards set forth by the Court to designate gay men and lesbians as a suspect class, thereby requiring strict scrutiny of legislation that discriminates against them. Should this occur, the burden would shift to the government to demonstrate that the legislation at issue serves a compelling interest and utilizes the least restrictive means available to forward that interest.

Because the current Court is reluctant to extend suspect classification beyond race and alienage, it is unlikely that this reasoning regarding the classification of gay men and lesbians will soon be adopted. One implication of granting suspect classification to gay men and lesbians would be guaranteed access to the fundamental right to marry. Except for a single short-lived exception, courts across the country have consistently refused to grant gay men and lesbians this right. Thus, the provision of equal protection in cases of same-sex domestic violence is better approached through another means.

B. Intermediate Scrutiny Analysis

Within the past twenty-five years, the Supreme Court has adopted an intermediate standard of review for certain classifications. This standard is not as difficult for government to meet as is the strict scrutiny analysis, but intermediate scrutiny does not give the broad deference to legislation found under the rationality test. To date, the Court has only applied intermediate scrutiny to classifications based upon gender and illegitimacy. Domestic violence legislation which does not apply equally to opposite-sex and same-sex couples violates the Equal Protection Clause and triggers intermediate scrutiny for two reasons: first, gay men and lesbians should be afforded quasi-suspect classification based on the traditional analysis used by the Court to determine such classifications, and second, the exclusion of same-sex couples is a form of gender-based discrimination, already subject to intermediate scrutiny.

1. Quasi–Suspect Classification

Under intermediate scrutiny, the Court utilizes many of the same criteria used in strict scrutiny analysis and has not drawn bright-line distinctions between what qualifies one group as suspect and another as quasi-suspect. The quasi-suspect classifications of gender and illegitimacy share with the suspect classifications of race and alienage certain immutable characteristics which have been the occasion of irrational stereotyping and prejudice, resulting in historically unjust treatment of the groups in question. In *Equality Foundation of Greater Cincinnati v. City of Cincinnati*,[143] the U.S. District Court for the Southern District of Ohio held that sexual orientation is a quasi-suspect classification. In making this determination, the court found that gay men and lesbians "have been stigmatized throughout history based on erroneous stereotypes and mischaracterizations regarding their sexual orientation." The court also found that sexual orientation in no way affects a person's ability to contribute to society. The court recognized, however, that as a result of these inaccurate stereotypes, gay men and lesbians experience unique disabilities, including vicious physical attacks. In addition, the court recognized the immutability of sexual orientation. Finally, in determining that gay men and lesbians are a quasi-suspect class, the court considered the significant political impediments that gay men and

---

143.   860 F.Supp. 417 (S.D.Ohio, 1994).

lesbians face. For all of the reasons set forth by the court in *Equality Foundation of Greater Cincinnati*, gay men and lesbians meet the criteria for quasi-suspect classification.

2. *Gender-based Discrimination*

Gender-based classifications are already subject to intermediate scrutiny, as declared by the Supreme Court in *Reed v. Reed*[150] and *Frontiero v. Richardson*[151] because these classifications are inherently suspect. In order for legislation which discriminates upon the basis of gender to be declared valid, the state must show a fair and substantial relationship between the discrimination and the interest being forwarded. All legislation that discriminates against gay men and lesbians rests upon a gender-based classification, since the applicability of such legislation depends upon the gender of the parties. The domestic violence statutes being analyzed here are therefore inherently suspect, since they discriminate against gay men and lesbians. Although the gender argument may initially appear to be abstract and difficult, one state supreme court has already adopted and employed this argument.

* * *

A domestic violence statute that provides or denies protection based upon the genders of the parties likewise violates the Equal Protection Clause. For example, if John and Barbara, an opposite-sex couple, and Jill and Julie, a same-sex couple, are experiencing domestic violence of exactly the same sort, Barbara will be protected from John's abuse because John is male, but Julie will be denied protection because Jill is female. Therefore, just as it is race-based discrimination to deny equal protection to a white woman because of her marriage to a black man, so it is gender-based discrimination to deny equal protection to a woman because her abusive partner is female or to a man because his abusive partner is male.

C. *Rational Basis Analysis*

The most deferential standard of review utilized in equal protection challenges is rational basis analysis. In order to withstand an equal protection challenge at this level of scrutiny, a legislative classification need only be related to a legitimate state interest. When a state statute is challenged for violating an individual's right to due process under the law, the burden is on the individual to establish that the legislature has acted in an arbitrary and irrational way. In an equal protection challenge, on the other hand, the burden is on the state to provide a justification for its actions. While a state has no duty to enact comprehensive domestic violence legislation, once it has done so, it must apply the legislation equally to all. As Chief Justice William Rehnquist stated in *DeShaney v. Winnebago County Dep't of Soc. Serv.*, "[t]he State may

---

150. 404 U.S. 71 (1971).   **151.** 411 U.S. 677 (1973).

not, of course, selectively deny its protective services to certain disfavored minorities without violating the Equal Protection Clause."[186]

While it is not common for the Supreme Court to invalidate legislation under the rational basis test, the decisions in which it has done so indicate that invidious discrimination based on nothing more than irrational fear and prejudice will not be upheld. Even under this minimum level of scrutiny, "mere negative attitudes, or fear" do not constitute a rational basis for a legislative classification. In *Cleburne v. Cleburne Living Center*,[189] the Supreme Court held that, under a rational basis analysis, a city zoning ordinance was invalid as applied. When the Cleburne Living Center submitted an application for a zoning permit to operate a group home for the mentally retarded, the city informed the Center that a special use permit would be required, which the city refused to grant. The Court found that the permit would have been granted but for the fact that the home was to be occupied by mentally retarded persons. The burden fell on the state to show that it was rational to treat the mentally retarded differently, but the Court held that the characteristics of the intended occupants of the home did not provide the city a justification rationally related to the denial when a similar permit would be granted to others occupying the same site. The Court concluded that "some objectives—such as a bare desire to harm a politically unpopular group—are not legitimate state interests."[194] Thus, a domestic violence statute that offers protection only against abuse by "a person of the opposite sex" should be invalidated if a state's only justification is the fear and prejudice its citizens feel toward gay men and lesbians.

Domestic violence statutes are criminal statutes that should be applied in such a way as to provide for the prosecution of all persons who violate the law. The legislation most commonly reviewed under the rationality standard, on the other hand, involves economic or social welfare benefits. Given the wide deference afforded to legislation that does not affect a fundamental right or draw upon a suspect or quasi-suspect classification, states may put forth almost any economic argument with some confidence that courts will accept it as rational. Unlike economic legislation, domestic violence legislation is enacted for the purpose of criminalizing violent acts. Only if financial resources are insufficient to fund criminal prosecution of all persons who commit acts of domestic violence, government actors could maintain that they have a rational basis for exempting gay men and lesbians who abuse their partners. In this way, discriminatory domestic violence statutes might be upheld under a rational basis analysis.

IV. No Private Matter: Policy Considerations

The equal protection challenge to domestic violence statutes that deny protection to same-sex partners does not rest upon privacy issues

---

186. DeShaney v. Winnebago County Dep't of Soc. Serv., 489 U.S. 189, 197 n. 3 (1989). * * *

189. 473 U.S. 432, 435 (1985).

194. City of Cleburne v. Cleburne Living Ctr., 473 U.S. 432, 446–47 (1985).

regarding sexual conduct. In general, issues of privacy have no place at all in considerations of domestic violence. Distinctions that have been drawn between those areas of law deemed public and those areas deemed private certainly should not inform the policies upon which domestic violence legislation is grounded. In codifying the intent of its domestic violence statute, the Florida legislature explicitly stated that "it is the intent of the Legislature that domestic violence be treated as an illegal act rather than a private matter."[204] Domestic abuse is an appropriate matter for public concern and a reasonable occasion for public interference, not a private activity in which victims engage voluntarily or an issue of domesticity traditionally deemed private.

* * *

VI.   CONCLUSION

* * *

Battered women endured generations of abuse at the hands of their fathers and husbands. When the women's movement brought this problem to the public eye, legislatures finally responded with domestic violence statutes that condemned abusers and protected victims. Significant societal change only comes as the result of a long and arduous struggle for recognition by an unpopular group. Gay and lesbian victims of domestic violence are now engaged in just such a struggle, yet their voices alone are not strong enough to be heard. All of us must join in their effort by criminalizing domestic violence without regard to gender or sexual orientation.

State domestic violence legislation that discriminates, either *de jure* or *de facto*, against gay and lesbian couples cannot withstand an equal protection challenge. Courts should either grant quasi-suspect classification to gay men and lesbians or recognize that discrimination against them is gender discrimination. The Supreme Court's unwillingness to protect homosexual sodomy as a fundamental right is irrelevant, because domestic abuse does not involve issues of privacy, morality, or tradition. Domestic violence legislation must provide all persons with equal protection under the law.

RUTHANN ROBSON, LAVENDER BRUISES: INTRALESBIAN VIOLENCE, LAW AND LESBIAN LEGAL THEORY
20 Golden Gate U. L. Rev. 567–591 (1990).

INTRODUCTION

Intra-lesbian violence is not a new phenomenon, although the legal reaction it has provoked has at times penalized lesbian sexuality rather than violence. A 1721 German trial transcript, for example, documents intra-lesbian violence: the "two women did not get along. Because the

---

204. 1994 Fla. Sess. Law Serv. ch. 94–134, § 741.2901 (West).

codefendant complained that she did not earn anything, the defendant beat her frequently."[4] However, it was not the violent expressions that prompted judicial intervention, but the sexual ones. The women were on trial for the crime of lesbianism. Found guilty, the defendant Catharina Linck was sentenced to death. The codefendant Catharina Muhlhahn received the lesser sentence of three years in the penitentiary and then banishment, not because she was the victim of physical abuse, but because she was "simple-minded." The violence between the women was superfluous from the legal perspective: what was criminalized was sexuality.

This Article seeks to elucidate the confusion between sexuality and violence that confounds legal treatments of intra-lesbian violence. This confusion is both explicitly and implicitly revealed in judicial decisions and legislative enactments. A distinct but intertwined task of this Article is to situate intra-lesbian violence within the development of a lesbian legal theory. It is intra-lesbian violence that makes equally untenable either a separatist lesbian legal theory (eschewing all reference to a patriarchal legal system) or an assimilationist lesbian legal theory (advocating lesbianism as an irrelevant factor in legal determinations).

Before broaching legal discourse or the development of a lesbian legal theory relating to that discourse, it is necessary to clarify certain terms. While lesbians are often defined with exclusive reference to their sexuality, lesbians—like other humans—cannot easily be demarcated. As I am using the term "lesbian," it denotes a woman who primarily directs her attentions, intimate or otherwise, to other women. Lesbianism is the theoretical grounding for such attentions. Lesbian theory is not limited to sexual orientation; thus it is not co-extensive with gay rights ideologies. Similarly, lesbian theory is not limited to gender; thus it is not co-extensive with feminism. Lesbian theory, as it is being generated by lesbians in works of philosophy, literature, art and experimental forms, is a discrete body of discourse relating to lesbian life. The development of lesbian theory in relation to law is emerging. This Article is an attempt to begin to develop a lesbian legal theory relating to intra-lesbian violence.

Intra-lesbian violence primarily involves physical and emotional violence between lesbians, although it also encompasses expressions of lesbian sexuality between women who may not identify themselves as lesbians as well as violence between women whose lesbianism is at issue. Intra-lesbian violence may consist of three types of possible relationships between the lesbians. The first type of relationship, a "non-relationship" of strangers, is apparently a very rare form of violence between lesbians. The second type of possible relationship is that of acquaintances or friends within the lesbian community. The third type of relationship is that of lovers, and in this form of intra-lesbian violence the dynamics often parallel the patterns of domestic violence that have been so well

4. A Lesbian Execution in Germany, 1721: The Trial Records, 6 *J. Homosexuali-* *ty* 27, 32 (1980/81) (translated by Brigitte Eriksson).

documented in heterosexual relationships. The latter two types of relationships, of course, are not mutually exclusive, for the boundaries between "friend" and "lover" may be fluid among lesbians. Another example of intra-lesbian violence that straddles the latter two categories is violence revolving around a love triangle. In a recent situation, a woman murdered her former lover who ended the relationship and had found a new lover. In a famous historical trial in the Netherlands, two lesbian lovers were convicted of conspiring and committing the murder of a former lover. Whatever the type of intra-lesbian violence, however, such violence poses problems for the development of a lesbian legal theory. Intra-lesbian violence also proves problematic for the present legal system as it attempts to address the violence.

II.   INTRA-LESBIAN VIOLENCE AND THE LAW

The legal sanctions in cases of intra-lesbian violence have often been directed more at the "lesbian" sexual component than at the act(s) of violence. The punishment of sexuality may be explicit, as it was in the *Linck* case in which a lesbian was executed. The punishment of sexuality may also be implicit, as it was in the Netherlands "love triangle scandal," in which the crime was sensationalized in a manner in which sexuality eclipsed murder. The legal response to such sensationalism was not increased prosecutions for murder, but increased prosecutions for lesbianism.

In addition to sensationalizing, another legal response to intra-lesbian violence which implicitly privileges sexuality over violence is the insistence on the erasure of lesbianism. While this appears paradoxical, this strategy operates to insulate lesbianism from candid consideration as it relates or does not relate to the violence. Thus, the lesbianism may be denied or it may be "hetero-relationized." In modern American cases in which judges refer to lesbianism, lesbianism is often an issue of the defendant's "character." For example, in a recent Florida appellate opinion, the court rejects the defendant's claim that her lesbianism was improperly before the jury:

> Wiley further contends on appeal that her character was impermissibly placed in issue when the State elicited the fact that she was a "bull dagger"—a lesbian that assumes the male role during intercourse. This contention is without merit. The record undeniably shows that the question of Wiley's sexual preferences came into the trial as a part of her own confession. According to Wiley, the victim hurled this invective at her during the quarrel that occurred between them on that fateful evening. This accusation perhaps constitutes an explanation for the flailing received by the victim some moments later. The State's only crime here was to try to explain to the jury exactly what a "bull dagger" is.[22]

Thus, the court conceptualizes the defendant's lesbianism in a hetero-patriarchal manner ("male role") and disparages it ("invective")

22.   Wiley v. State, 427 S0.2d 283, 285
(Fla. Dist. Ct.App., 1983).

even while trivializing it ("the State's only crime"). Interestingly, in *Wiley* the appellate court does not reveal the relationship between the defendant and the victim: they could have just met in the "local night spot" near where the incident occurred; they could have been casual acquaintances arguing; they could have been best friends; they could have been lovers. In an earlier Texas case in which the victim is the defendant's putative lover although the defendant denies she is a lesbian, the appellate court is more straightforward about rejecting the defendant's claim that evidence of her lesbian relation with the murder victim was prejudicial. What is troublesome, however, is that during the Texas trial the "evidence" of the relationship consisted in part of photographs and testimony that the defendant "dressed like a man; kept her hair cut like a man; wore men's clothing, including men's shoes."[24] The appellate court is comfortable in relying on heterosexual stereotypes to confirm the defendant's lesbianism, despite the defendant's denials.

The judicial discourse relating to lesbian violence thus finds it relevant to denominate the male-identified lesbian, even absent a partner-relationship as in *Wiley*. Perhaps this denomination is a cipher for categorizing the defendant as the aggressor. It is not necessary for courts to engage in hetero-relational analogies to name the aggressor. For example, in a 1957 case involving a lesbian's murder of her partner's child, the court is rather circumspect in relating testimony of prior violent activity while avoiding heterosexism.[25] Nevertheless, most courts are at least implicitly heterosexist. In a 1985 case, the appellate court repeats trial testimony of prior violence, but also finds it relevant that the defendant "was physically larger than the decedent."[26] Even in a recent California case which might be considered a model, the appellate court's recitation of the facts is revealing: We learn that the defendant became involved with her lesbian lover after the defendant "left her husband because he had been beating her."[27] The relevance of the prior violent relationship is tangential at best, the defendant's defense was apparently based on diminished capacity due to alcohol intake on the day of the crime rather than abuse. We are left wondering why the appellate court found this fact relevant enough to include in its opinion.

Determining the aggressor in a violent lesbian relationship becomes especially crucial when the defense to murder is self-defense. In *Crawford v. State*, the appellate court provides excerpts of the defendant's interrogation in which the law enforcement officers unceasingly reiterate disbelief that the defendant was beaten by her lover and that defendant was not the "aggressor."[28] The appellate court reversed, on the basis of the prejudicial nature of the trial admission of the law enforcement officer's statements during the interrogation, after categorizing the

24. Perez v. State, 491 S.W.2d 672, 673 (Tex.Crim.App.1973)* * *.

25. People v. Steward, 156 Cal.App.2d 177, 318 P.2d 806 (1957). * * *

26. People v. Huber, 131 Ill. App. 3d 163, 165, 475 N.E.2d 599, 601 (1985).

27. People v. Gibson, 195 Cal. App. 3d 841, 843, 241 Cal. Rptr. 126, 127 (1987).

28. Crawford v. State, 285 Md. 431, 449, 404 A.2d 244, 253 (1979).

victim as the one who had assumed "the dominant role" in the lesbian relationship. While the court's conclusion that the admission of the officer's statements during interrogation was prejudicial error seems a fair one, one wonders to what extent this conclusion is buoyed by the finding that the victim was the "dominant" one.[29] The court does not relate any prior incidents of violence for its conclusion of "dominance." What I am suggesting is that "dominance" is a hetero-relational concept that may not be applicable to lesbian relationships; the operative consideration in murder trials in which self-defense is raised should be related to abuse rather than heterosexist notions of dominance that are based on stereotypical gender roles.[46]

Not only does hetero-relationality impact upon legal responses to intra-lesbian violence, but homophobia does as well. In a very recent and unreported trial apparently involving the first use of the "battered woman syndrome" defense in a lesbian relationship, Annette Green was convicted of the first degree murder of her lover Ivonne Julio by a Palm Beach County, Florida, jury. The trial judge allowed the "battered woman syndrome defense," construing it as a "battered person defense." The prosecutor had argued that the defense was inappropriate, despite his admission that defendant Green had been "battered. She was shot at before by the victim. She had a broken nose, broken ribs." Nevertheless, even with the complicated issues presented by the "battered person" defense before the jury, it took only two and one-half hours to return a guilty verdict. Green's defense attorney attributed this to homophobia, noting that it usually takes a jury much longer to deliberate, even in routine cases. One jury member related an incident to the judge in which two venire members spoke in the women's restroom about their desire to be selected as jurors in order to "hang that lesbian bitch." The court personnel also exhibited what the defense attorney termed homophobic conduct. Further, the defense attorney attributes homophobia to the first degree murder charge, although the situation of battering and self-defense was a "classic murder-two case."

* * *

III.   DEVELOPING A LESBIAN LEGAL THEORY OF INTRA-LESBIAN VIOLENCE

Intra-lesbian violence in all forms presents a complex and vital issue for resolution by any attempts to articulate a lesbian legal theory. Lesbian legal theory could, of course, embrace either of two extremes: eschewing the "patriarchal" legal system altogether; or embracing the legal system as if lesbianism was irrelevant. The first alternative is based upon the politics of lesbian separatism and upon the realistic suspicion of a disenfranchised group. The second alternative is based upon the politics of the domestic violence movement which has stressed that the "legal response to family violence must be guided primarily by the

---

29. Id. at 451, 404 A.2d at 254.   **46.** Fla. Stat. § 741.30 (*l*)(a) (1988).

nature of the abusive act, not the relationship between the victim and the abuser."[66]

Both of these extremes are unsatisfactory, yet the tension between these extremes appears again and again in lesbian discourse about intra-lesbian violence. In a fictional example, the lesbian characters discuss the relative merits of using the legal system as opposed to a lesbian arbitration to redress the trashing of the victim's apartment by two lesbians whose acts were motivated by politics. In another example, a battered lesbian relates:

> The response of the local lesbian community to the arrest of my former lover was demoralizing. Lesbians were upset—even angry—that I had called the police. "I can see turning in a batterer and calling the cops," said one woman. "But a lover? What does that say about your ability to be intimate with anyone?".... Several women put a lot of pressure on me to drop the charges. They said things like: "Oh, come on. Haven't you ever hit a lover? It wasn't all that bad." "You're dragging your lover's name through the mud. It was in the newspapers." "Do you realize that the state could take away her children because of what you have done?" They suggested setting up a meeting between my former lover and me. They volunteered to mediate so we could reach an "agreement."
>
> I can think of few crueler demands on a woman who has been attacked than to insist she sit down with her attacker and talk things out. I would guess that none of the lesbians who wanted me to do that would consider demanding such a thing from a straight woman who had just been attacked by her boyfriend.... The lowest blow came when a friend called me the day before a pre-trial hearing. "You should drop the charges," she said. "We in the lesbian community can take care of our own." "But what about me? Who's going to guarantee my safety and see that my house doesn't get trashed?" She had no response.[68]

In this instance, the battered lesbian went to court and related her story, but the "story" was partial. The defendant's lawyer "covered up the relationship" stating that the lesbian lovers were "just two good friends" and the battered lesbian "did not say we had been lovers." In addition to erasure of lesbian existence, another cost of resort to legal adjudication could be hetero-relationizing (and thus also erasing) lesbian existence. In yet another instance, the battering lesbian availed herself of the judicial procedure to contest the restraining order, resulting in the order being made mutual, and thus confirming unarticulated suspicions of the legal system. As the battered lesbian explains:

> I found virtually no support within the lesbian community. Of the many people who supported her [the batterer] those years, I know of

---

66. U.S. Attorney General's Task Force on Family Violence, Final Report 4 (Sept. 1984). * * *

68. Dietrich, Nothing Is The Same Anymore, in *Naming the Violence, supra* note 13, at 155, 159–60.

only one woman who actually confronted her on her violent behavior against me or herself. In fact it was through the help of friends that she brought me to court, seeking to revoke the restraining order I had obtained against her. Why didn't one of those friends simply tell her I had every right to a restraining order? Given her violence against me, the order obviously could not be revoked, no matter how justified she felt in her actions. The courtroom exposure of our abusive relationship was a horrendous and humiliating experience. Clearly not knowing what to do, the judge made an absurd, inappropriate and insulting ruling to make the restraining order mutual.[70]

Because we are only beginning our attempts to formulate a lesbian legal theory, the problem of intra-lesbian violence has not been addressed. Domestic violence in feminist legal theory is not necessarily applicable to lesbian legal theory because feminist legal theory is often based upon heterosexist assumptions. If lesbianism is mentioned at all, it is distorted. For example, feminist theorist Catharine MacKinnon explicitly connects domestic violence to heterosexual activity and heterosexualized (and sadomasochistic) lesbianism:

> Marital rape and battery of wives have been separated by law. A feminist analysis suggests that assault by a man's fist is not so different from assault by his penis, not because both are violent, but because both are sexual. Battery is often precipitated by women's noncompliance with gender requirements. Nearly all incidents occur in the home, most in the kitchen or bedroom. Most murdered women are killed by their husbands or boyfriends, usually in the bedroom. The battery cycle accords with the rhythms of heterosexual sex. The rhythm of lesbian sadomasochism is the same. Perhaps violent interchanges, especially between genders, make sense in sexual terms.[72]

The extent that lesbian sadomasochism is or is not violent is beyond the scope of this article, yet the simplistic equation of lesbian sadomasochism with heterosexual domestic violence does not elucidate the issues involved in intra-lesbian violence. Many lesbians in the battered women's movement whose work included daily confrontations with heterosexual battering theorized that domestic abuse could be attributed to disparities in gender. Yet, it soon became obvious that inextricably linking intimate violence with sexuality is problematic for lesbian legal theory. For, if lesbian legal theory were to adopt such a view, it would hetero-relationize itself in the same manner in which the legal system often hetero-relationizes lesbian relationships. To sanction MacKinnon's view would be to make relevant an inquiry into "who is the man" in order to determine the identity of the batterer. Obviously, lesbian legal theory cannot countenance such a result.

---

70. Corimer, Coming Full Circle, in *Naming the Violence, supra* note 13, at 124, 127–28.

72. C. MacKinnon, *Towards a Feminist Theory of the State* 178 (1989).

Intimate intra-lesbian violence threatens the very gendered foundations of explanations for domestic violence. To name the batterer as "male-identified" does not solve the problem. Lesbian therapists have been engaged in much work involving intra-lesbian violence, and these insights are certainly useful for the development of a lesbian legal theory. Likewise, some sociological work is beginning in the area of intra-lesbian violence. Nevertheless, neither psychology nor sociology can produce the political grounding necessary for a lesbian legal theory of intralesbian violence: what is necessary are multi-disciplinary and complex approaches.

Perhaps also useful is the work that is beginning in lesbian moral philosophy on intra-lesbian violence. In the recent work: Lesbian Ethics, Sarah Hoagland addresses intra-lesbian violence, but her focus is on its prevention:

> [S]uch actions did not come from nowhere, "out of the blue." A series of events took place, a series of actions; and finally one act or series of acts crossed a limit. When our interactions cross a limit, it is because there has been increasing and compounded failure in our relationships up to that time. And the function of the ethics I am attempting to outline concerns our interactions before they reach that point.[78]

Concerning extended harassment, in a situation in which the relationship has ended, Hoagland provides no solution even as she specifically rejects legal recourse:

> Ultimately, any words I have here are inadequate. This is a crisis, and lesbians in crisis have to use all our wit, ingenuity, skill, and resources to get through it. But there is a difference between making choices in crisis and reaching for community social justice.
>
> The problem with crises is that they interrupt all else that we're doing and rivet us on someone else's agenda which we didn't agree to, often one we wanted to ignore. However, a system of punishment ... structures our agendas too....
>
> If, instead, we attend the crisis, asking for help from friends, doing whatever is necessary to take care of ourselves, and go through the time it takes to dissolve it (sometimes years, if one can't let go), as has been happening, we may begin gaining understanding of ways to keep similar situations from reaching crises in the future.[79]

The rejection of concepts such as "social justice" and legalism is consonant with Hoagland's lesbian separatist politics, yet "doing whatever is necessary to take care of ourselves" does seem to allow legal intervention as a potential. What I find more problematic from a lesbian legal theory perspective, however, is the emphasis on structuring future actions to prevent "similar situations from reaching crises." While

---

78. S. Hoagland, *supra* note 14, at 266.   **79.** Id. at 270.

Hoagland is very explicit about rejecting the concept of "blame," such an emphasis does seem to me to intensify the tendency to blame the victim, who had she been more "understanding" could have prevented the crises.

Another critique of Hoagland's work from an intra-lesbian violence perspective is from Claudia Card. Card notes that Hoagland's conceptualization of "attending" can encompass a hostile attending by batterers who monitor another's actions: "Those who batter focus inordinately, in ludicrous detail, on those who they batter. Monitoring, more than acute battering incidents, is their great source of control." Card does not explicitly address the role of law, but she seems to eschew legal intervention. For example, she states:

> Let us see how an ethic of attending might respond effectively and well to horizontal violence among lesbians.... Counselling withdrawal of the battered is unhelpful when batterers pursue or when battering disables lesbians from withdrawing. Withdrawal of outsiders from batterers can facilitate battering. For, battery of intimates is often a highly private affair; some who would not dream of violence in the presence of outsiders will do incredible things to intimates in private. Attendance of outsiders can disempower batterers, an exploitable strategy. We may need emergency outside attendance in relationship crises to interrupt scripts, disengage, intimidate without ulterior threats, thereby controlling—i.e., checking—without punishments and without domination.[83]

The nonpunishing, nondominating "outsider" is probably not a patriarchal legal authority. Yet Card's treatment of intra-lesbian violence does implicate some sort of theory that might allow an external force—a community or a public—to prevent and censor violence. The nature of this public is unspecified, but both Card and Hoagland conceptualize a lesbian community in which the lesbian violence occurs.

Presupposing an ideal lesbian community does not usually include the fantasy of a lesbian "police force" to enforce the authority of the community's "philosophical discourse." Instead, the lesbian community may exercise its "police power" in the form of ostracism. Although ethicist Hoagland specifically rejects the concept of ostracism, as attorney Barbara Hart conceptualizes it, the issue is one of "safe space." Hart contends that the community and the battered women's movement take responsibility for providing a safe space for battered women by excluding all "lesbians who have battered and who have not been accountable to the person battered and to their community of friends." While it is unclear whether Hart is defining community with reference to the "battered women's community" or the "lesbian community," what is intensely interesting is the insistence on accountability not only to the woman battered but also to "their community of friends." For batterers who have been "accountable," the exclusion is less automatic but is exercised at the option of the battered lesbian.

83. Id. at 97–98.

While the concept of community responsibility is a vital one, the existence or not of a lesbian community and the degree of intimacy experienced within that community by lesbians involved with violence, seem to me to be crucial variables in the expression of any lesbian legal theory that addresses intra-lesbian violence. Even if one were to adopt the extreme that resort to patriarchal legal mechanisms is unacceptable in situations of intra-lesbian disputes because lesbians "can take care of our own," such a position is nonsensical if there are no available lesbians to accomplish the taking care. Many lesbians do not live within lesbian communities. Even battered lesbians who live within lesbian communities, even small lesbian communities, may be isolated. Any reference to lesbian community within lesbian legal theory to solve battering situations must be cognizant of the tendency of the batterer to isolate her lover, and must also acknowledge the segregation that the violence itself causes. Thus, lesbian legal theory cannot assume the existence of a lesbian community.

Lesbian legal theory cannot assume the character of lesbian community, even presupposing that one exists. For although much lesbian discourse posits politically sensitive groups of lesbians, for many other lesbian communities, this is simply not the case. Further, there is no guarantee that individuals within such communities will act according to their pronounced politics. Even given the variability in available lesbian communities, I think it is nevertheless possible to attempt some principles that might guide the development of lesbian legal theory in the area of intra-lesbian violence. These principles are derived from reading much experiential material on intra-lesbian violence as well as speaking with many lesbians who have experienced intra-lesbian violence and with many lesbians who devote their considerable energies to working, in legal and nonlegal capacities, on the issue of intra-lesbian violence.

A necessary foundation for lesbian legal theory in the area of intra-lesbian violence, especially as it confronts the extant legal system, is an insistence on recognition. Recognition for lesbians and lesbianism in the law is paradoxical: it demands both relevance and irrelevance. Recognition is that which does not privilege sexuality over violence by punishing sexuality, by erasing sexuality, or by distorting sexuality.

Thus, lesbianism must be recognized by including intimate lesbian violence in legal discourse and enactments relating to domestic violence. Statutes that deny lesbians the ability to obtain judicial protective orders on the same basis as married persons, related persons, or heterosexuals are discriminatory and limiting. Further, the judicial enforcement of such statutes should preclude mutual restraining orders except in those instances in which "fighting" truly occurs. The evidentiary standard should not be different in cases involving two persons of a shared gender from cases involving persons of different genders. To do otherwise is not only to erase lesbian sexuality, but also to punish the expression of that sexuality by deeming it sufficient to deserve violence.

Lesbianism must also be recognized as lesbianism. Heterorelationism disguises intra-lesbian violence in ill-fitting heterosexist apparel. Lesbian relationships are not synonymous with heterosexual relationships. This is not to say that lesbian relationships, whether violent or not, are completely dissimilar from all other relationships. Violence occurs in heterosexual, gay and lesbian relationships, and in many ways this violence may be remarkably similar. Nevertheless, attempting to adapt lesbian relationships to heterosexual ones brutalizes and erases lesbian existence. It also distorts, provokes, maintains and justifies intralesbian violence.

Intra-lesbian violence presents one of the most important issues for a lesbian legal theory to confront. Intra-lesbian violence makes impossible a separatist lesbian jurisprudence that eschews all involvement with the extant legal system. Intra-lesbian violence also makes impossible an assimilationist position that lesbians should participate in the legal system as if they were not lesbians. Intimate intra-lesbian violence exhibits the incompleteness of both the extant legal system and feminist attempts to reform that system. As we begin to confront these issues, we come closer to not only acknowledging the problem but attempting to use the law and legal theory for the benefit of all lesbians, including lesbian victims and lesbian defendants. Meanwhile, lesbians are being beaten, punched, kicked, strangled, terrorized and murdered—by other lesbians.

VALLI KANUHA, COMPOUNDING THE TRIPLE JEOPARDY: BATTERING IN LESBIAN OF COLOR RELATIONSHIPS

Diversity and Complexity in Feminist Therapy 176–184 (1990).

For all of the reasons previously discussed, and perhaps others, lesbians of color take enormous risks to come out in lesbian, feminist, or ethnic communities, and of course, in society-at-large. For lesbians of color who are in violent relationships, "coming out" about being battered is further compromised due to the history that many of the communities mentioned above have had in dealing with the problem of domestic abuse in male-female relationships. For battered lesbians of color, their abusers, and all of us who are concerned about violence and its relationship to complex institutions of oppression, we are facing the uncovering of another class of people whose presence blatantly reminds us of the continuing impact of sex, race, class, and other forms of oppression in our society.

The acknowledgement of lesbians of color in battering relationships will threaten many of us in the communities that we have so carefully nurtured over the years to protect us from those painful effects of oppression. For feminists, the existence of violence in lesbian of color relationships will represent the failure of the mainstream women's movement to adequately address the interface of sexism, racism, violence, and homophobia. If the women's movement over the last 25 years has built a credible base against White, male patriarchy at least in part by minimizing non-White and lesbian perspectives in the early development of feminism, acknowledging lesbians of color in battering relationships will surely shatter some of that stability.

For the battered women's movement, the discussion of violence in lesbian of color relationships will raise the same questions and criticisms as did the acknowledgement of lesbian battering, about our heretofore well-founded analysis of sexism and male violence. In addition, the progressive sexual assault and battered women's movements will undoubtedly be forced to confront the role of lesbians of color—as clients, residents, participants, staff, and as leaders—in our local, state, and national programs.

For lesbian communities, the exclusion of lesbians of color in many of the lifestyle norms of lesbian culture will become more apparent when battering in lesbian of color relationships is recognized. While domestic abuse is now more widely viewed as a social problem, it still has implications of deviancy not only for the victim ("Why does she stay?") but also for the abuser ("Batterers are sick"). With the stigma of pathology that is still attached to homosexuality, as well as the growing conservative backlash which has marked the U.S. social-political climate in the 1980s, the fear of increased homophobic retaliation towards the entire lesbian and gay community will surely be intensified by lesbians of color coming out about their abusive relationships.

Finally, for communities of color that have built strong ties based on ethnic pride and solidarity against racism, dealing more openly with lesbians of color in battering relationships will make those communities more vulnerable to racist attacks by attributing lesbian violence in non-White populations to "problems in the race." In addition, those communities will have to confront the sexism and homophobia in their own neighborhoods that continue to hurt lesbians of color who are their mothers, daughters, and sisters.

* * *

If we consider the racist society in which we live, and place within it the heterosexist attitudes and practices of some communities of color, lesbians of color have good reason to believe that their ethnic communities will not provide them safety from the domestic violence they are experiencing. While escape from racism in society-at-large usually reinforces among people of color loyalty to one's ethnic community, the sense of belonging and protection for lesbians of color in battering relationships is usually compromised due to their sexual preference. In addition, many lesbians of color who are experiencing relationship violence express a need to protect both their communities and themselves from the retaliation of the dominant White and heterosexual society that would use lesbian battering to further stigmatize and oppress them.

In the final analysis, the conflicting loyalties to their community, to their relationships, and to themselves become so overwhelming that lesbians of color are oftentimes trapped into remaining in battering situations. Dealing with these conflicts by clearly delineating the multiple issues involved in "coming out" about being women of color, being lesbians, and experiencing violence, along with identifying appropriate responses to each of those situations would empower lesbians of color to alleviate the violence in their relationships.

A number of lesbians of color who have been in battering relationships with White women have suggested that the power issues inherent in biracial relationships had an effect on the violence with their partners. One battered lesbian of color stated that her partner, who was White, verbally abused her using racial epithets and negative racial stereotypes while also physically abusing her. Another woman of color described an S & M ritual based on a master-slave scenario with her White partner that eventually deteriorated into non-consensual sexual and physical abuse.

Since there are no studies of the effect of racism on the dynamics of relationship violence (in either heterosexual or lesbian couples), we can only speculate on its impact and/or meaning. For White lesbians who are in battering relationships, the power implied in White privilege may manifest itself either by rationalizing the use of violence to control their partners, or by justifying the battering by their partners who are women of color as an irrational attempt to "equalize" the relationship. For lesbians of color who are in battering relationships with White partners, one of the results of institutionalized racism could be a form of internalized oppression where violence is well understood as one of the behaviors that people of color are accustomed to experiencing. This is not to imply that lesbian relationships with/between women of color are more violence-prone, since there is absolutely no evidence to support such a conclusion. Rather, lesbians of color who are in biracial relationships have often reported that the use of violence to control others is part and parcel of racism and therefore is sometimes used to explain why one could batter, or be battered. In our work with lesbians of color who are either abusers or survivors, clinicians need to be aware of the possible effects that racism has on the dynamics of violence and control in intimate relationships.

Many of the public agencies that deal with domestic abuse—police, courts, social services—have notoriously poor training or sensitivity not only about women, but certainly about women of color and lesbians. The rampant heterosexism and racism of these key service providers in domestic abuse intervention always jeopardizes women, but even more so women of color and lesbians. For lesbians of color in battering relationships, their legitimate fear of these systems cannot be underestimated. Many lesbians of color will refuse to call the police, obtain orders for protection, or press charges against their abusers due to the retaliation that they will have to endure by those agencies. It is important to understand the critical role of systems advocacy, in addition to supportive counseling when working with lesbians of color who are attempting to access these services. Clinicians must be careful and thorough in assessing the inherent dangers to lesbians of color who utilize traditional institutions that work with heterosexual battered women, and should respect the choices that lesbians of color must make with regard to those systems.

Finally, the role of psychotherapy in the "treatment" of domestic abuse has received mixed reviews by many feminists due to the traditional tendency of the male-dominated mental health profession to blame women who are the victims of violence (Bograd, 1984; Schecter, 1982). Over the last five years, training and monitoring of therapists who work in the area of domestic abuse has given therapy more credence as an option for battered women and their families (Edelson, 1984; Walker, 1984). However, there is still an absence of training on issues related to women of color, lesbians of color, and lesbian battering throughout the various mental health disciplines. Therapy for lesbians of color in battering relationships requires that the therapist not only be competent in evaluating the appropriateness of psychotherapy (vs. support, advocacy, or self-help), but that she have an understanding of all areas that affect the lives of lesbians of color, i.e. racism, sexism, and domestic abuse.

Conclusion

The multiple issues that affect lesbians of color in violent relationships are complex, confusing, and always painful. Therapists working with lesbians of color must not only be able to acknowledge this myriad of issues, but more importantly to understand the interface between them. The isolation, silence, and fear that many lesbians of color must live with daily can only be broken through that acknowledgement and understanding. By continued research, analysis, and clinical observation, the feminist therapy profession can make significant contributions in ending violence in the lives of this vulnerable group of women.

Chapter 5

SUING BATTERERS IN
TORT ACTIONS

Moving away from an overview, introduction, and examining some of the particular groups affected by domestic violence, this chapter begins the exploration of how the civil part of the legal system has dealt with domestic violence through a focus on interspousal torts.

The chapter starts with a look at the history of interspousal immunity laws and their impact on suits between victims and perpetrators of domestic violence. But as this antiquated and unconstitutional doctrine is eroded, new questions arise, such as whether there should be a separate cause of action for such abuse, and how to prove the abuse, given the fact that victims typically cover up and hide the abuse rather than documenting it. Additionally, the materials raise the issue of joinder with divorce actions—i.e. should tort and divorce cases sometimes or always be joined, and if so, under what conditions, or should they always be separate? Statutes of limitations are often a bar in domestic violence tort cases; the materials discuss how courts should handle this, including the possibility of defining domestic violence as a continuing tort.

Another article notes that the definition of "outrage" in marital relationships is inconsistently defined and based in sexist beliefs, and proposes that violation of a restraining order should be grounds for finding that the violator has acted outrageously, the basis for a claim of intentional infliction of emotional distress.

The chapter concludes with a recent case brought under the civil rights provision of the federal Violence Against Women Act, the most controversial aspect of the Act. While the Act will be discussed more in Chapter 14, this case raises the same statute of limitations issue in federal court which is often raised in state tort claims for domestic violence, and includes a novel solution.

CLARE DALTON, DOMESTIC VIOLENCE, DOMESTIC TORTS AND DIVORCE: CONSTRAINTS AND POSSIBILITIES

31 New Eng. L. Rev. 319–395 (1997).

I. INTRODUCTION

Reading from the latest editions of most torts casebooks would lead you to believe that interspousal immunity is now a dead letter, leaving spouses free to sue one another in tort almost as if they were strangers. It would be a mistake to assume, however, that this makes a tort suit by an abused spouse against an abuser a straightforward affair. Far from it. This Article explores the remaining formidable obstacles to such suits, and what might be done to overcome or dismantle those obstacles, at the level of daily practice or through further legal reform.

A significant problem confronting any plaintiff who is considering a tort claim arising out of domestic violence is her batterer, and the potential danger involved in challenging his abusive behavior. My suggestions strive to be consistently attentive to this reality, but proceed from the premise that further problems inhere first in the tort system itself, and then in the juncture between tort law and the law of divorce, as that interface is currently managed by the legal system. They also proceed from the premise that there is a world of difference between simply removing the overt discrimination against such plaintiffs embodied in the interspousal tort immunity, and making the tort system genuinely hospitable to them. Achieving this latter goal involves significant redesign of a system not developed with such claims in mind. It involves committing the system to assist plaintiffs who have been victims of a partner's violence as they pursue a somewhat particularized set of goals within the particular limitations imposed by their situations. And to the extent that it involves compromising other goals or values usually promoted or accommodated by the system, it necessitates some hard choices. Finally, the suggestions are directed as much toward practitioners as they are toward judges or legislatures. This is an area in which the legal profession can no longer expect to escape responsibility for failing to identify victims of domestic abuse, but rather must exploit existing opportunities for redress, and push for the creation of new ones.

* * *

II. THE TORT CONTEXT

A. Domestic Torts in Historical Perspective

From the perspective of many modern commentators, interspousal tort immunity has long seemed an anachronism. This has perhaps obscured from modern audiences just how durable the immunity has proved to be in many states, and how very recent its demise. Georgia and Louisiana are still hanging on stubbornly to their immunities. Florida's Supreme Court capitulated, finally, to the demand for its total abolition only in 1993. In the same year Delaware abolished the immunity for negligence cases, with the implication that cases involving intentional torts would be treated similarly, and Hawaii passed legislation generally abolishing the immunity. Missouri made the move only in 1986, in a case discussed in more detail below. Other states could be added to this list of late and reluctant abolitionists, while still others, like Massachusetts, have taken confusingly piecemeal steps toward reform, with the first steps coming early, but the last coming late. When you add to this the crucial fact that not many domestic tort suits are brought, for some obvious and some not-so-obvious reasons, it becomes apparent that there has been relatively little opportunity for state courts to "develop" their domestic tort law to fit current understandings and needs, or to tinker creatively with the fit between domestic tort litigation and divorce proceedings, even if inclined to do so.

It is also important to reflect on the ideologies that have supported interspousal immunity at different times, and those that have provided the arguments for its demise. Back in the nineteenth century the immunity was understood to flow from the even earlier idea that a woman was merged with her husband in marriage, so that as an indivisible marital unit, neither partner could sue the other on any cause of action, tortious or otherwise. The husband, of course, was the legal representative of this marital unit, and the only partner endowed with legal capacity to pursue its goals or protect its interests in court. This highly legalized explanation served to distance the legal profession from another enduring ideology—that as the head of the household, the husband, father and master was in fact privileged to discipline those under his sovereignty, whether wife, children or servants, which privilege extended to the use of reasonable physical "chastisement."

By the end of the nineteenth century, however, the Married Women's Property Acts and Earnings Acts, supported by an energetic women's movement, had made significant inroads on the "marital unity" ideology, endowing women with legal personality and capacity, and thereby recognizing their individuality. It would have been a conceptually easy matter at this point to allow spouses to sue one another in tort, as well as in contract, or with respect to property rights. And yet most states resisted that interpretation of their new laws. Missouri provides a magnificent example of this reluctance, detailed by the State's Supreme Court in *Townsend v. Townsend*, the 1986 case that finally recognized the right of one spouse to sue another for intentionally inflicted injury.[25] In a lower court Mrs. Townsend was able to recover for the damage to her clothing when her husband aimed a shotgun at her back and fired, but not for the damage to her person—under the prevailing rules that allowed her the property claim, but not the personal injury claim.

While it was possible to hang on to interspousal tort immunity simply through obdurately restrictive interpretations of Married Women's Property Acts or related legislation, reformulated policy arguments were usually brought in to provide a second line of defense. The two

---

25. See 708 S.W.2d 646, 650 (Mo.1986)   (en banc). * * *

most crucial arguments, often used in tandem, were the "domestic harmony" argument and the "privacy" argument. Domestic harmony, the argument goes, requires that a state committed to the institution of marriage—as all states are—should encourage the maintenance of marital relationships, and not provide discontented partners with opportunities for blowing their domestic grievances out of all proportion, exacting revenge for minor slights and injuries, rather than kissing and making up. Family life, the privacy argument goes, is an essential feature of society, but at the same time fragile, requiring protection from the incursions of the state. To some extent, both arguments propose, we are better off tolerating abuses within that private sphere than we would be trying to micromanage family relationships.

Both domestic harmony and privacy arguments have proved vulnerable, over time, to the feminist critique that they privilege men over women in relationships in which privacy can too easily become a license for abuse, and in which the illusion of "harmony" is too frequently maintained by male dominance and female subservience. In the often extreme cases in which state Supreme Courts have done away with interspousal tort immunity, it would have been preposterous to argue that there was any "harmony" left to preserve, and recognizing the "privacy" argument would have made a mockery of the state's power to protect its citizens against private predation. Nonetheless, these arguments, unlike the older "marital unity" argument, still exert residual influence on the legal system, just as they do on popular thinking, complicating the impetus for reform.

Because reforming zeal has until very recently remained focused on the outmoded patriarchal values and assumptions underlying interspousal tort immunity, the emphasis has necessarily been on the threshold issue of access to the tort system, rather than the deficiencies of that system as applied to domestic claimants. Their somewhat specialized experiences of injury or violation were previously excluded from the courts: remaining unheard and unconsidered by the judges who built modern tort law, necessarily, out of the cases that came before them. A parallel could be drawn here with women's experiences in the workplace. The first goal of reformers was to overcome the discrimination that kept women out of so many work environments. The second phase of reform has been to work for changes in those environments to make them practically, rather than merely theoretically, accessible to women. In both cases the first step must, of necessity, precede the second, and has enormous symbolic importance. But in both cases, the second step may turn out to be the harder struggle, requiring a level of change that stirs up resistance, and offers resisters many fronts on which to fight.

* * *

C. Stating the Claim

1. Using Existing Causes of Action

From the preceding account it becomes clear that while broken bones, black eyes, burns, and lacerations may be evidence of battery, and threats levelled directly at a partner may constitute assault, this just begins the list of abuse-related injuries. In many cases a more potent cause of action may be intentional infliction of emotional distress, especially when the emotional toll the abuse has taken is measurable in the symptomatology of post-traumatic-stress disorder. The isolating strategies may be extreme enough to constitute false imprisonment. When an abuser verbally humiliates his partner in public, making false accusations of infidelity, or substance abuse, or tries to poison his partner's professional relationship with a school or an employer by blackening her reputation, she may have an action in defamation. Illegal wiretapping may be civilly actionable.

If children are themselves abused or threatened, physically or sexually, they have their own assault and battery claims. If they witness a parent's violence, the psychological consequences for them may provide a basis for a claim of negligent, reckless, or intentional infliction of emotional distress. If their access to one parent is manipulated by the other as part of his campaign to control his partner, there may be claims, called by various names in different jurisdictions, such as child snatching, obstruction of visitation rights, or interference with custody. A child hurt accidentally by violence aimed at his or her parent can pursue a straightforward negligence action.

Could a direct victim of domestic violence argue negligence rather than battery? Why might she want to? Chiefly because negligence claims may find a deeper pocket than the batterer's own—if injuries negligently inflicted are covered by a household or an automobile insurance policy, as they usually are, while intentionally inflicted injuries are not, as is also common. Is it then worth a woman's while to argue that when her husband backed the car down the driveway, pinning her to the garage door, he was driving negligently, while the insurance company argues that his violence was deliberate, and therefore beyond the terms of the policy? I have to confess that my own enthusiasm for tort recovery for victims of battering falters when recovery depends on their participation in a "cover-up." "Covering-up," after all, is what most victims of domestic violence have done for too long before they are able to take action to challenge their abusers. In addition, all too often their abusers have tried to persuade them, after the fact, that they were hurt by accident, rather than deliberately. There is a good deal unsavory about a legal process that mimics this same distortion of reality. Nonetheless, if compensation is the priority, this may be a strategy to consider in some cases.

While it is important to be creative in considering potential tort claims, the ones most commonly employed in the domestic abuse context are certainly assault and battery on the one hand, and intentional infliction of emotional distress on the other. There is more to be said about the choice between these two. But it is worth pausing for a moment to note that the intentional infliction of emotional distress claim, so promising in many respects, has one vulnerability. It depends on a judge or jury finding that the defendant's behavior is "extreme and outrageous," or "beyond all possible bounds of decency," or "utterly intolerable in a civilized community." This community-based standard provides a good test of how far America has come today in condemning cruel and abusive behavior between intimate partners.

On the one hand, the Idaho Supreme Court, in 1993, in *Curtis v. Firth*,[60] upheld a million dollar verdict, which included a $225,000 sum for intentional infliction of emotional distress and $725,000 in punitive damages, for behavior ranging from forcing the plaintiff to participate in sexual activity that she found "repugnant," to anal rape, to mental abuse:

> [O]n numerous occasions Curtis would publicly and loudly scream at Firth if she displeased him. On some occasions she could identify the conduct which displeased him, such as Curtis not liking her cooking; but frequently she had no idea what made him angry or when he might start using profanities toward her. She also identified incidents where Curtis physically shook her so hard she feared she would fall off a boat dock, placed his foot in her back and kicked her out of bed, slapped her on the buttocks hard enough to leave a hand print, and pulled her hair as he threw her against the sink.

On the other hand, the New Mexico Supreme Court, in 1991, in *Hakkila v. Hakkila*, reversed a damage award entered on behalf of a wife who claimed intentional infliction of emotional distress.[62] The husband's behavior, as summarized by the court in its findings, included assaulting and battering his wife; insulting his wife in the presence of guests, friends, relatives and foreign dignitaries; screaming at his wife at home and in the presence of others; on one occasion locking his wife out of the residence over night in the dead of winter, while she had nothing on but a robe; making repeated demeaning remarks about his wife's sexuality; continuously stating to his wife that she was crazy, insane and incompetent, and refusing to allow his wife to pursue schooling and hobbies. The incidents of assault and battery included a time when the wife was putting groceries in their camper, and the husband slammed part of the camper shell down on her head and the trunk lid on her hands; throwing her face down across a room, twisting her wrist severely, and using excessive force during sex.

For the court, the decision was straightforward. "The merits of the wife's claim can be disposed of summarily. Husband's insults and outbursts fail to meet the legal standard of outrageousness." The court reasoned that:

> Conduct intentionally or recklessly causing emotional distress to one's spouse is prevalent in our society. This is unfortunate but perhaps not surprising, given the length and intensity of the marital relationship. Yet even when the conduct of feuding spouses is not particularly unusual, high emotions can readily cause an offended

---

60. 850 P.2d 749 (Idaho 1993).

62. See Hakkila v. Hakkila, 812 P.2d 1320, 1326–27 (N.M.Ct.App.1991).

spouse to view the other's misconduct as "extreme and outrageous." Thus, if the tort of outrage is construed loosely or broadly, claims of outrage may be tacked on in typical marital disputes, taxing judicial resources.

Decisions such as the one in *Hakkila* indicate the extent to which judges require further education in the dynamics of abuse, if they are to appreciate the difference between "feuding spouses" and a relationship in which one partner is systematically subverting the autonomy, and even the identity of the other, through cruel and terrorizing behavior designed to establish his dominance and her subordination, with measurable physical, as well as psychological consequences.

2. A New Cause of Action?

Although the injuries of abuse can be captured quite successfully through existing causes of action, especially if lawyers themselves have a good understanding of the dynamics of abuse, and use both lay and expert witnesses to good effect, an argument can be made for creating a new tort of "partner abuse," which would allow the entire history of combined physical and emotional abuse to be presented to the court in support of a single claim. Recognition of this cause of action, which would in turn support the presentation of cases not as a collection of unfortunate incidents, but as a coherent narrative of domestic abuse, might advance the goal of improving understanding of domestic violence among both lawyers and judges. New Jersey courts have taken this step, recognizing "battered-woman's syndrome as an affirmative cause of action under the laws of New Jersey."[69] In the first such case, the court explicitly held that "[b]ecause the battered-woman's syndrome is the result of a continuing pattern of abuse and violent behavior that causes continuing damage, it must be treated in the same way as a continuing tort."[70] Elsewhere the concept of a unique cause of action has been treated with suspicion, suggesting that increased understanding of abusive relationships may need to precede any such change, rather than being a consequence of it.

There is one additional danger associated with this strategy, which is that the elements of the new cause of action might be somewhat inflexibly conceived, creating a stereotype of the abusive relationship of which not all victims could take advantage. The unfortunate result of this might be to discredit the claims of some injured by abuse, leaving them in a worse position than they currently enjoy under the present "piecemeal" approach. This problem has hounded the efforts of battered women's advocates to make "battered woman syndrome" relevant to women's claims of self-defense, only to find their clients measured against an inflexible stereotype, and denied the status of "battered woman," with the new legal protection it affords, if they do not fit the stereotype. If the tort of partner abuse were recognized, would a woman who could not meet the elements of that claim, but sued her former

---

69. Cusseaux v. Pickett, 652 A.2d 789,   **70.** Id. at 794.
793 (N.J. Super. Ct. Law Div. 1994). * * *

partner instead for battery and intentional infliction of emotional distress, be met with the argument that she was merely trying to manipulate the system into providing relief for partner abuse under circumstances in which she did not qualify for that relief?

Ultimately, the strongest argument in favor of a new cause of action is that if partner abuse were understood as a continuing tort, victims of abuse would be free of the artificial constraints imposed by existing statutes of limitation. These issues of timing are treated in a later section.

3. Issues of Process

In the preceding pages I have been "fitting" the experience of abuse into the substantive categories of tort, as they presently exist, or as we might modify them. But long before a judge or jury decides on the substance of a claim, plaintiffs can be derailed by the procedural demands of the system. In this section I explore the procedural obstacles most commonly experienced by domestic violence plaintiffs, or the lawyers who would pursue their claims.

a. Identifying the Claim

Before a plaintiff can bring an action in tort he or she has to understand that what is happening to him or her is a tort, or at least can be plausibly argued to be a tort. For many plaintiffs in many tort cases this is unproblematic, so unproblematic that we do not even focus on the process by which the plaintiff reaches this conclusion. There are some cases, however, in which aspects of the process become visible as they become problematic.

A plaintiff exposed to an environmental toxin does not realize at the moment of exposure that he has been injured. * * * Sexual abuse by a therapist provides another somewhat different example. * * * Victims of childhood sexual abuse are another class given special assistance by the legal system in making their claims. * * *

For the victims of domestic abuse, the road from injury to suit is also a long one, with many potential detours and dead ends. A victim of emotional abuse may recognize that her abuser's constant put downs are painful, but may experience her pain—or depression—as associated with her own inadequacies, rather than his behavior. When the physical violence begins, she may feel that she has provoked it, and be more inclined to blame herself than him. In this sense, the batterer employs his own power in the relationship to disguise his responsibility, just as the abusive therapist does. In extreme cases, victims of domestic abuse can entirely lose their capacity to assess their own reality, and take on the perspective offered by their abusers, just as prisoners of war can come to identify with their captors. In many other cases, of course, women do appreciate, or come to appreciate, that their partners are abusive, and that the abuse is undeserved and wrong. But a woman may still feel committed to her partner, or her sense of herself as someone who can make a relationship work, and have some confidence that she can end the violence without ending the relationship. Or she may be too intimidated or psychologically depleted to take action against the abuse—whether practically or legally.

For the victim of domestic abuse who does ultimately bring her case to court, the question will be whether she can persuade a court to accommodate her situation, especially by allowing her some leeway in terms of the timing of her suit. But first, like the victim of therapist abuse or childhood sexual abuse, she has to get to the point of telling her story to someone who can help her frame it as a story of abuse for which someone is accountable. Disclosure, however, is problematic. Some women deny or minimize the violence even to themselves as a way of keeping their fear or shame under control. Many hide it from others, for a variety of reasons. What cannot be admitted to themselves surely cannot be admitted to others. But even if they are clear in their own minds about the abuse, shame or fear may stand in the way of sharing it with others. If the motivation is fear, it may or may not be a fear triggered by specific threats. Even without those threats, a woman may be hesitant to disturb the status quo or to initiate an intervention over which she may not have control, and which may backfire to her further injury. For some women, this fear will be based on prior experiences of seeking help, and finding that their situations worsen rather than improve.

It would be a mistake to conclude this discussion without acknowledging that while some of the pressures against disclosure are either internal to the woman, or to the relationship, others are external. There are injuries that are difficult to acknowledge—it is painful to think about children being sexually abused by adults in whom they trust, or adults being victimized by their partners. Society as a whole has a tendency to deny or minimize these injuries, and to mobilize to suppress the disclosures that would erode that denial, or undercut the minimization. Disclosures can undermine our faith in humanity, or the institution of family. Sometimes they will reverberate with our own experience, stirring up emotions that we have done our best to repress. Other people's stories can make us experience vicariously their pain, their vulnerability, and their powerlessness. They can also challenge us to become involved in situations in which involvement might put us personally or professionally at risk. A victim who is, quite independently, reluctant to disclose will be sensitive to cues that a listener is equally reluctant to hear.

All these factors decrease the likelihood that a woman will come forward to sue her abuser. But despite all the constraints, there are many women who do seek assistance in freeing themselves from violence, and among those, many who turn to the legal system. For those who seek protective orders, or invoke the criminal justice system, the abuse is the sine qua non of intervention, and will be exposed from the beginning. But if instead a woman chooses to initiate divorce proceedings to separate herself from her abuser, in a no-fault divorce system there is no requirement that the abuse be identified. It becomes critically important in this context that family lawyers stand ready, first to identify abuse, and then to assist their clients in deciding what responses are desirable. This issue will be discussed again in Part III.

b. Problems of Proof

The woman who reaches the point of bringing a civil suit will have to prove her injuries to support her action, and her damage claim. But this may not be easy. First, the same disclosure difficulties that stand in the way of her seeking legal assistance may make it difficult for her to document the abuse she has suffered. Have family members, neighbors or friends ever witnessed her partner's abuse, or its consequences? Has she confided in them? Have police ever been called to her home, and are there police reports documenting physical injuries or damaged property? Has she ever applied for a protective order, with a written affidavit documenting the abuse or the fear that qualifies her for the protection? Has her abuser ever been arrested or charged on a domestic violence offense, and if so has she confirmed his abuse, or rather sought to deny it, or share responsibility for the violence, so that the charges will be dropped? Have co-workers, or her children's teachers, ever noticed cuts or bruises? Have her physical injuries ever taken her to the doctor, or to an emergency room, or has she foregone medical attention out of shame, or because her partner forbade her to go, or because she was afraid of getting him into trouble? If she did seek medical attention, did she admit that her injuries were abuse related, and does that appear in her record, or did she attribute them to accidents—saying that she had fallen, burned herself while cooking, walked into a corner of the kitchen cabinet, or got her black eye playing baseball with her son in the yard? Has her batterer previously denied his abuse, and is he likely to make an effective witness in the future?

To the extent her injuries are emotional, there are further complications. While her batterer may have been less cautious about hiding some aspects of his emotional abuse, so that there are more witnesses, it may be harder to demonstrate the accumulation of emotionally abusive incidents that make his conduct "outrageous." The plaintiff will also have to prove the causal linkage between his abuse, and the symptoms of emotional distress she is manifesting. Courts may ask whether her symptoms are not the consequence simply of marital discord or the stress of separation. Alternatively, if she has also been the victim of physical or sexual abuse in the past, whether as a child or an adult, her abuser may argue that her symptoms are the residue of that experience, and that her characterization of his behavior is distorted by that earlier history.

To the extent her claims derive from sexual aggression on the part of her abuser—rape or sexual assault—she may be handicapped not only by the unwitnessed nature of these violations, but by the fact that she very quickly learned not to resist him strenuously, but instead tried to minimize her injuries by acquiescing in his demands. In this as in so many other contexts, courts may have trouble distinguishing between consensual and nonconsensual sexual activity.

While some of these problems of proof may be relatively intractable, there are steps that can be taken to help women build the record of abuse that may later support their efforts to hold the abuser accountable. First, whenever a woman is being interviewed, whether by police or by a service provider, in the context of abuse or suspected abuse, she should be interviewed separately from her abuser. She should be asked specific questions about abuse. All records of injuries sustained should be specific and detailed, and if possible accompanied by photographs taken while those injuries are still fresh. Second, even if the woman denies the abuse, and attributes her injuries to a different source, the reporter should have room within the report to note that in his or her opinion the woman's explanation is inconsistent with the physical evidence or symptoms. At the same time, care must be taken that the documentation of abuse-related injuries does not put the woman at greater risk of subsequent abuse by an angry partner; and that the confidentiality of her medical records is scrupulously maintained, so that she controls any subsequent access to them, or utilization of them.

At the time the woman is seeking to take action against her abuser, careful interviewing of both her and others may uncover more witnesses than she initially identifies. If, for a period of time, she was denying the fact of her abuse or minimizing it, she may have convinced herself that others were unaware, and those others may have acted as if they were indeed oblivious to what was going on, when in fact they saw and heard enough to corroborate her testimony of abuse. While using children as witnesses is always something to be approached with considerable care, children are almost always aware of abuse in their homes. Parents may need and want to think that their children are asleep, or out of earshot, but sympathetic questioning will usually dispel that illusion. Finally, a thorough psychological assessment will be invaluable in documenting the emotional consequences of abuse, and allowing their measurement on scales that should serve to distinguish these injuries from the less severe emotional wear and tear associated with marital conflict or separation.

c. Statutes of Limitation

Traditionally, statutes of limitation require that actions for battery or assault be brought within two, or at most three years after the incident on which they are based. The corresponding limitation periods for intentional infliction of emotional distress are sometimes a little more generous—ranging between one and six years. Based on what was said earlier about the nature of abusive relationships and the time it may take for an abused partner to take action, if these limitation periods are imposed without modification, she is likely to be able to sue for only a small portion of her total injury.

The most successful litigation strategy to date has been to argue that partner abuse should be understood as a continuing tort, and a cumulative injury, so that statutes of limitation begin to run only when the abuse stops, which will be when the partners separate, unless the abuser continues to terrorize his partner, either to punish her, or in the hopes of bringing her back into the relationship. But, and this is an important qualification, the argument appears to have been successful, at least at the appellate level, only for claims of intentional infliction of emotional distress, not for claims based on physical injury. With respect to these more concrete incidents of physical abuse, courts have tended to adhere to the shorter limitation periods associated with battery and assault, and to insist on viewing each incident separately.

The consequence of this approach is that the physical and emotional components of the relationship become artificially separated, whereas in truth the threat or reality of physical abuse is one potent source of the cumulative emotional impact of abuse. Do judges expect juries to distinguish, and exclude, emotional injuries associated with incidents of physical violence, while awarding damages based on other emotional injuries? If instead the theory is that all emotional injuries can be included, as part of the cumulative impact of the abuse, it seems illogical to exclude more tangible injuries flowing from the very same incidents. It may be that jury discretion is, in practice, what rescues this system from its own illogic. It may also be that judges view this position as a compromise that does rough justice by "splitting the difference" between the justice of plaintiffs' claims, and defendants' arguments that they deserve the traditional protection provided by statutes of limitation against fading memories, lost witnesses, and missing documentation. If it were the goal instead to bring judicial application of statutes of limitation into line with the reality of abusive relationships, some other possibilities might be worth exploring.

The first would be to push a little harder for the recognition of the cumulative and intimately connected impact of both the physical and emotional or psychological dimensions of abuse, so that both, in the particular context of an abusive relationship, could be considered continuing torts. From a conceptual point of view it might seem best to make this point by creating a new tort of partner abuse, which would be characterized precisely by its cumulative or "continuing" character. This has been the strategy followed by the New Jersey courts in recognizing "battered woman's syndrome" as creating an independent cause of action. In the *Giovine* case, the court dealt specifically with the impact of this new cause of action on existing statutes of limitation, holding that those statutes would be tolled, and the plaintiff "entitled to sue her husband for damages attributable to his continuous tortious conduct resulting in her present psychological condition," provided she could introduce expert testimony to prove that she did indeed suffer from the syndrome, as the court defined it, and could show that she had taken no previous action to remedy her situation. However, the potential rigidity introduced by these conditions, as well as the failure of other courts to adopt the New Jersey approach, suggest the wisdom of a diversified strategy.

Another alternative is to accept the "continuing-tort" fix for emotional injuries, but make some additional arguments, applicable to both physical and emotional injuries, for tolling otherwise applicable statutes of limitation in the context of abuse. One such argument would be that to the extent victims remain in abusive relationships out of the desire to make them work—seeking to end the violence without ending the relationship—they are expressing the very values that supported the old interspousal tort immunity. In essence, they are seeking to restore marital harmony to a relationship disrupted by violence. The immunity was flawed in imposing that value on marital partners, whether or not they shared it. But to the extent an abused partner embraces that value as her own, we should not penalize her by jeopardizing her ability to recover for her injuries if her efforts are sabotaged by further abuse. Rather, the legal system should recognize her efforts by preserving her right to sue.

If instead her failure to take action sooner is the result of intimidation, then her argument for tolling applicable statutes of limitation is an argument based on duress. Even if her abuser does not say in so many words: "Sue me and you are dead," or "Sue me and you'll be sorry," the underlying theory is the same. She fears, with reason, that any action taken to separate herself from her abuser, or confront him with his abuse, will result in serious injury or death to her, and for the time being chooses what appears to be the lesser of two evils. In *Giovine*, the New Jersey court linked its recognition of abuse as a continuing tort to earlier cases tolling statutes of limitation in the context of duress, when the duress "is either an element of or inherent in the underlying cause of action."[121] The court stated that "within certain limits, a prospective defendant's coercive acts and threats may rise to such a level of duress as to deprive the plaintiff of his freedom of will and thereby toll the statute of limitations." Other states have similarly held that duress can be an appropriate ground for tolling, although not in the specific context of abuse.

A third argument is that the abuser's power over his partner prevents her from being able to frame her abuse as a wrong for which he is responsible, and seek to hold him accountable. Like the sexual abuse victim of a therapist, she needs distance from this inherently unequal relationship to see the exploitation for what it is and to summon the independence to challenge it. In the context of therapist abuse, courts place great weight on the professional "tools" that make the patient vulnerable to exploitation, but the equally effective "tools" of the batterer give his victim's claim just as much force.

In *Giovine*, in addition to the duress analogy discussed earlier, the court analogized the plaintiff's situation to others in which "insanity," induced by the defendant's conduct, had been held to toll a statute of limitation. Insanity, according to the court, meant " 'such a condition of mental derangement as actually prevents the sufferer from understanding his (or her) legal rights or instituting legal action' " and was a concept broad enough to encompass "the status of a victim of repeated violence within the marital setting, who may 'sink into a state of

121. Giovine, 663 A.2d at 116.

psychological paralysis and become unable to take any action at all to improve or alter the situation.'" While this may be an argument applicable to the situation of some women, it should not be used to the exclusion of duress, which recognizes constraint without attaching a potentially pejorative label to its victim, or to the exclusion of a theory that emphasizes the emotional grip of the batterer, and his abuse of power, rather than his partner's impairment.

It would be possible to litigate these arguments separately, as seemed most appropriate in each individual case. It might be more effective, however, to urge that every abusive relationship of any dura- tion will fit into one or more category, and that litigation would be streamlined, and justice better served, by creating a tolling provision universally applicable in partner-abuse cases, whereby any applicable statute of limitation would begin to run only when the abuse ended, whether that occurred at the time of separation, or subsequently. This might be more likely to come from a legislature than from the judiciary. To adopt such a provision would be to recognize that merely abolishing the interspousal tort immunity does not in fact equip spouses to redress their grievances against one another, when those grievances arise out of abuse. The tolling provision recognizes that intimate relationships con- tinue to require somewhat special treatment within the legal system: room for partners with positive aspirations for their relationships to seek to work out their differences, without compromising their claims, and room for partners whose independence has been compromised in their relationship to recover sufficient autonomy to assert their rights as individuals.

III.   The Divorce Context

The reason the juxtaposition of domestic torts and divorce is so potent is that in so many cases the first time the victim of domestic violence will be able even to contemplate a tort action is when she decides to initiate a divorce action. At this stage, something has now happened to tip the balance, to make separation from her abuser feel either safe, or in any event less dangerous, physically and emotionally, than trying to maintain the relationship. Perhaps the level of violence has become life-threatening. Perhaps it is spilling over onto the children. Perhaps the police have come to the house, and through a restraining order or criminal process the woman has made contact with a victim- witness advocate who has expanded her sense of the options available to her. Perhaps a friend's patient insistence that she does not deserve to be treated this way has eroded her partner's hold on her. For whatever reason, she has shifted from efforts to minimize the abuse and contain it "at home," to invoking the legal system to help her put it behind her. If she has, in addition, retained the services of a family lawyer, she also has access to new information, not only about the dissolution of her mar- riage, but also about her rights and options with respect to a tort claim.

On the other hand, the barriers to suit we have already identified are still there. And a new set of questions about the relationship between the divorce proceedings and any cause of action in tort will have to be answered. Thus far, courts around the country have responded in a bewildering variety of ways to the question of whether, and under what circumstances, the civil cause of action can be pursued simultaneously with, or subsequent to, the divorce. And even when it can, the lawyer and her client will have to decide whether it provides a useful supplemental or alternative mechanism for sorting out her financial claims—measured against the financial settlement that will accompany the divorce.

In the sections that follow I first return to the questions of process already identified—asking how the context of divorce, and the relationship between a woman and her family lawyer, affects the identification of the tort claim, problems of proof, and the impact of statutes of limitation. Then I turn to the new question of how different states have regulated the relationship between the divorce proceedings and the tort claim, and the somewhat different question of what an optimal relationship might be.

A.   Issues of Process Revisited

1.   Identifying the Claim: The Crucial Role of the Family Lawyer

The fact that a woman is seeking a divorce because of physical and/or emotional abuse in her marital relationship does not mean that she will spontaneously share that information with her lawyer. Shame may still be a powerful inhibitor. Further, the very boldness of the step she is considering taking may exacerbate her fears about her partner's potential for future abuse. She may want to minimize her present danger by minimizing the extent to which the divorce exposes his abuse. She may hope that by appeasing him, to the extent that is possible, consistent with pursuing the divorce, she will be better positioned to achieve her goals, first among which are likely to be an end to the abuse, and custody of her children. Ultimately the decision about whether to disclose the abuse, first to her lawyer, and then to the court, must rest with the client. Nonetheless, there is plenty of room for the family lawyer to improve the chances that her client will at least take the first step of sharing the information with her, and plenty of reasons why working towards that initial disclosure can be crucial both to her client's safety, and to effective representation.

Are there reasons why a family lawyer may be reluctant to ask about abuse, above and beyond the issues we all struggle with, and which have already been described? An additional factor, in this context, may be that the family law system has traditionally organized itself without reference to partner violence. Even in the most recent editions of family law casebooks partner violence scarcely appears as a topic, and as a consequence many family law courses still ignore it. Neither practitioners nor judges, that is to say, have traditionally learned about domestic violence in the course of their law school training.

Even more significant may be the prevailing ideology of family courts, which emphasizes the mediated resolution of conflict, the desirability of minor children continuing to have significant relationships with both parents, and the development of stable post-divorce relationships between parents in the interests of children. In this context, the partner who seeks to avoid mediation on the grounds that her relationship with an abusive spouse precludes bargaining on a level playing field, and puts her at risk; or the parent who seeks to oppose shared custody or supervised visitation, on the grounds that it endangers her or her children, upsets the smooth functioning of the system, and is readily cast as a pariah. Such women are often suspected of manipulating the system for their own advantage, distorting the truth, or turning their children against their former partners out of vindictiveness. In this context it sometimes seems that the increased public attention and sympathy given to domestic violence victims nationally has produced a backlash, generating more intense suspicion and fear that "alleged" victims will play on public sympathy to gain unfair advantage. Anecdotal evidence abounds, although there are no reputable empirical studies to support either the proposition that women routinely fabricate stories of abuse themselves, or the proposition that they successfully "plant" such stories in their children.

* * *

Thus far the emphasis here has been on the lawyer's need for information about the abuse in order to adequately represent her client in the divorce proceedings. But in addition, my argument is that the lawyer must elicit sufficient information to be able to advise her client about the possibility of an action in tort, the potential value of such a suit, and how it would relate to the divorce proceedings. The extent to which the family lawyer would remain involved with the tort action, rather than referring her client to another attorney, would depend in part on her own expertise and choice, the timing of the two proceedings, and the extent to which the particular jurisdiction demanded coordination of the two.

* * *

2.   *Problems of Proof and Statutes of Limitation*

Again, the question here is how the family lawyer can help her client address the problems of proving abuse, and building a strong civil claim despite the barriers imposed by statutes of limitation. With respect to problems of proof there are two different contributions the lawyer may be able to make. The first, already suggested earlier, is to unearth, through careful questioning, sources of corroboration that the woman herself may initially overlook, for abuse that may have occurred over a lengthy period of time, in private, and never been officially documented. The second is to assist her client in planning to document any ongoing abuse. Because the woman's steps toward ending the relationship will put such pressure on her abuser to reassert control over her, the period during which the lawyer will be working with her will be a volatile one, and it is to be expected that the abuser will threaten her in various ways. He may show up at her home, her workplace, or at the children's school, and make scenes. He may threaten harm to her property, to her, to their children, to other family members or friends, or to himself. He may act upon those threats. At one level the purpose of safety planning is to minimize the chances that he will make good on any of those threats. But to the extent his threats, and any acts in pursuance of them, can be recorded, it will be that much easier to establish the abusive nature of the relationship. And the history of abuse will become more credible, even if the supporting evidence is thin, if it seems consistent with contemporary abuse.

With respect to applicable statutes of limitation, the lawyer may also have some role to play. If the fear or expectation is that periods of limitation will be strictly construed, then the most important goal will be to document thoroughly any contemporary abuse, and any abuse within the qualified period. To the extent that there may be judicial flexibility, then it will be important to build the case for tolling the limitation periods under whatever theories have already been successful in the jurisdiction, or seem to fit the case most comfortably. Certainly the lawyer should help her client develop a narrative that stresses the continuing and cumulative nature of the abuse and its associated injuries, whether physical or emotional.

B.   The Divorce/Tort Interface

Suppose now that the family lawyer has identified the abuse, and has determined that sufficient proof can be gathered to support a substantial claim likely to survive, at least in significant part, a statute of limitations challenge. Should that claim be brought? Must it be combined with the divorce proceedings or can it be pursued separately? If it can be brought separately, should it be brought contemporaneously with, or after the divorce proceeding? This is a problem that presents itself differently in different states—the one commonality seems to be that it puts stress on a system not designed for this combination of claims. As the lawyer assesses the available options her top priorities must be how best to preserve her client's physical and emotional safety, while trying to ensure that the ultimate financial settlement properly reflects the abuser's responsibility for the injuries he has inflicted.

1.   Together or Apart?

New Jersey provides an example of a state that insists on divorce and tort claims being joined, on the grounds that "all claims between the same parties arising out of or relating to the same transactional circumstances (should) be joined in a single action."[154] In New Jersey, it seems that an intentional tort committed by one spouse against the other is considered a "constituent element" of the divorce action, even when the divorce is not fault-based. New Jersey's position, which subsequent

---

154.   Brown v. Brown, 506 A.2d 29, 32   (N.J.Super.Ct.App.Div.1986); * * *.

caselaw has revealed to be less than absolute, is surely influenced by the fact that under state law, wrongful marital conduct can be considered in a divorce case, and an award made for that conduct. New Jersey courts have also been careful to preserve a claimant's right to jury trial when her tort claims are sufficiently divisible from the other claims in the divorce proceeding. Nonetheless, the courts' reasoning seems insufficiently attentive to the reality of divorce proceedings in the context of abusive relationships, as the remainder of this discussion will clarify.

A number of states, among them Arizona, Colorado, New Hampshire, Illinois, Utah and Vermont, forbid joining a tort claim with a divorce action. These states see tort actions and divorce proceedings as fundamentally distinct. Some emphasize that divorce statutes do not provide courts with the authority to award a spouse a money judgment for an intentional tort committed by the other. Divorce is about terminating the relationship, and allocating resources, generally on a no-fault basis. Torts are about compensation for an identified wrong. Moreover, divorce proceedings are equitable and tort claims legal; either a tort claimant forced into family court might lose her right to jury trial, or the very equitable nature of the divorce proceedings might be compromised by the inclusion of "matters of law." Yet other states, including Alaska, Arkansas, Idaho, Texas and Wisconsin, take the view that the tort claim may be combined with the divorce, but need not be. The same reasons articulated by courts that have forbidden joinder appear to guide those courts that permit but do not require it.

2. Simultaneous or Subsequent?

Typically, the issue of joinder arises when an abused partner seeks to bring a tort action after the divorce, and the defendant seeks to have the action dismissed, on the grounds that the divorce settlement has already provided a full and final disposition of all claims between the former partners. If joinder is required, as in New Jersey, the later tort claim will almost inevitably be dismissed. The most crucial consequence of allowing the claims to be brought separately, therefore, is that it opens the way for a subsequently filed tort claim. But not all such claims will be permitted to go forward. Courts have variously used doctrines of *res judicata*, equitable estoppel, and waiver to bar certain tort actions when brought by one divorced partner against the other.

If joinder is forbidden, it is hardly possible for the defendant in the tort action to argue *res judicata*. As the Connecticut Supreme Court recently explained in this context:

> [T]he doctrine of *res judicata*, or claim preclusion, [provides that] a former judgment on a claim, if rendered on the merits, is an absolute bar to a subsequent action on the same claim. A judgment is final not only as to every matter which was offered to sustain the claim, but also as to any other admissible matter which might have been offered for that purpose.[167]

---

167. Delahunty, 674 A.2d at 1294 (alter-   ations in original).

How can a claim that cannot be made in the context of the divorce proceeding be resolved by it? But arguments still may be advanced that the plaintiff is equitably estopped from pursuing the claim, or that the divorce judgment or settlement contained an express or implied waiver of the claim. Both these topics are developed further below. In those states that neither mandate nor prohibit joinder as a blanket rule, on the other hand, courts will inevitably be asked to determine whether principles of *res judicata* preclude some number of tort actions brought subsequent to divorce proceedings in which a partner's abuse was arguably already addressed. Issues of waiver or equitable estoppel will be relevant in this context as well.

a. *Res Judicata*

There are a number of decisions in which *res judicata* has been used to bar plaintiffs from bringing tort actions after their divorces on the grounds that the issue of their partners' abuse was fully addressed in the context of the divorce. The crucial question here is how ready a court will be to reach that conclusion. In the 1987 Tennessee case of *Kemp v. Kemp*,[168] for example, a Court of Appeals applied *res judicata* to bar an abused wife's tort claim, because the divorce court had ordered the husband to pay the past and future medical bills associated with his abuse. The court admitted that the two causes of action were not the same, but concluded that because of this award she had "in effect ... prevailed on a tort claim." While the court stopped short of saying that all tort actions must be joined to divorce actions when the injuries occur during marriage, it nonetheless espoused a broad application of *res judicata*, suggesting that "principles of *res judicata* apply not only to issues actually raised and finally adjudicated in prior litigation, but to 'all claims and issues which were relevant and which could reasonably have been litigated in a prior action.' " Similarly, in an Alabama case in 1988, an abused wife was precluded from bringing a tort suit subsequent to the divorce, on the grounds that the issues of continuing health insurance and payment of her medical bills had been central to the divorce settlement negotiations.[171] The divorce court had approved the settlement, and was aware of the wife's claims that her husband's abuse had resulted in a ruptured disc for which she required surgery.

On the other hand, the Eleventh Circuit, applying Alabama law in a 1989 case, found that a subsequent tort suit for battery, intentional infliction of emotional distress and outrage was not barred when the husband's abuse was not the basis of the no-fault divorce, even though the injunctive terms of an earlier protective order obtained by the wife were merged with the divorce decree.[173] In 1988, a Michigan Court of Appeals refused to bar a later-filed assault and battery and intentional infliction of emotional distress claim, even though the divorce court had

---

168. 723 S.W.2d 138, 139–40 (Tenn.Ct. App.1986).

171. See Smith v. Smith, 530 So. 2d 1389, 1391 (Ala.1988).

173. See Abbott v. Williams, 888 F.2d 1550, 1552–55 (11th Cir.1989).

divided marital property according to the parties' fault.[174] Also in 1988, the Idaho Supreme Court allowed a subsequent tort action, concluding that even though Idaho trial courts have the jurisdiction to address and resolve issues of intentional wrongful conduct occurring in the course of a marriage in the context of dissolution proceedings, an exception to the court's traditional interpretation of *res judicata* should be recognized in cases involving abuse.[175] And in the same year the Massachusetts Supreme Court declined to apply *res judicata* in a tort action in which evidence of the husband's abuse and the wife's resultant injuries were introduced during the earlier divorce proceedings, when the divorce was granted based on irretrievable breakdown of the marriage. The probate judge did not specify what factors had influenced his award of alimony and his division of marital property.[176]

b. Equitable Estoppel

Massachusetts, while roundly rejecting a mandatory joinder approach, and appearing sympathetic to arguments against the application of *res judicata* to subsequently filed tort suits, has nonetheless used the doctrine of equitable estoppel to create strong incentives for lawyers to bring divorce and tort suits simultaneously. This is the practical result of two defining decisions. In the first, *Heacock I*, the Supreme Court rejected the defendant's argument that his former wife's tort claim was precluded by their earlier divorce. On remand, however, the trial court found that the abusive husband had been disadvantaged by not knowing, at the time of his divorce, that his wife was planning the later tort claim. The claim was therefore disallowed, on the grounds of equitable estoppel, and this ruling was upheld on appeal in a case known as *Heacock II*.[178]

* * *

A dramatic contrast to *Heacock II* is provided by a 1987 Wisconsin case, *Stuart v. Stuart*, in which an abused wife brought a tort suit for assault, battery, and intentional infliction of emotional distress three months following the conclusion of a no-fault divorce proceeding.[185] The divorce and the division of the marital estate were based on a stipulation that there had been "a full disclosure of all assets, debts, and other ramifications of the marriage." As in *Heacock II*, the husband argued that the wife's failure to mention her potential tort claims in the context of the divorce proceeding should preclude the suit on the basis of *res judicata*, waiver, and equitable estoppel. The trial court agreed, concluding that it was " 'absolutely unconscionable' that she would negotiate ... her divorce and advise the court that it was based upon full disclosure when she knew a civil lawsuit would be filed immediately after

---

174. See McCoy v. Cooke, 419 N.W.2d 44, 46 (Mich.Ct.App.1988). * * * see also Karp & Karp, supra note 53, at 64.

175. See Nash v. Overholser, 757 P.2d 1180, 1180 (Idaho 1988).

176. See Heacock v. Heacock (Heacock I), 520 N.E.2d 151, 152 (Mass. 1988); * * *

178. Heacock v. Heacock (Heacock II), 568 N.E.2d 621 (Mass. App. Ct. 1991). * * *

185. See Stuart v. Stuart, 410 N.W.2d 632, 634 (Wis.Ct.App.1987).

the divorce was granted." So strong was the trial court's reaction that it described the tort suit as "an abuse of the judicial system," and agreed with the husband that it was "brought in bad faith and solely for the purposes of harassment and malicious injury." On the basis that the claim was frivolous, the court awarded the husband $10,000 for his legal expenses in responding to it.

The appeals court saw the case entirely differently. It saw no basis for the application of *res judicata*. The issues litigated in the divorce proceedings were: "the termination of the marriage and the equitable division of the marital estate," without regard to the fault of the parties. "Consequently, in making the financial allocation between the parties, the court could not consider one spouse's tortious conduct or, based upon that conduct, award the injured spouse punitive damages or compensatory damages for past pain, suffering, and emotional distress." Since "divorce and tort actions do not easily fit within the framework of a single trial," the objectives of *res judicata*, which the court identified as "judicial economy and the conservation of those resources parties would expend in repeated and needless litigation," would not be met by demanding a single trial in these circumstances. In addition, the appeals court believed that it would be fundamentally unfair to the wife to apply *res judicata*, because the divorce proceeding "did not provide an opportunity for a full and fair determination of (her) tort claim."

The appeals court was equally unimpressed with the equitable estoppel argument. "Failing to disclose a potential tort claim," it concluded, "cannot be interpreted as a representation that no such claim exists." Nor was there any evidence that the husband relied to his detriment on any such representation "in achieving the divorce stipulation and the division of the marital estate," because those were "achieved according to the dictates of state law." The Supreme Court of Wisconsin affirmed the appeals court, adopting its reasoning wholesale.[196]

c. *Waiver*

The appeals court in *Stuart* was also clear that neither the wife's decision to pursue divorce proceedings, nor her failure to mention her tort claim in those proceedings, could be construed as a waiver—a voluntary and intentional relinquishment—of her right to pursue the tort action subsequent to her divorce. There was no evidence of any such intent on the part of the wife, the court concluded, and the law of Wisconsin "will not force one party to a marriage to choose between commencing an action to terminate a marriage or one to recover compensation for injuries sustained as a result of spousal abuse." Nor could her stipulation that she had disclosed all "assets, debts and other ramifications of the marriage" be interpreted as a waiver of the tort claim, even though the court believed that the claim was indeed an asset that should have been disclosed.

196. See Stuart v. Stuart, 421 N.W.2d 505, 508 (Wis.1988).

While the requirement that waiver be both intentional and voluntary argues strongly against any findings of implied waiver in this context, a more difficult question is whether to interpret release clauses, which are routinely included in settlement agreements, and subsequently incorporated into divorce decrees, as explicit waivers of later tort claims. Many courts have so found, but the language of these releases is not uniform, and decisions about their scope must be made on a case-by-case basis.

* * *

d. Later Is Better

An increasing number of jurisdictions are allowing former marital partners to bring tort claims after divorce proceedings are concluded, resisting the application of any of the restrictive doctrines discussed above. * * *

The most crucial argument in favor of allowing a woman to wait until her divorce is resolved before she brings a tort action against her abuser is that unless the legal system preserves this option, a tort remedy will be foreclosed altogether for any woman who feels that pursuing a claim is simply too dangerous, until such time as her separation from her abuser has been successfully accomplished, and a structure has been put in place that sets limits to his interactions with her and her children. If she is forced to pursue the tort claim together with the divorce, or even to notify the probate court that she is bringing it, or plans to bring it in another court, she may well forfeit the claim to buy her safety. But if the legal system encourages or facilitates this choice, it rewards her abuser by reinforcing his belief that violence, or the threat of violence, is an effective strategy to secure his interests. As the court in *Delahunty* concluded: " 'The doctrines of preclusion ... should be flexible and must give way when their mechanical application would frustrate other social policies based on values equally or more important than the convenience afforded by finality in legal controversies.' "[220] The values furthered by allowing the abused partner to recover for her injuries, and holding the abuser accountable for his abuse, must weigh heavily in the balance.

Courts have not always acknowledged the unique constraints faced by a victim of abuse as she embarks upon the difficult and dangerous task of challenging her abuser's control, and breaking free of the coercive relationship in which she is trapped. Many courts have noted that separating tort claims from dissolution proceedings will reduce the level of acrimony attending the divorce, consistent with the goals of a no-fault system. Fewer have paused to consider what that may mean in the context of an abusive relationship. In the *Stuart* case, however, the

---

220. Delahunty v. Massachusetts Mut. Life Ins. Co., 674 A.2d 1290, 1295 (Conn. 1996). * * *

Wisconsin appeals court, in a portion of its opinion specifically endorsed by the Supreme Court, did pay attention to this reality:

> If an abused spouse cannot commence a tort action subsequent to a divorce, the spouse will be forced to elect between three equally unacceptable alternatives: (1) Commence a tort action during the marriage and possibly endure additional abuse; (2) join a tort claim in a divorce action and waive the right to a jury trial on the tort claim; or (3) commence an action to terminate the marriage, forego the tort claim, and surrender the right to recover damages arising from spousal abuse. To enforce such an election would require an abused spouse to surrender both the constitutional right to a jury trial and valuable property rights to preserve his or her well-being. This the law will not do.[222]

Similarly, in the *Nash* case, the Idaho Supreme Court reasoned that a divorce proceeding should not serve as a catalyst for additional abuse, and the Connecticut Supreme Court in *Delahunty* approvingly cited both.

3. *Managing the Money*

As courts have repeatedly emphasized, a divorce proceeding is usually not a suitable forum in which to present detailed accounts of abuse, with specific price-tags attached. Further, while the distribution of marital assets may be governed by a set of criteria broad enough to respond to past abuse, and support obligations may also be structured to account for continuing needs and disabilities, both physical and emotional, that are the consequence of abuse, both distribution and support decisions may legitimately be made on the basis of such an array of "factors," that the abuser never fully pays the bill associated with his abuse. This is problematic from both the perspective of justice, and the perspective of accountability. Furthermore, with respect to support, an award may be subsequently modified for reasons that have nothing to do with one partner's wrongdoing toward the other, or her legitimate claim for redress—seriously undercutting the message that he is responsible because of his past conduct, and the injuries he has inflicted. There is the further danger, in the context of a divorce proceeding, that an abuser will use the leverage of access to the children to make his partner scale down her financial claims. This is, of course, a charge against the family law system not limited to those interested in the issue of domestic violence—but it has particular poignancy in a context in which a woman may be very legitimately concerned for the physical safety of her children.

For all these reasons, the tort system may offer a more satisfactory process for collecting compensation. Here the only issues are the perpetrator's wrongdoing, and the injuries, physical and emotional, he has inflicted. The award can recognize pain and suffering, as well as the tangible elements, such as medical expenses and lost earnings; punitive

---

222. Stuart v. Stuart, 421 N.W.2d 505, 508 (Wis.1988) * * *

damages are also a possibility. However, some difficult questions remain about the precise relationship between the financial settlement, or judgment, that comes out of the divorce proceeding, and a tort recovery. Courts that have insisted that the claims be joined, or at least brought simultaneously, have sometimes suggested that the divorce proceeding, which would normally be concluded before the tort action, should be stayed, so that any tort recovery by the abused partner can be taken into account in distributing the marital estate and awarding support. * * *

One problem with this approach is the delay it imposes with respect to the divorce. Quite apart from the psychological importance of closure, which may provide some peace of mind for the abused partner, and an important message to the abuser that his claim on his victim has been finally and firmly annulled, there is a practical need to settle both the financial issues and issues about the custody of minor children. Courts that have forbidden joinder have frequently argued that this need for closure militates against tying the two claims together, and having the divorce be hostage to the timing of the tort claim.

An even more serious problem with this approach is the possibility that the abuser will be "rescued" from full responsibility for his abuse, if a court, looking at the issue of distribution subsequent to the tort award, when he is relatively poorer and his partner relatively richer, divides the marital estate in a fashion that favors him. * * *

If the tort action is brought simultaneously with, but concluded after, the divorce proceedings, the question will be how the probate court should address any potential overlap between the two judgments. One way in which that question is posed is whether the divorce court should try to factor the pending claim into the distribution, as an "asset" belonging to the abused partner, even though its value is uncertain. Some courts have opted for that strategy, while others have declined, on the theory that the value of an unliquidated claim is simply too speculative to warrant inclusion in the calculations. Again, the argument could be couched in terms of justice—why should the distribution favor the abuser, when his potential liability for the injuries he has caused are designed either to compensate his partner (not to make her richer, but only to make her whole) or in the case of punitive damages, to punish him for egregious behavior? The impact of those damages is surely cushioned in a troubling way if he is given more, by way of the distribution, to pay for them.

If the jurisdiction is one in which marital misconduct can be taken into account in the distribution, the probate judge who knows a tort claim is pending might choose nonetheless not to use fault as one of the factors guiding his allocation. Or he might want to use fault as one among the many relevant criteria, but indicate what influence it had on his decision, allowing the court in which the tort claim is tried to reduce its award to the abused partner by that amount, to prevent double recovery.

If the probate court does not know that a tort claim will be filed, because the abused partner has chosen to say nothing until after the divorce is concluded, the judge's options are somewhat different. The abuse may or may not be apparent. If the abused partner has chosen to disclose the abuse, and the jurisdiction allows the judge to use that conduct in calculating the distribution, then it would be safer for the judgment to specify how the abuse had influenced that calculation, on the theory that a suit might be brought subsequently. If the abuse is not disclosed, then it cannot influence the distribution, and the problem disappears from the probate court's view. It may resurface in the later tort action, if the abusive partner claims that a need-based distribution was in fact responsive to needs created by his abuse, and was to that extent, compensatory. The best answer to this problem may be that it is the responsibility of the partner who knows, or should know, that he may be vulnerable to a later tort claim to seek clarification from the probate court about the basis of the property allocation, if he wishes to preserve the possibility of reducing the tort award on a double-recovery theory.

The support obligation raises no double recovery concern, because it can be modified in the face of any material change in circumstance. This enables an abusive partner to go back into probate court seeking a downward modification of his support obligation in the event that his former mate later receives a substantial tort award. Thus, if the woman's claim in the divorce proceedings is that she is unable to support herself financially because of a temporary or permanent disability caused by her partner's abuse, her support award should reflect that current need. If the tort award then provides her with compensation for that same disability, her former partner can seek to have his support obligations reduced or eliminated. It is clearly preferable to modify the support obligation in light of the tort award, rather than to reduce that award to reflect current support payments, which can be changed for a variety of reasons having nothing to do with her need. It is also clearly preferable to leave the support order in place until the tort award is safely in the bank, because support payments are often substantially easier to collect.

As long as we have safeguards in place to deal with the limited kinds of "double recovery" issues that might arise there is little to support the idea that the Mr. Heacocks of the world are prejudiced by not anticipating a later tort action when they finalize their divorces. Could we not move to view the situation as one in which an abusive partner should be aware of that possibility as a matter of course, especially if his partner has not agreed, in the context of the divorce proceedings, to waive any other rights she may have against him? Given the prevalence of abuse, should not every divorcing partner be counseled to disclose any potential allegations of abuse against him, so that his lawyer can attend to the potential consequences of those allegations? Hopefully more and more courts will follow the lead of those who have already declared the legitimacy of the "divorce first, tort last" strategy, and those that have "managed the money" so that the abused partner can be fully compensated for the injuries she has suffered, while her partner is held fully accountable for his abuse.

IV. CONCLUSION

What more can the legal system do to facilitate tort actions by victims of domestic abuse who might choose to make their abusers accountable, and recover for their injuries, both physical and emotional?

I have suggested, first, that the legal profession needs to do all it can to create a climate in which women entering the legal system in search of any kind of legal assistance are encouraged to disclose, and feel secure enough to disclose, a history of abuse. This goal is particularly relevant to family lawyers who may not immediately recognize their divorce clients as victims of abuse.

I have suggested, second, that attention be paid both to telling women's stories of abuse in ways that make creative use of existing causes of action, and to developing descriptions of the underlying structure of abusive relationships that will encourage judicial or legislative recognition of partner abuse as a continuing tort characterized by cumulative physical and emotional injury.

I have suggested, third, that other issues of process require attention, from individual lawyers, and then also from judges and legislatures. It is the task of lawyers to assist their clients in pulling together the sometimes elusive proof needed to support their claims. It is also the task of individual lawyers to urge judges in individual cases that justice requires the tolling of conventional statutes of limitation. But it may be the larger task of the profession to urge a more generic recognition of the injustice of strict adherence to those periods of limitation in cases involving abuse, and to advocate change.

Finally, I have suggested that women are still, in many jurisdictions, foreclosed from suing their abusers civilly, because they are not permitted first to secure their safety and the safety of their children through divorce proceedings. Those states that have permitted such suits offer the model for others to follow, although each state provides a somewhat different framework in which the model must be adapted to fit.

My proposals fall far short of providing a detailed blueprint, not least because of the many variations in state law—both substantive and procedural—with respect to both family law and actions in tort. My hope, rather, is to suggest some directions for future efforts, and provoke further critical consideration of existing constraints and possibilities.

JESSIE E. THOMPSON v. CHARLES N. THOMPSON

Supreme Court of the United States (1910).
218 U.S. 611–624, 31 S.Ct. 111, 54 L.Ed. 1180.

This case presents a single question, which is involved in the construction of the statutes governing the District of Columbia. That question is, Under that statute may a wife bring an action to recover damages for an assault and battery upon her person by the husband?

The declaration of the plaintiff is in the ordinary form, and in seven counts charges divers assaults upon her person by her husband, the defendant, for which the wife seeks to recover damages in the sum of $70,000. An issue of law being made by demurrer to the defendant's pleas, the supreme court of the District of Columbia held that such action would not lie under the statute. Upon writ of error to the court of appeals of the District of Columbia, the judgment of the supreme court was affirmed.

At the common law the husband and wife were regarded as one,— the legal existence of the wife during coverture being merged in that of the husband; and, generally speaking, the wife was incapable of making contracts, of acquiring property or disposing of the same without her husband's consent. They could not enter into contracts with each other, nor were they liable for torts committed by one against the other. In pursuance of a more liberal policy in favor of the wife, statutes have been passed in many of the states looking to the relief of a married woman from the disabilities imposed upon her as a feme covert by the common law. Under these laws she has been empowered to control and dispose of her own property free from the constraint of the husband, in many instances to carry on trade and business, and to deal with third persons as though she were a single woman. The wife has further been enabled by the passage of such statutes to sue for trespass upon her rights in property, and to protect the security of her person against the wrongs and assaults of other.

It is unnecessary to review these statutes in detail. Their obvious purpose is, in some respects, to treat the wife as a feme sole, and to a large extent to alter the common-law theory of the unity of husband and wife. These statutes, passed in pursuance of the general policy of emancipation of the wife from the husband's control, differ in terms, and are to be construed with a view to effectuate the legislative purpose which led to their enactment.

It is insisted that the Code of the District of Columbia has gone so far in the direction of modifying the common-law relation of husband and wife as to give to her an action against him for torts committed by him upon her person or property. The answer to this contention depends upon a construction of § 1155 of the District of Columbia Code. That section provides:

> Sec. 1155. power of wife to trade and to sue and be sued.—Married women shall have power to engage in any business, and to contract, whether engaged in business or not, and to sue separately upon their contracts, and also to sue separately for the recovery, security, or protection of their property, and for torts committed against them, as fully and freely as if they were unmarried; contracts may also be made with them, and they may also be sued separately upon their contracts, whether made before or during marriage, and for

wrongs independent of contract, committed by them before or during their marriage, as fully as if they were unmarried; and upon judgments recovered against them execution may be issued as if they were unmarried; nor shall any husband be liable upon any contract made by his wife in her own name and upon her own responsibility, nor for any tort committed separately by her out of his presence, without his participation or sanction: Provided, that no married woman shall have power to make any contract as surety or guarantor, or as accommodation drawer, acceptor, maker, or indorser.

In construing a statute the courts are to have in mind the old law and the change intended to be effected by the passage of the new. Reading this section, it is apparent that its purposes, among others, were to enable a married woman to engage in business and to make contracts free from the intervention or control of the husband, and to maintain actions separately for the recovery, security, and protection of her property. At the common law, with certain exceptions, not necessary to notice in this connection, the wife could not maintain an action at law except she be joined by her husband. For injuries suffered by the wife in her person or property, such as would give rise to a cause of action in favor of a feme sole, a suit could be instituted only in the joint name of herself and husband.

By this District of Columbia statute the common law was changed, and, in view of the additional rights conferred upon married women in § 1155 and other sections of the Code, she is given the right to sue separately for redress of wrongs concerning the same. That this was the purpose of the statute, when attention is given to the very question under consideration, is apparent from the consideration of its terms. Married women are authorized to sue separately for "the recovery, security, or protection of their property, and for torts committed against them as fully and freely as if they were unmarried." That is, the limitation upon her right of action imposed in the requirement of the common law that the husband should join her was removed by the statute, and she was permitted to recover separately for such torts, as freely as if she were still unmarried. The statute was not intended to give a right of action as against the husband, but to allow the wife, in her own name, to maintain actions of tort which, at common law, must be brought in the joint names of herself and husband.

This construction we think is obvious from a reading of the statute in the light of the purpose sought to be accomplished. It gives a reasonable effect to the terms used, and accomplishes, as we believe, the legislative intent, which is the primary object of all construction of statutes.

It is suggested that the liberal construction insisted for in behalf of the plaintiff in error in this case might well be given, in view of the legislative intent to provide remedies for grievous wrongs to the wife; and an instance is suggested in the wrong to a wife rendered unable to follow the avocation of a seamstress by a cruel assault which might destroy the use of hand or arm; and the justice is suggested of giving a remedy to an artist who might be maimed and suffer great pecuniary damages as the result of injuries inflicted by a brutal husband.

Apart from the consideration that the perpetration of such atrocious wrongs affords adequate grounds for relief under the statutes of divorce and alimony, this construction would, at the same time, open the doors of the courts to accusations of all sorts of one spouse against the other, and bring into public notice complaints for assault, slander, and libel, and alleged injuries to property of the one or the other, by husband against wife, or wife against husband. Whether the exercise of such jurisdiction would be promotive of the public welfare and domestic harmony is at least a debatable question. The possible evils of such legislation might well make the lawmaking power hesitate to enact it. But these and kindred considerations are addressed to the legislative, not the judicial, branch of the government. In cases like the present, interpretation of the law is the only function of the courts.

An examination of this class of legislation will show that it has gone much further in the direction of giving rights to the wife in the management and control of her separate property than it has in giving rights of action directly against the husband. In no act called to our attention has the right of the wife been carried to the extent of opening the courts to complaints of the character of the one here involved.

It must be presumed that the legislators who enacted this statute were familiar with the long-established policy of the common law, and were not unmindful of the radical changes in the policy of centuries which such legislation as is here suggested would bring about. Conceding it to be within the power of the legislature to make this alteration in the law, if it saw fit to do so, nevertheless such radical and far-reaching changes should only be wrought by language so clear and plain as to be unmistakable evidence of the legislative intention. Had it been the legislative purpose not only to permit the wife to bring suits free from her husband's participation and control, but to bring actions against him also for injuries to person or property as though they were strangers, thus emphasizing and publishing differences which otherwise might not be serious, it would have been easy to have expressed that intent in terms of irresistible clearness.

We can but regard this case as another of many attempts which have failed, to obtain by construction radical and far-reaching changes in the policy of the common law, not declared in the terms of the legislation under consideration. * * *

Nor is the wife left without remedy for such wrongs. She may resort to the criminal courts, which, it is to be presumed, will inflict punishment commensurate with the offense committed. She may sue for divorce or separation and for alimony. The court, in protecting her rights and awarding relief in such cases, may consider, and, so far as possible, redress her wrongs and protect her rights.

She may resort to the chancery court for the protection of her separate property rights. Whether the wife alone may now bring actions against the husband to protect her separate property, such as are cognizable in a suit in equity when brought through the medium of a next friend, is a question not made or decided in this case.

We do not believe it was the intention of Congress, in the enactment of the District of Columbia Code, to revolutionize the law governing the relation of husband and wife as between themselves. We think the construction we have given the statute is in harmony with its language, and is the only one consistent with its purpose.

The judgment of the Court of Appeals of the District of Columbia will be affirmed.

Mr. Justice Harlan, dissenting:

This is an action by a wife against her husband to recover damages for assault and battery. The declaration contains seven counts. The first, second, and third charge assault by the husband upon the wife on three several days. The remaining counts charge assaults by him upon her on different days named,—she being at the time pregnant, as the husband then well knew.

The defendant filed two pleas,—the first that he was not guilty, the second that, at the time of the causes of action mentioned, the plaintiff and defendant were husband and wife, and living together as such.

The plaintiff demurred to the second plea, and the demurrer was overruled. She stood by the demurrer, and the action was dismissed.

The action is based upon §§ 1151 and 1155 of the Code of the District, which are as follows:

> Sec. 1151. All the property, real, personal, and mixed, belonging to a woman at the time of her marriage, and all such property which she may acquire or receive after her marriage from any person whomsoever, by purchase, gift, grant, devise, bequest, descent, in the course of distribution, by her own skill, labor, or personal exertions, or as proceeds of a judgment at law or decree in equity, or in any other manner, shall be her own property as absolutely as if she were unmarried, and shall be protected from the debts of the husband, and shall not in any way be liable for the payment thereof: Provided, That no acquisition of property passing to the wife from the husband after coverture shall be valid if the same has been made or granted to her in prejudice of the rights of his subsisting creditors.

> [dissent then quotes Sec. 1155.] * * *

The court below held that these provisions did not authorize an action for tort committed by the husband against the wife.

In my opinion these statutory provisions, properly construed, embrace such a case as the present one. If the words used by Congress lead to such a result, and if, as suggested, that result be undesirable on grounds of public policy, it is not within the functions of the court to ward off the dangers feared or the evils threatened simply by a judicial construction that will defeat the plainly-expressed will of the legislative department. With the mere policy, expediency, or justice of legislation the courts, in our system of government, have no rightful concern. Their duty is only to declare what the law is, not what, in their judgment, it ought to be, leaving the responsibility for legislation where it exclusively belongs; that is, with the legislative department, so long as it keeps within constitutional limits. Now, there is not here, as I think, any room whatever for mere construction, so explicit are the words of Congress. Let us follow the clauses of the statute in their order. The statute enables the married woman to take, as her own, property of any kind, no matter how acquired by her, as well as the avails of her skill, labor, or personal exertions, "as absolutely as if she were unmarried." It then confers upon married women the power to engage in any business, no matter what, and to enter into contracts, whether engaged in business or not, and to sue separately upon those contracts. If the statute stopped here, there would be ground for holding that it did not authorize this suit. But the statute goes much farther. It proceeds to authorize married women "also" to sue separately for the recovery, security, or protection of their property; still more, they may sue separately "for torts committed against them, as fully and freely as if they were unmarried." No discrimination is made, in either case, between the persons charged with committing the tort. No exception is made in reference to the husband, if he happens to be the party charged with transgressing the rights conferred upon the wife by the statute. In other words, Congress, by these statutory provisions, destroys the unity of the marriage association as it had previously existed. It makes a radical change in the relations of man and wife as those relations were at common law in this District. In respect of business and property, the married woman is given absolute control; in respect of the recovery, security, and protection of her property, she may sue separately in tort, as if she were unmarried; and in respect of herself, that is, of her person, she may sue separately as fully and freely as if she were unmarried, "for torts committed against her." So the statute expressly reads. But my brethren think that, notwithstanding the destruction by the statute of the unity of the married relation, it could not have been intended to open the doors of the courts to accusations of all sorts by husband and wife against each other; and therefore they are moved to add, by construction, to the provision that married women may "sue separately . . . . for torts committed against them, as fully and freely as if they were unmarried," these words: "Provided, however, that the wife shall not be entitled, in any case, to sue her husband separately for a tort committed against her person." If the husband violently takes possession of his wife's property and withholds it from her, she may, under the statute, sue him, separately, for its recovery. But such a civil action will be one in tort. If he injures or destroys her property, she may, under the statute, sue him, separately, for damages. That action would also be one in tort. If these propositions are disputed, what becomes of the words in the statute to the effect that she may "sue separately for the recovery, security, and protection" of her property? But if they are conceded,—as I think they must be,—then Congress, under the construction now placed by the court on the statute, is put in the anomalous position of allowing a married woman to sue her husband separately, in tort, for the recovery of her property, but denying her the right or privilege to sue him separately, in tort, for damages arising from his brutal assaults upon her person. I will not assume that Congress intended to bring about any such result. I cannot believe that it intended to permit the wife to sue the husband separately, in tort, for the recovery, including damages for the detention, of her property, and at the same time deny her the right to sue him, separately, for a tort committed against her person.

I repeat that with the policy, wisdom, or justice of the legislation in question this court can have no rightful concern. It must take the law as it has been established by competent legislative authority. It cannot, in any legal sense, make law, but only declare what the law is, as established by competent authority.

My brethren feel constrained to say that the present case illustrates the attempt, often made, to effect radical changes in the common law by mere construction. On the contrary, the judgment just rendered will have, as I think, the effect to defeat the clearly expressed will of the legislature by a construction of its words that cannot be reconciled with their ordinary meaning.

I dissent from the opinion and judgment of the court, and am authorized to say that Mr. Justice Holmes and Mr. Justice Hughes concur in this dissent.

MORAN v. BEYER

U.S.Ct. of Appeals, 7th Cir. (1984).
734 F.2d 1245–1248.

At issue on this appeal is the constitutionality of Illinois' interspousal tort immunity statute. The district court, on a motion for summary judgment, rejected the constitutional challenge to the statute and dismissed those portions of Deborah Moran's suit against her husband in which she alleged that he had beaten her. We reverse.

I.

Ms. Moran alleges in her complaint that, a short time after she was married to Daniel Beyer, he became increasingly hostile towards her. Her complaint details a number of disputes between the two which ended in physical injury to her. The injuries included cuts, bruises and a broken nose. Beyer's answer admits his part in the violence Moran describes, but replies that his actions were justified. He claims extreme provocation and self-defense. By Christmas of the year after the marriage, Moran had moved away from Beyer. At the time this action was commenced, the two were no longer married. In her suit, Moran alleged one count of assault and battery and one count of intentional infliction of emotional distress. Beyer counterclaimed, alleging the same.

Had the paths of these two individuals crossed under any circumstances other than marriage, the district court[2] would have proceeded to weigh their allegations and decide who, on the basis of the evidence, should win the case. However, since Moran and Beyer were married, the district court was confronted with Ill.Rev.Stat., ch. 40, § 1001 (1980), which was controlling at that time, and which commanded that:

> A married woman may, in all cases, sue and be sued without joining her husband with her, to the same extent as if she were unmarried; provided, that neither husband nor wife may sue the other for a tort to the person committed during coverture.[3]

Beyer moved for summary judgment on the ground that Moran's action was barred by this provision of Illinois law. The trial court was persuaded, summary judgment was granted in Beyer's favor, and this appeal was commenced. The thrust of Moran's appeal is that her Fourteenth Amendment right to equal protection of the laws is violated by a statute which prohibits a married person from pursuing the same remedy for the same kind of injuries which an unmarried person is free to pursue.

II.

In evaluating ch. 40, § 1001 under the Equal Protection Clause, "we must first determine what burden of justification the classification created thereby must meet, by looking to the nature of the classification and the individual interests affected." Moran argues that the statute is constitutionally suspect under both the "strict judicial scrutiny" standard and the less rigorous "rational relationship" test.

A.

We decline the invitation to declare that the interests upon which ch. 40, § 1001 impinges are so fundamental that they justify the protections of strict judicial scrutiny. It is true, as Moran argues, that the courts have come to confer this heightened protection upon certain decisions relating to marriage.

However, not every choice made in the context of marriage implicates the privacy and family interests which make certain marital decisions fundamentally important. The decision to bring suit against a spouse does not so strategically advance privacy or family interests that the decision itself accedes to the status of a fundamental right. Nor does a statute limiting the exercise of this choice constitute a direct legal obstacle to marriage. Also, the statute does not so significantly discourage marriage that it merits the "rigorous scrutiny" which has been applied to other regulations qualifying marital rights. Accordingly, strict scrutiny of the statute is not required.

---

2. Most cases of this sort would, of course, be resolved in state court. This one is in the federal system because the parties, at the time the suit was commenced, lived in different states.

3. The statute has since been altered to abrogate interspousal immunity in cases of intentional tort. * * *

B.

Thus, we turn to Moran's second line of argument. She contends that there is no rational relationship between the statutory classification and the Illinois legislature's purpose in enacting it. The pertinent inquiry is whether the scheme, which prevents a married person from seeking a remedy which is available to an unmarried person, "advances a reasonable and identifiable governmental objective." The analysis breaks down into two questions: (1) whether the statute's purpose is reasonable, and (2) whether the statute rationally advances that purpose.

Without question the purpose behind creating interspousal tort immunity is reasonable. Maintaining marital harmony is an admirable goal, especially considering the numerous social problems to which marital strife gives rise.

However, we cannot agree with the district court that ch. 40, § 1001, is rationally related to this goal. It truly would take "something more than the exercise of strained imagination," to find some objective basis for believing that depriving a physically battered spouse of a civil remedy for her injuries will advance some sense of "harmony" with the person who inflicted the injury. Dean Prosser eloquently dismantled this justification when he observed that the "domestic harmony" rationale rests upon

> the bald theory that after a husband has beaten his wife, there is a state of peace and harmony left to be disturbed; that if she is sufficiently injured or angry to sue him for it, she will be soothed and deterred from reprisals by denying her the legal remedy—and even though she has left him or divorced him for that very ground[.]

Prosser, Torts, 863 (4th ed. 1972). The immunity rule confuses cause and effect. Because the immunity rule leaves unchecked the actual cause of marital discord—such as the assault and battery committed in this case—it can do absolutely nothing to further marital harmony. Indeed, for a knowledgeable couple leery of marriage, the statute may do more to retard the institution than further it: unmarried persons living together can still resort to the courts for protection from a "partner", while a married person has no such protection against his or her spouse. Finally, added to these inconsistencies is the fact that nothing in the statute prevents one spouse from undermining domestic tranquility altogether by swearing out a criminal complaint against the other.

Other rationales which have been advanced in support of the statute are even less tenable under the circumstances of this case. While there is a danger of fraud or collusion between spouses where insurance proceeds or the like are at stake, as there is in almost every case involving third party insurance, that danger is very low in the case of intentional torts involving serious physical injury. Similarly, the fear of a flood of frivolous suits wasting limited judicial resources is unfounded. This flood does not appear to have materialized in states which permit suits between spouses.

For his part, Beyer urges us to yield to the wisdom of the Illinois legislature. This is the restrained position which Illinois courts have taken in construing ch. 40, § 1001. We do not share the reluctance of these state courts. To begin with, we are faced with facts of a more egregious character than *Steffa*, which arose out of an automobile accident. Furthermore, we cannot find it at all rational to believe that the Illinois legislature's desire to protect marital harmony is fulfilled by ch. 40, § 1001, which does little more than grant one spouse almost unconditional license to make his marriage partner a sparring partner. We are, therefore, compelled to declare it unconstitutional.

Accordingly, the decision of the District Court is REVERSED, the judgment entered on behalf of Beyer is VACATED, and this action is REMANDED to the district court for further proceedings.

JEAN MARIE CUSSEAUX v. WILSON PICKETT, JR.

Superior Court of New Jersey, Law Division, Bergen County (1994).
279 N.J.Super. 335, 652 A.2d 789.

I. INTRODUCTION

This matter is before the court on defendant's motion to dismiss the first count of plaintiff's complaint for failure to state a cause of action pursuant to R. 4:6–2(e). The defendant argues that the "battered-woman's syndrome" is not recognized as an affirmative cause of action by the courts of this State. This court denies the motion to dismiss and holds that the "battered-woman's syndrome" is now a cognizable cause of action under the laws of New Jersey.

II. FACTS

Plaintiff, Jean Marie Cusseaux, lived with the defendant, Wilson Pickett, Jr., for a period of about ten years, from 1982 to 1992. Plaintiff alleges that, during this time period, defendant severely mistreated her, jeopardized her health and well-being, and caused her physical injuries on numerous occasions. Plaintiff further alleges that defendant's actions were part of a continuous course of conduct and constituted a pattern of violent behavior, frequently associated with his being intoxicated. Plaintiff alleges that the acts of abuse and violence are too numerous to detail with specificity; however, on a number of occasions, she was required to seek medical attention. As a result of the defendant's behavior, plaintiff alleges that she was caused to suffer the condition of the battered-woman's syndrome, which includes serious personal and emotional injuries that will require medical and other attention. On April 15, 1992, defendant's final assault allegedly caused plaintiff finally to end the relationship.

III. LAW

A. *Standard*

Pursuant to R. 4:5–2, a pleading which sets forth a claim for relief, whether an original claim, counterclaim, cross-claim or third-party claim, shall contain a statement of the facts on which the claim is based, showing that the pleader is entitled to relief, and a demand for judgment for the relief to which he deems himself entitled. * * * However, the New Jersey Supreme Court has expressly held that trial courts must accord any plaintiff's complaint a "meticulous" and "indulgent" examination. Accordingly, it is in keeping with this clear signal from the Supreme Court to seek to preserve a plaintiff's cause of action that this trial court will consider the present application.

B. Battered–Woman's Syndrome

The battered-woman's syndrome was first recognized by the courts in New Jersey in *State v. Kelly*, 97 N.J. 178, 478 A.2d 364 (1984), where the Court acknowledged it as an element of self-defense. The Court held that expert testimony on the battered-woman's syndrome was admissible because it is relevant and material to establish the honesty and reasonability of the defendant's belief that she was in imminent danger of serious bodily injury or death.

The *Kelly* Court relied heavily on the then recently enacted Prevention of Domestic Violence Act, N.J.S.A. 2C:25–1 to 2C:25–16.

The Legislature finds and declares that domestic violence is a serious crime against society; that there are thousands of persons in this State who are regularly beaten, tortured and in some cases even killed by their spouses or cohabitant; that a significant number of women who are assaulted are pregnant; that victims of domestic violence come from all social and economic backgrounds and ethnic groups; that there is a positive correlation between spousal abuse and child abuse; and that children, even when they are not themselves physically assaulted, suffer deep and lasting emotional effects from exposure to domestic violence. It is therefore, the intent of the legislature to assure the victims of domestic violence the maximum protection from abuse the law can provide.

* * *

... Further, it is the responsibility of the courts to protect victims of violence that occurs in a family or family-like setting by providing access to both emergent and long-term civil and criminal remedies and sanctions, and by ordering those remedies and sanctions that are available to assure the safety of the victims and the public. To that end, the Legislature encourages ... the broad application of the remedies available under this act in the civil and criminal courts of this state.... [N.J.S.A. 2C:25–18.]

The Court stated that there is a high incidence of unreported abuse because there exists a stigma against battered women that is institutionalized in the attitudes of law enforcement agencies, not to mention the stereotypes and myths concerning the characteristics of battered women and their reasons for staying in battering relationships. However, as the problem began receiving more attention, the focus turned to the effects a sustained pattern of physical and psychological abuse can have on a woman.

The *Kelly* Court stated that the battered-woman's syndrome is "a series of common characteristics that appear in women who are abused physically and psychologically over an extended period of time by the dominant male figure in their lives."

The abuse is cyclical. The first stage is characterized by minor battering incidents and verbal abuse while the woman, beset by fear and tension, attempts to be as placating and passive as possible in order to stave off more serious violence. The second phase is characterized by acute battering, which is triggered when the tension between the woman and the batterer becomes intolerable. The third phase is characterized by extreme contrition and loving behavior on the part of the battering male. "During this period the man will often mix his pleas for forgiveness and protestations of devotion with promises to seek professional help, to stop drinking, and to refrain from further violence."

It is this third phase that explains why more women simply do not leave their abusers.

Different women have different reactions to this cycle. Some perceive it as normal, some may not wish to acknowledge the reality of the situation and still others become so demoralized and degraded by the fact that they cannot predict or control the violence that they sink into a state of psychological paralysis and become unable to take any action at all to improve or alter the situation. There is a tendency in battered women to believe in the omnipotence or strength of their battering husbands and thus to feel that any attempt to resist is hopeless. Further, external social and economic factors often make it difficult for some women to extricate themselves from battering relationships. Women typically earn less money and are more responsible for child care than men.

"Thus, in a violent confrontation where the first reaction might be to flee, women realize soon that there may be no place to go. Moreover, the stigma that attaches to a woman who leaves the family unit without her children undoubtedly acts as a further deterrent to moving out."

In addition, these women are frequently unwilling to confide in others because of the shame, humiliation, and fear of reprisal by their husbands. Thus, they literally become trapped by their own fear.

The *Kelly* Court stated that

[t]he combination of all of these symptoms—resulting from sustained psychological and physical trauma compounded by aggravating social and economic factors—constitutes the battered-woman's syndrome. Only by understanding these unique pressures that force battered women to remain with their mates, despite their long-standing and reasonable fear of severe bodily harm and the isolation that being a battered woman creates, can a battered woman's state of mind be accurately and fairly understood.

Further, the *Kelly* Court noted that the battered-woman's syndrome is beyond the understanding of the average person. Accordingly, the *Kelly* Court held that expert evidence on the battered-woman's syndrome should be admitted when it is relevant to the defendant's claim of self-defense, specifically with respect to the honesty and reasonability of defendant's belief that she was in imminent danger.

Notwithstanding, there has yet to be a civil case in New Jersey that has recognized the battered-woman's syndrome. Thus, it is this case of first impression which now addresses whether the battered-woman's syndrome is a cognizable cause of action under the laws of New Jersey.

IV. ANALYSIS

It is well established in this State that an injured party may sustain a cause of action for serious personal and emotional injuries that are directly and causally related to the actions of another person. As discussed above, the Legislature has specifically found domestic violence to be a serious crime against society. More importantly, in enacting the Prevention of Domestic Violence Act, the Legislature recognized that our judicial and law enforcement system was insufficient to address the problem. If this Act had never become law, the ubiquitous deficiency of our legal system would continue in spite of the fact that the acts listed among those classified as "domestic violence" under the statute were already criminal offenses.

The efforts of the Legislature to this end should be applauded. However, they are but steps in the right direction. As is the case with the domestic violence statute where existing criminal statutes were inadequate, so too are the civil laws of assault and battery insufficient to redress the harms suffered as a result of domestic violence. Domestic violence is a plague on our social structure and a frontal assault on the institution of the family. The battered-woman's syndrome is but one of the pernicious symptoms of that plague. Though the courts would be hard-pressed to prescribe a panacea for all domestic violence, they are entrusted with the power to fashion a palliative when necessary. The underpinning of our common law and public policy demand that, where the Legislature has not gone far enough, the courts must fill the interstices. As the Legislature stated, "it is the responsibility of the courts to protect victims of violence that occurs in a family or family-like setting by providing access to both emergent and long-term civil and criminal remedies and sanctions...."

Thus, this court will recognize the battered-woman's syndrome as an affirmative cause of action under the laws of New Jersey.

In order to state a cause of action for the battered-woman's syndrome, the plaintiff must allege the following elements. The plaintiff must show 1) involvement in a marital or marital-like intimate relationship; and 2) physical or psychological abuse perpetrated by the dominant partner to the relationship over an extended period of time;[6] and 3) the aforestated abuse has caused recurring physical or psychological injury over the course of the relationship; and 4) a past or present inability to take any action to improve or alter the situation unilaterally.[7]

In *Laughlin v. Breaux*, 515 So.2d 480 (La.App. 1 Cir.1987), the court was faced with a similar application by a woman seeking affirmative damages based upon the battered-woman's syndrome. The Louisiana court rejected the argument that the battered-woman's syndrome constituted a continuing tort. Rather, the court stated that each incident of battery and assault was a separate cause of action. Thus, the plaintiff was precluded from recovering damages for incidents that occurred beyond the effective statute of limitations period. This Court totally rejects the *Laughlin* holding to the extent that it asserts that the incidents of assault and battery were individual causes of action rather than a continuing tort. Because the battered-woman's syndrome is the result of a continuing pattern of abuse and violent behavior that causes continuing damage, it must be treated in the same way as a continuing tort. It would be contrary to the public policy of this State, not to mention cruel, to limit recovery to only those individual incidents of assault and battery for which the applicable statute of limitations has not yet run. The mate who is responsible for creating the condition suffered by the battered victim must be made to account for his actions—all of his actions. Failure to allow affirmative recovery under these circumstances would be tantamount to the courts condoning the continued abusive treatment of women in the domestic sphere. This the courts cannot and will never do.

V. CONCLUSION

This court holds that the battered-woman's syndrome constitutes an affirmative cause of action under the laws of New Jersey. Defendant's motion to dismiss Count One of the complaint for failure to state a cause of action is denied.

JOY LEE STUART v. RONALD T. STUART

Supreme Court of Wisconsin (1988).
421 N.W.2d 505–510.

This is an appeal of a published decision of the court of appeals, *Stuart v. Stuart*, 140 Wis.2d 455, 410 N.W.2d 632 (1987), reversing the

---

6. In order to be classified as a battered woman, the victim must go through the battering cycle at least twice. Any woman may find herself in an abusive relationship with a man once. If it occurs a second time, and she remains in the situation, she may be a battered woman. Kelly, supra, 97 N.J. at 193, 478 A.2d 364 (citing L. Walker, supra, at xv).

7. Nothing in this opinion should be construed to limit the application of these principles only to women in traditional marital or marital-like relationships. Indeed, in any domestic intimate partnership, the victim, whether female or male, whether the union is heterosexual or homosexual, may plead a battered-person syndrome so long as the aforementioned requirements are met. It is the unhappy history of domestic violence against women in traditional marital relationships which has given this tort its name.

judgment of the circuit court for Sawyer county, Alvin Kelsey, circuit court judge. The circuit court entered judgment dismissing Joy Stuart's lawsuit against Ronald Stuart for intentional torts (assault, battery and intentional infliction of mental distress) allegedly committed during the Stuart marriage. We affirm the decision of the court of appeals allowing the wife to proceed with her tort action.

The issue in this case is whether the divorce judgment bars the wife's tort action. The facts are not disputed. Before the divorce judgment was entered the wife and her divorce attorney did not disclose to the husband, his divorce attorney or the circuit court that she intended to sue him for intentional torts allegedly committed during the marriage. During the divorce proceedings the wife had discussed with her divorce attorney the possibility of bringing a tort action against the husband. In negotiating maintenance, the wife's divorce attorney had discussed with the husband's divorce attorney the wife's health problems stemming from the alleged battery. Prior to the court approval of the stipulation, which divided the property and provided for no maintenance allowance, the wife's attorney represented in open court that there had been full disclosure "of all assets, debts and other ramifications of the marriage." The wife stated to the circuit court that she "wanted a full settlement from Mr. Stuart."

The circuit court is not to consider marital misconduct in granting a divorce or in determining property division or maintenance. The circuit court does, however, consider any health problem of either party, whatever its source, in dividing the property or awarding maintenance. In this case, the circuit court expressly stated that it had considered the physical and emotional health of the parties before approving the stipulation.

Three months after the divorce, the wife brought this tort action against the husband. The husband moved for summary judgment, and the parties agreed to the circuit court's deciding the summary judgment motion on the file, which includes pleadings, transcripts of the divorce proceeding, depositions, briefs, affidavits, and memoranda-correspondence.

The circuit court concluded that the wife's tort action was barred by the doctrines of *res judicata*, equitable estoppel and waiver, dismissed the wife's tort action as frivolous, and awarded the husband costs and attorney fees under § 814.025, Stats. 1985–86. The circuit court stated that "it seems absolutely unconscionable that a party could negotiate all aspects of a stipulated divorce and advise the court in open court that all aspects based on full disclosure and negotiations as to property, health and waiver of maintenance, et al. have been considered, knowing at that time that as soon as the divorce is granted a civil lawsuit such as this is going to be filed. This type of procedure is an abuse of the judicial system."

After reviewing the record in this case, the court of appeals determined that the husband was not entitled to judgment which dismissed the action as a matter of law.

The court of appeals ruled that the doctrine of *res judicata* does not bar the tort action, because the divorce and tort actions lack an identity of causes of action or claims.

The court of appeals further held that the doctrine of equitable estoppel does not bar the tort action, because the wife's failure to disclose the tort claim during the divorce proceedings cannot be interpreted as a representation that no tort claim exists, nor was there evidence that the husband relied to his detriment upon any such representation.

Finally, the court of appeals found no evidence that the wife's proceeding with a divorce action constituted a voluntary and intentional relinquishment of a known right to proceed with a tort action. Accordingly the court of appeals held that on this record the wife did not waive her right to bring the tort action.

We agree with the court of appeals' discussion of the legal principles underlying *res judicata*, equitable estoppel and waiver and the court of appeals' application of the legal principles to the undisputed facts of the case. We do not repeat the court of appeals' discussion here and adopt it as a correct statement of the law.

The court of appeals then discussed whether public policy requires the wife to join her tort action in the divorce action. The court of appeals aptly stated the factors to be considered in deciding this question and correctly concluded that although joinder of an interspousal tort action and a divorce action is permissible, it is contrary to public policy to require such a joinder. We agree with the following analysis presented by the court of appeals:

> If an abused spouse cannot commence a tort action subsequent to a divorce, the spouse will be forced to elect between three equally unacceptable alternatives: (1) Commence a tort action during the marriage and possibly endure additional abuse; (2) join a tort claim in a divorce action and waive the right to a jury trial on the tort claim; or (3) commence an action to terminate the marriage, forego the tort claim, and surrender the right to recover damages arising from spousal abuse. To enforce such an election would require an abused spouse to surrender both the constitutional right to a jury trial and valuable property rights to preserve his or her well-being. This the law will not do.

> Although joinder is permissible, the administration of justice is better served by keeping tort and divorce actions separate.... Divorce actions will become unduly complicated if tort claims must be litigated in the same action. A divorce action is equitable in nature and involves a trial to the court. On the other hand, a trial of a tort claim is one at law and may involve, as in this case, a request

for a jury trial. Resolution of tort claims may necessarily involve numerous witnesses and other parties such as joint tortfeasors and insurance carriers whose interests are at stake. Consequently, requiring joinder of tort claims in a divorce action could unduly lengthen the period of time before a spouse could obtain a divorce and result in such adverse consequences as delayed child custody and support determinations. The legislature did not intend such a result in enacting the divorce code.

We address the final two issues considered by the court of appeals but not briefed by the parties. The court of appeals concluded that the wife's "tort claim was an asset requiring disclosure because it represented a possible award of monetary damages based upon alleged incidents that occurred during the marriage." 140 Wis.2d at 464, 410 N.W.2d 632. See § 767.27(1). The court of appeals further concluded, "Any damages [the husband] would be obligated to pay as a result of the alleged tort are to be satisfied from his individual property or from his interest in the marital property."

We refrain from deciding these issues and disavow the court of appeals' discussion of them. These issues are best decided when they are essential to the disposition of a case and when the parties have briefed them.

Sec. 767.27(1) requires the parties to disclose information to each other and the court for purposes of property division and maintenance. This court has not decided whether a cause of action for intentional torts against a spouse is "an asset owned in full or in part by either party separately or by the parties jointly," or a debt or liability which must be disclosed under sec. 767.27(1). We recognized in *Richardson v. Richardson*, 139 Wis.2d 778, 784 n. 3, 407 N.W.2d 231 (1987), that personal injury claims raise numerous questions in divorce proceedings. We further noted that courts in other jurisdictions disagree whether an unliquidated personal injury claim of medical malpractice is so speculative that it cannot be considered as property under the property division statute. Similarly a court may conclude that an unliquidated personal injury claim by one spouse against the other is so speculative as not to constitute an asset or liability that need be disclosed in divorce.

We need not determine in this case whether the unliquidated interspousal tort claim is an asset or a liability. The issue has no bearing on this case. We have already determined that failure to disclose the tort claim in this case—whether or not the statute requires disclosure—did not bar the wife's tort action on the grounds of *res judicata*, equitable estoppel, or waiver. Moreover, under the Wisconsin statutes a party who fails to disclose an asset does not forfeit the asset, as the husband would have us hold in this case. Sec. 767.27(1) provides that "deliberate failure to provide complete disclosure constitutes perjury." Sec. 767.27(5) provides that "if any party deliberately or negligently fails to disclose information required under [§ 767.27(1)]," the aggrieved party may petition the court to declare a constructive trust as to the undisclosed assets. If the husband should request a court to grant relief for the wife's failure to disclose this tort claim as an asset, the court would have to decide the issue of disclosure in that proceeding.

The other issue that the court of appeals discusses without benefit of briefs—and that the court of appeals need not have reached—is which of the husband's assets may be used to satisfy the judgment, should the wife prevail in her tort action. The court of appeals refers to § 766.55(2)(cm), which states that an obligation incurred by a spouse during marriage resulting from a tort committed by the spouse during marriage may be satisfied from that spouse's individual property or interest in marital property. It is not entirely clear what the court of appeals had in mind or whether § 766.55(2)(cm) is applicable if the wife should prevail in her tort action. The question of which of the husband's resources are available for payment of a judgment should the wife prevail in her tort action is not before us, and we do not decide it.

For the foregoing reasons, we affirm the decision of the court of appeals that reverses the judgment of the circuit court and remands the case to the circuit court for further proceedings. Because we reach this conclusion we also conclude, as did the court of appeals, that the wife's tort action has a reasonable basis in the law and that the circuit court erred in concluding that the action was frivolous and in awarding costs and attorney fees pursuant to § 814.025, Stats. 1985–86.

The decision of the court of appeals is affirmed.

STEINMETZ, JUSTICE (concurring).

I agree with the majority opinion; however, I write separately to suggest that attorneys representing parties in a divorce action should make sure everything is out on the table if a settlement is being discussed. If the funds are to come from a third source, such as an insurance company, there could be no influence on a settlement of property or maintenance. We have already discussed the division of proceeds from a tort judgment as between the spouses in *Marriage of Richardson v. Richardson*, 139 Wis.2d 778, 407 N.W.2d 231 (1987). However, if the funds are to come directly from one spouse, as would occur in an intentional tort action brought by one spouse against the other, this is best discussed at the time of the settlement, because it may affect asset distribution to some degree.

If at all possible, the parties in a divorce should best be able to terminate their relationships. They will have enough problems with the care, custody and support of children without having wounds reopened after the marriage is terminated regarding prior existing claims.

MERLE H. WEINER, DOMESTIC VIOLENCE AND THE *PER SE* STANDARD OF OUTRAGE

54 Md. L. Rev. 188–195, 213, 219–224 (1995).

INTRODUCTION

This Article * * * inquires whether the tort of intentional infliction of emotional distress can provide a viable remedy for domestic violence victims. The Article begins by analyzing the current state of the law. The success of suits for intentional infliction of emotional distress generally turns on the plaintiff's ability to demonstrate that the defendant's conduct was "outrageous." In theory, such a showing should not be difficult for a domestic violence victim. Under traditional doctrine, there are four factors that arguably support a finding of outrageousness in cases involving domestic violence: a special relationship exists between the parties; domestic violence typically involves a pattern of harassment; an abuser usually exploits a known hypersensitivity of his victim; and a historic and gendered distinction between public and private spheres persists, which should make violence in the private sphere seem particularly outrageous.

Notwithstanding these considerations, the use of the tort by domestic violence victims is problematic under current law. Courts have applied the tort inconsistently in domestic violence cases. The meaning of the term "outrageous" is highly subjective, and allows courts to hold that domestic violence does not qualify. If fact, the ubiquity of domestic violence in our society presents a major barrier to labelling such violence "outrageous" under existing doctrine. Further, current law creates a dilemma for feminists who are reluctant to invoke various arguments that underscore the outrageousness of domestic violence—for example, traditional stereotypes of women's role in the home.

This Article argues for a *per se* standard of outrage whereby the defendant's conduct would be outrageous as a matter of law if he violated an injunction issued for a woman's protection. Such a rule would avoid the need for a subjective, ad hoc inquiry into the outrageousness of domestic violence. Upon proving that the defendant had in fact willfully violated a civil protection order, the plaintiff would establish conclusively the most important element of the tort.

By proposing a solution to the tort's current limitations for domestic violence victims, this Article hopes to provide a useful remedy to women who find the existing remedies (including the tort) inadequate. In general, the proposal may help victims shut out of the criminal justice system, either because the abuser's conduct is not criminal, or because the criminal process is ineffective for domestic violence victims. As a plaintiff can recover punitive damages for the tort of intentional infliction of emotional distress, the tort's punitive component can function like the criminal law, thereby discouraging violence. As one author wrote, "[P]unishment is a central feature of outrageousness. Defendants may be punished—stigmatized by the label 'outrageous' and made to pay damages—because of the obnoxious quality of their behavior alone. In this respect, the tort functions like the criminal law."[20] Yet the tort of intentional infliction of emotional distress also provides benefits beyond the punitive function of the criminal law, as it allows victims to receive compensatory damages. The tort can even be useful for a woman who has obtained a civil protection order and whose abuser has committed criminal contempt or another criminal offense by violating the order. The police often do not obtain an arrest warrant if the batterer has fled, and prosecutors and judges treat private complaints for contempt "less seriously." Even if the woman prosecutes the action for criminal contempt herself, she is faced with a more difficult burden of proof than in an ordinary civil action. She must prove every element of the offense beyond a reasonable doubt, and the successful criminal contempt prosecution will not provide her with compensation for her injuries or punitive damages. Nor will she receive the additional benefit of society labelling her abuser's conduct "outrageous," although a criminal contempt proceeding undoubtedly provides some form of censure.

The proposal similarly may assist women who otherwise would lack a civil remedy. This Article is less concerned with the domestic violence victim who can establish a battery (aided, perhaps by compelling physical evidence), than with the woman who cannot, for whatever reason, establish that she has been harmed in that manner. This Article focuses on the woman who has obtained a civil protection order, i.e., injunctive relief through a domestic violence remedial scheme, and yet continues to be abused, although perhaps not in a way that is readily actionable under current tort law. For example, the proposal would be useful to the woman who is not "assaulted" because she suffers only verbal threats of future bodily harm, or a woman who misses the statute of limitations for assault or battery. The proposal even benefits the woman who could successfully prosecute a civil contempt action for the violation of her civil protection order. The tort of intentional infliction of emotional distress affords her the opportunity to obtain punitive damages unavailable in a civil contempt action. It also guarantees her compensatory damages for her emotional distress, often not recoverable in a civil contempt action. In addition, it allows her to prove her case by a preponderance of the evidence, an easier evidentiary burden than the "clear and convincing evidence" standard which exists in a civil contempt proceeding.

The proposal provides the indirect victims of domestic violence with a civil remedy as well. The impact of domestic violence on children is often ignored. Yet, as one court has acknowledged, "In a large percentage of families, children have been present when the abuse occurred.... Even if the child is not physically injured, he [or she] likely will suffer emotional trauma from witnessing violence between his [or her] parents."[32] The child who witnesses an outrageous act could recover under

---

20. Givelber, supra note 12, at 55. * * *   **32.** State ex rel Williams v. Marsh, 626 S.W.2d 223, 229 (Mo.1982) (en banc).

the tort (and be benefitted by the proposal herein) because the child, a third party, is a close relative of the intended victim of the outrageous act. Similarly, other friends and relatives of the victim also may have a cause of action.

Finally, the proposal hopes to move society towards a recognition that all domestic violence is outrageous. A Comment to the Second Restatement, written over a quarter of a century ago, is still true: the law "is still in a state of development, and the ultimate limits of this tort are not yet determined."[36] By adopting the rule that violating a restraining order is per se outrageous conduct, the legal system would validate domestic violence victims' experiences of harm, and move closer to a recognition that domestic violence is itself "outrageous" conduct.[37]

> Law is a language of power, a particularly authoritative discourse. Law can pronounce definitively what something is or is not and how a situation or event is to be understood.... Legal language does more than express thoughts. It reinforces certain world views and understandings of events.

Tort law generally, and the tort of intentional infliction of emotional distress in particular, frames what interests we value as a society and prescribes how human beings should treat each other. Within the known and comfortable contours of the law, the per se standard of outrage for violation of a civil protection order will help mold society's thinking about domestic violence. The proposed standard takes the first step towards making all domestic violence *per se* outrageous.

* * *

II.   THE INADEQUACIES OF THE PRESENT APPROACH

A.   *Inconsistencies Exist*

Courts that have addressed the tort of intentional infliction of emotional distress in the context of domestic violence have taken inconsistent approaches that have resulted in inconsistent outcomes. A brief examination of six cases illustrates the various approaches, and illustrates that there is no consensus on at least one key issue: how to analyze the element of "outrageousness" in a domestic violence situation.

* * *

B.   *Domestic Violence Is the Norm*

As is evident from the above cases, some judges do not characterize domestic violence as outrageous conduct. Struggling with whether a

---

36. Restatement, supra note 12, § 46 cmt. c. See also Karp & Karp, supra note 33, § 1.24 ("Its limits ... are still only vaguely defined.").

37. Lucinda M. Finley, Breaking Women's Silence in Law: The Dilemma of the Gendered Nature of Legal Reasoning, 64 Notre Dame L. Rev. 886, 888 (1989). Cf. Sylvia A. Law, Rethinking Sex and the Constitution, 132 U. Pa. L. Rev. 955 (1984). * * *

defendant's conduct is "truly outrageous," judges have applied the tort to the domestic context in a manner that has been described as "somewhat controversial." The prevalence of domestic violence in our society explains, in part, the inconsistent case outcomes and presents a major obstacle for domestic violence victims who seek redress through use of the tort. Domestic violence is incredibly common, as is society's tolerance of it. Murray Straus has written, "[F]or many people a marriage license is a hitting license [and] physical violence between family members is probably as common as love and affection between family members...."[156] A survey conducted for the U.S. National Commission on the Causes and Prevention of Violence found that about twenty-five percent of the people interviewed approved of a spouse hitting the other spouse under certain circumstances. This figure is probably conservative due to underreporting. When one includes emotional abuse, domestic violence, as well as society's acceptance of it, is virtually epidemic. At least one court has acknowledged explicitly that the prevalence of domestic violence makes the tort's application problematic. The court in *Hakkila* stated, "Conduct intentionally or recklessly causing emotional distress to one's spouse is prevalent in our society. Thus, if the tort of outrage is construed loosely or broadly, claims of outrage may be tacked on in the typical marital disputes, taxing judicial resources."[160]

It appears that male judges exemplify and perpetuate, to some extent, society's tolerance of domestic violence, and this tolerance poses an obstacle for plaintiffs seeking to establish the outrageousness of the abuse. The New Jersey Supreme Court Task Force on Women in the Courts, while examining judicial attitudes in the context of the implementation of the Prevention of Domestic Violence Act, found that judges exhibited "gender-based biases, stereotypical attitudes and ... well intentioned ignorance."[163] In particular, judges were insensitive to the "dependency factors present in the abusive relationship." They also often "trivialized the plight of the female as victim" because it was a "domestic problem," and considered "what [the woman] did to earn her beating." Furthermore, they failed to punish violations of domestic violence orders in situations that "clearly would not be tolerated except in the domestic context." The offending judges' conduct supports one critic's opinion that "[t]here is a general belief [among judges] that if the woman was seriously abused, then she would leave; if she stays, then the abuse did not occur."[167] Anecdotal evidence indicates that judicial insensitivity is rampant. To make matters even worse, "[i]n the judicial system dominated by men, emotional distress claims have historically been marginalized: 'The law of torts values physical security and proper-

156. Murray A. Straus, Sexual Inequality, Cultural Norms, and Wife–Beating, in Women into Wives: The Legal and Economic Impact of Marriage 59 (Jane R. Chapman & Margaret Gates eds., 1977). * * *

160. Hakkila, 812 P.2d at 1324–25. * * *

163. Lynn H. Schafran, Educating the Judiciary About Gender Bias: The National Judicial Education Program to Promote Equality for Women and Men in the Courts and the New Jersey Supreme Court Task Force on Women in the Courts, 9 Women's Rts. L. Rep. 109, 150 (1986).

167. Cahn, supra note 8, at 1985; see also Blair v. Blair, 575 A.2d 191, 192–93 (Vt.1990) * * *.

ty more highly than emotional security and physical relationships.' "[169] Even if a case survives pretrial adjudication, the judge may give the issue of outrage to the jury, subjecting the domestic violence victim to lay misconceptions about domestic violence.[173] The judge may also give a jury instruction on outrage that is potentially detrimental to domestic violence victims.[174] In sum, the male-dominated judiciary is predisposed to disfavor civil claims by victims of domestic violence: "The legal system is dominated by members of the same group engaged in the aggression.[175] The practice is formally illegal but seldom found to be against the law. The atrocity is *de jure* illegal but *de facto* permitted."

C. The Current Doctrinal Approach Is Problematic for Feminism

Feminists face a dilemma when invoking the tort of intentional infliction of emotional distress as a remedy for domestic violence. We may find it strategically advantageous to portray the plight of victims in terms of traditional gender roles in order to emphasize the outrageousness of abusers' misconduct and enhance the chances for recovery. On the other hand, such stereotypes help to perpetuate legal and social disadvantages. By stressing women's moral purity, for example, society can justify keeping women out of some rough-and-tumble areas of the workforce. More insidiously, "lingering stereotypes reinforce gender hierarchy by obscuring its dynamics. The result is that sex-based subordination appears natural and necessary, rather than a consequence of societal construction and a subject for societal challenge." Stereotypes also perpetuate a world view that does not comport with the reality of most women's lives. For instance, many women are single heads of households, and a vast majority of women participate in both the private and public spheres. The traditional public/private sphere dichotomy ignores this reality, and allows courts to rationalize staying out of domestic violence issues altogether. It is similarly problematic to rely on doctrine that defines domestic violence victims as hypersensitive, evoking the stigma of abnormality that the prefix "hyper" implies. Additionally, the current doctrine creates perverse incentives for a victim who wants to increase her chances for recovery: A domestic violence victim is more likely to recover under current doctrine if she experiences repeated harassment or learned helplessness, rather than leaving an abusive relationship.

III. A NEW STANDARD FOR THE DOMESTIC VIOLENCE CONTEXT: *PER SE* OUTRAGE

A. A Description of the Standard

As noted above, almost all states have statutes authorizing civil protection orders for domestic abuse, and protective orders are also

169. Twyman, 855 S.W.2d at 642 (Spector, J., dissenting) * * *

173. Catharine A. MacKinnon, Reflections on Sex Equality Under Law, 100 Yale L.J. 1281, 1303 (1991) (referring to rape); * * *

174. See Finley, supra note 37, at 891 * * *

175. Id. at 1755.

available in criminal cases. This Article's modest proposal is that a willful violation of a civil protection order should constitute outrage *per se*. Whenever a woman, or the state on her behalf, has obtained a judgment for criminal contempt or a conviction for the violation of a civil protection order, that conviction or finding of contempt should suffice to establish the outrage element of the tort of intentional infliction of emotional distress. Alternatively, a woman should be able to prove to a civil court, without first having obtained an order of criminal contempt or a conviction, that the defendant willfully violated her civil protection order. This proposal would simplify the determination of outrage and reduce the plaintiff's burden in proving intent to inflict severe emotional distress, but would leave intact the elements of severe emotional distress and causation. Adoption of the *per se* standard would ensure that "the circumstances in which the tort is recognized [are] described precisely enough ... that the social good from recognizing the tort will not be outweighed by the unseemly and invasive litigation of meritless claims."[182]

This approach has an analogy in the tort law of negligence. The doctrine of *per se* negligence exists in most American jurisdictions and allows a court to use the violation of a safety statute to assist it in deciding one element of the tort. Negligence *per se* applies

> Where a statute or municipal ordinance imposes upon any person a specific duty for the protection or benefit of others, if he [or she] neglects to perform that duty he [or she] is liable to those for whose protection or benefit it was imposed for any injuries of the character which the statute or ordinance was designed to prevent, and which were proximately caused by such neglect.[185]

Under a negligence *per se* rule, a defendant can be liable for certain acts or omissions that might not qualify as negligence under the ordinary reasonable person test, and the issue of reasonable conduct need not go to the jury. Negligence *per se* is a bright-line rule. It supplants the jury's subjective determination of reasonableness with an objective standard. While negligence *per se* establishes the existence of the defendant's breach of a legally cognizable duty owed to the plaintiff, it does not establish liability. The plaintiff must still show that such negligence was a proximate cause of the injury or damage sustained.

* * *

DAISY ANNETTE SANTIAGO v. OSVALDO RIOS ALONSO

United States District Court, D. Puerto Rico (1999).
66 F.Supp.2d 269–274.

I. Statement of Claim Under VAWA

On December 21, 1998, defendant presented a motion seeking dismissal of the instant complaint for failure to state a cause of action

---

182. Hakkila v. Hakkila, 812 P.2d 1320, 1326 (N.M.Ct.App.1991).

185. Osborne v. McMasters, 41 N.W. 543 (Minn.1889); 57A Am. Jur. 2d Negligence § 727 (1981).

under the Violence Against Women Act, 42 U.S.C. § 13981 ("VAWA"). On June 28, 1999, this Court ordered plaintiff to "state which acts by defendant constitute 'crimes of violence' and, pursuant to § 13981(d)(2)(A), specify the predicate felony offense said acts qualify under." In addition, plaintiff was directed "to state sufficient facts to show that the alleged acts of violence were motivated by defendant's animus to plaintiff's gender."

On July 6, 1999, plaintiff adequately complied with the aforementioned order. Plaintiff's responding motion lists the felonies which defendant allegedly committed against her and states sufficient facts which, if believed, would allow a jury to make a reasonable inference that defendant acted out of animus against her gender. Accordingly, this Court finds that plaintiff has alleged sufficient facts to state a claim under VAWA and defendant's motion for summary judgment is hereby DENIED because said motion based on animus due to gender is fraught with issues of motive and intent not susceptible of disposition at this time via summary judgment standards.

II.

Also on December 21, 1999, defendant filed a motion seeking partial summary judgment of claims barred under Puerto Rico's statute of limitations and dismissal of alleged constitutional violations. We proceed to discuss each one of these separately.

A. *Plaintiff's Complaint Is Time Barred*

Both parties to this case agree that VAWA does not set forth an applicable statute of limitations, and that this being the case, the applicable statute is the one year limitations period set forth in Article 1868 of Puerto Rico's Civil Code, P.R. Laws Ann. tit. 31 § 5298 (1990). Both parties also agree that plaintiff's claim is based on incidents which occurred on February or March of 1996, May of 1996, September of 1996 and November 24, 1996. The parties do not agree, however, as to when the limitations period began to run and which incidents are barred from being asserted as elements of plaintiff's claim.

On the one hand, defendant asserts that plaintiff's claim is based on a series of independent events and that the statute of limitations applies independently to each one of them. Consequently, those events which occurred before November 20, 1996 are barred from consideration, leaving only a claim based on the events of November 24, 1996. On the other hand, plaintiff argues that the acts on which her claim is based were a "series of continuing unlawful acts which were part of an abusive relationship causing the battered woman syndrome." It was not until the last of these events, which occurred on November 24, 1996, that the statute of limitations began to run. Plaintiff filed her complaint on

November 20, 1997, hence, none of the events alleged in her claim are barred from consideration.

* * *

Application of Statute of Limitations

After considering both parties' positions as to the timeliness of plaintiff's complaint, this Court concludes that plaintiff's claim is not barred as to any of the incidents of violence for which she seeks compensation. Surprisingly, none of the parties in this case addressed the doctrine of "serial violations" delineated by the First Circuit in *Jensen v. Frank*, 912 F.2d 517, 522–523 (1st Cir.1990) and *Sabree v. United Broth. of Carpenters and Joiners*, 921 F.2d 396, 400 (1st Cir. 1990); and followed by this Court in *Borrero-Rentero v. Western Auto Supply Co.*, 2 F.Supp.2d 197 (D.P.R.1998). Nonetheless, these cases provide the applicable rule of law for this case.

> A serial violation is defined as "a number of discriminatory acts emanating from the same discriminatory animus, each constituting a separate wrong actionable.... [A]t least one act in the series must fall within the limitations period." Once a single claim in the series falls within the limitations period, a plaintiff may "reach back" to other past acts, at least as "relevant background evidence."

In the instant case there is no doubt, pursuant to the summary judgment standard, that an alleged crime of violence motivated by gender occurred within the 1 year limitations period set forth by Puerto Rican law. Thus, plaintiff's claim is certainly actionable as to the events which transpired on November 24, 1996. Further, because the events predating the limitations period are alleged to be part of the same series of discriminatory acts as the event which transpired on November of 1996, those previous events are also actionable under the doctrine of "serial violations." Thus, plaintiff's claim is not barred as to any of the events alleged in her complaint and defendant's motion for partial summary judgment is hereby DENIED.

B. Constitutional Claims

Plaintiff's complaint alleges that defendant violated her constitutional rights under the Fourth, Fifth, Eighth and Fourteenth Amendments. Plaintiff does not allege that defendant's acts involved state action, nor does she allege the violation of specific rights under any of the mentioned Amendments.

The safeguards against the deprivation of individual liberties contained in the Fourth, Fifth, Eighth and Fourteenth Amendments to the United States Constitution apply only to activities of either the state or federal governments. * * * Furthermore, even if plaintiff alleged that state action was present in this case, plaintiff's allegations are too vague to satisfy Rule 8(a) of the Federal Rules of Civil Procedure. * * * Defendant's motion to dismiss as to the quashing of causes of action under the Fourth, Fifth, Eighth, and Fourteenth Amendments is, therefore, GRANTED.

Chapter 6

CIVIL RESTRAINING ORDERS

This chapter continues the exploration of civil remedies for domestic violence, focusing on protective orders issued by civil courts, also called restraining orders. The first set of materials looks at issuance of orders, and the important question of access to the courts, for victims of domestic violence in general and for a deaf woman in particular. A national survey containing many recommendations for improvement in the way the legal system deals with restraining orders is summarized.

The next two pieces focus on mutual restraining orders, which are very problematic in domestic violence cases. They describe both how such orders come to be issued, why they are problematic, and how some states have passed statutes limiting or prohibiting such orders.

Enforcement has been called "the Achilles heel" of the civil protective order system, since issuance of an order without enforcement may actually put the victim in a worse position. Another national study is summarized, finding that overall these orders are beneficial, though improvements in enforcement need to be made. One writer advocates for more use of criminal contempt sanctions, initiated by the victim, rather than relying solely on prosecutors to enforce civil protection orders. Such suggestions raise questions of double jeopardy; the only US Supreme Court case to address this issue is included.

The chapter concludes with the new provision for interstate enforcement of restraining orders mandated under the Violence Against Women Act, yet based on an old constitutional concept, full faith and credit.

A. ISSUANCE, MUTUAL ORDERS

KIT KINPORTS AND KARLA FISCHER, ORDERS OF PROTECTION IN DOMESTIC VIOLENCE CASES: AN EMPIRICAL ASSESSMENT OF THE IMPACT OF THE REFORM STATUTES

2 Tex. J. Women & L. 167–168, 182–186, 210–220 (1993).

Our concern that the reform statutes might not be having their intended effect sparked our decision to evaluate the protective order statutes empirically. We therefore distributed a lengthy survey to 843 domestic violence organizations nationwide that help battered women obtain protective orders. The survey focused on three issues. The first issue was access to the courts: Is the protective order remedy accessible to battered women? The second issue related to the procedures for obtaining orders of protection: Are judges granting orders in appropriate cases, and are they awarding the full range of remedies contemplated by the reform statutes? The third issue involved the procedures for serving and enforcing protective orders: Are emergency orders being served promptly, and are the police, the prosecutors, and the courts responding adequately to violations? We were interested in discovering what types of problems exist in these three areas, and whether they are attributable to inadequacies in the domestic violence reform statutes themselves or simply to the way the statutes have been implemented by executive and judicial officials.

We received 326 completed surveys, for a reply rate of 38.7%. Responses came from all but three of the states and territories included in our mailing. Moreover, the answers to the survey questions fell along a broad spectrum, suggesting that the respondents—advocates who, admittedly, tend to be identified with only one of the parties in the proceeding—were not biased in any particular direction with respect to the strengths and weaknesses of the protective order system.

In general, the survey results show that while some statutory modifications would result in modest improvements, the domestic violence reform statutes are, on the whole, protective of battered women's interests. On the other hand, the responses uncovered serious implementation problems in all three areas of inquiry. In many instances, these problems are traceable to the attitudes of the judicial and law enforcement personnel charged with applying and enforcing the statutes. In addition, we found that ultimately the three issues are not quite so distinct; problems in one area spill over and create difficulties in the other areas as well.

* * *

I. ACCESS TO THE COURTS: IS THE PROTECTIVE ORDER REMEDY READILY AVAILABLE TO BATTERED WOMEN?

* * *

D. Recommendations

Although the domestic violence reform statutes intended that battered women could use the courts for protection, the protective order remedy is currently inaccessible for many women. Some women are not aware that the remedy exists, and others do not have the legal expertise or assistance needed to obtain relief. Logistical difficulties create additional barriers to access. Women may be required to travel significant distances to the courthouse, and judges typically do not issue protective orders during the hours when most abuse occurs. Most significant, the fact that women must spend a great deal of time away from their work and children to obtain an order of protection substantially reduces the chances that they will seek judicial relief. Finally, financial constraints may make protective orders inaccessible for women who are unaware of or ineligible for fee waivers.

Our recommendations for improving access to orders of protection fall into four categories: (1) further educate the public about the protective order remedy; (2) improve the sources of legal assistance available to battered women; (3) make emergency orders available after business hours and over the telephone; and (4) eliminate all fee requirements for orders of protection.

1. Educate the Public About Orders of Protection: Additional steps need to be taken to inform the community about the availability of protective orders so that battered women will realize they are an option. If a woman is not aware that orders of protection are available or does not know how to secure an order, even an ideal system for obtaining and enforcing protective orders will be under-utilized.

2. Improve Sources of Legal Assistance for Petitioners: Legal assistance needs to be made available to battered women seeking orders of protection. There are at least four ways to accomplish this goal. First, *pro se* filing can be facilitated by further simplifying the so-called "simplified" forms. The forms should be written in terms understandable to a person with no legal training who is experiencing a very traumatic event.

Providing written materials that explain the procedures and requirements for obtaining an order of protection would further assist those who file for protective relief *pro se*. Only about one-third (35.7%) of the respondents reported that the court currently provides petitioners with written guidelines that describe the procedures for obtaining protective orders, and fewer than one-fourth (24%) indicated that the court offers written guidelines outlining the requirements for obtaining orders or fee waivers. Our statistical analyses suggest that communities that do provide such guidelines tend to experience significantly fewer access and relief problems.

In drafting these guidelines, care should be taken to ensure that they are comprehensible, so as to avoid the situation described by one respondent from a rural western community: "Many times written guidelines are worse than the forms." In addition, all forms and materials should be available in languages other than English in areas with a significant non-English-speaking population.

Providing simplified forms and guidelines, thereby ensuring that the protective order process is conducive to *pro se* filing, may have the independent advantage of empowering battered women. As one respondent from a rural southern community noted:

> [B]eing able to fill the forms out, ... file them with the clerk, and talk[ ] with the judges makes a difference for women because it empowers them ... to complete the process. It may take a bit longer ... but we have seen this help break the cycle [of violence].

Second, court clerks should be required to help petitioners complete protective order petitions as part of their job. They should be given training and written guidelines concerning the state's domestic violence statute so that they do not misinform women about the requirements for obtaining orders of protection and do not unintentionally usurp the judge's function by rating the merits of the petition. Clerks should also be educated about domestic violence so that they understand, for example, why battered women find it difficult to leave an abusive relationship and why they may therefore drop their first request for protective relief only to return later to seek a second order. Refresher courses should be offered periodically. Additionally, court personnel should be instructed to provide special assistance to petitioners who are not literate or do not speak English. Finally, notices should be posted in conspicuous places in the courthouse informing potential petitioners of the services provided by the clerk's office.

Third, any battered woman who needs help filing for protective relief should have access to an advocate. Although advocates are already offering assistance in many communities, the demand for their time is high, and women in some areas may not be able to obtain this valuable service. Increasing funding for domestic violence organizations to enable them to hire additional legal advocates would help solve this problem.

Finally, *pro bono* programs operated by local bar associations or law schools can help provide legal assistance to petitioners. In New Mexico, for example, the Young Lawyers Division on Assistance to Victims of Domestic Violence has set up a toll-free telephone number that battered women can call to receive legal assistance with orders of protection. Similarly, Yale Law School has established a student-run legal assistance program to help battered women obtain protective orders. In any such program, providing attorneys to women whose abusers are represented by counsel should be the first priority. Given our inconclusive findings about the effects of involving lawyers in the process, however, caution should be exercised before dramatically increasing the role attorneys play in a protective order system. In any event, those who participate in such *pro bono* programs should be given special training regarding the dynamics of domestic violence.

3. Make Emergency Orders Available After Business Hours and Over the Telephone: Judges should be available to grant emergency orders of protection twenty-four hours a day. Currently, twenty-three domestic violence reform statutes authorize the issuance of emergency orders during non-business hours, but some jurisdictions have not established procedures to put those provisions into effect. Similar legislation should be passed in the remaining states and should be implemented in all areas that have not yet done so.

In addition, emergency orders should be available by telephone. Statutes in several states now authorize the issuance of short-term emergency orders of protection that can be obtained over the phone when the courthouse is closed. In these states, a police officer who responds to a battered woman's request for assistance calls the judge for the short-term order; the woman then has several days to go to the courthouse to obtain a regular emergency order before the short-term order expires.

Making emergency orders available twenty-four hours a day and over the phone would obviously alleviate the problem of judicial inaccessibility during non-business hours. It would also minimize access problems in areas where petitioners must travel long distances to reach the courthouse. In addition, issuing orders by phone during non-business hours rather than at the courthouse may not have an adverse effect on judicial attitudes and behavior because telephone orders require less of a judge's time and effort.

4. Eliminate Fees for Orders of Protection: Fee requirements should be abolished for all petitioners. Eliminating fees would ensure that no victim of domestic violence is prevented from seeking protection because of financial constraints and would also symbolize society's commitment to ending domestic abuse. Many states have already taken this step; the remaining jurisdictions should follow that lead.

* * *

II. Issuance and Scope of Orders of Protection: Are Judges Granting Orders Promptly in Appropriate Cases, and Are They Awarding the Full Range of Remedies?

* * *

D. *Recommendations*

The survey results suggest that the issuance of protective orders is often delayed. In addition, judges in a substantial number of jurisdictions deny orders even though women are entitled to protection under the terms of the statute. Even more frequently, they refuse to grant battered women at least some of the remedies contemplated by the statute. Finally, disrespectful and insensitive behavior by judges discourages battered women from turning to the judicial process for relief.

Our recommendations for addressing these relief problems and improving the procedures for issuing orders of protection fall into six categories: (1) increasing the judicial resources allocated to domestic violence cases; (2) educating judges about the dynamics of domestic violence and the state's domestic violence statute; (3) holding protective order hearings in the judge's chambers; (4) facilitating appeals of unfavorable judicial decisions; (5) expanding the role of advocates in the judicial process; and (6) limiting the use of mutual orders of protection. In addition, we suggest a number of miscellaneous statutory reforms.

1. Increase the Judicial Resources Allocated to Domestic Violence Cases: Crowded dockets and delays in issuing orders of protection discourage women from seeking protective relief and expose them to the risk of additional violence. Devoting more judicial resources to domestic violence cases should help minimize these problems.

2. Educate the Judges: To some extent, the relief problems confronting battered women may be corrected by educating judges about both the state's domestic violence statute and the dynamics of domestic violence. Taking steps to improve judicial understanding of domestic violence and the parameters of the state's statute may reduce the number of cases in which judges deny protective orders altogether, refuse to include specific remedies, or engage in insensitive, victim-blaming treatment of the women appearing before them.

Approximately three-fifths (60.9%) of the respondents reported that the judges in their county deny some orders or some remedies due to a lack of knowledge or training about domestic violence; almost one-third (29.2%) characterized this as a significant or very serious problem. Even more surprising, about two-fifths (40.9%) believed that the judges in their county deny some orders or remedies due to a lack of knowledge or training about the domestic violence statute itself; 12.9% thought that this was a significant or very serious problem. As one respondent from an urban northeastern county commented, judges "need training badly [because] as a whole, they are the weakest link in the system."

Training might alleviate these problems, educating judges on issues such as why it is hard for women to leave permanently, how a man who has beaten a woman can convince her that he's changed overnight, how to handle requests to drop the orders, how to handle repeated requests for protective orders by the same person, and why battered women are sometimes "nervous" wrecks in court while batterers are calm and collected.

Several respondents pointed to the benefits they had seen result from judicial training. One respondent from an urban northeastern county described the impact of a brief domestic violence training course recently conducted for the judges in her state: "Since the training I have noticed a greater effort on the judges' parts not to [victimize] and to explain the process in a more understandable way, as well as efforts to tell the defendant this is inappropriate behavior." Likewise, another respondent from a rural northeastern county reported, "More emotional abuse is being accepted [as the basis for protective relief] compared to one year ago. Our judges have had courses offered to them in domestic violence, [and] many have made themselves more aware of the issues."

Others, however, said that efforts to educate judges had not been particularly successful. Some respondents noted that judges were often unwilling to participate in training programs. As one respondent from the Midwest reported, "Some [judges] have done education on their own and a selected few have been open to education from us, but overall, in this rural area, the judicial system is reluctant to learn about domestic violence from us." Other respondents explained that judges resist training because "they already know it all" or because they "do not wish to visit with 'special interest groups.'"

Conversely, some respondents indicated that the judges in their community had undergone training, but with no noticeable improvement in their treatment of battered women. For example, one respondent reported that the judge in her rural midwestern county has been trained, but still denies remedies in protective orders; "training is not the problem," she concluded.

Judicial training programs might meet with less resistance if they were a collaborative effort involving both court personnel and domestic violence organizations and thus were legitimated in the eyes of the judges. In addition, refresher courses should be held periodically in order to maximize their effectiveness.

3. *Hold Protective Order Hearings in Chambers:* Holding protective order hearings in an informal setting may alleviate some of the problems women encounter when they become emotional or confused while testifying and may also encourage more women to seek relief. Currently, however, the hearings are often formal courtroom proceedings. Although more than four-fifths (83.5%) of the respondents indicated that some judges will issue emergency orders without seeing the petitioner at all or after holding an informal hearing outside the courtroom, about one-third (32.2%) reported that some judges will sign an emergency order only after a courtroom hearing. Most of the formal proceedings occur in open court: only 5.9% of the respondents indicated that the judge refuses to permit observers in the courtroom during the hearing. The plenary hearing is even more likely to be a formal courtroom proceeding. Even if the abuser does not appear for that hearing, only about one-third (33.7%) of the respondents indicated that the judge will sign the order without seeing the petitioner or after an informal hearing outside the courtroom.

Moving protective order hearings to a less formal setting may have two advantages. First, women may find the protective order process less intimidating and therefore may be able to testify more clearly if not forced to do so during a formal hearing in open court. As a result, judges may be more inclined to credit their testimony and less likely to treat them in an impatient or insensitive manner.

Second, a less formal process might encourage more women to seek relief. About three-fourths (75.8%) of the respondents reported that the public nature of the procedures for obtaining orders of protection and the embarrassment of going to court prevent some women in their county from seeking protective relief; more than one-fifth (22.2%) considered this a significant or very serious problem. Moreover, our interviews in Champaign County suggested that women who were required to publicly describe the abuse they had experienced in order to obtain an emergency order were significantly less likely to return to court to obtain a plenary order.

Admittedly, a *per se* policy of holding all plenary hearings in chambers is likely to run afoul of the First Amendment right of public access to trials. The right of access is only a "qualified" one, however, that may be overcome by "an overriding interest based on findings that closure is essential to preserve higher values and is narrowly tailored to serve that interest." Just as protecting the victims of sex crimes from "the trauma and embarrassment of public scrutiny may justify closing certain aspects of a criminal proceeding," allowing a battered woman to testify in chambers may be necessary to protect the woman or to fully elicit her testimony. Judges should therefore be required to make case-by-case determinations concerning the appropriateness of moving plenary hearings to less formal surroundings.

Holding emergency order hearings in chambers is much less likely to raise constitutional concerns. The qualified right of public access applies only when a certain proceeding has historically been open to the public and public access "plays a significant positive role in the functioning of the particular process in question." Civil courts have traditionally had the authority to conduct business other than trials in chambers. Moreover, the emergency order is only intended to protect the petitioner temporarily, until a plenary hearing can be scheduled; denying the public access at this preliminary stage of the proceedings therefore does not seem particularly problematic.

4. Facilitate Appeals of Unfavorable Decisions: Judicial oversight through the appellate process may help improve the courts' record in issuing orders of protection. Encouraging battered women to appeal unfavorable rulings might provide a check on those judges who circumvent the state's domestic violence statute by, for example, refusing orders in cases involving threats or non-physical abuse, enforcing informal rules, or denying remedies contemplated by the statute. The appellate process might also provide guidance to judges as to when orders of protection are appropriate and what remedies they ought to include.

Facilitating appeals by battered women requires, however, removing some barriers that hinder use of the appellate process today. Currently, it appears that very few protective order cases make their way to the appellate courts. Only 12.2% of the respondents indicated that both emergency and plenary orders can be appealed directly to the state court of appeals, and even fewer remembered actual instances when orders had been appealed. In addition, the few appeals that are filed are more likely to involve the abuser challenging the issuance of the order than the petitioner appealing its denial.

These figures are not particularly surprising. The denial of an emergency order may be a nonappealable interlocutory decision. Although there should be no comparable legal bar to appealing the denial of a plenary order or the judge's refusal to include certain remedies in that order, other factors make the appellate process unattractive. First, orders of protection last no longer than one year in most states; an appeal might still be pending at that time, and the petitioner might not see much benefit in ultimately being vindicated after the order would have expired anyway. Second, in many instances, no record is made of the rationale for the court's ruling, making it difficult to challenge the decision on appeal. In Champaign, for example, the judge refuses to provide written, and sometimes even oral, reasons for his decisions, even though the Illinois statute explicitly requires a written explanation.

Third, women who cannot afford to hire an attorney to represent them at the protective order hearing presumably cannot afford to retain appellate counsel, and filing a *pro se* appeal is much more difficult than using the simplified forms to petition for an order of protection without counsel. As one respondent from a rural northeastern community reported, "Victims rarely appeal due to cost and difficulty finding an attorney who will accept the case."

Finally, if, as our experience suggests, women who are denied an emergency order tend to choose not to seek a plenary order, an unfavorable outcome at the plenary hearing is similarly likely to discourage women from pursuing an appeal. As one respondent from a rural southern community noted, "Women are very reluctant to appeal denials as they are intimidated by the judges who deny [the orders]."

Petitioners must be afforded legal assistance if they are to overcome these barriers and appeal unfavorable decisions. Perhaps, then, this is one area where lawyers and *pro bono* programs can be of the greatest help. In addition, the legislature could authorize an expedited appellate process to provide some additional incentive to appeal the denial of a protective order. To further facilitate the appellate process, protective order hearings should be taped or recorded by a court reporter. At a minimum, judges should be required to explain in writing why they denied an order of protection or refused to include certain remedies in the order.

5. *Expand the Role of Advocates:* Allowing advocates to play a greater role in protective order hearings may help ensure that orders of protection are issued in all appropriate cases. First, the presence of an advocate may enhance the accountability of the judges. As one respondent from a rural southern community reported, "We believe our presence with women has made a significant difference—we know it's different when we're not there." For example, she said, "We have one magistrate that routinely tells petitioners they must file criminal charges before he will grant an order of protection. Often this is inappropriate. When we accompany a woman this doesn't happen. But many women come to us after such an experience and no order of protection." In

addition, she said, "Magistrates sometimes won't grant petitions—then we go and they do." Likewise, another respondent from a rural northeastern community concluded, "[W]e find when we write orders of protection ourselves and accompany victims before the judge, there is a much better chance that the order of protection will be granted."

Second, the presence of an advocate may reduce the risk that the petitioner will be intimidated or become confused or emotional during the hearing. The support provided by the advocate may help the petitioner feel more comfortable, and thereby minimize the adverse impact that her confusion or emotion can have on both the outcome of the case and the judge's treatment of her.

Almost all (93.5%) of the respondents indicated that domestic violence advocates accompany battered women to court for protective order hearings, and some said that judges welcome their presence and input. In many cases, however, the court places substantial limits on the role the advocate can play at the hearing. More than two-fifths (43.2%) of the respondents reported that judges impose restrictions on the advocate during protective order hearings, and 17.4% characterized these limitations as a significant or very serious problem. The restrictions imposed include barring advocates from the courtroom altogether, prohibiting them from sitting with the petitioner to provide emotional support, refusing to allow them to talk to the petitioner during the hearing, and denying them permission to speak in open court if the petitioner becomes upset or confused.

Some respondents reported that the judges in their counties were quite inconsistent in their treatment of advocates. One respondent from a rural northeastern community noted that, "[d]epending on the judge, the advocate's role changes. Sometimes advocates can speak for the client if the client is having a difficult time. Sometimes judicial behavior is insulting and demeaning to advocates...." Likewise, another respondent from an urban southern community commented that the advocate's role "[d]epends on the personal mood of that judge at that time of the day."

A number of respondents observed that the limits placed on advocates in these courts have had adverse consequences on both the petitioner and the protective order process. For example, one respondent from a rural midwestern county reported, "Judges will not usually allow an advocate to approach the bench area with the survivor. This sometimes leaves a survivor feeling very vulnerable and alone—especially if the advocate is seated far back in the courtroom." Another respondent from an urban southern community suggested that "victim advocates should be allowed to speak on behalf of victims during hearings as most victims are scared to speak out when the abuser is sitting across the table from them. They are very intimidated." Finally, one respondent noted that the judges in her rural western county refuse to permit the advocate to accompany the petitioner to the bar; as a result, she said, women are often "so frightened they will not go for the hearing."

In order to allay the petitioner's fears, the advocate should, at a minimum, be permitted to sit with the petitioner and provide her with information and support. In addition, the judge should have the discretion to allow the advocate to speak on behalf of a petitioner who is too upset or intimidated to present her case. The judge should be particularly open to the advocate's input at *ex parte* emergency order hearings, plenary hearings at which the alleged abuser does not appear, and any other hearings that do not strictly adhere to formal courtroom procedures. If the advocate merely tells the judge what the petitioner told her about the abuse she experienced and the relief she needs, the advocate functions essentially as a translator and therefore should not be guilty of practicing law without a license. Nevertheless, legislation may be required to authorize this reform, especially given the threats made in some states to charge domestic violence advocates with the unauthorized practice of law.

6. *Limit the Use of Mutual Orders:* Mutual orders of protection should not be issued unless both parties have filed petitions and have proved that they are entitled to relief under the statute. Use of the appellate process is one way to end the practice of issuing mutual orders as a matter of course. Alternatively, legislation can be passed abolishing mutual orders, or at least specifying the limited circumstances in which they are appropriate. A number of states have already enacted such provisions.

7. *Miscellaneous Statutory Reforms:* In addition to the suggestions described above, some of which can obviously be implemented by the legislature, a number of other statutory changes could be made to help refine the procedures for obtaining protective orders.

First, the likelihood that orders of protection will be issued in all appropriate circumstances might increase if each statute explicitly authorized protective relief in any case involving one of the following types of abuse: physical abuse in any form; threatened or attempted physical abuse; sexual abuse; and non-physical abuse, including verbal abuse, harassment, or psychological abuse, at least where that abuse creates a fear of physical harm. In addition, the legislature should make clear that the informal rules used to deny orders—most notably, delay in filing for relief and failure to pursue a prior petition—are not proper grounds for refusing orders of protection and that the history of the abusive relationship as well as the most recent assault is relevant in deciding whether to issue protective relief. Finally, in order to facilitate oversight of the judicial process, the courts should be required to keep separate records detailing the number of protective order petitions filed and their disposition.

Second, in terms of remedies, the statute should authorize a broad range of relief, including possession of the residence and temporary custody at the emergency order stage, and custody, as well as child support and other financial remedies, at the plenary stage. Visitation should be denied when there is evidence that the abuser's violence has been directed toward the children and should always be structured to safeguard the woman from further abuse. Therefore, if visitation is ordered, the judge should be instructed to impose conditions to protect the woman, such as limiting visitation to situations where a neutral adult is present, where arrangements are made for picking up and dropping off the children so as to avoid contact between the couple, and where the abuser agrees not to use drugs or alcohol before or during visitation.

Finally, judges should be required to communicate certain information to the parties. For example, the legislature could require judges to emphasize to abusers that their behavior was inappropriate and to inform them that an order of protection is a court order that the judicial system takes very seriously. In addition, the judge could be asked to instruct the petitioner to report any violations of the order to the police.

* * *

V.C. v. H.C., SR., ET AL.

Supreme Court, Appellate Division, First Department, New York (1999).
689 N.Y.S.2d 447, 449–451, 452–454.

At issue on this appeal is whether the Family Court, having found that a victim of domestic violence who has fled the marital home for her safety is entitled to an order of protection, should also have provided a remedy that could restore the victim to her home and exclude her abusers instead of leaving the home in the sole possession of the abusers.

On January 3, 1995, petitioner, a middle-aged deaf woman, filed petitions for orders of protection, alleging that she had fled her home in December 1994 because of escalating violence and abuse by her husband and their adult son and requesting that the orders provide that respondents be excluded from their common residence. Specifically, she alleged, *inter alia*, that her husband physically and verbally abused and threatened her, changed the locks on the marital home and refused to give her a key, and forced her to take drugs against her will, and that their son was verbally and physically abusive.

Following an initial *ex parte* proceeding, the Family Court denied the request that respondents be excluded from the home and issued temporary orders of protection pursuant to Family Court Act § 828 requiring respondents not to "assault, menace, harass or recklessly endanger petitioner" and "not to exclude petitioner from the marital residence."

At the fact-finding hearing, petitioner testified that she fled to her daughter's home in December 1994 after two incidents in which her husband, who is confined to a wheelchair, pointed a loaded gun at her and threatened to kill her. On November 18, 1994, while her husband was high on cocaine, he pulled a loaded gun out from under the seat of his wheelchair, pointed it at her, and said, "I am going to kill you". She ran into the bathroom and locked the door. On another day, he reached into the drawer in the couple's bedroom, placed his hand on his gun, and cursed at her. She called for their son to come help her, but when he entered the room he blocked the bedroom door and trapped her in the room.

Petitioner also testified that, in 1975, her husband, while intoxicated, shot her in the heat of a dispute, grazing her chest. He was not arrested because he told the police that someone else had shot her, and he threatened those present, including petitioner's oldest son, who is his stepson, not to contradict his story.

In addition to these specific incidents, petitioner testified that her husband constantly abused her by punching her in the face and pulling her hair. She also testified that he hit her twice on the back with a stick.

As to the petition against her younger adult son, petitioner testified that he punched and slapped her when she refused his demands to cook meals or do other errands for him, made at all hours of the day and night. On numerous occasions, father and son acted together to abuse her. In November 1994, they changed the locks on the home and refused to give her a key. It was only after she had left home, retained counsel, and obtained an *ex parte* order of protection that they eventually provided her with a key.

Petitioner's adult daughter corroborated her mother's account of her stepfather's abuse, providing details as to other incidents, including one in which he attempted to stab petitioner with a machete, and confirming that her stepfather always kept a gun near him. She also testified that when her mother arrived at her home in December 1994, she noticed that her mother, who said she was frightened, was severely bruised. Although petitioner's daughter's testimony was cut short, she also testified briefly to certain incidents during her childhood, including her stepfather's use of herself and her brothers and cousins to assist him in selling drugs until, as a teenager, she was placed in foster care.

Petitioner's oldest son also corroborated the abuse against his mother, stating that it was often precipitated by drinking. He recounted witnessing the 1975 shooting, and he also testified that his stepfather had sexually abused him from the time he was seven or eight until he was in ninth grade, at which time he left home to live on the streets to escape the abuse.

On August 18, 1995, the court informed counsel that it was terminating the fact-finding hearing because sufficient evidence had already been presented to show that respondents had committed the family offense of harassment. Petitioner's counsel objected, arguing that the remainder of the evidence would establish far graver offenses. The court overruled the objection and instead offered respondents the option of admitting to harassment, in which case they could remain in the marital residence pending disposition. In the alternative, it informed them that it would make a finding of harassment and would exclude them from the apartment pending disposition. Respondents admitted to harassment. The court thereupon extended the *ex parte* order of protection requiring them not to harass petitioner and ordered Mental Health Services

["MHS"] to evaluate the parties and render a recommendation as to disposition.

Although that report was prepared, it failed to make a recommendation as to disposition. The matter was set down for disposition, but was transferred several times to different judges for various reasons, including the failure of the court to provide an appropriate interpreter for petitioner, and the transfer to another county of an assigned judge. Ultimately, on July 17, 1996, 18 months after petitioner had fled her home to escape from the abuse and filed petitions, the matter appeared before Judge Cohen for a dispositional hearing. However, rather than hearing testimony, the court issued a ruling summarily denying a three-year order of protection and denying the request that the order of protection exclude the respondents from the marital home, and instead issued a one-year order of protection merely requiring respondents to stay away from petitioner. The court stated:

> It is my understanding that the main issue at this dispositional hearing is the apartment. I want it clear I am not ruling on who gets the apartment. I won't even consider it. at this point my understanding is that the mother moved out and is living somewhere else and she wants the apartment back.... if the petitioner wants the apartment she will have to take appropriate action in the appropriate court. This is not the court for this. You can have a hearing for 20 months and I will never rule on who gets this apartment. It's not before me.

We reverse.

* * *

Initially, we reject respondents' argument that petitioner's appeal is academic because the one-year order of protection has expired and has not been renewed. Petitioner's argument that the court improperly failed to exclude respondents from the marital home as a condition of the order of protection is obviously not academic. Petitioner, who has shown that she remains unable to return to her home based upon the court's failure to address the issue of whether respondents should be excluded is clearly continuing to suffer harm. Moreover, by removing herself from the family home for her own safety, petitioner obviated the need for a further order of protection, so her failure to seek one does not render academic her argument that the order was inadequate * * *.

Moreover, we find that Family Court erred in failing to hold a dispositional hearing to consider the issues of whether the order of protection should have included a provision excluding respondents from the marital apartment and whether it should have extended for three years.

We find no basis in law for the Family Court's action in refusing to even consider whether respondents should be excluded from the apartment as a condition of the order of protection, which it had found to be clearly warranted by respondents' behavior. As noted above, the Family

Court is unquestionably permitted to order a non-resident party to stay away from the home of the other spouse or to exclude a resident party from the common home. There is no logical rationale to limit the power of the court by prohibiting it from excluding a resident abusive spouse merely because the victim of the abuse has been forced by her abuser to flee their common home. Such a holding would reward the worst of abusers, i.e., those whose behavior was so violent or threatening that it forced their family members to leave home, with automatic possession of the home, and would obviously frustrate the intent of the statutory scheme, which seeks to protect, not punish, the victims of domestic violence.

For these reasons, it was clearly error for the Family Court to base its decision, as it intimated it was doing, on the fact that petitioner could theoretically seek exclusive occupancy of the marital home in a divorce action commenced in Supreme Court. The issue before the Family Court was not, as claimed by respondents, a permanent award of exclusive possession of the marital property incident to the divorce, but, instead, the propriety of an exclusion order to prevent further family disturbance. Regardless of the fact that the petitioner had already moved out, the Family Court not only has jurisdiction to determine this issue, but it is its very mandate to provide for this type of relief in matters involving family violence. Clearly, recourse to a divorce proceeding was of little or no use to petitioner. Not only would she not be entitled to counsel in a divorce proceeding, but the commencement of a new action would cause further delay, during which time petitioner would remain excluded from her home by the threat of violence.

Further, while we must remain sensitive to the fact that the Family Court must deal with the practical realities of the impact of its decisions on the safety and well-being of the litigants before it, we note that the court should not base its decision solely on the fact that one party has found another place to stay and the other has not.[2] A victim of the outrageous and life-threatening sort of abuse set forth in this matter cannot be held hostage to the potential homelessness of her abuser, who created the intolerable situation in the first instance.

Moreover, in addition to its failure to consider excluding respondents from the home, we find that the Family Court erred in not considering whether the order of protection should extend for three years. * * * We categorically reject respondents' argument that a petitioner must specifically state in the petition that "aggravating circumstances" exist in order for the court to issue a three-year order of protection upon disposition. There is certainly no such requirement in

2. In this context, petitioner argues quite compellingly that, if the court were going to base its decision on the fact that she had found another place to live and that her husband, who was in a wheelchair, had no place else to go, she should at least have been permitted to present evidence showing that he was not without other relatives in the area who could take him in and that the accommodations that she had since found, i.e., sharing a one-bedroom apartment that was not outfitted with special equipment for the hearing impaired with her daughter, her granddaughter and her daughter's boyfriend, were completely inadequate to her needs.

the statute. Clearly, it is for the court to determine, on the evidence before it, whether such circumstances exist, and the court is in no way barred from doing so merely because the petitioner did not use certain special language in her petition.

Respondents also argue that, regardless of whether the court erred in determining that it did not have the power to grant petitioner the relief she requested, petitioner has not demonstrated that she was entitled to a dispositional hearing because all of the facts relevant to her claim were presented in the fact-finding hearing and those facts demonstrate that the order issued by the court was the appropriate relief under the circumstances.

However, it is clear that, under the circumstances of this case, petitioner was entitled to present further evidence on the issue of disposition. In particular, we note that petitioner has demonstrated that the fact-finding hearing, which was held before a different judge from the one determining disposition, was abbreviated by respondent's admission to the family offense of harassment prior to petitioner having had an opportunity to present evidence that she claims would have been crucial to disposition. Most significantly, at the fact-finding hearing, the court terminated the case prior to the planned testimony of an expert on battered women's syndrome, who, according to petitioner's offer of proof, would have helped explain her delayed reaction to the abuse inflicted upon her, her inability to leave the marital home on her own, and the impact of her deafness on her ability to function under hostile circumstances. These were factors relevant not only to fact-finding but to disposition as well. While the court had already ruled that the expert's testimony was germane to the issues presented, it apparently concluded that it was able to reach a conclusion as to the fact-finding portion of the proceeding without the testimony. Under these circumstances, petitioner has demonstrated that she had further evidence relevant to disposition that she should have been permitted to set before the court. * * *

Finally, we note the absurdity of the argument set forth by respondents that there was no need for a dispositional hearing to explore whether an order of exclusion was necessary because the record is clear that respondents ceased harassing petitioner when ordered to do so in the original temporary order of protection. We can hardly require evidence of continuing harassment to be a condition to an order of exclusion in a situation where the respondents, who were found to have committed harassment, remain in the home while their victim has been forced to flee, thereby eliminating both their motivation and opportunity to further abuse her.

Under these circumstances, it is clear that a dispositional hearing was necessary in this matter. We therefore remand for a dispositional hearing before a different judge of the Family Court, to determine whether an order of protection excluding respondents from the apartment is warranted and whether it should extend for three years. * * *

JOAN ZORZA, WHAT IS WRONG WITH MUTUAL ORDERS OF PROTECTION?

4(5) Domestic Violence Report 67–68, 78 (June/July 1999).

Mutual orders of protection are protective orders issued against each of two parties by the other party. Typically they occur within the same document, but they need not do so. Indeed, they could be issued by two different courts at different times, provided that they are both in effect simultaneously. Usually mutual orders are issued after only one of the parties has sought a protective order, particularly when they are issued within the same document. Regardless of how the mutual orders are granted, they have many problems. They often deny due process to one or both of the parties, and they are more dangerous to the victim than having no order at all.

BASED ON MISCONCEPTIONS

Mutual orders are based on misconceptions, myths, gender bias and incorrect theories about domestic violence. Such misconceptions include: she pushes his buttons; she must have provoked the abuse; it is a family dynamic; it takes two to tango; the abuse will end when they get divorced; it couldn't have been that bad or she would have left long ago; it won't happen anymore because we have mediated all their disputes; it only happens in dysfunctional families; or they are co-dependent on each other. Sometimes mutual orders are issued upon the consent of both parties, or after the case is sent to mediation, usually because the abuser (or the abuser's attorney) intimidates the victim, or the judge or victim's attorney is lazy or feels rushed and does not want to hold an evidentiary hearing about whether either party perpetrated abuse that was not justified.

Domestic violence occurs by choice of the abuser, and when society does not hold the abuser fully accountable, the abuser benefits more by being abusive than he risks through societal sanctions. Almost never is abuse a mutual matter.

MUTUAL ORDERS SEND EVERYONE THE WRONG MESSAGE

Mutual orders send everyone the wrong message. They encourage society to trivialize the abuse, to consider the abuse too minor to determine the identity of the real abuser. At the same time, such orders also encourage people to blame the victim rather than hold the abuser accountable. People believe that the court would not have issued mutual orders if only one party was abusive, so both must have been at blame. Mutual orders reinforce all the misconceptions that justify having granted mutual orders in the first place.

Confuses Children: These wrong messages are particularly unfortunate for the victim's children, confusing the children about what the grownups and court system think is going on, what is acceptable behavior, who is at fault, what happens to those who abuse others, and what happens to victims who try to seek protection for themselves or their children. As a result, mutual orders contribute to perpetuating the intergenerational cycle of violence, the exact opposite of what domestic violence protection statutes are meant to accomplish.

Confuses and Further Empowers Abuser: Mutual orders reward the abuser and further empower him. They enable him to deny his actions and not take responsibility for them. Through mutual orders, the abuser is also able to get the entire system to focus on the victim. This is particularly true when the abuser falsely alleges, as abusers frequently do, that the victim abused him or violated the order. He will be able to endlessly accuse her of having violated one or more terms of the protective order, or force her to bargain away her rights in exchange for his not bringing charges against her for violating the order.

Stigmatizes and Further Disempowers Victim: The wrong messages sent by a mutual orders stigmatize the victim. Instead of being empowered by such orders, it further disempowers her. The enhancement of the power difference in the relationship, through the issuance of mutual orders, can only further confuse her.

Not Therapeutic: The stigmatization of the victim and enhancement of the abuser's power is not therapeutic for anyone. Without naming or recognizing the violence the victim cannot heal. Without holding the abuser accountable, the abuser cannot begin to heal. Children learn that violence works, that the abuser can largely (or completely) get away with the abuse, and that the system does virtually nothing to protect the victim. When the abuser's messages are reinforced by society, the children may feel safer if they take the abuser's side, even if this makes them feel guilty. If the children remain loyal to the victim, they worry about what the abuser will do and whether it is their fault. Mutual orders also prevent the children from understanding what is going on, and hence from beginning to heal.

Confuses the Community and Keeps Violence Private: Mutual orders reinforce society in ignoring domestic violence. The community is effectively told that domestic violence is a minor matter, one that is just between the parties involved, and that it is not important to know who abused whom or how serious the abuse was. Mutual orders keep the community as well as the family involved from recognizing the abuser's fault and holding him responsible. This judicial failure to hold the abuser accountable further encourages the community to not get involved and not help the victim, thus, guaranteeing that society will continue to encourage domestic violence.

Anthropologists have long told us that there are non-violent societies where men do not batter women. What distinguishes these societies is an atmosphere characterized by cooperation, commitment, sharing and equality. In societies where men do not beat women, women do not beat men, and although divorce is equally easy for both men and women to obtain, divorce is quite rare. If a woman is beaten in a nonviolent society, the entire community immediately intervenes, taking her side. The abuser gains nothing from his abuse, whereas his victim receives all of the support and sympathy, the exact opposite of what happens when mutual orders are issued. (Of course, a similar injustice happens if only one order is issued that is directed against the victim.)

MUTUAL ORDERS ARE WORSE THAN NO ORDER AND ENDANGER THE VICTIMS

Confuses Police: Mutual orders confuse the police and give them no guidance on which party is guilty. Unless the police have witnessed the entire transaction, it is often impossible for them to know which party violated an order that directs both parties to stay away from each other, not interfere with the personal liberty of the other, and not contact the other. Usually such orders give the police no guidance on how to enforce the order, with the result that when police are summoned, they either do nothing, or threaten to or actually arrest both parties.

Police Confusion Results in Inappropriate Responses: When police are confused and do not know how to respond, the results are problematical. When police tell the real victim that no help will be given regardless of the abusiveness of the batterer, the victim learns that nobody will help her, no matter how serious the danger. This leaves the victim with no one to rely on. It also teaches the abuser that nobody cares about or is going to help the victim, reinforcing the abuser's belief that it is acceptable to beat and terrorize the victim.

When police threaten to or do arrest both parties, the victim learns that help will only be given at an unfair and unacceptable price to the victim, i.e., the victim's arrest. Unfortunately, many batterers are quite willing to risk their own arrest if their victim will also incur punishment. For these abusers, arresting both parties is not a deterrence, but may actually encourage them to continue and even escalate their violence. This is a subversion of the legislature's intent in enacting the domestic violence statute.

Dual Arrests Are Much Harder on the Victim: When both parties are arrested, the victim is far more likely to spend more time in jail, particularly when the victim is female and the abuser is male. Victims are likely to have less money and less access to money than are abusers, and as a result are less able to be bailed out of jail. Victims are also less likely to have a support network of family or friends who can help bail them out of jail because abusers tend to isolate their victims from any potential emotional support (by, for example, being inhospitable to those who might support the victim).

Having less money, the victim is less likely to be able to afford a lawyer; even if the victim is indigent, the court will not appoint a defense attorney before the arraignment. As most gender bias studies have shown, women's jails are usually located further from the courthouse than are those housing men. Most attorneys practicing criminal law have far more clients in the men's jails and prisons, so it is usually less convenient for them to go to see their imprisoned women clients. Partly as a result of the distance and inconvenience factors, attorneys spend considerably less time interviewing their jailed female clients than their jailed male clients facing similar charges. Given that battered women are more likely to languish in jail awaiting trial than their male batterers, their cases are likely to seriously suffer as a result of less preparation.

In addition, those abusers who are out of jail while their victims remain locked up, are better suited to bolster their cases, threaten witnesses who might support the victims' side, or destroy exculpatory evidence. Because many attorneys do not take their female clients as seriously, they tend to believe the "mutual abuse" theory. Also, many attorneys become overconfident that a battered woman has a winning case, and as a result, they do not investigate or prepare the case and witnesses adequately.

At the same time, fear for their children will make most battered women far more concerned about just ending the ordeal, even if that means pleading guilty. If a battered woman becomes depressed or suicidal or engages in other self-destructive behavior, her case is further damaged as are her chances for custody of her children.

As a result of all these factors, the victim is far more likely to plead guilty or be found guilty, again reinforcing the "mutual abuse" theory.

Mutual Orders Endanger the Children: In families with minor children, a mutual order will cause the victimized parent to lose her advantage in a custody case, an advantage that the legislatures of more than 40 states have meant the victimized parent to have in a custody dispute with an abuser. Judges in these states are required to consider domestic violence in their custody determinations, and to favor the non-battering parent. However, when mutual orders are issued, the battered parent is considered as culpable as the other parent, and is generally given no advantage. If the battered mother was jailed and later convicted, she is further jeopardized in the custody case, especially if the abuser was acquitted.

When a battered mother is arrested, the children are likely to feel guilty, sabotaged and helpless, especially if one of the children called the police. When both parties are arrested, the children risk being placed in foster care. This is an emotionally devastating experience for children. While the police, child protection agency or courts are very quick to put children in foster care, it often takes months or years to return the children to their home. When just the victimized mother is arrested (or the abusive father is able to bail himself out quickly), the children are likely to end up in the care of their father. This is exactly the result that the legislature sought to avoid. It sends the wrong message to the children about which parent will be rewarded for the abuse. Also, it enables the abuser to have the children in his sole care if a divorce is filed, making it more likely that he will end up with permanent custody.

Even if the state in which the family lives does not require its judges to consider domestic violence in making a custody decision, the issuance of a mutual order or the arrest of the abused victim may jeopardize the victim's ability to seek custody in another state that does consider domestic violence.

Mutual Orders Help Abusers Manipulate and Blame: Mutual orders give abusers another tool for harassing their victims. Because the abuser has an order against his victim, the abuser can intimidate or force the victim into a situation where the victim is not in compliance with the order, or can falsely accuse the victim of violating the order in the hope that the police will arrest the victim or file charges in court against the victim. As a result, the abuser keeps shifting the blame back onto the victim, never taking responsibility for any of the abuse. In this way, the abuser can exhaust, demoralize, drain, and retaliate against the victim, rewarding the abuser for false or spurious claims and further reinforcing the system's mistaken belief that its "mutual abuse" theory is true.

May Jeopardize Immigration Claim: An undocumented battered women married to a U.S. citizen or permanent resident alien may well lose the right to obtain her green card as a battered spouse if an order of protection, including one issued as part of a mutual order, has been entered against her.

Victim Risks No Full Faith and Credit

The victim also may lose full faith and credit recognition of her order of protection if she flees to another state. The police may refuse to enforce the victim's order. The police may even be justified in not enforcing the victim's order if the abuser initially sought the protection and the victim never filed for protection. Such is also the case if both the victim and abuser filed for protection, but the court never made findings as to whether the abuser perpetrated the abuse justifying the victim's order. Even when the victim's order is entitled to enforcement, the state to which she fled may not understand its enforceability, due to insufficient facts or otherwise. Again, this puts the victim at risk for further abuse.

Many mutual orders are issued because of (1) incorrect notions about mutual abuse, (2) gender bias against women, (3) laziness on the part of attorneys, mediators, or judges who do not want to go through the court case and make a proper decision, (4) failure of the victim to have any or decent representation or knowledge of the dangers of mutual orders, or (5) direct or indirect intimidation of the victim by the abuser.

A problem with the lack of full faith and credit of mutual orders is that most battered women do not seek protection in other states unless they are fleeing their abusers out of desperation, with the knowledge that they were not protected where they were. Although Congress wanted to see all victims of domestic violence protected throughout the country, Congress recognized that some orders are issued without complying with minimum legal standards, and as a result exempted these orders from receiving full faith and credit. Congress hoped and expected that these federal standards would be picked up as minimum standards throughout the country. However, judges and law officers who are lazy or gender biased do not care, or may actively want to subvert battered women.

Mutual Orders Violate Due Process

Mutual orders of protection violate the due process rights of the person against whom they are sought, when the pleadings requesting such orders are not served on the person in advance of the hearing, or when they do not state the basis on which they are sought. This is why Congress exempted most mutual orders in its full faith and credit provisions of the Violence Against Women Act, 18 U.S.C. § 2265. Every court that has ruled on the issue has struck down a mutual order issued against the original petitioner if issued without some pleading having been served on her, at least if the original petitioner objected at the hearing. The original petitioner's due process rights were violated because no advance notice was given of any allegations. Without notice of the alleged wrongdoing, adequate preparation of a defense is impossible. That is why every state's domestic violence statute requires the person initially seeking the order to state the supporting allegations in the petition or complaint, and then to serve the pleading on the person against whom the order is sought.

* * *

KAREN ANN MECHTEL v. ALLEN DAVID MECHTEL

Court of Appeals of Minnesota (1995).
528 N.W.2d 916, 917–921.

Facts

On March 22, 1994, appellant Karen Mechtel applied to the Houston County District Court for an order for protection against her husband, Allen David Mechtel (respondent). In her affidavit, appellant alleged that respondent had stopped his psychiatric care for manic depression and quit taking his medication in August 1993. She alleged that on August 23, 1993, respondent became angry, smashed a coffee table, threw plants and furniture around the house, and threatened to kill her—all in front of the children. Appellant left the house and stayed with a neighbor for a week. She went home with the agreement that respondent would move out. Respondent moved out in mid-September.

The week before appellant filed the petition, she told respondent that she "wanted to move on with [her] life." On March 29, 1994 respondent appeared at the house and was "angry, hollering, and irrational." Appellant was advised by the sheriff who came to her house that day that she should get an order for protection. Appellant stated that respondent was "mentally unstable, and capable of killing me, when he has a rage. When [respondent] is out of control, I fear for my life."

On the same day that appellant applied for the order for protection, the district court issued an order for hearing and *ex parte* order for protection. The order provided that (1) a hearing was to be held on

March 28; (2) respondent must not harm appellant or cause her to fear harm; (3) respondent must not enter appellant's residence; (4) appellant shall have temporary custody of the children; (5) neither party shall sell or damage any real or personal property; (6) respondent must surrender his keys to the residence and the 1993 Dodge Caravan to a law enforcement official; and (7) "the parties shall meet with Kevin L. Siebold, Court Services Officer on Thursday, March 24, 1994, at 4:00 P.M., to discuss the issues at hand." The parties met with the court services officer on March 24 as ordered by the district court.

Respondent requested and was granted a continuance to obtain counsel and the hearing was held April 7, 1994. Respondent was represented by counsel. Before the hearing, James Schultz, an attorney appellant hired to start a dissolution action, gave respondent's counsel a copy of a summons and petition he had drafted. Schultz then left the courtroom and appellant appeared *pro se* at the hearing. No testimony was taken, and the court did not ask about the domestic abuse allegations.

On April 8, 1994, the court issued an order for protection. The court deleted the portion of the pre-printed order for protection form that read "Acts of domestic abuse have occurred, including the following" and substituted "The Court makes no determination of guilt or any violation but will issue this mutual Restraining Order." The court only ordered respondent not to commit acts of domestic abuse and to make and keep an appointment to be evaluated by the Counseling for Abusive Men Treatment Program. The court further stated that this was a mutual restraining order and directed that "[n]either party shall harass the other party hereto in any manner or form whatsoever."

On May 26, 1994, appellant was served with a criminal complaint, charging her with violations of the restraining order.

Issues

1. Did the district court err by ordering that appellant participate in mediation?

2. Did the district court err by issuing a mutual protection order when respondent did not request an order for protection, and there was no evidence of abusive acts by appellant?

3. Did the district court err by using the language of a dissolution summons as the basis for relief in a domestic abuse proceeding?

4. Did the district court err in not holding a "full hearing" and not making a finding whether domestic abuse occurred?

Analysis

I. Mediation

Appellant argues that, by requiring her to meet with respondent two days after the issuance of the *ex parte* order and four days before the full hearing, the district court improperly ordered her to participate in mediation with respondent.

"If a court determines that there is probable cause that one of the parties, or a child of a party, has been physically or sexually abused by the other party, the court shall not require or refer the parties to mediation or any other process that requires the parties to meet and confer without counsel, if any, present." Minn.Stat. § 518.619, subd. 2 (1992). The family court rules have a similar provision: "The court shall not require mediation when it finds probable cause that domestic or child abuse has occurred." Minn.R.Gen.Pract. 310.01(a).

The first question is whether there was probable cause that domestic abuse had occurred. In *Vogt v. Vogt*, 455 N.W.2d 471, 474 (Minn. 1990), the supreme court noted that "by issuance of the protective order" the court had "implicitly found * * * probable cause of physical abuse." In that case, however, the protective order was issued after a hearing was held. The question in this case is whether the issuance of an *ex parte* order should also be treated as an implicit finding of probable cause of physical abuse. We conclude that it should.

The reason for this rule is clear—a victim should not be required to go through mediation with an abusive spouse. If the court determines after a full hearing that no abuse occurred, then the court is free to order mediation. In cases in which the court does eventually make a finding of domestic abuse, it would be wrong for the victim to have been ordered to participate in mediation merely because the court had not yet held the statutorily required hearing or made the statutorily required findings.

The next question is whether the meeting with the court services officer "to discuss the issues at hand" constituted "mediation." The statute does not define the term mediation. The Supreme Court has cited to the following definition with approval in an order for protection case: "A forum in which an impartial person, the mediator, facilitates communication between parties to promote conciliation, settlement, or understanding among them." Since the meeting ordered by the district court is consistent with this definition, we conclude that the court improperly ordered appellant to participate in mediation.

II. *Mutual Restraining Order*

The district court's April 8, 1994 Order for Protection included a mutual restraining order. Appellant argues the district court erred in issuing a mutual restraining order since respondent did not file a petition for an Order for Protection and the court made no finding of mutual abuse.

In *FitzGerald v. FitzGerald*, 406 N.W.2d 52 (Minn.App.1987), the wife alleged that the district court erred in issuing a mutual restraining order when her husband did not seek a restraining order, there was no evidence to show that she was an abusing party, and she was not given notice and an opportunity to prepare an adequate defense. This court agreed that there was no evidence to support the issuance of a restraining order against the wife, and reversed the portion of the order that restrained her. Id. at 54.

At the brief hearing in this case, appellant was *pro se* and respondent was represented by counsel. There was no inquiry into the abuse allegations. The court asked appellant if a mutual restraining order was "in accordance with your understanding." She replied "No, it isn't." She also asked the court, "[C]an you explain to me what you mean a mutual restraining order?" and indicated that "I am being advised not to agree with a mutual restraining order." The following exchange took place:

> COURT: That would be mutual that you can't call him up and start calling him obscene names, for example. He cannot do that to you either. That's not any admission of any type of guilt on your part but if you would, if you were to call him up and call him names or threaten him or—[Appellant]: I certainly agree not to do that, Your Honor. THE COURT: Then you possibly could face criminal charges just the same as he could face them if he does that to you so is that clear, do you feel you understand that all right? [Appellant]: Yes.

Based on this exchange, the district court may have thought that appellant was agreeing to a mutual restraining order. Appellant, however, indicated twice before that she did not want a mutual restraining order. Appellant also indicated that she was confused about the concept of a mutual restraining order. Since appellant was *pro se*, the district court should have been very careful to make sure that she was agreeing to a mutual restraining order.

Since respondent did not ask for a protective order, no evidence of abuse by appellant was produced at the hearing, and appellant twice indicated that she did not agree to the issuance of a mutual restraining order, the district court erred in issuing a mutual restraining order.

III. *Relief in A Domestic Abuse Proceeding*

The order for protection provided that "This is a mutual Restraining Order to correlate with the Order in the dissolution proceedings. Neither party shall harass the other party hereto in any manner or form whatsoever." There was, however, no dissolution order. The court was apparently referring to a dissolution summons that had been handed to respondent's attorney just before the hearing. Appellant argues that the district court erred in using the summons in a dissolution action as the basis for relief in a domestic abuse proceeding.

Appellant properly notes under Minnesota law, every dissolution summons must, *inter alia,* contain a notice that, once the summons is served "[n]either party may harass the other party." Minn.Stat. § 518.091(a) (1992). Appellant argues that the district court erred in using this boilerplate relief provision from the standard dissolution summons rather than granting the relief of an order for protection.

The Domestic Abuse Act provides that the granting of relief is within the district court's discretion. See Minn.Stat. § 518B.01, subd. 6(a) ("Upon notice and hearing, the court may provide relief as follows"). Since we reverse on other grounds, we do not decide what relief should be ordered in a case such as this. Nevertheless, we note that judges considering actions brought under the Domestic Abuse Act should consider the uniqueness of the remedies available under the statute, as well as the potentially devastating consequences if such relief is not granted.

IV. Procedural Requirements of Domestic Abuse Act

Appellant argues that since the court did not ask any questions about the allegations of domestic abuse, she was denied her right to a "full hearing."

The Domestic Abuse Act provides that, upon the receipt of a petition for an order for protection, the court shall order "a hearing" within 14 days. When a petition alleges an immediate danger of domestic abuse, the court may grant an *ex parte* temporary order for protection, pending a "full hearing."

This court need not decide precisely what is a "full hearing" within the meaning of the Domestic Abuse Act since, under any definition, it is clear that the hearing in this case would not meet that definition. The transcript of the hearing is only five pages long. As appellant notes, the district court did not even ask whether the allegations in the petition were true. Thus, the district court did not hold a "full hearing" as required by the Act. Appellant also argues that the district court erred in failing to make a finding of domestic abuse. The court deleted the portion of the pre-printed order for protection form that read "Acts of domestic abuse have occurred, including the following" and substituted "The Court makes no determination of guilt or any violation but will issue this mutual Restraining Order."

In *Andrasko v. Andrasko*, 443 N.W.2d 228, 230–31 (Minn.App.1989), this court held that where the district court made no written findings, did not fill in the blank space for findings on the pre-printed order for protection form, and did not make any oral findings on the record, the court erred by failing to make any findings concerning domestic abuse.

Similarly, since the court in this case made no written or oral findings, and filled in the blank space for findings with a statement that it was not making a determination of guilt or any violation, the court erred in failing to make domestic abuse findings.

DECISION

The district court improperly ordered appellant to participate in mediation. The district court erred in issuing a mutual restraining order. The district court erred in failing to hold a "full hearing" and in not making any findings concerning domestic abuse.

Reversed and remanded.

B. ENFORCEMENT

JOAN ZORZA AND NANCY K. D. LEMON, TWO–THIRDS OF CIVIL PROTECTION ORDERS ARE SUCCESSFUL; BETTER COURT AND COMMUNITY SERVICES INCREASE THEIR SUCCESS RATES

2(4) Domestic Violence Report 51–52 (April/May 1997).

In 1994, the National Center for State Courts in Williamsburg, Virginia began a study in three communities of the effectiveness of restraining orders. Their findings, which include some surprises, have just been released. Susan L. Keilitz, Paula L. Hannaford, & Hillery S. Efkeman, Civil Protection Orders: The Benefits and Limitations for Victims of Domestic Violence (National Center for State Courts 1997). Their study builds on earlier studies that had shown that the effectiveness of protective orders depends on the specificity and comprehensiveness of the relief granted and how well the orders are enforced.

The researchers compared three factors: the accessibility of the court process; the linkages to public and private services and sources of support; and the criminal record of the abuser.

Participants included 285 battered women in Denver, Colorado; Wilmington, Delaware; and Washington, DC. The researchers also spoke with judges and court personnel, police, prosecutors, and victim services staff, and they checked court files and observed the civil protection order hearings. They interviewed all 285 women petitioners by telephone approximately one month after they received a temporary or permanent order, conducted follow-up interviews with 177 of the same women about six months later, and checked the civil case files and the criminal history records of the men named as abusers.

Many of the women had been severely abused. Over half of them had been threatened or injured with a weapon, over half had been beaten or choked, and 84% had been slapped, kicked or shoved. Almost a quarter of the women had been abused for more than five years and the women who had been beaten the longest experienced the most intense violence. This is consistent with battered women's observations that violence escalates in intensity, frequency and duration over time.

CRIMINAL HISTORY OF ABUSERS RELATED TO SEVERITY OF ABUSE

This study found that 64.8% of the abusers had prior criminal arrest histories, which is roughly similar to what has been found in other communities that have reviewed abuser's criminal histories. Furthermore, over half of these abusers' crimes (52.9%) involved violence (i.e., simple assault, weapons charges, domestic violence and other violence), 29.5% were drug and alcohol-related crimes, and 49.6% had histories of other crimes. When an abuser had a criminal history of both violent and drug or alcohol-related crimes, his abuse of his partner was likely to be far more severe and his partner was considerably less likely to be available for the second interview. These findings show the need to offer safety planning to every battered women the first time she appears in court, particularly if her partner has a criminal history involving prior violence or substance abuse.

The effectiveness of protection orders was measured on two scales: the petitioner's subjective feelings of well-being and safety, and whether the order was violated. Overall, the study found that nearly 75% of petitioners had increased feelings of well-being soon after the order was issued, rising to 85% after six months. At six months 92.7% of the women plaintiffs reported feeling better about themselves and 80.5% felt they were safer. At both interviews, 95% of the women stated that they would seek an order again.

SUCCESS RATES OF PROTECTIVE ORDERS

Though the results varied somewhat among the sites of the study, overall 72% of the petitioners stated that the order was not violated within the first month. While this decreased to 65% after six months, this is still a very significant success rate. In addition, at the follow-up interviews, only 8.4% of the women reported being physically re-abused (versus 2.6% at the initial interviews). In Denver, where the police were most likely to arrest abusers, physical re-victimization was only experienced by 2% of the women, considerably lower than the 10.9% and 11.9% rates reported by Delaware and District of Columbia women, respectively. Consistent with studies documenting that batterers attending intervention programs shift to using psychological abuse, 4.4% of the women in this study reported psychological abuse at their initial interviews, and 12.6% reported it six months later. Abuser stalking also increased from 4.1% at the initial interviews to 7.2% six months later.

The most common problem reported by the women at both interviews was that the abuser called the victim at home or work (16.1% and 17.4% respectively), or came to her home (9%). Only 5.4% of the victims reported more than two types of problems from their abusers.

Although abusive men with violent criminal histories were more likely to violate the protective orders, interestingly, their partners were more likely to report more positive feelings about themselves after obtaining the final orders. This suggests that more aggressive criminal prosecution may address the violence more effectively, whereas the civil restraining order may better bolster the victim's self-esteem and feelings of security.

INITIAL PROTECTIVE ORDERS ARE SUCCESSFUL EVEN WHEN PERMANENT ORDERS NOT OBTAINED

Many of the women who did not return for their permanent orders stated it was because their partner had stopped bothering them (35.5%)

or because the abuser had left the area (10%). While 17% claimed to have reconciled, only 2% said they had not returned to court because their abuser had threatened them and another 2% stated that they did not return because their abuser had persuaded them to drop their case. In addition, one-quarter of the women who did not return for permanent orders had help devising a safety plan at that first hearing; this should be standard procedure for all women seeking temporary orders of protection. The significant success from merely obtaining the initial protection order (i.e., the 45.5% of the cases where the abuser either stopped his abuse or left the area) and the safety plans devised at the temporary order stage, demonstrate the benefits of women coming to court even if they do not follow through in obtaining final orders. At a minimum, the courts need to stop viewing women who fail to return as abusing the court process, and instead recognize the power of the courts to deter merely as a result of the abuser knowing that his victim can return to court should he not stop his abusiveness.

Protection of Battered Women With Children

Women with children reported a higher number of problems with orders being violated than did women without children; at the follow-up interviews only 61.7% of women with children reported having no problems, compared to 79.4% of women without children. Sadly, large numbers of judges granted abusers visitation, usually without any restrictions at the final order stage, leaving the abusers free to go on legally abusing many of the women. Judges denied visitation in only 8% of the cases at the final order stage and ordered supervised visitation in only 4% of cases. In 4% of cases the court prohibited the abuser from contacting a child, yet it is unclear whether these abusers were the fathers of the children, or stepparents or the mothers' boyfriends. Few judges made the abuser vacate or remain away from the home (7.9% and 55.3%, respectively) at the final hearing. And despite federal law making gun possession illegal by the abusers, the court rarely ordered abusers to relinquish weapons (none in Denver and the District of Columbia and only 14.7% in Delaware).

[Editor's note in original: Because the study was conducted by an organization tied to supporting the judiciary, the researchers were constrained from criticizing the judges for inadequately protecting the women and children.]

Recommendations of Study

The study includes many useful recommendations. For example, it recommends informing domestic violence victims that the longer the abuse continues, the more severe it will probably become. It also recommends using the time during which the petitioner first comes to court to fill out forms to help her create a safety plan, since many battered women in the study did not return for the long-term order.

Another recommendation was that judges issue more orders requiring substance abuse counseling or batterer's counseling, especially in cases where the respondent has a history of arrest for substance abuse or violence, since these respondents are most likely to violate the protection order. Thus, judges issuing civil orders need access to this criminal information. Forms should be revised to reflect the full relief and enforcement options available.

Judges should also inform victims of the various ways to enforce their orders, including contempt actions. For example, the courts could provide easy information with each order on how to enforce the order. Battered women rarely used the contempt process to enforce their protection orders. In 87.7% of the cases, many of which involved violated orders, women never filed contempt motions. Even more disappointing was the fact that only 13 cases had one contempt motion filed and two cases had more than one contempt filed; only five of the nine contempt cases filed resulted in a finding of contempt.

In addition, courts should inform women of all the services available in the community to help them. While 77.5% of the women participants received some type of assistance either before or after they obtained their order, most depended on relatives and friends for this assistance, with few receiving other services. Furthermore, the assistance that the women received was usually in the month before they got their orders, and not afterwards. The only exceptions were counseling and support groups, which women utilized somewhat more often after they had obtained court protective orders. All of the community's services should be made available to women seeking court protection, including police, prosecutors, victim assistance, victim counseling, shelters, *pro bono* legal services, employment and education counseling, and housing services.

The marked discrepancy in police arrest rates of respondents (87.1% in Denver, 55.0% in Delaware and 41.2% in the District of Columbia) illustrates the need for better, more aggressive and consistent use of ascertaining probable cause to arrest abusers. The police must also be consistent in informing victims about obtaining civil protection orders and enforcing existing orders. The study criticized the District of Columbia police who got high marks for telling women about the availability of civil protection orders, but at the expense of seldom arresting the abusers. Similarly, the study stresses the need for more aggressive prosecution policies, and the need for domestic violence training as an integral part of law enforcement education (not just in the police academies).

This very interesting and useful study concludes by noting that "the effectiveness of civil protective orders is inextricably linked to the quality of the system of government and community services in which protection orders operate. Issuing a protection order is only one part of the remedy."

DAVID M. ZLOTNICK, EMPOWERING THE BATTERED WOMAN: THE USE OF CRIMINAL CONTEMPT SANCTIONS TO ENFORCE CIVIL PROTECTION ORDERS

56 Ohio St. L. J. 1190–1215 (1995).

IV. CIVIL PROTECTION ORDERS AND CRIMINAL CONTEMPT SANCTIONS

A. Civil Protection Orders Are a Core Component of Society's Response to Domestic Violence

1. An Overview of Civil Protection Orders

Civil protection orders are now available for battered women in all fifty states and the District of Columbia. They permit a victim of domestic violence to obtain a binding order from a court that at the minimum prohibits an abuser from committing further acts of violence. Such orders may also enjoin other conduct (e.g., all contact whatsoever with the woman), award custody of children to the woman, limit the batterer's visitation rights, grant the woman possession of the residence or other property, and award child support or other economic relief.

Obtaining a civil protection order is usually a two-step process. First, the victim petitions the court *ex parte* for a temporary order that provides emergency injunctive relief restraining the batterer from inflicting further violence. The emergency order will remain in effect for a short duration, usually only a few weeks. The emergency order must then be served on the batterer along with notice of an adversary hearing. Second, the court will hold a subsequent hearing during which the civil protection order may be made semi-permanent, lasting anywhere from several weeks to a year or longer.

Civil protection orders, as opposed to criminal sanctions, are prospective. They explicitly seek to alter the future behavior of the batterer. The remedies offered by protection orders are also broader than criminal remedies because they are available to deal with conduct that the police might otherwise overlook as not serious. In addition to providing a measure of protection, a civil protection order serves to bring the batterer and victim into the domestic violence system.

While civil protection orders were initially limited to certain classes of persons and were sometimes difficult to obtain, their availability and flexibility has grown dramatically in recent years. There is now near universal agreement that civil protection orders are an essential part of domestic violence reform. But while everyone agrees that greater enforcement of civil protection orders is necessary, lack of enforcement is still cited as the principal weakness of protection orders.

2. Civil Protection Orders Are Currently Enforced Through Contempt Sanctions and Criminal Prosecution

Varying state to state, a violation of a civil protection order is punishable as a misdemeanor, by civil or criminal contempt, or by both criminal and contempt sanctions. Approximately forty states currently have statutes criminalizing violations of protection orders. Just over thirty-two states and the District of Columbia specifically authorize either civil or criminal contempt as a remedy. About half the states permit violations to be prosecuted both as contempts and misdemeanors. However, even where not specifically authorized by statute, state judges generally retain the power to punish violations of court orders by contempt; thus contempt sanctions are available in most jurisdictions.

While statutes providing for criminal contempt vary, there are two major ways of seeking such sanctions—either through prosecutions by the state or through actions prosecuted by the battered women themselves, *pro se*, or with the assistance of private counsel. While this flexibility is certainly one feature that makes contempt sanctions an attractive remedy, it is more important that contempt sanctions offer an opportunity to empower women; further, they are more practical than criminal prosecutions for violations because they are faster and encounter less resistance from institutional actors.

B.　Criminal Contempt Sanctions for Violation of Civil Protection Orders Will Empower Battered Women

A civil protection order initially empowers the battered woman by giving her a written legal document that legitimizes her right to be free from violence at the hands of her abuser. Many orders boldly highlight that a violation of the order constitutes contempt of court or a criminal offense. Battered women believe that civil protection orders will be effective and are often told by police officers that nothing can be done for them without such an order. Furthermore, all institutional participants support orders and want them obeyed.

Under a civil protection order, the battered woman is placed at the center of the decision-making process. She can now fairly easily obtain a temporary order without counsel to provide much needed protection in emergency situations. However, the process also allows her to weigh her options before seeking a permanent order which can be tailored to her specific situation. From initiation of the process, civil protection orders empower women by legitimizing their claims of abuse and demonstrating to them that they have access to and the support of societal institutions.

If the order is violated in a jurisdiction in which the self-help system of private initiation and prosecution is permitted, the battered woman has the power to file the initial contempt motion and can conduct the hearing herself or through counsel. This route avoids reliance on over-burdened and often unsympathetic prosecutors' offices and provides an opportunity for battered women's groups to establish their own advocacy network. Even where only the state prosecutor may prosecute the contempt action, the battered woman is still empowered because it is the order she initiated that is the legal source of the conviction rather than the criminal law.

Providing criminal contempt as an option also increases the flexibility of a battered woman's available remedies. The very experience of having a choice can itself be empowering. For example, one battered woman might trust the court that issued the protection order and would prefer to have the issue litigated there. Another might prefer to force the batterer to face a jury in a criminal case. Multiplying their options empowers battered women while protecting them from further abuse. Regardless of the method used to obtain the criminal contempt sanction, the significant involvement of the victim in the civil protection order process and the potential for renaming the batterer's conduct as contemptuous make the criminal contempt route both an empowering and transformative experience for the battered woman.

C. *Practical Advantages of Criminal Contempt as the Immediate Remedy for Violation of Protection Orders*

1. *Contempt Is Faster and Faster Is Better*

In addition to the empowerment potential of criminal contempt sanctions, this route also offers practical advantages to the traditional criminal process. First and foremost, the criminal contempt route is often faster than the criminal justice system. Contempt orders can either be filed as emergency orders in the family court, or be transferred over to the criminal division, thus obtaining priority over other cases.

In the states that explicitly authorize contempt sanctions for violations of protection orders, contempt proceedings are often specifically given an expedited hearing under the statute. For example, in Connecticut, when a motion for contempt is filed for a violation of a protection order, a hearing must be held within five days of the service of the motion on the defendant. Even when no specific time period is stated in the statute, courts have required a speedy hearing to effectuate the legislative intent of ensuring the battered woman's safety.

When contempt motions can be heard in the issuing court, there can be additional time savings. While domestic court dockets are by no means under-utilized, they are usually less crowded than misdemeanor dockets. Also, because many jurisdictions permit victims to initiate the actions themselves, battered women need not wait for police to make an arrest or prosecutors to file charges.

Once initiated, contempt hearings can often be concluded faster than criminal trials. Since contempt is generally punishable by less than six months' imprisonment, contempt proceedings are tried before a judge, eliminating jury selection and other time-consuming aspects of jury trials. Bench trials also spare the victim the perils and stresses of a jury trial.

Granting a speedy hearing is essential because batterers are more likely to respond to a fast contempt mechanism than a slower criminal prosecution, because deterrence is generally more potent when a quick punishment follows an infraction. From a batterer's unique psychological perspective, however, contempt also offers distinct advantages. Batterers are manipulative individuals who think they can talk their way out of trouble or evade the constraints that society imposes on individual behavior. Also, because they tend to conceive relationships in terms of power, they tend to respond only to a specific threat from an identifiable person whom they perceive as more powerful. A directive from a family court judge that he or she will lock up the batterer for contempt, which is then followed by a contempt hearing before the same judge, is therefore more effective than the general threat of criminal prosecution—especially since many batterers do not regard their behavior as criminal.

2. Institutional Actors Are Less Resistant to Criminal Contempt Sanctions

Critics frequently complain that participants in the process (i.e., police, prosecutors, and judges) are unwilling to take violations of protection orders seriously and prosecute them vigorously. However, such criticism fails to differentiate among the various enforcement methods. In many cases, the criminal contempt sanction accommodates the needs of bureaucratic actors better than the other methods and thereby will result in more effective enforcement of protection orders.

Most significantly, implementation of criminal contempt sanctions can be tailored to the resources and commitment level of the various institutional actors. In jurisdictions where the prosecutor's office is willing to cooperate, separate domestic violence contempt units have been established with some success. Where prosecutors lack the resources or commitment, advocates can devote the financial and human resources of women's groups and request the *pro bono* efforts of sympathetic members of the domestic relations bar to provide legal assistance.

The police, prosecutors, and the courts are also more likely to support criminal contempt actions because they arise in contexts that do not overburden their resources or challenge their long-held notions about domestic violence. For example, police officers called to the scene of a battery by a repeat violator are more likely to arrest the offender if the complainant has obtained a civil protection order, or in the case of the persistent batterer, if she has subsequently filed contempt charges for additional incidents. Her behavior demonstrates her consistency and persistence, giving institutional actors' reason to believe she will follow through with the prosecution. The paper trail of repetitive violations signals to the officers that this offender is dangerous and does not respect the legal system.

There is also hope that courts will be more willing to punish contemnors than domestic violence defendants. Judges simply do not like being disobeyed, particularly when they have issued a direct order to someone, and studies suggest that judicial behavior can have profound effects on the outcome of domestic violence cases.

3. The System for Holding Batterers in Criminal Contempt for Violation of Protection Orders Can Be Improved

Despite the flexibility and empowerment advantages of the criminal contempt route, approximately twenty states have not yet authorized it as a remedy for violations of protection orders. To the extent these states have not acted due to perceived flaws in the criminal contempt delivery system, these problems actually can be addressed fairly easily through existing institutions or existing methods of reform.

For example, if judges are refusing to incarcerate domestic violence contemnors, sanctions for the violation of civil protection orders can be stiffened. Some states now require mandatory jail terms for repeat violators of protection orders. As with other areas of sentencing disparities, courts can be reined in by sentencing guidelines. For the police, a modified version of the mandatory arrest concept would limit the mandatory arrest scenario to situations in which a batterer has violated an order, a policy more consistent with their own discretionary judgments.

The most significant area, however, to ensure that criminal contempt sanctions work is the provision of legal services. If legislatures fund special units within state attorney's offices for these prosecutions, at least the financial aspect of this problem will be relieved. If battered women are to be responsible for bringing some or all of their own contempt actions, there is a definite need for more lawyers (both full-time and *pro bono*) to work in this field. However, rather than being seen as an obstacle, the provision of legal services for battered women should be perceived as an organizing tool for mobilizing sympathetic members of the bar. To the extent that *noblesse oblige* may be an insufficient motivation, legal aid rules can be altered to omit the income of the spouse from the eligibility calculation and provisions for payment of attorney's fees to the prevailing party can be added.

D. The Role of Substantive Criminal Charges for Violations of Civil Protection Orders

1. Feminists Are Mistakenly Advocating the Over–Criminalization of Protection Order Violations

Despite the many advantages of criminal contempt outlined above, some battered women advocates are now seeking the criminalization of violations of civil protection orders to the exclusion of other remedies. The most expansive proposals would convert protection order violations into misdemeanors that otherwise would not constitute substantive criminal behavior (i.e., violations of "stay away" and "no contact" provisions). Some jurisdictions, such as Florida, recently abolished use of the contempt sanction, requiring that all violations of civil protection orders be referred to the local state attorney's office for criminal prosecution as misdemeanors.

These advocates contend that criminalization of all acts of domestic violence will serve to transform cultural and institutional attitudes toward such violence, so that it will come to be seen as a crime in the ordinary sense. They also criticize the use of civil process (e.g., the contempt sanction), characterizing it as a "soft" approach that fails to treat battering as a crime worthy of punishment.

This overemphasis on criminal prosecution is misguided for many reasons. First, as discussed above, pursuing a contempt sanction for violation of a civil protection order can be an empowering experience for a battered woman if the system works properly. Second, the criminal justice system will resist the complete criminalization of civil protection order violations, despite hopes to the contrary. Third, past experience has shown that over-reliance on a single solution is a mistake. Fourth, a pure criminalization approach is overly optimistic about society's willingness to brand every protection order violation a criminal act.

Despite the wishes of these advocates, domestic violence does not behave like an "ordinary" crime and prosecutors and police have legitimate grievances about being forced to treat it as such. While police and prosecutors can be blamed for the reluctance of some victims to prosecute, the battering theory itself acknowledges that many battered women drop charges because they have not yet realized that the cycle will repeat itself or the batterer is able to manipulate them into dropping the charge. Even sympathetic prosecutors recognize that criminal prosecution alone is not going to provide the cure.

Further, prosecutors have credible institutional concerns with the pure criminalization approach. Overloading the criminal justice system with more, primarily misdemeanor cases will have several deleterious effects. More cases mean more delay. Misdemeanor cases, particularly in urban court systems, can take significant time to wend their way to trial. More delay and backlog invariably lead to more dismissals, as witnesses disappear or victims grow weary of endless court appearances. Dismissals demoralize victims and further frustrate police and prosecutors, who are generally interested only in cases with a high likelihood of success (which means a conviction). No-drop policies and subpoenas that compel battered women to testify against their will are time-consuming and have significant potential to further victimize women. Finally, delayed adjudication is a serious health risk for any woman whose batterer has already ignored a civil protection order. The first concern, therefore, should be a speedy adjudication of the civil protection order violation.

Pure criminalization advocates also ignore entrenched attitudes toward misdemeanor cases, particularly those tried before juries. Misdemeanor cases usually have the lowest conviction rate, as jurors are more willing to find a reasonable doubt for what they perceive as a minor crime. This is sure to be exacerbated when a jury is presented with criminal charges for incidents such as a violation of a stay-away or no-contact order. Further, rules of evidence, such as the general prohibition on the introduction of prior bad acts, will often exclude pertinent evidence of a prior battering relationship.

With respect to the courts, these arguments ignore the realities of bail and sentencing in criminal courts. Pretrial detention or high bail are usually reserved for defendants who have committed the most violent offenses or those persons likely to flee. Judges are reluctant to detain defendants who are employed, particularly if they are providing for minors. The pure criminalization approach is unlikely to result in immediate detention pending trial in all but the most violent cases.

In addition, criminal docket judges hear about an extraordinary amount of violence on a day-to-day basis. It is unrealistic to assume that incarceration rates for nonviolent violations of protection orders will be significant. As suggested, however, judges as a group tend to look particularly unfavorably on those who directly challenge their authority, such as by disobeying a civil protection order. Thus, pure criminalization advocates miss an opportunity to take advantage of an institutional bias in favor of incarceration by presenting the case as a contempt of court issue, preferably before the court that issued the protection order. Ultimately, criminalization advocates must recognize that single solutions for a complex social problem are bound to fail. Particularly in the criminal justice system, for which discretion is so fundamental a component, inflexible directives will be resisted. As with any crime, there is an upper limit on full enforcement of criminal laws against domestic violence.

On a theoretical level, the pure criminalization advocates are too far ahead of current cultural values. Given the high level of violence in our society, and especially in some communities, juries resist branding an individual a criminal when there is no act of violence, as in the violation of a stay-away order. Therefore, this attempt to transform public opinion through labeling all acts associated with a domestic violence as criminal simply goes too far. While words can open the door to change, those words must bridge existing beliefs with new facts, such as in the separation assault context. While more severe criminal penalties for domestic violence are necessary and the criminalization of protection order violations can be a useful step, alone they will not be effective. On the other hand, because the legal and everyday label of contempt is a better mesh with societal values, a resulting incarceration for violation of a protection order is more apt to be accepted as a just result.

Lastly, the pure criminalization approach is sometimes justified on the ground that successive prosecutions of the same act of domestic violence for contempt of a protection order and the criminal law might constitute double jeopardy. This was a particular concern after the Supreme Court's double jeopardy decision in *Grady v. Corbin*.[265] However, the Supreme Court reversed *Grady* in *United States v. Dixon*,[266] which specifically considered the double jeopardy consequences of successive prosecutions for contempt and a criminal offense arising from the same acts of domestic violence. In *Dixon*, a sharply divided Court reinstated serious felony charges against a batterer who had already been held in contempt for all but one of a series of acts. While ambiguous language in the *Dixon* decision may still present a double jeopardy issue, careful consideration of that issue before pursuing the contempt remedy can

265. 495 U.S. 508 (1990), overruled in part by United States v. Dixon, 113 S.Ct. 2849 (1993).

266. 113 S.Ct. 2849 (1993).

avoid a double jeopardy bar to criminal prosecution of serious incidents of domestic violence. In less serious cases, particularly non-violent cases where criminal prosecution is unlikely, the double jeopardy issue should not dissuade legislatures from authorizing both remedies for violations of protection orders.

V. CONCLUSION: THE PROPER CHRONOLOGICAL MIX: CONTEMPT FIRST, CRIMINAL PROSECUTION SECOND

While contempt sanctions have substantial benefits and a pure criminalization approach is unwise, the question that still remains is: What is the best approach for punishing violations of civil protection orders? Consistent with the current comprehensive approach, a system that includes a mix of contempt and criminal prosecution would likely produce the best results.

More specifically, contempt should be the preferred initial remedy because it can be faster and it offers a better chance of some sobering jail time before a sufficiently violent act yields the rare pretrial detention. Second, contempt sanctions as the initial remedy will serve the empowerment goal by enabling battered women to psychologically break the bonds to their batterers.

However, just as a pure criminalization approach will not work, contempt sanctions, while offering certain advantages, are not a panacea that will effectively punish and deter all batterers. The average maximum sentence under contempt statutes, of sixty to one-hundred-eighty days, will not always be sufficient to punish violations of protection orders. For cases involving assaultive conduct, traditional criminal charges such as assault and battery must be available to take advantage of the greater penalties for first degree misdemeanors and the substantial sentences for felonies. In some jurisdictions, newly created misdemeanors for violations of protection orders could serve the same function in some cases.

For the most hard-core violent batterer, severe criminal penalties will still be the only solution. Any domestic violence reform package must treat such batterers as the most violent criminals are treated, including preventive detention and high bail. On the other hand, in cases involving purely technical violations of specific provisions of a protection order such as a stay-away clause, criminal contempt sanctions alone should generally be sufficient and will offer the best chance for incarceration, if necessary. In cases involving violent acts, however, contempt can still be the first remedy pursued by the victim, independent of criminal prosecution, although cognizant of the potential double jeopardy issue. This strategy allows prosecutors to retain their traditional discretion without permitting the batterer to escape swift punishment.

An approach taking advantage of the speed and empowerment features of contempt and the stiffer penalties under criminal law is consistent with the comprehensive approach to domestic violence reform that seems to yield the best results. A contempt and criminal sanction approach also can be easily integrated with domestic violence courts and specialized prosecution units. Lastly, the need for attorneys to prosecute these actions in some jurisdictions can be seen as a positive avenue for concerned attorneys and advocacy organizations to take beneficial social action. Thus, in most significant respects, using contempt and criminal sanctions in unison is a winning proposition for battered women and the institutional actors involved in domestic violence control.

UNITED STATES v. ALVIN J. DIXON AND MICHAEL FOSTER

Supreme Court of the United States (1993).
509 U.S. 688–690, 113 S.Ct. 2849, 125 L.Ed.2d 556.

SYLLABUS

Based on respondent Dixon's arrest and indictment for possession of cocaine with intent to distribute, he was convicted of criminal contempt for violating a condition of his release on an unrelated offense forbidding him to commit "any criminal offense." The trial court later dismissed the cocaine indictment on double-jeopardy grounds. Conversely, the trial court in respondent Foster's case ruled that double jeopardy did not require dismissal of a five-count indictment charging him with simple assault (Count I), threatening to injure another on three occasions (Counts II–IV), and assault with intent to kill (Count V), even though the events underlying the charges had previously prompted his trial for criminal contempt for violating a civil protection order (CPO) requiring him not to " 'assault ... or in any manner threaten ...' " his estranged wife. The District of Columbia Court of Appeals consolidated the two cases on appeal and ruled that both subsequent prosecutions were barred by the Double Jeopardy Clause under *Grady v. Corbin*, 495 U.S. 508, 110 S.Ct. 2084, 109 L.Ed.2d 548.

Held: The judgment is affirmed in part and reversed in part, and the case is remanded.

JUSTICE SCALIA delivered the opinion of the Court with respect to Parts I, II, and IV, concluding that:

1. The Double Jeopardy Clause's protection attaches in nonsummary criminal contempt prosecutions just as it does in other criminal prosecutions. In the contexts of both multiple punishments and successive prosecution, the double jeopardy bar applies if the two offenses for which the defendant is punished or tried cannot survive the "same-elements" or "*Blockburger*" test. See, e.g., *Blockburger v. United States*, 284 U.S. 299, 304. That test inquires whether each offense contains an element not contained in the other; if not, they are the "same offence" within the Clause's meaning, and double jeopardy bars subsequent punishment or prosecution. The Court recently held in *Grady* that in addition to passing the *Blockburger* test, a subsequent prosecution must satisfy a "same-conduct" test to avoid the double jeopardy bar. That test provides that, "if, to establish an essential element of an offense charged

in that prosecution, the government will prove conduct that constitutes an offense for which the defendant has already been prosecuted," a second prosecution may not be had.

* * *

JUSTICE SCALIA, joined by JUSTICE KENNEDY, concluded in Parts III–A and III–B that:

1. Because Dixon's drug offense did not include any element not contained in his previous contempt offense, his subsequent prosecution fails the *Blockburger* test. Dixon's contempt sanction was imposed for violating the order through commission of the incorporated drug offense. His "crime" of violating a condition of his release cannot be abstracted from the "element" of the violated condition. *Harris v. Oklahoma*, 433 U.S. 682. Here, as in *Harris*, the underlying substantive criminal offense is a "species of lesser-included offense," *Illinois v. Vitale*, 447 U.S. 410, 420, whose subsequent prosecution is barred by the Double Jeopardy Clause. The same analysis applies to Count I of Foster's indictment, and that prosecution is barred.

2. However, the remaining four counts of Foster's indictment are not barred under *Blockburger*. Foster's first prosecution for violating the CPO provision forbidding him to assault his wife does not bar his later prosecution under Count V, which charges assault with intent to kill. That offense requires proof of specific intent to kill, which the contempt offense did not. Similarly, the contempt crime required proof of knowledge of the CPO, which the later charge does not. The two crimes were different offenses under the *Blockburger* test. Counts II, III, and IV are likewise not barred.

JUSTICE WHITE, joined by JUSTICE STEVENS, concluded that, because the Double Jeopardy Clause bars prosecution for an offense if the defendant already has been held in contempt for its commission, both Dixon's prosecution for possession with intent to distribute cocaine and Foster's prosecution for simple assault were prohibited.

JUSTICE SOUTER, joined by JUSTICE STEVENS, concluded that the prosecutions below were barred by the Double Jeopardy Clause under this Court's successive prosecution decisions (from In *re Nielsen*, 131 U.S. 176, to *Grady v. Corbin*, which hold that even if the *Blockburger* test is satisfied, a second prosecution is not permitted for conduct comprising the criminal act charged in the first. Because Dixon's contempt prosecution proved beyond a reasonable doubt that he had possessed cocaine with intent to distribute it, his prosecution for possession with intent to distribute cocaine based on the same incident is barred. Similarly, since Foster has already been convicted in his contempt prosecution for the act of simple assault charged in Count I of his indictment, his subsequent prosecution for simple assault is barred.

C. FULL FAITH AND CREDIT

SUSAN B. CARBON, PETER MacDONALD AND SEEMA ZEYA, ENFORCING DOMESTIC VIOLENCE PROTECTION ORDERS THROUGHOUT THE COUNTRY: NEW FRONTIERS OF PROTECTION FOR VICTIMS OF DOMESTIC VIOLENCE

50(2) Juvenile and Family Court Journal 39–43 (1999).

INTRODUCTION TO FULL FAITH AND CREDIT: SECTION 2265 OF THE VIOLENCE AGAINST WOMEN ACT (VAWA)

On September 13, 1994, President Clinton signed into law the Violence Against Women Act (VAWA) as Title IV of the Violent Crime Control and Law Enforcement Act of 1994. Among other things, VAWA provides legal protections to battered women and enhances prosecution of domestic violence crimes. One of the most important provisions of VAWA is the section that establishes nationwide enforcement of civil and criminal protection orders in state, tribal, and territorial courts. More specifically referred to as the full faith and credit provision, this section directs states, Indian tribes, and U.S. territories to honor "valid" protection orders issued by sister states, tribes, and territories and to treat those foreign orders as if they were their own (18 U.S C sec. 2265).

The full faith and credit provisions of VAWA pose some serious problems for those involved in the enforcement of orders from other jurisdictions. VAWA is an extraordinary piece of legislation—extraordinary in its brevity and the fact that it affects the entire country. It does not, however, answer serious questions about procedures for the enforcement of orders across jurisdictional lines.

Protecting Battered Women's Right to Travel

Section 2265 of VAWA is extremely important, not only because it identifies domestic violence as a national problem, but, more importantly, because it reaffirms a battered woman's right to travel and recognizes the necessity of affording her protection wherever she may be found. Mobility is essential to victims of domestic violence for a variety of reasons. For example, if an abused woman is establishing a household independent of her batterer, she may need to travel or move to another jurisdiction to pursue employment opportunities; she also may find it necessary to relocate to another state, territory, or tribe in order to be closer to her personal support network of family and friends. In addition, a victim may need to travel to protect herself from recurring violence. Indeed, enhancing victim safety is the primary rationale behind passage of the federal law. In short, Section 2265 of VAWA was enacted to enable victims of domestic violence to relocate quickly and frequently in order to protect themselves from further acts of violence and stalking behaviors.

Requirements for "Validity"

As mentioned above, the full faith and credit provision applies only to "valid" protection orders. An order is deemed "valid" if the court that issued it had both subject matter jurisdiction over the case or controversy in question and personal jurisdiction over the parties. In addition, the issuing court must have provided the defendant with reasonable notice and an opportunity to be heard before the order was entered. In the case of *ex parte* orders, notice and opportunity to be heard must be afforded in the time required by the state, tribal, or territorial law, and, in any event, within a reasonable period of time after the order is issued, sufficient to protect the defendant's right to due process.

Section 2265 of VAWA applies to "any injunction or other order, issued for the purpose of preventing violent or threatening acts or harassment against, or contact or communication with or physical proximity to, another person, including temporary and final protection orders issued by civil and criminal courts (other than support or child custody orders). . . ." (18 U.S.C. sec. 2266). In other words, the full faith and credit provision covers emergency and temporary *ex parte* orders, as well as final civil or criminal protection orders, provided all such orders meet the due process and jurisdictional requirements of "validity" as set forth in the Act.

As noted above, Section 2266 defines protection orders expressly to exclude "custody and support orders." Does this mean that custody provisions in protection orders are not entitled to interjurisdictional enforcement under the full faith and credit provision of VAWA? At present, there is a lack of consensus about whether the mandates of Section 2265 extend to custody provisions that are included as part of the relief in protection orders. On the one hand, a number of experts maintain that the plain language of the federal statute explicitly exempts custody and support provisions. On the other, a handful of scholars contend that Congress only intended to exclude custody and support orders that are issued pursuant to custody matters filed in a separate divorce proceeding.

Since the legislative history is silent and, thus, the answer remains unclear, attorneys and advocates for victims of domestic violence need to be aware of this potential problem when seeking relief under state, tribal, or territorial protection order codes. Beyond that, practitioners should refer to other laws that govern whether custody awards in protection orders are entitled to full faith and credit. in particular, they should review their state uniform child custody jurisdiction act (UCCJA) or uniform child–custody jurisdiction and enforcement act (UCCJEA) and the federal parental kidnapping prevention act (PKPA). if the custody provisions in a protection order are consistent with the jurisdictional requirements of these laws, then theoretically they should be entitled to interstate enforcement.

Under the full faith and credit provision of VAWA, mutual protection orders which generally are defined as protection orders that include prohibitions against both parties, are enforceable only on behalf of the plaintiff (or petitioner) in other states, Indian tribes, and U.S. territories, unless the defendant (or respondent) filed a cross or counter-petition seeking such an order and the court made specific findings that each party was entitled to such an order.

Enforcement of Foreign Orders

The full faith and credit provision of VAWA directs enforcing states, tribes, and territories to treat foreign protection orders as if they were their own. What does this mean for purposes of enforcement? Basically, it means the enforcing (non-issuing) jurisdiction must follow three rules:

- It must honor the foreign protection order, even if the protected party would not have been eligible for a protection order in that jurisdiction.

- It must enforce all of the terms of the foreign protection order, even if the order provides relief that would be unavailable under the laws of the enforcing jurisdiction.

- It must treat the foreign protection order as if it were issued in that (non-issuing) jurisdiction and apply whatever sanction or remedy is available under the laws of that (enforcing) state, tribe, or territory for violations of the foreign order.

Section 2265 is not self-executing. In other words, it does not prescribe the specific enforcement procedures that states, U.S. territories, and Indian tribes must adopt to comply with its mandate. In fact, pursuant to the full faith and credit provision, the only requirement for interstate or interjurisdictional enforcement of a protection order is that the foreign order be valid as that term is defined in the Act. Jurisdictions are free to establish their own procedures for enforcement of foreign protection orders provided those procedures do not frustrate or conflict with the intent of the federal law.

Registration/Filing and Certification of Foreign Protection Orders

A number of states and tribal nations currently have mechanisms for the registration or filing of foreign domestic violence orders of protection. The Act, however, does *not* require prior registration or pre-certification of an order of protection in an enforcing state or tribal court in order to receive full faith and credit. However, if a victim of domestic violence does want to register the order in another jurisdiction, it is imperative that the issuing court impart some information so that this process can be eased. The issuing court should inform plaintiffs that registration may be available in other jurisdictions and that they should contact the clerk of the court in the jurisdiction in which they may be planning to establish a residence.

The issuing court, at the time of the entry of the order of protection, should inform the parties that a certified copy (use of this term means the highest form of validation of the issuing state or tribe) should be obtained from the issuing clerk's office, if the order is not certified at the time of its issuance. The issuing court has an important role in informing the victim that if she chooses to relocate, for whatever reason—safety, economics, or proximity to family—or she crosses jurisdictional boundaries even temporarily, she should carry a certified copy of the order of protection at all times.

The victim also should be told that it would be beneficial to contact the state domestic violence coalition, local battered women's shelter, National Domestic Violence Hotline, or the Full Faith and Credit Project in the state, tribe, or territory to find out if there are any particular requirements for the registration of the foreign order that could be resolved before leaving the jurisdiction of the issuing court.

Service of Process Across State Lines

There currently remain many troubling issues as to service of protection orders across jurisdictional lines. While VAWA requires that all orders must be enforced across jurisdictional lines, there is no provision for the service of process across jurisdictional lines. The Act directs that victims of domestic violence not be liable for filing fees and costs related to criminal conduct and process, including the cost of service. However, many jurisdictions continue to charge for these services in violation of the Act.

After the passage of VAWA, many jurisdictions amended laws to waive service costs. Although most of these directives were silent on the question of whether service costs were to be waived for those seeking to have nonresidents served with orders of protection, many jurisdictions will not serve foreign orders without the payment of service fees. This creates a financial barrier to many persons seeking orders of protection. In many of these cases, the end result is that the temporary order of protection is terminated for failure of service, or that the order that is entered is invalid and unenforceable because due process has not been given to the batterer.

It has been suggested by many that the resolution to this dilemma might be to withhold VAWA grant funds from those jurisdictions that refuse to serve out-of-state orders or continue to charge filing fees for domestic violence victims. Another suggestion has been to allow grant funds to be used for the service of process. Whatever the final solution may be, it is imperative that victims of domestic violence not be charged any fees for any filing of petitions for orders of protection or for the service of process on those charged with committing acts of domestic violence.

IMPLEMENTING FULL FAITH AND CREDIT: STRATEGIES ACROSS THE COUNTRY

Albuquerque: A National Conference

In October 1997, the Department of Justice, in collaboration with the National Council of Juvenile and Family Court Judges, The Battered Women's Justice Project, and the National Center for State Courts, convened a national conference on full faith and credit in Albuquerque,

New Mexico. The Albuquerque conference brought together multi-disciplinary teams representing 45 states, 26 Indian tribes, and two US territories. Its purpose was two-fold: first, it provided education: and second, it served as a call to action.

Since the national full faith and credit conference, there have been numerous initiatives to try to resolve troubling issues with the enforcement of out-of-jurisdiction orders. A number of jurisdictions have convened statewide conferences with all participants in domestic violence cases attending to learn about the provisions of VAWA. Various jurisdictions have enacted enabling legislation so that violations of foreign orders of protection can be punished. Many jurisdictions have adopted uniform forms in domestic violence cases; training has increased, or at least been initiated in a great number of jurisdictions; and registries are being established in areas where they did not exist before. However, at the time of this writing, a handful of states still do not have enabling legislation and little information is available about enabling legislation from the tribal nations.

Overview of the Kentucky Pilot Project

One particularly exciting strategy the authors wish to highlight in this article comes from Kentucky, which is proposing an eight-state initiative for implementing the full faith and credit provisions of VAWA. The program builds upon Kentucky's first full faith and credit grant and plans to create a partnership between Kentucky and its seven surrounding states. The goal will be to provide a regional model, which ultimately will be expanded to the entire country, to demonstrate how orders of protection for domestic violence victims and their children can be enforced across jurisdictional boundaries. The Governor of Kentucky, the Chief Justice, and the United States Attorneys will be contacting their counterparts in each of the seven surrounding states and asking them to participate in the regional program. Each state will be asked to identify a state team comprised of advocates for battered women and key representatives from law enforcement and the court system.

Research is being conducted on the statutory provisions of each state's laws related to orders of protection and the current status of each state's criminal justice information system, specifically including the status of each state's data base for protection orders and their entry into the National Crime Information Center's (NCIC) Protection Order File. The specific forms currently being used by each state for orders of protection also will be analyzed for comparison purposes. The Kentucky project proposes to use this research to develop a recognizable form for domestic violence orders of protection, which each state in the eight-state area will be asked to adopt. If the development of one recognizable form is not feasible, a certification or confirmation form will be developed for each state to use in addition to its own form, thereby allowing each of the surrounding states to recognize the other states' orders as being valid orders of protection. If the proposal proves successful, and there is no reason for it not to succeed if each of the states participates fully, the proposal can be expanded regionally and then nationally.

State Registries and the National Crime Information Center's Protection Order File

Such proposals are necessary at this time because there isn't a registry in every jurisdiction; and the NCIC Protection Order File is not operating at full capacity. At the time of this writing, several states do not have a registry for orders of protection. If registries for protection orders were in existence in each state, territory, and tribal nation, and the NCIC Protection Order File had all of the orders from each of the registries entered, there would be fewer problems implementing the full faith and credit provisions of VAWA. Unfortunately, that has not been realized yet, and may not be for several more years.

Where registries exist, an order of protection is placed in the local, county, court, or state law enforcement database or registry. Registries historically were established to facilitate enforcement of local orders; they permit law enforcement to verify the existence and status of any order furnished by a victim, or enable confirmation of an order when the victim does not have a copy in her possession. With the advent of statewide protection order registries, some jurisdictions have eliminated local registries.

The purposes of the National Crime Information Center's Protection Order File are:

- to provide timely and accurate information to civil and criminal courts for use in stalking and domestic violence cases;
- to notify law enforcement agencies nationwide of the existence and terms of protection orders; and
- to support the identification of persons who are subject to a protection order and are prohibited from receiving or possessing a firearm pursuant to other federal laws.

Any order of protection that meets the requirements of VAWA may be eligible for entry into the NCIC file. The Department of Justice and Federal Bureau of Investigation have established such a file, but until every jurisdiction enters *all of its orders*, it is vital that other means of verification remain available.

Currently, only 23 states are participating to some extent in the NCIC Protection Order File registry; and as of April 12, 1999, there were 147,000 orders in that file. Until all states, tribes, and territories fully participate, it will be necessary for victims to know whether the issuing court participates, whether the issuing court or jurisdiction provides a 24–hour registry, and how law enforcement in other jurisdictions can access the state or local registry for verification of an order. Contact information related to state and local police registry access should be furnished to all victims who think they might seek to have an order enforced in another jurisdiction.

It should be noted that most tribal law enforcement departments currently do not maintain a 24–hour accessible registry and orders of tribal courts may not appear in the NCIC Protection Order File. Therefore, until there is a national registry which includes orders issued by tribal courts, the Bureau of Indian Affairs and tribal police will have difficulty verifying the validity of orders issued by other tribal courts. [Also it is important to note that tribal police are not granted electronic access to state and local registries in many jurisdictions.] It would, therefore, be important for state and tribal police and courts to establish procedures and protocols for verification of their respective orders so that protection can be afforded to victims outside of the usual business hours of the court.

Once the NCIC Protection Order File is implemented fully in every jurisdiction, the problems that enforcing states and tribes encounter will diminish dramatically. No longer will courts have to struggle to determine whether an order of protection still is in effect. No longer will law enforcement officers struggle in the middle of the night with the issue of whether the paper they are looking at is indeed an authentic order of protection issued by a court outside of the state or tribal nation. No longer will victims of abuse have to fear that an order issued by one state or tribe will not be enforced in another state or tribal court.

The National Instant Criminal Background Check System (NICS)

On November 30, 1998, the interim provisions of the Brady Bill ended and the permanent provisions became effective. The Brady Handgun Violence Prevention Act of 1994 required the Attorney General to establish a system for immediately identifying persons who are prohibited from purchasing a firearm under federal, state, or local laws. The system to be established was, and is, known as The National Instant Criminal Background Check System, or NICS. NICS was established by the Federal Bureau of Investigation, in cooperation with the Bureau of Alcohol, Tobacco, and Firearms, and state and local law enforcement agencies. The system will contain records provided by federal agencies and information voluntarily provided by states on persons who have been denied the purchase of a firearm or who are known to be disqualified from possessing a firearm under federal law. The individual state, tribal, and territorial courts will make the decision about whether orders of protection will have a Brady Indicator to prohibit receiving or possessing any firearm.

While the interim provisions of Brady applied only to handguns, the permanent provisions apply to *all* firearms. The interim provisions also allowed up to five days to process a background check—the permanent provisions are "immediate."

Chapter 7

CHILDREN IN HOMES WHERE DOMESTIC VIOLENCE TAKES PLACE

This chapter focuses on children of domestic violence. The first section deals with substantive custody and visitation decisions. Main issues include the dangers to children of living with batterers, the overlap between partner abuse and child abuse, how legislatures and courts can best protect such children while dealing fairly with their parents, and the nuts and bolts of supervised visitation orders and programs. The concept of a rebuttable presumption against custody to batterers, an emerging statutory trend, is discussed.

The second section looks at what courts should do when either the battered parent or the batterer takes the children to another location, sometimes crossing state or international lines. In some instances this is done as part of an abduction, in which case both the civil and the criminal aspects of the legal system may be implicated. In other cases, the battered parent and the children are fleeing from the abuse and requesting protection from courts in the new state or country (triggering the UCCJA/UCCJEA or the Hague Convention). In a third category of cases, the battered parent has been granted a custody order but is now petitioning the court for permission to relocate to a more distant location, which impacts the visitation rights of the batterer.

The third section focuses on the response of juvenile and criminal courts to children who have witnessed domestic violence or may have themselves been physically abused in the context of partner abuse. The issue of whether the battered parent "failed to protect" the child from the batterer, and the ability of the victim parent to stop the child abuse, is a central one. One article looks at a pilot program seeking not to punish such victim parents, but instead to provide services which will enable child protection to take place. Other solutions discussed range from termination of parental rights for the batterer or victim parent, to prison terms for the parent who allegedly failed to protect the child.

A. CUSTODY AND VISITATION

JOAN ZORZA, PROTECTING THE CHILDREN IN CUSTODY DISPUTES WHEN ONE PARENT ABUSES THE OTHER

April 1996 Clearinghouse Review 1113, 1115–1121, 1122–1125, 1126–1127.

I. INTRODUCTION

Domestic violence hurts children, both physically and emotionally. And the violence may not end even after the parties separate; indeed, separation may actually provide fathers with more opportunities to hurt their children. It is a myth that women most often win contested custody disputes; in fact, fathers who fight win either sole or joint custody a majority of the time. And, in part due to bias in the law and the courts, abusive fathers win custody disputes at least as often as nonabusive fathers. This article discusses these issues and suggests ways to protect mothers and their children better from abusive fathers in custody disputes.

* * *

III. DOMESTIC VIOLENCE AND CHILDREN

Men who abuse pose many dangers to their children. Over half of all men who beat their female intimate partners deliberately beat their children. Furthermore, many abusers inadvertently hurt their children as a result of their reckless violence directed at their partners, without regard for the children's safety. The youngest children sustain the most serious injuries, such as concussions and broken bones. But adolescent and teen sons, who almost always intervene to try to protect their mothers, are also frequently hurt. Many wife abusers also sexually abuse their children. At least half of the country's 350,000 child abductions every year occur in the context of domestic violence, most of them perpetrated by abusive fathers. These abductions are as traumatic to children as when strangers abduct them; children abducted by abusive parents frequently evidence posttraumatic stress disorder as a result of the kidnapping.

Even when the children are not physically injured, they are usually severely psychologically injured by witnessing their fathers abuse their mothers. Moreover, the abusers force these child witnesses to become part of the conspiracy of covering up the violence. Most child witnesses painfully learn that disclosure only gives their abusers another chance to further victimize them or their mothers. Sons who witness their mothers being abused are at increased risk of growing up to become woman abusers themselves or to commit violent crimes.

Furthermore, children's lives are often disrupted by household moves because of the violence. Half of all homeless women and children in America are fleeing domestic violence, which also costs the children considerable loss of school time.

Abused mothers who are suffering from the cumulative stress of their own victimization are at risk of neglecting or even abusing their children. Women generally perpetrate less child abuse as measured both in frequency or severity than do the men who batter their female partners; fathers perpetrate about three times as much actual abuse (although mothers are often held accountable, since many child protective service programs focus solely on mothers as possible child abusers). Children's Hospital in Boston has found that, regardless of which parent is abusing a child, the abuse virtually always ends if the father is removed from the home and the woman is protected from him.

The harm caused to children living in abusive homes is known to be far greater than the harm caused to children by their parents' divorce. All children who witness domestic violence are at serious risk of developing psychological trauma, including numerous psychological symptoms and syndromes, from earliest infancy throughout childhood. Posttraumatic stress disorder is quite common. So great is the harm to children who witness domestic violence that they actually do better in domestic violence shelters, especially the shelters that have special programs for child witnesses, than they do at home.

After separation, many abusers discover that using the children is the best way to hurt their former partners. Five percent of abusive fathers threaten during visitation to kill the mother, 34 percent threaten to kidnap their children (and 11 percent actually do abduct them); and 25 percent threaten to hurt their children. Their success in demoralizing the mothers cannot be ignored, as 20 percent of battered women return to their batterers at least once because of the abusive fathers' threats to take or hurt their children.

Abusive men are also far less likely than nonabusive men to pay child support. Furthermore, abusive fathers are far more likely to fight for custody of their children. This is so even though few abusive men were previously involved in caring for the children or taking any other adult responsibility during the marriage.

IV. FATHERS IN CONTESTED CUSTODY DISPUTES

Despite men's claims that fathers are discriminated against in custody disputes, in actuality fathers who fight for custody in America win sole or at least joint custody in 70 percent of these contests. As many state court gender bias studies have concluded, fathers often win because mothers are held to a far higher standard. In addition, since women's concerns are trivialized, mothers are believed less often than men.

Many factors favor fathers over mothers in custody fights. Although every state recognizes the best-interests-of-the-child standard in making custody determinations, few states except West Virginia consider that most children have a strong preference for continuity with their primary care giver. (Domestic violence, the only other custody factor that generally favors mothers, is discussed in the next section.)

In contrast, virtually all the factors that courts consider with regard to stability and economics favor men. Men still have greater access to better jobs, salaries, and perquisites; are more likely to have substantial assets; are more likely to obtain free services (most typically from their mothers or new female partners) to help them care for their children; and are more likely to reap the economic consequences of women's having foregone career opportunities to raise their children, whether by choice, socialization, or discrimination or forced on them (usually by their male partners). Proposed changes in the welfare system will only exacerbate these financial inequities, especially since, traditionally, fathers have seldom been penalized for not paying child support or for not paying it on time.

Courts simply do not hold fathers responsible for obvious foreseeable economic deprivations that their nonsupport and late support payments cause: evictions, costs to reconnect shut-off utilities, homelessness, moving expenses, interest on late credit payments. Few courts award or require fathers to pay interest costs or the mothers' legal fees to pursue these payments, and despite federal law many courts still reduce arrearages when fathers fall behind on support payments. Many states do not allow courts to make any negative inference in a custody case against a parent who does not pay child support although able to do so. Amazingly, many dissolution courts, which in every state have equity powers, actually penalize the mother of a deadbeat partner in the custody dispute by considering her less stable financially, effectively holding her responsible for the father's failure to pay court-ordered support. If women and their children are to be denied or permanently pushed off welfare after a limited time, as proposed welfare changes portend, deadbeat fathers will actually be further rewarded in custody disputes for driving their female partners into (or further into) debt, hardly the intention of the welfare proposals. Under these proposed changes, if the estranged male husband or partner raped or had consensual sex with his current or former wife or partner while she is receiving welfare and impregnated her, their new child might never be eligible for public assistance, even if the father paid no support. Yet it remains difficult for women to acknowledge or report marital rape and for police, prosecutors, courts, and administrative agencies to believe that a woman was raped by her husband or partner.

Most custody disputes are sent to mediation, a process that generally favors men and harms women. It may be that custody is just so important to mothers compared to fathers (on average) that it is not possible to mediate custody disputes. Mediation assumes that the spoils of a relationship are somehow large enough that a fair division is possible. Yet, for many mothers, keeping custody is far more important than everything else combined. This makes the whole mediation process seem unfair to mothers.

V. Custody for Abusive and Nonabusive Fathers

Given that abusive fathers are so likely to fight for custody, it is surprising that a larger proportion of batterers than nonbatterers actually win custody. At least 39 states, the District of Columbia, and the Virgin Islands have statutes requiring courts to consider at least domestic violence in custody determinations; every state has case law allowing courts to consider domestic violence in custody disputes; and the Congress unanimously passed a resolution calling on every state to enact a presumption that batterers not obtain sole or joint legal or physical custody but that they receive at most supervised visitation. Both the National Council of Juvenile and Family Court Judges and the American Bar Association's report to its president recommend passage of similar legislation.

A. *Most Professionals Lack Knowledge About Domestic Violence*

Unfortunately, most judges and mental health professionals (including those who do custody evaluations) lack training in, or deny or trivialize, the seriousness of domestic violence. Many wrongly believe that abuse is provoked, consensual, or mutual or that it ends when the parties have separated. Some who recognize the effects on the parents incorrectly believe that the abuse does not adversely affect the children. Dr. Peter G. Jaffe, executive director of the London (Ontario) Family Court Clinic and one of the world's experts on domestic violence and child custody, explains:

> Even mental health professionals, who should have benefited from several decades of research on domestic violence, still believe that as many as one in eight women are magnifying violence as a ploy in custody disputes (Johnston & Campbell, 1993). In my experience of over 20 years of completing custody and visitation assessments, the real problems lie in overlooking violence and most women underreporting out of embarrassment, humiliation, and lack of trust for legal and mental health professionals.[69]

Virtually missing from court records, reports, and transcripts is evidence of the marital rapes that at least 59 percent of battered women experience, usually repeatedly and more brutally than stranger rapes, and about 10 percent of which occur in front of their children.

Equally little acknowledged by judges and mental health professionals is the fact that batterers regularly deny, minimize, or blame the victim or circumstances for their violence, or lie about it. Batterers often manipulate the police and courts for their personal advantage or to hurt their victims, for example, by falsely reporting (or having a relative report) that a child is missing or abused (usually blaming the victim or the victim's new partner) or that the victim physically attacked the abuser. Studies of divorced men, whether or not abusive, have found that

---

69. Jaffe, supra note 29 (citing J.R. Johnston & L.E.G. Campbell, Parent–Child Relationships in Domestic Violence Families Disputing Custody, 31 Fam. & Conciliation Cts. Rev. 282–98 (1993)).

they greatly devalue their former wives and that they characterize them, but not themselves or their current partners, in highly negative and deviant terms.

Furthermore, by the time battered women go to court, they are finally aware of their anger at the unfairness of what their abusers have done to them and their children and comprehend the real dangers they and their children faced and still face, particularly since the danger probably will have increased and will have been redirected more at the children. The court's desire to "smooth things over" acts further to victimize the battered woman. The professionals involved in custody disputes, who often lack any real knowledge of domestic violence, frequently accept many gender bias notions that devalue women's concerns. They therefore may believe that battered women in custody disputes are being petty, angry, or vindictive, particularly when such women raise questions about whether their abusers may be physically or sexually abusing their children. Batterers who physically or sexually abuse their children are more likely to win full or joint custody than abusive fathers who have never physically or sexually abused a child. Although it is widely believed that women frequently make false accusations that children are being sexually abused in contested custody cases, in fact such allegations are raised in only 2 percent of all custody cases and are as likely to be true when custody is in dispute as at other times. Even when allegations of child abuse cannot be substantiated, they are usually made in good faith. But because the myths are so widely believed, many child protective service agencies fail to investigate any incest allegations made during the pendency of a custody dispute.

* * *

C. *Friendly Parent Provisions Penalize Battered Women*

So called friendly parent provisions in statutes or case law favor awarding custody to the parent who will foster the better relationship between the child and the other parent. Yet these provisions have the effect of negating or even overriding domestic violence considerations and of further victimizing the battered woman. Few courts even ask a mother why she may be discouraging the father's access to the children. Even if she manages to explain that she believes that she or her children are at risk, she will probably be disbelieved or her concerns ignored. Every abused mother walks a tightrope. On the one hand, she must protect her children at the risk of the state's removing them or her being criminally prosecuted if she fails to protect them. On the other hand, she risks losing custody to her abuser if she protects her children by restricting the abuser's access to them. Friendly parent provisions punish her and the children if she even raises concerns about his fitness or parenting ability (or, in many states, if she opposes joint custody) because her very concern can be used as a weapon against her to deny her custody. Friendly parent provisions actually encourage abusers to continue to use the children as pawns in custody fights because even false allegations that a father was denied access to the children frequently result in the abuser's winning custody. Thus, friendly parent provisions, rather than being the benevolent facilitator of better parenting, actually have the likely effect of rewarding the less fit parent with sole custody.

The need for friendly parent provisions is often justified by the popularly espoused parental alienation syndrome. But if the court credits Richard Gardner's parental alienation theory and his related "Sex Abuse Legitimacy Scale," which have never been subjected to peer review or accepted within the scientific community, the mother may be denied visitation as well.

The ultimate "unfriendly" behavior is to remove the children from the noncustodial parent's access, usually by going into hiding or fleeing the jurisdiction with the children. If the mother is so frightened by the abuser's actions or threats that she flees the country with her children, she can raise as a complete affirmative defense that she was fleeing "an incident or pattern of domestic violence." But she has no equivalent statutory defense in most states if she flees but remains within the country's borders.

Well-intentioned efforts to promote better parenting through the use of friendly parent provisions and court orders providing that neither parent should disparage the other parent in front of the children have the unintentional results of keeping the abuse secret, reinforcing the abuser's right to perpetuate the violence, not holding the abuser responsible for his abuse (the first necessary step before he can recover), further victimizing the abused parent and greatly increasing the chance that the children will be permanently psychologically abused and become abusers as adults.

The National Center on Women and Family Law is often told that the same courts that frequently deny women custody and even visitation for being "unfriendly" parents have never declared a father "unfriendly," even when he alienates the children or regularly denies the mother access. It is hardly surprising that father's rights groups strongly favor both joint custody and friendly parent provisions.

D.   That Joint Custody Is Best for Children Is a Myth

The first studies that examined joint custody arrangements suggested that joint custody was very promising, largely because they studied a highly unusual, select group of parents who insisted on sharing custody even when it was not legal to do so. That these parents generally were far more cooperative encouraged proponents of joint custody to hope that joint custody orders would create more amicable parents and children. Based on the apparent success of the first studies, California became the first state to enact a presumption in favor of joint custody. Yet, as more families started sharing custody, it became clear that the experiment was not a success. Ultimately, California rescinded its joint custody preference after realizing that it was not the easy solution to divorce and separation.

The main arguments advanced in favor of joint custody are that, as a result of joint custody, children do better, fathers are more involved with their children, child support is paid more willingly, the parents cooperate better, the number of children abducted by the noncustodial parent is decreased, and court time, especially the number of contempt citations, is reduced. Yet not one of these rationalizations has proved to be true. And, as California discovered, what may sound fair and even work reasonably well for some parents (particularly the fathers) may be a disaster for the children. After separation, fathers tend to fade from their children's lives, even when they have joint custody and are strongly encouraged to stay involved. Not only do separated fathers have less physical contact with their children, but also they become less altruistic over time, less likely to pay child support, and further likely to disengage from their children.

Use of the term "joint custody" results in lower child support awards, but even those much lower amounts are no more likely to be paid. Studies in Wisconsin showed that joint legal custody did not result in better compliance with payments. Joint physical custody arrangements do not result in the children's being better adjusted. A number of studies have found that the frequency of contact with fathers is unrelated to the children's adjustment after divorce. Joint legal custody does not increase the father's compliance with child support orders, does not result in his assuming greater child-rearing responsibilities, and does not increase the amount of time he spends visiting with the children, his involvement in decision making about his children, or the degree of cooperation between the parents. In addition, joint custody does not reduce the risk of parental abduction because fathers who have more frequent visitation with their children are more likely to abduct them. They do so as the most effective way to hurt the children's mother.

Joint custody does not work when it is imposed on parents over the objections of one or both parents. When joint custody is imposed by the courts, it is probably the worst possible arrangement for the children. Children in imposed joint custody do poorly and are more depressed and disturbed than children in sole custody. And even when parents genuinely chose joint custody, the children are no better off. Indeed, the negative effects of divorce or single parenting are not reduced or eliminated if children have considerable contact with the noncustodial parent.

But however bad joint custody is when parents argue about their differences, when one parent is abusing or terrorizing the other parent the arrangement becomes an absolute nightmare for the victimized parent and, often, for the children. Like couples counseling and mediation, joint custody, whether legal or physical, gives the abuser license to continue abusing his victim. It is likely to endanger the abused parent and any children in the family.

E. *Incorporating Safety Concerns for Women and Children Is Needed*

The unwillingness of most courts to provide real safety for women and children forces some mothers to conclude that they have no choice but to give up their children to their abusers for their own and their children's survival. Sometimes courts leave battered women so vulnerable to future violence that the court interprets the women's resultant stressed-out behavior as unfit or inadequate parenting. Similarly, precisely because abusers very likely have psychopathologies that enable them to appear calm, charming, and in control, courts may see them as the better parents and give them custody.

Courts that award joint physical or legal custody or "reasonable visitation" to batterers or fail to acknowledge the safety concerns of battered women and their children give batterers license to continue their abuse and control. Even supervised visitation, if not provided by those truly knowledgeable about domestic violence and able to protect (which few family members can do), will not fully protect most battered women and their children.

In extreme cases, courts should allow battered women and their children to relocate and even change their identities if they want to do so as the only way they perceive to be safe. At a minimum, battered women should be allowed to keep their whereabouts confidential so that their abusers cannot locate them. However, despite a recent recognition that domestic violence should be a concern in relocation decisions, courts are particularly hostile to mothers seeking to relocate, as gender-bias studies in many states have found.

* * *

VI. SOME CAUTIONS ABOUT GIVING CUSTODY TO FATHERS

Fathers generally have higher incomes than mothers, but children living with single fathers do not do better than those living with single mothers. Although sons have the same high school dropout rates whether living with single mothers or single fathers, daughters living with single fathers have a 37 percent chance of becoming teenage mothers, contrasted with a 30 percent chance if they live with single mothers. Since these rates do not take into account the likely income differences between the parents' households, and income differences account for approximately half of the detrimental effect of single parenting, it is likely that children would do far better living with mothers who have the same incomes as fathers. These facts indicate that the popular belief that children do better living with fathers than mothers is not true.

Perhaps a more sensible custody solution might be to equalize the economic differences after separation and divorce by setting child support award amounts considerably higher so that single mothers will be able to parent far more effectively, particularly as there are indications that fathers are, in fact, able to afford to pay considerably higher amounts. It is also possible that we have been looking at the problem the wrong way. Men who do not pay child support tend to stop visiting their children. Rather than trying to increase child support by giving men more visitation, we may need to order fathers to pay higher child support amounts so that they will visit.

VII. CONCLUSION

In a number of cultures, family violence does not exist. In these nonviolent cultures, family life is characterized by cooperation, commitment, sharing, and equality; there is no double standard about premarital sex for men and women; both husbands and wives do work (though, not necessarily the same work) that is highly valued by the culture and for which each is compensated; wives have some control over the fruits of the family labor; marriage is monogamous; husbands and wives share living quarters (i.e., sleep together and not in separate quarters); there are no menstrual taboos; wives can divorce their husbands as easily as their husbands can divorce them (although divorce is actually very rare in these cultures); and, if a woman is beaten, the entire community immediately intervenes, taking her side (which means that any potential abuser would gain nothing from his abuse).

Anthropologists have found that physical abuse of husbands never occurs in any culture unless wife-beating is present, and that husband beating is always far less serious than wife beating.

However, in violent cultures abusive men learn that they have little to risk from their abuse and often much to gain. If nothing else, their violence enables them to win every argument, feel important, and obtain compliance with whatever they want from their victims. Abusers rationally decide whether to batter, using a cost-benefit analysis. To end the violence, society's only hope is to make it too costly for abusers. It is very likely that, by encouraging fathers to fight their partners for custody of their children, rather than to have egalitarian, cooperative, close, committed relationships, we are encouraging family violence and eliminating the positive effects of domestic violence statutes and other efforts to end family violence. At a minimum we should be spending more time studying nonviolent cultures to learn more about how family violence can be eliminated.

But even in our violent culture, many people are basically reasonable, even when they are going through a divorce. Reasonable people, even when undergoing the pain of a separation and breakdown of a marriage, want to and mostly are able to cooperate reasonably well in their parenting for the sake of their children. Custody fights are rare among reasonable people. Both parents want the children to continue their involvement with the other parent. And while they probably feel some sadness at having to give up some time with the children, most reasonable parents who were not the primary care givers feel strongly that their children should continue living with the parent who has been their main care giver. Just as we need to study nonviolent cultures, we need to study the people who are reasonable.

As for the combative parents, we should not increase the danger and vulnerability of those who are already victimized by forcing them to continue submitting to their abusers' contact and control over them and their children, under such benevolent-sounding guises as mediation, couples counseling, parent education, joint custody, or shared parenting. Parenting programs that encourage shared parenting and minimize the reality of abuse and the need for protection will not help the victims, the children, or even abusers. For the sake of the children, we must protect victims of domestic violence from further abuse and allow them and their abusers to heal. If we do not do so, the cycle of violence will repeat itself endlessly, generation after generation.

STEPHEN E. DOYNE, JANET M. BOWERMASTER, J. REID MELOY, DONALD DUTTON, PETER JAFFE, STEPHEN TEMKO, AND PAUL MONES, CUSTODY DISPUTES INVOLVING DOMESTIC VIOLENCE: MAKING CHILDREN'S NEEDS A PRIORITY

50(2) Juvenile and Family Ct. Journal 1–12 (1999).

INTRODUCTION

The central thesis in this article is that the justice system needs to recognize better the special needs of children exposed to domestic violence. Even in cases where there are no observable injuries, children's adjustment and development can be jeopardized seriously by witnessing one parent abusing another parent. Being raised in a climate of fear, having poor models of conflict resolution, and observing abuse of power in intimate relationships can have long-term detrimental consequences for children and adolescents.

Domestic violence is a widespread and pernicious phenomenon. It consists of a pattern of behaviors including, but not limited to, the forms of abuse in Table 1 (omitted).

Courts in every jurisdiction decide custody disputes based on the best interests of the child. In determining best interests, family courts typically consider a broad spectrum of parental behaviors that affect children. California Family Code § 3011, for example, specifically requires courts to consider any history of abuse by one parent against the child or against the other parent in deciding issues of custody and visitation. California is not alone in this regard. Some 35 states have statutes which require courts to consider domestic violence as a factor in making custody determinations.

When considering domestic violence, the entire history of a battering parent's violence within the family—from verbal intimidation to homicide—should be considered by the court to assess properly what causes harm to children, either directly or indirectly. In the extreme case of spousal murder, some states, such as Pennsylvania, have statutes precluding an award of custody to a parent who murders the other. Even where there is no statutory directive, the detriment to children from loss of a parent should be considered if allegations are made that this loss is related to the actions of the surviving parent.

Because the psychological risks to children living with a batterer are high, there should be a rebuttable presumption against sole or joint custody for perpetrators of domestic violence, even if that parent never has abused the children directly.

* * *

Risks to Children From Living With a Perpetrator of Domestic Violence

The best available research has found that domestic violence can have dramatic and long lasting detrimental effects on children. * * *

A. Exposure to Abuse of Others as Emotional Abuse of Child

Although the term "violence" is usually associated with physical or sexual violence, most victims report that emotional or psychological abuse can have the most persistent long-term effects. Threats, demeaning or belittling comments, and an attempt to create a family climate of fear, terror, and insecurity characterize this abuse.

Although many parents within violent families think they have protected their children from the violence, between 80% and 90% of children indicate the opposite. In fact, a majority of children in violent families not only are aware of what happened, they also can give detailed descriptions about the pattern of escalating violence. Consequently, children who may be at their parents' bedroom door or who enter the room shortly after a violent episode, know all too well the reality of the violence including the emotional and physical consequences to their mothers. When men murder their wives, children are present in approximately 25% of the cases.

The term "witness," connoting exposure to violence, is not just the observation of discrete events, but rather, a child's total experience of fear and insecurity about what happens, what he anticipates happening, and the aftermath of physical, sexual, and emotional abuse in the family. Murder of one spouse by another—witnessed or not—represents the horrific extreme of exposing a child to family violence.

B. Impact of Exposure to Violence

Exposure to violence has both short-term and long-term consequences, depending on the children's age, gender, stage of development, and role within the family. Preschool children who are exposed to domestic violence may suffer from nightmares or other sleep disturbances. Often, this trauma may lead to great insecurity and confusion causing regressive behavior, such as excessive clinging to adults and/or fear of being abandoned. Constant fear and anxiety may polarize other children because the places and people who should afford them the greatest protection—their homes and parents—are the most dangerous. Moreover, children exposed to the abuse of their mothers by their fathers may exhibit a range of internalizing and externalizing emotional and behavioral problems. These symptoms can continue into adolescence.

Aside from the more dramatic or visible symptoms of being exposed to violence, children also can experience more subtle signs of this trauma, not apparent using traditional assessment and interview methodology. For example, children who are exposed to parental violence tend to hold beliefs that violence is an appropriate method of trying to resolve conflicts, especially in the context of an intimate relationship. Other children may see physical aggression as an acceptable means to gain respect or control in a relationship, excusable if a perpetrator is drinking, or if a victim supposedly has done something to "provoke" him (e.g., the house was messy or dinner not ready on time.)

Additionally, children tend to feel responsible and to blame themselves over time for the violence. Moreover, they can feel it is their duty to protect their mothers or even defuse their fathers' rage. Or, they may believe that if they were perfect in their own homes, their parents would not fight over them and cause more violence. In violent families, this pronounced sense of personal responsibility begins at an early age and can last into adulthood. These symptoms, as well as those previously mentioned, impede children's development and their academic and community involvement, and directly impact their self-esteem.

Many children may feel so responsible for their mothers' safety that they adjust their own lives in order to protect their mothers. For example, some children refuse to attend school and later receive the diagnosis of "school phobic" for this reason. Other fearful children may go to school but experience somatic symptoms such as headaches and stomach pains so that they can return home to their mothers. In some instances, abused mothers do not discourage this behavior because of their own isolation, depression, and inability to set limits for their children.

Adolescents who have been exposed to violence tend to develop their own unique coping strategies. At an adaptive level. with extended family or community supports, these young persons may attempt to separate and individuate from the family problems, seeking more independent living and school or vocational pursuits. Unfortunately, many adolescents do not have adequate skills and social supports in place and may attempt to cope through drug and alcohol abuse, or by running away to the street, a potentially more dangerous environment. Often, they become involved in abusive dating relationships and repeat the cycle they have witnessed. In this regard, adolescent boys who have been exposed to violence are more likely to be abusive themselves. On the other hand, girls who have been exposed to violence are less likely to question violence in a dating relationship. Unfortunately, many of these adolescents do not even realize that this violent behavior is criminal in nature and could lead to sanctions by the court system.

C. *Neurobiological Changes and Domestic Violence*

Children neurobiologically adapt to violence, exhibiting measurable change in the activity of their brainstems as a result of chronic traumatic stress in violent homes. However, the very neurobiological adapters that allow children to survive violence may, as they grow older, result in an increased tendency to be violent. Thus, living with a perpetrator of domestic violence makes it more likely those children will grow up to be violent themselves. In fact, in 14 of 16 studies, witnessing violence between one's parents or caretakers is a more consistent predictor of future violence than being the victim of abuse.

The long-term impact of being exposed to domestic violence is most apparent from retrospective studies of male perpetrators of violence and female survivors of violence in adult relationships. The majority of abusive husbands have grown up in families in which they were exposed to their fathers' abuse of their mothers. The landmark studies in this field suggest that sons of severe batterers abuse their wives at rates ten times the level of sons of non-violent fathers. Women are less likely to seek assistance when they are abused if they have been exposed to violence in their families of origin.

Several important issues and cautions need to be raised about the research on children who have been exposed to violence. Although exposure to violence is an important factor, it rarely happens in isolation from other stressors in a child's life, e.g., repeated separations and disruptions, financial hardships, and a lack of adequate housing or shelter. In many circumstances a child may experience several forms of violence aside from being exposed to his mother's victimization. The most conservative estimates suggest a 30% overlap between wife assault and physical child abuse. Some studies and recent reviews have estimated an overlap up to 70%.

Violence does not end with separation. Although the physical violence may terminate, ongoing issues of abuse of power and control may be played out in custody disputes, further compromising children's · emotional and behavioral adjustment.

PROBLEMS FOR VICTIMS CREATED BY CURRENT CUSTODY DISPUTE RESOLUTION SYSTEM

Children are a central focus in decisions battered spouses make about leaving their batterers or remaining in abusive relationships. Battered women often cite the children as a reason for staying with their spouses, in addition to other factors, such as fear, economic dependency, and lack of community support. Sometimes battered spouses are deprived economically to the point of being left homeless. They may be financially dependent on their abusers and may want the presence of a father, even if he is a poor role model. They also may fear losing the children, as many batterers threaten their partners with taking the children away and with proving them to be "unfit" mothers. These fears are well-founded, since some research suggests that perpetrators of domestic violence actually have a good chance of convincing judges they should have custody.

On the other hand, some battered women may decide to leave when they start to recognize the impact the violence has had on their children. Most often, this decision happens after an incident of physical or sexual abuse of the children, or when they recognize the impact exposure to the violence has had on their children.

The research on children of divorce and children exposed to domestic violence has developed separately, often leading to conflicting advice for battered spouses. The general literature on the impact of divorce stresses the negative influence of conflict on children and the positive influence of a co-parenting relationship in which the children maintain an ongoing, supportive relationship with both parents. This is often true for nonviolent families. In reality, however, contested custody cases often represent a high level of violence compared to the general population of divorcing adults. When domestic violence has been present, a co-parenting relationship and the impact of the ongoing conflict on the children often represent a negative influence on the children. Many battered spouses are advised to promote relationships and set aside past conflicts with ex-spouses who may be a danger to them and their children. If they do not comply, they may be deemed "unfriendly or unfit parents" and they can lose custody to abusive parents.

One of the most important issues, which often goes unrecognized by many legal and mental health professionals, is that the violence does not end with separation. A large-scale study of children of battered women in shelters in California showed that separation tends to lead to an escalation of violence and greater danger for their mothers. It is estrangement, not argument, which begets the worst violence, since a majority of spousal murders happen after women leave. In fact, many courts promote unsupervised visitation orders; and this may give abusive spouses an ongoing opportunity to expose children to violence or threats of violence. Recent clinical analysis in Canada points to ongoing psychological abuse whereby children become pawns in custody battles in order both to punish and devalue their mothers and to try to rewrite the history of abuse and parenting.

Paradoxically, women may not be believed when violence is reported because they are seen to be exaggerating incidents of violence as a way of manipulating the courts. Many of these women who suffer post-traumatic stress disorder have been labeled as histrionic or worse. For example, a recent article discussed a supposed "Malicious Mother Syndrome" in divorce to "explain" why some women hold animosity toward their former husbands, blame them for all the problems by accusing them of various behaviors, and attempt to keep them from seeing the children. The American Psychological Association Presidential Task Force on

Violence and the Family recently summarized the literature in this area, and expressed concerns about the labeling and pathologizing of battered women in divorce and custody cases. When such labeling occurs, men's violence may be minimized as only an emotional reaction to the separation.

DOMESTIC VIOLENCE SHOULD BE A PRIMARY CONSIDERATION IN CHILD CUSTODY DECISIONS

Domestic violence plays a significant part in many custody disputes and should be a primary consideration in questions of both best interests and detriment to children. An abusive parent often realizes, after separation or divorce, that the most effective way to hurt or destroy the other parent is through emotional or psychological abuse utilizing the family courts. Generalized notions of joint custody and two equal parents cooperatively planning for their children's future is impossible for many couples when there is family violence. In fact, this notion of shared custody may perpetuate the violence and abusive power and control in family relationships.

A.   *Domestic Violence and Legal Standards for Custody*

The best interest standard generally is applied in child custody determinations, with the underlying notion that there are two fit biological parents. In parent non-parent disputes, the detriment standard is generally used to counterbalance the biological parent's greater legal right to the child. Domestic violence frequently has been shown to be harmful to children, whether they are abused physically or not. Therefore. regardless of which legal standard is applicable, awarding batterers primary or joint custody should be viewed as being either detrimental to children or failing to satisfy their best interests.

Best Interests: In cases involving documented domestic violence, it is presumptively in the best interests of children to reside with a nonviolent caretaker, rather than a batterer. In many states, courts making determinations of best interests in custody proceedings are required to consider any history of abuse by one parent against the child or against the other parent.

In order to ensure the safety and well-being of children, however, a finding of abuse by one parent against the other needs more than just to be considered. It needs to be elevated over other best interest factors in disputed custody cases. This can be accomplished by a legal presumption denying joint or sole custody to a parent with a history of domestic violence. The National Council of Juvenile and Family Court Judges and the American Bar Association have recommended adopting such a presumption.

Because domestic violence rarely occurs as an isolated incident, application of such a presumption must be applied broadly. The court should consider the acts and patterns of physical abuse inflicted by the abuser on other persons, not limited to children and the abused parent, as well as the fear of physical harm reasonably engendered by this behavior. Even then, discrete acts of abuse do not convey accurately the risk of continuing violence, the likely severity of future abuse, or the magnitude of fear precipitated by the composite picture of violent conduct. Rather, the broader pattern of abusive and controlling behaviors must be considered in deciding whether to apply the presumption.

* * *

Current Practices: Research indicates that custody evaluators seldom consider domestic violence when they make child custody recommendations. A survey of psychologists from 39 states who conducted custody evaluations indicates that domestic violence was not considered a major factor in making custody determinations, except as a possible rationalization for not recommending joint custody. Even then, it was seldom listed as a determining factor. When the psychologists were asked for three to five reasons that would most support not recommending joint custody, family/domestic violence was the second least likely reason.

Of more concern was the finding that over three-quarters of the custody evaluators recommended denying sole or joint custody to a parent who "alienates the child from the other parent by negatively interpreting the other parent's behavior." This latter finding indicates that custody evaluators may be more likely to blame the parent seen as more hostile and uncooperative and, thus, deny that parent sole or joint custody even in cases where the hostile or uncooperative parent was leaving an abusive relationship.

Application of a rebuttable presumption against custody to perpetrators of domestic violence would help bring current practices more in line with our best knowledge about the effects of domestic violence on children. It also would prevent perpetrators of domestic violence from benefitting from their violent, abusive conduct in cases such as spousal murder where custody of the children may be awarded to the murderer.

B.   *Traumatic Bonding and Best Interests*

Judges in custody cases often are faced with a paradox inherent in the dynamics of domestic violence. On one hand, courts are presented with evidence showing special risks children face when they are placed in the custody of an abuser, risks not only to their physical safety, but also to their emotional and developmental needs. On the other hand, court-appointed experts, who may downplay domestic violence, may tell jurists that the children in a given case have a "close bond" with a parent who has committed domestic violence. In fact, the children even may say they "just want to go home."

The apparent closeness between perpetrators of domestic violence and their children, whether battered or not, can be explained by the concept of "traumatic bonding." Traumatic bonding occurs when intermittent maltreatment patterns produce strong emotional attachments. This phenomenon is the very reason some battered spouses stay in abusive relationships. Similarly, children may appear emotionally close to violent parents because they are afraid of them.

However, it is important to remember that living with domestic violence only makes it more likely children will repeat the cycle of violence themselves. In fact, children who grow up in abusive homes are more at risk for committing violence themselves, both within and outside their own families.

* * *

CONCLUSION

Children can be at great risk living with a perpetrator of domestic violence. Even if they have not been abused directly they may experience the same psychological fears and be traumatically bonded to the batterer, even expressing a preference to live with him. In the case of spousal murder, these children may suffer "secondary abuse," adopting a pattern of emotional compliance because they fear the penalty for misbehaving could be physical harm or death. However, the greatest future harm children face living with a batterer is that they may live to experience the abusive parent beat another partner, recycling the climate of fear that is so detrimental to children. Moreover, if they remain with a batterer, the same neurobiological adaptations that help them psychologically survive the traumas associated with domestic violence may increase the likelihood that they will grow up to be violent themselves. Daughters may be more likely to accept violence as an inevitable part of intimate relationships.

To prevent future detriment, children's safety and well-being should be elevated above the rights of violent parents. What is needed most to ensure children's protection in custody cases where there has been domestic violence is a new commitment to prioritize children's safety as an essential cornerstone of the justice system. This commitment must be indicated clearly by legislation, policy development, training, and specialized resources. If the justice system cannot assure children's safety, the cycle of violence will continue.

(This article is an outgrowth of an *amici curiae* brief submitted by the authors on behalf of themselves and several supporting organizations in the O. J. Simpson guardianship case reported at *Simpson v. Brown*, 67 Cal. App. 4th 914 (1998). The dispute in that case was between the father who allegedly had killed the children's mother and the mother's parents.)

LYNNE R. KURTZ, PROTECTING NEW YORK'S CHILDREN: AN ARGUMENT FOR THE CREATION OF A REBUTTABLE PRESUMPTION AGAINST AWARDING A SPOUSE ABUSER CUSTODY OF A CHILD

60 Alb. L. Rev. 1367–1374 (1997).

V. B. ANALYSIS OF OTHER STATES WITH A PRESUMPTION

Eleven states have enacted statutes creating a presumption against granting custody of a child to a spousal abuser. These statutes vary in many respects. Four of the states established presumptions, the other seven created rebuttable presumptions. The state statutes utilize different burdens of proof for establishing domestic violence as well as for rebutting the presumption. Another difference among states with a rebuttable presumption is the type of evidence required to rebut the presumption.

Of the eleven states containing presumptions, Louisiana has developed the most concise and specific statute that best serves to protect the child. The statute contains a presumption denying both sole and joint custody to an individual with a history of domestic violence.[157] In order to rebut the presumption, the parent must show by a preponderance of the evidence that he has "successfully completed a treatment program ... [and] is not abusing alcohol and ... drugs" and that it is in the best interests of the child to give the abusive parent custody.

The Louisiana Code also provides that if both parents have a record of domestic violence, sole custody should go to the parent least likely to be abusive. This parent must also complete a treatment program. The statute also states that if a parent is a spousal abuser, that parent must only be allowed supervised visitation and must complete a treatment program. However, the parent may have unsupervised visitation if he can show by a preponderance of the evidence that he has completed the program, is not abusing drugs or alcohol, is not a danger to the child, and that visitation is in the best interests of the child.

Of all the statutes, the rebuttable presumption created by Louisiana best addresses the effects domestic violence has on children. The child is automatically kept from the sole or joint custody of an abusive parent, unless the parent can rebut the presumption by showing he has satisfied a statutory condition. The code also protects the child during visitation, which is important because studies have shown that the violence may increase after divorce.

Florida's presumption statute directs that if a parent was convicted of a second degree felony or higher, that parent should not share custody of the child. The presumption does not cover serious violence or abuse

---

157. See La. Rev. Stat. Ann. § 9:364(A)   (West Supp. 1997).

that is not designated a second degree felony. Therefore, this statute does not afford enough protection to the child and should not be followed by New York. In Florida, "second degree felonies include attempted murder, manslaughter, aggravated battery, sexual battery, lewd and lascivious or indecent assault on a minor and aggravated child abuse."[166]

The language of the statute fails to account for the many battered women who never disclose their abuse to anyone, or who seek to keep their husbands away from themselves and their children, but do not necessarily wish to see them convicted and jailed. If there is no conviction, the statute treats evidence of domestic violence as a mere factor. The statute also does not consider batterers who may have pled down to a lesser charge from a second degree felony or higher.

The other nine statutes fall in between the extremes set out in Louisiana and Florida. North Dakota's presumption against awarding an abuser sole or joint custody is rebutted solely by clear and convincing evidence that it is in the best interests of the child to have the abusive parent participate in custody. While the strong evidentiary standard is appropriate, the court is still left to use its own discretion to decide what evidence qualifies to rebut the presumption.

In one North Dakota case, the trial court heard evidence regarding a husband who had abused his wife during their marriage.[170] The court nevertheless granted custody to the father, stating that the presumption was rebutted by evidence that the husband had not been violent towards the children and could give them a " 'more stable home environment.' " The appellate court upheld this decision. This type of holding best illustrates why rebuttable presumption factors should be explicitly laid out in the statute.

The dissenting opinion stated that the majority holding placed domestic violence in the context of a mere factor and had trivialized the statutory presumption. However, the dissent then opined that "the fact that [the husband] directed his physical abuse exclusively at his wife is irrelevant." It is this very attitude that the North Dakota code should have addressed.

The presumption against joint custody created by the Wisconsin statute is rebuttable by "clear and convincing evidence that the abuse will not interfere with the parties' ability to cooperate in the future decision making required." Although the high standard of clear and convincing evidence is adequate, the statutory language describing how the presumption may be rebutted solely addresses the parents and makes no mention of the child. Since domestic violence tends to increase after divorce, and because many spousal abusers also abuse their children, this statute is insufficient.

---

166. Lars Hafner, O.J.'s Case Puts Focus on Spouse Abuse, Largo–Seminole Times (Fla.), July 6, 1994, at 2.

170. See Schestler v. Schestler, 486 N.W.2d 509, 510 (N.D.1992). * * *.

In Colorado, a presumption against awarding an abuser joint custody is proven by credible evidence. However, if the court finds that the parties can share responsibility for their child without confrontation, joint custody will be awarded. There are no explicit factors laid out to evaluate this evidentiary standard to help the court make this determination. The court is instead left to its own discretion. This can be dangerous for the victim and her children if the court is unaware of or unsympathetic to the fact that domestic violence may escalate after divorce.

Delaware created a presumption that can be rebutted using the same factors as Louisiana. However, the Delaware Code fails to provide any evidentiary standards at all. The court is left to its own discretion in deciding whether the rebuttable presumption applies, and if so, what standard should be used in order to rebut the presumption. This is too much discretion to allow the court.

Minnesota and Oklahoma have each formulated a rebuttable presumption against awarding an abuser joint custody. However, those states' statutes fail to list the factors the legislators intended would rebut the presumption. These codes leave the court too much discretion to decide when the presumption has been rebutted.

Texas and Washington have each created presumptions which deny an abusive parent custody. The Texas code denies the parents joint custody if credible evidence demonstrates that one of the parents is an abuser. Washington does not mandate that a certain evidentiary standard be used to prove domestic violence. Instead the statute states that a parent's "residential time with the child shall be limited" if the parent is an abuser. If limiting the residential time is not enough to protect the child, the statute then prohibits the abusive parent from coming into contact with the child. Washington's code also provides that the court may limit or preclude an abusive parent from obtaining custody if there is evidence of spousal abuse.

The Wyoming statute finds evidence of domestic violence to be "contrary to the best interest of the child." There is no explicit standard given in the statute to prove domestic violence has occurred.

Iowa and Nevada have recently enacted laws which create rebuttable presumptions against awarding an abuser custody. Iowa's statute does not state an evidentiary standard, but it does list certain factors that will determine if a history of domestic violence exists, such as the previous issuance of a protective order. The statute also fails to define what evidence will rebut the presumption.

Nevada's law creates a rebuttable presumption that neither sole nor joint custody be granted to a spousal abuser. This statute creates a clear and convincing evidentiary standard for proving the violence. There is however, no guidance given to the court to determine what evidence will rebut the presumption.

In Massachusetts, a bill submitted to the legislature favors a rebuttable presumption against awarding an abuser joint or sole custody. An evidentiary standard of a preponderance of the evidence is needed to create this presumption. In order to rebut the presumption, the abuser must show by a preponderance of the evidence that it is in the best interests of the child to give the abusive parent custody.

C.   Arguments Against Establishing a Presumption

One popular argument against creating a presumption is the fear that the number of unfounded allegations of spousal abuse in custody proceedings will increase. Proponents of this contention believe that this presumption will then serve to open "a flood gate for false allegations and attempts to remove a person from the household or a part of an overall strategy . . . to eventually prevent the relationship of one parent with the child."[199]

It is reasonable to assume that some vindictive spouses may abuse this presumption, or that an over-zealous attorney may even urge a client to do so in order to gain an advantage over the other spouse. The use of a child as the pawn of a parent in order to gain an upper hand in the divorce is not, of course, in the best interests of the child. However, the protection a presumption affords the child far outweighs this argument. It is also for this reason that this Comment advocates the use of an explicit evidentiary standard to prove the existence of domestic violence.

The constitutionality of a presumption against awarding an abusive spouse custody has also been questioned. Some have argued that the presumption would infringe on a parent's due process rights. A presumption is never irreversible, even if the word 'rebuttable' does not appear beside it. The constitutionality of rebuttable presumptions has been upheld where "there is a rational connection between the facts needed to be proven and the fact presumed, and there is a fair opportunity for the opposing party to make his defense." A rebuttable presumption against awarding a spousal abuser custody is rationally related to protecting the best interests of a child. The abusive parent also has the chance to make a defense. If a parent who has been abusive can meet the evidentiary burden to prove he is a fit and able father, despite a history of abuse, the court will act accordingly.

Another argument against the use of a presumption is that a custody determination is best left to the discretion of the judges. For the many reasons outlined in this Comment which refute this argument, including a lack of education about the effects of domestic violence and the possible existence of personal biases which remain despite education, it must be dismissed.

Lastly, the Family Violence Project of the National Council of Juvenile and Family Court Judges recently suggested that statutory presumptions against awarding an abuser custody may not be more

199. Hearings, supra note 21, at 86   * * *.

successful in protecting the best interests of a child than codes which list domestic violence as a factor the court must consider. The Family Violence Project even suggested that a presumption may hurt parents who used violence to defend themselves or their children.

Unambiguous statutory language would prevent a parent who used violence solely as a means of defense from becoming an abuser under the presumption. Wording such as "a history of acts," "a history or pattern," or "the occurrence of ongoing domestic abuse" would prevent the victim from becoming the batterer within the code. The state should also create a specific statutory definition of domestic violence to further protect the battered victim.

MAUREEN SHEERAN AND SCOTT HAMPTON, SUPERVISED VISITATION IN CASES OF DOMESTIC VIOLENCE

50(2) Juvenile and Family Ct. Journal 13–21 (1999).

Over the past several years, researchers and practitioners have brought to public consciousness the devastating impact domestic violence has on its child witnesses. It is estimated that between 3 million and 10 million children witness one parent abusing the other parent, typically the father or partner of the mother abusing the mother. Children living in homes where there is domestic violence are affected profoundly by witnessing violence and are at risk of abuse themselves. Alarmingly, the dangers that perpetrators pose to their victims and children do not cease when the relationship ends. Rather, separation increases risk and creates a new set of threats to their emotional and physical well-being.

The ongoing risk perpetrators of domestic violence pose to victims and children after separation has led to the development of new laws and services designed to address one crucial area of concern: facilitating safe contact between perpetrators of domestic violence and their children. Specifically, many states have passed laws giving courts broad discretion to order supervised visitations in cases involving domestic violence. As supervised visitation becomes increasingly recognized as a potential tool for protecting battered women and their children, communities are mobilizing to develop supervised visitation services that are safe and appropriate for cases involving domestic violence.

* * *

POST-SEPARATION DANGERS POSED BY PERPETRATORS

A victim's move to separate from her abusive partner marks for the abuser the loss of control over his partner, often leading to an escalation of violence and increased risk for victims and children. The abuser will use more serious acts of violence as a way to retaliate against the victim for leaving him or to coerce her to return. Separation from a batterer puts a victim at risk of serious, even deadly violence. In fact, research shows that an important situational antecedent to a domestic violence homicide is attempting to break away from the perpetrator.

A key indicator of risk in domestic violence situations is the abuser's access to the victim; and visitation with the children in an unprotected visitation or exchange setting is a guarantee of continued access. Visitation can be a time of particular volatility as it provides the small window of opportunity, maybe the only opportunity, for a batterer to focus his desperate efforts to regain control. Judges and victims agree that visitation holds the greatest potential for renewed violence. Many battered women report threats against their lives during visitation and exchanges, and some, in fact, are killed in those contexts. The Commission on Domestic Violence Fatalities in New York found that of 57 deaths studied, custody disputes were at the root of three homicides, two of which were committed in connection with exchange of the children.

In addition to the risks of severe or lethal violence, child visitation and exchanges create opportunities for batterers to follow through on their threats to abduct their children. Research has proven a definite link between parental child abduction and domestic violence. In one study, family violence marked the relationships between abducting and left-behind parents in 54 percent of the sample cases of child abduction, with the abductor "reportedly the only violent partner 90 percent of the time."[13] Often abduction of the child, or refusal to return children after the scheduled visits, is a manipulative attempt by the perpetrator to coerce the victim into returning.

Aside from the risks of severe violence or homicide after separation, the risks posed by batterers to their children, alone, is enough to cause acute concerns about how safe children may be in an unprotected setting with a violent parent. Battered mothers often work diligently to protect children from battering parents and worry about the children's safety when they are not able to protect them. The concerns for safety are so great that many battered women contemplate violating a court order, or even fleeing with the child, to avoid the dangers of sending the child on an unsupervised visit with a battering father.

* * *

Drafters of the *Model Code [on Domestic and Family Violence]* also were sensitive to the increased danger victims of domestic violence and their children face during visitation. The *Model Code* sets forth conditions for awarding visitation in cases involving domestic violence, stating:

"A court may award visitation by a parent who committed domestic or family violence only if the court finds that adequate provision for the safety of the child and the parent who is a victim of domestic or family violence can be made."

13. Grief, G. and Hegar, R. (1992) When   the Headlines, p 36.
Parents Kidnap: The Families Left Behind

The *Model Code* also grants courts broad authority to impose such conditions as ordering exchange to occur in a protective setting, ordering that visitation be supervised, ordering the perpetrator to complete a counseling or intervention program, ordering the perpetrator to pay for supervision or post a bond for the return and safety of the child, and prohibiting overnight visitation. This section of the *Model Code* also allows the court to order the address of the child and victim be kept confidential, precludes the court from ordering the victim-parent to counseling relating to her status as a victim as a condition of receiving custody or as a condition of visitation; and requires the court to establish conditions to be followed during visitation if the court allows a family or household member to supervise the visit.

While states have been slower to act in placing limitations on visitation than they have on requiring the consideration of domestic violence in custody determinations, by December 1998, eight states had passed supervised visitation legislation patterned mostly or entirely on the *Model Code* § 405. Another 17 states have legislation specifically allowing supervised visitation in custody or protection order proceedings involving domestic violence. Those statutes vary. In Iowa, for example, the court is required to consider whether the safety of the child, other children, or the parent will be jeopardized by awarding unsupervised or unrestricted visitation when determining what custody arrangement is best for the child. Much stronger restrictions are placed on visitation with a perpetrator of domestic violence in Louisiana, where the court can allow only supervised visitation to a perpetrator-parent, conditioned upon that parent's participation in and completion of a treatment program. In Louisiana, unsupervised visitation is allowed only if it is shown by a preponderance of the evidence that the perpetrator-parent has met certain conditions and poses no danger to the child, and that such visitation is in the child's best interest. * * *

Even in states without specific legislation addressing supervised visitation in the context of domestic violence, courts generally have broad discretion to fashion visitation arrangements appropriate to a given case and thus the authority to require that contacts between a batterer and his children be supervised. * * *

Supervised Visitation Programs

The growing acknowledgement that in some situations the only safe visitation is supervised visitation has created a great demand for visitation services. These services are an essential element in a coordinated community intervention system designed to protect victims from abuse and eliminate violence.

* * *

Acknowledging the need for visitation services, the *Model Code* requires states to provide for visitation centers throughout the state in order to allow court-ordered visitation which protects all family members. If implemented, this section would require a state to ensure the existence of centers, but would not mandate that centers be owned or operated by the state or at public expense. The American Bar Association also supports the establishment of visitation centers. Additionally, many state and local violence councils and task forces have made establishment of such centers a priority.

Supervision of visitation or exchanges is not new. Child protection agencies have been supervising visitation between parents and abused or neglected children for some time as a way of maintaining ongoing parent-child contact pending reunification or termination of parental rights. Supervised visitation programs and the concept of supervised visitation as a social service, however, are relatively new.

Also new is the use of visitation centers in the context of domestic violence. The past few years have seen the emergence of new supervised visitation programs around the country, many of which have been established specifically to address the safety needs of battered women and their children. The Resource Center on Domestic Violence: Child Protection and Custody receives calls regularly from domestic violence programs attempting to establish supervised visitation programs. In one community, the murder of a battered woman was the impetus for developing a supervised visitation center when the victim's family donated her house for a visitation center.

As more centers develop to respond to the needs of battered women and their children and as existing programs, which developed from various approaches, work increasingly with families experiencing domestic violence, the unique demands domestic violence places on centers are coming into focus. Some special considerations brought on by domestic violence are detailed below.

Need for heightened security: Safety of the children and victim-parent are the overarching concerns in supervised visitation in the context of domestic violence. The dangers posed by batterers are well documented. Therefore, visitation centers working with cases involving domestic violence require procedures designed to reduce risks brought on by domestic violence. To enhance safety some centers establish such procedures as:

Ensuring that facilities and procedures preclude contact between the custodial and non-custodial parent. For example, centers can have parents arrive and leave at separate times, park in separate parking lots, enter through different entrances, and wait in separate areas. Assuming the non-custodial parent is the offending parent, safety can be enhanced by having the non-custodial parent arrive 15 minutes prior to the visit and wait 15 minutes after the visit before leaving the facility; and the custodial parent arrive and leave immediately prior to and after the visit.

• Providing on-site security.

- Screening all cases for domestic violence.

- Refusing cases too dangerous for centers to handle safely.

- Developing policies to enhance confidentiality, such as maintenance of separate files for the perpetrator-parent and the victim-parent.

Need for understanding the dynamics of domestic violence: Given the unique dynamics of domestic violence, visitation supervisors working with perpetrators and victims of domestic violence and their children should have an in-depth understanding of the dynamics of domestic violence. In Massachusetts visitation centers that receive funding from the Domestic Violence Unit of Massachusetts Department of Social Services "should be grounded in the belief that domestic violence is an attempt by one family member to gain control over other family members." Service providers are expected to understand the dynamics of domestic violence, "including the involvement of and impact on children," and the importance of batterer accountability.

For practitioners who work with both children of divorce and children of domestic violence, information about the dynamics of domestic violence is particularly important in helping them make the distinction between a battered mother's protective behavior and "unfriendly" or "alienating" behavior. A common factor included in custody statutes is which parent does a better job of facilitating the relationship between the other parent and the child. The presence of domestic violence often explains a mother's reluctance or inability to do this.

Similarly, a practitioner's ability to understand the characteristics and behavior of a batterer is important. For example, some men who batter minimize or deny their violence or project the blame for their violence onto others, primarily the victim, or on stressful circumstances. Because a batterer can appear quite charming, witty, and intelligent, practitioners may have a difficult time understanding that such a person could engage in violent and controlling behavior, especially in light of his often convincing denial or minimization.

In order to develop a better understanding of domestic violence and to ensure that programs are rooted in that understanding, it is recommended that visitation providers receive significant training in domestic violence and that visitation programs develop affiliations with domestic violence victim and perpetrator service agencies.

Need for case oversight: Dependency cases have child protection case workers and case or service plans. In contrast, domestic violence cases involved in supervised visitation programs and not involved in child protection proceedings seldom have case workers or mechanisms for ongoing case oversight other than judicial review. Child protection cases are marked by services designed to move families out of the dependency process. Traditionally, that is not the case in family court cases, including those with allegations of domestic violence. Given the lack of service plans and independent evaluations in family violence cases, judges often look to visitation supervisors to make more evaluative determinations than supervisors feel qualified to make. And, given the context of supervised visitation, the information visitation supervisors can provide to courts is of limited value to judges. What a visitation supervisor sees is a "snapshot" of a parent and child together for a brief moment in highly artificial circumstances where the parent is aware of the observation. This observation is not an adequate predictor of how the batterer will relate to the child in another setting and under other circumstances.

CAUTIONS AND CONCLUSIONS

While visitation centers and services are becoming important pieces in a coordinated response to domestic violence, a number of key considerations remain: visitation centers are not a guarantee of safety for vulnerable family members; they do little to improve the ability of a batterer to parent in a responsible, non-violent way; and funding for supervised visitation centers and services is uncertain.

Safety: Visitation centers can help reduce some of the risks of violence during parent-child contacts, but in no way eliminate all danger and in some circumstances actually increase danger. Some non-custodial parents attempt to use visitation centers as a vehicle for gaining access to their victims. For example, in December 1998, Carlton Edwards shot and killed his wife, Melanie Edwards, and their two-year-old daughter, Carli Edwards, in the parking lot of a visitation center following a scheduled visit. Prior to the murder, Melanie Edwards had taken several steps to protect herself from Carlton. She had moved out, filed for an order of protection, and entered an address confidentiality program. Despite Melanie's accessing protective services and tools available in the community, the exchange setting provided Carlton the access to her. This murder brings into sharp focus the limitations of visitation centers and the importance of taking those limitations into account when handling cases involving perpetrators of domestic violence. A range of community interventions, of which supervised visitation is only one, is necessary to enhance safety.

Perpetrators and Parenting: Supervised visitation allows a perpetrator-parent continued access to his child in a setting designed to enhance safety for the child and the victimized parent. But, do these cases enter visitation centers with any end in sight? What is needed to move a case from the point where the safety and well-being of the child and victimized parent necessitate that visitation or exchanges between the perpetrating parent and children be supervised to a point where supervision is not needed?

Many communities have batterer intervention programs and often batterers are ordered into those programs as a condition of visitation.

Yet, a batterer's involvement in an intervention program does not guarantee that the batterer will cease his abusive and violent behavior.

Even for batterers who do not abuse their children directly, battering and parenting are linked directly. As stated earlier, children experience maltreatment related to witnessing their father's abuse of their mother and the potential risks to children are well documented and significant. Yet, often a father who has abused his children's mother shows little awareness that his abusive behavior toward the mother impacts his parenting, assuming "he is not hurting the child if he primarily targets the adult." One study found that few battering fathers "acknowledge the need for, or understand their children's participation in, specialized domestic violence programs."

Challenging abusive men to take responsibility for the harm caused to their children by their abusive behavior is crucial. But, few programs and materials have been developed to address the parenting role of men who batter.

Resources: Visitation services are not available in many communities; and in communities where they are available, the demand for service far outstrips the capacity. One of the largest obstacles to developing or maintaining visitation services is funding. Many programs attempt to serve families regardless of their ability to pay. User fees make up about 30 percent of program budgets, leaving programs to make up for the rest of the budget with court contracts, grant funding, and charitable contributions. Lack of funding was cited as a "major problem" by 67 percent of surveyed administrators.

This has resulted in long waiting lists for services. Also, some programs report imposing limitations on the amount of time a client may use the center. This has families exiting services without regard to whether the circumstances necessitating the supervision had been ameliorated.

Supervised visitation as a social service and its application to cases involving domestic violence are still unfolding. Yet to be studied are the impact of visitation services on the lives of children and the value to a child of continued access with a violent parent. So while supervised visitation holds some promise for achieving a balance between safety and parent-child access, it does little to affect the circumstances bringing this issue to the scale: that the values of parent-child access and safety for vulnerable family members clash when domestic violence is involved. Getting at those circumstances requires a commitment from courts and communities not only to develop and sustain visitation programs, but also to develop and study other policies and services needed to address the core issues of battering parents.

B.   LEAVING WITH THE CHILDREN: ABDUCTION, UCCJA/UCCJEA, HAGUE CONVENTION, RELOCATION

BARBARA J. HART, PARENTAL ABDUCTION AND DOMESTIC VIOLENCE

Unpublished paper presented at American Prosecutors
Research Institute, Boston (1992).

There has been a change in consciousness about domestic violence over the course of the last ten years. We no longer believe that wife/partner beating is inevitable and private. We believe it is avoidable and criminal. We have all heard statistics that nearly 6 million women will be battered by their husbands in any single year and that that 28% of all the adult women in this country are likely to be the victims of woman abuse during an intimate relationship. We have learned that battery is the single major cause of injury to women in the U. S., more significant than auto accidents, rapes and muggings put together.

In one hour more than 200 women are battered by their husbands across the country; that's one domestic violence assault every 18 seconds. Three of four of these women may be injured in the assaults. During this seminar at least $6,000 will be paid in medical costs related to spouse/partner abuse. More than 70 adults will face a spouse wielding a knife or gun. Almost 400 children will have witnessed their fathers assaulting their mothers. Between 40 and 100 children will be abused by fathers, mothers, caretakers. More than 40 children will be abducted by a parent. All this in one hour. And in one day as many as four women are killed in this country by their husbands or partners.

CHILDREN OF DOMESTIC VIOLENCE

Virtually all children living in a home where one parent assaults and terrorizes the other are aware of the violence. The majority of children from violent families actually witness their fathers battering their mothers. In fact, some fathers deliberately arrange for children to witness the violence. Studies show that such role models perpetuate violence into the next generation. Boys who witness their fathers battering their mothers are three times more likely, as adults, to hit their own wives. And sons of the most violent fathers have a rate of wife-beating 1,000 times greater than sons of non-violent fathers. There is some evidence that girls from violent homes are at heightened risk of being battered as adults.

Children who witness abuse frequently evidence behavioral, somatic and emotional problems similar to those experienced by physically abused children. Pre-school children often become intensely fearful, experience insomnia, sleep walking, nightmares and bed-wetting, and suffer a variety of psychosomatic problems such as headaches, stomach aches, diarrhea, ulcers, asthma and enuresis. Older boys tend to become aggressive, fighting with siblings and schoolmates and have temper tantrums. Girls are more likely to become passive, clinging and withdrawn, and to suffer low self-esteem.

Research further reveals that more than half of men who batter their female partners also abuse their children. Child abuse usually begins after a pattern of wife abuse has been firmly established. The abuse inflicted on the child by a battering husband is likely to be serious. Seventy percent of injuries inflicted on children by male perpetrators are severe and eighty percent of child fatalities within the family have been attributed to fathers or father surrogates. The more severe the abuse of the mother, the worse the child abuse.

Older children are frequently assaulted when they intervene to defend or protect their mothers. Female children are at particular risk. Daughters are more likely than sons to become victims of the battering husband, and they are six and one-half times more likely than girls of non-abusive families to be sexually abused as well. When children both observe their mothers' beatings and are abused themselves, the risks of serious and long-lasting harm are accelerated.

While courts and the general public are often impatient with battered women for not leaving the abuser, assuming that the mother and children will be safer after separation, data reveal that leave-taking is fraught with danger. The abuse of children and the mother may sharply escalate at the time of separation and thereafter as the abusing father attempts to reclaim his family. Men, who believe they are entitled to an on-going relationship with their partners, or that they "own" them, view their partners' departure as ultimate betrayal which justifies retaliation.

> Abuse of children by batterers may be more likely when the marriage is dissolving, the couple has separated, and the husband and father is highly committed to continued dominance and control of the mother and children. Since ... abuse by husbands and fathers is instrumental, directed at subjugating, controlling and isolating, when a woman has separated from her batterer and is seeking to establish autonomy and independence from him, his struggle to ... dominate her may increase and he may turn to abuse and subjugation of the children as a tactic of ... control of their mother.[25]

Moreover, research confirms that the post-separation adjustment of children is not facilitated by joint custody or frequent visitation arrangements when there is chronic conflict and violence between the divorced parents. The more frequent the access arrangement between children and the non-custodial parent, the greater the level of physical and emotional abuse and conflict between the parents. The more severe the parental conflict, the greater the child's distress and dysfunctional behavior. Specific parental behavior particularly associated with troubled

---

25. Stark, E. and Flitcraft, A., "Women and Children at Risk: A Feminist Perspective on Child Abuse," *International Journal* *of Health Services*, 18(1), 1988, at pp. 97–118; Bowker, Arbitell and McFerron, *op cit.* at footnote 15.

post-divorce adjustment in children includes: "fighting in front of the children; demeaning the other parent in front of the children; asking the children to carry a hostile message to the other parent; asking intrusive questions about the other parent; and making the children feel the need to hide their feelings or some information about the other parent."[28] On the contrary, the adjustment of children seems to be associated with a warm relationship with a sole custodian who provides a predictable routine and consistent, moderate discipline and who buffers the child against the stresses of divorce.

Too many prosecutors and courts, uninformed about family violence and the danger it poses to adult and child victims, consider the abuse of wives or mothers by male partners as largely irrelevant to parenting, concluding either that men who are violent toward their partners may, nonetheless, be very good fathers or that domestic violence has little effect on the children or that even if the father was violent during cohabitation, he will cease beating and terrorizing the mother upon separation. All of these conclusions are erroneous.

Parental Abduction and Domestic Violence

The research literature on parental abduction is limited. The most illuminating recent study suggests that in about half of the instances of parental abduction, the abducting parent made prior threats of abduction. Only about 15% of the abductors used force or violence in abduction; yet almost 40% of the abductions by fathers involved force or violence as contrasted with 10% when the abducting parent was a mother. About 54% of the sample identified domestic violence as occurring during or after the marriage or relationship. This is substantially larger than the general population of divorcing couples. Approximately 55% of the parents abducting children were fathers and about 55% of the children abducted were boys. Another study reveals that about 69% of parental abductors are fathers or their agents.

Mothers are more likely to abduct children to protect themselves or a child from abuse or battering than are fathers; 20% of the women abductors and only 6% of the male abductors identified flight to avoid abuse as the reason for parental abduction. It appears to be generally true that men abduct out of revenge while women do so out of a desire to be with their children.

There are also differences between non-abducting mothers and fathers. Mothers whose children were abducted were more likely to have sole custody of the children, had fewer resources to seek return of the children, were less educated, were more apt to be unemployed or employed in lower status jobs and were earning significantly less than fathers whose children were abducted. Non-abducting mothers are more likely to be the victims of domestic violence perpetrated by the abductor

---

28. Kelly, J.B., "Parental Conflict: Taking the Higher Road," *Family Advocate,* Winter 1992, at p. 17.

than were men and were more likely to identify domestic violence as the reason for the divorce than were non-abducting men.

STRATEGIES TO PROTECT CHILDREN AND PREVENT PARENTAL ABDUCTION

Having identified the jeopardy to which children and battered women may be exposed in the context of domestic violence, it is imperative that professionals, including prosecutors and judges, identify strategies to safeguard against these risks.

1. Risk Identification and Safety Planning

A critical strategy for child protection is risk identification. Once battered women have recognized the abuse inflicted on them and the risk for child abuse and abduction, they can then design strategic plans to avert violence or abduction whether they elect to remain in residence with the batterer or separate from him. To accomplish this, criminal justice system personnel must consistently identify domestic violence and talk about safety planning with battered women. Most domestic violence programs will assist battered women with safety planning; referrals should thus be made to local shelters and domestic violence advocacy programs.

2. Supervised Visitation Centers

A practical and feasible strategy in most communities is the establishment of supervised visitation centers. These facilities can offer supervised exchange, on-site and monitored visits, protections against parental abduction, as well as education and counseling for abusing fathers on parenting and the impact of domestic violence on children.

3. Custody Law Reform

The Louisiana Code, amended in the summer of 1992, is likely to serve as a model for legal reform efforts. The statute is an extensive articulation of safeguards for abused parents and children. The Louisiana legislature set forth its intent as follows:

> The legislature ... finds that the problems of family violence do not necessarily cease when the victimized family is legally separated or divorced. In fact, the violence often escalates, and child custody and visitation become the new forum for the continuation of the abuse. Because current laws relative to child custody and visitation are based on an assumption that even divorcing parents are in relatively equal positions of power and that such parents act in the children's best interest, these laws often work against the protection of the children and the abused spouse in families with a history of family violence. Consequently, laws designed to act in the children's best interest may actually effect a contrary result due to the unique dynamics of family violence.[36]

36. La. Rev. Stat. Ann. §§ 9:361– 9:366B.

The new statute creates a rebuttable presumption against an award of sole or joint custody of children to a parent who has perpetrated physical or sexual abuse or other "offenses against persons" upon the other parent or against any of the children. The statute directs courts to award only supervised visitation with the abusing parent and conditions that visitation on the offending parent's participation in and completion of a treatment program specifically designed for perpetrators of domestic violence.

The code further states that the presumption against sole or joint custody awards to the perpetrating parent can only be overcome by successful completion of the treatment program, by refraining from abuse of alcohol or illegal drugs and by demonstrating that the absence or incapacity of the abused parent, or other circumstances, are such that it is in the best interest of the children to award custody to the abusing parent.

The code also directs that unsupervised visitation is only permissible if the abusing parent has "successfully completed (the) treatment program, is not abusing alcohol or psychoactive drugs, poses no danger to the child, and that such visitation is in the child's best interest."

The statute provides that the court must deny any visitation or contact of a parent who has sexually abused his or her child or children with the children until the offending parent has successfully completed a program particularly designed for sexual abusers and the court subsequently concludes that supervised visitation is in the child's best interest. Beyond this, where a parent is being prosecuted for any crime against a child or the other parent, if the state or the abused parent requests, the court must prohibit all contact between the accused and the other parent and all children of the family, except that supervised visitation may be authorized if the court concludes that it is in the best interest of the child.

The code defines supervised visitation as

> face to face contact between a parent and a child which occurs in the immediate presence of a supervising person approved by the court under conditions which prevent any physical abuse, threats, intimidation, abduction, or humiliation of either the abused parent or the child. The supervising person shall not be any relative, friend, therapist, or associate of the parent perpetrating family violence. With the consent of the abused parent, the supervising person may be a family member or friend of the abused parent. At the request of the abused parent, the court may order that the supervising person shall be a police officer or other competent professional.... In no case shall supervised visitation be overnight, or in the home of the violent parent.

The offending parent is required to pay any and all costs associated with the supervised visitation.

The code requires that an injunction against family violence be included in all divorce, separation, custody and visitation orders or judgments where family violence has been identified. The injunction must prohibit

> the violent parent from in any way contacting the abused parent or the children except for specific purposes set forth in the injunction, which shall be limited to communications expressly dealing with the education, health, and welfare of the children, or for any other purpose expressly agreed to by the abused parent.

It also must contain language prohibiting

> the violent parent, without the express consent of the abused parent, from intentionally going within fifty yards of the home, school, place of employment, or person of the abused parent and the children, or within fifty feet of any of their automobiles, except as may otherwise be necessary for court ordered visitation or except as otherwise necessitated by circumstances considering the proximity of the parties' residence or places of employment.

Codes in about one-third of the states specifically direct the courts to protect the child and/or the abused parent from further harm in crafting custody or visitation awards.

In Pennsylvania, the courts may not award custody or visitation to a parent who has been convicted of kidnapping, unlawful restraint, and enumerated acts of child abuse or endangering the welfare of children until the court has appointed a qualified professional to provide specialized counseling to the offending parent and has taken testimony from that professional regarding provision of counseling. Furthermore, if the court does award custody or visitation to the offending parent, it may

> require subsequent periodic counseling and reports on the rehabilitation of the offending parent and the well-being of the child ... (and) if ... the court determines that the offending parent causes a threat of harm to the child, the court may schedule a hearing and modify the order of custody or visitation to protect the well-being of the child.[48]

In Pennsylvania's protection order statute, a court may not grant an abuser custody or unsupervised visitation when it finds that the perpetrator of domestic violence has abused the minor children or has been convicted of interference with the custody of children within two calendar years prior to the application for the protection order. The court must consider and may impose conditions on custodial access to assure the safety of the abused parent and minor children.

Certainly, even rigorous adherence to these protective custody codes will not immunize abused parents and children from parental abduction,

---

48.   23 Pa. Cons. Stat. Ann. § 5303(c).

but they are prevention strategies that merit implementation and evaluation.

4. Child Protective Service Reforms

At the present time, state child abuse prevention and protection statutes do not authorize the exclusion of a child-abusing parent or a perpetrator of adult domestic violence from the family residence as one of the enumerated remedies that may be imposed to protect children. Furthermore, few squarely address parental abduction or the threat thereof as child abuse. A minority of codes direct that the abusing parent may only be given access to an abused child or a child at risk in secure and supervised visitation programs.

Child protective services agencies and prosecutors should begin to identify domestic violence against mothers as a significant risk marker for child abuse and parental abduction. They must also recognize that protection of the battered mother is an effective remedy for protecting the abused child and preventing abduction. Therefore, child abuse intervention plans (in child protection proceedings) and conditions imposed on release and in sentencing (in criminal cases) should be routinely constructed to protect battered mothers so that they can more effectively protect children and prevent abuse and abduction.

Abused mothers are frequently held accountable for the violence perpetrated by batterers and child abusers. They may be held responsible for the violence perpetrated by the father, yet are not provided with the power to avert the risks posed to children in the context of domestic violence. Research reveals that when battered women apprehend that the abuser is also violent to the children or poses a risk of abduction, they increase help-seeking efforts to escape the abuse and protect their children. In fact, there is strong evidence that battered women's efforts to utilize community resources to end the violence are greater when child abuse is present, demonstrating that battered women may be most motivated to change their circumstances when they conclude that it is critical to protect their children from the risks of abuse. Research further reveals that child abuse, whether by fathers or mothers, is likely to diminish once the battered mother has been able to access safety services and achieve separation from the violent father.

CONCLUSION

Parental abduction can be prevented. Early intervention by justice system personnel can avert the risks posed to children and their mothers in the context of domestic violence, can erect barriers to parental abduction, and can assist battered women in establishing stable and secure households independent of battering men. Prevention efforts may offer children the best hope for violence-free, stable and loving families.

[Chart Omitted]

BILLIE LEE DUNFORD–JACKSON, THE UNIFORM CHILD CUSTODY JURISDICTION AND ENFORCEMENT ACT: AFFORDING ENHANCED PROTECTION FOR VICTIMS OF DOMESTIC VIOLENCE AND THEIR CHILDREN

50(2) Juvenile and Family Ct. Journal 55–60 (1999).

Legislators around the nation soon will have the opportunity, if they have not already, to decide whether to adopt the new Uniform Child Custody Jurisdiction and Enforcement Act (UCCJEA) as replacement for their states' enactment of the old Uniform Child Custody Jurisdiction Act (UCCJA). For a number of reasons, the UCCJEA is superior to the act it seeks to replace, especially in the protections it affords victims of domestic violence and their children.

BACKGROUND ON UNIFORM ORDERS PERTAINING TO CHILD CUSTODY

Prior to 1968, no uniform laws existed concerning jurisdiction of child custody issues involving more than one state. As a result, multiple contrary rulings on the same facts involving the same parties were common, as were races to the courthouse and forum-shopping. In that year, and because of these problems, the National Conference of Commissioners of Uniform State Laws (NCCUSL) promulgated the UCCJA; and all fifty states, the District of Columbia and the Virgin Isles in due course adopted the Act with few variations.

Although the UCCJA partially solved the problems it had been designed to address, it did not entirely take care of conflicts; and its effectiveness lessened over the years with the enactment of subsequent federal legislation. One of the problems with the Act is that its goals were mutually incompatible. It sought first to prevent parental kidnapping of children by attempting to provide clear rules of jurisdiction and enforcement; and second to provide that the forum which decided the custody determination would be the forum which could make the most informed decision. Because the court having jurisdiction under the UCCJA was not always the court able to make the most informed decision, courts divided doctrinally as they accorded primacy to one or the other of the goals.

A second problem with the UCCJA is that it established four bases of jurisdiction and did not prioritize them. On occasion, therefore, multiple courts were able to demonstrate jurisdiction over the same case and reached inconsistent results. For instance, one state might qualify as the home state because the child had lived there for the six months immediately prior to the filing; another might qualify as a state with significant contacts in that the same child had lived there for years, and maintained strong social, family, school, church, counseling and other contacts there.

A third problem with the Act is its inconsistency with the subsequently passed Parental Kidnapping Prevention Act (PKPA), 28 U.S.C. § 1738A, and with the Full Faith and Credit requirements of the Violence Against Women Act (VAWA), 18 U.S.C. § 2265, which were enacted by Congress in 1980 and 1994, respectively. The PKPA accords full faith and credit to the custody determinations of other jurisdictions made in conformity with the PKPA itself, that is, which give priority to home state jurisdiction. Inconsistencies in the interpretation of the UCCJA, with its multiple bases fur jurisdiction, and the PKPA over the years reduced the uniformity the UCCJA was intended to achieve.

To complicate matters even further, the PKPA accords full faith and credit only to those custody decisions made after notice and a reasonable opportunity to be heard. VAWA, by contrast, accords full faith and credit to *ex parte* order provisions where there will be notice and a reasonable opportunity to be heard. Moreover, it expressly excludes custody orders from its definition of protective order. 18 U.S.C. § 2266. Victims of domestic violence frequently receive *ex parte* protective orders, which also grant temporary custody of the children. PKPA and VAWA, taken together, produce the result that, while the protection order provisions of such an order merit full faith and credit should a victim then flee with the children across state lines, the custody provisions of the same order do not, unless the court interprets those as safety provisions rather than as pure custody rulings. The UCCJA is of no help in reconciling these results.

As a result of the thirty years' worth of deteriorating uniformity under the UCCJA, NCCUSL undertook in 1994 to draft a replacement act for the UCCJA, a replacement act which it hoped would resolve these inconsistencies. Although the new act, the UCCJEA, is not the perfect solution, it does recognize at least tacitly what the UCCJA did not, that a majority of the time when interstate custody disputes arise, domestic violence is at the root of the trouble; and it does offer a number of tools which, used effectively, will drastically enhance protections for such victims and their children.

Specific improvements in the UCCJEA

In a number of ways, the UCCJEA affords both better protection for victims of domestic violence and their children and better protection for the due process rights of all parties than did its predecessor. Sections 108 and 109, for example, serve both goals. The former allows notice to persons outside the state by any method allowed by either of the states involved, the one issuing the notice or the one where notice is received. Thus the party to be served is more likely than previously to get actual notice of the proceeding. For battered women, this should prove to be an improvement over the typical situation where she takes the children and flees to the refuge state for safety; the abuser files in the home state for an award of custody; the victim, with no actual notice, fails to appear; the court awards custody to the abuser; and the victim then discovers that she is in peril of federal kidnapping charges.

The second of these, § 109, allows a person not subject to a court's personal jurisdiction to make a special appearance in a custody proceeding or enforcement action without subjecting him/herself to the general jurisdiction of the court. While this provision safeguards the due process rights of all parties, in the case of the domestic violence victim, it is likely to be especially helpful where the abuser takes the children, flees with them in an attempt to coerce the victim back into his control and files for custody in the new state. If the victim chooses to engage in the custody contest in that court, she can do so without according that court jurisdiction over the other aspects of the case, a divorce proceeding, for example.

New Protections for Victims of Domestic Violence

Other sections of the new act especially protective of the safety of battered women and their children are:

Section 204, the temporary emergency jurisdiction section, which offers three major improvements over the emergency jurisdiction afforded in the UCCJA. First, unlike the old act, which gave a court emergency jurisdiction only if a child were in need, this new provision accords a court emergency jurisdiction if a child, a sibling, or a parent is threatened with or subjected to mistreatment or abuse. Second, an order entered by a court having emergency jurisdiction becomes a final order if it so provides, no other order has been entered or proceeding started in another court, and the state becomes the child's home state. Third, this section empowers the court having emergency jurisdiction to take evidence in each case and make a determination, based upon the victim's needs and the limitations imposed by the docket of the home state court, of how long the order should remain in effect. The aim is to afford the victim, given her personal circumstances, a reasonable opportunity to file for a permanent order in the court which would have original jurisdiction and to avoid placing her in the predicament where her emergency order expires before her case can be docketed in the home state. Because in a typical case, a victim fleeing for safety with the children has few if any financial resources, especially shortly after her flight, and generally is coping with the inconveniences and expenses of relocating—finding housing for herself and the children, arranging for employment and transportation, getting the children enrolled in school, and so forth—this power of the court to enter an order good for a length of time tailored to her needs is especially helpful.

Section 207, the inconvenient forum section, establishes the circumstances under which the home state court can decline to take jurisdiction because it constitutes an inconvenient forum. In performing an inconvenient forum assessment, the court is to take into account all relevant factors, including eight enumerated ones. Numbers two through eight are standard jurisdictional factors such as the length of time the child has been gone from the state, the distance of the parties from the court and so forth. Number one, however, a new factor, is whether domestic violence has occurred and is likely to continue and which court can best protect the parties and child.

Section 208 is the section under which a court may decline jurisdiction by reason of the conduct of the petitioner, the so-called "unclean hands doctrine." The language instructs the court to decline jurisdiction if the person seeking to invoke it has engaged in unjustifiable conduct. The provision specifically exempts cases brought under § 204 emergency jurisdiction and calls for deference to those state statutes which provide that a victim fleeing domestic violence shall, as a matter of law, be deemed not to have engaged in unjustifiable conduct, even if she is technically noncompliant with terms of an existing order. The Comments to this section explain further the intent of the section to exempt victims of domestic violence from application of the unclean hands doctrine.

Section 209 deals with information which is to be submitted to the court and how identifying information which would endanger the parties or child can be kept confidential. Salient features especially helpful to battered women are the requirement that the parties must inform the court of any proceedings in the past involving violence between them or relating in any way to the child and have an ongoing duty to inform of any additional such proceedings; and the provision that, upon the request of a party under sworn pleadings or an affidavit that disclosure would endanger a child or party, identifying information will be sealed unless ordered otherwise after a hearing in which the court takes into consideration the health, safety or liberty of a child or party and determines that disclosure is in the interest of justice.

Additional Due Process Protections

Sections 201 through 203 of the UCCJEA establish a framework of jurisdictional priorities designed to ensure that the court has personal jurisdiction over all parties. In that regard, if complies with the PKPA. Under the construct of these sections, home state jurisdiction is given priority; and home state is defined as the state where the child has been for at least six months before any proceeding is filed and where a parent or person acting as a parent continues to live (§ 201). Exclusive, continuing jurisdiction remains in the home state so long as the child or the child and a parent or person acting as a parent continue to reside there, and substantial evidence concerning the child's care, protection, training, and personal relations remain there. The home state court is the only court authorized to determine when it no longer has such jurisdiction, unless neither the child nor any parent or person acting as a parent remain there; once everyone has moved, any state can make the determination that the former home state no longer has jurisdiction (§ 202). Jurisdiction to modify a determination remains with the home state exclusively so long as it has exclusive, continuing jurisdiction, except where emergency jurisdiction is invoked (§ 203).

The UCCJEA further complies with the PKPA in its § 205 requirement, that in order for an order to be valid and merit full faith and credit, each party be given notice and an opportunity to be heard. The Comments to this section say that a temporary *ex parte* order may be enforceable, against due process objections, for a short period, if issued as a temporary restraining order to protect a child from harm. Even if that is true, this statutory scheme leaves unresolved the predicament where a victim of domestic violence obtains an *ex parte* protection order which is valid under VAWA and which contains as well temporary custody provisions. Such a victim still has an order enforceable in other jurisdictions as to certain of its provisions and not as to others. However, model state legislation cannot repair what will take an amendment of the federal PKPA to achieve: a domestic violence exception according full faith and credit to *ex parte* temporary custody provisions within protection orders, where there will be notice and a reasonable opportunity to be heard.

New Tools for Judges

Even with its limitations, the UCCJEA affords judges much needed new tools which, used appropriately, will enhance safety for battered women and their children. For example, the new Act contemplates unprecedented communication and cooperation among courts and provides a mechanism for achieving that end. Under this mechanism, the court of the refuge state functions as an adjunct of the home state court, obviating the need for a battered woman to put herself back in the realm of physical danger by attending proceedings in the same courthouse with her abuser.

Three sections, §§ 110, 111 and 112, establish the means for communication and cooperation between courts. Section 110 generally authorizes communication between the court of the home state and that of the refuge state and sets up the parameters within which it is to occur. Parties may either attend the telephone communication sessions between the courts and present facts and legal arguments before any ruling on jurisdiction; or, if they do not attend, have access to the record which must be kept of any such communication, again with an opportunity to be heard before any ruling. Several sections in the Act require the courts to employ the communication mechanism established in this section, including the emergency jurisdiction provisions of § 204; and the inconvenient forum provisions of § 207 strongly recommend it.

Section 111 authorizes a court to require testimony to be taken in a court of another state and preserved for its use. The UCCJA contains this same provision. However, in light of new provisions contained in § 112 of the UCCJEA, § 111 becomes more significant. Section 112 authorizes a court to require the assistance of the court in another state to hold evidentiary hearings and preserve records of them; order child custody evaluations; order the production or giving of evidence under its discovery procedures; order a custodial party to appear; and forward all records, evaluations, and so forth to be made part of the record of the case. Courts can provide the best service to victims of domestic violence and their children by using these provisions as they were intended—

talking to each other; as home state courts, seeking the cooperation of refuge state courts in order to obtain all pertinent evidence before rendering rulings; and, as refuge state courts, making themselves available willingly to assist home state courts in that endeavor.

In numerous other ways, courts can use the provisions of the UCCJEA to enhance the safety of battered women and their children. They can grant emergency jurisdiction under § 204 where it appears a victim and her children may not be safe if they have to return to the home state without the protections which temporary rulings can buy for them. They can provide that the temporary order will become permanent if the statutory requirements are met; and they can give the temporary order a lifespan calculated to shield the victim for so long a time as she reasonably needs to get to her home state court and on its docket, considering her circumstances and the limitations that docket imposes.

Courts can relinquish jurisdiction under the inconvenient forum provisions of § 207 when it appears that continued jurisdiction may put victims and children at risk of further harm. They can remember that abusers tend to be determined and manipulative; and, since victims of domestic violence are the best estimators of their abusers' lethality, they can avoid assuming that they can protect victims in cases where the victims themselves believe otherwise.

Courts can be mindful that abusers use every tool available to maintain their control over their victims, including abusing the court process if they are permitted to. One of the most common of their tactics is to prolong litigation and make it as costly and inconvenient as possible for their victims, who usually do not have the same financial resources available to the batterers. Another is to take control of the children and use them to coerce reconciliation. If it appears that an abuser is attempting these tactics, the court can deny jurisdiction under § 208. By the same token, if it appears that according a victim access to the court can best protect her or her children, even in a case where she may be in noncompliance with an order, the court can refrain from imposing the unclean hands doctrine to deny her access.

Courts can keep in mind that batterers often try to manipulate gatekeepers of information into making disclosures. They can use the confidentiality provisions of § 209 to guard protected information and make sure a process is in place so that court employees are aware of these issues and are not in a position inadvertently to release shielded information to a batterer or a source where a batterer might obtain it.

CONCLUSION

As a society, we encourage victims of domestic violence to leave their abusers. We recognize the harm which witnessing domestic violence causes children, and we pressure non-violent parents to remove their children from the arena of combat. Sometimes, in fact, if they do not leave their abusers, we find them guilty of failing to protect their children; and we remove the children from their custody. For many women, separating from their batterers means leaving the state. Some of them can achieve safety only by putting distance between themselves and their abusers; others can afford to live independently of their abusers only by relying on support systems offered by families in another state. Such victims must not be forced back into close physical proximity with their abusers. The UCCJEA provides tools for courts which, if used effectively, can curtail the abusive power of batterers and enhance safety for victims and children and, if disregarded, can produce tragic results. It needs to be enacted, and judges need to use it wisely and well.

REGAN FORDICE GRILLI, DOMESTIC VIOLENCE: IS IT BEING SANCTIONED BY THE HAGUE CONVENTION?

4 Sw. J. L. & Trade Am. 71–75, 77–78, 82–86 (1997).

I. Introduction

In 1992, Stephanie Tice–Menley, an American woman, moved to Mexico and married Enrique Nunez–Escudero, a Mexican citizen.[1] They had a child, Enrique Nunez–Tice, in Mexico in July, 1993. Six weeks after giving birth, Tice–Menley left Mexico with the baby, and returned to the home of her parents in Minnesota. She said that Nunez–Escudero had physically, emotionally and sexually abused her. Tice–Menley stated she was not allowed to leave the family home without being accompanied by either her husband or her father-in-law, and that the men had "treated [her] as a prisoner." She alleged that her husband and his family had objected to her nursing the baby, and that her husband had refused to buy a car safety seat for the child. Tice–Menley recounted other incidents of violence in the family home, including witnessing her father-in-law striking his youngest son with a wooden plunger. Tice–Menley stated that she feared for her own safety and the safety of her child if she remained in Mexico.

Nunez–Escudero filed a petition for return of the child pursuant to the Hague Convention on the Civil Aspects of International Child Abduction, in the United States District Court for the District of Minnesota, alleging that Tice–Menley wrongfully removed the baby from Mexico, his place of habitual residence. The district court, without reaching a conclusion about the child's habitual residence, found that there was a grave risk that the return of the baby to Mexico would "expose him to physical and psychological harm and place him in an intolerable situation." The district court denied Nunez–Escudero's petition for return of the child. Nunez–Escudero appealed to the Eighth Circuit. The Eighth Circuit reversed the district court's ruling, and remanded the case for a determination of the Article 13(b) risk and the habitual residence issue.

* * *

---

1. Nunez–Escudero v. Tice–Menley, 58   F.3d 374 (8th Cir.1995). * * *

II. HAGUE CONVENTION

A. An Overview of the Hague Convention

The Hague Convention is an international treaty, designed to deter parents from abducting a child to a more favorable jurisdiction to resolve or escape from custody disputes. It mandates the return of children to their place of habitual residence to restore the status quo prior to the abduction, so that a custody determination can be made. Although the drafters of the Convention created an exception that the return is not required if there is a grave risk of danger to the child if he is returned, American courts have not interpreted this exception to include victims of domestic violence. Furthermore, with the elusive and complicated concept of habitual residence, it is difficult for an "abductor" to prevail in a situation such as Tice–Menley's in the Nunez–Escudero case, despite the fact that the reason behind the "abduction" was to escape a potentially deadly domestic violence situation.

The express purpose of the Hague Convention is to facilitate the return of children who have been wrongfully removed or retained in any Contracting State and to "ensure that rights of custody and of access under the law of one Contracting State are effectively respected in the other Contracting States." The petitioner bears the burden of proving by a preponderance of the evidence that the removal of the child from the Contracting State was wrongful under Article 3 of the Convention. However, if respondent can show by clear and convincing evidence that one of the Article 13 exceptions apply, the judge has the discretion to refuse to issue return orders. Therefore, even though a Hague Convention proceeding is a jurisdictional proceeding and not a determination of the underlying custody suit, the drafters of the Convention allowed the contracting states "to retain some autonomy in custody disputes and protect the best interests of the child in particular fact situations."

B. Interpretation of Habitual Residence

A "curious feature" of the Convention is the term "habitual residence." The term was intentionally left undefined in the Convention, and there is only a small amount of case law in the United States that involves the Hague Convention and interpretation of the term. However, interpretation of the term is a critical step in determining individual cases and exceptions under the Convention. If the child was not removed from a place that was his habitual residence, then the Convention and ICARA may not be invoked. "The intent [of the writers of the Convention] is for the concept [of habitual residence] to remain fluid and fact based, without becoming rigid."[26] The purpose is to keep the idea of habitual residence free from technical rules, which can be the cause of inconsistent rulings in different countries.

* * *

26. Levesque v. Levesque, 816 F. Supp.   662, 666 (D.Kan.1993).

2. *The Application of Habitual Residence in the* Nunez-Escudero v. Tice–Menley *Case*

In the *Nunez-Escudero v. Tice–Menley* case, Tice–Menley argued that the appellate court should uphold the judgment of the trial court, because due to the coercive nature of her stay in Mexico, neither she nor the baby were habitual residents there. She argued that the Convention does not apply because her detention in Mexico removed the elements of choice and "settled purpose" from her decision to reside in Mexico with her husband and their child. In fact, she was being held there against her will. Furthermore, since it was not her intention to remain in Mexico, it could not have been the child's intention either. The Eighth Circuit factually distinguished Tice–Menley's case from *Ponath*, because in *Ponath*, the child was born and lived in the United States, prior to being retained in Germany. In Tice–Menley's case, the child was born in Mexico and lived in Mexico until his mother brought him to the United States. However, this analysis is shortsighted, because had Tice–Menley been free to travel at her will, she may have left Mexico weeks earlier, and the child would have been born in the United States. Additionally, the court should have weighed the amount of time the child had spent in Mexico with the amount of time he spent in Minnesota. In Bates, the court said that at least three months was required for habitual residence to be established. Furthermore, the dissent in the *Feder* case points out that under an Article 12 exception, a return may be thwarted if it can be demonstrated that after a year, a child is "settled."[50] "Thus in [a different] context, the Convention recognizes that at least one year must pass before a child can be sufficiently 'settled' so as to affect the location where custody will be adjudicated."[51] In Tice–Menley's case, the baby had lived in Mexico for only six weeks; not nearly enough time under Bates or the Convention's definitions to become settled. Since leaving Mexico, the child has spent all but six weeks of his life in Minnesota. Thus, Minnesota is the only home he has ever known and been settled in, and to return the child to Mexico would seriously disrupt his life.

Because the trial court did not clearly state that Nunez–Escudero had not met his burden of proving the baby's habitual residence, it left the question unanswered, and the appellate court had no choice but to remand it for a determination of habitual residence. Instead, the trial court refused to order the return of the child based on an Article 13 exception. The appellate court could not uphold the lower court's ruling on the grave risk exception, because of the unanswered habitual residence question.

C.   *The Grave Risk Exception, Article 13(b)*

If the petitioner can establish that the child was wrongfully removed from his place of habitual residence, the respondent must use one of the exceptions of the Convention as a defense against a return order. Under

---

50. Feder v. Evans–Feder, 63 F.3d 217, 230 (Sarokin, Circuit Judge, dissenting).   **51.** Id.

Article 13(b) of the Hague Convention, the reviewing judicial authority is not required to order the return if the person opposing the return establishes that "there is a grave risk that [the child's] return would expose the child to physical or psychological harm or otherwise place the child in an intolerable situation." In applying this exception, the court will not consider evidence that would be appropriate in a plenary custody hearing. However, the court has the discretion to evaluate the safety, propriety and nurturing character of the environment.

* * *

2. *Application of the Grave Risk Exception in the* Nunez-Escudero v. Tice–Menley *Case*

Tice–Menley provided affidavits that stated that the environment in the Nunez–Escudero home was unstable. She stated that there had been physically and sexually violent acts perpetrated against her, verbal and physical violence toward other children in the home, and that her husband refused to purchase a car seat for the baby. While this evidence was not substantiated by eyewitness or expert testimony, the affidavits of Tice–Menley, her parents and a psychologist, as well as oral arguments by counsel suffice to create a realistic uneasiness concerning the physical safety of the child, and the integrity of the home environment. However, the district court based its no return order on the age of the child, the impact the separation from its mother would have on the child, and the potential of institutionalization. The district court erred by not articulating a no-return order that detailed the surroundings of the home in Mexico, and the types of violent behavior engaged in by the people who lived there. This type of order would have fit squarely within the grave risk exception. Not surprisingly, the appellate court found that the evidence in the trial record was irrelevant to an Article 13(b) exception. "It is not relevant to this Convention exception who is the better parent in the long run, or whether Tice–Menley had good reason to leave her home in Mexico[.]" The appellate court said the type of evidence in the trial record concerned the relationships she had with her husband and father-in-law, and not the grave risk of harm to the child should he be returned. Nevertheless, the appellate court acknowledged that "to ensure the child is adequately protected, the Article 13(b) inquiry must encompass some evaluation of the people and circumstances awaiting the child in the country of his habitual residence."

Both the trial court and the appellate court failed to acknowledge that the behavior of Nunez–Escudero and his father directly correlates to the environment, circumstances and types of people in the home in Mexico. However, even though the appellate court may have drawn factual conclusions that differed from those of the trial court, it should have upheld the trial court's ruling unless it could definitively state that the trial court had committed an error. The appellate court erred in failing to use its discretionary power to affirm the order based on a 13(b) exception.

D. Safe Harbor

A different approach to the no return policy would be a so-called "safe harbor" exception.[92] This is a solution that has the potential to protect the health and safety interests of a child while his parents and the courts determine the underlying custody issues. Under the safe harbor approach, "so long as the courts of the 'Habitual Residence' can assure the courts of the Responding country that the child will be protected, ... a 'safe harbor' is created in the 'Habitual Residence.' "[93] Therefore, even if the judge decides the habitual residence is in the abusive parent's country, the judge can still fulfill the jurisdictional obligations of the Convention and order that the custody dispute be determined in the habitual residence. However, instead of ordering the immediate return of the child to the habitual residence itself, the judge can order that the child be sent to a safe place until the custody dispute can be resolved. The judge can even order that the child remain with the abducting parent until the question of custody is resolved in the habitual residence. The judge has the discretion to determine that the safest harbor is with the "abducting" parent. An additional option would be to order the child back to his habitual residence accompanied by the abducting parent. These types of "safe harbor" orders do not sanction the abduction, because the abducting parent must still return to the habitual residence, have custody determined there, and abide by that court's ruling. Rather, it allows the child to be safe during the proceedings, while the court in the habitual residence takes evidence of the domestic violence, and the subsequent abduction, into consideration during the custody proceedings.

III. Public Policy

In non-violent situations it is critical that judicial authorities use the Convention and its exceptions in a way that maximizes its purpose of deterring international forum shopping in child custody disputes. The Convention was not designed to give either parent a jurisdictional advantage, and if the courts of the contracting states indiscriminately allow invocation of the exceptions to avoid returning children, the effectiveness of the Convention will be degraded. The judicial authorities of the contracting states must allow their international counterparts to decide whether to return children in the Hague cases that are in their jurisdictions, when there is insufficient cause to invoke an exception. However, there is a very important and overriding issue on the agenda: protecting victims of domestic violence. This cannot be achieved by returning children to dangerous situations they were removed from.

92. William H. Hilton, Dreaming the Impossible Dream: Responding to a Petition Under the Convention on the Civil Aspects of International Child Abduction, Done at the Hague on 25 Oct 1980, North American Symposium on International Child Abduction: How to Handle International Child Abduction Cases 6, at 13 (Sept. 30, 1993).

93. Id.

A. Domestic Violence

The real issue in *Nunez-Escudero*, domestic violence, does not fit squarely within the limited interpretations of existing case law under the Hague Convention. However, in cases of international abduction, where escaping domestic violence is the cause of the abduction, the judicial authorities that are applying the Convention must consider the exceptions available to them before sending a child back to a dangerous habitual residence. The drafters accounted for cases of grave risk, and provided a limited exception for those legitimate cases where "the child [himself], and not the abductor, would be placed in an intolerable situation."

* * *

As the judicial system of a world leader, the courts of the United States need to take a bold approach in interpreting the elusive language of the Hague Convention, and not hesitate to apply the appropriate exceptions in domestic violence situations. "[T]he United States has an obligation to educate others regarding the Convention." The courts have a responsibility to interpret the procedural requirements of the Convention to promote and encourage the return of abducted children, but more importantly to protect those that are in grave risk of danger of further domestic violence if returned.

This note is not suggesting that the way to resolve domestic violence issues in an international setting is to abduct a child and flee to another country. However, if the last resort for a parent in a domestic violence situation is to flee the perpetrator, and thus, the country of the child's habitual residence, she should be entitled to invoke the limited defense of grave risk if a proceeding is filed against her. Courts have been reluctant to allow respondents to utilize the exceptions, because in most cases, respondents have wrongfully removed the child. However, in domestic violence situations, a woman is not often left with many choices. Furthermore, the Hague Convention is still in its early stages, and the courts have not had much opportunity to interpret the exceptions and apply them to precedent setting cases such as the *Nunez-Escudero v. Tice–Menley* case.

IV. CONCLUSION

Nunez-Escudero has a "happy" ending. After the appellate court remanded the case, the parties agreed to settle. The child stayed with Tice–Menley in Minnesota, and they arranged a visitation schedule for Nunez–Escudero. However, not all stories end as well. Children, especially infants, are often powerless to articulate the horrors they have seen in their own homes, nor seek help in keeping themselves safe from dangerous situations. Their fears, and the fears of their parents are often exacerbated by living in a foreign country. Citizenship and international law issues only add to the confusion and fear of their domestic situations. Thus, in international child abduction cases, the judicial authority needs to be well versed in the discretionary powers available under the

Convention and to be able to protect the victims of domestic violence. They need to read between the lines of the black letter law of the Convention, and independently evaluate each and every claim of grave risk, before returning a child to a potentially dangerous or deadly environment.

JANET M. BOWERMASTER, RELOCATION CUSTODY DISPUTES INVOLVING DOMESTIC VIOLENCE

46 U. Kan. L. Rev. 433–444, 449–463 (1998).

I. INTRODUCTION

The unrelenting question in domestic violence cases, "why doesn't she just leave," has a surprising answer in some child custody cases. Custodial parents attempting to escape abusive situations may actually be prevented from moving to another state, city, or even school district by state laws restricting the removal of minor children without the noncustodial parent's permission. These laws, which were designed to protect noncustodial parents' access to children after divorce or separation, contain no generally recognized exception for those custodial parents who are fleeing from domestic violence. Violation of these removal restrictions can result in custody being transferred to the violent parent.

Consider the case of Deb C. Her husband beat her and sexually and verbally abused her. In December 1993, when he beat her in front of their four-year-old son, Deb called 911. Two sheriff's officers responded to the call. Her husband violently resisted the officers. He injured one of the officers so severely that the officer was taken to the hospital and was unable to work for three weeks. The authorities removed Deb's husband from the home and arrested him for two counts of battery against police officers, resisting arrest, battery against Deb, and domestic violence without a weapon. Deb filed for divorce ten days later and believed the horrors were behind her.

In March 1994, Deb's husband was convicted of violently resisting his December arrest. The other charges, including the charge of battery against Deb, were dropped. In April 1994, he attacked her at her bank and was arrested again. Frightened at having been attacked in public, Deb asked the court's permission to remove a restraint that prevented her from leaving the state with her son. She wanted to take her family to Florida where her parents and her brother and his wife were living. She had a job offer there starting at $42,000 a year. She had no friends or family in California, no job, and she lived in constant fear for her life. Her eighteen-year-old daughter from a prior marriage was so frightened she neither slept in her own room nor stayed in the house alone. Deb's now ex-husband had informed her daughter that he had peeked in her windows. He also had broken into their home on many occasions.

In November 1994, Deb's ex-husband pled "no contest" to the battery of Deb at the bank. But arrests, restraining orders, and incarceration were no deterrent to his bizarre, violent behavior. He was subsequently arrested for felony stalking, peeping, violation of a court order, annoying telephone calls, trespass, and felony terrorist threats. Deb and her children were chosen to participate in Sacramento County's AWARE program. The program involves an alarm system provided to "high risk" families who are considered to be in clear and present danger for their lives. In November 1995, Deb's ex-husband pled guilty to stalking and was sentenced to jail.

During this time, Deb was unable to work because of her ex-husband's death threats, batteries, and stalking. She could leave her home only when someone was with her. Because of these circumstances, her only means of support was through Aid to Families with Dependent Children (AFDC).

Pursuant to a court order, Deb's son continued to have "supervised" visits with his father. The boy's mental health suffered to the point that, at age five, he entered weekly therapy that lasted for a year and a half. The son's therapist strongly recommended he be allowed to leave the state with his mother.

During the many months that Deb feared for her life, she went to Family Court Services three different times for court-ordered mediation and still was not allowed to remove her son from the state. A psychological evaluation was ordered, which cost $6,000. The psychologist recommended Deb be allowed to take her son to Florida as soon as possible with only minimal visitation by his father. When her husband challenged the evaluation, two more follow-up evaluations were ordered. Deb's evaluation fees now totaled nearly $15,000. Each evaluator recommended Deb be allowed to take her son to Florida.

Because Deb and her ex-husband could not agree on custody, a hearing was set for November 2, 1995. Witnesses were subpoenaed and Deb's parents flew to California from Florida. On the morning of the hearing, Deb was informed that neither a courtroom nor a judge was available, and the next available trial date would be January 12, 1996. Meanwhile, Deb was not allowed to move. A representative from the District Attorney's office advised her that if she took her son to Florida without the court's approval, she would be prosecuted for federal kidnapping, and her son would be returned to California and placed in his father's custody. When Deb, her parents, and her other witnesses appeared on January 12, 1996, there was another shortage of judges and courtrooms. The hearing was rescheduled again, this time for April 4, 1996. This hearing went forward as scheduled. A week later, the State of California granted Deb's request to remove her son from the state. On May 22, 1996, after a thirty-day stay, the court allowed Deb and her son to fly to safety in Florida. This finally occurred two-and-a-half years after Deb filed for divorce from her violent husband.

When Deb filed for divorce she was a successful business woman, she now owes her family law attorney $50,000, owes her parents $50,-

000, and has filed for bankruptcy. Yet, she considers herself fortunate to have made it out alive and with her child.

People confronted with stories like Deb's ask how such things can happen. The pervasiveness of domestic violence and its high social costs are well known. Progress in combating domestic violence has been made in many areas. In the family courts, however, stopping violence is not a priority.

There are many professional participants in child custody proceedings and each professional constituency has its own focus. Judges are concerned with fairness between litigants, mental health professionals with healing, mediators with problem solving/shared parenting, and lawyers with client interests. Only domestic violence advocates have protection of abused women and their children as the top priority.

At a recent program for women lawyers, a well-regarded family court judge was asked to address issues of domestic violence. She passionately recounted familiar statistics on the frequency and severity of injuries to women by their intimate partners. She fervently cited research demonstrating the harmful effects of domestic violence on children. But, when she addressed the responsibility of local family courts, she sighed fatalistically and said, "Children need their fathers—what can we do?"

* * *

II. Historical Context

When it comes to determining the custody of children, the commitment to ending domestic violence often becomes entangled in and obscured by complex social issues that coexist with domestic violence. Disputes arising when custodial parents seek to relocate with their children are one such social issue.

Although lack of research makes it difficult to determine the prevalence of domestic violence in relocation custody cases, it is clear that the two are significantly interrelated. Experts estimate that at least one-half of all contested custody cases involve some history of family violence. There is also evidence that domestic violence is frequently found among "high conflict" custody cases. Because "high conflict" couples are less able to negotiate custody disputes without court intervention, abused women are likely to be overrepresented in relocation custody cases.

Part of the reason why domestic violence and relocation restrictions frequently occur together is because violence against wives and the desire to control where they live share similar historical and cultural origins. The roots of violence against wives have been traced back to early marriage laws.

* * *

Until recently, the American common law and statutes also openly recognized the husband's legal right to control where his wife and children would live. Like the right to physically chastise wives, the right for husbands to control where their wives would live was based on the legal marriage relation and changed form as marriage laws evolved.

Under the unities doctrine of marriage, there was little question that the husband had the right to dictate where his wife would live. A famous English case decided in 1840, for example, affirmed a husband's right to use force to compel his wife to cohabitate with him. The wife in that case had run away from her husband to live with her mother and was later "forcibly taken captive" by her husband, who kept her "lest she flee again." The husband was thus allowed to kidnap, beat, and keep his wife prisoner in his house to enforce her marital obligation to cohabitate with him.

In America during the latter half of the nineteenth century, the unities doctrine of marriage gave way to the "traditional" marriage model as married women gradually attained separate legal identities from their husbands. Constitutional and statutory provisions, referred to collectively as "Married Women's Property Acts," removed the common law disabilities imposed on women by the law of coverture, one by one. Although married women thus acquired the legal capacity to act independently outside of their families, the dominant/subordinate relationship of husband and wife inside the family remained unchanged.

Similarly, although the husband was no longer the sole legal being under the traditional marriage model, he was still the legal head of the family. As such, the law gave him the legal right to choose where the family would live, and his wife was expected to submit to his authority and follow him to his choice of domicile. The Montana Supreme Court explained the husband's authority to choose where the family would live as part of his role as head of the family. * * *

The law's deference to the husband's prerogatives in this area is reflected in the language of a 1963 Pennsylvania court opinion that, while requiring the wife to follow her husband, supported the husband's right to "change his home if his business, his comfort or his convenience requires it."

By the time the traditional marriage model was firmly in place, husbands were no longer legally entitled to use force to compel their wives to live with them. The law's coercion, however, was still available for that purpose. A wife who would not yield to her husband's choice of domicile was vulnerable to charges of desertion. A finding of desertion, in turn, gave the husband fault-based grounds for divorce. In a 1965 case, for example, an Illinois court determined that the wife was at fault for refusing to leave her teaching position and tenure in the Atlanta school system, the home she owned in Atlanta, her pension rights, and her pursuit of a master's degree in library science to follow her husband in his decision to move to Chicago to attend graduate school in business administration. The court granted the husband a fault-based divorce based on the wife's desertion. A fault-based divorce typically meant that the guilty party was deprived of the rights to alimony, property division, and custody of the children.

This type of legal coercion was no longer available with the advent of no-fault divorce and the transition from the "traditional" to the "egalitarian" marriage model during the period from 1969 to 1985. Under the egalitarian model, the ideal of gender equality replaced the dominant/subordinate paradigm of the traditional marriage model. This model gave wives equal rights to the management of community property, equal responsibility for supporting their children, liability for their husbands' necessaries, and equal footing with their husbands with regard to custody of their children.

Today's laws no longer give husbands the explicit right to choose their wives' domicile, nor do they expressly condone wife beating. However, the historical male prerogatives traditionally associated with marriage are ingrained in contemporary social attitudes and continue to be reflected in American laws and behaviors. Sexual relations, for example, are part of the traditional marital obligation. Marital rape exemptions suggest that men continue to be legally entitled to use force to extract a wife's sexual services when she is unwilling. Household services were also traditionally part of the wife's marital duties. The fact that wife-battering incidents are often directed towards enforcement of household chores suggests that men continue to consider themselves entitled to these services.

Similarly, the husband's prerogative to control where his wife and children live is still embedded in the American culture. Couples still tend to live in the place chosen by the husband, usually to accommodate his employment. At marriage, women typically move to where the husband lives rather than vice versa. Even after couples divorce, most jurisdictions have limitations on the ability of custodial parents to move away with their children without the noncustodial parents' permission. Because women continue to be the primary custodial parents in most cases, they are the ones whose mobility is restricted. Evidence suggests custodial fathers are less likely to be geographically restricted than custodial mothers.

III. THE BASIC MOVEAWAY CASE

A. *Rationales for Geographic Restrictions on Custodial Parents*

Even though the legitimacy of the legal doctrine has been successfully challenged, the husband's ancient prerogative to control where his wife would live continues to influence custody cases. Judges, of course, no longer insist that the husband has the legal right to choose the wife's domicile. Rather, they talk about the best interests of children after separation or divorce and the importance of keeping both parents involved in their children's lives.

* * *

IV. THE DOMESTIC VIOLENCE MOVEAWAY CASE

A. Relocation Restrictions as a Tool for Batterers

This trend toward emphasizing continuity in primary caretaking relationships, rather than geography or frequent and convenient visitation, is helpful in relocation custody cases. It is not sufficient, however, to protect women and children who are victims of domestic violence. When Deb C. finally got a hearing before a judge, she was allowed to move with her son away from her violent ex-spouse to the safety of her family in Florida. But, because of the legal approach to these cases, she was not able to flee with her children until she had endured two-and-a-half more years of severe abuse at the hands of her violent ex-husband. Had she been able to move after the violent beating that precipitated her filing for divorce, she would not have been attacked at her bank, would not have lived in constant fear for her life, would not have experienced the helplessness of being unable to protect her children, would not have suffered the humiliation of losing her ability to earn a living and becoming dependent on AFDC, and would not have had to declare bankruptcy.

To avoid playing into the hands of batterers, it is important for those involved in child custody decision-making to understand the role that custody disputes play in domestic violence. In the mix of factors that prevent women from leaving their abusers, one of the most powerful barriers to their escape is the fear of losing custody of their children. This fear may be well-founded. There is evidence that violent men seek custody more often than non-violent fathers and are frequently successful. Visitation is rarely denied. When visitation with a violent father is ordered, it is not supervised as a matter of course. This allows violent men to use custody and visitation as the continuing arena for their domination and control once women have succeeded in leaving their marriages or relationships.

Moveaway cases are a microcosm of the broader domestic violence dynamic. Moveaway restrictions give violent men the power to prevent their ex-partners from escaping and to continue controlling essential aspects of their lives after separation and divorce. Batterers use social isolation to maintain their power over their intimate partners. Moveaway restrictions often prevent custodial mothers from returning to their families of origin for support and protection. Batterers keep tight control of the families' money and interfere with women's efforts to become financially self-sufficient. Moveaway restrictions often prevent custodial mothers from moving to take new jobs or to continue their educations in preparation for new jobs. Batterers are often irrationally jealous. When custodial mothers seek to move in order to remarry or to accompany their new husbands, relocation restrictions allow the violent ex-husbands to wreak havoc on the mothers' new relationships. Because batterers are exceedingly dependent on their intimate partners as the only source of their sense of control, they often go to great lengths to prevent their partners from getting away. Moveaway restrictions allow batterers to use the legal system to keep their ex-wives from leaving and to continue their domination through control of the children.

B.   *Special Problems for Abused Parents*

1.   *Fleeing Without the Children*

Abused parents who try to escape their abusers without losing custody of their children face a variety of relocation custody problems. Some parents have to flee without the children because of the emergency nature of their flight, the lack of resources to provide for the children, or the fear that their abusers will hunt them down and hurt them or the children if the children are removed without the protection of a court order. When this occurs, their flight without the children may be characterized as abandonment and used against them by the abusive parents in subsequent custody proceedings.

2.   *Fleeing With the Children*

a.   *Interfering With Noncustodial Parents' Rights*

Abused parents who manage to flee with their children may not fare much better. Abused mothers may find themselves penalized in subsequent custody proceedings when their relocation to escape the violence interferes with the fathers' access to the children. In *Desmond v. Desmond*,[94] for example, the court directly considered "whether, in a custody case, the legal position of a repeatedly and severely abused spouse should be considered weakened as a result of her abrupt, out of state move with the children." Although ultimately supporting the mother's move, the court's analysis was a tortured study in ambivalence. The court found that the father had "so severely abused his wife physically, emotionally, and sexually that there is little hope that their relationship can, for the foreseeable future, be an umbrella of security necessary for these children's emotional peace." The court found the mother was "completely justified in escaping from the marital home, with the children, to protect their respective safety and best interests" and that she "had more than reasonable cause to be frightened by any prospect of her taking up residence locally after the proven history of petitioner's abuse."

All the same, the court was concerned with "the mother's inappropriate conduct toward the father" when she interfered with his access to the children. The court noted:

> [A]fter she fled the state with the children she secreted them from their father for almost two months. While her reasons for leaving her husband are clear and more than understandable, there was no justification for her depriving the children of any contact with their father for such a long period of time.

The court also emphasized that the mother was at fault for not actively facilitating the father's relationship with the children. Among the enumerated acts of the mother's misconduct were that she did not

94. 509 N.Y.S.2d 979 (N.Y.Fam.Ct. 1986).

promote the needed harmony with petitioner. For example, since August, 1985, she has not sufficiently communicated with the father concerning the children's performance in school, their activities, and their health care. She failed to react appropriately against petitioner's illegal drug use in the marital home. Finally, there is insufficient evidence that respondent has actively encouraged the children to call, write, or visit their father since she left with them in August, 1985.

Never mind that the mother had been terrorized over the years by the father's abuse and that she had fled his violence and still feared him. She was nevertheless blamed for interfering with his access to the children for two months and for failing to adequately encourage the children's relationship with him. Although the court expressed concern for the safety and welfare of the mother and children, their safety was not a high enough priority to justify interfering with the father's access to his children.

In *DeCamp v. Hein*,[104] the trial court similarly focused on the father's visitation rights. After a six-year marriage marred by violence, the mother and her two young children left their home in Florida and returned to the mother's birthplace in New Jersey where she had extended family. She then filed for divorce in Florida. Over eight months later, when the final judgment of divorce was entered, the court awarded custody to the mother but only if she agreed to return to Florida to live near the father's residence. The reviewing court reversed and allowed the mother to retain custody in New Jersey. In deciding to reverse, the reviewing court wrestled with "the vexing problem of moving out of state and what havoc that wreaks on the visitation rights of the noncustodial parent." Thus, while it noted that the opportunity for arguments and violence was obviously reduced by a thousand-mile hiatus, it was ultimately persuaded to reverse by the fact that the "record makes it abundantly clear that the wife approves of her husband's right of access to the children and contemplates lengthy visitation in the summer." This solicitude for fathers' visitation rights, particularly when used to restrict mothers to the fathers' chosen domicile, is reminiscent of fathers' historical marriage prerogatives.

b. *Thwarting the Court's Authority*

Mothers who move away with their children to avoid abuse may also be penalized if their relocation is perceived as offending the court's authority. Domestic violence researchers Walker and Edwall report that some battered women flee their homes without court permission because they are afraid to tell the court where they are going. They tell the story of one such woman: * * *

The use of custody decisions to punish mothers who are unwilling to trust the courts with their safety and the safety of their children can also be seen in reported cases. * * * The irony of these cases is that while judges often blame battered women for not leaving their abusers, they

---

104. 541 So. 2d 708 (Fla.Dist.Ct.App. 1989).

are punitive towards battered women who flee from the jurisdiction to protect themselves and their children without permission from their abusers or the courts.

3.   *Seeking Court Permission Before Moving*

Abused parents who neither flee with the children nor challenge the authority of the court may avoid the court's rancor, but they do not always succeed in securing permission to relocate with their children. With the courts' growing awareness of domestic violence, more and more of these abused parents are eventually able to relocate without losing custody. As in the case of Deb C., however, their families may be financially and emotionally devastated in the process.

V.   SOLUTIONS AND RECOMMENDATIONS

A.   *Fleeing Without the Children*

Relocation custody disputes that involve domestic violence consist of numerous related problems. Each requires a different legal response to adequately protect abused parents and their children. The Model Code on Domestic Violence has provisions directed at improving the legal position of abused parents in custody cases. The overall theme is to create a child custody regime in which the safety and well-being of the child and abused parent are elevated above other best-interest factors when there has been a finding of abuse by one parent against the other. The Code contains, for example, a presumption that it is detrimental to the child and not in the best interest of the child to be placed in sole custody, joint legal custody, or joint physical custody with the perpetrator of family violence. It also directs courts to give primary consideration to the safety and well-being of the child and of the parent who are victims of domestic violence.

The Code specifically addresses the concern that abused parents' flight from abuse without the children might be viewed as abandonment and might put them at a disadvantage in subsequent custody proceedings. Section 402 of the Code was intended to prevent abusers from benefitting from their violent or coercive conduct by giving the abused parents an affirmative defense to allegations of child abandonment. A few state statutes have incorporated similar protections.

There may be unstated, practical time limitations on this protection. If the fleeing parent remains away for too long, the abusive parent may establish a continuity of care that the courts are loathe to disturb, especially if the children appear to be flourishing in the abuser's care. This can be problematic for abused parents who may need time to find a job, secure appropriate housing, and obtain legal assistance before seeking custody of the children. However, widespread adoption of the Model Code would be a positive step towards protecting abused parents in situations where they have been forced to flee without the children.

B. Fleeing With the Children

The Model Code does not specifically address situations in which abused and battered women flee with their children. Sudden, long-distance moves are sometimes necessary to adequately assure their safety. Legal remedies, such as restraining orders, are helpful tools for law enforcement, but they are insufficient protection against violence. Media reports after women have been shot or killed by their intimate partners often quote law enforcement officials and victim advocates reminding the public that "restraining orders are not bulletproof." Indeed, recent research suggests that having a permanent restraining order does not deter most types of abuse.

Judgments of divorce are incorporating residence restrictions into child custody provisions with increasing frequency. This makes it increasingly likely that custodial parents who flee the jurisdiction, will do so in violation of a court order. Even when there is no custody order in place, there is a danger that courts will be negatively disposed towards abused parents who conceal their whereabouts to avoid further violence. Yet there are situations in which distance or concealment are a battered woman's only safety. Women who have left their abusers report that the abusers continue to follow, harass, and intimidate them and that the violence continues. Like Deb C., some abused parents are not safe in the same locale as their abusers. As one commentator noted, "[i]f the wife does manage to escape, her husband often stalks her like a hunted animal. He scours the neighborhood, contacts friends and relatives, goes to all the likely places where she may have sought refuge, and checks with public agencies to track her down."[144]

Protection in child custody statutes similar to those in parental kidnapping statutes would be helpful for abused parents who relocate in this type of situation. Such provisions would direct courts not to penalize abused parents who suddenly move away in violation of a court order or who temporarily conceal the whereabouts of the children if they were fleeing domestic violence. Analogous to criminal provisions for parental kidnapping, such protection might require that abused parents notify the authorities of the reason for their move, produce credible evidence of the danger, and promptly take action to adjust their legal status with regard to custody and visitation. Even if some family courts already take the conditions of flight into account informally in custody proceedings, the impact that such a provision would have on less well-informed courts would be salutary.

C. Seeking Court Permission Before Moving

1. Priority of Custodial Parent's Needs

The Model Code contains a general provision that would assist abused parents in many kinds of relocation disputes. Section 403 articulates a rebuttable presumption that non-abusive parents should be the

---

144. Lisa G. Lerman, A Model State Act: Remedies for Domestic Abuse, 21 Harv. J. on Legis. 61, 79 n.64 (Winter 1984).

custodial parents and that they should be free to move with the children to the location of their choice. This presumption was designed to counteract custody awards conditioned on the abused parents remaining within the jurisdiction of the marital domicile to facilitate convenient visitation by noncustodial parents. It recognizes that the enhanced safety, personal and social supports, and economic opportunities available to the abused parent in another jurisdiction are in the best interests of both that parent and the child.

The majority of states have included domestic violence as a statutory factor that courts must consider when making custody determinations. Many fewer have mandated that courts consider evidence of domestic violence as contrary to the best interests of the child or to a stated preference for joint custody, or expressly prohibit an award of joint custody when a court makes a finding that domestic violence has occurred. An even smaller number of jurisdictions have established a presumption against the award of sole or joint custody of children to perpetrators of domestic violence. No state has followed the Model Code by adopting a special statutory provision for relocation cases involving domestic violence.

2. *Speeding Things Up*

Such a statutory scheme would definitely assist abused parents in being able to relocate without losing custody of their children. The recent state court trend towards supporting custodial parents' ability to relocate has already begun the movement in this direction. However, even a presumption that the custodial parent is entitled to move with the children does not go far enough in preventing abusive parents from using the right to contest proposed relocations as a tool for continued abuse.

Deb C. eventually was allowed to relocate, but not until her financial ability to provide for her children was severely impaired and she and her children sustained significant psychological harm. Anecdotal evidence indicates abused parents are prevented from obtaining employment in other jurisdictions because they are given short time frames for accepting the employment (typically 30 days) while it may take many months to get a hearing on the relocation issue. Other parents report that they cannot afford the several thousand dollars in attorney fees needed to mount full-blown moveaway custody cases. Indeed, the strategy of preventing custodial parents from being able to relocate by deliberately protracting the litigation has been dubbed as "winning through financial attrition." Some abused parents, like Deb C., find themselves relying on public assistance in the jurisdiction where the father lives when there is protection, family support, and employment for them in another jurisdiction.

Structural analysis of battering reveals that the scope of behaviors involved in the battering of women ranges far beyond the physical violence to which the legal system has begun to respond. Batterers employ a wide range of violent, manipulative, coercive, and controlling behaviors to establish dominance including isolation, economic abuse, emotional abuse, and abuse through women's attachments to their children. Understanding the entire array of tactics the abuser uses to control the other parent should be as important to the legal system as the specific acts of physical violence. The law may not be able to prevent domestic violence, but it certainly should not be in the business of providing the tools for abusers to continue their abuse in the legal arena.

Minnesota's approach to moveaway cases would limit the abusive parent's ability to use relocation custody disputes to deplete the custodial parent's financial and emotional resources that are needed to care for the children. Custodial parents in Minnesota are presumptively entitled to remove their children to another state unless the party opposing removal establishes, by a preponderance of the evidence, that the move is not in the best interests of the children or is sought for the purpose of interfering with visitation. Central to this reasoning is that the custodial parent and the children are a new family unit. What is best for the children is considered in the context of what is best for this new family. Decisions concerning the welfare of the child are thought to be best left to the custodial parent who, because of his or her day-to-day relationship with the child, is best suited to judge the child's needs. The courts thus take the view that the custodial parent's decision about where the family unit will live should be second-guessed only where it would present a "clear danger to the child's well-being."

The unique aspect of the Minnesota formulation is that permission for relocation with the children may be granted without an evidentiary hearing unless the parent resisting the move makes a *prima facie* case against removal. Establishing that *prima facie* case requires more than a showing of the natural adjustments and difficulties of moving to a new community and away from one parent. It takes a showing of some unique detriment to the child involved in the move. Absent such a showing, the parent opposing the relocation is not entitled to an evidentiary hearing on the removal issue.

Dispensing with the hearing except in cases where the noncustodial parent makes a *prima facie* showing of unique detriment to the child would obviate the need for many relocation hearings. Most resistance to relocation is based on the increased distance between the child and the noncustodial parent. Under the Minnesota approach, so long as reasonable alternative visitation can be arranged, the presumption favoring relocation requires that custodial parents be free to go where their best interests lie. Removal of the children from the jurisdiction may not be denied simply because the move may require an adjustment in the existing pattern of visitation.

Permission to relocate without hearings would spare custodial parents the time, expense, and emotional trauma of defending custody challenges. This would leave them free to focus their time, energy, and finances on smoothing the transition for their children to the new location. Eliminating hearings would also prevent abusive parents from being able to continue their tactics of coercion, intimidation, and control through the legal system. Adopting such an approach would send a strong message to abused and abusive parents alike that family courts will no longer participate in the continued abuse of women and children after separation and divorce.

VI. Conclusion

The truth is that some victims of domestic abuse do not leave their damaging and dangerous situations because the legal system will not let them. Stopping violence is not the highest priority in family courts. The legacy of the patriarchal marriage law still influences the way disputes between the genders are handled. This is particularly evident in custody relocation disputes, and it plays into the hands of perpetrators of domestic violence.

Modern family law doctrine is in rapid transition. Solicitude for noncustodial father's rights has often been the real rationale behind moveaway restrictions claimed to be in the "best interests of the child." Recent decisions by many state supreme courts, however, are moving society to a stance more focused on the custodial family unit. The rest of the legal system is slowly being pulled along in the process.

Unfortunately, there is still a lack of consensus about the appropriate balance of interests in relocation custody disputes. This creates an especially difficult situation for victims of domestic violence, because their abusers can use the confusion of the legal system to continue perpetrating violence. Custody and visitation are often used by violent men to dominate and control former wives.

Abused custodial parents who leave, with or without their children, are often chastised by courts for interfering with noncustodial parents' convenient access to their children. Courts, unaware of the dynamics of domestic violence, actually award custody to abusive parents when victims leave to escape the violence and intimidation. Abused parents who wait for a court to give them permission to leave with their children must often endure continuing violence, oppressive legal costs, and emotional devastation while they wait. Even then, they are not assured of being allowed to move with their children.

The collection of problems encountered in relocation custody disputes in which domestic violence is involved can only be addressed by a collection of legal responses. The Model Code on Domestic Violence holds some of the solutions. Child custody statutes prohibiting courts from penalizing abused parents who move away in violation of court orders would also assist in solving the problem. And, if society is to significantly ameliorate the financial and emotional burdens imposed by the legal system onto the already troubled shoulders of abused custodial parents, it must embrace Minnesota's compassionate approach to relocation custody disputes, which protects the new custodial families without abandoning the legitimate concerns of loving noncustodial parents.

C. RESPONSE OF JUVENILE AND CRIMINAL COURTS TO "FAILURE TO PROTECT"

G. KRISTIAN MICCIO, A REASONABLE BATTERED MOTHER? REDEFINING, RECONSTRUCTING, AND RECREATING THE BATTERED MOTHER IN CHILD PROTECTIVE PROCEEDINGS

22 Harv. Women's L. J. 91–94, 98, 101–121 (1999).

While political discourse locates intimate violence within the sphere of state accountability, such conceptions remain outside the lexicon of legal discourse—particularly as the discourse pertains to battered mothers, their children and conceptions of a maternal duty to protect. State and federal courts protect a social contract where the state is not accountable for contributing to woman battering within the family. Because intra-familial violence is viewed as "private," the state is shielded from accountability. Under this conception of state accountability, there is no need to examine how state nonfeasance constructs and perpetuates the harm to battered mothers and to witnessing children.

Nonetheless, state abuse and neglect statutes hold battered mothers responsible for harms they have neither created nor perpetrated. Such statutes craft a system of laws that punish battered mothers while failing to protect children from abusive paramours and fathers. Most jurisdictions have codified a failure-to-protect standard in their child protective statutes and apply such provisions to battered mothers. In such cases, states bring charges against abused mothers, via the theory of failure to protect, for failing to stop the abuse to themselves. Indeed, courts permit state removal of children from homes where the sole charge is violence against the mother.

Using a theory of derivative abuse combined with a reasonable parent standard, courts find battered mothers neglectful because witnessing such abuse is deemed harmful to the child. Furthermore, according to the courts, mothers should know of such injury. Under this construction, mothers have an affirmative duty to intervene. There is no inquiry, however, into how state inaction contributes to continuation of the violence. In fact, evidence of state inaction is irrelevant. In jurisdictions that impose a strict liability standard in failure-to-protect cases, the question of state nonfeasance is irrelevant as a matter of law. Since conceptions of state accountability fall outside the ambit of judicial inquiry, they are invisible before the law.

CONSTRUCTING THE PARADIGM

Domestic violence conditions the survivor's existence upon the good will of the batterer. Survivors exist below the surface, where life is a day-to-day struggle and where violence is the only constant. In a world where terrorism is a daily occurrence, notions of privacy, bodily integrity and personal autonomy are illusory.

Such violence distorts reality. An "Alice through the looking glass" logic prevails, where conceptions of right, wrong and indifference hold no tangible meaning. Within this construct, the survivor's life is recast to fit perceptions set by the batterer. This re-formation is done to survive. To the battered woman, life is conditional and living is about subtle acts of survival.

Yet, the socially constructed paradigm of mothering leaves no accommodation for the battered mother. Within this construct, the "good mother" is selfless and deferential. The needs and desires of fathers and children define her existence. The "bad" or "evil" mother is one who insinuates her independent self into the familial picture, permitting her needs to co-exist with those of familial members.

Cultural inscriptions of the "good mother" require women to place themselves outside the ambit of self-concern. Consequently, a woman who constructs a self independent from that of her children or from the father or husband does not conform to socially accepted notions of mothering or of motherhood. Battered women, then, who struggle for individual survival, as well as for the survival of their children, are bad mothers and transformed into cultural pariahs.

Furthermore, the cultural norm of mothering shapes both legal lexicon and legal terrain. Statutes that regulate and form familial relationships construct the maternal duty of care along the cultural fault line. Mothers are responsible for harms to children—harms that they had no hand in creating. In many states, mothers are responsible even when they are the targets of intra-familial violence and not the perpetrators of such violence.

Failure to protect provisions, applied through objective standards, transform domestic violence into a sword to sever the mother-child relationship, regardless of the mother's non-culpability. In jurisdictions that impose strict liability, maternal harm rather than maternal conduct becomes the basis for state removal. Thus, the law treats battered mothers and battering fathers or paramours equally.

Such statutes do more than perpetuate notions of the "good mother," however. They shape conceptions of mothering that are at once isolating and harmful. In this isolating social construct, society or the collective "we," has neither responsibility for nor accountability to mothers and children. When viewed through this prism, domestic violence itself is suspended—having neither social consequences nor roots within the community. However, we know this is wrong. VAWA creates a construct that explodes the isolationist myth surrounding intra-familial violence. Yet such perceptions not only continue, they guide judicial inquiry and shape judicial rulings that rupture the mother-child bond.

Additionally, this construct is harmful because it sends the not-so-subtle message to the batterer that his conduct and her pain are structurally equal. Such formalized equality renders accountability moot, while placing battered mothers and witnessing children at further risk. Under this schema, neither the batterer nor society is culpable for creating and sustaining the violence; hence, the source of the violence is left unabated and unchecked.

* * *

II. THE SHADOW STATE OF BATTERED WOMEN

Intimate violence is not seen as violence. It is viewed as private, personal and domestic and as a consequence of marital discord. Such conduct is obscured through characterizations as "subtle chastisement" or as discipline. Ironically, in child abuse proceedings this violence is the sword that severs the tie between mother and child.

A. Cathy G's Story

* * *

In *DeShaney*, the Rehnquist Court found no constitutional violation on the part of Wisconsin when it returned four-year-old Joshua DeShaney to his abusive father after an emergency state removal. The Court characterized Joshua's severe beatings by his father as private. Because the Court found that Joshua's injuries were not directly inflicted by the state nor inflicted while the child was in state custody, the Court concluded that the state owed no particularized duty of protection to the child.

Justice Rehnquist, writing for the majority, affirmed the lower federal court decisions and reinscribed a narrow conception of due process. According to Rehnquist, the Due Process Clause confers no affirmative right to governmental aid in the absence of a special relationship between the victim and the state A special relationship is triggered only when the victim is in the custody of the government. Consequently, when actor and situs of the harm are private, the state is shielded from constitutional liability. Under this conception of state action, there is no need to examine how state nonfeasance constructs and perpetuates the harm.

As in *DeShaney*, the violence in *Cathy G.* is "private"—beyond public control and not the creation of the state. But as the dissenting Justices in *DeShaney* suggest, "violence itself is public as well as private—that law is part of the violence and that law itself can be violent." Here, as in *DeShaney*, law and legal actors were complicit in perpetuating violence.

B. Systemic Failure to Protect

1. Social Systems' Failure to Respond

The response of New York and Georgia in the *Cathy G.* case reflects an historic norm of inaction. As this case illustrates, the state's failure to protect results in a multitude of harms to mother, to child and to society.

Cathy visited a private New York hospital on numerous occasions. She presented injuries that at the very least suggested domestic violence.

Indeed, her injuries and explanation for the cause of such injuries parallel symptoms and excuses closely associated with child abuse—specifically, the repeated use of accidental injury as the cause, the location of the injuries and the frequency of emergency room visits. Moreover, the assailant's continued presence during hospital visits comports with intra-familial abuse.

Despite evidence of intra-familial violence and ample opportunity to intervene, the hospital failed to either investigate or to offer any assistance. Rather than involve itself in the "private" affairs of their patient, the hospital released her into the custody of the abuser—to be abused again. By conflating traditional notions of familial privacy with that of a social duty of care, domestic violence is met with little social intervention. For Cathy G. one avenue of escape was blocked.

The hospital's dismissive conduct placed Cathy in more than an untenable position—it placed her at greater risk of harm. During Cathy's last hospitalization, she disclosed the abuse to a doctor and the hospital social worker. Studies indicate that battered women make multiple attempts to leave the violence. Because safety is paramount, battered women are forced to make repeated attempts to leave. The response of social systems is critical since "leaving" is not carried out in isolation. Institutional, social, community, and governmental responses contribute to shaping survivor conduct. Social neglect reinforces an inability to leave. Hence, at the stage where leaving is perceived as an option, systemic inaction diminishes severely the survivor's chance of following through with leaving. And, since a third party knows about the violence, retaliation on the part of the perpetrator increases dramatically.

Conceptions of safety, however must be contextualized and individualized. What constitutes a safe option for one woman may be a deadly alternative for another. Thus, requiring that every battered mother flee the batterer as a condition of "reasonable conduct" may be signing a death warrant for a specific class of battered mothers.

At the point that Cathy initiated contact with the hospital, the initial response of the hospital shaped her decision to either exit or to stay in the relationship. Her ability to leave depended on direct support provided by external sources. Such support required staff to actively facilitate the decision to leave, not merely to suggest exit options. Instead of assisting her, the hospital merely provided advice. Indeed, the hospital's actions marginalized Cathy's act of disclosure and the attendant risks that such disclosure creates for the unprotected battered woman.

Moreover, when confronted by Thomas, hospital staff acquiesced in his demands—further empowering the abuser rather than the abused. The hospital's discharge telegraphed a dual message. First, Thomas' right to exercise control and Cathy's submission to his control were appropriate. Second, there was no safe haven from the abuse. For Cathy G., leaving Thomas was not a viable option since it could not be exercised with support or in safety. Realistically, there was no means of escape.

2. State Failure to Protect

In understanding how domestic violence flourishes, our analysis must extend beyond the "individual characteristics of the man, the woman and the family and look to the structure of the relationships, the role of the state and law in underpinning that structure." Women are subjects of a system of familial terror, supported by state inaction where the veil of familial privacy shields the perpetrator and the state from accountability.

A shadow state exists where the power of the patriarch is enforced through state acceptance of domestic violence. Such state condonation is evidenced in failing to arrest in domestic violence cases, in mitigating murder to manslaughter in cases where the victim is the wife or heterosexual partner of the perpetrator and in decriminalizing non-consensual sex acts committed by husbands on their wives. Where the state turns a deaf ear or blind eye to such violence, the state is transformed into an accomplice in creating the harm. Such was the case in *Cathy G.*

There was ample opportunity for the state to intervene. When the police first arrived at the G. home, arrest was an appropriate response. Indeed, under New York law, it was mandated unless the survivor requested otherwise. Here, the police refused to arrest because Cathy would not file a police report. Yet, filing such reports is not a predicate for an arrest in general and certainly not in domestic violence matters in particular.

If, however, there was any question concerning Cathy's resolve to have Thomas arrested, it was put to rest on the following day. Once physically separated from Thomas and in a safe space, Cathy called the police and requested an arrest. Rather than make an arrest at this point, the police refused, conditioning their responsibility to arrest on the actions of the survivor. Cathy missed her "chance" the night before. Hence, her inability to comply with procedures was transformed into a power that did not exist—an ability to construct police policy and shape police conduct.

The combined response of New York and Georgia law enforcement created an environment where the assailant's conduct went unchecked and unabated. Georgia could have arrested Thomas for stalking or harassment, and New York could have arrested him for felonious assault on at least two occasions. Nonetheless, both jurisdictions chose to take no action.

Such conduct on the part of the state has devastating effects on mothers and children. Through police avoidance of arrest, the assailant learns that his conduct is outside state concern and state reach. Violence within the home is extraneous to state concern and, for the survivor, the private sphere functions as a movable prison. Consequently, the response of New York and Georgia in the *G.* case reflects a norm of inaction. As this case demonstrates, states' failure to protect results in harms to mother, child and society.

For Cathy G., the harms were particularized to both mother and child, compromising their right to bodily integrity and to the society of parent and child. Here, the state's failure to take affirmative action resulted in further abuse, escalation of the terror and the eventual rupture of the mother-child relationship. The state's refusal to intercede as an affirmative protector of the mother-child relationship, while being altogether too willing to separate the child from her, makes the mother a disengaged stranger to the law. Such state inaction contributes to the continued cycle of abuse.

* * *

3. *Judicial Inquiry and Rulings: Reifying Myths and Dislocating Harms*

The court in the *G.* case did not examine how state inaction shaped Cathy's conduct and Thomas' behavior. There was no analysis on the part of the court of the nexus between systemic failure to protect Cathy G. and the continuation of the violence. Furthermore, there was no judicial inquiry into how structural inaction (for example, police failure to arrest and hospital failure to call police) created Cathy's "inability" to exit the relationship. The court's ruling obscured the nature of the violence, dismissed Cathy G.'s attempts to get help and minimized the effects of systemic inaction. And finally, the court's conduct was reductionist in that it distilled a complex set of individual and collective interactions into a cultural and inexact stereotype of the passive battered woman.

4. *The Move to Strict Liability*

Cathy G. was charged with neglect under New York's child protective statute. Specifically, Cathy was charged with failure to protect. In the *G.* case, domestic violence against Cathy formed the basis for allegations of neglect using the theory of derivative abuse. Derivative or secondary abuse constructs harm from witnessing traumatic events such as intra-familial violence. Because the child is within the zone of psychological, emotional or psychic danger, imminent harm flows from the effects produced when witnessing such events. The target of the violence then is as culpable for creation of the harm as is the perpetrator.

In finding neglect, the court articulated a strict liability standard when it held that domestic violence is *per se* neglect. Under this standard, conduct is irrelevant. The critical issues are legal relationship and existence of the harm. Once these two criteria are met, neglect is established. Conduct then falls outside the ambit of judicial inquiry.

The *Cathy G.* case is rooted in the evolving position of the courts concerning battered mothers and failure to protect. In 1992, a New York family court decision articulated what courts had been doing for eight years, applying a strict liability standard in failure to protect cases.

In *In re Glenn G.*,[105] the court explicitly rejected strict liability as the standard in abuse proceedings, but adopted it for neglect. Reasoning that one who is abused cannot be abusive, the court did not apply strict liability within the context of abuse. In reaching this conclusion, the court considered evidence of domestic violence including expert testimony on "Battered Woman's Syndrome" (BWS). Within the context of abuse, the court refused to hold a battered woman equally liable with an abusive father when the mother did not create the harm to the child. The family court did find, however, that Patty G. was neglectful.

Since abuse and neglect findings trigger similar consequences, a mother adjudicated neglectful can lose custody of her children to state control as quickly as one adjudged abusive. State interference with a mother's fundamental right to her child occurs regardless of the label ascribed by the court. Practically, the distinction between abuse and neglect is meaningless.

Strict liability as a legal standard is dangerous because it apportions responsibility based on status, not on conduct. The abused mother suffers the same consequences as the abusive father; therefore, the perpetrator and the victim are legally indistinguishable. Such reductionism obscures violence against the mother and the root causes of the harm to the child remain unchallenged and unchanged.

Finally, such treatment of the mother further legitimates male power over women and children in the family and fails to adequately identify the social and legal structures that perpetuate the violence. When strict liability is applied in cases such as *Cathy G.* and *In re Glenn G.*, focusing only on harm without analyzing cause places the mother in an untenable position.

Strict liability requires prevention of the harm to the child. Yet, where intra-familial violence exists, there are two harms—the harm to the mother and the harm to the child. In fact, the child's harm is directly linked to the mother's abuse. One cannot eliminate the resulting harm without first addressing the underlying violence. Thus, a standard that fails to address the constitutive nature of perpetrator and state conduct in forming the harm does little to stop child abuse or neglect.

Further, imposition of strict liability requires the mother to do what society is incapable of doing—displace domestic violence from social behavior. She must do this even where social supports are nonexistent or illusory. In the case of Cathy G., police protection from assault, harassment and stalking were unrealistic expectations. In New York, the police suggested that Cathy move rather than arrest in a case where they had direct knowledge of the violence and were mandated by statute to act. Under these circumstances, using strict liability to determine maternal neglect obscures police arrest avoidance, thereby contributing to the state's continued failure to protect mothers and children.

105. 154 Misc. 2d 677 (N.Y.Fam.Ct. 1992).

Similarly, in *In re Dalton*,[116] an Illinois family court found a mother neglectful because she remained with the abusive husband. The court found irrelevant evidence that the mother's attempts to leave were frustrated by police arrest avoidance and the batterer's repeated threats to kill the children. Additionally, the court dismissed uncontroverted evidence that when the mother attempted to intervene on behalf of the children, she was beaten severely. In *Dalton*, as in *Glenn G.* and *Cathy G.*, the abused mother was expected to act on behalf of her children, without regard for herself or for the potential harm that exists to the children. Such a standard is emblematic of the fatuous social expectation that the "good mother" will sacrifice her own life for her child's.

We know that violence against mothers and children escalates at the point of separation from the batterer. Homicides and serious injury to mothers and children occur when battered mothers attempt to leave or to assert a self independent from that of the batterer. Thus, a mother's decision to remain in an abusive relationship may be based strategically on the inherent dangers that leaving the abuser may pose to both mother and child. The "positive valence placed on leaving, ignores the fact that domestic violence is a struggle for control and overlooks the extreme dangers of separation." Yet, judicial inquiry that focuses solely on "the results of [maternal] efforts" rather than on efforts made to protect children within the context of the violence, places mothers and children at greater risk of harm—harms that society is still loathe to prevent.

Finally, by focusing on the mother's conduct, the father's assaultive behavior is viewed in the context of what the mother failed to prevent. Accountability is defined and culpability assessed in terms of maternal failure thereby viewing assailant and survivor equally liable.

By failing to hold the assailant accountable for injuries, violence left unchallenged will most likely be repeated. Studies indicate that abusive males are pattern abusers. As pattern abusers, it is probable that they will abuse every woman with whom they are intimate. If children are located within the family structure, such abuse affects them as well. Thus, failure to eradicate the roots of familial violence insures its recurrence within successive familial constellations.

Further, strict liability denies the nexus between perpetrator conduct and state inaction. Systemic failure to respond shapes both perpetrator conduct and survivor behavior. Thus, maternal accountability cannot be assessed without inquiry into how these two factors combine to form maternal conduct. Finally, because of the frequency and unpredictability of violence against women by intimate partners, strict liability portends a culture in which removal of children, the break-up of the family (mothers and children) and state control over mothers and children become the rule and not the exception.

116. 424 N.E.2d. 1226 (Ill. App. Ct.   1981).

C.　Objective and Subjective Standards: Marginalizing the Violence

Purely objective tests do not particularize circumstances unique to either the battered woman or her environment. Yet in reality, the yardstick used to measure conduct is situated along axes of gender, race, class and sexual orientation since dominant cultural norms construct the standard. Thus, in spite of neutral language, the reasonable parent or person is white, male, heterosexual and middle class.

Additionally, since reasonable parent standards lack particularity as to environment, evidence of how domestic violence influences that environment is missing. Consequently, factors that shape maternal conduct are removed from the legal equation.

Although a hybrid subjective-objective standard includes limited particularity, male norms still construct the yardstick against which battered mothers' conduct is measured. Thus, mothers' voices are muted and their reality is distorted. The confluence of environmental generality with (dominant male) identity particularity molds standards that exclude battered women's experience as individual women and as survivors of domestic violence.

1.　Objective Tests

In *Katherine C.*,[131] a New York family court articulated an objective standard in finding a battered mother abusive because she failed to stop the stepfather from engaging in inappropriate sexual conduct with her daughter. The court held that a reasonable prudent parent would have both known of the abuse and stopped such conduct.

What is instructive about *Katherine C.* is the court's utter failure to recognize domestic violence and account for its effects on both maternal conduct and familial environment. Co-respondent mother was a battered woman. Her husband used force, both psychological and physical, as a means of control. In fact, the court mentions as an aside that the husband menaced the mother with a knife. It also alluded to the frequency of violence. Yet in its analysis, the court dismissed the consequences of such violence and how it effaces and distorts life.

Interestingly, the court in *Katherine C.* noted the presence of wife battering in the home, but only insofar as existence of the violence marked further maternal failure. According to the court, because co-respondent mother did not file for an order of protection, such an omission evinced an inability to protect. Additionally, notwithstanding evidence to the contrary, the court insinuated that her failure to file for an order of protection vitiated the existence of violence, its severity and its consequences.

The position taken by the court then underscores judicial inability to adequately account for and assess the nature and scope of domestic violence, particularly when maternal conduct is compared with that of the reasonable parent. The yardstick that measures maternal conduct is

131.　122 Misc. 2d 276　(N.Y.Fam.Ct.　1984).

inappropriate because the objective test filters out violence. Within the context of child abuse such de-formation can have deadly and far reaching consequences.

2. Hybrid test

The difference between a wholly objective standard and a hybrid test is the subjective qualification of the objective person. The objective "reasonable prudent parent" is qualified subjectively by evaluating circumstances particular to the respondent. Thus "under like circumstances" permits infusion of characteristics particular to the respondent and her environment. Yet even with a subjective qualification, the hybrid test is an ineffective measure of maternal conduct because the standard is gendered and underparticularized.

In *In the Matter of Q. Children*,[139] the mother, an undocumented nineteen-year-old Ecuadorian woman, was kicked, hit, bruised and threatened with knives by her twenty-eight-year-old American-born husband. Additionally, because the mother was undocumented, did not speak English and had neither friends nor relatives residing in New York, she was entirely dependent on her husband. All information was filtered through the husband, and all contacts with the outside world were monitored by him. She was a captive in her own home.

In this case, domestic violence came to the attention of New York City's Child Welfare bureaucracy because the mother was arrested for "stabbing" her husband. Although criminal charges were subsequently dropped, the district attorney notified the Child Welfare Agency (CWA) of domestic violence in the home. In spite of the district attorney's decision to withdraw criminal charges because the stabbing was in self-defense, CWA filed civil charges against the mother in family court. Paradoxically, the violence that exculpated the mother in the criminal forum was used as the basis to disengage mother from child within the context of child-protective proceedings.

The family court treated the mother as neglectful for failing to protect her children from witnessing the violence. In crafting its position, the court relied on a hybrid test. Thus, the mother's conduct was evaluated against the standard of a reasonable prudent person under like circumstances. Although the court deviated from the practice of imposing either a strict liability or a wholly objective test, the outcome was consistent with other such standards because of the focus of judicial inquiry.

The court concerned itself with the mother's parenting skills as defined by her continued presence in the home. Judicial inquiry was framed by her failure to adequately parent, as evidenced by her remaining with the batterer. Her failure dominated, overshadowing his conduct of abuse and the attendant harm such abuse inflicts upon mother and child.

---

139. Case handled by the legal center.

In *In re A.D.R.*,[141] there was no evidence of direct abuse to the child. Indeed, there was no evidence that the child suffered any harm. In fact, the court described her as a happy and contented baby. However, the battered mother was found neglectful because she did not extricate herself and her child from the abusive home. In ruling that the mother was unable to care for the child, the court opined, [w]e need not wait until ADR herself becomes a victim nor wait until the repeated beatings of her mother cause so much emotional damage, that ADR is permanently affected."

The courts' failure to apply a textured analysis to either mother's situation in *In the Matter of Q. Children* and *In re A.D.R.* is troubling. In both cases, the courts did not examine how violence shaped the mothers' decisions to remain. Indeed, in *Q. Children*, the mother was young, undocumented and isolated. If anyone needed access to community and state support, she did. Accessibility to resources that would support her decision to leave safely, however, was no part of the court's inquiry. Moreover, there was no judicial examination of the state's responsibility to assist the battered mother in extricating herself and her child from the batterer and whether such assistance would facilitate a decision to leave. In *Q. Children*, the state utilized its resources only to prosecute the mother for criminal assault or for civil abuse.

In *A.D.R.*, the mother visited the same emergency room sixty times over a seven-year period and repeatedly described her injuries as accidental. Yet, there was no inquiry into why the mother used accident as an excuse or into the hospital's responsibility to recognize and treat the domestic violence. Consequently, notwithstanding a particularized standard, neither the New York nor the Illinois court considered the issue of leaving within the context of safety. Perhaps if social reality were part of the calculus, decisions to use accident as an explanation for injuries or to remain in an abusive environment would be viewed as strategic. Because mothers are held to a different cultural standard regarding parenting, however, maternal safety is irrelevant. It is that cultural standard that configures judicial inquiry.

III. CONSTRUCTION OF A REASONABLE BATTERED MOTHER TEST: THE ANTIDOTE TO SYSTEMIC MISOGYNY

Current legal standards fail to address the complexity of battered mothers' lives. Rather, such standards reify a cultural standard of mothering that is at once gendered and oppressive. Moreover, the lexicon of neutrality filters out how gender, violence and mothering shape responses of both mother and state. There is no recognition of the social context of the violence.

Domestic violence in the context of child abuse and neglect proceedings requires an understanding of a more complex version of social reality where maternal conduct is constructed by social experience. A battered mother's material existence is formed by the batterer, by failure

---

141. 542 N.E.2d 487 at 492.

of social systems to respond and by failure of the state to adequately protect. Yet, the tests employed by the courts filter out her social reality and, as in *DeShaney*, reinscribe privatization of the harm and state inaction. Thus, it is impossible for courts to situate maternal responsibility absent inquiry into her social reality.

The reasonable battered mother test has legal and political currency, unlike contemporary standards that create critical voids and operate on gendered assumptions. The RBMT permits a textured and contextual inquiry by the court and corrects the cultural myopia that neutrality constructs. Such neutrality obscures the gendered nature of domestic violence, the state's failure to respond and the construct of mothering. The RBMT functions then as both a legal and social corrective.

A.   *The Gendered Nature of the Violence and State Response*

1.   *Domestic Violence as Gender Violence*

The liberty to beat wives, as granted to husbands through the common law doctrine of coverture, is still part of our common culture. In the context of the family, male power over women's bodies and lives is evident in legal and social structures that protect the power of the patriarch. And this power has expanded to heterosexual relationships not involving marriage.

The studies and statistics submitted to Congress during the VAWA hearings demonstrate that battering is pervasive and that it disproportionately affects women. As illustrative of domestic violence nationwide, VAWA cited various state reports. In New Jersey, wives and girlfriends were victims in 85% of all reported domestic violence cases. In Massachusetts, a study of court records indicated that 91% of petitioners in domestic violence cases were female. In New York, over 80% of reported domestic violence cases involved female complainants. According to FBI statistics, more than one-third of women murdered in America were murdered at the hands of their boyfriends or husbands. VAWA documents that domestic violence is not only gendered, it is universal.

2.   *The Gendered Nature of State Inaction*

In concluding that state remedies were inadequate to address crimes against women, the Senate Judiciary Committee found that "crimes disproportionately affecting women are treated less seriously than comparable crimes affecting men." In a 1989 study conducted in Washington, D.C., 85% of family violence cases in which a woman was found bleeding from wounds did not result in the arrest of her male abuser, simply because the violence occurred between intimates. Relying upon a United States Department of Justice report, the Senate Judiciary Committee noted that one-third of domestic violence attacks, if reported, would be classified as felony rapes, robberies or aggravated attacks. Of the remaining domestic attacks, two-thirds were classified as simple assaults, although nearly one-half involved "bodily injury at least as serious as the injury inflicted in 90 percent of all robberies and aggravated assaults."

State judicial systems did not remain unscathed. The Senate report cited the Iowa Courts Task Force Report as an example of systemic neglect. The report noted that a majority of judges question the character of survivors of domestic violence or tend to doubt the seriousness of the abuse. Judicial incredulity was expressed even in the face of bruises, knife wounds and broken bones.

Such judicial disbelief is framed by two assumptions. The first assumption is that it is women's nature to lie. In *Illinois v. Phillips*,[159] decided in 1989, the Court permitted a Hale instruction in a rape case, opining that "his statement has been approved by this court ... it is just as accurate and viable today as it was when ... first uttered by Lord Hale." Women's narrative then was presumed untrustworthy.

In domestic violence cases that involve allegations of physical abuse, visible injuries as a precondition to judicial believability are the functional equivalent of the Hale instruction. Thus, the underlying assumption that gender determines credibility shapes judicial inquiry in cases where males perpetrate violence against women.

The second assumption concerns the battered woman's continued presence in the home or in the relationship. Here, the court conditions existence of the harm on her decision to leave or to stay with the batterer. And where she remains with the batterer, courts minimize the violence or dismiss it completely.

Gender bias then contributes "to the judicial system's failure to afford protection of the law to victims of domestic violence." Simply put, battered women are treated as second-class citizens because of the states' failure to investigate, arrest, prosecute and punish the gender-based crime of intimate violence.

3. How Gender and Cultural Attitudes of Mothering Shape State Intervention

While the state is loathe to intercede on behalf of battered mothers, it readily insinuates itself in cases of failure to protect. Here gender and cultural attitudes of mothering conflate to shape both state response and judicial inquiry.

In cases where mothers are criminally charged with failure to protect, the severity of the charges may be greater then those faced by their male counterparts. In *State v. Williquette*, the Wisconsin Supreme Court held that a mother's failure to stop the father's abuse of the children constituted sufficient conduct to support a conviction for aiding and abetting child abuse.[165] By finding that an omission to act establishes aiding and abetting, the court cast the mother's behavior as a direct cause of the harm even though she did not affirmatively abuse the children.

159. 536 N.E.2d 1242 (Ill. App. Ct. 1989).

165. 385 N.W.2d 145 (Wis.1986).

In *State v. Danforth*,[168] a case decided the same day as *Williquette*, a live-in boyfriend's conviction for perforating the child's intestine was affirmed by the Wisconsin Supreme Court. Notably, both defendants in *Williquette* and *Danforth* faced the same sentence for palpably different conduct.

In *Danforth*, the defendant caused undeniably life-threatening harm to the child, while in *Williquette*, the mother failed to protect her children from a known abuser. Yet the State of Wisconsin, in charging the male abuser in *Danforth*, chose to indict on a lesser felony even though the harm created met the elements of more serious crimes. Here, equality of treatment by the state belies the actual differences in the defendants' conduct.

Gender and conceptions of mothering framed the state's response in *Williquette* and *Danforth*. It is presumed that a mother will protect her children at all costs, even if it results in further risk to herself. Personal and disempowering sacrifices are expected of mothers while expectations of fathers, real or surrogate, are defined by a thin cultural standard. The perception of woman-as-mother is relational, not individual; her existence is contrived by her proscribed role within the family. Thus, in *Williquette*, the state extracts a higher price for maternal failure to protect because such failure violates social norms of mothering.

Finally, even though the child in *Danforth* perceived the boyfriend as his father, because the state treated the defendant as a disengaged stranger to the child, expectations concerning child-caring were diminished further. Consequently, the defendant in *Danforth* was held to a lower standard of care then a mother, despite far more culpable conduct.

B. *The Reasonable Battered Mother as Legal and Cultural Standard*

A reasonable battered mother test enlightens our thinking by declaring that women in general and battered mothers in particular are rational distinct beings, worthy of a voice. By qualifying "battered mothers" with the term "reasonable," I am proposing that femaleness neither disqualifies nor disrupts notions of reasoned behavior. Thus, gender, child-rearing and survivor status do not render one incapable of rational choice. Finally, this standard recognizes the constitutive nature of these categories in shaping maternal responsibility.

As a legal yardstick, the RBMT requires the discarding of a male standard of measurement. The particularity of battered mothers' experiences forms the backdrop against which the contours of maternal responsibility are identified. The social circumstances of battering and of mothering within a violent environment shape judicial inquiry. Thus, state and social inaction to intra-familial violence is relevant in determinations of failure to protect.

Because the RBMT particularizes experience, specific facts of the violence and its perpetration give shape to the environment where the

---

168. 385 N.W.2d 125 (Wis.1986).

abused mother and child live. Moreover, it permits inquiry into how environment constructs maternal choices to control and minimize harm to herself and her child.

If such a standard had been imposed in the *Cathy G.* case, it is likely that the court would have found that the mother had taken all reasonable steps to protect herself and her child. Cathy G. made repeated attempts to disclose the violence to the police and to hospital personnel. She also left the abusive relationship and moved to an undisclosed jurisdiction. When Thomas located Cathy, she immediately contacted the police and requested an arrest only after retelling the history of abuse. Yet the police neither arrested the assailant nor provided Cathy with any assistance. Consequently, each contact with the system not only failed to produce the desired result, that of cessation of the harm, but placed Cathy and her family at greater risk of injury. Thus, when confronted with the choice of staying in Georgia or returning to New York with the abuser, Cathy chose the latter.

In *Cathy G.* the battered mother's return to the abusive environment was constructed by her social reality: state inaction and social neglect shaped her decision to return to the abuser. When viewed contextually, Cathy G.'s behavior was not only proactive and strategic, it was reasonable.

Similarly, in *Glenn G.*, if the court had examined the abused mother's circumstances and evaluated her responses in light of her reality, it would have recognized that her attempts to escape and minimize the harm were shaped by the system's failure to respond and the abuser's ability to control and manipulate her immediate environment.

Finally, the Reasonable Battered Mother Test challenges the belief that mothering takes place in a social vacuum. The social vacuum idea ignores the dynamics of domestic violence and the reality of the abused mothers' struggle for survival. There are two actors in creating and sustaining domestic violence: the perpetrator and the state. Where the state fails to protect against domestic violence, it is an accomplice. Thus, unlike in *DeShaney*, state inaction contributes to the harm. Such conduct must be factored into the court's failure to protect analysis.

CONCLUSION

A reasonable battered mother test not only re-configures the terrain of judicial inquiry, it re-forms conceptions of equality so that difference is a legitimate part of the calculus. Traditional liberal conceptions of equality, which call for universal norms to be applied to all individuals and groups regardless of difference, fail to account for how difference is shaped by and formative of law. Further, the use of universal norms as performative legal standards presumes sameness. Such sameness denies the existence of gender asymmetry and how it structures power relationships in the family and women's right to bodily integrity and personal autonomy.

Moreover, sameness-as-equal obscures how gender, race and class construct universal norms and the legal yardstick that measures behavior. Thus, notwithstanding neutral language, reasonable-parent standards are constructed along an axis of domination.

The creation of a standard that recognizes gender, child-rearing and survivor status identifies critical differences that constitute reality and shape choices. Moreover, the RBMT neither destroys notions of equality nor stigmatizes battered mothers. Rather, it contextualizes maternal conduct so that the contours of maternal and state responsibility can be identified. Thus, a reasonable battered mother test situates maternal responsibility within a particularized social reality. Because the RBMT is a hybrid standard, it accounts for differences in race and class, thereby not essentializing gender, child-rearing or survivor status. Consequently, such a differentiated standard further textures judicial inquiry.

Finally, a reasonable battered mother standard contextualizes the abuse of mothers in a way that neither minimizes the violence nor uses it to penalize. Moreover, the RBMT situates maternal responsibility within a constellation of social conditions that transforms maternal conduct. By contextualizing mothering, it is possible that courts charged with the protection of children can identify the individual and systemic actors that perpetuate the harm. Perhaps then we can craft protection paradigms that keep children safe, empower mothers and locate the contours of maternal and state responsibility.

LESLEY E. DAIGLE, EMPOWERING WOMEN TO PROTECT: IMPROVING INTERVENTION WITH VICTIMS OF DOMESTIC VIOLENCE IN CASES OF CHILD ABUSE AND NEGLECT; A STUDY OF TRAVIS COUNTY, TEXAS

7 Tex. J. Women & L. 313–317 (1998).

V. B. 2. INSTITUTIONAL CHANGES

In order to support battered women's efforts to protect themselves and their children, the CPS system should work to increase awareness of domestic violence issues among parties to CPS litigation and develop a coordinated community response to family violence through the provision of more direct services for battered mothers.

This research has indicated that all parties to CPS litigation in Travis County should raise their awareness of the impact of domestic violence on their client's behaviors and needs, particularly considering the high estimate of CPS cases in the county involving domestic violence. Inquiries into the presence of domestic violence should be a routine part of intake assessments and initial interviews conducted by CPS caseworkers and attorneys. All parties should be discussing specific legal and practical strategies with their clients to increase the clients' safety at home, at work, at school, and in visitation with family members. Practitioners who do not assess for the presence of domestic violence cannot be effective advocates for their clients, nor can they argue accurately in a party's best interest.

Empowering women to protect children requires long-term, continuous support of their efforts to become independent. Different strategies have been implemented in other jurisdictions to address this need for an intensive, coordinated community response to family violence. The Massachusetts Department of Social Services (DSS), the government agency charged with intervening when there are reports of child abuse and neglect, initiated a domestic violence program to integrate battered women's services with child protection efforts. Since the program's inception in 1991, the Domestic Violence Unit of DSS has hired eleven domestic violence specialists who work in DSS field offices, consulting on specific cases and serving as liaisons between DSS and other services for battered women. The unit specialists also provide training for DSS social workers and members of the community on the impact of domestic violence, as well as methods of investigating and assessing domestic violence in child abuse cases. Furthermore, the DSS adopted a domestic violence protocol for investigation, assessment, and service planning, which maintains child protection as its focus and relies on nonviolent mothers as a key element of the child protection effort:

> The primary focus of DSS intervention in domestic violence cases is the ongoing assessment of the risk posed to children by the presence of domestic violence. The preferred way to protect children in most domestic violence cases is to join with mothers in safety planning and to hold offenders accountable. It is important to work closely with battered women's programs, the criminal justice system and batterer's treatment providers.

The Domestic Violence Unit serves to bridge the work of domestic violence advocates and child protective workers, which has led to less conflict and suspicion between the two groups. One result of this coordinated response is that out-of-home placements for abused children whose mothers also are battered appear to be reduced in areas of the state that have received support from the Domestic Violence Unit.

At Boston Children's Hospital, the staff of Project AWAKE (Advocacy for Women and Kids in Emergencies) works with the hospital's child protection team and other health and social service centers in the community to provide advocacy for battered women. Once AWAKE receives a referral, battered women are assigned an advocate. Very few of the abused children in these cases require out-of-home care. The project's director attributes AWAKE's success primarily to the longevity and comprehensiveness of its services for battered women.

AWAKE accesses long-term counseling for women in their communities and provides a range of support groups for women, such as a substance abuse group and a Spanish-speaking group. Its staff members also do in-person advocacy at myriad agencies, including immigration, housing, and welfare. For battered women involved in child abuse and neglect proceedings, AWAKE staffers coordinate with advocates at the

Domestic Violence Unit of the Massachusetts DSS, accompany women to any legal proceedings, and, if needed, speak on the women's behalf. In addition, AWAKE works on broad-based public information and education on domestic violence.

Although intensive coordination between CPS and battered women's advocates has been effective in increasing the rates at which children in Massachusetts remain with nonviolent mothers, simply providing mothers with access to battered women's advocates goes far toward achieving the financial and emotional stability and physical security that the CPS system typically requires of parents. In San Diego, The Family Violence Program, a nonprofit organization affiliated with the Children's Hospital's Center for Child Protection, has developed a community-based model of support services for battered women. Like AWAKE, the program receives referrals from all community sectors, including self-referrals. Services provided by the program include accompanying women to court hearings, coordinating counseling and group therapy for women and their children, and offering legal consultations and referrals. Although affiliated with a hospital, the program is located in a separate building in the community, which the program's director believes increases the access of typically underserved populations to their services. Interfacing with the community also affords the program the ability to monitor the effectiveness of various services and programs that battered women access so that its staff are in a better position to recommend areas for improvement in service delivery to local domestic violence advocacy groups.

* * *

V.   CONCLUSION

Empowering battered women to protect their children involves more than creating complex legal strategies to counter the failure to protect doctrine. Empowering women to protect requires the development of legal and social service tools, such as a reasonableness defense to the charge of failure to protect and the assignment of battered women's advocates, that incorporate into the state's child protection effort the women's existing efforts to keep themselves and their children safe. It also requires developing a CPS system that provides incentives for battered women to seek this assistance. Currently in Texas, the fact that women are held accountable for failing to separate from a batterer and failing to protect, while less attention seemingly is focused on the batterer's violent conduct, creates many disincentives for mothers to come forward.

* * *

The child protective system has continuously evolved, reflecting a greater appreciation of the plight of abused children and an understanding of the effective ways in which government and the private sector can ensure their basic needs are being met. Parties to CPS litigation should continue to act in this spirit of collaboration. Working to treat family violence as a whole, by including comprehensive domestic violence assessment and service planning in CPS cases, increases children's protection from violence while providing for safe relationships with parents, both equally essential to a child's healthy development.

BRYAN A. LIANG AND WENDY L. MacFARLANE, MURDER BY OMISSION: CHILD ABUSE AND THE PASSIVE PARENT

36 Harv. J. on Legis. 440–445 (1999).

D.   Battered Woman Syndrome and Public Policy

The parent/child relationship exhibits a unique paradox—children are most vulnerable to abuse by the very persons who have the highest duty to protect them, their parents. As one court has stated:

> [A] parent's failure to take appropriate steps to protect their child from the abuse of the other parent is tantamount to neglect of that child, not to mention moral complicity with the base crime being perpetrated upon the child by the other parent. In a situation where it is the other parent perpetrating the abuse upon the child, the non-abusing parent is under an even greater duty to take steps necessary to prevent the abuse. First, the parent has a higher probability of knowing about the abuse because he or she lives with both the victim and the abuser. Second, the relationship of the child-victim to the parent-abuser presents additional problems that do not arise when the abuser is a stranger. Due to the added problems inherent in a parent-child abuse situation, the non-abusing parent, as the only advocate for the child, has a greater responsibility to prevent such abuse when it becomes or should have become evident to that parent.[313]

Scientific support for BWS is weak. To allow BWS to exculpate a parent who breaches her legal duty to protect her child simply vitiates that duty. Proponents of an imperfect duress defense seek to excuse the battered woman from her omission because her perception was distorted. According to these advocates, sufferers of the syndrome cannot form the requisite intent because their free will is compromised.

Duress, however, is rarely recognized as a complete defense to homicide. In at least seventeen states, it is unavailable. At common law, duress was not a defense to intentional killing. Case law, in the absence of statutes, has generally held that duress cannot excuse an intentional killing or an attempt to kill. Even those jurisdictions that recognize a duress defense for murder hold that the defense is unavailable if the actor intentionally, knowingly or recklessly places herself in a situation in which it is probable that she would be subject to duress. The duress defense is also unavailable if the actor does not take advantage of a

---

313. Muehe, 646 N.E.2d at 983–84.

reasonable opportunity to escape. This requirement applies uniformly, even if the charge is felony child-abuse.

By submitting to abuse or allowing her child to be abused, a woman seems to place herself in a situation in which she is likely to be subject to duress. It is a weak argument that such a woman is trying to protect the child from some greater harm. If BWS is characterized by increasing cycles of violence, the battered woman should arguably realize that submission will not result in less abuse, but more—just as it has previously.

No one except the abuser himself benefits when a woman fails to protect her child. Indeed, use of the duress defense neither discourages the mother from entering another battering relationship nor encourages her to protect the child from further abuse. To deter passive acceptance of known child abuse, the duress defense should not be permitted in cases when a child dies as a result of the abuse. To require otherwise would create the bizarre incentive to let the child die before seeking help. Such a result is unconscionable.

In *Hernandez*, Gabriela might have been afraid to come to her daughter's aid because of the fear that Rogelio would harm either herself or Joselin. Initially, there were no negative consequences of Gabriela's failure to act. She had regained custody of her daughter, despite the abuse. Gabriela might even have had a relatively clear conscience, as she was not doing the beating. Further, Gabriela might have feared losing her other child if she reported the abuse.

To allow BWS to excuse Gabriela's breach, however, would protect no one. It would create no incentive for battered women to report abuse, and it could subject her son and any future children to a fate similar to Joselin's. Gabriela breached her duty to protect Joselin when she failed to take steps to protect the toddler from Rogelio's abuse. Further, Gabriela knowingly and recklessly remained in a situation likely to subject her to duress. Gabriela was fully aware of the potential consequences of not taking advantage of the many opportunities to report Rogelio's further abuse to CPS, and of choosing to remain living with him while he abused their daughter. But ultimately, whether she reasonably or unreasonably believed that she was in imminent harm, duress does not excuse homicide.

The parent who fails to protect her child must be held accountable for her omission. When there is a history of child abuse, BWS should be no defense. The law holds much more attenuated parties, such as physicians, educators and other third parties, responsible for not reporting child abuse. Those with the highest duty and the most special relationship to the child should be accountable as well.

Heather Skinazi, a proponent of BWS, states that "[c]onvicting a non-abusing battered mother for failure to protect will not benefit children, rather it only serves to revictimize both mother and child who have suffered enough abuse. No child should be wrenched from a loving and good parent simply because that parent has been battered."[325] However, this argument mislabels the non-battering parent. A parent who fails to protect her child from abuse is no more a "loving and good parent" than the abuser. Further, as Skinazi herself notes, "in homes where mothers are victims of domestic violence, about seventy percent of fathers or father-substitutes also beat the children." One who intentionally places herself in an abusive relationship should not be characterized as a victim of that relationship. By focusing on the rights of the parent, Skinazi ignores the child's rights. Such a view only re-victimizes the child by failing to create an incentive for the parent to report or stop the abuse. Thus, in the absence of a clear legal pronouncement, such a perspective sacrifices the rights of the child for the rights of the parent.

In one of the first cases considering duress where a battered woman was charged with failure to protect her child, *United States v. Webb*,[327] the court refused to admit expert testimony explaining why a battered woman might not be able to leave her batterer and seek protection. In that case, June Webb was convicted on two counts of injury to a child by failing to obtain medical care for her six-year-old son, Steve. The evidence revealed that Keith, June's husband, repeatedly beat her and their son Steve. Their son finally succumbed to the beatings and scaldings he had endured, and Keith buried his body in the desert. Almost one month later, June reported Steve's death to the authorities and accused Keith of causing her son's death. In court, June claimed she did not report the death sooner because Keith had threatened to kill her, her other children, and her family in Delaware if she reported him.

Skinazi argues that the jury's verdict in *Webb* hinges on the court's use of an objective standard of reasonableness. She contends that BWS would explain why June Webb was unable to report the child abuse until one month after her son's death. However, Skinazi omits from her analysis certain facts that might very well explain the verdict independently of the objective reasonableness standard. For example, June did not continuously live with or even near Keith. She enlisted in the Army and lived alone in Germany for two years. Despite Keith's prior physical abuse, the two reconciled when June returned from Germany. Leaving her children in Delaware, June moved with Keith to Texas, and the beatings resumed. After a few months Keith's legal wife and her four children arrived, as did June's two children. These nine lived together in a three-bedroom house, June being the sole source of support. Meanwhile, Keith continued to abuse June and began to abuse their six-year-old son.

There is no evidence that June was forced to reconcile with Keith after she returned from Germany, nor is there evidence that she was forced to bring her own two children to live in the home. And as June was the household's sole source of monetary support, she was not financially dependent on Keith. It is arguable whether June was emo-

---

325. Skinazi, supra note 295, at 999. **327.** 747 F.2d 278 (5th Cir.1984).

tionally dependent on Keith—indeed, she lived alone for two years prior to moving to Texas.

Texas law states that duress is unavailable as a defense if the actor intentionally, knowingly, or recklessly placed herself in a situation in which it was probable that she would be subjected to compulsion. In light of the facts, it is understandable how a jury might believe that June's feelings of duress, whether or not her apprehensions were reasonable, were nonetheless self-imposed. BWS may explain why June was unable to leave her situation, but it can not explain why she placed herself in such a situation initially.

AMY HADDIX, UNSEEN VICTIMS: ACKNOWLEDGING THE EFFECTS OF DOMESTIC VIOLENCE ON CHILDREN THROUGH STATUTORY TERMINATION OF PARENTAL RIGHTS

84 Calif. L. Rev. 760–762, 814–815 (1996).

* * * Although forty-four states and the District of Columbia currently allow or require evidence of domestic violence by one parent against the other to be considered in custody disputes between the parents, state legislatures and courts have been reluctant to allow such evidence to be introduced in termination proceedings, which are a more severe form of intervention. Unlike custody proceedings, which frequently preserve a parent's rights to visitation and continued legal control over the child, termination proceedings are geared toward permanently severing the parent/child relationship and placing the child with state agencies or private third parties.

The California case *In re James M.*[10] presents a striking example of the way in which courts ignore crimes of domestic violence against the mother when evaluating a father's parental fitness. In *James M.*, Sergio and Judith Marks were married and living together with seven children, four of whom were Sergio's. Judith left Sergio for another man and took the children with her. Sergio attempted to reconcile with Judith. When she refused to return to him, he stabbed her twenty-two times, killing her. Sergio pled guilty to second-degree murder and was sentenced to five years to life in prison.

Following the murder, the department of public welfare filed a petition to terminate Sergio's parental rights. In denying the petition, the appellate court upheld the trial court's determination that Sergio's murder of his wife was a "crime of passion" and that Sergio's acts were "not the product of a violent and vicious character." The court further reasoned that depriving the children of their mother was analogous to separation through divorce and did not constitute neglect of the children's needs. The court finally concluded that, because Sergio's actions

10.   135 Cal. Rptr. 222 (Ct. App. 1976).

toward Judith did not amount to cruelty toward his children, and because the children did not want to be separated from each other or from their father, Sergio should retain his parental rights.

Similarly, in *Bartasavich v. Mitchell*,[18] the Pennsylvania Superior Court reversed a trial court's decision to terminate a father's parental rights where evidence of domestic abuse was presented. In that case, the father stabbed and killed the mother during a domestic dispute, took his two-year-old daughter to a neighbor's home, and then attempted suicide by stabbing himself with a fork. Despite findings that the child feared her father and suffered from anxiety during her visits with him in prison, the court held that the father's killing of the mother and its attendant consequences for the child were not sufficient, standing alone, to terminate the father's parental rights as a matter of law.

Although some state courts have found that, in particular instances, killing a child's mother justifies termination of a father's parental rights, they have generally refused to recognize a *per se* connection between domestic violence and parental unfitness. As a recent Florida custody case indicates, courts may even determine that a lesbian mother poses a more dangerous influence on her child than does a homicidal father.

Terminating the rights of an abusive father becomes even more difficult when the child is a newborn with whom the father has had little or no contact. This is particularly true in cases where the mother attempts to "thwart" the father's parental involvement, either by failing to inform him of the pregnancy or by hiding the child from him after birth, while she seeks adoptive placement for the child. If the biological father has no true interest in raising his child, judicial intervention may be necessary to provide the child with a stable, permanent adoptive home. In such cases, however, the courts have consistently refused to terminate the father's parental rights in favor of a third-party adoption. For the child, who will likely reach the age of two before the conclusion of any appeals, moving from a stable adoptive home to live with a father she has never known could be both emotionally and physically devastating, particularly if a close relationship with the biological father fails to develop.

* * *

CONCLUSION

* * *

Courts have mistakenly resisted acknowledging the connection between domestic violence and parental unfitness. Any concern they may have over the strength of that connection dissipates in the face of the sociological evidence. Based upon this evidence, and the legislative findings by Congress and the majority of state legislatures, a statute including domestic violence by one parent against the other as a ground for

18. 471 A.2d 833 (Pa. Super. Ct. 1984).

termination likely would survive a due process challenge under intermediate scrutiny.

During a termination proceeding, the petitioning party would be required to establish the abusive parent's acts of domestic violence by clear and convincing evidence. Although this is a lesser standard of proof than previously has been required by states that allow use of past felony convictions to indicate unfitness, the lesser showing does not raise constitutional concerns. Because the connection between domestic violence and parental unfitness has been determined to exist as a matter of law and is statutorily codified, the legislature need not require a higher level of proof.

Evidence of domestic violence would create a presumption of unfitness, which the father could then rebut by showing his rehabilitation by clear and convincing evidence. Thus, admission of domestic violence evidence in and of itself would not automatically terminate a father's rights. Rather, the judge would retain ultimate discretion to determine unfitness, according to legislative guidelines for finding rehabilitation. In those cases where rehabilitation is not feasible, the proposed model termination statute would help to place children in supportive environments before their lives are irreparably damaged by domestic violence. The statute, however, would not serve as a sword against the victimized woman by terminating her parental rights for not removing herself and her children from the abusive environment.

The model statute I have proposed is designed to alleviate the social epidemic facing our children. Children are entitled to live in a loving and supportive environment where they may experiment and grow free from the stress inherent in a violent household. The state, as *parens patriae*, has not only the right but the obligation to protect children from abusive parents. If the state fails to intercede, children likely will mature into mirror images of their parents, perpetuating the cycle of domestic violence into future generations. Admittedly, termination is a drastic means by which to achieve the goal of child protection. However, in light of batterers' high rates of recidivism and post-separation violence, termination is the only sure way to protect children from chronically abusive parents.

AUDREY E. STONE AND REBECCA J. FIALK, CRIMINALIZING THE EXPOSURE OF CHILDREN TO FAMILY VIOLENCE: BREAKING THE CYCLE OF ABUSE

20 Harv. Women's L. J. 210–213 (1997).

III.   REASONS TO CRIMINALIZE DOMESTIC VIOLENCE
COMMITTED IN A CHILD'S PRESENCE

The criminal justice system has made tremendous strides in responding to domestic violence within the past twenty years. Currently, every state has enacted statutes that protect direct victims of domestic violence. These statutes uniformly protect married and formerly married persons; nearly all cover persons living together and close relatives. Cities such as San Diego, California; Quincy, Massachusetts; Duluth, Minnesota; Knoxville, Tennessee; Newport News, Virginia; and Seattle, Washington have reported significant reductions in repeat offenses and in domestic violence homicide rates as a result of implementing aggressive arrest and prosecution policies.

Despite these significant advances, prosecutors by and large do not focus on the holistic nature of domestic violence, leaving to family courts and child welfare agencies the task of confronting the needs of and the dangers to children who reside in violent homes. No state laws currently identify child witnesses of domestic violence as a class of persons in need of specific legal protection, unless the child has been physically abused or neglected. In light of the vast amount of research supporting the harmful consequences child witnesses suffer, current criminal statutes should explicitly protect these children. Criminalizing the exposure of a child to domestic violence holds the batterer accountable for abusive conduct. Furthermore, criminalizing the exposure of a child witness to domestic violence can serve as a critical step in the process of ending the intergenerational transmission of violence. Criminal sanctions send a message to child witnesses that the violence they observe in their homes is a criminal act that brings negative consequences to the perpetrator and should not serve as a model for their future relationships.

Within the broader social context, the legal system perpetuates the traditional, stereotypical notion that it is the mother's sole responsibility to protect her children. When courts intervene to protect the child, they typically blame the mother for not removing the child from the abusive household, instead of focusing on the husband's obligation to cease the violence. This blaming is especially common where the child has been abused, and the mother has not reported the abuse. However, courts also blame women for staying in abusive relationships where only the mothers, not the children, are the physical victims of the batterer. When the system responds by removing children from the abused mother, it discourages women from reporting domestic violence to authorities. Women learn that reporting violence inevitably leads to the removal of their children from their homes. Courts that separate victim mothers from their children reinforce the negative social stereotype of blaming battered women for not escaping abusive situations. More disturbingly, by blaming the battered victim, courts, as well as society at large, may disregard the legitimate efforts of these women to protect their children. Yet battered women know that by keeping their families intact they could be preventing an escalation of the domestic violence. When a woman leaves a batterer, the violence can intensify from abusive hostility to homicidal rage that creates even more danger for the entire family. Given this reality, criminal codes should focus on the batterer's conduct and hold him accountable, rather than focusing on the victim's inability to free herself and her children from the abusive environment.

Abusive husbands have been surprisingly successful in gaining custody. Although many states have begun to address the dangers of granting custody to perpetrators of spousal abuse through custody and visitation statutes, current child custody and visitation laws are "based on an assumption that ... parents are in relatively equal positions of power, and that such parents act in the children's best interest."[42] In reality, these laws do not reflect the dynamics of families experiencing domestic violence. Criminalizing the exposure of a child to domestic violence would have a positive effect on civil custody proceedings. It seems logical that abusive husbands are also unfit parents because they have exposed their children to unhealthy home environments; however, not all judges agree. A father's assault conviction against the mother does not necessarily become a factor in determining the best interests of a child. In contrast, a father's conviction for harming a child would be difficult for courts to ignore in custody or visitation proceedings. A conviction for endangering the welfare of a child by exposing him or her to domestic violence would be compelling evidence for the court to find that the best interests of the child do not lie with the batterer.

Another compelling reason to criminalize exposing children to abuse is to provide prosecutors with a new tool for combatting domestic violence. Often prosecutors find complainants in domestic violence cases unwilling to assist in prosecuting their batterers. Where insufficient evidence exists for prosecuting a batterer on assault charges, a case for harming the child may still be viable. Of course prosecutors must continue to exercise their discretion in charging offenders. The facts and circumstances of the individual case should guide the prosecutor in charging this offense. However, fathers who batter commit an egregious act against the children in their homes to whom they owe a special duty of care. Society must consider the impact of spousal abuse on child witnesses and move toward criminalizing this conduct.

42. La. Rev. Stat. Ann. § 9:361 (West Supp. 1997).

Chapter 8

ALTERNATIVE DISPUTE
RESOLUTION

This chapter looks at alternative dispute resolution in the context of domestic violence. It concludes the section of this book dealing with civil courts, and immediately precedes the section on criminal courts; this is because alternative dispute resolution can occur in either type of domestic violence case, though it is more typically found in custody disputes in the civil court.

The materials start with a case example to illustrate how this issue typically arises in the context of a custody and visitation dispute, when the parties are referred to court-connected mediation. The materials then outline how mediation works generally, and the arguments for and against its use in domestic violence settings. An example of guidelines which one state has adopted for mediators handling this type of case follows, along with examples of typical behaviors which abusers may demonstrate during mediation. Next is the summary of a national survey looking at how administrators of court-based mediation programs say their programs are dealing with domestic violence cases, and recommendations for improvement, including domestic violence training for all their staff.

The chapter concludes with a description of traditional dispute resolution in the Navajo community, known as "peacemaking," along with an analysis of whether this practice is beneficial in preventing future abuse in intimate relationships. Note that in this context the criminal aspects of domestic violence are being resolved along with the civil.

VOGT v. VOGT

Supreme Court of Minnesota, (1990).
455 N.W.2d 471, 472–475.

This case discusses the manner in which temporary visiting rights should be determined when one spouse is seeking an order for protection in a domestic abuse proceeding.

On January 30, 1989, Cindy Vogt filed a *pro se* petition with the Steele County District Court for an order for protection pursuant to the Domestic Abuse Act, Minn.Stat. ch. 518B (1988). In the space provided in the petition for her affidavit, petitioner wrote how a few days before her husband, Thomas Vogt, had physically abused her in front of their two small children. An *ex parte* order of restraint was issued and served on Thomas Vogt.

On February 6, 1989, a court hearing was held on the petition with both parties appearing *pro se*. Thomas Vogt filed no counter-affidavit. When asked what his position was, Thomas Vogt replied, "I did go and seek professional help to deal with my problem." The court then issued that same day an order restraining Thomas Vogt from harassing his wife and awarding custody of the two children (3 and 6 years old) to Cindy Vogt, "subject to reasonable visitation [*sic*] in accordance with the plan developed by Steele County Court Services." Thomas Vogt asked when he might visit the children, and, when the parties indicated they then had time available, the court told them to see Mrs. Durst in Court Services. Mrs. Durst met separately with the Vogts. Both then signed a handwritten agreement setting out a temporary visiting schedule, which was then attached to the court's order.

Two days later, on February 8, the parties were back in court, apparently for Thomas Vogt's arraignment on fifth degree assault charges. The husband was represented by counsel and the wife appeared *pro se*. Thomas Vogt's attorney took the occasion to serve Cindy Vogt with the husband's petition for a marriage dissolution. When the attorney expressed concern about the children, the court responded that Court Services' recommendation on visiting would be followed unless something came up that indicated it should not be. The court then added, "It's not their [the parties'] decision to make, it's up to Court Services."

A few days later Cindy Vogt retained a Legal Aid attorney who wrote a letter to the husband's attorney "revoking" the visiting agreement. On March 13 the parties were back in court on a variety of motions, namely, Cindy Vogt's application for temporary relief in the dissolution proceeding, Cindy Vogt's motion to vacate the February 6 visiting agreement, and Thomas Vogt's motion that his wife be found in contempt of court for failing to abide by the court's order on visiting. Cindy Vogt filed an affidavit claiming that when she met with Mrs. Durst of Court Services she felt "overpowered and confused"; that Mrs. Durst told her she was being "selfish" and "greedy" and that a written agreement had to be signed that day. No affidavit from Mrs. Durst was filed.

At the hearing on the motions, Cindy Vogt argued that the visiting schedule agreement obtained by Court Services was the product of mediation, which was unauthorized because there was probable cause of physical abuse. The trial court stated that mediation had not been ordered and had not been involved, and ruled that Court Services had been properly used.

The motion to vacate the visiting agreement was denied. So was Thomas Vogt's motion to hold Cindy Vogt in contempt. The domestic abuse proceeding was consolidated with the marriage dissolution proceeding, and an order for temporary relief was issued incorporating the same visiting schedule that was in the Court Services' agreement. On May 11 these orders were reduced to judgment, and from this judgment Cindy Vogt now appeals. In an unpublished opinion, the court of appeals affirmed, concluding that "court services personnel were appropriately used" in fixing the visiting schedule. We granted Cindy Vogt's petition for further review.

In this appeal, only the legality of the procedures used by the court in establishing the visiting schedule in the domestic abuse case is being questioned. Cindy Vogt is not seeking review of the visiting schedule itself, nor is she questioning the manner in which the court set visiting rights in the dissolution proceeding. Later in the dissolution proceedings, interestingly enough, Cindy Vogt proposed a visiting schedule more liberal for Thomas Vogt than was set out in the court services handwritten agreement. Thomas Vogt was subsequently acquitted of the fifth degree assault charges. Two weeks before we granted review here, the Vogts stipulated to a custody and visiting agreement.

Broadly stated, there are two main issues: (1) Is compulsory mediation of visiting rights permissible in a domestic abuse case? and (2) What is the role of Court Services in establishing visiting rights? There is also a threshold question whether these issues are moot on appeal.

I.

The Vogts were told by the trial court they should see Mrs. Durst in Court Services to work out a visiting schedule. Appellant Cindy Vogt chooses to characterize this occurrence as an order for compulsory mediation. She then argues that this mediation was unauthorized, and the ensuing agreement consequently invalid.

The trial court quite correctly pointed out that it had not ordered mediation and that Cindy Vogt was raising a non-issue. Unfortunately, to reinforce its position, the trial court suggested in *dicta* that the statutes disallow mediation outside dissolution and separation proceedings, and also disallow where only visiting, not custody, is being contested. Appellant Cindy Vogt seeks to challenge this interpretation of the statutes.

Although the Vogts are no longer concerned about visiting rights, *amicus* argues that the issue of statutory construction is not moot because it raises an issue capable of repetition yet evading review. The issue is not, however, capable of repetition. The current session of the legislature has amended the applicable statutes to provide that court-ordered mediation is available in any child custody determination (except, of course, where there is probable cause of domestic abuse), and that a contest over visiting rights is included in a custody determination. The issue is moot.

II.

The second issue raised is whether the trial court properly used Court Services in establishing visiting rights. While moot as to the Vogts, we conclude we should entertain this issue on appeal. Unlike the first issue, the use of Court Services is a question capable of repetition yet unamenable to review. The Domestic Abuse Act authorizes a court to establish "temporary visitation [*sic*]" as relief in a proceeding for an order for protection. Minn.Stat. § 518B.01, subd. 6(3) (1988). These proceedings occur frequently. The relief provided is transitory, usually for not more than 1 year. Minn.Stat. § 518B.01, subd. 6(8)(b) (1988). The parties, usually *pro se*, are unfamiliar with extraordinary writs, and the proceedings move quickly. These conditions conspire to insulate issues that may arise from effective review.

What complicates this case is that the record lends itself to different interpretations of what occurred. Appellant argues that the trial court ordered compulsory mediation. Arguably, the parties, at the court's suggestion, voluntarily agreed to use the auspices of Court Services to negotiate a visiting schedule. Arguably, too, the court ordered visiting and directed Court Services to work out the scheduling details.

Plainly, mediation was not used in this case. The trial court never said this was what it was doing; rather, as the court stated at the February 8 hearing, "It's not their [the parties'] decision to make, it's up to Court Services." In its order following this hearing, the court expressly stated it had not used mediation to establish visiting rights, but that it had asked Court Services to "arrang[e] the details" for the visits. Even if the trial court had thought court-ordered mediation was available in domestic abuse proceedings, it would not have used it here because the court had implicitly found (by issuance of the protective order) probable cause of physical abuse. See Minn.Stat. § 518.619, subd. 2 (1988) (court-ordered mediation not available when there is a finding of probable cause of physical or sexual abuse); accord Minn.R.Fam.Ct.P. 9.01.

Mediation is "[a] forum in which an impartial person, the mediator, facilitates communication between parties to promote reconciliation, settlement, or understanding among them." "A mediator may not impose his own judgment on the issues for that of the parties." *Id*. Mediation requires a trained neutral. It can be a useful technique, especially in the family law area, to help people help themselves in solving their disagreements. If Cindy Vogt's version of the meeting at Court Services is correct (and it is the only version we have), an agreement was forced upon her, a process clearly at odds with mediation.

As we read the record, the trial court determined Thomas Vogt was entitled to visit his children and then referred the visiting arrangements to Court Services for its recommendation. The trial court may ask Court Services for "an investigation and report concerning custodial arrangements." Minn.Stat. § 518.167, subd. 1 (1988). In this case Court Services went beyond consulting the parties separately and submitting a report. Instead, it overrode the misgivings of one of the spouses and exacted a signed written agreement from the parties. The trial court appears to have initially accepted this agreement not as a recommendation from Court Services requiring the court's independent appraisal and decision, but simply as the consensual agreement of the parties which the court might incorporate in its order without further inquiry.

Trial courts have a difficult task in these domestic abuse cases. The parties are often *pro se*. The parties may differ sharply in describing events and assigning motives; their positions may be ill-defined and their arguments may lack focus. Yet the issues themselves, such as when and how one party may visit the children, involve the welfare of children and basic parental concerns. The law is expected to provide immediate, temporary relief, yet time for courts to decide a case fairly and thoughtfully is often in short supply.

Nevertheless, it is the court's job to decide cases, these cases no less than others, and it is important, too, that the court, not some agency, is perceived by the parties as the decision-maker when it decides. The trial court has wide discretion in dealing with these matters. Ordinarily, consideration of any affidavits and some brief questioning of the parties will suffice for issuance of an order for temporary relief; the order is, of course, subject to revision if more information subsequently comes to light. Or Court Services can conduct an abbreviated preliminary investigation, at least interviewing the parties, sorting out their respective positions and making recommendations to aid the court in arriving at its decision. If both parties are represented by counsel, the court's job is made easier. Only when there is no probable cause of domestic abuse may court-ordered mediation be used.

We conclude that the manner in which the temporary visiting arrangements were established in the protective order was improper for the reasons stated in this opinion. This issue arises within the context of the trial court's order denying Cindy Vogt's motion to vacate the visiting agreement. Accordingly, that order and the judgment entered thereon, though now moot, are reversed. No costs on appeal will be awarded either party.

Reversed.

HOLLY JOYCE, MEDIATION AND DOMESTIC VIOLENCE: LEGISLATIVE RESPONSES

14 J. Am. Acad. Matrim. Law. 447–448, 450–458, 465–467 (1997).

I. Introduction

In the emotionally charged arena of family law, mediation seeks to serve as a more conciliatory and subjective process than the traditional legal process which is grounded in adversity, abstract rules, and objectivity. Where the adversarial system focuses on individual rights, mediation focuses on individual responsibility. Mediation in contrast, can be defined as a dispute resolution process

> by which the participants, together with the assistance of a neutral person ... systematically isolate disputed issues in order to develop options, consider alternatives, and reach a consensual settlement that will accommodate their needs. Mediation ... emphasizes the participants own responsibility for making decisions that affect their lives. It is therefore a self-empowering process.[4]

Mediation has become a widely accepted alternative to traditional divorce and child custody proceedings in the United States and around the world. Thirty-two states have passed legislation implementing court supervised mediation programs in response to both the public outcry for a non-adversarial environment in which to decide family law issues and the need to lessen the burden on courts' overflowing dockets.

Since California enacted the first mandatory child custody mediation legislation in 1981, commentators have been embroiled in a debate over the appropriateness of mediation in cases involving domestic abuse. Currently, court-connected mediation plans vary widely from state to state, with no consensus among jurisdictions on the role mediation should play when domestic violence somehow taints the process. Some jurisdictions leave the decision to mediate to the parties, others vest discretion in the court to order mediation, and still others prohibit mediation in cases with a history of domestic violence. The legal community, including lawyers, mediators, judges, and legislators must decide the best manner in which to handle family law disputes with a history of domestic violence. This decision should include consideration of the best manner in which to protect violence victims from future violence while empowering them to gain control over their lives.

* * *

III. IS MEDIATION APPROPRIATE IN CASES INVOLVING DOMESTIC VIOLENCE?

In every case involving domestic violence there are two overriding interests which should be guarded carefully—protecting the victim from further abuse and empowering the victim to take back control over her life. Commentators disagree on whether mediation is a process which protects these interests. Those opposed to mediation where domestic violence is present argue that mediation legitimizes violence rather than punishing abusers, places victims at risk for further violence and abuse, and results in unfair agreements for the abused who have been stripped of their ability to advocate for their own interests. Commentators who support mediation in cases involving domestic abuse argue mediation can succeed in areas in which the traditional court system has failed in responding to domestic violence; mediation empowers participants to end violence within their relationship by serving as a model of conflict

---

4. Jay Folberg & Alison Taylor, Mediation: A Comprehensive Guide to Resolving Conflicts Without Litigation 7–8 (1984).

resolution; and empowers both abusers and victims by allowing them to create guidelines to govern future interaction.

A. Why Mediation May Fail to Protect and Empower Victims of Domestic Violence

First, commentators argue that mediation fails to protect and empower domestic violence victims because its methods and objectives are incompatible with those necessary to end domestic violence within a relationship. Domestic violence can be described as "a tool of coercion and control." The abuser uses the threat of violence to maintain power over every detail of his victim's life, from how she dresses to her choice of friends to how she asserts herself in a mediation conference. The goal of mediation is to resolve conflict through a process where each party assumes the responsibility for making decisions that affect his life.

Critics argue if violence is caused by control issues rather than genuine conflict, "both the ideology and the practice of mediation are incompatible with a culture of battering." Mediation may be ineffective and inappropriate in cases with overtones of domestic violence because while the objective of mediation is to resolve conflict or disagreements between parties, domestic violence is rooted in a struggle for power and control. When a victim is forced into mediation her fear of her abuser may prevent her from asserting her needs. In fact, batterers admit they want to "scare their partners into obeying and will lie, deny, and minimize the effects of their violence." Commentators argue that it will be dangerously disempowering to force a battered woman into a dispute resolution scheme where there may be no conflict to resolve, only a pattern of domination and control by her abuser.

Another factor making mediation incompatible with domestic violence is that mediation requires cooperation. Barbara Hart argues "cooperation by a batterer with his wife/partner is an oxymoron.[44] Cooperation ... means to act or work together for mutual benefit.... A batterer understands mutual benefit as synonymous with his exclusive self-interest."

In sum, because domestic violence results from a struggle for control, it is incompatible with mediation's goal of resolving conflict, and is therefore inappropriate in cases where domestic violence is an issue.

A second reason critics oppose mediation in cases involving domestic violence is that it potentially places victims at risk for future violence. The most dangerous time for a battered woman is when she separates from her partner. Forcing abused women to mediate will in most cases subject them to face-to-face contact with their abusers, thereby potentially exposing them to further violence. For example, in states where mandatory mediation is the practice, a woman who has been evading her batterer might be forced by court order to come out of hiding, giving her batterer an opportunity to discover her location and harass or attack

---

44. Barbara J. Hart, Gentle Jeopardy: The Further Endangerment of Battered Women and Children in Custody Mediation, 7 Mediation Q. 317, 317 (1990).

her. In addition to the risk imposed by the face-to-face interaction the mediation process generally imposes, mediated agreements may give the batterer frequent access to his victim under the terms of child custody and visitation provisions.

In sum, mediation generally requires contact between the victim and abuser which places the victim's safety at risk. Therefore, the commentators argue, mediation is inappropriate in such cases.

Third, although mediation is ideally an empowering process for all participants, mediation arguably risks disempowering abused women by invalidating the seriousness of the abuse inflicted upon them. This disempowerment can hinder a victim's ability to negotiate for an agreement to serve her best interests. Society seeks to preserve the sanctity of marriage by protecting the home from intrusion by the government. In the past, police departments and courts have been hesitant to get involved in domestic violence, viewing it as a personal matter between husband and wife rather than a crime.

Critics have argued mandatory mediation of cases involving domestic violence is another example of the courts shirking their responsibility to treat domestic violence as a crime. Mandatory mediation dilutes the message that violence in any context is unacceptable. Instead, sending cases to mediation sends a message to the batterer and the battered that "violence is not so serious as to compromise the parties' ability to negotiate as relative equals" which "blurs the message of offender accountability."

Further, the procedural structure of mediation can work counter to meditation's goal of empowerment in cases involving domestic violence for several reasons. First, because mediation is a future oriented process, mediators might discourage discussion of past abuse to preserve the prospective approach of the process. When an abused woman cannot talk about the abuse she suffered in the past, her anger and pain are invalidated and the abuser is excused from accountability. In fact, in some cases the victim may feel she shares responsibility for the abuse. Second, mediator neutrality can also disempower the abused. If the mediator does not condemn the abuse, the batterer's belief that the behavior is acceptable is maintained. Third, unless a jurisdiction requires strict confidentiality forbidding the mediator from making recommendations to the court, "a frightened battered woman may disclose information . . . that the abuser may use in court against her."

In sum, in cases where domestic violence is present, mediation will fall short of its goal of empowerment and may actually be detrimental to domestic violence victims.

A fourth argument against mediating cases with a history of domestic violence is that a battered woman's fear of violent retribution prevents her from asserting her own best interests, which results in agreements which are unfair to victims. Fear, the defining emotion in a violent relationship, is always present when battered wives encounter their abusers. Even in relationships where violence has not been constant, the victim may still feel threatened. The batterer's control over the abused is maintained by this threat of future violence which impedes the abused woman's ability to be her own advocate. As a result, reaching a fair and voluntary agreement is impossible.[67] One victim described the impact that her fear of her abusive husband had on her participation as follows:

> Mediation does not take into account the fear that I as a battered woman have about voicing my needs in the presence of someone who has pushed me and belittled me for expressing any needs at all.... I endured two months of weekly meetings with the man who had knocked me to the ground, raped me and repeatedly violated me.... I felt forced to comply, to attend those sessions and thus avoid greater pain. It reminded me of the nights spent silently weeping as he raped me. If I complied, the pain ended more quickly.... In mediation, if I let my ex-husband verbally intimidate me and emotionally abuse me, I wouldn't have to go to court. The trade off was not a fair one.[68]

In summary, some commentators argue mediating cases involving domestic violence fails to protect victims from future abuse and fails to empower victims with the ability to take control over their lives for four reasons. First, the methodology of mediation, which is designed to deal with conflict is ill-equipped to deal with violence. Second, bringing the abuser and victim together in close proximity to bargain face-to-face places victims at risk of further abuse. Third, the future-oriented nature of mediation runs counter to mediation's goal of empowerment in the context of domestic violence. And, fourth, mediation results in unfair agreements for battered women, who as a result of the abuse they have suffered, are unable to negotiate for their own self-interests.

B. Why Mediation Protects and Empowers Victims of Domestic Violence

The commentators who support mediation in cases involving domestic violence offer several bases for their position. First, although they concede mediation is not a perfect form of dispute resolution, it is better suited than the courts to cases where domestic violence is present. The courts and mediation have the same purposes: to divide the assets of the marriage and to establish guidelines for the parties to follow after their marriage is ended. However, some aspects of the adversarial system may render it less suitable to divorce cases and child custody disputes where domestic violence is present. Under the traditional adversarial system, as the parties draw their battle-lines and the conflict between them escalates, each party is encouraged to blame the other for the problems in the relationship rather than taking individual responsibility for their actions. This blaming game can lead to an escalation of abuse. In addition, the adversary process risks failing to impress upon the abuser the criminality of his behavior because the system encourages him to

67. Hart, supra note 44, at 320.   **68.** Id. at 157.

deny his past abusive behavior. In contrast, by being focused on the future rather than past behavior, mediation empowers couples to take responsibility for their past and rise above it by setting boundaries for future behavior.

Further, victims will often take a passive role in their relationship with their attorney which can reinforce the domination she has suffered under her abuser. In mediation however, both parties are forced to take responsibility for shaping their future. And, mediation is much less structured and locked into formality than the courts. Unlike a judge, a mediator can shape the mediation process on a case by case basis to serve the needs of battered women through measures such as including mental health professionals, using telephone conferences and private caucusing.

Second, keeping in mind that the most dangerous time for a victim is immediately after leaving her abuser, mediation can mitigate the increased risk of violence a victim faces after separating from her abuser. "Mediation by definition is adaptable to meet the individual needs of the negotiating parties." The mediator can customize the process to serve the best interests of the parties. For example, she can employ methods such as shuttle mediation or telephone conferences to keep the parties separated. Or, she can assist the parties in setting ground rules for how the mediation will be conducted. For example, one ground rule could prohibit the parties from engaging in degrading behavior such as yelling or name calling. The consequence for breaking the rules could be terminating the mediation. These are just a few illustrations of ways in which mediation can be tailored to protect and empower the victim. In sum, mediation proponents argue these steps will help protect victims from immediate and future danger.

Commentators favoring mediation also argue mediation can provide a model of "positive post-divorce interaction." Mediation by definition is a process which requires cooperation. The mediator as a neutral third party can guide the parties through this process and spark cooperation between the abused and the victim. This model of dispute resolution can be mirrored in future interaction between the parties, which may be inevitable if they have children, in place of the former method of domination and submission. Mediation becomes an additional tool to break the cycle of abuse. The mediator models communication and dispute resolution skills, which can serve as an alternative way to "solve problems without resorting to threats." In sum, by serving as a model of effective communication, mediation assists batterers and victims change their behavioral patterns which in turn decreases the risk of future violence.

Third, mediation proponents are concerned that many of the arguments in opposition to mediation in domestic violence situations are focused on the worst-case scenario battering relationship. However, not every instance of domestic violence occurs as part of a cycle of violence. The violence between the parties may have been an isolated incident or have occurred only rarely over the course of their marriage. Many mediation proponents concede that not every case is appropriate for mediation, especially where a cycle of abuse has completely paralyzed a victim by fear and stripped her of her ability to negotiate for her own interests or where the relationship is so volatile, the victim's safety cannot be assured. But commentators argue, in cases where both parties consent to the process, a successful and safe mediation can occur if thorough screening measures are employed to determine whether or not the violence between the parties rises to a level which renders the process inappropriate. In addition, the mediator in such a case should be specially trained in domestic violence and the use of techniques to balance any power differential between the parties.

To conclude, mediation can provide a supportive, empowering environment for women who in many cases have been stripped of their identity, dignity, and self-esteem. Ann Yellot, an experienced mediator argues we should not deny these women an opportunity to participate in a process which can empower them to reclaim what they have lost. She writes, "[w]hen women express a desire to meet with their abusive partner ... it seems disempowering to categorically refuse to afford them that option under the guise of protecting them."[94]

* * *

V. CONCLUSION

There are no easy solutions to the problems associated with mediation in the context of domestic violence. States must seek to strike the delicate balance between the interests in protecting victims from further abuse and empowering victims to take control over decisions which will affect the rest of their lives. Jurisdictions such as Florida, Illinois, Iowa, Louisiana, Minnesota, Montana, North Dakota, and Pennsylvania, which have strict prohibitions against mediating cases involving domestic violence go a long way in protecting victims from further violence. However, these jurisdictions are denying victims for whom mediation would be appropriate the opportunity to participate in an empowering process. On the other hand, states such as Maine, Oregon, Rhode Island, South Dakota, and Washington, which offer no guidance to courts on the appropriate manner in which to handle cases involving domestic violence, may fail to protect certain victims who should never be required to mediate.

However, there is a trend emerging in the mediation arena which fills the gaps left by the statutes listed above. Five states, Alaska, Hawaii, Kentucky, New Hampshire, and New Mexico, have enacted court-connected mediation statutes which both protect and empower victims of domestic violence. These statutes could be labeled "victim's choice" statutes. All of these provisions prohibit the court from referring

94. Ann W. Yellot, Mediation and Do-   Mediation Q. 39, 45 (1990).
mestic Violence: A Call for Collaboration, 8

the parties to mediation unless the violence victim consents to or specifically requests participation in the process. In addition, Alaska, Hawaii, New Hampshire, and New Mexico require additional safety precautions to ensure the victim's well-being throughout the mediation process. For example, some safety precautions include a requirement that the mediator be notified that the case involves domestic violence, that the mediator have special training in domestic violence and that she uses special techniques to protect the victim from future violence including allowing the victim to bring a support person or attorney to mediation conferences. Other requirements include a finding by the court that the abused party is capable of participating in negotiations without being adversely affected by an imbalance of power resulting from the violence.

In conclusion, the legal community must develop methods to effectively deal with domestic violence in the context of family law. In many divorce and child custody cases, mediation conducted with special sensitivity to the dynamics of abusive relationships can be a viable option. Policy-makers should be encouraged to implement court-connected mediation programs modeled after the "victim's choice" method. Although such programs are not the panacea that will end domestic violence, they will go a long way in protecting and empowering victims of abuse.

JOANNE FULLER AND ROSE MARY LYONS, MEDIATION GUIDELINES

33 Willamette L. Rev. 922–929 (1997).

APPENDIX B: GUIDELINES FOR THE USE OF MEDIATION IN FAMILY LAW

Preface

The following recommendations have been developed by the Mediation Work Group of the Oregon Domestic Violence Council. They are the result of many hours of discussion and review which took place over more than a year. The work group has attempted to find common ground between the concerns of mediators and concerns for the safety of survivors of domestic violence. The work group recognizes that mediation is a useful process, enabling many families to design their new form following separation. The group also recognizes, however, that mediation is not appropriate for all cases. It can present particular problems for survivors of domestic violence.

Mediation is a process that presumes that participants can maintain a balance of power with the help of a mediator. It can be misused if the imbalance is great, and/or the imbalance is unrecognized. As this imbalance of power is characteristic of relationships in which there is domestic violence, mediation can be a dangerous process for those subjected to domestic violence (see Appendix for examples of imbalance of power). Mediation is especially dangerous when the person who has experienced domestic violence has recently made a move out of the relationship, a time known to be particularly hazardous.

Where domestic violence is present, the case should be presumed inappropriate for mediation, unless compelling reasons justify the use of mediation. The decision of whether to enter into mediation should be made on a case-by-case basis. These guidelines are intended to assist mediation programs and independent mediators in the development of appropriate protocols, in order to enable the parties to make the appropriate use of the mediation process while maximizing safety for all participants.

While mediation can be useful to some parties, it is not always beneficial, and in some cases is harmful. Mediators should disclose to parties who are considering mediation the disadvantages as well as the advantages of using the process. Exposure to information about the mediation process, screening for mediation, resource information and referral, and related services may be made mandatory. Exposure to information about the mediation process may also appropriately be made mandatory, but mediation should not be initiated, and if initiated should not continue, unless both parties and the mediator believe that a fair, non-coercive process will occur.

Guidelines

Domestic violence poses a serious threat to the safety, health, and well-being of a significant number of families. A high incidence of such violence occurs during and following separation and divorce. The Oregon Domestic Violence Council, therefore, recommends that every family mediator and family mediation program, whether court-connected or private, formulate and follow a domestic violence protocol that includes the following elements:

1. All programs/mediators shall recognize that mediation is not an appropriate process for all cases and an agreement is not necessarily the appropriate outcome of all mediation. *Commentary:* The mediator's job includes continuous assessment of whether a case is better resolved in mediation, or by other means. Factors in this assessment include whether the participants can stand up for what they believe is good for their children and themselves and what alternatives to mediation exist. There may be a conflict of interest when mediators are paid per session in that ending mediation would reduce the mediator's income. Furthermore, mediators and programs should not be evaluated on the basis of the number of agreements, as a high rate of agreement may indicate that many cases are being resolved in mediation because one participant is unable or unwilling to stand up for what he or she believes. The assessment process should identify these cases as not appropriate for mediation.

2. Neither the existence of nor any of the provisions of a FAPA restraining order shall be mediated. *Commentary:* Oregon law prohibits courts from ordering or providing mediation of a

FAPA restraining order. This provision, of course, applies only to court-connected mediation but it is the position of this Council that mediation of restraining orders should not be provided in the public or private setting. ORS 107.755, however, provides that " ... the circuit court ... may provide mediation under ORS 107.755 to 107.785 for child custody and visitation disputes in a domestic relations suit, or for child custody and visitation disputes in filiation suits...."

The question arises whether it is appropriate to mediate domestic relations cases when one party has obtained a FAPA restraining order, even when the restraining order itself is not mediated. All mediation cases should be carefully screened for domestic violence. It is the presence of domestic violence, and not the type of case the parties filed, which should be the focus of the screening process. Where domestic violence is present, the case should be presumed inappropriate for mediation unless compelling reasons justify the use of mediation, and the decision of whether to enter into mediation should be made on a case-by-case basis. Under no circumstances should the restraining order itself ever be mediated.

A domestic relations case which has been screened and determined to be appropriate for mediation may also involve a FAPA order. In this case, although the FAPA order is not mediated, the domestic relations case may be. The court may determine that the resulting agreement affects the provisions of the FAPA order.

3.   All programs/mediators shall develop and implement a screening and ongoing evaluation process of domestic violence issues for all mediation cases. *Commentary:* In all mediation cases, screening and ongoing evaluation of domestic violence are essential. A domestic violence survivor who has left the abusive relationship has taken a very important step. However, the dynamics of power and control which existed in the abusive relationship may continue to dictate the way the parties relate to each other during the course of mediation.

To screen and evaluate appropriately, all programs/mediators must provide:

- Safety in arrival, seating, and departure

- Separate orientations for the parties if both are not comfortable with attending orientation together

- Separate and private individual conferences with each party prior to mediation to explore concerns about domestic violence, safety of parents and children, and issues concerning communication, comfort, and the ability to negotiate

- A policy that mediation may be initiated, and if initiated may continue, only if the following occur:

   1) Each party chooses to participate; and

2) Each party and the mediator believe that a fair, non-coercive process resulting in an informed discussion will occur.

If concerns regarding safety, ability to negotiate, or informed discussion exist, the mediator should advise the party to seek the guidance of an attorney.

- Procedures for terminating mediation at any point if either party or the mediator deem this appropriate. The mediator should emphasize to the clients that mediation has not failed if an agreement has not been reached.

4. When mediators explain the process to the parties, the explanation shall include the disadvantages of mediation and the alternatives. *Commentary:* Mediators should inform participants in advance about the drawbacks of the mediation process so they do not experience pressure from the mediator or the judicial system to participate or to reach agreement. Mediation is a process that presumes that a mediator can help maintain a balance of power between parties. Mediation can be misused if there is a significant or unrecognized imbalance of power. The mediator's initial explanation of mediation must cover this presumption and include a specific example of the misuse of mediation with parties who have been in a violent relationship.

5. All programs/mediators shall develop and implement a provision for opting out of mediation which allows either party to decline mediation once they have been informed of the advantages and disadvantages of mediation or at any time during the mediation. *Commentary:* It is important that participants understand clearly that it is appropriate to decide mediation is not the best process for them. Participants should be assured that exposure to mediation fulfills the requirements of a court-ordered referral. They need to understand it is not a "failure" to terminate mediation and there are no legal repercussions for doing so.

It is the mediator's responsibility to terminate mediation if he or she believes either of the participants is unable to mediate safely, competently, and without fear of coercion. Monitoring is a continuous responsibility throughout the mediation process. The manner in which a mediator terminates mediation can be critical to a participant's continuing safety. To avoid creation of further danger for the survivor, the mediator needs to be careful in explaining the reason for termination to the parties. The mediator should, as much as possible, take responsibility for the decision.

6. All programs/mediators shall develop and implement a set of safety procedures aimed at minimizing the likelihood of intimidation or violence in orientation, during mediation, or on the way in or out of the building. *Commentary:* Attendance at separate orientations should be allowed. Separate seating and separate arrival and leaving times should be arranged, if necessary. The parties should leave separately if a restraining order is in effect, if there has been any indication of discomfort or conflict, or if either party requests this. The abused should arrive last and leave first with a reasonable lag in time for safety purposes.

Parties should be allowed to have a support person accompany them to the office. It is desirable to have two exits from the mediator's office. The availability of Security staff is most helpful. Separate meetings and conference calls should be used when appropriate. Shuttle mediation, with the mediator going between the parties who are in separate rooms, can also be useful. At the outset of mediation, both parties should agree to ground rules for behavior, which should be explained to them by the mediator. Rules should include:

- Parties are not to interrupt one another;
- Parties are to refrain from the use of blaming or hurtful language and intimidating behavior;
- The continuation or dismissal of restraining orders is not an appropriate discussion for mediation, and Parties are to maintain a businesslike and respectful attitude.

7. All mediators shall obtain continuing education regarding domestic violence and related issues. *Commentary:* Mediation in cases in which there is or has been domestic violence is complicated and can be dangerous to the participants and the mediator. Therefore, family mediators must be knowledgeable about domestic violence. In the context of mediation, it is easy to overlook or misread the signs of domestic violence, perceiving the victim as the uncooperative party. Mediator misconceptions about domestic violence can result in domestic violence not being identified or not being reported, and/or in victim-blaming. A single training on domestic violence is not sufficient exposure to maintain mediator awareness. Continuing education on domestic violence issues is necessary and should be required.

OAR 718–30–060 (1) requires court-connected domestic relations mediators to have completed seminar or graduate level course work which substantially covers domestic violence and child abuse. Training required of court-connected mediators should be required of all family mediators and should include:

- The dynamics of domestic and family violence, including familiarity with the power and control model;
- Issues related to physical and psychological abuse and their effects on family members;
- The impact of family violence, including the witnessing of violence, on children;
- Effective techniques for screening, implementing safety measures and safe terminations;
- Knowledge of appropriate referral resources used in addition to or instead of mediation;
- Sensitivity to cultural, racial, and ethnic differences that may be relevant to domestic violence. Mediators should have an understanding of and sensitivity to cultural, political, economic, and family value differences enabling them to:

1.   Be aware of personal and global cultural biases and how these biases and stereotypes may influence screening for abuse and the mediation process itself.

2.   Avoid assumptions about clients' values, habits, interests, needs, and socialization.

3.   Consider the effects of social and/or cultural isolation related to:

a) Culture shock, health care, isolation, fear of or threats of being deported.

b) Fear of or threats of having sponsorship for employment withdrawn.

c) Levels of community contact and access to services.

d) Personal rights under the law.

4.   Recognize how cultural differences can affect the meaning of nonverbal body language.

5.   Understand the impact of housing, public assistance, immigration laws, refugee and legal aid policies on assaulted women.

Cross-cultural curriculum content, process, and design ought to include the support and participation of providers of services to culturally diverse and minority populations.

* * *

8.   Mediation programs shall collect appropriate data. The determination of what data to collect shall be made with sensitivity to domestic violence issues.

APPENDIX TO GUIDELINES FOR THE USE OF MEDIATION IN FAMILY LAW

Examples of How an Imbalance of Power Can Be Manifested in Mediation:

1.   Past history has taught her to know that a certain benign look from him means that she is saying something that is making him angry. This simple look can easily pass from him to her without the mediator being aware.

2.   He complains to the mediator that she never had enough baby food, diapers and other supplies on hand, therefore she is not the best parent for the child. The reality is that he had her on an unreasonable allowance and had total control of the family finances.

3.   He tells the mediator how he attempts to visit the children or to talk to them on the telephone because he is a concerned and caring parent. He is rebuked by her for these attempts and she is angry that he wants to see the children. She knows however that he is using these visits and calls to monitor her activities.

4. He tells the mediator he is willing to allow her to keep the station wagon for transporting the children and says that she should also be allowed to have the family cat. She says simply "No." The mediator perceives her as uncooperative and him as generous and willing to be reasonable and looking out for the well being of the children. She is afraid to say that he has removed the distributor cap from the car and has killed the family cat.

5. He tells the mediator that he "gave" her the house so that his children would have a home. The reality is that he threatens her with not making the payments if she does not do as he wishes.

JESSICA PEARSON, MEDIATING WHEN DOMESTIC VIOLENCE IS A FACTOR: POLICIES AND PRACTICES IN COURT–BASED DIVORCE MEDIATION PROGRAMS

14(4) Mediation Quarterly 319, 332–333 (1997).

This article looks at how mediators and court administrators say they are handling domestic violence cases in their caseloads. It is based on the reports of administrators of court-based divorce mediation programs and in-depth study of practices in five settings using qualitative interviews and observation techniques. We focus on whether and how mediators and court staff attempt to gauge the level of domestic abuse and the capacity of the parties to mediate; we also describe common adjustments to the mediation process that they make in order to enhance safety. Since the study did not include feedback from victims and batterers, we offer no reading on whether remedial strategies developed by courts have had their intended effects. Rather, we document trends in the evolution of mediation practice in U.S. courts.

* * *

CONCLUSIONS

This research confirms that court mediation programs are grappling with the issue of domestic violence in their caseloads. Administrators seem more aware of the problem today than in the past, estimating that it is a problem for 50–80 percent of the divorcing couples referred to their programs. They report that most mediation services have changed how they do business as a result of thinking and discussion prompted by advocates for victims. They estimate they only exclude about 5 percent of referred families because of concerns about power imbalances, safety, and other factors related to domestic violence.

The debate about mediating in cases with domestic violence is far from decided. Moreover, the patterns we report are based on responses by program administrators—a method that can be tainted by social desirability. The other techniques we relied upon—qualitative interviews and observations in five jurisdictions that are leaders in the mediation field—are also subjective. The study did not include feedback from victims and batterers. Thus, we have no reading on whether the remedial strategies developed by court mediation programs have had their intended effects.

More to the point, we cannot assume that all mediation programs are as attentive to safety and as committed to adopting policies aimed at minimizing the dangers associated with domestic violence as are the programs examined in this research. Fully 20 percent of the program administrators we surveyed reported no use of screening procedures to detect domestic violence; only 50 percent reported the use of private face-to-face screening interventions preferred by mediators and advocates. Similarly, 30 percent of responding administrators reported that their mediation staff had received no training on domestic violence. Six percent reported no use of special techniques and at least 30 percent reported no use of the special mediation techniques most favored in domestic violence cases: shuttle approaches and co-mediation.

Mediation programs should be taking several steps to accommodate the inevitable incidence of domestic violence in their caseloads. One is to involve their mediators in continuing training on the dynamics of families in which there is domestic violence and techniques of managing a safe environment. Mediation program directors should involve their local advocacy community in the training effort too. The collaboration affords mediators with the best opportunity to learn about the scope and nature of the problem from frontline workers. It also helps to dispel misconceptions about the process that many advocates may hold.

Another key feature of program response is the adoption of screening prior to mediation. It has been suggested that legislatures require all family law participants to engage in screening for domestic violence. This would include lawyers, clerks of the court, judges, and mediators. Whether or not screening procedures become statutorily required, they are regarded as the cornerstone of safe mediation. The features of a credible screening effort are contained in the guidelines adopted by various organizations for mediation practitioners or the screening tools available in the published literature. They include use of separate and private interviews to screen prior to mediation; reliance on more than one method of identification; eliciting information in a neutral, safe atmosphere; and making assessments that lead to the conduct of mediation as usual, the conduct of mediation with special conditions, or case referral for alternative treatments.

Still another component of desirable program practice is review of current procedures and their assessment for their potential safety impacts. Among the accommodations to conventional mediating practice that are recommended to maximize safety are use of security personnel, shuttle techniques, co-mediation procedures, nonagreement, and safe termination of the mediation process.

Finally, the debate about mediation and domestic violence should prompt communities to recognize the need for better coordination between and among the criminal justice, court, and support agencies that assist families and the need for key legal and treatment interventions. This is an era of declining resources for social programming. Advocates for victims of domestic violence, the judiciary, the legal community, and the mediation profession must all work together to prevent domestic violence from occurring and, following its identification, to develop community resources for safe living and parenting.

DONNA COKER, ENHANCING AUTONOMY FOR BATTERED WOMEN: LESSONS FROM NAVAJO PEACEMAKING

47 UCLA L. Rev. 32–38, 101–107 (1999).

I. DOMESTIC VIOLENCE CASES IN PEACEMAKING

* * *

B. Peacemaking: Theory and Practice

Ultimately ... the greater necessity is that [tribal court] decision-making craft a jurisprudence reflecting the aspiration and wisdom of traditional cultures seeking a future of liberation and self-realization in which age-old values may continue to flourish in contemporary circumstances.[132]

Though the Peacemaker Courts were first established in 1982, they were largely ignored until 1991, when the Supreme Court of the Navajo Nation began a push to reinvigorate modern Navajo law with Navajo common law. In an endeavor to bring about cultural and social reform as well as legal reform, the Navajo Supreme Court is attempting to integrate traditional Navajo law into all adjudicatory functions. The general premise is that Anglo justice, described as hierarchal and "win-lose," has failed the Navajo. They argue that the only hope for Navajo people is a return to the problem-solving methods that worked in early Navajo history.

The Honorable Robert Yazzie, Chief Justice for the Supreme Court of the Navajo Nation, contrasts the Navajo concept of "horizontal" justice with the Anglo "vertical" system of justice. The latter uses coercion and power, focuses on finding "truth," and limits standing to parties who claim direct injury, and its criminal law focuses on establishing guilt. In contrast, horizontal justice systems have a much wider "zone of dispute" and rely on moral suasion rather than coercion and power. The emphasis in horizontal justice systems is on healing rather than on guilt. Yazzie argues that the term " 'guilt' implies a moral fault which commands retribution," but the end goal of Navajo law is not fault finding but "integration with the group" accomplished through "nourishing ongoing relationships with the immediate and extended family, relatives, neighbors and community."[141] Thus, Peacemaking is

132. Frank Pommersheim, Liberation, Dreams, and Hard Work: An Essay on Trib- al Court Jurisprudence, 1992 Wis. L. Rev. 411, 413.

141. Yazzie, Life Comes from It, supra

premised on traditional Navajo jurisprudence in which "law is not a process to punish or penalize people, but to teach them how to live a better life. It is a healing process that either restores good relationships among people or, if they do not have good relations to begin with, fosters and nourishes a healthy environment."[142]

Traditional Navajo thinking does not separate religious and secular life; rather, all of life is sacred and imbued with spiritual meaning. The concept of *k'e*, fundamental to Navajo common law, expresses an interdependence and respect for relationships between humans, the natural world, individuals and family, and individuals and clan members. This interdependence operates to define Navajo common law, which derives from relational frameworks in which "responsibilities to clan members are part of a sophisticated system that defines rights, duties, and mutual obligations." "The individual and the community are part of the kinship that exists among all life forms and the environmental elements. Harmony is the desired result of the relationship with all life forms, including humans, animals, and plants."[145] Relational justice does not necessitate the subordination of the individual, however. Traditional Navajo thought and law are radically egalitarian and eschew coercion. Individuals do not speak for others, not even for members of their own family.

These concepts of relational justice provide the foundation for the practice of Peacemaking. In Peacemaking, parties meet with a peacemaker and others who have either a special relationship to the parties (e.g., family and friends) or relevant expertise (e.g., alcohol treatment counselors and hospital social workers). Each participant is given a chance to describe the problem that the petitioner has identified as the reason for the session. The peacemaker then leads the group in developing recommendations and agreements designed to ameliorate or solve the problem.

Peacemaking is structured around procedural steps. It begins with an opening prayer in both Navajo and English. After the peacemaker has explained the rules, the petitioner is allowed to explain his or her complaint. The respondent is then asked to respond to the petitioner's complaint. Next, the peacemaker provides a "[b]rief overview of the problem as presented by the disputants." Family members and other participants, including traditional teachers, may then join the discussion, providing their description or explanation of the problem(s).

The peacemaker, usually chosen by his or her chapter, is a respected person with a demonstrated knowledge of traditional Navajo stories. He or she must be someone who possesses the power of persuasion, because peacemakers do not judge or decide cases. Their power lies in their words and their influence. Peacemakers "show a lot of love, they use encouraging words, [when you] use [Navajo] teaching to lift [participants] up you can accomplish a lot, [if you] are very patient."

note 21, at 182. * * *

142. Yazzie & Zion, *supra* note 2, at 160–61.

145. Valencia–Weber & Zuni, *supra* note 50, at 87.

Peacemaking may be hard for outside observers to understand, because it seems to combine so many different things: mediation, restorative justice, therapeutic intervention, family counseling, and Navajo teaching. Understanding is also made more difficult because of the significant differences in the practice of various peacemakers and the different approaches used for different kinds of problems. Peacemaking practice is fluid, flexible, and thoroughly practical, fitting the process to the situation. As Phil Bluehouse, coordinator for the Peacemaker Division, relates:

> [I]f there's no flexibility [in peacemaking], we'll be doing a disservice.... [I] prefer [the] middle ground leaning more towards flexibility, because to me, that's the nature of the human being.... I encouraged fluidity over the process. Be dynamic, be explorative.... The court[s] compartmentalize, it's this kind of case or that kind of case. I say, we're dealing with human beings.... [166]

The Peacemaker Court Manual also stresses the need for flexibility:

> It cannot be stressed, repeated or urged enough that the Peacemaker Court ... is not frozen in its present form forever. As an experiment which has been carefully built upon Navajo custom and tradition, we will have to see whether it meets the needs of the Navajo people ..., and we will have to see what changes need to be made.[167]

Peacemaking is a formal part of the Navajo legal system, developed and overseen by the Navajo Nation judiciary. There are two primary routes by which cases reach Peacemaking: court referral and self-referral. Criminal cases may be referred by the court as the result of diversion or as a condition of probation. The Domestic Abuse Protection Act creates special rules for domestic violence protection order cases: A referral to Peacemaking must be approved by the petitioner, and the peacemaker must have received special domestic violence training. In all other civil cases, the rules allow courts to refer cases to Peacemaking over a party's objection, but in practice judges seldom refer civil cases involving allegations of domestic violence unless both parties agree to the referral. In addition to court referral, Peacemaking may be initiated by a petitioner on a claim that he or she has been "injured, hurt or aggrieved by the actions of another." Self-referred cases make up the majority of Peacemaking cases. In a self-referred case, the peacemaker liaison seeks authorization from the district court to subpoena the respondent and all other necessary parties identified by the petitioner.

* * *

CONCLUSION: LESSONS FROM NAVAJO PEACEMAKING

This Article moves back and forth between a study of the specifics of Navajo Peacemaking in domestic violence cases and an exploration of

---

166. Interview with Philmer Bluehouse, supra note 15.

167. Zion & McCabe, supra note 56, at 157.

Peacemaking's theory of adjudication and its lessons for intervention strategies in domestic violence more generally—even when those possibilities are imperfectly realized in current Navajo practice.

In the struggle for greater autonomy and for some measure of safety against male violence, women choose methods and resources, discarding those that fail to work and refining those that, while not perfect, provide some advantage. Women's experiences of battering are framed by their experiences of other subordinating experiences: racism, childhood abuse, and economic deprivation. These experiences are also framed by women's political and cultural ideals and commitments. While there is no one intervention strategy that will work for all women, one critical measure of the effectiveness of any strategy is its capacity for placing resources—material, emotional, spiritual—in the hands of battered women. In some locales, this may best be accomplished through informal mechanisms that engage intentional communities, such as churches or civic organizations, in assisting battered women.

As developed in this Article, the Navajo Peacemaking model may increase a woman's material resources through *nalyeeh* and referrals to social services. It may increase her familial, emotional, and spiritual resources through its assistance in reconnecting her with family, redefining for her in-laws her relationship with their abusive son, providing referrals to counseling (both secular and spiritual), and through demonstrating care and support.

Peacemaking offers other potential benefits for some women. It may assist in disrupting familial supports for battering because family members are subpoenaed and peacemakers confront familial denial and minimizing. Peacemaking may directly address the abuser's victim blaming, excusing, or minimizing statements. Peacemaking may allow for the recognition of the impact of oppressive systems in the lives of men who batter without resort to excuse or victim blaming. Peacemaking thus avoids the "responsibility versus description" dichotomy of formal adjudication that limits its ability to address the complexity of battering behavior.

Peacemakers value relationships, even relationships with a batterer. Because peacemakers do not presume that separation is the best course of action, women are free to see Peacemaking as their last hope for saving a marriage. Peacemaking may provide women with tools to change the balance of power within their relationships.

Peacemaking also provides partial remedies for the problems that plague other informal adjudication. Rather than mediation's neutral ideal, peacemakers see themselves as fair but interested intervenors whose role is to instruct and to guide. Thus, Peacemaking has the potential to operate with a clear and overt antimisogyny norm. This antimisogyny norm may be strengthened by the use of traditional Navajo stories that emphasize the importance of gender balance and complementariness.

The Navajo Peacemaking experience underscores the necessity of an antimisogyny norm. Peacemakers who equate battering with a conflict or disagreement may domesticate the abuse. When peacemakers are clear that the abuse is an important object of intervention and that it is harmful and the responsibility of the abuser, it provides the possibility for real change in the batterer's thinking. It can reframe the battering. It may force the batterer to listen to " 'his family tell of the ordeal and ... what they went through during this time of terror.' "

Despite these potential benefits, Peacemaking is no more ideal at meeting the goal of promoting women's autonomy than are other imperfect interventions. Indeed, as described in this Article in some detail, Peacemaking's current practice creates real dangers for some women, primarily because it coerces participation in self-referred cases. Additionally, safety is compromised because Peacemaking does not routinely provide battered women with the information they need to make an informed decision about whether to enter Peacemaking. Some peacemakers appear biased against divorce, thus sandwiching women between the separation focus of formal adjudication and a stay-married focus in Peacemaking. But this is not always the case. Some peacemakers routinely assist women in obtaining a divorce, some women come to Peacemaking expressly to use the process to gain a divorce, and a significant number of women take their case to family court when they are unhappy with Peacemaking's results (or with their partners' failure to change).

What are the lessons of Navajo Peacemaking for designing informal domestic violence intervention strategies? First, such a process must have safeguards to limit the abuser's ability to use the process to locate and continue to abuse the woman. Cases should be screened to identify battering. Respondent victims should be able to opt out. They should be given full information regarding the pros and cons of the process (as compared with others), and should be assisted with safety planning. Such a process would borrow from Navajo Peacemaking the understanding that fairness need not mean neutrality. This is particularly true with regard to the facilitator's understanding of violence and controlling behavior. The facilitator should use not only an antiviolence norm but also an antimisogyny norm. Peacemaking demonstrates the power of stories used in the furtherance of such a norm. In pluralistic American culture, stories compete. The facilitator in the informal process I imagine would, much as the most common batterer's treatment programs now do, support a story that values women's autonomy.

Like Peacemaking, this process should allow for a description of the oppressive structures that operate in the life of the batterer without reinforcing his sense of "victimhood" or entitlement. This underscores the process's link to social justice, spirituality, and the capacity for individual change. It allows women to affirm cultural and political identity—their solidarity with men in antiracist, anticolonialist work—without sacrificing their right to be free of gender-related violence. Such a process should value connection and relationships but should equally value choice—enlarging women's ability to choose by increasing women's resources.

The remedies available might include those currently available in restraining-order processes. For those who are separating, this might include such remedies as stay-away provisions, child custody and visitation, and child support. For those who live together, it might include prohibitions against violence, harassment, stalking, and phone calls at work. It might also include affirmative agreements to share housework or childcare, to express anger in noncontrolling and nonthreatening ways, to seek alcohol and batterer's treatment, and to cease certain battering-supporting friendships. As proposed by Braithwaite and Daly, it should include changes in the distribution of family assets so as to provide the woman with greater economic independence.

Without a sense of clan and familial responsibility, it may be difficult to persuade an abuser's family to provide the victim with goods and services. However, agreements involving victim reparations will often, in actuality, draw on familial assets. The process should encourage the attendance of the victim's family members as well, which will sometimes strengthen frayed family relationships.

Drawing on Yamamoto's work on intergroup race apologies as well as Navajo Peacemaking theory, such a process should encourage the batterer and his family and other support systems to recognize the harm caused by his behavior. Peacemaking supports this recognition through the use of the victim's stories and those of her family and friends. It also supports this recognition through the peacemaker's confrontation of denying and minimizing statements made by the batterer and his family. Yamamoto's second step, "taking responsibility," will often require more extensive inquiry into the various tactics used by a batterer to control, intimidate, and harm his partner or ex-partner. This requires confrontation not only of statements that deny or minimize the violence, but also of statements that attempt to excuse or blame the violence on the victim's bad behavior. It requires a cataloguing of controlling behaviors. This process cannot be accomplished solely through the use of an informal process, but it can begin there. Referrals to batterer's treatment, alcohol treatment, and spiritual healers or counselors must continue the process. The third step, "reconstruction," requires the concrete measures described above. *Nalyeeh*, or reparations after this thorough searching process, is much more than victim compensation. Reparations should include the resources, within the limits of availability, required to broaden the victim's autonomy. More than a therapeutic intervention, such a process would seek to restructure the power relationships between a man who batters and the woman he batters.

The Navajo "art and science of dealing with crime" provides some valuable lessons for thinking about the future of anti-domestic violence work. Intervention strategies that broaden women's choices, that address their material and context-specific needs, are the strategies that will be most effective. Peacemaking is not perfect—no domestic violence intervention is perfect—but Peacemaking offers possibilities for women that are largely unavailable in other intervention strategies.

Chapter 9

RAPE OF INTIMATE PARTNERS

This chapter begins an examination of how the criminal justice system treats domestic violence. The topic, intimate partner rape, sometimes falls "between the cracks" of sexual assault laws, policies, and programs on the one hand, and domestic violence laws, policies, and programs on the other. However, it belongs in both areas, as rape is a frequent aspect of domestic violence.

The chapter begins with the history of the marital rape exception, which lasted for centuries in Anglo–American law. The materials discuss the rationales for this exception, as well as its recent demise, including a landmark case in which it was held unconstitutional. They also note that even in jurisdictions which criminalize marital rape (which now include all US states, federal lands, the District of Columbia, and the Navajo Nation) there are still major problems in terms of identifying, reporting, charging, and obtaining convictions. Some of these problems are statutory, while others are based on long-held beliefs that this type of case does not belong in the criminal justice system.

The chapter ends with two contrasting pieces: first, the relevant sections in the Model Penal Code, which surprisingly still include this antiquated exemption, and second, a short summary of how marital rape statutes have evolved in the last twenty years, with recommendations for further legislative change.

LISA R. ESKOW, THE ULTIMATE WEAPON?: DEMYTHOLOGIZING SPOUSAL RAPE AND RECONCEPTUALIZING ITS PROSECUTION

48 Stan. L. Rev. 677–698, 703–709 (1996).

I can see a lot of women taking advantage of [marital rape laws].... I think too many women use sex as a weapon already. Why give them another round for their arsenal? It's the ultimate weapon. since a woman's ultimate weapon is sex, a man's ultimate weapon has to be his strength. Ross, 38, divorced, college-educated businessman[1]

The idea that marriage implies or requires perpetual consent, under all circumstances, to sex is grotesque. . . . But it is a grave business when the law empowers one partner to charge the other with a felony punishable by 20 years in prison. George F. Will[2]

Virtuous women, like young girls, are unconsenting, virginal, rapable. Unvirtuous women, like wives and prostitutes, are consenting, whores, unrapable. Catharine A. Mackinnon[3]

The "Battle of the Sexes" conjures up mass media images of celebrity sports challenges or TV game shows. This cliche, though tired, remains tried and true. Tensions between the sexes escalate as more women abandon the traditional roles of housewife and full-time mother to enter the "real world" and compete with men for jobs, educational opportunities, and equal social status. Affirmative action quotas and sexual harassment policies have sparked divisive debates over the role of gender in the workplace. Yet, nowhere are the battle lines drawn more clearly than in the domestic sphere.

The age-old problem of domestic violence is finally gaining recognition, both in our culture and under the criminal law. However, domestic sexual violence remains an elusive concept. While the marital home no longer provides an impenetrable sanctuary for batterers, the marital bedroom stands as a questionable arena for state intervention. Sex has always been perceived as an integral component of "domestic bliss," both for procreative and romantic reasons. For some, sex is the quintessence of privacy rights, triggering the Fourteenth Amendment's guarantee of freedom from state intrusion. For others, sex is the systematic means through which men subjugate women. Legal responses to sexual violence often shift within a domestic context, suggesting that forced marital sex is something other than rape. Long perceived as a crime of sexual passion, rape is now widely regarded as an act of violence and is prosecuted as such. Rape within marriage, however, falls into a gray area of the American criminal justice system.

* * *

I. RAPE IN MARRIAGE

A. A Historical and Legal Overview of Spousal Rape

Early Judeo–Christian tenets established rape as a legitimate means of acquiring wives. Florence Rush writes:

Judaism ordained that a bride could be legally acquired by contract, money, or sexual intercourse, but since the church eschewed materi-

---

1. David Finkelhor & Kersti Yllo, License to Rape: Sexual Abuse of Wives 68 (1985).

2. George F. Will, When Custom Doesn't Work Anymore, Wash. Post, Dec. 28, 1978, at A23, quoted in Helen Benedict,

Virgin or Vamp: How the Press Covers Sex Crimes 67 (1992).

3. Catharine A. MacKinnon, Toward a Feminist Theory of the State 175 (1989).

alism, sexual intercourse emerged as the validating factor. As early as the sixth century, Pope Gregory decreed that "any female taken by a man in copulation belonged to him and his kindred." And since copulation with or without consent established male possession of the female, vaginal penetration superseded all impediments.[8]

Legal theorists followed suit, advocating unimpeded male sexual access to women. Lord Matthew Hale, Chief Justice of England in the seventeenth century, set the tone for rape prosecutions with his infamous, and shockingly enduring, observation that "rape ... is an accusation easily to be made and hard to be proved, and harder to be defended by the party accused, tho never so innocent."[9] Hale's comment, casting the alleged rapist as a likely victim, is far from a jurisprudential relic; it remained a mandatory jury instruction in California rape trials until as recently as 1975 and can still be introduced in many jurisdictions at a judge's discretion. In addition to his legendary status as the progenitor of rapists' rights generally, Hale made a crucial contribution to marital rapists' rights specifically, proclaiming: "[T]he husband cannot be guilty of a rape committed by himself upon his lawful wife, for by their mutual matrimonial consent and contract the wife hath given up herself in this kind unto the husband, which she cannot retract." The notion that marriage entails the wife's "irrevocable" or "implied" consent to sex formed the basis for the common law marital rape exemption, which shielded sexually abusive husbands from criminal prosecution. Like Hale's rape instruction, this contract-based, "irrevocable consent" theory endures as a defining principal in states' marital rape laws.

Another historical rationale for the marital rape exemption roots its approach in property rights. Traditional proscriptions against rape protected female chastity as a valuable asset—not of the chaste woman, but of her father, who could trade his daughter's virginity for economic or social gain from a prospective suitor. Husbands, too, had a property interest in their wives' fidelity. Consequently, no legal basis existed to prosecute husbands for raping their own wives, since the husband infringed no man's property rights. According to Blackstone's common law "unities" doctrine, husband and wife merged into a single legal entity upon marriage, with the husband assuming complete control of their joint existence. The unities doctrine thus "legitimate[d] the propertization of women through marriage." Under this marital construct, "a man could no more be charged with raping his wife than be charged with raping himself." Perhaps Lawrence Friedman puts it best: "Essentially, husband and wife were one flesh; but the man was the owner of that flesh."

Although Western culture almost uniformly perpetuated the assumption that forced intercourse is a woman's matrimonial duty, the

8. Florence Rush, The Best Kept Secret: Sexual Abuse of Children 32 (1980).

9. 1 Matthew Hale, The History of the Pleas of the Crown 634 (Sollom Emlyn ed., 1st Am. ed. 1778) * * *.

common law marital rape exemption nonetheless drew some early critics. John Stuart Mill, for example, observed:

> [A] female slave has (in Christian countries) an admitted right, and is considered under a moral obligation, to refuse to her master the last familiarity. Not so the wife: however brutal a tyrant she may unfortunately be chained to—though she may know that he hates her, though it may be his daily pleasure to torture her, and though she may feel it impossible not to loathe him—he can claim from her and enforce the lowest degradation of a human being, that of being made the instrument of an animal function contrary to her inclinations.[23]

Mill, however, espoused a minority view, and the marital rape exemption endured, unchallenged, for centuries. As recently as 1958, Encyclopedia Britannica's definition of rape stated: "A husband cannot commit rape upon his wife unless she is legally separated from him." According to Sally Mariko Lorang, a criminal appeals attorney, domestic violence volunteer, and member of the California State Bar Committee on Women in the Law:

> "The assumption that a man has a proprietary right to his wife's sexuality and reproductive capacity is so well entrenched in common law that it has only recently been challenged by such rulings as *Roe v. Wade.* . . . It has always been presumed that men should have unlimited sexual access to their wives." Susan Estrich, author of the groundbreaking Real Rape, agrees that a husband's right to sex is rarely challenged: "Men in appropriate relationships enjoy a broad right to seduce. Men in the most appropriate relationship of all, marriage, have enjoyed an absolute right." Because marriage is a proxy for unlimited male sexual access, David Finkelhor and Kersti Yllo conclude that "the marriage license can indeed be called a 'license to rape.' "

Contemporary rape statutes reflect the tenacity of the marital rape exemption. The classic legal definition of rape is: "an act of sexual intercourse accomplished with a person not the spouse of a perpetrator. . . ." In 1981, ten states barred prosecutions of husbands for marital rape. By 1990, no state retained an absolute marital rape exemption, although thirty-five states placed limits on the prosecution of marital rapists. Such prosecutorial restrictions included non-cohabitation or aggravated force requirements, ceilings on punishment, specifications on when—and to whom—marital rape must be reported, and the creation of alternative, frequently misdemeanor, sexual assault statutes that applied when criminal behavior otherwise classifiable as felony rape happened to be perpetrated by a spouse. Within one year, ten of those thirty-five states revoked or revised these provisions. By 1994, twenty-four states had abolished any form of marital rape exemption—either through legislative reform or judicial interpretation of existing statutes. Nevertheless, at least thirteen states still offer preferential or disparate treat-

---

23. John Stuart Mill, The Subjection of Women, in John Stuart Mill & Harriet Taylor Mill, Essays on Sex Equality 123, 160 (Alice S. Rossi ed., 1970).

ment to perpetrators of spousal sexual assault. Marital rape laws are in a constant state of flux; in March 1995, Laura X, Director of the National Clearinghouse on Marital and Date Rape, estimated that marital rape related bills were pending in twenty-eight states.

However, not all recent legislative reform aims to revoke the marital exemption's "raping license." Several states have actually extended their exemptions to include non-married, cohabiting couples. For example, cohabitation is an affirmative defense to rape in Connecticut, regardless of the legal status of the relationship between the victim and the defendant. One of the more egregious examples of a legal "raping license" appears in Delaware, where a "voluntary social companion" exemption impedes prosecution of men who engage in non-consensual sex with "a victim who is in the defendant's company on the occasion of the offense as a result of the victim's exercise of rational intellect and free will, without trick, coercion or duress" and who has engaged in consensual sex with the defendant within the past year. Such expansions of the marital rape exemption into other forms of domestic and social relationships reveal the persistent legal and cultural obstacles to securing women's sexual autonomy, not only in marriage, but also in society generally.

B. The Reality of Marital Rape

The marital rape exemption does not exist in a legal vacuum; it reflects, and aggravates, the daily abuse experienced by married women whose husbands claim an absolute right of access to their bodies. The exemption also reinforces many wives' belief that duty compels compliance with their husbands' every sexual desire. According to Ross, the divorced businessman quoted at the outset of this note, sex in marriage is the "ultimate weapon." But while Ross, and many men, view sex as a tool women use to manipulate and undermine their husbands, far too many women experience sex in marriage as a weapon with which husbands dominate and batter their wives. As Susan Brownmiller maintains: "[I]f women are to be what we believe we are—equal partners—then intercourse must be construed as an act of mutual desire and not as wifely 'duty' enforced by the permissible threat of bodily harm or of economic sanctions."[42]

Domestic violence has gained increasing recognition due to the efforts of the feminist and battered women's movements. Rape, too, has been reconceptualized to some degree, with more widespread acknowledgment of date and acquaintance rapes that do not fit the traditional "stranger rape" profile. But spousal sexual abuse, which combines the elements of domestic violence and rape, has failed to attract the same attention or support. Diana Russell, author of the seminal work Rape in Marriage, contends that feminist discourse on both domestic violence and stranger rape has excluded wife rape as a pressing concern. Neglect by mainstream feminists and domestic violence activists is a tragic

42. Susan Brownmiller, Against Our Will: Men, Women, and Rape 381 (1975).

omission, considering that wife rape may well be the most prevalent form of rape. According to Russell's widely cited 1978 study of 930 women in San Francisco, 14 percent of all married respondents reported at least one incidence of spousal rape. In a 1980–81 survey of 323 Boston-area married women, David Finkelhor and Kersti Yllo reported that 10 percent had experienced sexual coercion involving force or threat of force by their husbands. Catharine MacKinnon recently stated that 24 percent of women are raped during marriage. Regardless of which statistics we accept, the prevalence of spousal rape presents an urgent issue that lobbyists, legal reformers, and women's rights activists must address.

Debate continues, however, over how to define and contextualize spousal rape. In particular, scholars and activists disagree on the extent to which marital rape and battering are distinct phenomena. Some, like Finkelhor and Yllo, locate spousal rape primarily within the battered woman's experience. Others go even further, contending that "[m]arital rape doesn't occur without other forms of domestic violence." In contrast, Russell's study suggests that for at least some women, spousal rape poses a distinct threat: Of the 644 ever-married women in her San Francisco sample, 10 percent (63) reported being victims of both spousal rape and battering; 4 percent (24) reported rapes only; and 12 percent (75) reported beatings only. Other studies indicate a closer link between battering and sexual abuse in marriage. Using a sample of 137 battered women, Irene Frieze found that 34 percent had been raped at least once. Russell quotes an oft-cited figure that 40 percent of battered women in shelters have been raped by their husbands. The highest statistic comes from a Denver survey cited by Finkelhor and Yllo: Fifty-nine percent of self-identified battered women reported instances of marital rape.

Despite the demonstrated link between domestic physical violence and sexual abuse, theorists like Russell contend that treating spousal rape as a subset of domestic violence excludes too many women who experience coercive sex in marriage without accompanying non-sexual abuse: "Taking wife rape out of a violent, battering context . . . ," she argues, "highlights the connections between wife rape and other prevalent negative marital sexual experiences reported by women." Furthermore, incorporating spousal rape within domestic violence may unnecessarily complicate the issue. Within Russell's study, beating was the primary or sole problem in 54 percent of abusive marriages; rape played a pivotal role in only 23 percent of those relationships. Thus, locating spousal rape within the domestic violence context is both over-and underinclusive: It includes marriages in which rape plays a minor role, while ignoring marriages in which rape, as opposed to non-sexual battering, is the crucial problem. Hence, Russell concludes:

> Recognizing wife rape requires recognition of a new group of abused wives, as well as of another form of abuse suffered by wives whose other abuse already has gained some recognition. Hence, wife rape cannot and must not be subsumed under the battered woman rubric.

The tendency to see wife rape as the exclusive problem of battered women has led to an important segment of wife rape victims being overlooked—those who are never beaten, or those for whom wife beating is a much less significant problem than sexual abuse. Instead, Russell advocates conceptualizing a spectrum of marital sex outside the domestic violence model. She positions marital rape at one end of a continuum, with voluntary, mutually desired sex at the other pole; in between falls "rape-like" behavior (such as coercive sex without force or threat), unwanted sex, or sex where women are passive and servicing their husbands. In addition to encompassing a broader range of non-consensual marital sex, removing marital rape from the battering context may help debunk notions that the domestic sphere is a private sexual realm beyond state control.

Practicality may also favor separating spousal rape from domestic violence, particularly in providing counseling and intervention services. According to a 1987 study by Lynn Thompson–Haas, Executive Director of the Austin Rape Crisis Center, only 40 percent of battered women's programs included staff training on marital rape; in contrast, 72 percent of rape crisis centers educated their staff of this issue. Thompson–Haas also found that rape crisis centers provided better services to marital rape victims than did battered women's shelters. They were more likely to initiate discussion of marital rape at the crisis intervention stage (97 percent versus 69 percent for shelters), and they were nearly twice as likely to raise the issue of marital rape in a follow-up session (86 percent versus 46 percent). Rape crisis centers were also more than doubly effective as advocates for marital rape victims during interviews with hospitals and law enforcement officials (84 percent versus 32 percent). Finally, they were more than three times as likely to offer marital rape support groups (54 percent versus 17 percent).

One serious drawback of rape crisis centers, however, is their inability to provide a marital rape victim with emergency housing; unlike most other rape victims, wives have no safe haven at home. In this respect, battered women's shelters offer a distinct advantage. Unfortunately, many shelters are reluctant to deal with victims of marital rape who have not suffered accompanying physical abuse; these shelters fail to acknowledge rape alone as a life-threatening problem. Their perception, however, is severely mistaken. Among batterers, those who rape are particularly brutal and violent. Russell suggests that at least one-third of women murdered by their husbands have also suffered marital rape. In her San Francisco sample, approximately 12 percent of wife rape victims believed they stood a substantial risk of being killed by their abusers. Furthermore, the wife's life may not be the only one in danger: Marital rape victims are not only more likely to be murdered by their husbands, but also to murder their husbands in self-defense. In Faith McNulty's The Burning Bed, Francine Hughes describes the final act that precipitated her own violent response to her husband's sexual abuse: "I hated it worse than I ever had before. The idea of him inside me, owning even my insides, shoving deep into me, made my flesh crawl.... There is no way to describe how I felt: a helpless, frozen fury; a volcano blocked just before it erupts." After her husband fell asleep, she doused the room with gasoline and burned him alive on the bed where he had raped her.

Battering and spousal rape often go hand-in-hand in the cycle of violence. While these acts involve important differences, they also share some dynamics. Ignoring these overlapping symptoms is as damaging as conflating the two phenomena; both oversimplifications hinder efforts to understand, and eradicate, misconceptions about marital rape. In addressing both forms of abuse, two similarities emerge: First, husbands' acts of physical and sexual violence escalate when their wives attempt to leave the marriage. These "separation assaults," as Martha Mahoney terms them, reflect the abusive husband's "quest for control." In Finkelhor and Yllo's study, one-quarter of divorced or separated women reported a past incident of forced marital sex. Over two-thirds were raped shortly after ending a previous separation or when making plans to leave. These findings prompted Finkelhor and Yllo to conclude that "[a] wife's leaving or threatening to leave her marriage frequently provokes a marital rape."

Second, wives' economic dependency on their husbands may fuel both physically and sexually abusive marriages. Russell identifies a pervasive "notion that the male breadwinner should be the beneficiary of some special immunity because of his family's economic dependence on him." In her study, 90 percent of wives who stayed with their husbands following a rape depended on the husband for money, whereas only 24 percent of those who left faced this financial constraint. Russell also makes the striking observation that 100 percent of those women who were the sole providers for their households at the time of the rape left their husbands following the act. Economic independence, apparently, gave these women not only the financial means, but also the emotional and psychological capacity, to break free from an abusive marriage cycle.

While Russell offers compelling reasons for analytically separating marital rape from the larger domestic violence context, one cannot ignore the aspects of domestic violence that infiltrate many sexually abusive relationships. Without question, marital rape reform requires solutions tailored to the unique characteristics of a sex crime. But, ignoring symptoms suggesting a larger domestic violence context will ultimately undermine the effectiveness of reforms adopted solely from a sex crime model. Only by demythologizing domestic privacy taboos and acknowledging the complex dynamics of marital rape can legal reform effect a viable strategy for prosecuting marital rapists.

The next Part explores common myths about marital rape, identifying the cultural attitudes activists must address, and transform, in order to insure women's sexual and physical security at home.

II. Marital Rape Myths

Myths, both about sex in marriage and about the crime of rape, hinder mainstream acceptance of the pervasive reality of marital rape.

As Part I explained, three popular and interrelated myths render wives "unrapable." First, many women feel duty-bound to submit to sex in marriage. Second, many husbands believe they have an absolute right to sex on demand. Third, many individuals view marriage as constituting perpetual, even contractual consent.

Widespread cultural myths about marital rape in turn infiltrate the criminal justice system, creating an ancillary set of prosecutorial myths. Prosecutorial myths influence strategies for trying marital rape cases before jurors who presumably hold at least some preconceptions about rape and, in particular, rape in marriage. For example, prosecutors who believe jurors subscribe to the popular myth that marital status negates, or at least mitigates, the crime of rape may be reluctant to charge a marital rape case from the outset, anticipating inevitable defeat at trial. Hence, only by demythologizing marital rape in our culture can we effectively reconceptualize the prosecution of that crime.

A. *Popular Myths*

"I don't think this should be a crime," said the mother of a convicted wife rapist in 1984, "because after all, this is what men get married for." "I would never think of taking it by force—except from my wife," stated a respondent in Shere Hite's 1981 study on male sexuality; "It so appalls me that I couldn't do it"—except, apparently, to his wife. "A woman who's still in a marriage is presumably consenting to sex," argued defense attorney Charles Burt during the first nationally publicized marital rape trial in 1978; "[m]aybe this is the risk of being married, you know?" "If you can't rape your wife," asked California State Senator Bob Wilson in 1979, "who can you rape?"

Statements and images endorsing marital rape pervade not only press reports, but also popular culture. One of the most celebrated romantic movie scenes of all time is the moment in Gone With the Wind when Rhett sweeps up a protesting Scarlett and forcibly carries her off to bed. She wakes up the next morning, aglow. As Margaret Mitchell wrote in the novel: "He had humbled her, hurt her, used her brutally through a wild mad night and she had gloried in it." Feminists never failed to catch the underlying message: Scarlett was raped—and she loved it. That message was not lost on mainstream audiences either, although they processed it quite differently. As Finkelhor and Yllo maintain:

> We may disapprove of his methods, but we cannot help approving of his ends: conjugal relations.
>
> ... [I]t would be a travesty of the highest order if Rhett Butler ... ended up facing a five-year jail term for [his] excess of passion. No wonder people are startled by the idea of criminalizing marital rape.

Cultural myths about the importance of facilitating conjugal relations and the absurdity of criminalizing marital rape influence many wives' perceptions of their own trauma. These myths foster a false consciousness of consent in women experiencing coercive marital sex. Of the women identified as survivors of marital rape in Russell's study, only 7 percent (6 out of 87) responded affirmatively when asked directly if they had been "raped." Another 6 percent acknowledged incidents of forced sex, but tempered their characterizations of the experience, saying "[i]t was almost like rape"; or "[h]e pinned me down like he was raping me"; or "[i]t was just like a rape, except I was on [my own] bed." These women believed they had experienced an act that would otherwise constitute rape, but for the fact that it was perpetrated by their husbands and in their own homes.

Societal myths equating conjugal relations with domestic bliss enhance women's reluctance to admit wife rape, since such admissions might suggest sexual inadequacy and an inability to please one's husband. Notions of a "normal marriage" stem from society's construction of what Martha Fineman terms a "sexual family": a mythical conception assuming a "horizontal" sexual relationship between husband and wife that overrides all other familial connections.

The sexual family myth creates confusion over what constitutes rape in marriage and underscores the gendered hierarchy of the marital institution. As one respondent to Finkelhor and Yllo's survey put it: "I know I was feeling coerced and not doing it willingly most of the time.... But in a way I'm not sure it was done by him. It was really my own upbringing and the things that I'd been taught. It came from me. He couldn't have really raped me. I was allowing my own body to be violated, and that's not rape. My allowing it is what makes it not rape." Whether this woman accurately assesses her situation or suffers from false consciousness, her self-analysis illustrates the influence of socializing forces and societal constructions of marital norms on women's sexual autonomy. Consequently, Fineman endorses the abolition of the legal institution of marriage as we know it, observing that disbanding the sexual family "would remove the justification for the defense of marriage to a charge of rape."

Women's views of marital sexual norms are not·the only ones molded by societal forces. Society treats male sexual supremacy as a source of pride and a measure of self-worth. Consequently, when that supremacy is challenged, men need to reassert their dominant position in the gender hierarchy. Ross, quoted previously, admits to forcing his now ex-wife to have sex. He explains the motivation behind one particular assault following a verbal fight:

> I guess subconsciously I felt she was getting the better of me. it dawned on me to just throw her down and have her ... which I did.... I grabbed her by the arms and she put up resistance for literally fifteen seconds and then just resigned herself to it. There were no blows or anything like that. it was weird. I felt very animalistic, and I felt very powerful.... I'm not proud of it, but, damn it, I walked around with a smile on my face for three days.

Ross continued:

You could say, I suppose, that I raped her. But I was reduced to a situation in the marriage where it was absolutely the only power I had over her. . . .

Subconsciously I think she kept egging me on because she wanted to be dominated. . . . [S]he just completely emasculated me. It was the only thing I had left.

Ross used rape as a weapon to reassert his sexual dominance and bolster his waning self-worth. An admitted rapist, he ironically perceives himself both as a victim of his wife's castrating personality and as her sexual savior, providing the rape she craves. Interestingly, Ross admits that had spousal rape been a crime for which he could have been prosecuted at the time of this act, he probably would have resisted the forced encounter. But, had Ross realized how deeply marital rape myths pervade not only the bedroom but the courtroom, he might have reconsidered his reluctance to rape.

B.   Marital Rape Myths in the Courtroom

As the preceding section illustrates, myths about marital rape pervade our culture. At best, marital rape is a crime distinct from—and lesser than—rape; at worst, it is a legal impossibility. Media coverage of marital rape trials both reflects and reinforces these popular myths.

The media cannot resist a good sex crime. Unfortunately, reporting frequently relies on cliches, sensationalism, and shallow analyses of complex domestic scenarios. According to media analyst Helen Benedict, "[s]ex crimes have a unique ability to touch upon the public's deep seated beliefs about gender roles ... call[ing] into play age-old myths and assumptions about rape and sex. . . ." Tapping into these stereotypes, the media associates sex crime victims with one of two archetypal images: the pure and innocent "virgin" or the sexually provocative (and thus culpable) "vamp." According to Benedict, a woman who knows her alleged assailant typically falls into the "vamp" category. And who could know the assailant better than his own wife?

The media's virgin-or-vamp paradigm is central to a number of pervasive courtroom myths affecting rape prosecutions. These myths contend that: the victim provoked her rapist; she could have prevented the rape; the victim deserved it; she cried rape to extort money or to punish a man for dumping her. An enduring classic is that only "bad" women get raped. Most rape myths apply equally to marital and nonmarital rape, reflecting a Matthew Hale-esque suspicion of women and a sympathy for men's fragile reputations. Marital rape scenarios, however, blur the lines in the virgin-or-vamp paradigm. Wives fit the virgin profile when raped by strangers, but they become "unrapable" vamps when the assailant is their husband.

In 1978, the media swarmed to Oregon for the first nationally publicized marital rape prosecution. John and Greta Rideout's marriage had a history of domestic violence and coerced sex. Greta pressed charges of rape two days after a particularly violent incident, during which John beat her and forced sex in front of their daughter. After a brief separation, the couple reconciled and engaged in consensual sex; but Greta could neither stay in the relationship nor ignore the rape that occurred days before.

Greta availed herself of Oregon's new spousal rape statute; John responded by challenging the law on the ground that it violated a fundamental right to marital privacy. As the sordid details of the Rideout marriage began to surface, receiving more press than the legal issues, the story made headlines nationwide. John effectively put Greta on trial, and the media readily participated in her prosecution, circulating reports that she falsely reported rape to further the feminist political crusade against traditional family values. As Benedict observes, it was "the old myth with a new twist: the 'rape lie' as a weapon with which to subordinate the foundation of society, the institution of marriage."

Charles Burt, John's attorney, masterfully manipulated rape myths to portray John as the victim of Greta's vindictive scheming. By characterizing rape as a crime of lust rather than violence, the defense intimated that Greta was frigid and thus to blame for John's irrepressible sexual desires. Burt also played on the myth that only "bad" women are raped, introducing testimony concerning Greta's alleged heterosexual—and lesbian—extra-marital affairs. Finally, he suggested that Greta cried rape for revenge. Reporters covering the trial "fell into Burt's mythmaking like wasps into honey."

Cast as the quintessential vamp—a sexually aggressive, adulterous woman with lesbian tendencies, withholding sex from the one man deserving it—Greta did not have a prayer. Despite the fact that evidence clearly demonstrated a physically abusive pattern in their marriage, John was acquitted on the rape charge. Roughly one year later, John and Greta Rideout announced their reconciliation, shocking the nation. The media ridiculed the spousal rape activists who had rallied to Greta's cause, heralding the case as the triumph of privacy in the bedroom. Invoking a classic, pop-cultural rape myth, columnist Art Buchwald, initially sympathetic to Greta, now wrote: "I'll never take sides in another husband-wife rape case again without thinking of Gone With the Wind."

Inevitably, John resumed his violent behavior and the couple filed for divorce. Later, the court issued a restraining order issued against John; he violated it and served a term in jail. The Rideouts were a classic example of a couple trapped in a domestic violence cycle. Greta's post-trial reconciliation with John is not evidence of a rape hoax, but rather the classic behavior of a battered woman. Had the Rideout prosecutor made a more explicit domestic violence link, the case might have escaped the media's ridicule and may have even educated people. Instead, the debacle reinforced popular myths about marital rape, both through the courtroom drama and the media's depiction of events. As Benedict recalls, "Greta went down in history as a woman who accused her husband of raping her and then went back to him—a woman, like Scarlett O'Hara, who likes rape."

If the Rideout episode lent credence to male paranoia that wives cry rape, Lorena Bobbitt's trial for the "malicious wounding" of her alleged rapist husband, John Wayne Bobbitt, sent signals that manipulative wives may just skip the false rape report and instead cut off their husbands' penises. Alan Dershowitz claims that Lorena Bobbitt's " 'insanity' defense had been a cover for the real defense of 'the sexist son-of-a-bitch had it coming'. . . . Bobbitt was an angry, vengeful woman," the equivalent of "Dirty Harry in a dress." Dershowitz acknowledges that "[s]he claimed that he had raped her, though he was acquitted," suggesting that the acquittal implies the falsity of the charge.

Dershowitz offers the FBI's misleading statistic that 8.4 percent of reported rapes each year are "unfounded"; he then translates this figure into 8,000 false rape reports annually. In reality, the term "unfounded" refers specifically to cases in which police determine they have insufficient evidence to proceed with a rape investigation; the designation has no bearing on the alleged victim's veracity. Contrary to Dershowitz's figure, studies indicate that the statistic for false rape reports is only 2 percent, the same as for most other felony crimes. Nonetheless, like Greta Rideout, Lorena Bobbitt now stands as a media creation with mythological significance: living proof to rebut statistics and confirm that married women's rape reports must not be trusted.

Many rape statutes reflect suspicion of women's credibility and motives by instituting reporting and fresh complaint requirements and by demanding corroboration or demonstrated force in order to classify a forced sexual encounter as rape. Susan Estrich views these laws as "a response to a man's nightmarish fantasy of being charged with simple rape" and the "institutionalization of the law's distrust of women victims through rules of evidence and procedure." Wives are, in fact, even more suspect than unmarried women. For example, in California, a husband can be prosecuted for raping his wife, but only if she files a formal report within one year, eclipsing the six-year statute of limitations for non-marital rape. Criminal procedure theorist Yale Kamisar endorses such fresh complaint requirements, fearing wives will file false rape reports to gain leverage during divorce or custody battles.

Pernicious myths about both marital and non-marital rape influence lawmakers and the potential pool of jurors in the population at large. Even supposedly neutral judges are susceptible to cultural cues. One male judge who presided over several rape trials in the early 1970s endorsed the view that victims provoke rape: "I believe biologically it is wrong to entice a man knowing the situation you're creating and then saying 'no.' There is a button a man has that cannot be turned off and on like a light switch. And a man can go to prison for a very long time because of it." In 1993, Baltimore Circuit Judge Thomas J. Bollinger justified imposing a probation sentence on a convicted acquaintance rapist with a property rights analogy: "[I]f I grab your purse, its [sic] robbery, but if you leave your pocketbook on the bench and I take it, its [*sic*] larceny, which is less serious." Under Judge Bollinger's analysis, if acquaintance with one's rapist connotes assumption of the risk, marriage to one's rapist no doubt qualifies as estoppel.

III.   CALIFORNIA'S SPOUSAL RAPE LAW: A CASE STUDY OF LEGISLATIVE AND PROSECUTORIAL PRACTICES

This Part presents a case study of California's legislative and prosecutorial responses to marital rape in order to gauge the degree to which both cultural and courtroom myths affect the enactment and enforcement of spousal rape laws.

A.   *Legislating Section 262*

Analysis of California's efforts to reform marital rape prosecution must begin with the law itself. California presents an intriguing case study of legislative reform; the state criminalized spousal rape in 1979, but it did so under the rubric of a distinct sex crime. To this day, section 261 of the California Penal Code defines "Rape" as a crime committed against someone "not the spouse of the perpetrator...." Marital rape falls under section 262 of the California Penal Code, entitled "Rape of Spouse." Until 1993, section 262 was distinct from section 261 not only in name, but also in substance: While Rape was a felony, Rape of Spouse was a "wobbler," giving prosecutors discretion to charge either a felony or misdemeanor offense.

In 1992, legislative efforts to eliminate the misdemeanor option sparked heated debates. The California District Attorney's Association (C.D.A.A.) opposed the bill, arguing three main grounds: The wobbler provided greater flexibility in plea bargaining; it facilitated victim cooperation, giving reluctant wives an alternative to sending their husbands to prison; and it created a palatable option for juries who, C.D.A.A. believed, simply would not convict husbands of felony rape of their wives. Despite these practical rationales, C.D.A.A. ultimately withdrew its opposition after the defense bar expressed support for the misdemeanor option and lobbyists agreed to incorporate less stringent probation and sex offender registration requirements in the spousal rape statute.

In the California legislature, some of the Senators opposing the bill expressed less articulate objections than C.D.A.A.'s initial tactical criticisms. Ed Davis, a former police chief and a Republican Senator from Santa Clarita, denounced the bill as "preposterous" and "without justification whatsoever," adding, "We get beaten up by the women lobbyists.... Let's face it, we've been a little terrorized of late...." Davis characterized the bill's lobbyists as "a bunch of grim-faced women glowering at me, most of them women that men would never touch."

Nancy Lemon, Lecturer at Boalt Hall School of Law and lobbyist for statutory marital rape reform, identifies herself as one of those "glowering women." She drafted the legislation that Governor Pete Wilson ultimately signed into law on September 30, 1993. Lemon remembers the Senate hearings as a forum for promoting pervasive myths about spousal rape. She recalls that even liberal Senator Barry Keane supported retaining spousal rape as a lesser crime, suggesting that "if [hypothetically] he was charged with section 261, it might ruin his career even if he was acquitted; but if he was charged with section 262, people wouldn't take it seriously." According to Lemon, male Senators' paranoia that they might become marital rape defendants impedes legislative reform. The Senate debates demonstrated "a prevalent fear that wives are angry, vengeful, and will lie about anything."

Although continuing reform efforts have made section 262 nearly identical, in effect, to section 261, Lemon nonetheless advocates a single, all-inclusive rape statute in "the hope ... that prosecutors, jurors, and judges would then say 'yes, this is rape.' " Laura X, Director of Berkeley's National Clearinghouse on Marital and Date Rape, points out that as long as California retains two separate statutes, the legislature creates a marital rape exemption every time it amends section 261 without enacting comparable changes to section 262. On March 28, 1995, Lemon testified before a Senate committee regarding a clean-up bill designed to bring section 262 in line with 1994 amendments to section 261 concerning administration of intoxicating substances and disability of victims. The bill passed within minutes, to Lemon's surprise. Following Assembly approval, California enacted the corrective legislation on July 24, 1995. One easy victory, however, is no panacea. Lemon notes that the section 261/262 split requires courts to inquire into legislative intent whenever one statute, but not the other, has been amended on a specific issue.

Although recent legislation removes most distinctions between sections 261 and 262, the statutes still diverge substantively in one crucial respect: reporting requirements. Under section 262, a wife must report the rape to "medical personnel, a member of the clergy, an attorney, a shelter representative, a counselor, a judicial officer, a rape crisis agency, a prosecuting agency, a law enforcement officer or a firefighter within one year after the date of the violation." Section 261 contains no parallel requirement. Both statutes carry a statute of limitations of six years, but the reporting requirement under section 262 effectively diminishes that parameter to one year for spousal rape. Lemon finds the disparity particularly troubling, since marital rapes typically occur in a series of assaults over long periods of time. Besides misconceiving the nature of marital rape, the reporting provision of section 262, in Lemon's view, serves as a legislative reflection of the myth that "vengeful wives will lie" and that husbands, therefore, need protection.

Consequently, Lemon's lobbying efforts to combine the two statutes aim at debunking these persistent myths. A single statute encompassing all rape, regardless of the relationship between victim and perpetrator, would send the message that rape prosecutions are "policy decisions made by society, not just one woman who wants one man to go to prison."

* * *

IV. A MODEL FOR COMPREHENSIVE REFORM

As preceding Parts demonstrate, myths about marital rape pervade both our culture and our courts. Popular attitudes regarding consent, marital duty, and family privacy—as well as widespread ignorance of the complex dynamics of domestic violence and marital rape—present constant hurdles for prosecutors. As the California case study suggests, legislative reform and prosecutors' enhanced awareness of the need to educate jurors is already reshaping the treatment of marital rape under the criminal law. However, substantial reform must take place before prosecutors, judges, and the public fully accept marital rape as a serious crime.

Marital rape prosecutions involve the intersection of three distinct aspects: the terms of the statute defining the crime; the methods utilized by prosecutors to debunk myths in the courtroom; and the tenacity of cultural misperceptions about marriage, rape, and domestic violence—particularly as reinforced by the media. Hence, reform efforts must address each of these interrelated elements.

A. Statutory Reform

The terms of a marital rape statute set the tone for trial. In California, activists fear that the statutory separation of marital and nonmarital rape, even if merely technical, signals that marital rape is, conceptually, a lesser offense. Although the prosecutors interviewed all agree that the distinction bears little practical significance in the courtroom, the separate statutes create a need for judicial determination of legislative intent whenever one provision is updated without a corresponding change to the other. Discrepancies resulting from uneven amendments to the two laws create mini marital rape exemptions that prosecutors must weigh in deciding whether to charge, and to try, section 262 cases.

Nonetheless, there actually may be some conceptual advantages to the statutory separation of marital rape. Given the pervasive myths that wives are unrapable and untrustworthy, and husbands vulnerable to false accusations, enacting a statute that specifically criminalizes coercive sex with one's wife may help reluctant jurors accept the notion that marital rape is neither excusable nor a private family matter. As Martha Mahoney contends, "naming" is a valuable means of establishing the validity of "assaults on women that were not cognizable until the feminist movement named and explained them." By making spousal rape a crime in its own right, the law names the phenomenon and signals that society not only condemns, but prosecutes, such acts.

Still, treating marital rape as a separate crime from rape does send a mixed message about the crime's severity. Instead of taking California's two-law approach, a legislature might affirmatively include wives in the statutory definition of rape, thereby eliminating any express or implied marital rape exemption. A statutory definition might then read: "Rape is an act of sexual intercourse accomplished with a person including the spouse of a perpetrator." Such an inclusionary approach, however, might inadvertently exempt other classes of non-strangers from prosecution unless specifically named within the crime's definitional terms.

Alternatively, the rape statute might omit all references to the victim-perpetrator relationship, neither excluding nor including spouses in the definition. The abolition of marriage as an affirmative defense to rape could then be acknowledged in a separate provision, such as North Carolina's "No defense" statute, which reads: "A person may be prosecuted under this Article whether or not the victim is the person's legal spouse at the time of the commission of the alleged rape or sexual offense." One drawback to this approach is that the affirmative "naming" of spousal rape as a crime occurs in a statute distinct from the primary definition of rape, diminishing the connection between the two provisions.

The best solution would therefore combine these various approaches in a single statutory framework. Utah's rape statute provides an excellent example of this comprehensive strategy:

> "RAPE: 1) A person commits rape when the actor has sexual intercourse with another person without the victim's consent.
>
> 2) This section applies whether or not the actor is married to the victim . . . . "

Here, a single statutory provision accomplishes both goals: The first paragraph sets forth a definition of rape that neither affirmatively includes nor excludes spouses as potential victims, while the second paragraph clarifies that marriage is no defense to rape.

B. Reforming Prosecutorial Strategies

Prosecutors' first task is to combat rape myths in the courtroom by introducing victim syndrome evidence. In spousal rape prosecutions, expert testimony on Rape Trauma Syndrome and Battered Woman Syndrome provides a vital means of explaining numerous behavioral irregularities, such as victim recanting and late reporting. In *Arcoren v. United States*,[165] Brave Bird, a victim of spousal rape, recanted in the midst of testifying against her husband. The prosecution introduced evidence of Battered Woman Syndrome in an attempt to explain Brave Bird's behavior. The Eighth Circuit determined that:

> A jury naturally would be puzzled at the complete about-face she made, and would have great difficulty in determining which version of Brave Bird's testimony it should believe. . . . [battered woman syndrome evidence] would help it to determine which of Brave Bird's testimony to credit. If the jury concluded that Brave Bird suffered from battered woman syndrome, that would explain her change in testimony—her unwillingness to say something damaging

---

165. Arcoren v. United States, 929 F.2d 1235 (8th Cir.), cert. denied, 502 U.S. 913 (1991).

against her husband. Jurors unfamiliar with the cyclical dynamics of domestic violence may misperceive late reports of spousal rape or retracted allegations as indicative of a wife's false claim. In fact, such acts are textbook indications of abusive relationships. Prosecutors should introduce victim syndrome evidence to bolster spousal rape victims' credibility and thus increase the odds of success at trial.

Jurors in marital rape cases may misinterpret lack of evidence of physical force as a sign of victim consent. Introducing evidence about the dynamics of abusive domestic relationships can help explain any seeming lack of resistance. As sociologist Diana Russell observes, this lack of evidence typically stems not from the wife's consent, but from the reality that she must coexist with her rapist under the same roof. When wives routinely are battered as well as raped, they may not resist forced sex for fear that resistance will provoke a more severe beating. Finkelhor and Yllo emphasize the "special problems of resistance to sexual assault in a marriage. These women frequently stressed the need to keep things civil and maintain the facade of a marriage. . . . A victim of marital rape ha[s] to face her assailant the next morning over breakfast." Expert testimony on Battered Woman Syndrome can explain not only why there may be fewer physical signs of struggle, but also why, if he raped her, the wife cooked pancakes for her husband the next day.

Although rape is unquestionably traumatizing no matter who perpetrates it, prosecutors must counter the prevailing myth that wife rape is less traumatic than stranger rape, and thus worthy of lesser punishment. If anything, wife rape may compound the trauma inflicted by the act's violence with an additional sense of betrayal by a loved-one. Russell's study bolsters this proposition: Fifty-two percent of women raped by a husband or other relative reported experiencing long-term trauma as a result, as opposed to 39 percent of women raped by strangers. In one unusual California opinion, the court in *People v. Salazar* departed from traditional stereotypes about stranger and acquaintance rapes, observing that "a person in a private residence, especially that of her attacker, is more vulnerable than a woman fending off a rapist in a car on a dark street or in a public restroom."[173] When the rapist is the father of your children, pays your rent, and provides your sole means of economic support, the vulnerability to attack increases, as does the trauma of rape. As Finkelhor and Yllo conclude: "When you are raped by a stranger you have to live with a frightening memory. When you are raped by your husband you have to live with your rapist." By introducing evidence about the reality of marital rape, prosecutors can help ensure that spousal rapists receive sentences commensurate with their non-spousal rapist counterparts.

Assuming that the four Bay Area prosecutors I interviewed provide a representative sample, the decision whether to introduce victim syndrome evidence through an expert witness—such as a psychiatrist or

---

173. 144 Cal. App. 3d 799, 813.

professor—or through a "nuts-and-bolts" police officer is largely a matter of prosecutorial style. Regardless of the tack taken, prosecutors must assess the twelve personalities in the jury box and gauge how best to contextualize marital rape for those jurors. Frank Passaglia stresses the reality that twelve individuals, not any statute or constitution, ultimately are the law. Thus, if a prosecutor senses that jurors might nullify the criminality of marital rape, she should follow Ray Mendoza's approach and ask for a special marital rape instruction.

Finally, most District Attorney offices currently assign domestic violence and sexual assault cases to separate units. Following Nancy O'Malley's suggestion, a combined unit comprised of attorneys with specializations either in sexual assault or domestic violence, supervised by a team leader with expertise in both areas, would ensure a comprehensive approach to marital rape prosecutions, acknowledging both the overlapping and the distinct dynamics of domestic violence and marital rape.

C. Reforming Potential Juror Pools Through Public Education and Media Savvy

Prosecutors' contributions to marital rape reform should not end at the courtroom door. They must help educate potential jurors in the population at large by taking a proactive stance with the media. Prosecutors can publicize their marital rape trials and give interviews about domestic violence and Rape Trauma Syndrome. As Mary Coombs observes, "litigation and its attendant publicity . . . are among the primary vehicles through which we create and test our cultural understandings of sexual violations." Rather than allow defense attorneys like Charles Burt and Alan Dershowitz to dominate media discourse, prosecutors should develop their own sound bites, adding their voices to the debate. Such enhanced participation could fundamentally alter the nature of sex crime reporting and hence public perceptions of those crimes. Of course, prosecutors must never endanger a victim's physical, psychological, or emotional security for the sake of promoting public awareness; nor should they coerce marital rape survivors to publicize private trauma.

However, when desired by the victim, prosecutors should enhance victim access to the media as a forum in which to share their stories. Mary Coombs contends that "telling stories of sexual violation increases the chances for all honest claims to be believed; these effects in turn increase support for legal reform." No doubt, many wife rape victims will not want to publicize their experiences. However, their reluctance to speak out may be overestimated. In Finkelhor and Yllo's study, many women wanted to discuss their marital assaults

> as a way of overcoming the suffering and isolation and embarrassment. . . . They wanted to tell the story of how they had finally escaped from the impossible marriage, how they had overcome timidity and fear and learned to act in their own behalf. The

accounts of some of these women had an almost inspirational quality.

One woman in this survey said, "If one word or one sentence I would say to you could keep one young woman from making the same mistake I did, give one woman the courage to leave such a marriage, or open one man's eyes to what he was doing and why, it would be worth the pain of opening healed wounds."

Despite the picture painted by the O.J. Simpson trial and its attendant media frenzy, the larger trend suggests that "[t]he rich and famous are being accused, charged and found guilty. This makes people more aware, and makes victims feel less like it is happening only to them." Virginia Commonwealth Attorney Paul Ebert, who tried both Bobbitt cases, contends that "[t]he whole explosion in publicity and communication about [domestic violence] has altered people's perception of what is happening."

Still, Nancy Lemon cautions that increasing awareness about domestic violence may not necessarily enhance sensitivity to marital rape. This next step in public education may require aggressive community outreach programs, as envisioned by Nancy O'Malley, or mandatory high school classes, as suggested by Linda Eufusia.

Yet, using domestic violence as a baseline against which to contextualize marital rape may be a useful educational tool. As previously mentioned, Helen Benedict observes that had the media explicitly linked domestic violence with rape in its reporting of the *Rideout* trial, the case might have educated mainstream America, rather than ridiculing and re-victimizing a marital rape survivor. Interestingly enough, in the twelve years following the *Rideout* trial, Greta educated herself about domestic violence and Battered Woman Syndrome, attended college, and studied journalism. Perhaps some day she will provide a marital rape victim with more sensitive press coverage than she herself received, debunking the persistent myths that still plague marital rape prosecutions.

V. Conclusion

Legislative and prosecutorial efforts to combat marital rape will not succeed until pervasive myths about sex, rape, and marriage are eradicated from our culture. A charge of marital rape has never been the "ultimate weapon" some men fear: a tool of vindictive, scheming women used to punish and manipulate their husbands. Nor should marital rape remain the ultimate weapon by which men dominate, humiliate, and subjugate their wives. Legislatures must affirmatively negate the marital exemption from rape statutes, and prosecutors must become educators, not only in the courtroom, but also in society at large, communicating the realities of marital rape through effective use of the media.

As Susan Estrich concludes, "[i]t may be impossible—and unwise—to try to use the criminal law to articulate any of our ideal visions of male-female relationships.... The challenge ... is to use the legitimizing power of law to reinforce what is best, not what is worst, in our changing sexual mores.''[186] Archaic notions of irrevocable consent and male property interests in their wives' sexuality have no place in modern relationships. The institution of marriage remains sacred in our society, but it must no longer constitute a sanctuary for rapists.

THE PEOPLE OF THE STATE OF NEW YORK v. MARIO LIBERTA

Court of Appeals of New York (1984).
485 N.Y.S.2d 207, 209–220.

The defendant, while living apart from his wife pursuant to a Family Court order, forcibly raped and sodomized her in the presence of their 2 1/2 year old son. Under the New York Penal Law a married man ordinarily cannot be prosecuted for raping or sodomizing his wife. The defendant, however, though married at the time of the incident, is treated as an unmarried man under the Penal Law because of the Family Court order. On this appeal, he contends that because of the exemption for married men, the statutes for rape in the first degree (Penal Law, § 130.35) and sodomy in the first degree (Penal Law, § 130.50), violate the equal protection clause of the Federal Constitution (U.S. Const., 14th Amdt.). The defendant also contends that the rape statute violates equal protection because only men, and not women, can be prosecuted under it.

I.

Defendant Mario Liberta and Denise Liberta were married in 1978. Shortly after the birth of their son, in October of that year, Mario began to beat Denise. In early 1980 Denise brought a proceeding in the Family Court in Erie County seeking protection from the defendant. On April 30, 1980 a temporary order of protection was issued to her by the Family Court. Under this order, the defendant was to move out and remain away from the family home, and stay away from Denise. The order provided that the defendant could visit with his son once each weekend.

On the weekend of March 21, 1981, Mario, who was then living in a motel, did not visit his son. On Tuesday, March 24, 1981 he called Denise to ask if he could visit his son on that day. Denise would not allow the defendant to come to her house, but she did agree to allow him to pick up their son and her and take them both back to his motel after being assured that a friend of his would be with them at all times. The defendant and his friend picked up Denise and their son and the four of them drove to defendant's motel.

When they arrived at the motel the friend left. As soon as only Mario, Denise, and their son were alone in the motel room, Mario attacked Denise, threatened to kill her, and forced her to perform fellatio on him and to engage in sexual intercourse with him. The son was in the

---

186. Estrich, supra note 26, at 101.

room during the entire episode, and the defendant forced Denise to tell their son to watch what the defendant was doing to her.

The defendant allowed Denise and their son to leave shortly after the incident. Denise, after going to her parents' home, went to a hospital to be treated for scratches on her neck and bruises on her head and back, all inflicted by her husband. She also went to the police station, and on the next day she swore out a felony complaint against the defendant. On July 15, 1981 the defendant was indicted for rape in the first degree and sodomy in the first degree.

II.

Section 130.35 of the Penal Law provides in relevant part that "A male is guilty of rape in the first degree when he engages in sexual intercourse with a female * * * by forcible compulsion". "Female", for purposes of the rape statute, is defined as "any female person who is not married to the actor" (Penal Law, § 130.00, subd. 4). Section 130.50 of the Penal Law provides in relevant part that "a person is guilty of sodomy in the first degree when he engages in deviate sexual intercourse with another person * * * by forcible compulsion". "Deviate sexual intercourse" is defined as "sexual conduct between persons not married to each other consisting of contact between the penis and the anus, the mouth and penis, or the mouth and the vulva" (Penal Law, § 130.00, subd. 2). Thus, due to the "not married" language in the definitions of "female" and "deviate sexual intercourse", there is a "marital exemption" for both forcible rape and forcible sodomy. The marital exemption itself, however, has certain exceptions. For purposes of the rape and sodomy statutes, a husband and wife are considered to be "not married" if at the time of the sexual assault they "are living apart * * * pursuant to a valid and effective: (i) order issued by a court of competent jurisdiction which by its terms or in its effect requires such living apart, or (ii) decree or judgment of separation, or (iii) written agreement of separation" (Penal Law, § 130.00, subd. 4).

Defendant moved to dismiss the indictment, asserting that because he and Denise were still married at the time of the incident he came within the "marital exemption" to both rape and sodomy. The People opposed the motion, contending that the temporary order of protection required Mario and Denise to live apart, and they in fact were living apart, and thus were "not married" for purposes of the statutes. The trial court granted the defendant's motion and dismissed the indictment, concluding that the temporary order of protection did not require Mario and Denise to live apart from each other, but instead required only that he remain away from her, and that therefore the "marital exemption" applied.

On appeal by the People, the Appellate Division, 90 A.D.2d 681, 455 N.Y.S.2d 882, reversed the trial court, reinstated the indictment, and remanded the case for trial. The Appellate Division held that a Family Court order of protection is within the scope of "[an] order * * * which by its terms or in its effect requires such living apart" even though it is directed only at a husband, and thus found that Mario and Denise were "not married" for purposes of the statute at the time of the incident.

The defendant was then convicted of rape in the first degree and sodomy in the first degree and the conviction was affirmed by the Appellate Division, 100 A.D.2d 741, 473 N.Y.S.2d 636. Defendant asserts on this appeal that the temporary order of protection is not the type of order which enables a court to treat him and Denise as "not married" and that thus he is within the marital exemption. Defendant next asserts, assuming that because of the Family Court order he is treated just as any unmarried male would be, that he cannot be convicted of either rape in the first degree or sodomy in the first degree because both statutes are unconstitutional. Specifically, he contends that both statutes violate equal protection because they burden some, but not all males (all but those within the "marital exemption"), and that the rape statute also violates equal protection for burdening only men, and not women. The lower courts rejected the defendant's constitutional arguments, finding that neither statute violated the equal protection clause in the Fourteenth Amendment. Although we affirm the conviction of the defendant, we do not agree with the constitutional analysis of the lower courts and instead conclude that the marital and gender exemptions must be read out of the statutes prohibiting forcible rape and sodomy.

III.

We first address the defendant's argument that, despite the order of protection, he was within the "marital exemption" to rape and sodomy and thus could not be prosecuted for either crime. Until 1978, the marital exemption applied as long as the marriage still legally existed. In 1978, the Legislature expanded the definition of "not married" to include those cases where the husband and wife were living apart pursuant to either a court order "which by its terms or in its effect requires such living apart" or a decree, judgment, or written agreement of separation. We agree with the Appellate Division that the order of protection in the present case falls squarely within the first of these situations.

The legislative memorandum submitted with the original version of the 1978 amendment, after referring to the situations brought within the scope of "not married", stated: "In each of the alternatives set forth in this bill, there must be documentary evidence of a settled and mutual intention to dissolve the marital relationship, or a court determination that the spouses should, for the well-being of one or both, live apart."

Although the language of the amendment was subsequently changed to the form in which it was enacted, this legislative memorandum was submitted with the final version of the bill. In addition to this clear statement of legislative intent, the plain language of the statute indicates that an order of protection is within the meaning of an order "which by its terms or in its effect requires the spouses to live apart". This language would be virtually meaningless if it did not encompass an order of protection, as the statute separately provides for the other obvious situation where a court order would require spouses to live apart, i.e., where there is a decree or judgment of separation.

Accordingly, the defendant was properly found to have been statutorily "not married" to Denise at the time of the rape.

IV.

The defendant's constitutional challenges to the rape and sodomy statutes are premised on his being considered "not married" to Denise and are the same challenges as could be made by any unmarried male convicted under these statutes. The defendant's claim is that both statutes violate equal protection because they are underinclusive classifications which burden him, but not others similarly situated. A litigant has standing to raise this claim even though he does not contend that under no circumstances could the burden of the statute be imposed upon him. This rule of standing applies as well to a defendant in a criminal prosecution who, while conceding that it is within the power of a State to make criminal the behavior covered by a statute, asserts that the statute he is prosecuted under violates equal protection because it burdens him but not others. Thus, defendant's constitutional claims are properly before this court.

A.   The Marital Exemption

As noted above, under the Penal Law a married man ordinarily cannot be convicted of forcibly raping or sodomizing his wife. This is the so-called marital exemption for rape. Although a marital exemption was not explicit in earlier rape statutes treatise stated that a man could not be guilty of raping his wife. The assumption, even before the marital exemption was codified, that a man could not be guilty of raping his wife, is traceable to a statement made by the 17th century English jurist Lord Hale, who wrote: "[T]he husband cannot be guilty of a rape committed by himself upon his lawful wife, for by their mutual matrimonial consent and contract the wife hath given up herself in this kind unto her husband, which she cannot retract." Although Hale cited no authority for his statement it was relied on by State Legislatures which enacted rape statutes with a marital exemption and by courts which established a common-law exemption for husbands.

The first American case to recognize the marital exemption was decided in 1857 by the Supreme Judicial Court of Massachusetts, which stated in dictum that it would always be a defense to rape to show marriage to the victim. Decisions to the same effect by other courts followed, usually with no rationale or authority cited other than Hale's implied consent view. In New York, a 1922 decision noted the marital exemption in the Penal Law and stated that it existed "on account of the matrimonial consent which [the wife] has given, and which she cannot retract."

Presently, over 40 States still retain some form of marital exemption for rape. While the marital exemption is subject to an equal protection challenge, because it classifies unmarried men differently than married men, the equal protection clause does not prohibit a State from making classifications, provided the statute does not arbitrarily burden a particular group of individuals. Where a statute draws a distinction based upon marital status, the classification must be reasonable and must be based upon "some ground of difference that rationally explains the different treatment."

We find that there is no rational basis for distinguishing between marital rape and nonmarital rape. The various rationales which have been asserted in defense of the exemption are either based upon archaic notions about the consent and property rights incident to marriage or are simply unable to withstand even the slightest scrutiny. We therefore declare the marital exemption for rape in the New York statute to be unconstitutional.

Lord Hale's notion of an irrevocable implied consent by a married woman to sexual intercourse has been cited most frequently in support of the marital exemption. Any argument based on a supposed consent, however, is untenable. Rape is not simply a sexual act to which one party does not consent. Rather, it is a degrading, violent act which violates the bodily integrity of the victim and frequently causes severe, long-lasting physical and psychic harm. To ever imply consent to such an act is irrational and absurd. Other than in the context of rape statutes, marriage has never been viewed as giving a husband the right to coerced intercourse on demand. Certainly, then, a marriage license should not be viewed as a license for a husband to forcibly rape his wife with impunity. A married woman has the same right to control her own body as does an unmarried woman. If a husband feels "aggrieved" by his wife's refusal to engage in sexual intercourse, he should seek relief in the courts governing domestic relations, not in "violent or forceful self-help."

The other traditional justifications for the marital exemption were the common-law doctrines that a woman was the property of her husband and that the legal existence of the woman was "incorporated and consolidated into that of the husband." Both these doctrines, of course, have long been rejected in this State. Indeed, "[n]owhere in the common-law world—[or] in any modern society—is a woman regarded as chattel or demeaned by denial of a separate legal identity and the dignity associated with recognition as a whole human being." Because the traditional justifications for the marital exemption no longer have any validity, other arguments have been advanced in its defense. The first of these recent rationales, which is stressed by the People in this case, is that the marital exemption protects against governmental intrusion into marital privacy and promotes reconciliation of the spouses, and thus that elimination of the exemption would be disruptive to marriages. While protecting marital privacy and encouraging reconciliation are legitimate State interests, there is no rational relation between allowing a husband to forcibly rape his wife and these interests. The marital exemption simply does not further marital privacy because this right of privacy protects consensual acts, not violent sexual assaults. Just as a husband cannot invoke a right of marital privacy to escape liability for beating his wife, he cannot justifiably rape his wife under the guise of a right to privacy.

Similarly, it is not tenable to argue that elimination of the marital exemption would disrupt marriages because it would discourage reconciliation. Clearly, it is the violent act of rape and not the subsequent attempt of the wife to seek protection through the criminal justice system which "disrupts" a marriage. Moreover, if the marriage has already reached the point where intercourse is accomplished by violent assault it is doubtful that there is anything left to reconcile. This, of course, is particularly true if the wife is willing to bring criminal charges against her husband which could result in a lengthy jail sentence.

Another rationale sometimes advanced in support of the marital exemption is that marital rape would be a difficult crime to prove. A related argument is that allowing such prosecutions could lead to fabricated complaints by "vindictive" wives. The difficulty of proof argument is based on the problem of showing lack of consent. Proving lack of consent, however, is often the most difficult part of any rape prosecution, particularly where the rapist and the victim had a prior relationship. Similarly, the possibility that married women will fabricate complaints would seem to be no greater than the possibility of unmarried women doing so. The criminal justice system, with all of its built-in safeguards, is presumed to be capable of handling any false complaints. Indeed, if the possibility of fabricated complaints were a basis for not criminalizing behavior which would otherwise be sanctioned, virtually all crimes other than homicides would go unpunished.

The final argument in defense of the marital exemption is that marital rape is not as serious an offense as other rape and is thus adequately dealt with by the possibility of prosecution under criminal statutes, such as assault statutes, which provide for less severe punishment. The fact that rape statutes exist, however, is a recognition that the harm caused by a forcible rape is different, and more severe, than the harm caused by an ordinary assault. "Short of homicide, [rape] is the 'ultimate violation of self.' " Under the Penal Law, assault is generally a misdemeanor unless either the victim suffers "serious physical injury" or a deadly weapon or dangerous instrument is used (Penal Law, §§ 120.00, 120.05, 120.10). Thus, if the defendant had been living with Denise at the time he forcibly raped and sodomized her he probably could not have been charged with a felony, let alone a felony with punishment equal to that for rape in the first degree.

Moreover, there is no evidence to support the argument that marital rape has less severe consequences than other rape. On the contrary, numerous studies have shown that marital rape is frequently quite violent and generally has *more* severe, traumatic effects on the victim than other rape.

Among the recent decisions in this country addressing the marital exemption, only one court has concluded that there is a rational basis for it (see *People v. Brown*, 632 P.2d 1025 [Col.]). We agree with the other courts which have analyzed the exemption, which have been unable to find any present justification for it. Justice Holmes wrote:

It is revolting to have no better reason for a rule of law than that so it was laid down in the time of Henry IV. It is still more revolting if the grounds upon which it was laid down have vanished long since, and the rule simply persists from blind imitation of the past (Holmes, The Path of the Law, 10 Harv.L.Rev. 457, 469).

This statement is an apt characterization of the marital exemption; it lacks a rational basis, and therefore violates the equal protection clauses of both the Federal and State Constitutions.

B.   The Exemption for Females

Under the Penal Law only males can be convicted of rape in the first degree. Insofar as the rape statute applies to acts of "sexual intercourse", which, as defined in the Penal Law (see Penal Law, § 130.00) can only occur between a male and a female, it is true that a female cannot physically rape a female and that therefore there is no denial of equal protection when punishing only males for forcibly engaging in sexual intercourse with females. The equal protection issue, however, stems from the fact that the statute applies to males who forcibly rape females but does not apply to females who forcibly rape males.

Rape statutes historically applied only to conduct by males against females, largely because the purpose behind the proscriptions was to protect the chastity of women and thus their property value to their fathers or husbands. New York's rape statute has always protected only females, and has thus applied only to males. Presently New York is one of only 10 jurisdictions that does not have a gender-neutral statute for forcible rape.

A statute which treats males and females differently violates equal protection unless the classification is substantially related to the achievement of an important governmental objective. This test applies whether the statute discriminates against males or against females. The People bear the burden of showing both the existence of an important objective and the substantial relationship between the discrimination in the statute and that objective. This burden is not met in the present case, and therefore the gender exemption also renders the statute unconstitutional.

The first argument advanced by the People in support of the exemption for females is that because only females can become pregnant the State may constitutionally differentiate between forcible rapes of females and forcible rapes of males. This court and the United States Supreme Court have upheld statutes which subject males to criminal liability for engaging in sexual intercourse with underage females without the converse being true. The rationale behind these decisions was that the primary purpose of such "statutory rape" laws is to protect against the harm caused by teenage pregnancies, there being no need to provide the same protection to young males.

There is no evidence, however, that preventing pregnancies is a primary purpose of the statute prohibiting forcible rape, nor does such a purpose seem likely. Rather, the very fact that the statute proscribes "forcible compulsion" shows that its overriding purpose is to protect a woman from an unwanted, forcible, and often violent sexual intrusion into her body. Thus, due to the different purposes behind forcible rape laws and "statutory" (consensual) rape laws, the cases upholding the gender discrimination in the latter are not decisive with respect to the former, and the People cannot meet their burden here by simply stating that only females can become pregnant.

The People also claim that the discrimination is justified because a female rape victim "faces the probability of medical, sociological, and psychological problems unique to her gender". This same argument, when advanced in support of the discrimination in the statutory rape laws, was rejected by this court in *People v. Whidden*, and it is no more convincing in the present case. "[A]n ' "archaic and overbroad" general-ization' * * * which is evidently grounded in long-standing stereotypical notions of the differences between the sexes, simply cannot serve as a legitimate rationale for a penal provision that is addressed only to adult males."

Finally, the People suggest that a gender-neutral law for forcible rape is unnecessary, and that therefore the present law is constitutional, because a woman either cannot actually rape a man or such attacks, if possible, are extremely rare. Although the "physiologically impossible" argument has been accepted by several courts, it is simply wrong. The argument is premised on the notion that a man cannot engage in sexual intercourse unless he is sexually aroused, and if he is aroused then he is consenting to intercourse. "Sexual intercourse" however, "occurs upon any penetration, however slight" (Penal Law, § 130.00); this degree of contact can be achieved without a male being aroused and thus without his consent.

As to the "infrequency" argument, while forcible sexual assaults by females upon males are undoubtedly less common than those by males upon females this numerical disparity cannot by itself make the gender discrimination constitutional. Women may well be responsible for a far lower number of all serious crimes than are men, but such a disparity would not make it permissible for the State to punish only men who commit, for example, robbery.

To meet their burden of showing that a gender-based law is substan-tially related to an important governmental objective the People must set forth an " 'exceedingly persuasive justification' " for the classifica-tion, which requires, among other things, a showing that the gender-based law serves the governmental objective better than would a gender-neutral law. The fact that the act of a female forcibly raping a male may be a difficult or rare occurrence does not mean that the gender exemption satisfies the constitutional test. A gender-neutral law would indisputably better serve, even if only marginally, the objective of deterring and punishing forcible sexual assaults. The only persons "benefitted" by the gender exemption are females who forcibly rape males. As the Supreme Court has stated, "[a] gender-based classification which, as compared to a gender-neutral one, generates additional benefits only for those it has no reason to prefer cannot survive equal protection scrutiny."

Accordingly, we find that section 130.35 of the Penal Law violates equal protection because it exempts females from criminal liability for forcible rape.

V.

Having found that the statutes for rape in the first degree and sodomy in the first degree are unconstitutionally underinclusive, the remaining issue is the appropriate remedy for these equal protection violations. When a statute is constitutionally defective because of under-inclusion, a court may either strike the statute, and thus make it applicable to nobody, or extend the coverage of the statute to those formerly excluded. Accordingly, the unconstitutionality of one part of a criminal statute does not necessarily render the entire statute void.

This court's task is to discern what course the Legislature would have chosen to follow if it had foreseen our conclusions as to underinclusiveness. As Judge Cardozo wrote over 50 years ago, " 'The question is in every case whether the Legislature, if partial invalidity had been foreseen, would have wished the statute to be enforced with the invalid part exscinded, or rejected altogether.' " These principles of severance apply as well where elimination of an invalid exemption will impose burdens on those not formerly burdened by the statute and where the exemption is part of a criminal statute.

The question then is whether the Legislature would prefer to have statutes which cover forcible rape and sodomy, with no exemption for married men who rape or sodomize their wives and no exception made for females who rape males, or instead to have no statutes proscribing forcible rape and sodomy. In any case where a court must decide whether to sever an exemption or instead declare an entire statute a nullity it must look at the importance of the statute, the significance of the exemption within the over-all statutory scheme, and the effects of striking down the statute. Forcible sexual assaults have historically been treated as serious crimes and certainly remain so today. Statutes prohibiting such behavior are of the utmost importance, and to declare such statutes a nullity would have a disastrous effect on the public interest and safety. The inevitable conclusion is that the Legislature would prefer to eliminate the exemptions and thereby preserve the statutes. Accordingly we choose the remedy of striking the marital exemption from sections 130.35 and 130.50 of the Penal Law and the gender exemption from section 130.35 of the Penal Law, so that it is now the law of this State that any person who engages in sexual intercourse or deviate sexual intercourse with any other person by forcible compulsion is guilty of either rape in the first degree or sodomy in the first degree. Because the statutes under which the defendant was convicted are not being struck down, his conviction is affirmed.

Though our decision does not "create a crime," it does, of course, enlarge the scope of two criminal statutes. We recognize that a court should be reluctant to expand criminal statutes, due to the danger of usurping the role of the Legislature, but in this case overriding policy concerns dictate our following such a course in light of the catastrophic effect that striking down the statutes and thus creating a hiatus would have. Courts in other States have in numerous cases applied these same principles in eliminating an unconstitutional exception from a criminal statute and thereby enlarging the scope of the statute. The decision most similar factually to the present one comes from the Alaska Supreme Court in *Plas v. State*, 598 P.2d 966 (Alaska). That court addressed an equal protection challenge by a female prostitute to a statute which criminalized prostitution, and defined it as a female offering her body for sexual intercourse for hire. The court agreed with the defendant that the statute violated equal protection because it covered only females, but chose to remedy this underinclusion by striking the definition, thereby expanding the statute to cover any person who engaged in prostitution, and affirmed her conviction.

The defendant cannot claim that our decision to retain the rape and sodomy statutes, and thereby affirm his conviction, denies him due process of the law. The due process clause of the Fourteenth Amendment requires that an accused have had fair warning at the time of his conduct that such conduct was made criminal by the State. Defendant did not come within any of the exemptions which we have stricken, and thus his conduct was covered by the statutes as they existed at the time of his attack on Denise.

Neither can it be said that by the affirmance of his conviction the defendant is deprived of a constitutionally protected right to equal protection. The remedy chosen by our opinion is to extend the coverage of the provisions for forcible rape and sodomy to all those to whom these provisions can constitutionally be applied. While this remedy does treat the defendant differently than, for example, a married man who, while living with his wife, raped her prior to this decision, the distinction is rational inasmuch as it is justified by the limitations imposed on our remedy by the notice requirements of the due process clause (U.S. Const., 14th Amdt.), and the prohibition against *ex post facto* laws (U.S. Const., art. I, § 10). Thus, for purposes of choosing the proper remedy, the defendant is simply not similarly situated to those persons who were not within the scope of the statutes as they existed prior to our decision.

To reverse the defendant's conviction would mean that all those persons now awaiting trial for forcible rape or sodomy would be entitled to dismissal of the indictment. Indeed if we were to reverse, no person arrested for forcible rape or sodomy prior to the date of this decision could be prosecuted for that offense, and every person already convicted of forcible rape or sodomy who raised the equal protection challenge would be entitled to have the conviction vacated. As the equal protection clause does not require us to reach such a result, we decline to do so.

Accordingly, the order of the Appellate Division should be affirmed.

CASSANDRA M. DELAMOTHE, *LIBERTA* REVISITED: A CALL TO REPEAL THE MARITAL EXEMPTION FOR ALL SEX OFFENSES IN NEW YORK'S PENAL LAW

23 Fordham URB. L. J. 868–883 (1996).

B. *Barriers to Prosecuting Marital Rape in the Aftermath of Liberta*

Although New York's highest court unequivocally declared that marital rape is a crime in New York, many factors prevent this crime from being adequately addressed. First, courts do not uniformly agree with *Liberta*, most notably the U.S. Court of Appeals for the Second Circuit, which failed to follow the *Liberta* holding on the unconstitutionality of the marital rape exemption. Second, case law suggests that the courts ambiguously define the required element of "force" in spousal rape cases. Third, because of credibility and proof problems, prosecutors often choose not to prosecute spousal rape cases. Fourth, marital rape prosecutions often fail to convict because of an entrenched gender bias in the judiciary, documented by the 1986 New York Task Force on Women in the Courts.

1. *Federal Court Equivocation*

The defendant in *People v. Liberta*, Mario Liberta, filed a *habeas* petition in federal court, seeking to overturn his conviction. The case, *Liberta v. Kelly*,[73] reached the Second Circuit, which declined to find the marital rape exemption unconstitutional.[74] Liberta argued that the New York Court of Appeals denied him due process when it struck down the marital rape exemption, in effect, creating a new statute, while affirming his convictions. The Second Circuit did not address the constitutionality of the marital rape exemption, the privacy issue, or any of the modern justifications for the exemption as addressed by the New York Court of Appeals. Instead, in *dicta*, the court noted that the Penal Law's "distinction between married men who are subject to protective orders and those who are not 'rationally furthers a legitimate state purpose.'" The rational basis is that those husbands subject to orders of protection are more dangerous than those who are not subject to orders of protection. The court further noted the availability of coercion statutes to prosecute

---

73. 657 F. Supp. 1260 (W.D.N.Y.1987), aff'd, 839 F.2d 77 (2d Cir.1988), cert. denied, 488 U.S. 832 (1988).

74. 839 F.2d at 77. * * *

husbands who raped their wives. Nonetheless, the Second Circuit affirmed Liberta's conviction, and found that he had received due process.

A fair reading of the Second Circuit in *Liberta* is that the court simply did not feel it necessary to consider the constitutionality of the marital exemption. The court's focus was narrower: whether it was appropriate for the State to single out those like Liberta, who were subject to protection orders. Nonetheless, the Second Circuit did not go out of its way to embrace the New York court's facial invalidation of the exemption. This has caused confusion among lower courts and scholars, and has unfortunately led to continued reliance by some courts on the marital exemption, at least where the defendant is not subject to an order of protection.

Despite the New York Court of Appeals' decision to strike down the marital rape exemption, courts continue to apply the exemption, even when evidence of force or physical injury exists. *Liberta* is subject to narrow construction since the Court of Appeals addressed the marital rape exemption only within the context of first degree rape and first degree sodomy. This narrow construction has caused procedural confusion among lower courts with respect to *Liberta's* application to other sex offenses. Courts have been forced to decide, based on the facts of each case, whether the marital exemption is applicable.

For example, in a recent unpublished opinion, a prosecutor presented medical evidence that a husband had raped his wife, seriously injured her during several attacks, and charged him with sexual misconduct. Nevertheless, relying upon the marital exemption, the judge dismissed the charges. According to the prosecutor, the judge narrowly construed the *Liberta* decision to apply to rape and not sexual misconduct, a misdemeanor under the Penal Law.

In another case, a jury acquitted a man of the rape and sodomy of his common-law wife after the trial court instructed the jury that a rape "victim" was "any female not married to the actor."[89] In a dissenting opinion, one justice inferred that the jury charge on the issue of rape probably led the jury to acquit.

2. *A Definition of "Force"*

The common-law approach to rape focused not on the offender's forceful conduct but on the victim's lack of consent. A victim had to show that she resisted her attacker to the "utmost" to prove that she did not consent to unwanted sex. Although force, or the threat of force, was generally an element of the crime of rape, cases often turned on the thorny issue of the victim's lack of consent.

The authors of the Model Penal Code, in drafting the Code's proposed sex crimes laws, attempted to shift the emphasis from the victim's lack of consent to the offender's forceful conduct. The New York Legislature followed the Model Penal Code's lead, repealing the common law "resistance" requirement in 1982. Despite the shift in focus from

---

89. People v. Guzman, 559 N.Y.S.2d   550, 552 (App. Div. 1990). * * *.

the victim's to the offender's behavior, most rape statutes still require both elements of nonconsent and force.

Some have argued that the standard of force used in rape cases is a standard defined by men. This male standard offers the predominantly male legal system little insight into the trauma suffered by rape victims.

The element of force is generally more difficult for the state to prove in nonstranger rape cases. In marital and acquaintance rapes, a defendant is usually acquitted unless his conduct was unquestionably brutal.

Some commentators advocate a standard based solely on the victim's nonconsent. Undoubtedly, a standard of force for rape based solely on the victim's lack of consent presents unique problems in marital rape cases.[103] One commentator notes that reformers have "characterize[d] as marital rape occasions when the wife is 'coerced' into unwanted sex by threats to leave, to cut off her source of money or to humiliate her in some way."[104] He suggests that reformers who advocate characterizing rape as any intercourse to which the wife does not expressly consent, shift the focus from an act of violence to one of "unwanted sex." Critics must distinguish between the stereotypical scenario in which a wife first declines to have sex and later indulges her husband, and those situations in which women suffer from real harm and violence. The legal system can, however, effectively protect victims without opening the floodgates to frivolous litigation. In *People v. Naylor*,[109] for example, a jury convicted an estranged husband of sexual abuse in the third degree after he sexually assaulted his sleeping wife. Although the act involved no force, the court found that the victim's lack of consent was sufficient to constitute a crime.

3. *Prosecutorial Discretion and Marital Rape*

"Prosecutorial discretion" refers to a prosecutor's power to decide whether to seek a conviction in a given case. Several factors might influence a prosecutor's decision not to prosecute a marital rape case. Those factors include the victim's reluctance to proceed, lack of corroboration, victim credibility, and public skepticism about the crime of marital rape. When prosecutors continually refuse to prosecute marital rape cases, law enforcement concludes that these acts are not worth the time and effort required to make arrests. Moreover, prosecutorial reluctance to proceed with these cases diminishes judicial exposure to the recurrence of spousal rape.

Prosecutors often choose not to file charges in marital rape cases because the victim refuses to testify against her husband. Although a victim's reluctance to testify is generally a problem in most rape cases, marital rape victims are even more reluctant to proceed for many reasons. Unsuccessful prosecution, they often assume, will leave them living unprotected with an angry spouse. Many women depend on their

---

103. See John D. Harman, Consent, Harm, and Marital Rape, 22 J. Fam. L. 423, 429 (1983–84) * * *.

104. Id. at 430.

109. 609 N.Y.S.2d 954.

husbands for financial support. Marital rape prosecutions also often founder because the victims themselves fail to perceive marital rape as a crime.

Victim credibility also persuades many prosecutors not to prosecute marital rape cases. The general suspicion is that vindictiveness motivates victims who seek prosecution. In acquaintance rape cases, which account for more than eighty percent of rape cases, the defense focuses on the victim's credibility. Without corroborating evidence, a prosecutor's decision to press charges becomes complicated. Prosecutors often require a greater amount of evidence in cases involving victims of domestic violence than in those cases involving violence between strangers. Marital rape, like domestic violence, rarely occurs in the presence of witnesses. Prosecutors face the difficult task of convincing a jury that a rape occurred. If additional evidence boosts the victim's credibility, the prosecutor might then proceed.

The public perception that marital rape is less severe than nonmarital rape also factors into a prosecutor's decision not to go forward with the case. Many people differentiate between marital and nonmarital rape, and would more likely accept a law criminalizing marital rape that punished it less severely than stranger rape. Many who would stop short of invoking Hale's notion of "implied consent" to rape would nevertheless consider a marital rape victim who remains with an abusive spouse, to have taken some responsibility for her situation, and are accordingly less sympathetic to her plight than to that of stranger rape victims. Although marital rapes are easier to investigate because victims can readily identify their assailants, victims undoubtedly face a more difficult process in the criminal justice system because of public attitudes.

4. Gender Bias in New York's Courts

Judges should decide cases without bias or prejudice. In 1986, however, the New York Task Force on Women in the Courts ("Task Force") concluded that women litigants, especially poor and minority women, lacked full access to the courts, encountered judges and juries that questioned their credibility, and faced a judiciary that had no knowledge of issues that were important to women. The Task Force concluded that gender bias pervades New York's court system.

Task forces across the country discovered that gender bias undermines women's credibility. "[B]oth women and men perceive females, as a group, as less credible than males." In rape cases, the victim's credibility suffered if she knew the rapist. In New York, for example, juries were found to be extremely skeptical of the alleged rape victim's credibility. This led juries to make decisions, not based wholly on the merits of the case, but on prejudicial views about sex roles and women's subordination to men in marriage. Although thousands of battered women seek protection from abuse each year, they face courts that trivialize the abusive situation.

The New York Task Force also found that judges lacked an understanding of the nature of domestic violence. Some judges even required visible physical injuries before granting orders of protection to victims of spousal abuse. This lack of understanding, coupled with the victim's psychological state, prevented women from receiving the relief they sought.

Prosecutors continue to treat rape victims as if they are on trial. Judges allow improper questioning of the victim's sexual behavior and lifestyle. The New York Task Force recommended that judges understand the difference between cross-examination that protects defendants' rights and improper questioning and harassment of rape victims.

Community bias against rape victims translates into juror bias in the courtroom. The defense attorney's stereotypical portrayal of the victim often influences jurors. Moreover, judges occasionally allow their own biases to appear in a jury charge.

To ensure that New York's marital rape victims receive the full protection *Liberta* affords, courts must eliminate the gender bias that pervades the legal system. Gender bias affects not only judicial decisions but the treatment of domestic violence and rape victims in the courts. Gender bias impedes the efficacy of major law reforms affecting rights for women. Cultural stereotypes that sanction abuse and treat wives as chattel influence judicial decisions. Similarly, bias against domestic violence victims reflects the historical treatment of women as property. Although rape laws that historically discouraged the prosecution of rape offenders have changed, bias against victims, especially victims of marital rape, remains. One way to ensure that judges do not rely on the statutory language to dismiss sexual assault cases involving married persons, is to explicitly repeal the marital exemption for all sex offenses.

GARTH E. HIRE, HOLDING HUSBANDS AND LOVERS ACCOUNTABLE FOR RAPE: ELIMINATING THE "DEFENDANT" EXCEPTION OF RAPE SHIELD LAWS

5 S. Cal. Rev. L. & Women's Stud. 591–592, 600–608 (1996).

I. Introduction

Almost one-third of all women who are victims of rape are attacked by someone they know. These women, victims of nonstranger rape, face many obstacles in seeking justice against an attacker who is, or was, very likely their husband or lover. These women will face juries that are prejudiced against victims whom they believe engaged in contributory behavior, such as dating. They will be viewed as victims of a less serious crime because their attacker was their husband or lover rather than a stranger. They will encounter prosecutors who are reluctant to bring charges. Finally, because these women had a prior relationship with the men who are charged with raping them, they are much less likely to see him convicted of rape.

The "defendant" exception to rape shield laws is one of the barriers to prosecuting and convicting a man of rape when that man is the husband or lover of his victim. While rape shield laws preclude a defendant from admitting the victim's prior sexual history with third persons to prove her consent, the defendant exception allows the court to admit such evidence when the victim's prior sexual conduct is with the defendant. This Article recognizes that this defendant exception is a serious obstacle to the successful prosecution and conviction of rapists who are the husband or lover of their victims, and proposes the elimination of this exception.

* * *

IV. Eliminating the Defendant Exception

There are several reasons to eliminate the defendant exception of rape shield laws. First, evidence of the victim's prior sexual conduct with the defendant is not relevant to whether she consented on the occasion in question. Second, even if such evidence is relevant, it must be excluded because it poses a serious danger of unfair prejudice. Third, eliminating the defendant exception advances the goals of rape shield legislation.

A. A Woman's Prior Consent Is Irrelevant to the Existence of Her Present Consent

Evidence is relevant when it tends "to make the existence of any fact that is of consequence to the determination of the action more probable or less probable than it would be without the evidence." Thus, in the context of the defendant exception, the victim's prior sexual conduct must make it more probable that she consented on the occasion in question in order to be relevant. This is simply not the case.

The fact that a woman consented to sexual intercourse with a man in the past does not make it more likely that she consented to have sex with that same man at a later time. Although proponents of the defendant exception argue that such prior sexual conduct does make it more likely that a victim consented on the occasion in question, their arguments employ the same archaic stereotypes and invidious inferences used to justify the now-prohibited admission of a victim's prior sexual history with third persons. Specifically, these arguments in favor of relevance fail because they make critically incorrect assumptions concerning the nature of a woman's sexuality. These flaws seriously weaken the claim that prior sexual conduct with the defendant is relevant to consent at a later time.

1. Women Are Not Slaves to Their Emotions

Proponents of the defendant exception argue that when a woman consents to sex she evinces an emotion toward her partner that would make it likely that she would allow him to have sex with her again. This argument fails because it makes two crucially incorrect assumptions. First, it assumes that a woman must be emotionally involved with someone to have sex with him. This is not true. Many women simply choose to have sex because they enjoy it physically and attach little or no emotional significance to it. Second, the argument also assumes that if a woman does show emotion toward a man during a sexual encounter, that this emotion will not only endure until a future sexual encounter with that man, but also that this emotion will cause the woman to consent to sex at a later date. This also is not true. Women are thinking, intelligent and rational beings capable of making decisions based on factors other than their emotions, or even in spite of them. Women are not bound by their emotions, nor do they require them to engage in consensual sexual intercourse.

Even if a woman did feel love toward a man she later claims has raped her, the presence of this emotion during a previous sexual encounter does not make it more likely that she consented on the occasion in question. This is because her expression of love during the previous encounter is evidence of nothing more than the emotion that she felt toward him at that time. More importantly, even if the emotion of love was still present on the occasion in question, its presence bears no relation to the existence of her consent. Women do not automatically consent to have sex simply because they love someone. Being in love with someone, and consenting to have sex with him, are not as integrally related as some people might presume. Many women choose not to have sex with the men they love, and some of those men force them to do so anyway.

2. *Past Lack of Force Is Not Relevant to Present Lack of Force*

Proponents of the defendant exception also argue that prior consensual sexual conduct is relevant because it increases the likelihood that a man who was able to persuade a woman to have sex once is unlikely to have to force her to have sex again. The crucial error of this argument is its focus on the one thing that is least relevant to whether or not a woman consented to sex: a man's power of persuasion. That a man was successful in persuading a woman to have sex on an earlier occasion does not mean that his tactics would again prove successful. Moreover, a man who was able to persuade a woman to have sex on an earlier occasion is not necessarily a man who would not resort to force on a later occasion if his normal strategy of obtaining consent were to fail. In fact, his failure to elicit the woman's consent a second time may anger and insult him to the point that he would take through force what he previously obtained through persuasion.

3. *A Woman's Mindset Is Not Static*

Supporters of the defendant exception also argue that a victim's prior sexual conduct with the defendant is relevant to present consent based on the assumption that the woman's state of mind is unchanged from the occasion on which she originally consented. This argument misses the obvious reality that a woman's state of mind can, and often does, change. The fact that a woman's state of mind indicated a willingness to have sex with a particular person on one occasion does not make it more probable that her state of mind was the same on a later occasion. Simply put, evidence of a mindset of consent on one occasion cannot be presumed to prove a mindset of consent at a later occasion just because the two occasions involve the same man. To argue otherwise is to invoke the very stereotypes and inferences that lead to and supported the admission of a woman's prior sexual history with third persons.

   4. Arguing the Relevance of Prior Consent: Archaic Stereotypes and Invidious Inferences

   The arguments in favor of the relevance of a victim's prior sexual conduct with a defendant to prove consent on a particular occasion fail because they are based on the same archaic stereotypes and invidious inferences about women that instigated the enactment of rape shield laws in the first place. The utility of the defendant exception depends on the archaic notion that when a woman has sex with a particular man, she impliedly gives consent to have sex with him at a later time. In that regard, the reasons for admitting evidence of prior sexual conduct under the defendant exception are no different from the reasoning employed in admitting a woman's prior sexual history with third persons to prove consent.

   Before rape shield laws were enacted, a defendant could admit a victim's prior sexual history with third persons because her prior consent to sex was considered relevant, in that it indicated an ever-present willingness to have sex with men. Similarly, by arguing that a woman's prior consent increases the likelihood of the existence of present consent, advocates of the defendant exception imply that a woman's prior consent also indicates an ever-present willingness to have sex. The only difference between this assumption and those now prohibited by rape shield laws is that the willingness applies to a single individual rather than to men in general. To characterize a woman as "ever-willing" to have sex, regardless of the number of men it applies to, is insulting and inaccurate.

   Proponents of the defendant exception insist, however, that their reasoning is different from that employed by those who supported admission of a victim's prior sexual history with third persons. Yet the deficiency of the reasoning is virtually identical to that of the earlier regime; the inference that a woman who consents to sex once is more likely to do so again by virtue of her earlier consent is no less invidious when it is drawn from her sexual encounter with one man than when it is drawn from her unrelated sexual encounters with three men. A woman's prior consent simply does not constitute permission to have sex with her on a later occasion.

   5. Limited Instances Where Prior Consent Could Be Relevant

   There are several contexts where the victim's prior sexual conduct with the defendant should be admitted to avoid abridging his constitutional right to present a defense.

   a. History of Violent Consensual Sex: The defendant should be permitted to admit evidence of his prior sexual conduct with the victim in cases where their prior sexual conduct involved acts normally associated with non-consensual sex. Such cases, presumably rare, exist where the victim's and the defendant's prior sexual conduct included the use of weapons, restraints, physical violence or statements of resistance by the victim. The prior sexual conduct, because it is factually similar to rape, may corroborate the defendant's account of what transpired on the occasion in question, but only if it involves the same conduct as the violent conduct which the two previously engaged in consensually. Such evidence may explain the presence of physical injury or weapons, as well as the sounds of resistance. More importantly, this evidence bears heavily on the defendant's belief that the victim was consenting to his use of force.

b.　The Defendant's Reasonable Mistake of Fact: If a victim's prior consent to sex with the defendant is evidence of anything, it is evidence of the defendant's perception regarding her consent, and could thus form the basis of a mistake of fact defense. However, when a defendant employs a mistake of fact defense he admits that the victim may not have consented. Because such a defense requires establishing the reasonableness of the defendant's mistaken belief in consent, the victim's prior sexual conduct with the defendant would be relevant. This evidence would not be admitted because of its bearing on the victim's actual consent, however, and as such is beyond the scope of this Article.

c.　The Victim's Motivation: When a woman is raped by her husband or lover there is a prior relationship with her attacker, during which she may have engaged in consensual sexual conduct. However, a prior relationship and prior sexual conduct are not the same thing. While a prior relationship encompasses everything—sexual and nonsexual—which transpired between the victim and the defendant, sexual conduct only pertains to their sexual activities together. Supporters of the defendant exception argue that a victim's prior sexual conduct with the defendant might be relevant because it may be probative of the victim's motivation for bringing her charge of rape. It is certainly possible that some aspects of the couple's prior relationship—such as physical abuse, unpaid debts, property disposition, living arrangements or child custody—could be used to show bias, prejudice or a motive to lie. These issues, however, are only tenuously connected, if at all, to the couple's prior sexual conduct. Therefore, the defendant should be required to make some offer of proof that the victim's sexual conduct with the defendant specifically relates to her motivation for bringing the charges if the defendant is to be allowed to introduce evidence that would otherwise lack probative value and be highly prejudicial.

B.　Prejudicial Effect of Prior Sexual History Evidence

Even if the victim's prior sexual conduct with the defendant is relevant to the existence of her consent, eliminating the defendant exception is still necessary because sexist attitudes among judges and juries still persist. Because of these attitudes, the probative value of the victim's prior sexual conduct with the defendant would be overwhelmed by the danger of unfair prejudice and confusion of the issues. Clearly, evidence that a woman consented to have sex with a particular man on a prior occasion is equally, and probably more, prejudicial than evidence that she had sex with several different men on prior occasions. The fact that traditional stranger-rape prosecutions are so much more successful than prosecutions of rape where the victim is either a friend of, or romantically involved with, her attacker is the most glaring proof that the current system cannot be relied upon to adequately screen the victim's prior sexual conduct with the defendant.

C. Furthering the Goals of Rape Shield Laws

Eliminating the defendant exception would advance all four of the purposes behind the passage of rape shield laws. First and foremost, eliminating the exception would require recognition that a victim's prior consent to sex with the defendant has no probative value as to whether she consented to have sex with him on a later occasion. As such, this would also accomplish the first goal of rape shield laws: the exclusion of evidence of a rape victim's prior sexual history when it is irrelevant and prejudicial. The accomplishment of this goal would signal a repositioning of the evidentiary focus of a rape trial on the facts of the event in question: namely the words said, the force used and the damage done. In so doing, the elimination of the defendant exception would expand the protection provided by rape shield laws to include not just women who are raped by strangers, but also the multitude of women who are tragically raped by lovers and husbands.

The expansion of rape shield laws through the elimination of the defendant exception would also serve to advance the second purpose of rape shield laws: the protection of rape victims' privacy. While one might believe that asking a woman about her sexual life with her spouse would lack the embarrassing or painful character that questions regarding casual sexual encounters might entail, this is not necessarily the case. Confronting a rape victim with the fact that she willingly—or unwilling-ly—repeatedly had sex with the man who she now claims is a rapist, then recounting the intimate details of those sexual encounters, and then finally questioning the honesty of her claim that she did not want or consent to have sex with him on the occasion in question because of their sexual history together, could prove to be the most painful invasion of privacy.

The prospect of having to face such invasive and painful question-ing, not to mention the resulting decrease in the likelihood of a convic-tion, is part of the reason that there are so few prosecutions of nonstranger rapes. Eliminating the defendant exception decreases the chance of undergoing painful and invasive questioning and, as a result, satisfies the third goal of rape shield laws by encouraging women who have been raped by their lovers and husbands to come forward.

Finally, eliminating the defendant exception serves the fourth goal of rape shield laws by protecting, and with the force of law serving to enhance, the autonomy of women. It enables every woman to say "no" to any man, even if she has said "yes" to him in the past.

MODEL PENAL CODE, PART II. DEFINITION OF SPECIFIC CRIMES, OFFENSES INVOLVING DANGER TO THE PERSON, ARTICLE 213. SEXUAL OFFENSES

Current Through Annual Meetings of American Law Institute (5/98).

§ 213.0. DEFINITIONS.

* * *

Deviate sexual intercourse means sexual intercourse *per os* or *per anum* between human beings who are not husband and wife, and any form of sexual intercourse with an animal.

§ 213.1. RAPE AND RELATED OFFENSES.

(1) Rape. A male who has sexual intercourse with a female not his wife is guilty of rape if:

(a) he compels her to submit by force or by threat of imminent death, serious bodily injury, extreme pain or kidnapping, to be inflicted on anyone; or

(b) he has substantially impaired her power to appraise or control her conduct by administering or employing without her knowledge drugs, intoxicants or other means for the purpose of preventing resistance; or

(c) the female is unconscious; or

(d) the female is less than 10 years old.

Rape is a felony of the second degree unless (i) in the course thereof the actor inflicts serious bodily injury upon anyone, or (ii) the victim was not a voluntary social companion of the actor upon the occasion of the crime and had not previously permitted him sexual liberties, in which cases the offense is a felony of the first degree.

(2) Gross Sexual Imposition. A male who has sexual intercourse with a female not his wife commits a felony of the third degree if:

(a) he compels her to submit by any threat that would prevent resistance by a woman of ordinary resolution; or

(b) he knows that she suffers from a mental disease or defect which renders her incapable of appraising the nature of her conduct; or

(c) he knows that she is unaware that a sexual act is being committed upon her or that she submits because she mistakenly supposes that he is her husband.

§ 213.2. DEVIATE SEXUAL INTERCOURSE BY FORCE OR IMPO-SITION.

(1) By Force or Its Equivalent. A person who engages in deviate sexual intercourse with another person, or who causes another to engage in deviate sexual intercourse, commits a felony of the second degree if:

(a) he compels the other person to participate by force or by threat of imminent death, serious bodily injury, extreme pain or kidnapping, to be inflicted on anyone; or

(b) he has substantially impaired the other person's power to appraise or control his conduct, by administering or employing without the knowledge of the other person drugs, intoxicants or other means for the purpose of preventing resistance; or

(c) the other person is unconscious; or

(d) the other person is less than 10 years old.

(2) By Other Imposition. A person who engages in deviate sexual intercourse with another person, or who causes another to engage in deviate sexual intercourse, commits a felony of the third degree if:

(a) he compels the other person to participate by any threat that would prevent resistance by a person of ordinary resolution; or

(b) he knows that the other person suffers from a mental disease or defect which renders him incapable of appraising the nature of his conduct; or

(c) he knows that the other person submits because he is unaware that a sexual act is being committed upon him.

§ 213.3. CORRUPTION OF MINORS AND SEDUCTION.

(1) Offense Defined. A male who has sexual intercourse with a female not his wife, or any person who engages in deviate sexual intercourse or causes another to engage in deviate sexual intercourse, is guilty of an offense if:

(a) the other person is less than [16] years old and the actor is at least [4] years older than the other person; or

(b) the other person is less than 21 years old and the actor is his guardian or otherwise responsible for general supervision of his welfare; or

(c) the other person is in custody of law or detained in a hospital or other institution and the actor has supervisory or disciplinary authority over him; or

(d) the other person is a female who is induced to participate by a promise of marriage which the actor does not mean to perform.

(2) Grading. An offense under paragraph (a) of Subsection (1) is a felony of the third degree. Otherwise an offense under this section is a misdemeanor.

§ 213.4. SEXUAL ASSAULT.

A person who has sexual contact with another not his spouse, or causes such other to have sexual contact with him, is guilty of sexual assault, a misdemeanor, if:

(1) he knows that the contact is offensive to the other person; or

(2) he knows that the other person suffers from a mental disease or defect which renders him or her incapable of appraising the nature of his or her conduct; or

(3) he knows that the other person is unaware that a sexual act is being committed; or

(4) the other person is less than 10 years old; or

(5) he has substantially impaired the other person's power to appraise or control his or her conduct, by administering or employing without the other's knowledge drugs, intoxicants or other means for the purpose of preventing resistance; or

(6) the other person is less than [16] years old and the actor is at least [4] years older than the other person; or

(7) the other person is less than 21 years old and the actor is his guardian or otherwise responsible for general supervision of his welfare; or

(8) the other person is in custody of law or detained in a hospital or other institution and the actor has supervisory or disciplinary authority over him.

Sexual contact is any touching of the sexual or other intimate parts of the person for the purpose of arousing or gratifying sexual desire.

§ 213.5. INDECENT EXPOSURE.

A person commits a misdemeanor if, for the purpose of arousing or gratifying sexual desire of himself or of any person other than his spouse, he exposes his genitals under circumstances in which he knows his conduct is likely to cause affront or alarm.

§ 213.6. PROVISIONS GENERALLY APPLICABLE TO ARTICLE 213.

(1) Mistake as to Age. * * *

(2) Spouse Relationships. Whenever in this Article the definition of an offense excludes conduct with a spouse, the exclusion shall be deemed to extend to persons living as man and wife, regardless of the legal status of their relationship. The exclusion shall be inoperative as respects spouses living apart under a decree of judicial separation. Where the definition of an offense excludes conduct with a spouse or conduct by a woman, this shall not preclude conviction of a spouse or woman as accomplice in a sexual act which he or she causes another person, not within the exclusion, to perform.

(3) Sexually Promiscuous Complainants. * * *

(4) Prompt Complaint. No prosecution may be instituted or maintained under this Article unless the alleged offense was brought to the notice of public authority within [3] months of its occurrence or, where the alleged victim was less than [16] years old or otherwise incompetent to make complaint, within [3] months after a parent, guardian or other competent person specially interested in the victim learns of the offense.

(5) Testimony of Complaints. No person shall be convicted of any felony under this Article upon the uncorroborated testimony of the alleged victim. Corroboration may be circumstantial. In any prosecution before a jury for an offense under this Article, the jury shall be instructed to evaluate the testimony of a victim or complaining witness with special care in view of the emotional involvement of the witness and the difficulty of determining the truth with respect to alleged sexual activities carried out in private.

MARNIE SHIELS, SPOUSAL RAPE LAWS: 20 YEARS LATER

5(4) Victim Policy Pipeline 5–6 (2000).

INTRODUCTION

Until the late 1970's, most states did not consider spousal rape a crime. Typically, spouses were exempted from the sexual assault laws. For example, until 1993 North Carolina law stated that "a person may not be prosecuted under this article if the victim is the person's legal spouse at the time of the commission of the alleged rape or sexual offense unless the parties are living separate and apart." These laws are traceable to a pronouncement by Michael Hale, who was Chief Justice in England in the 17th century, that a husband cannot be guilty of rape of his wife "for by their mutual matrimonial consent and contract the wife hath given up herself in this kind unto the husband which she cannot retract." In the late 1970's, feminists began efforts to change these laws. Currently, rape of a spouse is a crime in all 50 states and the District of Columbia.

The states used three different techniques for criminalizing spousal rape. The majority of states simply removed the marital rape exemption, without adding any other language. Other states replaced the exclusionary language with text specifying that marriage to the victim is not a defense. A few states created a separate offense of "spousal rape."

While spousal rape is now considered a crime, victims often have to overcome additional legal hurdles to prosecution not present for other victims of rape. These include time limits for reporting the offense, a requirement that force or threat of force be used by the offender, and the fact that some sexual assault offenses still preclude spousal victims.

EXEMPTION REMOVED, NO LANGUAGE ADDED

The most common approach states took to eliminate the spousal rape exemption was to simply remove the language which provided it.

Pennsylvania initially had a separate offense of spousal rape, which was a lower level offense than non-spousal rape. The law was repealed in 1995 to remove any language which indicated that the relationship between victim and offender was relevant, so that now in Pennsylvania "rape is rape."

Maine is another state which removed its exemption. During the legislative battle to change the law, one legislator even stated, "Any woman who claims she has been raped by her spouse has not been properly bedded." While the law has been revised, attitudes have been slower to change. Advocates report that many people still do not recognize spousal rape as rape.

Marriage Explicitly Excluded as a Defense

Several states have amended their laws to specify that marriage is not a defense to certain crimes. For example, the North Carolina law mentioned above was amended to read: "A person may be prosecuted under this Article whether or not the victim is the person's legal spouse at the time of the commission of the alleged rape or sexual offense." This law makes it clear that sexual offenses by spouses should be treated the same as sexual assault by others.

Another example is from Washington, D.C., where the law states that a person can be prosecuted for sexual assault against a spouse. Even though prior to the enactment of this law, the law did not differentiate between spousal rape and non-spousal rape, this approach was chosen as a way to address the societal presumption that rape cannot happen in marriage.

Spousal Rape as a Separate Crime

In seven states, rape of a spouse is a separate crime from rape where the victim and offender are unmarried. For example, in West Virginia, spousal sexual assault is defined as unconsented sexual penetration or sexual intrusion of the perpetrator's spouse. In addition, the perpetrator must use forcible compulsion or a deadly weapon or inflict serious bodily injury upon anyone. This offense is a felony, punishable by imprisonment for two to ten years. The same acts against a person who is not married to the perpetrator result in a sentence of ten to thirty-five years.

An example of a similar statute comes from California. The offenses of rape and spousal rape mostly parallel each other, but with some differences. For instance, a person who commits non-spousal rape by means of force, violence, duress, menace, or fear of immediate and unlawful bodily injury may not be sentenced to probation or suspended sentence. However, this prohibition does not apply to those who use the same means to commit spousal rape.

Additional Barriers for Spousal Rape Victims

Reporting Requirement

While all states recognize spousal rape as a crime, still, there are ways in which spousal rape is treated differently than non-spousal rape.

One difference in some states is a reporting period which is shorter for spousal rape than for other crimes. In Illinois, "prosecution of a spouse of a victim under this subsection . . . is barred unless the victim reported such offense to a law enforcement agency or the State's Attorney's office within 30 days after the offense was committed, except when the court finds good cause for the delay."

Prior to 1993, California victims were required to report the offense to a peace officer or prosecutor within 90 days of the crime. In 1993, the state's law was amended to expand the reporting period to one year (as opposed to at least three years for non-spousal rape). The amendment also broadened the professionals to whom the report could be made to include medical personnel, clergy, attorneys, shelter representatives, counselors, judicial officers, rape crisis agencies, and firefighters. The reporting requirement does not apply if the victim's allegation is corroborated by independent evidence that would be admissible during trial. A suggested reason for this and other restrictions on spousal rape victims is that the legislators are afraid people will make up stories of rape for use in a custody proceeding, or to harm their spouses.

Force or Threat Required

Another way that some states treat rape of a spouse differently than non-spousal rape is the requirement that force or threat of force must be used by the spouse. For instance, in Tennessee, a person commits rape or sexual battery of a spouse only when the person is armed with a weapon or credible decoy, causes serious bodily injury to the victim, or when the spouses live separate and apart and one of them has filed for a divorce or separation. Similarly, in Nevada, marriage is a defense to sexual assault of a spouse except where "the assault was committed by force or by the threat of force." In contrast, many non-spousal sexual assault laws refer to lack of consent, rather than the use of force.

Offenses Precluded for Spouses

Still, in many states, there are some offenses which are unavailable to victims who are married to the offender. In some, offenses which involve sexual acts other than penetration are precluded for spouses. For example, in Kansas, sexual battery consists of "the intentional touching of the person of another who is 16 or more years of age, who is not the spouse of the offender and who does not consent thereto, with the intent to arouse or satisfy the sexual desires of the offender or another." In Ohio, the offense of "sexual battery" does not apply to a spouse, and the offense of "rape" by the use of a drug or intoxicant which impairs the victim's ability to resist only applies to a spouse who is living separate and apart from the victim.

Conclusion

The states made progress in the past 20 years toward eliminating exemptions for sex offenders who are married to their victims. However, differences in the treatment of rape of a spouse from that of non-spousal rape remain. These include: reporting requirements, requirements that the offender use force or threat of force, and the fact that some offenses contain exemptions for spouses. States may want to consider the status of their spousal rape laws and amend them to create protections for victims of spousal rape equal to those for other victims of sexual assault.

Chapter 10

LAW ENFORCEMENT

This chapter opens with an overview of why law enforcement response to domestic violence—i.e. arrest—is key, but should always be seen in the context of a larger coordinated community response, and not relied on as an end in itself. Then comes an in-depth discussion of mandatory arrest studies and policies, including two authors who come to very different conclusions about the usefulness of such policies. A third argues that the emphasis on mandatory arrest policies ignores the circumstances in which poor women and women of color find themselves.

The next part of the chapter focuses on police liability for failure to arrest batterers, which was greatly limited by a 1989 US Supreme Court case, *DeShaney v. County of Winnebago Dept. of Social Services*. In spite of that case and its progeny, two cases in the materials illustrate situations in which courts ruled that there were grounds for such suits, based on the issuance of a protective order and on the civil rights provision of the Violence Against Women Act, respectively.

The chapter concludes with the concept of the "primary aggressor," first illustrated in a state statute mandating that officers make this determination whenever they encounter evidence that both parties in a domestic violence incident may have been violent. Second is a study which found that women in two cities were getting arrested in domestic violence cases at surprisingly high rates, and recommended that officers or prosecutors closely examine the cases to ensure that the right person is actually being arrested.

A. OVERVIEW

BARBARA J. HART, ARREST: WHAT'S THE BIG DEAL

3 Wm. & Mary J. Women & L. 207–211 (1997).

For the last twenty years, activists in the battered women's movement have been urging the criminal justice system to take action against domestic violence. They want the system to treat it like a crime, to recognize that its perpetrators are chronic, high-risk offenders, and to acknowledge that this violence is costly in both human and social terms. Arrest is one type of intervention that advocates for battered women have universally promoted as a fundamental underpinning of an effective response to violence targeted at women in intimate relationships.

Yet, activists have not seen arrest as a panacea. They have not identified it as a unitary action, sufficient unto itself. Rather, activists have been calling for coordinated, comprehensive, and specialized intervention by all components of the legal and human services systems. Experience has demonstrated that arrest, when effected in a system designed to protect the victim and hold the perpetrator accountable, may interrupt patterns of violence; avert life-imperiling injuries, homicide and suicide; and prevent the most frequent and endangering of "copycat" crimes. On the other hand, activists assert that when arrest is a singular intervention, the transitory nature of the beneficial effects and the chance that offenders will seek retribution may place battered women and children at an escalated risk.

Thus, when activists seek mandatory, preferred, or presumptive arrest policies and practice in domestic violence cases, it must be understood that the demand is for the employment of multiple, synchronized strategies by the legal system. The demand is based on a conviction that the death, dismemberment, destruction, and denigration of women are intolerable occurrences in society. Moreover, they are preventable.

SIX PRIMARY GOALS

Effective intervention, arrest, or other actions, must be measured in light of explicit goals. In the context of domestic violence, there are six primary goals. The first and overarching goal is safety for battered women and children. Every intervention should be measured against the yardstick of safety. Arrest may well serve this goal in the immediate future. A batterer who is in secure custody is significantly restrained from perpetrating acts of violence and intimidation (except as he is able to persuade third parties to act on his behalf).

A second goal of domestic violence intervention is to stop the violence. Arrest seemingly works best to stop the violence, at least in the immediate-term, when perpetrators are firmly connected to the community, that is, when men are employed, affiliated with social or religious organizations, have a stake in preserving their reputations and/or maintain close connections to friends, family, co-workers, et cetera. For these "connected" men, arrest alone may serve to stop the violence, at least temporarily. Long-term cessation or desistance is more likely when arrest is merely the first of numerous, concerted interventions by the legal system.

A third goal of legal system intervention is accountability of perpetrators—accountability to victims and to the community. Arrest draws the line. It informs the batterer that he has transgressed the principles safeguarding liberty and justice embodied in law. Arrest calls the batterer to account for his wrong doing in compromising community standards. It apprises him that continued violent conduct will be met with severe, adverse consequences. Accountability, thereafter, is a plan, either devised by the batterer or mandated by a court, for adherence to law, conditions of sentencing, and limitations imposed by victims as to future contact or relationships.

A fourth goal of legal intervention against domestic violence is divestiture by perpetrators. Most batterers believe that they are fundamentally and irrevocably entitled to relationships with battered women; entitled to the services, loyalty, obedience, and fidelity of a battered partner and entitled to superimpose his will upon her. Arrest gives notice that entitlement (this perceived inalienable right) is a fallacy. Arrest challenges a batterer's notion that he may do with a battered woman as he pleases and that the battered woman is without recourse or remedy related to his authority and ownership. Arrest profoundly challenges the beliefs of batterers that they have the right to control their battered partners.

A fifth goal of effective legal system intervention is restoration of battered women. The construct of restoration is complex. It includes restitution; timely compensation for losses sustained as a result of the violence, for example, replacement of destroyed clothing, household goods, eyeglasses, cars, and computers. Restitution involves compensation for loss of work related to court appearances occasioned by the violence. Restitution entails payment of all violence-precipitated medical costs. Restitution involves compensation for tuition or fees forfeited by battered women when these losses are directly caused by the coercive conduct of the perpetrator. Losses suffered by battered women are extensive. Compensation for the losses may be formidable as a consequence. All the more reason that these costs should be squarely assigned to the person responsible for them. Losses should not be borne by the victim. But restoration goes beyond restitution. It also anticipates that battered women must be restored to health, must live again without fear, must be accorded the opportunity to restore relationships with family, friends, neighbors, and co-workers, all of which may have been compromised by the batterer, his violence, and coercive controls. Arrest may merely permit battered women and children to sleep for the night. Arrest may permit battered women to escape from the house and seek shelter. Arrest may permit battered women to seek medical attention for their injuries. Arrest may eradicate the barriers that prevent battered women from accessing community resources and support.

Finally, the sixth goal of effective intervention is to enhance agency in the lives of battered women. Agency is the power to make informed decisions and implement them without interference by the batterer. Agency is the power to organize one's life. Agency is the power to establish stable, nurturing homes for children. Agency is the power to participate, without batterer impediment, in work, education, faith, family and community. Battered women cannot fully participate in the justice system or act as an advocate for themselves and their children in the community unless they are fully informed about what they can do and are able to act. Agency is the power to employ the legal options, community resources, economic remedies, housing opportunities, and educational programs available in order to escape the violence and achieve lives that are free of intimidation, degradation, and violation. Arrest facilitates agency when it both informs battered women of the social and legal options essential for sustained agency and when it brokers access to these legal and human services options.

COORDINATED COMMUNITY INTERVENTION

Arrest practice that is grounded in these intervention goals can make all the difference in the lives of men who employ violence against women in their intimate relationships. It is critical that law enforcement, particularly those who are the first to respond, "first-responders," are fully cognizant of the goals of domestic violence intervention. Those officers imbued with a rich understanding of the profound difference that their actions can make in the lives of adult and child victims, as well as perpetrators, will approach each of the tasks, which are associated with domestic violence intervention, equipped with a critical perspective—a perspective that informs each task undertaken at the scene of the domestic violence incident.

The perspective (the knowledge, beliefs, values, and departmental culture) of the first-responder is the engine that drives the intervention strategies selected. Perspective shapes the amount of caution exercised when approaching the scene, any identification of injuries, the assessment of probable cause, the decision about whether to arrest one or both parties, the brokering of community resources for the victim, and whether any emergency safety planning should be undertaken with the victim.

Without this perspective, first-responders in "mandatory arrest" or "preferred/presumptive arrest" jurisdictions will devise their own rationale for chosen responses to domestic violence. If an officer's perspective is that "women provoke violence" or "it takes two" or "domestic violence is nuisance behavior," then that perspective will shape intervention. Experts in the field of domestic violence, both sworn and civilian, agree that these perspectives convey an attitude of tolerance toward the violence, fail to call the perpetrator to account, and jeopardize both the safety of the officer and the victim.

When a department imposes a mandatory or preferred arrest directive, officers who embrace these victim-blaming, perpetrator-exculpating perspectives routinely resist the directive and either arrest both parties or conclude that probable cause does not exist to believe that the accused has committed the crimes alleged. Too often, then, the perpetrator gains further license for his behavior. Certainly, close supervision and monitoring by police management and the community can restrain the most egregious of these compromising practices, but resistance will be unremitting without a change in perspectives that embraces the six goals of intervention—safety, desistance, accountability, divestiture, restoration, and agency. Similarly, perspective is the engine that drives the practices of the other components of the legal and human services systems. It shapes policy and practice guidelines; it informs decision making; it shapes resource allocation; it bolsters or erodes the resolve to end violence against women. Perspective shapes institutional and individual practice. Without shared perspective, a coordinated community intervention plan to end domestic violence cannot work. Without shared goals, institutions will lapse into easy solutions or regressive practices. Without shared perspectives, law enforcement will retreat from policies and practices that favor arrest of domestic violence perpetrators. Without corresponding perspective and practice by other components of the criminal legal system, law enforcement will soon conclude that arrest is a worthless, if not endangering, intervention. Thus, it is critical that those engaged in coordinated community intervention against domestic violence periodically revisit and affirm their shared goals and their perspective, evaluating whether the policies and practices currently employed are consistent with the goals of safety, desistance, accountability, divestiture, restoration, and agency.

CONCLUSION

Police officers are the gatekeepers of the criminal legal system. Effective action by first-responders in police and sheriff departments may serve to open the gate both for victims and perpetrators. So, the big deal about mandatory, presumptive or preferred arrest policies is that they are the first link in a vital chain of institutional interventions that save the lives of battered women and children, restore the community, and invite batterers to accountability.

B. MANDATORY ARREST

LAWRENCE W. SHERMAN, THE INFLUENCE OF CRIMINOLOGY ON CRIMINAL LAW: EVALUATING ARRESTS FOR MISDEMEANOR DOMESTIC VIOLENCE

83 J. Crim. L. & Criminology 1–45 (1992).

I. INTRODUCTION

On September 19, 1986, the U.S. Food and Drug Administration approved the sale of a new drug, AZT, for the treatment of patients with AIDS. The drug had been in development for several years, and had been tested in a randomized clinical trial involving 282 patients. Using a standard medical research trial design, 137 patients were chosen by lottery to receive placebo (sugar) pills, and 145 were chosen to receive pills containing the real drug. In a followup period lasting up to six months, nineteen of the placebo group and one of the AZT group died. The experiment was halted ahead of schedule, although not nearly as soon as demanded by doctors and AIDS patients who wanted the drug to be approved before the research was completed. The FDA held fast to the policy it had adopted after the thalidomide disaster of the early 1960s, refusing to allow any drug to enter the market until it has been tested in a randomized clinical trial. The drug immediately became the standard treatment for all AIDS patients.

On May 27, 1984, the U.S. National Institute of Justice announced the results of a randomized clinical trial of the use of arrest for misdemeanor domestic violence. The 314–case experiment, conducted with the Minneapolis Police Department, used a lottery method that assigned about one third of the probable cause suspects to be arrested, one third to be advised, and the rest to be sent away from the home on threat of arrest. Over a followup period lasting at least six months, about ten percent of the arrested suspects and about twenty percent of the suspects not arrested were officially detected to have committed one or more repeated domestic assaults. Citing these results, the Attorney General of the United States four months later issued a report recommending that arrest be made the standard treatment in cases of misdemeanor domestic assault. Within two years, "preferred" arrest became the most common urban police policy for those cases. By 1989, mandatory or preferred arrest policies were reported by eighty-four percent of urban police agencies. By late 1991, fifteen states and the District of Columbia had passed mandatory arrest statutes for cases in which there was probable cause to believe that misdemeanor domestic violence had occurred.

The parallels between AZT for AIDS and arrest for domestic violence seem obvious. Both ailments are serious, afflicting millions of people and killing thousands each year. Victims of both ailments had strong political constituencies pressing to put the treatment into widespread use as soon as possible. Both treatments were carefully evaluated by scientists in collaboration with clinical practitioners, using the most advanced research design available for inferring cause and effect (the randomized, controlled experiment). Both evaluations, by the basic sciences of biochemistry and criminology, respectively, had an apparently strong influence on the respective professional practices. Unfortunately, both treatments were shown only to reduce the suffering associated with the target problems, but not to cure those problems.

A final parallel is less obvious. Both experiments raised basic questions about the relationship between science and professional practice, generating intense controversy. Both of them led to clear recommendations to change the standard procedures governing scientific influences on policy-making. Both of them led to charges that scientists were morally insensitive to the interests and suffering of victims. The irony of this final parallel is that the two respective controversies went in opposite directions. Critics of the FDA charged that it used too *much* science, caution and delay before adoption of the new treatment. Critics of the NIJ experiment charged that it used too *little* science, caution and delay before recommending adoption of the new treatment. The FDA responded by considering faster procedures for approving new drugs, possibly including approval without waiting for the results of controlled experiments. The NIJ responded by funding replications of the Minneapolis experiment in six new cities (Atlanta, Charlotte, Colorado Springs, Metro–Dade [Miami], Omaha, and Milwaukee), which are the subject of this symposium issue.

Explaining this irony is easy, but important. Over the preceding half-century, field experiments in biochemistry had become the basis for regulating the use of drugs as "dangerous commodities." The common wisdom in medicine was that it was unsafe to approve new drugs without large-scale controlled tests. The common wisdom in criminal law was just the opposite: penalties were a philosophical matter of just deserts, not an empirical question of effectiveness. Despite the pleas of some legal scholars to take questions of sanctioning efficacy more seriously, legislatures generally went about the process of making criminal law without much concern about its "safety." And while the FDA had never before encountered such a politically volatile disease, field experiments in criminology had never before achieved such influence over the course of the criminal law. As one observer put it, "the Minneapolis experiment probably reached the high water mark of research impact: in view of the publicity that the research received and the climate in which it was released, one can probably expect that social research will seldom have as much impact as this experiment did."

Just as some AIDS patients were shocked to discover that they could not have legal access to any new drug they chose even though they were dying, some criminologists were shocked to discover that criminology could have a clear impact on the shape of the criminal law. While that possibility is arguably one of the basic purposes of this journal, the lack of precedent for the dramatic impact of the Minneapolis experiment left criminology understandably unprepared to deal with the many moral and technical questions that impact raised. Is criminology a mature enough science—especially compared to biochemistry—to be guiding public policy at all? How much research is enough to support a policy recommendation? Should policy research results be publicized before they have been replicated? Should criminologists report only the average effect of a criminal law policy on a given sample, or must they also examine any systematic differences in the effects of the punishment on different kinds of people? Is crime control the only metric by which criminal law should be evaluated, or should other quality of life criteria—family unity, offender employability, children's trauma at seeing parents arrested—also be considered? Should the burden of proof lie more heavily on criminologists recommending changes in current practice than on those supporting the status quo, even when no research is available to justify current practices?

In choosing the Minneapolis experiment and its replications as the subject of this symposium volume, the editors have two goals. One goal is to report the most comprehensive information available about the effects of arrest for this most pervasive problem of violence. With some 2,000 murders and over four million police encounters each year in the United States alone, the subject of domestic violence needs little justification for a journal of criminal law and its basic science. The other goal is equally important: to explore the concrete problems of using criminology to influence the criminal law, with the domestic violence arrest experiments as a case study. These problems become especially complex when a crucial experiment is replicated, and generates conflicting results in different cities. Interpreting those diverse findings poses a substantial challenge for the science of criminology; determining how the criminal law should respond to them is an even greater challenge.

This introduction attempts to guide the reader towards accomplishing both goals. Starting with a review of the rationale for conducting controlled experiments in criminal sanctions, it shows why police policy on domestic violence was ripe for such an experiment in 1980. The Minneapolis experiment is then described in some detail, including its policy recommendations against mandatory arrest laws and its relative influence in the passage of such laws. The five replication experiments are also described in some detail, so as to make possible an accounting for their diverse results. The foreword concludes with an assessment of the teachings of the past decade about both of this Volume's concerns: policing domestic violence more effectively, and using experimental criminology more wisely.

II. CONTROLLED EXPERIMENTS IN CRIMINAL SANCTIONS

The importance of controlled experiments in criminal law derives largely from our ignorance of the true nature of criminal deterrence. As Professor Norval Morris has observed, every criminal law system in the world (except Greenland's) has deterrence as its "primary and essential postulate." As Sir Arthur Goodhart once observed, if punishment "cannot deter, then we might as well scrap the whole of our criminal law." Yet for most of human history, the evidence of the deterrent effects of criminal law has been little more than what Morris calls "a surfeit of unsubstantiated speculation."

In the past quarter century, substantial strides have been made toward filling the knowledge gap about the deterrent effects of criminal sanctions. A series of theoretical treatises was followed by a prestigious National Academy of Sciences panel report on the methodological limitations of existing deterrence studies, a series of survey studies published in this Journal and elsewhere, cross-sectional analyses of the relationship of criminal sanctions to crime rates, and quasi-experimental (before and after) evaluations of the effects of sudden changes in sanctions like capital punishment, mandatory prison sentences, and police crackdowns. None of these research methods, however, has been able to resolve the lingering problems of distinguishing mere correlations from true causation. As a result, our knowledge of the deterrent or other consequences of criminal sanctions—including a possible increase in crime—remains sketchy and uncertain.

Controlled experiments are fundamentally different from all other kinds of research. They are uniquely capable of eliminating alternative causes for observed effects, or plausible rival hypotheses also consistent with the evidence. In all other research designs the scientist must specify which rival theories must be tested and eliminated. In controlled experiments, even theories that the scientist never considered can usually be eliminated automatically. By making two groups comparable with respect to virtually all characteristics (within the limits of sampling error) *except* the factor under study (like AZT or arrest), a controlled experiment leaves very little doubt about inferring causation from any observed correlations—at least within the particular sample under study. As we shall see, however, generalizing from one sample to other populations is quite another matter.

The power to infer cause and effect has made controlled experimentation especially prominent in medical research, which has been blessed with far greater financial resources than criminological research. It has used those resources and the experimental method to accomplish the testing and approval of the Salk vaccine for polio, the use of penicillin to control infections, and the use of streptomycin to treat tuberculosis. Of equal importance is the role that controlled experiments have played in putting a stop to harmful medical practices, like blindness-causing oxygen treatments for premature infants, bleeding as a standard medical treatment, removal of intestinal parts to cure epilepsy, removing teeth to cure a pitcher's sore arm, and extended bed rest after heart attacks. It is largely because of the demonstrated dangers of treatments introduced without controlled tests that such tests became mandatory for new drugs in 1969, and why they continue to be used to expose established treatments that in fact make patients sicker.

The power to determine what works and what doesn't has not been lost on scholars of the criminal law. As early as 1959, Professors Zeisel, Kalven and Buchholz advanced the case for conducting controlled experiments in law. Their argument overruled the standard objection to such research: the claim that the Constitution prohibits random assignment of punishment options as discriminatory. They pointed out that present decisionmaking in criminal justice is already so shot through with arbitrary and discriminatory practices that, if anything, controlled experiments tend to make decisionmaking less discriminatory. By creating equal probability for each subject to receive each of the alternative treatments, random assignment formulas in controlled experiments remove the influences of race, sex, class and demeanor. The only disparity left is between the experimental and control groups, a disparity which constitutes no discrimination against any class protected under the Fourteenth Amendment. While the disparity is arguably unjust for those particular subjects, that cost is balanced against the benefits of the knowledge that a controlled experiment can produce.

This argument later led Chief Justice Burger's advisory committee on legal experimentation to endorse controlled experiments in criminal law. The committee's logic rested heavily on the benefits that were presumed to result from completion of a well-designed, statistically powerful experiment. Their report created a special ethical burden to guard against methodologically weak criminology or research designs that were doomed from the start (from such problems as inadequate sample size) to be unable to accomplish their objectives; these would impose the cost of disparity with no countervailing benefit. But as a report of the Social Science Research Council observed, it is extremely difficult to conduct controlled experiments properly. The organizational complexity of controlled experiments far exceeds that of standard social science research methods, and fits in very uneasily with the social science research culture of universities.

It is not surprising, then, that controlled experiments in criminal law got off to a slow start. Lack of funding, ethical objections, and organizational demands combined to discourage would-be experimenters. These obstacles were not impossible to overcome, however, either in the U.S. or in England. In state correctional agencies like the California Youth Authority, and in private "think tanks" like the Vera Institute of Justice in New York, controlled experiments began to thrive in the early 1960s. In perhaps the most famous of these, the Vera Institute developed and tested an alternative to money bail called "release on recognizance" (ROR). In a random assignment of persons with "community ties" to either money bail or ROR, virtually all those assigned to ROR appeared at court as scheduled. The influence of this experiment was widespread, resulting in the adoption of ROR by legislatures across the U.S. and in several other countries.

Even bolder experiments followed, although with less fame and influence. In the early 1970s, the California Department of Corrections conducted an experiment of a reduction of the time served by inmates in prison. The experiment randomly assigned 1,135 prisoners to either "full" or "reduced" prison terms, which represented a six month reduction. The average full term was 37.9 months; the average reduced term was 31.3 months. The researchers structured the data analysis to show that there was no significant difference between the two groups in the rate of "unfavorable" parole outcomes. But Duke University Professor Philip Cook's reanalysis of the data found a significantly higher prevalence of recidivism measured by arrest after release of the reduced prison term group, compared to the full prison term group.

Given our general ignorance about the effects of various types and doses of criminal sanctions, such experiments clearly meet the threshold justifications for randomized experiments recommended by the Federal Judicial Center. Those requirements provide that

     1.   The present practice must either need substantial improvement or be of doubtful effectiveness.

     2.   There must be significant uncertainty about the value of the proposed innovation.

     3.   There must be no other practical means to resolve uncertainties about the value of the proposed innovation.

4. The experiment must be seriously intended to inform a future choice between retaining the status quo or implementing the innovation.

A further ethical requirement suggested by Professor Morris was not included in the Federal Judicial Center's list. Writing in the 1960s, Morris suggested a principle of "less severity" than the status quo in any innovations to be tested by randomized experiments. At that time, most of the policy options under debate, such as deinstitutionalization of juvenile delinquents, were pointed in the direction of less severity. By the 1980s, however, the tide was running the other way, with most interest groups demanding greater severity in criminal justice responses. The choice in that context was to accede to greater severity without any evaluation, or to conduct a randomized experiment in which punishments of greater severity were randomly assigned. Nowhere, perhaps, was that choice more clearly framed than in the question of police responses to misdemeanor domestic violence.

III. Police Responses to Domestic Violence

The historical custom of police in the U.S. was to make arrests only rarely in cases of misdemeanor domestic violence. In the later 1960s, this custom was reinforced by federal sponsorship of training in police mediation of domestic "disturbances," including those in which minor assaults had occurred. By the late 1970s, women's advocates used litigation and legislation to press for a policy innovation: much greater use of arrest. From the 1980s to the present, the innovation many have recommended is mandatory arrest (required by state law) whenever police have probable cause to believe that a domestic assault has occurred. This recommendation clearly constitutes a substantial increase in the severity of criminal sanctions for this particular offense. What is less understood is that it constitutes a departure from, rather than an equalization with, the level of enforcement severity for most other misdemeanors and many felonies.

A. Under–Enforcement: Domestic and Other Violence

As recently as 1967, the leading police professional organization, the International Association of Chiefs of Police, declared in its training manual that "in dealing with family disputes, the power of arrest should be exercised as a last resort." This position was endorsed by the American Bar Association, whose 1973 *Standards for the Urban Police Function* said that police should "engage in the resolution of conflict such as that which occurs between husband and wife ... in the highly populated sections of the large city, without reliance upon criminal assault or disorderly conduct statutes." In 1977, police in three metropolitan areas were observed to take slightly longer to respond to domestic disturbance calls (4.65 minutes) than non-domestic disturbances (3.86 minutes). Police in these areas openly told observers it was the officers' policy (not the department's) "to proceed slowly in the hope that the problem would be resolved or that a disputant would have left before they arrived." The expression of such policies led many to conclude that male police officers practice discriminatory enforcement in such cases because they side with male offenders.

The evidence is far from clear, however, that police practiced more under-enforcement in domestic situations than in other cases in general, or in cases of interpersonal violence in particular. By the 1970s, the best evidence from observations of police work suggested that there was no less enforcement in domestic violence cases than in other cases of personal violence, although there was less enforcement in cases involving a male and a female than in cases involving two males. The evidence remains inconclusive largely because of imprecise data on the levels of injury involved in the different categories of cases.

The pattern of under-enforcement itself is clear. In 1966, Professors Albert J. Reiss, Jr. and Donald J. Black conducted the first multi-city study of police arrest decisions using systematic personal observations. This study of thousands of police-citizen encounters in Boston, Chicago and Washington found that, in cases where both victim and offender were present when police arrived, only forty-five percent of all felonies involving family members resulted in arrest; the proportion was fifty-five percent if the victim asked police to make an arrest. The arrest rate was about the same with respect to family misdemeanors overall (47%), although police were more likely to comply with victim requests for misdemeanor arrest (80%). In 1977, a similar study was conducted by Indiana University Professor Elinor Ostrom and her colleagues in twenty-four police departments in three metropolitan areas: Rochester (NY), Tampa–St. Petersburg (FL) and St. Louis (MO). One analysis of these data found that arrests were made in only twenty-two percent of all family assault cases (including those where one party had left the scene). Another study of over 3,000 family violence records in an Ohio county in 1978 found that arrests were made in twelve percent of cases involving current or former spouses or lovers.

Many reasons may account for this low level of enforcement. One is the common law in-presence requirement for misdemeanor arrests generally, which technically barred officers in many states from making warrantless arrests unless they had witnessed the offense. Other reasons include the muddy practical distinctions between felony and misdemeanor assaults, possibly erroneous police perceptions of domestic violence situations as extremely dangerous to police, frequent victim preferences against arrest, and possibly even support by some police for the practice of spouse-beating. What is poorly understood by most policy activists in this area, however, is that police under-enforce the laws generally, for a very wide range of offenses.

The myth of full enforcement has been demolished by several careful field studies of police arrest behavior. These studies show clearly that full enforcement is not standard police practice. They also show mixed evidence on whether police take family matters less seriously than crimes among acquaintances or strangers. The 1966 study for the

President's Commission on Law Enforcement and Administration of Justice found that, in 176 encounters in which both a suspect and a complainant were present, and in which there was legally sufficient evidence for making an arrest, arrests were made in only fifty-eight percent of the reported felonies and forty-four percent of the reported misdemeanors. Similar evidence comes from Ostrom's 1977 study of policing in sixty neighborhoods in three major metropolitan areas. Of the 742 cases (of all kinds of offenses) in which police had a legal basis for an arrest of a single suspect present at the scene, arrests were made in forty-two percent of the felonies and fourteen percent of the misdemeanors. There was no victim present in over half the cases. The victim expressed a clear preference for arrest in only ten percent of these cases, yet police still failed to make arrests in over half (53%) of those. *Across all types of observed encounters in the summer of 1977, police in three metropolitan areas chose not to make an arrest in eighty-three percent of the cases where there was legal basis to do so.* Even where the suspect and victim were strangers, police failed to make arrests in sixty-six percent of the cases (compared to eighty-three percent of cases where the parties were acquainted).

Observation studies have also witnessed police officers ignoring burglary, larceny, malicious destruction of property, drunk driving, hit and run accidents, and a broad range of other offenses. If there is a police agency that practices full enforcement anywhere in this country, researchers have yet to find it.

B. *Doing Something: Mediation vs. Arrest*

In the late 1960s, clinical psychologists like Professor Morton Bard recommended that police try to do more than walk away from domestic calls. They developed and trained officers in techniques of conflict mediation, a concept later found offensive by those who see assault as crime, not "conflict." These techniques taught police to be more on-the-spot marriage counselors than assessors of possible law breaking. The techniques quite sensibly included separation of the man and woman from each other and, if possible, other members of the household. Each party would then be able to give the officer her or his version of what happened without fear of being contradicted by the other party, leading to more shouting or worse. After hearing the two versions, police were supposed to consult with each other to discuss alternative actions. A preferred method was to get the two parties to calm down, sit down, and rationally discuss what would happen next. If that was not possible, officers would often advise one of the parties to leave for a cooling off period. Another option Bard stressed was referral to counseling or other social service agencies. Consistent with past practice, arrest was reserved for cases of serious injury or assaults on police.

This training resulted in some cities in a decrease in arrests. Some training explicitly made this a goal. This 1977 observation of a police encounter shows how the mediation training was carried out in many cases:

The officer received a call for family trouble. A woman met us at the door. she was crying and very upset. she had some bruises on her face and her lip was swollen and bleeding. She said that her husband had hit her, that she was not going to take it any more, and that she wanted him arrested. the officer had her sign a complaint form. At this point the man upstairs began yelling and cursing at the woman. It turned out that the man and the woman are not married but have been living together for some time and have a small baby. The woman thought that they were married, but the man is in the process of getting a divorce from his wife. The officer went upstairs [with the woman] to try to talk to the man who was very angry and yelled at the woman and the officer. the officer threatened him with arrest. Finally, the officer shut the door to keep out the woman. She got very upset and felt that the officer was taking the side of the man. The back-up officer arrived and found the woman in the corner of the small room, still crying. She told the second officer that she thought she was legally married to the man. The officer told her that she could not be legally married to him, since he was still legally married to his wife. When the man came downstairs with the first officer, he said he was going to his mother's house. The officer asked if everything would be okay. the man said yes. the woman remained sitting in the corner crying. the officers left.[63]

In this example, mediation was substituted for a legally valid arrest. It also consisted primarily of a one-on-one discussion with the suspect. As Professor Oppenlander's analysis of the 1977 data points out, police discussions with one party are more frequent than those that engage both parties simultaneously. Yet it is hard to call such methods "mediation" if they do not involve consultation with both parties about the solutions being reached, regardless of whether there are face-to-face discussions.

In the majority of cases in which no crime has been committed, mediation techniques might make a great deal of sense in the short run. They are clearly focused on the immediate "crisis," and not on any long-term pattern or future risks of violence in the relationship. The implicit objective is to minimize the risk of harm while police are present at the scene, rather than to prevent a recurrence of violence. Since police mishandling of interpersonal relationships in the encounter can arguably escalate the risk of violence rather than defuse it, their mediation skills are important targets for training. Whether accomplishing the objective of minimizing violence at the police encounter will reduce domestic violence overall, however, is debatable. Unfortunately, no rigorous evaluation of mediation training was ever done that adequately addressed the key question of violence reduction.

The mediation approach also hypothesized that arrest should be avoided, even when a misdemeanor had been committed, because of the danger that arrest might backfire. This reflected a widespread belief

63. Oppenlander, supra note 51, at 460–61.

among police at that time. As one observer summarized the views of police he interviewed:

> An arrest in a family squabble does not resolve the underlying problems, and it may simply aggravate matters, especially if the husband is arrested. he will eventually get out of jail, and he may return home, angrier than before, to pick up where he left off.[65]

In the 1970s, however, women's advocates clearly rejected that hypothesis. As Joan Zorza's article in the present volume amply documents, the women's movement adopted a full enforcement position. This position implicitly hypothesizes that more arrests (and prosecution, and sentencing) would help to reduce male violence in the home against women. The first line of attack on police under-enforcement was through litigation. But litigation alone could not address the underlying statutory problem of the in-presence requirement for warrantless misdemeanor arrests. Accordingly, legislation was sought and obtained in several states in the late 1970s granting a specific exception to the in-presence requirement for domestic violence misdemeanors. One of the states in which this occurred was Minnesota, in 1978. Predictably, however, Minnesota police made little use of the expanded arrest powers that the legislature had granted them.

In this context, a controlled experiment was clearly justified under Federal Judicial Center guidelines. Practitioners had great uncertainty about a proposed innovation they were being asked to adopt, an innovation in practice if not in black letter law. Two competing hypotheses about the effects of arrest, at least in specific cases, could be set against each other on the criterion measure of repeat domestic violence. While a controlled experiment in arrest would not be able to address the *general* deterrent effects of arrest, it could examine the *specific* deterrent effects in which individual victims would have the greatest personal stake. Fortunately, Minneapolis appointed a new police chief in 1980, Anthony V. Bouza, who was willing to undertake the risk of conducting the first random assignment experiment in field arrests.

IV. The Minneapolis Experiment

A. *Design and Implementation*

In order to find which police approach was most effective in deterring future domestic violence by the same offender against the same victim, the Police Foundation and the Minneapolis Police Department agreed to conduct a controlled experiment with the support of the National Institute of Justice. The design of the experiment called for a lottery selection of three treatments for all suspects legally eligible for arrest under the 1978 Minnesota warrantless arrest statute. The lottery selection, as noted above, minimized the pre-existing differences among the three groups of suspects, and helped eliminate any other possible

---

65. Brown, supra note 61, at 204.

cause of observed differences in repeat violence rates besides the three treatments themselves. The treatments included the following:

1. arrest (with at least one night in jail)

2. sending the suspect away from the scene of the assault for eight hours (or arresting the suspects if they refused)

3. giving the couple some form of advice, which could include mediation at an officer's discretion.

The criterion for comparing the relative success of the three treatments was the frequency and seriousness of any future domestic violence over the next six months.

The experiment involved only simple (misdemeanor) domestic assaults, where both the suspect and the victim were present when the police arrived. Thus, the experiment included only those cases in which police were empowered, but not required, to make arrests. The police officer needed to have probable cause to believe that a cohabitant or spouse had assaulted the victim within the past four hours. Police did not need to witness the assault. Cases of life-threatening or severe injury, usually labeled as felonies (aggravated assault), were excluded from the design. So were cases in which the victim demanded an arrest, cases in which a court order of protection was in effect, cases in which the suspect assaulted a police officer, or any case in which a police officer believed an arrest was necessary due to an imminent threat of harm to the victim.

The design called for each participating officer—all of whom were volunteers—to carry a pad of report forms, color coded for the three different police responses. Each time the officers encountered a situation that fit the experiment's criteria, they were to take whatever action was indicated by the top report form on the pad. The forms were numbered and arranged for each officer in an order determined by the lottery. The consistency of the lottery assignment was to be monitored by research staff observers riding on patrol for a sample of evenings. After a police action was taken at the scene of a domestic violence incident, the officer was to fill out a brief report and give it to the research staff for follow-up. As a further check on the lottery process, the staff logged in the reports in the order in which they were received and made sure that the sequence corresponded to the original assignment of responses.

The experiment employed two key measures of repeat violence: official police records and victim interviews. A predominantly minority, female research staff was employed to contact the victims for a detailed, face-to-face interview, to be followed by telephone follow-up-interviews every two weeks for twenty-four weeks. The interviews were designed primarily to measure the frequency and seriousness of victimizations caused by a suspect after police intervention. The research staff also collected criminal justice reports that mentioned suspect's names during the six-month follow-up period.

As is common in field experiments, the actual research process in Minneapolis differed somewhat from the original plan. None of these differences, however, seriously threatened the experiment's validity. There is little doubt that many of the officers occasionally failed to follow fully the experimental design. Some of the failures were due to forgetfulness, such as when officers left report pads at home or at the police station. Other failures stemmed from confusion over whether the experiment applied in certain situations. Whether any officer intentionally subverted the design is unclear. The plan to monitor the lottery process with ride-along observers broke down because of the unexpectedly low frequency of cases meeting the experimental criteria, a problem that also affected the replications. Thus, the possibility existed that police officers finding the upcoming experimental treatment unpalatable may have occasionally decided to ignore the experiment. They may have chosen, in effect, to exclude certain cases in violation of the experimental design. Such action would have biased the selection of the experiment's sample of cases, but not the results of the experiment among the cases included.

Moreover, the plans assumed that there would be legitimate reasons why the three treatments were not always delivered as designed. Ninety-nine percent of the suspects targeted for arrest actually were arrested; seventy-eight percent of those scheduled to receive advice did; and seventy-three percent of those who were to be sent out of the residence for eight hours actually were sent (most of those who were not were arrested, as planned). One explanation for this pattern, consistent with experimental guidelines, is that mediating and sending off were more difficult ways for police to control a situation.

This pattern could have biased estimates of the relative effectiveness of arrest by removing uncooperative and difficult offenders from mediation and separation treatments. Any deterrent effect of arrest could be underestimated and, in the extreme, arrest could be shown to increase the chance of repeat violence. In effect, the arrest group could have received too many "bad risks" relative to the other treatments. Fortunately, Professor Berk's statistical analysis of this process shows that the delivered treatments conformed very closely to the experimental design, with no problems of bias.

More substantial problems arose with the interviews of victims. The majority of the victims could not be followed up for the full six months, and less than two-thirds even granted an initial interview. Many of the victims simply could not be found, either for the initial interview or for the follow-ups. They had left town, moved somewhere else, or refused to answer the phone or doorbell. The research staff made up to twenty attempts to contact these victims and often employed investigative techniques (asking friends and neighbors) to find them. Sometimes these methods worked, only to have the victim give an outright refusal, or break one or more appointments to meet the interviewer at a "safe" location for the interview. Fortunately, the experimental treatment assigned to the offender did not affect the victim's decision to grant initial interviews. Statistical tests showed the victims' willingness to give interviews did not depend upon what police did, the race of the victim, or the race of the offender.

Despite these limitations, the experiment succeeded in producing an experimental sample of 314 cases with complete official outcome measures and an apparently unbiased sample of responses from the victims in those cases.

B. Results

Consistent with the kinds of cases coming to police attention in most big cities, the sample contained a disproportionate number of unmarried couples with lower than average educational levels, minority couples, and couples who were very likely to have had prior violent incidents with police intervention. The sixty percent unemployment rate among the experiment's suspects was strikingly high. The suspects' fifty-nine percent prior arrest rate was also strikingly high, suggesting (with the eighty percent prior domestic assault rate) that the suspects generally were experienced law-breakers who were accustomed to police interventions. But with the exception of the heavy representation of Native–Americans due to Minneapolis' proximity to many Indian reservations, many of the sample's characteristics were probably close to those of domestic violence cases coming to police attention in other large U.S. cities.

The results, based on both official records and victim interviews, showed that arrest produced the lowest prevalence of repeat violence of any of the three treatments. The results taken from the police records on subsequent violence showed ten percent of the *arrested* suspects with at least one repeat incident, nineteen percent of the *advised* suspects, and twenty-four percent of the suspects sent away for eight hours. The arrest treatment was clearly an improvement over sending the suspect away, which produced two and a half times as many repeat incidents as arrest. The advise treatment was statistically not distinguishable from the other two police actions.

The victim interviews showed a somewhat different picture. According to the victims' reports of repeat violence, nineteen percent of the suspects in the *arrest* group, thirty-three percent of those in the *send* group, and thirty-seven percent of those in the *advise* group committed at least one repeat attack on the victims (defined as including assaults, threats or property damage). This ranking varies from the official measure results by reversing the send and advise groups. In this measure, sending the suspect away produced results that were not statistically distinguishable from the results of the other two actions. It is not clear why the order of the three levels of repeat violence was different for these two ways of measuring the violence. But it is clear that arrest worked best by either measure, at least in comparison to the two most common police alternatives as they were currently practiced by patrol officers. This does not mean that arrest was superior to more powerful alternatives; it only means that it worked better than the alternatives then in use.

C. Limitation

The experiment generally won high praise for the quality of the research design. It has been described as "a landmark study," and as "arguably the best field experiment on a criminal justice policy problem to date." Nonetheless, the study had a number of limitations, many of which were pointed out by the authors, and some of which were later identified by other commentators.

Perhaps the most important limitation was that the study was unable to say *why* arrest had the lowest rate of repeat violence. While the authors presented it as a specific deterrent effect, it may also have been a displacement effect, meaning that the suspects moved on to abuse new victims. The low completion rate of victim interviews also made it difficult to estimate the rate of breakup in relationships across treatment groups, which may also have reduced the risk of repeat violence. It was, however, large enough to refute the hypothesis that arrested suspects' victims were intimidated into remaining silent about new violence, since the interview completion rates did not vary by treatment group.

The study's summary report for practitioners identified several problems involved in generalizing from the study's results to other cities. One was the sample size, which was too small to yield information regarding the possibility of different effects among different kinds of people. Another was the automatic night in jail attendant to domestic violence arrest in Minneapolis, which is not true of all cities; without it, a deterrent effect might not be achieved. A third was the unusual combination of sixteen percent Native–American and thirty-six percent African–American suspects in the sample, which might not allow generalization to cities with, say, large proportions of Hispanics. A fourth was the fact that interviewers attempted to contact all the victims, which attention might have artificially enhanced the effects of the police actions.

Other critics have attacked the methods of analysis used in the original report, although a subsequent analysis addressed the purely statistical issues and found similar results no matter how the data were analyzed. The major debate about the limitations of the experiment concerned its appropriateness for serving as the basis of any national policy recommendations. One commentary, for example, called the experiment a mere "pilot study," and described using its results for national policy-making as "foolishness bordering on irresponsibility." Another suggested that the limitations implied a need for "some caution in rushing to a policy recommendation on the strength of these findings alone." These comments raise the distinct questions of what the authors actually recommended on the basis of the results, and what others recommended on the basis of the findings that the authors actively helped to publicize.

D. *Recommendations*

The authors actually recommended three policies. One was that the estimated twenty-two states then barring warrantless arrest for misdemeanor domestic violence not committed in the officer's presence change their laws to allow such arrests. This recommendation seemed to be amply supported by the research, and was the least controversial among both researchers leaning against drawing strong inferences from the study and women's advocates leaning in favor of drawing strong inferences. Professor Lempert, the first to call for caution in making innovations based on the results, concurred that "if I were a police chief I would change a 'do not arrest' policy because of the study's results, although I would not mandate arrest."

The Minneapolis experiment's authors concurred in cautioning against *mandatory* arrest, although they did write that, "on the basis of this study alone, police should probably employ arrest in most cases of minor domestic violence." They went on to cite the Minneapolis police department's policy (which I drafted) as the kind that "did not make arrest 100 percent mandatory. The policy did, however, require officers to file a written report explaining why they failed to make an arrest when it was legally possible to do so." The authors' opposition to mandatory arrest statutes stemmed primarily from the study's small sample size. This meant that, "because of the relatively small numbers of suspects in each subcategory (age, race, employment status, criminal history, etc.), it is possible that this experiment failed to discover that for some kinds of people, arrest may only make matters worse. Until subsequent research addresses the issue more thoroughly, it would be premature for state legislatures to pass laws requiring arrests in *all* misdemeanor domestic assaults."

In making this recommendation, the authors ran afoul of both academic critics and women's advocates. The academic critics argued, in the spirit of the Federal Judicial Center guidelines, that the experiment had too many limitations to justify a national policy innovation in the direction of greater severity. Women's advocates, in contrast, generally argued that the research showed the value of arrest, and that police would not make more arrests without a state statute requiring it. Having offended critics on both ends of the spectrum, the authors may claim to have taken the middle road. And judging by the standards for the approval of new drugs by the FDA, the case can be made that the Minneapolis experiment would have been sufficient evidence for the FDA to approve a "preferred arrest" policy of the kind the authors recommended.

The FDA analogy breaks down, however, with the authors' third recommendation: that the Minneapolis experiment be replicated in other cities. It appears to be unusual for randomized clinical trials to continue after the FDA has authorized a new drug, in part because it would mean withholding a treatment of proven effectiveness from a patient in need. This was the position taken by some opponents of the Minneapolis replication program, who argued for leaving well enough alone. The authors again took a middle ground, suggesting that the research results should be used provisionally. The authors stressed that more research was needed to insure that the findings would apply to other cities and that arrest would not create more violence among any particular sub-groups. As the results reported in this Symposium issue demonstrate, both concerns were valid.

E.   The Experiment's Influence

It is not clear exactly how much influence the experiment had in changing police policies and state laws, nor is it clear that those changes created substantial changes in police practice. What is clear is that the policies and laws governing police responses to domestic violence under-went a radical change in the years following the extensive publicity reporting the experiment's results.

In 1984, on the eve of the announcement of the final Minneapolis results, a national telephone survey of a sample of police departments serving cities of over 100,000 found that only ten percent of them encouraged their police officers to make arrests in misdemeanor domes-tic violence cases. By 1986, a repeat survey found that forty-six percent of a (slightly different) sample of those cities encouraged arrest in those circumstances. There is some evidence that cities were more likely to have made that change if the respondents could properly identify the results of the Minneapolis experiment, but some might read those results as showing only a modest direct influence of the experiment on policy.

What may have had greater influence on the policy change was the highly publicized $2.5 million jury verdict against the Torrington, Con-necticut Police Department for repeatedly failing to make arrests of an abusive husband who ultimately caused serious injury to his wife, Tracey Thurman. The threat of civil liability is often mentioned when police discuss this issue, even among police officers who have never heard of the Minneapolis experiment. The indirect influence of the experiment, however, might have come from Professor James Fyfe, who cited its findings as an expert witness testifying on behalf of plaintiff.

Whatever the relative contributions of the experiment, the Duluth mandatory arrest demonstration project, the Attorney General's Task Force on Family Violence, documentary and dramatized television pro-grams, and other attention paid to the issue in the mid–1980s, police policies continued to change. By 1989, a sample of big city police agencies found that eighty-four percent had adopted at least a preferred arrest policy, and seventy-six percent had adopted mandatory arrest policies. A sample of rural and urban police agencies in 1988 found that the Minneapolis experiment was ranked last among eight possible influences on police policies for domestic violence, but the authors of that survey argued that the experiment had indirect influence through lobbying on state legislatures. Whatever the influence on the state legislatures, all but one of the fifteen states with mandatory arrest statutes adopted them in the period after the Minneapolis experiment was released.

In recommending against such mandatory arrest laws and policies, the authors of the Minneapolis experiment warned that such laws would merely "invite circumvention" by police officers resistant to policy constraints. According to the available research on the implementation of such policies, that is generally what happened. Professor Ferraro's study of the Phoenix Police Department's field practices after the adoption of a mandatory arrest policy found that police made arrests in only forty-three percent of the cases where there was probable cause and the offender was present. Professor Balos, in her review of police compliance with the Minnesota mandatory arrest statute for violations of court orders of protection (about which the Minneapolis experiment was silent), found that police in Hennepin County, which includes Minneapolis, made arrests in only twenty-two percent of the cases where arrest was required by state law. Only Milwaukee, of all cities studied to date, appears to have achieved a high level of compliance with a mandatory arrest policy. Yet despite the resistance to full implementation of these policies, the national arrest rate for all simple assaults (most of which are probably domestic) rose by seventy percent from 1985 to 1989. In states where such laws were passed, moreover, it became legally impossible to replicate the Minneapolis experiment with a control group of non-arrested suspects, regardless of the *de facto* circumvention.

Fortunately, misdemeanor domestic violence arrests remained legally discretionary in enough states to allow the National Institute of Justice to sponsor a series of replications of the experiment—perhaps the clearest and most direct influence of the Minneapolis experiment on public policy.

V. The Replications

The five completed replications of the Minneapolis experiment have produced two key findings. One finding is that, in cases of arrest for probable cause, misdemeanor domestic assault has different effects in different cities. Specifically, the results in three cities (including Minneapolis) show evidence of a deterrent effect, while those in three others show evidence of increased violence overall. The second finding is that such arrests have different effects on different kinds of people, with a consistent variation depending on the employment status of the suspect. Employed suspects tend to be deterred by arrest, while unemployed suspects tend to become more frequently violent following arrest. These findings are drawn from the six experiments funded to replicate the Minneapolis experiment, all but one of which (Atlanta) has produced research reports as of this writing.

Understanding these results requires some appreciation of the differences among the experiments in their research designs and their implementation, as well as some of the possible reasons for the findings. It also requires special attention to the details of the Metro–Dade

(Miami) experiment, which alone among the completed experiments is not reported by its authors in this volume. Finally, the question of what influence the replications have had on the criminal law to date reveals important differences between them and the Minneapolis experiment.

A. Research designs

None of the replications was an exact reproduction of the Minneapolis research design. Rather than slavishly following the model of the physical sciences, the new experiments all improved upon the Minneapolis design in basic ways, and most of them tested different combinations of treatments against arrest. These changes in research design made the results arguably more powerful and interesting. The cost of those benefits, however, is some complication in our ability to make direct comparisons and draw conclusions across the studies.

The most basic improvement was the separation of police screening of cases for eligibility in the experiment from the application of the randomized treatment. That is, all five replications assigned the treatments after the police officer declared the cases eligible, and the officers had no idea of what the treatment would be at the time they made the eligibility decision. This was a potential problem inherent in the use of the color-coded report sheets that officers were issued in Minneapolis, due to the possible bias it could introduce into the officers' decision to include a case in the experiment. A "nice" suspect, for example, might have been excluded if the officer knew that arrest was the next treatment in his randomized sequence. By requiring officers to call headquarters to find out the treatment, the design greatly reduced the potential for such bias in sample selection.

Another improvement benefitting all but Omaha was a substantial increase in funding to allow much larger sample sizes. The larger sample sizes had several benefits. One was an increased number of treatments that could be tested in some experiments (Miami and Colorado Springs). Another was greater statistical power for examining different effects of arrest on different types of suspects. A third was greater power overall for detecting effects of arrest that are less substantial than the large differences found in Minneapolis.

The treatment innovations responded well to Professor Reiss's comment about comparing arrest to rather weak alternatives. The Colorado Springs experiment included immediate counseling at police headquarters, as well as police issuance at the scene of an emergency protection order legally ejecting the offender from the premises. The Metro–Dade experiment compared arrest with and without followup police counseling some days later to no arrest with and without counseling. The Charlotte experiment compared arrest to a ticket-style citation at the scene, which did not require the suspect to leave. Milwaukee pursued the question of jail time associated with arrest, randomly assigning three-hour and twelve-hour arrests to see what difference the variations in jail time across police agencies might make in the generalizability of the findings.

Only Omaha repeated the three Minneapolis alternatives, providing the closest replication of any of the five.

Eligibility criteria varied somewhat, sometimes unavoidably. In Metro–Dade, for example, warrantless arrest was illegal for unmarried couples, even if they were cohabiting, until near the end of the experiment. Thus, their sample has the highest proportion of married couples (79%) of any of the experiments, although it was closely followed by the sixty-nine percent married couples in the Colorado Springs sample—the only two experiments with a majority of married couples. The inclusion of non-spouse-like cases, such as homosexual lovers and other cohabitants, an issue raised by Ms. Zorza in this symposium, represented a trivial difference across the cities. While Charlotte, Colorado Springs and Metro–Dade excluded such cases, they constituted only eight percent of cases in Milwaukee, ten percent of cases in Omaha, and fifteen percent of the cases in Minneapolis. Alone among the six experiments, Charlotte excluded male victims entirely.

Perhaps the most striking difference was in the legal threshold of eligibility. While misdemeanor assault (or battery) was the only offense eligible in four of the experiments, Omaha and Colorado Springs accepted other "domestic" offenses. Such cases constituted only twenty-three percent of the Omaha cases, but they constituted over half (59%) of the Colorado Springs cases. It is not clear, then, that the Colorado Springs results are directly comparable to the other experiments, since most of its cases involved criminal "harassment" without evidence of physical contact. One experimental case I observed in Colorado Springs led to the arrest of a man who had been assaulted by a woman, on the rationale that he had come to her apartment that evening against her wishes. Under such circumstances in the Milwaukee experiment, and probably elsewhere, the woman would have been the experiment's suspect.

These variations, however, are also largely true of the police environment to which the results of these experiments must be generalized if they are to inform policymaking. What all six experiments had in common was that they all randomly assigned arrest and some sort of non-arrest. This alone made them among the most comparable studies of the effects of police practices ever undertaken.

B. Implementation

The comparability of results was further limited, however, by the diversity in actual implementation of the experiments. Table 1 summarizes these differences, along with the differences in the design elements. The Table reveals how much information we still lack on some key aspects of comparability of the experiments, such as the length of time arrestees are held in custody. Most of the important characteristics for comparison of the designs have been reported, however. They show great variance on some issues, and much less on others. What is most striking is that there is no consistent difference in any of these characteristics that matches the division of the six experiments into the two different substantive findings of deterrence or escalation effects.

The greatest variation across the experiments was in the demographic characteristics of the samples, which is exactly what the Minneapolis authors had recommended. Such variations helped to reveal whether arrest would have the same effects in different kinds of cities.

What was less variable, although far from consistent, was the nature of the arrest treatment. While the average number of hours spent in custody after arrest varied in percentage terms, it was generally reported to be in the range of nine to fifteen hours. Judging by the relatively small difference between the effects of short (three hour) and long (twelve hour) arrest in Milwaukee, these variations in custody time made little difference—assuming that they were measured accurately, which may not have been the case. Greater variability is found in the percentage of suspects who were handcuffed during arrest. While generally high where it was reported, Table 1 shows that Colorado Springs was again extremely different from the other experiments in having a rate of handcuffing four-fifths lower than those in the other cities. The greatest variability is found in the percentage of cases with prosecution leading to convictions and some sort of sentence which ranged from one percent in Milwaukee to sixty-four percent in Omaha. While the Minneapolis experiment, which had four percent convictions, could eliminate prosecution as a contributing influence on the effects of arrest, that was clearly not the case in Charlotte and Omaha.

More reassuring from a research design standpoint is that all six experiments had relatively high levels of compliance with the randomized designs. All of them improved on the Minneapolis compliance rate of eighty-two percent, ranging up to the Milwaukee rate of ninety-eight percent. While none of the experiments is perfect, in the historical experience of both medical and criminological experiments the compliance levels are substantial.

The most important methodological question, however, is whether the misassignment rate exceeded the base rate of recidivism, since that could severely distort an analysis of the results according to how each was *supposed* to have been treated, rather than to what actually happened. That approach to analysis is the standard for medical experiments, and was the method NIJ instructed the replication experiments to employ in the analyses summarized in Tables 1 and 2. Based on the current reports alone, it is impossible to tell how much statistical power each experiment may have lost from a high ratio of recidivism to the misapplication of randomly assigned treatments.

What is easier and equally important to assess is the effect of differences in response rates to the six-month followup victim interviews. These varied from twenty-three percent in Minneapolis to the seventy percent range in Omaha and Milwaukee. Where the response rates were under sixty percent (Charlotte, Metro–Dade, and Colorado Springs), there is a substantial likelihood of the interview sample having substantively different characteristics from the full sample. At the very least, this may account for any differences between the victim interviews and official records, which were found in all three replication cities with low response rates.

C. Results

The replication results, just like the Minneapolis results, were examined in several different ways. The logic of employing multiple analyses is to increase our confidence in results that are consistent across different approaches and criteria. The difficulty this approach can create, however, is in the interpretation of conflicting results even within experiments. As Table 2 summarizes, that is what occurred in almost all of the replications.

One of the key questions about a treatment is how long the effects last. As Table 2 shows, there was evidence of short-term deterrence followed by a longer-term decay in Milwaukee, and evidence that the effects of arrest worsened over time in both Omaha and Charlotte. A major contribution of Dr. Dunford's article in this symposium, in fact, is his demonstration that the conventional six-month followup period, driven largely by funding agencies' needs to contain costs, can substantially distort the measurement of the treatment effects. It is not clear why the effects of arrest worsen over time, but it is clear that the finding is not due to the idiosyncracies of any one experiment.

Another difference in the results concerns the suspects' repeat violence against the same victim or any other victim. The hypothesis that arrest displaces repeat violence onto new victims has its adherents, and so the Milwaukee experiment tested it. The results of both approaches were essentially the same, but there was admittedly little deterrent effect to explain away with displacement. As Table 2 shows, most of the other research reports stuck to the focus of the Minneapolis design, which examined repeat violence only against the same victim.

The most basic difference in the analysis of these results is the method of measuring recidivism: official records versus victim interviews. Low response rates in the latter, however, can make these two measures inappropriate for comparison. Even where response rates are relatively high, they can still capture different populations. For example, the sample represented in victim interviews might generally consist of couples who are more socially bonded and therefore easier to locate than those on the full sample captured by official measures. This disparity produces some striking differences in results between the official and interview measures, but in highly consistent ways.

For example, *all of the evidence of escalation effects are found in the official data, and not in the victim interviews.* The evidence in Omaha, Milwaukee, and Charlotte that the arrested suspects became significantly more violent than those not arrested is only found in the full samples, and not in the reduced portions of the sample granting interviews. While this may be due to inherent differences between interviews and official records, it is equally plausible that escalation effects are more pronounced among the less socially bonded couples who are harder to interview. It is also important that the reader note this before reading the individual experimental reports, since the authors do not put their own findings in the context of these other results. Thus the Charlotte experiment reported in this issue, for example, makes little of the significant escalation effect it found in one measure because it was not confirmed by the other. The replication of this difference in two other cities, however, gives the finding much more prominence as a clue to the overall puzzle of these diverse results.

Another striking fact about the two different measures is that *interviews generally show better results from arrest than does official data.* In both Colorado Springs and Miami, for example, at least one official measure shows no deterrent effect, while the victim interviews in both cities show a clear deterrent effect. This is again consistent with the hypothesis that the interviewed victims were different in important respects from the full sample. It is somewhat complicated, however, by the appearance of a deterrent effect as measured by one of the official measures in Miami.

These differences in the "main effects," or overall results for each randomly assigned treatment group, may mask underlying differences in the effects of arrest within each group. Ideally, such differences would be hypothesized in advance and built into the random assignment design by randomization within each subgroup, such as employed versus unemployed suspects. The political difficulties of obtaining approval for such a design in 1986, however, were insuperable. Thus, the experiments had an advance hypothesis that less socially bonded persons would react to arrest differently, but the full statistical power of the research design was not built around that hypothesis. This creates, in effect, some of the same problems of correlation versus causation which randomized experiments were designed to resolve. Some statisticians, however, endorse such sub-analyses as merely constituting experiments within experiments.

The results of these tests with regard to interaction effects are, so far, consistently in support of the social bonding hypothesis. *Arrest has consistently more crime reduction effect on employed suspects than it does on unemployed suspects. That is the good news. The bad news is that the weaker a suspect's social bonds, the more likely it appears to be that arrest will backfire by causing increased violence.* The initial data analysis demonstrating this effect is found in the article by Sherman and his colleagues in this issue. That analysis was subsequently confirmed with more powerful analytic techniques, which showed in particular that the greatest escalation effect was among suspects who were both unmarried and unemployed. An identical analysis was performed on the Omaha data, which showed even stronger differences (although not statistically significant ones, due to the smaller sample.) The interaction of unemployment and arrest was later replicated by Professor Berk and his colleagues, as reported in this symposium, although without taking marriage or other social bonding indicators into account. Finally, this pattern is consistent with the differences in Miami and Colorado Springs between the official and victim interview recidivism data.

Whether the pattern of interaction between social bonds and the effect of arrest holds up in Charlotte and Metro–Dade still remains to be seen. The fact that the interaction has been found in three very different cities, however, is a strikingly consistent finding no matter what the other experiments show. It demonstrates that in at least some cities, arrest does have different effects on different kinds of people. Under those conditions, it seems unlikely that the FDA would approve the marketing of mandatory arrest for all suspects.

Metro-Dade Details: While the statistical details of the other five experiments are published and accessible either in this issue or elsewhere, that is not true of the Metro–Dade experiment. Therefore, a full understanding of the replications is served by a brief summary of the Miami–Dade details.

The Miami Metro–Dade experiment randomly assigned four different treatments. Arrest and no arrest were each divided into two groups: those with and without followup counseling by a special police unit. These followup visits occurred within about a week after the call to police during which arrest was randomly assigned. There were no significant differences associated with the counseling treatments. The effects of arrest in Miami are clearest when we collapse the four groups into two, comparing all arrest cases to all non-arrest cases.

The Miami victim interviews clearly show deterrent effects of arrest, although we must recall that the victim interview response rate of forty-two percent of the full sample suggested very different characteristics of that sub-sample compared to the full sample of 907 cases on which official records were gathered. At the time of the initial interview, eighteen percent of the non-arrest victims reported at least one incident in which the suspect hit, slapped, hurt, or tried to hurt the victim. This compares to only ten percent of the arrest group victims. The frequency differences are similar: a rate of 345 per 1,000 suspects in the non-arrest group, compared to 182 in the arrest group. The differences in both measures are statistically significant, reducing the risk of repeat violence by about half. At the six month interviews, the prevalence effect was about the same. Twenty-seven percent of the non-arrest victims were hurt at least once compared to fifteen percent of the arrest group victims. The frequency difference was also of the same magnitude: 527 repeat incidents per 1,000 no-arrest suspects compared to 281 repeat incidents per 1,000 arrested suspects. These results were confirmed by significant differences in the results of three different tests of time to "failure," or the date of the first repeat incident of violence.

Repeat arrests for domestic violence also showed deterrent effects in Miami. While the number of repeat arrests in all groups was low, the prevalence rates were still significantly different among the suspects arrested and those not arrested. Out of the 465 arrested suspects, five

(1.1%) were re-arrested for at least one new offense against the same victims within six months. Among the 442 suspects randomly assigned to non-arrest, the comparable number was seventeen (3.8%) subsequent arrests, or almost four times the prevalence rate. The difference in frequency was of about the same magnitude as the difference in prevalence (although possibly due to chance): twenty-two subsequent arrests per 1,000 arrested suspects, compared to seventy-seven per 1,000 among the suspects not arrested. Once again, all three tests of the difference in average time to first repeat offense showed significant benefits of arrest.

The one measure that showed no statistically significant difference was the offense reports naming the same suspect as the offender against the same victim. At six months, the prevalence rates of this measure were almost identical for the arrest and non-arrest suspects. This was true whether the repeat offense was aggravated or non-aggravated battery, or if it was any other offense. The frequency of any offense, however, was still somewhat higher among those suspects who had not been arrested (342 per 1,000) than among those who had been (290 per 1,000). The time to first repeat offense also showed no differences.

Why the two official measures should disagree is unclear, although we can speculate that there was greater measurement error—or variability in police recordkeeping—in the offense reports than in the arrest reports. Had they been combined, as they were in Minneapolis, they would have probably shown no differences by treatment, given the far greater volume of offense reports than of arrests. Citing the Miami experiment as a strong confirmation of the Minneapolis results must therefore be done with some caution. Nonetheless, there is still support for positing a deterrent effect in at least one official measure, and very strong, consistent support in all five ways of analyzing the victim data— consistent with the social bonding hypothesis.

D. Explaining Diverse Results

Unfortunately, the social bonding hypothesis does not yet fully explain the differences in findings across cities. In order to give that hypothesis a full and fair test, the raw data from all of the six experiments must be merged and analyzed together. Different combinations of risk factors, for example, must be calculated, such as unmarried and unemployed (a category very rare in Colorado Springs) versus married and unemployed. Since not all of the raw data are yet publicly available, that analysis has not been possible. When it is, however, it may allow an explanation of the diverse results that goes beyond a simple bivariate inspection of the demographic differences portrayed in Table 1.

Taken by itself, Table 1 shows no clear demographic correlates between the deterrence and the escalation cities. Even where some differences appear, they apply to only two out of three cases. For example, the deterrent effect cities had a much lower average proportion of black suspects (38%) than the escalation-effect cities (63%). The almost identical proportions of black suspects in escalation effect Omaha and deterrent-effect Miami, however, seriously weakens race as an explanation for the diverse results. The raw data might, however, reveal other characteristics correlated with race in the different cities, which may in turn support a social bonds theory or some other interpretation of differential reactions to domestic violence arrests.

One such characteristic, for example, may be the social structure of the community setting in which the suspects reside. Unemployment or social bonds may simply be a correlate of a more powerful neighborhood effect on suspects' reactions to arrest. As Professors Sampson and Wilson have observed, much social science has a tendency towards the "individualistic fallacy" of assuming that all causation is located in characteristics of individuals rather than of their social settings. Given the strong ecological correlates of crime rates, it is equally plausible that there are structural characteristics of neighborhoods—such as the proportion of unemployed males or of unmarried couples or of persons with criminal histories—that could determine how neighborhood residents react to arrest for domestic violence.

This hypothesis would predict very different effects of unemployment on arrest reactions in Colorado Springs, for example, and in Milwaukee. The neighborhood proportions of unemployed persons, like the sample proportions reported in Table 1, are likely to be far higher in Milwaukee than in Colorado Springs. Thus we would expect more of an escalation or labeling effect in Milwaukee than in Colorado Springs. Similarly, we would expect more of a deterrent effect of arrest among employed persons in Colorado Springs than in Milwaukee, assuming the same ecological differences. As this issue reports, that is exactly what has been found to date. What remains to be done is to collect census tract and block level data for all the cases in the six experiments and test the ecological hypothesis. While such an analysis may be years in coming, it would be well worth the investment in unraveling the puzzle of the diverse results.

VI. The Symposium Issue

The main articles in this symposium make several contributions to the evolution of our knowledge about policing domestic violence. The gracious agreement of the authors to prepare papers for the issue has led, for the first time, to an assembly in one place of the original reports of research on most of the experiments. This will greatly simplify the task of policymakers and advisors seeking to digest the findings of the entire research program, and it will increase the odds that criminology may have an appropriate influence on the criminal law. The many requests for information on the experiments from state legislative counsel, even while the issue was in preparation, suggests the great need for such a compendium.

This symposium also allows comparison of the ways in which different researchers interpret the same data. The authors of neither the Omaha nor the Charlotte report would say that their experiments found that arrest caused an overall escalation in domestic violence, although that is how this introduction has characterized them. The reader is urged to attend to the reasons for these differences in interpretation, such as the consistent showing of escalation in official data, but not in victim interviews, in three experiments. Only by interpreting the experiments in relation to each other, which this symposium invites us all to do, can we fully understand the results.

The article by Ms. Zorza lays an excellent criminal law foundation for the significance of these criminological experiments. It comprehensively reviews the history of litigation and legislation that helped to frame the key questions to which the entire research program responded. It clearly demonstrates the significant stimulus that criminal law reform movements can have in shaping criminology, which in turn may shape criminal law. And as a representative statement of the reaction of many domestic violence victim's advocates to the results of the replication studies, Ms. Zorza's commentary on the experiments illustrates the great divide in language, epistemology, treatment of scientific evidence, values and assumptions separating criminologists and activists on this issue.

While the flaws of the Minneapolis experiment were substantial, they go unmentioned in the advocates' critique. The flaws of the replications—at least those of the first three reported, which do not support a deterrent effect—are highlighted instead, because of what Zorza describes as the researchers' appearance of seeming "intent on returning to the old do-nothing or even blame-the-victim practices." Such *ad hominem* comments are unfortunately frequent in the attacks on the replication results, but they go with the territory. An assistant attorney general of the United States once told this writer it was a good thing that the Minneapolis experiment had found a deterrent effect, for otherwise that official would have been compelled to attack the experiment's methodology. It is unfortunate that so many advocates cannot accept the concern of criminologists with the plight of domestic violence victims, apparently because we do not always reach politically correct conclusions.

It is even more unfortunate that the battered women's movement in Milwaukee and elsewhere has shown little concern for the evidence that arrest positively harms black women in at least one poverty ghetto, where the majority of the suspects are unemployed and unmarried. Zorza's characterization of those results typically obscures the issue:

> [E]ven if arrest may not deter unemployed abusers in ghetto neighborhoods, arrest still deters the vast majority of abusers ... [w]e do not consider eliminating arrest for other crimes (e.g., robbery), however, because it may not deter a particular individual or class of individuals.

The Milwaukee finding is not the failed deterrence of arrest, but the substantial *increases* arrest produces in the total volume of violence against victims of the ghetto poor unemployed. We have no evidence that arrest for robbery increases the total number of robbery offenses robbers commit, nor is arrest without prosecution the typical response to robbery—as it is in the realm of domestic assault. If we had evidence that the typical criminal justice response to robbery backfired, we might respond to it with longer prison sentences upon conviction in order to counteract higher recidivism rates with greater incapacitation effects. Whether such a response makes sense when applied to a crime as pervasive as domestic violence—either for the families involved or for society—is another question altogether. What seems clear is that prosecutors are generally unwilling to do much with domestic violence cases, especially in cities with high volumes of such arrests (like Milwaukee). As long as that is true, we must soberly assess the wisdom of an "arrest-and-nothing-else" policy, since that is all we seem likely to get.

The comment that "most abusers" are deterred by arrest also misses a key point. While most abusers may be white, married and employed, the abusers *coming to police attention* may not be. Most of the crime, most of the police, and most police responses to reports of domestic violence in this country are found in cities of over 100,000. Most of those cities, in turn, have substantial minority populations, in which victims disproportionately call on the police for assistance. Disregarding these facts in order to pursue a policy beneficial to women who do not live in poverty stricken ghettoes—primarily white women— displays an unfortunate racial and economic insensitivity to the overall effects of mandatory arrest. Even if most abusers coming to police attention are not ghetto dwellers, we cannot write off as unimportant the victims of those who are.

Professors Hirschel and Hutchison have provided an exemplar of a comprehensive report on a randomized experiment in criminal law. Their careful, cautious and thorough analysis provides ample detail to answer a wide range of questions about how the experiment was done and why it might have found what it found. One may take issue with their conclusions, but not with the admirable way in which they present their data.

Their conclusion that Charlotte showed no difference in the effects of the arrest, citation, and separate-or-advise treatments seems difficult to support. The fact is that offenders who were arrested and issued citations (tickets to appear in court) showed significantly higher rates of violence than did other offenders, at least as measured by the official data. The authors attempt to explain the discrepancy between the data obtained in official reports and that obtained in victim interviews by citing the under-reporting of repeat violence in the former, and the much higher rate of reported violence in the latter. We must recall, however, a more serious and profound difference between the official and victim data: the one-hundred percent coverage of the official data compared to the fifty percent coverage of the sample with the victim interview data. The two measures, in effect, compare a fruit basket (the full sample) to a group of oranges (the victim interviews). The differences between them may be just as plausibly related to the samples as to the method of measurement. The official data showing that arrest increased violence cannot be discounted, since it was the only measure for the entire fruit basket that constituted the randomized experiment. The causal inference value of the random assignment for such a small and possibly biased victim interview sample of what was randomized is highly questionable at best, just as it was in Minneapolis.

One point in the presentation of the Charlotte findings should also be clarified. The analyses taking into account race, prior record and other variables might be read as showing that there is no interaction effect between those variables and arrest. That is not what the article says. The authors actually state that there was no two-way correlation between repeat domestic violence and the respective predictor variables of race, age, marital status and employment status. That does not mean that there is no three-way association between employment, arrest and repeat violence, which is what is reported in the Milwaukee, Omaha and Colorado Springs studies. A three-way interaction may be present even when there is no two-way correlation, just as it was when no two-way correlation was found in Milwaukee. Thus, the Charlotte experiment does not falsify the prediction of such an interaction, at least as reported in this symposium. The three-way analysis still remains to be reported.

As the first to begin and report a Minneapolis replication experiment, Dr. Dunford has already detailed many of his results elsewhere. In this symposium, however, he contributes new and vital information. In the original report of the Omaha replication experiment, for example, he reported only the first six months' follow-up data, none of which showed any differences in repeat violence rates between arrest and non-arrest treatments. In this analysis, however, Dr. Dunford includes data covering a full year's follow-up (and more), and while he concludes that these extended data do not alter the finding of no deterrent effect for arrest, they clearly support an alternative interpretation: that arrest causes more repeat violence than non-arrest.

Dr. Dunford's Table 1 indicates that the frequency rate of repeat violence (measured by new arrests) in a one year follow-up was 248 incidents per 1,000 suspects among those who had been arrested, but only 154 incidents per 1,000 among those who had not been arrested. This difference is substantial: arrest caused a relative increase of sixty-one percent more repeat incidents than no arrest. The odds that this finding is not due to chance are ninety-three percent. This just barely misses the conventional standard of ninety-five percent, and clearly satisfies a widely used standard of ninety percent. A not quite as large difference found in the other official measure (39% more violence with arrest than non-arrest) has an eighty-four percent likelihood of not being a chance result. These substantial differences are thus very good bets to be more than mere flukes.

Dunford's main conclusion is that longer time periods are needed to assess the full effects of arrest and other interventions. While the victim interview data show no differences at twelve months, they showed non-significant differences in favor of deterrence at six months. Thus both the interview and the official data show the same trend in effects from six months to twelve months: a decreasing benefit and an increased cost associated with arrest. This prompts us to ask how much more repeat violence would be associated with arrest in an eighteen month follow-up. Viewed in the context of Milwaukee's and Charlotte's results, the Omaha findings are consistent with the pattern of official measures showing that arrest increases recidivism.

Equal time requires a comment on the article about the Milwaukee experiment, for which I bear the principal responsibility. An objective commentator should raise the question of a "shotgun" approach to data analysis in which a lack of significant differences in the main experiment leads the analysts to search anywhere for differences within subgroups, just to find some significant differences to report. An objective commentator would also have to note, however, that a "rifle shot" hypothesis that zeroes in on a few theoretically driven variables produces a far more compelling set of findings, less likely to be spurious or chance correlations. The commentator might concede that that was what happened in the Milwaukee analysis, given the publication of the "rifle shot" hypothesis in another law review symposium some eight years earlier. A more skeptical writer than the present one might still harbor lingering doubts, however, and tend to place greater reliance on the outcome of attempts to replicate the employment interactions in other experiments. That skeptic might then seize upon Professor Berk's analysis as evidence that the increase in violence among the unemployed suspects caused by arrest has been exaggerated by the Milwaukee writers. In doing so, the skeptic would be basing a conclusion on less than the full story.

In the article by Professor Berk and his colleagues, we are once again treated to that which he has so often provided: the application to a criminological problem of a cutting-edge statistical technique. The lawyers who read this volume should take comfort in the fact that Bayesian analysis is not only unfamiliar to them, but to most criminologists as well. The technique consists of analyzing data in one study—Colorado Springs—based on findings from two prior experiments in which interactions between arrest and unemployment had been found (Milwaukee and Omaha). The conclusion that an interaction effect is found in all three experiments is consistent with the social bonds hypothesis discussed above. The conclusion that an increase in domestic violence among the unemployed is not replicated warrants further comment.

Professor Berk's analysis of the effects of arrest in this symposium are limited to the *prevalence* of recidivism, or the percentage of suspects with one or more detected acts of repeat domestic violence. Of greater significance to both victims and police, however, may be the *frequency* of repeat violence, or the total number of attacks. As the report on the Milwaukee experiment in this symposium demonstrates, prevalence and frequency can lead to somewhat different interpretations. Indeed, the conclusion that arrest increases repeat violence among unemployed suspects is based primarily on the results for frequency, not for prevalence. Yet Professor Berk does not report the frequency results for Colorado Springs, and does not incorporate the frequency results for Omaha and Milwaukee.

As it happens, we do have the frequency results for both Milwaukee (reported in this issue) and Omaha (reported elsewhere). In both experiments, the frequency data show that arrest produces a pronounced increase in repeat violence among the unemployed. While Berk correctly reports a small prevalence difference in Omaha among unemployed suspects (57% among those arrested and 53% among those not), the frequency difference is in the same direction but much larger. The Omaha frequency data show that arrest reduces the rate of future violence among the employed from 280 to 176 incidents per 1,000 suspects per year (a 37.1% reduction). Among the unemployed, arrest increases the rate of future violence by 52.2% from 412 to 627 incidents per 1,000 suspects per year. Given the small number of cases in the Omaha sample (sixty-four unemployed and 175 employed persons), these differences do not achieve statistical significance. Yet the differences between these point estimates of the rate of future violence are larger than in Milwaukee (which had a forty-three percent increase in frequency caused by arrest among the unemployed), and in the same direction. It seems hard to justify a conclusion that arrest does not backfire for unemployed suspects, at least in those two cities. Frequency data for Colorado Springs may well show similar results.

Even if they do not, however, we must again note the differences between Colorado Springs and the other experiments: most of the suspects there were married and most of the offenses involved not physical violence but verbal harassment. Furthermore, Colorado Springs apparently has no poverty-stricken ghettoes with high proportions of persons with low marriage rates, long-term unemployment, low prevalence of high school education, high prevalence of prior arrests, and other similar characteristics. Thus, the "good risks" seem better and the "bad risks" seem not so bad in "hi-tech" Colorado Springs as in "rust belt" Milwaukee and Omaha. Given the major differences between the samples in the three cities, it is arguably impressive that the employment interaction results are as similar as they are.

I will not be commenting on the other commentaries in this issue. Suffice it to say that the Journal editors have chosen a distinguished group of commentators representing a broad range of viewpoints, from police to women's advocates to legal scholars.

VII. What Have We Learned?

After more than a decade of evaluating arrest for misdemeanor domestic violence, we still have much to learn. The jigsaw puzzle of diverse results in different cities has not been put together, and too many pieces are still missing. Many alternate approaches still remain untested or unreplicated, such as the impressive Omaha result that issuing warrants for *absent* offenders reduced repeat violence by fifty percent. Nonetheless, it is time we took stock of what we have learned, both about the substance of the problem and about the process of doing policy-relevant criminology.

A. Domestic Violence Arrests

One response to the replication results is that it is too early to reach any policy recommendations. This view implies that the burden of proof must be on any argument to undo mandatory arrest laws, or stop them from being passed. Such a view, however, runs contrary to the principles laid down by the Federal Judicial Center's Advisory Committee on Experimentation in the Law, as cited above. The question as of 1984 was whether an innovation of greater severity should be adopted—preferred or mandatory arrest. The initial experiment supported the innovation, but with reservations. On balance, the subsequent experiments have not.

Even if we disregard the evidence of increased domestic violence caused by arrest in some cities and with some kinds of offenders, the weight of the evidence fails to justify an innovation of greater severity— at least on specific deterrent grounds alone. Yet it is those grounds, alone, which have morally justified the entire program of research. If the FDA had to make a decision about allowing mandatory arrest to go on the market based on these experiments, it seems doubtful that it would. On the other hand, if it were asked to allow some doctors to use arrest on a selective basis when it was most likely to be effective, they might well do that.

Arrest is not a drug, of course, and it is constrained by principles of justice. The unfairness of arrest guidelines based on employment status would be unthinkable, regardless of its effectiveness. What may ultimately be acceptable, under the existing principles of community policing, is different police policies or practices for different neighborhoods. Police discretion already varies widely by neighborhood, and community policing is trying to make it vary even more explicitly in response to community preferences. A local option approach, informed by research on the specific deterrent effects of arrest in different communities, might be the best way to develop a workable policy from the findings.

This possibility can be fully assessed, however, only after further analyses explore the neighborhood basis for the interaction effects observed to date. Whether that analysis can predict the likely effects of arrest based on census tract characteristics remains to be seen. It may well be more effective at that task, however, than we have been in predicting city-level effects so far.

Whatever approach may be taken on structuring discretion to use arrest, the key question is whether any discretion should remain in the hands of the police. This question has both a philosophical and a practical dimension. On philosophical grounds, it is clear that large segments of the legal and advocacy communities want no discretion invested in the police; they can cite legions of horror stories in support of their positions. On the practical side, no one has ever figured out how to eliminate police discretion. As Ms. Zorza quite correctly points out, we have learned that mandatory arrest laws are widely circumvented. That is all the more reason, it would seem, to develop an alternative approach.

The available research cannot say what that approach should be. All it can say is what the results of the six experiments show. Therein lies the lesson for the influence of criminology on the criminal law.

B. *Experimental Criminology and Criminal Law*

The domestic violence experiments show that criminology can provide factual information about the criminal law and its consequences. That is about all it can do. It cannot, for example, control the ways in which participants in the political process describe (or distort) research results in advancing a point of view. It cannot ensure that its recommendations will be heeded, or that its conclusions will be believed. It cannot speak to value judgments about "just deserts," even when they are conveniently raised as a fallback position when evidence of deterrence is weakened. It cannot guarantee that its findings will resonate with the prevailing ethos of the age, as the Minneapolis findings did but the replication findings did not.

The Minneapolis findings stirred enormous interest by a wide range of writers and editorialists, who hailed the results as a breakthrough. The replication results received grudging acceptance in some of those quarters, and complete silence in most others. They were even attacked editorially by the Milwaukee newspapers. It is clear that our *zeitgeist* in the 1990s still favors "getting tough," and that greater severity is more politically correct than lesser severity among a broad coalition of both liberal and conservative groups. This carries a sobering lesson: provisional policy recommendations made on initial research results may be widely accepted in support of that broad coalition, but subsequent findings that run against it may have far less influence. Undoing the effects of initial results may be much harder than some criminologists imagined, largely because there is less rational interest in minimizing violence than one might have assumed. It appears that preferences for punishment have more ideological than pragmatic foundations, and that criminology can only speak to the pragmatic.

This is a sad commentary for a system of criminal law founded on the presumption of deterrence. It suggests that as criminology unravels the deterrence hypothesis in its full complexity, the criminal law is unlikely to respond to that information in ways that will maximize crime control. Rather, the principle of appropriate vengeance, already so strong in the sentencing guidelines movement, may become even stronger, making deterrence irrelevant. If this keeps up, we will have no need for a Journal of Criminal Law and Criminology; a Journal of Just Deserts will do just fine.

But times change, and knowledge takes a long time to accumulate. By the time we have fully assembled the puzzle of diverse effects of domestic violence arrests, perhaps the political culture may become more open to adopting columnist Ellen Goodman's point of view:

What is progress after all in the course of sexual politics? is it marked by an increase in the number of men in jail? or by a decrease in the number of assaults? I don't want to choose between law enforcement and "crime prevention," but I would chart the long run of progress by the change in men's behavior.[139]

JOAN ZORZA, THE CRIMINAL LAW OF MISDEMEANOR DOMESTIC VIOLENCE, 1970–1990

83 J. Crim. L. & Criminology 46–72 (1992).

I. BACKGROUND

Domestic disturbance incidents constitute the largest category of calls received by police each year. This is not surprising given the number of women who are abused by their intimate partners. Half of all married women will be beaten at least once by their husbands. Many of these women are beaten as frequently as once a month, once a week, or even daily. The U.S. Surgeon General found that battering of women by husbands, ex-husbands or lovers "is the single largest cause of injury to women in the United States," accounting for one-fifth of all hospital emergency room cases. The injuries women sustain in these attacks are at least as serious as those suffered in violent felony crimes. Weapons are used in thirty percent of all domestic violence incidents. Thirty-one percent of all women murdered in America are killed by their husbands, exhusbands, or lovers.

Woman abuse profoundly affects children living in the home. It imperils children psychologically even when they themselves are never beaten. Frequently children are also victims of abuse. Between fifty-three and seventy percent of men who abuse women also beat their children, and a significant number sexually abuse the children, especially daughters. Many children also suffer serious injuries as a result of the reckless conduct of their fathers while beating their mothers. In families where the mother is beaten, sixty-two percent of sons over the age of fourteen are injured trying to protect their mothers. A son who sees his father beat his mother is more likely to become a delinquent or a batterer himself than if his father beat him instead.

In most communities police officers may be the only meaningful contact citizens have with "the law." The evidence suggests, however, that police are largely indifferent to domestic violence, and that they attach to it a very low priority. Throughout the 1970s and early 1980s, officers believed and were taught that domestic violence was a private matter, ill suited to public intervention. Police departments also consider domestic violence calls unglamorous, nonprestigious, and unrewarding. Until recently, police frequently ignored domestic violence calls or pur-

---

139. Ellen Goodman, I'd Have Let Him Walk, Wash. Post, Dec. 14, 1991, at A27.

posefully delayed responding for several hours. Even when they eventually arrived on the scene, police rarely did anything about domestic violence, and some actually responded by laughing in the woman's face. Other officers talked to the abuser, possibly removing the batterer from the home temporarily to cool off. Some police officers removed the abused woman from "his" home. Yet, in conformity to traditional practice, police virtually never arrested the abuser. In rural areas, police who frequently know both parties or at least the abuser, were even more reluctant to respond in a manner that would protect the victim.

Indeed, those police departments that had policies on handling domestic calls in the 1970s had a clear non-arrest policy. The Oakland Police Department's *1975 Training Bulletin on Techniques of Dispute Intervention* explicitly described

> [t]he police role in a dispute situation [as] more often that of a mediator and peacemaker than enforcer of the law.... [T]he possibility that ... arrest will only aggravate the dispute or create a serious danger for the arresting officers due to possible efforts to resist arrest ... is most likely when a husband or father is arrested in his home.... Normally, officers should adhere to the policy that arrests shall be avoided ... but when one of the parties demands arrest, you should attempt to explain the ramifications of such action (e.g., loss of wages, bail procedures, court appearances) and encourage the parties to reason with each other.[25]

Detroit Police Commander James Bannon, in his address to the 1975 American Bar Association convention, described the manner in which his police officers respond to domestic violence calls. According to Bannon, the dispatcher would screen calls from battered women to respond only to those women who appeared in the most imminent danger. If the woman had only minor injuries when they arrived, the police became angry and would not respond quickly the next time. Women often learned to report that a stranger was attacking them or that their abuser had a gun. While such a desperate ploy might have worked once for a woman, police simply declared her not credible if they found no serious injuries. Lacking credibility, she was deemed unworthy of police protection if she called again. Police treated poor women and women of color with less concern than they did middle class and white women, even when they were severely injured.

Michigan's policy, as taught in its Police Training Academy, directed officers to:

> a. Avoid arrest if possible. Appeal to their [complainant's] vanity.
>
> b. Explain the procedure of obtaining a warrant.
>
> (1) Complainant must sign complaint.
>
> (2) Must appear in court.

25. Martin, supra note 14, at 93–94.

(3) Consider loss of time.

(4) Cost of court.

    c. State that your only interest is to prevent a breach of the peace.

    d. Explain that attitudes usually change by court time.

    e. Recommend a postponement.

(1) Court not in session.

(2) No judge available.

    f. *Don't* be too harsh or critical.[28]

Michigan's policy also failed to provide for sufficient education. While almost half of all Michigan police calls are for domestic disturbances, only three to five out of the 240 hours of police recruit training are devoted to the manner in which police should answer these calls. Training in other police departments has been similarly inadequate. Prior to 1980, when police academies were still uncommon, those who received on-the-job training were generally assigned to those experienced officers who were seen as most successful. Unfortunately, these officers were precisely those least likely to have challenged the standard practices for responding to domestic violence incidents. Rookies looked up to their experienced partners and were rewarded for imitating them.

With the advent of police academies, new recruits were trained by men generally "chosen" as instructors, not because of their academic ability or interest in teaching, but because of their advancing age or temporary disability, or because they were on leave or special duty restriction pending departmental investigation. New officers were often trained first and foremost as men, and the ethic of masculinity was seen as being of the utmost importance. Seeing anything from a woman's perspective was, if not almost taboo, at least so completely foreign that it did not happen.

In this light, it is hardly surprising that the police who did respond to domestic violence calls almost always took the man's side. And because abusers, when they did not or could not deny their abuse, tried to shift the blame onto others, especially their victims, the police frequently joined in blaming the victim. The responding officer often admonished the woman to be a better wife or asked, or at least wondered, why she did not leave. Some officers concluded that she must enjoy the beatings, or at least not mind them. These officers conveniently ignored the fact that their failure to protect the woman, her lack of money, and the far greater risk of being beaten or killed if she tried to separate herself from her abuser all combined to make her decision logical. Women's fears of retaliation for leaving are rational; divorced and separated women, who comprise only ten percent of all women, account for fully seventy-five percent of all battered women, and they

---

28. Martin, supra note 14, at 93.

report being battered fourteen times more often than do women still living with their partners.

Battered women who reported assaults have typically represented a small portion of the total number of victims. One 1970s study of 109 battered women revealed that of every 32,000 assaults, only 517, or less than two percent of the total, were actually reported. Victims sadly learned that reporting spouse abuse was futile.

In 1970, American law did not recognize marital rape as a crime. Though twelve percent of married women are raped by their husbands, and from thirty-four to fifty-nine percent of battered women report that their male partner rapes them, laws in most states continued to define rape as intercourse with a woman other than the rapist's wife. Marital rape is one of the strongest predictors of whether one of the spouses will kill the other. The injuries that wives receive from marital rape are more severe than those received from rape at the hands of a stranger, yet if a wife was raped by her husband before 1970, the strongest charges she could bring were assault charges or a divorce on cruelty grounds. In states like New York, where adultery was the only ground for divorce until 1966, the wife could not get a divorce regardless of how many times or how brutally her husband had raped her. Following the law, police throughout the United States largely ignored marital rape.

In 1981, the supreme courts of Massachusetts and New Jersey declared that a husband could be criminally liable for raping his wife. Several years later, New York, Florida, and Georgia followed suit. As of January 1985, twenty states permitted a wife to prosecute her husband for rape, although most of these states limited the situations in which she could do so. Even as recently as July 1991, only nineteen states had completely abolished the marital rape exemption. In those states where marital rape was not a crime, however, it was usually grounds for divorce. Furthermore, at least twenty-eight states currently specifically allow sexual abuse of a spouse as grounds for the issuance of an order for protection. These changes in the law have made police more able and willing to intervene in situations involving marital rape.

Police frequently rationalized their refusal to intervene in domestic violence cases on the ground that domestic violence work was highly dangerous.[59] Restoring peace while maintaining control was seen as the best way to minimize the risk to the responding officer with an emphasis on maintaining control.

> Arrests were actively discouraged as a waste of time except when disrespect or threats by an offender or victim indicated that the officer might lose control of the situation. arrest is therefore the assertion of authority rather than a response to the demands of the situation.[60]

59. Buzawa & Buzawa, supra note 15, at 32.

60. Id. at 33.

The reality, however, is that domestic disturbance incidents, which account for thirty percent of police calls, account for only 5.7% of police deaths, making domestic disturbances one of the least dangerous of all police activities. In addition, training police to better handle domestic violence incidents can reduce assaults against officers. Nevertheless, the myth that domestic violence work is dangerous is still used to justify police discrimination against battered women.

Another factor makes police education and training difficult. Beyond dismissing woman battering as a real crime, far too many police officers either engage in it themselves or tolerate it within their ranks. Like the general population, policemen are often socialized to regard women as inferior and subordinate. Even now, advocates of battered women know that a policeman's battered wife is their most difficult case since most other officers will fail to protect her or enforce any protective order that she may have obtained, and many will help trace her to any shelter where she has sought refuge.

In addition to police indifference, battered women faced a harsh body of civil law. Prior to 1972, the only civil remedy which a battered woman had was an injunction against her abuser pursuant to a divorce or a legal separation. These injunctions were quite limited. First, in order to even file such an action, a battered woman had to be married to her abuser. Second, the injunctions were available in only some states. Third, most injunctions expired automatically by law within a fairly short time or when the court concluded the case. Finally, there was no criminal penalty for violating such an injunction. The woman had to resort to filing a contempt action against her husband to bring criminal enforcement. Such actions usually required a new petition and another filing fee, with another order for her husband to appear in court and further costs to have him served. Even then, the woman had little hope that the man would get more than an admonishment from the judge. There was also always the chance that the contempt hearing would be turned against her, and the judge would examine her behavior to see what she had done to upset the husband, or what new court order would make him feel less aggrieved and therefore less likely to abuse her in the future. One thing, however, was certain; police were seen as having no role in enforcing these injunctions since the injunctions were purely civil matters.

II. COURT CHALLENGES

In the 1970s, Americans gradually became aware that millions of women were being brutally abused by their husbands. A few women had started organizing around the issue of battered women. Some opened their homes to victims or started shelters. Others proposed legislation to assist battered women. It was clear, however, that neither of these approaches would have much effect if the police did not enforce the new laws. As women, increasingly frustrated by the failure of police to arrest even husbands who committed felony assaults, it became clear that they needed to concentrate their efforts on forcing the police to enforce the few laws that did exist to help battered women.

In 1972, the executor of Ruth Bunnell's estate filed a wrongful death action against the San Jose Police Department.[78] Mrs. Bunnell had called the police at least twenty times in the year before her death to complain that her husband was abusing both her and her two daughters. Only once did they arrest her husband. In September of 1972, she called the police for help, telling them that her husband was on his way to the house to kill her. They told her to wait until he arrived. By the time police came in response to a neighbor's call, her husband had stabbed her to death. The California Court of Appeals upheld the trial court's dismissal of the case, reasoning that the police had never "induced decedent's reliance on a promise, express or implied, that they would provide her with protection."

Legal aid and legal service lawyers, who had always known that the vast majority of their female divorce clients were being violently abused by their husbands, were experiencing the same frustrations. Fearing that another tort action for damages against the police would probably meet with little success, two groups of legal services lawyers on opposite shores of the country decided to adopt a different approach. They filed for declaratory and injunctive relief against the police in order to force them to do what the law empowered them to do to protect battered women.

The first to file suit was a group of five attorneys in the Legal Aid Society of Alameda County in Oakland. They filed a complaint in October of 1976 in the Northern District of California. The suit which was captioned *Scott v. Hart*, was in the form of a class action against George T. Hart, Chief of the Oakland Police Department. They filed on behalf of "women in general and black women in particular who are victims of domestic violence." All five of the named plaintiffs were black women who had repeatedly called the Oakland police for protection when they were beaten up by their husbands, ex-husbands or boyfriends. The officers had either failed to respond or had responded in an ineffectual or, in one case, a threatening manner. By bringing their suit on behalf of black victims of domestic violence who were getting less adequate police responses than were white victims, the legal aid lawyers were able to allege a denial of the equal protection mandated by the Fourteenth Amendment. They also claimed that the police had breached their duty to arrest the abusers "when a felony [had] been committed such as felony wife beating" and that a "police policy that de-emphasizes and discourages arresting assailants ... is arbitrary, capricious, discriminatory, and deprives plaintiffs and the plaintiff class of the right to equal protection of the laws." The complaint asked the court to: (1) permanently enjoin the police from refusing to respond adequately to battered women's calls; (2) affirmatively order the police to respond adequately; (3) order the police "to arrest when they know that a felony has been

---

78. Hartzler v. City of San Jose, 46 Cal. App. 3d 6, 120 Cal. Rptr. 5 (1975).

committed or when the woman requests the arrest of the assailant"; (4) order the police to "advise women of their right to make citizens' arrests and [of the fact] that the police [will] effectuate those arrests by taking the assailant into custody"; (5) order the police to "take assailants to a mental facility for 72–hour observation" when appropriate; (6) order the police to train officers in "how to best handle these incidents"; (7) order the police to start a batterer treatment program; (8) order the city to establish a shelter for women; and 9) force defendants to pay plaintiffs' "court costs, expenditures and reasonable attorneys fees."

The first hurdle which plaintiffs needed to overcome was posed by the Supreme Court's ruling in *Rizzo v. Goode*.[97] In that case, the Court held that supervisory officials must have actual knowledge of and responsibility for promulgating discriminatory polices before an aggrieved party could get injunctive relief in federal court. This hurdle, however, proved to be not much of an obstacle in *Scott*. The existence within the Oakland Police Department of a clear arrest-avoidance policy which was known to the watch commanders and other supervisors persuaded the court to allow the case to survive a motion to dismiss. Not until November 14, 1979, however, more than three years after the class had filed its complaint, did the parties agree to a settlement. The settlement granted most of the plaintiff's requested relief: the police agreed to a new policy in which they would respond quickly to domestic violence calls. The police also agreed to make an arrest whenever an officer had probable cause to believe that a felonious assault had occurred or that a misdemeanor had been committed in his presence. This new policy required the police to make their arrest decisions without looking to factors traditionally used to justify inaction. The police also agreed not to use the threat of adverse financial consequences for the couple to justify inaction or to urge the victim not to pursue the case. The settlement also required police to inform each battered woman that she had a right to make a citizen's arrest, and required police to help her to do so. Officers would thereafter refer victims to supportive agencies for counseling and other assistance. Furthermore, the department acknowledged that it had an affirmative duty to enforce civil restraining and "kick out" orders. While Oakland was not required to provide a shelter and counseling for victims (or assailants), the city agreed to apply for federal funding for any support services available to battered women, and to pay the plaintiffs' attorney fees and court costs.

The *Scott* settlement decree could be modified by agreement of the parties, or by a showing by either party that modification was necessary "to avoid irreparable injury to a party, or to accommodate unforeseen or changed circumstances." The police department agreed to continue to give the plaintiffs crime and assignment reports and anything else they possessed regarding their response to domestic violence situations. The court retained jurisdiction of the case to ensure compliance, and neither party was allowed to apply to the court for dismissal of the case until at

97. Rizzo v. Goode, 423 U.S. 362 (1976).

least three years had passed and further supervision of the case was no longer necessary.

In December 1976, approximately six weeks after the *Scott* case was filed, three New York legal services programs and the Center for Constitutional Rights filed a similar class action suit on behalf of married battered women against the New York City Police Department and the New York Family Court. In their complaint, captioned *Bruno v. Codd*,[110] twelve named plaintiffs alleged that the police failed to arrest husbands who battered their wives and that New York Family Court personnel denied battered wives access to the court. The complaint, filed in the Supreme Court of the State of New York, named the New York City Police Department, the Family Court, the Probation Department, and sixteen others as defendants. They claimed thirteen causes of action on behalf of battered wives who had repeatedly been denied police protection or given endless runarounds. During the pendency of the case, affidavits from forty-eight more women were received, supporting all of the charges.

Thirteen months before the complaint was filed, two New York lawyers had decided to "institute a lawsuit challenging the legal system's treatment of battered wives" there. They interviewed numerous battered wives and collected information about the policies of the New York City Police Department. The affidavits that they collected showed a blatant disregard for women's welfare. The affidavits also showed that the women were desperate to stop the abuse, had tried numerous times to do so, and had failed due only to the system's faults. The women explained in their affidavits the economic and societal pressures that kept them from leaving their husbands. They outlined the obstacles each encountered, such as a lack of day care, shelter beds or housing, and increased violence from their husbands, which, along with the absence of police protection, combined to prevent them from leaving their husbands. They described how, even when women managed to obtain orders of protection, the police refused to enforce them.

The Administrative Judge of the Family Court stated to the *Bruno* court that he was unaware of the problems described in the plaintiffs' complaint, and that the Family Court had a right to address the changes which the plaintiffs' sought. The Director of the New York City Probation Department issued an order setting forth procedures for processing oral or written complaints against any probation employee who failed to advise women of their right to reject offers of mediation and instead appear immediately before a judge on a petition for an order of protection. In addition, the legislature amended the Family Court Act to prohibit officials from discouraging or preventing anyone wishing to file for a protective order from having access to the courts for such purposes. Accordingly, the New York Court of Appeals dismissed the causes of

---

110. Complaint, Bruno v. Codd, 90   1977) passim.
Misc. 2d 1047, 396 N.Y.S.2d 974 (Sup. Ct.

action against the Family Court and Probation Department. Even in dismissing the causes of action against the Family Court, however, New York's highest court praised "the welcome efforts of plaintiff's counsel" to alert and sensitize the courts to their responsibility to respond to the brutality inflicted upon battered women.

After the Court of Appeals dismissed the counts against the Family Court and the Probation Department, several counts against the Police Department remained pending in the trial court. Judge Gellinoff, the trial judge, was troubled by the allegations supporting these counts. "For too long," he wrote in denying a motion to dismiss,

> Anglo–American laws treated a man's physical abuse of his wife as different from any other assault and, indeed as an acceptable practice. if the allegations of the instant complaint—buttressed by hundreds of pages of affidavits—are true, only the written law has changed; in reality, wife beating is still condoned, if not approved, by some of those charged with protecting its victims.

The police department, concerned that the ruling on the motion to dismiss was a precursor of things to come, entered into a consent judgment with the plaintiffs. The judgment provided that the police would thenceforth have a duty to respond and would respond to every woman's request for protection against someone she alleged to be her husband if she said he was beating her or had violated an order of protection. If the officer has reasonable cause "to believe that a husband has committed a misdemeanor against his wife or has committed a violation against his wife in the officer's presence, the officer shall not refrain from making an officer arrest of the husband without justification." When the officer has reasonable cause to believe that a husband committed a felony against his wife or violated an order of protection, the officer must arrest him and should not attempt to reconcile the parties or mediate. When a husband who allegedly committed a crime against her is not present when the police arrive and the wife wants him arrested or to make a civilian arrest, the officer must locate the husband just as with any other crime. Officers must hereafter assist the wife in obtaining any needed medical assistance, and inform her of her right to get a protective order from the family court. The police department must promulgate new policies and training materials in conformance with the decree, and a supervising officer must promptly investigate any allegation that a provision of the consent decree was violated and, if it was, cause it to be immediately complied with as soon as possible. The court retained jurisdiction of the police action and allowed either party to apply for further relief as may be necessary or appropriate.

The Oakland and New York City lawsuits made clear to police departments throughout the United States that they were vulnerable to being sued if they failed to protect the rights of battered women. Battered women's advocates soon learned how many police chiefs knew that both of the departments had "lost." As a result, police departments in many towns and cities agreed to revamp their policies and practices without any suit having to be filed. The possibility that the town or city might be liable for attorney fees and even for damages in a case by injured women became a persuasive bargaining chip to many battered women's lawyers and advocates.

The caselaw took one more important step forward in *Thurman v. City of Torrington, Conn.*,[138] where a federal jury awarded Tracey Thurman and her son $2.3 million because the police were negligent in failing to protect her from her abusive husband.[139] The court found that Torrington's policy of indifference amounted to sex discrimination.[140]

The effect of the case was dramatic. As one commentator observed,

> The *Thurman* case was widely reported in the popular press and in academic journals. it graphically confirmed the extreme financial penalty that could be imposed on police departments when they abjectly fail to perform their duties. In addition, it confirmed that in appropriate cases, these massive liability awards would be upheld.[141]

Many police departments that did not get the message from *Scott* and *Bruno* were forced by *Thurman's* threat of huge liability to change their policies.

III. INCREASING ARREST POWERS

A. *Enforcing Protective Orders*

Although prosecutors, the judiciary, and probation offices must all play a role in protecting women from abusive partners, it is the role of the police, who are the first to respond, that usually determines whether victims ever get to a courthouse. Police are the actors who must decide whether to arrest the abuser or to tell the victim about her rights. Without police help, few victims will even realize what their options are.

Women who have civil protection orders fully believe that the orders will be enforced. The order frequently contains a warning printed on its face indicating that it is a criminal offense to violate the order. Court personnel lead victims to believe that the order will be enforced by the police. The police themselves, by urging victims to get civil orders, and by explaining that they cannot do anything without such orders, also lead victims to believe that the orders will be enforced.

Failure to enforce a protective order "increases the victim's danger by creating a false sense of security. Offenders may routinely violate orders, if they believe there is no real risk of being arrested." Ultimately, without arrest, domestic violence laws could be violated with impunity. Yet even a police force willing to enforce a law is limited by the arrest powers which they have.

---

138. 595 F.Supp. 1521 (Dist. Conn. 1984).

139. Buzawa & Buzawa, supra note 15, at 75.

140. Id. at 74–75.

141. Id. at 75.

B. *Warrantless Misdemeanor Arrest*

Realizing that the Oakland and New York City suits were time-consuming and that judgments were difficult to enforce, battered women's advocates soon turned to other approaches to changing police handling of woman abuse cases. One approach included efforts to get each police department to develop an effective domestic violence policy. Another centered on getting state legislatures to change the laws to enable police to arrest woman abusers when responding to domestic incidents.

At the same time, police organizations, following the success of the *Scott* and *Bruno* cases, were rethinking their policies. In 1980, the Police Executive Research Forum published *Responding to Spouse Abuse and Wife Beating: A Guide for Police*, which informed police that other police agencies were already "reevaluating their policies, procedures and training programs in order to improve" how they "handle spouse abuse and wife beating," and which proposed models for police in making effective changes.

Inadequate policies still were in place in most departments. While officers could arrest when they had probable cause to believe that a felony offense had been committed, in most, but not all, jurisdictions police could not make an arrest for a misdemeanor assault unless the assault occurred in the police officer's presence. Because most police charge domestic violence offenses only as misdemeanors, the law, in order to enable an officer to arrest the abuser when the offense was not committed in the officer's presence, has to permit the arrest without a warrant. Changes must be made.

Empirical research on police response to domestic abuse was beginning to be available. By 1984, the Minneapolis police domestic violence experiment was widely cited as proof that arrests had a deterrent effect on men who beat their wives. The movement to expand police arrest powers was already well established by 1984, however, and it was generally unopposed by police who established department policies. While many law enforcement officers still did not want to arrest batterers, they certainly had no objection to being given the discretion to make warrantless misdemeanor arrests upon probable cause. Many police chiefs and policymakers who knew that their departments would be vulnerable to police suits like the ones in Oakland and New York City sought these changes or instituted mandatory arrest policies.

Legislative action began somewhat earlier. The enactment of domestic violence legislation had actually begun in the 1970s. By 1976, the District of Columbia and Pennsylvania had each enacted such legislation. In 1978, Pennsylvania amended its domestic violence act to permit warrantless arrests if the officer had probable cause to believe that a protection order had been violated. In the eighties, progress continued. By October of 1981, thirty-six states and the District of Columbia had enacted domestic violence acts.[158] By 1983, forty-three states and the District of Columbia had passed such legislation.[159] Indeed, the only states without domestic violence statutes in September of 1983 were Arkansas, Idaho, Michigan, New Mexico, South Carolina, Virginia and Washington.[160] According to two commentators, by that time,

> [t]hirty-three states ha[d] expanded police power to arrest in domestic abuse cases. In twenty-eight states, arrest without a warrant [wa]s permitted where a police officer ha[d] probable cause to believe that an abuser ha[d] committed a misdemeanor. In nineteen states, police may arrest without a warrant if they ha[d] probable cause to believe that an abuser ha[d] violated a protection order. (Fourteen states allow[ed] probable cause arrest in both cases.)[161]

Furthermore, almost half of the states have now imposed duties on responding officers to, *inter alia*, remain with the victim until the danger passes, transport the victim to a hospital or shelter, or inform the victim about her legal rights.

In the mid-eighties, the Victim Services Agency, as part of an effort to encourage police chiefs to adopt effective domestic violence policies, ran workshops around the country. In September 1988, the agency published a compilation of each state's arrest law as interpreted by the state's Attorney General. The report showed that all but two states, Alabama and West Virginia, allowed misdemeanor arrest. These remain the only states where misdemeanor arrest is not allowed for offenses committed outside the officer's presence.[77]

C. Mandatory Arrest

The Oregon Coalition Against Domestic and Sexual Violence (hereinafter "OCADSV") took a different approach. It proposed a bill imposing a mandatory duty on the police. The bill required police officers to arrest anyone in a domestic violence incident whom the officer had probable cause to believe had committed an assault or had placed a victim with an order of protection in fear of imminent serious physical injury. This bill was enacted in 1977, making Oregon the first state to require police to arrest. A provision in the Abuse Prevention Act which allowed police not to arrest when the victim objected was eliminated in 1981 because police were using it to circumvent the law.

Although the OCADSV sent every police department a detailed explanation of the new law before it took effect, two years later the Oregon Governor's Commission on Women found that one third of all law enforcement agencies had not changed their policies to comport with the requirements of the law. One commentator reported that officers continued to think of their responsibilities in domestic disturbance situations as that of mediation and reconciliation. Police training had

158. Lerman & Livingston, supra note 150, at 1.

159. Id.

160. Id.

161. Id. at 4.

77. 295 Or. 702, 670 P.2d 137 (1983).

not changed. The police were still instructed to respond in terms of "crisis intervention" rather than "crime intervention."

In response to police inaction, Henrietta Nearing filed a tort suit in Oregon State Court against the police in the fall of 1980. The trial court granted summary judgment to the defendant police, and the Oregon Court of Appeals affirmed. The Oregon Supreme Court, however, reversed, holding in *Nearing v. Weaver* that the police may be held liable for harm resulting from their failure to enforce a restraining order. The court ruled that police did not have discretion in enforcing restraining orders issued pursuant to the Abuse Prevention Act. The *Nearing* decision virtually required every police department in Oregon to adopt a mandatory arrest policy.

Similar developments occurred elsewhere. By the middle of 1982, the domestic abuse laws of five states mandated that police arrest batterers upon probable cause to believe that a crime had been committed or a restraining order violated. Currently, fifteen states require the police to arrest for a domestic violence incident. In addition, nineteen states require police to arrest if the batterer has violated a protection order. Because some police departments have punitively arrested both parties in an attempt to circumvent the intent of mandatory arrest laws, eight states have enacted language directing the police to arrest only the primary physical aggressor or the party not responding in self-defense. Finally, one state, Louisiana, has a statute that appears to mandate arrest when a domestic violence offense has been committed, but it is not being so interpreted.

IV. QUESTIONS RAISED ABOUT THE POLICE ARREST EXPERIMENTS

Advocates of battered women have generally presumed that, until the entire system takes woman abuse seriously, men will go on abusing women with impunity. Advocates were encouraged by the suggestion of the original arrest experiment in Minneapolis that mandatory arrest alone had a significant deterrent effect on batterers. As more police departments adopted mandatory arrest policies, however, advocates were struck by the number of departments that failed to implement the policies. Even when the policies were implemented, others in the system continued to undermine the message that domestic violence is a crime not to be tolerated. Prosecutors who chose not to prosecute, judges who threw the cases out of court or refused to impose more than token punishment, or probation officers who never bothered to ensure compliance with probationary terms all left the batterer with the last laugh. This left the abuser free to flout to his victim the reality that society allowed him to beat her, or at least would do nothing effective to intervene.

Six studies were later funded to see whether arrest alone would have the deterrent affect it had in Minneapolis. The results of three of those studies, conducted in Omaha, Charlotte, and Milwaukee, indicated that arrest alone did not deter abusers. While these three newer studies cast some doubt on whether arrest alone is an effective deterrent with all abusers, there are a number of points to consider.

First and most important, even if arrest may not deter unemployed abusers in ghetto neighborhoods, arrest still deters the vast majority of abusers. That a few hours under arrest fails to deter the abusers who are generally considered to be society's failures is hardly surprising. In some subcultures of ghettoized people, where imprisonment is all too common, a few hours in jail may be seen as only minor irritation, or even a rite of passage. We do not consider eliminating arrest for other crimes (e.g., robbery), however, because it may not deter a particular individual or class of individuals. The studies may suggest that to deter more batterers, the stakes may need to be higher, not lower or nonexistent.

Second, when police arrested the offender, far fewer victims were beaten at their first subsequent encounter with their abuser. This was true even among those least likely to be deterred in the long run: in Milwaukee two percent of arrested batterers reassaulted as opposed to seven percent of those who received a warning.

Third, the Charlotte experiment found that informing both parties that an arrest warrant would be issued for the abuser was no less effective than an immediate arrest. Since only 0.9% of those who were arrested or for whom citations were issued served prison time after sentencing, the long period of uncertainty awaiting arrest may have reinforced the message that abuse is wrong.

Fourth, the Milwaukee, Omaha and Charlotte studies did not take into account how the female victims' responses to the various police actions may have affected the overall results. In contrast, other recent research into the effectiveness of batterer treatment programs has found that fifty-three percent of women plan to reconcile with a batterer-in-treatment but that only nineteen percent of abused victims plan to do so if the batterer is not in treatment. Although completing batterer treatment made no difference in stopping future violence or in the seriousness of future attacks by the abuser, women whose partners were sent to court-ordered treatment were more likely to call police and bring new charges if they were subsequently assaulted. While sending batterers to treatment has no deterrent effect on the batterer and may actually deceive many victims into reconciling with their abuser on the assumption that treatment must be effective, the victim is more likely to use that system in the future, knowing that the criminal justice system acted once in the past to support her. Clearly, victims' response can greatly affect how often police are called back or new charges are brought. The police studies replicating the Minneapolis experiment, however, like the original experiment itself, are flawed by their failure to take victim response into account.

Also marring these police studies is the amalgamation of numerous cases that may have far different dynamics that were lumped together. Although women victimized by male partners comprise ninety-four percent of domestic violence victims, the Milwaukee police study included

all cases of domestic violence. While in no way minimizing the seriousness of violence committed by a woman against a man or by one
homosexual or lesbian partner against the other, we know so little about
the dynamics of such cases that they should have been either excluded or
examined separately. Similarly, the minority of cases where women
battered men should have been excluded or examined separately. As
David Adams, the director of the country's first batterer's treatment
program, testified before the Gender Bias Study of the Court System in
Massachusetts, virtually every woman who was ever referred to his
program was in fact a victim wrongly accused by the batterer of being
the aggressor. The accused women who are actually victims should have
been excluded. Since we do not know whether the same factors motivate
and deter those few women who are abusers, the female abusers were
also inappropriately included with the male batterers in the Milwaukee
study.

Furthermore, the experiments to replicate the Milwaukee police
data introduced some aspects that were almost certain to influence the
results by discouraging women from recontacting the police. The Minneapolis experiment compared the effect of three police responses to
domestic violence: arrest, advice, and sending the abuser from the home
for eight hours. The advice given by the police officer was entirely left to
the officer's discretion. In Charlotte and Omaha the police actually asked
the victim to leave the home in forty percent and thirty-two percent of
the cases respectively when separation was the goal.

In Milwaukee, the three responses studied included arresting abusers for the "usual" average of 11.1 hours (full arrest), arresting abusers
for only a short average of 2.8 hours (short arrest), and giving only a
warning to the abuser. Each group was chosen at random and heard a
statement made by the officer. The officers for both arrest groups were
instructed to state the following:

1. You are under arrest for battery.

2. Battery is a crime against the state.

3. We are pressing charges against you, not the victim (cuff
suspect before conveyance).

Only for those in the short arrest group were officers instructed to
add:

4. If you cooperate, you may be released in a few hours.

Thus, some of the difference between the two groups might depend
upon the apparent empowerment given to offenders who were promised
a reward for cooperative behavior. In contrast, the warning was written
so that both abusers and victims would receive the same lecture:

1. We're not going to arrest anyone here tonight.

2. If we have to return, someone will go to jail.

3. This is a list of people who can help you, both of you, with
your problem.

4. The D.A.'s office is on that list and you can contact them if you want to press charges.

The warning, by failing to differentiate the abuser and the victim, or by failing to indicate that the police saw through the apparent equal treatment, could have only a chilling effect on any victim. This makes it far less likely that the women would ever call the police again or bring charges. Although the warning does clearly convey that the police see the situation as serious and will arrest at least one of the parties if they have to return, the neutral tone almost surely made many victims fear that they might be arrested. Likewise, the invitation to the abuser to file charges against the victim may have deterred many victims from either calling the police again or bringing charges against the abuser. Even the statement that they both have a problem and need help tended to disempower the victim and make the victim feel more shame, blame and possibly guilt. Of course, we do not know how the script was delivered. If the officer looked sternly at the abuser while stating that one of the parties would go to jail next time, the message could have been perceived very differently from the way it would be perceived if the officer said the same thing while looking sternly at the victim. Nonetheless, that such a dangerously inadequate message should have formed the basis of the control group renders the results entirely suspect.

Another weakness of these later studies was the experiment design. In some of the cities, the studies apparently called for subsequent police encounters to be treated as first encounters, with new random assignment to one of the three groups. That some abusers, who were told to expect arrest the next time the police were called, received only the same warning surely conveyed the message that the warning was empty rhetoric. That some abusers who were once arrested received only a warning a subsequent time (or possibly a short-term arrest) makes it almost impossible to track the reasons for their subsequent behavior. Victim response is again the key.

Another troubling aspect was the large number of calls excluded from the Charlotte experiment. Only 686 of 591,664 calls for domestic disturbance help were ultimately included, amounting to only .116% of the calls received (or .128% of the calls where an officer was dispatched). All cases where the women requested that the abuser be arrested were inexplicably excluded. Thus, the only cases studied were those few ones in which the woman was either ambivalent about or opposed to having her abuser arrested.

An equally disturbing feature of the Charlotte study was the assumption that women victims who were not interviewed were assumed not to have been victims of subsequent crimes. This assumption is especially suspect given the large discrepancy in uncompleted follow-ups in victim interviews between cases where an arrest was made or a citation issued and cases where advice and separation were used. In most of the cases that lacked follow-up interviews, the women could not be located. In a few, they were afraid to cooperate. In cases where their abusers were given citations or arrested on the spot, only 13.3% and 13.6% of the women, respectively, failed to complete the six-month follow-up interview. Yet 20.4% of the women (150% more than in the other groups) whose cases were mediated and who were temporarily separated from their abusers did not complete the six-month interview.

We also need to know how many victims and abusers heard about other police responses to domestic disturbances. The twenty-four percent of abusers and nineteen percent of victims who knew about Milwaukee's mandatory arrest policy should have been excluded from the study, particularly if no arrest was made. Others who learned of other possible police responses also should have been excluded. An inherent weakness in this experiment was the assumption that abusers would expect police to respond in the same way the next time.

It would be helpful to know in all of these studies whether and for how long the parties separated and whether and where any of them moved. Did the victim's behavior vary with the police response? If one or both of the parties (and especially the victim) moved out of the city, the abuser would be less likely to show up again in the city's police and court records, at least as repeating his violence against the same victim. Rather than asking abusers if they knew that the city had a mandatory arrest policy, it would have been more helpful to ask what policy they thought the police had. If it included arrest, then on what basis? Learning what the abuser believed to be the outcome of his actions might better explain his motivations in the first place. Someone who believes that arrest is an unlikely possibility will probably assess that risk very differently from someone who believes that arrest is a certainty.

That the prosecution outcome was not seriously monitored or examined in the replication experiments is also distressing. Battered women's advocates expect that an arrest, followed by a speedy trial with a real sentence whose terms are enforced, sends the strongest message. The message communicated when a person is arrested, but never prosecuted (as happened to ninety-five percent of those arrested in the Milwaukee experiment) might so weaken any long-term deterrent effect of the arrest as to explain the results. The same could be true of a low conviction rate (only one percent were convicted in Milwaukee) and lenient or unenforced sentences (only 0.9% in Charlotte spent time in prison after sentencing) or enforced.

We also need to explore the manner in which different arrest, prosecution and sentencing policies affect the children in homes where there is domestic violence. Even if it turned out that an arrest policy has no effect on either the offender or the victim, if it has a deterrent effect on the sons, the policy might still be worthwhile, because they are at danger of growing up to be abusers themselves. Similarly, if fewer daughters who grow up in homes where they see their abused mothers stay in abusive relationships as adults, the deterrence would be a success. Yet, society is unlikely to know any of this for many years.

We should not forget the results of the Duluth experiment, which studied different police policies. That study revealed that minority males comprised thirty-three percent of those arrested when arrest was encouraged but left completely to officers' discretion, thirteen percent of those arrested when officers were encouraged to arrest and required to submit written reports explaining failures to do so, but only 8.5% of those arrested under a policy mandating arrest. Thus, the more discretion officers had, the more they arrested individuals whom the Milwaukee experiment found were less likely to be deterred. Importantly, when police officers are given wide discretion, they frequently use that discretion to not arrest those abusers who would most likely be deterred by arrest.

It should also be remembered that advocates of battered women should be involved in designing any domestic violence experiments. That family counseling and mediation, both of which are known to increase domestic violence and thus to be contraindicated in cases of domestic violence, were included in the police replication experiments flaws the results. The same is true for the Milwaukee warnings suggesting that the victim risked being arrested. Likewise, the victim-blaming tactic that presumptively assumed that the victim should leave the home could only have increased some victims' guilt and self-blame, making them less likely to call the police in the future. Just because a police tactic successfully deters future calls to police does not mean that it did so by successfully deterring future criminal behavior.

At any rate, it seems problematic to single out domestic violence as the focus of a study whether arrest has any deterrent effect on offenders, since domestic violence crimes have been trivialized, if not ignored, for so long. Although advocates of battered women welcome the opportunity to learn what stops criminal behavior, we remain somewhat skeptical when so much of the research seems intent on returning to the old do-nothing or even blame-the-victim practices.

BARBARA FEDDERS, LOBBYING FOR MANDATORY–ARREST POLICIES: RACE, CLASS, AND THE POLITICS OF THE BATTERED WOMEN'S MOVEMENT

23 N.Y.U. Rev. L. & Soc. Change 281–282, 286–287, 290–296 (1997).

During my three years as a volunteer with a community-based organization for battered women, we tried, through education and grass-roots organizing, to convince police departments to implement policies that would lead to more arrests of men who perpetrate domestic violence. We believed that the problem of violence between intimate partners persisted in part because the police viewed it as a personal problem inappropriate for criminal sanction.

While we assumed that a battered woman would feel relief if not elation when her batterer was taken to jail, none of us knew whether an arrest would actually make a batterer stop being violent. Our support for a tougher arrest policy, however, was not based only on the deterrence effect it might have on an individual batterer. Criminalization, we trusted, expressed societal condemnation of domestic violence and thus could both force would-be batterers to reconsider the appropriateness of using force and intimidation and empower women in abusive relationships.

Contrary to our beliefs, recent research suggests that arrest actually may be ineffective in deterring domestic violence among low-income men, and that women of color may have reasons not shared by white women for being dubious about tougher arrest policies. Yet many white, middle-class feminists who consider themselves advocates for battered women continue to support such policies, including mandatory-arrest laws. These laws typically require police officers to arrest a man who violates an order of protection or whom police have probable cause to believe has committed a criminal offense against an intimate partner.

In congressional hearings on the Violence Against Women Act, white, middle-class advocates for battered women lobbied for a federal provision on mandatory-arrest laws. Their lobbying illustrates a central tension that this article attempts to explore: Although typically representing themselves as advocates for the needs and interests of all battered women, mandatory-arrest advocates are from a limited demographic base, ascribe to a narrow theoretical framework, and have an advocacy agenda that reflects this homogeneity.

* * *

II. ESSENTIALIZING THE BATTERED WOMAN

"The problem of domestic violence cuts across all social lines ... domestic violence is prevalent among upper middle-class families."[26] * * *

"Battered women come from all types of economic, cultural, religious, and racial backgrounds.... They are women like you. Like me. Like those whom you know and love."[27] * * *

"[C]ontrary to common misperceptions, domestic violence is not confined to any one socioeconomic, ethnic, religious, racial or age group."[28] * * *

"An estimated 3–million women are currently victims of domestic violence. [And] they [are not] all lower-middle class trash like the Bobbitts."[29] * * *

---

26. Natalie Loder Clark, Crime Begins at Home: Let's Stop Punishing Victims and Perpetuating Violence, 28 Wm. & Mary L. Rev. 263, 282 n.74 (1987).

27. Lenore E. Walker, Terrifying Love: Why Battered Women Kill and How Society Responds 101–02 (1989).

28. Women and Violence: Hearings Before the Senate Comm. on the Judiciary,

101st Cong., 2d sess. 139 (1990) (Statement of Susan Kelly–Dreiss).

29. Sheryl McCarthy, Look Around: Lorena's Life of Abuse Far from a Rare Occurrence, Newsday, Jan. 24, 1994, at 5.

"It's important that abuse not be seen as a blue-collar issue."[30]
* * *

In their written and oral testimonials such as those above, battered women's advocates typically argue that domestic violence does not occur primarily in one social group. While often subtly emphasizing the victimization of middle-and upper-class women, advocates describe domestic violence as a universal experience and minimize the significance of racial, class, and other differences among battered women. While their essentialist rhetoric seems to have been effective in forcing society to recognize the widespread nature of the problem, advocates have simultaneously ignored—to the detriment of many battered women—the salient difference that race, class and other differences make in determining appropriate remedies for domestic violence.

The remedies for domestic violence typically supported by advocates are consistent with the movement's theory that patriarchy is at the root of domestic violence. The movement has long objected to counseling for couples in which men are battering women, because counseling often does not adequately hold accountable the man and the male privilege he exercises. On the other hand, the movement supports shelters, because they accommodate a woman's need to escape from an abusive mate and to learn to live independently. One remedy favored by the movement is harsher criminal penalties for batterers. As the following account will show, its advocacy in this area has highlighted the problems that result from minimizing race and class differences among battered women.

* * *

Battered women's advocates' support for mandatory arrest also grows out of the belief that such a policy can empower the battered woman. Because battered women so often lack the ability, physically and psychologically, to extricate themselves from their abusive relationships, advocates argue, state intervention must be through a policy of mandatory rather than discretionary arrest. Allowing the woman to decide whether the batterer should be arrested leaves too much room for him to pressure her not to have him arrested.

Advocates argue that if law enforcement treats abusive conduct consistently as a crime against the state, rather than as a personal problem, individual battered women will have less to fear from their batterers. When the power and resources of the State, in the person of police officers, are placed squarely behind the battered woman in this manner, she will come to feel more valued as a member of society. Ultimately, advocates argue, she will be able to avoid, and protect herself from, further violence.

B. *Mandatory Arrest: A Universal Solution?*

Battered women's advocates rest their support for mandatory arrest on the deterrence of batterers and empowerment of women they believe

30. Cynthia Sanz, Shelter in the Storm: Denise Brown Backs a University's Refuge for Battered Women, Time, Oct. 23, 1995, at 63.

the policy can achieve. Subsequent criminological studies, however, suggest that any beneficial effects produced by mandatory arrest may not be universal across race and class.

* * *

Some police statistics seem to support the contention that mandatory-arrest policies prevent incidences of domestic violence. Following the enactment of Connecticut's mandatory arrest law in October 1986, for example, the Hartford Police Department reported a 28% drop in the number of calls for assistance in domestic violence incidents. However, such statistics do not prove conclusively that mandatory-arrest policies have a deterrence effect. Instead, they may indicate a greater hesitation on the part of battered women to report incidents of violence to the police.

After an incident of domestic violence, for example, a woman might wish to call the police and have them come to her home. She might reason that a police officer could diffuse an explosive situation or frighten her batterer into ceasing his abuse. She may engage in a careful cost-benefit analysis and determine that, while police presence would be useful, an arrest would not. A woman may be dependent on the income of her batterer, for example, or she may not want their children to witness their father's arrest. Such a woman, if aware of a mandatory-arrest policy in her jurisdiction, would likely refrain from calling the police at all, and would thereby be deprived of a potentially useful tool in her struggle to end the violence in her life.

While battered women's advocates may dismiss these concerns, they are nonetheless compelling to many battered women, who might well perceive a mandatory-arrest policy as paternalistic. While such concerns cannot be precisely correlated with the race and class of a woman or her batterer, they do indicate that women have individualized responses to the problem of domestic violence that are not respected by mandatory-arrest policies.

Advocates argue that mandatory arrest symbolizes the support of the state to a battered woman. However, for significant numbers of women, the state is not a source of comfort but a cause for mistrust or anger. Women in relationships with Black men, for example, confront a legacy of police brutality and disproportionately harsh prosecutorial treatment of Black arrestees. Particularly when these women are also Black and have grown up in a community with an excessive police presence, they may view the police with great suspicion and may not find the arrest of their batterer to embody support for them. Thus, any feelings of relief that an arrest of their batterers might otherwise bring may be trumped by feelings of guilt, fear and concern about the fate of their partners in the criminal justice system.

Some advocates have attempted to address the concerns about racism in the criminal justice system by arguing that a mandatory-arrest policy leads to less police racism than does a discretionary-arrest regime, where there is more room for the prejudices of individual officers to operate. However, even in a mandatory-arrest regime, the police still must make probable-cause determinations about whether violence has occurred; probable cause is not a colorblind calculation. That is, police racism and classism may operate to make them more incredulous of the testimonies of women of color and low-income women than of white and middle-class women, such that what is in fact a situation mandating arrest may not be perceived as such, and vice versa. The argument that police racism is less a factor in mandatory-than a discretionary-arrest jurisdiction is therefore incomplete.

Illustrating the particular difficulties posed by the intersection of race and sex, many Black women active in domestic violence research, policy advocacy, and organizing have warned battered women against allowing themselves to be "guilt-tripped" by abusive men who accuse them of racism and betrayal for reporting them to the police. One scholar argues, "We have paid our dues, and black men must be held responsible for every injury they cause."[68] An activist asserts: "It's a copout for brothers to use the issue of racism to make us feel bad."[69]

Women must have the right to receive effective police assistance when they are suffering abuse, no matter from whom. This assertion is particularly important for Black women, who face a historic presumption by police that their race predisposes them to enjoy violence. My argument is not that arrest for domestic violence in communities of color is always an inappropriate response. Rather, I am arguing that a mandatory-arrest policy presents unique problems for women of color and poor women that have been largely overlooked by mandatory-arrest advocates.

During congressional hearings on the Violence Against Women Act (VAWA), for example, feminist prosecutors of domestic violence cases, domestic violence policy advocates, and psychiatrists lobbied for language that would indicate federal approval of mandatory arrest. In their lobbying, the overwhelmingly white and middle-class advocates discussed the issues of class and race only to argue that they were insignificant factors in the formulation of policy. Sarah Buel missed the point when she argued that law enforcement officials consider race only to excuse the conduct of abusive men:

> I would encourage that a mandatory component of [training issues included in the bill] be on multicultural and antiracism issues. I am constantly hearing from police and D.A.'s and judges, whenever the defendant is of color, that somehow that is relevant to the abuse ... [They do this] because of the denial and because of the desire to distance themselves from the abuser, that if they can say this is part of the latino culture or this is something that foreigners do, because

68. Beth Richie–Bush, Facing Contradictions: Challenge for Black Feminists, Aegis 17–18 (1983).

69. Lynora Williams, Violence Against Women, Black Scholar, Jan.-Feb. 1981, at 18, 23 (quoting Nkenge Toure of Washington's Rape Crisis Center).

he is from Iran, that this is how this man behaves, and I can point out nine Italians and nine Irish, nine people from our community who they view as their children, their friends, and they do not want to see them in the same context. [A]buse, as others have testified, cuts across all race and class lines.[74]

Buel's comments dismissed the fact that while domestic violence may be universal, its causes and treatment may not.

Battered women's advocates have not demanded further studies of possible correlations between race, class, and other individual characteristics and the rate at which domestic violence occurs. One African–American activist and scholar describes an encounter with the Los Angeles Police Department in which a department spokesperson told her that battered women's advocates strongly opposed release of any statistics that would indicate the number of domestic violence incidents in communities of racial minorities.

The reason for this perspective by the battered women's movement is undoubtedly its legitimate concern about stereotypes. Linking a batterer's race and his propensity to be violent, or a woman's race and the length of time she spends with her batterer, may perpetuate racist stereotypes that men of color are more violent than white men, and that women of color are masochistic. The numerous battered women's advocates with experience in the anti-rape movement were criticized for insensitivity to the historically racist use of rape charges, and undoubtedly resolved not to leave themselves open to similar criticisms. Advocates neatly avoid this potentially dangerous political position by virtue of their oft-stated belief that domestic violence is universal, and that race and class differences affect neither the causes of nor the remedies for domestic violence. Because of this view, they argue that studying possible correlations between particular races and classes and domestic violence before enacting law enforcement remedies is not worthwhile.

For similar reasons, the battered women's movement has failed to survey the broad spectrum of battered women to determine whether mandatory-arrest laws and other remedial measures actually reflect their needs and interests. Instead, without having found out from the women themselves what they want, the movement has spoken on behalf of all of them.

C. SUING THE POLICE

JOAN ZORZA, SUING THE POLICE AFTER *DESHANEY*

Unpublished, National Center on Women and Family Law (1995).

* * *

II. THE *DESHANEY* DECISION

In 1989, the U.S. Supreme Court decided *DeShaney v. Winnebago*

---

74. Women and Violence: Hearings Before the Senate Comm. on the Judiciary, 101st Cong., 2d Sess. 124 (1990) (statement of Sarah Buel).

County Department of Social Services, a case which made suing the police considerably harder for battered women. Ironically, the case did not involve either the police or a man abusing his female partner. The tragic *DeShaney* case was brought as a section 1983 civil rights action by the mother of Joshua DeShaney, a child whose father so severely beat him that the child was left permanently brain damaged and profoundly retarded. Joshua's mother brought the case in her own name and on behalf of Joshua against the Winnebago County Department of Social Services (DSS) and several of its social workers who had received a number of complaints that the father was abusing the child. Although DSS took various steps to protect the child, it never removed the child from the father's custody, leaving the father able to nearly kill the son. The mother alleged that DSS's failure to act denied her son of his liberty rights in violation of the due process clause of the Fourteenth Amendment.

Joshua was born in 1979, and in 1980, a Wyoming divorce court had awarded custody to his father. The father then moved to Wisconsin with Joshua, remarried and again divorced. At the time of her divorce in January of 1982, the second wife informed the police that Joshua's father was abusing the son. DSS interviewed the father but took no further action. In January of 1983, a hospital notified DSS that Joshua had been admitted with multiple bruises and abrasions which appeared to be the result of child abuse. DSS placed Joshua in the temporary custody of the hospital, but decided three days later at a Child Protection Team meeting that there was insufficient evidence to retain Joshua in the court's custody. However, at that time DSS obtained a voluntary agreement with Joshua's father that required him to enroll Joshua in a preschool program, get himself into counseling, and have his girlfriend move out. The juvenile court dismissed the case and returned Joshua to his father's custody.

One month later Joshua was again treated by the hospital for suspicious injuries, but the caseworker declined to do anything. For the next six months, the caseworker made monthly visits to Joshua's home and observed that he had more suspicious head injuries, that he had never been enrolled in school, and that the girlfriend remained living in the home. Although the caseworker continued to suspect that someone in the house was physically abusing Joshua, she continued to do nothing. Joshua was again treated in the emergency room in November 1983 for suspicious injuries. The caseworker still did nothing, even though she was told on her next two home visits that Joshua was too sick to see her. In March 1984 the father beat the child so severely as to cause permanent brain damage. Joshua is now reduced to spending the rest of his life in an institution for the profoundly retarded. The father was finally tried and convicted of child abuse.

In addition to what the DSS caseworker had learned from the home visits and hospital staff, DSS staff had received a number of reports from neighbors, who at various times reported that they had seen or heard Joshua's father or his lover beating the boy. Perhaps most revealing of her mismanagement of the case, the social worker, upon learning of the final beating, acknowledged, "I just knew the phone would ring some day and Joshua would be dead."

Nonetheless, U.S. Supreme Court Chief Justice Rehnquist concluded in the majority opinion that the mother was not entitled to any damages because the purpose of the due process clause of the Fourteenth Amendment is to protect people from the state, not from each other's private violence. The Court held that the due process clause limits the state's power to act. It does not establish a minimum standard that the state must provide for safety and security, even when the state knows of the danger and her expressions of willingness for such protection. However, as Justice Rehnquist observed, had Joshua and his mother established that the state had created or assumed a "special relationship," the state would then have had an affirmative duty to assume some responsibility for Joshua's safety and general well-being.

Rehnquist justified holding the state not liable because his view was that Joshua's father—not the state—was responsible for Joshua's injuries. The state did nothing either to create the dangers to Joshua, or to increase his vulnerability. To Justice Rehnquist, the fact that the state had previously taken temporary custody of Joshua was irrelevant, because when the state returned Joshua to his father's custody, it placed him in no worse a position than he would have been in had the state not acted at all.

Yet Rehnquist explained that there are certain limited circumstances when the due process clause does impose an affirmative duty to act: cases where someone is deprived of his liberty to care for or protect himself. For example, the state is obligated to provide adequate medical care to incarcerated prisoners and to ensure adequate food, shelter, clothing, and medical care to involuntarily committed mental patients. But Rehnquist distinguished Joshua's situation from these on the ground that Joshua was not in the state's custody against his will. However, Rehnquist noted that Joshua might have been entitled to tort damages had the plaintiffs sued under state tort law. Similarly, had the plaintiffs claimed and established that Joshua was selectively denied services because he was a disfavored minority in violation of the Equal Protection Clause of the Fourteenth Amendment, they would have won.

Other court decisions, including those which Rehnquist cited, have upheld a victim's Section 1983 due process claims based on the individual's personal liberty's being restrained in a way similar to incarceration. These cases involve people who are in foster care, school or detainee status. Had Joshua actually been in foster care, the state would have had a duty to protect him from his father's violence; it would have been enough to establish a special relationship.[29]

Justice Brennan, in a dissent joined by Justices Marshall and Blackmun, would have had the court focus not on what Wisconsin failed to do, but on what it undertook to do with respect to Joshua and other children. Brennan cited *White v. Rochford*,[35] a case which did not involve physical restraints but, nonetheless, found that police officers had violated due process when, after arresting the guardian of three young children, they abandoned the children alone at night on a busy stretch of the highway. When the state "cuts off private sources of aid and then refuses aid itself, it cannot wash its hands of the harm that results from its inaction." Brennan's dissent would hold that when the state's action is a monopolization of a particular path of relief, that imposes positive duties on the state. Because Wisconsin gave DSS the exclusive authority to protect children from abuse, Brennan would have held DSS liable for its failure to protect Joshua. Citizens and governmental entities, including the police, must depend on the local DSS to protect children from abuse. Only DSS has control over the decision whether to take steps to protect a child when abuse is suspected. A person or non-DSS governmental worker reporting abuse to DSS is relieved of any further duty. Under Wisconsin law, no one except DSS will step in to fill the gap if DSS ignores or dismisses the abuse allegations. As Brennan observed, DSS "thus effectively confined Joshua DeShaney within the walls of Randy DeShaney's violent home until such time as DSS took action to remove him." In collecting all the reports of abuse and in making twenty home visits, the state gained ever more certain knowledge that Joshua was in grave danger. By failing to do their job, the persons and entities charged with providing child protective services may have put children like Joshua in worse circumstances. Accordingly, Brennan would have allowed "Joshua and his mother the opportunity to show that the respondents' failure to help him arose not out of the sound exercise of professional judgment that we recognized in *Youngberg* as sufficient to preclude liability ... , but from the kind of arbitrariness that we have in the past condemned." Brennan concluded that state "inaction can be every bit as abusive of power as action, that oppression can result when a State undertakes a vital duty and then ignores it."

Unfortunately, however more sympathetic Brennan's view is, it is Rehnquist's view that was the majority opinion adopted by the U.S. Supreme Court, and thus determines when the state can be sued under the Due Process Clause of the Fourteenth Amendment to the U.S. Constitution.

III. How The *Deshaney* Decision Affects Battered Women

The *DeShaney* case does not by its terms affect many of the legal causes of action that battered women can bring against the police. Those actions are discussed later in this paper, in sections IV through VII.

---

29. 489 U.S. 189, 109 S. Ct. 998 (1989).   **35.** 592 F.2d 381 (7th Cir.1979).

However, before the *DeShaney* decision, battered women had a much easier time suing the police and municipalities in federal court for failing to protect them under Section 1983 of the Federal Civil Rights Act. That section was enacted in 1871 to give people in the United States a civil cause of action when their constitutional rights are violated by someone acting as an officer of the state. The section provides specifically that: "Every person who, under color of any statute, ordinance, regulation, custom, or usage of any State or Territory or the District of Columbia, subjects or causes to be subjected, any citizen of the United States or other person within the jurisdiction thereof to the deprivation of any rights, privileges, or immunities secured by the Constitution and laws, shall be liable to the party injured in an action at law, suit in equity, or other proper proceeding for redress." Anyone winning such a suit is also entitled to an award of attorneys fees, making it more likely that an attorney will be willing to bring such a case. Furthermore, federal civil rights actions are not as limited as state tort actions often are. Many states insulate government officials against civil tort damage claims, thereby curtailing the victim's ability to be completely or at all compensated for her injuries.

Before the *DeShaney* decision, a battered woman could sue the responsible individual police and municipal officers under a claim that her substantive due process rights had been violated when the police failed to protect her, knowing of her need for protection, when they had a duty to do so. She would have had to show that the officer's act or failure to act deprived her of a constitutionally protected right. To be able to recover from the city or town, she had to show (1) that the policy, ordinance, or custom caused the deprivation and (2) that a reasonable officer would have understood that what he was doing would have violated her right. When a state has enacted legislation to protect battered women, such as a mandatory arrest law or a statute providing for orders of protection, a battered victim could sue a law officer who did not protect her or enforce her protection order, claiming that a "special relationship" existed between her and the officer which required him to protect her.

Because of the *DeShaney* decision, a battered woman can no longer expect to win a substantive due process civil rights case against the police for failure to act to protect her unless she fits under one of the exceptions which will be discussed later in this section. However, she can still sue under another theory, such as a state tort, equal protection violation, and/or a procedural due process violation claim, as will be discussed in sections IV to VI of this paper. A battered woman can also sue the police for declaratory relief, as was done in the *Scott* and *Bruno* cases; or she can try to fit herself in to one of the *DeShaney* exceptions. The *DeShaney* exceptions protect (a) victims in custodial relationships, (b) those whom the state actor puts in increased danger, and (c) those who are injured as a result of inadequate police training.

A. *The Custodial Relationship Exception to Deshaney*

Until there are significant changes in the composition or opinions of the U.S. Supreme Court, or unless another legislative exception is provided, it is unlikely that a battered women not in an actual custody situation will be successful in fitting herself into the custodial relationship exception.

After the *DeShaney* decision was released, the Ninth Circuit Court of Appeals withdrew and amended one of its prior decisions, *Balistreri v. Pacifica Police Department.*[44] The new decision in *Balistreri* held that even though the police knew both of the danger to Jena Balistreri, a battered woman, and that she had an outstanding restraining order against her ex-husband, the *DeShaney* decision barred her claim that she had established a special relationship with the police. Jena had been severely beaten by her ex-husband, yet the police refused to do anything except remove him from her home. They even refused to offer her any obviously needed medical assistance. After she and her husband separated and she had obtained a divorce and restraining order against him, she complained repeatedly to the police of his many acts of vandalism and harassing telephone calls. The police continued to refuse to assist her even after he crashed his car into her garage and later firebombed her house. But the court believed the *DeShaney* opinion prevented her from recovering from the police for their failure to assist her.

In *Duong v. County of Arapahoe,*[45] another court refused to find that a custodial exception existed when the wife's estranged husband killed her outside the courtroom, despite the fact that the state had compelled her to attend court and had promised to protect her when she did. When a court holds that a battered woman is not in custody when the state has required her to appear in court, it is unlikely that other battered women not actually in custody will prevail in their claims that they are in custody.

Borgmann, however, has suggested that a battered woman could argue that an order of protection constitutes a form of state custody because it creates a zone of safety where the state promises to protect her. The eviction or vacate (or possibly the no-contact or stay away from) terms of the protective order create the zone in which the woman is effectively put in custody and where the court tells her that she will be kept safe.

Another argument which a battered woman could raise would be to claim that a state law or a judicial order preventing her from moving herself and/or children without prior court permission puts her in custody. Her claim would be even stronger if she had already received a judicial opinion denying her request to move, particularly when she based her claim, at least in part, on her need for safety for herself and/or her children. Many women are compelled by the court deciding the custody issue to remain in a particular area (e g., within the state, or

44. 855 F.2d 1421, *amended and withdrawn*, 901 F.2d 696 (9th Cir.1988).

45. 837 P.2d 226 (Colo.Ct.App.1992), *cert. denied*, No. 92–SC–318 (Oct. 13, 1992).

within 50 miles of her current home). Yet, as mentioned above, these types of arguments are by no means sure to prevail, even if police enforced the statute or court order forbidding her to relocate.

Supporting such an argument is the Fifth Circuit decision in *Doe v. Taylor Independent School District*.[51] That decision found that the compulsory school attendance laws created a special relationship between school officials and their students which gave rise to an affirmative duty under the Due Process Clause to protect those students from a known danger. The school superintendent and principal had failed to protect a 14–year old student from her teacher's sexual molestation. The school officials who knew of the asserted danger and failed to act were therefore liable for injuries linked to the state agents' nonfeasance. The court concluded that public school officials have a duty to police their subordinates' misconduct and to protect students from dangers when the officials know or should know about them. The officials' deliberate indifference to these duties can form the basis of liability against them. However, this does not mean that school officials are liable in the ordinary course for injuries to students inflicted by fellow students, the court warned.

Another federal appellate court, the Third Circuit Court of Appeals, rejected the argument that compulsory school attendance laws mean that students are in state custody. In that case, *D.R. by L.R. v. Middle Bucks Area Vocational Technical School*,[53] the municipality was sued for failing to protect two female high school students from several male classmates who repeatedly physically, verbally and sexually assaulted them in a unisex bathroom and darkroom in the graphic arts room. But, as the dissent noted, the substantial compulsion associated with schooling should "qualify as the type of state restraint on personal liberty which gives rise to a duty to protect." The state significantly contributed to the girls' harm by assigning them to a chaotic classroom supervised by an unqualified student teacher where they were prevented from using anything but the unisex lavatory, the dissent noted.

Interestingly, the U.S. Supreme Court denied *certiorari* in both of these cases, leaving unresolved whether compulsory school attendance creates a duty on the part of school officials to protect students attending school. Also unresolved is the question of whether, if such a duty exists, it covers only injuries inflicted by school officials or also covers those inflicted by fellow students. The fellow student situation is more closely analogous to the predicament of a battered woman restricted from leaving the area by statute or court order. Although the need to supervise minors is more recognized than the need to protect an adult, the fact that the state can deny a victim of domestic violence the right to flee the area and then fail to give her and her children adequate police

---

51. 975 F.2d 137 (C.A.5), *cert. denied sub nom.* Caplinger v. Doe, 113 S.Ct. 1066, *reh'g denied*, 113 S.Ct. 1436, *reh'g granted*, 987 F.2d 231 (5th Cir.1993).

53. 972 F.2d 1364 (C.A.3 1992), *cert. denied*, 113 S.Ct. 1045 (1993).

protection may convince some judges that such a failure does violate her substantive due process rights.

B. The Increased Danger Exception to Deshaney

The second exception which the *DeShaney* decision envisioned was the situation in which a government actor placed the victimized person in greater danger. The *DeShaney* majority opinion emphasized that the state did nothing to increase Joshua's danger.

One post-*DeShaney* case was not dismissed because it presented a *prima facie* claim of increased danger. In that case, *Estate of Sinthasomphone v. City of Milwaukee*,[56] the estate of one of the boys whom Jeffrey Dahmer killed alleged that the city police had ignored the pleas of two bystanders who tried to tell them that the bloodied boy had been sexually abused by Dahmer and was trying to escape from him. In addition, the bystanders had tried to tell the police that Dahmer was calling the boy names and trying to control him. The complaint alleged that the police not only refused to investigate their claims, but actually threatened to arrest the two bystanders and, believing that Dahmer and the boy were adult homosexual partners, returned the child to Dahmer's apartment, with the result that Dahmer was not prevented from killing the child. The court reasoned that, if the claims were true, not only had the police actively prevented the private bystander citizens from helping the small 14-year old Laotian boy, but the officers had even acted to deliver the boy back to the unrelated adult, who had no legitimate claim to custody of the child. Although the court did not find that any special relationship existed between the boy and the officers, it was unwilling to hold that, if the facts alleged were true, the police had not increased the danger to the boy. Accordingly, the court did not dismiss his estate's claims. But the court did dismiss the claims regarding Dahmer's later victims, refusing to hold the police liable on the theory that had they arrested Dahmer for the Laotian boy's assault, Dahmer would not have been able to kill his subsequent victims.

In *Wood v. Ostrander*,[57] another increased danger case, the Ninth Circuit Court of Appeals held that a state trooper had placed a rape victim in greater danger when he abandoned her in a high crime neighborhood at 2:30 A.M. after arresting her driver companion and seizing the car. After the car was towed away, she was left stranded and eventually accepted a ride from a stranger who raped her.

In another case, *Cornelius v. Town of Highland Lake Ala.*,[58] the Eleventh Circuit Court of Appeals held that a town clerk had been placed in increased danger, resulting in her being abducted from her job and terrorized for three days by dangerous prison inmates assigned to work squads within the community. The court noted that the prison and town officials knew that many of the prisoners whom they regularly

56. 785 F.Supp. 1343 (E.D.Wis.1992).

57. 879 F.2d 583 (9th Cir.1989), *cert. denied*, 111 S.Ct. 341 (1990).

58. 880 F.2d 348 (11th Cir.1989).

placed in the town were dangerous. Yet they placed them in the community and even gave them access to knives, axes, machetes and the town car to drive. The court held that close nexus between the crime perpetrated and the town and prison officials' actions "create a triable issue as to special danger."

The Eighth Circuit Court of Appeals allowed the administratrix of the estates of a woman and her daughter to amend her complaint in *Freeman v. Ferguson*[60] to allege that the police chief had placed them in greater danger by directing other officers not to stop her husband, the police chief's close friend, from abusing his wife. The husband killed his wife and 18–year old daughter despite being restrained by a protective order "from harassing, coming about, intimidating, bothering or in any manner interfering with" his wife.

In *Gibson v. City of Chicago*,[62] the Seventh Circuit Court of Appeals, while finding some liability, absolved the police superintendent and city of some due process liability for the murder perpetrated by an officer on medical leave using a police issued firearm and ammunition. The department had put the officer on "medically unfit" status following several public complaints that he had used excess force and an evaluation that he suffered from atypical impulse control disorder, which caused him to use excessive force. In addition, the department had ordered the officer not to carry his weapon. Because he was stripped of his authority to perform any police duties, he was not acting under color of law. But because the department never removed his gun and had no policy about recovering deadly weapons and ammunition from mentally unfit officers, the court held that the department had increased the danger to the decedent. The department had not only armed and trained its employee, it had also allowed him to retain his weapon and ammunition after stripping him of the rest of his police authority, further endangering the decedent.

Yet not all cases involving allegations that police have increased a later victim's danger have been successful. The case of *Hilliard v. City and County of Denver*[64] is factually very similar to the *Wood* case, above. Kathy Hilliard's male companion was arrested after a minor traffic accident, the car impounded, and Kathy, who was intoxicated, was ordered not to drive. She was effectively stranded by the police in a high-crime area. Unable to summon help from a telephone in a nearby convenience store, she returned to the car, where a stranger attacked her. Although she was robbed, sexually assaulted and left naked, bleeding, and barely conscious, the court refused to hold that the police had put her in any increased danger.

In *Brown v. City of Elba*,[65] the district court held that because the police officer was no more than ordinarily negligent, he was not liable for allowing a husband to ride in the front seat of the patrol car next to the

---

60. 911 F.2d 52 (8th Cir.1990).

62. 910 F.2d 1510 (7th Cir.1990).

64. 930 F.2d 1516 (10th Cir. 1991).

65. 754 F.Supp. 1551 (M.D.Ala.1990).

officer, thereby enabling the husband to seize the officer's gun, which he used to shoot and kill his wife and then himself. But because there were no facts before the court indicating that the officer knew of the husband's prior violence towards the wife or that the husband then intended to harm her, the court ordered that the constitutional claims be dismissed.

Despite the *Hilliard* and *Brown* decisions rejecting increased danger claims, a battered woman with a protection order who is later injured by her abuser could argue that she faced increased danger because of state action. For example she could argue that she reasonably relied upon the established law enforcement agency to help protect her, and thus that she gave up various self-help remedies that she might otherwise have pursued. Similarly, a battered woman who is forced by state law (e.g., the state's version of the Uniform Child Custody Jurisdiction Act, which requires that she list her address in order to obtain a custody order) or by a court order requiring her to give her abuser her current address to have contact with him for visitation, joint counseling, or mediation can argue that the state increased her danger if her abuser makes use of that information to harm her. But, as the *Hilliard* and *Brown* cases show, it is by no means clear that a court will agree with her argument or hold that the state placed her in greater danger, even when she had argued that she needed more protection but the court had denied her request.

C. The Failure to Adequately Train Exception to Deshaney

Six days after the U.S. Supreme Court decided *DeShaney*, it upheld a Section 1983 municipal liability case on a due process claim in *City of Canton v. Harris*.[67] The *Canton* decision found the city liable for its failure to adequately train its police officers to recognize when someone who was in police custody required medical assistance. In *Canton*, the Supreme Court never invoked the special relationship doctrine or custodial relationship exception carved out of its *DeShaney* decision. Instead, it treated the theory of failure to adequately train theory as a distinct substantive due process claim. To succeed, the plaintiff detainee had to show that the city's failure to train amounted to "deliberate indifference to the rights of persons with whom the police come into contact." The Court established the deliberate indifference standard to protect municipalities from "unprecedented liability under Section 1983 ... and engaging the federal courts in an endless exercise of second-guessing municipal employee training programs ... an exercise ... that would implicate serious questions of federalism."

A battered woman could argue under *Canton* that the municipality becomes liable "when it maintains, or persists in following, a policy of lesser protection for domestic violence victims with deliberate indifference to the policy's disproportionate impact on women."[70] She could still

---

67. 109 S. Ct. 1197 (1989).

70. Laura S. Harper, "Battered Women Suing Police for Failure to Intervene: Via-ble Legal Avenues after *DeShaney v. Winnebago County Department of Social Services*"

claim that she was deprived of her liberty under the due process clause since this claim circumvents the special relationship doctrine. Likewise, she can argue a failure-to-train claim if the municipality's domestic violence training program was so inadequate that it "amounted to deliberate indifference to the need for heightened protection for ... victims" of domestic violence. However, she must show that her injury resulted from the city's policy of not adequately training—not because some particular officer was unsatisfactorily trained. Obviously, factors other than the city's policy may be responsible for the inadequacies of a particular officer.

IV. EQUAL PROTECTION CLAIMS

In *DeShaney*, the Supreme Court explicitly noted that its decision did not affect equal protection claims. "The State may not, of course, selectively deny its protective services to certain disfavored minorities without violating the Equal Protection Clause" of the Fourteenth Amendment, the *DeShaney* court stated. As a practical matter, proving an equal protection violation is often difficult without some clear proof, such as a written policy which makes clear on its face its discriminatory intent. However, through discovery or the testimony of other victims, one or more battered women may be able to convince the fact finder that the police did discriminate against her or the class of battered women. Tracey Thurman won her case based solely on her own testimony regarding the inadequacies of the police responses to her desperate calls to them over an eight-month period, during which she repeatedly sought their assistance in protecting her from her husband.

The case will be made harder because individual police officers can claim a qualified immunity defense to claims of gender discrimination or discrimination against victims of domestic violence. This defense protects individual state officers who are performing discretionary functions unless they violate "clearly established statutory or constitutional rights of which a reasonable person would have known." Discretionary functions, unlike ministerial tasks, are "almost inevitably influenced by the decisionmaker's experiences, values, and emotions." However, suing the municipality, instead of its officers in their individual capacities, enables the plaintiff to sue on a "policy or custom" claim, because the municipality cannot evoke the qualified immunity defense. Such claims are generally far easier to win.

Courts apply different levels of scrutiny to different types of discrimination claims. Claims based on disparate treatment on account of race, ethnic background or national origin are easiest to win, with the court applying a strict standard of scrutiny. In contrast, cases based on deliberate gender discrimination are examined by an intermediate level of scrutiny; the government will win if it can show that the challenged practice or policy is substantially related to an important government objective or interest. Finally, cases that involve other sorts of allegedly

in *Women and the Law*, Carol H. Lefcourt
& Adria S. Hillman Eds., 9B–31 (1991).

discriminating classifications are the easiest for the government to win. The government must show merely that the classification is "rationally" related to a valid governmental purpose.

Courts apply a rational basis for review when a plaintiff bases her case on being discriminated against as a victim of domestic violence. This is true because courts are generally unwilling to accept evidence of extreme disparate impact on women as sufficient evidence of discriminatory intent against a victim of domestic violence, since victims can be either males or females. If the practice or policy is race and gender neutral, the plaintiff must prove that it has a discriminatory intent or purpose before the court will invoke a higher level of scrutiny. However, just because the practice or policy has a disproportionate impact, the court will not infer that the policy's intent was to discriminate. Yet the court may consider circumstantial evidence, such as a policy's historical background or the extreme disparate impact, or the extreme discriminatory effect that a facially neutral policy has on a particular class of people, to show the policy's discriminatory purpose. This was the claim made by Tracey Thurman, who argued that Torrington, Connecticut had an administrative policy to implement the domestic violence law in a discriminatory fashion.

In the *Sinthasomphone* case, the estate of one of Jeffrey Dahmer's victims was able to prevent dismissal of its equal protection claims against the Milwaukee police because it claimed that the officers intentionally discriminated based on race, color, national origin, or sexual orientation in failing to protect the 14–year old Laotian boy. The estate alleged that the city's police had discriminated against minorities since 1958. It further alleged that the custom was evident from the reaction of police union officials and the prior police chiefs to the new police chief's disciplining of the officers involved.

V. PROCEDURAL DUE PROCESS CLAIMS

Procedural due process claims are considered to arise from state law and not under the U.S. Constitution. As a result, the *DeShaney* decision does not affect a battered woman's procedural due process claims against the police.

Under *Goldberg v. Kelly*[89] and *Board of Regents v. Roth*,[90] without adequate procedural safeguards the state cannot deny to any individual an interest to an entitlement that it has created, even when the state has voluntarily undertaken to provide the interest. In a procedural claim, the entitlement can be created by the combined effect of the battered woman's having an order of protection and a law or policy requiring the police to enforce the order. However, where the state leaves to the responding officer the ultimate determination of whether to enforce the order or make an arrest, then the battered woman has no entitlement to expect that the state-mandated procedures be followed. Thus a pro-arrest domestic violence statute probably does not create such an entitle-

89. 397 U.S. 254 (1970).   **90.** 408 U.S. 564 (1972).

ment, but a mandatory arrest domestic violence statute does if the conditions triggering the mandatory arrest are present. In like manner, a battered woman can seek enforcement of a law requiring police to give victims certain information about where they can go to get help (e.g., information about shelters, prosecution of abusers, and civil protection orders). In contrast, laws requiring the police to be trained in domestic violence may trigger an entitlement in the officers who are not being trained, but they probably do not trigger an entitlement in an uninjured battered woman who, as a result of the police's lack of training, is less likely to get an adequate police response if she has to call them in the future. In this last case, the battered woman is not yet even able to show that she has been injured. (But she would have a good cause of action if she was injured as a result of the police's not being trained.)

Another problem that a battered woman may encounter occurs when the individual responding officer acted against a department's established policy. In this situation, her remedy is to sue the individual officer if the officer did not follow the policy and/or, if the policy was not disseminated, the officer's superiors (e.g., the police chief). That happened in *Thurman* where the policy sat on a shelf.

A battered woman may still pursue any procedural due process claims that she may have despite the U.S. Supreme Court's *DeShaney* ruling.

VI. State Claims

A battered woman can file state tort claims against any governmental actor (e.g., the police) who failed to protect her. Many battered women have successfully brought tort suits against the police in state courts. But battered women may face some obstacles unrelated to *DeShaney* in bringing state tort claims against the police. While no states have absolute sovereign immunity to being sued, every state has retained restrictions or limitations on its amenability to suit. The laws and judicial decisions in each state determine what these restrictions or limitations are. In addition to these restrictions, most state actors, including the police, enjoy a qualified immunity for even negligently performed public or discretionary functions. About half of the states, especially those with mandatory arrest laws, give law enforcement officers immunity when intervening in a domestic violence crisis, but others immunize any act, or act or omission, by the officer. Statutes or case law which grant the officer immunity, particularly for any failure to act, will make it harder for the battered woman to successfully sue a law officer who failed to intervene appropriately to protect her from her abuser.

State law will also determine when a law officer's actions are considered discretionary functions. For example, Oregon's highest court held in *Nearing v. Weaver*[103] that police had no discretion in arresting when orders of protection were violated because the state's mandatory arrest law required them to arrest if they had probable cause to believe

---

103. 670 P.2d 137, 142 (Or.1983).

that a protective order had been violated. In *Irwin v. Town of Ware*,[105] Massachusetts' highest court held that an officer's function was not discretionary unless the officer had to weigh alternatives and make choices with respect to public policy. Thus, immunity is irrelevant when the police have a mandatory duty to arrest.

B.   State Constitutional Claims

Many state constitutions include provisions that are identical or similar to some or all of those in the U.S. Constitution or Bill of Rights. Many of these protections are interpreted more expansively by the state's courts than the corresponding U.S. Constitution protections are now interpreted by the federal courts, especially by the U.S. Supreme Court. Furthermore, some state constitutions contain specific protections which are not included in the U.S. Constitution, such as victims' rights, the right to individual dignity, or (in at least eighteen states) the right to not be discriminated against because of gender. Battered women can bring state constitutional claims along with state tort claims in state court. If a battered woman also raises federal claims, she can raise her state tort and/or state constitutional claims in federal court as ancillary to her federal claims.

VII.   DECLARATORY AND INJUNCTIVE CAUSE OF ACTION

A group of battered women in one community can sue the police on an injunctive or declaratory cause of action in a class action if they can show that the police are not following the law or a police policy. If the police are applying the law or policy in a discriminatory way, those suing can get relief for the entire class which is receiving inadequate or discriminatory treatment. The purpose of such a suit is to make the court issue an order which requires the police department to follow the existing laws and procedures.

The declaratory and injunctive action can be brought in state court if state law is involved. Or it can be brought in federal court if a federal law or any U.S. Constitutional issues are involved. Or it can be brought in either state or federal court if both state and federal issues are involved.

Suing for declaratory and injunctive relief was the approach so successfully pursued in the *Scott v. Hart* and *Bruno v. Codd* cases, discussed above. When the suit is brought as a class action, courts usually want a fair amount of documentation from a number of people or something in writing from the police to convince them that the police department is not applying the laws and policies which govern their domestic violence responses. It is also important to document that the police were informed of any problems but did not correct them.

CONCLUSION

The *DeShaney* decision of the U.S. Supreme Court has made it considerably harder for a battered woman to sue the police for tort

---

105.   467 N.E.2d 1292 (Mass.1984).

damages when the police have failed to protect her and she was injured as a result of that failure. Nonetheless, there are a number of exceptions that still enable battered women to successfully sue them.

A battered woman can sue based on state tort and/or state constitutional claims. She can still sue based on procedural due process claims. If the state legislature has created a legitimate expectation of entitlement pursuant to its domestic violence or police response law, she can claim a procedural due process violation if the state denied her that entitlement without adequate procedural benefits. She can sue based on a denial of equal protection if she can show she was treated differently because she is female or a member of a protected minority, or if she can establish that there was a discriminatory administrative classification. Even if her claim is a substantive due process one, she may fit into one of the exceptions to *DeShaney*: that the municipality (1) increased her danger, (2) owed her a higher duty because she was in its custody, or (3) failed to adequately train the police. If the police are not following their own laws and policies, she can also sue for *mandamus* or for declaratory or injunctive relief to force them to enforce the laws and policies which are supposed to protect her.

ANTHONY MASTROIANNI v. COUNTY OF SUFFOLK

Court of Appeals of New York (1997).
668 N.Y.S.2d 542, 543–546.

Plaintiff's complaint seeks damages stemming from an alleged failure to provide plaintiff's decedent with protection after the police department had been directly notified that decedent's husband had violated an order of protection. We conclude that a special relationship between the police department and the decedent arose from the circumstances presented. We further conclude that a question of fact has been raised concerning the department's duty of care owed to plaintiff's decedent due to the existence of this special relationship. Accordingly, summary judgment should not have been granted to the defendants and the order of the Appellate Division should be reversed.

Based on the papers submitted on defendants' motion, the record contains the following evidentiary allegations. On June 12, 1985, Family Court granted a petition filed under article 10 of the Family Court Act by the Child Protective Agency of the Suffolk County Department of Social Services on behalf of decedent's children against her estranged husband. Based upon the husband's alleged history of abuse toward his wife and her children, the court issued a permanent order of protection pursuant to Family Court Act § 842(a). The order provided that "[Anthony Swiggett] shall not have any contact with children or Mrs. Parker (Swiggett) and he is to remain away from their residence, to wit: 39 Pine Street, Central Islip, New York." Thereafter, the court sent a copy of the order to the Third Precinct of the Suffolk County Police Department. The husband was arrested for violating the order of protection on June 24, 1985, less than two weeks after it was issued against him.

At approximately 9:06 P.M. on September 5, 1985, Suffolk County police officers responded to a 911 call from decedent that her husband had violated the order of protection by entering her residence and throwing her furniture out into the yard. The officers met decedent at her mother's house where she accompanied the officers to her house located nearby. Upon arriving at the decedent's residence, the officers noted several pieces of furniture strewn about the lawn including some chairs, a couch and a washing machine. At this point, the officers were presented with the order of protection by the decedent. The officers described the decedent as "very upset" and she stated that she wanted her husband "locked up."

The officers discovered that the husband was visiting decedent's next door neighbors located between 20 to 30 feet away from decedent's residence. When the officers requested that the husband come outside to speak with them, they smelled alcohol on his breath but did not find him intoxicated. Upon questioning, the husband denied entering his wife's residence and removing the furniture. The officers questioned everyone present but no one, including the decedent, had actually seen who had moved the furniture. Although one person on the scene had seen the husband leaving the decedent's residence earlier that day, she did not tell this to the officers. She later explained that she had not seen the husband move the furniture and she felt that that was all the officers were asking about.

The officers discovered that there were no outstanding warrants for the husband's arrest. The officers were unsure how to proceed and called their supervisor for guidance. The supervising officer was asked whether it was necessary to see the subject within the premises "on an order of protection." The supervisor responded that it "depends how the order of protection reads ... but for you to arrest him he has to be there at the scene of his action." The officers then asked, "So you can't just do it on her say so that he was in the house prior?" The supervisor answered "Negative ... it's not like a warrant. He has to be there and ... otherwise her complaint should be for the court ... and you make a Field Report."

Based upon this advice, the officers told decedent that "according to the information [they] had, there was no justification to arrest him on the violation of the Order of Protection." According to one officer, "She was upset to the point she was crying, and she didn't really understand why he wasn't being arrested." The other officer claimed that the decedent "began crying and pleading that we arrest him" and told the officer that she was "afraid of this man." The officer told the husband "that I believed what [the wife] had told me, and ... if I had to come back here again tonight, if there were any further problems, that he would be arrested and taken to jail."

The officers remained on the scene for over an hour and watched while the wife moved her furniture back into her house. The officers did not enter the house itself or do any further investigation to ascertain who had moved the furniture. At approximately 10:25 P.M., the officers investigated an unrelated missing juvenile report they had received from a residence located across the street from decedent's home. After investigating this report, the officers left the area for a meal break at around 10:46 P.M. At the time the officers left, they did not know where the husband was.

At 10:54 P.M., the officers received a call to return to the area. The decedent had been stabbed. The same officers who had investigated the wife's earlier report then canvassed the area looking for the husband. When they found him, he was covered in blood and his pocket contained a copy of the same order of protection which the officers had seen earlier. The wife died from her wounds and a jury later convicted the husband for the stabbing of his wife.

Plaintiff commenced the instant action to recover damages for decedent's death. Defendants moved for summary judgment and Supreme Court denied the motion. The court found that the "order [of protection] satisfies proof of an affirmative duty to act, knowledge that inaction could lead to harm and justifiable reliance on the defendants' affirmative undertaking." The court also found sufficient questions of fact relating to the reasonableness of the actions of the officers which precluded summary judgment.

The Appellate Division reversed and dismissed the complaint. The Court held that the "unrebutted evidence submitted in support of the defendants' motion for summary judgment established that the defendants did not owe a special duty to the plaintiff's decedent." The Court also found that the record established "that the actions of the police department were reasonable under the circumstances." (228 A.D.2d 483, 643 N.Y.S.2d 1017.) This Court granted leave to appeal. We reverse.

DISCUSSION

As a general rule, a municipality may not be held liable for injuries resulting from a failure to provide police protection. As we have stated, "a different rule 'could and would inevitably determine how the limited police resources of the community should be allocated and without predictable limits.'" However, we have recognized potential liability stemming from the presence of a "special relationship existing between the municipality and the injured party."

In *Cuffy*, we stated:

The elements of this "special relationship" are: (1) an assumption by the municipality, through promises or actions, of an affirmative duty to act on behalf of the party who was injured; (2) knowledge on the part of the municipality's agents that inaction could lead to harm; (3) some form of direct contact between the municipality's agents and the injured party; and (4) that party's justifiable reliance on the municipality's affirmative undertaking (69 N.Y.2d, at 260).

The first two elements are satisfied by the issuance of an order of protection under the Family Court Act which provides that an order "shall constitute authority" for an officer "to arrest a person charged with violating the terms of such order of protection." Clearly, a duly issued order of protection constitutes an "assumption" of an "affirmative duty" of protection coupled with an awareness that "inaction could lead to harm" (*Id*).

The third element which must be satisfied to establish a "special relationship"—some form of direct contact between the municipality's agents and the injured party—depends upon the peculiar circumstances of each case (*Id* at 262). Although, this element of the test outlined in *Cuffy* may not be satisfied by the existence of the order of protection itself, we have generally utilized a flexible approach in analyzing this element when such an order is presented. It can hardly be disputed that this element is satisfied under the facts presented here. Not only was there direct and immediate contact between the officers and the decedent concerning a violation of the order of protection, but the police department had separate and verifiable knowledge of the husband's violent history through his prior convictions and arrests—which included an arrest a few months earlier for violating the same order of protection.

The remaining element which must be demonstrated to constitute a special relationship is that of justifiable reliance. The mere existence of an order of protection, standing alone, will not prove justifiable reliance. However, upon an examination of all of the circumstances here, we conclude that the victim's justifiable reliance on the officers' undertaking to protect her was established.

As noted above, after reviewing the order of protection, the officers, in response to her pleas for assistance, assured decedent that although they could not presently make an arrest, they "would do whatever [they] could" if she had any further problems with her husband. The officers then waited in front of the residence, observing decedent while she brought her furniture back inside her home. Thereafter, the officers remained on the scene, across the street from the Parker home, handling a report of a missing juvenile. Within minutes of their departure from the immediate area, the officers were directed to return to decedent's residence, where they found her fatally stabbed. Additionally, the victim had sought and obtained police intervention on a previous occasion when her husband had violated the very same protective order. The direct contact between the wife and the officers coupled with the circumstances giving rise to the officers' own belief that the order of protection had been violated support the conclusion that the wife justifiably relied upon the officers' "aid in securing the protection such order was intended to afford" (Family Ct. Act § 168[1]). Under these circumstances, the fact that the officers informed decedent that they would not make an arrest does not, alone, render her reliance unjustified, given their other affirmative undertakings on her behalf.

Thus, we conclude that the elements of a special relationship as set forth in *Cuffy* were present here. The existence of the order of protection, the direct contact of the police with the decedent and the decedent's justifiable reliance on the officers' affirmative undertaking on her behalf all serve to demonstrate that a special relationship was established here.

The question remains whether the record presents a question of fact concerning the reasonableness of the actions of the municipality's police department. The Appellate Division found that the officers' actions were reasonable as a matter of law. We disagree. Construing the record in plaintiff's favor, as we must on defendants' motion for summary judgment, we conclude that a question of fact has been raised regarding whether the actions taken by the officers were reasonable in securing protection for the decedent under the circumstances presented. Such questions concerning reasonableness are properly left for the fact finder under an examination of all the evidence.

The order of the Appellate Division should be reversed, with costs, and defendants' motion for summary judgment denied.

DEBRA CULBERSON v. VINCENT DOAN

United States District Court, S.D. Ohio (1999).
65 F.Supp.2d 701, 702–706, 714–717.

The Estate of Clarissa Culberson and Clarissa Culberson's parents, Debra and Roger Culberson, and her sister, Christina Culberson (collectively referred to as "Plaintiffs") bring this action against Vincent Doan ("Defendant"), Lawrence Baker, Tracey Baker, Richard Payton, and the Village of Blanchester ("Blanchester") (collectively referred to as "Defendants").

The facts as alleged by Plaintiffs in their Complaint concerning the disappearance and subsequently-ruled death of Clarissa Culberson ("Carrie") are sketchy, yet they tell a grim tale of domestic abuse.

Carrie lived with her mother and sister in Blanchester, Ohio. During 1995, Carrie and Defendant dated on a regular basis. Plaintiffs allege that, in the Fall of 1995, Defendant began to physically abuse Carrie. Plaintiffs contend that on one occasion Defendant "tightly clamped his hand over the nose, mouth and throat of [Carrie], who injured her face trying to pry his fingers off her mouth." Plaintiffs maintain that the abuse continued in 1996, pointing to an incident in which Defendant smashed the windows of Carrie's car as she sat in the vehicle. Although Carrie allegedly reported the incident to the Blanchester police, Plaintiffs assert that no charges were filed against Defendant.

Plaintiffs also allege that Defendant subsequently attacked Carrie in April, July, and August of 1996. As a result of the April attack, Plaintiffs contend that Defendant injured Carrie's head and kidneys. Thereafter, Carrie allegedly filed a police report with the Blanchester police; however, the police did not bring any charges against Defendant. On July 5, 1996, Plaintiffs allege that Defendant forced his way into Carrie's home and threatened her to prevent her from having any contact with other men. During this incident, Defendant allegedly pushed Plaintiff Debra Culberson in an unsuccessful attempt to assault Carrie. Debra Culberson also filed a criminal report with the Blanchester police department regarding the incident, but asserts that the police did not respond to the report. On July 28, 1996, Plaintiffs allege that Defendant attacked Carrie again when she came to his house while on an errand. Plaintiffs assert that, during this assault, he threw Carrie across a room and struck her in the head with a metal object, causing her to need surgical staples in her scalp. Carrie again sought criminal charges after this attack through the Blanchester police department. However, according to Plaintiffs, her attempt to get help was again unsuccessful. On August 26, 1996, approximately three days before Defendant allegedly murdered Carrie, Plaintiffs assert that he held her at gunpoint in a barn within the Blanchester area.

On August 29, 1996, at approximately 12:20 a.m., Defendant's neighbor witnessed him hitting Carrie in the head. At approximately 1:30 a.m., Defendant spoke with Lawrence Baker on the telephone. At 3:15 a.m., Defendant arrived at Tracey Baker's residence with blood on his chest, arms and pants. He then took a shower and left the residence with Tracey Baker, who was carrying a handgun and garbage bags.

At approximately 11:00 a.m., Debra Culberson reported her daughter missing to Blanchester Police Chief Richard Payton ("Chief Payton"). Debra Culberson also reminded Chief Payton at that time of the threats Defendant made to Carrie and the criminal reports made by Carrie during the preceding weeks. Plaintiffs contend that Chief Payton responded, "Why does she keep going back to it?" Plaintiffs assert that Chief Payton did not investigate Defendant, but went to Lawrence Baker's home later that day and warned him that Carrie had been reported missing and that Defendant would be a suspect.

On September 3, 1996, the Blanchester police department performed a search of Lawrence Baker's junk yard. During the search, a blood hound and a cadaver dog brought a small pond to the attention of the search party indicating that the dogs may have detected Carrie's scent. The search team officers informed Chief Payton that they wanted the pond drained; however, Chief Payton declined to proceed with the search that day and advised everyone to leave the premises. Lawrence Baker was present during the search. When the pond was drained the next day, footprints were visible on the bottom of the pond and a muddy path of weeds lead away from the pond.

Carrie's disappearance was ruled a homicide even though her body was never found. Subsequently, Defendant was charged with Carrie's murder. Tracey Baker was charged with obstruction of justice, tampering with evidence, and gross abuse of a corpse. Lawrence Baker was also charged in Carrie's disappearance.

On August 7, 1997, a jury found Defendant guilty of aggravated murder with one capital offense specification, and three counts of kidnapping in the Clinton County Common Pleas Court. He was sentenced to life imprisonment without parole. Tracey Baker's trial began in the Clinton County Court of Common Pleas on May 20, 1998. On June 4, 1998, a jury found Tracey Baker guilty of two counts of obstruction of justice and one count of tampering with evidence. Tracey Baker was found not guilty of gross abuse of a corpse. The trial of Lawrence Baker began in the Clinton County Court of Common Pleas on August 18, 1998. On August 25, 1998, the jury returned three not guilty verdicts against Lawrence Baker.

On October 24, 1997, Plaintiffs filed a complaint against Defendants Vincent Doan, Lawrence Baker, Tracey Baker, Richard Payton, and the Village of Blanchester, seeking both monetary and injunctive relief. In their Complaint, Plaintiffs claim that Defendant's actions toward Carrie were based primarily on account of her gender in violation of the Violence Against Women Act, 42 U.S.C. § 13981 (the "VAWA"). Furthermore, Plaintiffs assert that the actions of Defendants Vincent Doan, Lawrence Baker, Tracey Baker, and Police Chief Richard Payton "were willful, wanton, malicious or in reckless disregard or indifference to the safety of Carrie Culberson and to the peace of mind, rights, including rights of familial association of Debra Culberson, Roger Culberson, and Christina Culberson." Plaintiffs also claim that the Defendants violated their rights under 42 U.S.C. § 1983, as protected by the Fourteenth Amendment of the Constitution. Additionally, Plaintiffs assert state law claims of emotional distress, wrongful death, obstruction of justice and conspiracy.

In the instant matter, Defendant Vincent Doan has moved to dismiss this case on the grounds that Plaintiffs' Complaint fails to state a claim upon which relief can be granted. Defendant also challenges the constitutionality of the VAWA on its face and as applied. Furthermore, Defendant argues that Plaintiffs' claim under 42 U.S.C. § 1983 should be dismissed because their complaint fails to state a claim upon which relief can be granted and that the state law claims should be dismissed for lack of supplemental jurisdiction.

Plaintiffs filed a Response to Defendant's dismissal motion. Specifically, Plaintiffs assert that an examination of Defendant's abusive language and actions toward Carrie reflect his *animus* toward women in general. The Government has intervened pursuant to 28 U.S.C. § 2403(a) and argues in support of the constitutionality of the Act. The National Organization of Women Legal Defense and Education Fund ("NOW") also moved to intervene and file an *amici curiae* brief in support of the constitutionality of the Act.

* * *

DISCUSSION

I. *Plaintiffs' Claim Under the Violence Against Women Act*

The civil provisions of the Violence Against Women Act of 1994 (hereinafter the "VAWA" or "the Act"), provide a claimant with a civil right to be free from crimes of violence motivated by gender and provides a federal civil rights cause of action for victims of crimes of violence motivated by gender. See 42 U.S.C. §§ 13981(a)-(c). In order to establish a cause of action under the VAWA, the claimant must show (1) that she was a victim of a cause of violence and (2) that the crime was motivated based on her gender. The claimant does not need to show that there has been a prior criminal complaint, prosecution, or conviction against the defendant.

The Act defines a "crime of violence" as "an act or series of acts that would constitute a felony ... whether or not those acts have actually resulted in criminal charges, prosecution, or conviction," 42 U.S.C. § 13981(d)(2)(A), or acts that would constitutes a felony "but for the relationship between" the parties, i.e., marriages in states where laws exist to provide spousal immunity. 42 U.S.C. § 13981(d)(2)(B). Additionally, the Act defines the term "crime motivated by gender" as being done by the defendant "because of gender or on the basis of gender, and due, at least in part, to an *animus* based on the victim's gender...." 42 U.S.C. § 13981(d)(1). "Gender motivation" is to be determined through the use of circumstantial evidence in light of the totality of the circumstances similar to the manner determinations are made in cases of race and gender discrimination claims. S.Rep. No. 102–197 at 50 (1991). Finally, the types of civil damages that the claimant may seek under the Act are compensatory and punitive damages as well as attorneys' fees and injunctive relief.

In the case at bar, Plaintiffs point to Defendant's allegedly violent attacks on Carrie, asserting that those attacks were motivated primarily based on Carrie's gender and support a cause of action under the VAWA. Defendant does not dispute that Plaintiffs' allegations of Carrie's murder satisfies the definition of a crime of violence under § 13981(d)(2). However, Defendant argues that Plaintiffs fail to show that his actions were in any way motivated by Carrie's gender to satisfy the second element of "gender-based violence" under the VAWA.

As we noted earlier, the appropriate determination as to whether a particular act of violence is gender-motivated is based on the totality of the circumstances. In viewing the totality of the circumstances, we note that the extent or *animus* of the perpetrator is a question of fact. *Heights Community Congress v. Hilltop Realty, Inc.*, 774 F.2d 135, 140 (6th Cir.1985). Having reviewed the totality of the allegations made in Plaintiffs' Complaint, we believe that the Complaint does sufficiently set forth a claim under the VAWA. Moreover, we conclude that the allegations by Plaintiffs, if proven, are consistent with a showing that Defendant's actions toward Carrie were gender-motivated. For instance, on one occasion, Defendant allegedly forced his way into Carrie's home and attempted to assault her. Although the assault was unsuccessful, Defendant allegedly threatened Carrie to stay away from other men. We believe these allegations of Defendant's attempted assault and simultaneous threat to Carrie in order to prevent her from dealing with other men are sufficient to allege gender *animus* under the VAWA. Accordingly, we DENY Defendant's Motion to Dismiss Plaintiffs' Complaint on this ground.

(* * * In part II, the court ruled that VAWA was constitutional.)

III. *Plaintiffs' Claim Under 42 U.S.C. § 1983*

Next, Defendant Doan argues that Plaintiffs' Complaint should be dismissed because Plaintiffs fail to sufficiently allege a claim that Defendants violated 42 U.S.C. § 1983. Specifically, Defendants assert that Plaintiffs fail to show how Defendants' actions were under the color of law or deprived them of some right or privilege secured by the Constitution or laws of the United States. Defendant also asserts that the theory of *respondeat superior* is inapplicable under § 1983 and that Plaintiffs cannot base their claim of state action against Defendants under a conspiracy theory solely on basis of Defendant Payton's conduct, but must show that Defendant Village of Blanchester is itself liable for condoning a policy or custom within the police department that led to the deprivation of Plaintiffs' constitutionally protected rights. Defendant asserts that, at best, the only claim Plaintiffs can make is that Defendant Village of Blanchester failed to act to prevent Defendants' actions, not that Defendant Village of Blanchester condoned any policy or custom that caused the alleged cover-up of Carrie's murder. Absent any allegations that Defendants intended to cause Plaintiffs injury or that Defendants engaged in some type of conspiracy, Defendant contends that Plaintiffs' claim under § 1983 must be dismissed.

In response, Plaintiffs assert that they have sufficiently alleged a § 1983 claim against Defendants in their Complaint. Plaintiffs argue that it is not necessary for an individual to be an officer of the state in order to act "under the color of law" if it is shown that the person was a willful participant in a concerted action with the state or its agents. Plaintiffs maintain that Defendant Doan engaged in a conspiracy with Defendants Lawrence Baker, Tracey Baker and Chief Payton to ensure that Carrie's body would not be found and that any type of investigation into her disappearance would be thwarted. Plaintiffs contend that, because the question of whether a person acted "under the color of law" is a question of fact for the jury, the Court should allow the conspiracy allegations to be addressed during discovery and/or at trial. Plaintiffs argue that Defendant's assertion that there is no conspiracy falls more in line with a motion for summary judgment, not a motion to dismiss. Thus, Plaintiffs contend that Defendant's attack on the conspiracy claim is premature and his motion to dismiss should be denied.

In order to establish a claim under § 1983, a plaintiff must show that: (1) she was deprived of a right secured by the Constitution or laws of the United States, and (2) she was subjected to or caused to be subjected to this deprivation by a person acting under color of state law. Although a municipality may be held liable under § 1983 if the municipality itself caused the constitutional deprivation, a municipality does not incur § 1983 liability for an injury inflicted solely by its agents or employees. In other words, a municipality is only liable under § 1983 when the injury is caused by the execution of its policy or custom. "A 'custom' for the purposes of *Monell* liability must 'be so permanent and well settled as to constitute a custom or usage with the force of law.'" *Doe v. Claiborne Cty., Tenn.*, 103 F.3d 495, 507 (6th Cir.1996). Moreover, the supervisor through which § 1983 *respondeat superior* liability is being applied must have "encouraged the specific incident or misconduct or in some way directly participated in it." *Bellamy v. Bradley*, 729 F.2d 416, 421 (6th Cir.1984).

While § 1983 does not itself grant any substantive rights, it does provide a remedy for the deprivation of constitutional and federal rights. In this case, we first find that Plaintiffs, being Carrie's next of kin, have a protected property interest in the remains of Carrie's body under the Due Process Clause of the Fourteenth Amendment. Secondly, we conclude that Plaintiffs sufficiently allege in their Complaint that Defendants intentionally engaged in the activity of "selective enforcement" in violation of § 1983 by failing to act upon her reports of abuse and beatings by Defendant Doan. Such actions of "selective enforcement" based on race, nationality, religion, or gender can give rise to a claim under § 1983. Plaintiffs also sufficiently allege in their Complaint that Defendant Payton, the Chief of the Blanchester Police Department, acted under a policy or custom of the Blanchester Police Department to engage in "selective enforcement" in this case. While Defendant asserts that Plaintiffs cannot show that a conspiracy existed between the named Defendants, this Court believes that the matter should be addressed after discovery and through motions for summary judgment on this issue. In order to state a claim based on the existence of a conspiracy under § 1983, a plaintiff need only plead with some degree of specificity that the conspiracy occurred. "Vague and conclusory allegations unsupported by material facts will not be sufficient to state a claim under 1983." In Plaintiffs' Complaint, they allege that Defendant Payton warned Defendant Lawrence Baker that Defendant Doan would be a suspect in Carrie's disappearance. Plaintiffs also allege that Defendant Payton called off the search and investigation when the cadaver dogs discovered Carrie's scent at the edge of the pond; an inference that Defendant Payton enabled Defendants Lawrence Baker, Tracey Baker and Vincent Doan to remove her body from the pond that night. Thus, finding Plaintiffs' Complaint does sufficiently allege a violation of § 1983 by Defendants, we hereby DENY Defendant's motion to dismiss Plaintiffs' claim for a failure to state a claim under § 1983.

IV. State Law Claims

Finding that Plaintiffs' claims under the VAWA and § 1983 should not be dismissed, this Court believes that it is appropriate to continue to exercise supplemental jurisdiction over Plaintiffs' state law claims.

Nevertheless, Defendant Doan also maintains that Plaintiffs' state law claims of intentional infliction of emotional distress and conspiracy should be dismissed for failure to state a claim.

First, we acknowledge that courts in the State of Ohio have permitted family members to bring claims to recover emotional distress damages without a showing of physical injuries. Further, Plaintiffs' allegations sufficiently allege emotional distress in this case due to Carrie's disappearance and subsequently-ruled death.

Secondly, we reiterate that Plaintiffs have sufficiently alleged that a conspiracy occurred between the named Defendants. Accordingly, we deny Defendant's motion to dismiss Plaintiffs' state law claims.

Recognizing that a grant of a motion to dismiss is appropriate only if "it appears beyond doubt that the plaintiffs can prove no set of facts in support of his [or her] claims which would entitle him [or her] to relief." *Conley*, 355 U.S. at 45–46, 78 S.Ct. 99, we hereby DENY Defendant Doan's motion to dismiss Plaintiffs' Complaint.

D. DUAL ARREST

WISCONSIN STATUTES ANNOTATED, CRIMINAL PROCEDURE, CHAPTER 968, COMMENCEMENT OF CRIMINAL PROCEEDINGS

SECTION 968.075. DOMESTIC ABUSE INCIDENTS; ARREST AND PROSECUTION

* * *

(2) Circumstances requiring arrest.

(a) Notwithstanding § 968.07 and except as provided in par. (b), a law enforcement officer shall arrest and take a person into custody if:

  1. The officer has reasonable grounds to believe that the person is committing or has committed domestic abuse and that the person's actions constitute the commission of a crime; and

  2. Either or both of the following circumstances are present:

   a. The officer has a reasonable basis for believing that continued domestic abuse against the alleged victim is likely.

   b. There is evidence of physical injury to the alleged victim.

(b) If the officer's reasonable grounds for belief under par. (a)1 are based on a report of an alleged domestic abuse incident, the officer is required to make an arrest under par. (a) only if the report is received, within 28 days after the day the incident is alleged to have occurred, by the officer or the law enforcement agency that employs the officer.

(3) Law enforcement policies.

(a) Each law enforcement agency shall develop, adopt and implement written policies regarding arrest procedures for domestic abuse incidents. The policies shall include, but not be limited to, the following:

1. Statements emphasizing that:

    a. In most circumstances, other than those under sub. (2), a law enforcement officer should arrest and take a person into custody if the officer has reasonable grounds to believe that the person is committing or has committed domestic abuse and that the person's actions constitute the commission of a crime.

    b. When the officer has reasonable grounds to believe that spouses, former spouses or other persons who reside together or formerly resided together are committing or have committed domestic abuse against each other, the officer does not have to arrest both persons, but should arrest the person whom the officer believes to be the primary physical aggressor. in determining who is the primary physical aggressor, an officer should consider the intent of this section to protect victims of domestic violence, the relative degree of injury or fear inflicted on the persons involved and any history of domestic abuse between these persons, if that history can reasonably be ascertained by the officer.

    c. A law enforcement officer's decision as to whether or not to arrest under this section may not be based on the consent of the victim to any subsequent prosecution or on the relationship of the persons involved in the incident.

    d. A law enforcement officer's decision not to arrest under this section may not be based solely upon the absence of visible indications of injury or impairment.

* * *

ANDREA D. LYON, BE CAREFUL WHAT YOU WISH FOR: AN EXAMINATION OF ARREST AND PROSECUTION PATTERNS OF DOMESTIC VIOLENCE CASES IN TWO CITIES IN MICHIGAN

5 Mich. J. Gender & L. 254, 271–272, 279–289, 292–294, 297–298 (1999).

INTRODUCTION

I distinctly recall waiting one day in court for a law school clinic case to be called and noticing that of the six or seven domestic violence cases, three or four of the defendants were women. I thought that odd, but it had, after all, been a long time since I had spent any time in misdemeanor courts. Maybe women were doing more abusing than I remembered, or maybe it was just an aberrational day. But then I saw similar patterns on several other days.

I became curious: was this a pattern? If it was, why was it? I decided to look at six months of data on arrests for domestic violence. I chose the cities of Ypsilanti and Ann Arbor, because although they are the two largest cities in Washtenaw County and both house major universities, their populations are quite different. Ypsilanti has a much more significant minority population than Ann Arbor. Also Ann Arbor has a "must arrest" ordinance, while Ypsilanti has the milder "should arrest" statute. I looked at all of the domestic violence police reports from June through December of 1996.

* * *

III.   Results of the Investigation

Ypsilanti has a "should arrest" policy, while Ann Arbor has a "must arrest" policy. The following research regarding the effect of these laws is based upon redacted police reports from Ann Arbor and Ypsilanti police departments from June through December 1996.

These results should be read with caution. First, there is no way to know if records were purposely hidden or if records were not coded as domestic violence because another crime took precedence, so that flaw is an intrinsic part of the study. Second, there are significant differences between Ann Arbor and Ypsilanti arrest policies, which do not appear to be based on the difference in arrest standards. As I will discuss later, I believe another factor is creating the differences between the cities. Third, small sample size affects the results. In the studied time period, there were only 157 domestic violence calls, meaning police officers arrived at the scene, and out of those, only nineteen women were arrested. The data reveal that in slightly over twelve percent of the calls a woman was arrested. The breakdown is 9.5% in Ann Arbor and 15.9% in Ypsilanti. While it appears that race does not seem to be a significant predictor for whether a man, a woman, or either is arrested, there is one exception. Men are less likely to be arrested if they are in a mixed race relationship, but more likely to be convicted once they are arrested. The major statistically significant result is that if the police find out about a prior history of abuse, they are less likely to arrest a woman; however, if they have actually been called to that residence before, they are more likely to arrest a woman.

A.   Statistical Summaries—Arrest Patterns

* * *

1.   Prior Self–Reported History of Abuse

An analysis of arrests and self-reported history of abuse shows that prior history affects the chances of male arrest, but not female arrest. The fact that there is no significantly cognizable difference in the effect of self-reported history for women might be explained by the number of women in the sample. Combining the women arrested in Ann Arbor and Ypsilanti gives a number closer to 0.05. In other words, self-reported history of domestic violence may have the same effect on arrest rates for women, but it is hard to tell here without a larger sample size. On the other hand, one could argue that men are arrested if there is a previous self-reported history of domestic violence because that shows the police are doing their job. Whereas, when women are arrested, the police are not really arresting abusers, but rather arresting the women on the basis of some other motivation.

2. Prior Phone Calls

Overall, across all the data, when a woman is arrested, it does not matter if there have been calls to the police from that residence before. However, when you separate the data for Ann Arbor and Ypsilanti, the results change. In Ypsilanti, the effect of prior calls is not significant, similar to the overall result, while in Ann Arbor, prior phone calls to the police becomes a significant factor. Possibly, there is either conscious or unconscious retaliation by the Ann Arbor police against women for staying in an abuse situation. It is interesting that there are so few prior calls in Ypsilanti. Either people are not calling the police, or once the police are called, they rarely get repeat calls; it is unclear whether this is because the problem is solved, or calling the police does more harm than good. Looking at the cases where only a man is arrested (i.e. excluding dual arrests), whether police have been called before is not significant. It seems that if a woman says she has been hit before, the police are more likely to arrest the man, but if she has actually called the police before, they are not. Again, when there are prior calls to the police, the police appear less likely to believe the woman.

3. Compared By City

The statistics also show that whether the police have been called before significantly depends on the city. The difference between cities may be in the nature of the abusive relationships (i.e., in Ypsilanti the abuse is usually first time), the likelihood of people in that city to call the police, or in record-keeping procedures. When women are arrested or only men are arrested, there is a significant correlation between prior calls and arrest. Whether or not history is reported when women are arrested depends on the city. This may be because of better questioning techniques in Ann Arbor, or because there really is more prior abuse in Ann Arbor. The same result holds when men only are arrested. The result still holds when men and women are combined. There is also a correlation between whether or not an abuse history is reported and the offender's gender. This chart includes all calls, not just those where someone was arrested.

4. Mixed Race Couples

Examining the effects of race in more detail, we find that a woman's arrest is not significantly predicted by the fact that the woman is in a mixed race couple. However, being in a mixed race couple is a significant predictor of whether a man is arrested. The difference from the result for women may be a sample size problem (only three of the arrested women were in a mixed race couple), or it may be showing the intersection of racism and sexism. Further, the arrests of men were not significantly affected by their own race alone. The city is likewise not a significant predictor of whether a man will be arrested.

5. Harms

Following are breakdowns of the harm caused compared to arrest patterns. I have excluded harm levels not represented in the cases. The first table shows the results for women arrested; the only harm level that is significant for predicting arrest of women is hitting with an object, i.e., lamp, chair, glass, etc. The second shows the corresponding results for men; the category of slapping, hitting with fists, kicking, etc. is the only significant predictor for arrests of men. These results seem counter-intuitive, but I cannot say with certainty that certain harm levels were significant predictors while others were not, since each group (harm level) contains so few cases.

B. Logistic Regression—Arrest Patterns

* * *

1. Women Arrested Overall

The first test I ran examined the factors predicting whether a woman would be arrested. * * * These results demonstrate that prior calls and prior history are the variables that matter in explaining why a woman is arrested. Prior calls is negatively associated. Thus, if someone has called the police before, the woman is more likely to get arrested. Prior history is positively associated, meaning if the police find out about a prior abuse history, they are less likely to arrest the woman. These results are interesting and can perhaps be attributed to the way police in the two cities are trained, whether the prosecutors pursue the arrests, or a combination of both.

So, overall, we know that prior history, mixed race, and the city predict why men are arrested for domestic violence. The correlations tell us that when prior abuse history is reported, a man is more likely to be arrested; when the couple is of different races, the man is less likely to be arrested; and when the city is Ypsilanti, a man is more likely to be arrested.

* * *

3. Final Disposition

I also ran tests for final disposition results. In these tests, I excluded the dual arrest cases to simplify the analysis. I ran six groups of chi-square tests. First, I looked at either whether the case was dropped or not, and then whether the case resulted in some sort of guilty verdict or not. In other words, cases where there was some follow-up, but not a guilty verdict, or the information was not recorded were characterized as not dropped and also not guilty. Within both of those two major groups, I ran tests of cases overall, cases in Ann Arbor, and cases in Ypsilanti.

The factors that showed a significant correlation with a case not being dropped were prior history for male and female arrestees in Ann Arbor and calls for male and female arrestees in Ann Arbor. For guilty verdicts, the significant factors were for both cities combined, prior history for male and female arrestees, prior history for male arrestees, prior calls for male and female arrestees, and prior calls for female arrestees; and for Ann Arbor, prior calls for female arrestees.

Thus, overall, for both men and women, the only thing that predicts whether a case will not be dropped is the city. In other words, a case is more likely to be dropped in Ann Arbor.

CONCLUSION

That day I saw what appeared to me to be a disproportionate number of women in misdemeanor court charged with domestic violence turned out to be less of a pattern than I originally surmised, although the overall rate of women being arrested, twelve percent, is much higher than one would expect, given who is harmed most by domestic violence. It is also interesting that the items of statistical significance relate to location of prior calls and to race more than to gender.

The Ann Arbor Police Department is more likely to drop cases with its "must arrest" policy, while cases tried in Ann Arbor have a statistically significant correlation with acquittals. It may be that the police exercise discretion better in Ypsilanti, or it may be that there is more post-arrest prosecutorial discretion in Ann Arbor.

Many saw these "must arrest" and "should arrest" statutes as a major answer to the problem of domestic violence, but clearly they are not; domestic violence is still endemic in society. Between twenty-two and thirty-five percent of all women who seek treatment in hospital emergency rooms are there because of abuse by a man with whom they either are, or were, intimately involved. Forty percent of the injuries come from deliberate assaults by partners, and nineteen percent of those women have a previous history of abuse-caused injury.

Nonetheless, the high incidence of women arrested, as well as the negative response of the police to women when they have previously called the police, suggests some need for re-evaluation of policy. My suggestions are twofold. First, the "should arrest" policy is the better policy. If the police feel that they are not trusted to determine when an arrest should be made, they will inevitably become resentful and may end up "retaliating" by arresting a battered woman who returns to her batterer and once again needs help.

Second, I propose that after there has been an arrest, but before there is a prosecution, that the prosecuting authority set up a review team to look at each case to discern whether the "right" person has been arrested, to determine if there is a history of violence in this relationship, and to monitor what the police are doing. In this way, the prosecutorial and law enforcement agencies can learn from each other and can see to it that those who should be prosecuted are prosecuted.

Chapter 11

PROSECUTORIAL RESPONSE

This chapter starts by looking at the role of the prosecutor in domestic violence cases. It opens with a debate between two opposing viewpoints in terms of "no-drop" prosecution policies: the first writer advocates for such policies generally, arguing that this approach empowers victims of domestic violence, while the second writer opposes them as disempowering for victims. Along the same vein, another piece calls for prosecutors to modify such practices when dealing with battered immigrant women, stating that the prosecutorial role needs to change in such cases, from obtaining convictions to providing safety for victims.

The second part of the chapter looks at specific strategies being used by increasing numbers of prosecutors in obtaining convictions of batterers. These include introducing various types of evidence to corroborate the victim's testimony, to substitute for such testimony if the victim is unavailable or unwilling to testify, or to contradict the testimony if the victim recants. The use of expert witnesses is one such technique which is discussed, as is the inappropriateness of the term "battered woman syndrome." Two cases illustrate new legislative responses to the special issues raised in domestic violence prosecutions; in both cases, the appellate courts uphold laws allowing previously inadmissible evidence to be brought before the jury.

The chapter closes with two pieces looking at issues sometimes raised by alleged batterers who are being charged with domestic violence. The first article deals with prosecutions of men who have killed their partners, and then have claimed a "heat of passion" defense. It asks whether these defendants are in fact exercising the ultimate control, rather than losing control, and notes that the rationales advanced by the defendants are often the all too familiar refrains used by batterers to justify their behavior. The second article discusses the concept of a "cultural defense," which some immigrant men have asserted when charged with domestic violence crimes, and which raises very complex questions, including what culture is, who defines it, how static or changing it is, whether it should be taken into account in the US legal system, etc.

A. OVERVIEW, NO DROP POLICIES

DONNA WILLS, DOMESTIC VIOLENCE: THE CASE FOR AGGRESSIVE PROSECUTION

7 UCLA Women's L. J. 173–182 (1997).

I. INTRODUCTION

Prosecutors throughout the country, and especially in the State of California, have begun taking a more aggressive stance towards domestic violence prosecutions by instituting a "no drop" or "no dismissal" policy. Based on my experience as a veteran prosecutor who specializes in these cases, I firmly believe that this policy is the enlightened approach to domestic violence prosecutions. Fundamentally, a "no drop" policy takes the decision of whether or not to prosecute the batterer off the victim's shoulders and puts it where it belongs: in the discretion of the prosecutors whose job it is to enforce society's criminal laws and hold offenders accountable for their crimes. The prosecutor's client is the State, not the victim. Accordingly, prosecutorial agencies that have opted for aggressive prosecution have concluded that their client's interest in protecting the safety and well-being of all of its citizens overrides the individual victim's desire to dictate whether and when criminal charges are filed.

Aggressive prosecution is the appropriate response to domestic violence cases for several reasons. First, domestic violence affects more than just the individual victim; it is a public safety issue that affects all of society. Second, prosecutors cannot rely upon domestic violence victims to appropriately vindicate the State's interests in holding batterers responsible for the crimes they commit because victims often decline to press charges. Third, prosecutors must intervene to protect victims and their children and to prevent batterers from further intimidating their victims and manipulating the justice system.

II. DOMESTIC VIOLENCE IS A PUBLIC SAFETY ISSUE

Domestic violence is a societal, not merely an individual, problem; it is not just about two people in a private relationship working out their "family problems." The harm caused by this violence refuses to be neatly confined between the abuser and the victim. Rather, domestic violence impacts everyone: children, neighbors, extended family, the workplace, hospital emergency rooms, good samaritans who are killed while trying to intervene, and the death row inmates who cite it as a reason not to be killed. The State has a legitimate interest in maintaining public safety, especially by ensuring that domestic violence offenders are not allowed to flourish unabated.

Domestic violence advocates were correct in supporting laws that codified domestic violence as both a crime against the individual and a crime against the State. When prosecutors file charges, we enforce these laws and reinforce the fact that domestic violence is criminal conduct. In California, the Penal Code explains why special attention should be devoted to the prosecution of batterers: "The Legislature hereby finds that spousal abusers present a clear and present danger to the mental and physical well-being of the citizens of the State of California."[4] Besides being "an unacknowledged epidemic in our society," domestic violence is the leading cause of injury to women, a major factor in female homicide, a contributing factor to female suicide, a major risk for child abuse, and a major precursor for future batterers and violent youth offenders. The State cannot ignore the human tragedies that are caused by domestic violence.

The primary duty of government is to protect its citizens from assault as vigorously in the home as on the streets. The victims subject to domestic abuse are often not the only people who suffer. Most notably, children are secondary victims of violence in the home. The link between domestic violence and child abuse, both emotional and physical, cannot be ignored. Each year, between three and ten million children are forced to witness the emotional devastation of one parent abusing or killing the other. Many are injured in the "crossfire" while trying to protect the assaulted parent, or are used as pawns or shields and are harmed by blows intended for someone else. Some are born with birth defects because their mothers were battered during pregnancy. Children of domestic violence are silent victims who suffer without the options available to adults. Thus, aggressive prosecution furthers the State's goal of protecting not only the victim, but also the children in homes where domestic violence occurs.

Researchers have yet to determine the extent to which aggressive prosecution actually combats the problem of domestic violence. Although some recent studies have questioned whether mandatory arrest of batterers is beneficial in deterring domestic violence, such studies are misleading. No studies have focused on the incremental effects that aggressive prosecution has had on controlling, if not eliminating, recidivism. Nor has current research addressed the role of aggressive prosecution in decreasing the public's tolerance of domestic violence. Prosecutors realize all too well that criminal intervention alone may not be the ultimate "cure" for domestic violence any more than it is a complete solution to gang violence, carjackings, sexual assaults, child abuse, or any other kind of anti-social violence perpetrated by one human being against another. Indeed, criminal intervention does not guarantee that a batterer will forever refrain from further violence. However, failure to try to achieve this goal is not an acceptable alternative. Research notwithstanding, aggressive prosecution of batterers is a criminal justice decision predicated on what is best for the common good, not a scientifically formulated antidote guaranteed to transform batterers into peaceful spouses or model partners.

---

4. Cal. Penal Code § 273.8 (West 1988) (amended 1994).

III. Domestic Violence Victims Routinely "Refuse to Prosecute"

Domestic violence is not confined to any one segment of the population; it crosses race, social class, gender, and vocational lines. However, no matter how heinous the assault, the great majority of domestic violence victims have one characteristic in common: after making the initial report, they have neither the will nor the courage to assist prosecutors in holding the abusers criminally responsible.

Prosecutors and the courts have taken a long time to accept that a domestic violence victim's "refusal to press charges" is the norm in domestic violence prosecutions. Indeed, prosecutors traditionally are reluctant to charge batterers because victims frequently change their minds and later drop the charges. Faced with having to testify in court, domestic violence victims, especially battered women, routinely either recant, minimize the abuse, or fail to appear.

A domestic homicide case I prosecuted in 1987, *People v. Houston*, illustrates the battered woman's dilemma. Donna Houston, a twenty-nine year old mother of two, was shotgunned to death at her place of employment by the defendant, her thirty-year old estranged husband. During their brief one-year marriage, Donna reported escalating attacks by her jealous husband on three separate occasions. Early in the marriage, Donna's ten-year old son witnessed the defendant push his mother into a bookshelf, causing a heavy statue to fall and lacerate her head. Donna later "minimized" this incident by telling police that her injury was an accident and no charges were filed. Months later, after another argument, Donna's husband stabbed her in the face with scissors, causing a serious jagged laceration. Only after she pleaded with him for medical help and promised not to report his behavior to authorities did he take her to the emergency room for sutures to close the gaping wound. When Donna told the hospital staff what had happened, they called the police who arrested the defendant when he returned to the hospital to pick her up. The defendant had no prior record, but due to the seriousness of Donna's injury, the stabbing incident was filed as a felony spousal assault. A few days before the preliminary hearing, Donna came to the District Attorney's Office and insisted that she wanted to drop the charges. She had reconciled once again with the defendant and wanted to give their marriage another chance. When told that the prosecution would not be dismissed, Donna made herself "unavailable" to testify by going to New Jersey for an unscheduled "family visit." The case was dismissed for insufficient evidence to proceed.

Donna's girlfriend later testified that the parties subsequently separated and that when Donna refused to talk to him, the defendant tried to run Donna and the girlfriend off the road. Donna did not report this incident. Later, the defendant went to the baby-sitter's residence, grabbed their five-month old daughter from Donna's arms, and then led the police on a high speed chase, with the baby unrestrained in his van. He was apprehended and arrested and the child was safely returned to her terrified mother. Despite Donna's pleas, the defendant's wealthy family promptly posted his bail. On the same day he was released, the defendant bought a 12-gauge shotgun and ammunition from the local gun store. The next morning, he waited in the parking lot where Donna worked. As she walked out the back door, she saw him emerge from his hiding place and tried to run back into the building, but it was too late. The defendant shot Donna, delivering a fatal wound to her neck, in broad daylight, at close range, in front of six horrified co-workers. The defendant was convicted of first degree murder while lying in wait and is currently serving a sentence of life without possibility of parole. Donna's two minor children, now orphaned, are being raised by their maternal grandparents.

The defendant's escalating attacks on his wife and her initial refusal to cooperate with his prosecution demonstrate a classic scenario in domestic violence cases. Regrettably, many battered women fail to see that criminal intervention can assist in the shared goal of getting their abuser to stop the violence. Too often, they will seek to jettison prosecution of their batterer in favor of concerns inconsistent with their safety and the safety of their children. Too frequently, they are desperate to forgive and forget and to placate the abuser. Instead of criminal intervention, they dare hope to ease the violence by well-learned methods of coping. However, prosecutors have learned from the carnage and despair we have witnessed in domestic violence cases that victims cannot afford to forgive and forget and that the only thing worth negotiating is how much incarceration and how much mandated counseling is necessary to stop the batterer.

Cases like Donna Houston's remind prosecutors that while we wait for the battered woman to garner her "inner strength" to decide whether to press charges, harm continues to occur. Children are psychologically damaged from witnessing the battering, a child is placed in danger of physical injury or death, hospital emergency rooms are filled by injured women, and innocent third parties are endangered by assaults intended for someone else. Domestic violence prosecutors are haunted by tragedies like Donna Houston's. We need to be able to say that despite a battered woman's ambivalence, we did everything within our discretion to rein in the batterer, to protect the victim and her children, and to stop the abuser before it was too late.

IV. BATTERERS MUST NOT BE ALLOWED TO CONTROL JUSTICE

Batterers are "master manipulators." They will do anything to convince their victims to get the prosecution to drop the charges. They call from jail threatening retaliation. They cajole their victim with promises of reform. They remind her that they may lose their jobs and, hence, the family income. They send love letters, pledging future bliss and happiness. They have their family members turn off the victim's electricity and threaten to kick the victim and her children out into the street. They pay for the victim to leave town so that she will not be subpoenaed. They use community property to pay for an expensive lawyer to try to convince the jury that the whole thing was the victim's fault and that she attacked him. They prey on the victim's personal weaknesses, especially drug and alcohol abuse, physical and mental disabilities, and her love for their children. They negotiate financial and property incentives that cause acute memories of terror and pain to fade dramatically. Prosecutors watch with practiced patience as these vulnerable victims succumb to their batterers' intimidation and manipulation. Then, "no drop" prosecutors try to hold the batterers responsible regardless of the victims' lack of cooperation by using creative legal maneuvering.

Supporters of "no drop" domestic violence policies realize that empowering victims by giving them the discretion to prosecute, or even to threaten to prosecute, in actuality only empowers batterers to further manipulate and endanger their victims' lives, the children's lives, and the safety and well-being of the entire community. By proceeding with the prosecution with or without victim cooperation, the prosecutor minimizes the victim's value to the batterer as an ally to defeat criminal prosecution. A "no drop" policy means prosecutors will not allow batterers to control the system of justice through their victims.

Some critics of aggressive prosecution worry that "no drop" policies endanger victims by angering already volatile batterers. They argue that "jail doesn't do the batterer any good." However, arrest and prosecution of batterers does not endanger victims; batterers who attempt to control their mates through threats and violence endanger victims. Sentencing batterers to jail does not endanger victims; batterers who believe there is no higher authority than themselves endanger victims. Truly, it is the batterer who is responsible for the violent acts he chooses to commit, *with or without criminal justice intervention.* Even if jail does not guarantee rehabilitation, we would certainly rather incarcerate batterers than continue to "intern" their victims by forcing them into shelters to be safe.

Victims who shield their batterers from criminal sanctions naively accept responsibility to stop the batterer on their own, primarily by verbal persuasion. This approach is risky because the victim may be less objective in recognizing the lethal potential of everyday batterers. The criminal justice system, on the other hand, sees a wide spectrum of batterers. It also has more resources to assist in evaluating the danger a batterer poses to the victim. In addition, the criminal justice system can back up its intervention with incarceration to make the batterer understand that there is a price to pay for hurting a spouse or intimate partner and an "I'm sorry, I didn't mean it" may not suffice. Incarceration is a legitimate "therapy" to persuade the abuser to reconsider before resorting to violence. In addition to incarceration, *mandatory* rehabilitative counseling can be imposed, because very few batterers would voluntarily submit to counseling without the threat of jail.

When the 911 call is made to law enforcement, the criminal justice system is triggered. When the report of violence is made, that moment signifies that the victim is *without the power to get the batterer to stop the violence*. However, the criminal justice system is not without power to encourage the batterer to cease and desist. Arrest and prosecution, however temporary, serve notice on the batterer that what he did was wrong and warrants his immediate removal from the community. It also gives the victim a breather—time and opportunity to access counseling services, to investigate alternatives to life with a violent partner, to form a plan for safety, and to have authority focused on the batterer to stop the violence.

Prosecutors are aware of complaints that "no drop" policies make battered women feel "powerless" to keep the government, specifically the courts, from "interfering" in their lives. Some object to the court "dictating" what will happen to the case and the abuser in the aftermath of reporting the abuse. However, prosecutors must seize the "window of opportunity" given to us by the report of violence to get the batterer's attention. Working closely with victim advocates, prosecutors try to convince battered women to see the wisdom of criminal justice intervention. We tell the victims that we proceed with the prosecution because we cannot allow the batterer to believe that physical abuse is acceptable. We tell them that left without intervention, the violence may increase both in frequency of occurrence and severity of injury, often leading to the tragic scenario where he kills her or she kills him while defending herself against his aggression. We tell victims that the children suffer when they see their mother hurt and that the children need their mother to stay alive and well. We try to help them form a safety plan and deal with their fear, financial concerns, and future uncertainties, *with or without the batterer*.

V. CONCLUSION

Aggressive prosecution of domestic violence offenders rejects the notion that victims should be given the choice of whether to press or drop charges. No humane society can allow any citizen, battered woman or otherwise, to be beaten and terrorized while being held emotionally hostage to love and fear or blackmailed by financial dependence and cultural mores. As guardians of public safety, prosecutors must proceed against domestic violence offenders *with or without victim cooperation* as long as there is legally sufficient evidence. This policy of aggressive prosecution adopts the wisdom that "[t]here is no excuse for domestic violence." It tells batterers that violence against intimate partners is *criminal*, that offenders can and will go to jail, and that their victim's refusal to press charges is not a "get out of jail free" card.

LINDA G. MILLS, INTUITION AND INSIGHT: A NEW JOB DESCRIPTION FOR THE BATTERED WOMAN'S PROSECUTOR AND OTHER MORE MODEST PROPOSALS

7 UCLA Women's L. J. 183–199 (1997).

I. INTRODUCTION

Many battered women's lawyers and advocates believe that the most effective method for eradicating domestic violence is to arrest, prosecute, and jail perpetrators of intimate abuse, regardless of a battered woman's preference to avoid criminal intervention. While this response may be appropriate for a small, or even growing number of battered women, I contend in this Essay that these essentializing policies do not respond to the unique needs of individual battered women. Instead, I propose alternative methods to the one-size-fits-all mandatory prosecution strategy which, in Irigaray's words, help to "avoid the risks of hierarchy and submission," and facilitate the battered woman's ability to recapture her identity. My goal is to design a criminal process that is flexible enough to help battered women realize their need to take affirmative steps to reduce the violence in their lives.

Domestic abuse affects each person differently. Many women stay in abusive relationships because they are culturally pressured to endure violence. An Orthodox Jewish woman who files for divorce could be accused of violating Jewish law, even if she wishes to divorce her husband because he abuses her. When experiencing abuse at the hands of men of color, African–American women, Asian Pacific women and Latinas must confront the layered identities of gender and culture in the context of a racist society prepared and ready to label or blame. African–American women and Latinas who complain that their partners are violent fear they will be ostracized for contributing to racial stereotypes. Cultural pressures to identify with the larger Asian Pacific community may influence Asian Pacific women to fear rejection for revealing their secret. Violence is all too often the price women may pay for preserving their cultural identity. In other cases, women stay because they are too scared, poor, or unskilled to leave, or because they love a man who is only occasionally violent. In addition, women who are sympathetic to the traumas of their violent partners, especially those who are aware of a history of abuse in the batterer's family, may experience their lovers' violence differently than those of us who are less tolerant or understanding.

Mandatory arrest and prosecution policies, which are emblematic of a "law and order approach," are designed to fit a stereotypical battered woman's conundrum. Generally speaking, supporters of mandatory criminal interventions are most concerned with punishment under the guise of safety. As a result, they are less attentive to the often overriding financial, cultural, or emotional issues that plague battered women's lives.

Mandatory prosecution, like mandatory arrest, disempowers women by forcing a decision upon them without taking into account their individual needs. "Mandatory arrest" forces the police to detain a perpetrator of intimate abuse when there is evidence of violence such as bruises, cuts, or stab wounds. The battered woman's claims no longer matter—the police arrest regardless. "Mandatory prosecution," sometimes called a "no-drop" policy, requires a prosecutor to bring charges against the batterer regardless of the desire of the battered woman to pursue the prosecution. Some variation among no-drop jurisdictions does exist. A "hard" no-drop policy never takes the victim's preference into consideration. A "soft" no-drop policy permits victims to drop the charges under certain limited circumstances, such as if the victim has left the batterer. In a hard no-drop jurisdiction, the battered woman's preference is irrelevant, except to the extent that she helps, or does not help, win the prosecutor's case. In these situations, prosecutions are pursued against the batterer by forcing the woman to testify, sometimes leading to recantation, blurring, or rearrangement of the facts by the victim.

If current abuse patterns continue, 50% of all women will be victims of domestic violence at some point in their lives. Statistics aside, I too have been a victim. I never reported these incidents to the police, nor would I have prosecuted the two men who were abusive to me. If I had, I would have wanted the choice to proceed, or not to proceed, as I wished. Indeed, had anyone forced me to bring charges, I would have resisted them. When I shared my resistance to criminal intervention with other women, professional and non-professional, poor and middle class, of color and white, inside prison and out, far too many had never considered involving law enforcement, although they too had been stalked, struck, and even sexually tortured. These invisible faces compel me to take this controversial stand in their (our) defense.

This Essay explores three correlative themes. First, I contend that far too many battered women silently suffer at the edge of love's cliff and that their silence should be met with love, not fear, and connection, not rejection. Second, I argue that domestic violence advocates and prosecutors should begin to understand that each battered woman's story demands a specialized and tailored response. Finally, I suggest, within the limited context of the American criminal justice system, a model for rethinking prosecution strategies in intimate abuse cases.

II. THE NEED FOR A FLEXIBLE APPROACH TO DOMESTIC VIOLENCE

The multifaceted nature of domestic violence demands that we adopt a more flexible approach to this problem. I begin with the assumption that many battered women deny that their intimate relationships are violent. For some women, a police response to a domestic violence call or prosecution forces them to realize that they have been abused and have legal recourse. However, for other women, such criminal intervention reinforces their denial by sending them further underground. In the 1980s, one study revealed that less than 15% of battered women report severe incidents of violence. My concern is that the other 85% of battered women never report the abuse for fear that they will be met with a response which takes the violence "out of their control."

A small but growing number of feminists are beginning to worry that universally applied strategies, such as mandatory prosecution, cannot take into account the reasons women stay in abusive relationships or the reasons for their denial. These feminists fear that the State's indifference to this contingent of battered women is harmful, even violent.

Ironically, results from studies which focus on mandatory interventions, such as arrest and prosecution, are indeterminate. The first study to assess the effectiveness of arrest on recidivism revealed that arrest did, in fact, reduce future violence. This study inspired a national response as mandatory arrest became the call of battered women's advocates across the country. Despite this initial finding, however, none of the subsequent arrest studies confirmed these results. Although the studies revealed that arrest deterred "good risk perpetrators," the studies documented that arrest actually increased violence to some women, particularly for those whose batterers were unemployed or had previously been arrested.

The sole study of mandatory prosecution was done by Ford and Regoli ten years ago and involved 480 cases in Indiana. It also revealed that mandatory prosecution may be harmful to women in some cases. Indeed, the researchers found that a battered woman was most likely to ensure her subsequent safety when she could drop the charges and yet chose not to. Ford and Regoli explained that under these conditions, the battered woman could express her power in the situation and such expression had a positive effect on the battering relationship by actually decreasing the violence in her life.

So why have we implemented policies that actually increase the violence in some battered women's lives? Such policies largely are in effect due to the lobbying efforts of battered women's and feminist organizations. They believed a strong stance taken by the State would deter violence. They believed that a policy where the State prosecutes men for beating their neighbors, but does not prosecute men for beating their wives, is unfair. Until prosecutor's offices are willing to cooperate in studies which will reveal whether no drop prosecution policies actually decrease or increase violence to all women, and until we have evidence that state intervention is in fact a deterrent to all intimate abuse, we must implement a more flexible approach when criminalizing domestic violence.

Mandatory prosecution might initially appear to be a simple and preferable solution to domestic violence because it is easier to follow and forces police and prosecutors to take domestic violence seriously. However, the problem is that the policies backfire. When we force arrest and prosecution on battered women, they often recant and lie. One prosecutor in Los Angeles, who will remain anonymous, estimated that most battered women are reluctant witnesses who are willing to perjure themselves when they are put on the stand against their will. Perversely, in all too many cases, the effect of mandatory policies is to align the battered woman with her batterer, to protect him, and to further entrench her in the abusive relationship. The State, even with a policy of mandatory prosecution, cannot ensure that the batterer will be locked away forever, nor can it ensure that the battered woman will be free from his violence. Therefore, it is critical we teach the battered woman to yearn for her safety and to take whatever internal and external steps are necessary to achieve it.

Ironically, the opportunity to make that choice may be just the power the battered woman needs to stop the violence in her life. The decision regarding whether to prosecute may be her first opportunity to take an affirmative step in a relationship in which she previously has felt powerless. A system is needed that allows her this control, rather than replacing, as so often seems to be the case, the control of the batterer with the control of the prosecutor.

I suggest inflexible policies must be reformed to reflect the diversity of battered women's experiences and to expose the possibility that some battered women will need a legal response that does more than arrest and prosecute the batterer. Some battered women need a response that is intuitive to and insightful of their personal conundrum. I believe we should have a system that is flexible enough to respond to these varying needs when necessary. We need to recognize the hidden strengths of battered women and to acknowledge the need for legal interventions that help them find ways to reduce the violence in their lives.

Under such a system, women would be invited to file complaints in informal and confidential settings: with social workers in hospital emergency rooms, at women-run police facilities, or on battered women's hotlines. These reports could be retained for verification of patterns of abuse. For women who want them, restraining orders and other legal remedies would be available. Other safety measures, including shelter stays and house surveillance, would be available on request through battered women's service centers. Criminal or civil actions could be provided, but would be pursued only when and if the battered woman is physically and emotionally prepared to take that step. This kind of flexible system could effectively combat domestic violence by empowering battered women to design their own course of action to eradicate violence from their lives. Battered women need an array of options and a timeline that respects the uncertainty generated by conflicting loyalties. If they are not given the opportunity to leave their batterers at their own pace, then they may face more abuse, and possibly death.

Such a flexible approach, which I term an "affective" approach, requires that our intervention strategies proceed without the prejudgment pervading current policies. It demands we accept that a battered woman may not yet be ready to acknowledge her denial and that we embrace her regardless of her desire to return to the abuse. It means we must take the time to nurture and empower the battered woman toward her own decision, rather than to compel her to do something she may not be ready to do.

III.   PERSONAL OBSERVATIONS OF PROSECUTORIAL AGENCIES

Through my thirteen years of experience as a public interest lawyer and four years of experience in working on domestic violence issues, I have gained several insights into the work of prosecutors. Such reflections and observations are valuable in order to determine the best way to reform domestic violence criminal policy.

First, I have observed that prosecutorial agencies usually have difficulty responding in an individualized manner to domestic violence crimes, or to any crimes for that matter. Typically, prosecutors are trained to use a strategy of prosecution and jail time as a bargaining tool. As one prosecutor put it, she "had a bigger stick than the batterer" (the threat of incarceration), and she intended to use it. This approach assumes incarceration is the only effective deterrent to future crime. Ironically, most batterers receive, on average, only a few days or a few weeks in jail.

Second, prosecutors and other attorneys are trained in law schools which encourage unidimensional responses to social problems. Law students are taught to value reason over emotion and objectivity over subjectivity. They are taught to value the written word, the law, more than the welfare of their clients. Indeed, after three years of education and several more of working in a legal setting, some lawyers become even less comfortable addressing their clients' feelings. This training has the unwitting effect of hardening prosecutors to the individual narratives of the victims who rely on them.

Third, and most compelling, I have observed that prosecutors are profoundly constrained by their work environments. Budget and time limitations can force prosecutors to become mechanical, legalistic, and uninterested in those victims who are unwilling to help pursue a perpetrator. Prosecutors often are reluctant to take valuable time from their already overburdened schedules to help the victim come to terms with her abuse. After all, the State, not the victim, is the prosecutor's client. Their goal is to prosecute the defendant and to win. Therefore, their solutions to the problems of domestic violence are limited by these deeply ingrained constraints. Prosecutors have sometimes incorporated alternative remedies, such as mental health treatment, into their repertoire of solutions. However, they generally are unwilling to radically transform the legal system to address the unique nature of intimate abuse. To them, intimate abuse is just another crime.

Prosecutors generally oppose the suggestion that they should use more affective strategies when lawyering. Their most vigorous response is that "it's not our job." Furthermore, they contend that they are trained as lawyers and advocates for the State, not as social workers or therapists for the victims of crimes. Because of this lack of training, they argue that they are not equipped to address the trauma of a victim's suffering. These arguments reject the notion that emotional aspects of lawyering are relevant or useful when prosecuting perpetrators of crime, especially intimate abuse crimes. In addition, each of these arguments parallels my observations discussed in this section regarding the prosecutor's approach to domestic violence.

In prosecuting perpetrators of crimes, especially intimate abuse crimes, the attorneys should deliberately embrace affectivity as a method for providing individualized treatment of victims and for understanding their particular circumstances. Lawyers cannot both compartmentalize their feelings and be effective advocates—prosecutors should commit to nurturing the victim emotionally, with the overall goal of reducing domestic violence. Prosecutors must recognize that domestic violence patterns will continue if the battered woman does not realize, in her own language, how she can "manage" or escape the violence in which she is ensnared. Prosecutors' offices can no longer be solely concerned with prosecuting individual crimes. Law enforcement should be focused on seeing the larger criminal picture and its victims. Prosecutors should be committed to a grander vision of taking steps which have the possibility of helping women imagine a life without violence. An approach which takes into account the relationship between the two parties, perpetrator and victim, batterer and battered woman, is the only system likely to engage the parties long enough to have any long-lasting and significant effect.

The affective approach which I advocate has been successfully implemented in other countries. For example, in Great Britain and Australia, victims of juvenile crime are given the chance to confront their perpetrators and to impose their own sentences. In a recent example in England, a victim confronted a 16–year old burglar. After some initial resistance, the victim felt sympathetic toward the youth and asked only for an apology and a promise that he stay in school. On reflection, the burglar felt he had done something wrong and felt badly about it. "I promised [the victim] that I would try and be a better person." In New South Wales, Australia, where the program was first pioneered, they have seen a 50% reduction in the number of juvenile offenders in court and a 40% reduction in recidivism.

IV. Proposals for Change

My observations of prosecutorial agencies demonstrate the limitations on what seems institutionally plausible. Hence, I begin with an interim proposal, a limited project which could be adopted by prosecutors who are interested in incremental change. Ultimately, however, a systemic change, one which suggests a dramatic restructuring of the prosecutor-victim relationship and which transforms the lawyer and the battered woman through a process of empowering the victim through her relationship with her attorney should be adopted.

A. An Interim Proposal

Given the resistance described above, an interim proposal for reform would involve only minimal change on the part of prosecutors. Prosecutors should move toward affectivity by connecting with the victims of the crimes they prosecute. Prosecutors should use the emotional involvement which comes naturally to a "sensitive" lawyer rather than remaining emotionally detached. I suggest that the prosecutor working on domestic violence cases become aware of the special emotional issues battered women are likely to face. These needs are apparent because battered women enter the system particularly vulnerable and shattered, and because the perpetrators often are inextricably intertwined in most, if not all, aspects of their lives. This change towards affectivity is necessary for reasons other than the laudable goal of helping the victim heal; it will also help obtain the victim's honest testimony. Without taking the time to work with the victim and to understand her unique dilemma, the prosecutor may alienate her—making her a reluctant or even perjurious witness. Clearly, then, the affective dimensions of lawyering should be recognized and enhanced, ultimately making the prosecutor more effective in both prosecuting criminals and deterring future crime. By connecting with the victim emotionally, the prosecutor can create the possibility of having both a committed and credible witness, as well as a safer victim.

So what does it mean that prosecutors should be more emotional? I have previously argued that "counter-transference," a technique for critical self-reflection, is necessary when working with battered women. Counter-transference, a Freudian and Jungian invention, forces psychoanalysts and therapists to reflect on how their own life experience or story is evoked by the patient or client. In the legal context, prosecutors should rely on this technique to explore their own preconception or history of violence. This process would force prosecutors to feel what the victim evokes in them, emotionally speaking, to reflect on how those feelings become enmeshed in their reaction to the battered woman, and to understand why they might emotionally resist engaging the victim. Counter-transference is helpful because, through its use, the prosecutor comes to understand how her unconscious assumptions and judgments about the victim may alienate her from the prosecutorial process and allows the prosecutor to engage the survivor to really begin the process of helping her help herself. Indeed, the ability to reflect on one's own history and to lend insight and intuition to the prosecution of a victim's batterer is so important that such qualities should be considered when hiring prosecutors to work with victims of domestic abuse.

Prosecutors working in domestic violence units should have access to therapists who could help them manage their own complex emotions which are likely to arise when working with victims of intimate abuse. The therapist could assist the battered woman in becoming a credible and involved witness, as well as help the prosecutor who lacks the tools to work more directly with battered women. Together, the lawyer's more emotional response and the resources of a trained therapist should accomplish the limited goal of engaging the victim. They also should be able to better involve her in the process of prosecuting the batterer. They could thereby initiate the healing process rather than adding to the victim's suffering by inflicting institutional violence.

B. A More Radical Proposal

This alternative therapeutic lawyering I have previously described is the ideal to which we should all strive. My next proposal goes beyond the counter-transference, intuition, and insight suggested by the more modest proposal. Instead, it involves training prosecutors in social work or psychoanalytic techniques so that they can fully incorporate these ideas into their practice. Under this model, prosecutorial agencies would require their deputies either to have joint degrees or to attend a semester-long training course in therapeutic techniques.

This training course must include skills in working through the following complex issues: the battered woman's need for flexibility, the challenge she faces in the conflict between her love or commitment to her batterer, her cultural identity, her need to forego safety in the face of seemingly more pressing concerns, and her desire to maintain a family despite the violence she tolerates. Issues such as racism and financial dependence should also be seen as relevant considerations that warrant attention. Therefore, prosecutors should be trained in techniques which would enable them to identify the specific conflict of a particular victim and to understand how this complex picture affects a victim's willingness or reluctance to testify against her batterer. The prosecutor's ultimate goal should be deterring future violence, not just prosecuting *this* crime.

If this radical proposal were to be adopted, prosecutors would be ready and able to represent both the State and the victim. They would be trained to make prosecutorial decisions based on the many voices a truly democratic process demands, in a way that is empowering and likely to help the battered woman actually avoid future violence. Thus, the prosecutors would be able to participate in effective crime prevention and in preventing violence against women.

V. Conclusion

The criminal justice system must be overhauled to respond to the changing complexion of our class, cultural, and emotional landscape. The issue of domestic violence provides an opportunity to rethink how prosecutors work with victims, to rework the whole system of criminal justice, and to retool institutions to be prepared for the evolving environment. * * * [T]he prosecution of domestic violence should capture the battered woman's identity instead of losing it, and should avoid the fusion or "impersonality of one" that violence against women so often fosters.

SUSAN B. BREALL AND DEBORAH ADLER, GUIDE-BOOK FOR PROSECUTORS WORKING WITH BATTERED IMMIGRANT WOMEN

Volcano Press (2000).

Throughout the past decade, District Attorney's offices nationwide have begun to aggressively prosecute all cases of domestic violence. Current prosecutorial philosophy is to hold the perpetrator accountable and to prove the case—with or without the participation of the victim. This trend in prosecution is the result of countless effort by victims' right supporters, women's right activists and individuals both inside and outside the criminal justice system who realized the value of taking the onerous responsibility for prosecution out of the victim's hands and redirecting the focus of the case back where it belonged—both on the perpetrator and on the legal duty of the prosecutor to represent the state.

It is this very philosophy of aggressive prosecution without the participation of the victim, however, that we must now critically examine on behalf of battered immigrants. It is important to take a step back from our aggressive victimless prosecutorial stance of the past decade and examine how we are actually going to define successful and effective criminal justice intervention on behalf of immigrant women. Successful intervention and successful prosecution strategies can no longer be defined simply in terms of conviction rates and jail sentences for perpetrators. If our ultimate goal is victim safety, prosecuting the perpetrator and obtaining a conviction in the case without the input of the victim may endanger the victim.

For example, a conviction for domestic violence can result in deportation of the batterer, even if he is a lawful permanent resident. If the batterer loses his lawful permanent residence status as a result of the conviction before the INS approves the battered immigrant victim's self-petition to stay in this country, she may lose her ability to remain in the United States with her children. A battered immigrant woman's right to self-petition under the Violence Against Women Act to become a lawful permanent resident is tied to her marital status to a spouse who is currently a lawful permanent resident. Thus, the timing of the prosecution, as well as the input of the battered immigrant, can be crucial in this regard. Prosecuting a case without consulting with, or working with the victim, and helping her obtain an immigration attorney, may cause the abuser to retaliate against the victim by reporting her as undocumented to the INS. The end result may be her deportation without her ever having been notified of her right to apply under the Violence Against Women Act for legal status. If she is deported at any time prior to her batterer's conviction, she will likely lose custody of her children, who will then be placed in the hands of their abusive parent. Ultimately, if the battered immigrant victim is deported, and her spouse's subsequent conviction causes his deportation, both may end up in a country with few effective laws or protections against domestic violence. Even in those countries where domestic violence laws exist, such laws may not be enforced in any way to effectively protect her.

What can we as a community of assistant district attorneys and law enforcement officials do to effectively protect battered immigrant women? We must talk to these women in their own language. We must listen to their concerns. We must hear their voices. Above all else, we must educate ourselves and our colleagues about the complex and at times competing interests of the INS, victim advocacy groups and law enforcement agencies. We must do a complex analysis of the safety concerns of the victim. How realistic is her fear of loss of child support and her inability as an immigrant woman to get a job or to become in any way economically self sufficient? Has she been told by an immigration expert that she can apply under the Violence Against Women Act to obtain legal status? Has she been told that by merely making such an application, she can have access to public benefits and work authorization? Does she know that she has the right to obtain a protective order and police protection, regardless of whether or not she is a citizen? Is she concerned that her husband will go back to their home country and harm her family members, with little or no consequences?

Exploring a battered immigrant woman's choices and the consequences of those choices is vital to a truly successful prosecution which attempts to protect the victim and her family. Helping battered immigrant women access the services and immigration help they need is a critical step in overcoming the many barriers these victims face everyday in cooperating in the prosecution. This responsibility is as much that of a prosecutor as it is of every battered women's advocate, and will ensure trust and cooperation in the many immigrant communities in which we work.

* * *

What role should prosecutors play when handling cases involving battered immigrant women? This question has haunted prosecutors specializing in family violence cases since the domestic violence movement began. A prosecution is traditionally focused upon the suspect of a crime, not on the victim. Conceptually speaking, prosecutors lack individual clients. The people of the community as a whole are our clients. Victims are only witnesses, not necessarily people whose wishes must be heeded. In this traditional model of criminal justice prosecution, judges, defense attorneys and even prosecutors themselves are often wary of prosecutors becoming advocates on behalf of the complaining victim.

In this guidebook, we have taken the position that prosecutors should abandon the traditional model of "clientless" prosecution. We must view battered immigrant women as people whose needs and desires must be taken into consideration whenever possible during the prosecution of a case. We must educate ourselves about the risks each victim faces, as well as the barriers that often prevent them from leaving abusive situations or from accessing the criminal justice system. It is only by hearing the voices of battered immigrant women that we will begin to effectively eliminate violence in their lives and help create peace in their own homes.

B. EVIDENTIARY ISSUES

HEATHER FLENIKEN COCHRAN, IMPROVING PROSECUTION OF BATTERING PARTNERS: SOME INNOVATIONS IN THE LAW OF EVIDENCE

7 Tex. J. Women & L. 101–110 (1997).

V. Safety Planning

Before embarking on the prosecution of domestic batterers, the prosecutor has an obligation to ensure that the victims will be safe. The prosecutor should determine if these victims have access to information about social services and other legal options that might be available. In addition to exposing them to counseling and information, this initial stage is the time at which the prosecutor should weigh the victim's needs and desires against the benefits of prosecution. The prosecutor should ask direct questions about both the current incident of violence and any pattern of abuse the perpetrator has inflicted on the victim. These initial interviews with the victim will give the prosecutor information regarding the victim's safety and help prosecutor make better trial decisions.

Prosecutors should work closely with domestic violence advocates and counselors and should direct victims to these trained professionals, who will be able to help the victims make decisions about their safety. Even if victims are unable to call the police for intervention when abuse occurs, there are usually ways for victims to help themselves stay safe. Some counselors focus on addressing the victim's future needs by having the victim complete a preprinted safety plan, which is then reviewed with the victim so that the plan may be tailored to her specific situation. Other counselors may assist women in crisis by helping them to address their present needs. Most importantly, this is the time to encourage victims to take action for themselves. The victim must be the originator of much of the plan; otherwise, she may not use it.

Initial information sessions with the victims can also improve subsequent prosecutions of domestic crime. Even if the victim is unwilling to testify about the abusive incident that prompted her to file criminal charges or seek other help, such sessions allow the prosecutor or counselor to educate the victim about preserving evidence when future battering occurs. The victim should be instructed to keep a written record of all the abuse that occurs, which will help focus her testimony if she testifies at a later trial. Her account of specific incidences of abuse, such as, "He threw me down the stairs in March 1997," is apt to be more convincing than general allegations, such as, "He has been abusive in our marriage." Victims should also have friends, family members, or coworkers take photographs of their injuries to preserve the evidence for a future trial. Teaching victims about their potential role in the prosecution of their case can help victims empower themselves as they decide to leave the abusers.

VI. PROSECUTING THE BATTERER WITHOUT THE VICTIM'S TESTIMONY

Several jurisdictions have started domestic violence task forces that coordinate the police department, emergency medical personnel, battered women's advocates, and the district attorney's office. The combined efforts of these professionals can make it possible to preserve sufficient evidence to result in the conviction of batterers without the victim's testimony. For example, when responding to a domestic violence incident, law enforcement officers can gather statements from the victims and any eyewitnesses at the scene, and these out-of-court statements may be admissible at trial through the excited utterance exception to the hearsay rule. In addition, statements that the police are able to elicit from the batterer are admissions by a party-opponent, which are not hearsay and, therefore, admissible in court. Officers may also produce at trial photographs they took while investigating the domestic assault; these photographs illustrate the injuries and demeanors of the victim, the batterer, and any children who were present, and they portray the nature of the crime scene. Health care providers may also obtain the statements of victims, which the court can accept into evidence if the statements were made for the purpose of obtaining medical treatment. Advocates for victims of domestic violence can also facilitate the conviction of batterers by encouraging victims to secure evidence on their own. Moreover, these advocates may testify as experts on the behavior of battered women, helping the jury to understand the victim's absence from the courtroom by confronting jurors' stereotypes of battered women. Finally, the district attorney's office can improve its prosecution of batterers by formulating comprehensive *voir dire* questions that will better ensure an unbiased jury. If these professionals work together, the cases against domestic violence perpetrators can prevail without the battered victims' testimony.

A. *Voir Dire Examination*

When prosecuting a batterer without his victim's testimony, the prosecutor should begin the trial process by carefully preparing *voir dire* examinations that take into account the victim's absence from the courtroom. There are many misconceptions about domestic violence, and *voir dire* is the appropriate time to discover whether potential jurors are biased against prosecuting domestic violence perpetrators. Furthermore, *voir dire* can prepare juries for the victim's absence in the courtroom, pave the way for expert testimony on the behavior of battered women, and explain the victim's fear of retaliation. Most importantly, obtaining an impartial jury sets the stage for a successful trial, resulting in the batterer's conviction.

B. Photographs

Photographs can show the jury the crime scene better than any testimony can. "Batterers don't look like criminals, and, consequently, juries hesitate to convict. A photo can change their mind," states William Delahunt, District Attorney for Norfolk County, Massachusetts. For this reason, all police cars should carry instant cameras for immediate processing. Photographs are easily admissible in the courtroom if the photographer or another witness testifies, stating that the snapshot is an accurate depiction of the person or scene portrayed in the photograph. Therefore, it is important that the officers responding to a domestic violence call capture the images of the victim, the batterer, and any children present (whether or not any of these people appear physically harmed), and the nature of the crime scene.

Officers should take photographs of the victim from three perspectives—a full-body shot, a medium-range shot, and close-range shots of particular injuries. If the victim is female, a female officer should photograph the victim's injuries that clothing covers. Evidence gatherers should also examine the battered victim for injuries in various stages of healing; if found, photographs of such injuries serve as evidence of the perpetrator's pattern of battering behavior. Lastly, photographs of the victim's injuries should be taken again a few days after the abusive incident because bruising often will be evident by that time.

The injuries and demeanor of the victim are not the only images that should be captured on film, however. The responding officers also should take photographs of the batterer and any injuries that he might have. Photographs of children at the crime scene may further aid in the batterer's conviction, since they tend to show the jury the perpetrator's disregard for the children's well-being. Finally, law enforcement personnel should capture on film the site of the crime as well, paying particular attention to any broken furniture, remnants of alcohol or drug use, weapons, or signs of struggle. Without the testimony of the battered victim at trial, all of these recorded images become especially important in illustrating the crime for the jury.

C. Statements of the Victim, Eyewitnesses, and the Batterer

Many cities have prosecutors who make use of the exceptions to the hearsay rule to introduce as trial evidence the out-of-court statements of victims and other witnesses who do not testify, although some prosecutors have encountered judges who are hesitant to admit such statements. However, many of the statements made by victims or other witnesses are admissible under various exceptions to the hearsay rule, such as present sense impression, excited (or spontaneous) utterance, or medical diagnosis. Also admissible at trial are out-of-court statements made by the defendant, for such statements are not considered to be hearsay since they are made by the party-opponent. For instance, courts have routinely admitted 911 call recordings as exceptions to hearsay because the courts generally agree that these calls have a virtual guarantee of reliability.

An accurate and detailed police report of the domestic violence incident often provides the prosecutor with easily accessible sources of evidence. If responding officers carefully record the demeanor of the victim and her exact statements, officers then have a great tool that aids their trial testimony regarding the details of the crime scene. In these situations, statements made to the officer may be admissible through the officer's testimony, even if the person who gave the statement is available to testify, but does not do so.

In 1992, the U.S. Supreme Court held that the Confrontation Clause does not require the prosecution to produce at trial the victim of the crime, nor does it require that the trial court find the victim unavailable in order for her out-of-court statements to be admissible, thereby paving the way for the prosecution of batterers without the victim as a trial witness. *White v. Illinois*[133] involved the prosecution of the sexual abuser of S.G., a four-year-old girl. In that case, the child's babysitter heard her scream and rushed to her room, at which time S.G. told her babysitter about the abuse. Shortly afterward, S.G. repeated her accusations to her mother and again to a police officer, who investigated the abusive incident forty-five minutes after it occurred. At trial, the babysitter, mother, and police officer testified to S.G.'s statements, which the trial court admitted into evidence under the excited utterance (or spontaneous declaration) exception to the hearsay rule. The U.S. Supreme Court agreed, reasoning that spontaneous declarations likely are more reliable than in-court statements: "A statement that has been offered in a moment of excitement—without the opportunity to reflect on the consequences of one's exclamation—may justifiably carry more weight with a trier of fact than a similar statement offered in the relative calm of the courtroom."

In similar fashion, Texas courts have favorably interpreted the excited utterance exception to the hearsay rule, allowing prosecutors to try domestic violence cases without requiring that the victim testify at trial. In *McFarland v. State*,[140] the court stated that

> [w]hile the period of time that lapsed between the occurrence of the startling event and the making of the statement is a factor to consider in determining the admissibility of such statements, the critical factor is whether the declarant was still dominated by the emotions, excitement, fear, or pain of the event.

In *Short v. State*,[142] the victim's out-of-court statement was admissible as an excited utterance, despite the fact that it was made four and one-half hours after the startling event.

---

133. 502 U.S. 346 (1992).

140. 845 S.W.2d 824 (Tex.Crim.App. 1992).

142. 658 S.W.2d 250 (Tex.App.—Houston [1st Dist.] 1983), aff'd, 671 S.W.2d 888 (Tex.Crim.App.1984).

Around the country, a growing number of prosecutors now use the excited utterance exception to the hearsay rule when attempting to prove their cases without the testimony of the victim. One survey found that prosecutors used excited utterance statements in sixty-four percent of the domestic violence cases in which the victim did not appear as a trial witness. Therefore, law enforcement officers responding to calls involving domestic violence should make careful records of everything the victims, or others who are present, tell the officers, as well as make note of the speaker's demeanor because such documentation aids later efforts to prove that the declarant was in an excited state when she made the statements.

Unlike the time constraints relating to present sense impression or excited utterance statements, there are no time constraints to consider for statements made to health care providers in the course of seeking medical treatment. In *White*, the child's statements to medical personnel, in which she described the sexual abuse, were admitted under this hearsay exception, and it was irrelevant that the statements were made four hours after the abusive incident occurred. If health care providers routinely make inquiries about injuries they suspect may result from domestic violence, the victim's responses likely will be admissible at a criminal trial against the batterer. Therefore, it is essential that prosecutors train and coordinate with emergency room and other health care personnel, particularly in cases where the battered victim does not testify at trial.

Often, the batterer will admit the assault to the police at the scene, and the police should carefully detail that admission in their report. Later, if criminal charges are filed and the perpetrator pleads not guilty, this earlier statement could undermine his defense. Such a statement is an admission by a party-opponent, which the trial court may allow into evidence through the testimony of any witness who heard the batterer make the statement.

Some observers assert that gathering statements at the crime scene prepares the prosecution so well for trial that perhaps abusers would be more likely to plea bargain or admit their guilt. Such trial preparation has other benefits, as well. In the words of one attorney who represents battered victims, " 'The beauty of good investigative work . . . is that if it gets done routinely, defendants begin to realize that intimidating the victim accomplishes nothing. . . . You don't need to bring her to trial, she doesn't need to testify.' " At least one prosecutor agrees, claiming that good investigative work prevents the battered victim from attempting to persuade him to drop the charges against her abuser.

THE PEOPLE v. MARK ANTHONY HOOVER

Court of Appeal, Fourth District, California (2000).
77 Cal.App.4th 1020, 1023–1030.

1. INTRODUCTION

Defendant Mark Anthony Hoover appeals from a judgment against him for enhanced aggravated assault under circumstances involving domestic violence. Defendant was sentenced to a total prison term of 21 years.

The California Supreme Court granted review of the original published decision in this case. After rendering its decision in *People v. Falsetta* (1999) 21 Cal.4th 903, upholding the constitutionality of Evidence Code section 1108, the court ordered us to vacate our decision and to reconsider it in light of *Falsetta*.

Based on *Falsetta*, we again reject defendant's constitutional challenge to Evidence Code section 1109, which permits the admission of defendant's other acts of domestic violence for the purpose of showing a propensity to commit such crimes. We also reject defendant's contentions regarding instructional and sentencing error and affirm the judgment.

2. FACTS

Mary Theresa Seals (Seals) testified that she had dated and lived with defendant for several years. On September 18, 1996, she accompanied defendant to a Riverside motel room because she wanted to explain that she was involved in another relationship. Shortly after they entered the room, defendant made a comment about Seals' new boyfriend and then hit her in the nose. When she yelled and tried to leave the room, he grabbed her arms to prevent her. Seals went into the bathroom and screamed for help. Defendant opened the motel room door. Seals then called 911 and defendant left the motel room.

Seals also testified to several other incidents, beginning in 1993, in which defendant hit her in the face or choked her or threatened to kill her. She also told how on one occasion defendant attacked her male companion with a beer bottle. During her testimony, the court briefly admonished the jury that evidence of defendant's past conduct could only be considered for a limited purpose.

On cross-examination and redirect, Seals admitted to being a convicted felon, who was often in legal trouble. She also admitted that, in order to help defendant, she had not always told the truth about previous incidents involving him. She acknowledged that, when she testified at the preliminary hearing, she had blamed the subject incident on a dispute involving the motel room's bed sheets. She had also previously testified that she and defendant had shoved one another before he hit her.

On September 18 at 6:30 p.m., Joseph Miera (Miera), a Riverside police officer, responded to a call from the motel regarding a possible assault with a deadly weapon. When he arrived at the location, Seals was standing outside room 19 holding a bloody towel against her nose. She was crying and had difficulty speaking because of her injury. She told Miera that defendant, her former boyfriend, had punched her in the face. Seals also stated that she and defendant had been drinking beer with some friends. She told defendant that she had met someone else while defendant was in prison and she no longer wanted to date defendant. Defendant became angry, pushed her around, and then hit her. Miera observed fresh blood spattered throughout room 19. Miera arrested defendant, who was in the motel parking lot.

Dr. Greg Michaels, a radiologist, testified that he reviewed Seals' X-rays and observed a multiple fracture of her nasal bones, which had been caused by a blunt trauma.

Defendant did not testify.

3. THE CONSTITUTIONALITY OF EVIDENCE CODE SECTION 1109

During trial in January 1997, the prosecution sought to have admitted evidence of other acts of domestic violence by defendant against Seals under section 1101, subdivision (b), as evidence of and relevant to the issues of intent, motive, common scheme or plan, knowledge, and absence of mistake or accident. After the court had admitted such evidence, subject to a preliminary limiting instruction, the prosecutor discovered that section 1109 had recently been enacted. He asked the court to admit the same evidence of defendant's past conduct under that code section. The court did so but did not give the jury any further instruction regarding how to treat evidence of other acts of domestic violence.

The thrust of defendant's appeal is composed of various challenges to section 1109. That code section, enacted in 1996 and effective January 1, 1997, provides that evidence of previous acts of domestic violence may be admitted in a current prosecution for a domestic violence offense. Section 1109 was modeled on section 1108, which provides an identical exception for the admission of other sexual offenses in a prosecution for a sexual offense. In pertinent part, section 1109 states:

> (a) Except as provided in subdivision (e), in a criminal action in which the defendant is accused of an offense involving domestic violence, evidence of the defendant's commission of other domestic violence is not made inadmissible by Section 1101, if the evidence is not inadmissible pursuant to Section 352.

> . . . .

> (c) This section shall not be construed to limit or preclude the admission or consideration of evidence under any other statute or case law.

> (d) As used in this section, "domestic violence" has the meaning set forth in Section 13700 of the Penal Code.

Section 1109 thus supplants the usual rule of evidence that evidence of past conduct is not admissible to prove a defendant's conduct on a specified occasion.

Defendant does not deny that he hit Seals in the face. But defendant contends that section 1109 is unconstitutional on its face, and particularly as applied in this case, because it could not be used to show that defendant had the propensity to commit an aggravated assault involving great bodily injury rather than a lesser crime.

We first observe that it was probably unnecessary for the prosecution to have sought recourse in either section 1101 or section 1109. Even before the enactment of section 1109, the case law held that an uncharged act of domestic violence committed by the same perpetrator against the same victim is admissible: "Where a defendant is charged with a violent crime and has or had a previous relationship with a victim, prior assaults upon the same victim, when offered on disputed issues, e.g., identity, intent, motive, *et cetera*, are admissible based solely upon the consideration of identical perpetrator and victim without resort to a 'distinctive *modus operandi*' analysis of other factors." (*People v. Zack* (1986) 184 Cal.App.3d 409, 415.) That rule was not altered by *People v. Ewoldt* (1994) 7 Cal.4th 380, which sets forth the general principles governing the use of character evidence. The evidence of defendant's previous attacks on Seals was therefore admissible to show that he intended to inflict great bodily injury upon her on this occasion.

In the alternative, however, the subject evidence was also admissible under section 1109. In determining the constitutionality of section 1109, we adopt the reasoning of the California Supreme Court as put forth in *Falsetta*. In *Falsetta*, the court held that, under section 1108, evidence of two previous rapes by defendant could be used to show his propensity to commit the present rape. Similarly, the history of defendant's acts of domestic violence against Seals could be used to show that, on this occasion, defendant had the propensity to cause Seals great bodily injury.

Falsetta noted evidence of prior acts is generally inadmissible to prove conduct, but the Legislature relaxed this constraint with respect to sex offense cases, by enacting section 1108. *Falsetta* emphasized the difficulty of raising a due process challenge to a state criminal evidence statute: "To prevail on such a constitutional claim, defendant must carry a heavy burden. The courts will presume a statute is constitutional unless its unconstitutionality clearly, positively, and unmistakably appears; all presumptions and intendments favor its validity. In the due process context, defendant must show that section 1108 offends some principle of justice so rooted in the traditions and conscience of our people as to be ranked as fundamental. The admission of relevant evidence will not offend due process unless the evidence is so prejudicial as to render the defendant's trial fundamentally unfair."

The *Falsetta* court noted, however, that "Evidence Code section 1101 has long been subject to far-ranging exceptions, e.g., evidence admitted to show intent and other matters specified in Evidence Code section 1101, subdivision (b). *Falsetta* said legislative enactment of a further exception applicable in sex offense cases may not necessarily offend fundamental historical principles. *Falsetta* said it was unclear whether the rule against 'propensity' evidence in sex offense cases should be deemed a fundamental historical principle of justice, but even if the rule was deemed fundamental from a historical perspective, the court would nonetheless uphold section 1108 because it did not unduly 'offend' those principles, in light of the substantial protections afforded to defendants.

The same reasoning applies in the instant case. As in sex offense cases, the use of character evidence in domestic violence cases is more justified than in a murder case or a forgery case. The legislative history of section 1109, which recognizes the special nature of domestic violence crime, supports this point:

> The propensity inference is particularly appropriate in the area of domestic violence because on-going violence and abuse is the norm in domestic violence cases. Not only is there a great likelihood that any one battering episode is part of a larger scheme of dominance and control, that scheme usually escalates in frequency and severity. Without the propensity inference, the escalating nature of domestic violence is likewise masked, if we fail to address the very essence of domestic violence, we will continue to see cases where perpetrators of this violence [w]ill beat their partners, even kill them, and go on to beat or kill the next intimate partner. Since criminal prosecution is one of the few factors which may interrupt the escalating pattern of domestic violence, we must be willing to look at that pattern during the criminal prosecution, or we will miss the Opportunity [*sic*] to address this problem at all. (Assem. Com. on Public Safety report (Jun. 25, 1996) pp. 3–4.)

"Based on the foregoing, the California Legislature has determined the policy considerations favoring the exclusion of evidence of uncharged domestic violence offenses are outweighed in criminal domestic violence cases by the policy considerations favoring the admission of such evidence."

Defendant makes an additional argument that the admission of other acts of domestic violence dilutes the due process requirement of proof beyond a reasonable doubt of every fact necessary to constitute the charged crime. The jury was instructed that the question it was to decide was whether defendant committed the crime charged and that he could be found guilty only if the jury was convinced beyond a reasonable doubt that he committed the crime. While the admission of evidence of other acts of domestic violence "may have added to the evidence the jury could consider as to defendant's guilt, it did not lessen the prosecution's burden to prove his guilt beyond a reasonable doubt. 'The courts specifically addressing the question of *Winship's* application to uncharged misconduct uniformly hold that the admission of uncharged misconduct does not undermine *Winship*.' "

Furthermore, section 1109, like section 1108, has a safeguard against the use of other acts of domestic violence "where the admission of such evidence could result in a fundamentally unfair trial. Such evidence is still subject to exclusion under Evidence Code section 352. By subjecting evidence of uncharged sexual misconduct to the weighing process of section 352, the Legislature has ensured that such evidence cannot be used in cases where its probative value is substantially outweighed by the possibility that it will consume an undue amount of time or create a substantial danger of undue prejudice, confusion of issues, or misleading the jury. This determination is entrusted to the sound discretion of the trial judge who is in the best position to evaluate the evidence." With this check upon the admission of evidence of other offenses in prosecutions for crimes of domestic violence, section 1109, like section 1108, does not violate the due process clause.

We also conclude that section 1109 did not violate due process as applied. Defendant bases this argument on two points. First, defendant challenges the trial court's balancing determination as made under section 352. We do not agree that the trial court abused its discretion in admitting the evidence under section 1109. Particularly in view of the fact that the subject evidence involved defendant's history of similar conduct against the same victim, the evidence was not unduly inflammatory. The subject evidence was also not remote; its presentation was not confusing or time-consuming. Instead, the evidence was highly relevant and probative of the issues in this case.

Second, defendant argues that the jury was confused because it was incorrectly instructed with CALJIC No. 17.01 and not instructed at all regarding the use of the evidence permitted under section 1109, although during trial the jury had been given a preliminary limiting instruction based on section 1101.

We agree that the procedures followed in this case were somewhat irregular, due in part to the prosecution's sudden discovery during trial of the newly enacted section 1109. It would certainly have been better if the trial court had explained to the jury that its preliminary limiting instruction was wrong and that the evidence of past conduct could be considered to show that defendant had a present disposition to commit domestic violence offenses.

Furthermore, the jury was apparently confused by CALJIC No. 17.01 and its reference to other acts. A question from the jury during deliberations indicated that the jurors initially did not understand that they were not supposed to consider CALJIC No. 17.01 at all. The jury's note to the court said: "17.01 seems to state that all acts presented into evidence may be considered. [] Does this mean that if we agree that 'force likely to produce bodily injury,' was used in an incident other than the motel incident (namely, the incident where the plaintiff was struck with a cast) we can find the defendant guilty of Count 1?" The court, with agreement from both counsel, responded tersely and simply to the jury's inquiry, "No." Therefore, we must assume the jury followed the court's instructions.

Since it was ultimately proper for the jury to consider defendant's past conduct as evidence bearing on his present conduct, any errors committed at the trial level were clearly harmless.

Finally, we agree with the People that the proper standard for proving past conduct is by a preponderance of the evidence, not beyond a reasonable doubt, as defendant proposes. Therefore, the evidence of defendant's past conduct was sufficiently established by the testimony of Seals.

THE PEOPLE v. GABRIEL LOUIS HERNANDEZ

Court of Appeal, Fourth District, California (1999).
71 Cal.App.4th 417, 419–425.

A jury convicted Gabriel Louis Hernandez of inflicting corporal injury upon a cohabitant possessing methamphetamine and being under the influence of methamphetamine. The jury further found that Hernandez had suffered two prior strike convictions. He was sentenced to prison for two consecutive 25–year-to-life terms and appeals, claiming evidence was improperly admitted and his trial counsel was incompetent. We reject his contentions and affirm.

FACTS

Hernandez and the victim had been married, divorced, reconciled and had been cohabiting for five years since reconciliation. At the time of trial, she was unavailable to be a witness. During the early morning hours of August 17, 1996, the victim called 911 from a convenience store, reporting that Hernandez had battered her. An officer arrived and she told him that Hernandez had "tripped out," accusing her of having an affair, and when she told him he was crazy, he got mad and wrestled her to the floor. When she got up, he hit her about eight times in the face. Hernandez then ordered her out of the apartment they shared.

The victim's eyes were swollen and bruised. Her left shoulder was scratched and red. The officer was unable to locate Hernandez at the couple's apartment that morning, but saw his car parked there early the following morning. The officer then went to the apartment, where the victim falsely told the officer that Hernandez was not present. However, she did consent to the officer entering to see if everything was all right. When the officer went into the bedroom, he found Hernandez lying on a mattress, holding a rolled-up dollar bill. Under the mattress was a mirror containing methamphetamine. Hernandez appeared to be under the influence of the drug and testing of a urine sample taken from him at jail showed the drug in his system.

Hernandez told the officer that he had gotten into an argument with the victim over her alleged infidelity and he became very angry with her. He confronted the victim and hit her hard six times in the face because he was angry. He did not say that the victim had ever struck or assaulted him. He said he was embarrassed about the way her face looked. He had no injuries.

Hernandez took the stand at trial and claimed that it appeared as though a man had sneaked out of the couple's apartment after he arrived home from work late on August 16. When Hernandez accused the victim of "bring[ing her] business" into their home, the victim jumped on his back and began clawing him. He knocked her off with his elbow. She fell back, scraping her back. When Hernandez attempted to put their son on the bed, she attacked him again, scratching his face.

Hernandez shoved her to the floor. While she was on the ground, he hit her three or four times with his right hand. He picked her up, they wrestled and he pushed her out the door.

Hernandez testified that the victim invited him to return to their apartment the morning the police found him there. He joined the victim in the bedroom where she obtained a dollar bill from him which she rolled up before snorting some drugs. When the officer knocked on the front door, she threw the rolled-up bill on the floor near Hernandez. Hernandez saw the mirror bearing the drugs and he threw a blanket over it.

ISSUES AND DISCUSSION

1. *Admission of the Victim's Statements*

Before trial began, the prosecution moved to admit statements made by the victim to the police officer pursuant to Evidence Code section 1370. That section provides:

(a) Evidence of a statement by a declarant is not made inadmissible by the hearsay rule if all of the following conditions are met:

(1) The statement purports to narrate, describe or explain the infliction or threat of physical injury upon the declarant.

(2) The declarant is unavailable as a witness pursuant to Section 240.

(3) The statement was made at or near the time of the infliction or threat of physical injury. Evidence of statements made more than five years before the filing of the current action or proceeding shall be inadmissible under this section.

(4) The statement was made under circumstances that would indicate its trustworthiness.

(5) The statement was made in writing, was electronically recorded, or made to a law enforcement official.

(b) For purposes of paragraph (4) of subdivision (a), circumstances relevant to the issue of trustworthiness include, but are not limited to, the following:

(1) Whether the statement was made in contemplation of pending or anticipated litigation in which the declarant was interested.

(2) Whether the declarant has a bias or motive for fabricating the statement, and the extent of any bias or motive.

(3) Whether the statement is corroborated by evidence other than statements that are admissible only pursuant to this section.

(c) A statement is admissible pursuant to this section only if the proponent of the statement makes known to the adverse party the intention to offer the statement and the particulars of the statement sufficiently in advance of the proceedings in order to provide the adverse party with a fair opportunity to prepare to meet the statement.

The defense objected to admission of the statements, contending that Evidence Code section 1370 violated the confrontation and due process clauses of the Constitution and the right of counsel in that "it does not ... allow ... us to cross-examine the hearsay declarant about the events ... that resulted in the ... charges." The trial court granted the prosecution's motion, finding that Evidence Code section 1370 promotes an important public policy and assures the reliability of the statements, therefore, it does not violate the confrontation clause.

(1) Hernandez here contests the trial court's ruling, arguing, first, that Evidence Code section 1370 denies due process because it provides no reciprocity. Hernandez waived this argument by not asserting it below. Moreover, it is meritless.

The only case Hernandez cites in support of his position is *Wardius v. Oregon* (1973) 412 U.S. 470. However, *Wardius* concerned a discovery statute that required the defense to notify the prosecution of alibi witnesses it intended to call, but it did not provide for the prosecution to notify the defense of any witnesses it intended to call to refute the alibi. The United States Supreme Court concluded that it was fundamentally unfair to force the defense to divulge the details of its case to the prosecution while subjecting the defense to the hazard of surprise concerning refutation of the very evidence it was obliged to disclose.

As the People correctly point out, Evidence Code section 1370 is not one-sided—it permits the defendant to utilize it to the same extent the People may. Also, as the People point out, in *Whitman v. Superior Court* (1991) 54 Cal.3d 1063, 1082, the California Supreme Court rejected an identical challenge to Penal Code section 872, which permitted probable cause findings for bindovers to be made on the basis of out-of-court statements related to experienced law enforcement officers. The high court said,

> We find no similar unfairness here for, properly construed, the new hearsay statute contains no broad grant of authority to the prosecutor to rely on hearsay evidence. The section merely specifies a further, limited exception to the general hearsay exclusionary rule of Evidence Code section 1200, by allowing a probable cause finding to be based on certain hearsay testimony by law enforcement officers having specified experience or training. in light of the specialized nature of the exception, we see nothing fundamentally unfair in failing to provide some similar hearsay exception favoring the defense. (Indeed, although we leave the question open, the new provision might be interpreted as permitting the defendant to call a law enforcement officer to relate statements which might rebut a finding

of probable cause.) Defendants continue to enjoy the benefits of all preexisting hearsay exceptions.

Similarly, in *People v. Brodit* (1998) 61 Cal.App.4th 1312, the California Court of Appeal rejected an identical challenge to similar provisions (which apply to declarations by child abuse victims), saying:

[W]e disagree with appellant's premise that the new hearsay exceptions may only be used to benefit prosecutors. Nothing in the statutes explicitly limits the hearsay exceptions to evidence which is inculpatory and, as we explain below, occasions may arise in which the defense may find it useful to introduce hearsay testimony under these new exceptions. [] ... [] Here, we do not perceive ... unfairness in [the provisions]. First, as we have noted, nothing in those sections limits the exception to "inculpatory" evidence. in fact, cases may frequently arise where the defense will find it useful to introduce evidence under these exceptions.... Thus, both the prosecution and defense may make use of these new exceptions to the hearsay rule. contrary to appellant's assertion, [these provisions] do not create a one-way street in favor of the prosecution.

Brodit also relied on *Whitman* to declare that even if the hearsay provisions there pertinent did create "a one-way flow of evidence in favor of the prosecution," they did not violate due process.

Hernandez provides no persuasive argument that the analysis in *Whitman* and *Brodit* should not apply here.

Next, Hernandez reiterates the argument he made below, that Evidence Code section 1370 violates the confrontation clause because the statements are admitted without the opportunity for cross-examination of the declarant. However, he admits that with a particularized guaranty of trustworthiness or adequate *indicia* of reliability, such statements may be admitted without violating the confrontation clause. Alternatively, statements admitted under a firmly rooted exception to the hearsay rule do not violate the confrontation clause.

The People correctly assert that Evidence Code section 1370 is similar to the hearsay exception for spontaneous statements, which is firmly rooted. Additionally, Evidence Code section 1370 contains particularized guarantees of trustworthiness and adequate *indicia* of reliability by requiring the statement to be made (1) at or near the time of the incident (similar to a spontaneous declaration) by a person who experienced the incident, firsthand, (2) under circumstances indicating its trustworthiness, including whether it had been made in contemplation of litigation, whether the declarant had a bias or motive to fabricate and whether it is corroborated by other evidence not admissible under Evidence Code section 1370 and (3) to have been recorded in writing or electronically, or to have been made to a police officer (who normally makes a written report of such statements). While we agree with Hernandez that, under *Idaho v. Wright*, supra, 497 U.S. 805, corroboration by other evidence is not a legitimate component of trustworthiness, its presence in Evidence Code section 1370 does not render the statute unconstitutional because the section still requires the essential *indicia* of trustworthiness and it suggests other legitimate factors which may establish that. Absent a case where the trial court relied heavily upon the presence of corroborating evidence in making its determination that the statement bears *indicia* of reliability, the confrontation clause would not be violated. Therefore, we cannot agree with Hernandez that Evidence Code section 1370 violates the confrontation clause.

(2) Finally, Hernandez contends that even if Evidence Code section 1370 is constitutional, the trial court here abused its discretion in admitting the statements because they did not bear sufficient *indicia* of reliability. However, Hernandez ignores the fact that he failed to object to the statements below on this ground, and, therefore, he waived any such objection. Moreover, he is incorrect.

In arguing below that the statements should be admitted under Evidence Code section 1370, the prosecutor asserted that there were no circumstances suggesting the victim had a motive to lie, that she had been involved with Hernandez for 15 years, including having been married to him, having had his child and having resumed a relationship with him after they had been divorced. Additionally, the victim was upset and crying when she made the statements and made them to obtain help rather than to "connive." Finally, there existed corroboration for the statements in the form of the victim's recorded 911 call, which was admissible as a spontaneous statement, the admission of Hernandez that he punched the victim several times in the face and two sets of photographs of the victim, documenting her injuries. Hernandez did not dispute any of these representations below.

The trial court agreed with the prosecutor, finding there was sufficient *indicia* of reliability in " . . . [the prosecutor's] offer of proof [that] there is no indication of bias by the victim who is now deceased [and] the physical injuries that were photographed as well as statements made by the defendant himself."

After his silence on the subject below, Hernandez now points to facts, adduced at trial after the motion was heard, indicating that the statement was rendered under circumstances indicating it was not trustworthy. He is too late. We may assess the trial court's ruling only on the facts made known to it at the time it made that ruling. To do otherwise would require us to hold the trial court to an impossible standard. At the time this motion was decided, Hernandez pointed to no facts which would undermine the trustworthiness of the victim's statements. Therefore, we cannot conclude that the trial court abused its discretion, that is, acted unreasonably, in admitting the statements.

PAULA FINLEY MANGUM, RECONCEPTUALIZING BATTERED WOMAN SYNDROME EVIDENCE: PROSECUTION USE OF EXPERT TESTIMONY ON BATTERING

19 B. C. Third World L. J. 610–619 (1999).

B. Renaming Battered Women's Syndrome: Expert Testimony on Battering and Its Effects

When battered woman syndrome testimony was first used to support claims of self-defense, it had a substantial impact on the criminal process. Its use demonstrated a judicial recognition of the depth and severity of the problems of sex-stereotyping in the traditional conception of self-defense law. Almost all of the courts to first consider the issue of expert testimony on battered woman syndrome focused on Lenore Walker's work. Courts came to recognize the battered woman syndrome rubric, and states incorporated it in statutes governing the admissibility of such testimony. As battered woman syndrome became widely accepted, the term became a kind of descriptive shorthand for referring to the scientific and clinical literature dealing with the dynamics of a battering relationship.

However, there is a downside to assigning a shorthand explanation to the dynamics of domestic violence and battered women's experiences, particularly when that shorthand term is imprecise and misleading. In the twenty or so years since the introduction of battered woman syndrome theory, the conceptualization and understanding of domestic violence has continued to change. Not only have the limitations and inaccuracies of battered woman syndrome been exposed, but the body of scientific literature concerning domestic violence has grown at a rapid rate. This knowledge base, incorporating new and revised theories, empirical findings, and clinical observations, has developed greatly since battered woman syndrome was originally defined. Thus, although for many years battered woman syndrome was the rubric under which expert testimony was offered, it is no longer an adequate characterization of the breadth of available knowledge regarding battering and its effects.

A more accurate representation of this knowledge is expressed by language that is now recommended by many expert witnesses and commentators: "expert testimony on battering and its effects." The renaming of this testimony is not merely a verbal distinction; it unmasks images and inaccuracies attached to the "battered woman syndrome" nomenclature. Thus, the use of a newer, more accurate term, "expert testimony on battering and its effects," is critical to understanding a new and emerging trend in the use of this testimony.

IV. PROSECUTORIAL USE OF EXPERT TESTIMONY ON BATTERING AND ITS EFFECTS

The most striking trend in the acceptance of expert testimony on battering and its effects is its emerging use in the prosecution of batterers. At the beginning of the 1990s, courts paid little attention to the use of such expert testimony by the prosecution, and very few addressed its admissibility. However, by 1999, twenty-seven states have admitted or discussed with favor expert testimony on battering and its effects in the prosecution of certain cases.

Introducing expert testimony to describe the lives and experiences of battered women has a potentially broader application in the prosecution of batterers than in the defense of battered women. While the introduction of expert testimony on battering and its effects by prosecutors is still an uncommon practice in many state courts, the greater opportunity for the use of this evidence, by numbers alone, lies with prosecutors. The use of expert testimony on battering and its effects can assist in the successful prosecution of batterers, particularly in those cases where convictions may be otherwise unlikely. Furthermore, its use may result in a reduction in the number of prosecutions of battered women who resort to killing in self-defense.

A. Framework for Admitting Expert Testimony on Battering and Its Effects

In order to admit expert testimony on battering and its effects on behalf of the prosecution, a court must find that the testimony is relevant and that it meets general standards governing admissibility of expert testimony. Thus, a framework for introducing such testimony should address the following issues: (1) relevance of the evidence to issues in the prosecution's case; (2) usefulness of the evidence to the trier of fact; (3) acceptance of the scientific basis for admission of the evidence; and (4) qualifications of the expert.

1. Relevance of the Evidence to Issues in the Prosecution's Case

The admission of evidence about battering and its effects becomes an issue in a case in which a batterer is being prosecuted for a crime of domestic violence and the battered victim's behavior or conduct is raised as part of the batterer's defense. The prosecution may then seek to introduce expert testimony about battering and its effects in order to explain the victim's prior inconsistent statements, to rehabilitate the victim's testimony if her credibility is attacked, to corroborate her testimony after an impeachment attempt, or to prove an element of the state's case against the batterer.

Two fact patterns typify those cases in which expert testimony on battering and its effects is relevant to issues in the prosecution's case. In the first, a battered woman gives an initial statement to the police, a grand jury, or in a deposition, but recants her earlier statement at trial. In rebuttal, the prosecution may offer testimony on battering and its effects to explain the witness' inconsistent statements. In the second example, the defense attacks a battered woman's credibility by targeting her behavior or conduct, questioning why she remained in the battering relationship, delayed reporting the incident, or changed her story. In this situation, the prosecution may offer testimony on battering and its effects to rehabilitate the victim's credibility by explaining her conduct. In both examples, the expert testimony about battering and its effects can help judges and jurors understand the experiences, beliefs, and perceptions of women who have been beaten by their intimate partners.

2. Usefulness of the Evidence to the Trier of Fact

In spite of, or because of, increased public awareness of domestic violence, jurors come to a trial with assumptions and preconceptions about crimes of domestic violence, perpetrators, and victims.[124] Jurors may expect victims and batterers to fit certain stereotypes and may have certain expectations regarding a battered woman's behavior in a battering situation.[125] Whether a battered woman recants at trial or testifies willingly, much of the prosecution's case against a batterer is focused on the victim, and much of the batterer's defense is focused on challenging her credibility:

> [T]he focus of the case remains on her—her actions before, during, and after the assault, her appearance, her demeanor on the stand, her lifestyle, income, companions, race, and religion. The principal questions remain: what did she do to deserve or provoke the violence, or, why is she making all this up? If any of this had happened as she described it, then why didn't she leave? Why did she stay with him so long before moving? Why did she wait so long to report it? why didn't she tell her family and friends? Why is she still with him if he had beaten her?[126]

Expert testimony identifying the dynamics of domestic violence and the patterns of behavior in battering relationships is relevant to explaining these issues and is crucial to assist the factfinder in understanding the reasonableness of a battered woman's actions. Such expert testimony is particularly important for evaluating credibility when the victim's actions in court do not comport with the jury's expectations.

a. Establishing the Usefulness of the Evidence by Voir Dire Questions

The prosecution must establish that the trier of fact will be assisted by the proposed expert testimony on battering and its effects. In jurisdictions where the scope of *voir dire* questioning permits it, the jury should be questioned to elicit responses which reflect jurors' misconceptions and assumptions about domestic violence and battered women. *Voir dire* questions should address jurors' stereotypical perceptions of domestic violence and the limitations on their information about, and understanding of, the problem.

b. Establishing the Usefulness of the Evidence With Research Literature

The prosecution may also cite research studies to support its assertion that the proposed expert testimony on battering and its effects will

---

124. See Bowman, supra note 110, at 242. * * *.

125. See id. at 242.

126. Id. at 241.

assist the trier of fact. Numerous studies document findings that most people are misinformed about domestic violence and hold misconceptions about battered women.

3. *Acceptance of the Scientific Basis for Admission of the Evidence*

Courts in all fifty states have accepted the scientific basis for admission of evidence about battering and its effects in cases in which the battered woman is the defendant, and therefore have established a basis for allowing the admission of such evidence on behalf of a victim or a witness who is not a defendant. Additionally, some jurisdictions have allowed expert testimony concerning the reactive behavior of the victim in rape and child sexual abuse prosecutions. By analogy, the acceptance of the scientific basis for admission of expert evidence about rape and child sexual abuse victims suggests the admissibility of expert evidence on battering and its effects on behalf of a victim of battering.

4. *Qualifications of the Expert*

A court has discretion to qualify an individual as an expert witness based upon the individual's "knowledge, skill, experience, training, or education." The expert witness may testify to "scientific, technical, or other specialized knowledge [that] will assist the trier of fact to understand the evidence or to determine a fact in issue . . . ."

The jury should also learn how the expert is qualified to give an opinion about battering and its effects. Although opposing counsel may offer to stipulate to the expert's qualifications to prevent the jury from hearing the details of the expert's experiences and credentials, the prosecution should turn down the offer with an explanation that the expert's qualifications are critical to the jury's consideration of the weight to be given to the expert's testimony.

B. *The Introduction of Expert Testimony on Battering and Its Effects on Behalf of the Prosecution*

Expert testimony on battering and its effects may be introduced as soon as an attack on the victim's credibility is made by the defense. Thus, the testimony may be offered either during the prosecution's case-in-chief when the victim's credibility is attacked by the defense on cross-examination, or in rebuttal after the defense has directly attacked the victim's credibility.

Although expert testimony in cases involving battered women may be either general or case-specific, when the prosecution calls an expert witness, that expert will usually testify generally about battering and its effects. The expert's opinion or conclusions may be framed in response to hypothetical questions posed by the prosecution about typical victims of battering, but the expert should not testify to opinions or conclusions about the specific victim or the specific facts of the case. Indeed, in most prosecutorial situations, the expert will not have met, examined, or evaluated the battered woman who is the victim in the prosecution's case.

C. HEAT OF PASSION, CULTURAL DEFENSES

VICTORIA NOURSE, PASSION'S PROGRESS: MODERN LAW REFORM AND THE PROVOCATION DEFENSE

106 Yale L. J. 1331–1338 (1997).

How do we understand the death of loved ones at the hands of those with whom they are most intimate? In life as well as law, we say that murders of husbands, wives, and lovers are "crimes of passion." Thus we explain the event in a way that bridges the gap between love and murder as it separates them, that distances violence from our own homes as it bows to human frailty. This intellectual juggling act yields a law full of ambivalence toward those homicides it describes by the name of "passion." Doctrine condemns the killings, but with sympathy for the defendant's situation; theory excuses and justifies the killer, but only partially; verdicts do not acquit, but reduce the sentence from murder to manslaughter. This ambivalence has led to legal reforms promising greater humanity and consistency, promises that have moved lawyers to reject the older talk of "heat of passion" in favor of the more modern "emotional distress." However well-intentioned, these reforms have led us to change our understandings of intimate homicide in ways that we might never have expected. Our most modern and enlightened legal ideal of "passion" reflects, and thus perpetuates, ideas about men, women, and their relationships that society long ago abandoned.

Based on a systematic study of fifteen years of passion murder cases, this Article concludes that reform challenges our conventional ideas of a "crime of passion" and, in the process, leads to a murder law that is both illiberal and often perverse. If life tells us that crimes of passion are the stuff of sordid affairs and bed side confrontations, reform tells us that the law's passion may be something quite different. A significant number of the reform cases I studied involve no sexual infidelity whatsoever, but only the desire of the killer's victim to leave a miserable relationship. Reform has permitted juries to return a manslaughter verdict in cases where the defendant claims passion because the victim left, moved the furniture out, planned a divorce, or sought a protective order. Even infidelity has been transformed under reform's gaze into something quite different from the sexual betrayal we might expect—it is the infidelity of a fiancee who danced with another, of a girlfriend who decided to date someone else, and of the divorcee found pursuing a new relationship months after the final decree. In the end, reform has transformed passion from the classical adultery to the modern dating and moving and leaving. And because of that transformation, these killings, at least in reform states, may no longer carry the law's name of murder.

Reform's understanding of the passion defense reflects deeper roots in modern theories of criminal culpability. Staunchly defended by traditional legal scholarship, these theories center around the notion that defendants are less culpable when they lose "self-control." This sounds plausible and humane, but leaves unanswered an important question: Which losses of self-control merit the law's compassion? By systematically surveying how courts have answered that question, this Article argues that adherence to the self-control rationale masks a different, more pernicious, tendency. The law in practice does something more than protect self-control. Courts and lawyers have not measured claims of passion by "quickened heartbeats" or "shallow breathing," but by judgments about the equities of relationships, judgments disguised—and therefore rendered more powerful and resistant to change—by a jurisprudence pretending to make no judgments at all.

Because reform's ideas about intimate loyalties do not lie on the surface, they have survived in the face of obvious conflicts with well-accepted reform movements. Elsewhere, reform has acknowledged, indeed encouraged, women's freedom to divorce or separate. Reform of the passion defense, however, has yielded precisely the opposite result, binding women to the emotional claims of husbands and boyfriends long ago divorced or rejected. Reform in other areas of the law has encouraged battered women to leave their victimizers. Reform of the passion defense, however, discourages such departures, allowing defendants to argue that a battered wife who leaves has, by that very departure, supplied a reason to treat the killing with some compassion. In this upside-down world of gender relations, it should not be surprising to learn that the common-law approach toward the provocation defense, deemed an antique by most legal scholars, provides greater protection for women than do purportedly liberal versions of the defense.

Reform not only breeds conflict where gender is concerned; it also breeds conflict within the criminal law itself. Rarely, if ever, does the criminal law embrace defendants who kill in response to a lawful act or trivial slights, and yet passion's reform seems to permit defendants to argue that acts such as leaving or "dancing with another" constitute a "reasonable" explanation meriting our compassion. Rarely, if ever, does the criminal law embrace defendants who are to blame for creating their own defense, and yet some trial courts applying reform's passion defense have found mitigating stress in the defendants' own violent acts, even their own battering. These conflicts have gone largely unnoticed by scholars. Although students of the provocation defense have noted the odd case in which the defense generates absurd results, they have reserved their concern for the lawyer's unlikely hypothetical rather than the real-life lovers' quarrel. Scholarship has focused on different questions, questions about the characteristics of those who kill in these situations. In its focus on identity, this scholarship has made rather obvious normative conflicts within the criminal law all but impossible to see.

Reform's legacy affects both sexes, not one, and any effort to grapple with the defense's weaknesses must acknowledge the complexity of its gender effects. In the cases I have studied, men are by far the most frequent victimizers, and women the most frequent victims. But that does not mean that only women are killed; indeed, it is often the man helping the women leave—the sheriff or the mover or the lover—who dies. Reform often seems to tie women to relationships that they do not want, in effect, enforcing a rule of "emotional unity." But reform exacts a price from male defendants as well, albeit one of agency rather than blood. To obtain the law's compassion, men must forsake a claim that they are acting as moral agents and, instead, play the role of the helpless female: dependent, victimized by inarticulate impulse, and utterly incapable of freely determining a proper course of action. One need not celebrate female "states of injury" to see that passion's reforms have imposed upon men and women a "veil of relationship" that neither may have deliberately chosen.

I raise these issues in stark terms not to recommend abolition of the provocation defense but to advocate reconstruction—reconstruction based on a new theory of the law's ambivalence toward some passions. In the end, we do not solve provocation's problems by giving up the law's compassion for sincere emotion, nor by endorsing an abolitionist "ethics of autonomy." We must finally come to terms with the essential difficulties of the defense—why the law partially excuses some, but not all, emotional defendants and defines some, but not all, passions as rational. In Part I, I present my empirical findings, focusing on the role of departure in the practice of the provocation defense. In Part II, I consider the conventional arguments for the defense, finding that each leaves us with the same question: Why are some emotions worthy of protection (jealous rages), while others are not (till-inspired greed)? In this Part, I try to show how a defense committed to the idea that it protects the "choosing self" turns out to protect something quite different. In the face of repeated efforts to banish normative decisionmaking from the defense, liberal theorists have actually helped to entrench norms about relationships. The intellectual move here is one I call the "personification" of the defense, a move that places all of the normative questions into the form of questions about the qualities and attributes of persons and thus disguises both the essential normativity of the inquiry and the fact that the Model Penal Code's concealed normative commitments are to relationships rather than persons. In Part III, I explain that move and investigate the theoretical underpinnings of reform's approach, arguing that provocation's defenders and its critics are doomed to talk past each other. As long as reform's defenders start from the position that the freedom of individuals is measured in their distance from relationships, they will find little common ground with those who maintain that law must consider our relationships to each other.

Finally, in Part IV, I present a new, more limited, version of the defense that seeks to honor equality as well as autonomy. The passion defense should be retained as a partial excuse but only in the limited set of cases in which the defendant and the victim stand on an equal emotional and normative plane. When a man kills his wife's rapist, his emotional judgments are inspired by a belief in a "wrong" that is no different from the law's own: *Ex ante*, there is no doubt that rape is wrong both for the defendant and the victim and that the defendant's "outrage" is "understandable" from this perspective. When a man kills his departing wife, claiming that her departure outraged him, this normative equality disappears. There is no reason to suspect that the victim would have agreed to a regime in which "leaving" was a wrong that the law would punish. To embrace the defendant's emotional judgments in these latter circumstances not only allows the defendant to serve as judge and executioner, but also as legislator. It allows the defendant to stand above the victim and enforce at penalty of death a set of emotional judgments that are, at best, partial.

My proposal for a "warranted excuse" is likely to be controversial from a variety of perspectives: It declines to recommend abolition as some feminists have urged, rejects the traditional idea of emotion upon which current theories of self-control depend, and calls for a merger of excuse and justification that may appear oxymoronic to some. Moreover, it would change the practice of the defense substantially, barring manslaughter verdicts in most intimate homicide cases. The old scholarly questions may remain, but I offer my own view as a beginning to a new debate. We punish those who stand in emotional judgment not because of their character or their self-control, but because they have replaced the state as the normative arbiter of violence, and when we partially excuse, we excuse not because reasonable men kill but because the law sees reason in the defendant's emotion, reason that mirrors the law's own sense of retribution. In short, we partially excuse when coherence demands it, when the defendant appeals to the very emotions to which the state appeals to rationalize its own use of violence.

LETI VOLPP, (MIS)IDENTIFYING CULTURE: ASIAN WOMEN AND THE "CULTURAL DEFENSE"

17 Harv. Women's L. J. 57–62, 64–78, 93–101 (1994).

I. INTRODUCTION

The "cultural defense" is a legal strategy that defendants use in attempts to excuse criminal behavior or to mitigate culpability based on a lack of requisite mens rea. Defendants may also use "cultural defenses" to present evidence relating to state of mind when arguing self defense or mistake of fact. The theory underlying the defense is that the defendant, usually a recent immigrant to the United States, acted according to the dictates of his or her "culture," and therefore deserves leniency. There is, however, no formal "cultural defense"; individual defense attorneys and judges use their discretion to present or consider cultural factors affecting the mental state or culpability of a defendant. In my discussion of this strategy, I focus on the significance of its use for Asian women.

When examining the "cultural defense" and its effect on Asian women, I write from the subject position of an Asian–American woman. I also write with the benefit of collective insight of Asian American women working with the Asian Women's Shelter in San Francisco, who created the "Cultural Defense" Study Group. The Study Group arose from concern about the use of the "cultural defense" and from the pressing need for Asian American women to articulate a position on its use.

The "cultural defense" presents several complex problems inherent in essentializing a culture and its effect on a particular person's behavior. I analyze the use of the defense in two cases in order to illustrate problems with the defense and situations in which allowing cultural information into the courtroom might be appropriate. I argue that any testimony about a defendant's cultural background must embody an accurate and personal portrayal of cultural factors used to explain an individual's state of mind and should not be used to fit an individual's behavior into perceptions about group behavior.

Presentation of cultural factors must also be informed by a recognition of the multiple, intersectional layers of group-based oppression that may be relevant to understanding any particular case. The concept of intersectionality, which in this context refers to the interplay of racism and sexism in the experiences of women of color, provides a useful analytical tool. Because of our identity as both women and persons of color within discourses shaped to respond to one categorization or the other, women of color exist at the margins of both discourses. Because intersectionality is a methodology that disrupts the categorization of race and gender as exclusive or separable, I argue that an intersectional analysis is essential to an understanding of the relationship of the "cultural defense" to Asian women.

I also explore why the choice of whether or not to support the use of the "cultural defense" is difficult and suggest a strategy for making this choice. I ultimately argue that the value of antisubordination should be used to mediate between a position that totally rejects the defense and a position that embraces a formalized "cultural defense" from the perspective of cultural relativism. I conclude that the formalization of a "cultural defense" should not be promoted, and that a commitment towards ending all forms of subordination should inform the decision of whether or not to support the informal use of cultural information on behalf of a defendant in a given case.

I discuss two cases, *People v. Dong Lu Chen*[10] and *People v. Helen Wu*,[11] in detail because they are representative of the two kinds of cases in which "cultural defenses" involving Asian women have most often been attempted. The first type of case, exemplified in *Chen*, involves an Asian man seeking a "cultural defense" for his violence towards an Asian woman. The second factual pattern, seen in Wu, features an Asian

---

10. No. 87–7774 (N.Y. Sup. Ct. Dec. 2, 1988).

11. 286 Cal. Rptr. 868 (Cal.Ct.App. 1991), rev'g No. ICR 12873 (Super. Ct. Riv-

erside Co. 1990), review denied Jan. 23, 1992.

woman seeking to admit cultural factors to explain her mental state when she attempted to commit parent-child suicide.

Both of the cases I examine involve Chinese Americans. I hesitate to focus on these cases because Chinese Americans are frequently used to synecdochically represent all Asian Americans, and I repeat that process here by describing my project as one about "Asian women." Yet, paradoxically, because of the homogeneity into which the dominant community crushes the vast diversity of Asian America, the legal system's treatment of two cases affecting Chinese Americans does reflect popular and legal conceptions of other Asian American communities.

I use the terms "Asian" and "Asian American" at different points throughout this piece in order to emphasize how communities are identified in different contexts. The concept of a "cultural defense" rests on the idea of a community not fully "integrated" into the United States and assists "Asians in America," or "immigrants," as opposed to "Asian Americans." Asian Americans are those whom American society generally assumes to have assimilated into "American culture" to the extent that we do not require a special defense.

Drawing this distinction relies on the problematic positioning of recent immigrants from Asia as "not American." Reserving the term "American" for those who seem fully assimilated erases two important and related factors. The first is the fluid and shifting nature of American identity. The second is the fact that both immigrant and Asian experiences are integral and formative components of American identity. This failure to acknowledge the multiplicity of American identity leaves American identity, and specifically the identity of United States law, a neutral and unquestioned backdrop. One is left with an image of a spoonful of cultural diversity from immigrants ladled onto a flat, neutral base. Creating a "cultural defense" for immigrants in the United States thus rests on the implication that U.S. law is without a culture.

The flawed conception, inherent in a "cultural defense," that recent immigrants have a "culture" while U.S. law does not, promotes an anthropological relationship between the court and the immigrant defendant. The court, through testimony of "experts," conducts an examination of communities not considered to "fit" within the borders of U.S. law. This anthropological relationship is characterized by "expert" presentations of Asian culture that depict Asian communities as static, monolithic and misogynist. This dynamic distances the subject of study by creating an unrecognizable "other" and allows the dominant anthropologist "expert" to subordinate members of the foreign culture through descriptive control. * * *

II. INVISIBLE WOMAN: THE *PEOPLE V. DONG LU CHEN*

In 1989, Brooklyn Supreme Court Justice Edward Pincus sentenced Chinese immigrant Dong Lu Chen to five years probation for using a claw hammer to smash the skull of his wife, Jian Wan Chen. The defense sought to demonstrate that the requisite state of mind was lacking by introducing evidence about Chen's cultural background. After listening to a white anthropologist "expert," Burton Pasternak, provide a "cultural defense" for Dong Lu Chen, Pincus concluded that traditional Chinese values about adultery and loss of manhood drove Chen to kill his wife.

The defense introduced most of the information about Dong Lu Chen's cultural background through Pasternak's expert testimony. Defense Attorney Stewart Orden presented Pasternak with a lengthy hypothetical designed to evoke a response about the "difference" between how an "American" and a "Mainland Chinese individual" might respond to a particular set of events. This hypothetical was in fact a history of Dong Lu Chen and provided the defense's explanation for why he killed Jian Wan Chen.

As Orden set forth in this "hypothetical," Dong Lu Chen was fifty-four years old at the time of trial. Since 1968 Dong Lu Chen believed he was hearing voices around him; doctors told him there was something wrong with his mind.

In September, 1986, the Chen family immigrated to the United States. While Dong Lu Chen worked as a dish washer in Maryland, Jian Wan Chen and the three children stayed in New York. During a visit when Jian Wan Chen refused to have sex with him and "became abusive," Dong Lu Chen became suspicious she was having an affair. He returned to Maryland, burdened with the stress of his wife's assumed infidelity.

In June, 1987, Dong Lu Chen moved to New York. On August 24 he rushed into his wife's bedroom and grabbed her breasts and vaginal area. They felt more developed to him and he took that as a sign she was having affairs. When he confronted her the next day, she said she was seeing another man. On September 7, when he again confronted her and said he wanted to have sex, "she said I won't let you hold me because I have other guys who will do this." His head felt dizzy, and he "pressed her down and asked her for how long had this been going on. She responded, for three months." Confused and dizzy, he picked something up and hit her a couple of times on the head. He passed out.

After presenting the above "facts" as part of his hypothetical, Orden asked Pasternak if this history was consistent with reactions "under normal conditions for people from Mainland China." Pasternak responded:

> Yes. Well, of course, I can't comment on the mental state of this particular person. I am not a psychiatrist. I don't know this particular person. But the events that you have described, the reactions that you have described would not be unusual at all for Chinese in that situation, for a normal Chinese in that situation. Whether this person is normal or not I have no idea.... If it was a normal person, it's not the United States, they would react very violently. They

might very well have confusion. It would be very likely to be a chaotic situation. I've witnessed such situations myself.[39]

Orden also asked Pasternak to verify that a "normal Chinese person from Mainland China" would react in a more extreme and much quicker way than an "American" to the history as given in the hypothetical. Pasternak answered:

> In general terms, I think that one could expect a Chinese to react in a much more volatile, violent way to those circumstances than someone from our own society. I think there's no doubt about it.[41]

This initial testimony highlights some important issues. First, the distinction Orden and Pasternak draw between "American," "someone from our own society," and "Chinese" implies that "Chinese" and "American" are two utterly distinct categories: "American" does not encompass immigrant Chinese. This dichotomy rests on the lingering perception of Asians in America as somehow "foreign," as existing in "America" while not being "American." Importantly, the perspective that Chinese living in the United States are not "American" is the very basis for the assertion of the "cultural defense," on the grounds that someone from a distinctly "non-American" culture should not be judged by "American" standards.

Perceiving Chinese living in the United States as American, as part of our policy, significantly affects our responses to Dong Lu Chen. Referring to Dong Lu Chen's identity as a hyphenated identity—Asian–American—recognizes the specific histories of people of color in the United States while emphasizing the existence of a community of other Asian Americans that is best situated to evaluate and judge his actions. For reasons discussed further below, members of Asian American communities, particularly community organizations aware of internal power dynamics, should determine the use and content of the "cultural defense."

After dichotomizing "American" and "Chinese," Orden and Pasternak's second step in creating a "cultural defense" was to assert that a man considered "normal" in the category "Chinese" would react very differently from someone in the category "American" to the belief that his wife was having an affair. Their third step collapsed the history of a particular person with specific mental problems into the category "normal person from Mainland China." Finally, Orden's and Pasternak's description of Dong Lu Chen's reaction was predicated on the "stress theory" of violence: abuse happened because the batterer experienced stress. This is a theory much criticized by battered women's advocates who note that batterers choose to abuse power over their victims and that violence is not an automatic stress-induced response beyond batterers' control. As the prosecuting attorney pointed out, Chen waited from August 25, when he was allegedly informed by his wife that she was having an affair, until September 7 to confront his wife violently.

39. Record at 68–69.   **41.** Id.

To bolster Pasternak's assertions about Dong Lu Chen's behavior, Orden asked him to testify about the particularities of family life in China. Pasternak spoke of the "extraordinary" difference between "our own" ability and the ability of "the Chinese" to control the community through social sanctions. He added to the "voices" that Dong Lu Chen heard in his head, earlier presented as a sign of mental difficulties, another set of "voices" controlling Chen. Pasternak testified that his "Chinese friends" often said "there is no wall that the wind cannot penetrate," meaning that the voices of social control "will be heard everywhere." Orden and Pasternak repeated these "voices of the community" throughout the trial to signify that in a tradition-bound society like Mainland China, social control is more strict and unchanging than in the West, and that a "Chinese individual" carries these "voices" of social control wherever he goes.

Continuing his description of Chinese familial life and values, Pasternak asserted that "casual sex, adultery, which is an even more extreme violation, and divorce" are perceived as deviations from these social mores. "In the Chinese context," adultery by a woman was considered a kind of "stain" upon the man, indicating that he had lost "the most minimal standard of control" over her. Pasternak contrasted the condemnation of adultery in China with the United States, "where we take this thing normally in the course of an event." He claimed that the Chinese woman was likely to be "thrown out" and that both parties would have difficulty remarrying.

Pasternak proceeded to delineate the ramifications of a woman's adultery for the Chinese man and Chinese woman in the context of the United States. Pasternak relied on his perception of the prevalence of "yellow fever" among white males and the desexualization of Asian men in America to assert that a Chinese "adulteress" would have no problem establishing a relationship with a white man, while the Chinese male cuckold would have no chance of finding a white woman. The Chinese male would be considered a "pariah" among Chinese women because he would be viewed as having been unable to "maintain the most minimal standard of control" within his family.

Pasternak's bizarre portrayal of divorce and adultery in China in fact had little basis in reality. When Assistant District Attorney Arthur Rigby pressed Pasternak for his sources during cross-examination, Pasternak mentioned fieldwork he did between the 1960s and 1988 (he could not remember the title of his own article), incidents he saw, such as a man chasing a woman with a cleaver, and stories he heard. He admitted he could not recall a single instance in which a man in China killed his wife or having ever heard about such an event, yet he suggested that this was accepted in China. Pasternak's description of "Chinese society" thus was neither substantiated by fact nor supported by his own testimony. The description was in fact his own American fantasy.

During his cross-examination of Pasternak, Rigby attempted to undermine Chen's "cultural defense" by deconstructing Pasternak's identification of "American," his description of Chinese as insulated from Western influence and his depiction of Chinese Americans as completely non-assimilated. Rigby began his questioning by asking, "What would you consider your average American?" Pasternak responded, "I think you are looking at your average American."

With this statement Pasternak situated his own subjective position as the definition of the "average American." In other words, Pasternak defined the "average American" to be a white, professional male. By situating himself as the "average American," Pasternak exposed his subjective identification as the "average American" against whom the "foreigner," Dong Lu Chen, was to be compared. He also demonstrated his identification with masculinity. He thereby abandoned any pretensions towards "objectivity" he might have claimed as an anthropologist and revealed his personal investment in his identity as dominant anthropologist and white male, vis a vis the subordinated Chinese male and female objects of study.

When Rigby pressed Pasternak about whether he meant "Anglo Saxon male" by "average American," Pasternak responded by positioning "us"/"American" and "them"/"Chinese" as "two extremes." When asked to identify what he meant by "American," he replied by describing American as not "Chinese." With this explanation, Pasternak followed a tradition, identified as Orientalism, of dichotimizing the human continuum into "we" and "they" and essentializing the resultant "other." When a dominant group essentializes a subordinated group by focusing on selected traits to describe the group as a whole, the dominant group defines its own characteristics in contrast to the subordinated group. This fetishization of "difference" enabled Pasternak's creation of a "cultural defense" for Dong Lu Chen by depicting gender relations in China as vastly different from gender relations in the United States. The resulting image erased the prevalence of gendered violence in the United States and distanced the United–States-based spectator from both Dong Lu Chen and Jian Wan Chen in a way that rendered them unrecognizable and inhuman.

After challenging Pasternak's definition of "average American," Rigby attacked his depiction of Chinese culture as insular and impermeable by outside influence. Rigby asked whether in the last ten years, since Nixon opened relations with China, China had "embraced Western culture" and if this had a "liberalizing" or "awakening" effect. "No," said Pasternak. This question demonstrated that Rigby as well as Pasternak accepted a construction of China as a "closed" or "conservative" nation slumbering away, as compared to the "advanced" West. Rigby's method of attack thus depended in part on the same stereotypes he attempted to undermine.

Rigby, trying another approach, then asked:

"Now in a situation where someone from China comes to the United States, let's say, for instance, comes to New York City, how quickly do they assimilate, if at all, the American culture?" Pasternak answered, "Very slowly, if ever.... Of all the Asians who come to this country, from my experience, ... the people who have the hardest time adjusting to this society are Chinese. The Japanese do a lot better."[68]

Pasternak's statement obviously served his construction of Dong Lu Chen as inassimilable alien. His response failed to problematize the concept of assimilation, and its complete lack of historical or contextual specification unmasked ludicrous generalizations. Which "Chinese" was Pasternak referring to? Which "Asians?"

Although Orden attempted to point out some of the flaws inherent in Pasternak's characterizations of Chinese culture and its relationship to Jian Wan Chen's death, Justice Pincus was swayed by the "persuasiveness" of Pasternak's testimony about the "cultural" roots of Dong Lu Chen's actions. He held:

> Were this crime committed by the defendant as someone who was born and raised in America, or born elsewhere but primarily raised in America, even in the Chinese American Community, the Court would have been constrained to find the defendant guilty of manslaughter in the first degree. But, this Court cannot ignore ... the very cogent forceful testimony of Doctor Pasternak, who is, perhaps, the greatest expert in America on China and interfamilial relationships.[70]

Pincus specifically found significant Pasternak's testimony that Chen lacked a Chinese community to act as a "safety valve" to keep Chen from killing his wife. Yet the alleged motivation for Chen's actions was his "shame" and humiliation before this very same community. The inconsistency in this reasoning is self-evident.

Pincus attempted to incorporate his newly acquired, inaccurate and essentialized understanding of Chinese culture into his sentencing decisions. At the probation hearing Pincus tried to integrate these lessons about the "Chinese" and how a "Chinese" is motivated by "honor" and "face":

> And I must have a promise from the defendant on his honor and his honor of his family he will abide by all of the rules and conditions that I impose.... And if he does not obey and he violates any of these conditions, not only does he face jail, but this will be a total loss of face.[73]

In his decision to grant probation rather than impose a jail sentence, Pincus also took other unrelated "cultural" considerations into account. Pincus believed that the possible effect of Chen's incarceration on his daughters' marriage prospects should be a factor in determining Chen's sentence. Pincus told a reporter, "Now there's a stigma of shame on the whole family. They have young, unmarried daughters. To make them marriageable prospects, they must make sure he succeeds so they suc-

68. Id. at 102.   **73.** Id. at 311.
70. Id. at 301–02. * * *

ceed." In the sentencing colloquy Pincus indicated that he also learned that Dong Lu Chen was a "victim":

> Based on the cultural background of this individual he has also succeeded in partially destroying his family and his family's reputation.... There are victims in this case: the deceased is a victim, her suffering is over. The defendant is a victim, a victim that fell through the cracks because society didn't know where or how to respond in time.[75]

Thus Pincus was able to justify his probationary sentencing: Dong Lu Chen did not serve time for killing his wife because in balancing this action and the surrounding circumstances he was just as much a "victim" as she was.

But where was Jian Wan Chen in this story? The defense strategy rendered her invisible. She was most notably present in the testimony as a dead body and as a reputed "adulteress," bringing a "stain" upon her husband. Jian Wan Chen did not exist as a multi-faceted person but was instead flattened into the description "adulteress." Any discussion of her at trial was premised upon her characterization as a woman who provoked her husband into jealousy. How should this flattening be interpreted? This invisibility and erasure of the woman, Jian Wan Chen?

Jian Wan Chen's invisibility involved more than the disappearance of a victim in a trial focused on the guilt or innocence of a defendant. The defense presented a narrative that relied on her invisibility as an Asian woman for its logical coherence. This invisibility was manifest through the absence of Jian Wan Chen as a subject, a void that was filled only by stereotypes of the sexual relationships of "Chinese women" and an image of her silent physicality. She appeared as an object, whose silence devalued her humanity to the extent that the taking of her life did not merit a prison sentence.

Jian Wan Chen's invisibility is a legacy of an intersection of race and gender that erases the existence of women of color from the popular consciousness. Because white male citizens personify what is considered "normal" in the United States, a status as "other" that is more than one deviation away from the "norm" rarely exists in popular consciousness. The exclusion of Jian Wan Chen exemplifies the difficulty that women of color have when attempting to express themselves as holistic subjects, as Asian women whose identity lies at the intersection of multiple forms of subordination.

Applying an intersectional analysis, it is clear that what Pasternak presented as "Chinese culture" privileged race over any consideration of gender oppression. Pasternak's perspective was "male," obviating the possibility that a woman, and specifically a Chinese immigrant woman, might describe divorce, adultery and male violence within "Chinese culture" very differently. The perspective, was, of course, also "white." The "whiteness" of Pasternak's perspective allowed him to situate Dong

---

75. Id. at 355. * * *

Lu Chen in a category labelled "Chinese" diametrically opposite to Pasternak's own "average," white, male citizen position. Yet this placement ignored that Jian Wan Chen was, in fact, the person categorically opposite to Pasternak: she was Chinese, immigrant and female. Thus, the "cultural defense" served in this case to legitimize male violence against women by glossing over the gendered aspects of Pasternak's testimony about "culture."

The *Chen* trial suffered from a complete absence of any female perspective: Dong Lu Chen, Pasternak, Orden, Rigby and Pincus were all male. Jian Wan Chen was dead, symbolizing how ideologies that subordinate groups of people literally transpire over the body of an "other." Thus, Jian Wan Chen's invisibility is not only the product of the racist notion that "Asian life is cheap," it also is a remnant of the indifference with which many in the United States treat the epidemic of violence against women. Furthermore, the complete disregard for her life also reflected the way racism and sexism intersect to render insignificant violence against women of color, and here specifically, Asian immigrant women.

The impact of the trial and probationary sentencing resonated beyond the courtroom, sending a message to the wider community. Jian Wan Chen's life was not valued; her life was worth less than other lives; her murderer did not deserve punishment in jail. Other Chinese immigrant women living with abuse at the hand of their partners and husbands identified with Jian Wan Chen and clearly understood that violence against them by their partners and husbands had the implicit approval of the state.

The *Chen* decision sent a message to battered immigrant Asian women that they had no recourse against domestic violence. One battered Chinese woman told a worker at the New York Asian Women's Center, "Even thinking about that case makes me afraid. My husband told me: 'If this is the kind of sentence you get for killing your wife, I could do anything to you. I have the money for a good attorney.' "[85] In other words, her husband could afford to hire someone to testify as an expert to bolster a "cultural defense" that legitimized his violence. The New York Asian Women's Center co-director reported that battered women who had previously threatened their husbands with legal sanctions also lost this threat as a means to stop the abuse: "For some women this has worked, but no more. They tell me their husbands don't buy it anymore because of this court decision."[87]

III.   RESPONSE TO THE CASE: LIMITED POSITIONS

After Pincus's decision in the *Chen* case, a coalition of Asian American community activists and white feminists protested and planned to file a complaint against Pincus with the state Commission on

85. See Alexis Jetter, Fear is Legacy of Wife Killing in Chinatown, Battered Asians Shocked By Husband's Probation, Newsday, Nov. 26, 1989, at 4.

87. Id.

Judicial Conduct. The coalition, however, rapidly fragmented. White feminists like Elizabeth Holtzman and the National Organization for Women wanted to completely ban any consideration of culture from the courtroom, while Asian American activists from the Organization of Asian Women, the Asian American Legal Defense and Education Fund and the Committee Against Anti–Asian Violence were unable to agree with that position. Asian American groups wanted to be able to retain the possibility of using the "cultural defense" in other contexts. Francoise Jacobsohn, president of the New York City National Organization for Women chapter, said that she understood the concerns of the Asian American organizations but felt frustrated:

> They were afraid that we were going to go around with a battering ram and destroy the whole concept of a cultural defense. But the judge needed to know that we did not find his statements acceptable.[91]

The philosophical division that fragmented this coalition is symptomatic of the split that exists between white feminists and feminists of color. White feminists saw the case as indicating that a defendant's cultural background should never be taken into account in deciding a sentence: according to Holtzman, we should have only "one standard of justice."

Holtzman's position is one example of a number of different responses to the "cultural defense" taken by legal scholars. As yet, none has effectively navigated between the extremes of condemning the defense in all cases or promoting the defense in the interest of cultural pluralism. Neither of the extremes is satisfying because they both fail to acknowledge that the multiple subordinations existing within immigrant communities are relevant to the choice of whether to support the use of the "cultural defense" in any one case.

* * *

V.   THE RISK OF A FORMALIZED DEFENSE

* * *

Discourse about "race" or "culture" must not obliterate the intersectional oppressions of Asian women, who exist at a nexus of societal racism and sexism in multiple contexts. "Cultural defenses" that focus solely on "cultural difference" with no analysis of gender subordination serve to block out gender oppression and gender difference within Asian American communities. Thus, in the *Chen* case, the "cultural defense" masked the fact that Jian Wan Chen suffered subordination as a woman and as a victim of gendered violence. The deployment of the "cultural defense" where gender subordination is at issue requires that we examine not only the way that "cultural practices" among Asian men and Asian women are an expression of particular power arrangements, but

91. Id.

also the different means by which these practices are maintained and legitimated.

For example, the fact that domestic violence in Asian communities is frequently explained by both Asians and non-Asians as caused or promoted by "Asian culture" is particularly troublesome. This explanation was precisely the "cultural defense" given to Dong Lu Chen. Popular conception in the United States too often understands Asians to be governed by cultural dictates. This misconception is related to the association of "Asian" with "foreign" and "culture" with "other," and leads to dehumanizing descriptions of Asians. I do not mean to deny that there is something we can call "culture" that may explain behavior. My concern is that domestic violence among Asian American communities is explained as "cultural," when a similar description is rarely given to domestic violence in the heterosexual white community. This masks the severity of violence against Asian women by describing it as a "practice" rather than as a political problem. Moreover, to explain behavior as "cultural" implies that it is insular to Asian communities and that the dominant society bears no relationship to that behavior. This hides the fact that Asian women are also subject to oppression from forces outside of Asian communities.

While a formalized "cultural defense" is problematic because it will force defendants' actions to be defined through a group-based identity and reify cultural stereotypes, in some circumstances a defense that presents cultural background will be appropriate. In formulating a legal recourse to the predicament of a particular individual whose behavior was influenced by forces such as racism, sexism and subordination in the form of violence, admission of cultural factors should not function as a reductive "explanation" of that individual's actions as fitting into group behavior or "culture." Rather, the choice to provide an individual defendant with cultural information should be made for the purpose of explaining that individual's state of mind, in much the same way that the criminal law allows other information about a defendant's life history to mitigate sentences or charges in a criminal trial. Even when we attempt to use cultural information to explain an individual's oppressions or her state of mind, we are forced to label and define, in other words, to essentialize, certain behavior as "cultural." This can be done in the spirit of what might be called "strategic essentialism"—consciously choosing to essentialize a particular community for the purpose of a specific political goal. Strategic essentialism ideally should be undertaken by the affected community, which is best situated to undertake the process of selecting the appropriate circumstances in which to offer cultural information.

The defendant's community may be an important resource to provide the court with a "subjective" perspective that serves to explain her actions in the context of their own norms. In *State v. Chong Sun France*,[164] for example, a Korean woman who left her small children

164. 379 S.E.2d 701 (N.C.App.1989).   * * *

alone at night and returned to find one dead was sentenced to twenty years for second degree murder and felonious child abuse. The trial transcript demonstrates a hearing rife with gender, race, and cultural biases, as well as incredible communication difficulties between France and the court. Throughout the hearing, the prosecution portrayed France as a bad mother—irresponsible and negligent—and as an opportunistic and promiscuous immigrant woman. The court found France guilty, adopting the prosecution's argument that she deliberately placed her son in the bureau drawer and shut him inside, crushing him.

Chong Sun France would have benefited from "cultural information" from her community. Expert testimony could have provided information to the judge and jury, interpreting her actions as those of a caring but poor Asian woman with few resources to adequately care for her children. France was released on parole on December 31, 1992, after a massive campaign organized by Korean women, who pointed out the lack of culturally specific information in her representation. The campaign's petition provides "cultural information" explaining France's actions from the perspective of other Korean immigrant women and offering information about child care in Korea. While the community's presentation of cultural information runs the risk of essentializing Korean immigrant women in the eyes of the court and of popular culture, the risk can be justified in that it was the affected community of Korean immigrant women who made that strategic choice and also made the choice of what characteristics to present as "cultural information."

VI. Moving Towards Home

The juxtaposition of the cases of Dong Lu Chen and Helen Wu flushes into view what may seem to be a number of contradictions. How can one argue that the "cultural defense" for Dong Lu Chen was inappropriate while approving the use of cultural information for women like Helen Wu? Both defendants were accused of killing someone over whom they had power. Both alleged feelings of great stress. Both pointed to cultural determinants as a reason for their actions. I reconcile my divergent positions on the two cases by proposing that the value of antisubordination must be a criterion in the decision as to when and how cultural factors should be presented as a defense.

Antisubordination is a value that the legal system must factor into whether to present testimony as to a defendant's cultural background. Valuing the principle of antisubordination is more than a game of hierarchical rankings of "who's most oppressed"; it means a serious commitment to evaluating and eradicating all forms of oppression. In the cases of Helen Wu and Dong Lu Chen, it can involve making identity-based claims to knowledge about the appropriate political choices to make in balancing the risks of perpetuating stereotypes against fairness to the parties involved. As described above, this process can be called strategic essentialism.

Antisubordination does not posit that those who suffer oppressions lack agency due to their victimization and therefore are not responsible for their crimes. Rather, the agency of an Asian American woman, or of anyone who is the subject of multiple oppressions, exists within a complex arena of fractured structural forces and pressures. A fair presentation of her situation should evaluate her agency within this context. In cases like Chen and Wu, such an evaluation reveals these to be cases about Jian Wan Chen and Helen Wu, both subordinated on the basis of gender as well as impacted by dynamic forces from within and without their communities. The point of antisubordination is not to read every story as a "subordinated woman's story"; rather, it is that one must never explain or close off any story into being just one story.

One step in an antisubordination analysis can be to examine whether the defendant acted with a consciousness of her position within the social structure of her community. Helen Wu resisted what she perceived as subordination out of a set of very narrowly defined choices; Dong Lu Chen acted to constrain his wife's choices further. Understanding someone's location as marginal is crucial to understanding her actions. While I do not intend to justify Helen Wu's killing her son, an antisubordination analysis would consider her position in relation to her family and the narrow options she perceived to ameliorate her suffering.

Antisubordination, as premised on the vastness of oppression along unidirectional lines, such as male oppression of women, and xenophobic oppression of immigrants, must be the value on which we base our choices of whether to support the use of cultural factors in a defense and what information should be presented. Because the use of a "cultural defense" reflects the myriad problems of identity politics, including the perpetuation of stereotypical notions that can operate to exclude other people from benefitting from its use, this tactic will be a complex one to follow. Using a goal of antisubordination, however, to evaluate the appropriateness of these factors both combats decision-making premised on problematic descriptions of Asian women, and reflects a normative vision of what is valuable in our communities. Such a framework will also help dislodge the backdrop of "neutrality" as it exposes the relationship between the dominant and immigrant communities. The baseline from which the "uses and abuses" of "culture" are evaluated must be examined: we must question the unstated presuppositions about the American political and cultural character.

A coherent position on the presentation of "cultural information" that highlights its effect on Asian women thus requires an intersectional analysis, which implicates the use of antisubordination as a value to determine how the defense should be presented and when it should be used. Questions of identity and assimilation, of "strategic essentialism" and self-determination are important elements of the discussion. In making choices about the use of cultural testimony it is difficult to maneuver among complicated and sometimes contradictory strategic moves within a system that relies on its lack of flexibility as a means of deriving authority.

Creation of a formalized "cultural defense" will result in fossilizing culture as a reductive stereotype, and lead to inquiries into whether a defendant's identity sufficiently matches that stereotype to merit expert testimony. Cultural information should be allowed only as an informal factor to be considered in deliberations, with the following caveats.

Clearly, an awareness that "culture" is something that affects everybody's actions is essential in consideration of a "cultural defense." There must be an acknowledgement of the fluid and interdynamic nature of cultures. Information that explains the actions of a defendant should be articulated by community members who are sensitive to the dynamics of power and subordination within the community of the defendant. For example, in cases involving women who are abused, such as Jian Wan Chen or Helen Wu, input from organizations that work with battered Asian women is imperative, whether in the form of expert testimony or in amicus briefs. Information about the defendant's culture should never be reduced to stereotypes about a community but rather should concretely address the individual defendant's location in her community, her location in the diaspora and her history. The information should be provided so as to give insight into an individual's thoughts, and should not be used for purposes of explaining how an individual fits into stereotypes of group behavior.

Moreover, advocates should be wary lest the presentation of cultural factors does more harm to Asian women defendants than good, given the ease with which Asian behavior slips into stereotype. There may often be sufficient evidence to show that a defendant lacked the requisite mental state, without admitting special cultural testimony. In fact, a careful distinction must be made between assuming that cultural factors are relevant because Asians are governed by culture, and presenting an individual defendant with pertinent cultural background.

Highlighting the problematic aspects of "cultural defenses" should engender greater awareness of the complications connected to their use. It should also elucidate the difficult yet imperative nature of committing to a future that fights the subordination of Asian women, whether in forms material or descriptive.

Chapter 12

JUDGES AND COURTS

In this chapter, we examine the role of the judge in domestic violence cases. The first article looks at sentencing practices, arguing that the current trend toward batterer treatment programs is not justified and that types of criminal sentences should vary more, depending on the circumstances of each case. It also notes that sentencing practices show the fundamental conflicts between many of the goals of the criminal justice system, as well as the sometimes-conflicting values in the domestic violence community. The second article describes domestic violence courts, a recent development throughout the country. It points out that courts alone cannot stop domestic violence, but must be part of a larger coordinated community response, describing the necessary components of that response. The third article calls attention to problems stemming from the creation of domestic violence courts and from the way courts treat domestic violence generally, and lists several recommendations for more effectively implementing the legislative reforms of the last few decades.

The chapter closes with a brief description of a judicial training program which sought to reach judge's hearts as well as their minds, through using a short story to illustrate the realities of domestic violence.

CHERYL HANNA, THE PARADOX OF HOPE: THE CRIME AND PUNISHMENT OF DOMESTIC VIOLENCE

39 Wm. & Mary L. Rev. 1505–1514, 1526–1527, 1538, 1548–1550, 1558–1559, 1583 (1998).

INTRODUCTION

In 1995, a Chicago district court judge allowed Samuel Gutierrez to enroll in a batterer treatment program in exchange for pleading guilty to choking his girlfriend Kelly Gonzalez. This was one of nine incidents of abuse documented by Chicago police reports.

Then, in August 1996, after failing to appear for a status hearing, the police again arrested Gutierrez for beating Gonzalez. Five days later, the judge imposed, then stayed, a 120–day sentence, again ordering Gutierrez to enroll in treatment. One month later, in September 1996, the same judge continued the case. For the third time, Gutierrez was told to get counseling or face jail. In February 1997, Kelly Gonzalez's body was found; Gutierrez admitted to killing and hiding her body back in September 1996. If Gutierrez is telling the truth, then he killed Gonzalez when he should have been in treatment.

The criminal justice system arguably "did the right thing" in this case. The defendant was arrested, prosecuted, and sentenced to a batterer treatment program intended to aid him in unlearning his violent behavior. A probation officer even followed up to ensure that Gutierrez met his conditions of release. An aggressive state response from arrest to post-disposition was expected to keep Kelly Gonzalez alive. Why did the promise of punishment go unfulfilled in this and other instances?

This case illustrates a challenge to those of us who have argued for aggressive criminal intervention in domestic violence cases. The criminal justice system has made enormous strides in treating domestic violence as a serious crime. We have developed a better understanding of the relative costs and benefits of arrest and prosecution policies in these cases, but there has been little discussion on sentencing theory and practice. A critical look at sentencing suggests that many in the criminal justice system operate under faulty assumptions about the effectiveness of treatment and the futility of incarceration. Unless we take a harder look at punishment in domestic violence cases, we fool ourselves into thinking that well-intentioned arrest and prosecution policies alone will sufficiently curb domestic violence.

This Article argues that the preference for treatment as punishment for domestic violence offenders is misguided. First, empirical data have not shown that most domestic abusers can be rehabilitated through treatment programs as they are currently designed. Rather, the criminal justice system's reliance on batterer treatment programs is driven by politics, not science. Second, the politics of punishment in these cases are symptomatic of a greater debate among both practitioners and academics as to who can provide the "right answer" to why men abuse women and what the best legal response ought to be. Third, we need better interdisciplinary research that examines the causes of violent behavior, paying closer attention to the differences as well as to the similarities among men who abuse women. Finally, until we have this better and more nuanced understanding, the criminal justice system must explore sentencing alternatives that condemn intimate violence more generally, while at the same time impose sentences that specifically deter the most violent offenders, given the particulars of each case, rather than over-rely on therapeutic sentences, which are currently the trend.

As a former domestic violence prosecutor, I was continually frustrated with the unwillingness of judges to sentence domestic violence offenders to incarceration, opting most often for batterer treatment as a condition of probation. A commitment to gender equality originally brought me to work on women abuse. To me, the emphasis on treatment over punishment reflected a historically sexist system that treated domestic violence as a private family matter. Low sentences equated to gender bias. I blamed the judge.

Yet, at the same time, I found myself recommending probation with a condition of attending a batterer treatment program in cases that, had they involved a stranger, I would have recommended a prison term without hesitation. I justified my sentencing recommendations on the wishes of the victim or the likelihood of obtaining a plea if I recommended jail. My commitment to holding abusive men criminally responsible for their behavior often faltered, particularly at sentencing.

In an attempt to make greater sense of sentencing practices in these cases, I found the absence of legal scholarship about punishment puzzling. Popular media abounds with stories like the *Gonzalez* case. Pressure mounts on district attorneys and judges to handle domestic violence cases with greater sensitivity and understanding. Debate continues about domestic violence arrest and prosecution policies. Sentencing of other crimes, particularly sex and drug offenses, receives enormous attention. Why then have legal scholars written so little about the merger of punishment and domestic violence?

One might assume that the field of domestic violence and crime is too new for meaningful scholarship on punishment to yet evolve. Upon closer examination, however, I conclude that the silence subverts a more difficult issue of control—not control of the victim by the abuser—but control over the solution to domestic violence.

A deep and growing schism exists between feminist lawyers and advocates, who are largely responsible for legal reform in this area, and social scientists who continue to research this phenomenon. Debate centers around the causes and cures of domestic violence. Feminist theory continues to be rich, dynamic, and often contradictory in its conclusions; yet, the unequal power relationship between men and women is the common thread that runs through feminist discourse on domestic violence. Feminism is the primary paradigm that explains why women constitute the vast majority of domestic violence victims. In contrast, the social science community traces domestic violence to a violent culture that manifests itself in family conflict and violence. Social scientists respond that the feminist primary emphasis on gender does not explain why so few, as opposed to so many, men batter, nor does it account for why women also engage in violence against family members. Some psychologists locate the causes of domestic violence in individual pathologies, rather than in larger social structures. Behavioral biologists and evolutionary psychologists argue that male violence against women is deeply rooted in reproductive strategies particularly aimed at controlling women's sexuality, and thus we need to understand the biological, as well as social, causes of intimate violence.

When neither empirical data nor individual experience supports theoretical arguments, a tendency exists for each discipline to reject outright the arguments of the other. As Kersti Yllo argues: "Feminist scholars and activists with strong convictions are labeled ideologues.... At the same time, feminists deepen the chasm by dismissing nonfeminist insights too quickly and hastily deciding who 'gets it' and who doesn't."[22] What is happening in the domestic violence field is analogous to the parable of the blind men touching the elephant. Each discipline not only feels something different, but also claims to possess what it touches. We blindly hold on to our own piece of the elephant without fully appreciating how difficult a creature it is to grasp.

No single theoretical construct can account for the violence that afflicts women in their intimate relationships. Nor can any single course of punishment provide a perfect solution. In fact, our search for a perfect solution may have become counterproductive. Those of us who work in this field must base sentencing policy and decisions on both empirical data and descriptive information provided by those who "do law." Our propositions must be tested by their consequences. A discussion of punishment in domestic violence criminal cases presents an opportunity for feminists, social scientists, and researchers from other fields to develop interdisciplinary insights into the phenomenon of battering. To do so, however, we each have to relinquish ownership of the problem. In turn, it is my hope that sentencing practices will emerge that actually deliver the promise of punishment.

Part I of this Article reviews current sentencing practices in domestic violence cases. Despite increased attention to domestic violence, there is still a deep reluctance to incarcerate domestic violence offenders. Rather, most receive probation with mandated treatment regardless of the severity of the offense or their past violent histories. This trend continues despite empirical research that questions whether there is any direct causal link between participation in a batterer treatment program and recidivism.

Part II explores both the theoretical and practical reasons that have led to the emphasis on treatment over other forms of punishment. Many argue that sexist attitudes on the part of prosecutors and judges have led to disproportionately low sentences. This is partly true, but feminists are also responsible for the overemphasis on treatment. Furthermore, I explore the practical difficulties that often prevent even the most enlightened from imposing severe, yet appropriate sanctions.

Part III argues that there is no such thing as a "batterer profile." I draw from the emerging social science literature that suggests that men who abuse women do not have uniform characteristics or motivations. This research can help us better decide who is most likely to benefit from treatment and who is most deserving of long-term incapacitation. I then suggest practical measures for the criminal justice system to develop better, although imperfect, sentencing practices.

22. Kersti A. Yllo, Through a Feminist Lens: Power, Gender and Violence, in Current Controversies, supra note 17, at 47, 59.

Part IV concludes with an optimistic but cautionary note that the most effective way to reduce violence against women is to continue to study male battering and base our sentencing decisions on both theory and experience. Finally, we need to accept the limitations of any criminal justice strategy. This is, perhaps, the greatest challenge of all.

* * *

I.   A Critical Look at Sentencing Practices: The Disconnection Between Perception and Reality

B.   The Practice of Punishment

In 1984, the Attorney General's Task Force on Family Violence wrote that "the most successful treatment occurs when mandated by the criminal justice system." Although the report recommended incarceration for serious offenses, it encouraged the use of batterer treatment programs in cases where the injury to the victim was not serious. Most states and the federal government have since adopted faith in treatment as a matter of policy. Some states, such as California, Alaska, and Florida, require courts to order attendance in a treatment program as a condition of probation in a domestic violence case. Montana requires an offender convicted of partner assault to "complete a counseling assessment with a focus on violence, dangerousness, and chemical dependency." Connecticut requires anyone convicted for a lesser family violence offense to participate in a "family violence education program." South Carolina allows court-ordered counseling for domestic violence offenses but forbids a court from sentencing the offender to more than thirty days in jail. The VAWA also endorses batterer treatment programs for violations of its criminal provisions.

Domestic violence offenders can complete a pretrial treatment program to avoid conviction in some jurisdictions. These programs are generally not available for other violent offenses. For example, Louisiana has a pretrial diversion program available only to domestic offenders. Dade County, Florida has a specialized domestic violence court that permits pretrial diversion for first-time offenders if the offenders complete a batterer treatment program.

Some jurisdictions are moving away from pretrial diversion and instead require a conviction before treatment can be ordered. The rationale for disallowing diversion programs is that they fail to demand that the batterer acknowledge any wrongdoing. Drop-out rates are high; once an abuser stops attending, the prosecution rarely obtains a conviction.

* * *

II.   Who's to Blame?: The Complex Motivations That Drive Sentencing Decisions

A.   Theories of Punishment and the Privacy of Rehabilitation

In this section, I explore different theories of punishment and how they relate to domestic violence offenses. Too often, judges and legal scholars feel compelled to justify punishment on a particular theory without examining the underlying tensions of those theories when applied in practice. I argue that rehabilitation, the most common theoretical rationale for punishing domestic offenders, disguises the subversive notion that abuse is private and pathological; embracing rehabilitation will likely destroy the public goals of criminalization. Nevertheless, although other rationales for punishment, such as general and specific deterrence, therapeutic jurisprudence, incapacitation, and retribution, are not so laden with notions of privacy, they too are an imperfect fit when applied to domestic violence. Thus, rather than search for perfect punishment theories, ultimately we should be pragmatic, justifying decisions based on both general policy goals and the particulars of individual cases.

* * *

B. Feminist Approaches to Punishment

One might assume that incarceration, which ultimately removes male control over women, would drive feminist punishment agendas. But we ought to be careful not to stereotype feminists as wanting all bad men behind bars. A complicated dynamic keeps advocates for battered women from rejecting outright faith in treatment despite the lack of empirical evidence that mandated counseling works. Feminist advocates have not only accepted treatment but have embraced it. Despite feminist criticism of low sentences in particular cases and calls for increased probation supervision, the preference for treatment over incarceration has largely gone unchallenged.

There are many reasons why feminists might prefer treatment over more, arguably male, modes of punishment. The first is largely pragmatic. The domestic violence advocacy community is painfully aware of the reluctance of judges and prosecutors to take these cases seriously, let alone incarcerate offenders. Treatment programs offer at least some state supervision over the offender. Because most of these offenses are misdemeanors, the length of any jail stay would be short; unless some treatment option is available, the offender never learns the skills to change his behavior. Treatment is not perfect, but something is better than nothing.

Treatment also caters to the "upside" of privacy for women. Many in the feminist community argue that autonomous aspects of privacy can further women's equality and freedom. Privacy need not be confined to its historical meaning—as a separate domestic sphere where men are left alone to oppress women—but rather can refer to a preservation of autonomy over important life decisions. Because many women want their partners to change their behavior but do not want to end the relationship with incarceration, treatment is entirely consistent with the feminist notion that the law ought to protect "basic decisions of one's life respecting marriage, divorce, procreation, contraception, and the education and upbringing of children." The availability of treatment thus empowers women to shape their intimate relationships.

A feminist acceptance of treatment might also be explained in part by what Carol Gilligan calls the "ethic of care."[182] Through research on psychological theory, Gilligan argues that women resolve moral dilemmas differently from men.[183] Boys resolve conflict by employing a hierarchy of values; girls focus on preserving relationships.[184] Women see "a world comprised of relationships rather than of people standing alone, a world that coheres through human connection rather than through systems of rules."[185] Treatment, which resolves the problem of battering by focusing on improving the relationships between men and women, is entirely consistent with Gilligan's ethic of care. Women are rehabilitationists; men retributionists.

It is just as plausible that a feminist endorsement of treatment raises the issue of who controls the solution to domestic violence. If men are gender-motivated to use violence, then one way to correct this imbalance is to re-educate them to view women as equals. Treatment programs turn the tables of control from misogynist men to profeminist women and men whose agenda it is to restructure gender relations. This shifting of power from patriarchy to matriarchy, however, does not necessarily equalize the power balance between men and women; it may have the unintended consequence of reinforcing dominance and control of one group over another—precisely the problem that we are trying to solve by criminalizing domestic violence.

Feminist treatment programs are as political as they are therapeutic. They have much vested in the idea that treatment can restructure gender relations. These programs are not without merit. But just as some men find it difficult to give up control of women through violence, so too will feminist advocates face challenges relinquishing control over offenders through treatment.

* * *

D. The Paradox of Hope

"Evil" motivations alone cannot account for bad sentencing decisions. All of us who work in this field experience the paradox of hope—the optimistic but unrealistic belief that abusers can unlearn their violence through treatment. This might be true in individual cases, but it does not hold true universally. The challenge, then, is to develop a better understanding of when to maintain hope and when to abandon it.

Ironically, the most often asked question in these cases is why the woman does not leave. Women "stay" for many reasons: financial dependence; fear of separation assaults; concern for the children; low self-esteem; a perception that there is no place to go; and hope. Many

---

182. Carol Gilligan, In a Different Voice 164 (1982).

183. See id. at 24–63.

184. See id.

185. Id. at 29.

women believe that the violence will stop and the relationship will improve if only ... (fill in the blank). The wish list can include: he gets a job; he stops drinking; I keep the kids from crying; I pay more attention to him; I clean the house; or I love him more. Occasionally, women stay until it is too late. This hope masks a deeper sense of powerlessness. Nothing a woman does can stop the violence unless her partner wants and is able to change. In my own work with abused women, I find these conversations painful as I have come to appreciate that it is the visionary part of people, not the blind part, that believes personal transformation is possible.

This same sense of hope among criminal justice personnel is partially what motivates the preference for treatment. Faith in treatment reflects as much our naive idealism about the power of change as it does our deeply ingrained reluctance to criminalize violence against women. Legal decision making in this context is not so different from personal decision making by women to remain with abusive men. Recognizing the "good" as well as "evil" motivations that drive sentencing decisions should temper our arrogance about who "gets it" and who doesn't.

* * *

C. *Recommendations for the Future*

(Author calls for improving case screening, providing for an array of treatment programs, incarcerating when appropriate, establishing specialized probation departments, educating criminal justice personnel, and undertaking more collaborative research efforts.)

* * *

IV. CONCLUSION

This Article suggests that those responsible for the solutions to domestic violence have much to learn from each other before claiming to have found "the answer." As the criminal justice system's misguided preference for batterer treatment as "punishment" illustrates, until we can distinguish among men, we risk overpoliticizing domestic violence and foregoing opportunities to develop a richer understanding of intimate violence. Interdisciplinary insights and close attention to both empirical and descriptive data can illuminate our search for punishment alternatives that serve both social goals and the particulars of each case.

I am not prepared to abandon my optimism that we can make a difference. The criminalization of domestic violence plays a crucial, albeit not solitary, role in curbing family violence. Like any solution to a problem as complex as battering, progress will have its price. If we institute more comprehensive risk assessments along with more aggressive arrest and prosecution policies, then we are likely to find that more men are incarcerated rather than treated. Some jurisdictions may not pursue minor cases, concentrating resources on the serious ones. Batterer treatment programs as we now know them may no longer be the preferred punishment alternative. Women victimized by violence may find themselves struggling economically and emotionally if their partners go to jail. Children in these homes face a no-win situation. All of these strategies will require an investment of time and resources. And there are no guarantees that in every case we can ultimately deter violence and keep women safe.

Nevertheless, we must be honest. All men are not alike. Some can and want to change their behavior through some form of treatment. Others cannot or will not change. As we continue to struggle to do the right thing, we ultimately have to accept the paradox of hope.

AMY KARAN, SUSAN KEILITZ, AND SHARON DENARO, DOMESTIC VIOLENCE COURTS: WHAT ARE THEY AND HOW SHOULD WE MANAGE THEM?

50(2) Juvenile and Family Court J. 75–86 (1999).

INTRODUCTION

Day after day in courthouses across the country, judges, court managers and court staff face significant and difficult challenges: How can the court ensure safety for victims of domestic violence, hold perpetrators accountable for their actions, and administer justice fairly in complex and interrelated domestic violence cases? As domestic violence cases have become the fastest growing portion of their domestic relations caseload, courts are struggling to keep pace with profound institutional changes in how the criminal justice system, legislatures, and communities respond to domestic violence. Some of the major influences on how courts manage and adjudicate domestic violence cases include mandatory arrest statutes, victimless prosecution policies, specialized police and prosecutor domestic violence units, and full faith and credit for protection orders.

Three major challenges to establishing effective case management systems for cases involving domestic violence are jurisdictional limitations; lack of capacity to identify, link, and track cases; and the need to coordinate the court's operations with the initiatives and resources of other agencies and the community. First, domestic violence potentially can be an issue in a variety of cases that span different jurisdictions within the court system, including civil protection orders, misdemeanor and felony prosecutions, divorce, child custody and support, and dependency and juvenile delinquency. Second, the majority of state courts lack a consistent method for identifying and flagging cases where domestic violence is present in criminal and civil caseloads. They also lack data systems that can track the various case types that may be related to an individual domestic violence case. Third, the scope of domestic violence cases extends beyond the courtroom as the court interacts with other components of the justice system, social service systems, and community service providers that offer an array of programs and services addressing the complex problems encountered by domestic violence victims, perpetrators, and their families.

A growing number of courts have instituted a variety of special systems and procedures to help address these challenges. In a 1998 survey, over 200 courts reported having some specialized processing practices for domestic violence cases, including, for example, centralized intake processes, separate calendars for civil protection order petitions and criminal domestic violence cases, and domestic violence units. This trend toward specialized court management of domestic violence cases has been accompanied by the designation of these courts as domestic violence courts.

The use of "domestic violence court" is handy for conveying the idea that the court recognizes the distinct nature of domestic violence cases and the need for special attention to them. However, the great variation in what these specialized processes are and what they seek to achieve diminishes the utility of "domestic violence court" to describe a commonly understood court classification, such as we use for family courts, juvenile counts, and drug courts. We also do not yet have systematic empirical evidence of the wisdom of using the constellation of processes, practices, and services that are becoming known as domestic violence courts. Consequently, defining any type of specialized process or calendar for domestic violence cases a "domestic violence court" has raised concern among judges, court managers, domestic violence advocates, and others seeking to assure that public and private resources are allocated to domestic violence responses that are effective as well as innovative.

Despite these concerns, the number of courts implementing some type of specialized process for domestic violence cases is growing, and the designation of these processes as domestic violence courts probably is here to stay. Until research-based information about the effectiveness of domestic violence courts is available, judges and court managers need to learn from the experiences of those who have implemented and managed a domestic violence court to guide them toward better practices and away from expedient but unsafe practices. Therefore, the purposes of this article are to discuss the potential benefits that domestic violence courts can achieve if they are designed and managed well, to propose a model integrated systems approach to achieving those benefits, and to describe the judge's role in ensuring a fair and effective domestic violence case management system.

The Potential Benefits of Domestic Violence Courts

Domestic violence courts hold great promise to improve the responses of the judicial system to individual domestic violence victims. For example, many domestic violence courts include specialized intake units that orient victims to court procedures, provide more extensive legal assistance for victims, and refer them to court-related or community-based assistance programs. Specialized intake units also can facilitate the coordination of case management by linking the present case to any related case currently pending or filed subsequently. Some courts may not have an intake unit, but they coordinate case processing through a case manager or other staff assigned to search court files for related cases and to coordinate the scheduling of court hearings for these cases.

Another common feature of domestic violence courts is the dedication of one or more calendars for domestic violence matters, including *ex parte* protection order petitions, hearings on final protection orders, and proceedings in criminal cases. The availability of a central location for hearing domestic violence cases provides greater access to the judicial process, which is particularly valuable to victims seeking protection orders because the vast majority of these litigants proceed without counsel. Dedicated calendars also promote the use of uniform procedures by judges and court staff. Another advantage of dedicated calendars is that they facilitate case management for prosecutors and defense counsel. Counsel can handle higher caseloads and adhere to the court's scheduling more easily if all the cases are heard in one or more dedicated courtrooms.

Perhaps the most significant characteristic of a domestic violence court is the designation of specialized judges or teams of judges to hear domestic violence cases exclusively or as their primary assignment. Specialized judges have an opportunity to develop expertise in domestic violence issues and to improve their skills in adjudicating cases where one or both parties do not have counsel. Specialized judges also are better able to monitor the behavior of abusers and their compliance with court orders, including the terms of protection orders and orders to batterer intervention programs. Greater judicial oversight of perpetrator behavior and imposition of significant sanctions for violations of court orders should be the hallmark of a domestic violence court.

Finally, the court's focus on domestic violence emphasizes to the community both the seriousness of domestic violence and the dedication of the justice system to addressing the problem. This demonstrated commitment should help victims feel safer and more confident in pursuing their civil remedies and assisting the prosecution of criminal behavior. It also should encourage the other components of the criminal justice system and community-based services to collaborate in a systems approach to reducing domestic violence.

To achieve optimum benefits for victims and courts, many practitioners advocate an integrated approach for domestic violence courts that combines both the protection order and criminal calendars within the court's jurisdiction as well as employing various methods of coordination with intake and other processes. One new example of this integrated approach was launched in November 1996 by the Superior Court for the District of Columbia. The Domestic Violence Unit (DVU) within the court's Family Division is a fully integrated system that handles both civil protection orders and criminal domestic violence cases.

In addition, the DVU attempts to link related civil cases involving the parties to the domestic violence cases.

Dade County, Florida provides perhaps the most well-known example of an integrated model of a domestic violence court. Like the District of Columbia Court, Dade County's Domestic Violence Division hears all criminal misdemeanors involving domestic violence and petitions for civil protection orders. Dade County addresses domestic violence from a community-wide perspective and incorporates into the court process referrals for counseling, batterer intervention programs, and other resources for victims, batterers, and their families. The Court has four intake centers around the county to assist with civil protection order filings as well as a victim hotline.

A significant concept in the rationale for domestic violence courts is the integrated adjudication of all issues related to the domestic violence occurring in a victim's environment. For example, one of the services that many victim advocates view as crucial to increasing the chances of a victim with children successfully leaving an abusive partner is the establishment and enforcement of child support orders. Economic oppression is one of the primary reasons many victims stay in abusive relationships. When victims try to break from these relationships, courts can encourage their success by ordering child support, preferably through the federal Title IV–D agency. A fully integrated domestic violence court that handles both protection orders and criminal domestic violence cases and systematically links these cases to the processing and adjudication of related civil matters (e.g., paternity, child support, and divorce) holds perhaps the greatest potential to address domestic violence effectively and remove it from the lives of victims and their children.

DEVELOPING DOMESTIC VIOLENCE COURTS WITHIN
AN INTEGRATED SYSTEMS MODEL

The Need for an Integrated Systems Model

Victims of domestic violence, unlike other victims of crime, share a special relationship with the perpetrator. By definition, the parties are related by blood, are married, have been married in the past, are living, or have lived together, or have a child in common whether or not they have ever lived together. Some states have included dating relationships in their statutory scheme. In addition to this special relationship, domestic violence involves violent crime.

For these and other reasons, domestic violence cases present complex legal, psychological, and sociological challenges to our communities. Half measures to stop the violence actually may place the victim at greater risk than doing nothing. One recent Florida study of 328 domestic violence homicides suggests that there are certain predictors that occur prior to the victim's death. Among them are several that the justice system can and should document and heed: a prior history of domestic violence, prior law enforcement calls to the residence, prior criminal histories of victims and perpetrators, a history of mental illness or medical treatment of mental health problems, threats to kill and attempts by the victim to break away from the perpetrator, including obtaining a protection order. The study does not suggest that women should stop getting protection orders but rather that we as communities must do much more to assist women who choose to exercise this particular resistive option.

The nature of domestic violence cases and available research indicate the necessity for coordinated case processing and monitoring by all involved units of government and community service providers. However, until very recently, this has not been the practice in most communities. Although legal issues and remedies intertwine, these cases are typically adjudicated in separate courts before different judges and involve several criminal justice and community advocacy agencies with little or no coordination.

The following case scenario illustrates the complexity of domestic violence cases. The victim is raped and beaten by her boyfriend in the presence of their four-year-old child, who has also been beaten by the boyfriend. The boyfriend has a gun and flees. The victim's 14–year-old son by her estranged husband chases after the boyfriend and stabs him in the leg with a kitchen knife. The victim files a criminal complaint and requests an emergency protection order and child support. A warrant is issued: city police arrest the boyfriend, who is charged with a felony. Bond is set. The boyfriend posts bond, is released, and files a criminal complaint against the victim's son who is arrested by the county police. Child protective services files an abuse case against the boyfriend, and the victim's estranged husband files for divorce and custody of their 14–year-old son.

In the majority of jurisdictions across the United States, disposition of the cases arising from this scenario could involve numerous judges, a family court, a court of limited jurisdiction, a court of general jurisdiction, a series of prosecutors and victim advocates from different prosecutors' offices (felony, misdemeanor, and juvenile), various law enforcement departments, child protective services, numerous state and local advocacy agencies, various treatment providers, and state and community advocacy groups. Data relating to case histories and disposition could be entered into several different court data systems and numerous other data systems maintained by law enforcement, prosecution, child protective services, and other agencies involved in the case. Case coordination among and within the various agencies and courts involved most likely would be limited or non-existent.

Despite the efforts of committed judges, criminal justice system professionals, victim advocates, and service providers, the door to the courthouse in most jurisdictions is still a revolving one. Too often victims learn not to trust the system, and perpetrators learn that there will be few, if any, consequences for re-offending. Change is gradually occurring, however. Within the last few years, a growing number of jurisdictions have concluded that the cost of domestic violence in their community is too high in dollar terms and human misery. In these jurisdictions, the court, the criminal justice components, and the community have combined their collective resources to create a system where each component has a carefully defined role and each faithfully executes its responsibilities to safeguard its citizens.

COMPONENTS OF THE INTEGRATED SYSTEMS MODEL

There are many system models that may work to achieve the desired outcomes for domestic violence victims and their families. For example, the movement toward a coordinated community response to violence against women has generated several approaches that have met with success in different jurisdictions. similarly, different jurisdictions have implemented various types of specialized court processes, units, or courts for domestic violence cases. as long as positive outcomes are achieved, the particular method or process used may vary according to the resources of each component of the system and services available in the community. however, in each model there are certain recurring themes and goals that should be included in an effective systems response to domestic violence. these are reflected in the following components of an integrated systems model:

- Interagency collaboration
- Comprehensive victim advocacy
- Effective pre-arrest procedures
- Effective post-arrest procedures
- Multi-agency intake
- Integrated case processing
- Effective prosecution and defense
- Effective treatment programs
- Monitoring and judicial review
- Integrated data collection and distribution

Interagency collaboration

Over the past decade, communities have been learning that no one agency or special interest group alone can solve the community problem of domestic violence. System change requires multi-agency cooperation and collaboration. The more comprehensive the collaboration among agencies, the greater the possibility of success. The first step toward achieving this goal is to establish a multi-agency planning team composed of leaders and policymakers. Team members should include representatives of the following offices and agencies:

- The executive branch of government (mayor, county manager, governor's offices)
- The legislative branch (state and local representatives)

- The judiciary (chief judges and division judges)
- The clerk's office (family, juvenile, and criminal)
- The administrative office of the court (court managers from the various divisions of the court)
- Legal advocacy (legal clinics, area law schools, *pro bono* attorneys, private attorneys)
- Victim advocacy (state and non-profit agencies)
- The police department and/or sheriff's department
- The department of corrections
- The pretrial services agency
- The prosecutor's office
- The public defender's office and defense bar
- The probation department
- The department of parole
- Treatment providers
- Public governmental agencies
- Private non-profit agencies

Once the planning team is established, the next step is to develop a plan for an integrated system. There are several tasks involved in developing a plan which we do not elaborate here. These tasks include documenting the existing system; identifying system successes, system failures, and gaps in service; developing a comprehensive plan for the new system; identifying funding sources; and developing an implementation plan with written agency and interagency procedures. The team will be most effective if one of its members serves as a facilitator for the planning and implementation process.

Comprehensive Victim Advocacy

Effective victim advocacy is critical at every sage of adjudicating domestic violence cases, including the criminal and family court process. To best achieve continuity between the victim advocacy community and the justice system the community should:

- Develop "public-private" partnerships between the victim advocacy community and traditional criminal justice components such as local police, prosecutors, and probation agencies;
- Establish a formal link between the victim advocacy community and chief executive of local and state government, i.e., the mayor (or county manager) and the governor; and
- Develop advocacy programs such as shelter, victim support, and court advocacy initiatives, sustained by continuous institutional funding and private grants, sufficient to meet the needs of victims

of domestic violence who find themselves enmeshed in the justice system.

EFFECTIVE PRE-ARREST PROCEDURES

Law enforcement agencies represent the first link in the criminal justice process. Every law enforcement agency should have homicide prevention as its primary goal. The state attorney general's office should assist local law enforcement agencies by establishing statewide domestic violence law enforcement policies and practices and maintaining data on all domestic violence crimes in the state. Local law enforcement agencies should:

- Organize departments to include specialized domestic violence units as part of community-oriented policing initiatives;
- Develop written protocols and policies designed to effectively reduce domestic violence;
- Mandate and enforce domestic violence training for every police recruit and in-service training for officers and commanding officers;
- Develop "public/private" partnerships with local community advocacy groups;
- Work in close association with the prosecutor's office to develop evidence-gathering techniques that enhance the prosecutor's case at trial;
- Have the ultimate responsibility to serve both protective orders and warrants; and
- Ensure that accurate information regarding service and validity of protection orders is transmitted to the state's protection order registry.

Effective Post–Arrest Procedures

The department of corrections has the responsibility to book the defendant and to notify the victim prior to the defendant's release. The pretrial services agency typically performs a complete background check on defendants, performs drug testing in the jail, establishes conditions of release, and monitors the release conditions prior to trial. The pretrial services agency also should apprise the judge at the first-appearance hearing of the defendant's prior criminal history, outstanding warrants, and existing protection orders.

Multi–Agency Intake

Effective case processing begins with a comprehensive multi-agency intake center. A model intake center should be a collaborative effort designed to achieve "one stop shopping" for the victim. Victims should not be forced to navigate through complicated, redundant, ineffective procedures that confuse and discourage participation and ultimately place the victim at greater risk. Research consistently tells us that victims are in the most danger immediately after they leave their abusers. Multi-agency coordinated intake therefore may be the most critical component in any model system because it functions as the main doorway into the court system. The intake center should provide intake and coordination for all cases, criminal and family, between the parties where domestic violence is the underlying issue.

Multi-agency staffing contemplates support from the clerk, the court administrator, the prosecutor, law enforcement, probation and victim advocates. In this one location, a victim should be able to file for a protection order, for child support, a criminal complaint, and a motion for contempt. At the same time, prosecutors and their victim advocates should be available to interview the victim, make a charging decision and obtain a warrant to arrest the perpetrator. Victim advocates should be available to explain the court process and provide the victim with immediate referrals for services. There should be a close connection with law enforcement and probation from the intake center. If other related family cases are not actually filed in the intake center, a comprehensive cross-check of related cases between the parties should be done at the same time.

Integrated Case Processing

Integrated case processing is the responsibility of the bench, the court administrator, and the clerk's office. All three components of the court's case management team must work together to design and implement an integrated case processing system and to maintain it in the face of high volume caseloads, inadequate resources, and shifting priorities.

Judges: Domestic violence cases are more difficult than others for judges because they involve a complex dynamic between the parties and the parties often have multiple cases in the system simultaneously. In addition to a criminal case or civil protection order petition, the parties could be involved in paternity, child support, divorce or custody cases, abuse and neglect cases, termination of paternal rights cases, juvenile delinquency petitions, and eviction cases. Usually, judges in other divisions of the court hear these cases and they typically have little, if any, knowledge of the other cases between the parties. The probabilities therefore are high that they will enter inconsistent, ineffective, and sometimes dangerous orders because of this lack of knowledge. Adjudication of cases takes on a revolving door quality with little accountability from the offender or the system components in general.

To avoid these negative outcomes for the parties and the court, one judge or team of judges should be assigned to hear all related cases between the parties whenever possible. If the court's jurisdiction, organization, or judicial resources preclude assignment of all related cases to one judge or team, all the judges assigned to the different cases should have information about the other cases between the parties. The benefits of this assignment system are that judges are better able to:

- Provide meaningful access to the court;

- Fashion solutions that provide a complete remedy;

- Impose accountability on the offender and the other system components;

  - Provide coordination where multiple agencies or multiple judges are involved with the parties; and

- Instill confidence in the system.

Office of the court administrator: The planning and implementation process for an integrated system requires leadership within each agency and a facilitator for the entire project to organize, maintain momentum, and see the project through to completion. The court administrator is critical to this process and often is the most appropriate choice for the planning team facilitator. The administrator can organize and lead the countless meetings that ultimately are required to achieve a workable plan. This role allows the court administrator to bring the judicial perspective to the table and negotiate on behalf of the court for specialized prosecutors, public defenders, probation officers, police, treatment slots, advocates and all other system elements that must be in place when jurisdictions seek to develop a domestic violence court. To serve competently in this position, the court administrator must have the confidence and support of the judge. In addition to facilitating the planning process, the court administrator also may need to reallocate court resources, including physical space, staff, operations, management and computer technology.

The clerk's office: In most jurisdictions, the clerk's office performs its case processing functions according to case type rather than the relationship of the parties. Thus, for example, criminal cases are processed separately from family cases. Unless a jurisdiction has an established Family Division, even individual family cases are processed separately. Often case types have their own discrete computer systems, which are not integrated with other systems. For example case histories for divorce, juvenile, and child support cases may all be stored in separate systems. Even in those jurisdictions where there is coordinated case processing in family cases, rarely is there any coordination between family and criminal cases even though the parties are the same and the cases arise from the same incident.

Coordinated case processing is pivotal in domestic violence cases. The clerk's office should have a domestic violence unit that works in cooperation with the intake center. (In larger jurisdictions more than one clerk's office staff may be assigned to the unit, whereas in smaller jurisdictions one staff member will constitute the unit.) This unit of the clerk's office should be responsible for case processing of all related cases between the parties. These responsibilities should include:

- cross-checking and identifying all related cases between the parties and their children;

- assigning related cases to the same judge or team of judges if possible under the court's jurisdiction and organization;

- performing case processing for all related cases including scheduling, docketing, and data entry; and

- preparing the service of process packages for all petitions for protection orders and all Title IV–D paternity and child support petitions.

Effective Prosecution and Defense

A fair and balanced process that ensures both vigorous prosecution and due process for the accused is essential for the system to have credibility with the victims, perpetrators and society as a whole. Prosecutors should establish specialized units that thoroughly investigate their cases, are staffed by trained domestic violence prosecutors and victim advocates who handle the case from its inception though disposition, and employ procedures that stress victimless prosecution and vertical prosecution. These special units should have written domestic violence protocols and procedures and should establish linkages with community advocacy programs.

Defense counsel must vigorously defend their clients, yet they also should counsel them regarding all the implications of the criminal allegations against them. These include not only the possible outcomes of criminal prosecution, but also civil processes that could be instituted, including petitions by the victim for protection orders, child support, and child custody. Defense counsel also should seek services for their clients such as legal assistance for civil matters, employment services, mental health services, and batterer intervention programs. Although the concept of providing organized services for offenders on its face may conflict with the goal of maximizing resources for victims, offender services hold significant potential for making victims safer. First, offender services can provide the batterer with resources necessary to help break the cycle of violence. Second, the defense attorney has additional options to intervene with his or her client to stop the violence. Third, the batterer may come to see the system as an ally rather than as an unfair intrusion in the batterer's life, and the batterer may be more inclined to participate in and change through the process.

Standardized Treatment Programs

An integrated systems model includes the development of sufficient and meaningful treatment programs for offenders, including batterer intervention programs and substance abuse treatment. The content, duration, and quality of these programs as well as the educational requirements and training of the therapists should be standardized and subject to state certification and de-certification when appropriate. Program content should be monitored locally to ensure quality control. Communities may choose to use a private treatment model in which individual therapists trained to treat batterers contract with the court. In this mode, the cost of private treatment is borne by the batterer on a sliding fee scale. In other communities, treatment may be provided or connected with the department of probation or other government funded agencies. In these cases, the cost of treatment may be subsidized by these agencies. Communities should determine the existence and extent of treatment services before creating or expanding a system that will depend upon the availability of treatment as an alternative to incarceration.

Monitoring and Judicial Review

Jurisdictions should establish specialized domestic violence units in their departments of probation and parole with officers trained in domestic violence. These officers monitor compliance with conditions of probation, including treatment orders. Compliance with treatment orders issued in civil protection orders also must be monitored, and some systems may choose to have the probation department monitor both. In some jurisdictions, the probation department also offers batterer intervention programs or provides oversight of other treatment providers. To achieve maximum effectiveness in holding domestic violence perpetrators accountable, one central agency should coordinate monitoring of conditions of probation and compliance with the terms of protection orders, including treatment orders.

Domestic violence courts or courts with specialized domestic violence calendars should consider strongly establishing a judicial review docket. These dockets allow the judge who entered an order or accepted a plea to monitor periodically the perpetrator's compliance with the court's orders and puts the perpetrator on notice that the court will enforce its orders. The monitoring procedure should incorporate a system for increased criminal sanctions for repeated non-compliance with court orders and subsequent acts of violence against the victim.

Integrated Data Collection and Distribution

Every agency involved in the processing of domestic violence cases should develop the ability to identify, track, and analyze domestic violence cases. This is as true for the court as it is for law enforcement, prosecution, and the advocacy community. Only through data analysis can individual agencies and the system as a whole effectively manage cases, identify trends, measure progress, and make meaningful changes. The implementation of integrated data collection systems, capable of collecting and synthesizing data from all system participants, is the ultimate goal.

THE ROLE OF THE JUDGE IN PROMOTING A FAIR AND EFFECTIVE CASE MANAGEMENT SYSTEM

The role of the judge in a domestic violence court is complex. Effective domestic violence court judges must understand the dynamics of domestic violence, consider the effects of the violence that go beyond the legal issues in the individual case before the judge, and apply the concepts of therapeutic jurisprudence in decision-making and case management. Exercising these skills requires the judge to step out of the traditional judicial role. At the same time, the judge must remain true to the goal of administering justice, which requires the judge to safeguard the rights of all the parties, including access to justice and due process.

The complicated nature of domestic violence cases has been a significant force in altering this role. In a typical domestic violence case, the victim and the batterer have a current or past intimate relationship. The batterer often has unique access to the victim, either through a continuing relationship with the victim or through children the parties have in common. There often is a prior history of violence, and prior encounters with the justice system may have resulted in little or no accountability of the batterer for his behavior. In addition, neither the victim nor the batterer usually is represented by counsel in any civil matters between them.

Today's domestic violence court judge sees victims reluctant to come to court for fear of further abuse, victims who recant to stay with their battering partners, children who are abused or who witness violence, and batterers who will continue battering without effective intervention. The domestic violence court judge often will see the same parties back in court again and again as violence escalates, interventions fail, family resources and relationships deteriorate, and victims become increasingly less committed to the legal process.

These factors compel the judge to seek a complete remedy, which includes judicial involvement after the sentence has been pronounced or the protection order issued. The judge no longer is in the position of merely calling "balls and strikes" on legal maneuvers, as he or she does in other criminal and civil proceedings. Instead, the judge in a domestic violence case constantly is under the twin pressures of ensuring due process for the defendant or respondent and holding the perpetrator accountable. However, holding the perpetrator accountable often is far more complex than handing down a prison sentence. Not only is punishment needed, but the perpetrator also must undergo behavioral change. This requires integrated system procedures and resources for the victim, the victim's children, and the perpetrator.

The need for information about the victim and the batterer raises another dilemma unique to domestic violence court judges. To fashion remedies with purpose, the judge must be in a position to see the totality of the case in all of its dimensions. The judge cannot execute this responsibility when he or she hears one case in isolation with no knowledge of the multiple related cases possibly in the system or understanding of the complex dynamic between batterer and victim. On the other hand, there may be some information the judge should not know if he or she is to maintain judicial neutrality. This dilemma can best be addressed through an integrated case processing system designed to optimize the flow of information about related cases while it safeguards the confidentiality of information that would compromise due process and victim safety. To achieve the domestic violence court's goals of ensuring victim safety, stopping the violence in the lives of victims and their children, protecting the rights of all parties, and instilling confidence in the justice system, the judge's role should include these responsibilities:

- Ensuring that all of the parties understand the process, the power and the limitations of the court;

- Adhering to due process for all parties while establishing zero tolerance for further violence;

- Having knowledge of all related cases between the parties;

- Issuing orders that do not conflict with one another;

- Monitoring and enforcing compliance with the court's orders, including treatment conditions or conditions of release, through judicial review; and

- Providing leadership for collaboration among justice system practitioners, service providers for the victim and the children, and treatment providers for offenders.

CONCLUSION

The integrated systems model for domestic violence courts proposed here may appear to be too difficult for many jurisdictions to implement. However, the court working on its own or in partnership with only one or two other components of the system will not be able to provide the comprehensive remedies that domestic violence cases require. As with any innovation, there are methods for proceeding incrementally toward a fully integrated system as technology improves and resources change. Judges and court managers also need not adopt every component of the model we describe. In fact, every jurisdiction will have constraints that may preclude implementing one or more of the components. These could include jurisdictional limitations for hearing certain types of cases, lack of facility space, and a shortage of judicial resources.

Therefore, to create an effective system for managing and adjudicating domestic violence cases, each jurisdiction should evaluate its resources, needs, and the role each agency and community partner can best play to ensure that the system accomplishes the jurisdiction's objectives. The evaluation, planning, and implementation process requires the leadership commitment of agency heads and the time commitment of key agency personnel. It can pose political challenges and usually requires each agency to contribute or relinquish something, such as budget, staff, or authority, to make the final plan work. Navigating these waters and negotiating agreements between agencies requires time, skill, continuity and players who are willing to understand the whole system. As the process continues, the partners teach each other the entire system and build trust with one another. The ultimate result will be an integrated system that withstands and improves through the pressures and conflicts that inevitably arise.

Experimentation with specialized processes for domestic violence cases continues to gain momentum in jurisdictions across the country, and the concept of a domestic violence court is becoming a reality.

Although we lack a common understanding of what constitutes a domestic violence court, we are developing a consensus that the ultimate goals of a domestic violence court should be victim safety and batterer accountability. To achieve these goals, the court must become a component of an integrated system for reducing domestic violence in the community. Operating alone and without support from other system components, a domestic violence court can place victims at greater risk than they would be in a traditional court process. Creating an integrated system begins with and is sustained by the interagency collaboration needed to ensure that the system does not entice victims in but ultimately leave them unprotected and defenseless.

DEBORAH EPSTEIN, EFFECTIVE INTERVENTION IN DOMESTIC VIOLENCE CASES: RETHINKING THE ROLES OF PROSECUTORS, JUDGES, AND THE COURT SYSTEM

11 Yale J. L. & Feminism 35–49 (1999).

IV. C. CONCERNS RAISED BY AN INTEGRATED INTAKE AND CALENDARING PROCESS

There are several drawbacks to moving domestic violence cases into a specialized court. Insufficient physical space and personnel can result in a lack of privacy for victim interviews and lengthy intake waiting periods. Incompatible data processing systems can obstruct case coordination. Judicial training may be insufficient and overburdened judges may become subject to burnout. Inadequate resources can prevent the provision of comprehensive services for batterers, survivors, and their children.

In addition, several policy concerns loom large. Perhaps the foremost of these is that an integrated domestic violence court may exacerbate a deeply-ingrained tension between those communities primarily concerned about domestic violence and those primarily concerned about child abuse and neglect.

An integrated court system creates an environment in which victims with children are more likely to have extensive contact with government attorneys and paralegals. This, in turn, means that government workers are more likely to hear about abuse that occurred in the presence of children or where children themselves actually were harmed. In the District of Columbia, this has led to an increase (albeit a small one) in the rate of government reports to Child Protective Services.

These reports can result in two scenarios which may undermine the effective enforcement of domestic violence laws. In one, the victim herself is charged with child abuse. In the second, the perpetrator is charged with child abuse and the victim is charged with "failure to protect" the children. In either case, there is a substantial possibility that the children will be removed from the home and separated from both parents. These cases point to a long-standing historical conflict between the domestic violence community and the children's rights community—a largely unnecessary one, given how much common ground they actually share.

Child advocates have focused primarily on the rapid removal of children from the violent home. But this approach underestimates the influence of adult-on-adult domestic abuse on the family dynamic. If battered women learn that seeking protection from their abusive partner increases the risk that their children may be taken away, they will be greatly deterred from coming forward. As more women become reluctant to pursue legal assistance, both they and their children, who are dependent on them to escape, ultimately will remain trapped in violent families.

Moreover, in many "failure to protect" cases, the victim stays with the perpetrator not because she does not care about the children, but because she believes that staying is the best way to do so. Statistically, the moment of leaving is frequently the most dangerous and the most likely to result in death—of both the victim and her children. Adult victims are acutely aware of this possibility and, in addition, frequently report that the batterer threatens that if she leaves, he will take the children and she will never see them again. To stay and offer the children what protection she can may at times be a better option than to allow the perpetrator to abduct and mistreat the children.

* * *

As (the above) case demonstrates, children right's advocates, in their fight to protect young children from injury and death, too often fail to consider the dynamics of spousal abuse. However, domestic violence activists, desperate to bring the problem of woman abuse into public awareness and engender concern, have felt compelled to insist that all battered women are completely innocent victims. They have resisted recognizing that some victims belong to families where each member relates to one another through violence and threats of violence. I have repeatedly had experiences where a battered woman is seated in my office, telling me in detail about her husband's brutal assaults and her terror when he threatened to kill her. When her child gets too noisy playing in the waiting room outside, she pokes her head out of my door and yells, "If you don't quiet down, I'm going to kill you!" On some occasions I have seen a client hit her child or twist his arm, in a way that in my view exceeded acceptable disciplinary action. These moments are chilling.

It is time for domestic violence and children's rights advocates to take a more honest look at the relationship between woman abuse and child abuse, and to come up with more sophisticated solutions than automatic removal. These groups need to share their different areas of expertise so that everyone can do a better job of reducing violence in the family, in all its forms.

A handful of jurisdictions have brought domestic violence advocates and child welfare workers together to create long-term strategies to empower women to protect their children. Specialists in both fields exchange information, provide cross-training, and develop protocols for case handling and service provision. In some places, in-house domestic violence experts are placed at each child protective service office, to provide ongoing training and consultation. Child advocates provide services to the non-violent parent that are not contingent on the filing of failure to protect charges. Domestic violence advocates incorporate services for abused children into their programs, recognizing that a child may have needs independent of those of the non-violent parent. Where these multi-faceted services are provided on a long-term, continuous basis, there appears to be a reduction of out-of-home placements for abused children whose mothers have also been abused. Such programs are beginning to build the bridges needed to protect and support women and their children.

Another source of hope is this: When survivors learn about the intergenerational effects of domestic violence, they frequently react with a sense of epiphany about what has happened in their own lives and what may now be happening to their children. They often decide to seek counseling both for themselves and their children, to stop the injury inflicted by intimate abuse once and for all. Advocacy groups would do well to identify ways to encourage and extend this impulse because of its potential to improve the lives of all of those victimized by domestic abuse.

The creation of an integrated court raises a fundamental and related policy concern that the court may become overly systematized. Although integration and coordination can maximize battered women's access to services, it also can reduce their ability to decline such services if they wish to do so. For example, a woman who enters a comprehensive Intake Center seeking only a civil protection order is likely to also be automatically routed to a prosecution advocate to initiate criminal charges without being asked whether she wishes to do so. As discussed in Part III.B, *supra*, a battered woman may have many reasons to decline participation in a criminal case, but the coordinated intake process may push her into that arena without analysis of her personal concerns.

The more systematized a domestic violence court becomes, the more likely it is that a shift will occur away from woman-centered advocacy, in which each battered woman works with an advocate to define the assistance she needs, and toward service-defined advocacy, where advocates focus on providing available services regardless of whether they fit into a particular woman's risk analysis or safety plan. As in the domestic violence/child abuse and neglect context, it is crucial that expansion of the options available in intimate abuse cases occurs within a broader context of responsiveness to the particular needs of individual victims.

V. FAILURES OF NEUTRALITY: THE HOSTILITY
OF JUDGES AND COURT PERSONNEL

The problems caused by ineffective or overzealous prosecutorial policies and the information-sharing failures of the conventional courts are not the only systemic obstacles victims of domestic violence must surmount. In addition, intimate abuse complainants must face a deeply-ingrained hostility often exhibited by court clerks and judges.

A. Explanations for Judicial and Clerical Hostility Toward Battered Women

Most judges come to the bench with little understanding of the social and psychological dynamics of domestic violence and, instead, bring with them a lifetime of exposure to the myths that have long shaped the public's attitude toward the problem. The most persistent of these myths is the belief that battered women could leave their relationships if they simply chose to do so. But this belief ignores the real-life obstacles facing women who wish to end their relationships. These may include fear of retaliation; lack of economic resources; concern for children; emotional attachment to the perpetrator; perceptions of the availability of social support; and religious and culturally-based values and norms. In addition, this belief ignores the fact that many women make numerous unsuccessful attempts to leave before they actually are able to do so, and are punished with a more severe beating or even homicide.

Lack of knowledge about this basic aspect of domestic violence causes many judges and clerks to become frustrated with petitioners whom they perceive as "refusing" to leave the abusive relationship. Operating under this erroneous perception, they find the victim's behavior enormously frustrating. Clerks across the country complain bitterly about domestic violence cases, claiming that they require too much work and that too often the victims drop their suits anyway. This view results in clerks regularly refusing to provide assistance to petitioners and often actively discouraging them from filing for civil protection orders. Some clerks refuse to tell battered women about the availability of such orders; others refuse to assist victims in completing the necessary forms or refuse to make the forms available. Others will inform a petitioner (incorrectly) that she can only get one protection order in a lifetime, "so she had better be sure this [is] the time she really need[s] it." Some clerks arrogate to themselves the right to screen cases to determine which will be presented to a judge.

Judges similarly mistreat domestic violence victims. When cases are brought by women who have dropped charges on previous occasions, judges have made such comments as: " 'oh, it's you again,' or 'how long are you going to stay this time,' or 'you want to go back and get beat up again.' " Others have gone so far as to threaten victims with sanctions for repeated use of the court system. A particularly egregious example occurred in North Dakota, where a judge is reported to have told a domestic violence petitioner, "If you go back [to the perpetrator] one more time, I'll hit you myself."

In addition to their failure to understand the complexities of leaving abusive relationships, untrained court personnel and judges can and do misinterpret victim behavior that is symptomatic of the psychological trauma induced by extended abuse. Survivors of prolonged or severe domestic violence often exhibit some symptoms or meet the full diagnostic criteria for post-traumatic stress disorder (PTSD). This diagnosis, first constructed to explain the long-term psychological impact of traumatic combat on war veterans, produces three major categories of symptoms: "hyperarousal" (being in a constant state of alertness for and expectation of danger); "intrusion" (reliving the violent experience as if it were continually recurring in the present, through flashbacks and nightmares); and "dissociation" (a numbing response that includes repressing memories of violent incidents).

These symptoms can profoundly affect the way a battered woman appears in court and, in turn, how she is perceived by a judge. Dissociation may cause many survivors to testify about emotionally charged incidents with an entirely flat affect, or to be unable to remember dates or details of violent incidents. Hyperarousal can cause a victim to seem highly paranoid or subject to unexpected outbursts of rage in response to relatively minor incidents. The psychological phenomenon of intrusion may cause a witness to have vivid flashbacks on the witness stand that interfere with her ability to testify. But these explanations of battered women's behavior are not intuitively obvious, and because they differ greatly from the behavior and demeanor that a judge encounters in his normal experience, they often are incorrectly interpreted as indications of her lack of credibility. As former prosecutor Cheryl Hanna puts it, in court, "batterers can appear charming, respectful, and persuasive; by contrast, abused women can appear hysterical, vindictive, or prone to exaggeration."

This can lead judges to identify with the batterer, distance themselves from the victim, and apply artificially heightened standards of proof. A judge may refuse to issue civil protection orders when documentary or other physical evidence is absent; when unbiased eyewitnesses are not available; when the only witnesses are the parties and, therefore, a credibility determination is required; or when the petitioner has failed to follow through with a protection order case on a prior occasion. These kinds of standards have no basis in law and are not applied in other family law cases.

Judges and court personnel, like many laypeople, also frequently underestimate the seriousness and potential danger inherent in family abuse cases. A National Institute of Justice survey found that many judges report the belief that domestic violence consists of "verbal harassment, or a rare shove" and approach the issue as a " 'relationship problem' amenable to marital counseling." Virtually every study of gender bias in the courts corroborates this finding. A widespread attitude exists that cases involving large financial interests and crimes perpetrated on non-intimates are the "real" cases, while domestic violence is an inferior assignment or even a hazing ritual for junior judges. Too many judges call these cases "unimportant work" and make it known that they do not want them in their courtrooms. They view criminal prosecutions of intimate abuse as "family matters" that do not belong in criminal court.

* * *

Judges who do not understand the seriousness of family abuse often issue civil protection orders that fail to include the comprehensive relief necessary to stop future violence. Forty-three percent of domestic violence service providers across the country report that judges are unwilling to consider awarding remedies clearly authorized by statute, especially custody, child support, and other forms of financial relief. Similarly, gender bias task force reports indicate that judges impose lighter sentences on defendants convicted of domestic violence crimes than those involving violence against strangers.

Finally, many judges find it frustrating to deal with *pro se* litigants. Because the vast majority of domestic violence petitioners appear without counsel, this problem is pervasive. Examples of this problem include a California judge who denied a petition in which a woman had stated that the batterer hit her "upside the head," claiming that he did not understand the allegation. A Connecticut judge is reported to yell at *pro se* battered women for filing their court papers incorrectly and to actually throw the papers at them.

Judicial hostility toward domestic violence petitioners is particularly disturbing given the positive impact a judge can have. Studies have shown that judicial warnings or lectures to defendants about the inappropriateness and seriousness of their violent behavior can improve some defendants' future conduct. And victims report that receiving official affirmation from judges that they do not deserve to be abused helps them gain the strength to separate from their batterers.

B. *Judicial Education as a Force of Change*

As the stories above illustrate, judges often do not understand either the psychological dynamics of relationships involving domestic violence or the obstacles facing battered women who seek legal protection. To remedy this deficit, judges need to receive the education necessary to adequately perform their jobs. Education can be a highly effective tool for reclaiming judicial neutrality. For example, after attending a national interdisciplinary conference on domestic violence sponsored by the State Justice Institute, Nevada District Court Judge Terrance P. Marren disclosed that he had grown up in a family where his father abused his mother, and that "although he once perceived that he was dealing fairly with the abuse cases that came before him, his experience with judicial education showed him that he had a great deal to learn...." He has since persuaded the Nevada Supreme Court to require every judge to attend a two-day local conference on family violence.

In Washington, D.C., judges assigned to the new Domestic Violence Court are required to undergo formal training on intimate abuse and accept a long-term (one-year) assignment, to allow them to build a reservoir of experience. Although the training opportunities have been limited, the community already has witnessed substantial differences in judicial treatment of these cases.

A telling example lies in the change in judicial response to requests for custody and child support in civil protection order cases. As discussed in Part II, *supra*, rapid resolution of these issues is of extreme importance in domestic violence cases, where perpetrators commonly use financial leverage and threats of child kidnapping to manipulate and control their victims.

Prior to the Court's formation, D.C. judges awarded temporary custody in less than half of the civil protection order cases, despite clear statutory authorization to grant such relief. They awarded child support in only 2.6% of civil protection order cases where the parties had a child together, and 4.9% of those cases involving a custody order, although such an award also is authorized by statute and case law. This kind of track record is typical nationwide; forty-three percent of domestic violence service providers report that judges are unwilling to consider awarding these kinds of remedies.

In the new Court, however, judges now routinely award custody based on the best interest of the child standard as well as child support based on D.C.'s financial guidelines. They even occasionally take the time to talk to perpetrators about the harmful impact that witnessing adult-on-adult abuse can have on children and the intergenerational nature of domestic violence.

C. *Maintaining Judicial Neutrality*

In those few jurisdictions that have implemented domestic violence courts, the defense bar consistently has complained that judicial education about family abuse and extended tenure on a calendar devoted to such cases creates a pro-victim, anti-defense bias. Although this criticism is based solely on anecdotal evidence, most litigants and attorneys agree that these courts create a substantial change in judicial attitudes toward domestic violence cases. Given the extensive history of anti-victim bias among judges, however, it is difficult to believe that a newly-organized court could have an impact so fundamental as to not only level the playing field, but to regrade it in the opposite direction—against perpetrators.

The existence of a judicial bias created by domestic violence training can be empirically detected, and initial data from the District of Columbia experiment indicate that no such bias exists. Since the inception of the new domestic violence court, the percentage of civil protection orders issued in contested cases has actually decreased, from 86% in 1989 to 78.6% today. If the newly-trained judges have developed a bias in favor of victims, why has the overall victim success rate decreased?

Similarly, judges' extended exposure to and experience with a domestic violence calendar does not appear to erode their impartiality. The percentage of civil protection order trials in which domestic violence judges grant the petitioner's request for relief remained fairly constant during the first six months of the D.C. Domestic Violence Court's operation, with cyclical fluctuations between seventy-one percent and eighty-three percent. No trend of increased sympathy for alleged victims is apparent. The same is true for non-jury trials in criminal misdemeanor prosecutions, where the government success rates fluctuated between sixty-nine percent and seventy-six percent.

Of course, any judicial bias that is created—or simply perceived to exist—must be taken seriously. Although some victim advocates are perfectly comfortable with the idea of an anti-defense bias, it is in fact an issue that should be of equal concern to victims as it is to perpetrators.

Recent social science research demonstrates that defendant compliance with court orders depends more on the "procedural justice" with which the sanction is delivered than on the certainty and severity of the sanction itself. Unlike deterrence theory, which dictates that people obey the law when the benefits of compliance outweigh the costs, the procedural justice model recognizes that in many instances compliance occurs out of a sense of duty or morality, rather than self-interest. The obligation to comply arises when the courts imposing orders are viewed as moral and legitimate—when they treat people fairly. The perceived fairness of court proceedings has a direct impact on the likelihood that a person will comply with the court's ultimate decision—regardless of whether he considers that decision to be right or wrong.[251]

If people feel unfairly treated by a court, they will perceive it as less legitimate and as a consequence obey its orders less frequently.[252] A crucial element of this body of research, according to one of its pioneers, Tom Tyler, is that:

> [P]eople want to be treated fairly by authorities independent of any effect on favorable outcomes. [A]dhering to fair procedures will cement persons' ties to the social order because it treats them with dignity and worth and certifies their full and valued membership in the group. [B]eing treated fairly by authorities, even while being sanctioned by them, influences both a person's view of the legitimacy of group authority and ultimately that person's obedience to group norms.[253]

Researchers have identified several building blocks of procedural justice. One is the extent to which a person has the opportunity to state his case and be heard. Another is the impartiality of the relevant legal authority. Finally, respectful, ethical treatment by legal authorities is "directly related to perceptions that authorities are moral, legitimate, and [ ] deserving of compliance."

The provision of procedural justice has a demonstrable impact on compliance in the domestic violence arena. In a recent study, researchers considered the effect of a batterer's perception of police fairness on

---

251. See Tom R. Tyler, Why People Obey the Law 108 (1990).

252. See id. * * *.

253. Id. at 165.

intimate abuse recidivism rates. The pre-existing literature on this subject had focused exclusively on the impact of different police-imposed sanctions (warning, mediation, and arrest) on recidivism; the results were equivocal.

The principal investigators in the original police arrest experiment concluded that their study "strongly suggest[ed] that police should use arrest in domestic violence cases," because arrest was most highly correlated with low recidivism rates. But when six replication studies were conducted in different jurisdictions, the findings ranged from arrest having no effect, to a deterrent effect, to an escalation effect. And even within the same jurisdiction, the effect of arrest often varied based on the length of detention and certain offender characteristics, such as employment and other ties to the community.

What these studies ignored was the possibility that the procedures employed by the police might have affected the results. In 1997, researchers revisited the data from all seven studies to determine whether "the manner in which sanctions are imposed has an independent and more powerful effect on spouse assault than the sanction outcome itself." They found that perceptions of procedural justice have a statistically significant impact. The frequency of recidivist domestic abuse was lower for those perpetrators given only a warning than for those who were arrested, in cases where the arrested offenders perceived that they had been treated in a procedurally unfair manner. The frequency of subsequent abuse was far lower, however, when arrestees believed they had been treated fairly.

This study (and others like it) has substantial implications for judicial proceedings. Issuance of a civil protection order means little if the batterer views the order as illegitimate and therefore feels free to ignore it. By ensuring that all parties are provided with procedural justice, judges can influence responsiveness to their orders. Judges who recognize and respond to people's normative concerns can exercise their authority more effectively; their rules and decisions are more likely to be voluntarily accepted and complied with. As a result, judicial training must be targeted toward the eradication of existing anti-victim biases within a larger framework of promoting procedural justice.

JACQUELINE ST. JOAN, SEX, SENSE, AND SENSIBILITY: TRESPASSING INTO THE CULTURE OF DOMESTIC ABUSE

20 Harv. Women's L. J. 263–266, 307–308 (1997).

I. Introduction

In 1989, I was a judge presiding over a busy municipal courtroom in Denver, Colorado. I had a docket full of petty criminal matters and overflowing social problems—small precursors to a life of crime for some, one-time bad judgment calls for others—everything from domestic violence to prostitution, from trespass to urinating in public.

That year I was appointed to the planning committee for the state judicial conference and was charged with organizing a training session on domestic violence. Domestic violence was a subject with which I was well acquainted, having spent the eight previous years specializing in the field, first as an attorney and then as a judge. Domestic violence cases increasingly filled the dockets in Denver as a result of a series of reforms which had been instituted over the preceding five years—mostly as a result of coalition-building among feminists, legal organizations, and mental health agencies in the Denver community.

In 1984 the Denver police had instituted a "mandatory" or "preferred arrest" policy in domestic violence cases whenever an officer's investigation showed probable cause. Arrests in Denver for domestic violence increased sixfold in the next ten years, largely as a result of this policy: in 1994, Denver police made nearly 7000 arrests. The Denver County Court rules were also amended in 1985 to exclude domestic violence cases from the bonding schedule. This policy led to the need for bond hearings in all domestic violence cases. The demand for more domestic violence trials, dispositional hearings, and sentencings led to a near doubling of court personnel in the courtrooms where these cases were predominantly assigned. The increased numbers of domestic violence cases and a growing concern about the need for closer supervision also led to more probation supervision by the courts. As a result, judges held more hearings for review, ordered more probation revocations, and began to actively use new restraining order laws. All of these new judicial practices increased the amount of time judges spent listening to survivors, perpetrators, and witnesses of domestic violence.

By 1990, some judges were already being trained at judicial conferences in "Domestic Violence 101" through formal lectures and panels presented by domestic abuse survivors, advocates, treatment providers, and perpetrators. These conferences taught judges to identify the dynamics typical of domestic violence cases and to recognize that there are certain "myths" to question or disbelieve. Speakers encouraged judges to avoid certain judicial practices, such as making on-the-record statements that blame the victim for the abuse. Judges observed that many domestic violence victims recant, but confessed that they didn't really understand the complex reasons why. Judges expressed frustration with victims who did not want to testify or who did not want serious penalties imposed on criminal violators. Judges were also concerned that they might be blamed for the subsequent death of a victim if they made an error in judgment in a domestic violence case. The judges tended to blame the victim for the crime: Why does she stay? Why doesn't she call the police? Why doesn't she testify? How can she love a man who treats her this way?

In addition to confusion and frustration, these questions resulted in judicial counter-transference, "the surfacing of a psychotherapist's own repressed feelings through identification with the emotions, experiences, or problems of a person undergoing treatment." Counter-transference can lead judges—male or female—to make serious mistakes in evaluating cases before them. For example, Judge Paul Heffernan "turned to a man accused of choking and beating his wife and said: 'You want to gnaw on her and she on you, fine, but let's not do it at the taxpayers' expense.'"

Whether caused by judicial counter-transference, insensitivity and lack of empathy, or a superficial understanding of how victims and perpetrators of domestic violence behave, serious errors in judges' perceptions, thinking, speech, and practice occur every day. Literature, which holds the power to place a reader in the position of a narrator, can be an effective tool in training judges to realize these errors and to move to correct them. By encouraging an empathetic response to the harms caused by violence, literature can help judges learn to put themselves in another's place—even someone very different from themselves. Women's literature in particular challenges dominant cultural notions about domestic violence that construct judges' thinking about battered women.

In this Article, I argue for exposing judges to outsider literature—novels, short stories, and poetry—in order to improve their understanding of domestic violence. This exposure will help judges reduce their reliance on stereotypes, deepen the questions they ask themselves and others, and respond in a more just and effective manner to victims of abuse. In Part II, I describe a judicial education program that used literature to train judges to interpret domestic violence cases with improved sensitivity and deeper understanding. In this program the judges were exposed to a short story, "Trespass" by Sandra Scofield, and a courtroom drama, After Trespass, which was based on "Trespass." Here I analyze "Trespass" using findings of domestic violence research and literary criticism and focusing on narrative strategies writers use in order to influence readers. In Part III, I examine some of the theoretical bases for using literature to train judges about domestic violence. In particular, I introduce theories about three independent subjects: the role of passion in the law, the use of narrative in feminist literary and legal studies, and the value of increasing empathy in the law. In Part IV, I compare narrative elements such as theme, structure, imagery, character development, and subtext to demonstrate the kinds of information that are revealed in the short story. I then contrast this information with the more limited facts that are available in the narrative of a trial. In Part V, I examine how the rules of evidence and the interrogatory format of the trial process suppress the female voice and suggest remedying this problem by broadening the scope of judicial inquiry at trial and loosening restrictions on narrative-style testimony. In Part VI, I conclude that judicial education programs on domestic violence should target both sides of the brain as well as the heart by using the combined elements of literature, law, and domestic violence empirical research.

* * *

VI. Conclusion

In this Article, I have applied emerging theories in three legal subjects to argue that the use of literature in training judges can clarify perceptions and deepen responses of judges to domestic violence cases. I have examined the role of passion in law, feminist use of narratives in legal scholarship and practice, and theories of empathy as a source of knowledge. I have described one judicial education program, which combined elements of literature, law, and domestic violence research. Analyzing the short story, "Trespass," with theories developed in law, in literature, and in social science research emphasizes how these multiple approaches to interpreting human stories can provide judges with valuable perspectives for weighing evidence.

One way humans try to make sense of their lives is by organizing knowledge into stories. The tragic stories of domestic violence are unfolding in our courtrooms daily. The need for courts to improve responses to domestic violence is urgent, and more judges are responding to that urgency. Combining our understanding of law, literature, and domestic violence research is one profound and creative way for society to revise the endings of similar stories.

Chapter 13

VICTIMS OF DOMESTIC VIOLENCE AS CRIMINAL DEFENDANTS

This chapter concludes the section of this book which focuses on the criminal justice system's response to domestic violence, and looks at victims of domestic violence who are charged with crimes (other than "failure to protect" their children, dealt with in Chapter 7).

The chapter starts with two overviews of the subject area from a federal government report; the first outlines the issues generally, discusses how evidence of domestic violence is relevant in different types of criminal cases, and cautions against the use of the term "battered woman syndrome." The second piece briefly describes how the state appellate courts have dealt with this type of evidence. Then comes an article describing the relevance of domestic violence evidence to negate specific intent, an often overlooked issue.

The second half of the chapter focuses on victims of domestic violence who have been charged with killing their abusers. It starts with a landmark case in which the California Supreme Court overturned two appellate cases and announced a new standard regarding expert testimony. The chapter closes with two articles discussing the difficulties faced by victims of same-sex domestic violence and African–American battered women when members of these groups plead self-defense to killing an abuser.

MARY ANN DUTTON, VALIDITY OF "BATTERED WOMAN SYNDROME" IN CRIMINAL CASES INVOLVING BATTERED WOMEN

Edited by Malcolm Gordon, in National Institute of Justice, The Validity and Use of Evidence Concerning Battering and Its Effects in Criminal Trials, U.S. Department of Justice 1–5, 7–30 (1996).

Criminal Case Contexts in Which Battering Is an Issue

In criminal court proceedings the dynamics and effects of battering can become issues in:

- The self-defense or insanity defense of a battered woman accused of murdering or assaulting the perpetrator.

- Charging and sentencing in such cases.

- The duress defense of a battered woman accused of criminal or illegal conduct through the instigation or coercion of a perpetrator.

- The prosecution of cases of domestic violence.

- Addressing misconceptions about domestic violence that might be held by judge or jury.

To Support a Plea of Self–Defense

Battered women sometimes use physical force, including the use of weapons, in response to their batterers' violent behavior toward them and other family members. These women may be charged with a criminal offense. In such cases, the legal defense of self-defense is often introduced. Of course, not all women who use violence against an intimate partner do so in self-defense.

The elements of self-defense in situations where the effects of battering are particularly relevant require that the defendant reasonably believed (a) that deadly force was necessary to protect herself or others against death or serious bodily harm used or threatened by the batterer and (b) that the use of force was immediately necessary to protect against death or serious bodily injury. Most state courts do not require a duty to retreat, but factfinders may, nevertheless, find this issue to be relevant in their deliberations. Thus, evidence and testimony may be introduced to assist the triers of fact in deliberations concerning the specific elements of self-defense.

To Support a Defense of Insanity

The defense of insanity requires a defendant to have had a severe mental illness, defect, or disorder at the time of the alleged criminal acts. Further, this condition must have impaired the defendant's mental capacity to such an extent that either (s)he did not understand the nature and consequences of what (s)he was doing or did not understand that what (s)he was doing was wrong. Although this defense is used infrequently in cases involving battered women, it may apply in some instances.

An insanity defense claims that the battered victim's mental capacity was impaired, in contrast to a defense of self-defense or duress, which offers that the battered victim acted in response to a reasonable perception of danger. When the condition of legal insanity is related to domestic violence, testimony by experts can be offered to explain how traumatic reactions and their associated symptoms may preclude the victim from knowing right from wrong or appreciating the consequences of her actions at the time of the criminal acts.

To Support Mitigating Factors in Charging and Sentencing

Information about battering and its effects has been used by prosecutors in determining the severity of the charge that a battered woman should face in a trial and, during the sentencing phase, to show the existence of mitigating factors in the battered woman's criminal behavior. Information considered in charging and sentencing may include the history of violence against the battered woman, the battered woman's efforts to protect herself and obstacles to those efforts, the social and psychological impact of violence on her, and the context in which the violence occurred.

To Support a Defense of Duress

Batterers use physical force, intimidation, and coercion to control their victims' thoughts, feelings, and behaviors. Some women, in an attempt to avoid further violence and abuse, comply with the batterer's explicit or implicit demands. For some, compliance means being an accomplice to or actively engaging in illegal behavior, perhaps involving drug-related activity, fraud, theft, or even violence toward others. When a battered woman has participated in these and other criminal acts in response to the batterer's coercion, threats, or actual violence, a defense of duress is often introduced.

In order to successfully argue a defense of duress, the judge or jury must find that the defendant reasonably believed that participating in a crime (a) was necessary to avoid a specific and immediate threat of serious harm to self or others and (b) was the only way to avoid this harm. Thus, for a battered woman to prove duress, she must demonstrate her reasonable belief that criminal behavior was necessary in order to avoid the batterer's violent or abusive behavior. Describing the pattern, over the course of the relationship, of a battered woman's compliance in the context of the batterer's violence or threats can provide a framework for jury evaluation of whether the alleged criminal conduct resulted from duress or coercion.

To Support the Prosecution of Crimes Involving Domestic Violence

District attorneys may introduce evidence and testimony on battering and its effects in efforts to prosecute domestic violence perpetrators. Testimony may be used to explain a battered victim's recantation of an earlier statement, lack of cooperation with the prosecution, or other conduct of the victim. A battered victim may recant an earlier statement of abuse, often at the point when she reconciles with the batterer or when she is coerced by the batterer by threats of violence or withdrawal of economic support. In some cases, a battered woman may recant a self-incriminating statement only after the batterer has been arrested, and it is safer to do so. Testimony can be useful for explaining to the factfinder the various reasons why battered victims may respond in these ways.

To Explain Misconceptions Related to Domestic Violence

Both prosecution and defense attorneys may introduce testimony to explain to the factfinder what may be misconceptions about battering and its effects. It has been shown that lay persons generally hold misconceptions related to domestic violence. These misconceptions, when held by the triers of fact, can negate either the occurrence or seriousness of violence, as well as the victim's response of fear and intimidation.

Determining potential misconceptions relevant to a particular case depends, obviously, on the facts of that case. For example, a victim's alcohol or drug-abuse history may lead the jury to believe, erroneously, that the victim caused the battering. In another example, when a battered woman fights back against the batterer, her behavior could be construed as evidence of mutual battering, or even that she was the primary aggressor. Evidence and testimony can be useful to assist the factfinders in sorting out these issues.

The Relevance of Scientific and Clinical Knowledge Concerning Battering and Its Effects in Criminal Court Proceedings

Following is a brief review of the current "scientific, technical, or specialized knowledge" relevant to criminal cases involving battered women. As discussed above, battering and its effects have become an issue primarily in criminal cases in which (1) a battered woman is being tried for a crime and introduces a defense of self-defense, coercion, or insanity, (2) a battered woman has been charged or convicted of a crime, and evidence of battering or its effects is offered to reduce the seriousness of the charges or the severity of the sentence, or (3) a batterer is being tried for murder or assault and the battered woman's behavior or responsibility for the abuse is raised as part of the defense of the batterer. In these instances research studies of battering and its effects are relevant. Research on the dynamics of battering relationships and on a woman's perception of danger in such relationships is pertinent to the defenses of self-defense and coercion. Studies of the consequences of battering on a woman's state of mind, including traumatic stress reactions and disorders associated with battering, are relevant to an insanity defense and issues of diminished capacity. Research identifying patterns of coercive behavior in battering relationships and a victim's coping behaviors is relevant to explaining the seemingly dysfunctional behavior of battered women—an issue raised in charging and sentencing battered women and prosecuting batterers.

This review is representative of the breadth of current and relevant information. By its nature, knowledge is in a process of continual revision, based on new observations and empirical research findings. The information presented here is drawn from the interdisciplinary fields of domestic violence and traumatic stress, which reflect work in psychology, psychiatry, sociology, nursing, criminal justice, and other disciplines.

* * *

Battered Woman's Appraisal of Danger

Psychology offers a guide to understanding the processes by which an individual appraises a situation as threatening—a matter central to the legal elements of both self-defense and duress. Understanding an individual's appraisal of a situation as dangerous involves consideration of the actual threat behavior, the dangerousness of the situation, and the resources at hand for responding to that threat. Thus, most people would consider that a woman is endangered in situations in which a batterer is physically assaultive or directly threatens an imminent assault; in other situations, where the threat is not immediate, a woman's history of being battered is relevant to her perception of the dangerousness of the situation and its likely outcome. Analysis of the influence of a history of battering on a woman's appraisal of danger can contribute to understanding her reaction to a threatening situation. Where the appraisal of threat by a woman is high and/or her appraised resources for responding to threat behavior are low, an expected response would include fear or anxiety, physiological arousal, and behaviors intended either to avoid or alter the situation. Thus, testimony can be offered to assist the factfinder in understanding the battered woman's appraisal of threat, i.e., her perception of danger at the time of a criminal act, as well as her response to that threat.

Threat behavior may be considered dangerous based solely on its objective nature, considering the disparity between two individuals in size, weight, strength, and/or skill in using physical force. Examples of such threat behavior include explicit or implicit threats to harm (e.g., threats to injure, maim, kill, or sexually assault) as well as actual violent behavior (e.g., punching, pushing down a flight of stairs, sexual assault, or use of a weapon). In addition, a batterer's unique history of abuse and violence may provide his victim with added information against which to determine the meaning of his subsequent behavior. For example, intimate partners generally learn to read the subtle nuances of each other's behavior more clearly than can others. Persons who are oppressed or victimized, such as prisoners of war or hostages, have a great incentive to read their oppressor's behavior accurately. This principle applies to battered women in their abusive relationships. That is, a battered woman's appraisal of the threat implicit in a batterer's behavior is based on his pattern of prior violence and abuse. When she has been exposed to severe violence by her partner on previous occasions, she has had the unfortunate opportunity to learn the behavioral clues that signal danger. Thus, the meaning of threat behavior can best be understood in light of a woman's unique history and her knowledge of her partner's prior behavior, as well as by the objective properties of the threat behavior.

Generally, the severity of threat behavior influences the extent to which that behavior is reasonably appraised as dangerous. "Actual or threatened death or serious injury, or a threat to the physical integrity of self or others" is defined as a traumatic event within the medical and psychological community. However, once a batterer has engaged in severe violence toward his partner, any implied or low-level violence can be understood as, potentially, a reasonable and imminent threat to her physical integrity. Even in situations where minor violence or threats do not actually escalate to serious violence, it is the batterer, not the battered woman, who determines to what point the violence escalates and at what point it ceases.

The timing of threat behavior also influences the extent to which such behavior is appraised as dangerous. Sometimes the batterer's threat is perceived as certain or inevitable, but not necessarily as immediate. Some battered women report as credible their batterers' threats to kill, maim, or seriously injure them at some point in the future. Sometimes, these threats are in connection with the battered woman's stated intention or actual attempts to leave; at other times they arise from a batterer's knowledge that his partner is no longer available to him (e.g., when she has begun a new relationship or filed for divorce). This pattern of violence has been referred to as "separation abuse." In these instances, the incubation, or period of anticipation, heightens the stress or fear associated with the threat. That is, if a batterer has made threats to kill the battered woman, and she perceives this outcome to be inevitable, the passage of time since the threat serves to enhance the level of fear. Even when a battered woman attempts to cope with or in some way reduce that fear (e.g., denial, minimization, substance abuse, attempts to leave, and reports to the police), any renewed indication that the batterer is willing to act out the threat can trigger the full intensity of her fear reaction.

A battered woman's threat appraisal also can be influenced by her state of mind at the time the threat is made. Her prior exposure to violence can result in negative psychological *sequelae*, altering her state of mind in such a way as to enhance the salience of the batterer's threat. Specifically, domestic violence can lead to posttraumatic stress reactions, including posttraumatic stress disorder (PTSD), in which certain behaviors or events can cause the battered woman to act or feel as if prior severe violence were recurring, even if it is not. This experience may include "reliving the experience, illusions, hallucinations, and dissociative flashback episodes, including those that occur on awakening or when intoxicated." Additional research supports the conclusion that violence negatively impacts battered women in other ways, for example, economic loss, loss of employment, and increased health-care utilization. The scholarly literature documents the negative emotional, social, educational, and physical impact of domestic violence on children. The negative effects on children of witnessing violence can serve as an additional stressor for battered women, thus increasing their distress and/or decreasing their capacity to cope effectively.

To summarize, a battered woman's appraisal of the batterer's threat behavior can best be understood in terms of her unique history with the batterer. Of course, in some cases, an understanding of the threat is obvious, even without knowledge of such history. Knowledge about factors that influence an individual's appraisal of threat can assist the jury in determining whether a battered woman perceived a specific situation as dangerous, particularly in cases in which self-defense or the duress defense are raised. In self-defense, the battered woman claims that her use of force was justified as a response to danger; in a duress defense, the claim is that the battered woman's criminal activity was a means to avoid such danger.

Negative Psychological Consequences of Domestic Violence

An extensive and continually expanding research literature supports the assertion that domestic violence is associated with a wide range of traumatic psychological reactions. Recognition of the effects of trauma dates back more than 200 years. Trauma theory explains the psychological and physical impact of traumatic experiences, including violence, on victims. Research on a wide variety of both acute and chronic trauma has established that exposure to serious traumatic events can lead to exceptional mental states both during and following the trauma. Such altered mental states during trauma exposure can include amnesic states, in which aspects of traumatic events cannot be recalled or are otherwise blocked from consciousness, and dissociative states, in which no awareness exists of the self or of events during the course of exposure to the traumatic event. Some altered mental states following trauma exposure can include flashbacks and other forms of reexperiencing the trauma, a generalized flattening of affect to avoid overwhelming emotions associated with the trauma, and pathological feelings of shame or guilt ("survivor guilt"). Such exceptional mental states associated with psychological reactions to trauma exposure can explain puzzling aspects of the battered woman's state of mind and behavior, either during the abusive relationship or in relation to alleged criminal behavior associated with the trauma of battering. In criminal cases in which a woman is accused of assaulting her abuser, the woman's psychological reactions to chronic or acute battering during the period preceding or during the assault may so impair mental capacity as to support a defense of insanity: the claim that a battered woman's mental condition impaired her capacity to such an extent that either she did not understand the nature and consequences of what she was doing, or she did not understand that what she was doing was wrong. Similarly, traumatic psychological reactions can explain some puzzling patterns of behavior following assaults that may create an impression of culpability, such as an inability to remember events and their sequence, the absence of emotional reactions to the events, hostile or angry reactions, or a wish to be punished for the assault.

A woman's mental state during an assault on her abuser can be determined by her immediate intense reaction to perceived danger or by posttraumatic reactions to prior trauma. Traumatic stress reactions are initiated when an individual's normal coping processes are overwhelmed during exposure to events that threaten physical harm or an individual's life, psychic identity, or integrity. Traumatic stress reactions can be initiated by such threats to self or valued others. Traumatic stress responses during traumatic events can include fear or terror, dissociation, and amnesia. Altered mental states and dysfunctional behavior can continue in the aftermath of exposure to traumatic events as posttraumatic stress reactions. Chronic forms of posttraumatic stress reactions may meet the criteria for the psychiatric diagnosis of posttraumatic stress disorder, the symptoms of which include persistent reexperiencing of the traumatic events in such forms as flashbacks, distressing dreams, or reenactments of the traumatic events; persistent avoiding of stimuli associated with the traumatic event and/or a numbing of general responsiveness; and persistent symptoms of heightened physiological arousal as manifested in, for example, hypervigilance, irritability, or sleep difficulties.

As described briefly in the preceding section, a battered woman's perception of danger in certain circumstances can reflect previous experience of psychic trauma. Thus, when a battered woman suffers from posttraumatic stress disorder based on previous violence in either a current or former relationship, she may experience a new situation as dangerous due to *reexperiencing* prior trauma through flashbacks and similar psychological reactions. In this example, the battered woman's experience of fear is genuine. However, it is based not on the objective reality of the current situation but, rather, on her psychological reaction, triggered by an event similar to or symbolic of a previously traumatic (e.g., violent) experience. In some cases, the triggering process may occur upon awakening or while intoxicated. Consider an example where, on a prior occasion, a battered woman had been severely beaten by her husband following an argument about her work. At some later point when her husband begins to talk about her work, the woman may experience the situation, specifically the fear, as though the beating was recurring. In this example, the fear may be due not to any actual danger of the moment but, rather, to a triggering of fear that originated from previous danger or harm. This situation must be distinguished from the more common one described earlier in which the battered woman's perception of danger is based on her ability to detect cues in her partner's behavior that signal actual impending danger. Similarly, physiological *hyperarousal*, which can be manifested as hypervigilance for signs of danger in the environment, physical exhaustion and psychic confusion from sleep deprivation, and paranoid states, can affect her perception of events or her ability to cope with perceived threats.

In criminal proceedings in which a woman is accused of assaulting her abuser, posttraumatic psychological reactions and accompanying behavioral responses can affect the woman's demeanor and response to the offense and her ability to aid in her defense. Such reactions and behavior can include nightmares and flashbacks, avoidance of thoughts and feelings associated with the trauma, difficulty with concentration or memory, sleep disturbance, depression, low self-esteem, suicidal thoughts, anxiety, dissociation, anger or irritability, somatic or health problems, social withdrawal, and substance abuse. Thus, presence of a posttraumatic stress reaction may explain a battered woman's apparent lack of, or atypical, emotion when testifying or talking about her experience with violence. In some cases, the battered woman may report these events as though she has no feeling or emotion related to them, as if on "automatic pilot." The post traumatic psychological response of dissociation, or the separation of feelings about an event from the knowledge of it, can account for this behavior. In other cases, a woman's flat affect may be explained by attempts to avoid thinking or experiencing emotions associated with her traumatic experiences. In other instances yet, the battered woman may talk about her battering experience with anger or hostility. This behavior may be misinterpreted to suggest that she is an aggressor or, at least, an unlikely victim. This explanation fails to account for the normal reaction of anger as part of the psychological *sequelae* to the experience of a traumatic event. In fact, it can be an indication of progress in the health process following victimization when a battered woman recognizes her anger at her partner for his violent behavior toward her.

Some women are unable to remember traumatic aspects of the battering or their actions during such episodes even when they want to, due, in part, to a dissociative amnesia resulting from exposure to violence—or even to neurological damage associated with head injuries resulting from the battering. Therefore, they are unable to participate effectively in their own defense. In other cases, posttraumatic guilt, shame, or depression may seriously weaken a woman's desire to avoid punishment for the assault.

Although a framework for describing negative psychological consequences of battering that focuses on traumatic stress reactions may explain many of the behavioral and psychological responses of battered women, especially those who have experienced chronic and severe violence, it should be emphasized that a wide range of other responses may be involved. Many battered women have the personal resources to cope with their battering experience, ensure eventual safety for themselves and their children, and function with minimal mental health problems. Another common mental health outcome of battering is acute or chronic depression. In many cases, symptoms of depression (or of many other mental health problems experienced by battered women) will be maintained during the battering relationship but will quickly or gradually remit after the woman has been able to terminate the abusive relationship. It is also often the case that mental health problems will emerge after termination of an abusive relationship due to stress (e.g., serious loss of income from leaving the relationship, locating employment and child care, and lack of an intimate relationship) associated with establishing an independent life for the woman and any children.

Offering evidence of posttraumatic stress reactions or other mental health problems or disorders as an explanation for the reactions or behavior of a particular battered woman, of course, requires that an individual, face-to-face evaluation be made by a qualified expert. Possible clinical diagnoses relevant to diminished mental capacity that, if sufficiently serious, have been associated with battering include anxiety disorders (including PTSD and acute stress disorder (ASD)), dissociative disorders, brief psychotic disorder, disorders of extreme stress not otherwise specified (DESNOS), depressive disorders, and substance-related disorders. Of course, symptoms of these disorders may exist prior to the traumatic experience and, therefore, are not caused by it. However, preexisting disorders may be exacerbated by the traumatic experience of violence.

Behavioral Patterns of Victims of Domestic Battering

One consequence of the negative psychological and social *sequelae* to battering is that victims sometimes engage in patterns of behavior that may be misinterpreted if not considered within the context of a battering relationship. Among such behavior patterns are continued involvement in an abusive relationship, use of physical aggression toward an abuser, and lack of cooperation in the prosecution of an abuser. These behaviors may be misinterpreted in legal proceedings as indicating that the alleged abuse was not serious or that the abused woman is primarily or partly responsible for the abusive behavior that occurred.

Continued Involvement in an Abusive Relationship: A frequently raised issue in legal proceedings is why a battered woman did not terminate an allegedly abusive relationship or, if she did leave, why she returned to the abuser. An implication that may be drawn is that the abusiveness of the relationship is being exaggerated by the victim, as demonstrated by her failure to terminate the relationship. A number of factors or obstacles make terminating an abusive relationship difficult. Major factors addressed here include a lack of economic and other tangible resources, fear of retaliation, and emotional attachment. Other factors include the desire to provide children with a father in the home, shame and embarrassment, and denial of the severity of abuse.

Economic Factors: The lack of economic and other tangible resources makes leaving or staying away difficult for some battered women. Without money, transportation, shelter, child care, and a source of income or support, a woman leaving an abusive relationship has no means of providing for herself and her children. Without these resources, she may risk losing custody of her children to the batterer or some other family member with more adequate means. Resources, such as shelters and advocacy services, to aid battered women in leaving abusive relationships and establishing independent households are severely limited in most communities throughout the country.

Separation Abuse and Fear of Retaliation: Another reason that may keep battered women from leaving abusive relationships has been termed "separation abuse"—retaliation for a woman's efforts to separate from the abuser or to end the relationship. The battered woman may fear retaliation through harm to herself, her children, other family members, friends, or coworkers. Even when a battered woman is able to secure safety for herself, she may not be able to do the same for parents or coworkers; when the batterer is unable to attain access to the battered woman, he may turn to other important people in her life.

When battered women are killed, they are more likely than not to be separated from their batterers at the time of death. Jealousy and possessiveness on the part of the batterer are common in domestic homicides. Thus, a battered woman's fear that her abusive partner will escalate his violence toward her at the point she attempts to separate from or end the relationship with him is validated, generally, by homicide statistics.

A battered woman may fear retaliation through the batterer's threat to seek custody of her children or to keep them from her by kidnapping or other means. It has been shown that batterers seek custody at higher rates and are awarded custody no less often than nonbatterers. There is often no more powerful obstacle to terminating an abusive relationship than when a woman faces the possibility that her children will be taken from her either through custody decisions that favor the batterer, kidnapping, or homicide. A threat that the batterer will continue his coercion of the battered woman through manipulation of the courts in custody battles and other litigation can represent a significant barrier to terminating a violent relationship.

Emotional Attachment: Emotional attachment is yet another significant factor in explaining why battered women are often reluctant to leave an abusive relationship. In spite of past violence, some women hope that their abusive partner's violence will cease, much in the way that marital partners maintain hope that difficulties in a troubled marriage will be resolved. For battered women, the hope is often built on the batterer's apologies, promises, kindnesses, and gifts during the contrite phase of the cycle of violence. Another explanation for a battered woman's emotional attachment to an abusive partner is based on traumatic bonding, a process similar to that which occurs in captive prisoners of war or hostage victims. In traumatic bonding, a battered woman who experiences chronic and escalating violence can come to see the batterer as all-powerful, on the one hand, and to believe that she cannot survive without him, on the other.

Understanding these and other obstacles to leaving or staying away from a battering relationship assists the factfinder in considering the context of a battered woman's efforts to resist, escape, and cope with a violent relationship. Without an appreciation of this context, the factfinder's deliberations may rest on faulty assumptions, for example, that a woman who remains in an alleged abusive relationship has exaggerated or lied about the fact of violence.

Victim's Use of Physical Aggression Toward the Abuser: Stereotypes and misconceptions about battered women interfere with the factfinder's ability to consider relevant issues in a criminal case involving domestic violence. One common stereotype is the view that battered women are passive or helpless, that they do not call the police, fight back, or actively resist the violence against them. Although early observations portrayed battered women as passive and suffering from learned helplessness, more recent work documents that many battered women engage in active efforts to resist, avoid, escape, and stop the violence against them.

A recent Bureau of Justice Statistics study reported that 40 percent of battered women fought back physically, and another 40 percent fought back verbally. Results from other studies support the conclusion that it is not uncommon for battered women to resist the batterer's violent behavior. However, battered women's efforts to protect themselves have been shown to make the situation worse at times, escalating the batterer's violent behavior and increasing the odds of injury to the victim. Thus, evidence of a battered woman's use of physical or verbal aggression does not necessarily imply that she was the primary aggressor or that battering was mutual.

The National Crime Victimization Survey found that more than 50 percent of women in the interviewed sample who had been assaulted by an intimate partner had reported at least one assault to the police, although police response to domestic violence (as opposed to stranger violence) is slower and less likely to result in a written report or a search for evidence. Many battered women, however, are reluctant to call police based on concerns about racial or ethnic discrimination against their male partners by police or court systems. Further, social norms maintaining that violence in the home is a private matter are also obstacles to calling the police.

Thus, it should not be assumed that a battered woman who has remained in an abusive relationship has been passive or helpless in that situation. Rather, the battered woman's efforts to respond to the violence against her and her children in the past and the outcome of those efforts should be examined in a criminal case involving a battered woman. However, based on a number of factors outside of the battered woman's control (e.g., police response, court decisions regarding custody and visitation, economic resources), and, in spite of the battered woman's previous efforts, the threat of violence may continue or even escalate.

Battered women actively respond to violence and abuse in many other ways, both during an ongoing assault and subsequent to it. These include telling family or friends about the violence, fleeing from the batterer, legally separating and divorcing, seeking shelter residence, filing for civil protection orders, complying with the batterer's demands, hiding from the batterer, and others. Ironically, maintaining contact with the batterer, in order to minimize or more accurately gauge the level of danger, is a strategy employed by some battered women. This type of information can inform the factfinder's analysis about a particular battered woman's response to violence and abuse in the criminal case at hand.

Lack of Cooperation in Prosecuting the Abuser: Battered women may recant previous reports or testimony about the batterer's violence or may not cooperate with a district attorney in prosecuting a batterer. Various factors may explain this behavior, including the victim's psychological reactions to violence. For example, fear of the batterer can explain why a battered woman may attempt to "protect" him from negative legal consequences of his violent behavior. Even when a battered woman has called the police, she may attempt to avoid the batterer's retaliation by refusing to pursue criminal charges or to testify against him at trial.

Another explanation of a battered woman's reluctance or refusal to be involved in the prosecution derives from her avoidance reactions associated with PTSD. She may miss appointments to talk with the prosecutor or fail to appear in court. By avoiding having to remember or to talk about prior violence, the battered woman may also effectively postpone experiencing painful and distressing emotions.

CRITIQUE OF "BATTERED WOMAN SYNDROME"

Evidence and testimony in criminal cases concerning battering and its effects have often been presented in an attempt to establish that the behavior of an alleged victim falls within the parameters of the "battered woman syndrome." However, the term "battered woman syndrome" does not adequately reflect the breadth or nature of knowledge concerning battering and its effects. The scientific and clinical literature offers a large body of information relevant to various issues considered by the factfinder in criminal cases involving battered women, and the term "battered woman syndrome" has been used to signal a shorthand reference to that body of knowledge. However, use of the term "battered woman syndrome," in the context of the knowledge developed within the past 20 years, is imprecise and, therefore, misleading. The knowledge pertaining to battering and its effects does not rest on a singular construct, as the term "battered woman syndrome" implies. Thus, the term "battered woman syndrome" is not adequate to refer to the scientific and clinical knowledge concerning battering and its effects germane to criminal cases involving battered women.

There is no "battered woman defense," *per se*. Offering evidence of the effects of battering does not, in itself, constitute a legal defense. That is, the question of "battered woman syndrome" is not the ultimate issue in a criminal case involving a battered woman. Rather, testimony about battering and its effects is offered to assist factfinders in their determination of the ultimate issues, which are case-specific and are reflected in questions such as:

- Did a battered woman reasonably believe she was in danger of harm when she assaulted her abuser?

- Did a batterer threaten or coerce the battered woman into participating unwillingly in a crime?

Following is a discussion of the problems that exist with use of the term "battered woman syndrome" in criminal cases involving battered women.

As conceptualized in the late 1970s, "battered woman syndrome" encompassed a condition of "learned helplessness" in the battered woman that was hypothesized to explain her inability to protect herself against the batterer's violence. Application of the learned helplessness theory to situations involving battered women who face actual danger has been challenged as a misinterpretation of the original learned helplessness theory. Further, as discussed above, empirical evidence contradicts the view of battered women as helpless or passive victims; rather, it supports the idea that battered women continue to make active efforts to resist, escape, or avoid violence.

Another early formulation of "battered woman syndrome" incorporated the cycle of violence theory. The cyclical pattern of the batterer's behavior, including phases of tension building, acute battering, and contrition, was cited to explain women's reluctance to leave battering relationships. Where the cycle of violence is identified within a particular battering relationship, it may be useful to explain why, in spite of repeated occurrences of violence, the battered woman remained in, or returned to, an abusive relationship. Alternatively, it may be useful to explain why she was able to recognize the inevitability of a subsequent violent episode. Nevertheless, the scientific literature does not support a universal "cycle-of-violence" pattern in battering relationships, although this pattern is recognized in some relationships. As discussed previously, some battered women report violence that occurs suddenly with no observable tension-building phase prior to a beating. Nor are all battering relationships characterized by a contrite, loving phase following a beating. Some women report no history of apologies or acts of kindness, while others report that, over time, these behaviors following a beating have diminished. Perhaps most importantly, a "cycle of violence" is not necessary to define a battering relationship or explain why a battered woman remains within it.

More recently, "battered woman syndrome" has been construed as indicating that a battered woman suffers from PTSD as a reaction to her experience of physical violence. A diagnosis of PTSD requires a specific constellation of symptoms. These include intrusion of the traumatic memory into the individual's consciousness, avoidance of thoughts and feelings associated with the traumatic experience or numbing of general responsiveness, and symptoms characterized by increased arousal (e.g., difficulty sleeping or concentrating, hypervigilance). Prevalence studies of battered women have found the rates of PTSD range from 31 to 84 percent. Diagnosed in a particular case, PTSD may be relevant to a number of issues in that case. For example, indication that the battered woman suffered PTSD at the time of an alleged criminal act may help the factfinder to understand her state of mind. However, nothing in the scholarly literature suggests that PTSD is necessary, generally, to establish the relevance of battering and its effects to the various elements of criminal cases involving battered women.

Restricting the definition of "battered woman syndrome" to PTSD is problematic. Within the last decade, the scientific and clinical literature has documented a broad range of emotional, cognitive, physiological, and behavioral *sequelae* to traumatic events such as battering. Our understanding of the complexity and variability of traumatic response to violence continues to increase rapidly. Any of these reactions to trauma, when characteristic of the battered woman, may be relevant to the factfinder in considering the various issues in the case. Limiting the scope of consideration of the mental health consequences of battering to PTSD alone excludes other potentially relevant and important information necessary for the factfinders in their deliberations.

Finally, the term "battered woman syndrome" evokes a stereotypic image of battered women as pathological or maladjusted. Accordingly, expert testimony can mistakenly suggest to the factfinder that it is a battered woman's aberrant psychological condition that explains, for example, her acting in self-defense, committing a crime under duress, or recanting her testimony about her partner's battering. While psychological trauma associated with battering may be central to this explanation by the expert witness, the battered woman's greater acuity in detecting danger from an abusive partner, in some cases, is the more salient factor. Generally, the term "battered woman syndrome" fails to incorporate the social and psychological context necessary to "see what she sees and know what she knows" in considering the defendant's actions.

In sum, "battered woman syndrome" is an inadequate term to represent the scientific and clinical knowledge concerning battering and its effects. Nevertheless, evidence and testimony on battering and its effects serves an important function in assisting the factfinder to consider the context of a battered woman's actions.

Expert Testimony in Cases Involving Battered Women

Expert testimony on battering and its effects is introduced in criminal cases involving battered women by both defense counsel and prosecuting attorneys. It is used by defense counsel to support various types of criminal defenses including self-defense, duress, and insanity. Expert witness testimony may also be used by the defense in conjunction with the sentencing phases of a trial for purposes of mitigation. Prosecutors use expert testimony in domestic violence prosecution cases to explain such matters as the battered victim's recantation or lack of cooperation with the prosecution. Further, both the prosecution and defense use expert witness testimony to provide an explanation for what may be misconceptions about battered women, battering, and its effects. It is not the role of the expert witness to determine the ultimate issues (for example, whether it was reasonable for the battered woman to have held the perception that she was in danger). However, expert testimony is offered to assist in the determination of these issues.

A general framework for admissibility of expert testimony in criminal cases is provided in Rule 702 of the congressionally enacted Federal Rules of Evidence:

If scientific, technical, or other specialized knowledge will assist the trier of fact to understand the evidence or to determine a fact in issue, a witness qualified as an expert by knowledge, skill, experience, training, or education, may testify thereto in the form of an opinion or otherwise.

It follows, therefore, that the framework for expert testimony in criminal cases involving battered women rests on the "scientific, technical, and other specialized knowledge base" concerning battering and its effects. Thus, information based on the expert witness' "knowledge, skill, experience, training, or education" provides the basis for his or her expert testimony.

A 1977 Supreme Court of Washington decision, *State v. Wanrow*,[91] ruled in a self defense case involving a woman defendant that she was "entitled to have the jury consider her actions in the light of her own perceptions of the situation." Counsel successfully argued that the jury instructions offered at trial did not take into account the woman's perspective, thereby failing to correctly apply the existing standard of self-defense: "requiring the jury to consider the defendant's action seeing what (s)he sees and knowing what (s)he, knows,' taking into account all the circumstances as (s)he knew them at the time."

In addition to testimony offered by the defendant, evidence concerning a battered woman's perceptions and the relevant circumstances in a situation in which she has been charged with a crime can be introduced through expert testimony. Such expert testimony has been introduced in criminal cases involving battered women since the late 1970s. Based on a recent analysis, "expert testimony on battering and its effects is admissible, at least to some degree, or has been admitted (without any discussion of the standards for admissibility) in every state." Expert testimony in criminal cases involving battered women was developed initially to explain "the common experiences of, and the impact of repeated abuse on, battered women." That is, expert testimony is offered to show the trier of fact the context of a battered woman's actions. This type of expert testimony, generally, has been referred to as social framework testimony: "employing social science research . . . to provide a social and psychological context in which the trier can understand and evaluate claims about the ultimate fact."

Expert testimony offered in cases involving battered women is either general or case-specific. A number of considerations influence which form of expert testimony is offered in a particular case. These include the facts of the case, case law or state statutes governing expert evaluation and testimony, available resources, and case strategy. General testimony is based on an understanding of the scientific and clinical knowledge about domestic violence and its effects on battered women. In this type of testimony, there is no attempt to form opinions or conclusions related to a specific case.

91. 88 Wash. 2d 221, 559 P. 2d 548   (1977).

Case-specific testimony provides information about a particular battered woman and the context in which domestic violence occurred; it places the unique facts of a specific case in a framework of what is known in the literature about battering and its effects. Case-specific testimony, or conclusions about a particular battered woman, requires a face-to-face evaluation of the battered woman, in addition to a review of relevant documents and other information. A suggested approach to case-specific expert testimony about battering and its effects is patterned after a clinical hypothesis-testing model of assessment. Based on consultation with the attorney, an expert can generate a set of questions, or hypotheses, related to battering and/or its effects relevant to a particular case. The expert can then analyze data pertaining to the particular battered woman, relying on all the information obtained in the evaluation process. This information is later distilled either to support or refute the questions to which the expert will be asked to respond. This approach fits a model of clinical assessment routinely used in empirically based clinical practice. Furthermore, the process is straightforward and makes explicit the relevant questions for inquiry by the expert witness.

CONCLUSIONS

The body of relevant scientific and clinical knowledge in the scholarly literature strongly supports the validity of considering battering as a factor in the reactions and behavior of victims of domestic violence. Evidence and testimony about battering and its effects provide information germane to factfinders' deliberations in criminal cases involving battered women. There exists an extensive body of scientific and specialized knowledge derived from the disciplines of the social, behavioral, and health sciences, that contributes to an understanding of domestic violence and traumatic stress reactions.

Although the term "battered woman syndrome" is inadequate to characterize either the reactions or behaviors of battered women, much progress has been made under this rubric toward the admissibility of battering and its effects as considerations in criminal trials. A more accurate representation of battering and its effects includes a range of issues on the nature and dynamics of battering, the effects of violence, battered women's responses to violence, and the social and psychological context in which domestic violence occurs. These issues are relevant in charging, trying, and sentencing battered women in criminal cases involving battering and in prosecuting batterers.

Expert testimony on battering and its effects is supported by an extensive body of scientific knowledge on the dynamics and consequences of domestic violence; this knowledge base will continue to expand with advances in the fields of social, behavioral, and health sciences. An effective framework for expert testimony must permit both general and specific application of research findings to cases involving battered women.

JANET PARRISH, TREND ANALYSIS: EXPERT TESTIMONY ON BATTERING AND ITS EFFECTS IN CRIMINAL CASES (HIGHLIGHTS)

In National Institute of Justice, The Validity and Use of Evidence
Concerning Battering and Its Effects in Criminal Trials, U.S.
Department of Justice ix-xii (1996)

An analysis of 238 state court decisions, 31 federal court decisions, as well as 12 state statutes addressed the admissibility of expert testimony on battering and its effects in criminal trials, the types of cases in which expert testimony was admitted, the showing necessary to introduce such testimony, the scope and relevance of expert testimony, the circumstances under which such testimony triggers an adverse psychological examination, and the disposition of cases on appeal.

With respect to admissibility, expert testimony on battering and its effects is admissible, at least to some degree, or has been admitted (without any discussion of the standards for admissibility), in each of the 50 states plus the District of Columbia.

● Of the 19 federal courts that have considered the issue, all but three have admitted expert testimony on battering and its effects in at least some cases.

● Twelve states, moreover, have enacted statutes providing for admissibility of expert testimony, although in two states, the courts have interpreted these statutes in a restrictive fashion, limiting the admissibility of expert testimony to cases in which self-defense is claimed.

● However, 18 states have excluded expert testimony in some cases. Only in Wyoming is there still doubt under case law as to the testimony's admissibility, but Wyoming provides for the admissibility of expert testimony by statute.

While the types of cases in which expert testimony on battering and its effects is admitted can vary, it is most readily accepted by state courts (i.e., in 90 percent of the states) in cases involving traditional self-defense situations.

● A substantial number of state courts have also admitted expert testimony in nontraditional self-defense situations (e.g., when a battered woman kills her batterer when he is asleep or hires a third party to kill him), in non-self-defense cases (e.g., where duress is asserted as a defense), and when offered by the prosecution (e.g., to explain a battered woman complainant's prior inconsistent statements).

● Of the 19 federal courts admitting expert testimony, two-thirds have done so in a duress case, while more than one-third have done so in traditional self-defense cases.

With respect to the showing necessary to introduce expert testimony, nearly 40 percent of the states require that the defendant raise a self-defense claim in order to introduce expert testimony on battering and its effects; one third of the states have explicitly required that the proffered expert must be properly qualified as such.

Although there is significant consensus among the courts as to the issues on which expert testimony on battering and its effects is relevant and admissible, case-by-case variations also exist within a given jurisdiction that depend on the nature of the case, the specific facts of the case, or the specific issues raised by the defendant on appeal.

● Over three-quarters of the states have found expert testimony admissible to prove the defendant is a battered woman or that she "suffers from 'battered woman syndrome.' " Almost 70 percent of the states have found "generic" expert testimony admissible in order to explain battering and its effects generally, without reference to a specific defendant. Twenty percent of the states, however, explicitly preclude experts from testifying that the defendant is a battered woman or "suffering from 'battered woman syndrome.' "

● Nearly 70 percent of the states have found expert testimony relevant to supporting a self-defense claim; nearly 70 percent of the states also agree that expert testimony is relevant to the issue of the defendant's state of mind at the time of the charged crime.

● Two-thirds of the states consider expert testimony on battering and its effects relevant to the question of why the defendant did not leave the battering relationship or to explain other conduct, such as acts performed under duress. A similar proportion of the federal courts have found the testimony relevant for these purposes.

● A significant minority of the states have explicitly noted that the testimony is admissible to rebut common myths and misperceptions about battered women (33 percent), to prove a defendant's diminished capacity or lack of intent (30 percent), to bolster the defendant's credibility (25 percent), or to show the existence of mitigating factors in the defendant's favor at the sentencing phase of the trial (20 percent). A similar proportion of the federal courts admitting such expert testimony have also found it relevant for these purposes.

Twenty-two percent of the states have ruled on the issue of whether offering expert testimony on battering subjects a defendant to an adverse psychological examination by the prosecution's expert. All but one found that introducing expert testimony does trigger an adverse examination. Of the three federal courts that have considered this question, two have found that introduction of expert testimony does subject the defendant to an adverse examination.

With respect to case disposition on appeal, the appeals of 152 battered women defendants in state courts were analyzed for this study; 63 percent resulted in affirmance of the conviction and/or sentence, even though expert testimony on battering and its effects was admitted or found admissible in 71 percent of the affirmances.

• These findings are considered strong evidence that the defense's use of, or the court's awareness of, expert testimony on battering and its effects in no way equates to an acquittal on the criminal charges lodged against a battered woman defendant.

• Moreover, of those appeals in state courts that resulted in reversals, less than half were reversed because of erroneous exclusion of, limitation of, or failure of counsel to present, expert testimony.

• Of the 22 appeals of battered women's cases heard in federal courts, more than three-quarters resulted in affirmances of convictions and/or sentences.

ELLEN LEESFIELD & MARY ANN DUTTON–DOUGLAS, "FAITH AND LOVE": USE OF THE BATTERED WOMAN SYNDROME TO NEGATE SPECIFIC INTENT

The Champion 9–12 (1989).

Q. Did Jane Doe report to you, as a part of your examination, her attitude or consciousness towards John Smith?

A. Yes.

Q. What was that attitude or consciousness?

A. The attitude about John Smith, initially, was one of faith and love.... She reported that she had great confidence in him—trust in him, and believed that he had her best interest at heart and would not harm her even though at the time he was in fact reported to be physically abusing her.

THE BACKGROUND

Jane Doe and John Smith were once lovers and friends. But by the time Jane Doe reached my office, her lover is a cooperating witness against her in a check fraud case. Apparently, he had stolen blank money orders from packages at his work at Eastern Airlines and brought them home to Jane. Jane tells me that John had instructed her to fill out the money orders in the name of anyone she pleased and endorse the backs accordingly. I ask her whether she had thought it strange that John had brought home blank money orders, that any name could be filled in on the blank forms, or that he did not fill them in himself. She answers that John had told her that the money orders were repayment for a loan from his friend and that money orders were "good," no matter whose name was on them.

Although Jane doesn't strike me as dull or stupid, her actions appear to be either stupid or knowingly criminal. In fact, she appears quite bright and worldly at times. Therefore, I try a bright and worldly approach that goes something like this:

"This is really a probationable offense. You are a first offender and the sum total here does not amount to much more than $3,000. John is testifying against you, and a third co-defendant is pleading guilty. We have a fairly kind sentencing judge—so long as we don't go to trial and aggravate him. Now, are you sure you didn't know these checks were stolen?

Her answer: a flat "no. John told me they were all right," she says.

I don't know why I ask this question. Perhaps it is her poor eye contact. Maybe it's the way she hangs her head, which bobs and bounces like the heads on one of those dolls that, when touched, bobs incessantly. Moreover, she seems to be a somewhat intelligent women; how could a somewhat intelligent women be fiercely loyal to a dumb idea—that it was reasonable to have believed that the kind of behavior she was led into had been "all right" and that this man who is now testifying against her—would not have done anything to "hurt her?"

I ask whether John had been physically abusive to her. Her answer is slow in coming. With an ironic smile, she replies, "I guess you could say that." "How often?" I inquire.

"Regularly."

Upon further inquiry, I learn that during their last year together, John had broken her nose on one occasion and had bruised her fairly badly on others. Sometimes, there were periods when he did not physically abuse her, but he had always screamed and threatened her. Now, I *think* I understand: "So, he *forced* you to sign the checks," I conclude.

"No," she answers flatly, "John said the checks were O. K., so I believed the checks were O.K."

I decided to have Jane evaluated, for I felt a little "out of my field." I conferred with Dr. Lenore Walker and Dr. Mary Ann Dutton–Douglas—two psychologists who are experts in the field of battered women. Since these experts were both unavailable at the time of trial, I called on Dr. Leonard Haber, a Miami forensic psychologist, who has examined patients for the defense, the prosecution, and the courts on hundreds of occasions concerning family violence.

I asked Dr. Haber to evaluate Jane Doe, generally looking for any abnormalities and particularly focusing on whether Jane exhibited patterns associated with Battered Woman Syndrome (BWS).

The answer to my inquiry concerning Battered Woman Syndrome was positive. Dr. Haber also confirmed that Jane was, as I had guessed, above-average in intelligence. What, if anything, was the relationship between my client "qualifying" as a battered woman and any defenses she may have to a non-violent crime of specific intent (fraud)? Was it possible that the psychological effect of being consistently physically and psychologically battered had had such an impact on her judgment that she believed her batterer, despite certain "red flags" of reality?

The specific theory, which evolved after a re-evaluation of my client and consultation with the experts, was that my client, as a victim of Battered Woman Syndrome, more readily adopted the reality offered by her batterer. It was a concept that would not be easily understood by a jury unless an expert walked them through it. For a jury to decide this issue accurately, they should have a chance to hear the testimony of an expert.

The Motion

I filed Notice of Expert Testimony, as required by Fed. R. Crim. Proc. 12.2(b). The government objected by Motion in Limine. Citing *U.S. v. Bright*[2] the gravamen of the government's objection to such testimony was that it should be precluded, absent the presence of a mental disease or defect. Moreover, the government argued that such testimony would violate Fed. R. Evid. 704(b)'s ban on expert opinion as to ultimate issues and that, in any case, the testimony of the expert would be cumulative for the defendant and merely confusing to the jury.

I responded that the testimony was properly admissible under Fed. R. Evid. 702's "assist the jury" standard; I found no cases directly on point but a handful of "expert" cases were helpful, and I could look forward to an intelligent judge, mindful of the defendant's rights.

The hurdles of admissibility lined up as the following questions: (1) Does the testimony regarding BWS meet the *Frye*[7] test? (2) Is the testimony needed to assist the trier of fact? (3) Will the testimony violate Rule 704(b)? To get over the first two hurdles of admissibility—acceptance in the scientific community and helpfulness to the trier of fact, I prepared for the hearing by arming myself with full knowledge of Battered Woman's Syndrome and the expert's role in testifying at trial. Dr. Dutton–Douglas's expertise was very helpful in this preparation.

BWS

What Is It?

Battered Woman Syndrome (BWS) refers to the psychological *sequelae* of victimization by physical, sexual, and psychological abuse from an intimate partner. Effects of abuse can be conceptualized to include the emotional, cognitive, physiological, and behavioral responses that follow each abuse occurrence and are presumably related to it.

Battered women engage in specific behaviors that represent efforts to avoid, escape, or otherwise cope with the abuse as well as its effect. Some efforts to cope with the abuse include compliance with the batterer's demands, assertion of the unacceptability of violence, and addictive use of food, alcohol, and drugs, including prescription medications. Self-destructive behavior, such as bulimia and suicide may occur. Ultimately, fighting back, including self-defense by homicide, can occur.

Why an Expert Should Testify

Use of an expert witness to testify about Battered Woman Syndrome is potentially useful in a variety of legal contexts. An expert will likely

---

2. United States v. Bright, 517 F.2d 584 (2d Cir.1975).

7. Frye v. United States, 293 F. 1013 (D.C.1923).

render an opinion about three issues: (1) Is the woman likely a battered woman? (2) Does she exhibit indicators of Battered Woman Syndrome? (3) What is the relationship between Battered Woman Syndrome and the alleged criminal behavior with which she is charged? The question of whether the battered woman actually engaged in the specific behavior for which she is criminally charged is often not at issue. More often issue is the question of whether she was justified in engaging in such behavior (in the case of justifiable homicide), whether she did so under duress, or whether she formed the intent necessary to define the action as criminal.

The first question, whether or not the defendant is a battered woman, is often aided by evidence such as police reports, hospital records, or the testimony of witnesses or those who had prior knowledge of the abuse.

Although important, the second question, whether the battered woman suffers from Battered Woman Syndrome, is also really the primary issue at hand.

It is with regard to the third question, concerning the functional relationship between the alleged criminal activity and the experience of battering, that the expert witness is most needed. Although a particular woman may be battered and, additionally, may suffer from Battered Woman Syndrome, these phenomena may or may not be useful in explaining her alleged criminal behavior. The expert witness can provide an important understanding of this connection—a connection that the lay juror, without help, may not see. The central issue is how the alleged criminal behavior is within the battered woman's psychological reality and whether her battering experience and its aftermath is functionally related to it. Of particular importance in providing this explanation is understanding the battered woman's perception of impending danger, her learned response of compliance—even with behaviors that are objectionable to her—as a means of surviving or reducing even more threatening consequences, and *her tendency to adopt the reality of her batterer, even in the face of obvious cognitive distortions.* Only by placing the criminal activity in the context of these phenomena can one clearly understand the battered woman's behavior.

Acceptance in Scientific Community

The American Psychological Association filed an *amicus* brief in the case of *Hawthorne v. State.*[8] The APA's *amicus* provided a clear statement supporting the contention that Battered Woman Syndrome is accepted within the scientific community. There are hundreds of articles available in professional journals describing the effects of various forms of family violence, including woman battering, on its victims. Expert testimony on BWS is now widely accepted in criminal defense cases.

Moreover, Post–Traumatic Stress Disorder is a formal diagnostic term used to identify symptoms associated with having experienced

---

8. Hawthorne v. State, 470 So.2d 770 (Fla.Dist.Ct.App.1985). The APA's Amicus Brief is available from Bruce J. Ennis, Washington, D.C.

trauma. These symptoms are the result of the physical, sexual, and psychological abuse experienced by women from their intimate partners.

How Is BWS Evaluated?

A complete evaluation of BWS requires a combination of an extensive clinical interview as well as psychological testing. Interviews of significant other persons (family, neighbors) and review of documents (police reports, hospital records) are also useful.

The clinical interview is necessary to establish the history and patterning of victimization experienced by the battered woman as well as a developmental history of the relationship between the victim and her batterer generally.

How Does BWS Distort Perceptions?

Cognitive distortions are commonly found in trauma victims of all kinds, including battered women. One particular type of distortion is the minimization or denial of the severity of violence or likelihood of its recurrence. This distortion likely functions to reduce the fear and anxiety that would be present were there a realistic appraisal of danger.

Another type of distortion of reality is when the battered woman adopts the reality as presented to her by her abusive partner. The abuser may attempt to control his victim by challenging the reality of her feelings or thoughts. Further, he may even distort reality based on knowledge or sensation (having seen or heard certain events). One actual example involved the batterer's tying a string across a doorway through which his wife walked and consequently tripped. It was only after his death and several months of counseling that she realized he had deliberately placed the obstacle in her path in an attempt to make her feel as though she were clumsy. Another very common example is the distortion in the battered woman's perception of herself, such as her body or her abilities, created by the batterer's seemingly deliberate actions in this direction. In spite of the social validation received for her physical appearance or the fact that she may have financially supported the household by her successful employment, the battered woman may believe her batterer's contentions about these matters. The psychological control that the batterer is often able to achieve is very similar to the effects of brainwashing seen in examples of hostage or prisoner of war situations.

In the hearing on the Government's motion, the judge admitted the expert testimony and allowed the defense of Battered Woman Syndrome to negate specific intent. Citing *U.S. v. Frisbee*,[13] he cautioned the defense, as does *Frisbee*, to avoid leading the expert down the path toward the "ultimate issue."

Defendant may offer expert testimony concerning whether [she] could have possessed the requisite mental intent to have committed

13. United States v. Frisbee, 623 F.Supp. 1217, 1222–24 (D.Cal.1985).

[the crimes] knowingly and willfully. However, this testimony may not include an opinion or inference on the ultimate issue of specific intent. Moreover, the Court will instruct the jury that the testimony may only be considered on the issue of whether the defendant possessed the specific intent necessary for conviction (i.e. did she commit the crimes knowingly and willfully).

In reaching this conclusion, the Court has fully followed the mandate and intent of Federal Rules of Evidence 704(b), while at the same time, providing the defendant with her opportunity to offer full explanation, through expert testimony, of the mental state of the accused at the time of the offenses.

These are the issues which arose in *Jane Doe*, using a psychologist-expert in the field of battered women. However, many of these same issues will arise in any case in which an expert-psychologist is presented to give evidence that negates specific intent. Additionally, it was argued by the prosecution that the defendant was trying to "back door" the insanity defense. In contemplating the use of any psychological or "state of mind" expert, a careful reading of *U.S. v Gold*[14] will take you beyond the argument by the prosecution that "if it isn't insanity, you can't use it." Moreover, a careful review of the case of *U.S. v. Levi* will help you to avoid improperly framing your issue.

CONCLUSION

While the use of expert testimony concerning Battered Woman Syndrome has been widely used to defend women who ultimately kill or assault their mates in defense of themselves or for the complex reasons described by the experts, no cases report presenting evidence of BWS to defend against a non-violent crime by negating specific intent. Obviously, such a defense should be used with great caution and only after a careful examination of the defendant and the facts of the case. There are several cases allowing for the admissibility of psychologists' and psychiatrists' testimony for various other mental disabilities; these may be useful to the reader in similar circumstances.

Although "duress" would have been an easier concept to explain to the jury, in *Jane Doe* this was simply not Jane's position. Therefore, it was necessary to use expert testimony to aid the jury in understanding that her reality had been distorted due to the physical and psychological abuse known as Battered Woman Syndrome.

THE PEOPLE v. EVELYN HUMPHREY

Supreme Court of California (1996).
13 Cal.4th 1073, 1076–1090, 1092–1093, 1100–1103.

The Legislature has decreed that, when relevant, expert testimony regarding "battered women's syndrome" is generally admissible in a criminal action. (Evid. Code, § 1107.) We must determine the purposes

---

14. United States v. Gold, 661 F.Supp. 1127 (D.D.C.1987). * * *

for which a jury may consider this evidence when offered to support a claim of self-defense to a murder charge.

The trial court instructed that the jury could consider the evidence in deciding whether the defendant actually believed it was necessary to kill in self-defense, but not in deciding whether that belief was reasonable. The instruction was erroneous. Because evidence of battered women's syndrome may help the jury understand the circumstances in which the defendant found herself at the time of the killing, it is relevant to the reasonableness of her belief. Moreover, because defendant testified, the evidence was relevant to her credibility. The trial court should have allowed the jury to consider this testimony in deciding the reasonableness as well as the existence of defendant's belief that killing was necessary.

Finding the error prejudicial, we reverse the judgment of the Court of Appeal.

I. The Facts

A. *Prosecution Evidence*

During the evening of March 28, 1992, defendant shot and killed Albert Hampton in their Fresno home. Officer Reagan was the first on the scene. A neighbor told Reagan that the couple in the house had been arguing all day. Defendant soon came outside appearing upset and with her hands raised as if surrendering. She told Officer Reagan, "I shot him. That's right, I shot him. I just couldn't take him beating on me no more." She led the officer into the house, showed him a .357 magnum revolver on a table, and said, "There's the gun." Hampton was on the kitchen floor, wounded but alive.

A short time later, defendant told Officer Reagan, "He deserved it. I just couldn't take it anymore. I told him to stop beating on me." "He was beating on me, so I shot him. I told him I'd shoot him if he ever beat on me again." A paramedic heard her say that she wanted to teach Hampton "a lesson." Defendant told another officer at the scene, Officer Terry, "I'm fed up. Yeah, I shot him. I'm just tired of him hitting me. He said, 'You're not going to do nothing about it.' I showed him, didn't I? I shot him good. He won't hit anybody else again. Hit me again; I shoot him again. I don't care if I go to jail. Push come to shove, I guess people gave it to him, and, kept hitting me. I warned him. I warned him not to hit me. He wouldn't listen."

Officer Terry took defendant to the police station, where she told the following story. The day before the shooting, Hampton had been drinking. He hit defendant while they were driving home in their truck and continued hitting her when they arrived. He told her, "I'll kill you," and shot at her. The bullet went through a bedroom window and struck a tree outside. The day of the shooting, Hampton "got drunk," swore at her, and started hitting her again. He walked into the kitchen. Defendant saw the gun in the living room and picked it up. Her jaw hurt, and she was in pain. She pointed the gun at Hampton and said, "You're not going to hit me anymore." Hampton said, "What are you doing?" Believing that Hampton was about to pick something up to hit her with, she shot him. She then put the gun down and went outside to wait for the police.

Hampton later died of a gunshot wound to his chest. The neighbor who spoke with Officer Reagan testified that shortly before the shooting, she heard defendant, but not Hampton, shouting. The evening before, the neighbor had heard a gunshot. Defendant's blood contained no drugs but had a blood-alcohol level of .17 percent. Hampton's blood contained no drugs or alcohol.

B.   Defense Evidence

Defendant claimed she shot Hampton in self-defense. To support the claim, the defense presented first expert testimony and then nonexpert testimony, including that of defendant herself.

1. Expert Testimony

Dr. Lee Bowker testified as an expert on battered women's syndrome. The syndrome, he testified, "is not just a psychological construction, but it's a term for a wide variety of controlling mechanisms that the man or it can be a woman, but in general for this syndrome it's a man, uses against the woman, and for the effect that those control mechanisms have."

Dr. Bowker had studied about 1,000 battered women and found them often inaccurately portrayed "as cardboard figures, paper-thin punching bags who merely absorb the violence but didn't do anything about it." He found that battered women often employ strategies to stop the beatings, including hiding, running away, counterviolence, seeking the help of friends and family, going to a shelter, and contacting police. Nevertheless, many battered women remain in the relationship because of lack of money, social isolation, lack of self-confidence, inadequate police response, and a fear (often justified) of reprisals by the batterer. "The battering man will make the battered woman depend on him and generally succeed at least for a time." A battered woman often feels responsible for the abusive relationship, and "she just can't figure out a way to please him better so he'll stop beating her." In sum, "It really is the physical control of the woman through economics and through relative social isolation combined with the psychological techniques that make her so dependent."

Many battered women go from one abusive relationship to another and seek a strong man to protect them from the previous abuser. "[W]ith each successful victimization, the person becomes less able to avoid the next one." The violence can gradually escalate, as the batterer keeps control using ever more severe actions, including rape, torture, violence against the woman's loved ones or pets, and death threats. Battered women sense this escalation. In Dr. Bowker's "experience with battered women who kill in self-defense their abusers, it's always related to their perceived change of what's going on in a relationship. They become very sensitive to what sets off batterers. They watch for this stuff very carefully. [] ... Anybody who is abused over a period of time becomes sensitive to the abuser's behavior and when she sees a change acceleration begin in that behavior, it tells them something is going to happen...."

Dr. Bowker interviewed defendant for a full day. He believed she suffered not only from battered women's syndrome, but also from being the child of an alcoholic and an incest victim. He testified that all three of defendant's partners before Hampton were abusive and significantly older than she.

Dr. Bowker described defendant's relationship with Hampton. Hampton was a 49–year-old man who weighed almost twice as much as defendant. The two had a battering relationship that Dr. Bowker characterized as a "traditional cycle of violence." The cycle included phases of tension building, violence, and then forgiveness-seeking in which Hampton would promise not to batter defendant any more and she would believe him. During this period, there would be occasional good times. For example, defendant told Dr. Bowker that Hampton would give her a rose. "That's one of the things that hooks people in. Intermittent reinforcement is the key." But after a while, the violence would begin again. The violence would recur because "basically ... the woman doesn't perfectly obey. That's the bottom line." For example, defendant would talk to another man, or fail to clean house "just so."

The situation worsened over time, especially when Hampton got off parole shortly before his death. He became more physically and emotionally abusive, repeatedly threatened defendant's life, and even shot at her the night before his death. Hampton often allowed defendant to go out, but she was afraid to flee because she felt he would find her as he had in the past. "He enforced her belief that she can never escape him." Dr. Bowker testified that unless her injuries were so severe that "something absolutely had to be treated," he would not expect her to seek medical treatment. "That's the pattern of her life...."

Dr. Bowker believed defendant's description of her experiences. In his opinion, she suffered from battered women's syndrome in "about as extreme a pattern as you could find."

2. *Nonexpert Testimony*

Defendant confirmed many of the details of her life and relationship with Hampton underlying Dr. Bowker's opinion. She testified that her father forcefully molested her from the time she was seven years old until she was fifteen. She described her relationship with another abusive man as being like "Nightmare on Elm Street." Regarding Hampton, she testified that they often argued and that he beat her regularly. Both were heavy drinkers. Hampton once threw a can of beer at her face, breaking her nose. Her dental plates hurt because Hampton hit her so often. He often kicked her, but usually hit her in the back of the head because, he told her, it "won't leave bruises." Hampton sometimes threatened to kill her, and often said she "would live to regret it." Matters got worse towards the end.

The evening before the shooting, March 27, 1992, Hampton arrived home "very drunk." He yelled at her and called her names. At one point when she was standing by the bedroom window, he fired his .357 magnum revolver at her. She testified, "He didn't miss me by much either." She was "real scared."

The next day, the two drove into the mountains. They argued, and Hampton continually hit her. While returning, he said that their location would be a good place to kill her because "they wouldn't find [her] for a while." She took it as a joke, although she feared him. When they returned, the arguing continued. He hit her again, then entered the kitchen. He threatened, "This time, bitch, when I shoot at you, I won't miss." He came from the kitchen and reached for the gun on the living room table. She grabbed it first, pointed it at him, and told him "that he wasn't going to hit [her]." She backed Hampton into the kitchen. He was saying something, but she did not know what. He reached for her hand and she shot him. She believed he was reaching for the gun and was going to shoot her.

Several other witnesses testified about defendant's relationship with Hampton, his abusive conduct in general, and his physical abuse of, and threats to, defendant in particular. This testimony generally corroborated defendant's. A neighbor testified that the night before the shooting, she heard a gunshot. The next morning, defendant told the neighbor that Hampton had shot at her, and that she was afraid of him. After the shooting, investigators found a bullet hole through the frame of the bedroom window and a bullet embedded in a tree in line with the window. Another neighbor testified that shortly before hearing the shot that killed Hampton, she heard defendant say, "Stop it, Albert. Stop it."

C. Procedural History

Defendant was charged with murder with personal use of a firearm. At the end of the prosecution's case-in-chief, the court granted defendant's motion under Penal Code section 1118.1 for acquittal of first degree murder.

The court instructed the jury on second degree murder and both voluntary and involuntary manslaughter. It also instructed on self-defense, explaining that an actual and reasonable belief that the killing was necessary was a complete defense; an actual but unreasonable belief was a defense to murder, but not to voluntary manslaughter. In determining reasonableness, the jury was to consider what "would appear to be necessary to a reasonable person in a similar situation and with similar knowledge."

The court also instructed:

Evidence regarding Battered Women's Syndrome has been introduced in this case. Such evidence, if believed, may be considered by you only for the purpose of determining whether or not the defendant held the necessary subjective honest [belief] which is a requirement for both perfect and imperfect self-defense. However, that same evidence regarding Battered Women's Syndrome may not be considered or used by you in evaluating the objective reasonableness requirement for perfect self-defense.

. . . .

Battered Women's Syndrome seeks to describe and explain common reactions of women to that experience. Thus, you may consider the evidence concerning the syndrome and its effects only for the limited purpose of showing, if it does show, that the defendant's reactions, as demonstrated by the evidence, are not inconsistent with her having been physically abused or the beliefs, perceptions, or behavior of victims of domestic violence.

During deliberations, the jury asked for and received clarification of the terms "subjectively honest and objectively unreasonable." It found defendant guilty of voluntary manslaughter with personal use of a firearm. The court sentenced defendant to prison for eight years, consisting of the lower term of three years for manslaughter, plus the upper term of five years for firearm use. The Court of Appeal remanded for resentencing on the use enhancement, but otherwise affirmed the judgment. We granted defendant's petition for review.

II. Discussion

A. Background

With an exception not relevant here, Evidence Code section 1107, subdivision (a), makes admissible in a criminal action expert testimony regarding "battered women's syndrome, including the physical, emotional, or mental effects upon the beliefs, perceptions, or behavior of victims of domestic violence. . . ." Under subdivision (b) of that section, the foundation for admission is sufficient "if the proponent of the evidence establishes its relevancy and the proper qualifications of the expert witness." Defendant presented the evidence to support her claim of self-defense. It is undisputed that she established the proper qualifications of the expert witness. The only issue is to what extent defendant established its "relevancy." To resolve this question we must examine California law regarding self-defense.

For killing to be in self-defense, the defendant must actually and reasonably believe in the need to defend. If the belief subjectively exists but is objectively unreasonable, there is "imperfect self-defense," i.e., "the defendant is deemed to have acted without malice and cannot be convicted of murder," but can be convicted of manslaughter. To constitute "perfect self-defense," i.e., to exonerate the person completely, the belief must also be objectively reasonable. As the Legislature has stated, "[T]he circumstances must be sufficient to excite the fears of a reasonable person. . . ." Moreover, for either perfect or imperfect self-defense, the fear must be of imminent harm. "Fear of future harm-no matter how great the fear and no matter how great the likelihood of the harm-will not suffice. The defendant's fear must be of imminent danger to life or great bodily injury.''

Although the belief in the need to defend must be objectively reasonable, a jury must consider what "would appear to be necessary to a reasonable person in a similar situation and with similar knowledge. . . .'' It judges reasonableness "from the point of view of a reasonable person in the position of defendant. . . .'' To do this, it must consider all the " 'facts and circumstances . . . in determining whether the defendant acted in a manner in which a reasonable man would act in protecting his own life or bodily safety.' '' As we stated long ago, " . . . a defendant is entitled to have a jury take into consideration all the elements in the case which might be expected to operate on his mind. . . .''

We recently discussed this question in a different context. In *People v. Ochoa* (1993) 6 Cal.4th 1199, the defendant was convicted of gross vehicular manslaughter while intoxicated. The offense requires "gross negligence,'' the test for which is " 'objective: whether a reasonable person in the defendant's position would have been aware of the risk involved.' '' The defendant argued that, "because the test of gross negligence is an objective one . . . , evidence of his own subjective state of mind was irrelevant and unduly prejudicial.'' We disagreed. "In determining whether a reasonable person in defendant's position would have been aware of the risks, the jury should be given relevant facts as to what defendant knew, including his actual awareness of those risks.'' "[A]lthough the test for gross negligence was an objective one, '[t]he jury should therefore consider all relevant circumstances. . . .' ''

What we said in *Ochoa* about the defendant's actual awareness applies to this case. Although the ultimate test of reasonableness is objective, in determining whether a reasonable person in defendant's position would have believed in the need to defend, the jury must consider all of the relevant circumstances in which defendant found herself.

With these principles in mind, we now consider the relevance of evidence of battered women's syndrome to the elements of self-defense.

B.   Battered Women's Syndrome[3]

Battered women's syndrome "has been defined as 'a series of common characteristics that appear in women who are abused physically

---

3. We use the term "battered women's syndrome'' because Evidence Code section 1107 and the cases use that term. We note, however, that according to *amici curiae* California Alliance Against Domestic Violence *et al.*, " . . . the preferred term among many experts today is 'expert testimony on battering and its effects' or 'expert testimony on battered women's experiences.' Do-

mestic violence experts have critiqued the phrase 'battered women's syndrome' because (1) it implies that there is one syndrome which all battered women develop, (2) it has pathological connotations which suggest that battered women suffer from some sort of sickness, (3) expert testimony on domestic violence refers to more than women's psychological reactions to violence, and psychologically over an extended period of time by the dominant male figure in their lives.' "

The trial court allowed the jury to consider the battered women's syndrome evidence in deciding whether defendant actually believed she needed to kill in self-defense. The question here is whether the evidence was also relevant on the reasonableness of that belief. Two Court of Appeal decisions have considered the relevance of battered women's syndrome evidence to a claim of self-defense.

People v. Aris, supra, 215 Cal.App.3d at page 1185, applied "the law of self-defense in the context of a battered woman killing the batterer while he slept after he had beaten the killer and threatened serious bodily injury and death when he awoke." There, unlike here, the trial court refused to instruct the jury on perfect self-defense, but it did instruct on imperfect self-defense. The appellate court upheld the refusal, finding that "defendant presented no substantial evidence that a reasonable person under the same circumstances would have perceived imminent danger and a need to kill in self-defense."[4] The trial court admitted some evidence of battered women's syndrome, but the defendant argued that it erred "by excluding expert testimony (1) that defendant was a battered woman based on the expert's psychological evaluation of the defendant and (2) 'explaining how the psychological impact of being a battered woman affected her perception of danger at the time she shot her husband.' "

Although the trial court did not instruct on perfect self-defense, the appellate court first concluded that battered women's syndrome evidence is not relevant to the reasonableness element. "[T]he questions of the reasonableness of a defendant's belief that self-defense is necessary and of the reasonableness of the actions taken in self-defense do not call for an evaluation of the defendant's subjective state of mind, but for an objective evaluation of the defendant's assertedly defensive acts. California law expresses the criterion for this evaluation in the objective terms of whether a reasonable person, as opposed to the defendant, would have believed and acted as the defendant did. We hold that expert testimony about a defendant's state of mind is not relevant to the reasonableness of the defendant's self-defense."

The court then found the evidence "highly relevant to the first element of self-defense—defendant's actual, subjective perception that she was in danger and that she had to kill her husband to avoid that danger.... [] The relevance to the defendant's actual perception lies in the opinion's explanation of how such a perception would reasonably follow from the defendant's experience as a battered woman. This relates

(4) it focuses attention on the battered woman rather than on the batterer's coercive and controlling behavior and (5) it creates an image of battered women as suffering victims rather than as active survivors."

4. This case presents no issue as to when the instructions are necessary be-

cause the court did instruct on both perfect and imperfect self-defense. Unlike *People v. Aris*, there was substantial evidence here that defendant reasonably feared imminent harm.

to the prosecution's argument that such a perception of imminent danger makes no sense when the victim is asleep and a way of escape open and, therefore, she did not actually have that perception." The trial court thus erred in not admitting the testimony to show "how the defendant's particular experiences as a battered woman affected her perceptions of danger, its imminence, and what actions were necessary to protect herself."

Concerned "that the jury in a particular case may misuse such evidence to establish the reasonableness requirement for perfect self-defense, for which purpose it is irrelevant," the *Aris* court stated that, "upon request whenever the jury is instructed on perfect self-defense, trial courts should instruct that such testimony is relevant only to prove the honest belief requirement for both perfect and imperfect self-defense, not to prove the reasonableness requirement for perfect self-defense." The trial court gave such an instruction here, thus creating the issue before us.

In *People v. Day* (1992) 2 Cal.App.4th 405, the defendant moved for a new trial following her conviction of involuntary manslaughter. Supported by an affidavit by Dr. Bowker, she argued that her attorney should have presented evidence of battered women's syndrome to aid her claim of self-defense. Relying on *Aris*, the appellate court first found that the evidence would not have been relevant to show the objective reasonableness of the defendant's actions. It also found, however, that the evidence would have been admissible to rehabilitate the defendant's credibility as a witness. Finding that counsel's failure to present the evidence was prejudicial, the court reversed the judgment.

The Attorney General argues that *People v. Aris* and *People v. Day* were correct that evidence of battered women's syndrome is irrelevant to reasonableness. We disagree. Those cases too narrowly interpreted the reasonableness element. *Aris* and *Day* failed to consider that the jury, in determining objective reasonableness, must view the situation from the defendant's perspective. Here, for example, Dr. Bowker testified that the violence can escalate and that a battered woman can become increasingly sensitive to the abuser's behavior, testimony relevant to determining whether defendant reasonably believed when she fired the gun that this time the threat to her life was imminent. Indeed, the prosecutor argued that, "from an objective, reasonable man's standard, there was no reason for her to go get that gun. This threat that she says he made was like so many threats before. There was no reason for her to react that way." Dr. Bowker's testimony supplied a response that the jury might not otherwise receive. As violence increases over time, and threats gain credibility, a battered person might become sensitized and thus able reasonably to discern when danger is real and when it is not. "[T]he expert's testimony might also enable the jury to find that the battered [woman] ... is particularly able to predict accurately the likely extent of violence in any attack on her. That conclusion could significantly affect the jury's evaluation of the reasonableness of defendant's fear for her life."

The Attorney General concedes that Hampton's behavior towards defendant, including prior threats and violence, was relevant to reasonableness but distinguishes between evidence of this behavior—which the trial court fully admitted—and expert testimony about its effects on defendant. The distinction is untenable. "To effectively present the situation as perceived by the defendant, and the reasonableness of her fear, the defense has the option to explain her feelings to enable the jury to overcome stereotyped impressions about women who remain in abusive relationships. It is appropriate that the jury be given a professional explanation of the battering syndrome and its effects on the woman through the use of expert testimony."

The Attorney General also argues that allowing consideration of this testimony would result in an undesirable "battle of the experts" and raises the specter of other battles of experts regarding other syndromes. The Legislature, however, has decided that, if relevant, expert evidence on battered women's syndrome is admissible. We have found it relevant; it is therefore admissible. We express no opinion on the admissibility of expert testimony regarding other possible syndromes in support of a claim of self-defense, but we rest today's holding on Evidence Code section 1107.

Contrary to the Attorney General's argument, we are not changing the standard from objective to subjective, or replacing the reasonable "person" standard with a reasonable "battered woman" standard. Our decision would not, in another context, compel adoption of a " 'reasonable gang member' standard." Evidence Code section 1107 states "a rule of evidence only" and makes "no substantive change." The jury must consider defendant's situation and knowledge, which makes the evidence relevant, but the ultimate question is whether a reasonable person, not a reasonable battered woman, would believe in the need to kill to prevent imminent harm. Moreover, it is the jury, not the expert, that determines whether defendant's belief and, ultimately, her actions, were objectively reasonable.

Battered women's syndrome evidence was also relevant to defendant's credibility. It "would have assisted the jury in objectively analyzing [defendant's] claim of self-defense by dispelling many of the commonly held misconceptions about battered women." For example, in urging the jury not to believe defendant's testimony that Hampton shot at her the night before the killing, the prosecutor argued that "if this defendant truly believed that [Hampton] had shot at her, on that night, I mean she would have left.... [] If she really believed that he had tried to shoot her, she would not have stayed." Dr. Bowker's testimony " 'would help dispel the ordinary lay person's perception that a woman in a battering relationship is free to leave at any time. The expert evidence would counter any "common sense" conclusions by the jury that if the beatings were really that bad the woman would have left her husband much earlier. Popular misconceptions about battered women would be put to rest.... ' ' "[I]f the jury had understood [defendant's] conduct in light of [battered women's syndrome] evidence, then the jury may well have concluded her version of the events was sufficiently credible to warrant an acquittal on the facts as she related them."

As *Day* recognizes, *People v. McAlpin* (1991) 53 Cal.3d 1289, supports this conclusion. There we held that expert testimony regarding parental reluctance to report child molestation was admissible to bolster a witness's credibility: "Most jurors, fortunately, have been spared the experience of being the parent of a sexually molested child. Lacking that experience, jurors can rely only on their intuition or on relevant evidence introduced at trial. . . . [Evidence that parents often do not report child molestation] would therefore 'assist the trier of fact' by giving the jurors information they needed to objectively evaluate [the witness's] credibility." As in *McAlpin*, the expert testimony in this case was " 'needed to disabuse jurors of commonly held misconceptions. . . .' " It was relevant "to explain a behavior pattern that might otherwise appear unreasonable to the average person. Evidence of [battered women's syndrome] not only explains how a battered woman might think, react, or behave, it places the behavior in an understandable light." Thus, it was admissible under Evidence Code sections 801 and 1107.

We do not hold that Dr. Bowker's entire testimony was relevant to both prongs of perfect self-defense. Just as many types of evidence may be relevant to some disputed issues but not all, some of the expert evidence was no doubt relevant only to the subjective existence of defendant's belief. Evidence merely showing that a person's use of deadly force is scientifically explainable or empirically common does not, in itself, show it was objectively reasonable. To dispel any possible confusion, it might be appropriate for the court, on request, to clarify that, in assessing reasonableness, the question is whether a reasonable person in the defendant's circumstances would have perceived a threat of imminent injury or death, and not whether killing the abuser was reasonable in the sense of being an understandable response to ongoing abuse; and that, therefore, in making that assessment, the jury may not consider evidence merely showing that an abused person's use of force against the abuser is understandable.[5]

We also emphasize that, as with any evidence, the jury may give this testimony whatever weight it deems appropriate in light of the evidence as a whole. The ultimate judgment of reasonableness is solely for the jury. We simply hold that evidence of battered women's syndrome is generally relevant to the reasonableness, as well as the subjective existence, of defendant's belief in the need to defend, and, to the extent it is relevant, the jury may consider it in deciding both questions. The court's contrary instruction was erroneous. We disapprove of *People v. Aris* and *People v. Day* to the extent they are inconsistent with this conclusion.

---

5. If the prosecution offers the battered women's syndrome evidence, an additional limiting instruction might also be appropriate on request, given the statutory prohibition against use of this evidence "to prove the occurrence of the act or acts of abuse which form the basis of the criminal charge." (Evid. Code, § 1107, subd. (a); see CALJIC No. 9.35.01 (1996 new)(5th ed. Supp.).)

C. Prejudice

Defendant contends that the instructional error unconstitutionally deprived her of her rights to present a defense and to equal protection of the laws, thus requiring reversal unless the error was harmless beyond a reasonable doubt. We disagree that the *Chapman* standard applies. The erroneous instruction may have adversely affected the defense, but it did not deprive her of the right to present one or deny her equal protection. In effect, the court excluded some evidence as to one element of the defense. When the reviewing court applying state law finds an erroneous exclusion of defense evidence, the usual standard of review for state law error applies: the court must reverse only if it also finds a reasonable probability the error affected the verdict adversely to defendant.

Under this standard, however, we conclude the error was prejudicial. The jury found defendant guilty of voluntary manslaughter, not murder. Although the verdict may have been based on a finding of provocation, the arguments to the jury and the jury's request for clarification of the terms "subjectively honest and objectively unreasonable" suggest the question of unreasonable self-defense was critical. The jury likely concluded that defendant actually believed in the need to defend, but her belief was unreasonable. If so, guilt or innocence hinged on the precise issue—objective reasonableness—on which the court told the jury not to consider the battered women's syndrome evidence. As stated above, the prosecutor argued that defendant's actions were unreasonable because the last "threat that she says he made was like so many threats before. There was no reason for her to react that way." The testimony the court told the jury not to consider was directly responsive to this argument.

Although we do not know what weight the jury would have given the expert testimony in determining reasonableness, the testimony "was not only relevant, but critical in permitting the jury to evaluate [defendant's] testimony free of the misperceptions regarding battered women." Overall, the evidence, including defendant's corroborated testimony about the shooting the night before, presented a plausible case for perfect self-defense. The actual verdict was reasonable, but so too would have been a different one. Under all of these circumstances, it is reasonably probable the error affected the verdict adversely to defendant.

* * *

Brown, J., Concurring.—For years the lower courts, poised precariously upon the slippery slope of personalized defenses, have tried valiantly not to ski down it. Early cases focused on the general admissibility of evidence of battered woman's syndrome (BWS) to support claims of self-defense. By 1991, with that question answered by legislative fiat, concern shifted to a more nuanced discussion of relevance. Courts found expert testimony admissible to rehabilitate the defendant's credibility and to explain her subjective state of mind, but not relevant to the jury's determination of the objective reasonableness of her actions.

Today we hold that "evidence of battered women's syndrome is generally relevant to the reasonableness, as well as the subjective existence, of defendant's belief in the need to defend and, to the extent it is relevant, the jury may consider it in deciding both questions." But, this conclusion only begins, rather than ends, the discussion. As always, the devil is in the details.

Substantial questions remain unresolved: when, to what purpose, and to what extent can expert opinion concerning the defendant's mental state be used to assess the objective reasonableness of a claim of self-defense? If we go too far, accountability—the essential touchstone of the criminal law—is undermined; if we do not go far enough, the defendant is deprived of a defense the jury may find genuine. It is the struggle to find the balance point between accountability and justification that engenders confusion when a victim of battering kills her abuser and seeks to prove her claim of self-defense with BWS evidence.

While I agree with the general conclusions of the majority, concern with the specific application of these principles prompts me to examine more closely the links between the objective component of self-defense and BWS.

* * *

Turning to the facts of this case, for the most part defendant's account of events leading to the shooting did not require the filter of an expert's opinion to assist in determining the question of reasonableness. She presented a relatively straightforward claim of self-defense the jury could either accept or reject as such. According to defendant, Hampton had been physically and verbally abusive for most of the year they lived together. His threats and acts of violence had been increasing for several weeks prior to the fateful evening. Although he liked guns and owned several, he had never shot at her until the previous night. On the way home from the mountains the next day, he pointed out what he thought would be a good place to kill her because no one would find the body for awhile. Just minutes before the shooting with the gun lying within easy reach, he told her "[t]his time" he would not miss. She then grabbed the weapon as he appeared about to do the same. While she was holding him at bay, he reached for her arm at which point she apparently shot him. On their face, nothing in these facts lies beyond the experience of the average reasonable person or the ken of the average juror.

At the same time, defendant also testified to facts implicating characteristics of BWS that correspond to the objective element of self-defense. Consistent with his threats, Hampton began hitting her more frequently when he got off parole. The night before, he was "getting crazy" asking for the gun, which he then shot in her direction narrowly missing her. At that moment, he had a "look on his face" that defendant had seen before "but not this bad"; he "wasn't the same person." As to events surrounding Hampton's death, defendant related that shortly before she grabbed the gun, the two were screaming and arguing; "then all of a sudden, he got quiet for a minute or two, and, then, he just snapped." A few moments later, he moved from the kitchen toward the gun saying, "This time, bitch, when I shoot at you, I won't miss." At this point, she "knew he would shoot me" and was "scared to death" not only because of Hampton's threats and prior violence but also because of his "very, very heavy" walk indicating he was "mad." She had no doubt he would kill her if she did not kill him first. As they confronted each other in the kitchen, he "looked crazy." She assumed he was going for the gun when he reached for her arm and shot him.

As relevant to this testimony, Dr. Bowker explained generally that with the cycles of violence typifying BWS the "severity tends to escalate over time." Battered women develop a heightened awareness of this escalation as threats and physical abuse become increasingly menacing. A sense of the batterer's omnipotence due to his dominance may augment this hypervigilance, causing the woman to believe all the more he will act on his threats of violence.

Bowker also discussed some specifics arguably relating to defendant's objective perception of imminent harm:

> [T]he escalation had been such, particularly the night before, where [Hampton] actually shot at her that it would be pretty hard to doubt the seriousness.... A difference, I think, [between Hampton's last threat and previous ones] is that [defendant] felt for the first time that he really intended to do it and, you know, my experience with battered women who kill in self-defense their abusers, it's always related to their perceived change of what's going on in a relationship. They become very sensitive to what sets off batterers. They watch for this stuff very carefully. [] Anybody who is abused over a period of time becomes sensitive to the abuser's behavior and when she sees a change acceleration begin in that behavior, it tells them something is going to happen and usually the abuser said things specifically like "i'm really going to kill you this time," and, you know, they don't admit to that something happens that there's a label put on it by the abuser which was certainly true in Albert's case and that's intensification or an acceleration of the process is what leads to some self-defensive action which is beyond anything that the woman has ever done before.

This testimony could assist the jury in determining whether a reasonable person in defendant's situation would have perceived from the totality of the circumstances imminent peril of serious bodily injury or death. Absent the expert's explanation, the average juror might be unduly skeptical that a look, footstep, or tone of voice could in fact signal impending grave harm or that a reasonable person would be able accurately to assess the need to take self-defensive action on that basis. Accordingly, the trial court erred in categorically precluding consideration of evidence relevant to this purpose rather than giving a properly worded limiting instruction.

Prejudice

Notwithstanding the error, the question of prejudice is extremely close given the "miscarriage of justice" standard of review. * * * On balance, however, the scales tip marginally in defendant's favor in light of her limited burden of proof. Defendant does not have to prove the homicide was justified; she merely has to raise a reasonable doubt that it might have been.

DENISE BRICKER, FATAL DEFENSE: AN ANALYSIS OF BATTERED WOMAN'S SYNDROME EXPERT TESTIMONY FOR GAY MEN AND LESBIANS WHO KILL ABUSIVE PARTNERS

58 Brook. L. Rev. 1425–1436 (1993).

III.   C. Battered Woman's Syndrome and the Gay or Lesbian Defendant

The primary problem with battered woman's syndrome expert testimony for all defendants is that it often enforces the very stereotypes of women that it seeks to dispel. Courts, mimicking the experts' testimony, continue to describe battered women as helpless, passive and incapacitated victims, stereotypical attributes that have plagued women for centuries. In light of judicial use of battered woman's syndrome, the success of Walker's theory rests more on its emphasis of the stereotypical helplessness of women than on its illumination of the dynamics of intimate violence.

Gay and lesbian defendants, already the victims of stereotypes that portray them as gender-confused, will be forced to defend not only their action, but their ability to fit within the stereotyped female gender-role. Experts who explain intimate violence in the terms used for battered woman's syndrome will encourage the jury to try to fit the same-sex relationship into the mold of a heterosexual relationship. This can lead to increased stereotyping and confusion, as the expert and the jury will be forced to ask themselves who played the role of the man and who played the role of the woman. The chance that either the defendant or the batterer/victim will fit into stereotypical gender roles is minimal.

Furthermore, the harsh reality is that the popular image of the battered woman as small, meek and cowering will not translate to a defendant as large and strong as his or her partner. Although the gay or lesbian defendant may not be equal in size and strength to the abusive partner, generally the discrepancy between the two will not be as extreme as the discrepancy between men and women. This discrepancy between men and women has been, at least in part, the basis courts have used to liberalize the proportional force rule and to subjectivize the standard for the defendant's belief of imminent danger. Judges and jurors will have great difficulty understanding the dynamics of intimate violence when unable to view the defendant as the weaker, helpless victim described in Walker's model.

The description of the battered person as a helpless, passive victim also does not translate to defendants who on prior occasions fought back or attempted to flee. Despite the recognition from experts on heterosexual intimate violence that battered women engage in defensive actions (mutual battering), this aspect of intimate violence is antithetical to Walker's model of the passive victim. While it is not clear whether battered gay or lesbian victims engage in more mutual battering than heterosexual women, the fact that the partners are of the same gender and are likely to be of relatively the same size may suggest to the fact-finder that the defendant did fight back or at least had the capacity to fight back.

If the defendant did engage in mutual battering or any other non-passive behavior, as Annette Green did, the prosecution will be able to argue that the defendant is not a "battered woman" because he or she does not fit the model. In *State v. Anaya*[209] the expert recited the Walker model when she testified that "battered wives typically stay with their men out of economic dependency, and that they 'most frequently . . . react with passivity' to the violence of their mates." In this case, however, the defendant's boyfriend was unemployed throughout the time the couple lived together and the defendant had stabbed the victim on an earlier occasion. The prosecution was permitted to use the expert's characterization of battered woman's syndrome to refute the "battered wife defense."

Finally, both experts and courts have contributed to the creation of a new stereotype, the "good battered woman," that gay and lesbian defendants will have difficulty overcoming. Part of the problem arises from the characterization of the effects of intimate violence as a "syndrome." The word appears to connote an illness for which there are definitive symptoms subject to accurate diagnosis. "Expert testimony on the 'battered woman syndrome' . . . although intended to address damaging myths and misconcretions, also contributes in a subtle way to an image of maladjustment or pathology. Just the use of the term 'syndrome' connotes impairment to most people, including judges and jurors."[214] A battered gay man or lesbian who does not exhibit all or some of the "symptoms" (e.g., passivity, economic or emotional dependence, lack of education or total isolation from family or friends) will be categorized as a "bad battered woman" or not a battered woman at all. Thus, the focus of the cases tends to be on whether the defendant is entitled to call himself or herself a "battered woman," not whether the defendant's action was reasonable or justified.

Gay and lesbian defendants who try to use the battered woman's syndrome testimony are in for a double whammy. First, the theory is already flawed as it applies to heterosexual women. Second, the theory's procrustean bed may break under the tension of applying it to gay and

---

209. 456 A.2d 1255, 1266 (Me.1983); see also Mullis v. State, 282 S.E.2d 334 (Ga. 1981) * * *.

214. Browne, supra note 15, at 177.

lesbian relationships. In essence, the theory relies on gender stereotypes for its impact. Stereotypes, such as women's socialized passivity, their economic dependence and their lesser size, strength and fighting ability, are central to the explanation of why women are abused by men and why they have difficulty leaving or fighting back. Once battered woman's syndrome expert testimony is drained of these gendered notions, it offers little to no explanation of why intimate violence occurs in same-sex relationships or why battered gay men and lesbians have difficulty in separating themselves from the relationship.

D. TOWARD A MORE GENDER-NEUTRAL THEORY OF INTIMATE VIOLENCE FOR GAY AND LESBIAN DEFENDANTS

To avoid these problems, an expert witness in a battered gay man's or lesbian's self-defense case must present a theory of intimate violence that does not depend upon the gender of the batterer and victim. Since most of the current research on intimate violence is based on heterosexual women's experiences, however, there are no "genderless" theories of adult intimate violence available. Thus any expert on intimate violence must depend on theories that have been developed for heterosexual women. This problem is not insurmountable. At least two current theorists, Dr. Angela Browne and Dr. Julie Blackman, have authored studies on intimate violence that avoid many of the pitfalls associated with Walker's model. In particular, neither theorist's work depends on portraying the battered person as helpless or passive. Both characterize the battered woman's behavior in avoiding the violence and coping in other areas of her life as active. Since battered women have encountered such difficulty when experts used Walker's theory of learned helplessness to explain why the women failed to leave, this difference is significant.

Browne's study is particularly compelling because its focus is specifically on battered women who killed, rather than on battered women generally. When the two groups were compared, Browne found that there were no significant differences between the backgrounds of the women (i.e., education, employment status, violence in childhood), but there were very significant differences in the behavior of the batterer and in the frequency and severity of their violence against their spouses. By explaining these differences to a jury, the expert can lay the groundwork for the jury's interpretation of the defendant's act as reasonable:

> [A]knowledge of the history of the prior violence and the specific context within which the incident occurred is essential for understanding the woman's perceptions at the time of the homicide.... [T]he life of a battered woman is "replete with prior provocation, continuing apprehension, and the constant threat of impending danger." ... As we learn more about battered women ... those who kill ... seem to be reacting to the level of violence perpetrated against them.[222]

222. Id. at 175–76 * * *.

To explain why some battered women fail to leave the relationship, Browne looks at the battered woman's dim view of her alternatives. Here, she compares battered women with other victims of trauma. Like victims of disasters and wars, battered women focus on self-protection and survival during the impact phase.

> [B]attered women's affective, cognitive, and behavioral responses are likely to become distorted by their intense focus on survival. They may have developed a whole range of responses such as controlling their breathing or not crying out in pain, in an effort to mitigate the severity of the abuse during violent episodes, but have not developed any plans for escaping the abusive situations.[224]

They later "may be extremely suggestible or dependent and, during the period that follows, may minimize the damage or personal loss. This is often followed by a 'euphoric' stage, marked by unrealistic expectations about recovery."[225] Browne finds even a closer parallel between battered women and prisoners of war:

> "Fight or flight" responses are inhibited by a perception of the aggressor's power to inflict damage or death, and depression often results, based on the perceived hopelessness of the situation. The victims' perceptions of their alternatives become increasingly limited the longer they remain in the situation, and those alternatives that do exist often seem to pose too great a threat to survival.[226]

Belief that safe alternatives exist is still more unlikely for gay men and lesbians who in fact have even fewer alternatives than heterosexual battered women.

The victim's behavior and perceptions must be viewed in light of both factors: the level of violence perpetrated against them and their diminished ability to perceive escape opportunities. While the victim may initially remain with the batterer out of love or a sense of commitment or responsibility to the batterer or children, the victim's reasons for remaining change over the course of the relationship. Browne noted that

> as the severity and frequency of abuse increases, three additional factors have a major impact on the women's decision to stay with violent partners: (1) practical problems in effecting a separation [like the lack of access to shelters], (2) the fear of retaliation if they do leave, and (3) the shock reactions of victims to abuse.[228]

Browne's model creates a more stark and frightening portrait of the abusive relationship than the Walker model and, with the focus on the brutality of the abuser, permits a jury to interpret the defendant's reaction as reasonable more easily.

The most significant difference between Blackman's and Browne's study is Blackman's theory of why the battered woman remains in the relationship. One of Blackman's fundamental premises is that "intimate

224. Id. at 125–26.

225. Id. at 123.

226. Id. at 124.

228. Id. at 110.

violence does harm to victims' concepts of justice." Without a sense of what is just, a person is less able to perceive injustice and act on this perception. Damage to a person's justice concept "narrows the vision of the victim, diminishing the ability to perceive alternatives and leading to an unusual level of acceptance of cognitive inconsistency as a way of coping." Blackman argued:

> [T]his tolerance of inconsistency is a reflection of the fundamental inconsistency of their lives: that the man who supposedly loves them also hurts them. This characteristic of battered women is particularly important for jurors to understand, since it may cause her to describe the events of her life in ways that are seemingly contradictory and may be misinterpreted as signs of a generally poor memory or of bungled attempts to be deceptive.[232]

Thus, Blackman's research goes a little further than Browne's to explain the differences in perception that may result from long-term battering. such an explanation may aid the jury in understanding more fully why many battered victims are able to survive within the context of a relationship without becoming mentally impaired.

Both Browne's and Blackman's works are especially important to gay and lesbian defendants because both include research that can be applied in a gender-neutral manner. Browne's comparison between victims of trauma and battered women is particularly useful because of the connection between non-gender-specific victims and battered victims. In addition, because Browne's study reveals significant differences in the violence of the relationship of battered women who kill, the jury's attention is shifted away from the psychology and gender of the defendant, and toward the batterer and his or her acts of violence.

Although Blackman's work is primarily the result of research on women, her theories are not necessarily gender-specific. While more research needs to be done on same-sex intimate violence, it is likely that any victim of ongoing intimate violence will experience the cognitive reactions that Blackman found in battered women. Finally, it is important to note that neither researcher uses the term "battered woman's syndrome." The absence in their theoretical language of such gender-based terminology makes the adaptation of the theories to gay men and lesbians easier.

Yet, the simple presentation of a gender-neutral theory of intimate violence will not create by itself an environment free from damaging stereotypes, it merely will not add to those which already exist. Jurors who believe that homosexuals routinely sexually molest children or attempt to convert children to homosexuality may be predisposed to convicting a gay or lesbian defendant regardless of the case's merits. Jurors who believe that same-sex couples are incapable of sustaining long-term relationships may be unable to understand the impact of intimate violence on a gay or lesbian individual. They may assume that

232. See Blackman, supra note 15, at   194.

it is easier for a gay man or lesbian to leave the relationship merely because the relationship is not as important to them as relationships are to heterosexuals. Therefore, experts must also be prepared to educate the jury on the nature of same-sex relationships and to refute the stereotypes and prejudices that both the judge and jury bring with them into the courtroom.

In sum, an expert on same-sex intimate violence must be for the battered gay or lesbian defendant what experts on battered woman's syndrome are for battered women: a translator of their lives' experiences. Experts can "educate the judge and jury about the common experiences of battered [persons and] ... explain the context in which an individual battered [person] acted, so as to lend credibility and provide a context to [his or her] explanation of [the] action."[239] Expert testimony can also refute judges' and jurors' own stereotypes of both intimate violence and the gay and lesbian lifestyle as well as "answer specific questions that are in judges' and jurors' minds of why the battered [defendant] didn't leave home ... and most importantly, why [he or] she believed that the danger ... faced on the particular occasion was life-threatening."[240] Gay or lesbian defendants on trial for killing their intimate partners who are not availed of this opportunity lack a fundamental right to be judged fairly without regard to their sexual orientation.

LINDA L. AMMONS, MULES, MADONNAS, BABIES, BATH WATER, RACIAL IMAGERY AND STEREOTYPES: THE AFRICAN–AMERICAN WOMAN AND THE BATTERED WOMAN SYNDROME (PART II)

1995 Wis. L. Rev. 1068–1078 (1995).

V.   AFRICAN-AMERICAN WOMEN DEFENDANTS AT TRIAL AND THE USE OF BATTERED WOMAN SYNDROME TESTIMONY: A USEFUL TOOL OR A HINDERANCE?

* * *

We are considered evil, but self-sacrificing; stupid but conniving; domineering while at the same time obedient to our men; and sexually inhibited, yet promiscuous. Covered by what is considered our seductively rich, but repulsive brown skin, Black women are perceived as inviting but armored. Society finds it difficult to believe that we really need physical or emotional support like all women of all races.

Much has been written about battered women who commit crimes and claim self-defense or coercion, and the inability of jurors to understand the complexity of their cases because of social mores and gender bias. As discussed in Part I, courts have allowed experts to explain the impact of battering on the woman's actions, because although jurors

---

239. Schneider, supra note 36, at 201.   **240.** Id. at 202.

think they understand domestic violence, the abusive relationship and a person's response to battering is in some cases "beyond the ken of the jury."

The convergence of race and sex provides an interesting intersection from which to analyze whether scientific data about how an African–American woman responds to violence is useful, or, conversely, whether such data further disadvantage African–American female defendants. In addressing these issues, the following questions must be asked and answered. First, can a black woman who is beaten by her current or past intimate partner experience the psychological, physical, and sociological phenomena now labeled as battered woman syndrome (or is this designation exclusive to white middle class women?). Second, when an African–American woman commits a crime and claims that she acted in self-defense because she was battered, what are the pragmatic and/or political realities of characterizing a black woman as a battered woman syndrome survivor?

As has been previously discussed, the prerequisite for experiencing post-traumatic stress disorder, of which battered woman syndrome is a subcategory, is exposure to extreme physical or psychological violence. Clinical tests can be administered to determine if a woman has symptoms that indicate that she has suffered from trauma. One researcher has found that race was a "relatively unimportant variable in terms of defining difference" in the experiences between white women and black women who were battered. However, the psychologist did note that black women in her sample, although abused, were less passive, or tougher, than the white women tested.

Not all persons, including women who are battered, will respond to brutality in the same way. Nevertheless, one can reasonably conclude that a significant group of women, regardless of their race, can react in similar ways to violence. The commonality of humanity and the shared experience of being violated transcends the social constructs of race and class. While the psyche and the body can tolerate certain levels of abuse, coping with violence is supposed to be an abnormal experience.

The issue is not whether a battered black women can experience the trauma known as battered woman syndrome. The focus of the inquiry should be if she does, is her claim likely to be discounted even more than that of her battered white counterpart because of her race? In other words, while a black female defendant may be able to establish the clinical elements of post-traumatic stress disorder or battered woman syndrome, which results in learned helplessness, of what benefit is that diagnosis, when at trial she must compete with racial and cultural stereotypes that indicate that she is anything but "helpless?" Battered women who become defendants face an uphill battle in court. Under the law, when the claim is self-defense, the defendant must convince the jury that her actions were reasonable, that she believed that she was in imminent danger of death and/or bodily harm and that there was no other way of escape. The defendant's credibility is at issue because in cases where a woman has killed an intimate partner, juries often do not understand how an adult with the freedom to associate chooses to remain in a volatile relationship, or why the woman does not successfully cut all ties to the alleged abuser. Explaining the context of a woman's actions is important. Whether she defended herself in the midst of a violent confrontation, or struck back during a temporary lull in a beating episode (e.g., while he is asleep), jurors have believed that the woman was to blame for her battering and the death of her partner.

Expert testimony on the nature of intimate violence and why a given defendant responded in a particular way may be needed to bolster the credibility of the defendant. This testimony can be used to explain the reasonableness of the defendant's action or her perception of imminent danger.

When a black female is facing trial for a crime that she says was committed in connection with domestic violence, and the woman can legitimately claim self-defense, her defense team must decide, among other things, whether the diagnosis of battered woman syndrome is appropriate, and whether, as a strategic matter, the defense team should offer testimony to explain why the woman acted reasonably under the circumstances (i.e., did not, or could not leave or sever all ties to the abuser).

"Learned helplessness" may or may not be the issue. If the woman's response to the batterer's actions is understood as traditional self-defense, a helplessness claim may confuse the jury and cloud the issue. However, if the jury is going to hear an expert explain how the defendant was "helpless," (in that she could not get out of the relationship or that he would not stop beating her even after she had separated herself from him), the defense team should be aware that this categorization, however scientific it might be, could be at odds with the contrary, pre-existing, persistent images (i.e., stereotypes) of black women. Therefore, the expert must be capable of first understanding, and then explaining, the cultural nuances that may make the woman appear to be able to take a different course of action. In other words, the defense team must be culturally competent. One expert may not be capable of testifying about psychological and cultural factors. A second expert may be needed to testify as to how the mythology concerning African–American women operates because educating all jurors, regardless of race, is critical. The presence of blacks on a jury does not ensure that the black woman will not be subjected to myths that may have been internalized by members of her own group. Some African–Americans may hold to the notion that black women do not tolerate abuse. Upon closer examination, the facts and psycho-social reality may reveal that the woman had little or no alternatives under the circumstances.

In preparing for jury selection, juror questionnaires are one approach in screening potential jurors and their biases. The responses can also be used to show the relevancy of the expert's testimony. Among the questions that should be asked in the juror questionnaire are:

1. How do you believe that the race of the defendant will affect you?

2. Use four words to describe black people.

3. What have been your experiences with black people?

4. Do you have any black friends, co-workers, acquaintances?

5. Describe your relationship with each.

6. Describe the typical black family.

7. Use four words to describe black women.

8. True or False, black women are more likely than white women to become victims of domestic violence? Explain.

9. What does the phrase "racial prejudice" mean to you?

10. Do you think that racial prejudice no longer exists? If not, Why?

Once the defense team has the juror's answers, it can better determine whether the juror is likely to understand the theory of the case, or just how much the juror will have to be educated. In *voir dire*, jurors may be reluctant to reveal their biases because of the dynamics of being in a group and the desire to be accepted. Requesting individual *voir dire*, at the very least on racial-gender issues, may minimize that tendency. Questions about prejudices may signal jurors to give the politically correct response even though they may actually hold certain biases. However, it may be more important to run the risk of alerting a potential juror about the search for prejudice than not to attempt to remove biased jurors or at least educate those that remain. In a battered woman case with a black female defendant, not only is it appropriate to pose questions about gender biases, but attitudes concerning African–American women should be probed as well.

There may not be a one-to-one correlation between seeing a black woman as a strong matriarch; or as an alluring, provocative Jezebel; or as a punishing, provoking Sapphire; or as a welfare cheat, and seeing the defendant as violent. If one were to accept the common mythology about black males, a black female defendant on trial for murdering her partner should benefit from a juror's perception that black men are violent, assuming that the alleged aggressor was a black male. But, when a juror is trying to reconcile what he or she believes about African–American females and what is perceived as helplessness, the typical images of black women may be a barrier to seeing the defendant as not culpable (either because of her strength of character, or her suspect character) for the violent encounter(s). Jurors have to be educated about how a black woman can be economically independent and yet emotionally dependent or "trapped" in a relationship. An African–American female's psychological disposition or practical circumstances may run counter to the notion that she is in control.

Chapter 14

FEDERAL RESPONSES: VIOLENCE AGAINST WOMEN ACT, RESTRICTIONS ON FIREARMS

This chapter looks at federal government responses to domestic violence. The first half focuses on the Violence Against Women Act. The materials begin by outlining the Act's overall provisions, and looking at the opportunities and challenges VAWA presents in terms of seeing domestic violence as a civil rights issue, including alliance-building between feminist groups and civil rights organizations representing communities of color.

Several articles then examine the civil rights provision of the Act, its most controversial section. Among other questions, they ask how the courts should define gender-motivated crimes, and note that the old view that domestic violence is "private conduct" continues to show itself in the sometimes strenuous objections to opening federal courts to these new types of cases. The U.S. Supreme Court decision, *U.S. v. Morrison*, decided May 15, 2000, is then excerpted. In a 5 to 4 decision, the Court held this provision of VAWA unconstitutional under both the Commerce Clause and the Fourteenth Amendment to the US Constitution.

The second half of the chapter concerns federal restrictions on possession of firearms by batterers, either after a misdemeanor conviction or when the respondent is subject to a domestic violence restraining order. These materials include statistics on firearms and domestic violence, a description of the applicable federal statutes, and two federal district court cases. Again, one upholds such restrictions, while the other holds that the restrictions are unconstitutional.

A. OVERVIEW

GEORGE B. STEVENSON, FEDERAL ANTIVIOLENCE AND ABUSE LEGISLATION: TOWARD ELIMINATION OF DISPARATE JUSTICE FOR WOMEN AND CHILDREN

33 Willamette L. Rev. 855–860, 871–874, 881–882 (1997).

The tide of federal response crested with the landmark of modern comprehensive domestic violence and abuse legislation: The Violence Against Women Act of 1994 (VAWA). The VAWA has numerous components that will be discussed throughout this Article. Congressional intervention will continue and become more sophisticated with the creation of permanent administrative offices, such as the Violence Against Women Office. However, much of the current legislation is so new that its full impact is still unknown. Numerous federal bills discussed in this Article provide funding for study and research to better understand domestic violence, sexual assault, and child abuse. Accordingly, many of these bills mandate study and reporting in order to determine the most effective responses to domestic violence, and strategies for victim support, prevention of abuse, and apprehension, conviction, and rehabilitation of offenders.

The general objectives of federal domestic violence and abuse legislation include: (1) improved criminal justice response at all levels; (2) enhanced victim services, including services through private nonprofit entities; (3) encouraging tougher intervention by state and local governments; and (4) expanded and improved telecommunication and record-keeping systems for tracking and screening offenders. Congress has enacted comprehensive bills to implement what it perceives as the changes necessary to achieve its objectives.

II. COMPREHENSIVE LEGISLATION

The drafters of the Violent Crime Control and Law Enforcement Act intended it "to allow grants to increase police presence, to expand and improve cooperative efforts between law enforcement agencies and members of the community to address crime and disorder problems, and otherwise to enhance public safety...." The Act is another massive anticrime bill in the tradition of the 1968 Omnibus bill. It protects people of all ages from violence, abuse, and neglect. There is an underlying assumption that a correlation exists between domestic violence against women and child abuse. The most highly publicized portion of this legislation was the Violence Against Women Act (VAWA), which contains a number of independent sections that apply to all ages and genders of victims. The VAWA demonstrates an overt commitment to changing the criminal justice system's response to violence against women. Its provisions commit a significant amount of federal resources and attention to restructuring the criminal justice response to women and children who have been, or potentially could be, victims of violence.

* * *

A.   1.   *The Safe Streets for Women Act*

The Safe Streets for Women Act ironically has little to do directly with a vision of "safe streets" except for provisions granting money to localities for safety improvements in public transit and park facilities. The Act bears two themes: (1) support for women and child victims; and (2) high profile criminalization through apprehension, conviction, and imposition of stiffer sentences. The indirect impact of the Act could be "safer streets" by removing the offender from the street for a longer period of time.

* * *

2.   *The Violent Crime Control and Law Enforcement Act*

This comprehensive Act contains several domestic violence provisions that directly affect female victims of violence. The next part of this Article explores these hard intervention provisions.

Federal statutes now require life imprisonment for a person convicted in federal court of a serious violent felony after prior conviction in a state or federal court of two serious felonies or a serious violent offense and a serious drug offense—"three strikes and you're out." Qualifying prior felony convictions include assault with intent to commit rape, aggravated sexual abuse, sexual abuse, abusive sexual conduct, and any attempt, conspiracy, or solicitation to commit any of these offenses. The court also must consider any prior offense punishable up to ten years or more that has an element of use, attempted use, or threatened use of physical force against another person.

Sentencing options for other offenses include probation or post-prison supervision. Congress' action tightens the controls over offenders in probation or post-prison status, and limits the offender's opportunity for probation. Persons convicted of a federal domestic violence crime may receive probation unless: (1) the crime is a Class A or B felony; (2) no probation is allowed as a matter of law; or (3) the offender is sentenced to imprisonment for another offense at the same time. Therefore, probation is not available to those classes of persons prone to repeat violent conduct. The federal government protects potential victims by assuming this hard intervention will both reduce recidivism and remove the threatening offender from the streets.

The Violent Crime and Control Act requires the courts to sentence all first-time domestic violence offenders to a term of probation, if not imprisoned. Judges may order post-prison supervised release or may sentence the first-time offender up to five years for a felony or one year for a misdemeanor. Previously, first-time offenders received deferred or diverted prosecution. This new approach to sentencing conforms to and reflects the current concept of treating domestic violence as a crime.

One condition of first-time offender probation is participation in a private nonprofit rehabilitation program approved by the court in consultation with a State Coalition Against Domestic Violence. This condition applies only if an approved program is available within a fifty-mile radius of the offender's residence. Unique to this rehabilitation program, defendants with "organic brain damage or severe mental illness" are assured treatment; however, the treating program may refer back to court any defendant for whom a rehabilitative program is inappropriate. Preventive treatment is a token of lingering hope for the "non hardcore" offenders and is rarely a feature of recent legislation.

* * *

C. Legislation for the Protection of Women

1. Stalking

Stalking behavior constitutes a perplexing problem to victims and the criminal justice system because the behavior may consist of a series of noncriminal acts that, collectively, place a victim in a permanent state of physical and mental siege. Stalking can range from harassment to terrorization. National attention focused on stalking after the 1989 shooting death of actress Rebecca Shaeffer in California by a fan who stalked her for two years. As a result of the shooting, California adopted the first antistalking law.

The first federal legislation to address stalking was inconspicuously introduced in a massive 1992 fiscal appropriations act. This Act called for the Attorney General, through the National Institute of Justice (NIJ), to study and develop a model antistalking code for distribution throughout the states. The NIJ submitted a progress report to Congress in 1993 to justify further funding. The NIJ reported a significant lack of information regarding stalking behaviors, and suggested that further study was required. The NIJ studies examined both public figure and ordinary citizen victims.

The NIJ produced a Model Antistalking Code in October 1993 with the recommendation that the offense be considered a felony to emphasize the seriousness of the crime. In 1996, however, it seemed that felony treatment only would leave other less dangerous but offensive conduct unpunished as stalking. The Code punishes a course of conduct (maintaining proximity to the victim or communicating a threat verbally, in writing, or impliedly through conduct) that would cause a victim to reasonably fear for his or her life. The NIJ identified community policing, later endorsed and funded by the VAWA, as a limited front-line source of protection for victims and potential victims of stalking.

The Safe Homes for Women Act, created under the VAWA, encompasses much more than the mere concept of "safe homes"; it also provides law enforcement personnel with the authority to enforce civil protective orders from other states, as well as punish an offender who travels interstate. Theoretically, the Act should encourage women to obtain protective orders in one state even if they later leave that state to seek safety elsewhere.

Congress relied on its regulatory authority under the Commerce Clause to punish domestic abusers or stalkers who cross state lines, enter or leave Indian country, or cause a victim to do so. For the Act to apply, the victim, a spouse or intimate partner, must sustain bodily injury. Punishment of the abuser is increased according to the victim's degree of injuries, including death or life imprisonment if the victim dies.

In order to make the antistalking measures successful, the protective orders and offender's description must be verifiable nationwide. Federal statutes authorize the Attorney General to make funds available to improve processes for entering stalking and domestic violence data into local, state, and national databases, such as the NCIC. To be eligible for this program, a state or local government must enter into the database the warrants for arrest, protective orders, arrests of persons violating protective orders, and the offender's comprehensive criminal history. The program also includes funds to provide technical assistance and training for state and tribal judges handling stalking and domestic violence cases. The statute mandates that the Attorney General enter compiled data into the National Incident–Bases Reporting System (NIBRS). The ability to establish the suspect's identity and verify warrants or protective orders may allow police to head off a would-be assailant, make a pre-emptive arrest, track a fleeing suspect who may attempt to use an alias, enforce an out-of-state order before the new state can issue an order, or identify a potential suspect if a victim is missing, dead, or disabled. This federal effort would be ineffective if the protective orders possessed no interstate authority. Therefore, Congress requires every state or tribe to give full faith and credit to protective orders issued by any other state or tribe.

In addition, the VAWA amended the Family Violence Prevention and Services Act to establish the National Domestic Violence Hotline. The Act authorizes the Secretary of Health and Human Services to grant money to a private nonprofit entity to provide a national toll-free telephone hotline for a maximum of five years to inform and assist victims of domestic violence. An open line is especially needed by women and children isolated in rural areas or on Indian reservations where fewer resources are available. This toll-free line will help put victims who flee hurriedly to another state in touch with protective shelters and other resources. These provisions offer the hope to victims that "safe homes" will be available to them throughout the country.

* * *

2. *Equal Justice for Women in the Courts*

The VAWA expanded the State Justice Institute's authority and mission to study and eliminate gender bias in all criminal justice and court systems. To accomplish this goal, the Institute requires each federal circuit judicial council to form gender bias task forces to study gender bias and implement reforms in their circuit. These task forces will examine the treatment of all persons during the trial process, the interpretations and applications of law, treatment of violent crime victims, sentencing disparities, federal employment appointment and advancement opportunities and practices, and court rulings on the admission of past sexual conduct evidence.

The Institute has authority to award grants to develop model programs to be used in training state and Indian tribal judges and court personnel on dealing with rape, sexual assault, domestic violence, and other crimes of gender-motivated violence. The Administrative Office of the United States Courts receives the task force reports, and the Federal Judicial Center implements training and programs to overcome any deficiencies the reports may reveal. The overall purpose of these programs is to make court less foreboding to domestic violence victims and as a result, to overcome victim reluctance to report domestic violence and pursue judicial remedies.

JENNY RIVERA, THE VIOLENCE AGAINST WOMEN ACT AND THE CONSTRUCTION OF MULTIPLE CONSCIOUSNESS IN THE CIVIL RIGHTS AND FEMINIST MOVEMENTS

4 J. L. & Pol'y 464–467 (1996).

INTRODUCTION

The enactment of the Violence Against Women Act ("VAWA") in 1994 was, ostensibly, a success of historic proportions on various political and social fronts. It has significantly furthered efforts to legitimize a feminist anti-violence agenda within the political mainstream by providing federal criminal and civil legal remedies for female survivors of violence. Indeed, significant portions of the VAWA were originally viewed as highly controversial, in part because of their feminist origin. These provisions, and consequently the VAWA *in toto*, were politicized in a derogatory manner prior to the VAWA's passage. When the VAWA was finally signed into legislation, it marked the end of a protracted political and educational campaign conducted in Congress and across the country on gender-motivated violence.

While the enactment of the VAWA is undeniably a victory for feminism, and as such served as a vehicle for a sophisticated national discourse on violence between intimate partners, the passage of the VAWA is also a civil rights victory. This Article argues that, at a time when the hard-won gains of civil rights and feminist struggles are being challenged and dismantled, both movements must work together cooperatively. In order for cooperation to be successful, cooperation cannot be based or forged solely on the mutual need for a solid constituency. Rather, cooperation must be the acknowledged result of the application of civil rights and feminist doctrines to the issues and problems faced by women and people of color in society. The VAWA represents an important opportunity for civil rights activists and feminists to identify common goals and philosophies of their respective social and legal reform movements, and an opportunity to convert their doctrines into practice through joint action.

The recognition that the civil rights movement can be gender-conscious and gender-responsive, and that the feminist movement can speak to issues of race and ethnic discrimination—that both movements can be constructed in such a way as to account for and respond to the particular issues and concerns of women of all races and ethnic backgrounds—allows for collaboration between the proponents of these two movements. As a consequence, both movements will benefit and can fully pursue their mutual goals of equity and justice. The concept of a multiple consciousness which governs and informs these movements can be realized.

Part I of this Article provides a brief overview of the common, yet often conflicting, history of the civil rights and feminist movements and provides examples of why the current political climate threatens to dismantle the hard-won advances of both movements, and, simultaneously, serves as an impetus to unite the two around common goals. Part I concludes that, given the histories of the two movements and their relative positions in the current political landscape, the VAWA is a potential point of convergence where constituencies and representatives of both groups can construct a dialogue and strategy that furthers their mutual and respective goals. This is partly because, at least theoretically, the VAWA responds to the concerns of both communities of color and women. Part II discusses the VAWA in greater detail and identifies the VAWA provisions of particular interest for women of color, especially Latinas and immigrant women. In addition, part II identifies some of the potential problems foreseeable in the application of these provisions. Lastly, this Article concludes by urging civil rights and feminist activists to expand and equalize their collaborative efforts and apply their respective social reform doctrines to each others' struggles. It further encourages activists to maximize the VAWA's potential for reform by aggressively utilizing its remedies, calling for enactment and enforcement of those provisions which take account of the particular needs of women of color and immigrant women, and combining the two movements' considerable experiences and strengths to end the multiple forms of intimate partner violence against all women.

* * *

I. C. CURRENT BATTLEGROUNDS: THE POLITICAL AGENDAS OF PEOPLE OF COLOR AND WOMEN AT A CROSSROADS

Reconsideration and reformulation of traditional civil rights and feminist theories and strategies are of paramount importance to the survival and vitality of both these movements. They are at a doctrinal and political crossroads, coming under attack from critics within and outside of the two movements.

In recent years, civil rights and feminist theories have been criticized as outdated, outmoded, a failed attempt at political and social reform or, at best, unresponsive to the current political and social conditions of persons living in the United States. Indeed, both have been charged with failing to represent the majority of their constituents. Debates over the ability of these movements to represent their respective target constituencies are frequent and often peppered with vitriolic hyperbole.

Political and physical attacks on civil rights and feminist activists, and sometimes against women and people of color generally are at palpably high levels, and reflect a fear that traditional power dynamics are finally, gradually shifting. For example, angry mobs picket women's health clinics and, under the guise of "right to life" rhetoric, violent acts—including murder—are encouraged and, not surprisingly, proliferate against the supporters of women's right to choose. Indeed, aggressive attacks on feminism and civil rights advocacy are international in expanse and have escalated in the past few years.

Attempts to eradicate certain entitlement programs and affirmative action policies, in part the result of civil rights and feminist struggles, have placed women in the United States, particularly poor women and women of color, under both racial-and gender-based attack. For example, legislative and popular challenges to long-established state-or federally-funded programs that largely serve women seek the elimination of federal job training programs, public and private affirmative action initiatives, as well as entitlement programs. Supporters of these agendas come from both the Republican and Democratic political parties. They assert that a redefinition of government is necessary for the survival of United States economic and political systems. This process is marked by the downsizing of government and the elimination of government services without regard for—and sometimes with hostility toward—women and the resulting impact on their lives.

* * *

Demands to end affirmative action and the scaling-back of various entitlement programs, are similarly marked by gendered and racialized notions about relative roles and group market contributions. As in the debates about the elimination of entitlement programs on which women depend, calls for the discontinuance of affirmative action programs are devoid of analyses of the impact on women's economic status. The absence of such analysis in the affirmative action context perpetuates the myth that affirmative action programs are strictly designed for African American men. This is a clearly inaccurate representation of affirmative action initiatives and their beneficiaries, since significant numbers of women have made economic gains under affirmative action programs. Similarly, as the battle lines are drawn on the issue of entitlements for single parents, recipients are cast almost without exception as female, young, irresponsible, often Black and/or Latina, and who, moreover, must be pushed into the work force. Again, these characterizations are inaccurate and part of a larger agenda which portrays individuals who are the targets of social service cuts as marginal noncontributors.

One result of these political attacks on women and people of color has been the development and implementation of cooperative strategies by civil rights and feminist activists. The progressive ideologies of civil rights advocacy and feminism have coalesced and flourished globally in the international arena, where women's rights are receiving increasing attention and are being treated as human rights. This collective work, and the coalescing of resources for joint initiatives in furtherance of complementary agendas, are a natural progression of the struggles of the civil rights movement and the feminist movement. Both have used similar strategies in furtherance of their respective goals for equality and opportunity. Arguably, both have learned from one another's successes and mistakes. Despite a sometimes adversarial and contentious history of joint accommodation, more common ground than discord exists between these two movements.

* * *

II. B. The VAWA as Gender Conscious-Gender Responsive Civil Rights Legislation

The passage of the VAWA is an important victory for the combined efforts of civil rights and feminist movements, but it is only the beginning of a more complex set of historical events. The most telling aspects of the story behind the VAWA will ultimately be defined and developed in the implementation and enforcement of that legislation. This section explores the potential for activists and theorists from both movements to effectively continue their collaborative efforts, and highlights some of the problems they may encounter in making the VAWA's promises a reality.

The VAWA provides a unique opportunity for the fusion of the visions of civil rights and feminist struggles. With the establishment of a new cause of action in the VAWA, which provides a civil rights remedy, the opportunity for a civil action based on gender violence would appear at first glance to be the appropriate legal and analytical framework for such fusion. Nevertheless, it is more likely that the civil rights provision provides little practical relief from the complex multiple experiences of sexism, and race, ethnic and culture-based discrimination endemic to the lives of women of color. When considering those provisions of the VAWA which truly incorporate a gender responsive civil rights approach to violence against women, it is those sections which speak directly to the issues of women of color which reflect multiple consciousness. Moreover, it is not solely particular VAWA provisions working in isolation which make the legislation unique and uniquely applicable to women of color. Rather, it is the various sections of the VAWA working in tandem which make the VAWA a gender conscious-gender responsive civil rights law;

one which provides legal recourse to all women survivors of domestic violence, regardless of race, ethnicity, culture and/or language.

One of the primary aspects of the legislation is its ambitious attempt to respond to the particular ways women experience violence. First, it recognizes the prevalence of violence between intimate partners, and, because it applies to former intimate partners, it also recognizes that violence does not necessarily terminate when the relationship ends. Second, the VAWA avoids making the all too common mistake of judging women who stay in violent relationships by adversely characterizing them as "failing" to take aggressive steps to curtail the batterer's conduct, or otherwise blaming women for their abusers' conduct. Rather, the VAWA provides for the establishment of programs and law enforcement strategies that will, at least in theory, create an environment in which women can feel they have real options to negotiate the violence. If these programs and strategies are effectively established and enforced, women will have more resources, such as shelters and support services, and police will be better able to respond appropriately to domestic violence with education and enhanced resources.

Another way in which the VAWA incorporates the experiential and doctrinal foundations of civil rights and feminist antidiscrimination theory and activism is by providing for the installation and integration of programs and services responsive to the different situations faced by women of color. This ensures the applicability of particular VAWA projects to a diverse population of women, and also enhances the VAWA's overall vitality. For example, in several sections the VAWA mandates the inclusion of representatives from various communities, including communities of color, in the development and strategic planning of VAWA mandated or facilitated enforcement, education and research projects. Thus, the VAWA discretely, but effectively, recognizes that women of color have available to them different and often fewer options than do many White women because of their race, ethnicity, culture and language.

The experiences of women of color as survivors of domestic violence often differ from those of other women, therefore, *a fortiori*, the development and implementation of anti-violence strategies as applied to women of color must reflect those differences. The VAWA recognizes that within communities of color there are different issues and discrete culturally-based concerns. For example, law enforcement and prosecution federal grants are available for, *inter alia*, purposes of "developing or improving delivery of victim services to racial, cultural, ethnic, and language minorities...." Further, states must set forth in their grant applications the demographics of the service population, including information on "race, ethnicity and language background...." in order to qualify for a grant. Applicants for the National Domestic Violence Hotline grant had to provide a plan for servicing "non-English speaking callers," such as by employing Spanish-speaking hotline personnel, and had to demonstrate a commitment to "diversity, and to the provision of services to ethnic, racial, and non-English speaking minorities...."

Although the VAWA data collection provisions are less specific, they do require, in the development of a research agenda, inclusion of experts on services to ethnic and language minority communities, and a focus on the needs of underserved populations. Such data is critical because there is little information about domestic violence and its impact on women within communities of color. The collection of this data is an important step in designing appropriate preventive and protective anti-violence programs in ethnic communities.

* * *

1. Civil Rights Remedy—Subtitle C

Civil rights advocates and feminists generally recognize the historical benefits of civil litigation and the role civil rights and women's rights cases have played in improving the status of women and people of color. The VAWA civil rights remedy, however, contains certain difficulties related to its usefulness.

First, access to the legal system, including the courts, continues to be a major obstacle for women of color. There are too few Latino, African American and Asian officials in the legal system, serving as judges, lawyers, clerks, court officers and other court personnel. People of color, and women of color in particular, are isolated and have little faith in our legal system. Latinas, for example, carry the disproportionate burden of the lack of bilingual-bicultural personnel. Without sufficient translators and appropriate bilingual-bicultural providers available to them, Latinas are often reluctant to seek legal assistance, or unable to secure a legal remedy, even when they do turn to the courts for help. This situation is unlikely to improve as federal and state legislators ignore or reject the need for affirmative hiring and training programs which would increase the presence and employment of people of color in the judicial system. The likelihood of more representation in the legal system of historically excluded populations is minimal.

Second, the legal system has not always served as a positive vehicle for reform with respect to the struggles of women of color. Often, cases have furthered oppression or justified acts of injustice. Women of color are treated differently than men and other women. They are subject to both the sexism which pervades the judicial system, as well as the discrimination based on race and national origin which characterizes too many "judicial proceedings" and is found too often in the "halls of justice." It is with diminished expectations that many women of color turn to the courts.

Third, and perhaps the determinative factor in the equation, is the likelihood of obtaining satisfactory relief through this civil process. Since the scope of the civil rights provision is as yet untested, the extent of the relief courts will grant is unknown, and the possibility of securing financial compensation from the litigation is uncertain. In addition, the necessary financial and emotional investment in such litigation can be prohibitive for Latinas and other women of color survivors of domestic violence. Many do not have even sufficient financial resources to provide for their basic needs. Nor are the batterers who would be the subjects of these lawsuits, deep-pocket defendants. The incentive to sue an abuser is even lower when, as is true for many women, the abuser provides the only, or a necessary portion of, the family's income.

Undoubtedly there will be women who would nevertheless proceed with such litigation notwithstanding the lack of monetary compensation involved. However, it is unlikely that counsel could be secured in such cases. Although the VAWA civil rights remedy provides for attorneys' fees, the "judgment-proof" status of the defendant is a consideration for the private bar.

Fourth, there are too few attorneys interested in these cases and competent to develop the litigation required to succeed. The theoretical framework for the civil rights cause of action will be tested in the courts, but it will take several decisions before there is some semblance of judicial interpretation of the contours of the remedy. This process, as is the case historically for new legislation, will take years to develop and the decisions will take additional time to assess. In the interim, however, it is unlikely that women of color will be part of these test cases, for the reasons set forth above. In essence, the fact is that the survivor of domestic violence must be aware of the possible legal remedies in order to engage the system, and the survivor must have counsel available and ready to develop litigation in untested waters. Currently, the likelihood that women of color can be full participants in this litigation process is minimal.

Lest this analysis of the VAWA civil rights cause of action appear too pessimistic, I believe that there is also potential for reform based on utilization of this remedy. The ability to proceed in federal court has historically been a positive element in civil rights legislation. Perceptions of the likelihood of more just treatment in federal rather than state courts has been a factor in the decision of counsel and clients to proceed with federal litigation. The existence of a support network is also critical to the utilization of this remedy. As the first section of this article makes clear, such a support network already exists. The visibility of civil rights activists and feminists, including women of color from both movements, can greatly increase the likelihood of litigation against gender-based violence.

* * *

Conclusion

Recommendations for the increased utilization of all sections of the VAWA by women of color must promote the integration of women of color into the political system and into civil rights and feminist movements. The collaborative agenda that can be developed together by participants in the civil rights movement and the feminist movement is possible so long as women of color have an equal voice in the political dialogue. Any and all programs financed and promoted under the auspices of the VAWA must be designed and implemented with the assistance and under the direction of women representing diverse communities. Representational programs have long been integrated into various federal initiatives. *A fortiori* women of color and programs run by women of color must receive their fair share of VAWA allocations and decision-making power. Legislation that purports to address gender-based violence must also address the concerns and issues of women of color specifically. This requires addressing discrimination based on race, national origin, culture and language. The passage of the VAWA brings us part of the way towards addressing these issues. Through the cooperative efforts of civil rights activists and feminists, the VAWA can fulfill its obligation to all women, and can become part of a more fully collaborative activism that is the culmination of the struggles of women and people of color against violence as systemic oppression.

B.   VAWA'S CIVIL RIGHTS REMEDY

VICTORIA F. NOURSE, WHERE VIOLENCE, RELATIONSHIP, AND EQUALITY MEET: THE VIOLENCE AGAINST WOMEN ACT'S CIVIL RIGHTS REMEDY

11 Wis. Women's L. J. 1–6 (1996).

The 1994 signing of the Violence Against Women Act represented the culmination of a four-year struggle of politics, law, and understanding. Many stories could be written about this legislative effort: stories about political fortunes, personal perseverance, and daring backroom maneuvering. But the legal story, one now being played out in the federal courts, is a story of the law working against its own language and rhetoric, a law struggling to try to change its own understanding of violence against women.

When the Violence Against Women Act (the "Act" or "VAWA") was first introduced, drafters wrestled with the words that could be used to describe this violence, acknowledging openly that the standard expressions seemed not only inadequate but potentially destructive. The very categories the law directed them to use incorporated the problem that they were trying to solve. "Acquaintance rape" and "domestic violence," not to mention "marital rape" or "incest," all defined crime "by relationship." The crime did not exist without that relationship, and yet, it was that relationship that had helped to make the crime something "lesser," some "inferior" kind of crime, both in the eyes of the law and popular imagination. The legislative history of the Violence Against Women Act is a story, in the end, of using the idea of equality to challenge the "veil of relationship" shrouding this violence.

Today, it may seem as if this should not have been much of a struggle. The most controversial media events of this decade—the confirmation hearings of Justice Thomas and the trial of O.J. Simpson—have helped to change public attitudes about violence against women. At the time the Violence Against Women Act was introduced in 1990, however, it is fair to say that battering was still considered "natural" violence by many and, as a result, seen by mainstream politicians as a "fringe" issue trumpeted only by radical feminists. Within this atmosphere, it might have seemed downright foolhardy to challenge the power of relationship to diminish violence by invoking the idea of gender equality. And yet, that is precisely what its sponsor, Senator Joseph Biden, did when he introduced the bill in June of 1990.

The struggle of understanding that led to the Act's passage is important not only as history but also as prologue. Already, the Act's civil rights remedy is being challenged in the federal courts on constitutional grounds. This makes our understanding of the Act's history doubly relevant. First, the legislative history speaks directly to the constitutional questions (at least as then understood). Second, and perhaps more importantly, it was the organized federal judiciary, led by the Chief Justice of the United States, whose opposition to the bill's civil rights remedy delayed its passage. That opposition hinged upon a particular understanding of the nature of that remedy as a "domestic relations" statute and, therefore, unsuited for federal court adjudication. It was precisely this understanding, however, that drafters hoped that the Violence Against Women Act would alter—that crimes against women would no longer be lessened, diminished, and dismissed because of the relationships that had spawned them.

The Violence Against Women Act aimed at comprehensiveness, covering everything from domestic violence hotlines, to evidentiary matters in sexual harassment cases, to rape kit exams. Elsewhere, I have offered a more comprehensive history of the Act. Here, I tell the history of the Violence Against Women Act with special reference to its major attempt to change the legal terms in which we understand this violence—the civil rights remedy. Part I summarizes the overarching debate about the remedy. In Part II, the first drafts of the bill, along with its first hearings, are discussed. Part III tells the story of the controversy about the civil rights remedy and Congress' attempts to address the constitutional questions in light of the Supreme Court's recent decision in *United States v. Lopez*. Part IV discusses the final changes to the bill, including the *"animus"* language added to the "gender-motivation" requirement. Part V briefly describes the final passage of the Act in the Senate and House and the Conference Committee consideration.

PART ONE—THE CIVIL RIGHTS REMEDY: THE ISSUE

Our very first civil rights laws barred the use of violence to brand some men as inferior. In 1871, the Congress opened the federal courts in cases where state laws had failed to protect against violent racial discrimination. By 1990, then, it should have been well established that violence could also be discrimination. It should also have been well established that, where state laws and practices failed to protect the equal rights of citizens, the federal government had the power, and the obligation, to provide an alternate forum to resolve those disputes, even where the underlying conduct might also be barred by state law.

If these were well-established principles as a matter of law, they were not principles that the bill's sponsors expected would carry the day. They acknowledged, early on, that the touchstone of a civil rights remedy is its ability to redress the failures of State law. Not surprisingly, the Committee reports and hearings focus on law as much as personal harm; they tell a story of the "puzzling persistence of public policies, laws, and attitudes that treat some crimes against women less seriously than other violent crimes." In many ways, the story told was one of law veiled by the idea of the relationship, a law that perceived "marital disputes" where there were felonies; that refused to see force as force as long as it was tied to an acquaintance; that believed that there was something "personal" about rape when perpetrated by a husband; that said that violence was chosen by choosing a relationship. After decades of state law reform, "it was still easier to convict a car thief than a rapist and authorities were more likely to arrest a man for parking tickets than for beating his wife." As Senator Biden summed it up, the "criminal justice system had failed to do its part," it had given half of our citizens only "distrust, disbelief, and discrimination."

Despite this foundation, the analogy to existing civil rights protections would leave many unconvinced. Unlike the racially-motivated violence first outlawed by Congress in the Reconstruction era, violence perpetrated against women did not seem primarily conspiratorial, widely identified with organized political movements, or the product of publicly institutionalized slavery. Compared to America's shameful history of racial discrimination, the critics urged, violence against women seemed far less political and far more personal; the product of private relationships, not public discrimination. Indeed, its very commonness, its ubiquity, seemed to counsel against the idea that violence discriminated.

In a sense, these arguments might have been predicted. Once upon a time, the "whites only" sign on the door of the local diner was a private matter; once upon a time, sexual favors were the "trivial" price to be paid for a job; once upon a time, we believed that sex and race segregation at work and at school were part of the normal order of things. If arguments of triviality, privacy, and normalcy had proven poor predictors of injustice in the past, they found a new resonance in these circumstances. Critics argued that gender-based violence was "different": it wasn't employment, it wasn't race, it was "personal and private." There were, of course, counter-examples—no individual act of lynching nor of sexual harassment may seem "political" or "organized" to its victims and each is barred by state law, however ill-enforced. In the end, however, these examples of violent discrimination seemed more public, less emotional, and less close-to-home. What gave force to the critics' arguments was an implicit call to relationship: these were private matters precisely because they involved personal relationships, not public attacks by strangers. That, of course, joined the issue precisely: for it was the idea that relationship could automatically diminish the violence that the law's advocates sought to challenge.

By invoking an existing civil rights tradition, drafters were not engaging in an effort of principle alone. They sought to extend the protection of existing gender discrimination laws. Massive efforts had been made in the 1970s and 1980s to ensure equal opportunity for women: equal opportunity in employment, in education, in the application of family and criminal law. Experience had proven, however, that these formal advances were no match for private violence. Would a law guaranteeing equal pay mean much to a woman whose husband beat her when she tried to leave the house for a job interview? Would a sex-neutral divorce law help a woman who, when she tried to leave her husband, was stalked and threatened into returning? Would a gender-neutral rape law mean much to a woman, raped by a date, if the prosecutor refused to bring her case? In a sense, violence against women was the ultimate weapon against gender equality—it could wipe out in a single blow any and every advance in opportunity created by over twenty years of law reform.

Persuading the Congress to take the leap of imagination from existing civil rights laws to VAWA's civil rights remedy would not be legislatively or politically easy. When drafters decided to include the remedy, they invited controversy. Much of VAWA built upon significant reform efforts of the 1970s and 1980s: proposals for funding shelters, expanding rape shield rules, and strengthening special prosecutorial units covered familiar legal territory. The civil rights remedy, however, was unprecedented. It not only departed from traditional approaches toward violence against women, it also departed, in significant ways, from other civil rights remedies. As a result, it became controversial among private civil rights groups as well as federal and state judges, eventually yielding the public opposition of the Chief Justice of the United States. Not surprisingly, this controversy stalled the bill at various points on the road to final passage.

* * *

JULIE GOLDSCHEID, GENDER–MOTIVATED VIOLENCE: DEVELOPING A MEANINGFUL PARADIGM FOR CIVIL RIGHTS ENFORCEMENT

22 Harv. Women's L. J. 148–157 (1999).

IV. LIMITATIONS OF THE ANALOGY AND THE SPECIAL PROBLEMS OF GENDER

Enactment of the VAWA Civil Rights Remedy has established a threshold for how gender-based bias crimes will be assessed in the context of federal civil remedies. While the requirement of circumstantial evidence may be imperfect because it may preclude recovery if that evidence is not available in a particular case, it also imposes a limiting principle that addresses concerns about overwhelming federal judicial resources. As the first cases litigated under that law indicate, a critical inquiry as to the presence of circumstantial evidence of bias in sexual assault and domestic violence cases may uncover the extent to which bias infuses those acts.

Nonetheless, questions about how to interpret the VAWA Civil Rights Remedy standard inevitably will be raised. For example, courts will be called on to address the meaning of the statutory requirement of *"animus"* here, as opposed to other anti-discrimination contexts. In the case of domestic violence, suggestions have been made that there is a difference between "ordinary" domestic violence and that which is motivated by gender. Some argue that domestic violence cannot be gender-motivated because of evidence that women batter men, notwithstanding evidence that women's violence frequently is committed in self-defense and occurs disproportionately less frequently. Critics argue that the fact that violence occurs in lesbian and gay as well as heterosexual relationships compels the conclusion that gender-motivation never animates domestic violence cases, although even the United States Supreme Court has recognized that sexual harassment can be committed regardless of the respective genders of the harasser and victim. Similarly, some objections invoke the incidence of male rapes of other men as dispositive of the non-gendered nature of all sexual assaults. In addition, commentators have objected that hate crime laws recriminalize already illegal conduct. Finally, the *Brzonkala* trial court decision reflects the oft-cited perception that it is difficult to discern when personality rather than bias underlies unwanted sexual assault. This section will address some of the issues underlying these objections.

A.   The Meaning of 'Gender *Animus*"

The language of the VAWA Civil Rights Remedy has introduced a wrinkle to the debate on establishing gender-motivation: whether use of the term *"animus"* differentiates the standard for proving gender-motivation from that used to establish discriminatory motivation in other contexts. As discussed above, in order to establish the "gender-motivation" element the statute requires, a plaintiff must prove both that the act was committed "because of gender or on the basis of gender," and that it was "due, at least in part, to an *animus* based on the victim's gender." Also as discussed previously, the legislative history shows that Congress intended the *"animus"* language to clarify that only gender-motivated crimes, rather than all violent crimes committed against women, or "random" acts of violence committed against women, would be covered.

The inclusion of the term *"animus"* does not change the nature or quantum of evidence required to establish gender-motivation. Congress used the term *"animus"* to mean "purpose," as in "an animating force," and it used the words *"animus,"* "purpose," and "motivation" interchangeably, dispelling any notion that disparate impact, i.e., proof that a violent act disproportionately affects women, alone would be sufficient to merit recovery. The first part of the gender-motivation definition arguably gives rise to that concern. The language requiring that the underlying violent act was committed "because of gender or on the basis of gender" tracks Title VII, which encompasses disparate impact as well as treatment cases. The *"animus"* language eliminates any question about whether disparate impact cases might be covered.

In the first cases interpreting the Remedy, courts have ruled consistently with Congress' direction and have treated the gender-motivation element as a single inquiry, rather than two separate questions about *animus* and whether the act was committed because of gender. That approach also comports with other bias crime case law, which treats circumstantial evidence the same way under a range of statutory formulations. For example, cases litigated under 42 U.S.C. § 1985(3) require proof that the conduct was motivated by "racial, or perhaps otherwise class-based, invidiously discriminatory *animus*" in order to prevail. Yet even under that apparently higher standard, the previous analysis of Section 1985(3) and other cases reveals that the same evidence establishes bias regardless of whether the standard for assessing *animus* is articulated as "because of" a protected category, based on *"animus"* or driven by "invidiously discriminatory *animus."*

As recounted above, the type of evidence used to show gender or other bias motivation does not vary, regardless of the particular statutory formulation. In addition, other federal civil rights cases also confirm that even under Section 1985(3), gender-based *animus* does not require proof of malice or hatred. As with other discrimination and bias crime cases, the essential inquiry is whether the crime was committed solely for random or non-discriminatory reasons. The use of the term *"animus"* in the Civil Rights Remedy does not alter that essential inquiry for gender-based bias crime cases.

B. Addressing Concerns Unique to Gender: the Prevalence of Domestic Violence and Sexual Assault and their Purported "Neutral" Motivations

Perhaps the principal or underlying objection to treating domestic violence and sexual assaults as civil rights cases is the staggering number of those crimes committed each year. Yet it would be an absurd perversion of our justice system if the prevalence of a problem became the justification for ignoring it. If the true problem is a lack of sufficient resources to cover all the cases that should be treated as civil rights violations, resources should be provided. Nonetheless, the Civil Rights Remedy's statutory requirements appear to be successfully limiting the number of cases actually brought.

In assessing whether violent acts are gender-motivated, courts inevitably will grapple with the question of whether an allegation of domestic violence or sexual assault alone provides enough evidence from which to draw an inference of bias motivation. It is difficult to imagine an act of rape, sexual assault, or domestic violence that is not in part fueled by the tradition of gender-motivated violence in this country. Given that history, perhaps acts of rape or domestic violence should be analogized to lynching or cross-burning, and viewed as symbolic acts that alone reflect gender-motivated bias. Indeed, any reluctance to recognize sexual assault or domestic violence as inherently bias-driven stands in stark contrast to the ease with which we recognize symbolic acts such as lynching or cross-burning as discriminatory.

Nonetheless, the Civil Rights Remedy's legislative history indicates that allegations of domestic violence, rape, or sexual assault may not presumably be considered to be gender-motivated for the purpose of federal civil rights intervention. In addition, social science data and some commentary reflect the view that not all acts of rape, sexual assault, or domestic violence are driven by a discriminatory motivation. In particular, discussions of the gendered nature of rape and sexual assault inevitably address acquaintance rape, which many find presents the quagmire of distinguishing those crimes based on "bias" from those based on "lust," "passion," or "personality." Recent scholarship and studies have begun to investigate a range of motivations that might drive rapists: some men rape because they want to have sex; others, to demonstrate their strength and masculinity; and still others, to establish their dominance over, or distinction from, other men. The assertion of power and anger also have been asserted to play a key role in rape. Similarly, recent research indicates that there are different motivations for domestic violence.

These theories arguably could support a contention that "neutral" psychological factors rather than bias fuel acts of domestic violence or sexual assault. However, the two should not be mutually exclusive because a particular act could be motivated by bias as well as by "neutral" psychological factors. In the context of other bias crimes and in some areas of anti-discrimination law, courts do not inquire whether psychological factors neutralized a bias motivation. To the contrary, psychology undoubtedly plays a role in all actions, and psychological factors may drive violent perpetrators in other bias crime contexts as well. Whether a perpetrator's conduct was driven by psychological factors in addition to bias should not matter as long as the statutory framework for establishing discriminatory conduct is satisfied. The same should be the case in assessing bias motivation based on gender.

Cases involving same-sex sexual harassment raise an analogous question to the inquiry as to whether all acts of sexual assault or domestic violence are gender-biased. In determining whether same-sex sexual harassment is actionable as a form of sex discrimination, some courts have looked to evidence of gender bias to conclude that conduct was discriminatory and prohibited under sexual harassment laws. In allegations of gender-motivated violence, circumstantial evidence of gender-bias similarly may resolve any doubt as to whether bias was at least a partially motivating factor to warrant civil rights remedies.

In practice, federal enforcement will be available only in cases in which the circumstantial evidence described above can be proved. That approach undoubtedly represents a compromise. It may preclude federal enforcement of sexual assaults or acts of domestic violence that may in fact be rooted in bias, but which lack sufficient circumstantial evidence of bias beyond an allegation of domestic violence or sexual assault. Nonetheless, the approach preserves an important advance by creating federal civil rights recognition for gender-motivated crimes. As a limitation that applies only to litigation, it in no way constrains complementary public education campaigns that recognize and seek to reform the generally misogynistic roots of sexual assault and domestic violence.

This standard makes it incumbent on civil rights practitioners and prosecutors (assuming the HCPA is enacted) to probe the facts of a particular case for evidence of gender bias. A case of domestic violence or rape that lacks additional circumstantial evidence of bias may not be subject to federal remedies. If it is true that some rapists are not acting out of a sexist motivation, but rather are expressing generalized sexually violent conduct that they direct toward everyone, or if some cases of domestic violence are not manifestations of gender-based bias, federal civil rights enforcement may be unavailable. Requiring circumstantial evidence of bias would weed out any violent but "neutral" nondiscriminatory acts, whether committed by people of the same or different genders.

Even if federal jurisdiction ultimately is not extended to each and every gender-motivated crime, the Civil Rights Remedy provides a crucial remedy—for example, it may be the only avenue of redress in cases in which both formal and informal biases preclude or limit civil and criminal enforcement in state courts. For example, marital rape exemptions may preclude or limit criminal prosecution for married or intimate partners. Remnants of interspousal immunities may limit civil recoveries as well. Further, local law enforcement officials, in some instances, still fail to prosecute domestic violence and rape cases, and legal remedies for compelling enforcement may be limited. In a small town, a batterer may be friends or business associates with the police, who may decline to prosecute as a result. Cases involving police officers who have been alleged to be batterers, but who escape prosecution, highlight the need for federal prosecution as an available option.

Moreover federal prosecution of gender-based bias crimes and civil rights recovery for damages recognize the special nature of the harm these bias crimes inflict. As the Supreme Court has acknowledged, bias crimes and other civil rights violations exact a special toll and impose a particular harm, which is deserving of enhanced attention and consideration. Current experience with the Civil Rights Remedy indicates that fears that these new laws will flood the courts are unfounded. Nonetheless, if numerous cases result, perhaps they will bring greater attention to the issue and assist in making headway toward eradicating the problem.

C. Purported Differences Between Gender–Based and Other Bias Crimes: Familiarity and Consent

Other arguments may be raised to distinguish gender-based bias crimes. For example, some argue that gender-based crimes are different from other bias crimes because in many instances, particularly in cases of domestic violence, the victim knows her attacker. However, the notion that familiarity between victim and perpetrator means a crime is not bias-motivated is inconsistent with other bias crime cases. Cross-burnings on a neighbor's lawn surely would qualify for hate crime prosecution even though the victim and perpetrator knew one another. An attack accompanied by racial epithets also would qualify, whether or not the victim and perpetrator were strangers or long-time acquaintances. Arguably, personality conflicts could fuel violence that transpired between two acquaintances who had a history of racial or other class-based animosity between them, but an attack marked by epithets or other evidence of bias might be considered bias-motivated all the same. The presence of non-bias-related evidence does not eviscerate evidence that bias also was a motivating force. Mixed-motive paradigms for discrimination cases offer a ready analogy for analyzing civil claims when more than one factor drives the conduct. Although "lack of familiarity" may characterize many bias crimes, it is but one of many factors rather than a requirement and should not be invoked as a bar to prosecution. Moreover, evidence indicates that victims of gender-based crimes may well be interchangeable, even when they have intimate relations with the perpetrators.

Similarly, the fact that the issue of consent may not arise in other bias crime contexts does not preclude the treatment of sexual assault or domestic violence as a bias crime. Sexual harassment cases offer a useful analogy. In those cases, a plaintiff must establish "unwelcomeness" as an element of her claim. Provided she establishes unwelcomeness as well as the other required elements, she can go on to prove that she suffered sexual harassment, a form of sex discrimination. Acquaintance rape is the context in which the consent issue is most likely to arise. Similar to sexual harassment cases, once a woman establishes that she did not consent there should be no bar to considering the attack a bias crime. As one court noted in discussing the Civil Rights Remedy: "Rape is rape, and it is doubtful that a woman ... who had been violently invaded and attacked, would take comfort in the fact that it was a date (or 'friend') who did it."[187]

REVA B. SIEGEL, "THE RULE OF LOVE": WIFE BEATING AS PREROGATIVE AND PRIVACY (PART II)

105 Yale L. J. 2196–2200, 2202–2203, 2205–2206 (1996).

IV.   C. Discourses of Affective Privacy Today: Interpreting the Violence Against Women Act

The Violence Against Women Act (VAWA) was enacted to provide resources to local authorities attempting to combat the types of violence women commonly suffer—in particular, assaults by spouses or other

---

187. Braden, 4 F. Supp.2d at 1362   * * *.

intimate partners and acts of rape. Concerned that states had historically failed to provide women adequate protection from violent, sexualized assault, and that little protection was provided by existing anti-bias crime laws, the Act's proponents also sought to create a federal civil rights remedy for victims of gender-motivated violence. The civil rights remedy contained in Title III of the bill was intended to effectuate federal constitutional guarantees of equal protection. But the proposed civil rights remedy was soon mired in controversy, drawing opposition in Congress that for some time threatened to prevent the Title's passage. Critics of Title III did not object to providing women relief from gender-motivated violence; instead they complained that the new civil rights remedy would federalize matters that had historically been regulated by the states. While opponents of Title III did not succeed in blocking its passage, they did play a role in shaping the civil rights remedy that Congress ultimately enacted into law.

A brief review of the controversy attending the enactment and interpretation of VAWA's civil rights remedy provides a fitting place to conclude this Article for at least two reasons. First, a strong case can be made that the controversy over the civil rights remedy reflects the continuing power of certain modes of reasoning about marital violence that began in the nineteenth century. Second, even those readers who remain unpersuaded that discourses of affective privacy have shaped the controversy over VAWA's civil rights remedy will be able to appreciate how interpretive conflicts over the provision have prompted the renewed modernization of discourses of gender status. In short, the controversy over VAWA's civil rights remedy illustrates that, even today, the rules and rhetoric of gender status relations continue to evolve in the face of recent civil rights initiatives. In the following sections, I recount briefly the controversy surrounding the civil rights remedy, and then demonstrate how it enacts, both substantively and methodologically, the modernization dynamic explored throughout this Article.

1. VAWA's Civil Rights Remedy for Gender–Motivated Violence

VAWA's civil rights remedy broke new ground. Title III analyzed violence against women as a form of sex discrimination. It was premised on the view that " 'crimes motivated by the victim's gender constitute bias crimes in violation of the victim's right to be free from discrimination on the basis of gender,' " that " 'existing bias and discrimination in the criminal justice system often deprives victims of gender-motivated crimes of equal protection of the laws and the redress to which they are entitled,' " and that " 'victims of gender-motivated violence have a right to equal protection of the laws, including a system of justice that is unaffected by bias or discrimination and that, at every relevant stage, treats such crimes as seriously as other violent crimes.' " The bill provided victims of rape and domestic violence protection under federal civil rights laws which heretofore they had not had.

While VAWA's civil rights remedy drew many critics, not one critic of the civil rights remedy disparaged the statute's goal of protecting women from rape and domestic violence. Rather, critics argued that creating a federal cause of action to vindicate such injuries usurped a traditional regulatory interest of the states and threatened to flood the federal courts with cases the federal judiciary was ill-equipped to handle.

For example, in January of 1991, the Conference of Chief Justices announced its opposition to Title III on the grounds that the provision could "cause major state-federal jurisdictional problems and disruptions in the processing of domestic relations cases in state courts."[292] The state chief justices reasoned that the "right will be invoked as a bargaining tool within the context of divorce negotiations and add a major complicating factor to an environment which is often acrimonious as it is." They continued:

> The issue of inter-spousal litigation goes to the very core of familial relationships and is a very sensitive policy issue in most states. It does not appear that S. 15 is meant to plunge the federal government into this complex area which has been traditionally reserved to the states, but this might well be the result if the current language stands. It should be noted that the volume of domestic relations litigation in state courts is enormous.
>
> It should also be noted that the very nature of marriage as a sexual union raises the possibility that every form of violence can be interpreted as gender-based. Observing that "the federal cause of action ... would impair the ability of state courts to manage criminal and family law matters traditionally entrusted to the states," The Conference of Chief Justices resolved that the provision should be eliminated.[295]

By September of 1991, the Judicial Conference of the United States joined the Conference of Chief Justices in opposing Title III. The federal judges complained that the new civil rights remedy would burden an already overcrowded federal docket; they also echoed the concern voiced by the state judges that the civil rights cause of action " 'will be invoked as a bargaining tool within the context of divorce negotiations [complicating] an environment which is often acrimonious as it is.' "[296] The Judicial Conference then observed that the "subject of violence based on gender and possible responses is extremely complex," and promised to work with Congress "to fashion an appropriate response to violence directed against women."[297] It was in this context that Chief Justice Rehnquist raised his objections to Title III, complaining that the "new private right of action [is] so sweeping that the legislation could involve the federal courts in a whole host of domestic relations disputes."[298]

---

292. Crimes of Violence Motivated by Gender: Hearing Before the Subcomm. on Civil and Constitutional Rights of the House Comm. on the Judiciary, 103d Cong., 1st Sess. 80 (1993) [hereinafter Crimes of Violence] * * *.

295. Id. at 83–84.

296. Id. at 75 * * *.

297. Id. * * *

298. See Rehnquist, supra note 216, at 1, 3.

Facing opposition to Title III, VAWA's original sponsor, Senate Judiciary Committee Chairman Senator Joseph Biden, joined with Senator Orrin Hatch (then ranking minority member of the Committee) to draft a version of the civil rights remedy that could allay the federalism concerns voiced by the bill's critics. In order to defer to the states' traditional role in regulating matters of marriage and divorce and to shield federal dockets from overcrowding, Senator Hatch sought to limit the range of assaults that might fall within the ambit of Title III's protections.

The statute that ultimately emerged from these negotiations provides that, "All persons within the United States shall have the right to be free from crimes of violence motivated by gender." It then defines "motivated by gender" as follows: "[T]he term 'crime of violence motivated by gender' means a crime of violence committed because of gender or on the basis of gender, and due, at least in part, to an *animus* based on the victim's gender." Victims of gender-motivated violence are entitled to compensatory and punitive damages, as well as declaratory and injunctive relief. The Act requires courts to determine which instances of rape or battery the civil rights remedy covers on a case-by-case basis. (It provides: "Nothing in this section entitles a person to a cause of action ... for random acts of violence unrelated to gender or for acts that cannot be demonstrated, by a preponderance of the evidence, to be motivated by gender....") Congress declared that it was enacting the new civil rights remedy pursuant to its power under Section 5 of the Fourteenth Amendment as well as its power to regulate commerce.

The same federalism concerns that critics raised in opposition to the civil rights remedy presumably will shape its interpretation, as courts attempt to identify which acts of violence are "gender-motivated" within the meaning of the act, and which are not. But how is it that courts are to determine which acts of rape and domestic violence are "gender-motivated" and which are not? Here the meaning given the phrase "an *animus* based on the victim's gender" will be pivotal in the interpretation of the new civil rights remedy. Will courts construe "*animus*" to mean something akin to "purpose" or "malice"? Those, such as Senator Hatch, who seek a more restrictive construction of the civil rights remedy will argue that *animus* means malice, while those more receptive to a federal role in remedying violence against women will construe *animus* as a form of purpose. To appreciate how the interpretive struggle will unfold in more concrete terms, it is helpful to consider how Senator Hatch described for the New Republic the injuries the statute covers:

> We're not opening the federal doors to all gender-motivated crimes. Say you have a man who believes a woman is attractive. He feels encouraged by her and he's so motivated by that encouragement that he rips her clothes off and has sex with her against her will. Now let's say you have another man who grabs a woman off some lonely road and in the process of raping her says words like, "You're wearing a skirt! You're a woman! I hate women! I'm going to show you, you woman!" now, the first one's terrible. but the other's much

worse. If a man rapes a woman while telling her he loves her, that's a far cry from saying he hates her. A lust factor does not spring from *animus*.[306]

* * *

2. *VAWA: Rule of Love Redux*

* * *

The claim that marriage is properly a matter of state-law concern has important roots in nineteenth-century deliberations of Congress and the Court. One prominent source of this notion is the "domestic-relations exception" to federal diversity jurisdiction, announced in the 1858 case of *Barber v. Barber*.[312] But if we read Barber closely, it turns out that the claim that husband and wife cannot be diverse for federal jurisdictional purposes was itself an outgrowth of the doctrine of marital unity. Under the common law of marital status, a wife's domicile was her husband's; thus, following the logic of the common law, the Supreme Court reasoned that husband and wife could not be diverse (i.e., citizens of different states) for federal jurisdictional purposes. Both the majority and dissenting opinions in *Barber* affirm that proposition. The *Barber* dissent then goes on to translate that precept of marital unity doctrine into the discourse of affective privacy:

> It is not in accordance with the design and operation of a Government having its origin in causes and necessities, political, general, and external, that it should assume to regulate the domestic relations of society; should, with a kind of inquisitorial authority, enter the habitations and even into the chambers and nurseries of private families, and inquire into and pronounce upon the morals and habits and affections or antipathies of the members of every household. . . .
> The Federal tribunals can have no power to control the duties or the habits of the different members of private families in their domestic intercourse. This power belongs exclusively to the particular communities of which those families form parts, and is essential to the order and to the very existence of such communities.[314]

This passage from *Barber* should sound somewhat familiar. It discusses the role of the federal and state government in regulating domestic relations much as the *Rhodes* opinion discussed the role of state government and "family government" in regulating domestic relations. As this passage from *Barber* might suggest, much of the idiom used to designate marriage as a "local" matter within discourses of federalism either echoes or can be traced to the common law doctrines of marital privacy of the sort examined in Part III of this Article.

* * *

---

306. Ruth Shalit, Caught in the Act, New Republic, July 12, 1993, at 12, 14. * * *

312. 62 U.S. 582, 584 (1858) * * *.

314. Id. at 602 (Daniel, J., dissenting).

Senator Hatch differentiates the roles of federal and state government in regulating intimate assaults by looking to the motivation animating the conduct. When such acts are motivated by hate, he reasons, they are properly matters of federal concern, but when they are motivated by love, they are not. As Senator Hatch succinctly put it: "If a man rapes a woman while telling her he loves her, that's a far cry from saying he hates her. A lust factor does not spring from *animus*." Restating this distinction, those acts of rape and domestic violence that are motivated by hate properly concern women's status as equal citizens of the United States, while those acts of rape and domestic violence that are motivated by love (or lust) are matters of purely local concern having no bearing on women's status as federal citizens or persons entitled to equal protection of the laws. The structure of this claim depends in part on an assumption that gender bias will manifest itself as race discrimination manifests itself: in an emotional state called "hate." But the claim also draws force from specifically gendered assumptions about intimate relations of the sort manifested in the discursive tradition of affective privacy. As in the nineteenth-century interspousal immunity cases, assertions about love and intimacy in a relationship rhetorically efface the violence of sexualized assault. We might distill the logic of this tradition to the following maxim: Where love is, law need not be. Intimacy occurs in a domain having no bearing on matters of citizenship.

* * *

UNITED STATES v. ANTONIO J. MORRISON ET AL.

Supreme Court of the United States (2000).
120 S.Ct. 1740.

In these cases we consider the constitutionality of 42 U.S.C. § 13981, which provides a federal civil remedy for the victims of gender-motivated violence. The United States Court of Appeals for the Fourth Circuit, sitting *en banc*, struck down § 13981 because it concluded that Congress lacked constitutional authority to enact the section's civil remedy. Believing that these cases are controlled by our decisions in *United States v. Lopez* 514 U.S. 549 (1995), *United States v. Harris* 106 U.S. 629 (1883), and the *Civil Rights Cases* 109 U.S. 3 (1883), we affirm.

I

Petitioner Christy Brzonkala enrolled at Virginia Polytechnic Institute (Virginia Tech) in the fall of 1994. In September of that year, Brzonkala met respondents Antonio Morrison and James Crawford, who were both students at Virginia Tech and members of its varsity football team. Brzonkala alleges that, within 30 minutes of meeting Morrison and Crawford, they assaulted and repeatedly raped her. After the attack, Morrison allegedly told Brzonkala, "You better not have any ... diseases." In the months following the rape, Morrison also allegedly announced in the dormitory's dining room that he "like[d] to get girls drunk and...." The omitted portions, quoted verbatim in the briefs on file with this Court, consist of boasting, debased remarks about what Morrison would do to women, vulgar remarks that cannot fail to shock and offend.

Brzonkala alleges that this attack caused her to become severely emotionally disturbed and depressed. She sought assistance from a university psychiatrist, who prescribed antidepressant medication. Shortly after the rape Brzonkala stopped attending classes and withdrew from the university.

In early 1995, Brzonkala filed a complaint against respondents under Virginia Tech's Sexual Assault Policy. During the school-conducted hearing on her complaint, Morrison admitted having sexual contact with her despite the fact that she had twice told him "no." After the hearing, Virginia Tech's Judicial Committee found insufficient evidence to punish Crawford, but found Morrison guilty of sexual assault and sentenced him to immediate suspension for two semesters.

Virginia Tech's dean of students upheld the judicial committee's sentence. However, in July 1995, Virginia Tech informed Brzonkala that Morrison intended to initiate a court challenge to his conviction under the Sexual Assault Policy. University officials told her that a second hearing would be necessary to remedy the school's error in prosecuting her complaint under that policy, which had not been widely circulated to students. The university therefore conducted a second hearing under its Abusive Conduct Policy, which was in force prior to the dissemination of the Sexual Assault Policy. Following this second hearing the Judicial Committee again found Morrison guilty and sentenced him to an identical 2–semester suspension. This time, however, the description of Morrison's offense was, without explanation, changed from "sexual assault" to "using abusive language."

Morrison appealed his second conviction through the university's administrative system. On August 21, 1995, Virginia Tech's senior vice president and provost set aside Morrison's punishment. She concluded that it was " 'excessive when compared with other cases where there has been a finding of violation of the Abusive Conduct Policy,' " 132 F.3d 949, 955 (C.A.4 1997). Virginia Tech did not inform Brzonkala of this decision. After learning from a newspaper that Morrison would be returning to Virginia Tech for the fall 1995 semester, she dropped out of the university.

In December 1995, Brzonkala sued Morrison, Crawford, and Virginia Tech in the United States District Court for the Western District of Virginia. Her complaint alleged that Morrison's and Crawford's attack violated § 13981 and that Virginia Tech's handling of her complaint violated Title IX of the Education Amendments of 1972, 86 Stat. 373–375, 20 U.S.C. §§ 1681–1688. Morrison and Crawford moved to dismiss this complaint on the grounds that it failed to state a claim and that § 13981's civil remedy is unconstitutional. The United States, petitioner in No. 99–5, intervened to defend § 13981's constitutionality.

The District Court dismissed Brzonkala's Title IX claims against Virginia Tech for failure to state a claim upon which relief can be granted. See *Brzonkala v. Virginia Polytechnic and State Univ.*, 935 F.Supp. 772 (W.D.Va.1996). It then held that Brzonkala's complaint stated a claim against Morrison and Crawford under § 13981, but dismissed the complaint because it concluded that Congress lacked authority to enact the section under either the Commerce Clause or § 5 of the Fourteenth Amendment.

A divided panel of the Court of Appeals reversed the District Court, reinstating Brzonkala's § 13981 claim and her Title IX hostile environment claim. *Brzonkala v. Virginia Polytechnic and State Univ.*, 132 F.3d 949 (C.A.4 1997). The full Court of Appeals vacated the panel's opinion and reheard the case *en banc*. The *en banc* court then issued an opinion affirming the District Court's conclusion that Brzonkala stated a claim under § 13981 because her complaint alleged a crime of violence and the allegations of Morrison's crude and derogatory statements regarding his treatment of women sufficiently indicated that his crime was motivated by gender *animus*. Nevertheless, the court by a divided vote affirmed the District Court's conclusion that Congress lacked constitutional authority to enact § 13981's civil remedy. *Brzonkala v. Virginia Polytechnic and State Univ.*, 169 F.3d 820 (C.A.4 1999). Because the Court of Appeals invalidated a federal statute on constitutional grounds, we granted *certiorari*.

* * *

II

* * *

As we discussed at length in *Lopez*, our interpretation of the Commerce Clause has changed as our Nation has developed. We need not repeat that detailed review of the Commerce Clause's history here; it suffices to say that, in the years since *NLRB v. Jones & Laughlin Steel Corp.*, Congress has had considerably greater latitude in regulating conduct and transactions under the Commerce Clause than our previous case law permitted.

Lopez emphasized, however, that even under our modern, expansive interpretation of the Commerce Clause, Congress' regulatory authority is not without effective bounds.* * *

As we observed in *Lopez*, modern Commerce Clause jurisprudence has "identified three broad categories of activity that Congress may regulate under its commerce power." "First, Congress may regulate the use of the channels of interstate commerce." "Second, Congress is empowered to regulate and protect the instrumentalities of interstate commerce, or persons or things in interstate commerce, even though the threat may come only from intrastate activities." "Finally, Congress' commerce authority includes the power to regulate those activities having a substantial relation to interstate commerce, ... i.e., those activities that substantially affect interstate commerce.''

Petitioners do not contend that these cases fall within either of the first two of these categories of Commerce Clause regulation. They seek to sustain § 13981 as a regulation of activity that substantially affects interstate commerce. Given § 13981's focus on gender-motivated violence wherever it occurs (rather than violence directed at the instrumentalities of interstate commerce, interstate markets, or things or persons in interstate commerce), we agree that this is the proper inquiry.

Since *Lopez* most recently canvassed and clarified our case law governing this third category of Commerce Clause regulation, it provides the proper framework for conducting the required analysis of § 13981. In *Lopez*, we held that the Gun–Free School Zones Act of 1990, 18 U.S.C. § 922(q)(1)(A), which made it a federal crime to knowingly possess a firearm in a school zone, exceeded Congress' authority under the Commerce Clause. See 514 U.S., at 551. Several significant considerations contributed to our decision.

First, we observed that § 922(q) was ''a criminal statute that by its terms has nothing to do with 'commerce' or any sort of economic enterprise, however broadly one might define those terms.''

* * *

The second consideration that we found important in analyzing § 922(q) was that the statute contained ''no express jurisdictional element which might limit its reach to a discrete set of firearm possessions that additionally have an explicit connection with or effect on interstate commerce.'' Such a jurisdictional element may establish that the enactment is in pursuance of Congress' regulation of interstate commerce.

Third, we noted that neither § 922(q) '' 'nor its legislative history contain[s] express congressional findings regarding the effects upon interstate commerce of gun possession in a school zone.' '' * * *

Finally, our decision in *Lopez* rested in part on the fact that the link between gun possession and a substantial effect on interstate commerce was attenuated. * * *

With these principles underlying our Commerce Clause jurisprudence as reference points, the proper resolution of the present cases is clear. Gender-motivated crimes of violence are not, in any sense of the phrase, economic activity. While we need not adopt a categorical rule against aggregating the effects of any noneconomic activity in order to decide these cases, thus far in our Nation's history our cases have upheld Commerce Clause regulation of intrastate activity only where that activity is economic in nature. See, e.g., id., at 559–560, and the cases cited therein.

Like the Gun–Free School Zones Act at issue in *Lopez*, § 13981 contains no jurisdictional element establishing that the federal cause of action is in pursuance of Congress' power to regulate interstate commerce.* * *

In contrast with the lack of congressional findings that we faced in *Lopez*, § 13981 is supported by numerous findings regarding the serious impact that gender-motivated violence has on victims and their families. * * *

In these cases, Congress' findings are substantially weakened by the fact that they rely so heavily on a method of reasoning that we have already rejected as unworkable if we are to maintain the Constitution's enumeration of powers. Congress found that gender-motivated violence affects interstate commerce "by deterring potential victims from traveling interstate, from engaging in employment in interstate business, and from transacting with business, and in places involved in interstate commerce; . . . by diminishing national productivity, increasing medical and other costs, and decreasing the supply of and the demand for interstate products." H.R. Conf. Rep. No. 103–711, at 385.

Accord, S.Rep. No. 103–138, at 54. Given these findings and petitioners' arguments, the concern that we expressed in *Lopez* that Congress might use the Commerce Clause to completely obliterate the Constitution's distinction between national and local authority seems well founded. See *Lopez, supra*, at 564. The reasoning that petitioners advance seeks to follow the but-for causal chain from the initial occurrence of violent crime (the suppression of which has always been the prime object of the States' police power) to every attenuated effect upon interstate commerce. If accepted, petitioners' reasoning would allow Congress to regulate any crime as long as the nationwide, aggregated impact of that crime has substantial effects on employment, production, transit, or consumption. Indeed, if Congress may regulate gender-motivated violence, it would be able to regulate murder or any other type of violence since gender-motivated violence, as a subset of all violent crime, is certain to have lesser economic impacts than the larger class of which it is a part.

Petitioners' reasoning, moreover, will not limit Congress to regulating violence but may, as we suggested in *Lopez*, be applied equally as well to family law and other areas of traditional state regulation since the aggregate effect of marriage, divorce, and childrearing on the national economy is undoubtedly significant. Congress may have recognized this specter when it expressly precluded § 13981 from being used in the family law context. See 42 U.S.C. § 13981(e)(4). Under our written Constitution, however, the limitation of congressional authority is not solely a matter of legislative grace.

We accordingly reject the argument that Congress may regulate noneconomic, violent criminal conduct based solely on that conduct's aggregate effect on interstate commerce. The Constitution requires a distinction between what is truly national and what is truly local. * * *

* * *

III

Because we conclude that the Commerce Clause does not provide Congress with authority to enact § 13981, we address petitioners' alternative argument that the section's civil remedy should be upheld as an exercise of Congress' remedial power under § 5 of the Fourteenth Amendment. As noted above, Congress expressly invoked the Fourteenth Amendment as a source of authority to enact § 13981.

The principles governing an analysis of congressional legislation under § 5 are well settled. Section 5 states that Congress may " 'enforce,' by 'appropriate legislation' the constitutional guarantee that no State shall deprive any person of 'life, liberty or property, without due process of law,' nor deny any person 'equal protection of the laws.' "
* * *

Petitioners' § 5 argument is founded on an assertion that there is pervasive bias in various state justice systems against victims of gender-motivated violence. This assertion is supported by a voluminous congressional record. Specifically, Congress received evidence that many participants in state justice systems are perpetuating an array of erroneous stereotypes and assumptions. Congress concluded that these discriminatory stereotypes often result in insufficient investigation and prosecution of gender-motivated crime, inappropriate focus on the behavior and credibility of the victims of that crime, and unacceptably lenient punishments for those who are actually convicted of gender-motivated violence. Petitioners contend that this bias denies victims of gender-motivated violence the equal protection of the laws and that Congress therefore acted appropriately in enacting a private civil remedy against the perpetrators of gender-motivated violence to both remedy the States' bias and deter future instances of discrimination in the state courts.

As our cases have established, state-sponsored gender discrimination violates equal protection unless it " 'serves "important governmental objectives and . . . the discriminatory means employed" are "substantially related to the achievement of those objectives." ' " However, the language and purpose of the Fourteenth Amendment place certain limitations on the manner in which Congress may attack discriminatory conduct. These limitations are necessary to prevent the Fourteenth Amendment from obliterating the Framers' carefully crafted balance of power between the States and the National Government. Foremost among these limitations is the time-honored principle that the Fourteenth Amendment, by its very terms, prohibits only state action.

* * *

Petitioners alternatively argue that, unlike the situation in the *Civil Rights* Cases, here there has been gender-based disparate treatment by state authorities, whereas in those cases there was no indication of such state action. * * *

But even if that distinction were valid, we do not believe it would save § 13981's civil remedy. For the remedy is simply not "corrective in its character, adapted to counteract and redress the operation of such prohibited [s]tate laws or proceedings of [s]tate officers." * * * Section 13981 is not aimed at proscribing discrimination by officials which the Fourteenth Amendment might not itself proscribe; it is directed not at any State or state actor, but at individuals who have committed criminal acts motivated by gender bias.

In the present cases, for example, § 13981 visits no consequence whatever on any Virginia public official involved in investigating or prosecuting Brzonkala's assault. The section is, therefore, unlike any of the § 5 remedies that we have previously upheld. * * *

Section 13981 is also different from these previously upheld remedies in that it applies uniformly throughout the Nation. Congress' findings indicate that the problem of discrimination against the victims of gender-motivated crimes does not exist in all States, or even most States. By contrast, the § 5 remedy upheld in *Katzenbach v. Morgan, supra,* was directed only to the State where the evil found by Congress existed, and in *South Carolina v. Katzenbach, supra,* the remedy was directed only to those States in which Congress found that there had been discrimination.

For these reasons, we conclude that Congress' power under § 5 does not extend to the enactment of § 13981.

IV

Petitioner Brzonkala's complaint alleges that she was the victim of a brutal assault. But Congress' effort in § 13981 to provide a federal civil remedy can be sustained neither under the Commerce Clause nor under § 5 of the Fourteenth Amendment. If the allegations here are true, no civilized system of justice could fail to provide her a remedy for the conduct of respondent Morrison. But under our federal system that remedy must be provided by the Commonwealth of Virginia, and not by the United States. The judgment of the Court of Appeals is Affirmed.

(Justice Thomas's concurrence is omitted.)

JUSTICE SOUTER, with whom JUSTICE STEVENS, JUSTICE GINSBURG, and JUSTICE BREYER join, dissenting.

The Court says both that it leaves Commerce Clause precedent undisturbed and that the Civil Rights Remedy of the Violence Against Women Act of 1994, 42 U.S.C. § 13981, exceeds Congress's power under that Clause. I find the claims irreconcilable and respectfully dissent.

I

Our cases, which remain at least nominally undisturbed, stand for the following propositions. Congress has the power to legislate with regard to activity that, in the aggregate, has a substantial effect on interstate commerce. See *Wickard v. Filburn,* 317 U.S. 111(1942); *Hodel v. Virginia Surface Mining & Reclamation Assn.,* 452 U.S. 264 (1981). The fact of such a substantial effect is not an issue for the courts in the first instance, but for the Congress, whose institutional capacity for gathering evidence and taking testimony far exceeds ours. By passing legislation, Congress indicates its conclusion, whether explicitly or not, that facts support its exercise of the commerce power. The business of the courts is to review the congressional assessment, not for soundness but simply for the rationality of concluding that a jurisdictional basis exists in fact. Any explicit findings that Congress chooses to make, though not dispositive of the question of rationality, may advance judicial review by identifying factual authority on which Congress relied. Applying those propositions in these cases can lead to only one conclusion.

One obvious difference from *United States v. Lopez*, 514 U.S. 549 (1995), is the mountain of data assembled by Congress, here showing the effects of violence against women on interstate commerce. Passage of the Act in 1994 was preceded by four years of hearings, which included testimony from physicians and law professors; from survivors of rape and domestic violence; and from representatives of state law enforcement and private business. The record includes reports on gender bias from task forces in 21 States, and we have the benefit of specific factual findings in the eight separate Reports issued by Congress and its committees over the long course leading to enactment. Compare *Hodel*, 452 U.S., at 278–279 (noting "extended hearings," "vast amounts of testimony and documentary evidence," and "years of the most thorough legislative consideration").

With respect to domestic violence, Congress received evidence for the following findings: * * * The evidence as to rape was similarly extensive, supporting these conclusions: * * *

Based on the data thus partially summarized, Congress found that

crimes of violence motivated by gender have a substantial adverse effect on interstate commerce, by deterring potential victims from traveling interstate, from engaging in employment in interstate business, and from transacting with business, and in places involved, in interstate commerce ... [,] by diminishing national productivity, increasing medical and other costs, and decreasing the supply of and the demand for interstate products.... H.R. Conf. Rep. no. 103–711, p. 385 (1994).

Congress thereby explicitly stated the predicate for the exercise of its Commerce Clause power. Is its conclusion irrational in view of the data amassed? True, the methodology of particular studies may be challenged, and some of the figures arrived at may be disputed. But the sufficiency of the evidence before Congress to provide a rational basis for the finding cannot seriously be questioned.

Indeed, the legislative record here is far more voluminous than the record compiled by Congress and found sufficient in two prior cases upholding Title II of the Civil Rights Act of 1964 against Commerce Clause challenges. * * *

While Congress did not, to my knowledge, calculate aggregate dollar values for the nationwide effects of racial discrimination in 1964, in 1994 it did rely on evidence of the harms caused by domestic violence and sexual assault, citing annual costs of $3 billion in 1990 and $5 to $10 billion in 1993. Equally important, though, gender-based violence in the 1990's was shown to operate in a manner similar to racial discrimination in the 1960's in reducing the mobility of employees and their production and consumption of goods shipped in interstate commerce. Like racial discrimination, "[g]ender-based violence bars its most likely targets— women—from full partic[ipation] in the national economy."

* * *

II

The Act would have passed muster at any time between *Wickard* in 1942 and *Lopez* in 1995, a period in which the law enjoyed a stable understanding that congressional power under the Commerce Clause, complemented by the authority of the Necessary and Proper Clause, Art. I. § 8 cl. 18, extended to all activity that, when aggregated, has a substantial effect on interstate commerce. As already noted, this understanding was secure even against the turmoil at the passage of the Civil Rights Act of 1964, in the aftermath of which the Court not only reaffirmed the cumulative effects and rational basis features of the substantial effects test, see *Heart of Atlanta, supra*, at 258; *McClung, supra*, at 301–305, but declined to limit the commerce power through a formal distinction between legislation focused on "commerce" and statutes addressing "moral and social wrong[s]," *Heart of Atlanta, supra*, at 257.

The fact that the Act does not pass muster before the Court today is therefore proof, to a degree that *Lopez* was not, that the Court's nominal adherence to the substantial effects test is merely that. Although a new jurisprudence has not emerged with any distinctness, it is clear that some congressional conclusions about obviously substantial, cumulative effects on commerce are being assigned lesser values than the once-stable doctrine would assign them. These devaluations are accomplished not by any express repudiation of the substantial effects test or its application through the aggregation of individual conduct, but by supplanting rational basis scrutiny with a new criterion of review.

Thus the elusive heart of the majority's analysis in these cases is its statement that Congress's findings of fact are "weakened" by the presence of a disfavored "method of reasoning." This seems to suggest that the "substantial effects" analysis is not a factual enquiry, for Congress in the first instance with subsequent judicial review looking only to the rationality of the congressional conclusion, but one of a rather different sort, dependent upon a uniquely judicial competence.

This new characterization of substantial effects has no support in our cases (the self-fulfilling prophecies of *Lopez* aside), least of all those the majority cites. * * *

B

The Court finds it relevant that the statute addresses conduct traditionally subject to state prohibition under domestic criminal law, a fact said to have some heightened significance when the violent conduct in question is not itself aimed directly at interstate commerce or its instrumentalities. Again, history seems to be recycling, for the theory of traditional state concern as grounding a limiting principle has been rejected previously, and more than once. * * *

C

The Court's choice to invoke considerations of traditional state regulation in these cases is especially odd in light of a distinction recognized in the now-repudiated opinion for the Court in *Usery*. In explaining that there was no inconsistency between declaring the States immune to the commerce power exercised in the Fair Labor Standards Act, but subject to it under the Economic Stabilization Act of 1970, as decided in *Fry v. United States,* 421 U.S. 542 (1975), the Court spoke of the latter statute as dealing with a serious threat affecting all the political components of the federal system, "which only collective action by the National Government might forestall." Today's majority, however, finds no significance whatever in the state support for the Act based upon the States' acknowledged failure to deal adequately with gender-based violence in state courts, and the belief of their own law enforcement agencies that national action is essential.

The National Association of Attorneys General supported the Act unanimously, and Attorneys General from 38 States urged Congress to enact the Civil Rights Remedy, representing that "the current system for dealing with violence against women is inadequate." It was against this record of failure at the state level that the Act was passed to provide the choice of a federal forum in place of the state-court systems found inadequate to stop gender-biased violence. The Act accordingly offers a federal civil rights remedy aimed exactly at violence against women, as an alternative to the generic state tort causes of action found to be poor tools of action by the state task forces. As the 1993 Senate Report put it, "The Violence Against Women Act is intended to respond both to the underlying attitude that this violence is somehow less serious than other crime and to the resulting failure of our criminal justice system to address such violence. Its goals are both symbolic and practical...." S.Rep. No. 103–138, at 38.

The collective opinion of state officials that the Act was needed continues virtually unchanged, and when the Civil Rights Remedy was challenged in court, the States came to its defense. Thirty-six of them and the Commonwealth of Puerto Rico have filed an amicus brief in support of petitioners in these cases, and only one State has taken respondents' side. It is, then, not the least irony of these cases that the States will be forced to enjoy the new federalism whether they want it or not. For with the Court's decision today, Antonio Morrison, like *Carter*

Coal's James Carter before him, has "won the states' rights plea against the states themselves."

III

All of this convinces me that today's ebb of the commerce power rests on error, and at the same time leads me to doubt that the majority's view will prove to be enduring law. There is yet one more reason for doubt. Although we sense the presence of *Carter Coal, Schechter,* and *Usery* once again, the majority embraces them only at arm's-length. Where such decisions once stood for rules, today's opinion points to considerations by which substantial effects are discounted. Cases standing for the sufficiency of substantial effects are not over-ruled; cases overruled since 1937 are not quite revived. The Court's thinking betokens less clearly a return to the conceptual straitjackets of *Schechter* and *Carter Coal* and *Usery* than to something like the un-steady state of obscenity law between *Redrup v. New York,* 386 U.S. 767 (1967) (*per curiam*), and *Miller v. California,* 413 U.S. 15 (1973), a period in which the failure to provide a workable definition left this Court to review each case *ad hoc.* As our predecessors learned then, the practice of such *ad hoc* review cannot preserve the distinction between the judicial and the legislative, and this Court, in any event, lacks the institutional capacity to maintain such a regime for very long. This one will end when the majority realizes that the conception of the commerce power for which it entertains hopes would inevitably fail the test expressed in Justice Holmes's statement that "[t]he first call of a theory of law is that it should fit the facts." O. Holmes, The Common Law 167 (Howe ed. 1963). The facts that cannot be ignored today are the facts of integrated national commerce and a political relationship between States and Nation much affected by their respective treasuries and constitu-tional modifications adopted by the people. The federalism of some earlier time is no more adequate to account for those facts today than the theory of *laissez-faire* was able to govern the national economy 70 years ago.

JUSTICE BREYER, with whom JUSTICE STEVENS joins, and with whom JUSTICE SOUTER and JUSTICE GINSBURG join as to part I–A, dissenting.

No one denies the importance of the Constitution's federalist princi-ples. Its state/federal division of authority protects liberty—both by restricting the burdens that government can impose from a distance and by facilitating citizen participation in government that is closer to home. The question is how the judiciary can best implement that original federalist understanding where the Commerce Clause is at issue.

I

The majority holds that the federal commerce power does not extend to such "noneconomic" activities as "noneconomic, violent criminal conduct" that significantly affects interstate commerce only if we "ag-gregate" the interstate "effect[s]" of individual instances. Justice Souter explains why history, precedent, and legal logic militate against the majority's approach. I agree and join his opinion. I add that the majority's holding illustrates the difficulty of finding a workable judicial Commerce Clause touchstone—a set of comprehensible interpretive rules that courts might use to impose some meaningful limit, but not too great a limit, upon the scope of the legislative authority that the Commerce Clause delegates to Congress.

A

Consider the problems. The "economic/noneconomic" distinction is not easy to apply. Does the local street corner mugger engage in "economic" activity or "noneconomic" activity when he mugs for money? * * *

The line becomes yet harder to draw given the need for exceptions. The Court itself would permit Congress to aggregate, hence regulate, "noneconomic" activity taking place at economic establishments. And it would permit Congress to regulate where that regulation is "an essential part of a larger regulation of economic activity, in which the regulatory scheme could be undercut unless the intrastate activity were regulated." Given the former exception, can Congress simply rewrite the present law and limit its application to restaurants, hotels, perhaps universities, and other places of public accommodation? Given the latter exception, can Congress save the present law by including it, or much of it, in a broader "Safe Transport" or "Workplace Safety" act?

More important, why should we give critical constitutional importance to the economic, or noneconomic, nature of an interstate-commerce-affecting cause? If chemical emanations through indirect environmental change cause identical, severe commercial harm outside a State, why should it matter whether local factories or home fireplaces release them? The Constitution itself refers only to Congress' power to "regulate Commerce . . . among the several States," and to make laws "necessary and proper" to implement that power. Art. I, § 8, cls. 3, 18. The language says nothing about either the local nature, or the economic nature, of an interstate-commerce-affecting cause.

This Court has long held that only the interstate commercial effects, not the local nature of the cause, are constitutionally relevant. Nothing in the Constitution's language, or that of earlier cases prior to *Lopez*, explains why the Court should ignore one highly relevant characteristic of an interstate-commerce-affecting cause (how "local" it is), while placing critical constitutional weight upon a different, less obviously relevant, feature (how "economic" it is).

Most important, the Court's complex rules seem unlikely to help secure the very object that they seek, namely, the protection of "areas of traditional state regulation" from federal intrusion. The Court's rules, even if broadly interpreted, are underinclusive. The local pickpocket is no less a traditional subject of state regulation than is the local gender-motivated assault. Regardless, the Court reaffirms, as it should, Congress' well-established and frequently exercised power to enact laws that satisfy a commerce-related jurisdictional prerequisite—for example, that some item relevant to the federally regulated activity has at some time crossed a state line.

And in a world where most everyday products or their component parts cross interstate boundaries, Congress will frequently find it possible to redraft a statute using language that ties the regulation to the interstate movement of some relevant object, thereby regulating local criminal activity or, for that matter, family affairs. See, e.g., Child Support Recovery Act of 1992, 18 U.S.C. § 228. Although this possibility does not give the Federal Government the power to regulate everything, it means that any substantive limitation will apply randomly in terms of the interests the majority seeks to protect. * * *

The majority, aware of these difficulties, is nonetheless concerned with what it sees as an important contrary consideration. To determine the lawfulness of statutes simply by asking whether Congress could reasonably have found that aggregated local instances significantly affect interstate commerce will allow Congress to regulate almost anything. Virtually all local activity, when instances are aggregated, can have "substantial effects on employment, production, transit, or consumption." Hence Congress could "regulate any crime," and perhaps "marriage, divorce, and childrearing" as well, obliterating the "Constitution's distinction between national and local authority."

This consideration, however, while serious, does not reflect a jurisprudential defect, so much as it reflects a practical reality. We live in a Nation knit together by two centuries of scientific, technological, commercial, and environmental change. Those changes, taken together, mean that virtually every kind of activity, no matter how local, genuinely can affect commerce, or its conditions, outside the State—at least when considered in the aggregate. And that fact makes it close to impossible for courts to develop meaningful subject-matter categories that would exclude some kinds of local activities from ordinary Commerce Clause "aggregation" rules without, at the same time, depriving Congress of the power to regulate activities that have a genuine and important effect upon interstate commerce.

Since judges cannot change the world, the "defect" means that, within the bounds of the rational, Congress, not the courts, must remain primarily responsible for striking the appropriate state/federal balance. Congress is institutionally motivated to do so. Its Members represent state and local district interests. They consider the views of state and local officials when they legislate, and they have even developed formal procedures to ensure that such consideration takes place. See, e.g., Unfunded Mandates Reform Act of 1995, Pub.L. 104–4, 109 Stat. 48 (codified in scattered sections of 2 U.S.C.). Moreover, Congress often can better reflect state concerns for autonomy in the details of sophisticated statutory schemes than can the judiciary, which cannot easily gather the relevant facts and which must apply more general legal rules and categories. Not surprisingly, the bulk of American law is still state law, and overwhelmingly so.

B

I would also note that Congress, when it enacted the statute, followed procedures that help to protect the federalism values at stake. It provided adequate notice to the States of its intent to legislate in an "are[a] of traditional state regulation." And in response, attorneys general in the overwhelming majority of States (38) supported congressional legislation, telling Congress that "[o]ur experience as Attorneys General strengthens our belief that the problem of violence against women is a national one, requiring federal attention, federal leadership, and federal funds."

Moreover, as Justice Souter has pointed out, Congress compiled a "mountain of data" explicitly documenting the interstate commercial effects of gender-motivated crimes of violence. After considering alternatives, it focused the federal law upon documented deficiencies in state legal systems. And it tailored the law to prevent its use in certain areas of traditional state concern, such as divorce, alimony, or child custody. Consequently, the law before us seems to represent an instance, not of state/federal conflict, but of state/federal efforts to cooperate in order to help solve a mutually acknowledged national problem.

I call attention to the legislative process leading up to enactment of this statute because, as the majority recognizes, it far surpasses that which led to the enactment of the statute we considered in *Lopez*. And even were I to accept *Lopez* as an accurate statement of the law, which I do not, that distinction provides a possible basis for upholding the law here. This Court on occasion has pointed to the importance of procedural limitations in keeping the power of Congress in check.

Commentators also have suggested that the thoroughness of legislative procedures—e.g., whether Congress took a "hard look"—might sometimes make a determinative difference in a Commerce Clause case, say when Congress legislates in an area of traditional state regulation. Of course, any judicial insistence that Congress follow particular procedures might itself intrude upon congressional prerogatives and embody difficult definitional problems. But the intrusion, problems, and consequences all would seem less serious than those embodied in the majority's approach.

I continue to agree with Justice Souter that the Court's traditional "rational basis" approach is sufficient. But I recognize that the law in this area is unstable and that time and experience may demonstrate both the unworkability of the majority's rules and the superiority of Congress' own procedural approach—in which case the law may evolve towards a rule that, in certain difficult Commerce Clause cases, takes account of the thoroughness with which Congress has considered the federalism issue.

For these reasons, as well as those set forth by Justice Souter, this statute falls well within Congress's Commerce Clause authority, and I dissent from the Court's contrary conclusion.

II

Given my conclusion on the Commerce Clause question, I need not consider Congress' authority under § 5 of the Fourteenth Amendment. Nonetheless, I doubt the Court's reasoning rejecting that source of authority. The Court points out that in *United States v. Harris* 106 U.S. 629 (1883), and the *Civil Rights Cases* 109 U.S. 3 (1883), the Court held that § 5 does not authorize Congress to use the Fourteenth Amendment as a source of power to remedy the conduct of private persons. That is certainly so. The Federal Government's argument, however, is that Congress used § 5 to remedy the actions of state actors, namely, those States which, through discriminatory design or the discriminatory conduct of their officials, failed to provide adequate (or any) state remedies for women injured by gender-motivated violence—a failure that the States, and Congress, documented in depth.

Neither *Harris* nor the *Civil Rights Cases* considered this kind of claim. The Court in *Harris* specifically said that it treated the federal laws in question as "directed exclusively against the action of private persons, without reference to the laws of the State, or their administration by her officers." 106 U.S., at 640; see also *Civil Rights Cases*, 109 U.S., at 14 (observing that the statute did "not profess to be corrective of any constitutional wrong committed by the States" and that it established "rules for the conduct of individuals in society towards each other, . . . without referring in any manner to any supposed action of the State or its authorities").

The Court responds directly to the relevant "state actor" claim by finding that the present law lacks " 'congruence and proportionality' " to the state discrimination that it purports to remedy. That is because the law, unlike federal laws prohibiting literacy tests for voting, imposing voting rights requirements, or punishing state officials who intentionally discriminated in jury selection, is not "directed . . . at any State or state actor."

But why can Congress not provide a remedy against private actors? Those private actors, of course, did not themselves violate the Constitution. But this Court has held that Congress at least sometimes can enact remedial "[l]egislation . . . [that] prohibits conduct which is not itself unconstitutional." *Flores*, 521 U.S., at 518; see also *Katzenbach v. Morgan*, supra, at 651; *South Carolina v. Katzenbach, supra*, at 308. The statutory remedy does not in any sense purport to "determine what constitutes a constitutional violation." *Flores, supra*, at 519. It intrudes little upon either States or private parties. It may lead state actors to improve their own remedial systems, primarily through example. It restricts private actors only by imposing liability for private conduct that is, in the main, already forbidden by state law. Why is the remedy "disproportionate"? And given the relation between remedy and violation—the creation of a federal remedy to substitute for constitutionally inadequate state remedies—where is the lack of "congruence"?

The majority adds that Congress found that the problem of inadequacy of state remedies "does not exist in all States, or even most States." But Congress had before it the task force reports of at least 21 States documenting constitutional violations. And it made its own findings about pervasive gender-based stereotypes hampering many state legal systems, sometimes unconstitutionally so. The record nowhere reveals a congressional finding that the problem "does not exist" elsewhere. Why can Congress not take the evidence before it as evidence of a national problem? This Court has not previously held that Congress must document the existence of a problem in every State prior to proposing a national solution. And the deference this Court gives to Congress' chosen remedy under § 5, suggests that any such requirement would be inappropriate.

Despite my doubts about the majority's § 5 reasoning, I need not, and do not, answer the § 5 question, which I would leave for more thorough analysis if necessary on another occasion. Rather, in my view, the Commerce Clause provides an adequate basis for the statute before us. And I would uphold its constitutionality as the "necessary and proper" exercise of legislative power granted to Congress by that Clause.

C.　FIREARMS RESTRICTIONS

MARIA KELLY, DOMESTIC VIOLENCE AND GUNS: SEIZING WEAPONS BEFORE THE COURT HAS MADE A FINDING OF ABUSE

23 Vt. L. Rev. 361–363 (1998).

II.　B.　Why Seize Firearms From Dangerous Abusers?: The Statistics

Firearm use in domestic violence incidents is becoming less and less unusual. In 1992, 62% of all murder victims killed by their partners or ex-partners were shot to death. Handguns were used in three-quarters of these deadly firearm encounters. It is important to note that while these statistics include both female and male victims, the two genders commit spousal murders for very different reasons. Women primarily kill their partners in self defense or in retribution for prior acts of violence, while men commonly kill in response to the woman's attempt to leave the abusive relationship. More than twice as many women are shot by their husbands or partners than are shot by strangers.

When a batterer possesses weapons he has used or has threatened to use, his access to them increases his potential to kill as well as the likelihood that he will. Abusers frequently use weapons such as firearms when victims decide to leave the violent relationship. Most domestic violence-related murders are committed with firearms. Firearm assaults are twelve times more likely to result in death than non-firearm assaults, three times more likely to result in death then assaults involving knives, and twenty-three times more likely to result in death than assaults involving non-firearm weapons or bodily force.

The majority of homicides within the home occur during arguments or altercations. In cases of assault, people tend to reach for the most lethal weapon readily available. In a large number of cases where assaults are committed with guns or knives, fatality seems to be an almost accidental outcome. Therefore, easy access to firearms may be particularly dangerous in households prone to domestic violence since there is a greater chance of fatality with firearms than with other types of weapons. If access to firearms were reduced, some domestic violence homicides would be prevented because abusers would be forced to substitute less lethal weapons.

Most handgun owners cite protection from crime as the single most important reason for keeping a gun in the home. This practice, however, may be counterproductive. Although forced entry followed by homicide is the most serious of household crimes, it occurs far less frequently than other types of household crime. The mere presence of a gun in the home, however, increases the risk of homicide among family members and other intimates.

Even if weapons were seized from abusers before conviction, abusers might still be able to purchase weapons illegally or to gain access to another individual's weapon. No statistics are available on how many domestic violence murders have been committed with illegal firearms. Arguably, if an abuser has a criminal history, he may be more inclined to obtain weapons illegally. In fact, half of the defendants who kill their spouses have criminal histories. Additionally, although an individual is currently subject to a Brady weapons check when he purchases a handgun from a dealer, if two individuals enter a private transaction, Vermont, like all states, will have no record that the transaction occurred.

Because domestic violence firearm attacks are three times more likely to be fatal than attacks with knives, and because studies show that violence in the home is independently associated with firearm assaults, legislation prohibiting dangerous and abusive individuals from possessing firearms is justified. A provision prohibiting dangerous abusers from owning firearms would not be infallible, but it would be a step in the right direction.

SUSAN CARBON, PETER MacDONALD AND SEEMA ZEYA, ENFORCING DOMESTIC VIOLENCE PROTECTION ORDERS THROUGHOUT THE COUNTRY: NEW FRONTIERS OF PROTECTION FOR VICTIMS OF DOMESTIC VIOLENCE (PART II)

50 Juvenile and Family Ct. Journal 43–48 (1999).

RELATIONSHIP BETWEEN VAWA FULL FAITH AND CREDIT AND FEDERAL FIREARMS LEGISLATION

Domestic violence has, at its roots, a threat or reality of bodily injury. Because firearms provide a vehicle by which to make such threat a reality, Congress has enacted legislation restricting the possession of firearms by certain classes of persons when the proposed recipient of the firearm has perpetrated domestic violence. It is important for judges to be aware of these federal laws when issuing protective orders.

The federal Violent Crime Control and Law Enforcement Act of 1994 provided significant amendments to the 1968 Gun Control Act (18 U.S.C. secs. 921–930). Title IV of the 1994 Act was the landmark VAWA of 1994. VAWA was enacted principally to help states, tribes, and local governments develop and strengthen law enforcement, prosecutorial, and judicial strategies to combat violent crimes against women.

Individual states also have enacted restrictions concerning firearms, which may be included in state court orders. These restrictions must be given full faith and credit by enforcing jurisdictions, just like any other portion of a protective order, even if the enforcing state's laws do not provide similar protection to a victim.

There are two primary federal gun control laws that contain restrictions on persons subject to valid protection orders. They are: 18 U.S.C. sec. 922 (g)(8)—which makes it a crime to possess a firearm (or ammunition) if one is subject to a qualifying protection order; and 18 U.S.C. sec. 922 (d)(8)—which makes it a crime to knowingly transfer or sell a firearm to a person who is subject to a qualifying protection order. Not only is it a federal offense for an individual subject to a qualifying civil protection order to possess a weapon, but it is also a crime to knowingly transfer a firearm to a person who is subject to a protection order.

Judges must understand these federal laws and their interrelationship with underlying civil orders. They also must understand how the full faith and credit provision of VAWA affects enforcement of their orders outside their jurisdiction, and orders from a foreign jurisdiction that they are asked to enforce.

18 U.S.C Sec. 922(g)(8)

This section of the Gun Control Act of 1968, as amended in 1994, makes it a federal crime for a person to possess a firearm or ammunition if that person is subject to a qualifying protection order.

Requirements: The protection order must restrain the defendant expressly from harassing, stalking or threatening an intimate partner or a child of the defendant and intimate partner, or it must restrain the defendant from engaging in other conduct that would place an intimate partner in reasonable fear of bodily injury to the partner or child.

The protection order *must* state that the defendant represents a *credible threat* to the physical safety of the victim (otherwise referred to as the defendant's intimate partner or child of the parties); *or* it must prohibit the defendant explicitly from using, attempting to use, or threatening to use force that reasonably would be expected to cause injury to the victim.

Although this statute does not say so explicitly, it is presumed that the perception of the threat would be from the victim's vantage point, as distinguished from a more generic "reasonable person" standard. This distinction is important for judges to understand, since events that may not appear "fearful" to the trial judge may be terrifying to a victim who has suffered a history of abuse at the hands of the defendant.

The protection order also must have been issued following a hearing. The defendant must have been provided with actual notice of the hearing and an opportunity to participate in the proceeding. Thus, a defendant will not be barred under federal law from possessing a firearm at the time of a temporary or *ex parte* hearing that does not provide for an actual opportunity to participate.

Protected persons: Section 921(a)(32) defines the class of protected persons. They include intimate partners of the defendant who are either a spouse of the defendant, an individual who is a parent to a child of the defendant, or an individual who cohabits or has cohabited with the defendant. Note that federal law is much more restrictive than many states' laws. Certain classes of persons who might be protected under state law are not afforded protection, namely persons who are or have been involved in a dating relationship, but never cohabited or bore a child together. While such persons still may be protected under a state's laws requiring dispossession of guns, they are not protected under this federal law.

Exemptions: There is one significant category of exemptions to the provisions of section 922(g)(8). Law enforcement officers and military personnel are *not* subject to this law. They may continue to possess and utilize their weapons while performing their work responsibilities. The exemption, however, only applies to service weapons, not to personal weapons. Thus, law enforcement officers are prohibited from possessing any weapons other than those issued by their departments/agencies for the performance of their official duties.

Provided these elements are satisfied, a defendant may be prosecuted for mere *possession* of a weapon, even if the defendant does not otherwise violate a protection order. In fact, even if the protection order does not prohibit possession (such as when relinquishment of firearms is not ordered), a defendant still may be prosecuted under federal law. It certainly would be appropriate for the court to advise the defendant of these ramifications, even if weapons are not ordered relinquished under state law.

Consider the interplay of the full faith and credit provisions of VAWA in the following example:

Plaintiff and defendant are married, therefore qualifying the plaintiff as a protected person under federal firearms legislation. A court in State A (the Issuing State) orders the defendant to relinquish all weapons on the date the final civil protection order is issued, following an evidentiary hearing where defendant had notice and the opportunity to participate. The weapons are to remain relinquished for the three-year duration of the protection order under this jurisdiction. The victim (plaintiff) lives in State A, but works in State B (the Enforcing State). The victim registers the protective order in State B, where civil protection orders are valid for only one year.

Under the full faith and credit provision of VAWA, State B must honor (enforce) State A's restriction on relinquishment of weapons for three years, even though its own law only would permit relinquishment for one year. Therefore, the defendant may not possess a weapon in State B (or elsewhere for that matter) as a consequence of the protection order from State A. Possession would violate both state and federal law.

18 U.S.C. Sec. 922(d)(8)

This section of the Gun Control Act, also added in 1994, makes it a federal offense to sell or transfer a firearm to a defendant who is subject to a qualifying protection order.

Requirements: The due process, procedural, and substantive requirements under section (d)(8) are identical to those set forth under section (g)(8), and a further requirement exists: the violation committed by the transferor must be *knowing*. Thus, even if all the due process requirements above have been satisfied, there may not be a prosecution against a transferor unless it can be demonstrated that the transferor knew the defendant was prohibited from possessing a weapon. This is a difficult burden in light of the absence of a nationwide, central registry. Furthermore, the requirement to complete a background check applies only to licensed dealers. Therefore, many people who sell guns privately may have no knowledge of these restrictions. As a result, it is likely that many victims will not have the full breadth of protection otherwise contemplated by this statute.

Exemptions: As under section (g)(8), law enforcement officers are exempt from this provision. It is not unlawful, therefore, to sell or transfer weapons or ammunition to a law enforcement officer, provided they are for the performance of official duties. It would be unlawful, however, to sell or transfer weapons and ammunition to law enforcement officers when the intended use is personal, not professional.

18 U.S.C. Sections 922(g)(9) and (d)(9)

There are two other related federal gun control laws that judges should know about, although not directly relevant to the issue of full faith and credit. In 1996, Congress enacted another significant amendment to the Gun Control Act of 1968. Known as the Lautenberg Amendment and enacted as part of the Omnibus Consolidated Appropriations Act of 1996, it prohibits a defendant from possessing a firearm or ammunition following conviction of a state or federal misdemeanor crime of domestic violence. (The amendment also prohibits defendants from shipping, transporting, or receiving firearms or ammunition.) The Lautenberg Amendment added "misdemeanor crime of domestic violence" into the definitions section (18 U.S.C. sec. 921(a)(33)(A)) in addition to sec. 922(g)(9).

Perhaps the most significant feature of the Lautenberg Amendment is its scope of coverage:

- It applies to convictions on and after September 30, 1996, the date of enactment.

- It applies retroactively, to convictions occurring prior to the effective date of the Act.

- Law enforcement officers and military personnel are subject to this law.

- It *forever* precludes defendants from possessing firearms or ammunition following a conviction, regardless of when the conviction occurred.

Requirements: Certain requirements must be satisfied before invoking this provision. First, the conviction must be for a "qualifying misdemeanor crime," as defined under sec. 921(a)(20). The crime must have, *as an element,* the use or attempted use of physical force or the threatened use of a deadly weapon. The crime also must have been committed by a current or former spouse, parent, guardian of the victim, or a person with whom the victim shares a child, or by one who is or has cohabited as a spouse, parent, guardian or person similarly situated to a spouse, parent or guardian. Furthermore, the definition includes all misdemeanors that involve the use or attempted use of physical force where the defendant falls into any of the defined categories of parties above. The term "misdemeanor" as used in section (d)(9) and section (g)(9) discussed below, includes any offense under federal or state law or local ordinance punishable by imprisonment not in excess of one year. Use of the term "misdemeanor" in the statute or ordinance is not required.

Second, the conviction must have been obtained with advice of counsel, or alternatively, only if the defendant executed an appropriate waiver of counsel. Finally, if the jurisdiction provides for a jury trial for the domestic violence misdemeanor crime, the defendant must have been afforded this right or, again, knowingly waived it.

It is important to note that under these sections, there is *no* law enforcement or military exemption. Thus, if a law enforcement officer or member of the military is convicted of a misdemeanor crime of domestic violence, he may *never* possess a weapon, for any reason, including in the line of duty. Section 922 (g)(9) thus provides a blanket prohibition against possession of a weapon, whether for a law enforcement officer, military official, or any other citizen.

It also is important to note that there need not be a civil protective order underlying the criminal conviction. Thus, a defendant charged and convicted of any misdemeanor crime of domestic violence, whether or not the victim ever obtained a civil restraining order, will be subject to this law and all its ramifications.

One also should be aware that state statutes define perpetrators and victims differently from federal legislation in certain respects. Careful analysis will be important to ensure that application of federal law is appropriate. For example, some states include those with a dating relationship among the class of protected parties for purposes of civil protection orders or in defining misdemeanor crimes of domestic violence, even if there has been no cohabitation or the parties do not share a child in common. Under the Lautenberg Amendments, a defendant who was convicted of sexually assaulting his girlfriend, with whom he had never cohabited, would not be subject to its provisions, because the defendant does not fall within the definitional scope. On the other hand, if the parties had a child together, sexual assault against the victim by the defendant would give rise to prosecution under the Act and the lifetime ban against possession of weapons.

Just as section 922(d)(8) complements section 922(g)(8), so, too, does section 922(d)(9) complement section 922(g)(9). Under section 922(d)(9), it is a federal crime to knowingly transfer or sell a firearm to any person.

Penalties: Penalties for violations of 18 U.S.C. sec. 922(d)(8), (g)(8), (d)(9), and (g)(9) are set forth in sec. 924(a)(2). An offender is subject to a ten-year term of imprisonment. For misdemeanor crime violations, an optional, additional fine of up to $250,000 also is provided. The Bureau of Alcohol, Tobacco and Firearms has jurisdiction to investigate.

* * *

The trial judge also has a duty to discuss prohibitions against access, use, and possession of firearms during the pendency of protective orders. In addition to explaining the state restrictions that may exist, it is important that defendants be admonished that under federal law they may not possess, use, or acquire a firearm if a qualifying order is in effect. They also should be warned that if convicted of a qualifying domestic violence misdemeanor, they will be prevented forever from owning, possessing, or using a firearm. It is important to make clear two points in this regard. First, these provisions are non-discretionary. It is not an option that the victim may request. The federal prohibitions are absolute. And second, guns used for hunting are included within these prohibitions. A defendant may not seek temporary access of hunting rifles, for example, during hunting season, whether it is for food or sport. The restrictions are absolute. * * *

UNITED STATES OF AMERICA v.
TIMOTHY JOE EMERSON

United States District Court, N.D. Texas (1999).
46 F.Supp.2d 598–602, 607, 610–612.

Defendant Timothy Joe Emerson ("Emerson") moves to dismiss the Indictment against him, claiming that the statute he is prosecuted under, 18 U.S.C. § 922(g)(8), is an unconstitutional exercise of congressional power under the Commerce Clause and the Second, Fifth, and Tenth Amendments to the United States Constitution. For the reasons stated below, the Court GRANTS Emerson's Motion to Dismiss.

I. BACKGROUND

On August 28, 1998, Emerson's wife, Sacha, filed a petition for divorce and application for a temporary restraining order in the 119th District Court of Tom Green County, Texas. The petition stated no factual basis for relief other than the necessary recitals required under the Texas Family Code regarding domicile, service of process, dates of marriage and separation, and the "insupportability" of the marriage. The application for a temporary restraining order—essentially a form order frequently used in Texas divorce procedure—sought to enjoin Emerson from engaging in various financial transactions to maintain the financial status quo and from making threatening communications or actual attacks upon his wife during the pendency of the divorce proceedings.

On September 4, 1998, the Honorable John E. Sutton held a hearing on Mrs. Emerson's application for a temporary restraining order. Mrs. Emerson was represented by an attorney at that hearing, and Mr. Emerson appeared *pro se*. Mrs. Emerson testified about her economic situation, her needs in the way of temporary spousal support and child support, and her desires regarding temporary conservatorship of their minor child.

During the hearing, Mrs. Emerson alleged that her husband threatened over the telephone to kill the man with whom Mrs. Emerson had been having an adulterous affair. However, no evidence was adduced concerning any acts of violence or threatened violence by Mr. Emerson against any member of his family, and the district court made no findings to that effect. Furthermore, the court did not admonish Mr. Emerson that if he granted the temporary restraining order, Mr. Emerson would be subject to federal criminal prosecution merely for possessing a firearm while being subject to the order.

II. ANALYSIS

As stated above, Emerson was indicted for possession of a firearm while being under a restraining order, in violation of 18 U.S.C.

§ 922(g)(8) ("the Act"). * * * Emerson argues that 18 U.S.C. § 922(g)(8) is an unconstitutional exercise of congressional power under the Commerce Clause and the Second, Fifth, and Tenth Amendments to the United States Constitution. The Court will address these arguments *seriatim.*

A. *Commerce Clause*

Emerson first argues that 18 U.S.C. § 922(g)(8) is an unconstitutional exercise of congressional power under the Commerce Clause of the United States Constitution. Pursuant to the Supreme Court's holding in *United States v. Lopez,* 514 U.S. 549 (1995), Emerson argues that the Act is unconstitutional because it does not regulate commercial activity.

However, the Fifth Circuit Court of Appeals has examined the validity of 18 U.S.C. § 922(g)(8) under a Commerce Clause challenge and has held that the Act is constitutional. *United States v. Pierson,* 139 F.3d 501 (5th Cir.1998). Accordingly, Emerson cannot sustain a Motion to Dismiss under a Commerce Clause challenge.

B. *Second Amendment*

Emerson claims that 18 U.S.C. § 922(g)(8) violates his rights under the Second Amendment to the United States Constitution. * * * Only if the Second Amendment guarantees Emerson a personal right to bear arms can he claim a constitutional violation. Whether the Second Amendment recognizes an individual right to keep and bear arms is an issue of first impression within the Fifth Circuit. Emerson claims that he has a personal right to bear arms which the Act infringes, while at oral argument on the Motion to Dismiss, the Government claimed it is "well settled" that the Second Amendment creates a right held by the States and does not protect an individual right to bear arms.

1. *Second Amendment Schools of Thought*

Two main schools of thought have developed on the issue of whether the Second Amendment recognizes individual or collective rights. These schools of thought are referred to as the "states' rights," or "collective rights," school and the "individual rights" school. The former group cites the opening phrase of the amendment, along with subsequent case law, as authority for the idea that the right only allows states to establish and maintain militias, and in no way creates or protects an individual right to own arms. Due to changes in the political climate over the last two centuries and the rise of National Guard organizations among the states, states' rights theorists argue that the Second Amendment is an anachronism, and that there is no longer a need to protect any right to private gun ownership.

The individual rights theorists, supporting what has become known in the academic literature as the "Standard Model," argue that the amendment protects an individual right inherent in the concept of ordered liberty, and resist any attempt to circumscribe such a right.

2. Textual Analysis

A textual analysis of the Second Amendment supports an individual right to bear arms. A distinguishing characteristic of the Second Amendment is the inclusion of an opening clause or preamble, which sets out its purpose. No similar clause is found in any other amendment. While states' rights theorists seize upon this first clause to the exclusion of the second, both clauses should be read *in pari materia*, to give effect and harmonize both clauses, rather than construe them as being mutually exclusive.

The amendment reads "[a] well regulated Militia, being necessary to the security of a free State, the right of the people to keep and bear Arms, shall not be infringed." Within the amendment are two distinct clauses, the first subordinate and the second independent. If the amendment consisted solely of its independent clause, "the right of the people to keep and bear Arms, shall not be infringed," then there would be no question whether the right is individual in nature.

Collective rights theorists argue that addition of the subordinate clause qualifies the rest of the amendment by placing a limitation on the people's right to bear arms. However, if the amendment truly meant what collective rights advocates propose, then the text would read "[a] well regulated Militia, being necessary to the security of a free State, the right of the States to keep and bear Arms, shall not be infringed." However, that is not what the framers of the amendment drafted. The plain language of the amendment, without attenuate inferences therefrom, shows that the function of the subordinate clause was not to qualify the right, but instead to show why it must be protected. The right exists independent of the existence of the militia. If this right were not protected, the existence of the militia, and consequently the security of the state, would be jeopardized.

The Supreme Court recently interpreted the text of the Second Amendment and noted that the phrase "the people" in the Second Amendment has the same meaning in both the Preamble to the Constitution and in the First, Fourth, Fifth, and Ninth Amendments. *United States v. Verdugo–Urquidez*, 494 U.S. 259, 265, 110 S.Ct. 1056, 108 L.Ed.2d 222 (1990). The Court held that the phrase "the people" "seems to have been a term of art employed in select parts of the Constitution." The Second Amendment protects "the right of the people to keep and bear Arms," and the Ninth and Tenth Amendments provide that certain rights and powers are retained by and reserved to "the people."

* * *

The Court has also held that given their contemporaneous proposal and passage, the amendments of the Bill of Rights should be read *in pari materia*, and amendments which contain similar language should be construed similarly. *Patton v. United States*, 281 U.S. 276, 298. The Court's construction of "the people" as used in the Second Amendment supports a holding that the right to keep and bear arms is a personal right retained by the people, as opposed to a collective right held by the States. Thus, a textual analysis of the Second Amendment clearly declares a substantive right to bear arms recognized in the people of the United States.

3. Historical Analysis

"[T]here is a long tradition of widespread lawful gun ownership by private individuals in this country." A historical examination of the right to bear arms, from English antecedents to the drafting of the Second Amendment, bears proof that the right to bear arms has consistently been, and should still be, construed as an individual right.

* * *

a. English History

* * *

In retrospect, the framers designed the Second Amendment to guarantee an individual's right to arms for self-defense. Such an individual right was the legacy of the English Bill of Rights. American colonial practice, the constitutional ratification debates, and state proposals over the amendment all bear this out. The American Second Amendment also expanded upon the English Bill of Rights' protection; while English law allowed weapons "suitable to a person's condition" "as allowed by law," the American right forbade any "infringement" upon the right of the people to keep and bear arms.

In his influential Commentaries on the Constitution, Joseph Story emphasized the importance of the Second Amendment. He described the militia as the "natural defence of a free country" not only "against sudden foreign invasions" and "domestic insurrections," but also against "domestic usurpations of power by rulers." He went on to state that "[t]he right of the citizens to keep and bear arms has justly been considered as the palladium of the liberties of a republic; since it offers a strong moral check against the usurpation and arbitrary power of rulers; and will generally, even if these are successful in the first instance, enable the people to resist and triumph over them."

* * *

7. Constitutionality of 18 U.S.C. § 922(g)(8)

18 U.S.C. § 922(g)(8) is unconstitutional because it allows a state court divorce proceeding, without particularized findings of the threat of future violence, to automatically deprive a citizen of his Second Amendment rights. The statute allows, but does not require, that the restraining order include a finding that the person under the order represents a credible threat to the physical safety of the intimate partner or child. If the statute only criminalized gun possession based upon court orders with particularized findings of the likelihood of violence, then the statute would not be so offensive, because there would be a reasonable nexus between gun possession and the threat of violence. However, the statute

is infirm because it allows one to be subject to federal felony prosecution if the order merely "prohibits the use, attempted use, or threatened use of physical force against [an] intimate partner."

However, prosecution based on such an order would be tautological, for § 922(g)(8)(C)(i) merely repeats in different wording the requirement in subsection (B) that the order "restrains such person from harassing, stalking, or threatening an intimate partner of such person or child of such intimate partner or person, or engaging in other conduct that would place an intimate partner in reasonable fear of bodily injury to the partner or child." All that is required for prosecution under the Act is a boilerplate order with no particularized findings. Thus, the statute has no real safeguards against an arbitrary abridgement of Second Amendment rights. Therefore, by criminalizing protected Second Amendment activity based upon a civil state court order with no particularized findings, the statute is over-broad and in direct violation of an individual's Second Amendment rights.

* * *

C. *Fifth Amendment*

Emerson also contends that 18 U.S.C. § 922(g)(8) violates his Fifth Amendment due process rights. He argues that the perfunctory, generic temporary orders issued in his divorce proceedings expose him to federal criminal liability for engaging in otherwise lawful conduct.

Firearm possession is a valuable liberty interest imbedded in the Second Amendment to the United States Constitution. "[T]here is a long tradition of widespread lawful gun ownership by private individuals in this country." Thus, Emerson has a protected liberty interest in firearm possession under the Fifth Amendment.

"It is wrong to convict a person of a crime if he had no reason to believe that the act for which he was convicted was a crime, or even that it was wrongful. This is one of the bedrock principles of American law. It lies at the heart of any civilized system of law." It offends both substantive and procedural due process for Emerson to be convicted of a crime he did not know existed. Because 18 U.S.C. § 922(g)(8) is such an obscure criminal provision, it is unfair to hold him accountable for his otherwise lawful actions.

The conduct this statute criminalizes is *malum prohibitum*, not *malum in se*. In other words, there was nothing inherently evil about Emerson possessing a firearm while being under a domestic restraining order. His conduct was unlawful merely because the statute mandated that it be. Section 922(g)(8) is one of the most obscure of criminal provisions. Here, Emerson owned a firearm, and knew or should have known that if, for example, he was convicted of a felony, he would have to relinquish ownership of his firearm. If by chance he did not know this, the sentencing judge or the probation officer would have informed him of the law. Nevertheless, when Emerson was made subject to the restraining order telling him to not harass his wife, Emerson could not have known of the requirement to relinquish his gun unless the presiding judge issuing the order told him. In this case, the state district judge did not tell Emerson about the requirement. Emerson's attorney did not tell him either, because Emerson did not have a lawyer. The fact that the restraining order contained no reference to guns may have led Emerson to believe that since he complied with the order, he could carry on as before.

* * *

Because § 922(g)(8) is an obscure, highly technical statute with no *mens rea* requirement, it violates Emerson's Fifth Amendment due process rights to be subject to prosecution without proof of knowledge that he was violating the statute. Accordingly, Emerson's Motion to Dismiss the Indictment as violative of the Fifth Amendment is granted.

D. Tenth Amendment

* * * While it is arguable that § 922(g)(8) may offend general tenth amendment principles of federalism, because congress was acting through an enumerated power in drafting the law, and the law does not command state activity in support of it, this statute does not clearly violate the Tenth Amendment under the supreme court's holdings in *New York* and *Printz.* accordingly, Emerson's Tenth Amendment challenge to the statute fails.

UNITED STATES OF AMERICA v. JAMES L. BOYD III

United States District Court, D. Kansas (1999).
52 F.Supp.2d 1233–1238.

INDICTMENT

On January 6, 1999, the grand jury returned a two-count indictment charging the defendant with two violations of 18 U.S.C. § 922(g)(9), that is, possession of a firearm by a person convicted of a misdemeanor crime of domestic violence. Count one charges that the defendant knowingly and intentionally received and possessed a .9 mm semi-automatic pistol on May 30, 1998, after having been convicted on March 31, 1995, in Shawnee County, Kansas, of a misdemeanor crime of domestic violence. Count two charges that the defendant knowingly and intentionally received and possessed a .380 caliber semi-automatic pistol on August 24, 1998, after having been convicted on March 31, 1995, in Shawnee County, Kansas, of a misdemeanor crime of domestic violence. Each count charges that the respective firearm "had been shipped or transported in interstate or foreign commerce."

MOTION TO DISMISS ON CONSTITUTIONAL GROUNDS

Interstate Commerce Clause Challenge

The defendant's argument relies extensively on *United States v. Lopez*, 514 U.S. 549 (1995), in which the Supreme Court held that

Congress exceeded its interstate commerce powers by criminalizing the knowing possession of a firearm in a school zone, 18. The Court noted that among its precedent even "the most far reaching example of Commerce Clause authority over intrastate activity, involved economic activity in a way that the possession of a gun in a school zone does not." The defendant keys on this observation and the Court's conclusion that § 922(q) had "nothing to do with 'commerce' or any sort of economic enterprise, however broadly one might define those terms." The defendant criticizes the lower court opinions subsequently applying *Lopez* as having narrowly construed *Lopez* and having failed to address this aspect of the Supreme Court's opinion. The defendant argues that § 922(g)(9) focuses not on the weapon and its movement in interstate commerce but rather on the regulation of domestic violence which has nothing to do with commerce. In short, the defendant contends it is not enough that the statute expressly makes interstate commerce an element of the crime.

If it were writing on a clean slate, this court might have more reason to discuss at length the defendant's arguments.[1] The slate, however, is not clean, and the court is bound to follow the Tenth Circuit precedent of *United States v. Farnsworth*, 92 F.3d 1001, 1006 (10th Cir.1996); though these precedent do not address the interstate commerce nexus within the particular context § 922(g)(9), they do address that nexus in other § 922(g) provisions and their reasoning cannot be distinguished on any legally relevant ground. In fact, § 922(g) imposes the same jurisdictional element for the nine different disabling statuses (e.g., felony conviction, fugitive from justice, illegal alien, unlawful user of controlled substance, and misdemeanor domestic violence conviction) listed in § 922(g)(1)-(9). Specifically, the statute makes it unlawful for a person fitting one of the nine listed statuses "to ship or transport in interstate or foreign commerce, or possess in or affecting commerce, any firearm ... or to receive any firearm ... which has been shipped in interstate commerce." This common jurisdictional element defeats the defendant's commerce clause challenge.

All of these cases have recognized that central to the Supreme Court's holding in *Lopez* was the "lack of a 'jurisdictional element which would ensure, through a case-by-case inquiry, that the firearm possession in question affects interstate commerce.'" "Unlike the statute at issue in *Lopez*, § 922(g) expressly requires some nexus to interstate commerce, reflecting the ability of Congress to exercise its delegated power under the Commerce Clause to reach the possession of firearms that have an explicit connection with or effect on interstate commerce." *United States v. Luna*, 165 F.3d at 321. Thus, it should come as no

---

1. * * * From its reading of this limited legislative history, the court's unmistakable impression is that the Lautenberg Amendment was an effort to regulate serious domestic violence, because the state criminal justice systems were perceived as ineffec-tive, too lenient, and outdated. The court is troubled when Congress can use the minimal interstate feature of firearms as a pretext for regulating activity that traditionally and historically has been considered a crime to be regulated by the states.

surprise that Commerce Clause challenges to § 922(g)(9) have had no success. Nor will this challenge prevail here.

Within his Commerce Clause challenge, the defendant weaves certain Tenth Amendment arguments and even comments that "[t]he major questions that arise in the interstate commerce area are the overarching Tenth Amendment issues." Most of this argument is aimed at giving *Lopez* a broad reading that would reject any federal criminal statute regulating traditional intrastate matters which really have little to do with business and commerce. Even so, if the defendant intended to make a separate Tenth Amendment challenge to § 922(g)(9), the court rejects the same based on sound reasoning found in *United States v. Bostic*, 168 F.3d 718, 1999 WL 74754, at 6. * * * In short, the court is compelled by binding precedent to find that § 922(g)(9), just like the other provisions of § 922(g), is a constitutional exercise of Congress's commerce power, and the court is convinced that § 922(g)(9) can be implemented by federal authorities without impermissibly infringing on the States' rights to regulate domestic relations.

Ex Post Facto Challenge

" 'A law violates the *Ex Post Facto* Clause when it punishes behavior which was not punishable at the time it was committed or increases the punishment beyond the level imposed at the time of commission.' " The defendant argues that § 922(g)(9) alters the definition of criminal conduct, increases the punishment for an earlier crime, and attaches unforeseeable consequences to a completed criminal case.

This court, as have all others deciding such a challenge, have concluded that because the illegal act in § 922(g)(9) is the possession of the firearm, not the misdemeanor domestic violence conviction, the illegal act was not completed until after § 922(g)(9) became effective. Consequently, this statute does not impose a heavier or additional penalty for the earlier domestic violence conviction, but rather imposes authorized punishment for criminal conduct that has occurred after the passage of the law. The defendant cites no legal authority, for the proposition that it must have been foreseeable to him at the time of his domestic violence conviction that Congress would create a disabling status based on this conviction. Indeed, such a claimed right far exceeds what are recognized as a defendant's due process rights. As this court said in *Hicks*, "§ 922(g)(9) plainly sets forth the conduct which it prohibits and to whom it applies." 992 F.Supp. at 1246. The defendant's *ex post facto* challenge fails.

Second Amendment Challenge

The defendant argues that the application of a firearm disabling statute to those convicted of misdemeanor crimes of domestic violence violates the Second Amendment to the United States Constitution. In the defendant's opinion, a misdemeanor crime of domestic violence provides an insufficient basis for depriving a person of his right to keep and bear arms. The defendant summarily contests the Supreme Court precedent which arguably restrict this right to militia matters and, alternatively, argues that 18 U.S.C. § 922(g)(9) even fails the most permissive "rational basis" review standard.

In *United States v. Oakes*, 564 F.2d 384, 387 (10th Cir.1977), the court held that "[t]o apply the [Second] [A]mendment so as to guarantee appellant's right to keep an unregistered firearm which has not been shown to have any connection to the militia, ... , would be unjustifiable in terms of either logic or policy." Relying on *Oakes*, the Tenth Circuit has summarily rejected all subsequent Second Amendment challenges. In *Lewis v. United States*, 445 U.S. 55, 65 n. 8, (1980), the Supreme Court held:

> These legislative restrictions on the use of firearms [prohibiting a felon's possession of firearms] are neither based upon constitutionally suspect criteria, nor do they trench upon any constitutionally protected liberties. See *United States v. Miller*, 307 U.S. 174, 178, 59 S.Ct. 816, 83 L.Ed. 1206 (1939) (the second amendment guarantees no right to keep and bear a firearm that does not have "some reasonable relationship to the preservation or efficiency of a well regulated militia").

The defendant has not presented this court with any argument that could justify this court departing from this binding precedent.

Equal Protection

The defendant argues first that he has a fundamental right to keep and bear arms under the Ninth and Second Amendments. This position is not supported by the case law. In *Lewis*, the Supreme Court said that the federal "firearm regulatory scheme is consonant with the concept of equal protection ... if there is 'some "rational basis" for the statutory distinctions made ... or ... they "have some relevance to the purpose for which the classification is made." ' " Besides *Lewis*, other courts also have relied on the rational basis standard in evaluating criminal statutes that disabled certain classes from possessing firearms. Because the statutory classification here does not involve a suspect class or bear on a fundamental right, § 922(g)(9) will be upheld if it is "rationally related to a legitimate government objective."

"Legislative penalties imposed on certain classes of persons must 'rest on real and not feigned differences,' must 'have some relevance to the purpose for which the classification is made,' and must not subject the class members to wholly arbitrary treatment." To prevail on his challenge, the defendant must establish "that no 'state of facts reasonably may be conceived to justify' the disputed classification."

The defendant's only equal protection argument is based on the public interest exception in 18 U.S.C. § 925 which was successful in *Fraternal Order of Police v. United States*, 152 F.3d 998, 1002–03 (D.C.Cir.1998), reh'g granted, 159 F.3d 1362 (D.C.Cir. Nov.12, 1998). The remedy granted in that decision was to hold "§ 925 unconstitutional insofar as it purports to withhold the public interest exception from those convicted of domestic violence misdemeanors." The court does not appreciate how that decision or its remedy has any applicability to the present case. For that matter, the defendant has presented no argument or evidence that even suggests the public interest exception could apply here. Unless the public interest exception is involved in the charged conduct here, the defendant is without standing to raise a claim that Congress violated his equal protection rights by irrationally excluding domestic violence misdemeanors from the public interest exception. The court finds the defendant lacks standing to challenge § 922(g)(9) on the equal protection grounds argued here.

* * *

CHAPTER 15

CONFIDENTIALITY ISSUES, INCLUDING MANDATORY REPORTING OF DOMESTIC VIOLENCE

This chapter deals with issues of privacy and confidentiality, which are key to safety for victims of domestic violence. The legal system has the potential to increase danger to victims or to decrease this, in a variety of ways. The chapter starts with an overview of the topic, focusing on how the legal system can help keep survivor's addresses confidential from the general public and the abuser. It also stresses the need for security in the courthouse, and concludes that until we offer battered women and their children true protection, we should not fault them for failing to leave their abusers.

The other articles in this chapter deal with the policy question whether intimate partner abuse should be reported over the wishes of the survivor, and if so, to whom. One article argues in favor of such reporting policies, stressing that this practice is helpful in stopping domestic violence, and arguing that those who are obligated but fail to report should be civilly liable. The other article argues that such policies are more likely to further endanger victims of domestic violence and to keep them from seeking help.

JOAN ZORZA, RECOGNIZING AND PROTECTING THE PRIVACY AND CONFIDENTIALITY NEEDS OF BATTERED WOMEN

29 Fam. L. Q. 273, 280–294, 308–311 (1995).

I. INTRODUCTION

There is an increasing understanding that battered women are at serious risk from their abusers and that their abusers spend much of their time monitoring and harassing them. Battered women must be given real protection that will keep them safe not only from the abuse, but also from their abusers' intrusion and harassment. This article will explore some of the obstacles that keep battered women from leaving, many of which derive from the failure of society and the legal system to protect women's privacy and confidentiality needs. The article urges the need for battered women to be able to keep their whereabouts confidential, examines victim-counselor confidentiality privileges and nondisclosure laws, discusses the need of battered women to be able to relocate with their children, and examines the security needs of the courthouse.

* * *

III. KEEPING LOCATION CONFIDENTIAL

If the victim is to be kept from being homeless, her home must be secure from her abuser, whether it is the home in which she alone has been living, the residence previously shared with her abuser, or an entirely new home. It is not enough to allow her to live somewhere and to ensure that she has adequate support to do so, including the cost to move and set up a new home. She must be allowed to have a real zone of safety where her abuser cannot harass her. This may mean far greater restrictions on where her abuser can go than most courts and laws have been comfortable with giving. In addition, we must listen to and respond to her fears based on what she knows or believes from her abuser's threats. We must also help her plan for likely contingencies based on other abusers' tactics.

Her greatest danger is if she is to continue living at an address known to her abuser. At a minimum, her safety requires that he not have access to the keys to the home. If he previously had access to the key to the home where she is to live, especially if she lacks the means to change the locks, the court should hold him responsible for paying the cost for her to have new, secure locks installed. In addition, the police must truly protect her, particularly if her abuser comes near her home, place of work, school, or wherever she goes. Similarly, police must protect the children. To be realistic, any visitation that her abuser gets should be supervised at a safe location by someone impartial.

Often a victim will feel so vulnerable or demoralized by her abuser's continued threats, violence, stalking behavior, and/or harassment that she will decide that she needs to move to a location unknown to her abuser. Whether she moves now or later, her safety and continued emotional well-being should be grounds for letting her move with the children to a place where she will feel, and hopefully be, safe. But, as Kirkwood found, any battered woman who considers leaving her abuser faces formidable hurdles. Many of these hurdles could be eliminated or dramatically reduced if she were given the full protection possible under our laws, and if these were enforced by the police and courts.

An abused woman must be able to keep her whereabouts confidential because many abusive and controlling men spend enormous amounts of time and effort spying on, seeking out, following, and harassing their victims. Such stalking behaviors can be especially lethal to the victim and children. Once her location is known to her abuser, he is very likely to go on battering her. And he may even kill her, and her children, as well.

A. Keeping Her Address Confidential

Given that most abusive men continue to search for and abuse their prior partners, for a battered woman to be safe, she has to be able to keep any new address confidential. Perhaps the most important addresses which must be kept confidential are those of battered women's shelters. Every woman and child who stays at the shelter is put in jeopardy if the shelter's location is compromised.

Some states have statutes in their domestic violence codes or elsewhere which mandate that courts keep the address of any battered women's shelter confidential. Other states require or allow courts to keep the victim's address confidential. Some courts rely on general provisions permitting them to order any other relief that is just to permit battered women to keep their addresses or that of shelters from public scrutiny. California's code has provisions for omitting the applicant's address, place of residence, school, employment, or the applicant's child's place of school or child care.

Federal law requires every domestic violence shelter that receives federal money to have confidentiality provisions, provisions which include keeping the address confidential. The Family Violence Prevention and Services Act provides that the address will not be made public to anyone except upon written authorization from the persons responsible for operating the facility. A similar provision protects any domestic violence shelter receiving Victims of Crime Act (VOCA) funding. Courts have not always protected this confidentiality. Some judges believe that a husband or father has an absolute right to know the address of his wife or children, even if release of a shelter's address may result in the termination of federal or state funding to domestic violence programs in the state.

Not only must the shelter's location be kept confidential, but also the woman's own new address, and possibly her place of school, employment, her children's places of child care and/or school, and any health-care facility where she or her children go. However, courts have often failed to protect the victim's address, even when their own state's law require them to do so. A survey of courts in three counties in Massachusetts, where the judges have no discretion to not impound the address of a petitioner seeking protection under the state's domestic violence act, found that the judges ordered impoundment for only 4 percent of the women who requested this relief, and in only 6 percent of the cases where the woman made clear in the pleadings that she had left her home to avoid the abuse.

While states often have provisions in their domestic violence codes to restrict or prevent disclosure of the victim's address, many other statutes and court practices encourage or even require disclosure of the very address which the victim must keep confidential for her security.

The Uniform Child Custody Jurisdiction Act notice requirements, which will be discussed in a later section, create serious obstacles to many victims. When an abuser misuses the system to gain access to his victim's address, the court should require him to fully pay for the victim to move to a new, nondisclosed address of at least comparable value, including her new security deposit and any necessary costs to break the existing lease.

1. *School Records:* By law, children are required to attend school if they are between certain ages. Many abusers locate their victims through their children's school records. The federal government and many states have provisions for making a child's school records available to both parents. Although some states allow courts to restrict access to some or all of the information to an abusive parent, it is rare for domestic violence victims to request such relief or to even know that such relief is available. Even when it is requested, courts are not always willing to grant it. Furthermore, the trend toward state registries of domestic violence orders has encouraged more uniform protective orders with fewer complexities that are unlikely to restrict the abuser's access to school records.

Other states give the public access to students' names and attendance records or attendance records and permanent records of each student's grades. Tennessee allows the public access to any student's name, age, address, dates of attendance, grade level completed, class placement, and degrees awarded. Restricting the abuser's access is meaningless if everyone else can obtain the desired information for him.

In addition, many states have provisions for flagging a child's school records and/or birth certificate when the child is reported missing so the parent who is left behind can be notified if one of the documents is requested to register a child in a new school or to apply for a passport. Notification better equips the parent to find the missing child. Abusers, who regularly deny or minimize their abuse and often lie, sometimes claim that their children are missing or abused as a way to punish and control their partners or gain access to their whereabouts. Some abusers have their family members make false accusations that the victim or child is missing or that the child is abused by the victim or her new partner. These efforts are almost always successful in getting a court to order the information turned over to the father. They also serve to shift the blame onto the mother, even when the accusation is blatantly false. When state custody laws or judges use "friendly parent" provisions, which factor in the effort made by each parent toward achieving a positive relationship with the other parent, such false accusations may further reward the abuser by resulting in a change of custody, further victimizing the victim and children and reinforcing the perpetrator's abusive behavior.

2. Medical Records: Mothers frequently utilize doctors and medical facilities on behalf of themselves or their children. If they do not get medical attention for their children, they may well be subject to being reported for child abuse. Yet battered women must make use of these medical services at their peril. As some health-care workers become more aware that children are harmed by witnessing their mother being abused, they file more child neglect and/or abuse reports. In some states, like California, health workers must file medical reports if they know or suspect that any adult is abused. Sometimes the abuser is actually contacted about the report that he abused the woman or the child. When he is notified, he is very likely to retaliate against his victim. But even if only the victim is notified, the abuser may learn of the report, and use it against her in a custody proceeding. Because even when he is the perpetrator of the abuse, the child protective agency usually substantiates the claim against the mother for allowing herself to be abused, even though she had no ability to stop or control his abuse.

Furthermore, the abuser may be able to learn further information to locate or use against his victim because many states allow both parents access to their child's medical records. Many states by statute or practice provide that a hospital must release records pursuant to a subpoena, *subpoena duces tecum*, or court order. Such orders are freely given out by most judges whenever a parent, particularly a father, alleges that a child is missing. This is true even when there is an order of protection in place that restricts his access to such data. Few courts consult even their own abuse prevention files, particularly when an emergency hearing is demanded. As previously noted, many abusive fathers make such allegations, even when they know that they are false. But few courts punish fathers who make such false allegations. Instead, most courts will treat his allegation as an emergency or a material change in circumstances and, if not give him custody, will at least order the victim not to leave the state with the children. States need to establish statewide registries for protective orders and keep such records even after orders expire. Courts should be required to check these records prior to transferring custody to any abuser, even if the victim has fled with the children. And courts must hold the abuser responsible when he manipulates the court personnel and the system to maintain power and domination over his victim.

3. Postal Service Records: Domestic violence programs usually rent post office boxes to receive mail while keeping their addresses confidential. Until recently, any citizen could request for a small fee under the Freedom of Information Act the forwarding address of anyone who had recently moved, or the name and address of anyone who had rented a post office box. But, at the suggestion of domestic violence advocates, a provision was included in the Violence Against Women Act, later incorporated into the Crime Bill, that required the Postal Service to prohibit access to the public of addresses of domestic violence programs and victims of domestic violence. Even before the bill was enacted, the Postal Service changed its policy, effective March 11, 1994, to prohibit the public's access to forwarding addresses and identifying information about holders of post office boxes. On January 1, 1995, the Postal Service confidentiality provisions of the Violence Against Women Act went into effect. But, although the public is prohibited from access to this information, the Postal Service will still provide boxholder information and forwarding addresses upon request to law enforcement agencies, courts, and other governmental programs when a Request For Boxholder Change of Address Information Needed for Service of Legal Process form is submitted. Because batterers frequently falsify facts and manipulate courts, agencies, and police for their personal advantage or to hurt their victims, these provisions may not adequately protect battered women, or even shelters, from disclosure of their addresses.

It is clear that tougher provisions must be put into effect to protect battered women and shelters from having their addresses disclosed. After consulting statewide registries to verify that no protective orders have ever been issued against the abuser, courts should still have to weigh the need for confidentiality of the shelter or a victim of domestic violence against the abuser's likely manipulation of the system and the need for disclosure, even before ordering the release of the information to a law enforcement agency.

4. Departments Of Motor Vehicle Records: Another section of the Crime Bill, the Driver Privacy Protection Act, was enacted to stop the widespread practice of states' registry of motor vehicles giving out or selling information about individuals or all licensed drivers or owners of registered motor vehicles. Individuals in the thirty-four states which released the names, addresses, and social security numbers of drivers and car owners, will be unable to get this information, although the restrictions do not become mandatory for three years. States have sold this information at considerable profit. According to testimony on the Driver Protection Act, New York State made more than $125 million in the previous year from selling its Department of Motor Vehicle records.

Under the new law, states will have to stop releasing any "individual's photograph, social security number, driver identification number, name, address (but not the five-digit zip code), telephone number, and medical or disability information."

5. Voter Registration Information: As political activists and candidates generally know, voter registration lists containing the voting record and party affiliation, if any, are readily available to the public. The easy access to these lists has long prevented many battered women from registering to vote. Consequently, battered women are forced either to endanger themselves and their children if they register to vote, or to forego their right to vote, one of the most precious and fundamental constitutional rights of America's democratic society.

At least two states will accommodate battered women who wish to vote without publicly disclosing their addresses. Rutgers Law School Professor Eric Neisser filed a suit in New Jersey on behalf of a battered women who unsuccessfully sought to register to vote by giving her post office box number instead of her street address. She alleged that her husband repeatedly abused her, including an incident in violation of a permanent restraining order, and that she suffered permanent neck and back injuries as a result of his abuses. She also stated that she had moved to her current address in order to escape him.

The Superior Court of New Jersey, Monmouth County, citing the legislature's intent to assure domestic violence victims the maximum protection from abuse which the law can provide, noted that the state's Prevention of Domestic Violence Act requires the court to "waive any requirement that the victim's location be disclosed to any person" in a court pleading. Although the act does not specifically provide for the confidentiality of the battered victim's address in other contexts, the court found that the voting rights of abused victims, as with other citizens, must be ensured. The New Jersey court held that the Superintendent of Elections is required to register the abused victim without making her address a matter of the public record. In order to be registered, the victim must submit a voter registration form excluding her street address, submit a copy of her domestic violence restraining order, provide a mailing address such as a post office box, inform the commissioner which election district she lives in after examining a map of the town's voting districts, and promise to promptly notify the commissioner in writing if she moves.

This court decision was later codified to permit a victim of domestic violence with a permanent restraining order to register to vote without listing the actual street address on the registration form. Instead, the registrant attaches a copy of the permanent restraining order, a note indicating that she fears further violent acts by her abuser, and any address, including a post office box, where the applicant can receive mail. If she later moves, the registrant will be deemed to have informed the commissioner or board if she completes a new permanent registration form in the manner described. The State of Washington has also enacted legislation to allow battered persons to register to vote without publicly disclosing their addresses as part of the program described in the next section.

B. The Washington State Address Confidentiality Program

The State of Washington has made provisions to protect its abused citizens through the Washington State Address Confidentiality Program. The program's goal is to keep secret the new location of domestic violence victims who have permanently left an abusive situation. One part of the law allows victims to use post office box addresses as their officially listed addresses. The other part stops the public's access to certain addresses. Confidentiality is given upon request in both voting and marriage records. Those in the program, which is administered by the Secretary of State's office, can submit documentation from that office in lieu of address information needed for access to various programs and assistance. The program costs its participants nothing. This program provides an ideal model to other states wishing to protect its victims, as does Florida's newly enacted law which permits victims of many crimes, including domestic violence, to request in writing that a state agency not reveal the victim's home or work address or telephone number; the request is valid for five years.

C. Name Change

When the victim and/or her children are at serious danger from her abuser and she wants to cut off all contact with him, she should have the ability to change her and her children's names without notifying the abuser of what their new names will be. Courts must keep such records absolutely confidential from the public and the abuser so that nobody can obtain access to their new names.

In addition, every state should have provisions to terminate the right of only one parent when that parent is a domestic violence perpetrator who is seriously endangering the health and well-being of the other parent or the child. In many states the state can only file an action to terminate parental rights against both parents, even when the parents are divorced. In cases of domestic violence the mother is usually a fit parent, or becomes fit once protected from her abuser, even without therapy. Terminating her rights makes little sense, given that she will almost certainly be able to recover once protected. But unless she is given adequate protection, she and the children will continue to be at risk.

If she is divorced from her abuser (or was never married to him) and the abuser's parental rights are terminated, she is free to change her and the children's names and to move, if she desires, to prevent being traced by her abuser. If she notifies her children's schools and health-care providers of the termination, the abuser should have no further access to these records. Because she is no longer married to him and he has no further parental rights, he will have no further responsibility for paying child support, even if she receives public assistance.

In the event that she is not yet divorced from her abuser, courts should seriously consider expediting her divorce. A study of over 551 battered women killed by their intimate partners in the Canadian province of Ontario over seventeen years, found that none of the women was killed after they were actually divorced from their abusers, although the time when they went through divorce proceedings was a time of very high risk. This suggests that protracted divorce proceedings, which are all too common in domestic violence cases, may be especially dangerous to battered women. Accordingly, courts should consider expediting divorce proceedings for battered women to see if this reduces their danger.

D. Social Security Numbers

The Social Security Administration issues to each U.S. citizen and certain aliens a social security number. These numbers are used to identify individuals throughout their lives for social security purposes. However, the numbers are used for many other identification purposes, including on records for obtaining public assistance, on tax returns, bank records, credit files, and more recently on marriage certificates and birth records of children. Often these numbers are used on driver licenses, medical insurance policies, and sometimes even on school records. These numbers are also used by abusers to track their victims.

The director of a social security office has the authority to issue a new social security number on behalf of a victim whose life, or that of a child in the victim's care, is in serious danger. Although new numbers are readily issued for people in the federal government's witness protection program, social security offices seldom issue them to battered women.

Even if the woman and her children obtain new numbers, her abuser may be able to track them down if they continue to use the same names, transfer money between bank accounts, use old credit records to obtain new ones, apply for public assistance (especially if the child support enforcement unit pursues child support on their behalf) or, after changing their names, notify schools or agencies that licensed or accredited them in any way. It is likely that the only victims who successfully escape homicidal lovers intent on tracking them, effectively had to abandon not only their friends and families, high school diplomas, credit records, medical records, employer references, and driver licenses, but also nursing degrees, beautician licenses, and other professional accreditation. Courts should order the Social Security Administration to issue new social security numbers to battered women and their children who are in serious danger, and to inform them of how they can minimize the risk that they will be located through other means.

E. "Good Cause" to Not Cooperate with Child Support Enforcement

An applicant or recipient of public assistance is expected to cooperate with the IV–D child support enforcement agency in her state so that child support can be obtained from the child's missing parent. However, an exception exists if the applicant/recipient is afraid that serious physical or emotional harm will come to her or her child if the agency locates the parent, takes him to court, or orders him to pay child support. She is entitled to receive benefits so long as her "good cause" claim is pending. If her claim is upheld, she will not have to supply any information about him (e.g., his name, address, social security number, parents' names, or place of employment) or go to court against her abuser. However, she may find that she receives a temporary determination and must reapply in a few months. Furthermore, the agency is still entitled to go after her abuser using information obtained from other sources, and will very likely succeed if paternity can be presumed because of their marital status or he is listed as the father on the child's birth certificate.

F. Paternity Establishment

In many states the mother of a nonmarital child may be free to relocate with her child or deny the father visitation if paternity has never been established. However, effective December 23, 1994, all birthing centers and hospitals will encourage and assist parents in establishing paternity of children born out of wedlock before the mother and child leave the facility. The regulations make it clear that establishing paternity is voluntary. Various welfare proposals will prohibit welfare eligibility when paternity is not established. But some mothers may choose to forego collecting welfare and/or child support in the hope of preventing further contact with an abusive partner. Yet she may find that he seeks custody, visitation, return of the child, and/or paternity, thereby defeating her efforts to protect herself and the child. Fairness requires that any welfare changes and programs to encourage establishing paternity should contain a "good cause" exemption for abused persons.

G. Telephone Technology Threat

Often, a battered woman obtains an unlisted telephone number in the hope that it will protect her from being located or harassed. Domestic violence shelters also want protection for their telephones to prevent abusers from calling staff or residents. However, new telephone technologies jeopardize what little security shelters and battered women expect from having unlisted numbers, particularly if a battered woman or her children are required to telephone her abuser, not an unusual requirement or consequence of court ordered visitation. Caller ID visually displays, and sometimes stores, the telephone number of an incoming call. In some parts of the country, Caller ID also shows the name of the caller. Some of the Caller ID equipment can store up to sixty-four telephone numbers, including unlisted and unpublished ones. Utility commissions often require telephone companies to block the telephone lines of any domestic violence program for free, and possibly those of any subscriber who asks. Even though the entire telephone line can be blocked in those states or a particular call can be blocked by dialing in a special code, Last Call Return service and various other services allow that number to be stored and later redialed, thereby effectively enabling the abuser to have permanent access to that telephone number. Many abusers readily admit that they frequently use Caller ID as a control tactic to monitor and track their victims' activities and whereabouts. Another technology they sometimes use enables them to repeatedly redial a victim's number.

Further jeopardizing a victim's safety, many telephone companies refuse to block a telephone line for Caller ID purposes if the phone service is in another person's name, most often the abuser's. Even when the victim has a court order excluding him from the home, some telephone companies refuse to transfer service to the victim unless she has her abuser's written permission and arrangements have been made to pay off arrearages, conditions to which the batterer is unlikely to agree and which may precipitate another beating. Some telephone companies have been known to telephone the abuser at his new listing to ask him for instructions, including whether to unblock her line, without telling her.

Errors have also foiled people who tried to block their numbers. Recently the press revealed that NYNEX, the telephone service for 90 percent of New York state lines, was unable to provide the line block protection it had promised to almost 30,000 subscribers who asked for it. NYNEX knew of the error for over a year, but did nothing until the press exposed the failure.

Battered women have also found that cellular and cordless telephones subject them to easy monitoring. Many new technologies will probably pose even greater risks to battered women.

H. Witness Protection Program

The federal witness protection program is best known for the new identities it gives to criminals who act as witnesses for the government against other criminals. These informants are known to be in great danger of retaliation by the criminals against whom they testify. Some battered women desire to change their identities to escape their abusers. They and their children often face as much danger in leaving as informants do by testifying. The witness protection program should be expanded to protect these domestic violence victims and their children.

* * *

VII. Security in the Courthouse

Battered women not only need good laws, they need safe courthouses so they will not be killed, abused, or followed home by their abusers. Assaults by their partners are not uncommon, even in courthouses. Family courts are the nation's most dangerous courts. According to one survey, former partners either physically or verbally assaulted at least seventeen of the 385 women granted protective orders in Colorado on the day that their orders were issued. However, when a batterer or his friends and family harass an abused woman or her children in the courthouse, especially when an order of protection is in effect, court officers present seldom do more than try to keep the parties quiet or suggest that one of them move, thereby trivializing the violence. This conveys the messages that (1) courtroom decorum is more important than the victim's safety, (2) even the court regards its own order as unimportant, (3) the victim is unworthy of protection, and (4) the abuser is justified in his behavior. The result is that the abuser is reinforced in his control of his victim, while she is left feeling more helpless and powerless, with little or no confidence in the court, thereby reinforcing the very cycle of violence that the court's intervention is meant to break.

* * *

Courts should develop protocols for minimizing the dangers to battered women, court personnel, lawyers, and the public, and for dealing with violent situations inside and near the courthouse. They should ideally use metal detectors or x-ray machines to screen for any weapons and have separate entrances, separate secure waiting rooms, and escape exits for victims. Courts should allow and encourage victims to come to court with advocates, particularly when they are not represented; their advocates are likely to know the layout of the courthouse so can minimize their risk when going, say, from the clerk's office to the courtroom, or to the rest room. Inside the courtroom the parties should be seated separately, with barriers (a table, if need be) separating the parties when their case is heard. Courts also need provisions for child care that insure that the children are protected from harm and abduction, and are not used by an abuser to gain access to the victim.

Courts should develop protocols that cover all situations, including those involving abusive law enforcement officers and even court personnel who are victimized by or are victimizing family or household members, because domestic violence can affect anyone. Court protocols should protect court personnel as well as parties, witnesses, jurors, and the public. An increasing number of courts use bullet proof barriers and have protocols for opening suspicious packages. Some judges protect themselves by obtaining unlisted telephone numbers, omitting any address on their checks, having unmarked reserved parking spaces, and having home security. Victims of abuse deserve the same type of protection.

VIII. Conclusion

Abusive men terrorize their victims into fearing death or serious injury for themselves or their loved ones if they leave. These threats are carried out all too often. In addition, society has created many hurdles that further endanger, or at least fail to protect, battered women who want to leave their abusers. These hurdles reflect misinformation and gender biased notions about domestic violence, its perpetrators and victims, what men and women deserve, and what is good for families and children. We need to rethink our laws and practices to be realistic about the safety of battered women and their children. Until we offer battered women and their children true protection and hold their abusers accountable, it is unreasonable and counterproductive to fault them for failing to leave.

MIA M. McFARLANE, MANDATORY REPORTING OF DOMESTIC VIOLENCE: AN INAPPROPRIATE RESPONSE FOR NEW YORK HEALTH CARE PROFESSIONALS

17 Buff. Pub. Interest L. J. 20–32 (1998–1999).

C. Arguments in Opposition to Mandatory Reporting

Many domestic violence organizations opposed Assembly Bill 4586 and sent position papers to the Governor and the Legislature voicing their concerns. These groups oppose the proposed mandatory reporting law for several well founded reasons: the law cannot guarantee women's safety, it fails to recognize that women are autonomous adults capable of making their own decisions, and it violates ethical considerations in the medical profession. These arguments apply not only to the New York bill but to mandatory reporting laws in general. Therefore, this section will focus both on the proposed New York legislation as well as the arguments for and against mandatory reporting in a broader context—including other states and national arenas.

One factor which is likely to have a powerful effect on current and proposed mandatory reporting laws is the official position of the American Medical Association, which in 1997 announced its opposition to such legislation. While the American Medical Association identified valid arguments on both sides of the mandatory reporting issue, it underscored the fact that in the absence of formal research on the benefits or harm of a mandatory reporting policy, these arguments are mostly conjectural and stem from the ideological beliefs of the supporters and opponents. Consequently, the American Medical Association based its position on the fact that mandatory reporting laws conflict with the profession's ethical tenets regarding patients' rights and physicians' responsibilities. The position officially adopted in 1997 was as follows: "The American Medical Association opposes the adoption of mandatory reporting laws for physicians treating competent adult victims of domestic violence if the required reports identify victims. Such laws violate basic tenets of medical ethics and are of unproven value." The ethical considerations of the medical profession and other concerns with mandatory reporting laws are addressed below.

1. Safety Concerns

When a victim of domestic violence tries to leave an abusive relationship, the batterer fears that he is losing power and control. Consequently, the violence usually escalates. When a woman makes a police report or seeks an order of protection, plans must be put in place to ensure her safety. Only the battered women fully understands her own particular situation, knows when and how she can be safe, and can decide when it is the right time to leave the relationship.

Although the criminal justice system has improved its response to domestic violence, it has failed to protect battered women in the past. Many victims have been seriously injured or killed after police reports have been made or orders of protection have been sought. These dangerous circumstances dictate that only the woman should be able to decide when a report should be made.

The inability of the system to protect domestic violence victims from retaliation by their abusers is one reason for opposing mandatory reporting. If a doctor reports domestic violence, the report does not guarantee that the woman will be safe when she leaves the emergency room. When batterers are arrested, they are often only in custody for a short time. In fact, they may even return to the home before the battered woman has returned from the hospital. Batterers are not always held without bail, and the criminal justice system cannot ensure around-the-clock protection. In these instances, instead of helping victims of domestic violence, the reporting law inadvertently places women in greater danger.

In addition to retaliation issues, a woman's health may be further jeopardized if the batterer denies a victim access to health care or if the woman does not seek medical attention for fear of reprisals. Because batterers attempt to control all aspects of their partner's lives, they also seek to control access to health care. If the batterer knows that he will be reported if abuse is detected by a health care provider, then he is likely to bar the woman from seeking medical attention. Even in instances where the abuser does not expressly forbid medical care, the battered woman may not risk seeing a physician for fear that a report will be made. Mandatory reporting laws pose particular concerns for immigrants who fear that a report could lead to their deportation.

Ariella Hyman, a San Francisco attorney who specializes in domestic violence, has written much on the subject of mandatory reporting, and she has compiled anecdotes about the effects of the mandatory reporting law in California. Several stories have been reported to Hyman of women seeking medical assistance from battered women's shelters, rather than hospitals, in order to avoid mandated reporting by a physician. In these cases, the women had suffered serious injuries and were in need of hospital care: one woman's husband burned her face by holding it against a hot grill; another woman's husband banged her head against the floor and a wall causing serious head injuries.

Although many of the arguments involving safety issues are based on mandating reports to law enforcement agencies, similar arguments can be made in opposition to laws mandating reports to social service agencies. In Kentucky, health care providers are required to report domestic violence to the Department for Social Services (DSS) which investigates the allegation of abuse by contacting the victim by phone, letter, or a home visit. The Kentucky Domestic Violence Association argues that "[t]his contact can be dangerous when dealing with an abuser who jealously guards his spouse or partner's every move." Furthermore, state social service agencies are overburdened, underfunded, and are not always sensitive to the needs of domestic violence victims.

2. *Violations of Autonomy*

One of the main arguments cited in opposition to mandatory reporting laws for domestic violence is that women are autonomous, competent, rational adults capable of making their own decisions. Concepts such as the battered women's syndrome and learned helplessness often lead people to believe that women are unable to make appropriate decisions in order to help themselves. This thinking often justifies paternalism and serves as an excuse to usurp the battered woman's right to make decisions affecting her own life. Given their situations and vulnerability, battered women often act in rational ways, and they are likely to be well aware of the consequences that will result from particular courses of action. Mandatory reporting laws, such as those currently proposed in New York State, deny women the right to make decisions that have serious consequences for their lives.

Many mandatory reporting laws for domestic violence are based on similar laws for child abuse and elder abuse. Part of the New York State Assembly's justification for bill 4586 is that "[t]here are laws to protect children in this state who are abused. There should also be laws to protect adults from physical harm." Opponents of the mandatory reporting laws argue that these laws perpetuate the stereotypes of battered women as being "helpless" and "childlike." Furthermore, mandatory reporting laws replicate the power and control dynamic that occurs in an abusive relationship, only here the state and physicians are the ones taking power away from the woman and making decisions for her.

Mandatory reporting laws in other states demonstrate a blatant disregard for a woman's autonomy. The portrayal of victims as helpless is evident in the legislative intent of some of these state statutes. For instance, the legislative findings and purpose of the New Mexico reporting statute indicate that the "legislature recognizes that many adults in the state are unable to manage their own affairs or protect themselves from exploitation, abuse or neglect." Almost identical language is found in the legislative intent of Kentucky's reporting statute: "The General Assembly of the Commonwealth of Kentucky recognizes that some adults of the Commonwealth are unable to manage their own affairs or to protect themselves from abuse, neglect, or exploitation."

Physicians should help battered women regain a sense of control by providing information, offering choices, and letting women decide when a report should be made. "Although tempting, practitioners should avoid the pitfall of 'rescuing' their patients." Some doctors have gone on record supporting such a stance. For instance, Dr. Howard Holtz testified:

> I don't think that competent women who have experienced violence, who go to their doctors and depend on that trust and confidentiality, should have the specter of mandatory reporting to some adult protective service agency. This isn't the model of child abuse. We're not dealing with developmentally or cognitively incompetent patients, and after thinking about it long and hard, I am very much against any kind of mandatory reporting other than for statistical purposes, on an anonymous basis, about domestic violence in clinical situations.[138]

Similar sentiments have been voiced by other professionals. Regina Podhorin, former Supervisor of the Office on Prevention of Violence Against Women, Division on Women, testified:

> I would prefer to look at that—to mandate them [physicians] to record, to put in the medical record, their suspicions, so that there is

138. Caroline W. Jacobus, Legislative Responses to Discrimination in Women's Health Care:A Report Prepared for the Commission to Study Sex Discrimination n the Statutes, 16Women's Rts. L.Rep., 153, 216.

documentation of it, but not that it be a reporting to officials, because I still also believe that women have the right to not have that reported to officials until they are ready. One of the most critical things about following through and making sure that women are able to be empowered and freed—it needs to be at their pace; it needs to be at their time. The danger level of doing it before that may help us to feel better, that we have done our part, but may put her in more danger. I don't know that is a good place for all of us to be. It almost feels like a salve. Instead of something that is helping that woman, it is something that is taking us off the hook by saying, "well, we reported it." that is not necessarily helping her.[139]

Many doctors are frustrated by domestic violence and are eager to do something about the problem, but mandatory reporting laws are not the answer. Reporting domestic violence may help health care providers feel that they have done their part, but there are safer and more effective ways for physicians to assist battered women.

3. Ethical Concerns

Another concern regarding mandatory reporting laws is that such requirements breach confidentiality between doctors and their patients. Some mandatory reporting laws in other states actually contradict the express policies of the American Medical Association which provide that "[f]or competent adult victims, physicians must not disclose an abuse diagnosis to caregivers, spouses or any other third party without the consent of the patient." "Similarly, the Council on Ethical and Judicial Affairs (CEJA) opinion 2.02 (Current Ethical Opinions) tells physicians to routinely screen patients for physical, sexual and psychological abuse, but not to disclose the diagnosis for an adult patient to anyone without the patient's consent." These medical ethics present a conflict for physicians who are mandated in certain states to report domestic violence. If New York adopts mandatory reporting legislation, the state will be placing all physicians in an ethical dilemma. In July of 1997, the AMA House of Delegates officially adopted the position that it opposed mandatory reporting of domestic violence.

When a person receives medical care, she is already in a vulnerable situation. Many people feel nervous during a physical examination; this situation is exacerbated when the patient does not trust the health care provider. Battered women, in particular, have experienced relationships with others in which their trust in that person has been shattered. They may not readily confide in other people, including doctors. Physicians may have to gain a battered woman's trust, and this trust would be destroyed if confidentiality is breached.

In order for a battered woman to receive the proper medical treatment, she must feel safe enough to completely disclose the abuse,

139. Id.

including information on specific symptoms and injuries. If a woman fears that the abuse will be reported, she may not be forthcoming with her physician. Inadequate information available to a physician could lead to inadequate medical treatment.

In addition to confidentiality concerns, other professionals have used the medical concepts of nonmaleficence and beneficence to argue against reporting laws. The doctrine of nonmaleficence states that above all else, the doctor should do no harm; the doctor should not risk engaging in any practice which would leave the patient worse off than before he or she intervened. Under this argument, physicians should not report domestic violence because there is no guarantee that the patient will not be harmed. A similar argument could be made under the beneficence doctrine which requires physicians to help their patients. The best way for a physician to help is to provide a safe and supportive environment in which the battered woman is free to discuss her abuse without repercussions. Health care providers should provide information, make referrals, and document the abuse so that it can be used in the future if the victim decides to prosecute. Effective assistance can be better achieved without the mandatory reporting requirements.

4. *Other Concerns*

A significant concern with the mandatory reporting of domestic violence is that criminal justice and social service systems already have difficulty serving the women that come forward on their own. Many argue that mandatory reporting will detect many more cases, but these women will be at greater risks of danger if the system is so overburdened that it cannot protect them all. For example, "in San Francisco, four out of five women are turned away from shelters due to lack of space." Other commentators have also voiced concerns regarding cases in which the batterer is a police officer.

An additional concern with the imposition of mandatory reporting is that of skewed data collection. Many supporters of mandatory reporting laws assume that the laws will lead to improved data on domestic violence. However, this assumption rests on the notion that doctors will always identify and report domestic violence. In reality, incomplete documentation and reporting may lead to skewed data. The American Medical Association has stated that domestic violence reporting may encounter problems similar to those found in the area of child abuse where reporting has been inconsistent and has reflected the cultural biases of physicians. Even the best-intentioned laws can have implementation problems. If physicians fail to report domestic violence, then the incidence of domestic violence would be underestimated, which in turn is likely to affect future policies and funding for domestic violence programs.

JAMES T. R. JONES, KENTUCKY TORT LIABILITY FOR FAILURE TO REPORT FAMILY VIOLENCE

26 N. Ky. L. Rev. 56–65 (1999).

TORT LIABILITY FOR FAILURE TO REPORT SPOUSE ABUSE

Various United States jurisdictions recognize that child abuse is not the only type of family violence which must be reported to the government if it is to be detected and properly handled. In particular, detection of domestic violence is a serious problem due to the reluctance of many victims to go to the police for help. Instead, they often turn to medical professionals for aid. For example, as many as thirty percent of women treated in hospital emergency rooms are there because of domestic violence. Physicians can help the increasing number of battered women by reporting, to the proper authorities, the numerous known or suspected abuse cases they see, yet they refuse in overwhelming numbers to do so. What can be done to cause these professionals to report?

As in the child abuse situation, civil liability can provide the incentive that inspires physicians to identify the otherwise unknown victims of insidious crimes, and thus the perpetrators as well. Although to date no United States courts have ruled on this point, the rationales of *Landeros* and the cases which impose liability for failure to report child abuse also should apply to spouse abuse.

When common law liability is the issue, it seems clear from cases like the infectious disease decisions or *Tarasoff* that physicians and related professionals owe a duty to the battered women they serve. When they have the requisite relationship with a battered spouse, they also should have the duty to report abuse of that person regardless of the existence of a mandatory reporting law. They should be civilly liable for any injuries the spouse suffers which are proximately caused by the physician's failure to discharge that obligation. Mandatory reporting has numerous salutary results; civil liability of non-reporters is justified notwithstanding the opposition of many who point to alleged problems due to breach of confidentiality, denial of patient self-determination, or various other concerns.

Review of the child abuse precedents demonstrates some of the problems in convincing tribunals to hold spouse abuse non-reporters liable on a common law basis. Courts which have rejected *Landeros* and *J.A.W.* may be even less likely to impose common law liability in domestic violence cases, which involve presumably competent adults rather than children. *Landeros* itself would seem to support such liability, although child and spouse abuse situations may be distinguishable.

Regardless of how United States courts view proclaiming a common law duty for physicians to report domestic violence, they should not hesitate to declare a reporting obligation in any of the many jurisdictions which have some version of statutorily-mandated reporting. These jurisdictions include the states, in particular Kentucky, with well-developed spouse abuse reporting requirements, as well as others with more general reporting laws. Typical of the general laws are those (1) requiring physicians to report injuries caused by firearms, knives, or other sources attributable to criminal acts, and (2) immunizing physicians from liability for their reports. Even the American Medical Association agrees that physicians should report violent acts committed against their patients when a statute mandates that they do so. The statutory negligence doctrine will provide the basis for holding the physicians negligent if they do not report as required by statute.

The recent child abuse precedents could be worrisome when statutory negligence for a failure to report domestic violence is the issue. All those cases involved specific child abuse reporting laws, which were focused in a relatively narrow way. Yet, as noted, some courts have refused to apply statutory negligence to those provisions. On the other hand, in all but a few states, the only reporting laws which apply to spouse abuse are general ones which extend to crimes across the board. These laws, accordingly, are even more vulnerable to attack than the child abuse provisions because at least the child abuse laws apply only to children. And even the laws in states, like Kentucky, with specific spouse abuse reporting laws similar to specific child abuse reporting statutes, are vulnerable to attack like the child abuse laws addressed in cases like *Borne v. Northwest Allen County School Corp.* Still, the statutory negligence doctrine ought to apply whether the statute in question is a specific spouse abuse reporting law or a general crime reporting provision. The public policy which favors mandatory reporting as a major initiative in the effort to protect domestic violence victims, as recently reiterated in *Commonwealth v. Allen*, equally should favor courts using the statutory negligence approach as a means for making reporting an even more effective tool. The judiciary ought freely to use it regardless of narrow decisions to the contrary.

Note that the reporting law, and potential liability for non-reporting, are not limited to the physician or other professional who does not report that a patient may be a battered spouse. It may apply to others, such as the pediatrician who notices that the adult who brings in a child for treatment is an apparent spouse abuse victim. It also applies to the physician/dentist/teacher/clergy whose patient tells her that the patient/student/parishioner is a spouse abuser. This clearly could raise problems for psychiatrists and other mental health providers, who view the confidentiality of their relationships with their patients as sacrosanct. As noted above, the Kentucky adult protection reporting statute waives any privilege that otherwise might apply here, and immunizes any good-faith reporter from civil or criminal liability for breach of confidence. In so doing, it follows the lead of numerous cases which have held that confidentiality concerns must give way to the public need to know about dangerous contagious diseases, child abuse, or potentially dangerous individuals. In these reporting cases, psychiatrists and other physicians are required by the Kentucky statute, on pain of potential civil and criminal liability, to report their reasonable suspicion of spouse abuse.

Strong policy reasons support imposing civil liability against non-reporters of family violence. The protective, preventive and social benefits of reporting, especially by physicians, are numerous. For example, such a requirement increases the number of abuse reports turned in to the authorities. This increase is advantageous because these reports help society detect and prevent crime (abuse); identify and offer protection, information and services to the victims of abuse, and collect data on the problem of family violence. Identification particularly is advanced since otherwise it is very difficult for the authorities to determine which individuals are abuse victims unless either the abuse is reported or the abuse is so bad for so long that it becomes obvious (and quite possibly causes permanent injuries or is fatal). Data collection is also a real issue, as without obligatory reports there is significantly less information available for measuring this type of criminal activity (and if statistics show abuse is a major problem, society is much more likely to respond to it both with attention and adequate resources).

If courts require reporting, they will demonstrate concern over family violence and a commitment to public action. Abusers who go unreported often continue their behavior, and ultimately may kill or severely injure their victims. Mandatory reporting reminds the many professionals who are reluctant to report abuse that they have to report whether they want to or not. Domestic violence is a crime which will not truly be curtailed until it is reported to the appropriate authorities as fully as any other offense. Once they learn of the violation, the authorities can take suitable steps, including offering voluntary protective services to the victims and possibly prosecuting the abuser. This can protect and empower the victim as well as hold the batterer accountable for his actions which, in turn, helps his victim (by stopping the abuse—hopefully forever). It also can aid the batterer himself by forcing him to obey the law, obtain any needed treatment services, and learn the consequences of not doing so.

Required reporting does other worthwhile things. It helps those victims who are too intimidated by their batterers to seek help. It gives physicians and others a means for having possible abuse cases investigated and provides a central place to send information about their battered patients. Required reporting can encourage some to report what they otherwise might fear to bring out absent the defense that mandatory reporting provides. Mandatory reporting lets the professional see that the authorities take reports of abuse seriously, and forces all physicians, not just the ones who report abuse voluntarily, to bear ratably the various economic and non-economic costs of reporting. Examples of these costs of reporting include time spent in filing reports and, perhaps, testifying in court; lost income for time spent on reporting rather than treating other patients; cost of office staff who help in the reporting process; and lost income from patients who change physicians as they do not want a physician who reports abuse to treat them or their victims—

probably not a problem if all physicians report pursuant to an obligatory rule.

The principal arguments against mandatory reporting, and thus against civil liability of non-reporters, focus on a woman's right of self-determination and the confidentiality of the physician-patient relationship. Both are serious issues, but neither justifies blocking a reporting requirement. The self-determination issue is whether reporting a battered spouse's condition to the state merely reflects appropriate governmental concern over the safety of its citizens or constitutes officious intermeddling in a competent adult's life which is intolerable in a free society. Its resolution requires a consideration of the nature of domestic violence.

Spouse abuse is a terrible social problem involving controlling, violent, criminal behavior against those often unable to protect themselves. If such conduct happened in any other context, society would not tolerate it. But, because it typically arises in a relationship, and with a woman as the victim, it has been treated differently—as a "private" concern, not for any, much less state, intervention. However, abusive acts are not "private," regardless of against whom they are directed. Spouse battering is as "public" a problem as any robbery or assault, rape or murder, and needs to be pursued just as vigorously whether or not the victim demands outside intervention. By keeping areas mostly involving women "private," society has kept them out of view, and also out of thought. Such treatment has meant that problems like child abuse, elder abuse, and spouse abuse have continued for centuries without serious interference or restriction from any outside source. Finally, the government is starting to get involved and is making a dent in these problems; claims that they are "private" matters can only hinder government's efforts.

When a problem is public, the government must try to deal with it, and that can mean—in addition to offering information and protective services—prosecuting or otherwise pursuing criminals regardless of the wishes of the victims, because crime is an offense against both individual victims and society, not just the victims alone. Victim safety and wishes must be considered, but cannot govern what society does. After all, the victim's "wishes" may not be her own at all, but rather those of the batterer who controls her. The state does intrude into the victim's life when it acts on mandatory abuse reports, but then it frequently meddles with people's lives (hopefully for valid reasons) pursuant to tax laws, motor vehicle registration, and drivers' licensing provisions without having these actions successfully challenged for violating individual independence and self-determination.

Requiring reporting, and follow-up investigations, is not so onerous for the victims that the community ought to ignore the abuse inflicted upon them in order to protect their right to be left alone. This is particularly true in light of society's distinct interest in preventing an ongoing pattern of violence from permanently injuring or killing its members, as domestic violence tends to be continuing behavior rather than an isolated criminal act. If victims cannot, or will not, protect themselves, then government must step in to prevent worse things from happening in the future. The victims' needs can be met through counseling and other spouse abuse resources after their physical safety is assured. Helping those in severe need is not really "paternalistic," or at least not in any negative sense. Society has to look after itself and its members, even if that entails occasional interference with someone's present perceptions, perhaps ill-founded, of her wishes. Although the issue is not without doubt, on balance, the fundamental right to self-determination should not overcome the state's obligation to protect its citizens and enforce the law. Mandatory reporting is a valuable, measured tool which must be upheld, although it certainly should be implemented so as to minimize any negative effects it may have.

The other major category of objection to mandatory reporting focuses on medical and legal concepts of confidentiality in the physician-patient relationship. A partial answer is that it is legally permissible to relate otherwise confidential information to the authorities when some compelling public purpose, such as protecting battered women from further abuse, is served by so doing (especially when, as in Kentucky, the confidentiality of such information is preserved). But that may not so completely resolve the ethical question of whether a breach of confidentiality truly is justified even in egregious domestic violence situations so that it precludes further discussion. Battered women face an ethical balancing process as their interest in confidentiality is measured against society's interest in protecting them from further abuse. There must be exceptions to confidentiality when they are necessary for the welfare of the patient or others. As noted, such exceptions are made in the United States when the issue is the reporting of child abuse or contagious disease (as in the HIV cases). Given the gravity of the violence problem, the public needs to identify its victims and perpetrators should resolve the confidentiality issue in favor of disclosure.

In the United States, medical professionals may face both common law and statutory negligence liability when they do not report domestic violence to the authorities, the abuse continues, and the victim suffers additional harm. Although unprecedented to date in spouse abuse situations, such liability has been imposed in child abuse situations and will further the policy of mandatory reporting. Kentucky courts can, and should, impose such liability in spouse abuse cases. Moreover, *Tarasoff* liability also is a real possibility in many cases. Just like child abusers, spouse abusers may voice their violent intentions to their therapists (indeed, the facts of *Tarasoff* itself closely resemble a spouse abuse/stalking situation). These twin liability theories will give professionals dual grounds for reporting lest they face a two-pronged complaint for damages.

Chapter 16

VICTIMS OF DOMESTIC VIOLENCE AS WELFARE RECIPIENTS AND WORKERS

This chapter looks at victims of domestic violence as welfare recipients and workers. These monetary issues, key to the survival of victims and their children, raise many legal questions.

The chapter starts with a discussion of theories underlying the recent push for welfare reform, and the implications of those theories for victims of domestic violence. The materials then describe the current state of welfare law under the federal Personal Responsibility and Work Opportunity Act of 1996, including the Family Violence Option (adopted by most states), with an emphasis on the impact of this law on domestic violence victims and their children. One of the authors points out that historically the domestic violence and anti-poverty movements have not worked together, and calls for a new collaboration between them in order to address this crucial issue more effectively. Excerpts from an *amicus* brief and a recent US Supreme Court case highlight the issue of state residency requirements for welfare recipients, an issue which particularly impacts victims of domestic violence and their children.

The second half of the chapter focuses on survivors of domestic violence as workers. This is a relatively new area of law, which employers and labor attorneys are beginning to address. The first article in this section advocates for the rights of employees who are battered. The other article complements the first by focusing on the responsibilities and liabilities of employers when one of their employees is either a victim or a perpetrator of domestic violence.

A. WELFARE ISSUES

JODY RAPHAEL, DOMESTIC VIOLENCE AND WELFARE RECEIPT: TOWARD A NEW FEMINIST THEORY OF WELFARE DEPENDENCY

19 Harv. Women's L. J. 215–220 (1996).

III. D. THE FACTOR OF DOMESTIC VIOLENCE

The impact of domestic violence on the lives of AFDC recipients reveals critical flaws within the main theories of welfare dependency and appears to account for much of the observed behavior of poor girls and women that these theories to date have been unable to explain.

1. *"Culture of Poverty" Theory*

The "culture of poverty" theory attempts to explain behavior of many poor women that is better diagnosed by domestic violence experts as post-traumatic stress disorder. Post-traumatic stress disorder describes the traumatic effects suffered by combat veterans and prisoners of war. It has become clear to many psychiatric professionals that this same psychological syndrome manifests itself in survivors of rape, domestic battering, and incest.

The similarities between "culture of poverty" behavior and the symptoms of post-traumatic stress disorder are startling. Vocational rehabilitation expert Patricia Murphy has annotated the diagnostic criteria for post-traumatic stress disorder to relate the aspects of the disorder to possible vocational impairments. The themes of passivity, hostility, and helplessness expounded by the "culture of poverty" theorists permeate her analysis of the effects of trauma. For instance, recurrent and intrusive recollection of the battering event may lead to difficulty in learning and poor concentration, avoiding thoughts or feelings associated with the trauma may result in suppression of creativity, loss of confidence, and fear of new challenges, and a sense of a foreshortened future may lead to a feeling that planning is futile and a predisposition against completion of classes and projects.

These effects on important work skills can explain the less tangible, and seemingly less curable, "culture of poverty." As one writer has expressed, when a person suffers from post-traumatic stress disorder, "[t]he whole apparatus for concerted, coordinated, and purposeful activity is smashed." Proper diagnosis of observed behavior in poor women is vitally important in providing appropriate and necessary therapy. Most importantly, experts recognize that identification of the trauma is central to the recovery process for domestic violence victims.

Also relevant to welfare policy is the relationship between low reading skills and domestic violence. Patterns of domestic violence often include verbal and emotional abuse that may extensively damage the intellectual development of the abused women. Abused women are told over and over that they are unintelligent, incompetent, or dumb. Over time, the effects of this upon potential skills or vocational development may be more detrimental than the consequences of physical abuse. Many verbally abusive partners, who perceive that the development of good reading skills means that their partners will have access to information that is not screened and controlled by them, convince the women that they are not good readers.

2. The "Rational Choice" Model

Although the "culture of poverty" theory may be consistent with domestic violence on some levels, the "rational choice" model is an inadequate predictor of behavior, given its failure to acknowledge the unique problems facing victims of domestic violence. Many women receiving welfare either do not think of themselves as participating in the labor market due to their financial dependence on men or are prevented from participating by men. Thus, it is very unlikely that enhanced education and training, tax reform, higher minimum wages, or any other labor market solutions promoted by the "rational choice" proponents, although necessary, will be adequate and effective in enabling women living with domestic violence to maintain employment. Indeed, domestic violence probably accounts for much of the pattern of cycling on and off welfare, as well as the puzzling inability of basic skills and job training programs to result in large scale employment for women on welfare. Faced with emotional coercion, physical violence, and outright sabotage, many women abandon their training and employment and return to the home.

3. Feminist Approach, Theories of Patriarchy

Reports of widespread domestic violence in relationships between single mothers on welfare and abusive men confront feminist welfare theory and disrupt its basic tenet. Evidence that many women receiving AFDC are in relationships with men suggests that most women are not using welfare to gain independence from patriarchy. Rather, the existence of AFDC with its low benefit structure has encouraged girls and women to become enmeshed in relationships with men who support them but are often controlling and abusive. Often these relationships permanently prevent low-income girls from developing a sense of themselves as independent persons. The seriousness of this problem cannot be overstated.

The problem of teenage pregnancy is one disturbing form of this phenomenon. Abusive relationships with controlling older men who promise to support them may permanently prevent low-income girls from developing as independent persons and gaining the skills they need to participate in the labor market. Trapped on welfare and in detrimental relationships, poor girls and women have an extremely difficult time extricating themselves from this situation. They and their children may face such a risk of physical harm that escape proves to be totally impossible. When abused women leave their partners, they often face heightened risk of harm. The scars from domestic violence, in the form of post-traumatic stress disorder, may also permanently prevent employment, especially through damage to intellectual development.

E.   *Toward a New Feminist Theory*

During the last ten years, "culture of poverty" and "rational choice" proponents have pushed the parameters of the welfare reform discussion and, in doing so, have set welfare research and policy in the wrong direction. Remedies under both theories have obviated the need for further research and investigation. For example, under the "rational choice" model, there is no further need to research the ways in which women on welfare live because the solution is to provide entry level jobs with higher wages in the economy for women on welfare with low basic skills.

To date, feminists have been unable to dislodge these theories because their own constructs of patriarchy have led to the defense of single-parent households as well as teen pregnancy. To state that teen-age parenthood is unhealthy and destructive to young girls does not mean embracing the stereotype of the nuclear family. Recognition of the dead-end nature of many of these girls' involvement with abusive men constitutes a strong anti-patriarchal statement and could lead to policies that truly enable young girls to develop and establish themselves without dependence upon men. The goal of feminist welfare policy should be the preservation of conditions of autonomy and independence for girls and women.

A new feminist theory requires a close look at the roles and behavior of men in the lives of low-income women. The caretaker allowances, advocated by Martha Fineman and others as an alternative to work, could only prevent dependence of women on men if they were generous enough to put women and their children well above the poverty line, a policy unlikely to happen in the current political climate. Moreover, these allowances could be dangerous, because they might attract low-skilled, low-income men to women possessing these stipends, and these men might use coercion and violence to maintain access to the funds. Skills development and labor market participation are critical ingredients for greater independence of women from abusive men. Women's employment remains threatening to many men because in earning a salary, women participate in the larger world, have access to new information and experiences, can obtain support from office mates, and may succeed well beyond the level of their male partners. Ultimately, it is doubtful that women can avoid or escape domestic violence unless they have the means to support themselves and their children on their own.

MARIA L. IMPERIAL, SELF–SUFFICIENCY AND SAFETY: WELFARE REFORM FOR VICTIMS OF DOMESTIC VIOLENCE

5 Geo. J. on Fighting Poverty 3–15 (1997).

I think if they are talking about reforming welfare, they should be talking about helping us build a foundation and keeping us safe....

Felicia, a resident at an emergency domestic violence shelter

INTRODUCTION

The problem of domestic violence has recently received increased national attention. The federal government's response to the problem—strengthening criminal justice policies and enacting the federal Violence Against Women Act of 1994—has coincided with an increased focus on welfare and the passage of the federal Personal Responsibility and Work Opportunity Reconciliation Act of 1996. These movements have been taking place separately. With little communication between domestic violence advocates and welfare reform proponents, there has historically been little consideration of the connection between these issues. Many domestic violence advocates do not know about welfare issues, and welfare advocates are generally not well versed in domestic violence issues. Because of the few acknowledged links between these two areas, discussions of welfare reform have barely recognized or acknowledged the relationship between welfare dependency and domestic violence, nor the profound impact that alterations in public assistance programs and policies will have on the lives of battered women and their children.

While domestic violence appears to know no socioeconomic boundaries, a study of female homicide victims between 1990–1994 by the New York City Department of Health found that women with the least financial resources made up the majority of those who were killed by their partners. Thus, it appears that the poorest women are in the most precarious relationships. These women are eligible for welfare and emerging data suggests that domestic violence may in fact be a key cause of their welfare dependency. Many women in violent relationships are economically dependent on their abusive partners. To ensure their victims' compliance, abusers often forbid their partners to pursue employment and undermine their efforts to keep their jobs. As a result, domestic violence victims are often unemployed or underemployed and must rely on public assistance.

Welfare may also be a battered woman's only bridge to freedom. When women, often with dependent children, leave their batterers, they frequently have no means of self-support other than welfare. Many battered women state that their ability to obtain welfare is a critical first step to becoming independent.

Because punitive welfare reform policies may create yet another barrier to a battered woman's ability to gain independence, the voices of domestic violence victims, together with an understanding of the complexity of their lives, must be injected into the public policy debates on welfare reform. Unfortunately, the media perpetuate stereotypes about women on welfare and these stereotypes are the basis upon which welfare legislation is passed. "[T]he exclusion of the diversity of poor women and the complexity and context of their experience . . . creates a deviant image of welfare recipients, perpetuating the concept of individual moral fault and driving legal debate."[8] Stereotypes of poor women, many of whom are domestic violence victims, need to be challenged. Alternative perspectives based on the reality of violence in the lives of women and girls are needed to inform public debate on welfare. Federal and state governments must listen to domestic violence victims and thoughtfully respond to their different circumstances with concern for their self-sufficiency and safety.

* * *

I. Overview of the Personal Responsibility and Work Opportunity Reconciliation Act of 1996: Provisions Relating to Domestic Violence

Prior to signing the Personal Responsibility and Work Opportunity Reconciliation Act into law on August 22, 1996, President Clinton had called for "an end to welfare as we know it." The Personal Responsibility and Work Opportunity Reconciliation Act (PRWORA) did end welfare as we knew it, by replacing the Aid to Families with Dependent Children (AFDC) program with the Temporary Assistance to Needy Families (TANF) block grant and eliminating the federal entitlement to public assistance. The underlying rationales of the Act are the misperceived causes of welfare dependency: Teenage girls choosing to have babies and women choosing not to work and to remain single heads of household. A major cause of welfare dependency, addressed only on a limited basis in the Act, however, is the effect of violence on the lives of women and girls.

Only two areas of the PRWORA specifically refer to domestic violence, reflecting the general lack of knowledge about the pervasive role of domestic violence in creating welfare dependency. First, under the time limit hardship provision, the Act permits states to exempt up to 20% of their caseload from the sixty-month limit for "reason of hardship or if the family includes an individual who has been battered or subjected to extreme cruelty." Second, the Act permits states to adopt the Family Violence Option, which allows states to implement domestic violence screening and counseling programs as well as permitting states to grant "good cause" waivers to certain PRWORA requirements.

Other parts of the PRWORA do not mention domestic violence victims, but will likely have a disproportionate effect on them. The

---

8. Lucy A. Williams, Race, Rat Bites and Unfit Mothers: How Media Discourse Informs Welfare Legislation and Debate, 22 Fordham Urb. L. J. 1159, 1196 (1995).

PRWORA prohibits states from using TANF funds to provide benefits to certain people, permits states to adopt other restrictions, and imposes social welfare mandates. While domestic violence victims seem not to have been considered when these provisions were drafted, they will likely be harmed when they are implemented.

A. Fund Restrictions: Limits on the Use of TANF

Several of the restrictions on funding could have a detrimental effect on battered women if exceptions are not granted. The Act prohibits the use of TANF funds for families who have received assistance for sixty months. However, states may "exempt" up to 20% of their population "for reasons of hardship or if the family includes an individual who has been battered or subjected to extreme cruelty." While this exemption may seem favorable for victims of domestic violence, the 20% cap forces the state to choose between providing relief to victims of domestic violence and families experiencing other types of hardship. It is unclear how states will make this choice.

Also restricted from receiving TANF benefits are unwed parents of children over twelve weeks, if the parents are under the age of eighteen and have not completed high school. The restriction does not apply, however, if the teen parent is attending school and living at home or in an adult-supervised setting. Such a provision is designed to encourage marriage and may result in live-in relationships between teenage mothers and abusive adult men. As outlined later in this article, this provision may lead a teenage mother to marry or move in with an abusive boyfriend to maintain her benefits, with dangerous consequences for the safety of the teen mother and the health of the child.

Another restriction on state use of TANF funds limits assistance to parents whose children do not attend school. Many states had already implemented these restrictions, termed "Learnfare," under waivers to AFDC from the Department of Health and Human Services (HHS). Under Learnfare, families on welfare are sanctioned if children miss school. Unfortunately, Learnfare provisions do not address the special circumstances faced by battered women and their children. Learnfare is especially unfair to domestic violence victims' families, who are forced to move repeatedly to remain safe. It is often difficult for children to attend school on the days that these moves are taking place, putting the family's benefits in jeopardy.

In addition, the PRWORA denies TANF support for individuals convicted of certain drug felonies. This provision is problematic for domestic violence victims in light of the correlation between substance abuse and domestic violence. Battered women are fifteen times more likely to be at risk for alcoholism than non-battered women and are three to eight times more likely to be at risk for drug abuse than non-battered women. The excess risk among battered women arises almost entirely after the first reported abusive episode indicating that domestic abuse is the context, not the consequence, for alcohol and drug abuse.

A final significant fund restriction is the prohibition on the use of TANF funds for most legal immigrants during the first five years of their residency. This provision is very troubling. Battered immigrant women are among the most vulnerable victims of domestic violence because they often lack crucial community and familial supports as well as the ability to communicate in English. While consideration of the particular effect of welfare reform on immigrant women is extremely important, an analysis of the special needs of immigrant domestic violence victims is beyond the scope of this article.

B. Options

In addition to the restrictions on the use of TANF funding, the PRWORA allows states to incorporate several optional provisions, many of which are relevant to battered women. First, states may adopt the Family Cap as part of their TANF programs. The Family Cap prevents the use of TANF funds for children conceived while a family is receiving public assistance, or for children born within ten months of the family's receiving public assistance. Family cap provisions can unfairly affect domestic violence victims whose partners may use force or the threat of force to have sex with them. A majority of states that have enacted Family Cap provisions have included a rape exception in their legislation. According to Rape in America, a survey conducted by the National Victim Center and the Crime Victim Research and Treatment Center, 36% of women raped in the United States are raped by a family member. Fear of their batterers may make it difficult for domestic violence victims to negotiate for protected sex. This sexual abuse then, may result in unplanned pregnancy. Under the TANF Family Cap, benefits may not be provided for this child, further punishing the already victimized mother.

States also have the option to lower the amount of cash assistance they provide to their new residents. States can choose to provide residents with only the assistance level of the state from which the residents moved. If the battered woman's home state provided less money than does her new state, the new state may provide her with the lower level of assistance. This provision will hurt battered women who escape from states that provide lower benefits to states with higher costs of living. For example, suppose a domestic violence victim flees to New York from Florida to hide from a violent partner. If friends and relatives are there to provide shelter and emotional support, fleeing to New York may be her only way to escape. But if Florida provides less money than New York, and New York chooses to provide its new residents with the amount of benefits paid by Florida, that battered woman now in New York will have to live on the Florida benefit payment. She may be forced to place financial burdens on her family and friends. She may be unable to provide for herself and children in New York with only the cash assistance at the Florida level. Faced with these obstacles, the battered woman who fled to escape her abuser may have to return home.

C. Mandates

PRWORA also imposes numerous mandates on states implementing TANF, several of which affect victims of domestic violence. One of the more troubling is a provision awarding a bonus to states that decrease their illegitimacy rates. One hundred million dollars are available for up to five states that demonstrate that they have decreased their rate of out-of-wedlock births as well as abortions, as measured against the entire state's population, not just TANF recipients. Because this bonus is tied not only to reductions in the state pregnancy rate, but also to a reduction in the number of abortions performed, some domestic violence advocates worry that states will attempt to achieve "better" numbers by restricting access to abortion. Women who want to terminate their pregnancies may be forced to travel out of state to obtain an abortion. But traveling is often dangerous for a battered woman because she may have to hide from her batterer that she is traveling, perhaps taking time off from work, and in some cases, staying away overnight. Traveling is especially difficult for a teenager, who faces the same problems as a battered woman, but also usually has fewer resources, such as money or a car. These young women are also less mature and thus more vulnerable. In many states teenagers face parental involvement laws that require the teen to notify or gain the consent of a parent(s) or seek a judicial bypass allowing the abortion.

In addition to adopting restrictive abortion policies, to win the bonus dollars states may seek to decrease out-of-wedlock births by promoting "shotgun" marriages. At least one state has begun to encourage teenage girls to marry the fathers of their children. Others may follow, and marriage may be encouraged despite evidence of abuse in these relationships. To further their efforts to prevent out-of-wedlock births, states are also required to give "special emphasis" to teenage pregnancy prevention and to implement a state-wide statutory rape education program.

PRWORA also requires states to increase their rates of paternity establishment and child support payment. States are required to increase the paternity establishment rate and to impose penalties on recipients who fail to cooperate in identifying the father of the recipient's child, unless the recipient has good cause not to cooperate. Cooperation is defined as providing the father's name and "other information," as defined by the state. States are also required to reduce or eliminate assistance to a recipient family if an individual member does not cooperate with child support enforcement, unless the individual has "good cause" not to cooperate. The penalty for non-cooperation with either paternity establishment or child support enforcement is a grant reduction of at least 25%, although states are given the option to deny the entire family cash benefits. A battered woman, however, is often unable to reveal the name of her child's father; if she does report his name, and child support enforcement or paternity establishment procedures are begun, the abuser may retaliate violently. The battered woman is thus forced to choose between losing her benefits, if she does not provide the paternity information, and maintaining her benefits but risking further abuse, if she reports the information.

D.　Provisions That Could Help Battered Women

While PRWORA as a whole appears insensitive to the special circumstances of domestic violence victims, it does contain some provisions that could benefit battered women who receive welfare. First, PRWORA grants states the authority to use TANF funds to create "individual development accounts" for recipients to use for specific purposes, such as post-secondary education, first home purchase, or business investment. The terms of the program are liberal: contributions must be from earned income, withdrawals are only allowed for the specifically designated purposes, and federal benefit programs must disregard funds in the account in determining eligibility and amount of aid. Although discussion of this new provision has been limited, the establishment of individual development accounts could provide an opportunity for those on public assistance to plan for a more financially secure future. This approach may be especially promising for domestic violence victims. The individual development accounts could become essential components of a self-sufficiency plan for domestic violence victims and their children.

Second, the Wellstone/Murray Family Violence Option, discussed in Part III *infra*, provides states with the option to screen for and identify domestic violence victims, to refer victims to services, and to waive some of the requirements that might put domestic violence victims in danger and prevent their wounds—both physical and emotional—from healing.

In drafting the PRWORA of 1996, legislators indicated an awareness of the importance of teenage pregnancy in causing welfare dependency. These legislators, however, stopped short by failing to discern the relationship between violence against women, teenage pregnancy, and the need for public assistance. A number of studies have documented that domestic violence acts as a barrier to getting off welfare. Violence in the lives of teenage girls and women leads many to become dependent on welfare. Rather than contributing toward alleviating violence in the lives of women and girls, the PRWORA may actually exacerbate the situation by punishing, re-victimizing, and placing battered women at additional risk.

II.　Violence in the Lives of Women and Girls as a Cause of Welfare Dependency

In adopting welfare reform, Congress stated that "marriage is an essential institution of a successful society which promotes the interests of children" and that "responsible fatherhood and motherhood" need to be promoted. Congress cited the growth in the number of children on welfare who were born to unmarried women and the increased rate of teenage pregnancy as bases to support its new law. The consequences of these phenomena were documented: Unmarried women with children spend more time on welfare, they have a higher risk of bearing children born at a low birth weight with lower cognitive scores, and there are increased chances that these children will be on welfare when they become adults.

To address these problems, PRWORA replaced the AFDC program with the TANF block grant system. As outlined in the federal law:

> [The purpose of PRWORA is to] increase the flexibility of states in operating a program designed to—(1) provide assistance to needy families so that children may be cared for in their own homes or in the homes of relative; ... (2) end the dependence of needy parents on government benefits by promoting job preparation, work, and marriage; ... (3) prevent and reduce the incidence of out-of-wedlock pregnancies and establish annual numerical goals for preventing and reducing the incidence of these pregnancies; ... and (4) encourage the formation and maintenance of two-parent families.

Although the stated goals of PRWORA include the reduction of teenage pregnancies and the maintenance of two-parent families, they do not include the pressing need to reduce violence in the lives of women. The role of male abusers in the welfare cycle was not addressed; marriage, rather than violence prevention, is encouraged as the solution to the complex problem of welfare dependency. Three of the four purposes cited for creating the TANF program are related to marriage and to controlling women's reproduction: end dependence on government benefits by promoting marriage, reduce out-of-wedlock pregnancies, and break the cycle of single parent families.

This part will explore the relationship between welfare dependency and violence in women's lives. Despite the strong link, little consideration was given to domestic violence when PRWORA was enacted. This part will first discuss violence in the lives of women as a cause of welfare dependency and an obstacle to getting off welfare. Next, this part will address violence in the lives of teenage girls that leads many of them to become dependent on public assistance. As the data below demonstrates, violence against women is a key cause of welfare dependency. A law that largely ignores the impact of violence is destined not only to fail to solve the problem of welfare dependency, but also to re-victimize and punish an enormous percentage of poor women and children in the United States.

A. Violence in the Lives of Women

In October 1995, Jody Raphael of Chicago's Taylor Institute convened a national group of domestic violence and welfare advocates, academics, and policy analysts to discuss how domestic violence interferes with women moving off welfare. At the time of that meeting, little data existed documenting the relationship between domestic violence and welfare or showing the number of welfare recipients who were past or current domestic violence victims. Since that meeting, however, a number of studies have documented the effects of violence on the ability of battered women to end their dependence on welfare, as well as the extent of the problem of domestic violence. The studies found that consistently high percentages of women on welfare are currently abused by their partners, and showed that the majority of women on welfare are past victims of domestic violence. The studies further indicated that domestic violence victims suffered from depression and other mental health problems, as well as post traumatic stress disorder, drug and alcohol abuse, and physical health problems at higher rates than did women who were never abused. These health problems often prevent women on welfare from moving to work.

In addition to these studies, surveys of welfare-to-work programs indicate that over half the women participants had been abused by male partners. In Prisoners of Abuse: Domestic Violence and Welfare Receipt, the Taylor Institute documented that current and past domestic violence creates barriers for women who are leaving welfare to join the workforce. The male partners of women in these programs not only physically and emotionally abused the women, but repeatedly interfered with their efforts to become self-supporting. In Report from the Front Lines: The Impact of Violence on Poor Women, the National Organization for Women Legal Defense Fund (NOWLDEF) found that between 30% and 75% of women in New York City's welfare-to-work training programs had been abused by their partners. In addition to physical violence, their abuse included efforts to sabotage the women's success in their educational or job training program. Some common tactics included withdrawing child-care offers at the last moment, keeping the woman up all night before a key exam or presentation, and disfiguring the victim the night before work so that she either needed medical help or was too ashamed to be seen at her job.

Domestic violence has been shown to interfere not only with women getting off welfare, but with women's employment generally. In the face of such abuse, self-sufficiency becomes increasingly difficult. A study by Victim Services surveyed fifty women who had both worked and been battered within the previous year and identified a broad range of barriers to employment for battered women, including the insidious ways that batterers actively prevent women from working. Almost two thirds of the women surveyed reported that they were late to work because of the abuse; specific reasons included being too exhausted after violent incidents occurring late the night before, needing extra time to cover up bruises, and waiting for pain killers to take effect. Twenty percent said that they were late for work because their partners, who opposed their employment, tried to sabotage their ability to keep a job by turning off the alarm clock, keeping them up all night, or refusing to babysit at the last minute. Three quarters of the women had been harassed by the batterer at work, either by phone or in person. Job loss was a common occurrence for these women, with 56% reporting that they had lost at least one job as a direct result of the violence.

Similar results were reported by Connie Stanley in a study of 118 battered female clients of the Domestic Violence Intervention Services of Tulsa, Oklahoma. More than 70% were telephoned excessively at work by their abuser, and more than 50% missed days of work because of the abuse. Thirty percent reported that the abuse had caused them to lose a job.

Studies of women in welfare-to-work programs, in programs for battered women, and of women in the workforce show that domestic violence is a significant impediment to work. Unable to maintain steady employment habits, battered women lose their jobs, cannot find new employment, and become dependant on public assistance.

B. *Violence in the Lives of Teenage Girls*

Research on violence in the lives of women has shown not only the link between domestic violence and welfare, but also that many women have been battered for years. Because abuse that begins in adolescence often continues into adulthood, any attempt to understand welfare dependency must take account of the abuse of teenage girls. A study conducted by the Better Homes Fund on patterns of welfare use among poor and homeless women in Worcester, Massachusetts, found that more than 40% of the women in the study had been sexually molested as children and that 60% had been severely physically or sexually abused in childhood. Violent victimization was shown to correlate both to long-term use of welfare and to cycling on and off welfare.

While it is commonly acknowledged that one in five girls has been sexually abused, the percentage of teen mothers who experienced such abuse is much higher; studies have shown that more than half have been sexually molested before their first pregnancy, most often by adult men related or otherwise known to them. Such sexual abuse has myriad short-and long-term effects on girls, not the least of which are a reduced sense of self-esteem, a feeling that they lack control over their futures, and the perception that their personal value is related to their sexuality. These effects of sexual abuse are risk factors for teen pregnancy. Studies have found that the survivors of incest and other forms of molestation and abuse are significantly more likely to become pregnant during adolescence than women who have not been abused. Thus, abuse is at the root of much teen pregnancy, driving many young women onto welfare.

While abuse is often the cause of teen pregnancy and welfare dependency, it is a common misunderstanding that the cause of the teenage pregnancy "epidemic" is the irresponsible behavior of teenage girls and boys. As a result, the primary approach advocated in PRWORA to stem this epidemic is abstinence from sexual activity by teenagers. To truly address the problem of teenage pregnancy, however, one must gain an understanding of the real factors underlying the problem.

Contrary to the view that teen pregnancy results from stereotypical licentious and irresponsible teenage boys, studies have demonstrated that the fathers of children born to teenage girls, more often than not, are adults. A study of births to teenage mothers in California found that three out of four births to high school girls were fathered by men older than high school age; men over the age of twenty-five accounted for twice as many teen births as did boys under the age of eighteen; and men over twenty years of age were responsible for five times as many births among junior high school girls as were junior high school boys, and for two-and-a half-times as many births among high school girls as were high school boys. National data points to similar patterns: Only 29% of babies born to teen mothers are fathered by teenagers, while 71% are fathered by men over the age of twenty. Many of these pregnancies result from abuse. Even when the adult male father is considered a "boyfriend" the relationship is often abusive; "consensual" sex between an underage youth and an adult presents a high risk of abuse. Developmentally, a teenager's understanding of her sexuality and self-determination are far inferior to those of an adult. The adult in the sexual relationship is therefore usually the one with power, and the teenager the victim. While perhaps not descriptive of every sexual relationship between a teenager and an adult, the power imbalance in the relationship, and the adverse physical and emotional consequences for the teenager, leads many experts to deem these relationships abusive. Further, under statutory rape statutes, the relationship, depending on the ages of the girl and man, is *per se* abusive. The conclusion that an enormous percentage of teen pregnancies result from abuse undercuts the assumption that irresponsible behavior and a choice to engage in early sexual activity are responsible for unwed teenage pregnancy. This assumption, though largely incorrect, is central to many of the PRWORA penalties on teenage welfare recipients.

Moreover, the asserted effects of teen pregnancy—a longer time on welfare, higher risk of low birth weight and lower cognitive scores—are actually more properly attributed to abuse than to the simple fact of the age of the mother. Like adult victims of domestic violence, teens are more likely to be battered when they are pregnant than when they are not. Abuse during pregnancy results in serious health consequences for the child. An informal survey of approximately 200 pregnant teens in several large metropolitan areas found that 26% were in a relationship with a male partner who was physically abusive. Of those girls being abused, 40% to 60% stated that their abuse began or escalated after they became pregnant. A study examining the possibility of a link between physical abuse and low infant birth weights found that 20.4% of the 589 postpartum surveyed had been victims of physical abuse. Of the women reporting abuse, 12.5% had a child with low birth weight. In contrast, only 6.6% of the women who were not abused had a child with a low birth weight. In one urban hospital's emergency department, 21% of pregnant women had been battered; this group had twice as many miscarriages as nonbattered women. Poor birth outcomes for children born to teenagers, then, are frequently due to the abuse experienced by teens during pregnancy. Furthermore, a relationship has been found to exist between a teenage mother's own victimization and the increased risk that her child will be abused. Young mothers who had themselves been abused were three times more likely to report that their children were abused. The PRWORA, however, ignores this reality.

Research shows that abuse of teen girls is the true cause of much teen pregnancy. It is this factor—abuse—that should be seen as the cause of a pregnant teen's longer time on welfare, the higher risk of her children being born at a low birth weight, the lower cognitive scores of these children, and the increased chance that they will be on welfare when they become adults.

III. WELLSTONE/MURRAY FAMILY VIOLENCE OPTION

A. *Description of the Family Violence Option*

Although abuse of teenagers and women by their partners leads to unplanned pregnancy and makes many women unable to remain in the workforce, the PRWORA does little to address the problem of violence in the lives of girls and women, nor to address the connection between this violence and welfare dependency. However, one provision of the Act, the Family Violence Option, does allow states to accommodate the difficulties faced by battered women in the new welfare system. This section will first compare the legislative history of the Family Violence Option with the Option as eventually enacted. Next, issues regarding implementation by those states that have adopted the Family Violence Option will be discussed.

Senator Paul Wellstone (D–MN), joined by Senator Patty Murray (D–WA) and Representative Lucille Roybal–Allard (D–CA), spearheaded efforts to include a provision in the new federal welfare legislation that would address the relationship between domestic violence and the receipt of public assistance. Senator Wellstone first introduced a legislative initiative to address the impact of domestic violence on welfare as an amendment to the welfare bill passed by the Senate in September 1995 that was later vetoed by President Clinton. It is important to note that this initial amendment had as its purpose "[t]o *exempt* women and children who have been battered or subjected to extreme cruelty from certain requirements of the Bill."

In May 1996, Senator Wellstone and Representative Roybal–Allard proposed a Sense of Congress Joint Resolution to address the relationship between domestic violence and poverty and to advocate for federal and state welfare legislation to address this issue. Unlike the 1995 amendment, the Joint Resolution called for providing referrals to "counseling and supportive services," and, most importantly, advocated for waivers from welfare requirements that would "stop the clock" for a period of time, rather than grant outright exemptions. Domestic violence advocates feared that exempting battered women from the Act's requirements would allow them to be excluded from job training and job placement opportunities; in contrast, granting waivers from certain requirements would allow a case-by-case consideration of each woman's circumstance, an approach strongly and repeatedly recommended by Senator Wellstone.

On July 18, 1996, after the PRWORA was introduced, Senators Wellstone and Murray offered the Family Violence Amendment to the welfare legislation based on the Joint Resolution. As originally proposed, the amendment mandated that states make flexible waivers and make appropriate supportive services available. The Conference Committee changed the Family Violence Amendment from a mandate to a state option.

The Family Violence Option as enacted allows states to develop a three-pronged strategy to help domestic violence victims who receive welfare become self-sufficient. Specifically, the Option allows states to: (1) establish procedures to screen and identify victims of domestic violence when they interact with the welfare system; (2) provide referrals for counseling and supportive services; and (3) waive certain program requirements if compliance with any of them would make it more difficult for victims to escape violence, unfairly penalize victims of domestic violence, or place the victims at risk of domestic violence.

It is not clear whether the Family Violence Option was intended to allow states to exempt more than 20% of their caseload from the time limits, as permitted in the body of the Act, for reasons of "hardship or if the family includes a member who has been battered or subject to extreme cruelty." Domestic violence advocates argue that the legislative history of the Family Violence Option shows that the 20% cap on hardship exemptions from the five-year time limit does not restrict in any way the ability of states to make an unlimited number of temporary good cause waivers of time limits under the Family Violence Option.

While states are not required by the PRWORA to adopt the Family Violence Option, on October 3, 1996, President Clinton issued a proclamation encouraging states to do so. He also urged the Departments of Health and Human Services (HHS) and Justice (DOJ) to work together to develop guidance for states to "assist and facilitate the implementation of the Family Violence provisions." On January 3, 1997, HHS and DOJ provided the President with a progress report on the agencies' efforts to implement his directive. The report highlighted the fact that HHS was consulting with a number of organizations regarding the implementation of the Family Violence Option. The report remained silent, however, about whether domestic violence victims waived from the time limits would be considered part of the 20% exempted under the hardship provision, or whether these waivers would be in addition to the 20% limit. HHS is currently developing regulations for implementing the Family Violence Option and has assured advocates that this issue will be addressed in those regulations.

In the absence of HHS guidance on this issue, Senators Wellstone and Murray introduced legislation in the spring of 1997 to clarify that Congress intends the temporary waivers available under the Family Violence Option to be separate from the 20% permanent exemptions available under the hardship provisions. Their bill provided that states will not be penalized for going over the 20% in order to give waivers to domestic violence victims. HHS took a contrary view when it finally published the promised regulations in late November, 1997. Noting that

"Congress chose not to amend the statute as part of budget reconciliation" (a reference to the failure of the Wellstone/Murray bill), the regulations interpret the statute to mean that waivers available under the Family Violence Option are included as part of the total 20% exemption under the hardship provision. The regulations state that HHS interprets the statute so as to encourage states to work with victims of domestic violence in securing jobs, rather than "divert resources and attention from these cases and unnecessarily prolong their dependence" by automatically and without penalty exempting them from the five-year requirement. However, HHS included a provision that would allow states to claim families granted waivers under the Family Violence Option as a "reasonable" basis for failing to comply with the five-year limit. This would allow states to avoid penalty by showing that the families who failed to meet the five-year limit possessed valid domestic violence waivers. By requiring states to pass the Family Violence Option in order to qualify for this "reasonable" basis consideration, the regulations may encourage more states to include the Family Violence Option in their TANF plans.

WENDY POLLACK AND MARTHA F. DAVIS, THE FAMILY VIOLENCE OPTION OF THE PERSONAL RESPONSIBILITY AND WORK OPPORTUNITY RECONCILIATION ACT OF 1996: INTERPRETATION AND IMPLEMENTATION

April/May 1997 Clearinghouse Review 1086–1095, 1097.

III.   IMPLEMENTATION OF THE FAMILY VIOLENCE OPTION

Good laws poorly executed can increase the risk of harm. The Family Violence Option is good law in need of thoughtful and sensitive policies and practices to ensure that no harm befalls survivors of domestic violence as a result of the adoption of this provision. Welfare and domestic-violence advocates must collaborate with state and local governments and agencies responsible for operating the Temporary Assistance for Needy Families (TANF) and child-support programs to ensure that their expertise guides the implementation of the Family Violence Option. First, we list six basic principles that should be reflected in all policies, programs, and procedures that seek to address the specific problems facing domestic-violence survivors. Second, we discuss the essential elements of successful implementation of the Family Violence Option.

A.   Basic Principles

Implementation of the Family Violence Option should be governed by these six basic policy principles:

First, domestic violence must be prevented and reduced.

Second, women must be trusted to tell the truth about the violence in their lives and to make the right decisions for themselves and their children. Their ability to evaluate their potential risk at the hands of an abusive partner must be given credence.

Third, safety is paramount. The safety of domestic-violence survivors and their children must be the first consideration of all public-assistance programs. Every interaction with a survivor and every decision about her case must consider whether that interaction or decision may result in actual harm or increase the risk of harm.

Fourth, disclosure of domestic violence must translate into survivors receiving the help and services they need. Disclosure is only the first step in helping domestic-violence survivors. It is not an end in itself.

Fifth, the individual applicant, recipient, and program personnel must be in a position to make informed decisions. All applicants and recipients need accurate information about their rights, responsibilities, and options under TANF and all public-assistance programs, including eligibility for waivers, extensions, or exemptions because of domestic violence, so that they make fully informed decisions about what is best for themselves and their children. This, in turn, will allow welfare agencies to make informed decisions about each person's case.

Sixth, recognizing differing degrees of crisis, differing consequences of violence, and, therefore, differing needs to be addressed, all public-assistance programs must have the flexibility to provide the amount of time and services needed by domestic-violence survivors.

B. Essential Elements of Successful Implementation

The essential elements of successful implementation of the Family Violence Option are: educating applicants and recipients about domestic violence; universal notification of the rights, responsibilities, and options of receipt of public assistance; universal screening to identify survivors of domestic violence; maintaining confidentiality; training for all personnel on domestic violence and its effect on victims and survivors; development of an integrated service delivery system for domestic-violence survivors; a clear and efficient waiver process; and flexibility in developing employability plans.

1. Education of All Applicants and Recipients of Public Assistance About Domestic Violence

All women would benefit from information about domestic violence and current information on where to go for help if and when it is needed. Many women are or have been victims of domestic violence, but because they never had a black eye or a broken bone they do not identify themselves as such. Women must understand that one does not have to end up in a hospital emergency room for the abuse to be considered domestic violence. Some women have difficulty coming to terms with their reality. After all, no one wants to think of herself as a victim. For still other women, they know they are survivors all too well but are too ashamed to tell anyone or too depressed to take any action that may help themselves.

* * *

2. Universal, Comprehensive Notification of the Rights, Responsibilities, and Options under Temporary Assistance for Needy Families

Universal, comprehensive notification of the rights, responsibilities, and options under the TANF program must be given. This notice must be presented in oral and written form before any questions are asked or forms completed at the interviews for initial screening, eligibility, assessment and employability plan, recertification, and paternity establishment and child-support enforcement. The oral notice may be given in groups as long as there is an opportunity for questions in a confidential setting afterward.

The notice should also include information about the availability of waivers under the Family Violence Option, the right to claim good cause for refusal to cooperate with paternity establishment and child-support enforcement, and other provisions to which waivers, extensions, or exemptions may be applied under the Personal Responsibility and Work Opportunity Reconciliation Act (PRA), such as the teen live-at-home requirement, the denial of assistance for minor children who are absent from the home for a significant period, and state-imposed restrictions such as the child exclusion policy.

The notice should describe rights and options, how to apply for the options, appeal rights and procedures, and privacy rights. It should include a warning that if child abuse is disclosed, this information must be reported to child protective services. For states where witnessing spouse or partner abuse is considered a form of child abuse subject to mandatory reporting, the warning should state that witnessing adult abuse is a form of child abuse, so that if the information that domestic violence took place in the presence of children is disclosed, it must be reported to child protective services.* * *.

In addition to a general notice as described above, written and oral notice that explains in depth the details of the paternity establishment and child-support enforcement requirement must precede any requests for information for this purpose, including the name of the father. This may need to be a separate notice.

This notice must state clearly what constitutes cooperation, the right to claim good cause for refusal to cooperate, and the evidence required to support a claim so that the applicant or recipient can make a fully informed decision regarding cooperation with paternity establishment and/or child-support enforcement. The notice must list all the parental rights and responsibilities the father would gain by establishing paternity, including the right to petition for visitation and custody. A woman who is unaware of the legal exposure she is incurring in naming an abusive man as the father of her child may not understand the need to invoke a good-cause exception. The notice should serve these functions.

The notice should also list the questions that will be asked for paternity-establishment purposes. These are highly personal questions, subject to abuse, particularly as applied to teens by welfare and child-support workers. The notice should inform applicants and recipients how to report if additional or inappropriate questions are asked.

3. Universal Screening for Domestic Violence

To encourage disclosure, opportunities to disclose domestic violence should be frequent, confidential, clearly voluntary, and easy for applicants and recipients to access. Survivors should have the opportunity and be encouraged to disclose domestic violence every time they interact with welfare workers or child-support workers. At the time of screening, disclosure should be limited to the minimum necessary information to identify an applicant or recipient as someone for whom domestic violence may be relevant to her ability to meet TANF requirements. This can be done with just a few questions along with an explanation of the reason for asking, and oral and written notification that responding is voluntary, that not responding or changing a response at a later date is not penalized, and that the information disclosed is confidential and will not affect the applicant's or recipient's eligibility. The following is suggested language: * * *

Many, perhaps most, domestic-violence survivors will not feel comfortable disclosing their situation within a public-assistance office and will answer "No" or "No comment" to these questions. That is why all applicants and recipients must be given a pamphlet or palm card with information about domestic-violence services within the community.

If any of the domestic-violence screening questions are answered "Yes" the individual has "screened positive." She should then be asked if she is interested in talking to someone in more depth about her situation and in exploring her eligibility for waivers of program requirements. If "Yes," then the survivor should be referred to a welfare worker who has received domestic-violence counselor training. Whatever the procedure for screening and identifying domestic-violence survivors, it must be integrated into the procedure for applying for benefits so that the initial contact date is the date of application for benefits.

4. Confidentiality

Privacy is key to safety. There must be a real commitment on the part of the state and all public-assistance agencies to maintain confidentiality and protect privacy throughout the system. The child-support section of the PRA has language on privacy safeguards that should be implemented for all public-assistance programs, including TANF:

> The state ... will have in effect safeguards, applicable to all confidential information handled by the state agency, that are designed to protect the privacy rights of the parties, including (A) safeguards against unauthorized use or disclosure of information relating to

proceedings or actions to establish paternity, or to establish or enforce support; (B) prohibitions against the release of information on the whereabouts of one party to another against whom a protective order with respect to the former party has been entered; and (C) prohibitions against the release of information on the whereabouts of one party to another if the state has reason to believe that the release of the information may result in physical or emotional harm to the former party.

* * *

5. *Trained and Educated Staff*

Welfare agencies and workers are already overburdened with a complex system that is undergoing enormous change. Because they cannot keep up, welfare workers are often a source of misinformation. To compound the problem, welfare agencies and workers are generally not knowledgeable about domestic violence and its effect on survivors. This must be addressed through training for all persons involved in administering and implementing TANF and child-support programs.

At least two types of training should occur, depending on the job responsibilities related to domestic-violence survivors and issues. The first is a basic domestic-violence training for all persons involved in running programs or administering assistance. * * *

A longer, more intensive domestic-violence counselor training program should be given to staff working with survivors on dealing with domestic violence and related issues. For example, workers who conduct any assessment and in-depth eligibility interviews and make referrals for services after an individual has screened positive, workers, including hearing officers, who review and decide requests for waivers, good-cause claims, extensions or exemptions based on domestic violence, and workers who help a survivor develop her employability plan, all should receive the more extensive training.

* * *

6. *An Integrated Service Delivery System*

The government has a responsibility to women who self-identify to ensure their safety and provide the services they need, whether or not a state adopts the Family Violence Option. States' commitment of financial and other resources for both in-house and independent domestic-violence services is necessary to build the capacity to respond to survivors' particular needs. An integrated service delivery system must be developed to accomplish this.

a. *System Components*

An integrated service delivery system should include a referral system, procedures for immediate assessment after disclosure of domestic violence and, of course, the inclusion of local domestic-violence advocates and service providers in the development and implementation of the service delivery system.

* * *

b. Service Delivery Models
i. Mentoring Model

* * *

The mentoring model should work as follows. The public assistance agency would identify the positions in which workers' responsibilities would include directly addressing domestic-violence issues, for example, workers who conduct the assessments after screening positive, development of employability plans, determinations on good-cause claims and waivers due to domestic violence. Separate domestic-violence units may be established to foster good case management. Local advocates should be consulted to help identify the workers with the most potential to make good domestic-violence counselors. Once these welfare workers are trained, the local advocates should be contracted with to serve as on-site mentors for one year, initially sitting in on interviews, responding to workers' questions, reviewing their work, etc. After the first year, the local advocates may need to supply ongoing monitoring and consulting to the welfare workers. This model does not preclude contracting with independent domestic-violence service providers for case management, including the development of the employability plan.

* * *

7. A Clear and Efficient Waiver Determination Process

A clear and efficient process for requesting waivers under the Family Violence Option and claiming good cause for refusing to cooperate with paternity establishment and child-support enforcement is needed so that survivors can gain and maintain safety, have the time needed to recover from the damage sustained, and receive the services that enable this to happen without delay and without the threat of sanctions or termination.

a. Interpretation of the Standard

The Family Violence Option states that a waiver may be granted if a requirement "would make it more difficult for individuals receiving assistance ... to escape domestic violence or unfairly penalize such individuals who are or have been victimized by such violence, or individuals who are at risk of further domestic violence."

* * *

8. Flexibility in Developing Employability Plans

The Family Violence Option gives states an opportunity to integrate greater flexibility into their TANF program for recipients who are survivors of domestic violence. This allows states to create welfare-to-work strategies that are responsive to recipients' strengths and limitations not merely at the initial assessment and development of an employability plan but throughout recipients' transition from welfare to self-sustaining employment.

The Individual Responsibility Plan (IRP) should outline individualized strategies for each recipient, put each on a path toward economic independence, set realistic short-and long-term goals, establish appropriate benchmarks to measure progress, and incorporate any waivers granted pursuant to the Family Violence Option. The IRP should be viewed as a fluid document, changing as a recipient's progress is assessed and reassessed over time, with each new activity building on the skills developed and barriers lessened from prior activities.

JOAN MEIER, DOMESTIC VIOLENCE, CHARACTER, AND SOCIAL CHANGE IN THE WELFARE REFORM DEBATE

19(2) Law & Policy 206–209 (1997).

INTRODUCTION

In the past two years of rapid activity concerning welfare reform, a small but growing chorus of activists in the anti-poverty and feminist movements has focused attention on the relationship between domestic violence and the poverty of women and children. While it is no surprise that some women become "poor" and in need of welfare when they separate from an abuser, another aspect of the link between domestic violence and welfare has been less well-understood, and has more fundamental implications for the continuing debate: For women seeking to get off welfare, the path from "welfare-to work" is frequently obstructed by abusive male partners. Such partners interfere with women's employment both directly, when they seek to prevent "their" women from gaining independence, and indirectly, when the secondary effect of domestic violence, that is, traumatization, prevents or greatly burdens women's abilities both to work and care for their children. Perhaps even more striking is the fact that this connection between welfare dependency and battering is far from rare: a series of recent studies have found with surprising consistency that 15% to 30% of welfare recipients are current—and a staggering 50% to 60% are past (as adults)—victims of domestic violence.

The link between battering and welfare has critical implications in this era of radical reform of welfare. Although we do not know precisely what percentage of battered women on welfare are there because of battering, the qualitative data documenting batterers' intentional sabotage of women's work efforts described in Section I below persuasively suggest that the link is not merely correlative, but is often also causal. At a practical policy level, this means that many of the stringent restrictions on public assistance, such as time limits, work requirements, residency restrictions, and others which the conservative movement for welfare reform has succeeded in incorporating into the federal Personal

Responsibility and Work Opportunity Act of 1996 ("PRA"), may threaten the survival of many battered women and children for whom the only choices may be welfare or physical abuse. At a more ideological level, the data challenge the reformers' moral critique of welfare and welfare recipients, that is, their beliefs that individuals' poverty is the result of a failure of character and moral virtue, reflected in laziness, lack of responsibility, substance abuse, and dependency on welfare. Implicit in the conservative critique is the assumption that many of the purportedly dysfunctional actions of the poor are freely "chosen," rational responses to the distorted incentives created by the availability of public assistance. However, the fact that many women depend on welfare because of men's intentional abuse potentially counters the widespread view that many women live off welfare purely because of their own failures of moral fibre or character.

At the same time, the new documentation of the linkage between battering and welfare raises a pressing question for thinkers and activists for the poor and for battered women. To many such as myself who work with poor battered women, while the statistics are somewhat surprising, the fact of the overlap between domestic violence and poverty is not. As longstanding participants in or observers of the battered women's and/or anti-poverty movements, we must then ask: why has this connection been ignored by activists of both movements for so long? There can be no doubt that there has been a historic disconnection between these movements: On the poverty advocacy side, it has been argued that both legal services lawyers and poverty theorists have marginalized family law in general, and domestic violence in particular. Conversely, until recently very little of the now voluminous scholarship, policy analysis, and activism against battering addressed the relevance of poverty to domestic violence. However, at root, it is my contention that the rift between these movements is due to more than mere historical happenstance or sexism; rather it is partly the product of a fundamental philosophical or ideological conflict between the philosophies and values of the two movements. It is this gulf which advocates for both the poor and battered women must now face: The insufficient integration of feminist—specifically domestic violence—perspectives into poverty advocacy, and of poverty concerns into advocacy for battered women, is in part what has allowed the nation's political culture to become so hostile to poor welfare mothers. The current welfare reform "crisis," which threatens the safety and well-being of many women and children, and which could not have occurred without the widespread belief that women on welfare are morally flawed, compels advocates from both the battered women's and poverty movements to come together on behalf of their poor constituents. Only when we understand the philosophical underpinnings of each movement and how they conflict, might we be able to move forward with new paradigms of both battering and poverty which can better answer the challenges of welfare reform.

This essay, then, explores the political and ideological ramifications both for policy and advocacy of the connection between domestic violence and poverty. I begin with a survey of the existing data, and a qualitative interpretation of those data to demonstrate a causal relationship between battering and welfare dependency. I discuss that relationship's implications for welfare reform policies and practices currently being considered or implemented under the PRA, as well as for the ideological premises of the welfare reform debate. I then examine its implications for the anti-poverty and battered women's movements themselves. I argue that the failure of activists and thinkers in the poverty and battered women's movements to address the interrelationship between domestic violence and poverty is due to a clash of ideologies that makes it difficult for their causes to be joined. The fundamental philosophy of the anti-poverty movement, the view that socioeconomic structural forces rather than individual bad character are to blame for poverty and dysfunctional behavior, is difficult to integrate with the fundamental philosophy of the battered women's movement, which calls for moral judgment against batterers, including criminal sanctions as a means of "moral education" or "character reform." The battered women's movement's emphasis on male domination of women is uncomfortable for anti-poverty activists who are reluctant to demonize half of the poor population. Conversely, the battered women's movement has avoided focusing on domestic violence among the poor in favor of the "universalist" premise that dramatic violence "cuts across race and class" and is a problem of sexist but universal, deeply-rooted norms condoning male domination of women. This movement has intentionally avoided discussing poverty in connection with domestic violence for fear that domestic violence would be viewed as "just another dysfunction of poor people," rather than the product of widely held sexist social and legal norms. Meaningful acknowledgment of the interaction between poverty and domestic violence thus threatens the fundamental tenets of both movements.

Ultimately I argue that the current welfare reform crisis demands that the battered women's and poverty movements join forces, incorporate the lessons of each, and reach a more unified position on the interaction of poverty and domestic violence. Such a synthesis is critical as a practical matter in policy development if poor victims of domestic violence are not to be put at even greater risk of violence by governmental welfare policies. Integration of the moral significance of domestic violence for welfare recipients is also the most effective weapon the Left currently has to counter the moral judgments against welfare mothers that are fueling the harshest aspects of welfare reform. While the current attack on the poor is unwarranted and unfair, welfare policy always has been and probably always will be in part a debate about gender roles, family structure and moral desert. That inherently moral debate needs to be informed by feminist, progressive values if there is to be some hope of achieving a more constructive perspective on the poverty and welfare crisis. The Left's alternative—refusal to engage in the moral debate—has simply meant abdicating the field to the conservative reformers.

Moreover, such a synthesis is also theoretically and philosophically compelled for both the battered women's and anti-poverty movements themselves. As a matter of intellectual honesty, both must come to terms with the increasingly prevalent data (both in welfare studies and others) that suggest that rates of battering are higher for lower income women. And as a matter of political efficacy, both movements stand to be revitalized by meaningful integration of the other's concerns. Both movements have been accused of late of sterility and stagnation. The poverty movement's lack of convincing moral power and failure to counter the gender stereotypes upon which both the welfare system and its conservative critics have relied suggests that incorporation of a meaningful gender analysis may offer some needed re-fueling for the anti-poverty cause. By the same token, integration of poverty and economic issues into the battered women's movement's approach can only improve our effectiveness with clients and communities of different classes and races: it may also offer a more sophisticated, nuanced approach to replace the simplistic stereotypes which have been destructive to many abused women and the cause as a whole.

ELOISE ANDERSON* v. BRENDA ROE AND ANNA DOE

United States Supreme Court *Amicus Brief* (1998).
1998 WL 847246 (pp 1–3, 11–12, 16–17, 25).

[*note: the name of the Supreme Court decision in this case is *Saenz v. Roe*.]

INTEREST OF *AMICI CURIAE*

Amici curiae are sixty-six organizations engaged in service delivery, advocacy, and research on behalf of survivors of domestic violence. They and their members include domestic violence shelters and counseling services from thirty-five states, public health professionals, and legal advocates committed to securing women's equality. Several *amici* are associations of low-income women, many of whom have suffered from family violence and who have needed Temporary Assistance for Needy Families ("TANF") in order to establish new homes away from abusive partners.

Amici are familiar with the needs of low-income families and have extensive knowledge of the plight of women and children struggling to escape their batterers. *Amici* have special expertise in the particular ways in which family violence traps women and children in poverty and dependency. *Amici* submit this brief to inform the Court of the harsh impact that durational welfare residency requirements will have on TANF families who move to another state to flee an abusive spouse or domestic partner. * * *

SUMMARY OF ARGUMENT

California's durational residency requirement for cash assistance harshly penalizes new state residents by denying them the very necessities of life: shelter, clothing, heat, food. The impact of welfare residency requirements is felt particularly keenly by women and children who migrate to another state to escape brutal, sometimes life-threatening domestic violence. This violence frequently escalates when the victim attempts to flee from her abuser, and can be so relentless that the victim must change her identity, move to another state, and abandon all ties to her former life. Welfare is a lifeline for these women and their children. Many have no other means of support and would otherwise be forced to choose between utter destitution and returning to their abusers.

Because abusers may control every aspect of their victims' lives and actively discourage their victims from holding jobs or completing their education, battered women face unique barriers to self-sufficiency. Most welfare recipients have work experience, but many have lost jobs or educational opportunities because of intentional interference or sabotage by abusive partners. Adequate levels of cash assistance are therefore essential if battered women are to survive on their own, apart from their abusers.

California's durational residency requirement does not rationally further any legitimate state interest in encouraging self-sufficiency. Its irrationality is particularly apparent in its impact on domestic violence survivors, for it punishes women who have courageously fled from their abusers in order to secure a safe and independent future for themselves and their children. The severe deprivation of basic necessities that this penalty inflicts on new residents is likely to deter some battered women from escaping from their violent partners, thus subjecting them to further injury and abuse.

ARGUMENT

I. Millions of Women are Victims of Domestic Violence, and Some Will Suffer Serious Injury or Death at the Hands of Their Abusers if They Cannot Flee to Safety.

* * *

In many cases, women will move to other states where they have family or friends who can provide at least some emotional and financial support. Without such support, these women risk being unable to secure basic necessities for themselves and their children—or being forced to return to dangerous and abusive relationships. For some women, the decision to flee a great distance to escape abuse is accordingly prudent and sometimes lifesaving. As set forth *infra* Part III, deterring victims from fleeing to another state or penalizing them for having done so places them and their children at grave risk of serious harm.

II. Domestic Violence Impoverishes Women by Depriving Them of Employment, Education, and the Supportive Relationships Necessary for Economic Independence.

Congress has expressly recognized that between 50% and 80% of women who received welfare through Aid to Families with Dependent

Children ("AFDC"), the predecessor to TANF, were survivors of domestic abuse. Recent research compellingly demonstrates this close relationship between domestic violence and poverty. This research indicates that, while domestic abuse afflicts women of all income levels, the incidence of abuse by a partner or former partner is higher among low-income women. U.S. Dep't of Justice, Bureau of Justice, Violence Against Women: Estimates from the Redesigned Survey 1 (Aug. 1995) (Women in families with incomes below $10,000 were more likely than other women to be victims of violence by an intimate.). Among low-income women who receive public assistance, the incidence of domestic violence is at its highest.

* * *

Adequate levels of public assistance are often the only way battered women can break free of their abusers and lead safe and self-sufficient lives. Financial security "often is the key factor that enables battered women and their children to leave and remain separated from their abusers. If public assistance were not available as a last resort, many battered women would be forced to remain in or return to dangerous or life-threatening situations."

III.   The California Durational Residency Requirement Will Harshly Penalize Domestic Violence Survivors and Actually Deter Some Women From Permanently Escaping Their Abusers.

The California durational residency requirement inflicts upon indigent families a substantial deprivation of "welfare aid upon which may depend the ability ... to obtain the very means to subsist—food, shelter, and other necessities of life." When every dollar is needed for rent, heating fuel, and winter clothing for the children, depriving desperately poor women and children of even a small amount of cash assistance has catastrophic consequences.

* * *

As this Court has previously held, a one-year welfare residency requirement does not rationally advance any legitimate state interest in encouraging employment. Its irrationality is poignantly apparent when its impact on domestic abuse survivors is considered. A law that deters women and children from escaping a life of violence and enforced dependency is directly at odds with the goal of fostering independent, self-sufficient families. It is also directly at odds with Congressional concern for the survival and safety of domestic violence victims and their children.

Because California Welfare and Institutions Code Section 11450.03 penalizes domestic violence survivors and will actually deter some battered women from permanently fleeing from their abusers, the judgment of the Ninth Circuit Court of Appeals should be affirmed.

RITA L. SAENZ v. BRENDA ROE AND ANNA DOE

Supreme Court of the United States (1999).
526 U.S. 489–491.

California, which has the sixth highest welfare benefit levels in the country, sought to amend its Aid to Families with Dependent Children (AFDC) program in 1992 by limiting new residents, for the first year they live in the State, to the benefits they would have received in the State of their prior residence. Cal. Welf. & Inst. Code Ann. § 11450.03. Although the Secretary of Health and Human Services approved the change—a requirement for it to go into effect—the Federal District Court enjoined its implementation, finding that, under *Shapiro v. Thompson*, 394 U.S. 618, and *Zobel v. Williams*, 457 U.S. 55, it penalized "the decision of new residents to migrate to [California] and be treated [equally] with existing residents," *Green v. Anderson*, 811 F.Supp. 516, 521. After the Ninth Circuit invalidated the Secretary's approval of § 11450.03 in a separate proceeding, this Court ordered *Green* to be dismissed. The provision thus remained inoperative until after Congress enacted the Personal Responsibility and Work Opportunity Reconciliation Act of 1996 (PRWORA), which replaced AFDC with Temporary Assistance to Needy Families (TANF). PRWORA expressly authorizes any State receiving a TANF grant to pay the benefit amount of another State's TANF program to residents who have lived in the State for less than 12 months. Since the Secretary no longer needed to approve § 11450.03, California announced that enforcement would begin on April 1, 1997. On that date, respondents filed this class action, challenging the constitutionality of § 11450.03's durational residency requirement and PRWORA's approval of that requirement. In issuing a preliminary injunction, the District Court found that PRWORA's existence did not affect its analysis in *Green*. Without reaching the merits, the Ninth Circuit affirmed the injunction.

Held:

1. Section 11450.03 violates Section 1 of the Fourteenth Amendment.

(a) In assessing laws denying welfare benefits to newly arrived residents, this Court held in *Shapiro* that a State cannot enact durational residency requirements in order to inhibit the migration of needy persons into the State, and that a classification that has the effect of imposing a penalty on the right to travel violates the Equal Protection Clause absent a compelling governmental interest.

(b) The right to travel embraces three different components: the right to enter and leave another State; the right to be treated as a welcome visitor while temporarily present in another State; and, for those travelers who elect to become permanent residents, the right to be treated like other citizens of that State.

(c) The right of newly arrived citizens to the same privileges and immunities enjoyed by other citizens of their new State—the third aspect of the right to travel—is at issue here. That right is protected by the new arrival's status as both a state citizen and a United States citizen, and it is plainly identified in the Fourteenth Amendment's Privileges or Immunities Clause, see *Slaughter-House Cases*, 16 Wall. 36, 80, 21 L.Ed. 394. That newly arrived citizens have both state and federal capacities adds special force to their claim that they have the same rights as others who share their citizenship.

(d) Since the right to travel embraces a citizen's right to be treated equally in her new State of residence, a discriminatory classification is itself a penalty. California's classifications are defined entirely by the period of residency and the location of the disfavored class members' prior residences. Within the category of new residents, those who lived in another country or in a State that had higher benefits than California are treated like lifetime residents; and within the broad subcategory of new arrivals who are treated less favorably, there are 45 smaller classes whose benefit levels are determined by the law of their former States. California's legitimate interest in saving money does not justify this discriminatory scheme. The Fourteenth Amendment's Citizenship Clause expressly equates citizenship with residence, and does not tolerate a hierarchy of subclasses of similarly situated citizens based on the location of their prior residences.

2. PRWORA's approval of durational residency requirements does not resuscitate § 11450.03. This Court has consistently held that Congress may not authorize the States to violate the Fourteenth Amendment. Moreover, the protection afforded to a citizen by that Amendment's Citizenship Clause limits the powers of the National Government as well as the States. Congress' Article I powers to legislate are limited not only by the scope of the Framers' affirmative delegation, but also by the principle that the powers may not be exercised in a way that violates other specific provisions of the Constitution.

B. WORKPLACE VIOLENCE

ROBIN R. RUNGE AND MARCELLENE E. HEARN, EMPLOYMENT RIGHTS ADVOCACY FOR DOMESTIC VIOLENCE VICTIMS

5(2) Domestic Violence Report 17–18, 26–29 (Dec/Jan 2000).

Kim (pseudonym) and her husband worked for the same large computer company. Kim's husband abused her at home and at work. One afternoon, he chased Kim down a hallway at work and assaulted her. Kim fled to a supervisor and told her that she was attacked in the office. In the next few days, Kim obtained a restraining order against her husband that included the workplace and told her employer about it, believing that the employer would enforce it in the workplace. At first, Kim was hopeful when the human resources director at her company met with her and then with her husband, assuring Kim that everything would be "taken care of"; however, no action was taken against her husband. A few weeks, Kim's husband assaulted her again at work, and she called the police who arrested him. Two days later, again failing to take any disciplinary action against her husband, the company revictimized Kim by firing her for "crying in the lobby."

Unfortunately, Kim's story is not unique. As advocates know, thousands of domestic violence victims each year face similar circumstances when abuse perpetrated by intimate partners affects their ability to find and keep employment. Batterers extend their pattern of abuse and control to the workplace by threatening a woman's ability to keep her job, using the employer as an accomplice in their abuse. The loss of economic independence often leads a domestic violence victim to remain in the cycle of violence. Employment rights advocacy can prevent job loss and, thus, is an important tool for domestic violence victim advocates. This article provides information about the employment rights of domestic violence victims and the ways in which advocates can help victims assert and enforce their rights so that they are not forced to choose between their jobs and their safety.

Link Between Domestic Violence and Employment

Several recent studies have documented the link between domestic violence and employment. In one study, 96% of employed domestic violence victims surveyed experienced some type of work-related problem due to the violence. Connie Stanley, Domestic Violence: An Occupational Impact Study, Tulsa, OK, (July 27, 1992). Between 35% and 56% of employed battered women were harassed at work by their batterers; 55% to 85% missed work because of the abuse; and 24% to 52% lost their jobs as a result of the abuse.

Domestic violence victims who lose their jobs may turn to welfare for income and training services; however, studies show that victims in welfare-to-work programs experience similar difficulties. For example, job training and education providers in welfare to work training programs in New York City estimated that 30% to 75% of their program participants were current or former victims of domestic violence. Other research found that between 15% and 30% of welfare recipients were currently being physically abused and 34% to 65% of welfare recipients have been abused as adults.

These statistics clearly show that batterers harass, stalk and even attack their partners in the workplace. Many women are forced to quit their jobs because they fear for their safety and that of their children. Moreover, injured domestic violence victims often lose their jobs after severe beatings force them to miss days of work while they heal. Finally, even more horrifying, employers frequently fire women who are victims of domestic violence simply because of their status as victims of violence, even when they competently perform their jobs.

Fortunately, employment laws can help domestic violence victims obtain job-protected medical leave, compensation for injuries, unemployment compensation or job reinstatement. Moreover, basic domestic violence advocacy, such as safety planning in the workplace, is highly effective and can enable a domestic violence victim to avoid job loss and to leave a violent relationship.

Employment Rights Advocacy for Domestic Violence Victims

One of the most important responsibilities of a domestic violence victim advocate is to help a victim develop a safety plan. A truly effective safety plan, however, must include the workplace, and basic employment rights advocacy is the key. As a domestic violence victim tells her story of abuse, an advocate should ask her whether the abuse has affected her ability to keep her job, whether the batterer knows where she works, if he works in the same place, and if the employer knows about the abuse. This information will inform the development of a safety plan to include the workplace. Advocates can also suggest possible workplace changes that will increase the victim's sense of personal safety, allowing her to focus on her job. For example, if the batterer is harassing her at work by calling her repeatedly, she could ask to have her telephone extension changed. If she has a restraining order against the batterer, it can be amended to include the workplace. A victim may also consider providing security personnel at work with a copy of the order and a picture of the batterer. In some cases, she may want to request a transfer to a different site or shift. Before making such a request, she should research whether the employer has a transfer policy or whether co-workers have recently transferred from one worksite to another. If so, she can raise these examples when advocating for her own transfer.

Many employers provide their employees with workplace policies. An advocate can review these policies to determine whether medical leave or personal time is available. If so, an employee may use such time to obtain a restraining order or to receive counseling for domestic violence. In addition, she may be eligible for paid time off to seek medical attention for an injury caused by domestic violence or to go to court. Many employers have sexual harassment policies prohibiting sexual harassment and assaults in the workplace. Moreover, some employers have adopted workplace or domestic violence policies that set forth how existing workplace policies apply in cases of violence.

Finally, if the domestic violence victim is a union member, the advocate can encourage her to contact her union representative and review her collective bargaining agreement for similar policies. The union may file a grievance on her behalf or represent her in any disciplinary proceedings for any violations of the union contract. However, if the batterer works for the same employer, the union also has a duty to represent him in any disciplinary or other proceedings that result from his violent behavior at work.

There are a few key issues to keep in mind when advising domestic violence victims of their employment rights. For a host of reasons, the domestic violence victim may not wish to disclose her abusive situation to her employer or union representative. It is incumbent upon the domestic violence advocate to warn the victim that she may be terminated by her employer just for disclosing the domestic violence and that this termination may be upheld in court, depending on state and federal law and the particular circumstances involved. In many circumstances, neither the union nor the employer is knowledgeable about domestic violence issues. With the employee's permission, domestic violence advocates can provide the employer or the union representative with valuable information about domestic violence that can help her keep her job. For example, the advocate may explain to the employer or union why a client's fear that her batterer will stalk her at work is reasonable. Advocates can also help employers and unions develop domestic violence policies and training programs to help ensure better treatment of their employees in the future.

Employment Legal Rights and Remedies for Battered Women

As employees, domestic violence victims are entitled to employment protections and remedies that may help them keep their jobs. The following are examples of legal theories under existing employment laws that can provide domestic violence victims with protection and remedies.

Family and Medical Leave Act: An employee who needs time off from work to seek medical attention and heal from a serious health condition resulting from domestic violence may be entitled to job-protected leave under the Federal Family and Medical Leave Act ("FMLA"), 29 U.S.C. § 2601 *et seq.* (1999); 29 C.F.R. § 825.100 *et. seq.* (1999). In order to be covered by the FMLA, the employee must have a "serious health condition." 29 U.S.C. § 2611(11)(1999). Domestic violence victims may experience many forms of physical and emotional abuse that may qualify as "serious health conditions" under the FMLA, such as post-traumatic stress disorder, depression, broken bones or sprains. The FMLA defines a serious health condition as "an illness, injury, impairment, or physical or mental condition that involves (1) inpatient care; or (2) continuing treatment by a health care provider." 29 C.F.R.§ 825.114. To be eligible for FMLA leave, 29 U.S.C. § 2611(4)(A)(i)(1999) requires that an employee must have worked for a "covered" employer for at least a year, and she must have worked at least 1250 hours for that employer in the last twelve months preceding the date she needs FMLA-qualifying leave. An employer is subject to the FMLA if it employs 50 or more persons within a 75 mile radius. If an employee is eligible for FMLA leave, § 2614(a) prohibits her employer from discharging her for taking up to 12 weeks of unpaid leave to care for her own serious health condition or that of her child. The employer is also required under § 2614(c) to pay any existing health insurance premiums during the leave.

The FMLA can be a powerful tool for domestic violence victims. For example, a domestic violence victim may request FMLA-qualifying leave after a severe beating for the period of time that her doctor indicates she will be incapacitated due to the injuries. At the end of her leave, her employer is required pursuant to § 2614(a) to return her to the same or an equivalent position. Although FMLA is unpaid, the employee may be able to take paid sick leave days concurrently or to collect state disability insurance while on leave. Moreover, an employer is prohibited by § 2615(a)(1)(2) from denying an eligible employee leave or discriminating against an employee for exercising her right to job-protected FMLA-qualifying leave.

Recognizing that the FMLA does not provide for job-protected leave to attend a civil protection order hearing or to make other arrangements to leave a batterer, Maine, and the City of Miami, Florida passed legislation that provides domestic violence victims with job guaranteed leave to obtain orders of protection, receive medical treatment, and obtain social services (providing leave to appear in court). In addition, federal legislation pending in Congress this year, H.R. 357, 106th Cong. (1999), would expand the FMLA to cover the same situations covered in Maine.

Americans with Disabilities Act: Disabilities caused by domestic violence may qualify domestic violence victims for protection from discrimination and wrongful termination as well as a reasonable accommodation in the workplace under the Federal Americans with Disabilities Act ("ADA"), 42 U.S.C. § 12102 (1999). In order to be subject to the ADA, the employer must have at least 15 employees.

A domestic violence victim must have a physical or mental impairment that "substantially limits a major life activity," must "ha[ve] a record of a substantially limiting impairment" or must "[be] regarded as having such an impairment" to access protections under § 12102(2)(A), (B), (C) of the ADA. Major life activities include such things as walking, sleeping, working, standing, thinking, lifting, and taking care of oneself. Although the Supreme Court recently ruled that mitigating measures must be taken into account when determining whether an individual is "substantially limited" under the first definition of disability, many long term injuries or illnesses caused by domestic violence may qualify as disabilities. Some forms of post-traumatic stress disorder, depression, or other physical injuries may "substantially limit a major life activity," thus qualifying women who have those conditions for protection under the ADA. Additionally, a domestic violence victim may be entitled to a reasonable accommodation, such as a modified work schedule, restructured job, transfer, modified work space or equipment or other changes to her job. Her employer is prohibited under § 12112(a) from discriminating against her by denying her employment or promotions or terminating her because of the disability.

Federal and State Gender–Based Discrimination Statutes: In some cases, battered women may be entitled to remedies under Title VII of the Civil Rights Act of 1964, 42 U.S.C. § 2000e (1999), or under state or local anti-discrimination laws. Title VII prohibits an employer from discriminating against an employee because of his or her gender. Employers violate sex discrimination laws when they treat battered women differently than similarly situated male employees on account of gender. For example, in Kim's case, her employer may have violated Title VII when it fired the female victim of the violence, but failed to discipline the male perpetrator. Similarly, if an employer allows male employees time off work to attend family court or child support proceedings, but refuses to allow female employees time off to seek protective orders from their batterers, the employer may be discriminating against the female employees because of their sex.

In addition, sexual harassment is a form of illegal sex discrimination. A batterer may create a "hostile environment" by sexually harassing or assaulting his partner at work. Two kinds of sexual harassment are prohibited by law (1) *quid pro quo* and (2) hostile environment. *Quid pro quo* is when a supervisor asks for sexual favors in return for a job benefit. Hostile environment sexual harassment occurs when harassment by a supervisor or another employee is so severe or pervasive that it creates an intimidating or abusive work environment. Hostile environment sexual harassment must be based on sex, unwelcome and severe or pervasive. The employer may be liable for sexual harassment, if it knew or should have known of the harassment and failed to take prompt remedial action. Since some anti-discrimination laws have strict procedural requirements and other filing deadlines, domestic violence victims who believe they have suffered from discrimination or have been sexually harassed in their workplace by their batterer should contact the local district office of the U.S. Equal Employment Opportunity Commission or the appropriate state or local agency that enforces the state or local anti-discrimination laws.

Victim Protection in Employment Laws: Many domestic violence victims reasonably fear that they will be fired from their jobs if they take time off to go to court to testify in a criminal case or to obtain a civil order of protection against their batterer, though 26 states make it illegal for an employer to do so with regard to a criminal case, as noted in the sidebar. In some cases the prosecuting attorney or the judge in the criminal case will assist women whose employers have threatened them with discipline or termination if they take time off work to go to court. Crime victim protection laws, however, generally do not protect women who need to take time off work to obtain a civil order of protection. Currently, only Rhode Island and California have laws that specifically prohibit an employer from terminating an employee for taking time off work to seek a protective order, although New York, Maine and Miami, Florida have laws that provide similar protections.

Unemployment Compensation: Many domestic violence victims who are forced to quit their jobs or who are fired from their jobs because of domestic violence may be eligible for unemployment benefits under their state's unemployment insurance system, a program that provides temporary wage replacement to people who lose their jobs through no fault of their own. Each state has its own rules concerning who is eligible, how much compensation the employee receives and for how long. Eligibility rules generally consider such factors as the time and hours worked, length of employment, wages earned, and why the employee lost her job. Generally, employees who quit their jobs are not eligible for unemployment benefits. However, many states will pay benefits to an employee who quits her job for "good cause." Each state has its own definition of what constitutes "good cause." In Maine, New Hampshire, California, North Carolina, New York, Connecticut and Wyoming, domestic violence victims who have left their jobs because of domestic violence are expressly eligible to receive unemployment compensation under a "good cause" provision that explicitly covers domestic violence. Domestic violence victims who live in other states may also be able to obtain unemployment compensation under their state's "good cause" provisions if they can show that they quit their jobs due to health and safety concerns or to protect their safety.

In order to be eligible for unemployment benefits, a domestic violence victim must be "able and available" to work which means that she is able to work and is seeking employment. If she resides in a shelter that prohibits her from working while she is in the shelter, she will not be able to meet this requirement.

If a victim is initially denied unemployment benefits, she can and should appeal that denial to an administrative law judge within the statutory time period, which is usually no more than 10 to 15 days. A hearing date will be set and she will have an opportunity to describe the reasons why she was unable to keep her job and the threat to her safety and health caused by the domestic violence. A domestic violence advocate can accompany a victim to the hearing. Job training and relocation assistance may also be available at the state agency that administers unemployment benefits.

Employment Rights in Welfare to Work Programs: Under the Federal Personal Responsibility and Work Opportunity Act of 1996 ("PRWORA"), 42 U.S.C. § 601, *et. seq.* (1998), a certain percentage of each state's welfare recipients are required to participate in a work activity. Since domestic violence victims who participate in welfare to work programs experience many of the same problems experienced by women working in other types of jobs, employment laws may help women in this context as well. The final regulations for the new welfare law stressed that federal employment laws such as Title VII, the Americans with Disabilities Act, and the Family and Medical Leave Act apply to welfare workers in the same manner as they apply to other workers. Thus, for example, a domestic violence victim whose batterer is sexually harassing her at her welfare to work placement, should be protected by Title VII to the same extent as other workers in her workplace.

In some cases, participating in a welfare to work program may be dangerous for a domestic violence victim. She may need to use the time to pursue an order of protection or to find safe housing in order to safeguard herself and her children from abuse. Also, her batterer may stalk her at her work placement. The Family Violence Option is a provision of the PRWORA that allows states to elect to waive domestic violence victims from welfare program requirements such as the work requirement when the program requirement would make it more difficult for the victim to leave the batterer or place her or her children at risk of harm. To date 37 states have adopted the family violence option.

Legislative Initiatives

Recognizing the limits of employment law protections available to domestic violence victims, advocates are working to enact a variety of federal and state legislative measures. At the federal level, the 1999 Violence Against Women Act (VAWA II), H.R. 357, 106th Cong. (1999), pending in the House of Representatives, includes two key sections that address domestic violence and employment. Under §§ 721–25 of the bill, the Victim's Employment Rights Act (VERA) would prohibit employers from discriminating against domestic violence victims in employment. The Battered Women's Employment Protection Act (BWEPA), which is currently pending in the House of Representatives, and the Battered Women's Economic Security and Safety Act (BWESSA) in the Senate would allow women to use their family and medical leave to address the domestic violence in their lives. In particular, the Acts would allow time off for medical appointments to treat injuries caused by domestic violence, for court appearances for civil order of protection hearings, and for preparatory meetings with attorneys. BWEPA and BWESSA would also make women who have quit their jobs due to domestic violence eligible for unemployment insurance.

At the state and local level, advocates are pushing to pass similar legislation. In New York City, for example, legislation was introduced that would make it an unlawful discriminatory practice for employers to discriminate against domestic violence victims in employment. In addition, several other states have considered legislation that makes it clear that domestic violence victims are eligible for unemployment compensation benefits if they are forced to leave their jobs because of domestic violence. * * *

All of these legislative efforts are extremely important to ensure that domestic violence victims do not have to choose between their jobs and their safety. Until these bills become law, however, domestic violence victim advocates can be extremely effective by advocating on behalf of victims' employment rights by using legal and non-legal strategies.

JILL C. ROBERTSON, ADDRESSING DOMESTIC VIOLENCE IN THE WORKPLACE: AN EMPLOYER'S RESPONSIBILITY

16 Law & Ineq. 639–642, 644–660 (1998).

I. E. RESPONDING TO WORKPLACE DOMESTIC VIOLENCE

The prevalence and resulting costs of domestic abuse-related problems in the workplace have forced many employers to confront this complicated issue. Several progressive companies have established guidelines on how to address workplace domestic violence; most corporations, however, have been slow to respond. While a National Institute of Justice survey of employee assistance program (EAP) counselors across the nation found that most counselors have worked with domestic abuse situations in the past year, many corporations remain ill-equipped to deal with the issue. Seventy-five percent of companies surveyed had workplace violence policies in place, but only 14% of the policies included domestic abuse.

In a 1994 survey conducted by Liz Claiborne, Inc., 96 out of 100 employers believed that domestic violence should be handled primarily at home. Even though 57% of employers surveyed identified domestic violence as a major societal problem and 49% recognized that the violence has harmful effects on job performance, only 12% of the corporations believed that workplaces should "play a major role in addressing the issue" of domestic violence.

II. THE DIFFICULTY OF COMBATING WORKPLACE DOMESTIC VIOLENCE

The underlying difficulty of addressing domestic violence in the workplace is twofold. Employers may not take the threat of workplace domestic violence seriously because they ignore the destructive effects, and employees may fear seeking help from or admitting abuse to employers. This section discusses why employers fail to address domestic violence, and why employees are reluctant to actively seek help.

A. Why Employers Avoid the Issue of Domestic Violence

The typical employer's "not my problem" attitude likely emanates from traditional views of domestic violence as a private, family affair. Under the often-cited "rule of thumb" concept, wife beating was once permitted if the stick used were no thicker than the husband's thumb. An 1874 court said that in cases of non-permanent injury, "it is better to draw the curtain, shut out the public gaze, and leave the parties to forget and forgive." These patriarchal views, though outdated, are not completely extinct. The sanctified home ideal has somehow sterilized abusive conduct into private "family problems." Indeed, the personal nature of domestic abuse, "committed by people the victim knows and trusts," sets it apart from other violent acts. But employers should realize that domestic violence attacks are no less harmful and feared than acts of non-domestic violence. The workplace mirrors societal attitudes about domestic violence as employers tend to ignore the troubling reflection.

Employers may blame victims for the abuse, wondering why they stay with their batterers. This common oversimplification ignores the debilitating cycle of domestic abuse. * * *

B. Why Abuse Victims Are Reluctant to Seek Help

Domestic violence victims are often unwilling to come forward with their abuse-related problems, and they may deny the violence when confronted. A victim's possible fears include: 1) that the batterer may seek revenge if he discovers that she revealed information to the employer; 2) that she may be responsible for the abuse; 3) that the abuser, whom she may still care about, will be harmed; 4) that her employer may not care about or have time for her problems; and 5) that she will be fired. Often, an abused woman isolates herself from family and friends, either because her abusive partner forces the separation with threats, or because the victim feels too ashamed to seek support. Without external motivation and overt support from employers, employees will likely keep the issue of abuse private and hidden.

Employees' tendency to avoid the issue of domestic violence may also result from societal attitudes that stem from a history of weak law enforcement and lax criminal prosecution of batterers. * * *

III. LEGAL AND POLICY INCENTIVES FOR EMPLOYER RESPONSE

In addition to the corporate and societal costs discussed above, the threat of legal liability and the motivation of sound public policy should convince employers to respond to workplace domestic violence issues. By protecting employees from domestic abuse, employers both safeguard their businesses and better their communities.

A. *Legal Liability for Failure to Address Domestic Violence*

Employers may be legally obligated to protect their employees from workplace domestic violence. Thus far, out-of-court settlements have limited relevant case law and the development of legal theories. The current settlement trend reflects employers' fear to go to court and face potential liability for third-party assaults against employees, according to Roberta Valente, Staff Director of the American Bar Association Commission on Domestic Violence. Valente believes courts will begin holding businesses liable if employers know about the threat of violence. For example, an employee may obtain a protection order against a domestic partner that includes a clause forbidding harassment at work. If the employer is aware of the order, or if the employee asks for help, Valente believes the employer has a duty to respond by protecting the employee.

By failing to protect their employees, employers may also violate the Occupational Safety and Health Act (OSH Act). And depending on the exclusivity of state workers' compensation laws, victims of workplace domestic violence seeking legal redress against their employers could raise common law tort or contract claims, or statutory claims.

1. *Osh Act's General Duty Clause*

Although domestic violence begins at home, employers may become legally responsible when it enters the workplace. The Occupational Safety and Health Administration (OSHA) could cite employers under the OSH Act's general duty clause, which requires that an employer provide a workplace "free from recognized hazards that are causing or are likely to cause death or serious physical harm." "Hazards" may be construed to include criminal acts of violence, such as domestic assaults. Industries should recognize workplace domestic violence as a hazard, particularly in light of the issue's recent publicity. Because employers are obligated to provide employees with a safe workplace, OSHA can issue citations if foreseeable violence endangers workers, and the employer does not attempt to prevent it.

Because citations invoke only limited penalties, employers may not be compelled to adhere to OSH Act standards. In addition, the OSH Act does not provide a private cause of action for injured employees. However, employers should be aware that employees may later use OSH Act violations as negligence *per se* or evidence of negligence in separate tort actions.

OSHA exemplified its concern over workplace violence by issuing federal advisory guidelines for preventing violent acts in health care and social service industries. Although OSHA constructed the guidelines only for the two industries where violent acts are most prevalent, employers from all areas can utilize the information and apply it to their respective workplaces. The guidelines suggest a zero-tolerance policy for workplace violence, including a prevention program that addresses: "(1) management commitment and employee involvement, (2) worksite analysis, (3) hazard prevention and control, and (4) safety and health training." Employers may want to implement similar guidelines to avoid citations under the OSH Act's general duty clause.

OSHA will not likely investigate noncomplying employers. Instead, the agency intends to encourage employers to address the important issue of workplace violence. However, if OSHA does not demand compliance, the potential effectiveness of the advisory guidelines is questionable.

Additional and more specific state safety regulations may encourage employers to address workplace domestic violence. Some states have issued requirements accompanying OSHA regulations that obligate employers "to do everything that is reasonably necessary to protect the life, safety and health of employees, including the furnishing of safety devices and safeguards, and the adoption of practices, means, methods, operations and processes reasonably adequate to create a safe and healthful workplace."

2. *Workers' Compensation*

Most states have adopted workers' compensation as the exclusive remedy for claims against an employer for an employee's injury or death at work. Workers' compensation covers medical bills, lost wages and rehabilitation costs resulting from workplace injuries. Injured employees may not sue under common law tort or contract theories, which provide considerably larger damage awards than workers' compensation provides. State workers' compensation statutes generally preclude civil actions against an employer who fails to provide a safe workplace free from third-person attacks.

An intentional tort exception to the workers' compensation exclusivity rule may arise if the employer's act is " 'genuinely' intentional, or the employer ... acted deliberately with the specific intent to injure the employee." Under New York's workers' compensation law, employees may choose to seek either civil damages or workers' compensation benefits for an intentional tort. Most courts are reluctant to undermine the expediency of the workers' compensation remedy, however, and thus construe the exception narrowly.

Under some states' workers' compensation statutes, cases may fall within an assault exception. If the attacker "intended to injure the employee for *personal* reasons," the victim may raise tort or breach of contract claims against the employer. For example, in Indiana, a woman's boyfriend entered the plant where she worked and killed her. Because the assault arose from the victim's personal life, the court deemed the case an assault exception to the exclusive remedy of workers' compensation. The death did not "arise out of" the employment. Workplace domestic violence attacks, by definition, involve attackers with personal vendettas against the victim. Therefore, in states with an assault exception, the court could excuse a plaintiff from workers' compensation and permit tort or contract claims if the victim is injured or killed on the job by a partner or ex-partner.

The following discussions of tort and contract claims assume that workers' compensation is not the exclusive remedy available to employees.

3. Tort Claims

Individuals may have a duty to protect others from third-party assaults where there is a special relationship between parties and where the harm is foreseeable. Case law is split regarding whether a special relationship exists between employers and employees, and courts have also been unclear on what constitutes foreseeable harm. Generally, it seems that an abuser must actually threaten an employee, and that the employer must be aware of the threat for the harm to be legally foreseeable. In *Clark v. Carla Gay Dress Co., Inc.*,[127] the plaintiff's husband entered the factory where she worked and shot her. The court affirmed a directed verdict for the employer, stating that the harm was not foreseeable in this situation, because the husband did not appear violent or angry when he entered the premises, nor did the wife communicate to her employer that she feared her husband. Based on this case, if a woman feels threatened by a batterer, she should inform her employer. Once notified, the employer may have a duty to protect the employee.

In cases where the perpetrator is also an employee, a plaintiff may have legitimate negligent hiring, negligent retention or negligent supervision claims against the employer if the employer is aware of potentially violent applicants or employees.[130] For example, in *Yunker v. Honeywell, Inc.*,[131] an employee had been employed by Honeywell before he was

---

127. 342 S.E.2d 468 (Ga.Ct.App.1986).

130. See, e.g., Yunker v. Honeywell, 496 N.W.2d 419 (Minn.Ct.App.1993).

131. Id.

imprisoned for five years for killing a co-employee. After the former employee's release, Honeywell rehired him as a janitor. Although the company knew that the employee was involved in violent workplace confrontations, Honeywell retained him. He then shot and killed another co-worker. The court held that Honeywell had a duty to maintain a safe workplace and remanded the case to determine whether retaining the worker constituted a breach of that duty. The *Yunker* result could apply to a similar action involving a workplace domestic violence attack.

To better compensate victims for violent attacks and to ensure that employers address the issue of workplace domestic violence, courts should consider adopting a new standard of liability based on what employers should have foreseen. An easier standard to meet, the foreseeability requirement could be satisfied by employees' expressed fears, by a record of threatening behavior by a potential perpetrator, or by the societal prevalence of workplace domestic violence in general. As with other workplace issues, courts should invoke this test on a case-by-case basis.

4. Contractual Claims

A workplace domestic violence victim may sue an employer for breach of contract under an implied contractual obligation theory. If employers outline their workplace violence policies in employee handbooks but do not follow them, they may be held liable for employee injuries based on breach of contract. If distributed throughout the workforce, an employee handbook could constitute a unilateral offer by the employer. Acceptance of the offer and consideration for the contract is assumed based on the employee's continued work under the handbook policies.

5. Additional Legislation

Workplace domestic violence may violate Title VII of the Civil Rights Act, which prohibits discrimination based on sex. In *Meritor Savings Bank, FSB v. Vinson*,[143] the U.S. Supreme Court found that harassment creating a hostile work environment is actionable under Title VII.

Domestic violence-related behavior is analogous to sexual harassment, implicating the same "hostile work environment." In a Ninth Circuit case, after their romantic relationship ended, a male police officer harassed his ex-girlfriend, a female co-worker, with phone calls, confrontations and attempts to run her car off the road. The court found that the city, as the employer, fostered a hostile working environment by failing to remedy harassment after becoming aware of it. Thus, the court placed an affirmative duty on the employer to address workplace harassment, even when it occurs between intimate, or formerly intimate, partners.

Sexual harassment claims may not be limited to co-worker or supervisor behavior; employers may also be liable for sexual harassment of employees by a non-employee. The Minnesota Court of Appeals found

143. 477 U.S. 57 (1986) * * *.

that, under the Minnesota Human Rights Act, employers must take "timely and appropriate action" to stop harassing behavior from non-employees as well as employees. The court relied partly on the federal Equal Employment Opportunities Commission Guidelines, which recognize that employers who know or should have known of the misconduct may be held liable if non-employees sexually harass employees.

Proposed federal legislation may force employers to address workplace domestic violence. A bill introduced in February 1997 would expand the Family and Medical Leave Act to allow battered employees to take unpaid leave for court appearances or counseling. The bill would also grant unemployment compensation to victims who leave their jobs because of domestic violence. The purposes of the proposed statute are to decrease incidents of domestic violence by providing victims with job opportunities to achieve the financial independence needed to leave abusive situations, to promote employee safety, and to reduce employers' economic losses from domestic violence.

B. Policy Reasons for Addressing Domestic Violence in the Workplace

In addition to the risk of legal consequences, sound public policy dictates the need for employers to address domestic violence in the workplace. More than just a criminal issue, domestic violence poses a public health risk. Rather than avoid the problem, which sends a clear and discouraging message to women that they will receive no help, employers, as part of their community responsibility, should help stop domestic abuse. Policy incentives for employers include strengthening families, reinforcing women's equal role in society, improving employee morale and portraying a positive corporate image.

First, employers have a "person-to-person obligation" to assist employees who are being threatened or harmed. Carrying out the moral duty of reducing workplace domestic violence will improve society by strengthening families. If the cycle of abuse goes uninterrupted, it furthers violence in homes and workplaces. Children also endure psychological harm from witnessing violent acts and are likely to be abused at home themselves.

Employers should encourage employees to report threats of abuse so perpetrators may be stopped from causing future injury to their families. In theory, this reporting practice will also deter potential abusers from committing violent acts.

Second, abuse perpetuates the societal subordination and objectification of women. Acts of domestic violence are gender-based. By controlling and victimizing their partners, men intend to "intimidate and terrorize" all women, reinforcing the traditional view of women's subordinate familial role. Employers can help hold batterers accountable for their crimes by identifying and refusing to tolerate domestic abuse.

Third, employers should send the important message to employees that they value their workers' safety by offering managerial and co-worker support. Addressing domestic violence in the workplace promotes individual well-being among workers by convincing abuse victims to seek needed help. Moreover, communicating a commitment to reducing domestic violence boosts employee morale and builds confidence, resulting in satisfied, healthy workers who contribute to overall workforce productivity. Employers will also directly benefit by retaining valuable employees.

Finally, addressing domestic violence portrays a positive image of the company to the public, thus attracting more quality employees and customers. Corporations with strong workplace domestic violence policies may be viewed as community leaders and organizations committed to fighting domestic violence for the betterment of their employees and of society. The workplace is a crucial link of support required to prevent detrimental effects of domestic abuse in the community.

IV. How to Address Domestic Violence in the Workplace

To satisfy the legal obligations of providing a safe workplace and policy incentives of bettering their communities and workplace environments, employers must take steps to end domestic violence. The Department of Justice suggests that employers take the following measures: 1) get management support; 2) establish policies, such as paid leave, for domestic violence victims; 3) include domestic violence services within employee assistance programs; 4) educate and train management and employees on domestic violence; 5) distribute materials and hotline referrals to all employees; 6) improve workplace security; and 7) support local domestic violence shelters. Employers should acknowledge the prevalence of domestic violence, detect warning signs in their employees, protect victims from abuse, and provide them with referrals for help. These suggested measures can be divided into three areas of employer action: awareness, protection and prevention.

First, employers must be aware of the prevalence of domestic violence and identify the tell-tale signs of abuse in typical situations. Consciousness-raising in the workforce requires education, which is satisfied simply by disseminating informational pamphlets or by requiring employees to attend educational workshops. For example, Target Stores has held education events and provided its 140,000 employees with awareness packets about domestic abuse. Likewise, Liz Claiborne, Inc. has hosted educational seminars at work to inform employees about domestic abuse issues. Regardless of what education methods are used, employees, as well as managers, should be able to recognize victims of abuse. Raising awareness helps eradicate outdated, traditional views of abuse as a purely private matter, thus opening minds to the importance of offering help.

Second, after identifying employees who are victims of abuse, employers must offer support. Doing the "right thing" for employees in need is not only socially beneficial, it may also be advantageous to the corporation. For example, a Texas business owner helped an employee who was attempting to leave her batterer. To ease the adjustment, he gave her paid leave and use of his vans and storage space during the move. The employer said, "It was the right thing to do ... and it made good business sense. She was a good, hard-working and dedicated employee." By helping the employee, the corporation retained a valuable worker. Similarly, when an employer noticed that one of her four-year employees was getting disturbing telephone calls at work, she gave the employee money and time off to obtain a restraining order. The employer found making accommodations worthwhile. Today the abuse survivor is one of the company's "most loyal and hard-working employees."

Domestic abuse support is not necessarily expensive or difficult to implement. Marshalls stores posted domestic abuse crisis hotline numbers in bathroom stalls and provided the company's EAP phone number. Liz Claiborne, Inc., inserted domestic violence brochures and referral telephone numbers in all paycheck envelopes. These inexpensive methods of communication assist employees in a confidential, nonconfrontational manner, and help create a climate in which employees feel comfortable seeking help.

Discreet approaches that respect a victim's need for confidentiality may be the most effective ways for an employer to address domestic violence. Companies should be sensitive to employees' privacy concerns, but "the employer must weigh the privacy rights of the employee against its own obligation to maintain a safe workplace." Co-workers, in addition to the victim, may be at risk in violent workplace situations, and employers are accountable for all employees' safety.

Finally, the unpredictable nature of domestic violence makes preventing violent workplace acts difficult, but taking action will help protect employees from harm and employers from liability. If women working at Polaroid fear abuse, employers may tap telephones, provide escorts, seek restraining orders to keep batterers away from the job site, and relocate domestic abuse victims to help them escape their abusers. Liz Claiborne, Inc., has provided battered employees with special parking spaces and escort services to promote safety. Other suggestions to prevent workplace violence include providing battered women with more flexible work hours and strengthening security measures, such as controlled access to the building, so that abusers would be unable to reach their victims.

Zero-tolerance policies require that employees report all threats and violent acts. Employers should then remove potential perpetrators from the workplace and assist in their prosecution. Employers must know their state's criminal statutes, so they can have the abuser arrested before a violent act occurs. Statutes may prohibit harassing telephone calls, stalking, and trespass by credible threat.

Government offices can help set an example by adopting their own policies. For example, Boston's zero-tolerance domestic violence policy provides counseling to city employees if they are domestic violence victims or potential abusers. Any of the mayor's appointees who are accused of domestic abuse will be suspended, and anyone convicted will be fired.

Similarly, Acting Massachusetts Governor Paul Cellucci signed an executive order authorizing state supervisors to discipline a worker if the court has found "probable cause" that the individual committed battery. The order also allows abused workers to take fifteen days of paid leave and six months of non-paid leave for domestic violence-related appointments or emergencies.

On the federal level, in response to recommendations by the Advisory Council on Violence Against Women, President Clinton ordered federal agencies to address the effects of domestic violence in the workplace. And recently, the President encouraged the private sector to join the nationwide alliance of combating violence against women. He emphasized the issue's broad scope: "Domestic violence is not simply a private family matter—it is a matter affecting the entire community."

CONCLUSION

President Clinton's message conveyed that the epidemic of domestic violence will not be stopped until it is ameliorated in all areas, including public and private workplaces. Preventing violent acts at work and reducing workplace effects from abuse inflicted at home requires employer awareness, attitudinal changes and action.

The malignancy of domestic violence, infecting all aspects of society, inflicts pain on many friends, relatives and neighbors. In essence, society feels the harmful repercussions of domestic abuse outside the home. The problem, too large to ignore, demands that employers recognize their moral, legal, and community responsibilities to address workplace domestic violence. Because the battlefield extends beyond the home, resulting in adverse societal and business effects, even those employers hesitant to infringe on a "private" affair will realize the importance of joining the frontlines of the fight to eradicate domestic abuse.

Chapter 17

IMMIGRATION AND HUMAN RIGHTS ISSUES

This chapter completes the book by bringing the topic back to the international aspects of domestic violence, which were touched on toward the beginning. The materials first focus on issues affecting battered immigrant women in the US, including authorization to work, receipt of public benefits, and self-petitioning for lawful permanent resident status under the Violence Against Women Act (VAWA). They also discuss the impact of a new federal law requiring deportation of convicted batterers, which can result in deportation of the victim, whose legal status is often dependent on the batterer. One article looks at the implications of this law on battered women, who are themselves sometimes arrested for domestic violence. Another notes the difficulties of obtaining VAWA relief for battered immigrants from Mexico, and advocates for legislative change in VAWA standards.

The second part of the chapter discusses domestic violence as an international human rights issue. This is still a new concept, given that human rights law, like most of the legal system, has viewed domestic violence as a private, not a state, issue. This concept is further developed in an excerpt from an *amicus* brief in a recent case, in which a battered Guatemalan woman requested asylum, arguing that domestic violence can be grounds for finding gender-based persecution. The chapter ends with a memo developed by the INS for asylum officers, training them on how to interview women who are requesting asylum based on gender-based persecution. This is a very hopeful development, which should result in more victims of domestic violence being able to escape from abuse.

A. IMMIGRATION

TIEN-LI LOKE, TRAPPED IN DOMESTIC VIOLENCE: THE IMPACT OF UNITED STATES IMMIGRATION LAWS ON BATTERED IMMIGRANT WOMEN

6 B. U. Pub. Int. L. J. 589–603, 606–621, 627 (1997).

I. INTRODUCTION

The devastating effects of domestic violence affect our entire society indiscriminately. Domestic violence is blind to distinctions based on class, race, ethnic, religious, and economic lines. However, the consequences are particularly overwhelming when the victim of abuse is an immigrant woman with conditional resident status. In addition to the fears that all domestic violence victims face, battered immigrant women live with fears that are unique to their situation—fear of deportation, a general distrust of authorities, and language and cultural barriers. All of these factors combine to increase their sense of isolation and create barriers that appear insurmountable, essentially trapping these women in violent relationships.

* * *

II. BARRIERS FACED BY BATTERED IMMIGRANT WOMEN

Cultural barriers present a major obstacle to a battered immigrant woman, often preventing her from seeking help. A battered immigrant woman's cultural and religious orientation may be one that instills a tolerance for domestic violence. A battered immigrant woman may have been raised in a society where it is acceptable for a husband to beat his wife and expect that she will endure it. For example, in many Asian cultures, Confucianism requires women to obey their husbands, while Buddhist women are prone to accept victimization as their fate. A Korean saying considers "women and dried fish ... alike. You have to beat them at least once a day to keep them good." According to Islamic law and the Koran, "men are in charge of women because Allah has made the one of them to excel the other and because they (the men) spend of their property for the support of women." The Koran's Sura IV. 34 further indicates that "good women are obedient" and instructs men on what steps to take in dealing with rebellious women: "admonish them, banish them to beds apart and scourge them."

Many cultures have different definitions of family and community. In some cultures, violence in a marriage is seen as a "private" problem. Discussion of such private affairs among family members, let alone with strangers humiliates the family and is a source of shame and family disgrace. Even if a woman does not willingly accept the abuse, she may not want to jeopardize her husband's standing in the community because of the importance placed on social status. Furthermore, an immigrant woman faces the possibility of ending her marriage and accepting the social consequences attendant to divorce. Divorce is particularly onerous in traditional families and communities that reject divorced women or women who have left their husbands. Thus, cultural mores often prevent women from ending their abusive relationships.

Furthermore, battered immigrant women live with a fear that is unique to their situation—fear of deportation. This is the single largest concern for battered immigrant women seeking to leave an abusive relationship. For some women who have fled persecution in their home country, deportation means torture, jail, or death. For others, it means a return to a life of extreme poverty, disease, and few or no opportunities. Fear of deportation does not imply that there was any duplicity in the acquisition of conditional status or that a woman entered into a fraudulent marriage to remain in the United States. Many immigrant women are undocumented despite the fact that they are in valid marriages to United States citizens or permanent residents. Fear of deportation is, in fact, a genuine concern which prevents battered immigrant women from leaving abusive marriages regardless of whether they have obtained legal immigration status. Many immigrant women are simply unaware that there are legal avenues available to stop the violence which will not affect their immigration status. This ignorance and unfamiliarity is largely due to incorrect information provided to battered women by their abusers. Large numbers of immigrant women are trapped in violent homes by abusive husbands who use the promise of legal status or the threat of deportation as a means to exert power and to maintain control over their wives. Immigrant women often fear that any sort of contact with governmental authority will expose their presence in the country and result in deportation. As a result, many women choose to stay in abusive relationships rather than face deportation.

Like most victims of domestic violence, battered immigrant women may hide the problem because of fear, shame and denial. Battered immigrant women unfamiliar with the ways of a new country may not have any friends or family, and may simply not know what to do. Many immigrant women may not even realize that domestic violence is against the law in this country. Battered immigrant women may often be afraid to call the police because of a basic distrust of law enforcement officials and government authorities. If a battered immigrant woman is from a country that views the police as repressive, it is difficult for her to have anything but terror of the police. Her experience with the legal system in her native country may make her reluctant to turn to the judicial system for help. In countries where the judiciary is an arm of a repressive government and does not function independently, those who prevail in court are the people with the most money or the strongest ties to the government. Against this background, battered immigrant women may find it difficult to believe that the legal system will protect or help them.

Battered immigrant women are often unfamiliar with ways to access the system or community resources. Seeking help from legal services or temporary safety at shelters is daunting for immigrant women who face significant language barriers. Most shelters do not have bilingual or multilingual staff or volunteers and therefore cannot accommodate non-English speaking women. Even if interpreters are available, many immigrant women may be reluctant to speak to an interpreter for fear of exposure, lack of confidentiality, and fear that their whereabouts may be disclosed to abusive spouses. Shelters may also be reluctant to provide assistance because immigrant women are less likely to have an income and may not be eligible for public benefits. Many shelters prefer to offer the limited numbers of spots to women who can theoretically make better use of all shelter services. Some shelters and legal services may even be unable to accept undocumented women because of government imposed funding restrictions.

Economic difficulties also make it difficult for immigrant women to leave abusive marriages. Battered immigrant women are often unemployed and have little social mobility. Many come to the United States with little or no independent financial resources. These women are often economically dependent on their husbands, lacking education or the marketable skills necessary to find higher paying employment which would enable them to live independently. This economic dependence is reinforced by the impact of immigration laws concerning employer sanctions and hiring practices. If the woman is undocumented she will not have authorization to work, and will be subject to deportation. As a result many women are forced to work in restaurants, garment factories, and other businesses that typically pay below minimum wage and provide no benefits. The lack of English further limits their employment opportunities, forcing them to remain within their ethnic community. Any decision to leave the community and seek shelter would thus result in an inability to support herself and her children. Without any means of achieving financial independence, escape from an abusive marriage will leave battered immigrant women and their children helpless and poverty stricken.

Cultural barriers, dependence on abusive husbands, fear of deportation, and language barriers all create a sense of isolation which leave battered immigrant women particularly vulnerable in situations of domestic violence. These factors create an environment in which immigrant women feel alone and powerless to escape abuse. Given the particular vulnerability and the additional difficulties that immigrant women face, a comprehensive statutory and regulatory framework is necessary to address the problems that are specific to battered immigrant women.

III.   THE STATUTORY AND REGULATORY FRAMEWORK

A. *Immigration Marriage Fraud Amendments of 1986*

United States immigration laws have presented the greatest obstacles to battered immigrant women. Under the Immigration and Nationality Act, marriage to a United States citizen or legal permanent resident ("LPR") confers certain immigration benefits on the immigrant spouse. In 1986, Congress passed the Immigration Marriage Fraud Amendments

("IMFA") in response to INS concerns about perceived increases in "sham" marriages. IMFA changed the status of immigrants who married United States citizens or legal permanent residents. Before the passage of IMFA, an immigrant spouse was granted permanent residency regardless of the length of the marriage. Under IMFA, the United States citizen or LPR had to petition the Immigration and Naturalization Service ("INS") for a two-year conditional residency for his immigrant wife. The conditional period commenced on the date she obtained conditional status, rather than at the beginning of the marriage. Legal permanent residency was only obtained when the immigrant woman and the sponsor-husband jointly petitioned the INS to adjust her conditional status to permanent residency before the end of the two years. The immigrating wife's conditional status automatically terminated and she became subject to immediate deportation if the couple failed to petition jointly, or if the marriage dissolved at any time during the conditional residency.

1. Waivers

IMFA however, provided a waiver of the joint petition requirement where the immigrant established that "extreme hardship" would result from deportation, or where the marriage had been entered into in good faith but had been terminated by the conditional resident for good cause, and the conditional resident was not at fault for failing to file the joint petition. These two waivers, however, did not adequately protect battered women with conditional residency status.

a. The "Extreme Hardship" Waiver

Under the "extreme hardship" waiver, a conditional resident was permitted to waive the joint petition requirement if she could prove that deportation would subject her to "extreme hardship." The "extreme hardship" waiver did not provide effective relief to battered immigrant women because such a showing was difficult to make, particularly since the INS was unlikely to find extreme hardship except in rare cases. Economic deprivation, lack of family assistance, or the fact that an immigrant woman would not be able to find work in her home country did not constitute "extreme hardship" by INS standards. Furthermore, an immigrant woman may have been the victim of domestic violence which undoubtedly created extreme hardship for the woman, but this did not qualify her for the waiver. This is because the focus of the hardship inquiry was on whether deportation would result in extreme hardship, and not on the extreme hardship endured during the marriage. Thus, according to INS standards, being a victim of domestic violence did not constitute "extreme hardship" sufficient to justify a waiver of the joint petition requirement. As a result, the "extreme hardship" waiver offered little protection to battered immigrant women.

b. The "Good Faith/Good Cause" Waiver

To obtain a "good faith/good cause" waiver to the joint petition phase of the process, a battered immigrant woman with conditional status had to demonstrate that she entered into the marriage in good faith, and that she initiated the divorce proceedings for good cause. The "good faith/good cause" waiver has since been modified, but this also proved problematic to immigrant victims of domestic violence. First, the waiver required the legal termination of a marriage; mere separation rendered the woman ineligible for a waiver. The immigrant woman also had to initiate the divorce—a requirement that essentially created a "race to the courthouse." This created additional problems for immigrant women. The lack of affordable family law services, particularly for those with limited English skills, made even the most simple dissolution difficult to obtain. Furthermore, although the INS recognized domestic violence as "good cause" for terminating a marriage, divorce proceedings in a "no-fault" jurisdiction created evidentiary problems for battered women.

The IMFA provisions created additional difficulties for immigrant women in domestic violence situations by providing a powerful weapon to the abusive husband to maintain complete control over a battered immigrant woman's status as an LPR. A battered woman could not gain legal immigration status if her sponsor-husband did not file the appropriate petitions, which he was free to withdraw at anytime. As a result, IMFA provisions created a framework under which a battered immigrant woman had to choose between remaining in an abusive marriage until the conditions of conditional status were removed, or leave and risk deportation if her sponsor-husband withdrew the petition or if the INS denied her waiver application. Thus, IMFA created a situation in which a battered immigrant woman's ability to remain in the United States depended exclusively on her husband's goodwill and the continued viability of her marriage. When faced with the choice of protection from batterers or protection against deportation, many battered immigrant women chose the latter. Many women were simply unwilling to leave even the most abusive of partners for fear of being deported.

B. The Immigration Act of 1990

Congress enacted the Immigration Act of 1990 ("the 1990 Act") in response to the negative impact that IMFA had on victims of domestic violence. Although the "extreme hardship" waiver established under IMFA was left unchanged, the 1990 Act contained two important provisions. First, the 1990 Act amended the "good faith/good cause" waiver by eliminating the requirement that the battered woman be the moving party in a divorce proceeding. This meant that "good cause" for termination of a marriage was no longer required and that either party could commence divorce proceedings. More importantly, the Act added a new waiver provision called the "battered spouse/child" waiver.

1. The "Battered Spouse" Waiver

The "battered spouse" waiver ensures that the threat of losing real residency status will not trap victims of domestic violence in abusive marriages. In contrast to the earlier "good faith/good cause" waiver, an immigrant woman could qualify for the "battered spouse" waiver even if she was divorced. A battered immigrant woman could qualify for the waiver if she could prove that she had entered into the marriage in good faith and that she or her children had been battered or subjected to "extreme mental cruelty" by the sponsor-husband. This meant that a battered immigrant woman could adjust her residency status to that of a permanent resident.

Although the 1990 Act made it easier for battered immigrant women to leave violent marriages and achieve legal permanent status, some major problems remained. Despite the "battered spouse" waiver, the Act left an abusive husband in control over the initial petitioning process. Even assuming that an initial petition was filed, the Act did not prevent an abusive husband from withdrawing the petition at any time before a battered immigrant woman's residency status was adjusted.

Withdrawal of the petition resulted in the loss of the immigrant woman's right to remain legally in the United States. As a result, the immigrant woman became an illegal alien, without work authorization and subject to deportation. Thus, in spite of the waiver, leaving an abusive situation was not a viable option for battered immigrant women. Furthermore, the Act only applied to battered women who had acquired conditional status and failed to take into account the large group of undocumented women whose husbands never filed an initial petition to commence their conditional status. The Act also failed to protect women who may have entered the United States as non-immigrants, married a citizen or LPR more than two years ago, but neglected to change their immigration status. As a result, these women became undocumented once their visa expired. The Act did not help these undocumented women who remained trapped in domestic violence situations due to their fear of deportation.

2. INS Regulations

The INS regulations interpreting and implementing the 1990 Immigration Act were unnecessarily burdensome on battered immigrant women. The regulations raised significant concerns with their stringent evidentiary requirements. The INS regulations separated the "battered spouse" waiver exception into two areas: physical battery and extreme mental cruelty. Under these regulations, battered spouses were required to prove abuse by providing the INS with certain types of evidence.

The INS regulations required proof of physical abuse including "expert" testimony in the form of reports and affidavits from police, medical personnel, school officials, and social service agency personnel. The regulations further mandated the INS' satisfaction with the credibility of the sources of documentation submitted in support of the application. However, getting the documentation required under the regulations proved burdensome for many battered immigrant women. Cultural and language barriers, embarrassment, and fear of deportation or reprisals from their batterers made available services such as shelters, police, and doctors unacceptable for many immigrant women who came from vastly different cultural backgrounds. Additionally, reporting abuse or seeking help of any sort, whether in the form of restraining orders, medical attention, or help from the police could be particularly frightening for these women. As a result, many battered immigrant women rarely had police records to help prove battery, especially if they did not call the police at the time of the assault.

The evidentiary requirements for "battered spouse" waiver applicants claiming "extreme mental cruelty" proved to be even more difficult to obtain. The INS regulations set out particularly stringent evidentiary requirements under this category. The regulations required applications to be supported by the evaluation of a professional recognized by the INS as an "expert in the field." However, the only professionals recognized by the INS for this purpose were "licensed clinical social workers, psychologists and psychiatrists." Personal affidavits from individuals who were not mental health professionals were unacceptable. The narrow application and documentation guidelines made qualification for the waiver difficult since many immigrant women did not have a medical report to help prove the injuries they suffered. These women often could not afford to or would not seek the services of a doctor, let alone a psychologist or psychiatrist to document their abuse. Furthermore, language barriers created additional problems. Bilingual professionals are often unavailable, and many women do not have the economic resources to have evaluations conducted through an interpreter.

Moreover, the evidence required to establish extreme mental cruelty focused entirely on the effect the abuse had on the victim, rather than on whether the abuser's behavior constituted extreme cruelty. A resilient woman who did not clinically show the debilitating effects of psychological cruelty would therefore not qualify for a waiver even if she deserved one based on the level of abuse she sustained. Thus, combined with the lack of resources to pay for medical attention or language assistance, a battered immigrant woman often found it difficult to meet the mental cruelty evidentiary requirement.

While the 1990 Immigration Act and INS regulations alleviated some of the problems faced by battered immigrant women, the statutory and regulatory framework remained flawed and incomplete. The framework left abusive husbands in control of the petitioning process and it established evidentiary requirements that the vast majority of immigrant women could never hope to meet.

C. The Violence Against Women Act of 1994

In an effort to close some of the gaps left by the 1990 Immigration Act, Congress passed the Violence Against Women Act ("VAWA") as part of the Violent Crime Control and Law Enforcement Act of 1994. Congress intended VAWA to make prevention of violence against women "a major law enforcement priority," and included provisions specifically designed to protect battered immigrant women.

VAWA contained several critical amendments. Immigrant victims of domestic violence with conditional status can now self-petition to adjust their immigration status without the co-operation and participation of their sponsor-husband. VAWA also provides a provision for the suspension of deportation for undocumented spouses and children who have been abused by their United States citizen or LPR husbands.

1. The Self–Petitioning Provision

As of January 1, 1995, a battered immigrant woman could file a petition with the Attorney General on her own behalf for unconditional permanent resident status without having to depend on her husband's participation or co-operation. The immigrant woman must demonstrate that: i) she is a person of good moral character; ii) she has lived in the United States with her citizen or LPR spouse; iii) she is currently residing in this country; iv) she married in good faith; v) during the marriage, the alien or her child was battered or subjected to extreme cruelty by her spouse; and vi) deportation would result in extreme hardship to her or her child. This self-petitioning provision protects women who fear that leaving an abusive spouse will subject them to deportation, or will jeopardize their chances of gaining legal status. It permits a battered immigrant woman to self-petition for nationality when her sponsor-husband refuses to cooperate in filing the joint petition to begin or remove conditional status. Most importantly, the self-petitioning provision prevents the abusive husband from using the petitioning process and immigration laws as a means to control or abuse the immigrant woman.

2. The Suspension of Deportation Provision

VAWA provides another avenue of relief through the suspension of deportation provision. To qualify for this form of relief, an applicant must first be "deportable," which usually means that they are present in the United States without legal immigration status. Under this provision, a battered immigrant woman may apply for suspension of deportation if she can prove that: i) she has been physically present in the United States for at least three years immediately prior to the application; ii) she was battered or subjected to extreme cruelty by her citizen or LPR spouse; iii) she is of good moral character; and iv) deportation would cause extreme hardship to her or her child. This avenue of relief is available to an undocumented battered woman who is subject to deportation as a result of her sponsor-husband's failure to file an initial petition to begin her conditional residency. Thus, the suspension of deportation provision gives undocumented women the freedom to more readily leave batterers without the threat of deportation.

3. Other Provisions of the Violence Against Women Act

Under the previous statutory and regulatory framework, divorce resulted in the automatic termination of conditional status and the ability to petition for permanent residency. In cases of domestic violence, VAWA includes a provision that an approved self-petition cannot be revoked solely because a marriage has been legally terminated. This provision allows a battered woman to end an abusive marriage without loss of her residency status. Thus, if a couple divorces after the INS approves a battered woman's self-petition, the INS cannot revoke its approval solely because of the divorce.

VAWA also relaxed the stringent evidentiary requirements of the 1990 Immigration Act's "battered spouse" waiver concerning proof of physical battery and extreme mental cruelty. VAWA did not explicitly repudiate the standards established in the previous INS regulations, but it directs the Attorney General to consider all "credible evidence" relevant to the petition.

Moreover, an INS memorandum issued after the release of the interim regulations specifically prohibited the INS from requiring that applications claiming extreme mental cruelty be supported by the evaluation of a licensed mental health professional. The relaxation of this requirement may ease the evidentiary burden placed on battered immigrant women and may also encourage women with limited resources and language skills to seek help.

* * *

IV. PROBLEMS IN THE CO-EXISTING FRAMEWORK

The statutory and regulatory framework that has evolved provides a baseline of protection for battered immigrant women. This framework allows battered immigrant women to leave abusive situations by providing for self-petitioning and the suspension of deportation. However, these provisions only address the problems created by immigration laws and the requirements of conditional residency. Battered immigrant women who leave abusive situations are, however, also confronted with critical crossover issues affecting their safety and economic status. These crossover issues must be addressed in the co-existing legal framework to ensure that the protections that were gained by VAWA are not undermined.

A. Work Authorization

Even if current laws enable battered immigrant women to remain in the United States, women still face the daunting task of finding housing and securing financial support for themselves and their children. Battered immigrant women are often subject to complete control and financial isolation by their husbands. Many do not have access to cash, checking accounts, or charge accounts. As a result, many immigrant women who are completely dependent on their husbands leave violent relationships with little or no independent financial resources. Furthermore, battered immigrant women often lack the education and skills necessary to find a higher paying job that would allow them to become financially independent. Thus, for immigrant women victimized by domestic violence, work authorization is of paramount importance.

1. VAWA Self–Petition Applicants

A battered woman's ability to receive work authorization as a self-petitioner depends on whether she is married to a United States citizen or an LPR. If a battered woman is married to a United States citizen, she can file an application for "adjustment of status" to legal permanent residency at the same time as her self-petition, and may obtain work authorization. This means that battered immigrant women, married to United States citizens, will have swift access to work authorization.

The situation is very different for self-petitioners who are married to abusive LPRs. These women may be forced to delay filing applications for "adjustment to status" to legal permanent residency because this category is subject to the visa allocation system which restricts the number of persons who may be granted legal permanent residency in any single year. Battered immigrant women whose eligibility is based on a relationship with a LPR cannot apply for "adjustment of status" until a visa is issued. A "priority" date determines an applicant's place in the waiting line and visa numbers are allocated in priority date order, which is typically the filing date of the application. It now takes approximately three years for the priority date to "become current" so that the visa can be issued. Women who are married to LPRs cannot request work authorization until they have properly filed an adjustment of status, but they cannot file to adjust their status until a visa is issued. Thus, battered immigrant women cannot even work despite the lengthy period that it takes to issue the visa. Without work authorization, a battered woman who has left her husband will have even greater difficulty achieving financial independence. She is likely to only find "under the table" jobs that are offered by unscrupulous employers who subject their workers to low wages, poor working conditions, and no benefits. Furthermore, if the INS discovers that a woman is working without work authorization, it will jeopardize the outcome of her pending application and subject her to deportation. Without work authorization these battered immigrant women will have no means by which to support themselves, and will be forced to return to their husbands and remain trapped in abusive relationships.

2. VAWA Suspension of Deportation Applicants

According to the INS, battered immigrant women who wish to file for suspension of deportation during immigration court proceedings may request work authorization. Battered immigrant women, however, cannot file affirmatively for suspension of deportation as the INS currently takes the position that a person cannot voluntarily go to the INS to file for suspension of deportation under the VAWA provision. This means that battered immigrant women cannot request work authorization until the INS initiates deportation proceedings against them. Thus, a battered immigrant woman is left with no legal means by which to work and to support herself and her children, precipitating a forced return to her batterer husband.

B. Public Benefits

Even if battered immigrant women are able to gain work authorization, it still may not be enough for them to survive independently. Circumstances often demand that battered women live, work, and care for their children in a location unknown to the abuser in order to escape violence. Many battered immigrant women have to leave their jobs and go into hiding from their abusive husbands. In many other situations, however, the lack of education or necessary skills prevents them from even finding employment. Such situations are further complicated if young children who require constant care are involved. Given these dismal circumstances, the period immediately after leaving an abusive relationship is when many battered immigrant women face an unavoidable need for public assistance.

Despite their dilemma, immigrant women are prohibited from receiving assistance from public benefits programs as a result of changes brought about by the Personal Responsibility and Work Opportunity and Reconciliation Act of 1996 ("The Welfare Reform Act"). The Welfare Reform Act specifically barred illegal immigrants from federal, state, and local public assistance. Even more significantly, it rendered legal immigrants ineligible to receive any assistance from most federally funded services, including food stamps and Supplemental Security Income (SSI). States are authorized to determine whether legal immigrants are eligible for a limited number of specified federal programs such as Medicaid. The states are also left to determine the eligibility of both illegal and legal immigrants for state and local public benefits. After the effective date, both legal and illegal immigrants are only eligible for emergency medical care, soup kitchens, and short term non-cash in-kind emergency disaster relief.

* * *

C. Resurgent Xenophobia and the Political Climate in an Election Year

As already evidenced by the Welfare Reform Act, the difficulties that battered immigrant women face have been exacerbated by conflicting laws that fail to take their situation into account. The protection extended by the legal framework was further threatened by vehement anti-welfare and anti-immigrant sentiment, as reflected by the flurry of restrictive immigration bills that emerged during the 104th Congressional term.

On April 26, President Clinton signed the Anti–Terrorism and Effective Death Penalty Act of 1996 ("AEDPA") into law. The AEDPA involved legislation that made drastic amendments to immigration laws, and had little to do with protecting the United States from terrorism. AEDPA eliminated certain avenues by which undocumented immigrants can stay in the United States, regardless of their citizen family members or length of residence. As a result, it deprived battered immigrant women of the relief intended by VAWA's suspension of deportation provisions. AEDPA essentially eliminated the availability of suspension of deportation for any non-citizens who entered the country without "inspection" by immigration authorities on arrival into the United States. By making all people who entered without inspection "excludable" rather than deportable, it eliminated suspension of deportation for undocumented immigrants. Suspension of deportation is not available to people in "exclusion" proceedings, since suspension of deportation is only available in a deportation hearing. Instead of a deportation hearing, an undocumented immigrant is subject to exclusion with an expedited exclusion interview. Thus, AEDPA makes undocumented battered women who are in the United States illegally, ineligible for VAWA suspension of deportation and subject to exclusion from the country.

* * *

V.   Recent Developments

A.   The Illegal Immigration Reform and Immigrant Responsibility Act of 1996

The protection offered by the legal framework was further undermined by legislation which threatened to make the most sweeping changes to immigration law in a decade. Congress ultimately passed the Illegal Immigration Reform and Immigrant Responsibility Act of 1996 ("the Immigration Reform Act") in response to the hostile anti-immigrant and anti-welfare sentiment that surfaced nationwide in an election year. Despite its generally restrictive nature, the Immigration Reform Act provided several exemptions for battered immigrant women, appearing to have actually considered the critical crossover issues that battered immigrant women face when they leave their batterers.

1.   The Public Benefits Ineligibility Exception

The Immigration Reform Act appeared to address the critical issues affecting battered immigrant women's safety and economic status by creating an exception to the public benefits ineligibility provision. The Immigration Reform Act amended the Welfare Reform Act by expanding the category of "qualified aliens" to include immigrant women who have been battered or subjected to extreme cruelty by a spouse. The exception also requires proof of a "substantial connection" between such battery or cruelty and the need for public benefits. In reality, the exemption does little to help battered immigrant women because of provisions already passed as part of the Welfare Reform Act in August 1996. The Welfare Reform Act previously restricted the eligibility of "qualified aliens" for federal benefits programs. Furthermore, qualified aliens may only receive state and local benefits, and Medicaid, if the states exercise their authority under the Welfare Reform Act to make immigrants eligible for such assistance. Thus, battered immigrant women who are lawfully present in the United States will be eligible for very limited assistance but only if the states choose to exercise their option to recognize their eligibility to receive such assistance. Thus, the exemption is extremely limited. It fails to acknowledge that women generally face poverty when they leave abusive relationships, and must be provided with some assistance to enable them to remain separate and independent from abusers.

There is also uncertainty surrounding the requirements that are necessary to meet the battered women exception to public benefits ineligibility. The exception requires proof of a "substantial connection" between the violence and the need for benefits. At this point, it is not clear what will constitute a "substantial connection," but hopefully the INS will promulgate regulations that do not impose onerous evidentiary burdens on battered immigrant women.

2. Exemptions From "Exclusion"

The Immigration Reform Act also provides an exemption for battered immigrant women who entered the United States without inspection. Under the exemption, a woman's undocumented presence in the country does not necessarily render her inadmissible for entry into the United States. However, the exemption is rather restrictive in the sense that it adds new qualifications for permanent residency. Battered immigrant women who enter the United States without inspection after April 1, 1997, must demonstrate that their entry without inspection was substantially connected to the abuse in order to qualify for lawful permanent residency. Abused women who have already entered the United States, or those who enter before April 1, 1997, continue to qualify for lawful permanent residency through VAWA without having to prove a "substantial connection."

The Immigration Reform Act also restored a modified version of the VAWA suspension of deportation provision that was undermined by AEDPA. The Immigration Reform Act contains a special provision for battered women that cancels the "removal" of undocumented women who meet essentially the same requirements as those under VAWA's suspension of deportation provision. Cancellation of removal is a form of immigration relief where immigration courts waive the grounds of removal. If cancellation is granted, a successful applicant is permitted to adjust his or her status to lawful permanent residency. However, the Immigration Reform Act restricts the number of aliens that the Attorney General may adjust to the status of permanent residency under this provision. According to the Immigration Reform Act, the Attorney General may not cancel the removal and adjust the status of more than four thousand aliens in any fiscal year. Efforts to extend protection to battered immigrant women will be undermined once again if battered immigrant women are denied protection solely because the quota limit has been reached.

3. Change in the Immigration Status of the Batterer

According to the INS interim regulations concerning the self-petitioning provision of VAWA, an abuser's change in immigration status will adversely affect a battered immigrant woman's self-petition. If an abusive LPR husband is deported before the approval of a self-petition, the battered immigrant woman's application will be denied since the abuser will lose his LPR status. Both AEDPA and the Immigration Reform Act include strict provisions concerning criminal offenses that have serious consequences for battered immigrant women in this context. AEDPA expands the grounds of deportability, making relief from deportation almost impossible for long term permanent residents who have criminal histories. This catch-all provision includes most felonies and misdemeanors, ranging from any drug offenses, such as marijuana possession, to crimes of moral turpitude and even shoplifting. Moreover, AEDPA makes no distinction between the seriousness of crimes, the length of time since the crime was committed, or whether the person served time in prison. If a woman is married to an abuser who is deportable under AEDPA because he may have been convicted of a minor crime in the past, her self-petition will be denied as he no longer has LPR status.

The Immigration Reform Act goes even further, by including provisions that require deportation for domestic violence offenses, stalking, and violations of civil protection orders. Ironically, the revocation of the batterer's immigration status will serve as a basis for denial of a self-petition. For women, the provisions expanding the grounds of deportability have even more far reaching consequences. Many women will be discouraged from seeking protection orders or from cooperating in criminal prosecutions for fear that it will result in the conviction and subsequent deportation of their LPR husbands. The termination of a husband's lawful permanent residency will ultimately adversely affect the woman's VAWA petitions. Thus, although aimed at sending a message that violence will not be tolerated, the AEDPA and the Immigration Reform Act have, in reality, seriously exacerbated the plight of battered immigrant women.

* * *

5. *Affidavits of Support*

The Immigration Reform Act also amended requirements concerning the legal obligations of batterers who may have provided signed "affidavits of support" when sponsoring their spouses for immigration into the United States. Before entry into the United States is granted, an alien must prove that he or she is not "likely at anytime to become a public charge." A common way to prove this was for the sponsor-husband to submit an "affidavit of support" stating that he would be financially responsible for her. These provisions created a sponsorship "deeming period" in which the income of the sponsor-husband who submitted the affidavit of support would be "deemed" as part of the sponsored-wife's income. Thus, it was assumed that for this period of time, the sponsored-wife had access to her husband's income. The Immigration Reform Act makes these affidavits of support legally enforceable as contracts and allows battered immigrant women to enforce them against their abusive sponsor-husbands. The remedies available to enforce an affidavit of support include judgment liens, writs of execution, installment payments, and garnishment provisions. As a practical matter, however, the remedies to enforce affidavits of support may prove daunting to immigrant women, overwhelmed by the complexities of an unfamiliar court system.

Although the Immigration Reform Act limited some of the adverse effects of anti-immigrant laws on battered immigrant women, it ultimately did little to extend protections to this group of women. The Immigration Reform Act failed to adequately address the most important crossover issues facing battered immigrant women and their ability to survive on their own. Unless battered immigrant women are given a means by which to support themselves and their children, the purpose of VAWA in extending protection to them will be rendered meaningless. The purpose of VAWA is to prevent battered immigrant women from being trapped in a violent relationship because they are completely dependent on their batterers. The framework will be undermined if it encourages battered immigrant women to leave their batterers but leaves them with no means to support themselves and their children. If these women are unable to make ends meet, they will be forced to return to their abusive husbands.

VI. RECOMMENDATIONS FOR CHANGE

Given the uncertainty and problems that battered immigrant women face, a comprehensive approach must be taken to ensure that serious efforts are made to address these concerns, and ensure continued protection for battered immigrant women. These remaining issues need to be addressed through a multi-faceted approach—through regulations, legislation, community based efforts, and training—in order to respond to the harrowing situation faced by immigrant women who are trapped in violent, abusive relationships.

A. INS Regulations

The flurry of immigration laws have created a number of uncertainties; thus, the promulgation of INS regulations concerning the implementation of VAWA and the Immigration Reform Act plays a crucial role in ensuring that the framework of protection is neither undermined nor rendered useless. Regulations could resolve many of these remaining uncertainties.

1. Regulations Implementing VAWA

Final regulations concerning the self-petitioning provision of VAWA need to address the problems surrounding work authorization for immigrant women who are married to LPRs. Under the interim regulations, only VAWA applicants who are married to United States citizens are guaranteed work authorization, while spouses of LPRs must wait for a visa before they can request an adjustment of status and work authorization. The final regulations should provide work authorization to all VAWA self-petitioners who file applications and who meet the self-petitioning requirements. The INS should create a simple unified system which could be used by all VAWA applicants to apply for work authorization simultaneously with their self-petition. The INS could process all the applications the same way it processes petitions filed by VAWA applicants who are spouses of United States citizens. Swiftly granting work authorization to self-petitioners will ensure that they overcome economic barriers and move quickly to independence. Battered immigrant women must be presented with realistic options that will permit them not only to leave, but to remain separated from their batterers.

The final INS regulations also need to address the problems concerning an abuser's change in immigration status. The regulations should be amended to ensure that battered immigrant women who otherwise qualify for VAWA protection obtain it as long as their abuser-husband is a citizen or LPR at the time they file VAWA self-petitions. This will not only protect battered immigrant women whose husbands become deportable because of criminal offenses, but it will also encourage women to cooperate in criminal prosecutions against their batterers. Through VAWA, Congress intended to provide protection to domestic violence victims from the earliest date possible. The final regulations should ensure that battered women remain eligible for VAWA protection even if the batterer's immigration status changes after the filing of a self-petition.

2. Regulations Implementing the Immigration Reform Act

Although the Immigration Reform Act reinstated VAWA suspension of deportation with the cancellation of removal provision, the latter provision must deal with essentially the same concerns as the VAWA provision. These concerns must be addressed by the INS when it promulgates regulations implementing the Immigration Reform Act. As cancellation of removal is only available to people in removal proceedings, the regulations must allow battered undocumented women to apply affirmatively for this kind of relief. The regulations must ensure that battered immigrant women have a means of survival, and must simultaneously allow them to apply for work authorization.

The regulations must also clarify how to interpret certain terms such as "extreme hardship" and "substantial connection." The phrase "extreme hardship" has acquired a settled meaning in the deportation context which is extremely difficult to meet. The forthcoming regulations must tailor the interpretation to the situation faced by battered immigrant women. Similarly, the INS regulations must also provide some guidance in the interpretation of the phrase "substantial connection" when evaluating the eligibility of battered women for both the public benefits and removal exemptions. The regulations must clarify the kinds of evidence that are sufficiently "substantial" to prove a connection between the abuse and the immigrant woman's situation. In light of the difficulties many battered immigrant women may have in gathering evidence to prove a substantial connection, the INS must adopt a generous interpretation that is tailored to the plight of battered immigrant women.

B. *Strengthening the Legislative Response at Federal and State Levels*

Legislation must also be passed to continue to extend protection to battered immigrant women. Given the desperate situations that many battered immigrant women face immediately after leaving their batterers, Congress must create a selective exemption restoring public benefits to battered immigrant women. This would allow them to receive assistance from federally funded programs. As the need for public assistance is at its greatest when battered immigrant women leave violent relationships, they must be given a realistic opportunity to start new lives and remain separate and independent from their batterers. Moreover, battered immigrant women's dependence on public assistance is likely to be temporary. The need for public assistance often arises directly out of the abusive relationship and the end of the relationship usually signals the beginning of the transition to independence. Moreover, most families who receive AFDC do so for no more than twenty-four months at a time, while over two-thirds of families headed by women under thirty receive benefits for an even shorter time period. Legislative efforts must recognize that poverty and the use of public benefits are endemic to the experience of domestic violence.

In the alternative, a narrow exemption restoring public benefits to battered immigrant women could alleviate the harsh impacts of the restrictive welfare and immigration laws at the state level, through a narrow exemption restoring public benefits to battered immigrant women. Under the Welfare Reform Act, states are authorized to determine whether legal immigrants are eligible for Medicaid. The Welfare Reform Act also gives power to the states to provide affirmatively any state or local benefits to both undocumented and legal immigrants. States must affirmatively recognize this eligibility by creating an exemption that allows battered immigrant women to receive state and local benefits, as well as Medicaid. Battered immigrant women must be provided with a way to gain financial independence or they will be forced to return to their abusive husbands.

If the federal or state governments create an exemption to allow battered immigrant women access to public benefits, coexisting laws must also be amended to ensure that the purpose of such an exemption is not undermined. Battered immigrant women must not face any danger in receiving public assistance. Under current immigration laws, applying for public benefits may affect the outcome of any pending immigration petition. Applicants for legal immigration status may be denied status if they fall into a category of exclusion, which includes becoming a "public charge." Thus, even if battered immigrant women have valid claims under VAWA, the INS could find that women who have received certain forms of public assistance, or those who need to receive public assistance will fall into this exclusionary category, which may serve as the basis for denial of their application to regularize their status in the United States.

Current immigration laws also make any immigrant who becomes a public charge within five years after entry deportable unless he or she affirmatively proves that the causes of dependency arose after entry. Thus, the public charge exclusionary category must also be amended to recognize that battered immigrant women may be forced to rely on public benefits and that such reliance should not affect any pending immigration petitions. The exclusionary category must be amended to ensure that the efforts to provide protection to battered immigrant women are not undermined.

C. Education, Outreach and Training

* * *

VII. Conclusion

As the issue of domestic violence has begun to receive more attention in the United States, the special problems faced by battered immigrant women have started to receive attention and recognition. However, a piece-meal approach to the difficulties faced by battered immigrant women will not alleviate the problem of domestic violence. A comprehensive framework that addresses the plight of battered immigrant women through regulations, legislation, and community based efforts is urgently needed.

* * *

CECELIA M. ESPENOZA, NO RELIEF FOR THE WEARY: VAWA RELIEF DENIED FOR BATTERED IMMIGRANTS LOST IN THE INTERSECTIONS

83 Marq. L. Rev. 163–166, 191–194, 196–197, 198, 201–202, 215–216 (1999).

I. Introduction

Congress adopted the Violence Against Women Act of 1994 (VAWA), in part, to provide relief to battered immigrant women. However, there is a substantial and increasing population of women who are precluded from relief by conflicting provisions within the Act. The punishment of perpetrators yields unintended consequences that harm battered immigrant women of color, undermining the effectiveness of affirmative immigration relief. By neglecting the circumstances where the woman is accused as the perpetrator, current provisions fail to address the cycle of violence that may generate false charges against battered women.

The underlying purpose of criminal and immigration laws against domestic violence is to protect victims of domestic abuse. The VAWA provides relief to immigrant victims by empowering them to obtain immigration status independent of their abusers. In order to qualify for this relief as a VAWA applicant, however, the applicant must meet statutory requirements that include proof that they have good moral character, a requirement that may not be met if the immigrant women are prosecuted as perpetrators of domestic violence. At the present time, no mechanism exists in either criminal or immigration law to evaluate whether a domestic violence conviction should lead to a loss of VAWA eligibility.

Furthermore, there is no guidance in either body of law to evaluate the woman's motivation. In addition, a further complication emerges because under the new immigration law's definition many domestic violence crimes constitute aggravated felonies.

While some women obtain relief under the current system, many more find themselves left in the shadows and precluded from relief. New methods of treating the issues presented by the victims must emerge to assist them in moving from the margins into a place where their interests can be met. This transition can only occur by confronting the limitations that emerge when their reality is overlooked.

This article focuses on the barriers to relief which emerge from well-intentioned, anti-domestic violence reforms adopted and implemented in the immigration and criminal law. * * *

IV. THE COLLISION COURSE FOR JUSTICE

Domestic violence advocates, and the policies that they urge, assume women are victims and men are perpetrators. In fact, domestic violence advocates note that ninety-four percent of abuse is male against female. The application of aggressive anti-domestic violence laws, however, has caught many unintended victims in its net. In jurisdictions which have adopted mandatory arrest policies, the arrests of women for domestic violence have increased dramatically.

In Tarrant County, Texas, ten to fifteen percent of the domestic violence cases each year involve female defendants. In Los Angeles, the rate has more than doubled in five years, and women accounted for 14.3% of the domestic arrests made in 1995. These findings are consistent with a 1998 study conducted by the National Institute of Justice that found between ten and fifteen percent of those arrested for battering are women.

In several jurisdictions, the Spouse Assault Replication Program (SARP) studies found an increase in the number of women arrested after the adoption of mandatory arrest policies. This trend has also adversely affected immigrant women, who are likely to be women of color. Given dual arrests occur when there is doubt about who is the primary aggressor, and because the police act in ways which discriminate against female complainants in low status areas where immigrant women of color reside, women of color are arrested more often than educated women who do not fit into stereotypes as abusers.

In fact, many immigrant women of color get caught in a no-win situation. The power dynamic precludes them from seeking outside assistance, and when they finally do affirmatively seek assistance, they are viewed as aggressive and considered the abuser. Their vulnerability is also exacerbated by the male partner's ability to negotiate the criminal justice system.

A. Case Studies: Demonstrating the Problems When the Immigrant Woman Is Arrested

As in any alleged criminal assault the actions of an accused immigrant may be characterized as self-defense, non-existent, mutual combat, or an outright assault. When the perpetrator is an immigrant, liability is complicated by the fact that there may simply be a lapse in understanding about the norm in the United States or a misinterpretation of her actions by neighbors and the police.

Notwithstanding, the underlying circumstance, an immigrant woman's involvement with the criminal justice system impedes her ability to qualify for VAWA relief because it creates problems in meeting VAWA eligibility requirements. Advocates foresaw some of the adverse effects, and argued against these provisions. As noted above, domestic violence as grounds for deportation was not adopted in the VAWA, but became so in the Illegal Immigration Reform and Immigrant Responsibility Act of 1996 (IIRIRA.)

1. Self Defense and Dual Arrest Policies

Mandatory arrest laws help women and men who are in danger of assault but at the same time they create a new category of victim, those unnecessarily arrested. Women are arrested even where the statutes limit arrests to "the primary aggressor." Additionally, in some states the statutes require an arrest of both parties when the "primary aggressor" cannot be identified. Finally, arrest is often predicated on physical injury rather than actual aggression.

Actions made in self-defense are often not considered at the initial point of contact and most arrests of women fail to evaluate when the women are acting in self-defense. Furthermore, domestic violence advocates who have "treated" female perpetrators report that most of the women in programs ordered by the court were in fact acting in self-defense. Immigrant women caught in these arrests cannot avoid adverse immigration consequences unless criminal charges are dismissed. In light of the heightened treatment of domestic violence cases this is not likely.

* * *

In the past many of these cases were handled by placing the woman into diversion or treatment programs. This form of relief was particularly helpful when dealing with women who are arrested "for defending themselves in the midst of a violent argument." Presently, many of these programs are unavailable or require admissions in criminal court which can be used against the women in immigration proceedings. In these circumstances, the possibility of arrest maintains the additional adverse consequence of reducing abuse reports. Studies indicate that it is unlikely that a woman will report further battering when they fear that they will be arrested.

* * *

2. *Non–Existent Conduct and the Retaliatory Spouse*

A second problem emerges for immigrant women who are falsely accused of criminal conduct. Abusive husbands may file false criminal charges against their spouses. In fact, some cases may be filed in retaliation for the woman leaving the abusive situation. Filing false charges against undocumented immigrants allows the abuser to show the woman that his threats to have the system work against her can be carried out. Alternatively, the husband may be the father of a mutual child with the woman. Consequently, he may use false criminal charges to obtain leverage against the woman, in child custody or support cases.

* * *

3. *The Woman as Aggressor and Mutual Conduct*

The feminist paradigm embraced by many domestic violence advocates, ignores or denies the existence of "mutual combat and female aggression." This creates a schizophrenic response which has advocates arguing that women should not be arrested regardless of probable cause. Researchers Murray Straus and Richard Gelles argue that one-half of all spousal violence is reciprocal.

Programs addressing domestic violence by women acknowledge that they act in mutual combat and as the primary aggressor. In light of this evidence, it is important to recognize that the traditional treatment of women as victims fails to appropriately deal with circumstances where the woman is in fact a perpetrator of domestic violence. Although this category of abusers is relatively small and immigrant women compose an even smaller portion within this group, the consequences for immigrant women who abuse are severe. The complexity of the woman's situation requires an analysis and approach which weigh adverse immigration consequences against the criminal justice system's goals.

* * *

V. Possible Solutions to the Problem

A. *Elimination of Good Moral Character Requirement*

The VAWA adopted procedures to allow immigrant victims of domestic abuse to terminate conditional residency status or self-petition for legal permanent residence status. In order to qualify for this relief, the victim must be a person with good moral character. A plea to either a crime of violence with a sentence of more than one year or a charge of domestic violence precludes a good moral character finding and adversely affects a prospective VAWA applicant.

This was an unforeseen consequence which has became a reality due to the intersections of competing provisions of the criminal and immigration law. To remedy this adverse consequence Congress should eliminate the good moral character requirement in the self-petitioning statute.

The absence of this requirement in self-petitioning cases will place the battered woman in the same position as any other visa holder.

An applicant under the traditional petitioning requirements need not affirmatively establish good moral character as a prerequisite to approval of the visa petition. Requiring good moral character of domestic violence victims is unreasonable and needlessly sets a barrier to relief. In advancing this amelioration, the removal of the requirement in cancellation cases is not promoted, as good moral character in cancellation cases serves a legitimate immigration control function. It does not, however, serve a legitimate function when applied to self-petitioning.

Some advocates argue that simply eliminating the new ground of deportability that was adopted in IIRIRA can resolve the good moral character problem. Even if the statute was amended to adopt this remedy, it would not provide sufficient relief. In light of the expanded aggravated felony definitions and the aggressive attitude of prosecutors of domestic violence cases the elimination of the domestic violence deportation ground is of little value. Undocumented women with spouses that use the system to lodge false complaints, and those whose conduct is not within the domestic violence provision remain unprotected.

The inequities that exist for self-petitioners arise because they are not placed in the same footing they would have been if their abusive spouses had not used immigration as an additional weapon of abuse. The elimination of the good moral character requirement places the self-petitioner on equal footing with other visa applicants. This remedy advances the goals set forth by Congress when it passed VAWA and ameliorates the adverse consequences to battered immigrant women.

B. Addressing Criminal Justice and Immigration Goals

For cases in suspension or cancellation of removal a different approach is required. The law should not perpetuate adverse consequences caused by the categorical approach. Instead immigration and criminal law goals should be evaluated and reconciled to promote protections for immigrant women who are victims of domestic violence. One manner of achieving this goal is to adopt a case by case analysis and allow criminal and immigration courts to grant judicial recommendations against deportation.

LEE J. TERAN, BARRIERS TO PROTECTION AT HOME AND ABROAD: MEXICAN VICTIMS OF DOMESTIC VIOLENCE AND THE VIOLENCE AGAINST WOMEN ACT

17 B. U. Int'l L. J. 1–9 (1999).

I. Introduction

The Immigration and Naturalization Service (INS) appealed the deportation relief of two Mexican women, Sara and Elena, arguing that the women had failed to meet the statutory requirements to forestall their deportation. The INS argued that the women did not demonstrate that their expulsion would result in extreme hardship to themselves and their children. The INS focused on the tender age of the women's children, their moderate but not lengthy residence in the United States, the absence of any involvement in their communities, and their ties to extended family in Mexico. The INS's arguments are not unusual and, in fact, are consistent with historical interpretation of hardship claims in deportation cases. However, the INS's opposition in the two women's cases is troubling because both women are victims of domestic violence and had relied on provisions of the Violence Against Women Act of 1994 (VAWA), which is designed to aid domestic violence victims.

Immigration judges had granted the applications based on findings of extreme hardship, on evidence that the women and their children had been subjected to severe physical and emotional abuse, and that they feared return to Mexico where the legal system would not afford them protection. In each case the INS appealed to the Board of Immigration Appeals (BIA), sharply criticized the courts' findings, and minimized the extent to which the women's abuse should be considered in the assessment of "extreme hardship." For example, the INS argued in Sara's case that "the immigration judge gave too much weight to the sole fact the respondent was a battered wife."

The decision of Congress to include "extreme hardship" as an eligibility standard and the INS responses in these and other cases threaten to undermine the advances made previously by VAWA to aid immigrant victims of domestic violence. Heralded as the most significant legislation to aid victims of domestic violence, VAWA was enacted in recognition of the fact that domestic violence is a serious national problem in the United States and that the undocumented immigration status of victims and their fear of deportation exacerbates domestic abuse. The immigration provisions of the law were significant because, for the first time, deportation relief was afforded specifically to battered and abused spouses and children of United States citizens and permanent residents. Additionally, undocumented victims of domestic violence were allowed to self-petition in order to become lawful residents without the assistance of their U.S. citizen or permanent resident spouse or parent. VAWA commands that immigration laws remedy rather than perpetuate violence in families of citizens and lawful permanent residents.

This article will address problems faced by undocumented women who are victims of domestic violence and who, as they seek the benefits of VAWA, attempt to prove they will suffer extreme hardship if deported. In passing the immigration provisions of VAWA, Congress intended to provide protection to battered immigrant women and to remove deportation as a tool of the abuser. The addition of "extreme hardship" as an eligibility standard is entirely inappropriate for this class of immigrants and is prone to interpretations which are unrelated to the problems and needs of domestic violence victims. Determinations in cases of battered immigrants must be based on consideration of the factors tied to domestic violence, including the nature and extent of abuse suffered by the victim and her need for support of U.S. social and legal systems.

The background of the "extreme hardship" standard and the dialogue between the agency and the federal courts over the construction and application of the term will be examined. Extreme hardship determinations mirror the struggle between the government's enforcement concerns and the ameliorative nature of the relief to which extreme hardship is tied. Historically, courts have deferred to the government's concern to control immigration by narrowly construing "extreme hardship." When the agency and reviewing courts consider whether a foreign national will suffer extreme hardship if expelled, they frequently assign little weight to the social, economic, and political conditions of the home country. Yet, for many battered immigrant women, the conditions they face abroad are a significant aspect of the hardship they and their families will suffer.

Mexican victims of domestic violence face considerable adversity if deported. This article will focus on the inappropriateness of the addition of "extreme hardship" as a requirement for VAWA applicants as illustrated by Mexican women, who account for a significant number of VAWA applicants. VAWA applications will be discussed in the context of the factors which Mexican women must set forth to convince the INS and immigration courts that they and their families will suffer "extreme hardship." For instance, Mexican women quite often cite the failure of their own country to protect victims as a major cause for their fear of deportation and their need to obtain the benefits of VAWA. While domestic violence is becoming a public issue in Mexico, it lags behind the United States in terms of providing substantive legal remedies and social services to deal with domestic abuse. Mexican women face significant barriers to protection from domestic abuse in their country. Undocumented Mexican women in the United States will encounter substantial risks if they fail in their efforts to convince government adjudicators of their concerns and they are deported.

This article concludes by offering several proposals. Congress should heed concerns raised by immigrants that the INS and immigration courts discount or ignore altogether factors relevant to undocumented victims of domestic violence. "Extreme hardship" should be removed as a standard for eligibility. Alternatively, the Department of Justice should define "extreme hardship" consistent with the purposes of the VAWA and take steps to eliminate disparate agency determinations of hardship. If retained as an eligibility standard, extreme hardship should be utilized not as a device for enforcement of immigration controls. Although the Department of Justice has recognized that "extreme hardship" should be broadly construed to encompass consideration of factors tied to domestic violence, the agency's measures are insufficient. Effective response to the needs of undocumented victims of domestic violence and the dangers posed by expulsion to countries that provide little or no protection could occur by Congress eliminating the requirement of "extreme hardship." In the alternative, the agency must adopt a new approach to making "extreme hardship" determinations in VAWA cases, one not based on a case by case consideration of multiple factors which may or may not relate to domestic violence, but one which embraces a rebuttable presumption that immigrant victims of domestic violence meet the "extreme hardship" criteria.

If Congress fails to remove "extreme hardship" as an eligibility factor in VAWA cases and the agency refuses to establish a group-specific definition of this ambiguous term, battered immigrants who are denied relief because they fail to individually prove "extreme hardship" will likely be left with few alternatives to expulsion from the United States. Avenues previously available to immigrants seeking to appeal denials of administrative decisions are now barred, as Congress has taken steps in recent legislation to drastically curtail litigation of immigration cases.

B. DOMESTIC VIOLENCE AS A HUMAN RIGHTS ISSUE

DOROTHY Q. THOMAS & MICHELE E. BEASLEY, DOMESTIC VIOLENCE AS A HUMAN RIGHTS ISSUE

58 Albany L. Rev. 1119–1134, 1140–1147 (1995).

Maria was brutally assaulted in her own kitchen in England by a man wielding two knives. He held one of the weapons at her throat, while raping her with the other. After he finished, the man doused her with alcohol and set her alight with a blow torch. Maria lived through the assault to prosecute the man, although seventy percent of her body is now covered with scars. But because they were married, he could not be charged with rape. He received a ten-year sentence for bodily injury, of which he will serve only five years.[1]

Between 1988 and 1990 in the Brazilian state of Maranhio, women registered at the main police station over 4,000 complaints of battery and sexual abuse in the home. Of those complaints, only 300—less than eight percent—were forwarded to the court for processing, and only two men were ever convicted and sent to prison.[2]

In Pakistan, Muhammad Younis killed his wife, claiming that he found her in the act of adultery. The court found his defense untrue, in part because the woman was fully dressed when she was killed, and sentenced him to life imprisonment. However, on appeal the Lahore High Court reduced his sentence to ten years at hard labor stating that the "accused had two children from his deceased wife and when accused took

---

1. Zelda Reynolds, *My Husband Had the Right To Rape Me,* The Independent, Feb. 23, 1990, at 14. It should be noted that since this case, England's House of Lords abolished the marital rape exception. *See*

Judges Nail "Lie" That Husbands Cannot Rape, The Independent, Oct. 24, 1991, at 3.

2. *Americas Watch, Human Rights Watch, Criminal Injustice: Violence Against Women in Brazil* 48–49 (1991).

the extreme step of taking her life by giving her repeated knife blows on different parts of her body she must have done something unusual to enrage him to that extent."[3]

It has been observed that "the concept of human rights is one of the few moral visions ascribed to internationally." Domestic violence violates the principles that lie at the heart of this moral vision: the inherent dignity and worth of all members of the human family, the inalienable right to freedom from fear and want, and the equal rights of men and women. Yet until recently, it has been difficult to conceive of domestic violence as a human issue under international law. We would like to explore some of the reasons why such a conceptualization has been so problematic, and how difficulties are beginning to be resolved through a combination of theory and practice. We stress that the methods of combating domestic under international law are still emerging and that the strategies set forth in this Article mark only one step in this process.

* * *

I. PROBLEMS WITH UNDERSTANDING DOMESTIC
VIOLENCE AS A HUMAN RIGHTS ISSUE

A. *The Scope of International Human Rights Law*

The concept of human rights developed largely from Western political theory of the rights of the individual to autonomy and freedom. International human rights law evolved in order to protect those individual rights from limitations that might be imposed on them by states. States are bound by international law to respect the individual rights of each and every person and are thus accountable for abuses of those rights. The aim of the human rights movement is to enforce states' obligations in this regard by denouncing violations of their duties under international law. The exclusive focus on the behavior of states confines the operation of international human rights law entirely within the public sphere.

B. *Gender–Neutral Law, Gender–Biased Application*

International human rights law is facially gender-neutral. The rights embodied in the Universal Declaration of Human Rights are defined as belonging to "all human beings," not just to men. All the major human rights instruments include sex as one of the grounds upon which states may not discriminate in enforcing the rights set forth.

Although international law is gender-neutral in theory, in practice it interacts with gender-biased domestic laws and social structures that relegate women and men to separate spheres of existence: private and public. Men exist as public, legal entities in all countries, and, barring an overt abuse by the state, participate in public life and enjoy the full extent of whatever civil and political rights exist. Women, however, are in every country socially and economically disadvantaged in practice and

3. Younis v. State, 1989 Pakistan Crim.
L.J. 1747.

in fact and in many places by law. Therefore, their capacity to participate in public life is routinely circumscribed. This gender bias, if unchallenged, becomes so embedded in the social structure that it often assumes the form of a social or cultural norm seemingly beyond the purview of the state's responsibility, rather than a violation of women's human rights for which the state is accountable. In some cases, even civil and political rights violations committed directly by state actors have been shrugged off as acceptable. For example, in 1986 a Peruvian prosecutor told an Amnesty International delegation visiting the state of Ayacucho that rape of civilian women by soldiers "was to be expected" when troops were conducting counter-insurgency operations.

When gender-neutral international human rights law is applied in these gender-biased social contexts, those making the application—both governments and nongovernmental organizations—do not necessarily challenge the gender bias embedded in the social structure or in the state's determination of its responsibilities. In past human rights practice, organizations often have not challenged the relegation of women and what happens to them in the private sphere, whether in law or in practice, and have allowed social or cultural justifications to deter them from denouncing restrictions on women's capacity to participate in public life. Even where abuses against women have occurred in realms they traditionally monitor, such as police custody, they have not consistently reported them. For example, only very recently have human rights organizations begun to report on rape of women prisoners as a form of torture. Thus, in the absence of a challenge to states' consistent relegation of women to the private sphere, application of international law can have the effect of reinforcing, and to some extent replicating, the exclusion of women's rights abuses from the public sphere and therefore from the state's international obligations. In a very real sense, gender specific abuses—even those directly attributable to states—have until recently been "privatized" internationally and either go unchallenged or are left out of human rights practice altogether.

Nowhere is the effect on international human rights practice of the public/private split more evident than in the case of domestic violence which literally happens "in private." States dismiss blatant and frequent crimes, including murder, rape, and physical abuse of women in the home, as private, family matters, upon which they routinely take no action. Moreover, the state's failure to prosecute violence against women equally with other similar crimes or to guarantee women the fundamental civil and political right to equal protection of the law without regard to sex have largely escaped international condemnation.

At least four interrelated factors have caused the exclusion of domestic violence in particular from international human rights practice: (1) traditional concepts of state responsibility under international law and practice, (2) misconceptions about the nature and extent of domestic violence and states' responses to it, (3) the neglect of equality before and equal protection of the law without regard to sex as a governing human rights principle, and (4) the failure of states to recognize their affirmative obligation to provide remedies for domestic violence crimes. These factors, independently and in relationship to one another, are beginning to change and, with them, so is the treatment of domestic violence under international law. The following sections attempt to trace the course and direction of this emerging change.

C.   The Concept of State Responsibility

The concept of state responsibility defines the limits of a government's accountability for human rights abuses under international law. Of course, all acts are done by real people, individually or with others, and not by the fictive "person" of the state. Therefore, responsibility is generally understood to arise only when an act by a real person or persons can be imputed to the state. Traditionally, the idea of vicarious responsibility for acts is a perfectly acceptable one: such responsibility flows from the authorized acts of agents of the state, or persons acting with the apparent authority or condonation of the state. In traditional human rights practice states are held accountable only for what they do directly or through an agent, rendering acts of purely private individuals—such as domestic violence crimes, outside the scope of state responsibility.

More recently, however, the concept of state responsibility has expanded to include not only actions directly committed by states, but also states' systematic failure to prosecute acts committed either by low-level or para-state agents or by private actors. In these situations, although the state does not actually commit the primary abuse, its failure to prosecute the abuse amounts to complicity in it. For instance, in three significant cases, *Velasquez*, *Godinez* and *Fairen*, and *Solis*, decided by the Inter–American Court on Human Rights in 1988–1989, the tribunal found that the government of Honduras was responsible for a series of forced disappearances carried out between 1981 and 1984 by members of be Honduran military who were acting as private individuals.

The test of the state's responsibility for an act differs depending upon whether the actor is the state or a private individual. To hold a state accountable for the actions of state actors, one of two things must be shown: (1) the state explicitly authorized the act (*i.e.*, a senior official committed or authorized it), or (2) the state systematically failed to prosecute abuses committed by its agent, whether or not these acts were ordered by senior officials. In the latter case, one must usually show a pattern of nonprosecution of acts that violate human rights, and that the state has agreed to enforce those human rights. For example, the state is responsible if it fails systematically to prohibit or prosecute torture, because the right to be free from torture is guaranteed under international law. Governments have agreed not to torture people themselves and have undertaken to ensure that no one else in the state tortures. If the state failed to prosecute torturers, it would violate its international obligations.

The test is different when the actors are private. For example, systematic nonenforcement of laws against armed robbery by private actors alone is not a human rights problem; it merely indicates a serious common crime problem. Nonprosecution of the crimes of private individuals becomes a human rights issue (assuming no state action or direct complicity) only if the reason for the state's failure to prosecute can be shown to be rooted in discrimination along prohibited lines, such as those set forth in Article 26 of the Covenant on Civil and Political Rights.

There are rights to bodily integrity in international human rights law which armed robbery appears to violate. However, these are rights *against the state*, not rights that states must enforce against all other persons. States *cannot* be held directly accountable for violent acts of all private individuals *because all* violent crime would then constitute a human rights abuse for which states could be held directly accountable under international law. The state's international obligation with regard to the acts of private individuals is to ensure that where it does protect people's lives, liberty, and security against private depredations, it must do so without discrimination on prohibited grounds. Therefore, there would have to be systematic, discriminatory nonenforcement of the domestic criminal law against murder or assault for domestic violence to constitute a human rights issue, not merely a showing that the victims' lives ended or their bodies were harmed.

The expansion of state responsibility to include accountability for some acts of private individuals as defined above is one of the factors necessary to permit analysis of domestic violence as a human rights violation. However, in many cases it is also necessary to show a pattern of discriminatory nonprosecution which amounts to a failure to guarantee equal protection of the law to women victims. The following section is an overview of new information about the vast extent of violence experienced by women and the frequency of its non-or discriminatory prosecution, which was revealed as a general characteristic, not merely a rare anomaly of domestic criminal law.

D.   Widespread Violence and a Pattern of Nonprosecution

As noted, domestic violence generally has been understood as a "private" matter in which governments should not interfere and for which they are not accountable. Traditionally the home has been idealized as a place of safety and security, a sanctuary from duty, responsibility, and work. The relationships between members of the family were also idealized as respectful and supportive. The reality is quite different. "[M]odern studies suggest ... that far from being a place of safety, the family can be [a] 'cradle of violence' and that much of this violence is directed at the female members of the family."

New information on domestic violence has surfaced as a result of a long international campaign by women's rights groups to raise consciousness about women's issues. After successfully pushing for the inclusion of a commitment to equal rights for women in the U.N. Charter and Universal Declaration of Human Rights, women's organizations worked for the establishment of the U.N. Commission on the Status of Women and other formal mechanisms for the advancement of women's status. The Commission and affiliated nongovernmental organizations (NGOs) drafted a variety of conventions to combat discrimination against women internationally and pressed for the General Assembly to declare a Decade for Women program. It was the international resurgence of women's activism in the 1960s and 1970s, and the pressure generated by women's organizations internationally, that made the U.N. Decade for Women (1975–1985) a reality. As the Decade unfolded, women's rights activists coordinated international efforts to study the position of women in all societies and the reasons for their subordinate status. In 1985, the participants at the Final Conference of the Decade for Women in Nairobi, Kenya, reached a consensus, that violence against women

> exists in various forms in everyday life in all societies. Women are beaten, mutilated, burned, sexually abused and raped. Such violence is a major obstacle to the achievement of peace and other objectives of the decade and should be given special attention.... National machinery should be established in order to deal with the question of violence against women within the family and society.[35]

In 1989, the U.N. Commission on the Status of Women in Vienna compiled a mass of domestic violence statistics and analyses by women's rights activists and academics, and published its report, *Violence Against Women in the Family*. The report's author reviewed over 250 articles, books, and studies of various aspects of domestic violence, of which only ten had been published earlier than 1971. Furthermore, the report is only a small sample of the huge amount of new material being published about this old problem. The report concluded:

> Women ... have been revealed as seriously deprived of basic human rights. Not only are women denied equality with the balance of the world's population, men, but also they are often denied liberty and dignity, and in many situations suffer direct violations of their physical and mental autonomy.

Domestic violence has been revealed as widespread and gender specific. For example, in the United States a 1984 National Crime Survey found that women were victims of family violence at a rate three times that of men, and that of all spousal violence crimes, ninety-one percent were victimizations of women by their husbands or ex-husbands. In Colombia during 1982 and 1983, the Forensic Institute of Bogota found that out of 1,170 cases of bodily injury, twenty percent were due to marital violence against women. The Forensic Institute also determined that ninety-four percent of persons hospitalized in bodily injury cases

35. Report of the World Conference To Review and Appraise Achievements of the U.N. Decade for Women: Equality, Development and Peace, ch. 1, § A, para. 258, U.N. Doc. A/CONF. 116/ 28/Rev:1 (1986).

were battered women. In Thailand, a study in Bangkok revealed that more than fifty percent of married women were beaten regularly by their husbands. And the reported number of women killed in dowry disputes in India almost doubled between 1985 and 1987, rising from 999 reports to 1,786 reports per year.

This is only a small sampling of the information emerging on domestic violence. Certain characteristics of the problem become clear from the overall research: domestic violence is not unusual or an exception to normal private family life; the vast majority of crimes against women occur in the home and are usually committed by a spouse or relative in the form of murder, battery, or rape; and, domestic violence is endemic to all societies. The immensity of the problem has led researchers to conclude:

> If you are one of only 500 women in a population of 50 million then you have certainly been more than unlucky and there may perhaps be something very peculiar about your husband, or unusual about your circumstances, or about you; on the other hand, if you are one of 500,000 women then that suggests something very different—that there is something wrong not with a few individual men, or women, or marriages, but with the situation....[45]

If violence against women in the home is inherent in all societies, then it can no longer be dismissed as something private and beyond the scope of state responsibility. Although information about government response to this problem is still minimal, the research suggests that investigation, prosecution, and sentencing of domestic violence crimes occurs with much less frequency than other, similar crimes. As the examples at the beginning of this Article indicate, wife-murderers receive greatly reduced sentences, domestic battery is rarely investigated, and rape frequently goes unpunished. Marital rape is often not seen as a crime. These examples stand in contrast to the treatment of violent crimes against male victims (a comparison now made possible by the new data on violence against women). The widespread absence of state intervention in crimes against women is not merely the result of governments' failure to criminalize a class of behavior (since the violent acts themselves usually *are* crimes), but rather is the result of governments' failure to enforce laws equitably across gender lines. The next section explains how gender discrimination in enforcement of criminal law constitutes a human rights issue and applies that analysis to domestic violence.

E. The Underlying Right to Equal Protection of the Law

As indicated above, the inclusion within the limits of state responsibility of failure to prosecute human rights abusers, whether by state agents or private individuals, is not—in and of itself—enough to position domestic violence within the human rights framework. Evidence of a state's failure to prosecute is not sufficient *unless a pattern can be shown*

45. Elizabeth Wilson, The Existing Research into Battered Women 5–6 (1976).

*that reveals the failure to be gender discriminatory and thereby a viola-
tion of the internationally guaranteed right to equal protection of the law.*
However, even though increased research into and understanding of
domestic violence indicated that states were discriminating against wom-
en in the enforcement of criminal laws, gender discrimination under
international law was not a central human rights concern.

Until recently, sex discrimination has been visibly absent from the
agendas of most governmental and nongovernmental bodies concerned
with human rights, with the exception of the Committee on the Elimination of All Forms of Discrimination Against Women, the U.N. body
which monitors state conduct under the Convention on the Elimination
of All Forms of Discrimination Against Women. The Committee and the
other women's rights bodies located in Vienna have undertaken landmark work in holding governments accountable for discrimination on
the basis of sex, whether by commission or omission. These organizations have made notable progress despite insufficient resources and
limited enforcement mechanisms in the instruments they oversee.

However and more importantly for the purposes of this Article, the
mainstream Geneva-based human rights bodies, which oversee instruments that have stronger protective mechanisms, have used the existence of this separate women's human rights regime as an excuse to
marginalize sex discrimination and most other women's human rights
violations, which nonetheless fall clearly within their own mandates.
Within the cumulative human rights practice of governments and governmental bodies, sex discrimination has been deemphasized and placed
outside the rubric of central human rights concerns. International non-
governmental human rights organizations, including the two largest
groups, Amnesty International and Human Rights Watch, have until
recently reflected and perpetuated this trend.

By failing to focus on the sex-discriminatory practices of governments, human rights organizations have neither challenged the broadest
form of sex discrimination that relegates women and what happens to
them to the "private" sphere, nor denounced one of its immediate
effects: governments' devaluation of women and their resulting failure to
prosecute violence against women equally with other similar crimes.
Instead, human rights organizations have allowed a pattern of discriminatory nonprosecution of such violence to flourish unchecked. This is
uncharacteristic because in other areas where governments discriminate
on a prohibited basis, such as race or ethnicity, NGO interventions have
been effective in exposing and reversing these violations. However, in
the case of domestic violence, the widespread failure by states to prosecute such violence and to fulfill their international obligations to guarantee women equal protection of the law has gone largely undenounced.

Ultimately, women's rights activists internationally condemned
many of the international governmental and nongovernmental human
rights bodies for gender bias and, among other things, for their failure to
adequately promote and protect women's rights to nondiscrimination

and equal protection of the law. Largely as a result of this increasing pressure from women's rights activists internationally, and heightened awareness of the extent of violence against women and government tolerance of it, the nongovernmental human rights of nations began to highlight these issues within their overall human rights practice.

These separate but interrelated developments have allowed domestic violence to be placed within the context of international human rights law and practice. Developments in the concept of state responsibility, new information about the gender-specific nature of domestic violence, its pervasiveness and frequent non-or discriminatory prosecution by governments, and a new emphasis on equal protection of the law as a central human rights concern have made it possible to conceptualize domestic violence as a human rights issue and to hold governments accountable for the pervasive abuse of women worldwide. In addition, there is a nascent movement to interpret international human rights law to assign accountability directly to governments for their failure to protect women from what has been revealed to be the leading form of violence experienced by women everywhere.

Although not all states have acknowledged that they have an underlying obligation to provide substantive protection to women from domestic violence, there is support in international human rights jurisprudence for the idea that states have an affirmative obligation to criminalize domestic violence. For example, in the case of *X and Y v. The Netherlands*, Y, a mentally handicapped girl was allegedly sexually assaulted by someone at the private facility where she lived. Her father, Mr. X, attempted to file a claim on her behalf with the local police, but they rejected it because the girl did not file it herself. Mr. X brought suit under the European Convention on Human Rights. The European Court on Human Rights found that "although article 8 [of the European Convention] is primarily concerned with protecting individuals from arbitrary interference by public authorities, it also may impose positive obligations on contracting states to insure effective respect for private and family life." Article 8 of the European Convention is equivalent to Article 17 of the Covenant on Civil and Political Rights and Article 12 of the Universal Declaration of Human Rights, which both contain the further guarantee of the protection of law against such interference or attacks. These provisions, if interpreted as was their sister provision by the European Court, would seem to provide direct shelter from domestic violence crimes, in addition to the indirect shelter already provided by the equal protection provisions contained in every human rights instrument.

This language would seem to indicate that there is some obligation under international human rights law to at least provide a real remedy for private violence that extends beyond the duty to provide equal protection. The European Court described the general parameters of that duty in the *X and Y* case, finding that while recourse to criminal law might not always be required to "ensure effective respect for private and family life," sexual assault "involved [such] fundamental values and essential aspects of private life" that effective deterrence was particularly crucial. Domestic violence might similarly be said to violate fundamental values of personal safety in one's private life, and thus similarly require that states provide recourse to victims through provisions of criminal law.

While states may not always bear responsibility for the violent acts of private individuals, this case implies that the rights contained in the major human rights documents do establish state responsibility for more than just equal protection with regard to abuse committed by private actors. This interpretation is borne out by Article 2 of the Covenant on Civil and Political Rights that requires each state party "to ensure to all individuals within its territory and subject to its jurisdiction the rights recognized in the present covenant" and provides that the state "adopt such legislative or other measures as may be necessary to give effect to the rights recognized in the present Covenant."

However, although approaches to combating domestic violence through the application of human rights law are still evolving, this point of view is far from universally held. So far, application of human rights law to domestic violence has used an equal protection framework. One practical application of this equal protection methodology, as explained above, is examined in the following section. It describes the first time an international human rights organization used human rights law to condemn a state's systematic nonprosecution of domestic violence crimes by analyzing that nonprosecution as a violation of the fundamental right to equal protection without regard to sex.

* * *

III.   Conclusions: the Limits and Value of the Equal Protection Human Rights Approach to Combating Domestic Violence

A.   *Practical Problems*

Human rights practice is a method of reporting facts to promote change. The influence of nongovernmental human rights organizations is intimately linked to the rigor of their research methodology. One typical method of reporting human rights violations in specific countries is to investigate individual cases of human rights violations through interviews with victims and witnesses, supported by information about the abuse from other credible sources.

Analysis of domestic violence as a human rights abuse depends not only on proving a pattern of violence, but also on demonstrating a systematic failure by the state to afford women equal protection of the law against that violence. Without detailed statistical information concerning both the incidence of wife-murder, battery, and rape, and the criminal justice system's response to those crimes, it can be difficult to make a solid case against a government for its failure to guarantee equal protection of the law. And inadequate documentation of human rights abuses against women is common to countries throughout the world.

As noted earlier, information about the nature and extent of domestic violence has only been available for a short time. For example, in Brazil, although anecdotal evidence of an overwhelming incidence of domestic violence exists, hard facts or large scale surveys of specific aspects of spousal murder, battery, or rape have often been hard to obtain, or altogether unavailable. At present, national homicide data by gender has not been collected, and statistics regarding battery and rape, where available, are usually compiled by hand and rarely in a systematic way. In addition, individual cases have not always been well documented or pursued beyond the original report that the abuse occurred—there is often no information about how the government responded, particularly as regards prosecution and sentencing.

Inadequate documentation is a function of another practical problem which is equally common internationally: the lack of cooperation between women's rights and human rights groups on both national and international levels. In Brazil, for example, the human rights and women's rights groups had no history at all of working together and, in fact, often saw their aims as antagonistic. For example, efforts to emphasize the equal rights of women in the context of the struggle against military dictatorship were often perceived by the human rights community as divisive and marginal to the central issue of creating a non-oppressive (and in this case, democratic) form of government. As a result of this split, human rights organizations lack information pertaining to violations of women's rights, and women's rights organizations often have neither the training nor the resources to document abuses as required to make a case under international law.

One of the important practical advances resulting from field work on women's human rights was the realization that to address abuses against women adequately in the context of international human rights practice, women's rights organizations and human rights organizations at national and international levels need to work together to locate and develop the data and methods necessary for the rigorous fact-finding and analysis on which human rights reporting is based.

Given attention and concerted effort, these and other emerging practical problems can be overcome. However, some profound methodological limits to the human rights approach must also be examined and addressed.

B. Methodological Limitations

In addition to the quality of its facts, the efficacy of the human rights method depends on the solidity of the legal principles on which arguments are made that governments are in violation of their international obligations and should change their practices. Consequently, changes in methodology must be developed from those legal principles or they will be ineffective to condemn states.

The most general methodological problem with applying human rights to domestic violence is not specific to domestic violence *per se*, but is a function of the general focus of human rights law: international human rights law is law that binds states, not law that binds individuals. As was discussed at length in Part I, the focus of human rights law on states and the fact that domestic violence, and other abuses of women's human rights, are often committed by private individuals, at present necessitates a complicated analysis to demonstrate state accountability. The requirements of building a case for state responsibility can appear daunting, particularly when coupled with the documentary problems detailed above.

Another limitation is that human rights practice tends to focus on individual acts (whether by state or non-state actors) and not on the causes of those acts. Documentation of a government's failure to prosecute domestic violence does not directly address the causes of that violence, which are rooted in social, economic, and legal structures that discriminate against women, and in widely-held attitudes about women's lesser status. The inability, in current human rights practice, to hold governments accountable for the broad economic and social inequities that underlie domestic violence has at least two consequences. First, it may lead governments to the false conclusion that all they need to do to eliminate domestic violence is prosecute aggressors equally with other violent criminals. Second, it largely limits human rights organizations to denouncing abuses after they have already occurred, when the victim is hurt or dead.

Put another way, it is very difficult to use the human rights approach to prevent domestic violence. Positive state responsibilities such as education or economic support programs, which might help eliminate the causes of domestic violence, are less clearly prescribed by international law than prohibitions against certain abuses, even where the state may be domestically obligated to undertake certain functions. It is one thing for a human rights organization to address the state's discriminatory application of law; it is quite another to direct a state to adopt a particular social program to change discriminatory attitudes. The first instance is, in a sense, a "negative" injunction, one to stop violations of international human rights law; the second is a "positive" exhortation to adopt a particular policy. The latter statement has a more amorphous basis in international legal principles and requires a less straightforward remedy. It is more difficult for an international human rights organization to be persuasive positively than negatively.

Increasingly, the positive responsibilities of states are being incorporated into international human rights law and practice. The Convention on the Elimination of All Forms of Discrimination Against Women (CEDAW), for example, requires governments to take positive measures to end legal, social, and economic gender inequality. The international human rights community has not yet reached a consensus about the ability of human rights organizations to advocate positions measures, or about states' responsibility under international law to take such actions. However, as the concept of state responsibility in international law evolves further, human rights organizations may more easily hold governments accountable for failing actively to counter the social, economic, and attitudinal biases which underpin and perpetuate domestic violence.

Finally, and perhaps most importantly, the current human rights approach to domestic violence and state responsibility only addresses the problem of equal protection; it usually cannot hold governments accountable for the domestic violence itself, just as it could not hold governments accountable internationally for other violent crimes committed by private individuals. Given the current state of international human rights jurisprudence, the nondiscrimination approach most closely resembles current thinking as regards state responsibility for private actions. However, it is possible to derive concepts of direct state accountability for private acts from human rights law, as we discussed above, and it might be preferable to undertake such an analytic endeavor.

Addressing the state's responsibility for domestic violence *per se* would entail investigating in more detail the particular characteristics of domestic violence, as distinguished from other violent crime. To some extent domestic violence is not random, that is, it is directed at women because they are women and is committed to impede women from exercising their rights. As such, it is an essential factor in maintaining women's subordinate status, as well as in the resulting domestic and international privatization of gender-specific abuse, the problem with which this Article began and which the integration of women's rights into human rights practice seeks to counter. In this sense, domestic violence is different from other violent crimes. Treating domestic violence as merely an issue of equal protection, and by inference therefore, setting up the treatment of men as the standard by which we ought to measure the treatment of women in our societies, may in fact disserve women and mask the ways in which domestic violence is not just another common crime. The norm of gender neutrality itself, embodied in the human rights treaties and international customary law, may unintentionally reinforce gender bias in the law's application and obscure the fact that human rights laws ought to deal directly with gender-specific abuse, and not just gender-specific failures to provide equal protection. The gender-neutral norm may appear to require only identical treatment of men and women, when in fact, equal treatment in many cases is not adequate.

These limitations to the approach used in the Brazil case study are grave. However, they should not obscure the viability of the equal protection approach and the important step that was taken in using human rights law in any capacity to address domestic violence. Nor should they detract from the real value to using human rights law in general as a tool to combating violence against women in the home.

C. *Value of the Human Rights Approach*

The practical and methodological problems outlined above are not an inherent deterrent to integrating domestic violence into human rights practice. To identify practical obstacles and understand the methodological limits of the current human rights approach is to expand human rights practice, which is far from static, that much further. Moreover, to understand the limits of the human rights approach is also to clarify the particular contributions it *can make* as part of broader local and international efforts to combat domestic violence.

"Human rights is a prominent subject of international diplomacy," and nongovernmental international human rights organizations have great prestige and influence. Heads of state pay significant attention to the findings, and recommendations of such NGOs, even if only to deny their validity, and states regularly monitor whether other states have successfully met their international obligations to uphold their citizens' human rights. Human rights activists have shown the effectiveness of prompting governments to curb human rights violations by aiming the spotlight of public scrutiny on the depredations. Therefore, the potential power of the human rights machinery to combat domestic violence is a strong incentive to use this approach.

The human rights approach employs a pre-existing international system to bring pressure to bear on governments that routinely fail to prosecute domestic violence equally, with other similar crimes. This provides an opportunity for local institutions and activists to supplement their efforts with support from the international community. The effect is twofold: local struggles are enhanced and domestic protections available to women may improve. For example, following the publication of the Brazil report discussed above, and the surrounding activism by local women's and human rights groups, the state of Rio initiated training programs in domestic violence with women's rights activists and local police. In addition, the report's release encouraged efforts in Sao Paulo to draft a state convention to eliminate discrimination against women. It also served as a catalyst to further research in Brazil on the "legitimate defense of honor" and on the criminal justice system's failure to punish domestic violence crimes. Finally, it provided an opportunity for local women's rights and human rights organizations to cooperate in these efforts.

The human rights approach to domestic violence may also have the effect of improving international protections for women. Although, until recently, "women's issues" have been seen as marginal to the "real" issues of human rights, placing domestic violence within the mainstream of the theory and practice of international human rights draws attention to the extent and seriousness of the problem. This not only points out the past failure of the human rights community adequately to counter the problem, but brings to light the urgent need for the international human rights system to function more effectively on behalf of women.

The most compelling advantage to utilizing a human rights approach to oppose domestic violence may be that it simultaneously raises women's issues in the mainstream of human rights practice, while it broadens the mainstream's perceived scope. Applying this approach to domestic violence produces the insight that the incorporation of women's rights issues into human rights practice is a revolutionary and evolutionary process, and that the process itself will provide new ideas and identify unsuspected obstacles at each step along the way. Together with developments in other areas of law and activism, this dynamic ultimately may help transform the international human rights system so that it honors the Universal Declaration of Human Rights and protects more than just the rights of man.

RADHIKA COOMARASWAMY, VIOLENCE AGAINST WOMEN IN THE FAMILY, INTEGRATION OF THE HUMAN RIGHTS OF WOMEN AND THE GENDER PERSPECTIVE: VIOLENCE AGAINST WOMEN

United Nations Commission on Human Rights.
Fifty-fifth session, E/CN, 4/1999/68, 10–11, 39, 10 March 1999.

IV. FINDINGS

A. *General Trends*

28. In the spring of 1998, the (UN) Special Rapporteur (on Violence Against Women) sent a note *verbale* to governments, requesting them to provide her with information about initiatives taken with regard to violence against women in the family. Subsequently, she sought the same information from non-governmental sources. In both governmental and non-governmental responses, there were common trends, positive and negative. Overwhelmingly, governments presented a picture which suggested that they are taking steps, as small as they may sometimes be, to address violence in the family. Governments have begun to acknowledge that violence against women in the family is a serious social issue that should be confronted. Formal provisions and policies have been adopted in many states.

29. The Special Rapporteur would like to highlight the encouraging trend in Latin America and the Caribbean to adopt specific legislation on domestic or intra-family violence. Thus far in the 1990s, 12 Latin American and Caribbean countries have adopted such legislation. The Special Rapporteur welcomes these initiatives and encourages governments to ensure effective implementation.

30. Generally, as testified to in non-governmental submissions from all regions, however, there is a lack of coordination between the state and civil society in working towards the effective implementation of formal provisions and policies. While some states make an active attempt to consult and include civil society representatives in the process of developing and implementing laws and policies, others have maintained a distant and, at times, antagonistic relationship with non–governmental organizations (NGOs). Overwhelmingly, governments lack the necessary expertise to develop and implement policy relating to violence against women. Government actors generally, and those within the criminal justice system in particular, continue to subscribe to outdated myths about the role of women in society and the family, and about causes of

violence in the family. Systematic training and gender awareness programmes are essential if policies are to be implemented by the criminal justice system.

31. Many states continue to make the erroneous link between alcohol and violence. While alcohol does in many cases exacerbate violence, alcohol does not itself cause violence against women. The focus on alcohol or drugs, rather than on male patriarchal ideology, which has as its ultimate expression male violence against women, undermines the anti-violence movement. Further, resources that should be allocated for support, training and systems' development in respect to family violence against women, is instead allocated to combat alcohol and drug use and provide services to alcoholics and drug-abusers. While such services may be necessary, they should not detract from resource support for violence against women programming.

32. Increasingly. states are using cultural relativist claims to avoid responsibility for positive, anti-violence action. The recognition of heterogeneous or multicultural communities is not at odds with developing comprehensive and multifaceted strategies to combat domestic violence. In all communities, the root causes of domestic violence are similar, even when the justifications for such violence or the forms of such violence vary.

33. Many Governments continue to classify women, children, the elderly, the disabled or any combination of these together as one social group. This arises from the paternal nature of the state, which seeks to protect "vulnerable" groups. While distinct measures must be developed to combat violence against women and provide remedies and support to victim-survivors, the emphasis must be on empowerment rather than care—on social justice rather than social welfare. Women must be treated, in fact and in law, as full citizens, endowed with rights and reason.

34. There is a continuing emphasis on mediation and counselling by police or mediation boards in cases of violence in the family. Police efforts to counsel victims in such cases, which often includes mediation between victim and perpetrator, may serve to undermine the seriousness of crimes of violence against women and, in many instances, may heighten the risk for the victim. While the police, as the gatekeepers to the criminal justice system, are in a unique position to link victims with support structures, police officers should not themselves serve as counsellors or mediators. This confuses the role of the police in the minds of the community and may send a message to the victim of domestic violence that the violence perpetrated against her is not serious enough to warrant the intervention of the criminal justice system.

* * *

V. Conclusion

242. Overwhelmingly, states are failing in their international obligations to prevent, investigate and prosecute violence against women in

the family. While there are encouraging moves to create and implement new policies, procedures and laws with respect to violence against women generally, and domestic violence specifically, such violence does not appear to command governments' attention. National policies continuously fail to give priority and force to women's human rights. Women continue to be viewed and treated as second-class citizens with a secondary rights status. Violence against women is overwhelmingly viewed as a "woman's" issue rather than a serious human rights issue which affects a large percentage of any country's population. With few exceptions, domestic violence continues, to varying degrees, to be treated by governments as a private family matter.

243. The non-governmental sector is charged with the double burden of undertaking their own programming, while simultaneously pressuring the government to fulfill its obligations with respect to women's human rights. The quest for effective mechanisms to combat violence against women in the family is not and cannot be the sole responsibility of women's NGOs. Rather, the eradication of violence against women is the responsibility of governments. Equality, political, social and economic participation, and development are all seriously undermined by the continuing and growing prevalence of violence against women generally and domestic violence specifically. Governments must take every possible step, in consultation and collaboration with activists, academics and other experts, to prevent, investigate and prosecute violence against women in the family and provide support and remedies to victim-survivors of such violence.

C. ASYLUM

IN RE R–A–, BRIEF OF *AMICI CURIAE* IN SUPPORT OF REQUEST FOR CERTIFICATION AND REVERSAL OF THE DECISION OF THE BOARD OF IMMIGRATION APPEALS

Before the United States Department of Justice, Attorney General Janet Reno, January 21, 2000, 1–12, 36–37.

This brief is submitted by one hundred *amici curiae* in support of the request by petitioner R–A–P that the Attorney General certify and reverse *In re R–A–* (Interim Decision No. 3403), a decision of the Board of Immigration Appeals (the "Board" or the "BIA") denying Ms. A–'s application for asylum despite an undisputed record of years of severe domestic violence and the failure of the government of Guatemala to respond to her repeated efforts to attain protection from this abuse. The Board's decision should be reversed because its refusal to acknowledge that domestic violence can be "on account of" gender represents a radical departure from both the Board's own asylum jurisprudence and the widely accepted understanding of domestic violence in international human rights and asylum law, domestic civil rights law, and the sociological and psychological literature.

STATEMENT OF INTEREST OF THE *AMICI CURIAE*

This brief is submitted on behalf of a coalition of 51 organizations and 49 law teachers who have experience as legal advocates and scholars in the immigration and domestic violence fields. Based on our extensive experience and expertise in these areas, we believe that the Board's approach to domestic violence is inconsistent with both well-established principles of international and domestic law and the realities of domestic violence as it is generally understood by professionals in various fields and directly experienced by its victims. Individual statements of interest on behalf of each of the organizations and individuals are attached as Appendix A to this brief.

THE BOARD'S DECISION

The material facts of this case are undisputed. Among the Board's own express findings with respect to the domestic violence inflicted on Ms. A– were that:

• Ms. A–'s husband was "domineering and violent" and "[f]rom the beginning of the marriage . . . engaged in physical and sexual abuse of" Ms. A–.

• "[T]he record strongly indicates that he would have abused any woman, regardless of nationality, to whom he was married."

• "There is little doubt that [Ms. A–'s husband] believed that married women should be subservient to their own husbands."

• Statements made by Ms. A–'s husband, such as "You're my woman and I can do whatever I want," and—in response to Ms. A–'s protests while being sexually assaulted—"You're my woman, you do what I say," "may well reflect his own view of women and, in particular, his view of the respondent as his property to do with as he pleased."

• The acts of violence occurred "whenever [Ms. A–'s husband] felt like it, wherever he happened to be: in the house, on the street, on the bus" and included such plainly gender-specific acts as "dislocat[ing Ms. A–'s] jaw bone when her menstrual period was 15 days late," "kick[ing] her violently in her spine" when "she refused to abort her 3–to 4–month-old fetus," "kick[ing her] in her genitalia, causing [Ms. A–] to bleed severely for 8 days," as well such acts as pistol-whipping her, breaking windows and a mirror with her head, "grab[bing] her head and strik[ing] furniture with it," throwing a machete at her hands, and whipping her with an electrical cord.

• Ms. A–'s husband raped her " 'almost daily' . . . caus[ing] her severe pain" and "would beat her before and during the unwanted sex" and "forcefully sodomize[ ] her."

• Ms. A–'s husband insisted that she "accompany him wherever he went, except when he was working" and he "escorted [her] to her workplace, and . . . would often wait to direct her home."

• When Ms. A– ran away to her brother's and parents' home, "her husband always found her" and, on at least one occasion, beat her unconscious. He reportedly has threatened to " 'hunt her down and kill her if she comes back to Guatemala.' "

• "[T]he level and frequency of [Ms. A–'s husband's] rage increased concomitantly with the seeming senselessness and irrationality of his motives" and "there [was] nothing the respondent could have done to have satisfied her husband and prevented further abuse."

• "He harmed her, when he was drunk and when he was sober, for not getting an abortion, for his belief that she was seeing other men, for not having her family get money for him, for not being able to find something in the house, for leaving a cantina before him, for leaving him, for reasons related to his mistreatment in the army, and 'for no reason at all.' "

Based on the record, the Board concluded that Ms. A– had suffered "severe injuries" that were "more than sufficient" to constitute persecution and that she was unable to avail herself of the protection of the government of Guatemala. Nevertheless, it rejected her claim that she had been persecuted "on account of" membership in a "particular social group" on two grounds. First, the Board rejected the social group that had been adopted by the Immigration Judge: "Guatemalan women who have been involved intimately with Guatemalan male companions, who believe that women are to live under male domination." It declined, however, even to address the other gender-based social groups that had been proposed by Ms. A–, merely making the conclusory assertion that it was unnecessary to do so because "each of them fails on this record under the 'on account of,' or nexus, requirement of the statute." The Board then found that the persecution of Ms. A– was not "on account of" her membership in the particular social group defined by the Immigration Judge because Ms. A–'s husband did not target women in that group but "would have abused *any* woman ... to whom he was married." (emphasis added). In addition, the Board found that Ms. A–'s testimony that the abuse was arbitrary, unprovoked, and often inflicted "for no reason at all" undercut her claim that her husband "sought to overcome" the characteristics of her proposed gender-based social groups. Rejecting the view that "societal attitudes" in Guatemala with respect to domestic violence and the status of women and wives might be relevant in construing the motivations of Ms. A–'s husband, the Board concluded that the severe abuse inflicted on Ms. A– had not been on account of her membership in a particular social group. The Board did not, however, propose any other plausible purpose for the violence, merely concluding that "some abuse occurred because of [her husband's] warped perception of and reaction to her behavior, while some likely arose out of psychological disorder, pure meanness, or no apparent reason at all."

SUMMARY OF ARGUMENT

The Board's approach to domestic violence in this case is fundamentally at odds with both its own prior jurisprudence and the widespread understanding that such violence is often—indeed, typically—directed at women "on account of" their gender. Gender-specific persecution, including domestic violence, has increasingly been recognized both internationally and in the United States as a human rights violation and a basis for asylum. However, the Board here refused to give any meaningful consideration to what its own findings make indisputably clear: that Ms. A–'s husband persecuted her because she was a woman, because she was his wife, and because she refused to conform to the gender stereotypes that he violently imposed on her.

Under the Board's own jurisprudence, persecution "on account of . . . membership in a particular social group" requires that the "particular social group" be defined by an innate or immutable characteristic, a past status that is unalterable due to its historical permanence, or a voluntary association that is entered into for reasons fundamental to the individual's dignity or identity. There can be no question that gender satisfies this test, either standing alone or in combination with either a past or present marital or other intimate relationship or a refusal to conform to socially sanctioned norms. Nevertheless, the Board failed even to consider these bases for Ms. A–'s "social group" claim.

Similarly, the Board, as well as federal courts, have recognized that a determination of whether persecution is "on account of" a statutory ground requires reasonable inferences from the nature and circumstances of the persecutor's conduct and a sensitivity to the social context and cultural meaning of those acts. In addition, a statutory ground—such as membership in a gender-based social group—need only be shown to be one of the persecutor's motivating factors. Here, by contrast, the Board simply closed its eyes to the overwhelming direct evidence that the persecution of Ms. A– was not only partly, but largely, gender motivated.

The Board's flawed analysis demonstrates the importance of requiring that fact finders in asylum proceedings be guided by the consensus of professionals across a wide variety of fields that domestic violence is a purposeful act, typically motivated by a desire to dominate and control a female intimate partner and to enforce and punish deviations from socially accepted gender stereotypes. As courts have done in applying the analogous requirement of the civil rights provision of the Violence Against Women Act, gender motivation should be readily inferred from the character and circumstances of the abuse itself. Thus, persecution in the form of domestic violence should be found to be "on account of" membership in a gender-based social group whenever the evidence fails to support some other plausible explanation that fully accounts for the nature, severity, or repeated character of the violence. No such explanation has—or could—be offered for the abuse of Ms. A–.

I. The Board's Approach to Gender–Based Violence Ignores Recent Developments in International and Domestic Human Rights and Asylum Law.

Both the United States and the international community have taken substantial steps in recent years toward recognizing the gravity of gender-related persecution and have specifically recognized that domestic violence can be a basis for an asylum claim. The position taken by the Board—that there is no nexus between Ms. A–'s persecution by her spouse and her membership in a gender-based social group—is inconsistent with this growing international consensus, as well as the Immigration and Naturalization Service's ("INS's") own recent efforts toward rectifying long-standing inequities in the treatment of male and female asylum claimants.

A critical element in the development of women's human rights has been the recognition that the serious harms women suffer typically are the result of cultural or customary practices and that these harms are often imposed at the hands of members of the woman's family or community. Consequently, the rights of women traditionally have been ignored or characterized as private and personal matters, often resulting in the exclusion of women from national and international protection altogether.

In recent years, however, those harms more typically perpetrated against women and girls have come to be viewed in the international human rights arena as important human rights concerns warranting the full protection accorded to other, more "traditional" human rights violations. As a result, many recent international human rights documents specifically address the concerns of women, and, in 1993, the United Nations General Assembly adopted a Declaration on the Elimination of Violence against Women that recognized that gender-based violence is an important human rights issue.

There has also been a parallel increase in awareness by the international community of the special needs of women and girls for protection under refugee and asylum law. In 1985, the United Nations High Commissioner for Refugees' ("UNHCR") Executive Committee first recognized that women may qualify for asylum based on membership in gender-based social groups, and it adopted a series of conclusions, throughout the late 1980s and early 1990s, aimed at affording more meaningful protection to women fleeing persecution in their home countries. More recently, the U.N. Special Rapporteur on Violence Against Women (the "Special Rapporteur") has expressed her support for the view that gender should be recognized as a "particular social group" for purposes of adjudicating asylum claims.

The tribunals of many countries—including the British House of Lords—have granted refugee protection to women based on membership in social groups defined by gender-based characteristics. Several countries, including the United States, have developed immigration policy and guidelines recognizing gender-based asylum claims, or have specifically adopted the position that gender is an appropriate characteristic defining a "particular social group" for asylum purposes.

In addition, there has been a growing recognition in the international community that domestic violence is an important human rights issue and a basis for asylum. For example, the 1993 Declaration on the

Elimination of Violence against Women expressly recognized the importance of eliminating domestic violence in order to advance the human rights of women. Similarly, in her 1996 *Report on Violence Against Women in the Family,* the Special Rapporteur specifically recommended that refugee and asylum laws be interpreted "to include gender-based claims of persecution, including domestic violence." As she observed, "[d]espite the apparent neutrality of the term, domestic violence is nearly always a gender-specific crime, perpetrated by men against women" and "*is directed primarily at women with the intention of depriving them of a range of rights and maintaining their subordination as a group.*"

Consistent with this view that domestic violence is targeted at women based on their gender, parties to the U.N. Convention/Protocol (from which United States asylum law is derived) have granted claims to refugee status based on domestic violence. For example, domestic violence as a ground for refugee protection is well established in Canadian case law, including decisions of the Canadian Immigration and Refugee Board, and the *Canadian Guidelines Update* allows for a grant of asylum based on gender-motivated domestic violence. More recently, the British House of Lords found that Pakistani women could establish claims to refugee status under the U.N. Convention/Protocol as victims of domestic violence.

Reflecting these developments in the international community, the INS took a major step toward redressing the discriminatory treatment of female asylum seekers within the United States with the issuance in 1995 of the *Consideration for Asylum Officers Adjudicating Asylum Claims for Women* (the "*INS Guidelines*"). The *INS Guidelines* set out both the procedural and substantive considerations to be applied when evaluating asylum claims brought by women applicants and explicitly state that "the evaluation of gender-based claims must be viewed within the framework provided by existing international human rights instruments and the interpretation of those instruments by international organizations." Although the *INS Guidelines* reflect important recent developments in asylum and human rights law, they do not represent a change in the law. Rather, they are an interpretation of existing law that takes into account the unique ways in which gender affects the asylum determination. Thus, they expressly recognize that women often experience types of persecution different from men and that among the types of persecution that are "particular to ... gender" and can serve as a basis for asylum is "domestic violence."

* * *

CONCLUSION

For the foregoing reasons, the *amici* respectfully request that the Attorney General grant Ms. A–'s request to certify and reverse the Board's decision in this case. Moreover, *amici* believe that the Board's failure to apply its own precedents to an asylum claim based on domestic violence and its refusal to credit the irrefutable evidence that Ms. A– was targeted for persecution because of her status as a woman and a wife demonstrates the need to set forth clear guidelines for asylum determinations based on domestic violence. These guidelines should make it clear that (*i*) persecution on account of membership in a "particular social group" defined by gender is a legally appropriate basis for asylum and (*ii*) domestic violence is gender-motivated whenever the evidence fails to support some other plausible explanation that fully accounts for the nature, severity, or repeated character of the violence.

MEMORANDUM

SUBJECT: Considerations for Asylum Officers Adjudicating
   Asylum Claims From Women
   DATE: May 26, 1995
   TO: All INS Asylum Office/rs, HQASM Coordinators
   FROM: Phyllis Coven, Office of International Affairs

pp. 1–8, 18–19

Recent international initiatives have increased awareness and suggested approaches to gender-related asylum claims. Enhancing understanding of and sensitivity to gender-related issues will improve U.S. asylum adjudications while keeping pace with these international concerns. This guidance will serve as a useful tool for new Asylum Officers, and will help to ensure uniformity and consistency in procedures and decisions. In–Service training at all Asylum Offices will be critical to using this guidance effectively.

Despite the increased attention given to this type of claim during the past decade, gender-based asylum adjudications are still relatively new developments in refugee protection. This "Considerations" memorandum is a natural and multi-faceted outgrowth of a set of gender guidelines issued by the United Nations High Commissioner on Refugees (UNHCR) in 1991, the 1993 Canadian gender guidelines, a proposed set of guidelines submitted by the Women Refugees Project of the Harvard Immigration and Refugee Program, Cambridge and Somerville Legal Services, in 1994, and recent (and still developing) U.S. caselaw. It is similar in approach to the Haiti "Considerations" memorandum of March 9, 1993 and other memoranda issued to maintain consistency among Offices and Officers. Additionally, this memorandum seeks to enhance the ability of U.S. Asylum Officers to more sensitively deal with substantive and procedural aspects of gender-related claims, irrespective of country of origin.

I.   Background and International Guidance

This section reviews the historical and human rights context in which guidance on gender-sensitive and gender-based adjudications have evolved internationally.

Human rights violations against women are not a new phenomenon. Yet, only recently have they risen to the forefront of the international agenda. Spurred by the United Nations and a handful of commentators, notably in Canada and the United States, understanding of gender-related violence in general is increasing.

The evaluation of gender-based claims must be viewed within the framework provided by existing international human rights instruments and the interpretation of these instruments by international organizations. The following international instruments and documents contain gender-related provisions that recognize and promote the principle that women's rights are human rights, and that women's rights are universal:

• CEDAW: The 1979 Convention on the Elimination of All Forms of Discrimination Against Women (CEDAW) is the most comprehensive international human rights instrument for women. CEDAW prohibits actions by States which are discriminatory and requires States to take affirmative steps to eradicate discriminatory treatment of women.

• UN DECLARATION: In June 1993, the United Nations World Conference on Human Rights emphasized the need to incorporate the rights of women as part of universal human rights, and called upon the General Assembly to adopt the Declaration on the Elimination of Violence against Women. On December 20, 1993, the United Nations General Assembly adopted the Declaration. The 1993 Declaration recognizes violence against women as both a *per se* violation of human rights and as an impediment to the enjoyment by women of other human rights.

• UNHCR CONCLUSIONS/GUIDELINES: In 1985, the UNHCR Executive Committee adopted Conclusion No. 39 noting that refugee women and girls constitute the majority of the world refugee population and that many of them are exposed to special problems. The Conclusion also recognized that States are free to adopt the interpretation that women asylum-seekers who face harsh or inhuman treatment due to their having transgressed the social mores of the society in which they live may be considered a "particular social group." In October, 1993, the UNHCR Executive Committee adopted Conclusion No. 73 on Refugee Protection and Sexual Violence. The 1993 Conclusion recognizes that asylum seekers who have suffered sexual violence should be treated with particular sensitivity, and recommends the establishment of training programs designed to ensure that those involved in the refugee status determination process are adequately sensitized to issues of gender and culture. In 1991, the Office of the High Commissioner issued its Guidelines on the Protection of Refugee Women (document EC/SCP/67). The 1991 UNHCR guidelines primarily address issues pertaining to women in refugee camps. However, the guidelines also address gender-related persecution and recommend procedures to make the refugee adjudication process more accessible to women.

• CANADIAN GUIDELINES: On March 9, 1993, the Canadian Immigration and Refugee Board (IRB) issued the ground-breaking "Guidelines on Women Refugee Claimants Fearing Gender–Related Persecution." The Canadian guidelines attracted considerable interest both in the United States and other countries because they are the first national guidelines to formally recognize that women fleeing persecution because of their gender can be found to be refugees. In developing the guidelines, the IRB carried out extensive consultations with interested governmental and non-governmental groups and individuals. More than two years after their release, the Canadian guidelines remain a model for gender-based asylum adjudications.

This is not intended to be a full compendium of international sources of gender-related instruments and documents, only illustrative of the types of initiatives which have taken place during recent years. All of these initiatives underscored and contributed to the development of international human rights and humanitarian law relating to women refugee claimants; and contributed directly to the formulation of the U.S. guidelines.

* * *

II. PROCEDURAL CONSIDERATIONS FOR U.S. ASYLUM OFFICERS

A. *Purpose and Overview*

The purpose of this section is to emphasize the importance of creating a "customer-friendly" asylum interview environment that allows women claimants to discuss freely the elements and details of their claims.

Asylum Officers should bear in mind the context of these human rights and cross-cultural considerations when dealing with women claimants:

• The laws and customs of some countries contain gender-discriminatory provisions. Breaching social mores (e.g., marrying outside of an arranged marriage, wearing lipstick or failing to comply with other cultural or religious norms) may result in harm, abuse or harsh treatment that is distinguishable from the treatment given the general population, frequently without meaningful recourse to state protection. As a result, the civil, political, social and economic rights of women are often diminished in these countries.

• Although women applicants frequently present asylum claims for reasons similar to male applicants, they may also have had experiences that are particular to their gender. A woman may present a claim that may be analyzed and approved under one or more grounds. For example, rape (including mass rape in, for example, Bosnia), sexual abuse and domestic violence, infanticide and genital mutilation are forms of mistreatment primarily directed at girls and women and they may serve as evidence of past persecution.

• Some societies require that women live under the protection of male family members. The death or absence of a spouse or other male family members may make a woman even more vulnerable to abuse.

● Women who have been raped or otherwise sexually abused may be seriously stigmatized and ostracized in their societies. They may also be subject to additional violence, abuse or discrimination because they are viewed as having brought shame and dishonor on themselves, their families, and their communities.

B.   Asylum Interviews/Officers

All INS Asylum Officers—men and women—will be expected to conduct interviews of women with gender-based claims. To the extent that personnel resources permit, however, Asylum Offices may allow women Asylum Officers to interview these cases. An interview should not generally be canceled because of the unavailability of a woman Asylum Officer. But we must also recognize that, because of the very delicate and personal issues arising from sexual abuse, some women claimants may understandably have inhibitions about disclosing past experiences to male interviewers.

Cases of this kind can often (but not always) be identified by a pre-interview reading of the Form I–589 application for asylum. Sometimes, only during the course of the asylum interview is it revealed that an applicant has suffered sexual violence. In such cases, Asylum Officers (men and women) must use their utmost care to assure that the interview continues in an atmosphere that allows for the discussion of past experiences.

C.   Interpreters/Presence of Family Members

Asylum Offices do not ordinarily have control over the interpreters chosen by asylum applicants. Testimony on sensitive issues such as sexual abuse can be diluted when received through the filter of a male interpreter. It is also not difficult to imagine the reluctance of a woman applicant to testify about sexual violence through a male interpreter, particularly if the interpreter is a family member or friend. We are hopeful that Non–Governmental Organizations (NGOs) will convey our openness to female interpreters. However, interviews should not generally be canceled and rescheduled because women with gender-based asylum claims have brought male interpreters.

Interviewing Asylum Officers should provide women with the opportunity to be interviewed outside the hearing of other members of their family, especially male family members and children. The testimonial process can be a highly stressful experience for anyone, and there is a greater likelihood that a woman applicant may more freely communicate a claim involving sexual abuse when family members are not present. Sexual violence is seen in some cultures as a failure on the part of the woman to preserve her virginity or marital dignity. Discussing her experience in front of family members may become a further source of alienation.

D. Interview Considerations

The atmosphere created during the non-adversarial asylum interview should allow for the full discussion of past experiences. Asylum Officers may have to build a rapport with an applicant to elicit claims and to enable the applicant to recount her fears and/or past experiences. Women applicants may have difficulty speaking about past experiences that are personally degrading, humiliating, or culturally unacceptable. Officers should begin interviews with questions that do not deal with sensitive matters, and should move on to issues such as sexual abuse and violence only when well into the interview. It should not be necessary to ask for precise details of the sexual abuse; the important thing is establishing whether it has occurred and the apparent motive of the perpetrator.

Keep in mind that, from the point of view of most applicants, Asylum Officers are authority figures and foreign government officials. Officers must also be culturally sensitive to the fact that every asylum applicant is testifying in a foreign environment and may have had experiences which give her (or him) good reason to distrust persons in authority, and a fear of encounters with government officials in countries of origin may carry over to countries of reception. This fear may cause some asylum applicants to be initially timid. Asylum Officers can overcome much of this nervousness by giving a brief "Opening Statement."

E. Demeanor/Credibility Issues

Inasmuch as Asylum Officers deal with people from a diverse array of countries, cultures and backgrounds, cross-cultural sensitivity is required of all Officers irrespective of the gender of the applicant. Nowhere is this sensitivity more needed than in assessing credibility and "demeanor." By "demeanor" is meant how a person handles himself/herself physically; for example, maintaining eye contact, shifts in posture, and hesitations in speech.

Women who have been subject to domestic or sexual abuse may be psychologically traumatized. Trauma can be suffered by any applicant, regardless of gender, and may have a significant impact on the ability to present testimony.

The demeanor of traumatized applicants can vary. They may appear numb or show emotional passivity when recounting past events of mistreatment. Some applicants may give matter-of-fact recitations of serious instances of mistreatment. Trauma may also cause memory loss or distortion, and may cause other applicants to block certain experiences from their minds in order not to relive their horror by the retelling.

In Anglo–American cultures, people who avert their gaze when answering a question, or seem nervous, are perceived as untruthful. In other cultures, however, body language does not convey the same message. In certain Asian cultures, for example, people will avert their eyes when speaking to an authority figure as a sign of respect. This is a product of culture, not necessarily of credibility.

It bears reiteration that the foregoing considerations of demeanor can be the products of trauma or culture, not credibility. Poor interview techniques/cross-cultural skills may cause faulty negative credibility findings.

F. *Derivative Status or Independent Claim*

Women in many cultures are viewed as completely subordinate to their husbands; that is, not having or deriving anything independently of their spouses. Asylum Officers of course do not make this assumption regarding the asylum eligibility of spouses. When a husband does not appear to have an approvable claim, an Asylum Officer should routinely review the merits of the wife's case even though she may be listed merely as a derivative on her husband's application and may not have filed a separate Form I–589 asylum application.

G. *INS Resource Information Center*

Asylum Officers must be able to rely on objective and current information on the legal and cultural situation of women in their countries of origin, on the incidence of violence, including both sexual and domestic, and on the adequacy of state protection afforded to them. To this end, the Resource Information Center (RIC) will be issuing papers ("alerts" and country profiles) dealing with these issues.

RIC will be working on a number of projects in an attempt to assure that information concerning violations of the rights of women are distributed regularly and systematically to all Asylum Offices.

* * *

IV. CONCLUSIONS: TRAINING & MONITORING/FOLLOW-UP

A. *Training*

This guidance is REQUIRED READING for all interviewing and supervising Asylum Officers. Photocopies should be made for the fullest possible distribution within the Corps. Upon receipt of this guidance, each Asylum Office must initiate four hours of in-Service training designed to help Officers to use this guidance, and reinforce their awareness of and sensitivity to gender and cross-cultural issues. Training materials will be provided by Headquarters and, in certain instances, trainers may be drawn from the ranks of concerned NGOs.

This guidance will be included in all future training sessions as a separate module. These training activities, and the information being gathered by the RIC, will enhance the ability of Asylum Officers to make informed, consistent and fair decisions.

Headquarters will continue to keep Office/rs abreast of the latest information on issues of gender and culture. Further training on these and related topics will take place as required. Training is critical to using this guidance effectively.

B. Monitoring

Asylum Officer interviewing and decision-making should be monitored systematically by Asylum Office Directors and Supervisory Asylum Officers. The latter will be held accountable for assuring that Asylum Officers fully implement this guidance.

As caselaw on gender-related persecution evolves, this guidance will be revised from time to time. Headquarters will keep track of all developments in the law of gender-related persecution, both in the United States and internationally. At the same time, procedures will be established to ensure collection of statistics on various aspects of gender-related claims adjudicated by the Asylum Officer Corps (AOC).